Islam
for
Nerds

500 Questions and Answers

Fully Revised First Edition

by
Gerald Drißner

Gerald Drißner (Drissner),

born 1977 in a mountain village in Austria, is an economist and award-winning journalist. He has been living in the Middle East and North Africa for more than ten years, where he has intensively studied Arabic.

He is the author of *Arabic for Nerds* (270 Questions about Arabic Grammar) and *Arabic for Nerds 2* (450 Questions and Answers).

IMPRINT/IMPRESSUM – Islam for Nerds

First edition, fully revised, November 2016 (130625)
Copyright © 2016 by Gerald Drißner (Drissner)
Cover design, layout: © 2016 by Gerald Drißner

Publisher: pochemuchka (Gerald Drißner)
Internet: https://pochemuchka-books.com
E-Mail: comment@pochemuchka-books.com
Address: Postfach 35 03 30, D-10212 Berlin, Germany
ISBN-13:   978-3-9819848-9-7 (paperback)
ISBN-13:   978-3-9819848-3-5 (hardcover)
ISBN-13:   978-3-9819848-4-2 (e-book)

Th. 4 □∃xG(x)

In words: "Necessarily, God exists."

Last line of Kurt Gödel's famous
ontological proof of God's existence

Disclaimer

"I saw that no one ever wrote a book
without, on the following day, saying:
'Had such-and-such been changed
it would have been better;
had such-and-such been added
it would have been more acceptable;
had such-and-such been stated earlier
it would have been preferable;
and had such-and-such been omitted
it would have been more elegant.'

Such a phenomenon is one of the great lessons and evidence of the
inherent insufficiency of all members of the human race."

al-Qāḍī al-Fāḍil ʿAbd al-Raḥīm al-Bisānī al-ʿAsqalānī
1135 (529 AH) - 1200 (596 AH)

Acknowledgements

This book consumed a huge
amount of work, research, and dedication.

I would like to express my gratitude to the many people
who saw me through this book;

to all those who taught me Arabic;

to all those who told me about Islam,

in Alexandria,
in Beirut, Cairo, Casablanca, Doha, Istanbul, Karachi, Kairouan,
Khartoum, Konya, Manama, Marrakesh, Ramallah, Sarajevo, Tunis;

and to all those who allowed me to quote their remarks.

Above all, I would like to thank

Ad Konings

for his countless comments
and profound and helpful remarks

and

my wife Mey
who supported and encouraged me
in spite of all the time it took me away from her.

Islam for Nerds

PART I: On the history of Muhammad

PART II: On the Qur'an

PART III: On the Hadiths

PART IV: On the history of Islam

PART V: On Fiqh (jurisprudence) and daily Muslim life

Appendix

Introduction

When I moved to Alexandria in Egypt to study Arabic, I ended up talking about religion all day long – which I hadn't expected. I realised how little I knew about Islam, and what I knew even differed from what the Arabs consider important. In my second Arabic lesson, having just learned how to say *hello*, we already studied the family tree of the Islamic prophet Muhammad. This particular lesson quickly turned out to be pretty useful for my daily conversations, since, in Egypt, everything starts and ends with religion.

I have lived in North Africa and in the Middle East for ten years, five years of this remarkable experience in Alexandria. By talking to my neighbours, my doormen, my Arabic teachers; by my daily encounters with taxi drivers, shopkeepers, people in the tram and by chatting with men in cafeterias, I gradually learned all the facts about the genesis of a world religion, the life of Muhammad, and who the most important Islamic figures were, as well as the dos and don'ts.

I took down notes and started to collect anecdotes and facts about Islam – 500 questions which I have now compiled into a book. In short: all the stuff kids in the Arab world already know but most people in other parts of the world have never heard of.

My aim is that people may gain a better understanding of what Islam means and what it is based on. Islam influences all aspects of a person's life. It is a religion that tries to provide a full life plan based on two main sources: the Qur'an, with 77,429 words, and thousands of Hadiths – the narratives relating deeds and utterances of the Prophet and his Companions.

Understanding the facts is helpful for discussions among Muslims, but more importantly between Muslims and non-Muslims. In my opinion, discussions about Islam often involve participants' lack of knowledge which can be tremendous. In my experience, most Westerners have never read the main Islamic sources and do not understand the mindset of Muslims. This leads to misunderstanding, misconception and perhaps to mistreatment. This book aims to fill this gap in understanding.

Every Muslim lives Islam differently. Every life lived by a Muslim is a statement about Islam. For example, Islam in Egypt is different from

Islam in Turkey. However, in the end they all share the same basis which is what I want to focus on in this book. While Islam is meant to be a complete plan for human life, the application of the Qur'an and the traditions and sayings of Muhammad to daily life is a challenge for every Muslim. Almost 1400 years have passed since the Archangel Gabriel - Jibrīl (جِبْرِيل) - appeared to Muhammad.

This book will show what Muhammad said in those days, what he did and why Muslims, until today, support and defend him loyally. Furthermore, this book will analyse the most important verses in the Qur'an and their impact on pious Muslims, and will explain why Islam, over the years, emerged as one of the world's biggest but also most misinterpreted religions.

By reading and understanding the principles of Islam, you will understand how people in predominately Muslim countries such as Egypt, Pakistan or Qatar think and live as most of their daily practices are rooted in Islam. According to research by the US-based Pew Forum on Religion & Public Life, Muslims will make up 26.4% of the world's total projected population of 8.3 billion in 2030. In Europe, the Muslim share of the population is expected to grow fast. In 2015, 1.3 million people - almost exclusively Muslims - applied for asylum in the 28 member states of the European Union.

Talking about religion is not an easy task. During my study of economics, when faced with a problem which did not have a clear solution, one of my professors told me: "If you want a simple truth, study mathematics. If you want one truth only, study theology." A religion cannot be right or wrong. A religion is by definition divine and therefore correct. It is impossible and pointless to prove its truth – you simply have to believe it.

The book consists of five parts: on Muhammad, on the Qur'an, on the Hadiths, on the history of Islam and on Fiqh (jurisprudence in Islam). It is a rough classification as some parts of this book could be placed in several other chapters.

In my discussions of the Qur'an, I use the early commentaries as well as the interpretation and commentaries of various scholars throughout history. I have almost exclusively used authentic (صَحِيح) sayings and traditions of Muhammad. Only in few cases, I refer to narrations which fulfil the minimal conditions of acceptability, so-called *hasan* (حَسَن), which I have marked as such.

I know from personal experience that for readers who don't know Arabic names can be confusing because they are difficult to read and easily mixed up. For that reason, I have repeated names and events frequently in an effort to help the reader getting used to Arabic names. In most cases, however, you can skip names, because the content is usually more important.

I have no intent to harm any believer. I respect all religions and I am convinced that it is more important to examine the shared, common ground than the few things that separate them. I tried to provide a neutral, objective view on Islam. For this reason, I will talk about the differences between Sunni and Shia Islam without taking a side. However, since I have lived only in countries with a Sunni majority, and since Sunnis are the majority of Muslims worldwide, I focus mainly on the Sunni view of Islam. Between 10 and 15 percent of all Muslims are of Shia faith.

I am not evaluating Islam, nor am I giving my opinion on Islam. There are rules and practices in Islam which are difficult to understand; some of them can be disturbing, but bear in mind that they were established 1400 years ago. Islam is not an open buffet from which you can pick and choose only what you like; instead it is all or nothing. Strictly speaking, in an Islamic framework, it is only possible to reform rules or practices which were established after Muhammad's death. Anything else is useless to discuss, as it undermines the core of Islamic faith – namely, to follow the Qur'an and the sayings and traditions of Muhammad.

However, I do believe that some parts of the Qur'an and the Hadiths should be read bearing their historic background in mind. I will provide significant historic facts as needed.

This book is neither scientific nor academic. It is a working paper which will be updated after some time. I am sure there are inaccuracies, since I have a mere practical view.

If you spot mistakes or have suggestions, please kindly let me know by e-mail: **comment@pochemuchka-books.com**

General remarks

Historic dates

Muslims use a lunar calendar. The so-called Hijri calendar is named after the migration of Muhammad from Mecca to Medina in 622. I mention the Islamic Hijri year if it helps to understand the time frame. It is denoted in Arabic with the letter hāʾ (ـه) as it is the first letter of the Arabic word Hijra (هجرة). Note that the shape of the letter is ـه (as it would be attached to another letter) and not ه which is the stand-alone version of the letter. I denote it in English by the abbreviations BH (before the Hijra) and AH (after the Hijra).

Salutations after certain names

After mentioning Allah, Muhammad, other Islamic prophets or companions of Muhammad, Muslims are supposed to praise them by uttering specific expressions. I don't use these expressions in the book, however, Muslims are supposed to say them. Here is a list of complimentary phrases that are used after certain names:

ALLAH (الله):
After mentioning Allah, Muslims say "subhānahu wa taʿālā" (سُبْحانَهُ وَتَعالَى) which means: "Glorious and exalted is He (Allah)". This is exclusively used with Allah. Abbreviation in English texts: SWT.

MUHAMMAD (مُحَمَّد):
After mentioning the Prophet's name, Muslims say "sallā Allāhu ʿalayhi wa sallam(a)" (صَلَّى اللهُ عَلَيْهِ وَسَلَّم). It means: "Allah bless him and grant him peace." Sometimes, you will also see: "(May) Allah pray for him and save him!" The abbreviation is, SAAS or SAAW or in its English translation: *peace be upon him* (PBUH).

This Arabic expression is used exclusively after saying the name of the Islamic prophet Muhammad. Note: In Arabic, the verbs are used in the past tense as it implies a wish. All other prophets receive honouring phrases of a lesser kind.

MESSENGERS, PROPHETS and ARCHANGELS – in short: people who are unerring according to Islam. After their names, Muslims say: *"alayhi al-Salām"* (عَلَيْهِ السَّلام) which means: *"Peace be upon him".* It is said after mentioning for example Noah (نُوح) or Gabriel (جِبْرِيل). Abbreviation in English: AS.

Shia Muslims, in addition to the prophets mentioned in the Qur'an, say *"alayhi al-Salām"* also after mentioning the name of members of Muhammad's household – especially after ʿAlī ibn ʾAbī Tālib (عَلِيّ بن أَبِي طالِب) and his wife Fātima (فاطِمة بِنْت مُحَمَّد), who was Muhammad's daughter, and their sons al-Hasan (الْحَسَن بن عَلِيّ) and al-Husayn (الْحُسَيْن بن عَلِيّ) and after mentioning any of the twelve Imams of Shia Islam.

Watch out: Islam teaches that it is in the very nature of humans to err and nobody seems to be exempted from this, including messengers and prophets. The story of Adam and Eve at the beginning of Sura 2 mentions the first error made by two of them. What follows from the story, though, is that erring is a necessary prerequisite for repentance, and repentance is a prerequisite for Allah's forgiveness. Throughout the Qur'an, there are multiple other accounts of prophets erring, then repenting and asking for forgiveness.

COMPANIONS (الصَّحابة) of the Prophet:
After mentioning one of Muhammad's companions, Muslims say the wish "radiya Allāhu ʿanhu" (رَضِيَ اللهُ عَنْهُ) which means: "May Allah be pleased with them." This is said for example after Muhammad's father-in-law ʾAbū Bakr (أَبُو بَكْر) or Muhammad's wife ʾĀʾisha (عائشة بِنْت أَبِي بَكْر). Abbreviation in English: RA.

Some remarks on the word *prostrating*

I use the word *prostrating* in this book as most Muslims use it in English. Islamic prayer (صَلَاة) includes both bowing (rukūʿ - رُكُوع) and prostration (sujūd - سُجود). Sujūd is a specific form of prostration where the forehead, nose, palms, knees, and toes touch the ground. It has always been a ritualised act.

Some remarks on the transliteration of Arabic words

I always give the Arabic source with vowels (تَشْكِيل) next to the English translation which might be helpful for readers who understand Arabic. For people who don't know Arabic, there is, in my opinion, nothing wrong in using translations especially as even a lot of Arabs are incapable of understanding classical texts properly. However, in order to understand the core of Islam, it is advisable to have a look at the Arabic meaning of words and concepts – which I do in this book when encountering controversial topics. The transliteration of Arabic words into English is tricky. I don't use a standardised system in this book. I focus on comprehensibility. For this reason, I do not use the correct Arabic plural in the English transliteration as this might be confusing for some readers. For example: Hadīth (حَدِيث) - 'Ahādīth (أَحادِيث). Instead, I use the word Hadiths to express the plural.

Sources for this book

I primarily use the Qur'an and (authentic) Hadith collections for this book. These two sources form the core of Islam; from these two sources, the Sharī'a (الشَّرِيعة) - the (sacred) Islamic law - is derived. The Sharī'a was developed and assembled during the first three centuries after the Prophet's death.

Regarding the English translation of the Qur'an, I found Muhammad Abdel Haleem's translation (Oxford-Press, 2004) appropriate, because it is a good mixture of traditional and liberal interpretations. He was born in Egypt and is currently the director of Islamic Studies at SOAS (School of Oriental and African Studies) in London.

Regarding the translation of the Bible, I use the New King James Version, an English translation of the Christian Bible for the Church of England.

Regarding dictionaries, I mostly use the *Arabic–English Lexicon* compiled by Edward William Lane (died 1876) as well as the Arabic-Arabic dictionary Lisān al-'Arab (لِسان الْعَرَب).

What about historical events? This is a difficult topic. Only few historical events are described in the Qur'an and in the Hadiths. There are no reliable historical accounts about the time of Muhammad which were written during his reign. All sources which Muslims use today were written dozens of years, even centuries later.

A biography of Muhammad, written by Ibn 'Ishāq (ابن إسحاق), is one of the few sources which details about the beginning of Islam. Ibn 'Ishāq was born in ~ 703 (85 AH) in Medina and died around 60 years later in ~ 768 (151 AH) in Baghdad. Islamic scholars say that most of his work is reliable, though they do disagree on the chronology and miraculous elements.

The original script, which was anyhow more of a collection of anecdotes, was lost. His work survived in the edited version of Ibn Hishām (ابن هشام), a scholar from Basra (الْبَصْرة) in present-day Iraq, who died in 833 (218 AH). He had edited the original version of Ibn 'Ishāq. Also, al-Tabarī (الطَّبَرِيّ), a Persian Islamic scholar who lived in the 9th century, had collected some facts of Muhammad's life.

Since Ibn Hishām died more than 200 years after the beginning of Islam, critics doubt that he got all the facts right. However, there are no other major sources about the early life of Muhammad or the beginning of Islam which mention so many details. Most other scripts are just fragments. For this reason, Ibn Hishām's work which is mainly based on Ibn 'Ishāq's notes is now considered one of the classic Arabic works on Muhammad and the early years of Islam.

In English, there is a translation of Ibn 'Ishāq's biography, enriched with the works of Ibn Hishām and others. It is called: "The Life of Muhammad". It was translated and edited by Alfred Guillaume (1888 - 1965), a Christian Arabist and scholar. I will mainly use his translation but will also mention the Arabic source of Ibn Hishām.

For Muslims, trying to find out what is lawful/permitted - so-called halāl (حَلال) - and what is prohibited - so-called harām (حَرام) - can be challenging. This is the reason for religious decrees - in Arabic called Fatwā (فَتْوى) - which tell Muslims the answer. Islam, on this matter, is different from other religions. Islam is trying to find a mandatory rule for every aspect in life. That makes it especially attractive to people who like following rules.

This also explains why the Islamic world, after having had a pioneering role in certain disciplines at the beginning of Islam, declined in the medieval ages. Islamic scholars were engaged with legal issues instead of investing time and manpower in natural sciences. Over the centuries, the world became very different compared to the time of Muhammad, furthermore, Muslims reached very different parts of the world compared to the Arabian desert and became exposed to foreign cultures. From an Islamic perspective, every invention, foreign food, clothes and habits - virtually everything which was new - had to be examined, i.e. is it halāl or harām for Muslims?

I do not focus in this book on Fatwas. Recently, with the rise of political Islamic and Salafi movements, I think there are too many Muslims who believe they are entitled to issue a Fatwa. I call it *Fatwa spam*. Some Fatwas are even bizarre.

However, it is difficult for Muslims to denounce them. In fact, it is not allowed for ordinary Muslims to discuss matters of Islamic law. Instead, Muslims must follow Islamic authorities by all means, so they might find themselves in a dilemma. An Egyptian friend once told me: "If he wasn't the Imam of the mosque, I would call him an idiot."

For readers who want to dig deeper into the sources of Islam, there are useful tools online to analyse the Qur'an and the Hadiths:

- http://library.islamweb.net – in Arabic. Resource for checking the origin and reliability of a Hadith. The site is administered by the Ministry of Endowments and Islamic Affairs in Doha, Qatar.

- http://www.sunnah.com – in English. Good collection of mostly authentic Hadiths. Some translations are bad and some are even wrong. So always try to double check with other reliable sources.

What you need to know for this book

Let's start with what you should know to be able to read this book. The following part is especially for people who have little or no idea about Islam.

When and where it all started

We have to go back in time, to the 6th century AD, to the hot desert of Arabia, Mecca, where events took place that shook world's history. Muhammad, who worked as a shepherd and later on as a trader, was born and raised there. He was born into the Banū Hāshim clan (بَنُو هاشِم) which belonged to the Quraysh tribe (قَبِيلة قُرَيْش).

Arabia was a place where several peoples mingled, e.g. Bedouins who believed in paganism, Jews and Christians. It is not entirely clear why there were Jewish clans and tribes. Some historians assume that they had migrated from Jerusalem in 70 AD when the Roman army besieged and conquered Jerusalem and eventually dismantled the famous Second Temple. Muslims say that the Arabs prior to Islam had lived in the *Days of Ignorance* – so-called Jāhilīya (جاهِلِيّة). The Arabic root of this term means *to be ignorant, irrational* or *stupid*.

When Muhammad was nearly 40, he liked to contemplate, he prayed and thought a lot about life, the typical main three W-questions: When did it all begin? Why are we here? What will happen after death?

Muslims believe that one day the Archangel Gabriel - in Arabic: Jibrīl (جِبْرِيل) - appeared before him and called upon him to read, but Muhammad replied: "I am unable to read."

This marks the beginning of Islam.

What are the two most important cities in Islam?

Mecca (مَكّة) and Medina (الْمَدِينة).

In pre-Islamic times Medina was called Yathrib (يَثْرِب) and was the city in which Muhammad sought refuge after he was driven out from his hometown Mecca. This event is called Hijra (الْهِجْرة) and marks the beginning of the Hijri calendar in 622 AD.

Are God and Allah the same?

Generally speaking, yes. The Arabic word Allah (الله) is the combination of the definite article al- (ال) and the Arabic word for *God* which is ʾIlāh (إله). So Allah literally means *The (one and only) God.*

For this reason, Christians who speak Arabic say Allah too, but they prefer the word *Lord* – in Arabic: Rabb (رَبّ). It is a difficult topic. Somehow, Muslims claim to have the copyright on the word Allah. Some Muslims even get angry when Christians say Allah.

Who is the leader of the Muslim nation?

The Caliph. After Muhammad's death, several Caliphs succeeded him as leaders of the Muslim nation. The Arabic word for *Caliph* is Khalīfa (خَلِيفة). It comes from the root kh-l-f (خ-ل-ف) which means *to be the successor; to follow.* The *Caliphate* is called al-Khilāfa (الْخِلافة). Islam has no popes, bishops or priests. All Muslims are equal. All Muslims have mutual rights and duties within Islam.

Battles during the time of the Prophet

There are two important terms which are used for these battles.

A **Ghazwa** (غَزْوة) - in English pronounced as "Razwa" without rolling the R - is a battle in which the Prophet went out with his companions and he himself led the battle. The number of these battles reached possibly 28.

A **Sarīya** (سَرِيّة) - literally *detachment; squadron; company* - is a battle in which the Prophet was not present and which he did not lead. The total number of these battles (which Muhammad had dispatched) reached at least 73. Note: 11 of these battles were sent out in the month of Ramadan.

Does Islam "accept" other religions?

They are subordinated. Muslims believe that Muhammad corrected and completed both Judaism and Christianity. They allege that Jews and Christians had corrupted the true message of God which had been transmitted by several prophets since Adam. That is why Muslims are convinced that they are superior to Christians and Jews.

Islam accepts the monotheistic *People of the Book* (Jews, Christians, Sabians) but rejects any other belief. Buddhism and Hinduism, for example, are treated as pagan beliefs in Islam, their followers and traditions are seen as a threat to Muslims. In Western countries, where religious freedom is a constitutional right, Muslim representatives try to withhold this fact in public discussions – fearing that people would show an unsympathetic reaction to this Islamic fact.

In most predominately Muslim countries, especially in the Arab world, religious minorities suffer severe discrimination.

What is the Qur'an?

The Qur'an is the central religious text of Islam. Muslims believe that the text in the Qur'an is a revelation from Allah. The Qur'an describes itself as a book of guidance. The Qur'an consists of 114 chapters, so-called **sūra** (سُورة). Each sura is divided into verses, so-called **'Āya** (آية) which literally means *sign*.

The suras are of unequal length. The shortest sura is 108 *Abundance* - in Arabic: al-Kawthar (سُورة الْكَوْثَر) - with only three verses; the longest sura is 2 *The Cow* - in Arabic: al-Baqara (سُورة الْبَقَرة) - with 286 verses. The suras are not arranged chronologically. Instead, they are arranged roughly in order of descending size. This makes it difficult to read the Qur'an. Without understanding the context or the historical background, without knowing the most important people in Islam, it is nearly impossible to understand the Qur'an.

Furthermore, non-Muslims may find several titles of suras strange and difficult to understand, for example sura 2 *The Cow*. Generally, the reader should not jump to conclusions about the content of a sura just because of its name.

Suras are classified as *Meccan* or *Medinan*, depending on whether the verses were revealed before or after the migration of Muhammad to the city of Medina.

What is a Hadith?

The Arabic word Hadīth (حَدِيث, plural: أَحَادِيث) basically means *statement*, *report* or *narrative*. The "ī" is pronounced as a long "ee"-sound – as in English *bee*. The "th" at the end is a "th" – as in English *think*. Make a small pause after the "a", and you will finally get: "Ha-deeth".

A Hadith is a report describing what the Prophet said, what he did, allowed, forbid, or recommended – in short: his traditions. It is a description of Muhammad's way of life, short episodes of his life which go as deeply as describing how he drank water, how he greeted people, what perfume he liked, how he cured diseases, what women are allowed to do during their menstruation, etc.

Without knowing the Hadiths it can be difficult to understand several parts of the Qur'an. For compiling the Islamic law - the so-called Sharī'a (شَرِيعة) - the Hadiths are second only to the Qur'an. Probably most of the daily habits of a pious Muslim are derived from the Hadiths and not from the Qur'an.

Muslims must follow both the Qur'an and all the sayings, teachings, deeds, permissions, and disapprovals of Muhammad. Muslims call the latter Sunna (سُنّة) which means *habitual practice*. The Sunna is basically just another word for the content of the Hadiths.

In the West, non-Muslims usually underestimate the importance and influence of the Hadiths on a Muslim's life. When they are discussing certain aspects of Islam, they usually ask: Is this found in the Qur'an? They simply don't know that most aspects of a righteous Muslim life are based on the Hadiths.

In the Arab world, however, Muslims know the value of the Hadiths. In fact, the Qur'an tells Muslims that Muhammad is the role model for their life. Let's have a look at sura 33 *The Joint Forces* - in Arabic: al-'Ahzāb (سُورة الأَحْزاب):

| 33:21 | The Messenger of God is an excellent model for those of you who put your hope in God and the Last Day and remember Him often. | لَّقَدْ كَانَ لَكُمْ فِي رَسُولِ اللَّهِ أُسْوَةٌ حَسَنَةٌ لَّمَن كَانَ يَرْجُو اللَّهَ وَالْيَوْمَ الْآخِرَ وَذَكَرَ اللَّهَ كَثِيرًا. |

This verse is not only a piece of advice – it is a command. Sura 4 *Women* - in Arabic: al-Nisā' (سُورة النِّساء) - issues a clear warning and tells Muslims what will happen if he or she does not follow both:

4:14	But those who disobey God and His messenger and overstep His limits will be consigned by God to the Fire, and there they will stay – a humiliating torment awaits them!	وَمَن يَعْصِ اللَّه وَرَسُولَهُ وَيَتَعَدَّ حُدُودَهُ يُدْخِلْهُ نَارًا خَالِدًا فِيهَا وَلَهُ عَذَابٌ مُّهِينٌ!

Every Hadith consists of two things:
- It has a **chain of narration** – in Arabic called ʼIsnād (إسناد) which literally means *ascription*.
- And there is of course the **content** of a Hadith, in Arabic called Matn (مَتْن) which literally means *board* or *deck*.

The Hadiths are based on spoken reports which were kept alive by retelling after Muhammad's death and were finally collected in the 8th century. There was no authority who decided which Hadith is correct. Instead, every Hadith was evaluated and eventually got a grade – depending on who had reported the saying or happening, how good the person knew the Prophet, and how it was transmitted.

There are mainly three grades or categories of Hadiths:
1. **Sahīh** (صحيح) means *authentic* or *correct*. It fulfils the highest conditions of acceptability.

2. **Hasan** (حَسَن) means *good, agreeable,* or *excellent.* It is used to describe a Hadith whose authenticity is not well-established, but sufficient for religious evidence. It fulfils the minimal conditions of acceptability.

3. **Daʻīf** (ضعيف) means *weak.* It fails to meet any of the conditions of acceptability. Only if there is no other information about a topic, Muslims may refer to a weak narration. However, most Muslim scholars reject these Hadiths. In most cases, a narration is weak because of the discontinuity in the chain of narrators.

The number of the Hadiths known in Islam is not entirely clear. There are several reasons: some narrations describe almost the same event or content, some may have different chains of narration but have the same content.

What is the difference between the Qur'an and the Hadiths?

- In the Qur'an, you will only find <u>Allah's words</u> which were transmitted by Archangel Gabriel to Muhammad.

- However, a Hadith usually contains <u>Muhammad's own words</u> or simply descriptions of his actions. Not every Hadith is of the same quality. Contrary to this, in the Qur'an every verse is con-sidered holy.

Are there contradictions and inconsistencies in Islam?

Yes, there are.

This makes Islam difficult to understand for non-Muslims. Even authentic Hadiths can contradict each other or are confusing although they refer to the same topic or the same event. Neverthe-less, Islamic preachers like to tell Muslims that there is a perfectly true answer for every question – but this is simply not true in Islam.

Some verses of the Qur'an and especially dozens of Hadiths are difficult to understand or simply illogical. For faithful Muslims, this is no problem as they are ordered to obey the commands of Allah by all means. In fact, the meaning of Islam implies nothing less than: *submission to Allah.*

Therefore, in Islam it is irrelevant whether a Muslim grasps the wisdom behind a command. A Muslim believes that Allah is the All-Knowing and that He knows what is good for his worshippers.

There are commands in Islam which are difficult to understand and accept. Sometimes Muslims can't find an explanation for the reasons behind certain rules.

For this reason, Muslims usually conclude with: "And Allah knows best" – in Arabic: "wa-llāhu 'a'lam[u]" (وَاللّٰهُ أَعْلَمُ).

Sunni (Sunnite) and Shia (Shiite) Islam

The history of Islam is overshadowed by the formation of the two major sects in Islam: Sunni and Shia.

The Arabic word Sunnī (سُنِّي) is derived from Sunna (سُنّة) which means *a way or path (for life)*; in Islam, it denotes *habitual practice*, basically what Muhammad did and said. Sunni therefore means *one of the path*. Sunni Muslims acknowledge the first four Caliphs to have been the rightful successors of Muhammad. Sunnis call themselves traditionalist.

The majority of Muslims are Sunni Muslims. In Arabic, the Sunnis as a whole are called 'Ahl al-Sunna wa al-Jamā'a (أَهل السُّنّة وَالْجَماعة) which means: *people of the tradition of Muhammad and the consensus of the 'Umma.* Usually, they are just called: 'Ahl al-Sunna (أَهل السُّنّة).

The main difference between Sunni and Shia Islam goes back to the time of Muhammad's death: Sunni Muslims insist that 'Abū Bakr (أَبُو بَكْر) was the legitimate successor and first Caliph, whereas Shia Muslims insist that it was Muhammad's son-in-law and cousin: 'Alī ibn 'Abī Tālib (عَلِيّ بن أَبِي طالِب).

Schools of jurisprudence

Islam is a complex system of rules. However, Allah has not delivered human kind a civil code and penal law ready for use. Scholars and jurists had to derive it first from the Qur'an and the sayings and teachings of the Prophet. Some rules and commands leave room for interpretation.

For this reason, different schools of jurisprudence were established – so-called Madhhab (مَذْهَب); pronounced in English like "Maz-hab". Madhhab means doctrine; in Islamic jurisprudence, it is a school of thought.

They are usually named after the scholar who taught them. They basically tell Muslims: what is allowed and prohibited? What are the punishments? Furthermore, they set the rules for Islamic rituals – for example the ablution ritual. In general, as they must follow the teachings of the Qur'an and the Hadiths, the differences are little.

Nowadays, Sunni Islam recognises four schools:

- The Hanafī School (حَنَفِيّ) was founded by 'Abū Hanīfa al-Nu'mān (أَبُو حَنيفة النُّعْمان). Most Sunni Muslims - the majority of Muslims - follow this school. It is mainly found in countries which were once part of the Ottoman Empire, thus, it is common in Egypt, Iraq, Turkey, Syria and Lebanon; but also in Pakistan, Afghanistan, and in the Caucasus.

- The Mālikī School (مالِكِيّ) was founded by Mālik ibn 'Anas (مالك بن أَنَس). It is common in most parts of North Africa (mainly in the Maghreb; but not in Egypt) and in West Africa.

- The Shāfi'ī School (شافِعِيّ) was established by Muhammad ibn 'Idrīs al-Shāfi'ī (مُحَمَّد بن إدْريس الشّافِعِيّ). It is followed by Muslims in East Africa, Indonesia, Malaysia, Brunei and Yemen.

- The Hanbalī School (حَنْبَلِيّ) was established by 'Ahmad ibn Hanbal (أَحْمَد بن حَنْبَل). It is the smallest and most traditional and conservative school. It is followed by Muslims in Saudi Arabia and Qatar. Furthermore, most Salafi Muslims use this school as a basis for their understanding of Islam's rules.

Remark: Shia Muslims use different schools of jurisprudence. The most important is called Ja'farī (جَعْفَرِيّ). It is named after Ja'far ibn Muhammad al-Sādiq (جَعْفَر بن مُحَمَّد الصّادِق).

Who were the Sahāba, the Muhājirūn, and the al-'Ansār?

The companions of the Prophet were called al-Sahāba (الصَّحابة). The most common definition of a companion - in Arabic: Sahābī (صحابِيّ) - is someone who met Muhammad, believed in him and died as a Muslim.

The first companions were subdivided into two groups:
1. The immigrants from Mecca - al-Muhājirūn (الْمُهاجِرُون) - were the followers of Muhammad who escaped from Mecca and went to Medina (then known as Yathrib). This event is called al-Hijra.

2. Al-'Ansār (الأَنْصار) were the locals of Medina. The Arabic expression al-'Ansār is usually translated as *the helpers*. They gave Muhammad and his followers - the Muhājirūn - a place to stay when they escaped from Mecca. The al-'Ansār embraced Islam.

Note: Without the definite article the word 'Ansār (أَنْصار) can mean *adherents, followers, sponsors, partisans*. The *Ansār al-Sharī'a* (أنصار الشَّريعة) - literally, *the followers of Islamic law* - is the name of various Islamic militia groups, for example in Libya and in Tunisia.

How do Arabic names work?

Names are constructed differently in the Islamic, mainly Arab world. A name is like a chain giving information about a person's descent. At the end of a name, you might find the name of the person's tribe, the name of a place where the family originated, or the name of a profession.

The important part is usually the second part. It gives you information about the father of a male or female person. It starts with the Arabic word ibn (ابن) which means *son of* or with bint (بِنْت) which means *daughter of*. What follows, is the name of the father. If you spot the word ibn after the first name, you can be sure that the person is a man.

Let's have a look at an example: Zaynab was a common name at the time of Muhammad. Watch out when people mention the name Zaynab and always look at the second part of the name which will give you the required information:

- Zaynab bint 'Alī (زَيْنَب بِنْت عَلِيّ). Literally: *Zaynab, daughter of 'Alī*. She was the third child of 'Alī and Fātima (فاطِمة). Fātima was Muhammad's daughter.
- Zaynab bint Jahsh (زَيْنَب بِنْت جَحْش). Literally: *Zaynab, daughter of Jahsh*. She was a cousin and wife of Muhammad.
- Zaynab bint Muhammad (زَيْنَب بِنْت مُحَمَّد). Literally: *Zaynab, daughter of Muhammad*. She is regarded as the eldest daughter of Muhammad and his first wife Khadīja (خَدِيجة).

Notice: The second Caliph in Islam, 'Umar ibn al-Khaṭṭāb (عُمَر بن الْخَطّاب), called upon the Arabs to say their <u>name</u> and not their origin as poor Bedouins used to do when someone asked them where they were from.

What did the Caliph mean by name? The Caliph meant the name of the family, the name of the clan or tribe. In Arabic culture, until today, the name of the family or clan bears a lot of information about the person: his wealth, power, courage, hospitality, etc.

Some remarks on the writing system of names in this book:

• Due to grammatical rules in Arabic, the word 'Abū (أَبو) - which means *father of* - might change into 'Abī (أَبِي). Both words mean the same; it is just a grammatical inflection. So don't get confused: 'Abū Bakr and 'Abī Bakr are the same person.

• In English texts, you occasionally read *bin* instead of *ibn*, for example: Osama bin Laden. Ibn (ابن or بن) is a tricky word in Arabic. At the beginning of an utterance, the correct pronunciation is: 'Ibn. In the middle of an utterance, it is either "ubn", "abn" or "ibn". But it can never be "bin". For this reason, I will always write *ibn*.

• What about names that are common in all Abrahamitic religions, for example Abraham ('Ibrāhīm) or Gabriel (Jibrīl)? In these cases, I normally use the common English form which is mostly based on the transliteration of the Bible. This will be much easier for people who don't know Arabic. Readers who know Arabic will stick to the Arabic sources in the book anyway. There is a conversion table in the appendix. Some stories of prophets and events are different in Islam compared to Judaism or Christianity. I will mention the differences and explain them when necessary.

• If Arabic names or expressions have entered the English language, I use these forms and don't pay attention to the Arabic transliteration.

PART I

On the history of Muhammad

1. When is Muhammad's birthday?

Answer: The exact date of his birth (مَولِد النَّبِي) is unknown.

Born	570 or 571 (~53 BH) in Mecca		Died	June 8, 632 (11 AH) in Medina, aged 61 or 62

There is only little information about the early years of Muhammad because no one expected that this little boy would eventually attend such a high profile and status. Muhammad was born into the Banū Hāshim (بَنُو هاشِم) clan which belonged to the Quraysh tribe (قُرَيْش). The Quraysh later became his enemy.

Muhammad was most probably 40 years old when Allah - as Muslims believe - sent the Archangel Gabriel to him. Then, Gabriel started to transmit what Allah wanted mankind to know.

Only when Muhammad started to preach, people became interested in his personal details. They tried to remember details, historical or personal events which would help them to determine the year of his birth. Most scholars agree that it was the year which is called *year of the elephant* – in Arabic: ʿĀm al-Fīl (عام الفِيل). This was either 570 or 571.

What Muslims know for sure is the day of the week: Muhammad was born on Monday. ʾAbū Qatāda (أَبُو قَتَادة الأَنْصارِئ) narrated that the Messenger of Allah said: "He was then asked about fasting on Monday, whereupon he said: It was the day on which I was born."[1]

What about the month? Most Sunni scholars agree that it was the lunar month called Rabīʿ al-ʾAwwal (رَبِيع الأَوَّل).

And the day? This is not entirely clear. The assumption is that Muhammad was born between the 8th and 12th of Rabīʿ al-ʾAwwal. Some astronomers have calculated that it must have been the 9th of Rabīʿ al-ʾAwwal what would correspond to the solar date of: 20th April in 571. But there is no proof for this.

Ibn ʾIshāq (ابن إسحاق) who wrote one of the most important biographies of the Prophet stated that Muhammad was born on the twelfth of the month.

---

1 ...أَنَّ رَسُولَ اللّٰه وَسُئِلَ عَنْ صَوْمِ يَوْمِ الإِثْنَيْنِ قَالَ: "ذَاكَ يَوْمٌ وُلِدْتُ فِيه." Sahīh Muslim 1162

Eventually, the majority of Sunni scholars nowadays say that Muhammad was born in the *year of the elephant* on Monday, 12th of Rabī' al-'Awwal – which could have been the 22nd of April in the year 571. Most Shia scholars believe it was the 17th of Rabī' al-'Awwal.

Interestingly, most scholars agree that Muhammad died on the 12th of Rabī' al-'Awwal in 632 (11 AH). So his birthday and his day of death could have happened on the same lunar day of the year.

In the end it doesn't really matter because Muhammad's birthday is not as important for Muslims as for example Jesus' birth is for Christians. The Prophet himself did not celebrate it, nor did he command anyone to do so.

Traditional Muslims say that the celebration of a birthday is an *innovation* - in Arabic called: Bid'a (بِدْعة) - which means: it should not be celebrated. However, most Sunni and nearly all Shia Muslims accept the celebration of Muhammad's birthday which is called: Mawlid al-Nabī (مَوْلِد النَّبِي).

Today, the Mawlid is recognised as a national holiday in most Islamic countries – except Saudi Arabia and Qatar. Among Sunnis, the celebration of the Mawlid became popular in the 12th century.

According to some historians the Mawlid was initiated by the Fatimids (الْفاطِمِيُّون). The Fatimids were of Shia believe – another reason, why traditional Sunni Muslims oppose the Mawlid.

When I was in Egypt, during the Mawlid, several shops offered sweets and pink coloured candies. They had the shape of a knight on horseback. In Tunisia and Libya, Muslims cook 'Asīda (عَصِيدة), a dough-based dessert which is made from wheat flour, butter and honey.

Note: The word Mawlid (مَولِد) is the so-called *noun of place* or *time* (إِسْم زَمان or إِسْم مَكان) in Arabic and is derived from the Arabic root w-l-d (و-ل-د) which means: *to give birth, bear a child*.

2. What is Muhammad's full name?

Answer: Muhammad ibn ʿAbd Allah ibn ʿAbd al-Muttalib (مُحَمَّد بن عَبْد الله بن عَبْد الْمُطَّلِب) – literally: Muhammad, son of ʿAbd Allah, son of ʿAbd al-Muttalib.

From this we see that ʿAbd Allah was his father and ʿAbd al-Muttalib his grandfather. The name Muhammad (مُحَمَّد) is derived from the Arabic root h-m-d (د-م-ح) which basically means *to praise*. The passive participle of the Arabic II-verb hammada (حَمَّدَ) - which means: *to praise somebody highly* - is Muhammad (مُحَمَّد). Therefore, Muhammad literally means: *praised; commendable; laudable*.

In the Qurʾan, the Prophet is called Muhammad and Ahmad. Both words more or less mean the same. The Arabic word ʾAhmad (أَحْمَد) is the comparative form (*more laudable, more commendable*) or, if used as a verb, it can express: *to become praiseworthy*.

The Prophet had several epithets. Jubayr ibn Mutʿim (جُبَيْر بن مُطْعِم) reported on the authority of his father that he heard Allah's Messenger say: "I have many names: I am Muhammad, I am Ahmad, I am al-Māhī through whom Allah obliterates unbelief, and I am al-Hāshir (the gatherer) at whose feet people will be gathered [on the Day of Resurrection], and I am al-ʿĀqib [who succeeds the other prophets in bringing good]."[2]

Note that Mustafā (مُصْطَفَى) - a common name among Muslims - is also an epithet of Muhammad. It means: *the chosen one*.

3. By which name was Muhammad nicknamed?

Answer: *The truthful* (الصَّادِق) and *the trustworthy* (الأَمِين) – in Arabic combined: *al-Sādiq wa al-ʾAmīn* (الصَّادِق وَالأَمِين).

Ibn ʾIshāq (ابن إسحاق) wrote in his biography of Muhammad: "He was the best and most noble of his people, the best of them in man-

---

2 قَالَ سَمِعْتُ رَسُولَ اللَّهِ يَقُولُ: "إِنَّ لِي أَسْمَاءً، أَنَا مُحَمَّدٌ، وَأَنَا أَحْمَدُ، وَأَنَا الْمَاحِي الَّذِي يَمْحُو اللَّهُ بِيَ الْكُفْرَ، وَأَنَا الْحَاشِرُ الَّذِي يُحْشَرُ النَّاسُ عَلَى قَدَمِي، وَأَنَا الْعَاقِبُ". Sahīh al-Bukhārī 4896.

ners, the most noble in character and the best neighbour and the greatest in standing and the most truthful in speech."[3]

Muslims believe that Muhammad never told a lie in his entire life. Even his enemies testify on his honesty and integrity. 'Abd Allah ibn 'Abbās (عَبْد الله بن عَبَّاس) narrated that the Messenger of Allah said to his companions: "If I inform you that cavalrymen are proceeding up the side of this mountain, will you believe me?" They said: "We have never heard you telling a lie."[4]

When I moved to Egypt, starting from leaving the plane at the airport in Cairo, people tried to rip me off telling me packs of lies. Most Egyptians pretend to be very faithful and at the same time they lie to you whenever they see an opportunity to get a (monetary) advantage. However, this contradicts entirely the teachings of Islam.

The characteristics of honesty and being truthful are of great importance for a Muslim. 'Abd Allah ibn 'Amr (عَبْد الله بن عَمْرو) narrated that Allah's Messenger said: "Whoever has (the following) four characteristics will be a pure hypocrite: If he speaks, he tells a lie; if he gives a promise, he breaks it; if he makes a covenant, he proves treacherous; and if he quarrels, he behaves in a very imprudent evil insulting manner (unjust). And whoever has one of these characteristics, has one characteristic of a hypocrite, until he gives it up."[5]

4. Who circumcised Muhammad?

Answer: Most probably his grandfather, 'Abd al-Muttalib ibn Hāshim (عَبْد الْمُطَّلِب بن هاشِم).

Born	~ 480 in Yathrib (Medina)	Died	~ 578 (45 BH), aged ~ 98 (!), buried in Mecca

---

3 ...كَانَ رَجُلاً, وَأَفْضَلَ قَوْمِهِ مُرُوءَةً وَأَحْسَنَهُمْ خُلُقًا, وَأَكْرَمَهُمْ حَسَبًا, وَأَحْسَنَهُمْ جِوَارًا, وَأَعْظَمَهُمْ حِلْمًا, وَأَصْدَقَهُمْ حَدِيثًا

4 ...فَقَالَ: "أَرَأَيْتُمْ إِنْ أَخْبَرْتُكُمْ أَنَّ خَيْلاً تَخْرُجُ مِنْ سَفْحِ هَذَا الْجَبَلِ أَكُنْتُمْ مُصَدِّقِيَّ." قَالُوا مَا جَرَّبْنَا عَلَيْكَ كَذِبًا. Sahīh al-Bukhārī 4971.

5 قَالَ رَسُولُ اللَّه: "أَرْبَعٌ جِلاَلٍ مَنْ كُنَّ فِيهِ كَانَ مُنَافِقًا خَالِصًا مَنْ إِذَا حَدَّثَ كَذَبَ, وَإِذَا وَعَدَ أَخْلَفَ, وَإِذَا عَاهَدَ غَدَرَ وَإِذَا خَاصَمَ فَجَرَ, وَمَنْ كَانَتْ فِيهِ خَصْلَةٌ مِنْهُنَّ كَانَتْ فِيهِ خَصْلَةٌ مِنَ النَّفَاقِ حَتَّى يَدَعَهَا ". Sahīh al-Bukhārī 3178.

The actual name of Muhammad's grandfather was Shayba al-Hamd ibn Hāshim (شَيْبة الْحَمْد بن هاشِم), commonly known as 'Abd al-Muttalib (عَبْد الْمُطَّلِب). It is not clear when he was born, most say in 480 AD, some say in the year 497.

Shayba means *the ancient one* or *white-haired*. There is a reason for this name: When he was born, he is said to have had a streak of white through his jet-black hair. Shayba al-Hamd (شَيْبة الْحَمْد) literally means: *the white streak of praise*.

After his father's death Shayba was raised in Yathrib (the pre-Islamic name for Medina) with his mother and her family until about the age of eight, when his uncle al-Muttalib (الْمُطَّلِب) went to see him and asked his mother Salmā (سَلْمَى بِنْت عَمْرو) to give him the right to care about Shayba. Al-Muttalib convinced her that the possibilities in Yathrib were not as good compared to Mecca. Salmā finally agreed to let him go. When al-Muttalib and Shayba arrived in Mecca, the people assumed the unknown child was Muttalib's slave, thus giving him the name 'Abd al-Muttalib which means: *slave of al-Muttalib*.

The word slave or servant - in Arabic: 'Abd (عَبْد) - is a very common first word of Muslim names for men. However, a Muslim must not be called for example *servant of al-Muttalib*. According to Islam, the word slave can only be used in combination with Allah or one of his attributes, for example: 'Abd al-Rahmān (عَبْد الرَّحْمـن), literally: *slave of The Entirely Merciful*. Or 'Abd al-'Azīz (عَبْد الْعَزِيز), literally: *slave of the Almighty*. However, this all happened prior to the formation of Islam.

When his uncle al-Muttalib died, Shayba succeeded him as the chief of the Hāshim clan. He took over the duties of providing water and food for the pilgrims. In pre-Islamic times, people went to Mecca and the Ka'ba (الْكَعْبة) to worship their deities.

The Banū Hāshim clan of the Quraysh, to which Muhammad was born into, was named after Shayba's father, who was called Hāshim.

Regarding the circumcision it is not clear what had happened:

- Hypothesis 1: Muhammad was born circumcised. Most of the Hadiths indicating this are weak (ضَعِيف).
- Hypothesis 2: The Archangel Gabriel circumcised Muhammad when he opened his chest. However, there is only an obscure Hadith which suggests this.

- Hypothesis 3: His grandfather, 'Abd al-Muttalib, circumcised Muhammad according to the Arab custom of circumcising their sons which was already common in pre-Islamic times. Some reports tell that his grandfather circumcised Muhammad on the seventh day after birth.

Remark: 'Abū Hurayra (أَبُو هُرَيْرة) reported that Allah's Messenger said that prophet Abraham - in Islam: 'Ibrāhīm (إِبْراهِيم) - had circumcised himself with the help of an adze when he was eighty (!) years old.[6] An adze is a carpenter's tool; Qadūm (قَدُوم) in Arabic. Muslims believe that Abraham was the first man who was circumcised.

5. Who is Muhammad's ancestor according to Muslims?

Answer: Ishmael, the son of Abraham.

There is no authentic, proven family tree of Muhammad. Most of the information is based on the work of Ibn 'Ishāq, mainly his biography of Muhammad. In the end, it is a matter of faith.

Judaism, Christianity and Islam are called the *Abrahamic religions*. Abraham - or 'Ibrāhīm (إِبْراهِيم) in Arabic - is regarded as the Patriarch of monotheism and the common father of the Jews, Christians and Muslims. Although all three religions agree on the role of Abraham, the role of his children is disputed.

In Islam, Abraham is a link in the chain of prophets that begins with Adam and ends in Muhammad – through Abraham's son Ishmael, in Arabic: 'Ismā'īl (إِسْماعِيل). Muslims believe that the Banū Hāshim clan of the Quraysh tribe can trace its origin to Ishmael's mother Hāgar (هاجر), the wife of Abraham. They find proof for this in the Hadiths.

Wāthila ibn al-'Asqa' (واثِلة بن الأَسْقَع) narrated that the Messenger of Allah said: "Indeed Allah has chosen Ishmael from the children of Abraham, and He chose Banū Kināna from the children of Ishmael,

---

6 قَالَ رَسُولُ اللَّهِ: "اخْتَتَنَ إِبْرَاهِيمُ النَّبِيُّ وَهُوَ ابْنُ ثَمَانِينَ سَنَةً بِالْقَدُومِ." ;Sahīh al-Bukhārī 3356
Sahīh Muslim 2370

and He chose the Quraysh from Banū Kināna, and He chose Banū Hāshim from Quraysh, and He chose me from Banū Hāshim."[7]

This is different to the narration of the Jews and is crucial in understand why the Jews in Arabia rejected Muhammad's claim to be a prophet. In Judaism, Abraham is the founding father of the Covenant, the special relationship between the Jewish people and God. Because of that, Jews believe that they are *The Chosen People* of God.

The Jews trace their origin to Jacob through Abraham's other son: <u>Isaac</u>, in Arabic: 'Ishāq (إسحاق), whose mother is <u>Sarah</u>. Jacob, Isaac's son and who later was named Israel, is regarded as a Patriarch of the Israelites.

6. Who were Muhammad's parents?

Answer: His mother was called 'Āmina (آمنة) and his father 'Abd Allah (عَبْد الله).

'Āmina bint Wahb (آمنة بِنْت وَهْب) was the mother of Muhammad. She was married to 'Abd Allah ibn 'Abd al-Muttalib (عَبْد الله بن عَبْد الْمُطَّلِب), a merchant and clay-worker who was neither poor nor rich.

After they got married, her husband 'Abd Allah went out to present day Syria (الشّام) for business – despite the fact that his wife 'Āmina was pregnant. He was absent for several months and also went to Gaza. On his return trip, 'Abd Allah fell sick and died before reaching Mecca.

' Āmina never recovered from this shock and loss. Approximately two months after 'Abd Allah's death, Muhammad was born. 'Āmina died in 577 (47 BH) when Muhammad was six or seven years old.

---

7 قَالَ رَسُولُ اللهِ: "إِنَّ اللَّهَ اصْطَفَى مِنْ وَلَدِ إِبْرَاهِيمَ إِسْمَاعِيلَ وَاصْطَفَى مِنْ وَلَدِ إِسْمَاعِيلَ بَنِي كِنَانَةَ وَاصْطَفَى مِنْ بَنِي كِنَانَةَ قُرَيْشًا وَاصْطَفَى مِنْ قُرَيْشٍ بَنِي هَاشِمٍ وَاصْطَفَانِي مِنْ بَنِي هَاشِمٍ." Jāmi' al-Tirmidhī 3964 (3605); Ṣaḥīḥ Muslim 2276

7. Who took care of the Prophet after his mother's death?

Answer: ʿAbd al-Muttalib (عَبْدُ الْمُطَّلِب), his grandfather.

ʿAbd al-Muttalib was most probably more than seventy years old when he was tasked to raise the orphan Muhammad. In 578 (45 BH) when Muhammad turned eight, just one or two years later, ʿAbd al-Muttalib died.

It is believed that he circumcised the Prophet and gave him the name Muhammad. Ibn Kathīr (ابن كَثِير), a respected Sunni scholar of the 14th century, said: "He used to sit on his cushion and ʿAbd al-Muttalib would not eat any food without saying: 'Bring me my son', and he would be brought to him."[8]

So who took care of Muhammad after the death of his grandfather? It was his paternal uncle ʾAbū Tālib (أَبُو طالِب) and ʾAbū Tālib's wife Fātima bint ʾAsad (فاطِمة بِنت أَسَد) in accordance with the last wishes of ʿAbd al-Muttalib. ʾAbū Tālib and Fātima were the parents of ʿAlī ibn ʾAbī Tālib (عَلِيّ بن أَبِي طالِب) who later became Muhammad's son-in-law and the fourth Caliph of Islam. ʿAlī is the reason for the split between Sunni and Shia Muslims.

Remark: Both - ʿAbd al-Muttalib and ʾAbū Tālib - died as <u>non-Muslims</u>; or, speaking in Islamic terms: as *unbelievers*.

• ʿAbd al-Muttalib, Muhammad's grandfather, died before Islam was founded.
• ʾAbū Tālib, his uncle, died about ten years after Muhammad had started his Islamic mission. Sunni Muslims say that ʾAbū Tālib had refused to embrace Islam. Shia Muslims see it differently, especially as he was the father of ʿAlī. They mostly say that he cared so much for the Prophet that he must have been at least a Muslim in his heart and can therefore be considered a Muslim.

---

8 ...وَكَانَ يَجْلِسُ عَلَى فِرَاشِهِ وَكَانَ عَبْدُ الْمُطَّلِبِ لا يَأْكُلُ طَعَامًا، إلّا قَالَ: عَلَيَّ بِابْنِي، فَيُؤْتَى بِهِ إلَيْهِ.
Ibn Kathīr

8. Who was Muhammad's first wet nurse?

Answer: Thuwayba (ثُوَيْبَة).

Born	in Mecca		Died	628 (7 AH) in Medina

Thuwayba was the first woman who suckled Muhammad after his mother: his first wet (milk) nurse. She was a slave of 'Abū Lahab (أَبُو لَهَب) who set her free. 'Abū Lahab was Muhammad's paternal uncle, but later became one of his fiercest enemies.

Thuwayba also suckled Muhammad's paternal uncle Hamza ibn 'Abd al-Muttalib (حَمْزة بن عَبْد الْمُطَّلِب) who thus became his brother through suckling. Therefore, Hamza was his uncle <u>and</u> his foster-brother. Scholars assume that Hamza was four years older than Muhammad.

Thuwayba became a Muslim and companion when Muhammad proclaimed prophethood. Her name means *deserving of Allah's reward*. After the Prophet had migrated to Medina, he continued to ask about her health and sent her clothes. When he returned from the Battle of Khaybar (غَزْوة خَيْبَر), Thuwayba had passed away.

9. Who was the famous foster mother of the Banū Sa'd tribe who took care of Muhammad?

Answer: Halīma al-Sa'dīya (حَليمة السَّعْدِيّة). Her full name was Halīma bint 'Abī Dhu'ayb (حَليمة بِنْت أَبِي ذُؤَيْب).

Born	unknown		Died	630 (8 AH) in Medina

In the first 14 months of Muhammad's life, Thuwayba (ثُوَيْبَة) took care of him. After that Muhammad's mother 'Āmina (آمنة) sent him into the desert as a baby as it was recommended and demanded by the old Arabian traditions which said that in the desert, one would learn self-discipline, nobility, and become hardened.

During this time Muhammad was nursed by a poor Bedouin woman called Halīma who nursed and breastfed him in the desert of Banū Sa'd (بادية بَني سَعْد) near al-Tā'if (الطّائِف).

Halīma told her husband to take the orphan boy because Muhammad's father, 'Abd Allah, had died before he was born. She is mentioned in several Islamic legends. According to Islamic narrations, immediately after accepting Muhammad, blessing came to her family. Her old camel, which had no longer given a drop of milk, was soon overflowing with milk.

When the usual period of 24 months had passed, Halīma brought Muhammad back to his mother in Mecca. 'Āmina was moved by her love and gave the child back to Halīma. She wanted that Muhammad was raised in the Banū Sa'd desert. It is said that Muhammad returned to Mecca again when he was about five years old. He lived with his real mother 'Āmina only for one more year.

According to another legend, Halīma once returned to Muhammad at Mecca when her family was starving. The Prophet's wife Khadīja (خَدِيجة بِنْت خُوَيْلِد) gave her 40 sheep as gift. Halīma is buried in the al-Baqī'-cemetery (جَنّة البَقِيع) in Medina.

In Islam, a woman who nurses a child (more than five times before the age of two) becomes mother by milk-relation with special rights under Islamic law. The suckled child is considered as a full sibling to the foster-mother's other children and as a Mahram (مَحْرَم) to the woman which in this case means that he cannot marry her. This is different to any other religion.

During the Battle of Hunayn (غَزْوة حُنَيْن) in 630 (8 AH), around 6000 war captives were released merely due to the milk-relation of the Prophet with many of his captives. Among them was an old woman in her sixties. Her name was Shaymāʾ (الشَّيْماء). She claimed that she was the sister of Muhammad; his foster sister, the daughter of Halīma. Muhammad recognised and welcomed her. She told him that when he was young, he had bitten her on the shoulder which became a scar. Shaymāʾ embraced Islam and went back to her tribe.

Later on, a lot of captives were released.

10. What happened to Muhammad in his infancy while he was in the steppe of Banū Saʿd?

Answer: The *"chest incision"*-incident (حَادِثَة شَقّ الصَّدْر).

According to several accounts, a strange and mysterious event happened to Muhammad when he was 4 years old.

ʾAnas ibn Mālik (أَنَس بن مالك) reported that Gabriel came to the Messenger of Allah while he was playing with his friends. He took hold of him and laid him prostrate on the ground, tore open his chest and took out his heart. He removed a blood-clot from it and said: "That was the part of Satan in you."

Then he washed it with the water of Zamzam (زَمْزَم) [a well at the Kaʿba] in a golden basin. Then it was joined together and restored to its place. His playmates ran to his mother, i.e. his nurse, and said that Muhammad had verily been murdered. They all rushed back to him [and found him all right]. "His colour had changed", ʾAnas said. "I myself saw the marks of needles in his chest."[9]

Another narration of the event mentions that Gabriel incised Muhammad's chest, took out his heart and removed a black leech from it. After this event his foster-mother Halīma (حَلِيمَة السَّعْدِيَّة) took the boy back to Mecca and told his mother what happened.

Around fifty years later something similar happened during the *night journey*. These events are called Laila(t) al-ʾIsrāʾ (لَيْلَة الإِسْراء) and al-Miʿrāj (المِعْراج). According to various reports, Muhammad's heart was opened and cleaned which made him capable of accomplishing the night journey to Jerusalem. Sura 17 is named after this event and therefore called *The Night Journey* – in Arabic: al-ʾIsrāʾ (سُورة الإِسْراء):

| 17:1 | Glory to Him who made His servant travel by night from the sacred place of worship (in Mecca: al-Masjid al-Harām) to the furthest place of worship (al-Masjid al-ʾAqsā in Jerusalem), whose surroundings We have blessed, to show | سُبْحَانَ الَّذِي أَسْرَى بِعَبْدِهِ لَيْلًا مِّنَ الْمَسْجِدِ الْحَرَامِ إِلَى الْمَسْجِدِ الْأَقْصَى الَّذِي بَارَكْنَا حَوْلَهُ |

---

9 ...أَنَّ رَسُولَ اللَّهِ أَتَاهُ جِبْرِيلُ وَهُوَ يَلْعَبُ مَعَ الْغِلْمَانِ فَأَخَذَهُ فَصَرَعَهُ فَشَقَّ عَنْ قَلْبِهِ فَاسْتَخْرَجَ الْقَلْبَ فَاسْتَخْرَجَ مِنْهُ عَلَقَةً فَقَالَ هَذَا حَظُّ الشَّيْطَانِ مِنْكَ. ثُمَّ غَسَلَهُ فِي طَسْتٍ مِنْ ذَهَبٍ بِمَاءِ زَمْزَمَ ثُمَّ لَأَمَهُ ثُمَّ أَعَادَهُ فِي مَكَانِهِ وَجَاءَ الْغِلْمَانُ يَسْعَوْنَ إِلَى أُمِّهِ - يَعْنِي ظِئْرَهُ - فَقَالُوا إِنَّ مُحَمَّدًا قَدْ قُتِلَ. فَاسْتَقْبَلُوهُ وَهُوَ مُنْتَقَعُ اللَّوْنِ. قَالَ أَنَسٌ وَقَدْ كُنْتُ أَرَى أَثَرَ ذَلِكَ الْمَخِيطِ فِي صَدْرِهِ. Saḥīḥ Muslim 162.

him some of Our signs: He alone is the All Hearing, the All Seeing.	لِنُرِيَهُ مِنْ آيَاتِنَا إِنَّهُ هُوَ السَّمِيعُ الْبَصِيرُ.

The ’Isrā’ and Miʿrāj are the two parts of a night journey which Muhammad accomplished during a single night around the year 621 (1 BH). The Arabic word ’Isrā’ is derived from the Arabic verb: *to travel by night* (أَسْرَى). The Arabic word Miʿrāj literally means *ladder*.

’Anas ibn Mālik narrated that ’Abū Dharr (أَبُو ذَرّ) heard the Prophet say: "The roof of my house was made open while I was at Mecca [on the night of Miʿrāj] and Gabriel descended. He opened up my chest and washed it with the water of Zamzam. Then he brought the golden tray full of wisdom and belief, and poured it in my chest and then closed it. Then he took hold of my hand and ascended to the nearest heaven. Gabriel told the gatekeeper of the nearest heaven to open the gate."[10]

Islamic scholars assume that it was a physical and spiritual journey. In the ’Isrā’, Muhammad went on al-Burāq (الْبُرَاق), a creature of unknown nature, to Jerusalem. He probably went to the al-’Aqsā mosque (literally, *the farthest mosque*) where he led other prophets in prayer. Then he ascended to heaven in the Miʿrāj journey where he spoke to Allah. According to legends, Allah told him about the amount of daily prayers. Burāq brought Muhammad back to Mecca.

The chest incision is mentioned in the Qur'an, in sura 94 *The Relief* – in Arabic: al-Sharh (سُورَة الشَّرْح):

94:1	Did We not relieve your heart for you [Proph.],	أَلَمْ نَشْرَحْ لَكَ صَدْرَكَ
94:2	and remove the burden	وَوَضَعْنَا عَنكَ وِزْرَكَ

Muslims see in the second opening of the chest (which is mentioned in the Qur'an) a metaphor for the blessings Muhammad had received and which enabled him to achieve all levels of perfection. In some Hadiths, narrators claim that Muhammad's chest was opened several times more, namely at the age of ten and when his mission began – but these Hadiths are weak.

---

10 ...قَالَ: "فُرِجَ سَقْفِي وَأَنَا بِمَكَّةَ، فَنَزَلَ جِبْرِيلُ فَفَرَجَ صَدْرِي، ثُمَّ غَسَلَهُ بِمَاءِ زَمْزَمَ، ثُمَّ جَاءَ بِطَسْتٍ مِنْ ذَهَبٍ مُمْتَلِئٍ حِكْمَةً وَإِيمَانًا، فَأَفْرَغَهَا فِي صَدْرِي، ثُمَّ أَطْبَقَهُ، ثُمَّ أَخَذَ بِيَدِي فَعَرَجَ إِلَى السَّمَاءِ الدُّنْيَا. قَالَ جِبْرِيلُ لِخَازِنِ السَّمَاءِ الدُّنْيَا افْتَحْ." Sahīh al-Bukhārī 1636

11. What was split into two halves during his reign?

Answer: The moon (الْقَمَر).

Muslims find evidence for this event in the Qur'an, sura 54 *The Moon* – in Arabic: al-Qamar (سُورة الْقَمَر). The title of this sura was taken from the first verse:

54:1	The Hour [Day of Judgement] draws near; the moon is split in two.	اقْتَرَبَتِ السَّاعَةُ وَانشَقَّ الْقَمَرُ.

This event is said to be one of the signs of the Day of Judgement or Day of Resurrection – in Arabic: Yawm al-Qiyāmā (يَوْم الْقِيامة). The Qur'an uses the past tense in Arabic. The verb is the first word in the sentence above: iqtarabat (اقْتَرَبَتْ), literally, *something* (i.e. The Hour) *got near/has approached*. The Qur'an occasionally uses the past tense for future events, and particularly so in passages which speak of the coming of the Day of Judgement, the Last Hour. In Arabic, the use of the past tense can stress the certainty of the happening of the event to which the verb refers to.

Traditional commentators assume that this verse in the Qur'an describes an event which really happened at the time of Muhammad and which was witnessed by several people around Muhammad. But in a broader meaning, they also think that it describes the end of the world. Let's have a look at a Hadith which indicates that something must have happened in the starry sky.

'Abd Allah ibn Mas'ūd (عَبْد الله بن مَسْعُود) narrated: "The moon was cleft asunder while we were in the company of the Prophet, and it became two parts." The Prophet said: "Witness, witness [this miracle]!"[11]

Modern scholars like Muhammad Asad (مُحَمَّد أَسَد), who translated the Qur'an in the 20th century, indicate that what had happened was an "unusual kind of partial lunar eclipse, which produced an equally unusual optical illusion". Nevertheless, he sees the cited verse of the Qur'an in a broader sense: "But whatever the nature of that phenomenon, it is practically certain that the Qur'anic verse does not

---

11 ...قَالَ انْشَقَّ الْقَمَرُ وَنَحْنُ مَعَ النَّبِيِّ فَصَارَ فِرْقَتَيْنِ، فَقَالَ لَنَا، "اشْهَدُوا، اشْهَدُوا." -Sahīh al-
Bukhārī 4865

refer to it but, rather, to a future event: namely, to what will happen when the Last Hour approaches."

12. Is Muhammad mentioned in the Bible?

Answer: Some Muslims say yes. This has to do with a verse in the Old Testament.

Muslims are convinced that Christians and Jews have corrupted the Biblical text with falsehoods. Muslims refer to a Bible verse of Moses, Deuteronomy 18:18: "I will raise up for them a Prophet like you from among their brethren, and will put My words in His mouth, and He shall speak to them all that I command Him."

Other Bible translators rendered the verse differently. In the so-called *New International Version*, instead of *brethren*, "from among their fellow Israelites" is used.

Since Muslims and Christians believe that all humans are descend-ants of Adam and Eve, then all of us are brothers and sisters. *Brethren* could include anyone who is a descendant of Abraham. Here comes the crucial point. Abraham had two sons. Muhammad is said to have descended from Ishmael (إشماعيل), while the Jews trace their ancest-ors to the other son, Isaac (إشحاق).

The *brethren* of the children of Israel are - as Muslims therefore claim - obviously the Arabs. Muhammad's tribe belonged to these descendants. Muslims believe that Muhammad was a descendant of Abraham's son Ishmael, so Muhammad can be viewed as a *brother* to the Israelites. Muslims conclude that he is therefore the prophet whom Moses foretold.

However, Jewish and Christian people don't see it that way. They say that the only interpretation for Moses' words is that the prophet, which was mentioned in the verse, must be an Israelite. The Jews say that Muhammad was not an Israelite and thus he could not have ful-filled the conditions Moses had told.

Christians, on the other hand, insist that Jesus is the prophet Moses foretold. Early Christian writers acknowledged that

Muhammad was predicted in the Bible – but as a forthcoming Antichrist, as a false prophet or false Messiah.

The earliest known advocate of this view was John of Damascus in the 7th century. The British historian Albert Hourani says in his monumental work *A History of the Arab Peoples* that initial interactions between Christians and Muslims were pretty hostile on the part of the Europeans because of their interpretation that Muhammad was the Antichrist. In the middle of the 9th century, in Islamic-ruled Andalusia, around fifty Christians were killed in Córdoba after a Christian priest said that Muhammad was one of the "false Christs" prophesied in the Gospels of Matthew.

Ricoldo da Monte di Croce, originally from Florence, was a Dominican father and missionary at the end of the Crusades. From 1288 onwards he travelled to Anatolia and the Middle East and stayed in Akkon, Erzurum and several years in Baghdad. Riccoldo's best known work, written in Baghdad, is *Contra legem Saracenorum* (*Confutatio Alcorani*). The book is a defamatory pamphlet against Islam and became popular among Christians over the centuries – thanks to the German priest Martin Luther, who translated the Bible from Latin into German and set the basis for the protestant church.

Luther had translated Ricoldo's work into German: *Bruder Richards Verlegung des Alkoran*, which was published in 1542. In one passage, Luther calls Muhammad (Mahmet) in his translation "ein Mensch, ja ein Teuffel, und ein erst gebornes Kind des Satans". In English: "A human, in fact a devil, and a first-born child of Satan". Luther's translation was used by many scholars and theologians to criticise Islam and the Qur'an.

A remark on the Biblical name *Deuteronomy*. It is the fifth book of Moses and roughly means *copy of the law*. This book was given to the Israelites; it was Moses' farewell address to them. A large part of it was a review of the laws between God and the Israelites and its reading was to prepare them to enter into the Promised Land.

13. Which of Muhammad's paternal uncles embraced Islam?

Answer: Two – Hamza (حَمْزة) and al-'Abbās (الْعَبّاس).

Let's have a look at these two important figures and start with Hamza ibn 'Abd al-Muttalib (حَمْزة بن عَبْد الْمُطَّلِب):

Born	~ 568 (54 BH) in Mecca	Died	625 (3 AH) in the mountains of 'Uhud

Hamza was a paternal uncle and companion of the Prophet. He was skilled in wrestling, archery, and swordsmanship. Reports also indicate that he liked hunting. Therefore various Islamic sources describe him as "the strongest man of the Quraysh and the most unyielding."[12] He died in the Battle of 'Uhud (غَزْوة أُحُد).

In classical Arabic, the meaning of the root h-m-z (ز-م-ح) is *to bite* or *to burn the tongue* (taste), i.e. a beverage *stung* or *bit the tongue* or *burned it by its strength and sharpness*. Hamza may also denote a special type of herb. It could mean *sourness in milk*. However, used with the Arabic definite article *al-*, the word al-Hamza (الْحَمْزة) normally denotes *the lion* (الْأَسَد).

Watch out: Do not confuse Hamza spelled with a ح with Hamza spelled with a ه because that is the term for the Arabic letter Hamza (هَمْزة). Both words are usually transliterated in the same way.

Let's continue now with the other uncle: al-'Abbās ibn 'Abd al-Muttalib (الْعَبّاس بن عَبْد الْمُطَّلِب):

Born	~ 567 (56 BH) in Mecca	Died	~ 653 (32 AH)

Like his brother Hamza, al-'Abbās too was a paternal uncle and a companion of Muhammad. Al-'Abbās was only three years older than his nephew Muhammad. After his father's death, al-'Abbās took over the Zamzam well (زَمْزَم) in Mecca and distributed water to the pilgrims. He became a spice-merchant in Mecca and was well off.

He protected his nephew Muhammad while he was in Mecca. However, he did that probably only because of his kinship. Some scholars claim that al-'Abbās did not follow his nephew's teachings

---

12 ...وَكَانَ أَعَزَّ فَتًى فِي قُرَيْشٍ وَأَشَدَّ شَكِيمَةً. Ibn Hishām

on Islam, at least not in the beginning. The fact that al-'Abbās fought on the side of the non-Muslims in the Battle of Badr (غَزْوَة بَدْر) suggests so. Al-'Abbās was captured in this battle by the al-'Ansār. Muhammad allowed al-'Abbās to ransom himself. 'Anas ibn Mālik (أَنَس بن مالِك) narrated: "Some men of the 'Ansār asked for the permission of Allah's Messenger and said: 'Allow us to not take the ransom of our nephew.' The Prophet answered: 'Do not leave [even] a dirham [of his ransom].'[13]

Some sources indicate that al-'Abbās became Muslim after the Battle of Badr in 624 (2 AH). This contradicts the view of other scholars who say that he did not formally profess Islam until January 630 (8 AH), just before the fall of Mecca.

Whatever the correct view is – al-'Abbās joined Muhammad's army in some of the most important battles of Islam, which were all fought in the year 630 (8 AH): Conquest of Mecca (فَتْح مَكّة), Battle of Hunayn (غَزْوَة حُنَيْن) and the Siege of al-Tā'if (غَزْوَة الطّائِف). It is said that he defended the Prophet at Hunayn when other warriors had abandoned him. Al-'Abbās had at least five wives. The Abbasid dynasty (الْخِلافَة الْعَبّاسِيّة) founded in 750 (132 AH) claimed the title of Caliph through their descent from al-'Abbās's son, 'Abd Allah.

14. About which of the Prophet's uncles exists an entire sura?

Answer: 'Abū Lahab (أَبُو لَهَب); real name: 'Abd al-'Uzzā (عَبْد الْعُزَّى).

'Abū Lahab was Muhammad's paternal uncle. 'Abū Lahab literally means: *father of a flame* or *flame man*. He got this name probably due to his red inflamed cheeks. The word لَهَب is also used to denote *shiny face*. 'Abū Lahab grew up in Mecca. When Muhammad was born, he sent his maid Thuwayba (ثُوَيْبَة) to suckle the child. However, the relationship changed dramatically when Muhammad started his mission as a prophet of Islam.

Muhammad Asad wrote in his commentary on the Qur'an that the "hostility (was) rooted in his ['Abū Lahab's] inborn arrogance, pride

---

13 ...أَنَّ رِجَالاً، مِنَ الأَنْصَارِ اسْتَأْذَنُوا رَسُولَ اللّهِ فَقَالُوا ائْذَنْ فَلْنَتْرُكْ لِابْنِ أُخْتِنَا عَبّاسٍ فِدَاءَهُ، فَقَالَ: "لا تَدَعُونَ مِنْهُ دِرْهَمًا." Saḥīḥ al-Bukhārī 2537

in his great wealth, and a dislike of the idea, propounded by Muhammad, that all human beings are equal before God and will be judged by Him on their merits alone."

'Abū Lahab and his wife 'Arwā bint Harb (أَرْوَى بِنْت حَرْب) opposed him fiercely. According to Islamic sources, it was known that she tied bunches of thorns with ropes of twisted palm fibre and threw them in Muhammad's way. She was the sister of another early enemy of Muhammad, 'Abū Sufyān (أَبُو سُفْيان), who later became Muslim.

'Abū Lahab is the only person from the enemies of Islam who has been cursed by name in the Qur'an. He and his wife are condemned in sura 111 *Palm Fibre* – in Arabic: al-Masad (سُورة الْمَسَد). This is one of the earliest suras. It was number six in the order of revelation and got its name from the last (Arabic) word of the sura. The whole sura deals with the hostility between Muhammad and his uncle.

Let's have a look:

111:1	May the hands of 'Abū Lahab be ruined! May he be ruined too!	تَبَّتْ يَدَا أَبِي لَهَبٍ وَتَبَّ
111:2	Neither his wealth nor his gains will help him:	مَا أَغْنَىٰ عَنْهُ مَالُهُ وَمَا كَسَبَ
111:3	he will burn in the Flaming Fire	سَيَصْلَىٰ نَارًا ذَاتَ لَهَبٍ
111:4	and so will his wife, the firewood-carrier,	وَامْرَأَتُهُ حَمَّالَةَ الْحَطَبِ
111:5	with a palm-fibre rope around her neck.	فِي جِيدِهَا حَبْلٌ مِّن مَّسَدٍ
Remark: The sura contains a kind of wordplay: In verse 1 you have the name 'Abū *Lahab* and in verse 3, *lahab* (لَهَب) denotes *Blazing Flames*.		

More details on the hostility between the two men and the emergence of the sura are found in the Hadiths. Muhammad went up the hill called al-Safā (الصَّفا) and called together all who could hear him from among his tribe, the Quraysh.

'Abd Allah ibn 'Abbās (عَبْد الله بن عَبّاس) narrated that one day the Prophet ascended Safā mountain and said: "Be on your guard!" All the Quraysh gathered round him and asked: "What is the matter?" He said: "Look, if I told you that an enemy is going to attack you in the morning or in the evening, would you not believe me?" They said: "Yes, we will believe you." He said: "I am warning you in face of a terrible punishment." On that 'Abū Lahab said: "May you perish ! Is it for this thing that you have gathered us?" So Allah revealed (in sura 111): "Perish the hands of 'Abū Lahab!"[14]

'Abū Lahab did not participate in the Battle of Badr (غَزْوة بَدْر) in 624 (2 AH), the first large-scale encounter between Muslims and their enemies from Mecca. When the news reached him that the Muslims won, he fell ill and developed the contagious disease of smallpox. He died a week later in 624 (2 AH).

Ibn 'Ishāq told: "They did not bury 'Abū Lahab, but he was put against a wall and stones were thrown upon him from behind the wall until he was covered. It is said that when 'Ā'isha [Muhammad's wife] passed the place, she used to veil her face."

According to some reports, after 'Abū Lahab's death, some of his relatives had a dream in which they saw him suffering in Hell. 'Umm Habība (أُمّ حَبِيبة) narrated: "When 'Abū Lahab died, one of his relatives saw him in a dream in a very bad state and asked him: 'What have you encountered?' 'Abū Lahab said: 'I have not found any rest since I left you, except that I have been given water to drink in this [the space between his thumb and other fingers] and that is because of manumitting [i.e. the release from slavery] Thuwayba.'"[15]

Remark: There were five fierce enemies at the beginning of Islam:

1. **'Amr ibn Hishām** (عَمْرو بن هِشام) better known by Muslims as 'Abū Jahl (أَبُو جَهْل), the flag-bearer of opposition towards Islam. He belonged to the Banū Makhzūm (بَنُو مَخْزُوم) of the Quraysh, one of the wealthy clans.

2. **'Abd al-'Uzza** (عَبْد الْعُزَّى بن عَبْد الْمُطَّلِب) better known by Muslims as 'Abū Lahab (أَبُو لَهَب), Muhammad's paternal uncle.

14... قَالَ صَعِدَ النَّبِيُّ الصَّفَا ذَاتَ يَوْمٍ فَقَالَ: "يَا صَبَاحَاهْ!" فَاجْتَمَعَتْ إِلَيْهِ قُرَيْشٌ قَالُوا مَا لَكَ قَالَ: "أَرَأَيْتُمْ لَوْ أَخْبَرْتُكُمْ أَنَّ الْعَدُوَّ يُصَبِّحُكُمْ أَوْ يُمَسِّيكُمْ أَمَا كُنْتُمْ تُصَدِّقُونِي." قَالُوا بَلَى. قَالَ: "فَإِنِّي نَذِيرٌ لَكُمْ بَيْنَ يَدَيْ عَذَابٍ شَدِيدٍ." فَقَالَ أَبُو لَهَبٍ تَبًّا لَكَ أَلِهَذَا جَمَعْتَنَا؟ فَأَنْزَلَ اللَّهُ {تَبَّتْ يَدَا أَبِي لَهَبٍ}.

Sahīh al-Bukhārī 4770

15... فَلَمَّا مَاتَ أَبُو لَهَبٍ أُرِيَهُ بَعْضُ أَهْلِهِ بِشَرِّ حِيبَةٍ قَالَ لَهُ مَاذَا لَقِيتَ قَالَ أَبُو لَهَبٍ لَمْ أَلْقَ بَعْدَكُمْ غَيْرَ أَنِّي سُقِيتُ فِي هَذِهِ بِعَتَاقَتِي ثُوَيْبَةَ.

Sahīh al-Bukhārī 5101

3. **Sakhr ibn Harb** (صَخْر بن حَرْب) better known by Muslims as 'Abū Sufyān (أَبُو سُفْيان), the leader of the Quraysh of Mecca. His mother was the paternal aunt of Muhammad's wife Maymūna.

4. **Hind bint ʿUtba** (هِنْد بِنْت عُتْبة), the wife of 'Abū Sufyān.

5. **Wahshī ibn Harb** (وَحْشِيّ بن حَرْب), an Ethiopian slave.

Later some of them became famous Muslims, some not. We will get to know them better in the following chapters.

15. What did Muhammad do with his right hand?

Answer: "Good" things only.

The right hand is the "good" hand in Islam. *Right hand* means everything that has to do with honour and nobility, for example: eating and drinking, using the tooth brush (Siwāk), shaking hands, shaving the head, touching the Black Stone, clipping nails, trimming the moustache, combing hair, and plucking the armpit hair.

ʿĀʾisha (عائشة بِنْت أبِي بَكْر) reported: "The Messenger of Allah loved to start from the right-hand side for performing ablution, for combing [hair] and putting on his shoes."[16]

Salama ibn-'Akwaʿ (سَلَمة بن الأَكْوَع) reported on the authority of his father that once in the presence of Allah's Messenger, a person ate with his left hand, whereupon he said: "Eat with your right hand!" The man said: "I cannot do that", whereupon the Prophet said: "May you never be able to do that!" It was vanity that prevented him from doing it and he could not raise it [the right hand] up to his mouth afterwards."[17]

In general, there is the *right-is-better*-rule in Islam. Muslims, for example, should enter a mosque or exit a toilet with their right foot.

---

16 ...قَالَتْ إِنْ كَانَ رَسُولُ اللَّهِ لَيُحِبُّ التَّيَمُّنَ فِي طُهُورِهِ إِذَا تَطَهَّرَ وَفِي تَرَجُّلِهِ إِذَا تَرَجَّلَ وَفِي انْتِعَالِهِ إِذَا انْتَعَلَ. Sahīh Muslim 268.

17 ...أَنَّ رَجُلاً أَكَلَ عِنْدَ رَسُولِ اللَّهِ بِشِمَالِهِ فَقَالَ: "كُلْ بِيَمِينِكَ!" قَالَ لاَ أَسْتَطِيعُ. قَالَ: "لاَ اسْتَطَعْتَ!" مَا مَنَعَهُ إلاَّ الْكِبْرُ. قَالَ فَمَا رَفَعَهَا إلَى فِيه. Sahīh Muslim 2021.

’Abū Hurayra (أَبُو هُرَيْرة) narrated that the Messenger of Allah said: "When one of you dons sandals, then let him begin with the right. And when he removes them then let him begin with left, so that the right will be the first to put on and the last of them removed."[18]

And what about the left hand?

The left hand is used by Muslims for things that are considered dirty. Muslims in the Arab world pay great attention with which hand you are eating, especially when you are invited to somebody's home. This happened to me a lot. When I started to grab some food from the table, all eyes had been upon my hands.

According to the Prophet, the Devil eats with his left hand. ‘Abd Allah ibn ‘Umar (عَبْد الله بن عُمَر) reported that Allah's Messenger said: "When any one of you intends to eat, he should eat with his right hand. And when he intends to drink, he should drink with his right hand, for the Satan eats and drinks with his left hand."[19]

Islam is regulating a Muslim's life in detail. There are even plenty of rules for going to the toilet. ’Abū Qatāda (أَبُو قَتادة) reported from his father that the Messenger of Allah said: "None of you should hold his penis with his right hand while urinating, or wipe himself with his right hand in privy and should not breathe into the vessel (from which he drinks)."[20]

16. Who was Muhammad's first wife?

Answer: Khadīja bint Khuwaylid (خَدِيجة بِنْت خُوَيْلِد).

Born	~ 556 (68 BH) in Mecca	Died	620 (3 BH) in Mecca

---

18 ... أَنَّ رَسُولَ اللَّهِ قَالَ: "إِذَا انْتَعَلَ أَحَدُكُمْ فَلْيَبْدَأْ بِالْيَمِينِ وَإِذَا نَزَعَ فَلْيَبْدَأْ بِالشِّمَالِ فَلْتَكُنِ الْيُمْنَى أَوَّلَهُمَا تُنْعَلُ وَآخِرَهُمَا تُنْزَعُ." Jāmiʿ al-Tirmidhī 1779

19 قَالَ: "إِذَا أَكَلَ أَحَدُكُمْ فَلْيَأْكُلْ بِيَمِينِهِ وَإِذَا شَرِبَ فَلْيَشْرَبْ بِيَمِينِهِ فَإِنَّ الشَّيْطَانَ يَأْكُلُ بِشِمَالِهِ وَيَشْرَبُ بِشِمَالِهِ." Sahīh Muslim 2020

20 قَالَ رَسُولُ اللَّهِ: "لاَ يُمْسِكَنَّ أَحَدُكُمْ ذَكَرَهُ بِيَمِينِهِ وَهُوَ يَبُولُ وَلاَ يَتَمَسَّحْ مِنَ الْخَلاَءِ بِيَمِينِهِ وَلاَ يَتَنَفَّسْ فِي الإِنَاءِ." Sahīh Muslim 267

Khadīja was a successful merchant. It is said that when the Quraysh trade caravans gathered for their summer journey to Syria or for their winter journey to Yemen, Khadīja's caravan alone was as big as all the others put together. Khadīja wanted to hire Muhammad to work for her and to trade on her behalf, which he did; and he did well.

Khadīja married three times and had children from all her marriages. Her first two marriages left her as a widow. Khadīja entrusted a (female) friend called Nafīsa (نَفِيسة بِنْت مُنَيّة) to approach Muhammad and ask if he would consider marrying her. Muhammad was hesitant because he didn't have the money to support a wife. Nafīsa asked if he would consider marriage to a woman who had the means to provide for herself.

Muhammad agreed to meet with Khadīja and after that, they both consulted their uncles. The uncles agreed to the marriage and Muhammad's uncles accompanied him to make a formal proposal to Khadīja. It is disputed whether it was only Hamza ibn 'Abd al-Muttalib (حَمْزة بن عَبْد الْمُطَّلِب) or only 'Abū Tālib (أَبُو طالِب) or perhaps even both who accompanied Muhammad. Khadīja's uncle accepted the proposal too – so they got married.

Some Islamic sources and historians say that she was 15 years older than Muhammad. She might have been 40 years old when she married Muhammad who himself was 25.

However, her age is a debate. Could a wife of that age have been capable of giving birth to six children over a period of ten years?
- Some Muslims believe that this was a wonder of Allah.
- Some historians say that she was much younger. They claim that Khadīja was only 3 years older when she married Muhammad, hence she was 28. But there is no reliable source for this.

Khadīja was the first person to accept Islam – which means that she accepted Allah as the One and only God and Muhammad as his messenger. Therefore, she was also the first female convert and is commonly regarded by Muslims as the *Mother of the Believers* (أُمّ الْمُؤمِنِين). Note that this term is applied to all wives of Muhammad.

Muhammad and Khadīja were married monogamously for twenty-five years. ʿĀʾisha (عائشة بِنْت أَبي بَكْر) said: "The Prophet did not marry any other woman until her [Khadīja's] death."[21]

This monogamous marriage contrasts with Muhammad's later practice of polygyny after Khadīja's death. Muhammad's youngest wife, ʿĀʾisha, was said to be very jealous of the affection and loyalty that Muhammad maintained for Khadīja even after her death. ʿĀʾisha said: "I was not jealous of any wife of the Prophet as I was jealous of Khadīja, and it was not because I saw her. It was only because the Messenger of Allah mentioned her so much, and because whenever he would slaughter a sheep, he would look for Khadīja's friends to gift them some of it."[22]

Muhammad and Khadīja had probably six children. Sources disagree about the exact number. Al-Tabarī (الطَّبَري), an Islamic historian from the 9th century, mentioned 8. However, most sources only identify 6:

1. Their first son was al-Qāsim (الْقاسِم بن مُحَمَّد) who died before his second birthday. That is why Muhammad's epithet - in Arabic called Kunya (كُنْية) - is ʾAbū al-Qāsim (أَبُو الْقاسِم) which literally means: *Father of al-Qāsim.*

Then, Khadīja gave birth to their daughters:

2. Zaynab (زَيْنَب بِنْت مُحَمَّد)

3. Ruqayya (رُقَيّة بِنْت مُحَمَّد)

4. ʾUmm Kulthūm (أُمّ كُلْثُوم بِنْت مُحَمَّد) and

5. Fātima (فاطِمة بِنْت مُحَمَّد)

and to their son:

6. ʿAbd Allah (عَبْد الله بن مُحَمَّد). He was known as al-Tayyib (الطَّيِّب) - literally, *the Good* - and as al-Tāhir (الطّاهِر) - literally, *the Pure* - because he was born after Muhammad had declared himself a prophet. ʿAbd Allah also died in childhood.

---

21 ...قَالَتْ لَم يَتَزَوَّج النَّبِيُّ عَلَى خَدِيجَةَ حَتَّى مَاتَتْ. Sahīh Muslim 2436.

22 ...قَالَتْ مَا غِرْتُ عَلَى أَحَدٍ مِنْ أَزْوَاج النَّبِيّ مَا غِرْتُ عَلَى خَدِيجَةَ وَمَا بِي أَنْ أَكُونَ أَدْرَكْتُهَا وَمَا ذَاكَ إِلَّا لِكَثْرَة ذِكْرِ رَسُولِ اللَّه لَهَا وَإِنْ كَانَ لَيَذْبَحُ الشَّاةَ فَيَتَتَبَّعُ بِهَا صَدائِقَ خَدِيجَةَ فَيُهْدِيهَا لَهُنَّ. -al-Tirmidhī 4249

17. What is meant by "the year of sorrow"?

Answer: The year 619 (3 BH); two important people in Muhammad's life died in this year.

First, his wife Khadīja (خَدِيجة بِنْت خُوَيْلِد) died in the month of Ramadan in 619 (3 BH). Thus, the Prophet lost his beloved wife and friend, the first person to accept Islam. Khadīja is said to have been about sixty-five years old when she died. She was buried in Mecca, in the cemetery called (in Arabic) Janna(t) al-Muʻallā (جَنّة الْمُعَلّى), where also Muhammad's grandfather and other ancestors were buried.

Soon after his wife's death, Muhammad's uncle and protector, ʼAbū Ṭālib (أَبُو طالِب), died too. ʼAbū Ṭālib had been one of the most respected men in Mecca because he was one of the Quraysh elders. Even though he had never (officially) converted to Islam, he had protected Muhammad. According to Arab customs anyone, who was under the protection of another, was safe as long as his protector lived. With the death of his uncle, Muhammad's protection was gone.

Muhammad later called this year the *year of sorrow*, in Arabic: ʻĀm al-Huzn (عام الْحُزْن).

18. Why was Muhammad called ʼAbū al-Qāsim?

Answer: Because of his first son whose name was al-Qāsim (الْقاسِم). ʼAbū al-Qāsim (أَبُو الْقاسِم) is Muhammad's Kunya (كُنْية) - his epithet -, which literally means *father of al-Qāsim*.

There is only little information about his son and first child. Most scholars say that al-Qāsim was born in 603 although this is vague. The boy died either 17 months or 2 years later – just when he had started to walk.

Jābir ibn ʻAbd Allah (جابِر بن عَبْد الله) narrated that the Prophet said: "Give the name after my name, but do not give my Kunya [ʼAbū al-Qāsim], for I am ʼAbū al-Qāsim [in the sense] that I distribute among you [the spoils of war] and disseminate the knowledge [revelation]."[23]

---

23 قَالَ رَسُولُ اللَّهِ: "تَسَمَّوْا بِاسْمِي وَلاَ تَكَنَّوْا بِكُنْيَتِي فَإِنِّي أَنَا أَبُو الْقَاسِمِ أَقْسِمُ بَيْنَكُمْ." Sahih
Muslim 2133

This means: Muslims are <u>not allowed</u> to give their child the name *'Abū al-Qāsim*. However, as seen in the Hadith above, there is nothing wrong with naming a child after Muhammad.

19. How many daughters did the Prophet have?

Answer: Four.

His two sons never witnessed to see adulthood and died as infants. So let's have a look at his daughters and start with the Sunni view.

They say that Muhammad had four daughters: Zaynab (زَيْنَب), Ruqayya (رُقَيّة), 'Umm Kulthūm (أُمّ كُلْثُوم), and Fātima (فاطِمة). All of them were daughters of Muhammad's first wife, Khadīja (خَديجة).

However, Sunni and Shia disagree about the number of daughters which the Prophet had. While most Sunnis accept that he had fathered four daughters with Khadīja, most Shia Muslims accept only Fātima as his daughter.

Why is that? Some Shia Muslims believe that the other three women were already living in the house of Khadīja prior to her marriage with Muhammad. The Sunni belief that he had other daughters with Khadīja denies 'Alī ibn 'Abī Tālib (عليّ بن أَبي طالب) the distinction of being Muhammad's only son-in-law.

20. Who was the only virgin Muhammad married?

Answer: 'Ā'isha bint 'Abī Bakr (عائشة بِنْت أَبي بَكْر). She was probably six years old when he married her and was nine when he consummated the marriage. All his other wives had been previously married.

After the death of his first wife Khadīja (خَديجة), Muhammad married Sawda bint Zam'a (سَوْدة بِنْت زَمْعة). Reports claim that she was an older woman and not very beautiful.

Four years later, Muhammad married the child 'Ā'isha. He was over fifty years old at that time. 'Ā'isha was the daughter of 'Abū Bakr (أَبو بَكْر), one of the most entrusted companions of Muhammad. Critics say that it was a "political marriage" which should seal the bond between the Prophet and the family of Abu Bakr.

'Urwa ibn al-Zubayr (عُرْوة بن الزُّبَيْر) narrated that the Prophet asked 'Abū Bakr for 'Ā'isha's hand in marriage. 'Abū Bakr said: "But I am your brother." The Prophet said: "You are my brother in Allah's religion and His Book, but she ['Ā'isha] is lawful for me to marry."[24]

The age difference and especially the fact that 'Ā'isha was a child and not yet a woman is disturbing, and Muslims find it difficult to accept and defend. The information about her age is recorded in several authentic Hadiths – most of them were reported by 'Ā'isha herself. According to her reports, the Prophet married her when she was six years old and he consummated the marriage when she was nine years of age, and then she remained with him for nine years [i.e. until his death].[25]

In some Hadiths, it is mentioned that she took her dolls with her for the marriage.[26] Most commentators say that the word *doll* here signifies 'Ā'isha's very young age.

About the day she got married, 'Ā'isha herself reported: "The Prophet married me when I was a girl of six years. We went to Medina and stayed at the place of Banū al-Hārith ibn Khazraj. Then I became ill and my hair fell down. Later on my hair grew (again) and my mother, 'Umm Rūmān, came to me while I was playing in a swing with some of my girl friends. She called me and I went to her, not knowing what she wanted to do to me. She caught me by the hand and made me stand at the door of the house. I was breathless then, and when my breathing became all right, she took some water and rubbed my face and head with it. Then she took me into the house. There in the house, I saw some women [from the 'Ansār] who said: 'Best wishes, Allah's blessing and good luck.' Then she entrusted me to them and they prepared me. Unexpectedly Allah's Apostle

---

24 ...أَنَّ النَّبِيَّ خَطَبَ عَائِشَةَ إِلَى أَبِي بَكْرٍ فَقَالَ لَهُ أَبُو بَكْرٍ إِنَّمَا أَنَا أَخُوكَ، فَقَالَ: "أَنْتَ أَخِي فِي دِينِ اللَّهِ وَكِتَابِهِ وَهْىَ لِي حَلَالٌ." Sahīh al-Bukhārī 5081

25 ...أَنَّ النَّبِيَّ تَزَوَّجَهَا وَهْىَ بِنْتُ سِتِّ سِنِينَ، وَأُدْخِلَتْ عَلَيْهِ وَهْىَ بِنْتُ تِسْعٍ، وَمَكَثَتْ عِنْدَهُ تِسْعًا. Sahīh al-Bukhārī 5133

26 وَلُعَبُهَا مَعَهَا. Sahīh Muslim 1422

came to me in the forenoon and my mother handed me over to him, and at that time I was a girl of nine years of age."[27]

So what were Muhammad's reasons to marry a child and how do Muslims defend the Prophet for doing this?

- Muslims believe that Muhammad saw a dream about marrying 'Ā'isha. She herself narrated that the Prophet told her: "You have been shown to me twice in my dream. I saw you pictured on a piece of silk and someone said [to me]. 'This is your wife.' When I uncovered the picture, I saw that it was yours. I said: 'If this is from Allah, it will be done.'"[28]

- Another reason is related to the fact that 'Ā'isha was the daughter of 'Abū Bakr who was said to be the most faithful follower of Muhammad.

However, both justifications don't really help that the Prophet had married a child. Let's have a look at Muhammad's other wives – which brings us to another point:

- Muhammad's spouses, at least a dozen, were a mixture of all kinds of types and ages: young, old, the daughter of a friend, the daughter of an enemy, a Jewish woman, a widow, etc. Muslims see this as an example of Muhammad showing the world how to deal with all kinds of people.

Finally, there is the biological hypothesis:

- Some Muslims try to prove that 'Ā'isha had already reached puberty at the age of nine. In hot climates, they say, girls can

---

27 ...قَالَتْ تَزَوَّجَنِي النَّبِيُّ وَأَنَا بِنْتُ سِتِّ سِنِينَ، فَقَدِمْنَا الْمَدِينَةَ فَنَزَلْنَا فِي بَنِي الْحَارِثِ بْنِ خَزْرَجٍ، فَوُعِكْتُ فَتَمَرَّقَ شَعَرِي فَوَفَى جُمَيْمَةً، فَأَتَتْنِي أُمِّي أُمُّ رُومَانَ وَإِنِّي لَفِي أُرْجُوحَةٍ وَمَعِي صَوَاحِبُ لِي، فَصَرَخَتْ بِي فَأَتَيْتُهَا لاَ أَدْرِي مَا تُرِيدُ بِي فَأَخَذَتْ بِيَدِي حَتَّى أُوقَفَتْنِي عَلَى بَابِ الدَّارِ، وَإِنِّي لأَنْهَجُ، حَتَّى سَكَنَ بَعْضُ نَفَسِي، ثُمَّ أَخَذَتْ شَيْئًا مِنْ مَاءٍ فَمَسَحَتْ بِهِ وَجْهِي وَرَأْسِي ثُمَّ أَدْخَلَتْنِي الدَّارَ فَإِذَا نِسْوَةٌ مِنَ الأَنْصَارِ فِي الْبَيْتِ فَقُلْنَ عَلَى الْخَيْرِ وَالْبَرَكَةِ، وَعَلَى خَيْرِ طَائِرٍ، فَأَسْلَمَتْنِي إِلَيْهِنَّ فَأَصْلَحْنَ مِنْ شَأْنِي، فَلَمْ يَرُعْنِي إِلاَّ رَسُولُ اللَّهِ ضُحًى، فَأَسْلَمَتْنِي إِلَيْهِ، وَأَنَا يَوْمَئِذٍ بِنْتُ تِسْعِ سِنِينَ. ‑Sahīh al-Bukhārī 3894

28 ...أَنَّ النَّبِيَّ قَالَ لَهَا: "أُرِيتُكِ فِي الْمَنَامِ مَرَّتَيْنِ، أَرَى أَنَّكِ فِي سَرَقَةٍ مِنْ حَرِيرٍ وَيَقُولُ هَذِهِ امْرَأَتُكَ فَاكْشِفْ عَنْهَا فَإِذَا هِيَ أَنْتِ فَأَقُولُ إِنْ يَكُ هَذَا مِنْ عِنْدِ اللَّهِ يُمْضِهِ." Sahīh al-Bukhārī 3895

reach puberty much earlier. Others say that she might have been an exception and might have reached puberty earlier than other girls. However, this doesn't really refute the accusation by non-Muslims that 'Ā'isha - at the age of nine - was too young for sex.

In fact, the debate is going nowhere. It is eventually simply a matter of faith when a Muslim is convinced that all actions done by the Prophet were righteous and correct.

However, the disturbing element about this episode of Muhammad is the sad reality that some Muslims justify having sex with children by the actions of the Prophet. While I was in Egypt, there were reports in the media that rich Saudi men came with suitcases full of money to literally buy under-aged virgin girls from poor families in the Nile delta – in order to marry and have sex with them. Just like the Prophet did, they claimed.

21. How many women did Muhammad marry in total?

Answer: At least twelve.

It is not entirely clear how many wives Muhammad had during his lifetime. Muslims call every wife of Muhammad *mother of the believers* – so-called: 'Umm al-Mu'minīn(أُمّ الْمُؤْمِنِين). Only two of his wives bore his children: Khadīja and Maria.

Note that there is not a lot of information available about the age of his wives and the time of marriage. The following numbers as well as the sequence are just rough estimates.

	Name	Year of death (wife)	Prophet's age at marriage	Wife's age at marriage	Year of marriage	Arabic name
1	Khadīja bint Khuwaylid	3 BH	~ 25	~ 40	28 BH	خَدِيجة بِنْت خُوَيْلِد
	Children: al-Qāsim (الْقَاسِم), 'Abd Allah (عَبْد الله), Zaynab (زَيْنَب), Ruqay-ya (رُقَيّة), 'Umm Kulthūm (أُمّ كُلْثُوم), Fātima (فاطِمة)					
2	Sawada bint Zam'a	54 AH	~ 49	~ 40	3 BH	سَوْدة بِنْت زَمْعة

3	ʿĀʾisha bint ʾAbī Bakr	56 AH	~ 52	6	2 BH	عائِشة بِنْت أَبِي بَكْر
4	Hafsa bint ʿUmar al-Khattāb	45 AH	~ 53	~ 19	2/3 AH	حَفْصة بِنْت عُمَر بن الخَطّاب
5	Zaynab bint Khuzayma	4 AH	~ 53	~ 28	3/4 AH	زَيْنَب بِنْت خُزَيْمة
6	ʾUmm Salama	58 AH	~ 55	~ 28	4 AH	أُمّ سَلَمة
7	Zaynab bint Jahsh	20 AH	~ 55	~ 37	4/5 AH	زَيْنَب بِنْت جَحْش
8	Juwayrīya bint al-Hārith	50 AH	~ 56	~ 20	5/6 AH	جُوَيْرِيّة بِنْت الحارِث
9	Maria al-Qibtīya	16 AH	~ 57	?	7 AH	مارية القِبْطِيّة
	Child: ʾIbrāhīm (إِبْراهِيم)					
10	ʾUmm Habība	44 AH	~ 57	~ 34	7 AH	أُمّ حَبِيبة
11	Safiya bint Huyayy	50 AH	~ 57	~ 16	7 AH	صَفِيّة بِنْت حُيَيّ
12	Maymūna bint al-Hārith	51 AH	~ 57	~ 35	7 AH	مَيْمُونة بِنْت الحارِث

Some remarks:

- The wives mentioned above were women with whom Muhammad consummated marriage. Two of them died during his lifetime: Khadīja and Zaynab bint Khuzayma. When the Prophet died, he left at least nine or ten wives behind.
- Safiya was of Jewish origin.
- ʿĀʾisha was six years old when Muhammad married her. But according to a Hadith which was narrated by ʿĀʾisha herself, Muhammad consummated the marriage when she was nine.

- Maria was a Coptic slave, born in Upper (southern) Egypt of a Coptic father and a Greek mother. The scholars differ whether she was a wife of the Prophet or just a concubine. However, she bore him a son, 'Ibrāhīm, who died at a very young age and is buried in the graveyard al-Baqīa' (الْبَقِيع).

Although Muslims would not see it in this way, Islam critics regard some of Muhammad's marriages as strategic decisions. They compare it to royal intermarriages which are known throughout history to enlarge, tighten or secure the empire.

It is true that some marriages indeed had a strategic impact, as Muhammad was now related to several clans and tribes. These clans were all of a sudden family to Muhammad and most considered themselves his allies.

For example, after the Battle of Khaybar, which was a Jewish stronghold, the Prophet married Safiya. The Prophet gave her a choice: She could remain a Jew and return to her people which were deprived of most of their wealth, power and rights, or she could marry him and become a Muslim – which she finally did.

22. Who was Muhammad's last wife?

Answer: Maymūna bint al-Hārith (مَيْمُونة بِنْت الْحارِث الْهِلالِيّة).

Born	594 (20 BH) in Mecca	Died	~ 680 (61 AH) or ~ 673 (51 AH) in Mecca

Maymūna married Muhammad in 629 (7 AH) in a village about ten miles away from Mecca, just after he had done the lesser pilgrimage – the so-called 'Umra al-Qadā' (عُمْرة الْقَضاء).

He was around 57 years old and she was probably in her early thirties. Maymūna lived with Muhammad for three years until his death in 632 (11 AH). Maymūna's name was originally Barra (بَرّة) which means *obedience* according to Edward Lane's dictionary. Muhammad, however, changed it to Maymūna which means: *lucky, fortunate.*

23. Muhammad married the daughter of which enemy?

Answer: Sakhr ibn Harb (صَخْر بن حَرْب), who is better known as 'Abū Sufyān (أَبُو سُفْيان).

Born	560 (63 BH) in Mecca	Died	between 652 (30 AH) and 656 (34 AH) in Medina

'Abū Sufyān was the leader of the Quraysh, the most powerful tribe of pre-Islamic Arabia in Mecca. He was a severe opponent of Muhammad at the beginning of the Prophet's mission.

The conflict between the two men escalated in 624 (2 AH). 'Abū Sufyān was leading a huge caravan carrying a fortune of the Quraysh's goods to Syria for trade. Forty to fifty soldiers guarded the caravan. Muhammad had learned that the caravan was passing near Medina en route to Syria and organised a Muslim force of 300 men to intercept and raid it. Muslims say that he wanted to get the goods back which the Quraysh had taken from the Muslims after they had left Mecca and migrated to Medina.

'Abū Sufyān had learned of the Muslims' plan from scouts and sent a crier to Mecca to alarm the Quraysh. The Muslims could not intercept the caravan, but instead had to confront the Meccan army, a force of around one thousand men, on the plains of Badr several days later. This was the first major battle between the Muslims and their enemies in Mecca. The Battle of Badr (غَزْوة بَدر), resulted in a Muslim victory.

'Abū Sufyān served as the military leader in the later Meccan campaigns against Medina, including the Battle of 'Uhud (غَزْوة أُحُد) in 625 (3 AH) and the Battle of the Trench in 627 (5 AH), but he could not achieve final victory.

During the Battle of 'Uhud 'Abū Sufyān's wife, Hind bint 'Utba (هِنْد بِنْت عُتْبة), had allegedly cut out the liver of Muhammad's uncle Hamza (حَمْزة بن عَبْد الْمُطَّلِب) and had chewed it raw before spitting it out over the remains of the battlefield. When the Muslims conquered Mecca in 630 (8 AH), both 'Abū Sufyān and his wife Hind converted to Islam.

After the Conquest of Mecca, 'Abū Sufyān became one of Muhammad's commanders - chief of staff (نَقِيب) - of the Muslim army in subsequent wars. During the Siege of al-Ṭāʾif (غَزْوة الطّائِف), he lost an eye. He also fought in the Battle of Yarmūk (مَعْرَكة الْيَرْمُوك) in 636 (15 AH), in which he lost his other eye.

- His grandfather was Umayya, the ancestor of the Umayyad dynasty (الأُمَويُّونَ).
- ʾAbū Sufyān's son, Muʿāwiya I (مُعاوِية بن أَبي سُفْيان), later founded the Umayyad dynasty.
- His other son, Yazīd ibn ʾAbī Sufyān (يَزيد بن أَبي سُفْيان), was one of the four Muslim generals who were ordered by Caliph ʾAbū Bakr (أَبُو بَكْر) to invade Roman Syria in 634 (13 AH). In the same year he became the governor of Damascus after the Conquest of Damascus.

Some sources say that ʾAbū Sufyān was more than ninety (!) years old when he died in Medina. His kinsman, ʿUthmān ibn ʿAffān (عُثْمان بن عَفّان), who became the third (*Rightly Guided*) Caliph in 644 (23 AH), led the prayer at his funeral.

So who was ʾAbū Sufyān's daughter whom Muhammad got married to? Her name was Ramla bint ʾAbī Sufyān (رَمْلة بِنْت أَبي سُفْيان) also known as ʾUmm Habība (أُمّ حَبيبة).

She was most probably born in 589 (35 BH) and died in 664 (44 AH). Before her marriage to Muhammad, she was married to ʿUbayd Allah ibn Jahsh (عُبَيْد الله بن جَحْش), and both became Muslims despite her father's opposition to Muhammad. ʿUbayd was a first cousin of the Prophet.

When the people of Mecca, after Muhammad had started to preach Islam, persecuted the first converts, some of them migrated to Christian Abyssinia (old name for Ethiopia) – among them were ʿUbayd and his wife Ramla. However, once they had arrived, ʿUbayd converted to Christianity. Due to his conversion, he separated from his wife. He eventually died in Abyssinia in 627.

Muhammad sent his widow, Ramla, a proposal of marriage which arrived on the day she completed her ʿIdda (الْعِدّة). ʿIdda is the period a widow must wait after the death of her spouse or after a divorce, during which she may not marry another man. The reason for this

waiting period is to ensure that the male parent of any child produced after the end of marriage would be known.

This period is also mentioned in the Qur'an in sura 2 *The Cow* – in
Arabic: al-Baqara (سُورة الْبَقَرة):

2:234	If any of you die and leave widows, the widows should wait for four months and ten nights before remarrying. When they have completed this set time, you will not be blamed for anything they may reasonably choose to do with themselves.	وَالَّذِينَ يُتَوَفَّوْنَ مِنكُمْ وَيَذَرُونَ أَزْوَاجًا يَتَرَبَّصْنَ بِأَنفُسِهِنَّ أَرْبَعَةَ أَشْهُرٍ وَعَشْرًا فَإِذَا بَلَغْنَ أَجَلَهُنَّ فَلَا جُنَاحَ عَلَيْكُمْ فِيمَا فَعَلْنَ فِي أَنفُسِهِنَّ بِالْمَعْرُوفِ وَاللَّهُ بِمَا تَعْمَلُونَ خَبِيرٌ.

Eventually, Muhammad married Ramla. The marriage ceremony
took place in Abyssinia even though the Prophet was not present.

Don't get confused: Muhammad also married ʿUbayd Allah's <u>sister,</u>
Zaynab bint Jahsh (زَيْنَب بِنْت جَحْش).

24. Did the Prophet like music?

Answer: Most probably not. He condemned musical instruments.

This is a challenging topic for Muslims. The Arab world has its
own pop stars, there are several TV channels similar to MTV. There
is loud music on weddings.

However, when I was living in Alexandria in Egypt, I witnessed
several times how traditional Muslims could easily convince shop or
cafeteria owners to turn off the loudspeakers, just by giving the
owner a telling-off using Islamic sources. In most cases, they forced
the owner to switch to a Qur'an channel. None of the visitors dared
to say anything against it. They simply accepted it.

Most kinds of amusement that are common in the West, such as
dancing, singing, and playing an instrument, are alien to Islam. In
Saudi Arabia, the religious police even hunts down musical instruments and smash them. They claim that this is a command in Islam.

Well, let's have a look.

The Qur'an does not mention music in particular, but gives a general warning to all Muslims who enjoy *idle talks*. This is found in sura 31 *Luqmān* (سُورة لُقْمان):

| 31:6 | But there is the sort of person who pays for distracting tales [some say: amusement of speech], intending, without any knowledge, to lead others from God's way, and to hold it up to ridicule. There will be humiliating torment for him! | وَمِنَ النَّاسِ مَن يَشْتَرِي لَهْوَ الْحَدِيثِ لِيُضِلَّ عَن سَبِيلِ اللَّهِ بِغَيْرِ عِلْمٍ وَيَتَّخِذَهَا هُزُوًا أُولَٰئِكَ لَهُمْ عَذَابٌ مُّهِينٌ! |

What does the Qur'an mean by *distracting tales*? A Hadith gives more information about it. According to ʿAbd Allah ibn ʿAbbās (عَبْد الله بن عَبَّاس), it means "singing and things like it."[29]

Some scholars indicate that this verse may accuse a specific person. Abdel Haleem, whose translation is mainly used in this book, said that this verse is a reference to al-Nadr ibn al-Hārith (النَّضْر بن الْحارِث), "who brought some ancient Persian stories to distract the people of Quraysh from listening to the Qur'an."

Al-Nadr was one of the fiercest enemies of Muhammad. Ibn Kathīr (ابن كَثِير) writes on al-Nadr in his commentary on the Qur'an (verse 8:31) that "al-Nadr visited Persia and learned the stories of some Persian kings, such as Rustum and Isphandiyar. When he went back to Mecca, he found that the Prophet was reciting verses of the Qur'an to the people. Whenever the Prophet would leave an audience in which al-Nadr was sitting, al-Nadr began narrating to them the stories that he learned in Persia, proclaiming afterwards, 'Who, by Allah, has better tales to narrate? I or Muhammad?' When Allah allowed the Muslims to capture al-Nadr in Badr, the Messenger of Allah commanded that his head be cut off before him, and that was done, all thanks are due to Allah."[30]

According to Muhammad Asad, a more liberal commentator of the Qur'an, the verse is "apparently an allusion to a pseudo-philo-

---

29 ...عَنِ ابْنِ عَبَّاسٍ، فِي قَوْلِهِ عَزَّ وَجَلَّ: ﴿وَمِنَ النَّاسِ مَنْ يَشْتَرِي لَهْوَ الْحَدِيثِ﴾، قَالَ: الْغِنَاءُ وَأَشْبَاهُهُ. al-'Adab al-Mufrad 1265

30 ...كَانَ قَدْ ذَهَبَ إِلَى بِلادِ فَارِس، وَتَعَلَّمَ مِنْ أَخْبَارِ مُلُوكِهِم رُسْتُم وَاسفِنديار، وَلَمَّا قَدِمَ وَجَدَ رَسُولَ اللهِ قَدْ بَعَثَهُ اللهُ، وَهُوَ يَتْلُو عَلَى النَّاسِ الْقُرْآن، فَكَانَ إِذَا قَامَ مِن مَجْلِسٍ، جَلَسَ فِيهِ النَّضْرُ فَيُحَدِّثُهُم مِنْ أَخْبَارِ أُولَئِكَ، ثُمَّ يَقُولُ: "بِاللهِ أَيُّهُما أَحْسَن قَصَصًا؟ أَنَا أَوْ مُحَمَّد؟" Ibn Kathīr

sophical play with words and metaphysical speculations without any real meaning behind them". He continues: "Contrary to what some commentators assume, the above statement does not refer to any one person (allegedly a contemporary of the Prophet) but describes a type of mentality and is, therefore, of general import."

What about the Hadiths?

Most narrations underline the view that Muhammad did not like music and that music is prohibited in Islam. ʾAbū ʿĀmir (أَبُو عَامِر) or ʾAbū Mālik al-ʾAshʿarī (أَبُو مَالِك الْأَشْعَرِيُّ) reported that he heard the Prophet say: "From among my followers there will be some people who will consider illegal sexual intercourse, the wearing of silk, the drinking of alcoholic drinks and the use of musical instruments as lawful.

And there will be some people who will stay near the side of a mountain and in the evening their shepherd will come to them with their sheep and ask them for something, but they will say to him: 'Return to us tomorrow.' Allah will destroy them during the night and will let the mountain fall on them, and He will transform the rest of them into monkeys and pigs and they will remain so until the Day of Resurrection."[31]

Let's have a brief look at the Arabic word which is used for musical instrument: Miʿzaf (مِعْزَف) or plural Maʿāzif (مَعَازِف). This is the so-called noun of instrument (اِسْم آلة) of the root ʿ-z-f (ع-ز-ف) which means: to *play* or *make music*. The plural form, which is used in the Hadith, denotes mainly instruments which are struck or beaten, for example drums, daff/duff, the tambourine.

There are a lot of Hadiths which clearly condemn singing. Some of them refer to the Prophet's companions.

ʿAbd Allah ibn Dīnār (عَبْد الله بن دِينار) said: "I went out with ʿAbd Allah ibn ʿUmar (عَبْد الله بن عُمَر) to the market. He passed by a small

---

31 ...وَاللَّهِ مَا كَذَبَنِي سَمِعَ النَّبِيَّ يَقُولُ: "لَيَكُونَنَّ مِنْ أُمَّتِي أَقْوَامٌ يَسْتَحِلُّونَ الْحِرَ وَالْحَرِيرَ وَالْخَمْرَ وَالْمَعَازِفَ، وَلَيَنْزِلَنَّ أَقْوَامٌ إِلَى جَنْبِ عَلَمٍ يَرُوحُ عَلَيْهِمْ بِسَارِحَةٍ لَهُمْ، يَأْتِيهِمْ يَعْنِي الْفَقِيرَ لِحَاجَةٍ فَيَقُولُوا ارْجِعْ إِلَيْنَا غَدًا. فَيُبَيِّتُهُمُ اللَّهُ وَيَضَعُ الْعَلَمَ، وَيَمْسَخُ آخَرِينَ قِرَدَةً وَخَنَازِيرَ إِلَى يَوْمِ الْقِيَامَةِ." -Sahīh al-
Bukhārī 5590

slave-girl who was singing and remarked: 'Satan! If he had left any-one, he would have left this girl!'"[32]

Children are allowed to sing only during the two Islamic feasts, the end of Ramadan - 'Īd al-Fitr (عيد الْفِطر) - and the Sacrifice Feast - 'Īd al-Adhā (عيد الأَضحى). This is based on a Hadith. 'Ā'isha reported that at one time her father 'Abū Bakr came to her on the day of 'Īd al-Fitr or 'Īd al-Adhā while the Prophet was with her. There were two girl singers with her, singing songs of the 'Ansār about the day of Bu'āth [a story, before Islam, about the war between the two tribes of the 'Ansār, the Khazraj and the Banū al-'Aws].

'Abū Bakr said twice: 'Musical instrument of Satan!' But the Prophet said: 'Leave them, 'Abū Bakr, for every nation has an 'Īd (i.e. festival) and this day is our 'Īd.'"[33]

Listening to music makes people forget about Allah, that is what traditional scholars say in order to justify the prohibition.

In Egypt, one of my teachers told me that I should stop listening to music. Instead, I should listen to the recitation of the Qur'an. She said that listening to the Qur'an is better than Aspirin. "When I have a headache", she told me, "I just listen to the recitation of the Qur'an, and the pain is gone after five minutes".

25. Did the Prophet like garlic?

Answer: No. He didn't like the smell of fresh garlic at all.

If a Muslim wants to eat garlic, he should cook it.

Ibn Mu'āwiya ibn Qurra (ابن مُعَاوِية بن قُرّة) narrated that the Messenger of Allah forbade these two plants [garlic and onions], because he said: "He who eats them should not come near our mosque. If it is

---

32 ...قَالَ: خَرَجْتُ مَعَ عَبْدِ اللهِ بْنِ عُمَرَ إِلَى السُّوقِ، فَمَرَّ عَلَى جَارِيَةٍ صَغِيرَةٍ تُغَنِّي، فَقَالَ: إِنَّ الشَّيْطَانَ لَوْ تَرَكَ أَحَدًا لَتَرَكَ هَذِهِ. al-'Adab al-Mufrad 784; hasan.

33 ...أَنَّ أَبَا بَكْرٍ، دَخَلَ عَلَيْهَا وَالنَّبِيُّ عِنْدَهَا يَوْمَ فِطْرٍ أَوْ أَضْحًى، وَعِنْدَهَا قَيْنَتَانِ {تُغَنِّيَانِ} بِمَا تَقَاذَفَتِ الأَنْصَارُ يَوْمَ بُعَاثَ. فَقَالَ أَبُو بَكْرٍ مِزْمَارُ الشَّيْطَانِ مَرَّتَيْنِ. فَقَالَ النَّبِيُّ: "دَعْهُمَا يَا أَبَا بَكْرٍ، إِنَّ لِكُلِّ قَوْمٍ عِيدًا، وَإِنَّ عِيدَنَا هَذَا الْيَوْمُ." Sahīh al-Bukhārī 3931

necessary to eat them, make them dead by cooking, that is, onions and garlic."[34]

If a Muslim eats garlic and one can smell it, he must not enter a mosque until he got rid of the smell. ʿAbd Allah ibn ʿUmar (عَبْد الله بن عُمَر) narrated that the Prophet said: "He who eats of this [offensive] plant must not approach our mosque until its odour dies."[35]

The consumption of garlic is not *forbidden*, so-called harām (حَرام). It is rather *disliked*, in Arabic called makrūh (مَكْرُوه). ʾAbū Saʿīd (أَبُو سَــعِيد) stated: "We made no transgression but Khaybar was conquered. We, the companions of the Messenger of Allah, fell upon this plant [garlic] because the people were hungry. We ate it to our heart's content and then made our way towards the mosque. The Messenger of Allah sensed its odour and said: 'He who took anything of this offensive plant must not approach us in the mosque.' The people said: 'Its [use] has been forbidden.' This reached the Messenger of Allah, thus he said: 'O people, I cannot forbid [the use of a thing] which Allah has made lawful, but this is a plant the odour of which is repugnant to me.'"[36]

26. What was the favourite perfume of the Prophet?

Answer: Musk (مِشك).

ʾAbū Saʿīd (أَبُو سَعِيد) recounted that when the Prophet had been asked about musk, he had answered: "It is the best of your perfumes."[37]

---

34 ...أَنَّ النَّبِيَّ نَهَى عَنْ هَاتَيْنِ الشَّجَرَتَيْنِ وَقَالَ: "مَنْ أَكَلَهُمَا فَلَا يَقْرَبَنَّ مَسْجِدَنَا." وَقَالَ: "إِنْ كُنْتُمْ لَا بُدَّ آكِلِيهِمَا فَأَمِيتُوهُمَا طَبْخًا." قَالَ يَعْنِي الْبَصَلَ وَالثُّومَ. Sunan ʾAbī Dāwūd 3827 (3818).

35 ...أَنَّ رَسُولَ اللَّهِ قَالَ: "مَنْ أَكَلَ مِنْ هَذِهِ الْبَقْلَةِ فَلَا يَقْرَبَنَّ مَسَاجِدَنَا حَتَّى يَذْهَبَ رِيحُهَا." يَعْنِي الثُّومَ. Sahīh Muslim 561.

36 ...قَالَ لَمْ نَعُدْ أَنْ فُتِحَتْ، خَيْبَرُ فَوَقَعْنَا أَصْحَابَ رَسُولِ اللَّهِ فِي تِلْكَ الْبَقْلَةِ الثُّومِ وَالنَّاسُ جِيَاعٌ فَأَكَلْنَا مِنْهَا أَكْلًا شَدِيدًا ثُمَّ رُحْنَا إِلَى الْمَسْجِدِ فَوَجَدَ رَسُولُ اللَّهِ الرِّيحَ فَقَالَ: "مَنْ أَكَلَ مِنْ هَذِهِ الشَّجَرَةِ الْخَبِيثَةِ شَيْئًا فَلَا يَقْرَبَنَّا فِي الْمَسْجِدِ." فَقَالَ النَّاسُ حُرِّمَتْ حُرِّمَتْ. فَبَلَغَ ذَاكَ النَّبِيَّ فَقَالَ: "أَيُّهَا النَّاسُ إِنَّهُ لَيْسَ بِي تَحْرِيمُ مَا أَحَلَّ اللَّهُ لِي وَلَكِنَّهَا شَجَرَةٌ أَكْرَهُ رِيحَهَا." Sahīh Muslim 565.

37 ...أَنَّ النَّبِيَّ سُئِلَ عَنِ الْمِسْكِ فَقَالَ: "هُوَ أَطْيَبُ طِيبِكُمْ." Jāmiʿ al-Tirmidhī 992.

Muhammad liked aromatic things and perfume. On waking up, he would relieve himself, perform the ritual washing - in Islam called Wuḍū' (الْوُضُوء) -, and apply fragrance on his clothing.

'Anas (أَنَس بن مالك) mentioned that the Messenger of Allah said: "In this world, women and perfume have been made dear to me, and my comfort has been provided in prayer."[38]

Muhammad is said to have had a vessel from which he perfumed himself, and it is said that it was a mixed perfume, a combination of several materials. In various texts, scholars say that it smelled so strong that when Muhammad had passed by a road in Medina, people would know and say that the Prophet had passed there – due to the perfume's effect.

If fragrance was presented to him, he would not refuse it. Thumāma ibn 'Abd Allah (ثُمَامة بن عَبْد الله) narrated: "Anas [a companion] never refused [a gift of] scent and used to say that the Prophet usually never refused [a gift of] scent."[39]

However, Muhammad forbade women to use perfume when they went out. It was recounted by Zaynab al-Thaqafīya (زَيْنَب الثَّقَفِيّة) that the Prophet said: "Any one of you [women] who wants to go out to the mosque should not go near any perfume."[40]

It was said that 'Abū Hurayra (أَبُو هُرَيْرة) met a woman who was wearing perfume. She was heading to the mosque. Her clothes were fluttering in the air. 'Abū Hurayra said: "O maid-servant of the Almighty, are you coming from the mosque?" She replied: "Yes." He said: "Did you use perfume?" She replied: "Yes." He said: "I heard my beloved 'Abū al-Qāsim [Muhammad] say: 'The prayer of a woman who uses perfume for [this] mosque is not accepted until she returns and takes a bath similar to that after sexual defilement.'"[41]

---

38 قَالَ رَسُولُ اللَّهِ: "حُبِّبَ إِلَيَّ مِنَ الدُّنْيَا النِّسَاءُ وَالطِّيبُ وَجُعِلَ قُرَّةُ عَيْنِي فِي الصَّلاةِ." -Sunan al-Nasā'ī 3939; hasan

39 ...أَنَّهُ كَانَ لاَ يَرُدُّ الطِّيبَ، وَزَعَمَ أَنَّ النَّبِيَّ كَانَ لاَ يَرُدُّ الطِّيبَ. Sahīh al-Bukhārī 5929.

40 ...أَنَّ النَّبِيَّ قَالَ: "أَيَّتُكُنَّ خَرَجَتْ إِلَى الْمَسْجِدِ فَلاَ تَقْرَبَنَّ طِيبًا." Sunan al-Nasā'ī 5262

41 ...قَالَ لَقِيَتْهُ امْرَأَةٌ وَجَدَ مِنْهَا رِيحَ الطِّيبِ يُنْفَحُ وَلِذَيْلِهَا إِعْصَارٌ فَقَالَ يَا أَمَةَ الْجَبَّارِ جِئْتِ مِنَ الْمَسْجِدِ قَالَتْ نَعَمْ. قَالَ وَلَهُ تَطَيَّبْتِ قَالَتْ نَعَمْ. قَالَ إِنِّي سَمِعْتُ حِبِّي أَبَا الْقَاسِمِ يَقُولُ: "لاَ تُقْبَلُ صَلاةٌ لِامْرَأَةٍ تَطَيَّبَتْ لِهَذَا الْمَسْجِدِ حَتَّى تَرْجِعَ فَتَغْتَسِلَ غُسْلَهَا مِنَ الْجَنَابَةِ." Sunan 'Abī Dāwūd 4174

According to another narration, Muhammad even compared a woman who uses perfume outside the house to an adulteress.

The prohibition is not surprising. In Islam, women should not attract men. Therefore, Muhammad has clarified the difference between perfumes for men and for women. It was reported by 'Abū Hurayra (أَبُو هُرَيْرَة) that the Prophet said: "The perfume for men is that the scent of which is apparent while its colour is hidden, and the perfume for women is that which colour is apparent, while its scent is hidden."[42]

27. Where are some hairs of Muhammad's beard stored?

Answer: In the mausoleum of Mevlana Rumi in Konya, Turkey.

Some Islamic dynasties as well as sects in Islam have a tradition of collecting relics which are said to be connected to the Prophet. Traditional scholars warn that this practice could lead to idolatry - in Arabic: shirk (شِرْك) - which is a sin. Most of these presumed relics are stored in Istanbul, in the Topkapı Palace.

Now let's return to Muhammad's beard, in Turkish called: *Sakal-ı Şerif.* The beard in question, as a legend has it, had been shaved from Muhammad's face by his barber Salmān al-Fārisī (سَلْمان الْفَارِسِيّ), in the presence of 'Abū Bakr and 'Alī, his son-in-law. Although some of the hair was taken away, parts of the beard were preserved and kept in a glass box in Konya. When I visited the museum, people were taking selfies in front of the box – although taking pictures is strictly forbidden there.

Remark: Salmān was a Persian-born barber who was taken into Muhammad's household. He became a model for spiritual adoption and mystical initiation. For Persians, he is one of the chains which link the Arabian world with Iranian tradition.

---

42 قَالَ: "طِيبُ الرِّجَالِ مَا ظَهَرَ رِيحُهُ وَخَفِيَ لَوْنُهُ وَطِيبُ النِّسَاءِ مَا ظَهَرَ لَوْنُهُ وَخَفِيَ رِيحُهُ." Sunan al-Nasā'ī 5118; hasan

28. How did the Prophet take a bath?

Answer: There are several reports that describe how he did it.

First of all, ritual cleanness is extremely important in Islam.

There are mainly two types of washing: The ablution - in Arabic: Wudū' (وُضوء) - done before praying; and taking a bath - in Arabic: Ghusl (غُسل) - done after certain events, for example sex. Both types are crucial for Muslims, especially for the validity of their prayers.

'Abū Salama ibn 'Abd al-Rahmān (أَبُو سَلَمة بن عَبْد الرَّحْمن) related on the authority of 'Ā'isha (عائشة بِنْت أَبي بَكْر) that when the Messenger of Allah took a bath, he started with the right hand, poured water over it and washed it, and then poured water on the impurity of the body with the right hand and washed it away using the left hand. And after having removed the impurity, he poured water on his head. 'Ā'isha said: "I and the Messenger of Allah took a bath from the same vessel, after sexual intercourse."[43]

On another occasion, 'Ā'isha further mentioned: "The prophet and I used to take a bath from a single pot called Faraq."[44]

Edward Lane describes a *Faraq* in his famous dictionary as a kind of vessel that could hold three Sā' (صاع), a measure of capacity.

29. How much water did the Prophet use for bathing?

Answer: In most cases it was one Sā' (صاع) which equals 4 times the quantity that could fill cupped hands, about 2.1 litre.

'Anas ibn Mālik (أنَس بن مالِك) reported that the Prophet used to take a bath with one Sā' up to five Mudds of water and used to perform ablution with one Mudd of water.[45]

---

43 ...قَالَتْ عَائِشَةُ كَانَ رَسُولُ اللَّهِ إِذَا اغْتَسَلَ بَدَأَ بِيَمِينِهِ فَصَبَّ عَلَيْهَا مِنَ الْمَاءِ فَغَسَلَهَا ثُمَّ صَبَّ الْمَاءَ عَلَى الأَذَى الَّذِي بِهِ بِيَمِينِهِ وَغَسَلَ عَنْهُ بِشِمَالِهِ حَتَّى إِذَا فَرَغَ مِنْ ذَلِكَ صَبَّ عَلَى رَأْسِهِ. قَالَتْ عَائِشَةُ كُنْتُ أَغْتَسِلُ أَنَا وَرَسُولُ اللَّهِ مِنْ إِنَاءٍ وَاحِدٍ وَنَحْنُ جُنُبَان. Sahīh Muslim 321

44 ...قَالَتْ كُنْتُ أَغْتَسِلُ أَنَا وَالنَّبِيُّ، مِنْ إِنَاءٍ وَاحِدٍ مِنْ قَدَحٍ يُقَالُ لَهُ الْفَرَقُ. Sahīh al-Bukhārī 250

45 ...يَقُولُ كَانَ النَّبِيُّ يَغْسِلُ أَوْ كَانَ يَغْتَسِلُ بِالصَّاعِ إِلَى خَمْسَةِ أَمْدَادٍ، وَيَتَوَضَّأُ بِالْمُدِّ. Sahīh al-Bukhārī 201

The measurement called Mudd (مُدّ) was - besides the Sāʿ - commonly known at the time of Muhammad. According to Edward Lane's dictionary, Mudd is a utensil with which grain is measured and therefore became a kind of measurement; it is equal to a pint (رِطل). According to Lane, a Sāʿ equals five pints and a third. We can imagine the Mudd as being about the same size as a medium-sized soup bowl. A Mudd is equivalent to the volume of two hands of an average man cupped together so that they are neither flat nor clasped.

Remark: In some Hadiths, also the word Makkūk (مَكُّوك) is used to denote the amount of water. Some narrations also indicate slightly different amounts of Sāʿ or Mudd.

Let's convert the ancient units to units we know:

- A Mudd is about 544 g (1.2 lbs) or 544 ml.
- A Sāʿ is about 2,176 g (4.8 lbs) or 2176 ml.

Watch out: The measurement differs dramatically in other places. In Palestine, a Mudd was defined by 18 litres; in Tangier it was 46,6 l.

30. On what day of the week did the revelation come down?

Answer: On the second day of the week, i.e. Monday (يَوْم الإِثْنَيْن).

The *revelation* is usually called al-Wahy (الوَحْي) in Arabic. The root w-h-a (و-ح-ى) means *to inspire; to reveal.*

Muslims believe that Allah used chosen individuals (messengers, prophets) to deliver his word to mankind. The Qur'an is considered a Wahy given to Muhammad.

Muhammad himself told his followers that he received his revelation on a Monday. This is found in a Hadith. 'Abū Qatāda (أَبُو قَتادة) reported that Muhammad was asked about fasting on Monday, whereupon he said: "It is [the day] when I was born and revelation was sent down to me."[46]

---

46 ...رَسُولَ اللَّهِ سُئِلَ عَنْ صَوْمِ الإِثْنَيْنِ فَقَالَ"فِيهِ وُلِدْتُ وَفِيهِ أُنْزِلَ عَلَيَّ". Sahīh Muslim 1162

31. For how many years did the revelation continue?

Answer: 23 years.

The Qur'an was revealed over 23 years. Muhammad was 40 years old when the first verse was revealed in Mecca. The duration of the revelation in Mecca extended for 13 years. In Medina, it continued for another 10 years. These two cities are also used to mark the suras. There are Medinan and Meccan suras.

32. Why do Muslims believe that Muhammad couldn't read?

Answer: Because it was told so.

There are no independent records saying that Muhammad was illiterate. Muslims like to say that Muhammad could not read and write. They use his illiteracy as evidence that the Qur'an was revealed to him by Allah since, as Muslims claim, Muhammad had simply not been capable of writing it by himself.

There is a Hadith that tells the story about Muhammad and his inability to read. 'Ā'isha (عائشة بِنْت أَبِي بَكْر) said: "The angel came to him in it [the cave of Hira] and asked him to read. The Prophet replied: 'I do not know how to read.'

The Prophet added: 'The angel seized me [forcefully] and pressed me so hard that I could not bear it any more. He then released me and again asked me to read, and I replied: 'I do not know how to read', whereupon he seized me again and pressed me a second time until I could not bear it any more. He then released me and asked me again to read, but again I replied: 'I do not know how to read.' [or, 'what shall I read?']

Thereupon he seized me for the third time and pressed me and then released me and said: 'Read! In the name of your Lord, Who has created [all that exists]. Has created man from a clot. Read! Your Lord is most generous...' [sura 96:15][47]

---

47 ...وَهُوَ فِي غَارِ حِرَاءٍ فَجَاءَهُ الْمَلَكُ فِيهِ فَقَالَ اقْرَأْ. فَقَالَ لَهُ النَّبِيُّ:" فَقُلْتُ مَا أَنَا بِقَارِئٍ فَأَخَذَنِي فَغَطَّنِي حَتَّى بَلَغَ مِنِّي الْجَهْدَ ثُمَّ أَرْسَلَنِي. فَقَالَ اقْرَأْ. فَقُلْتُ مَا أَنَا بِقَارِئٍ. فَأَخَذَنِي فَغَطَّنِي الثَّانِيَةَ حَتَّى بَلَغَ مِنِّي الْجَهْدَ، ثُمَّ أَرْسَلَنِي فَقَالَ اقْرَأْ. فَقُلْتُ مَا أَنَا بِقَارِئٍ. فَغَطَّنِي الثَّالِثَةَ حَتَّى بَلَغَ مِنِّي الْجَهْدَ، ثُمَّ أَرْسَلَنِي فَقَالَ اقْرَأْ بِاسْمِ رَبِّكَ الَّذِي خَلَقَ." حَتَّى بَلَغَ {مَا لَمْ يَعْلَمْ}. Sahīh al-Bukhārī 6982

33. Why do very pious Muslim men shorten their trousers?

Answer: Because Muhammad said that trousers should not go below the ankles.

When I first came to Egypt in 2006, it was a fashion for religious people to shorten their trousers (mostly blue jeans). People wanted to express that they are following Muhammad and are true believers of Islam. There was not a single Salafi in Alexandria who did not have his trousers shortened. Also, people from the *Muslim Brotherhood* did that.

Two Arabic terms are important to understand this phenomenon:

Al-'Izār (الإِزار): The lower garment (usually worn by men). Try to imagine something similar to a kilt, except that it is longer, lighter and thinner. 'Izār is defined in Arabic to be any garment tied to the waist covering the lower half of the body. It includes the Shalwar (traditional trousers used in Afghanistan, Iran, also by the Kurds, etc.), the Dhuti (a men's lower garment traditional in South Asia), and the Thawb (an ankle-length Arab garment, usually with long sleeves, similar to a robe).

Al-'Isbāl (الإِشبال): Letting the garment come below the ankles. This word is the infinitive noun (مَصدَر) of the Arabic IV-verb 'Asbala (أَسبَلَ). The active participle of this verb is used too: A musbil (مُسبِل) is a man lengthening his garment and making it hang down to the ground. It is also applied to women; a Musbila (مُسبِلة) is someone who has made her skirt to hang down to the ground. It can, however, also mean that a man has a long, ugly moustache.

So what about the rules? What is the correct length?

- 'Abū Hurayra (أَبُو هُرَيرة) reported that the Prophet said: "What is below the ankles of a lower garment ['Izār] is condemned to the Fire (Hell)."[48]
- 'Abd Allah ibn 'Umar (عَبد الله بن عُمَر) narrated a similar situation in which the Prophet said: "al-'Isbāl is in lower garment ['Izār],

---

48 ...مَا أَسفَلَ مِنَ الْكَعبَينِ مِنَ الْإِزَارِ فَفِي النَّارِ. Sahīh al-Bukhārī 5785.

shirt and turban. Whoever allows any part of these to trail on the ground out of arrogance, Allah will not look at him on the Day of Judgement."[49]

- Hudhayfa (حُذَيْفة) reported: "The Messenger of Allah took hold of the muscle of my calf (or his calf) and said: 'This is where the 'Izār should stop; if you insist, it may be lower, but it should not reach the ankles.'"[50]

- 'Abd Allah ibn 'Umar related: "I happened to pass before Allah's Messenger with my lower garment ['Izār] trailing [upon the ground]. He said: 'Abd Allah, tug up your lower garment!' I tugged it up, and he again said: 'Tug it still further!', and I tugged it still further and I went on tugging it afterwards, whereupon some people said: 'To what extent?' Thereupon he said: 'To the middle of the shanks.'[51]

This Hadith is the reason why very religious men occasionally wear their garment exactly to this length.

What were the reasons for this?

If we look at all the Hadiths that were recorded on this topic, we can say that the Prophet commanded the shortening of the clothes for men in all cases.

Around 1400 years ago, during the time of Muhammad, men probably tried to show off by wearing long clothes. Salafis use this point to justify the shortening (which is true according to Hadiths). Some say that they don't want their clothes to touch the ground because dirt is something very bad in Islam. They are afraid to become impure because of that or take dirt into their homes (but this is not the reason the Prophet stated).

There are few people who were exempted by Muhammad's command because they were free of pride according to Islamic sources.

---

49 قَالَ: "الإِسْبَالُ فِي الإِزَارِ وَالْقَمِيصِ وَالْعِمَامَةِ مَنْ جَرَّ مِنْهَا شَيْئًا خُيَلاَءَ لَمْ يَنْظُرِ اللَّهُ إِلَيْهِ يَوْمَ الْقِيَامَةِ". Sunan 'Abī Dāwūd 4094

50 ...هَذَا مَوْضِعُ الإِزَارِ فَإِنْ أَبَيْتَ فَأَسْفَلَ فَإِنْ أَبَيْتَ فَلاَ حَقَّ لِلإِزَارِ فِي الْكَعْبَيْنِ. Jāmi' al-Tirmidhī 1783

51 ...قَالَ مَرَرْتُ عَلَى رَسُولِ اللَّهِ وَفِي إِزَارِي اسْتِرْخَاءٌ فَقَالَ." يَا عَبْدَ اللَّهِ ارْفَعْ إِزَارَكَ." فَرَفَعْتُهُ ثُمَّ قَالَ: "زِدْ." فَزِدْتُ فَمَا زِلْتُ أَتَحَرَّاهَا بَعْدُ. فَقَالَ بَعْضُ الْقَوْمِ إِلَى أَيْنَ فَقَالَ أَنْصَافِ السَّاقَيْنِ. Sahīh Muslim 2086

'Abd Allah ibn 'Umar reported that the Prophet said: "Allah will not look, on the Day of Resurrection, at the person who drags his garment (behind him) out of conceit." On this 'Abū Bakr said: "O Allah's Messenger! One side of my lower garment ['Izār] hangs low if I do not take care of it." The Prophet said: "You are not one of those who do that out of conceit."[52]

And what about women?

The same is applied to women as indicated in a Hadith. 'Abd Allah ibn 'Umar narrated that the Messenger of Allah said: "Whoever drags his garment out of pride, Allah will not look at him." 'Umm Salama (أُمّ سَلَمة) said: "O Messenger of Allah, what should women do with their hems?" He said: "Let it down a handspan." She said: "But then their feet will show." He said: "Let it down a forearm's length, but no more than that." [Let them lengthen it by a cubit, but no more.][53]

How does Allah punish people whose clothes are too long?

The punishment for showing off may come to pass in this world, not in the Hereafter. 'Abū Hurayra (أَبُو هُرَيْرة) reported that Allah's Messenger said that there was a person who used to walk with pride because of his thick hair and fine coats. "He was made to sink in the earth and he would go on sinking in the earth until the Last Hour would come."[54]

It is related on the authority of 'Abū Dharr (أَبُو ذَرّ) that the Prophet said: "There are three [kinds of] persons with whom Allah would neither speak on the Day of Resurrection, nor would look at them nor would absolve them. There is a painful punishment. The one who wears his garment below his ankles, the one who reminds others

---

52 قَالَ أَبُو بَكْرٍ يَا رَسُولَ اللَّهِ إِنَّ أَحَدَ شِقَّيْ إِزَارِي يَسْتَرْخِي، إِلاَّ أَنْ أَتَعَاهَدَ ذَلِكَ مِنْهُ. فَقَالَ النَّبِيُّ: "لَسْتَ مِمَّنْ يَصْنَعُهُ خُيَلاَءَ." Sahīh al-Bukhārī 5784

53 قَالَ رَسُولُ اللَّهِ: "مَنْ جَرَّ ثَوْبَهُ مِنَ الْخُيَلاَءِ لَمْ يَنْظُرِ اللَّهُ إِلَيْهِ." قَالَتْ أُمُّ سَلَمَةَ يَا رَسُولَ اللَّهِ فَكَيْفَ تَصْنَعُ النِّسَاءُ بِذُيُولِهِنَّ قَالَ: "تُرْخِينَهُ شِبْرًا." قَالَتْ إِذًا تَنْكَشِفَ أَقْدَامُهُنَّ. قَالَ: "تُرْخِينَهُ ذِرَاعًا لاَ تَزِدْنَ عَلَيْهِ." Sunan al-Nasā'ī 5336

54 قَالَ: "بَيْنَمَا رَجُلٌ يَمْشِي قَدْ أَعْجَبَتْهُ جُمَّتُهُ وَبُرْدَاهُ إِذْ خُسِفَ بِهِ الأَرْضُ فَهُوَ يَتَجَلْجَلُ فِي الأَرْضِ حَتَّى تَقُومَ السَّاعَةَ." Sahīh Muslim 2088

of his favours, and the one who sells his products by means of making false oaths."[55]

34. Did the Prophet like red clothes for men?

Answer: No.

In principle, a Muslim may wear any colour which he likes – except for red and saffron colours (orange-yellow). These two colours were disliked by Muhammad.

- It was narrated that the Prophet's son-in-law ʿAlī (عَلِيّ بن أَبِي طالب) said: "The Messenger of Allah forbade me, but I do not say that he forbade you, from wearing rings of gold, wearing al-Qassī, wearing al-Mufaddam [garments dyed deep red] and al-Muʿasfar [garments dyed with safflower; yellowish], and from reciting Qurʾan while bowing."[56]

- ʾAbū Burda (أَبُو بُردة) said: "We asked ʿAlī: 'What is Qassī (الْقَسِّيّ)?' He said: 'These are garments imported to us from Syria or Egypt. They are slatted and marked like citrons.'"[57]

- ʿAbd Allah ibn ʿAmr ibn al-ʿĀs (عَبْد الله بن عَمْرو بن الْعَاص) reported: "Allah's Messenger saw me wearing two clothes dyed in safflower whereupon he said: 'These are the clothes worn by the Kuffār [disbelievers], so do not wear them.'"[58]

- Al-Barāʾ ibn ʿĀzib (الْبَراء بن عازِب) narrated: "He forbade us to wear silk, Dībāj [brocade], Qassī [cloths marked with patterns of citrons] and Istabraq [various kinds of silk clothes]; or to use red Mayāthir [saddle-cloths]."[59]

---

55 ...ثَلَاثَةٌ لَا يُكَلِّمُهُمُ اللهُ يَوْمَ الْقِيَامَةِ، وَلَا يَنْظُرُ إِلَيْهِمْ وَلَا يُزَكِّيهِمْ وَلَهُمْ عَذَابٌ أَلِيمٌ: الْمُسْبِلُ، وَالْمَنَّانُ، وَالْمُنَفِّقُ سِلْعَتَهُ بِالْحَلِفِ الْكَاذِبِ. Sahīh Muslim 106

56 ...قَالَ نَهَانِي رَسُولُ اللَّهِ وَلاَ أَقُولُ نَهَاكُمْ عَنْ تَخَتُّمِ الذَّهَبِ وَعَنْ لُبْسِ الْقَسِّيِّ وَعَنْ لُبْسِ الْمُفَدَّمِ وَعَنِ الْقِرَاءَةِ رَاكِعًا. Sunan al-Nasāʾī 5173

57 ...قُلْنَا لِعَلِيٍّ مَا الْقَسِّيَّةُ قَالَ ثِيَابٌ تَأْتِينَا مِنَ الشَّامِ أَوْ مِنْ مِصْرَ مُضَلَّعَةٌ فِيهَا أَمْثَالُ الأُتْرُجِّ. Sunan ʾAbī Dāwūd 4225

58 ...قَالَ رَأَى رَسُولُ اللَّهِ عَلَيَّ ثَوْبَيْنِ مُعَصْفَرَيْنِ فَقَالَ: "إِنَّ هَذِهِ مِنْ ثِيَابِ الْكُفَّارِ فَلَا تَلْبَسْهَا." Sahīh Muslim 2077

59 ...نَهَانَا عَنْ لُبْسِ الْحَرِيرِ، وَالدِّيبَاجِ، وَالْقَسِّيِّ، وَالإِسْتَبْرَقِ، وَمَيَاثِرِ الْحُمْرِ. Sahīh al-Bukhārī 5390

The **best colour** that a man can wear is **white**.

This is recorded in a Hadith narrated by 'Abd Allah ibn 'Abbās (عَبْدُ الله بن الْعَبَّاس) who has mentioned that the Prophet said: "Wear your white garments, for they are among your best garments, and shroud your dead in them."[60]

There are, however, some reports which indicate that it is permissible to wear red if it is mixed with another colour.

Al-Barā' ibn 'Āzib reported: "The Prophet was of a modest height. I saw him wearing a red Hulla and I did not see anything better than him."[61]

A Hulla (حُلّة) is a suit made of two Yemeni garments which are woven with coloured bands, mostly red and black or red and green. Most scholars agree that in the Hadith, the colour red indicates that the narrator meant red stripes. That's why scholars say it is okay to mix red with other colours regarding men's clothes.

Remark: There is no information why Muhammad disliked red-coloured clothes. Traditional scholars thought that it might have been because red is the adornment of women.

35. How did the Prophet sleep?

Answer: He lay down on his right side and put his right hand under his cheek.

'Abū Qatāda (أَبُو قَتادة) reported that when the Messenger of Allah was on a journey and he got down for rest at night, he used to lie down on his right side, and when he lay down for rest before morning, he used to stretch his forearm and place his head over his palm.[62]

'Abū Hurayra (أَبُو هُرَيْرة) narrated that the Messenger of Allah said: "When one of you goes to bed, he should undo the inside of his

---

60 قَالَ رَسُولُ اللَّهِ ﷺ: "الْبَسُوا مِنْ ثِيَابِكُمُ الْبَيَاضَ فَإِنَّهَا مِنْ خَيْرِ ثِيَابِكُمْ وَكَفِّنُوا فِيهَا مَوْتَاكُمْ وَإِنَّ خَيْرَ أَكْحَالِكُمُ الْإِثْمِدُ يَجْلُو الْبَصَرَ وَيُنْبِتُ الشَّعَرَ." Sunan 'Abī Dāwūd 3878

61 ...كَانَ النَّبِيُّ ﷺ مَرْبُوعًا، وَقَدْ رَأَيْتُهُ فِي حُلّةٍ حَمْرَاءَ مَا رَأَيْتُ شَيْئًا أَحْسَنَ مِنْهُ. Sahīh al-Bukhārī 5848

62 ...قَالَ كَانَ رَسُولُ اللَّهِ ﷺ إِذَا كَانَ فِي سَفَرٍ فَعَرَّسَ بِلَيْلٍ اضْطَجَعَ عَلَى يَمِينِهِ وَإِذَا عَرَّسَ قُبَيْلَ الصُّبْحِ نَصَبَ ذِرَاعَهُ وَوَضَعَ رَأْسَهُ عَلَى كَفِّهِ. Sahīh al-Bukhārī 683

lower garment and dust the bed with it. If he does not know what has come on his bed since he left it, he should lie down on his right side and say: 'In Your Name I have laid down on my side. If You take my soul, then have mercy on it. If You release it, then preserve it in the manner in which You preserve the men of right action.'"[63]

Al-Barā' ibn 'Āzib (الْبَراء بن عازِب) said: "When the Prophet went to bed, he laid down on his right side. Then he said: 'O Allah, I have turned my face to You and I have surrendered myself to You and I have committed my back to You out of fear and desire for You. There is no place of safety or refuge from You except with You. I have believed in Your book which You revealed and Your Prophet whom You sent.' He said: 'Whoever says it at night and then dies, dies in al-Fitra [natural state].'"[64]

However, sleeping on the left side is permissible. But if a Muslim dies on the left side in his bed, he will miss out a reward.

36. Why should Muslims close their doors at night?

Answer: The Prophet told them that Satan does not open a closed door.

Jābir ibn 'Abd Allah (جابِر بن عَبْد الله) narrated that the Prophet said: "When night falls, then keep your children close to you, for the Devil spreads out then. An hour later, you can let them free; and close the gates of your house [at night] and mention Allah's name thereupon, and cover your utensils and mention Allah's name thereupon. If you don't have anything to cover your utensil, you may place something over it [e.g. a piece of wood]."[65]

---

63 قَالَ رَسُولُ اللَّهِ: "إِذَا أَوَى أَحَدُكُمْ إِلَى فِرَاشِهِ، فَلْيَحُلَّ دَاخِلَةَ إِزَارِهِ، فَلْيَنْفُضْ بِهَا فِرَاشَهُ، فَإِنَّهُ لاَ يَدْرِي مَا خَلَفَ فِي فِرَاشِهِ، وَلْيَضْطَجِعْ عَلَى شِقِّهِ الْأَيْمَنِ، وَلْيَقُلْ: بِاسْمِكَ وَضَعْتُ جَنْبِي، فَإِنِ احْتَبَسْتَ نَفْسِي فَارْحَمْهَا، وَإِنْ أَرْسَلْتَهَا فَاحْفَظْهَا بِمَا تَحْفَظُ بِهِ الصَّالِحِينَ، أَوْ قَالَ: عِبَادَكَ الصَّالِحِينَ." al-'Adab al-Mufrad 1210

64 كَانَ النَّبِيُّ إِذَا أَوَى إِلَى فِرَاشِهِ نَامَ عَلَى شِقِّهِ الْأَيْمَنِ، ثُمَّ قَالَ: اللَّهُمَّ وَجَّهْتُ وَجْهِي إِلَيْكَ، وَأَسْلَمْتُ نَفْسِي إِلَيْكَ، وَأَلْجَأْتُ ظَهْرِي إِلَيْكَ، رَهْبَةً وَرَغْبَةً إِلَيْكَ، لَا مَنْجَا وَلاَ مَلْجَأَ مِنْكَ إِلاَّ إِلَيْكَ، آمَنْتُ بِكِتَابِكَ الَّذِي أَنْزَلْتَ، وَنَبِيِّكَ الَّذِي أَرْسَلْتَ، قَالَ: فَمَنْ قَالَهُنَّ فِي لَيْلَةٍ ثُمَّ مَاتَ مَاتَ عَلَى الْفِطْرَةِ. -al-'Adab al-Mufrad, 1211

37. Who was Muhammad's most famous servant?

Answer: 'Anas ibn Mālik (أنَس بن مالِك).

Born	612 (10 BH) in Yahtrib		Died	712 (93 AH) in al-Basra (Iraq), aged ~100 (!)

He was Muhammad's servant for many (perhaps ten) years. 'Anas ibn Mālik narrated: "I served the Prophet for ten years. He never said 'Uff' and never blamed me by saying: 'Why did you do so?' or 'why didn't you do so?' The Prophet had the best character among all people. I never touched a silk cloth nor silk, nor anything softer than the hand of the Messenger of Allah, nor have I smelled musk or a fragrance sweeter than the sweat of the Messenger of Allah."[66]

His epithet - in Arabic: Kunya (كُنْية) - was 'Abū Hamza (أَبُو حَمْزة). The Prophet nicknamed him after Hamza because 'Anas once was trying to pick some herbs. The word Hamza has several meanings, among others, it means a certain type of herb.

It is said that he fought 27 battles together with Muhammad. After the Prophet's death, 'Anas fought with 'Abū Bakr (أبُو بَكر) in the Ridda-wars (حُرُوب الرِّدَّة), the first inner-Islamic wars.

Because he was a servant of Muhammad, he got close to him and could observe how the Prophet lived, prayed or ate. 'Abū Hurayra (أبُو هُرَيْرة) said: "I have never seen anyone whose prayer resembles that of the Messenger of Allah so closely as the son of 'Umm Sulaym [='Anas ibn Mālik]."[67] Be careful: This was also said about other people, e.g.: 'Umar ibn 'Abd al-'Azīz (عُمَر بْن عَبْد العَزِيز).

---

65 النَّبِيُّ قَالَ: "إِذَا اسْتَجْنَحَ {اللَّيْلُ} أَوْ كَانَ جُنْحُ اللَّيْلِ فَكُفُّوا صِبْيَانكُمْ، فَإِنَّ الشَّيَاطِينَ تَنْتَشِرُ حِينَئِذٍ، فَإِذَا ذَهَبَ سَاعَةٌ مِنَ الْعِشَاءِ فَخَلُّوهُمْ وَأَغْلِقْ بَابَكَ، وَاذْكُرِ اسْمَ اللَّهِ، وَأَطْفِئْ مِصْبَاحَكَ، وَاذْكُرِ اسْمَ اللَّهِ، وَأَوْكِ سِقَاءَكَ، وَاذْكُرِ اسْمَ اللَّهِ، وَخَمِّرْ إِنَاءَكَ، وَاذْكُرِ اسْمَ اللَّهِ، وَلَوْ تَعْرُضُ عَلَيْهِ شَيْئًا."

Sahīh al-Bukhārī 3280

66 ...قَالَ خَدَمْتُ النَّبِيَّ عَشْرَ سِنِينَ فَمَا قَالَ لِي أُفٍّ قَطُّ وَمَا قَالَ لِشَيْءٍ صَنعْتُهُ لِمَ صَنعْتُهُ وَلاَ لِشَيْءٍ تَرَكْتُهُ لِمَ تَرَكْتَهُ وَكَانَ رَسُولُ اللَّهِ مِنْ أَحْسَنِ النَّاسِ خُلُقًا وَلاَ مَسِسْتُ خَزًّا قَطُّ وَلاَ حَرِيرًا وَلاَ شَيْئًا كَانَ أَلْيَنَ مِنْ كَفِّ رَسُولِ اللَّهِ وَلاَ شَمَمْتُ مِسْكًا قَطُّ وَلاَ عِطْرًا كَانَ أَطْيَبَ مِنْ عَرَقِ النَّبِيِّ. -Jāmi' al

Tirmidhī 2015

67 ...مَا رَأَيْتُ أَحَدًا أَشْبَهَ بِصَلاَةِ رَسُولِ اللَّهِ مِنِ ابْنِ أُمِّ سُلَيْمٍ يَعْنِي: أَنَس. Ibn Kathīr in al-Bidaya

wa al-Nihaya

'Anas is one of the major narrators of Hadiths (approximately two thousands). Shia Muslims, as well as some modern scholars, say that some of these are doubtful. However, the main Sunni transmitters of Hadiths - al-Bukhārī (الْبُجَارِئ) and al-Muslim (الْمُسْـلِم) - approved them as trustworthy. Shia Muslims don't like 'Anas very much. Some Shia sources claim that 'Alī ibn 'Abi Tālib denounced 'Anas as a liar.

It is said that 'Anas had vitiligo (skin condition) - in Arabic: al-Buhāq (بُهَاق) - and that he died of leprosy - in Arabic: al-Baras (الْبَرَص). Maybe the two diseases were mixed up, or maybe he had suffered both. Leprosy was a major disease at the time of Muhammad. 'Anas reported that the Prophet used to say: "O Allah, I seek refuge in You from leprosy, madness, elephantiasis and evil diseases."[68]

'Anas was probably the last of the companions to die; possibly at Basra (الْبَصْرة) in present-day Iraq. He died around the year 712 (~ 93 AH), aged probably above 100, some say even 103. The Islamic historian and scholar Muwarriq al-'Ijlī (مُوَرِّق الْعِجْلِيّ), who was born one hundred years after the Hijra, said that on the day 'Anas died: "This day, half of the knowledge left."[69]

Watch out: Do not confuse him with Mālik ibn 'Anas (مالِك بن أَنَس) - also known as Imam Mālik, who lived from 711 (93 AH) to 795 (179 AH). The Mālikī School of jurisprudence is named after Mālik ibn 'Anas and is one of the four schools of jurisprudence that are followed by Sunni Muslims to this day.

38. Which companion was adopted by Muhammad?

Answer: Zayd ibn Hāritha (زَيْد بن حارِثة).

Born	~ 581 (35 BH)	Died	629 (8 AH) in Mu'ta (مُؤْتة) in present-day Jordan

---

68 ...أَنَّ النَّبِيَّ كَانَ يَقُولُ: "اللَّهُمَّ إِنِّي أَعُوذُ بِكَ مِنَ الْبَرَصِ وَالْجُنُونِ وَالْجُذَامِ وَمِنْ سَيِّئِ الْأَسْقَامِ."

Sunan 'Abī Dāwūd 1554

69 ...ذَهَبَ الْيَوْمَ نِصْفُ الْعِلْم

Zayd ibn Hāritha belonged to the Banū Kalb (بَنُو كَلْب) tribe. In his childhood, he worked as a shepherd and was kidnapped one day by slave-traders. A nephew of Muhammad's wife Khadīja bought him at the slave market and brought him to Mecca where Khadīja took care of him and sheltered him in her home. Muhammad loved this child, thus, he manumitted Zayd and adopted him as his son. He was initially often called Zayd ibn Muhammad (زَيْد بن مُحَمَّد) which literally means: *Zayd, son of Muhammad.*

A verse in sura 33 *The Joint Forces* - in Arabic: al-'Ahzāb (سُورة الأَحْزَاب) - changed this:

| 33:5 | Name your <u>adopted sons</u> after their <u>real fathers</u>: this is more equitable in God's eyes if you do not know who their fathers are [they are your] brothers-in-religion and protégés. | ادْعُوهُمْ لِآبَائِهِمْ هُوَ أَقْسَطُ عِندَ اللَّهِ فَإِن لَّمْ تَعْلَمُوا آبَاءَهُمْ فَإِخْوَانُكُمْ فِي الدِّينِ وَمَوَالِيكُمْ وَلَيْسَ عَلَيْكُمْ جُنَاحٌ فِيمَا أَخْطَأْتُم بِهِ وَلَٰكِن مَّا تَعَمَّدَتْ قُلُوبُكُمْ وَكَانَ اللَّهُ غَفُورًا رَّحِيمًا. |

From that day on he was called Zayd ibn Hāritha. Sometimes the Arabic expression Mawlā Muhammad (زَيْد مَوْلَى مُحَمَّد) was added to his name. In Arabic, Mawlā (مَوْلَى) has many meanings, including *protégé, client,* and *companion.*

Zayd became a companion of Muhammad and was one of the very first converts to Islam. He led his final military expedition in September 629 (8 AH). A Muslim force of 3,000 men set out to raid the Byzantines. Zayd held the standard, Islam's banner, at the Battle of Mu'ta (سَرِيّة مُؤتة) until he was struck down by a spear and bled to death.

Zayd is the only companion whose name appears in the Qur'an. Why is this person so important that he made it into the Qur'an? It has to do with Zaynab bint Jahsh (زَيْنَب بِنْت جَحْش), the daughter of Muhammad's paternal aunt; thus a cousin. Zaynab was a skilled tanner and leather-worker.

She had a reputation for being prayerful. She prayed so much at night that she hung a rope between two pillars in the mosque and held onto it when she became too tired to prostrate. When the Prophet discovered the rope, he removed it and told her that if she became tired, she should stop praying.

Around 625 (~ 3 AH) Muhammad proposed to Zaynab that she should marry his adopted son: Zayd ibn Hāritha. But she refused, perhaps due to the difference in social status. Muslims believe that this was also the reason why Muhammad wanted her to do it. So what happened?

Muhammad announced a new revelation, which basically forced her to obey his command:

| 33:36 | When God and His messenger have decided on a matter that concerns them, it is not fitting for any believing man or woman to claim freedom of choice in that matter: whoever disobeys God and His messenger is far astray. | وَمَا كَانَ لِمُؤْمِنٍ وَلَا مُؤْمِنَةٍ إِذَا قَضَى اللَّهُ وَرَسُولُهُ أَمْرًا أَن يَكُونَ لَهُمُ الْخِيَرَةُ مِنْ أَمْرِهِمْ وَمَن يَعْصِ اللَّهَ وَرَسُولَهُ فَقَدْ ضَلَّ ضَلَالًا مُّبِينًا. |

Thus, Zaynab gave in to the marriage. But the story continues.

The 9ᵗʰ-century scholar al-Tabarī (الطَّبَرِيّ) gave two independent accounts of a visit that Muhammad paid to Zayd's house. The curtain that served as Zayd's front door was blown aside. Suddenly, Zaynab, who was only dressed in her shift, was accidentally exposed. Zaynab hurried to dress herself and informed Muhammad that Zayd was not home, but that he was welcome to visit. However, he did not enter. He exclaimed to himself: "Praise be to Allah, who turns hearts around!" and departed.

When Zayd came home, Zaynab told him what had happened. Zayd went to Muhammad, saying: "Prophet I have heard about your visit. Perhaps you admire Zaynab, so I will divorce her." Muhammad replied: "No, fear Allah and keep your wife."

After this there was conflict between the couple and eventually, Zaynab shut Zayd out of the bedroom. Their marriage, which had lasted less than two years, came to an end. He divorced her in 626.

Various Muslim scholars have rejected this story due to its vague sources. There is no authentic Hadith about this incident and the chain of narration of al-Tabarī's report is dubious. The scholars and commentators found it absurd that Muhammad would suddenly become aware of Zaynab's beauty after having known her for so long; if her beauty had been the reason for Muhammad to marry her, he would have married her himself in the first place rather than arranging her marriage to Zayd. However, Muhammad did marry her in the end.

The Prophet expected criticism if he married Zaynab. Pre-Islamic custom did not allow the marriage between a man and his son's former wife. Arab society would have viewed this union as profoundly wrong. They considered an adopted son to be a true *son*. This meant that a man who married his adopted son's wife - even if she was divorced - was considered committing incest.

Muhammad received another verse from Allah which mitigated this problem and made everything lawful. It mainly proclaimed that adoption does not create blood relations which would forbid marriage. In this verse, Zayd's name is mentioned:

| 33:37 | When you [prophet] said to the man who had been favoured by God and by you, 'Keep your wife and be mindful of God', you hid in your heart what God would later reveal: you were afraid of people, but it is more fitting that you fear God. When Zayd no longer wanted her, We gave her to you in marriage so that there might be no fault in believers marrying the wives of their adopted sons after they no longer wanted them. God's command must be carried out. | وَإِذْ تَقُولُ لِلَّذِي أَنْعَمَ اللَّهُ عَلَيْهِ وَأَنْعَمْتَ عَلَيْهِ أَمْسِكْ عَلَيْكَ زَوْجَكَ وَاتَّقِ اللَّهَ وَتُخْفِي فِي نَفْسِكَ مَا اللَّهُ مُبْدِيهِ وَتَخْشَى النَّاسَ وَاللَّهُ أَحَقُّ أَن تَخْشَاهُ فَلَمَّا قَضَى زَيْدٌ مِّنْهَا وَطَرًا زَوَّجْنَاكَهَا لِكَيْ لَا يَكُونَ عَلَى الْمُؤْمِنِينَ حَرَجٌ فِي أَزْوَاجِ أَدْعِيَائِهِمْ إِذَا قَضَوْا مِنْهُنَّ وَطَرًا وَكَانَ أَمْرُ اللَّهِ مَفْعُولًا. |

Western scholars, Orientalists and Islam critics use this verse as an example of a so-called *self-serving revelation*. They claim that some verses in the Qur'an rather express the Prophet's desires than the will of Allah.

According to some Hadiths, Zaynab herself used to boast about her marriage in front of the other wives of the Prophet. 'Anas ibn Mālik (أَنَس بن مالك) recounted that she would say: "You were given in marriage by your families, while I was married [to the Prophet] by Allah from above the Seven Heavens."[70]

70... قَالَ فَكَانَتْ زَيْنَبُ تَفْخَرُ عَلَى أَزْوَاجِ النَّبِيِّ تَقُولُ زَوَّجَكُنَّ أَهَالِيكُنَّ، وَزَوَّجَنِي اللَّهُ تَعَالَى مِنْ فَوْقِ سَبْعِ سَمَوَاتٍ. Saḥīḥ al-Bukhārī 7420.

'Anas ibn Mālik also narrated that 'Ā'isha (عَائِشَة بِنْت أَبِي بَكْر) said: "If Allah's Messenger were to conceal anything of the Qur'an he would have concealed this verse."[71]

After Muhammad's death, Zaynab never again left Medina. She continued to work at tanning and leather-crafts, and she gave away all her profits to charity. Zaynab died in the summer of 641 (21 AH) during the reign of the second Caliph, 'Umar ibn al-Khattāb (عُمَر بن الْخَطَّاب), being the first of Muhammad's widows to die after him. She was around fifty years old.

39. What was the secret place in Mecca where Muhammad gathered his followers at the beginning of his mission?

Answer: The house of al-'Arqam ibn 'Abī al-'Arqam (الْأَرْقَم بن أَبِي الْأَرْقَم).

Born	~ 597 in Mecca	Died	~ 675 (55 AH)

Al-'Arqam was a companion of Muhammad. He was the owner of the house where the early Muslim community held its meetings. There were good reasons for this, because people were not suspicious as al-'Arqam was not known for being a Muslim. Furthermore, he descended from a tribe called Banū Makhzūm (بَنُو مَخْزُوم) the leaders of which were fiercely fighting Muhammad.

The Banū Makhzūm was one of the wealthy clans of the Quraysh, the Arab tribe of Muhammad, which was divided into several sub-clans. Before Islam, the Banū Makhzūm were regarded as one of the three most powerful and influential clans in Mecca – the other two were Banū Hāshim (بَنُو هاشِم) and Banū 'Umayya (بَنُو أُمَيّة).

Al-Makhzūm was also the clan of Khālid ibn al-Walīd (خالِد بن الْوَلِيد), who played an important role in the Meccan victory at the Battle of 'Uhud (غَزوة أُحُد) against the Muslims. Later on, Khālid converted to Islam.

---

71 ...قَالَتْ عَائِشَةُ لَوْ كَانَ رَسُولُ اللَّهِ كَاتِمًا شَيْئًا لَكَتَمَ هَذِهِ. Sahīh al-Bukhārī 7420.

The house was located in a small street east of the hill called al-Safā (الصَّفا). We could say that this was the **first Islamic school** with Muhammad serving as the teacher and the first Muslims as the students. It was there that Muhammad's uncle Hamza (حَمْزة بن عَبْد الْمُطَّلِب) and 'Umar ibn al-Khattāb (عُمَر بن الْخَطَّاب) announced their conversion to Islam.

Remark: al-'Arqam is also the name of a Malaysia-based Islamic sect, founded by Ashaari Mohammad. The sect was banned by the Malaysian federal government in 1994.

40. For which king did the Prophet offer the first funeral prayer in absentia in Islamic history?

Answer: Al-Najāshī, king of al-Habasha (النَّجاشِيّ مَلِك الْحَبَشة). He is also known as: 'Ashama ibn 'Abjar (أَصْحَمة بن أَبْجَر). In some sources, you also find the name Negus.

Al-Najāshī had never met the Prophet in person. He was the king of Aksum in Abyssinia (Ethiopia) to whom Muhammad had sent around 80 Muslim men (and some women and children) because they were persecuted in Mecca. The historic accounts of the latter event are rather dubious regarding the dates and numbers. It probably happened around 616 (6 BH).

According to Islamic sources, the Meccan leaders and opponents of Islam eventually got word of the Muslim's exodus and sent 'Amr ibn al-'Ās (عَمرو بن الْعاص) - who had not yet converted to Islam at that time - to bring them back. 'Amr enjoyed good relations with 'Abū Sufyān (أَبُو سُفْيان), the leader of the Quraysh, and it happened that 'Amr was a friend of the Abyssinian king as well.

'Abū Sufyān wanted the king to expel the Muslims. His delegation arrived in Aksum with many valuable gifts. They tried to persuade the king in claiming that the Muslims were evil. Some stories state that they even bribed his bishops.

The king, however, listened to the Muslims and their message, and he believed them. The king ordered to dismiss the delegation and returned their gifts. This event is called the Hijra to Abyssinia (الْهِجْرَة إِلَى الْحَبَشة); some also call it *First Hijra*. Years later, when Muslims in Arabia felt secure, most of them in Ethiopia returned and went to Medina, where they reunited with the other Muslims.

The king al-Najāshī died in 630 (9 AH). Muhammad announced his death and held prayer in absentia (صَلاة الْغائِب). 'Abū Hurayra (أَبُو هُرَيْرة) said: "Allah's Messenger made them [the Muslims] stand in rows at the praying place and led the funeral prayer for the Negus and said four Takbīr [say: "Allāhu 'akbar!"]."[72]

Until today, a lot of Muslims speak favourably about Ethiopians – just because of this episode in Islamic history.

41. From where was the Prophet driven out before the Hijra?

Answer: From al-Tā'if (الطَّائِف).

Muhammad had started to preach his message only in Mecca. Historians say that the number of his followers was just around 170 men and women in Mecca during the first ten years. This was mainly because the leaders of the Quraysh opposed him. In 619 (3/4 BH), the *year of sorrow* (عام الْحُزْن), his wife Khadīja (خديجة) and his uncle 'Abū Tālib (أَبُو طالِب) died. This had consequences in Mecca. One of Muhammad's fiercest enemies, 'Abū Lahab (أَبُو لَهَب), took over control of the tribe Banū Hāshim (بَنُو هاشِم) from 'Abū Tālib – which meant that, according to Arabian tribal laws, Muhammad's protection by the Banū Hāshim tribe had ended.

Muhammad then decided to preach his message in another city. The nearest city was al-Tā'if, so he went there in late 619 together with his adopted son Zayd ibn Hāritha (زَيد بن حارِثة). Some other sources say that he went there by himself.

Al-Tā'if was an important place of ancient Arabia. Situated on the slopes of high and cool mountains and surrounded by many fertile gardens, it marks a spot on the road from Mecca to Yemen. At the

---

72 ...أَنَّ رَسُولَ اللَّهِ صَفَّ بِهِمْ فِي الْمُصَلَّى، فَصَلَّى عَلَيْهِ وَكَبَّرَ أَرْبَعًا. Sahīh al-Bukhārī 3881

time of the Prophet, people needed a three days' journey to get there from Mecca.

The ancient walled city housed the idol of the Arabian goddess al-Lāt (اللّت), who was known as *the Lady of Ṭā'if.*

The main leaders in al-Ṭā'if were three brothers. Muhammad talked to them, seeking protection and introducing his message. However, they kicked Muhammad out of the walled city. Some sources say, that they threw stones at him injuring his hands and feet. Eventually, he took refuge in an orchard beyond the city. Various Islamic reports say that when Muhammad later returned to Mecca, the people there opposed him more bitterly than ever.

Today, al-Ṭā'if is a city in Saudi Arabia, about 100 km (62 mi) south-east of Mecca. It is the unofficial summer capital due to its elevation of 1,879 m (6,165 ft) near the slopes of the Sarawāt Mountains (جِبَال السَّرَوات). The city has 1.2 million inhabitants and is known for its agricultural products, mainly grapes, figs and pomegranates. Al-Ṭā'if was little more than a medieval city when the Saudis took control and started to modernise it. Saudi Arabia's first public power generator was set up in al-Ṭā'if in the late 1940s.

In the 1991 Gulf War, al-Ṭā'if was chosen by the public relation company the *Rendon Group* to broadcast news to Kuwait during its occupation by troops of Saddam Husayn (Hussein).

42. What happened at al-ʿAqaba?

Answer: Twelve people accepted Islam and pledged the first oath of allegiance to Muhammad. This event is called Bay'a(t) al-'Aqaba (بَيْعَة الْعَقَبة الْأُولَى). The Arabic word Bay'a (بَيْعَة) means *deal; profession of loyalty; pledge of allegiance (to a ruler or head of state).*

When Muhammad started to preach Islam, the Meccans reacted with hostility. Muhammad's followers were persecuted, but some of them found refuge in Ethiopia. Muhammad wanted to spread his message beyond Mecca, especially as he faced strong opposition in his home town. 'Abū Lahab (أَبُو لَهَب) was fiercely opposing him calling him a liar and being insane.

Around 620, during the 11th year of revelation, six people from the tribe Banū al-Khazraj (بَنُو الْخَزْرَج) who were in a convoy heading to Yathrib (Medina) contacted Muhammad. Yathrib lies around 340 kilometres (210 mi) north of Mecca. At that time Yathrib suffered from the constant struggle between its two leading clans, the Banū al-ʾAws (بَنُو الأَوْس) and the Banū al-Khazraj. Muhammad told the group about Islam, and they became Muslims. They told him that they would return to Yathrib, that they would meet him again in the following year, and that they would bring more people.

When it was time for the next pilgrimage season to Mecca, a year after their first encounter with Muhammad, the six men set off in a caravan towards Mecca. One night twelve men met secretly with Muhammad in a narrow valley called al-ʿAqaba (العَقَبة). The meeting resulted in the **first Islamic agreement**. They all became Muslims. The whole delegation pledged their allegiance to Allah and Muhammad.

Ibn ʾIshāq told that ʿUbāda ibn al-Sāmit (عُبادة بن الصامِت) said: "There were twelve of us and we pledged ourselves to the Prophet after the manner of women and that was before war was enjoined, the undertaking being that we should associate nothing with God; we should not steal; we should not commit fornication; or kill our offspring; we should not slander our neighbours; we should not disobey him in what was right; if we fulfilled, the Paradise would be ours; if we committed any of those sins, it was for Allah to punish or forgive as He pleased."

43. Who was the first "ambassador" of Islam?

Answer: Musʿab ibn ʿUmayr (مُصْعَب بِن عُمَيْر).

Born	~ 595 (27 BH), in Mecca	Died	625 (3 AH), Battle of ʾUhud

When twelve people from Yathrib (which was later called Medina) met with Muhammad and pledged their allegiance to Allah and Muhammad in al-ʿAqaba, the delegation had asked the Prophet to send one of his students with them to teach the people the Qurʾan.

Muhammad sent Muṣʿab ibn ʿUmayr (مُصعب بن عُمَير). Musʿab is there-fore called the *first ambassador of Islam* (أَوَّل سَفِير فِي الْإِسلام). Eventu-ally, Islam began to spread in Yathrib and people started to convert.

These converts were known as al-'Ansār (الْأَنْصار) – *The Helpers*. Musʿab was also sent to prepare the city for the forthcoming migra-tion, the al-Hijra (الْهِجْرة).

44. What was the second pledge of al-ʿAqaba about?

Answer: The pledge of allegiance to Muhammad.

In the 12th year after the revelation, in June 622, three months before the Hijra, 73 men and 2 women from the clans of Banū al-'Aws (بَنُو الْأَوْس) and Banū al-Khazraj (بَنُو الْخَزْرَج) came from Yathrib to see Muhammad. They sat with the Prophet, offered the second oath of allegiance to the Prophet (بَيْعة الْعَقَبة الثّانِية) – which basically meant they converted to Islam.

But there was something else: They agreed on supporting his preaching and they pledged to protect him like they would protect their sons. All this happened in June 622 (13th of Dhū al-Hijja) when around 500 people of Yathrib, mainly from the tribe of al-Khazraj, went to Mecca for the annual pilgrimage. Don't forget that even before Islam, Arabs went to Mecca to worship their deities at the Kaʿba.

Musʿab ibn ʿUmayr (مُصعب بن عُمَير), who was sent to Yathrib as a teacher, had also accompanied the pilgrims. He he returned, he called on the Prophet and told him about the rapid progress of Islam in Yathrib. The idea of the migration to Yathrib was then born in the Prophet's mind. The delegation invited Muhammad to their city.

The Second ʿAqaba Pledge is sometimes (mostly by western schol-ars) referred to as the *Battle Pledge* or *Pledge of War* - in Arabic: Bayʿa(t) al-Harb (بَيْعة الْحَرْب) - because it contains terms and points referring to warfare. Yathrib is located at a strategic point that would lead to encounters with the Quraysh. Their caravans going to Syria and Iraq had to pass through this area. The second pledge at al-ʿAqaba is the most important event that preceded the migration to Medina, the Hijra (الْهِجْرة).

45. How did Muhammad manage to leave Mecca?

Answer: He tricked the Meccans.

Muhammad decided to leave his hometown Mecca because it became too dangerous for him. He had met secretly with influential people from Yathrib who pledged their allegiance twice, thus, he had a place to go with his followers, Yathrib, which later became Medina. After the second pledge of al-ʿAqaba, the Prophet had ordered his followers in Mecca to travel to Yathrib in secrecy – alone or in small groups. The first man who arrived in Yathrib was ʾAbū Salama ibn ʿAbd al-ʾAsad (أَبُو سَلَمة بن عَبْد الأَسَد).

Only Muhammad, ʾAbū Bakr (أَبُو بَكْر) and ʿAlī ibn ʾAbī Tālib (عَلي بن أَبِي طالِب) stayed in Mecca.

When the Quraysh realised that the Muslims were leaving, they feared that Muhammad would leave as well and wanted to prevent that. They gathered all clan and tribe leaders at a place called Dār al-Nadwa (دار النَّدوة) where the wise and elder people of the Quraysh usually met.

A spokesman, ʾAbū Jahl (أَبُو جَهْل), said that he had a plan; namely, that each clan should choose a young, strong, well-born fighter and to provide these men with swords, so that they could kill Muhammad. The idea behind his plan was that the responsibility for Muhammad's death would rest upon all clans.

What happened then? Most of the information about the Hijra is found in Ibn ʾIshāq's biography of Muhammad. Ibn ʾIshāq wrote that Gabriel came to Muhammad and said: "Do not sleep tonight on the bed on which you usually sleep." The Prophet told his cousin ʿAlī to sleep in his bed instead of him and that he should use his *Hadramī* layer (الْحَضْرَميّ) as Muhammad used to sleep in that. This should mislead his enemies. Muhammad was convinced that Allah would protect ʿAlī.

The Prophet told ʾAbū Bakr about the plot and Allah's order to leave Mecca. He asked him to get ready to leave for Yathrib.

The Meccans came to the Prophet's house at night and waited for him to come out, but they got sleepy. This was a chance for Muhammad to quietly leave the house on the night of Thursday, 9th September, 622. He went to ʾAbū Bakr who had prepared for their departure. Together, they rode south instead of going north towards

Yathrib. After some time, the Meccans outside the Prophet's house got suspicious and went in. They found only 'Alī – and rushed out to search for Muhammad. The Prophet and 'Abū Bakr hid in the cave of Thawr (غار ثَوْر). When the Meccan enemies came near the cave, the Prophet told 'Abū Bakr: "Do not be afraid, for Allah is with us." The chasers did not find them. Three days later, Muhammad and 'Abū Bakr left for Yathrib and arrived there on Friday, 27th September, in 622. Note: Modern scholars also give the date 24 September 622 CE.

Some scholars pointed out that the people of Yathrib had an ulterior motive when they invited Muhammad to migrate to their city. They wanted him to function as an arbitrator between the tribes which were each other's enemies.

When the Prophet settled in Yathrib, he arranged a pact of solidarity between the immigrants from Mecca - in Arabic: al-Muhājirūn (الْمُهاجِرُون) - and the Muslims of Yathrib, known as *The Helpers* – in Arabic: al-'Ansār (الأَنْصار). This alliance was not based on tribal but on religious solidarity. Muhammad wanted to change the social norms and traditions of Arabia. This was the first step. Yathrib was from now on called Medina (see question 47).

The *Constitution of Medina* was created to end the inter-tribal fighting between the rival tribes of Banū al-'Aws (بَنُو الأَوْس) and Banū al-Khazraj (بَنُو الْخَزْرَج). The Jewish groups were recognised too, which posed no problem at the beginning. But the peace did not last very long, not even for two years, when according to Islamic sources, a Jewish tribe broke the treaty.

The Prophet built Islam's first mosque in Medina. He used this place for preaching and for formation of new Muslims. He tried to mould a brotherhood of believers. Until today, Islam tries to unite all Muslims based on nothing more than its religious laws. Thus, in a perfect Islamic world, there would no longer be nations.

46. In which cave did the Prophet and 'Abū Bakr hide during the migration (Hijra) to Medina?

Answer: Ghār Thawr (غار ثَوْر); literally, *cave of the bull.*

The cave is located at Mount Bull (جَبَل ثَوْر) which is in the southern part of Mecca south of the Misfala (مِشْفَلة) district. The height of the mountain is 750 m (2,460 ft). For most Muslims, the cave is of great importance and is visited by thousands of pilgrims every year.

Muhammad and 'Abū Bakr took refuge there from the Quraysh during the Hijra to Yathrib. When the Quraysh came to pursue them, 'Abū Bakr was worried as they were just the two of them – but Muhammad assured him that Allah was the third in the cave. This is told in sura 9 *The Repentance* – in Arabic: al-Tawba (سُورة التَّوْبة):

| 9:40 | Even if you do not help the Prophet, God helped him when the disbelievers drove him out: when the two of them were in the cave, he [Muhammad] said to his companion, 'Do not worry, God is with us', and God sent His calm down to him, aided him with forces invisible to you, and brought down the disbelievers' plan. God's plan is higher: God is almighty and wise. | إِلَّا تَنصُرُوهُ فَقَدْ نَصَرَهُ اللَّهُ إِذْ أَخْرَجَهُ الَّذِينَ كَفَرُوا ثَانِيَ اثْنَيْنِ إِذْ هُمَا فِي الْغَارِ إِذْ يَقُولُ لِصَاحِبِهِ لَا تَحْزَنْ إِنَّ اللَّهَ مَعَنَا فَأَنزَلَ اللَّهُ سَكِينَتَهُ عَلَيْهِ وَأَيَّدَهُ بِجُنُودٍ لَّمْ تَرَوْهَا وَجَعَلَ كَلِمَةَ الَّذِينَ كَفَرُوا السُّفْلَىٰ وَكَلِمَةُ اللَّهِ هِيَ الْعُلْيَا وَاللَّهُ عَزِيزٌ حَكِيمٌ |

There is a long Hadith about the event, narrated by 'Ā'isha (بِنْت أَبِي بَكْر). Let's have a look at it step by step.

"At the time the Prophet was in Mecca, he said to the Muslims: 'In a dream, I've been shown your migration place, a land of date palms, between two mountains, the two stony tracts.' So, some people migrated to Medina, and most of those people who had previously migrated to the land of Ethiopia, returned to Medina. 'Abū Bakr also prepared to leave for Medina but Allah's Messenger said to him: 'Wait for a while because I hope that I'll be allowed to migrate also.'[73]

One day, while we were sitting in 'Abū Bakr's house at noon, someone said to 'Abū Bakr: 'This is Allah's Messenger with his head covered coming at a time at which he never used to visit us before.' 'Abū Bakr said: 'May my parents be sacrificed for him. By Allah, he

---

73 ...النَّبِيُّ يَوْمَئِذٍ بِمَكَّةَ، فَقَالَ النَّبِيُّ لِلْمُسْلِمِينَ: "إِنِّي أُرِيتُ دَارَ هِجْرَتِكُمْ ذَاتَ نَخْلٍ بَيْنَ لاَبَتَيْنِ." وَهُمَا الْحَرَّتَانِ، فَهَاجَرَ مَنْ هَاجَرَ قِبَلَ الْمَدِينَةِ، وَرَجَعَ عَامَّةُ مَنْ كَانَ هَاجَرَ بِأَرْضِ الْحَبَشَةِ إِلَى الْمَدِينَةِ، وَتَجَهَّزَ أَبُو بَكْرٍ قِبَلَ الْمَدِينَةِ، فَقَالَ لَهُ رَسُولُ اللَّهِ: "عَلَى رِسْلِكَ، فَإِنِّي أَرْجُو أَنْ يُؤْذَنَ لِي." Sahīh al-Bukhārī
3905

has not come at this hour except for a great necessity.' So Allah's Messenger came and asked permission to enter, and he was allowed to enter. When he entered, he said to 'Abū Bakr: 'Tell everyone who is present with you to go away.' 'Abū Bakr replied: 'There are none but your family. May my father be sacrificed for you, O Allah's Messenger!' The Prophet then said: 'I've been given permission to migrate.'[74]

'Abū Bakr replied: 'Shall I accompany you? May my father be sacrificed for you, O Allah's Messenger!' Allah's Messenger said: 'Yes.' 'Abū Bakr said: 'O Allah's Messenger! May my father be sacrificed for you, take one of these two she-camels of mine.' Allah's Messenger replied: '[I will accept it] with payment.' So we prepared the baggage quickly and put some journey food in a leather bag for them. 'Asmā', 'Abū Bakr's daughter, cut a piece from her waist belt and tied the mouth of the leather bag with it, and for that reason she was later referred to as Dhāt al-Niṭāqayn [i.e. the owner of two belts].[75]

Then, Allah's Messenger and 'Abū Bakr reached a cave on the mountain of Thawr and stayed there for three nights. 'Abd Allah ibn 'Abī Bakr, who was intelligent and a sagacious youth, stayed [with them] over night. He used to leave them before day break so that in the morning, he would be with the Quraysh as if he had spent the night in Mecca. He would remember any plot made against them and after dark he would [go and] inform them about it.[76]

After nightfall, 'Āmir ibn Fuhayra (عَامِر بن فُهَيْرَة), the freed slave of 'Abū Bakr, would bring the sheep [of his master, 'Abū Bakr] to them [their cave] in order to give the sheep some rest. So they always had fresh milk at night, which they warmed by placing heated stones in

74 ...قَالَتْ عَائِشَةُ فَبَيْنَمَا نَحْنُ يَوْمًا جُلُوسٌ فِي بَيْتِ أَبِي بَكْرٍ فِي نَحْرِ الظَّهِيرَةِ قَالَ قَائِلٌ لأَبِي بَكْرٍ هَذَا رَسُولُ اللَّهِ مُتَقَنِّعًا فِي سَاعَةٍ لَمْ يَكُنْ يَأْتِينَا فِيهَا فَقَالَ أَبُو بَكْرٍ فِدَاءً لَهُ أَبِي وَأُمِّي، وَاللَّهِ مَا جَاءَ بِهِ فِي هَذِهِ السَّاعَةِ إِلاَّ أَمْرٌ. قَالَتْ فَجَاءَ رَسُولُ." Sahīh al-Bukhārī 3905

75 ...فَقَالَ أَبُو بَكْرٍ الصَّحَابَةَ بِأَبِي أَنْتَ يَا رَسُولَ اللَّهِ. قَالَ رَسُولُ اللَّهِ: "نَعَمْ." قَالَ أَبُو بَكْرٍ فَخُذْ بِأَبِي أَنْتَ يَا رَسُولَ اللَّهِ إِحْدَى رَاحِلَتَيَّ هَاتَيْنِ. قَالَ رَسُولُ اللَّهِ: "بِالثَّمَنِ." قَالَتْ عَائِشَةُ فَجَهَّزْنَاهُمَا أَحَثَّ الْجَهَازِ، وَصَنَعْنَا لَهُمَا سُفْرَةً فِي جِرَابٍ، فَقَطَعَتْ أَسْمَاءُ بِنْتُ أَبِي بَكْرٍ قِطْعَةً مَنْ نِطَاقِهَا فَرَبَطَتْ بِهِ عَلَى فَمِ الْجِرَابِ، فَبِذَلِكَ سُمِّيَتْ ذَاتِ النِّطَاقَيْنِ. Sahīh al-Bukhārī 3905

76 ...ثُمَّ لَحِقَ رَسُولُ اللَّهِ وَأَبُو بَكْرٍ بِغَارٍ فِي جَبَلِ ثَوْرٍ فَكَمَنَا فِيهِ ثَلاَثَ لَيَالٍ، يَبِيتُ عِنْدَهُمَا عَبْدُ اللَّهِ بْنُ أَبِي بَكْرٍ وَهُوَ غُلاَمٌ شَابٌّ ثَقِفٌ لَقِنٌّ، فَيُدْلِجُ مِنْ عِنْدِهِمَا بِسَحَرٍ، فَيُصْبِحُ مَعَ قُرَيْشٍ بِمَكَّةَ كَبَائِتٍ، فَلاَ يَسْمَعُ أَمْرًا يُكْتَادَانِ بِهِ إِلاَّ وَعَاهُ، حَتَّى يَأْتِيهِمَا بِخَبَرِ ذَلِكَ حِينَ يَخْتَلِطُ الظَّلاَمُ. Sahīh al-Bukhārī 3905

it. 'Āmir would then call the herd away when it was still dark [before daybreak]. He did the same in each of those three nights.[77]

Allah's Messenger and 'Abū Bakr had hired a man from the tribe of Banū al-Dayl from the family of Banū 'Abd ibn 'Adī (عَبْد بن عَدِيّ) as an expert guide. He was allied with the family of al-'Āṣ ibn Wā'il al-Sahmī and he was of the religion of the infidels of Quraysh. The Prophet and 'Abū Bakr had trusted him and had given him their two she-camels, which he promised to bring to the Thawr mountain cave in the morning after the third night. And [when they set out], 'Āmir ibn Fuhayra and the guide went along with them and the guide led them along the sea-shore."[78]

There is a famous story which is circulating among Muslims, about a spider. The story of the spider's web was narrated by Imam 'Ahmad ibn Hanbal (أَحْمَد بن حَنْبَل الشَّيْبَانِي), a late 8th to mid-9th century conservative scholar and theologian, who is considered the founder of the Hanbalī School (الْمَذْهَب الْحَنْبَلِيّ) of Islamic jurisprudence.

"The polytheists [Meccan non-Muslims] spent the night waiting for 'Alī, thinking that he was the Prophet. When morning came, they pounced on him, and when they saw 'Alī, Allah thwarted their plot. They said: 'Where is that friend of yours?' He said: 'I do not know.' So they set out after him and when they reached the mountain, they were confounded. They climbed up the mountain, passed by the cave, and saw a spider's web over its entrance. They said: 'If anyone had entered here, the spider would not have spun a web over the entrance.' And it stayed there for three nights."[79]

---

77 ...وَيَرْعَى عَلَيْهِمَا عَامِرُ بْنُ فُهَيْرَةَ مَوْلَى أَبِي بَكْرٍ مِنْحَةٌ مِنْ غَنَمٍ، فَيُرِيحُهَا عَلَيْهِمَا حِينَ يَذْهَبُ سَاعَةٌ مِنَ الْعِشَاءِ، فَيَبِيتَانِ فِي رِسْلٍ وَهُوَ لَبَنُ مِنْحَتِهِمَا وَرَضِيفِهِمَا، حَتَّى يَنْعِقَ بِهَا عَامِرُ بْنُ فُهَيْرَةَ بِغَلَسٍ، يَفْعَلُ ذَلِكَ فِي كُلِّ لَيْلَةٍ مِنْ تِلْكَ اللَّيَالِي الثَّلَاثِ. Saḥīḥ al-Bukhārī 3905.

78 ...وَاسْتَأْجَرَ رَسُولُ اللَّهِ وَأَبُو بَكْرٍ رَجُلاً مِنْ بَنِي الدَّيْلِ، وَهُوَ مِنْ بَنِي عَبْدِ بْنِ عَدِيٍّ خِرِّيتًا وَالْخِرِّيتُ الْمَاهِرُ بِالْهِدَايَةِ قَدْ غَمَسَ حِلْفًا فِي آلِ الْعَاصِ بْنِ وَائِلٍ السَّهْمِيِّ، وَهُوَ عَلَى دِينِ كُفَّارِ قُرَيْشٍ فَأَمِنَاهُ، فَدَفَعَا إِلَيْهِ رَاحِلَتَيْهِمَا، وَوَاعَدَاهُ غَارَ ثَوْرٍ بَعْدَ ثَلَاثِ لَيَالٍ بِرَاحِلَتَيْهِمَا صُبْحَ ثَلَاثٍ، وَانْطَلَقَ مَعَهُمَا عَامِرُ بْنُ فُهَيْرَةَ وَالدَّلِيلُ فَأَخَذَ بِهِمْ طَرِيقَ السَّوَاحِلِ. Saḥīḥ al-Bukhārī 3905.

79 ...وَبَاتَ الْمُشْرِكُونَ يَحْرُسُونَ عَلِيًّا يَحْسَبُونَهُ النَّبِيَّ، فَلَمَّا أَصْبَحُوا ثَارُوا إِلَيْهِ، فَلَمَّا رَأَوْا عَلِيًّا رَدَّ اللَّهُ مَكْرَهُمْ، فَقَالُوا: أَيْنَ صَاحِبُكَ هَذَا ؟ قَالَ: لَا أَدْرِي. فَاقْتَصُّوا أَثَرَهُ، فَلَمَّا بَلَغُوا الْجَبَلَ خُلِّطَ عَلَيْهِمْ، فَصَعِدُوا فِي الْجَبَلِ فَمَرُّوا بِالْغَارِ، فَرَأَوْا عَلَى بَابِهِ نَسْجَ الْعَنْكَبُوتِ، فَقَالُوا: لَوْ دَخَلَ هَاهُنَا لَمْ يَكُنْ نَسْجُ الْعَنْكَبُوتِ عَلَى بَابِهِ، فَمَكَثَ فِيهِ ثَلَاثَ لَيَالٍ. Imam Ahmad 3241; al-Musnad 3251.

Although this story is often mentioned in books, Islamic scholars have doubts about the authenticity of the source. Some say that the chain of narration of the Hadith is good (حَسَن), for example Ibn Kathīr in al-Bidāya wa al-Nihāya (3/222). However, Muhammad al-'Albānī (مُحَمَّد الأَلْبَانِي), who died in 1999 (1420 AH), suggested that this Hadith is weak (ضَعِيف).

47. Why did the Prophet change Yathrib to Medina?

Answer: Probably because the word Yathrib has a bad meaning.

Muhammad did not like this name. The word Yathrib has a negative meaning. This is related to its Arabic root which is: th-r-f (ث-ر-ب).

The verbal noun/infinitive of the I-verb (which is rarely used) is tharb (ثَرْب) and can mean *corruption*. According to Edward Lane, it can also describe the *fat that is spread over the bowels or intestines*. The verbal noun of the Arabic II-verb is tathrīb (تَثْرِيب) which means *blame* or *rebuke*. Muhammad commanded his followers to use only names with good meanings. 'Abū Hurayra (أَبُو هُرَيْرَة) reported that Allah's Messenger said: "I have been commanded [to migrate] to a town which will overpower other towns. They [the people] call it Yathrib; its correct name is Medina. It eliminates [bad] people just as the blacksmith's furnace removes impurities from the iron."[80]

The Arabic word Medina (مَدِينة) simply means *city*. That is also why Muslims prefer to call the city al-Madīna al-Munawwara (الْمَدِينة الْمُنَوَّرة) – *the shining/enlightened city*. Sometimes, the adjective is used as an epithet for the city, i.e. Medina: al-Munawwra (الْمُنَوَّرة). The city is also called Medina(t) al-Nabī (مَدِينة النَّبِيّ) - *the city of the Prophet* – or as Tāba (طابة) which means *good*. 'Abū Humayd (أَبُو حُمَيْد) narrated: "We came with the Prophet from Tabūk and when we came near Medina, the Prophet said: 'This is Tāba.'"[81]

---

80 قَالَ رَسُولُ اللَّهِ: "أُمِرْتُ بِقَرْيَةٍ تَأْكُلُ الْقُرَى يَقُولُونَ يَثْرِبَ وَهِىَ الْمَدِينَةُ تَنْفِي النَّاسَ كَمَا يَنْفِي الْكِيرُ خَبَثَ الْحَدِيدِ." Sahīh Muslim 1382

81 ...أَقْبَلْنَا مَعَ النَّبِيِّ مِنْ تَبُوكَ حَتَّى أَشْرَفْنَا عَلَى الْمَدِينَةِ فَقَالَ: "هَذِهِ طَابَةُ." Sahīh al-Bukhārī

48. What is the name of the mosque which Muhammad founded when he came to Medina?

Answer: Qubā' (مَسْجِد قُباء).

The mosque lies in the south-western part of Medina and is located around 5 km (3.1 mi) from the Prophet's Mosque - in Arabic: al-Masjid al-Nabawī (الْمَسْجِد النَّبَوِيّ) -, which is the second most important in Islam. The Qubā' mosque was built in 622 (1 AH).

Notice the difference: Al-Masjid al-Haram in Mecca is the **first house** that Muslims **used as a mosque**. And Masjid Qubā' in Medina is the first mosque built by the Muslims.

The name of the mosque is said to be derived from the name of a well. The mosque is located in south-west Medina and within 30 minutes walking distance (~ 4 km; 2.5 mi) from the Prophet's Mosque (الْمَسْجِد النَّبَوِيّ).

Muhammad spent 14 days in this mosque during the Hijra praying a short prayer while he waited for 'Alī ibn 'Abī Tālib (عَلِيّ بن أبي طالب) to arrive in Medina. 'Alī had stayed behind in Mecca to carry out a number of tasks entrusted to him by the Prophet.

49. What was the first prayer direction in Islam?

Answer: Towards Jerusalem.

In Islam, the prayer direction is called Qibla (قِبْلة). During the thirteen years of his mission in Mecca, Muhammad used to offer his prayers facing towards Jerusalem. Muslims call Jerusalem *Bayt al-Maqdis* (بَيْت الْمَقْدِس) or simply *al-Quds* (الْقُدْس) which literally means *the holiness* or *the sacredness*.

Nevertheless, in the second year after the Hijra, in 624 (2 AH), in the middle of the lunar month of Rajab (رَجَب), the direction was changed to the Ka'ba (الْكَعْبة) in Mecca.

Muslims must face in the (shortest) direction of Mecca, as mentioned in sura 2 *The Cow* – in Arabic: al-Baqara (سُورة الْبَقَرة):

| 2:144 | Many time We have seen you [Prophet] | قَدْ نَرَى تَقَلُّبَ وَجْهِكَ فِي |

	turn your face towards Heaven, so We are turning you towards a prayer direction that pleases you. Turn your face in the direction of the Sacred Mosque [al-Masjid al-Haram at Mecca]: wherever you [believers] may be, turn your faces to it. Those who were given the Scripture know with certainty that this is the Truth from their Lord: God is not un-aware of what they do.	السَّمَاءِ فَلَنُوَلِّيَنَّكَ قِبْلَةً تَرْضَاهَا فَوَلِّ وَجْهَكَ شَطْرَ الْمَسْجِدِ الْحَرَامِ وَحَيْثُ مَا كُنتُمْ فَوَلُّوا وُجُوهَكُمْ شَطْرَهُ وَإِنَّ الَّذِينَ أُوتُوا الْكِتَابَ لَيَعْلَمُونَ أَنَّهُ الْحَقُّ مِن رَّبِّهِمْ وَمَا اللَّهُ بِغَافِلٍ عَمَّا يَعْمَلُونَطَاعُون.

Why was the direction changed? Muslim scholars think that there were mainly two reasons: First of all, Allah wanted to test his people and by changing the prayer direction, it became easy to distinguish Muslims from others. If someone prayed towards Mecca and not towards Jerusalem, it was clear whom this person was following.

Secondly, Muslims say that the idea behind this was to bring the two religions - the "old" one (Judaism) and the "new" one (Islam) - nearer to each other. According to some Islamic historians, the Jews were anxious that Islam would spread over the entire peninsula, which would have ended Jewish influence.

The Jews mocked Muhammad by asking how Islam could be a new religion with laws that superseded all previous (Jewish and Christian) laws, when the Muslims prayed in the same direction as the Jews? Muslim scholars say that this had hurt Muhammad a lot. One night, he walked out of his house and looked at the sky. He was awaiting a revelation, and an order was revealed to him – the change of the prayer direction.

Islam, and this is holds true until today, is based on the principle that Muslims should be recognisable. They should not be mistaken for Christians or Jews. From the very beginning of Islam, it was a fight which religion was stronger and had more rights to claim to be the one and only correct religion. The change of the Qibla was one of the signs that Islam used to prove to the others that they were wrong.

After this verse came down, it became apparent who was a Muslim and who was not – a fact which is mentioned in this verse:

| 2:143 | We only made the direction the one you [Prophet] used to face in order to distinguish those who follow the messenger from those who turn on their heels: that test was hard, except for those God has guided. God would never let your faith go to waste [believers], for God is most compassionate and most merciful towards people. | وَمَا جَعَلْنَا الْقِبْلَةَ الَّتِي كُنتَ عَلَيْهَا إِلَّا لِنَعْلَمَ مَن يَتَّبِعُ الرَّسُولَ مِمَّن يَنقَلِبُ عَلَىٰ عَقِبَيْهِ وَإِن كَانَتْ لَكَبِيرَةً إِلَّا عَلَى الَّذِينَ هَدَى اللَّهُ وَمَا كَانَ اللَّهُ لِيُضِيعَ إِيمَانَكُمْ إِنَّ اللَّهَ بِالنَّاسِ لَرَءُوفٌ رَّحِيمٌ. |

The Qibla is of great importance for many Islamic rituals:

- Muslims have to face (towards) Mecca when they pray. First of all, when all Muslims around the world pray towards the same point, it is symbolising the unity of the Muslims – the so-called 'Umma (أُمّة).

- The head of an animal that is slaughtered using halāl (خَلال) methods is usually aligned with the Qibla – although there is no authentic tradition commanding this.

- After death, Muslims are usually buried with the body at right angles to the Qibla and the face turned right towards Mecca. This helped archaeologists identifying Islamic necropolises.

The change of the prayer direction had a major impact in establishing of Islam as a religion with its own characteristics. The pilgrimage to Mecca all of a sudden became "Islamic". The legend of the Ka'ba (the story of Abraham/'Ibrāhīm) was now told from an Islamic viewpoint – starting at the very beginning of human kind.

From an Islamic point of view, the stories about Abraham who was commanded to clean and purify the Ka'ba were no tales or legends any longer, but historical facts (in the eyes of Muslims). This is all told in sura 22 *The Pilgrimage* – in Arabic: al-Hajj (سُورة الْحَجّ):

| 22:26 | We showed Abraham ['Ibrāhīm] the site of the House, saying, 'Do not assign partners to Me. Purify My House for those who circle around it, those who stand to pray, and those who bow and prostrate themselves.' | وَإِذْ بَوَّأْنَا لِإِبْرَاهِيمَ مَكَانَ الْبَيْتِ أَن لَّا تُشْرِكْ بِي شَيْئًا وَطَهِّرْ بَيْتِيَ لِلطَّائِفِينَ وَالْقَائِمِينَ وَالرُّكَّعِ السُّجُودِ. |

Islam understands itself as the continuation of the monotheism that started with Abraham ('Ibrāhīm) and which includes Judaism and Christianity.

Islam claims that both the latter religions corrupted the message of Allah. By changing the direction of praying to the Ka'ba, Islam corrected and completed the tradition of Abrahamitic monotheism. That is what Muslims believe.

They find proof for this in the Qur'an:

| 3:96 | The first House [of worship] to be established for people was the one at Mecca [in the Qur'an it is written Bakka]. It is a blessed place; a source of guidance for all people. | إِنَّ أَوَّلَ بَيْتٍ وُضِعَ لِلنَّاسِ لَلَّذِي بِبَكَّةَ مُبَارَكًا وَهُدًى لِّلْعَالَمِينَ. |

Some remarks:

- The mosque in Medina, where the change of the prayer direction happened, is called *the Mosque of the two Qiblas* - in Arabic: Masjid al-Qiblatayn (مَسْجِد الْقِبْلَتَين).
- Some Sunni Muslims describe themselves as the *People of the Qibla* (أَهْل الْقِبْلة).

50. Who made the Prophet laugh?

Answer: 'Abd Allah who was nicknamed *donkey* – Himār (جمار).

Non-Muslims occasionally imagine Muhammad as a man who did not laugh. Traditional Muslims usually try to imitate the Prophet by pretending to be very serious. However, there was at least one man during Muhammad's time who made him laugh.

It was narrated by 'Umar ibn al-Khattāb (عُمَر بن الْخَطَّاب): "During the Prophet's lifetime there was a man called 'Abd Allah whose nickname was donkey. He used to make Allah's Messenger laugh. [On several occasions] the Prophet had lashed him because of drinking [alcohol]. One day he was brought to the Prophet on the same charge and was lashed. Upon which, a man among the people [bystanders] said: 'O Allah, curse him! How frequently has he been brought [to the Prophet on such a charge]!' The Prophet said: "Do not curse him, for by Allah, I know he loves Allah and His Apostle."[82]

Scholars justify the joking of this man by saying that he wanted to make the Prophet happy: and because of that Muhammad had approved and didn't punish him even though he committed a sin [drinking alcohol] according to Islam. In some narrations, it was said that ʿAbd Allah [donkey] would gift the Prophet a vessel of ghee and honey. The Prophet then would refund him for what he had bought and given to him as a gift.

The above narration is interesting because it is forbidden in Islam to make fun of Hadiths, fun of prophets, and especially fun of Muhammad including his life and his traditions. So what was *donkey* joking about? Unfortunately, there is no source that relates how he actually made the Prophet laugh.

How about joking in general?

Islam is a very strict religion which has a very serious nature. Joking too much is, as most scholars say, not compatible with Islam. ʾAbū Hurayra (أَبُو هُرَيْرَة) reported that the Prophet said: "Do not laugh a lot. Laughing a lot kills the heart."[83]

If a Muslim tells a joke, it should not be based on lies. Bahz ibn Hakīm (بَهْز بن حَكِيم) mentioned that the Messenger of Allah had said: "Woe to the one who talks about something to make the people laugh, in which he lies. Woe to him! Woe to him!"[84]

51. What originated from between Muhammad's fingers?

Answer: Water.

---

82 ...أَنَّ رَجُلًا، عَلَى عَهْدِ النَّبِيِّ كَانَ اسْمُهُ عَبْدَ اللَّهِ، وَكَانَ يُلَقَّبُ حِمَارًا، وَكَانَ يُضْحِكُ رَسُولَ اللَّهِ، وَكَانَ النَّبِيُّ قَدْ جَلَدَهُ فِي الشَّرَابِ، فَأُتِيَ بِهِ يَوْمًا فَأَمَرَ بِهِ فَجُلِدَ، فَقَالَ رَجُلٌ مِنَ الْقَوْمِ اللَّهُمَّ الْعَنْهُ مَا أَكْثَرَ مَا يُؤْتَى بِهِ. فَقَالَ النَّبِيُّ: "لاَ تَلْعَنُوهُ، فَوَاللَّهِ مَا عَلِمْتُ أَنَّهُ يُحِبُّ اللَّهَ وَرَسُولَهُ." Sahīh al-Bukhārī 6780

83 ...النَّبِيُّ قَالَ: "لاَ تُكْثِرُوا الضَّحِكَ، فَإِنَّ كَثْرَةَ الضَّحِكِ تُمِيتُ الْقَلْبَ." Sahīh (al-ʾAlbānī), al-ʾAdab al-Mufrad 253

84 ...سَمِعْتُ رَسُولَ اللَّهِ يَقُولُ: "وَيْلٌ لِلَّذِي يُحَدِّثُ فَيَكْذِبُ بِهِ لِيُضْحِكَ بِهِ الْقَوْمَ وَيْلٌ لَهُ وَيْلٌ لَهُ." hasan; Jāmiʿ al-Tirmidhī 2315

The wonder of emerging water occurred several times during Muhammad's reign.

'Anas ibn Mālik (أَنَس بن مالِك) narrated: "A bowl of water was brought to the Prophet while he was at al-Zawra. He placed his hand in it and water started flowing from between his fingers. All the people performed ablution (with that water). Qatāda asked 'Anas: 'How many people were you?' 'Anas replied: 'Three hundred or nearly three hundred.'[85]

52. What was the Prophet's advice for people who felt sick?

Answer: To drink the milk and urine of camels.

This sounds strange but there are several authentic Hadiths which tell this story. The content of these narrations further indicate what Muhammad ordered to be done to people who betrayed him.

'Anas ibn Mālik (أَنَس بن مالِك) recounted: "Eight men of the tribe of 'Ukl (عُكَل) came to Allah's Messenger and swore allegiance to him on Islam, but found the climate of that land not agreeable to their health and thus, they became sick and complained to Allah's Messenger. The Prophet said: 'Why don't you go to [the fold] of our camels along with our shepherd and make use of their milk and urine?' They said: 'Yes.' They set out and drank the camels' milk and urine and regained their health. [However,] they killed the shepherd and drove away the camels.

This [news] reached Allah's Messenger. They were caught and brought to him. He commanded that their hands and feet were cut off and their eyes were gouged and then they were thrown in the sun, until they died."[86]

---

85 ...قَالَ أُتِيَ النَّبِيُّ بِإِنَاءٍ وَهُوَ بِالزَّوْرَاءِ، فَوَضَعَ يَدَهُ فِي الإِنَاءِ، فَجَعَلَ الْمَاءُ يَنْبُعُ مِنْ بَيْنِ أَصَابِعِهِ، فَتَوَضَّأَ الْقَوْمُ. قَالَ قَتَادَةُ قُلْتُ لِأَنَسٍ كَمْ كُنْتُمْ قَالَ ثَلاَثَمِائَةٍ، أَوْ زُهَاءَ ثَلاَثِمِائَةٍ. Sahīh al-Bukhārī 3572

86 ...أَنَّ نَفَرًا، مِنْ عُكْلٍ ثَمَانِيَةً قَدِمُوا عَلَى رَسُولِ اللَّهِ فَبَايَعُوهُ عَلَى الإِسْلاَمِ فَاسْتَوْخَمُوا الأَرْضَ وَسَقِمَتْ أَجْسَامُهُمْ فَشَكَوْا ذَلِكَ إِلَى رَسُولِ اللَّهِ. فَقَالَ: "أَلاَ تَخْرُجُونَ مَعَ رَاعِينَا فِي إِبِلِهِ فَتُصِيبُونَ مِنْ أَبْوَالِهَا وَأَلْبَانِهَا." فَقَالُوا بَلَى. فَخَرَجُوا فَشَرِبُوا مِنْ أَبْوَالِهَا وَأَلْبَانِهَا فَصَحُّوا فَقَتَلُوا الرَّاعِيَ وَطَرَدُوا الإِبِلَ فَبَلَغَ ذَلِكَ رَسُولَ اللَّهِ فَبَعَثَ فِي آثَارِهِمْ فَأُدْرِكُوا فَجِيءَ بِهِمْ فَأَمَرَ بِهِمْ فَقُطِعَتْ أَيْدِيهِمْ وَأَرْجُلُهُمْ وَسُمِرَ أَعْيُنُهُمْ ثُمَّ نُبِذُوا فِي الشَّمْسِ حَتَّى مَاتُوا. Sahīh Muslim 1671

Remark: In another Hadith, it is reported that "He [Muhammad] had their hands and feet cut, and their eyes were burned with pieces of hot iron and they were left in the Harra biting the dust [stones]."[87] The Harra (الْحَرَّة) is a land near Medina the soil of which consists of black stones. It is probably a lava field.

So is there any proof that the urine of camels is beneficial? Muslims told me that they believe that the camel's urine can be used as a treatment for several illnesses, such as hepatitis, digestive problems, ulcers and other skin diseases, even cancer. But I have to admit that I have never met a Muslim who actually had drunk it.

There is an anecdote about German soldiers during World War II, which concerns the excretions of camels. The soldiers, who were fighting in Egypt against British forces, had severe digestive problems. The doctors told them to eat the camel's dung because it contains a lot of useful microbes, and it got rid of the soldiers' stomach problems.

53. Did Muhammad have a sweet tooth?

Answer: Most probably, yes; at least, he loved honey.

'Ā'isha (عائشة بِنْت أَبِي بَكْر) narrated: "Allah's Messenger used to love sweet edible things and honey."[88]

Muhammad was not only very fond of eating honey. He also used it as medicine. 'Abū Sa'īd al-Khudrī (أَبُو سَعِيد الْخُدْرِيّ) narrated: "A man came to the Prophet and said: 'My brother has some abdominal trouble.' The Prophet said to him: 'Let him drink honey!'

The man came for the second time and the Prophet said to him: 'Let him drink honey.'

He came for the third time and the Prophet said: 'Let him drink honey.' He returned again and said: 'I have done that.'

---

87 ...فَقَطَّعَ أَيْدِيَهُمْ وَأَرْجُلَهُمْ وَسَمَرَ أَعْيُنَهُمْ، وَتَرَكَهُمْ بِالْحَرَّةِ يَعَضُّونَ الْحِجَارَةَ. Sahīh al-Bukhārī 1501

88 ...كَانَ رَسُولُ اللَّهِ يُحِبُّ الْحَلْوَاءَ وَالْعَسَلَ. Sahīh al-Bukhārī 5431

The Prophet then said: 'Allah has said the truth, but your brother's abdomen has told a lie. Let him drink honey.' So he made him drink honey, and he was cured."[89]

It was narrated that 'Anas ibn Mālik (أنَس بن مالك) said: "'Umm Sulaym had a wooden cup and she said: 'I gave the Messenger of Allah all kinds of things to drink from it; water, honey, milk and Nabīdh."[90]

Nabīdh (نَبِيذ) is an Arabic word which today is used for *wine*. So, did the Prophet drink wine? Certainly not. Muslims say that the Nabīdh Muhammed drank was just water sweetened with dates.

'Ā'isha said: "We prepared Nabīdh for Allah's Messenger in a waterskin, the upper part of which was tied and it [the waterskin] had a hole in its lower part. We prepared the Nabīdh in the morning and he drank it in the evening and we prepared the Nabīdh at night, and he would drink it in the morning."[91]

What did the Muslims use for the Nabīdh? It was narrated from Jābir ibn 'Abd Allah (جابر بن عَبْد الله) that "the Messenger of Allah forbade making Nabīdh with dates and raisins together, or with unripe and fresh dates together."[92]

54. What is the name of the Prophet's she-camel on which he migrated from Mecca to Medina?

Answer: Al-Qaswā' (الْقَصْواء).

He bought the she-camel (ناقة) from 'Abū Bakr for the Hijra to Yathrib (which later became Medina).

---

89 ...أَنَّ رَجُلًا، أَتَى النَّبِيَّ فَقَالَ أخِي يَشْتَكِي بَطْنَهُ. فَقَالَ: "اسْقِهِ عَسَلًا." ثُمَّ أَتَى الثَّانِيَةَ فَقَالَ: "اسْقِهِ عَسَلًا." ثُمَّ أَتَاهُ فَقَالَ فَعَلْتُ. فَقَالَ: "صَدَقَ اللَّهُ، وَكَذَبَ بَطْنُ أَخِيكَ، اسْقِهِ عَسَلًا." فَسَقَاهُ فَبَرَأَ.
Sahīh al-Bukhārī 5684

90 ...قَالَ كَانَ لِأُمِّ سُلَيْمٍ قَدَحٌ مِنْ عِيدَانٍ فَقَالَتْ سَقَيْتُ فِيهِ رَسُولَ اللَّهِ كُلَّ الشَّرَابِ الْمَاءَ وَالْعَسَلَ وَاللَّبَنَ وَالنَّبِيذَ. Sunan al-Nasā'ī 5753

91 ...قَالَتْ كُنَّا نَنْبِذُ لِرَسُولِ اللَّهِ فِي سِقَاءٍ يُوكَى أَعْلَاهُ وَلَهُ عَزْلَاءُ نَنْبِذُهُ غُدْوَةً فَيَشْرَبُهُ عِشَاءً وَنَنْبِذُهُ عِشَاءً فَيَشْرَبُهُ غُدْوَةً. Sahīh Muslim 2005

92 ...أَنَّ رَسُولَ اللَّهِ نَهَى أَنْ يُنْبَذَ التَّمْرُ وَالزَّبِيبُ جَمِيعًا وَنَهَى أَنْ يُنْبَذَ الْبُسْرُ وَالرُّطَبُ جَمِيعًا. Sunan ibn Māja 3520 (3395)

Edward Lane wrote that the word Qaswā' means "she that has split ears and nostrils."[93] It also describes a camel that has the end of an ear cut (for she-camels and ewes). In Pakistan, a military tank is named after al-Qaswā'.

Muhammad had other camels too. One was called al-'Adbā' (الْعَضْباء). Another one was called al-Jad'ā' (الْجَدْعاء). At the Battle of Badr (غَزْوة الْبَدْر), the Prophet took as booty a dromedary which had belonged to 'Abū Jahl (أَبُو جَهْل) - one of his biggest enemies - and had a silver ring in its nose. Muhammad sacrificed it on the day of the Treaty of Hudaybīya (صُلْح الْحُدَيْبِيّة) in order to annoy the non-Muslims.

55. How did the Prophet chose the location for his house?

Answer: Muhammad announced that wherever his she-camel kneels down, he will choose that place for building his mosque and his house.

Therefore, the place where his she-camel knelt down became the place of the Prophet's Mosque, al-Masjid al-Nabawī (الْمَسْجِد النَّبَوِيّ), which is the second most important in Islam.

Ibn 'Ishāq (ابن إسحاق), in his biography of Muhammad, told the following story. The camel returned to the place where it had knelt at first and knelt there again. It shook itself and lay exhausted with its chest upon the ground. It was a sort of open stable for camels and a yard for processing dates. Then Muhammad asked to whom the date-store belonged. He was told that the owners were two orphans, Sahal (سَهَل) and Suhayl (سُهَيْل), and that Muhammad could take it for a mosque. The young men were paid for it.

The mosque was founded in 622 (1 AH) in the month of Rabī' al-'Awwal (رَبِيع الْأَوَّل). The original mosque covered an area of 1,050 square metres (11,300 square feet) and had a height of 2 m (6.5 ft). The mosque was initially built with palm trunks; the roof was from palm fronds and the walls were covered with mud while the two doorposts were made of stone. The Prophet himself participated in its construction. A fire destroyed large parts of the mosque in the 13th century at the end of the Abbasid reign; the mosque was renovated. A second big fire occurred in the 15th century, and that renovation was finished in 1483 (888 AH).

The place originally belonged to the tribe Banū al-Najjār (بَنُو النَّجَّار). The Banū al-Najjār is the clan of Muhammad's maternal line which means that they were uncles of ʿAbd Allah (عَبْد الله بن عَبْد المُطَّلِب) who is Muhammad's father. They were a subdivision of the tribe Banū al-Khazraj (بَنُو الخَزْرَج). The Banū Najjār resided in Medina. After the Prophet's migration from Mecca, Muhammad settled with them in Medina, and it is at their settlement where the current mosque of the Prophet is located.

ʾAbū ʾUsayd al-Sāʿidī (أَبُو أُسَيْد السَّاعِدِيّ) narrated that the Prophet said: "The best family among the ʾAnsār is the Banū al-Najjār."[94]

A Hadith, narrated by ʾAnas ibn Mālik (أَنَس بن مالك) gives more details: "Later on the Prophet ordered that a mosque should be built and sent for some people of Banū al-Najjār. He said: "O Banū al-Najjār! Suggest to me the price of this [walled] piece of land of yours.'" They replied: 'No! By Allah! We do not demand its price except from Allah.'"

ʾAnas added: "There were graves of pagans in it and some of it was unlevelled, and there were some date palms in it. The Prophet ordered that the graves of the pagans be dug out and the unlevelled land be levelled, and the date palms be cut down. [So all that was done.]

They aligned these cut date palms towards the Qibla of the mosque [as a wall] and they also built two stone side-walls [of the mosque]. His companions brought the stones while reciting poetic verses. The Prophet was with them and he kept on saying: 'There is no goodness except that of the Hereafter, O Allah! So please forgive the al-ʾAnsār and the emigrants.'"[95]

94...قَالَ النَّبِيُّ: "خَيْرُ دُورِ الأَنْصَارِ بَنُو النَّجَّار." Sahīh al-Bukhārī 6053

95...وَأَنَّهُ أَمَرَ بِبِنَاءِ المَسْجِدِ، فَأَرْسَلَ إِلَى مَلَإٍ مِنْ بَنِي النَّجَّارِ فَقَالَ: "يَا بَنِي النَّجَّارِ ثَامِنُونِي بِحَائِطِكُمْ هَذَا."قَالُوا لاَ وَاللَّهِ، لاَ نَطْلُبُ ثَمَنَهُ إِلاَّ إِلَى اللَّهِ. فَقَالَ أَنَسٌ فَكَانَ فِيهِ مَا أَقُولُ لَكُمْ، قُبُورُ المُشْرِكِينَ، وَفِيهِ خَرِبٌ، وَفِيهِ نَخْلٌ، فَأَمَرَ النَّبِيُّ بِقُبُورِ المُشْرِكِينَ فَنُبِشَتْ، ثُمَّ بِالْخَرِبِ فَسُوِّيَتْ، وَبِالنَّخْلِ فَقُطِعَ، فَصَفُّوا النَّخْلَ قِبْلَةَ المَسْجِدِ، وَجَعَلُوا عِضَادَتَيْهِ الحِجَارَةَ، وَجَعَلُوا يَنْقُلُونَ الصَّخْرَ، وَهُمْ يَرْتَجِزُونَ، وَالنَّبِيُّ مَعَهُمْ وَهُوَ يَقُولُ: "اللَّهُمَّ لاَ خَيْرَ إِلاَّ خَيْرُ الآخِرَةِ فَاغْفِرْ لِلأَنْصَارِ وَالمُهَاجِرَة." Sahīh al-Bukhārī 428

56. What is the name of the first battle the Prophet had fought?

Answer: The Foray of al-'Abwā' (غَزْوة الْأَبْواء) or Waddān (غَزْوة وَدّان).

Poverty struck when Muhammad's followers were persecuted by the Meccan tribes and forced to flee Mecca. They lost nearly everything. The Quraysh confiscated all their belongings that they had left behind.

Muhammad was then around 53 years old. Beginning in winter 623, during the second year of the Hijra (الْهِجْرة), some Muslims started to raid Meccan caravans along the eastern coast of the Red Sea en route from Mecca to Syria.

The fourth raid, in August 623, is known as the Invasion of Waddān or al-'Abwā'. It is a place between Mecca and Medina. It was the first offensive in which Muhammad personally took part, with seventy men of the Muhājirūn (الْمُهاجِرُون). The village of al-'Abwā' (الْأَبْواء) is about 200 km (125 mi) south of Medina along the western coast of present-day Saudi Arabia. It was an important stop for pilgrims to Mecca because of its greenery – there is water and lots of vegetation.

Al-Sa'b ibn Jaththāma (الصَّعْب بن جَثّامة) has narrated: "The Prophet passed by me at a place called al-'Abwā' or Waddān and was asked whether it was permissible to attack the pagan warriors at night with the probability of harming their women and children. The Prophet replied: 'They [women and children] are from them [i.e. pagans].'"[96]

The battle lasted for fifteen days. The Muslims carried a white flag and were commanded by Hamza ibn 'Abd al-Muttalib (حَمْزة بن عَبْد الْمُطَّلِب). During the raid the Muslims did not really meet the enemy. Most of the fights were small encounters. Reports indicate that only arrows were launched most of the time and that there were no casualties. However, this event was a precursor to a bigger confrontation, i.e. the Battle of Badr (غَزْوة بَدْر).

Remark: Al-'Abwā' is also the place where the mother of Muhammad, 'Āmina bint Wahb (آمِنة بِنْت وَهْب), died in 577 (45 BH). She was twenty years old. Muhammad's mother possibly died somewhere near the old village on her way back from Yathrib to Mecca.

---

96 ...قَالَ مَرَّ بِي النَّبِيُّ بِالْأَبْواءِ أَوْ بِوَدّانَ وَسُئِلَ عَنْ أَهْلِ الدّارِ يُبَيَّتُونَ مِنَ الْمُشْرِكِينَ، فَيُصابُ مِنْ نِسائِهِمْ وَذَرارِيِّهِمْ قَالَ: "هُمْ مِنْهُمْ". Sahīh al-Bukhārī 3012

The tomb is among many on an old famous rocky hill, along the old path between Mecca and Medina.

57. What led to the Battle of Badr?

Answer: A raid by the Muslims on a caravan. The Battle of Badr (غَزوة بَدر) was the first military encounter between the Muslims and the Meccans.

Islam spread quickly in Medina. It was the time when Muhammad received very specific revelations – mainly of a legislative nature and regarding all aspects of individual and communal life – as for the first time in Islamic history, the Muslims had their own state.

During the second year in Medina, Muhammad received verses which had a dramatic impact, i.e. Allah allowed the Muslims to defend themselves militarily. These verses are told in sura 22 *The Pilgrimage* – in Arabic: al-Hajj (سُورة الْحَجّ):

22:38	God will defend the believers; God does not love the unfaithful or the ungrateful.	إِنَّ اللَّهَ يُدَافِعُ عَنِ الَّذِينَ آمَنُوا إِنَّ اللَّهَ لَا يُحِبُّ كُلَّ خَوَّانٍ كَفُورٍ
22:39	Those who have been attacked are permitted to take up arms because they have been wronged - God has the power to help them -	أُذِنَ لِلَّذِينَ يُقَاتَلُونَ بِأَنَّهُمْ ظُلِمُوا وَإِنَّ اللَّهَ عَلَى نَصْرِهِمْ لَقَدِيرٌ
22:40	those who have been driven unjustly from their homes only for saying, 'Our Lord is God.' If God did not repel some people by means of others, many monasteries, churches, synagogues, and mosques, where God's name is much invoked, would have been destroyed. God is sure to help those who help His cause - God is strong and mighty -	الَّذِينَ أُخْرِجُوا مِن دِيَارِهِم بِغَيْرِ حَقٍّ إِلَّا أَن يَقُولُوا رَبُّنَا اللَّهُ وَلَوْلَا دَفْعُ اللَّهِ النَّاسَ بَعْضَهُم بِبَعْضٍ لَّهُدِّمَتْ صَوَامِعُ وَبِيَعٌ وَصَلَوَاتٌ وَمَسَاجِدُ يُذْكَرُ فِيهَا اسْمُ اللَّهِ كَثِيرًا وَلَيَنصُرَنَّ اللَّهُ مَن يَنصُرُهُ إِنَّ اللَّهَ لَقَوِيٌّ عَزِيزٌ
22:41	those who, when We establish them in the land, keep up the prayer, pay the prescribed alms, command what is right, and forbid	الَّذِينَ إِن مَّكَّنَّاهُمْ فِي الْأَرْضِ أَقَامُوا الصَّلَاةَ وَآتَوُا الزَّكَاةَ وَأَمَرُوا

	what is wrong: God controls the outcome of all events.	بِالْمَعْرُوفِ وَنَهَوْا عَنِ الْمُنكَرِ وَلِلَّهِ عَاقِبَةُ الْأُمُورِ.

After this revelation, a number of severe battles against the hostile Meccan non-Muslims and their allies took place near Medina, starting with Badr. The economic survival of the Muslims in Medina was in principle based on constant raids on Meccan caravans.

So what happened during the famous Battle of Badr? There are several accounts; some are exaggerated, while others are contradicting. Let's focus on the main points:

- Muhammad was informed of a wealthy caravan travelling from Mecca to Syria. It was escorted by ʾAbū Sufyān (أَبُو سُفْيان). The Prophet organised a raiding force – and led it himself. The Muslim army consisted of 313 men, 70 camels, and 2 horses.

- By filling the wells with sand on the caravan route near Medina, the Muslims lured ʾAbū Sufyān's army to battle at Badr, near Medina, in March 624 (2 AH). Despite the superior number of Meccan forces (about one thousand men), the Muslims won. Many important Meccans were killed.

It was Muhammad's first military victory. It had a severe, negative impact on the position and the prestige of Mecca. Islam was now seen as a serious force on the Arabian Peninsula.

Many important tribal leaders of the Quraysh were slain, including ʾAbū Jahl (أَبُو جَهْل) whose head was brought to the Prophet.

Ibn ʾIshāq (ابن إسحاق) wrote about this incident in great detail: "I have heard that Muhammad had told them [his fighters] that if he [ʾAbū Jahl] was hidden among the corpses they were to look for the presence of a scar on a knee. When they both were young, they had been pressed together at the table of Abd Allah ibn Jadʿān (عَبْد الله بن جَذْعان). He was thinner than ʾAbū Jahl and gave him a push which sent him to his knees; one of them was scratched [cut] so deeply that it left a permanent scar."

ʿAbd Allah ibn Masʿūd said: "He [ʾAbū Jahl] said to me, you have climbed high, you little shepherd!' Then I cut off his head and brought it to Muhammad saying: 'This is the head of the enemy of

Allah, 'Abū Jahl.' He replied: 'By Allah, whom there is no other, is it?'[97] [This used to be his oath.] 'Yes', I said, and I threw his head before the apostle and he gave thanks to Allah."

'Abd Allah ibn Mas'ūd (عَبْد الله بن مَسْعُود) has narrated that "the Messenger of Allah turned his face towards the Ka'ba and invoked Allah's curse upon six men of the Quraysh [...] I swear by Allah that I saw them lying slain in the battlefield of Badr. It was a hot day; their complexion had changed [showing signs of decay]."[98]

What did the Meccan non-Muslims do after the Battle of Badr?

They prepared a strong army of 3000 men to take revenge. The Battle of Badr was extremely influential in the rise of two men who would determine the course of history on the Arabian Peninsula.

The first man was Muhammad who was transformed overnight from a Meccan outcast into a major leader. The other man was 'Abū Sufyān. After the battle, 'Abū Sufyān became chief of the Quraysh. They were fighting each other for six years until Muhammad conquered Mecca, when 'Abū Sufyān surrendered and eventually converted to Islam. He served as a general in the Islamic empire.

His son Mu'āwiya (مُعاوية) became even more powerful, as he later founded the Umayyad Caliphate (الْخِلافة الأُمويّة).

58. Did the first Muslims drink alcohol?

Answer: Yes, they drank alcohol. They drank al-Fadīkh (الْفَضِيخ).

First of all, at the beginning of Islam, even during the first battles, Muslims most probably drank alcohol. The prohibition of alcohol came many years after Muhammad had started his mission.

Jābir ibn Abd Allah (جابِر بن عَبْد الله) narrated: "Some people drank alcoholic beverages in the morning [of the day] of the 'Uhud Battle,

---

97 .فَقَالَ: "يَا رَسُولَ اللَّهِ، هَذَا رَأْسُ عَدُوِّ اللَّهِ أَبِي جَهْلٍ، فَقَالَ: "اللَّهُ الَّذِي لَا إِلَهَ إِلَّا هُوَ؟" Ibn 'Ishāq

98 ...قَالَ: اسْتَقْبَلَ رَسُولُ اللَّهِ الْبَيْتَ فَدَعَا عَلَى سِتَّةِ نَفَرٍ مِنْ قُرَيْشٍ. فِيهِمْ أَبُو جَهْلٍ وَأُمَيَّةُ بْنُ خَلَفٍ وَعُتْبَةُ بْنُ رَبِيعَةَ وَشَيْبَةُ بْنُ رَبِيعَةَ وَعُقْبَةُ بْنُ أَبِي مُعَيْطٍ فَأُقْسِمُ بِاللَّهِ لَقَدْ رَأَيْتُهُمْ صَرْعَى عَلَى بَدْرٍ. قَدْ غَيَّرَتْهُمُ الشَّمْسُ وَكَانَ يَوْمًا حَارًّا. Sahīh Muslim 1794

and on the same day they were killed as martyrs, and that was before wine was prohibited.”[99]

’Anas ibn Mālik (أَنَس بن مالك) narrated that the people said: “Some people [Muslims] were killed [in the Battle of ’Uhud] while wine was in their stomachs.' So, Allah revealed: 'For those who believe and do good deeds, there is no blame for what they ate [in the past].'” [sura 5:93][100]

’Anas ibn Mālik further reported: “I was pouring [wine] for ’Abū Talha, ’Ubayy ibn Ka‘b and ’Abū Dujāna among a group of ’Ansār when a man came in and said: 'Something new has happened; the prohibition of Khamr [alcohol] has been revealed!' ”[101]

What kind of alcohol did they most probably drink?

’Anas ibn Mālik narrated: “We had no alcoholic drink except that which was produced from dates and which you call Fadīkh.”[102]

What did the Prophet order to do after the prohibition of alcohol was revealed?

To spill it.

’Anas ibn Mālik narrated: “The alcoholic drink which was spilled was al-Fadīkh. [...] ’Abū Talha said to me: 'Go out and see what this voice [this announcement] is.' I went out and on coming back said: 'There is somebody announcing that alcoholic beverages have been prohibited.' ’Abū Talha replied: 'Go and spill it!' Then alcohol was seen flowing through the streets of Medina.[103]

---

99 ...قَالَ صَبَّحَ أُنَاسٌ غَدَاةَ أُحُدٍ الْخَمْرَ فَقُتِلُوا مِنْ يَوْمِهِمْ جَمِيعًا شُهَدَاءَ، وَذَلِكَ قَبْلَ تَحْرِيمِهَا. Sahīh al-Bukhārī 4618

100 ...فَقَالَ بَعْضُ الْقَوْمِ قُتِلَ قَوْمٌ وَهِيَ فِي بُطُونِهِمْ قَالَ فَأَنْزَلَ اللَّهُ {لَيْسَ عَلَى الَّذِينَ آمَنُوا وَعَمِلُوا الصَّالِحَاتِ جُنَاحٌ فِيمَا طَعِمُوا}. Sahīh al-Bukhārī 4620

101 ...قَالَ كُنْتُ سَاقِيَ الْقَوْمِ فِي مَنْزِلِ أَبِي طَلْحَةَ فَنَزَلَ تَحْرِيمُ الْخَمْرِ، فَأَمَرَ مُنَادِيًا فَنَادَى. فَقَالَ أَبُو طَلْحَةَ اخْرُجْ فَانْظُرْ مَا هَذَا الصَّوْتُ قَالَ فَخَرَجْتُ فَقُلْتُ هَذَا مُنَادٍ يُنَادِي أَلَا إِنَّ الْخَمْرَ قَدْ حُرِّمَتْ. فَقَالَ لِي اذْهَبْ فَأَهْرِقْهَا. قَالَ فَجَرَتْ فِي سِكَكِ الْمَدِينَةِ. قَالَ وَكَانَتْ خَمْرُهُمْ يَوْمَئِذٍ الْفَضِيخَ. Sahīh al-Bukhārī 4620

102 ...مَا كَانَ لَنَا خَمْرٌ غَيْرُ فَضِيخِكُمْ هَذَا الَّذِي تُسَمُّونَهُ الْفَضِيخَ. Sahīh al-Bukhārī 4617

103 ...فَقَالَ أَبُو طَلْحَةَ اخْرُجْ فَانْظُرْ مَا هَذَا الصَّوْتُ قَالَ فَخَرَجْتُ فَقُلْتُ هَذَا مُنَادٍ يُنَادِي أَلَا إِنَّ الْخَمْرَ قَدْ حُرِّمَتْ. فَقَالَ لِي اذْهَبْ فَأَهْرِقْهَا. قَالَ فَجَرَتْ فِي سِكَكِ الْمَدِينَةِ. Sahīh al-Bukhārī 4620

From that time on, alcohol was totally banned. Abd Allah ibn 'Umar (عَبْد الله بن عُمَر) related that the Prophet said: "Now then, O people! The revelation about the prohibition of alcoholic drinks was revealed; and alcoholic drinks are extracted from five things: Grapes, dates, honey, wheat and barley. And the alcoholic drink is that which confuses and stupefies the mind."[104]

What about the punishment?

Alcohol belongs to the so-called Hudūd (حُدُود) offences. These are severe crimes. The punishments are mandated and fixed by Allah. Islamic law, generally speaking, knows two kinds of offences: Those against Allah and those against man. Crimes against Allah violate his *boundaries* – which is what Hudūd literally means in Arabic.

'Anas ibn Mālik narrated that a man who had drunk wine was brought to the Prophet, so he beat him about forty times with two palm stalks. 'Abū Bakr did similarly, and by the time 'Umar became Caliph he sought counsel from the people. And 'Abd al-Rahmān ibn 'Awf said: 'I see that the lightest penalty is eighty lashes', so 'Umar ordered that."[105]

The fact that Muslims were sober (and their enemies probably drunk) gave them an advantage in battles. This could have been the reason why the Muslims, although most of the time outnumbered, were advancing so quickly and defeated the enemy rather easily.

---

104 ...قَالَ سَمِعْتُ عُمَرَ عَلَى مِنْبَرِ النَّبِيِّ يَقُولُ أَمَّا بَعْدُ أَيُّهَا النَّاسُ إِنَّهُ نَزَلَ تَحْرِيمُ الْخَمْرِ وَهِيَ مِنْ خَمْسَةٍ، مِنَ الْعِنَبِ وَالتَّمْرِ وَالْعَسَلِ وَالْحِنْطَةِ وَالشَّعِيرِ، وَالْخَمْرُ مَا خَامَرَ الْعَقْلَ. Sahīh al-Bukhārī 4619

105 ...عَنِ النَّبِيِّ أَنَّهُ أُتِيَ بِرَجُلٍ قَدْ شَرِبَ الْخَمْرَ فَضَرَبَهُ بِجَرِيدَتَيْنِ نَحْوَ الْأَرْبَعِينَ وَفَعَلَهُ أَبُو بَكْرٍ فَلَمَّا كَانَ عُمَرُ اسْتَشَارَ النَّاسَ فَقَالَ عَبْدُ الرَّحْمَنِ بْنُ عَوْفٍ كَأَخَفِّ الْحُدُودِ ثَمَانِينَ. فَأَمَرَ بِهِ عُمَرُ. قَالَ أَبُو عِيسَى حَدِيثُ أَنَسٍ حَدِيثٌ حَسَنٌ صَحِيحٌ. وَالْعَمَلُ عَلَى هَذَا عِنْدَ أَهْلِ الْعِلْمِ مِنْ أَصْحَابِ النَّبِيِّ وَغَيْرِهِمْ أَنَّ حَدَّ السَّكْرَانِ ثَمَانُونَ. Jāmi' al-Tirmidhī 1443.

59. What happened to the captives who were taken at the Battle of Badr?

Answer: According to Islamic sources, some were treated well, others were slaughtered.

It is said that the Quraysh (قُرَيْش) lost seventy men in the Battle of Badr (غَزْوَة بَدْر). Seventy were taken as prisoners. There are reports that after the battle was over, some prisoners were cruelly murdered.

There are Hadiths which tell more about the fate of some prisoners who were taken at the Battle of Badr by the Muslims. They give an indication why Muhammad was so mad at them.

'Urwa ibn al-Zubayr (عُرْوة بن الزُّبَيْر) narrated: "I asked 'Abd Allah ibn 'Amr: 'What was the worst thing the pagans did to Allah's Messenger?' He said: 'I saw 'Uqba ibn 'Abī Mu'ayt (عُقْبة بن أَبِي مُعَيْط) coming to the Prophet while he was praying.' 'Uqba put his robe round the Prophet's neck and tightened it severely. 'Abū Bakr came and pulled 'Uqba away from the Prophet and said: 'Do you intend to kill a man just because he says: 'My Lord is Allah and he has brought forth to you the Evident Signs from your Lord?'"[106]

So what about the prisoners? Muhammad commanded that two of them had to be executed. One of them was 'Uqba, the man who humiliated Muhammad while he was praying. 'Uqba was one of Muhammad's neighbours. He had assaulted the Prophet verbally and physically because he was preaching Islam.

Ibn 'Ishāq (ابن إسحاق) gave some details about the execution in his biography of Muhammad: "When the apostle ordered him to be killed, 'Uqba said: 'But who will look after my children, O Muhammad?' 'Hell!', the Prophet said."

Who was the other prisoner who was executed?

Ibn 'Ishāq wrote that it was al-Nadr ibn al-Hārith (النَّضْر بن الْحَارِث). According to Ibn 'Ishāq, he was killed by Muhammad's son-in-law, 'Alī ibn 'Abī Tālib (عَلِيّ بن أَبِي طَالِب).

---

106 ...قَالَ سَأَلْتُ عَبْدَ اللَّهِ بْنَ عَمْرٍو عَنْ أَشَدِّ، مَا صَنَعَ الْمُشْرِكُونَ بِرَسُولِ اللَّهِ قَالَ رَأَيْتُ عُقْبَةَ بْنَ أَبِي مُعَيْطٍ جَاءَ إِلَى النَّبِيِّ وَهُوَ يُصَلِّي، فَوَضَعَ رِدَاءَهُ فِي عُنُقِهِ فَخَنَقَهُ بِهِ خَنْقًا شَدِيدًا، فَجَاءَ أَبُو بَكْرٍ حَتَّى دَفَعَهُ عَنْهُ فَقَالَ أَتَقْتُلُونَ رَجُلًا أَنْ يَقُولَ رَبِّيَ اللَّهُ، وَقَدْ جَاءَكُمْ بِالْبَيِّنَاتِ مِنْ رَبِّكُمْ. Sahīh al-Bukhārī.

Why did Muhammad order to kill al-Nadr? Well, there is even a verse in the Qur'an about it, albeit quite abstract:

8:31	Whenever Our Revelation is recited to them they say, 'We have heard all this before - we could say something like this if we wanted - this is nothing but ancient fables.'	وَإِذَا تُتْلَى عَلَيْهِمْ آيَاتُنَا قَالُوا قَدْ سَمِعْنَا لَوْ نَشَاءُ لَقُلْنَا مِثْلَ هَذَا إِنْ هَذَا إِلَّا أَسَاطِيرُ الْأَوَّلِينَ

Ibn Kathīr (ابن كَثِير) wrote in his exegesis of this verse: "Whenever the Prophet would leave an audience in which al-Nadr was present, al-Nadr began narrating to them the stories that he had learned in Persia, and proclaiming afterwards: 'Who, by Allah, has better tales to tell, I or Muhammad?' When Allah allowed the Muslims to capture al-Nadr in Badr, the Messenger of Allah commanded that his head be cut off before him, and that was done, all thanks are due to Allah."[107]

War prisoners were a new phenomenon for the Muslims. The Prophet asked 'Abū Bakr (أَبُو بَكْر) and 'Umar ibn al-Khattāb (عُمَر بن الْخَطَّاب) what they thought about it. 'Abū Bakr suggested that he should ransom them. 'Umar opted for executing them. The Prophet preferred 'Abū Bakr's suggestion.

60. Was the Devil present at the Battle of Badr?

Answer: Most Muslims believe he was.

Muslims believe that the Devil (الشَّيْطَان) was present during the Battle of Badr. They say that he appeared in the person of Surāqa ibn Mālik (سُرَاقة بن مَالِك).

All this goes back to sura 8 *Battle Gains* (Bounties) – in Arabic: al-'Anfāl (سُورة الْأَنْفَال). This sura was revealed after the Battle of Badr. It received its name from the first verse.

---

107 ...إِذَا قَامَ مِنْ مَجْلِسٍ جَلَسَ فِيهِ النَّضْر فَحَدَّثَهُمْ مِنْ أَخْبَار أُولَئِكَ ثُمَّ يَقُول بِاللَّهِ أَيّنَا أَحْسَن قَصَصًا أَنَا أَوْ مُحَمَّد ؟ وَلِهَذَا لَمَّا أَمْكَنَ الله تَعَالَى مِنْهُ يَوْم بَدْر وَوَقَعَ فِي الْأَسَارَى أَمَرَ رَسُول الله أَنْ تُضْرَب رَقَبَته صَبْرًا بَيْن يَدَيْهِ فَفُعِلَ ذَلِكَ وَلِلّه الْحَمْد. Ibn Kathīr on this sura 8:31

| 8:48 | Satan made their foul deeds seem fair to them, and said, 'No one will conquer you today [the Battle of Badr], for I will be right beside you', but when the armies came within sight of one another he turned on his heels, saying, 'This is where I leave you: I see what you do not, and I fear God - God is severe in His punishment.' | وَإِذْ زَيَّنَ لَهُمُ الشَّيْطَانُ أَعْمَالَهُمْ وَقَالَ لَا غَالِبَ لَكُمُ الْيَوْمَ مِنَ النَّاسِ وَإِنِّي جَارٌ لَكُمْ فَلَمَّا تَرَاءَتِ الْفِئَتَانِ نَكَصَ عَلَى عَقِبَيْهِ وَقَالَ إِنِّي بَرِيءٌ مِّنكُمْ إِنِّي أَرَى مَا لَا تَرَوْنَ إِنِّي أَخَافُ اللَّهَ وَاللَّهُ شَدِيدُ الْعِقَابِ. |

The Islamic historian and scholar al-Tabarī (الطَّبَرِيّ) gave in his commentary some interesting details about this sura:

It was told that 'Abd Allah ibn 'Abbās (عَبْد الله بن عَبَّاس) said: "The Devil [Shaytān] came on the day of Badr bringing a troop of devils with him.

I saw him in the form of a man from Banū Mudlij (بَنو مُدْلِج), in the form of Surāqa ibn Mālik. The Devil said to the Mushrikūn [non-Muslims]: 'No one of mankind can overcome you this day [of the Battle of Badr] and verily, I will be your protector.'

"Then when the people had drawn themselves up in battle array, the Messenger of Allah picked up a handful of dust and threw it in the faces of the Mushrikūn, and they turned and fled. Gabriel came to 'Iblīs [Satan] and when he saw him, his hand was in the hand of one of the men of the Mushrikūn. 'Iblīs pulled his hand away, and turned and fled, he and his party.

The man said: 'O Surāqa, did you not say that you would protect us?' He said: 'Verily! I see what you see not. Verily! I fear Allah for Allah is severe in punishment.' That was when he saw the angels."[108]

---

108 ...قَالَ: جَاءَ إِبْلِيسُ يَوْمَ بَدْرٍ فِي جُنْدٍ مِنَ الشَّيَاطِينِ مَعَهُ رَأَيْتُهُ فِي صُورَةِ رَجُلٍ مِنْ بَنِي مُدْلِجٍ فِي صُورَةِ سُرَاقَةَ بْنِ مَالِكِ بْنِ جُعْشُمٍ، فَقَالَ الشَّيْطَانُ لِلْمُشْرِكِينَ: لَا غَالِبَ لَكُمُ الْيَوْمَ مِنَ النَّاسِ وَإِنِّي جَارٌ لَكُمْ، فَلَمَّا اصْطَفَّ النَّاسُ، أَخَذَ رَسُولُ اللَّهِ قَبْضَةً مِنَ التُّرَابِ، فَرَمَى بِهَا فِي وُجُوهِ الْمُشْرِكِينَ، فَوَلَّوْا مُدْبِرِينَ. وَأَقْبَلَ جِبْرِيلُ إِلَى إِبْلِيسَ، فَلَمَّا رَآهُ، وَكَانَتْ يَدُهُ فِي يَدِ رَجُلٍ مِنَ الْمُشْرِكِينَ، انْتَزَعَ إِبْلِيسُ يَدَهُ، فَوَلَّى مُدْبِرًا هُوَ وَشِيعَتُهُ، فَقَالَ الرَّجُلُ: يَا سُرَاقَةُ تَزْعُمُ أَنَّكَ لَنَا جَارٌ؟ قَالَ: (إِنِّي أَرَى مَا لَا تَرَوْنَ إِنِّي أَخَافُ اللَّهَ وَاللَّهُ شَدِيدُ الْعِقَابِ) وَذَلِكَ حِينَ رَأَى الْمَلَائِكَةَ. al-Tabarī.

61. What is the name of the second battle which was fought between the Muslims in Medina and their enemies in Mecca?

Answer: The Battle of 'Uḥud (غَزْوة أُحُد) which was fought in the month of Shawwāl (شَوّال) in March 625 (3 AH), one year after the Battle of Badr.

When talking about Islamic history or the time of the Prophet, you will encounter the Battle of 'Uḥud pretty often as it is one of the most important events for the shaping of Islam. It was the second battle between Muslim and Meccan forces. In Arabic, it is called Ghazwa(t) 'Uḥud (غَزْوة أُحُد).

A Ghazwa is a *military expedition*; a *raid* or *attack*; a *conquest*. Normally, Muslims use this term when they want to stress that the Prophet himself participated in the battle.

What happened? The Meccans wanted to avenge their losses they had suffered at the Battle of Badr (غَزْوة بَدْر). They marched out from Mecca towards Medina. The two armies met at a place outside Medina, five kilometres (3.1 mi) north of the city. The fighting took place in a valley at Mount 'Uḥud. The mount is 1,077 m (3,533 ft) high.

The Muslim army consisted of around 700 fighters, 50 archers, and 4 cavalries. The fighters from Mecca from the Quraysh and their allied tribes - Muslims call it the *Army of the Infidels* (جَيْش الْكُفّار) - had 3,000 men and 200 horses according to Ibn 'Isḥāq.

Although the Muslims were outnumbered, they gained the early initiative and pushed the Meccans back. The Meccan army fled, leaving behind their belongings. Thus, most of the Meccan camp was unprotected. When the battle was close to a Muslim victory, a serious mistake was committed by parts of the Muslim army.

Muhammad had asked fifty archers to station themselves on the mountain of 'Uḥud. They should protect the Muslim army from behind. He told them not to leave their position. However, forty of them breached his command, and left their posts – in order to despoil the Meccan camp. Khālid ibn al-Walīd (خالِد ابن الْوَلِيد), the leader of the Meccan horsemen (cavalry) and who later became a Muslim, noticed that the Muslim archers were leaving their posts. His men immediately attacked the Muslim army and thus caught them by surprise. The Muslims were confused; chaos broke out resulting in many casualties and injured soldiers. Muhammad was injured too and lost at least one tooth. There were even rumours that the Prophet had been killed.

The Meccans won the battle. Around 70 companions of Muhammad were killed. Among them was Muhammad's uncle, Hamza ibn ʿAbd al-Muttalib (حَمْزة بن عَبد الْمُطَّلِب).

In Islam, the defeat is seen as a day of disaster, as a trial by Allah. The two armies would meet again in 627 AD at the Battle of the Trench (غَزْوة الْخَنْدَق).

How did the Jews in Medina react to the outcome of the Battle of ʾUhud? Islamic historians say that some Jews were happy. It is not clear what they really said, but the following sentence is often quoted by Muslims who want to express the disloyalty of the Jews at the time of the Prophet: "If Muhammad was really a prophet, he would not have lost." The relationship between the Muslims and the three main Jewish tribes in Medina became tense.

62. Which tooth did the Prophet lose in the Battle of ʾUhud?

Answer: Not entirely clear.

Perhaps it was a lateral incisor (رَبَاعِية). There are four incisors in the upper jaw, and the lateral is the tooth between the central incisor (الثَّنِيَّة) and the (cuspid) canine tooth (النّاب).

Sahl ibn Saʿd al-Sāʿidī (سَهل بن سَعد السَّاعِدِيّ) narrated: "When the helmet broke on the Prophet's head and his face became covered with blood and his incisor tooth broke [i.e. during the Battle of ʾUhud], ʿAlī ibn ʾAbī Tālib brought water in his shield while Fātima washed the blood off his face. When Fātima saw that the bleeding increased because of the water, she took a wad [of palm leaves], burnt it, and stuck it [the burnt ashes] in the wound of Allah's Apostle; whereupon the bleeding stopped."[109]

---

109 ...قَالَ لَمَّا كُسِرَتْ عَلَى رَأْسِ رَسُولِ اللَّهِ الْبَيْضَةُ، وَأُدْمِيَ وَجْهُهُ، وَكُسِرَتْ رَبَاعِيَتُهُ، وَكَانَ عَلِيٌّ يَخْتَلِفُ بِالْمَاءِ فِي الْمِجَنِّ، وَجَاءَتْ فَاطِمَةُ تَغْسِلُ عَنْ وَجهِهِ الدَّمَ، فَلَمَّا رَأَتْ فَاطِمَةُ عَلَيْهَا السَّلَامُ الدَّمَ

There is some confusion about the type of the tooth.

In the Hadith, an Arabic IV-verb of the root r-b-' (ر-ب-ع) is used which means: *to lose the lateral incisor.* However, in many translations, the Arabic word رَبَاعِية is misinterpreted as *molar.* Maybe this is due to the following saying of the Prophet. It was narrated by 'Abd Allah ibn 'Abbās (عَبْد الله بن عَبَّاس) that the Messenger of Allah said: "Teeth are all the same; the incisor and the molar are the same."[110]

63. Did the Prophet kill anybody by himself in battles?

Answer: Yes. At least one person: 'Ubayy ibn Khalaf (أُبَيِّ بن خَلَف).

There are sources reporting that Muhammad sentenced people to death or, as some Hadiths indicate, even killed them himself. This is problematic for Muslims.

Muslims like to recite a verse of the Qur'an in order to prove that Islam is peaceful. This verse is found in sura 5 - *The Feast* - in Arabic: al-Mā'ida (سُورَة الْمَائِدَة):

5:32	On account of [his deed], We decreed to the Children of Israel that if anyone kills a person - unless in retribution for murder or spreading corruption in the land - it is as if he kills all mankind, while if any saves a life it is as if he saves the lives of all mankind.	مِنْ أَجْلِ ذَلِكَ كَتَبْنَا عَلَى بَنِى إِسْرَائِيلَ أَنَّهُ مَن قَتَلَ نَفْسًا بِغَيْرِ نَفْسٍ أَوْ فَسَادٍ فِى الْأَرْضِ فَكَأَنَّمَا قَتَلَ النَّاسَ جَمِيعًا وَمَنْ أَحْيَاهَا فَكَأَنَّمَا أَحْيَا النَّاسَ جَمِيعًا وَلَقَدْ جَاءَتْهُمْ رُسُلُنَا بِالْبَيِّنَاتِ ثُمَّ إِنَّ كَثِيرًا مِّنْهُم بَعْدَ ذَلِكَ فِي الْأَرْضِ لَمُسْرِفُونَ.

So what about the Prophet?

Let's try to answer this question step by step. There is a verse in sura 8 *Battle Gains* - in Arabic: al-'Anfāl (سُورَة الْأَنْفَال) – which various commentators link to the killing of non-Muslims during the Battle of Badr which was the first intense battle between the Muslims and the

---

Sahīh al- يَزِيدُ عَلَى الْمَاءِ كَثْرَةً عَمَدَتْ إِلَى حَصِيرٍ فَأَحْرَقَتْهَا وَأَلْصَقَتْهَا عَلَى جُرْحِ رَسُولِ اللَّهِ فَرَقَأَ الدَّمُ.
Bukhārī 5722

110 ...أَنَّ رَسُولَ اللَّهِ قَالَ: "الْأَسْنَانُ سَوَاءٌ الثَّنِيَّةُ وَالضِّرْسُ سَوَاءٌ." Sunan ibn Māja 2752

hostile Meccans. Sura 8 was revealed after the Battle of Badr. The Muslims had killed at least 70 men of the Quraysh (قُرَيْش):

| 8:7 | It was not you who killed them but God, and when you [Prophet] threw [sand at them] it was not your throw [that defeated them] but God's, to do the believers a favour: God is all seeing and all knowing | فَلَمْ تَقْتُلُوهُمْ وَلَكِنَّ اللَّهَ قَتَلَهُمْ وَمَا رَمَيْتَ إِذْ رَمَيْتَ وَلَكِنَّ اللَّهَ رَمَى وَلِيُبْلِيَ الْمُؤْمِنِينَ مِنْهُ بَلَاءً حَسَنًا إِنَّ اللَّهَ سَمِيعٌ عَلِيمٌ. |

Abdel Haleem wrote about this verse that "before the battle [of Badr], the Prophet prayed and threw a handful of sand at the enemy as a symbol of their being defeated."

'Abū Hurayra (أَبُو هُرَيْرَة) narrated that Allah's Messenger (pointing to his broken canine tooth) said: "Allah's Wrath has become severe on the people who harmed His Prophet. Allah's Wrath has become severe on the man <u>who is killed by the Messenger of Allah</u> in Allah's Cause."[111]

What does *in Allah's cause* (for the sake of Allah) in the above Hadith mean?

Al-Nawawī (النَّوَوِيّ), an influential Sunni Shāfi'ī (شافِعِيّ) jurist and Hadith scholar, mentioned that "*Allah's cause* excludes all people whom Muhammad had killed as a punishment (so-called Hadd or Hudūd) or by way of legal retaliation (Qisās)." The commentator concludes that whoever was killed by the Prophet during the battle, had intended to kill the Prophet."

This shows that in Jihād, killing for the sake of Allah is justified in Islam. However, it is not known that Muhammad killed any non-Muslim with his own hand except for 'Ubayy ibn Khalaf (أُبَيّ بن خَلَف). 'Ubayy was most probably killed in the second major battle at Uhud.

Muhammad ibn 'Abī Bakr (مُحَمَّد بن أَبِي بَكْر), also known as Ibn al-Qayyim (ابن الْقَيِّم), a commentator of the Qur'an from the 13th century, wrote a full account on the killing of 'Ubayy: "When they got close to the mountain, 'Ubayy ibn Khalaf, who was on his horse

---

111 ...قَالَ رَسُولُ اللَّهِ: "اشْتَدَّ غَضَبُ اللَّهِ عَلَى قَوْمٍ فَعَلُوا بِنَبِيِّهِ يُشِيرُ إِلَى رَبَاعِيَتِهِ اشْتَدَّ غَضَبُ اللَّهِ عَلَى رَجُلٍ يَقْتُلُهُ رَسُولُ اللَّهِ فِي سَبِيلِ اللَّهِ." Sahīh al-Bukhārī 4073.

whose name was al-'Iwadh, caught up with the Messenger of Allah. The enemy of Allah had claimed that he would kill the Messenger of Allah whilst riding this horse. When he got close to him, <u>the Messenger of Allah took a spear</u> from al-Hārith ibn al-Simma <u>and killed [fatally wounded] him with it</u>. It hit him in his collarbone and the enemy of Allah retreated in defeat."[112]

There is little known about 'Ubayy ibn Khalaf. He was a merchant in Mecca and became a strong opponent of Muhammad. The Prophet had been humiliated by the Meccans several times.

Therefore these people, among them 'Ubayy, were cursed by the Prophet as can be read in several Hadiths. 'Abd Allah ibn Mas'ūd (عَبْد اللهِ بن مَسْعُود) said: "While the Prophet was prostrating, surrounded by some men of the Quraysh, 'Uqba ibn 'Abī Mu'ayt (عُقْبة بن أَبِي مُعَيْط) brought the intestines of a camel and put them on the Prophet's back. The Prophet did not raise his head; then Fātima came and took them off his back.[113]

"'O Allah! Destroy [the pagans of] the Quraysh; O Allah! Destroy the Quraysh! O Allah! Destroy the Quraysh!', naming especially 'Abū Jahl (أَبُو جَهْل), 'Utba ibn Rabī'a (عُتْبة بن رَبِيعة), Shayba ibn Rabī'a (شَيْبة), al-Walīd ibn 'Utba (الوليد بن عُبة), 'Ubayy ibn Khalaf (أُبَيّ بن), (بن زَرِيعة), and 'Uqba ibn 'Abī Mu'ayt (عَقْبة بن أَبِي مُعَيْط).(خَلَف)"[114]

64. Did Jews live in Medina?

Answer: Yes. There were three main tribes.

---

112 ...فَلَمَّا اشْتَنْدُوا إِلَى الْجَبَلِ أَدْرَكَ رَسُولَ اللهِ أُبَيُّ بن خَلَف عَلَى جواد لَهُ يُقالُ لَهُ "العوذ" زَعَمَ عَدُوُّ الله أَنَّهُ يَقْتُلُ عَلَيْهِ رَسُولَ، فَلَمَّا اقْتَرَبَ مِنْهُ تَناوَلَ رَسُولُ اللهِ الْحَرْبَةَ مِن الْحارِث بن الصِّمَّةِ فَطَعَنَهُ بِها، فَجاءت فِي تَرقوته، فَكَرَّ عَدُوُّ الله منهزمًا. Ibn al-Qayyim; Zād al-Ma'ād 3/199.

113 ...قَالَ: بَيْنَا النَّبِيُّ ساجِدٌ وَحَوْلَهُ ناسٌ مِنْ قُرَيْشٍ جاءَ عُقْبةُ بْنُ أَبِي مُعَيْطٍ بِسَلى جَزُورٍ، فَقَذَفَهُ عَلَى ظَهْرِ النَّبِيِّ، فَلَمْ يَرْفَعْ رَأْسَهُ فَجاءَتْ فاطِمَةُ فَأَخَذَتْهُ مِنْ ظَهْرِهِ، وَدَعَتْ عَلَى مَنْ صَنَعَ فَقَالَ النَّبِيُّ. Sahīh al-Bukhārī 3854

114 ...فَقَالَ: "اللَّهُمَّ عَلَيْكَ بِقُرَيْشٍ، اللَّهُمَّ عَلَيْكَ بِقُرَيْشٍ، اللَّهُمَّ عَلَيْكَ بِقُرَيْشٍ!" لِأَبِي جَهْلِ بْنِ هِشَامٍ، وَعُتْبَةَ بْنِ رَبِيعَةَ، وَشَيْبَةَ بْنِ رَبِيعَةَ، وَالْوَلِيدِ بْنِ عُتْبَةَ، وَأُبَيِّ بْنِ خَلَفٍ، وَعُقْبَةَ بْنِ أَبِي مُعَيْطٍ. قَالَ عَبْدُ اللهِ فَلَقَدْ رَأَيْتُهُم فِي قَلِيبِ بَدْرٍ قَتْلَى. Sahīh al-Bukhārī 2934

Jewish tribes had settled in the western region of present-day Saudi Arabia - also called Hijāz (الْحِجاز) - after the Jewish-Roman wars in the year 70. The Jews introduced agriculture which gave them a culturally, economically, and politically dominant position.

When Muhammad arrived in Yathrib from Mecca with his followers, the Jews, in general, did not react with hostility. The Jews worked in agriculture, money lending, and traded weapons and jewellery. They had commercial relations with Arab merchants in Mecca.

Muhammad acted as a mediator between the two major Arab tribes who fought each other, the Banū al-'Aws (بَنُو الْأَوْس) and the Banū al-Khazraj (بَنُو الْخَزْرج), both had emigrated from Yemen in the 5th century. Each of the three main Jewish tribes was allied with either one of them. Muhammad set up the Constitution of Medina, between the Muslims, the 'Ansār, and the various Jewish tribes of Yathrib to regulate the governance of the city.

However, when Muhammad started to preach his message, this peaceful arrangement changed. And it definitely changed when the Prophet started to fight wars against the hostile Meccan non-Muslims. A power struggle emerged. The situation and fate of the Jews changed dramatically after the first three major wars.

Let's have a look at the three major tribes:

- **Banū Qaynuqā'** (بَنُو قَيْنُقاع). A dispute about a woman broke out between the Muslims and the Banū Qaynuqā' after the Battle of Badr. Soon after the altercation, they were the first Jewish tribe to be expelled by Muhammad. They were allied with the (Arab) Khazraj tribe.

- **Banū al-Nadīr** (بَنُو النَّضِير). Their fortresses were located half-a-day's march to the south of Medina. When the Muslims were defeated in the Battle of 'Uhud in 625 (3 AH), members of the Banū al-Nadīr challenged Muhammad as the leader of Medina. Islamic historians say that they even tried to kill the Prophet. It was the second Jewish tribe who had to leave Medina. Later, the Banū al-Nadīr sought revenge, and planned the Battle of the Trench together with the Quraysh. They also participated in

the Battle of Khaybar in 628 (7 AH). They were allied with the
'Aws tribe.

- **Banū Qurayza** (بَنُو قُرَيْظة). In 627 (5 AH), when the Meccans and
  their allies besieged Medina in the <u>Battle of the Trench</u>, the
  Qurayza are said to have violated a treaty with Muhammad by
  allying with the attacking tribes. Their conflict with Muhammad
  led to their extinction. Some Western historians even call it a
  genocide because the whole tribe was killed by the Muslims.
  They were allied with the 'Aws tribe.

65. What was the first incident between Muslims and Jews?

Answer: A Muslim woman was harassed by a Jewish goldsmith in
Medina.

The Banū Qaynuqāʿ (بَنُو قَيْنُقاع - in Hebrew: בנו קינקאע) was one of
the three main Jewish tribes living in the region of Medina in the 7th
century. It was the first Jewish tribe with whom Muhammad had a
warlike dispute.

They owned land and their jobs were mainly in the sectors of commerce, craftsmanship, and gold smithery. The Banū Qaynuqāʿ lived
in two fortresses in the south-western part of the city of Yathrib
which later became Medina. It is not clear when and in particular
why they had settled there.

After the Battle of Badr (غَزْوة بَدْر) in the year 624 (2 AH), the tensions
between Muslims and Jews escalated. Muhammad, strengthened by
victory, wanted to eliminate the Jewish opposition.

According to Ibn 'Ishāq (ابن إسحاق), a dispute broke out between
the Muslims and the Banū Qaynuqāʿ. A Muslim woman visited a jew-
eller's shop in the Qainuqāʿ marketplace, where she was harassed and
demanded to uncover her face.

The goldsmith, a Jew, pinned her clothing in such a way, that upon
getting up, she was stripped naked. A Muslim man, who came by,
killed the shopkeeper in retaliation. The Jews in turn killed the
Muslim man. This escalated to a chain of revenge killings, and hostil-

ity grew between Muslims and the Banū Qaynuqāʿ, which led to the siege of their fortress lasting for 15 days. Eventually, the tribe surrendered to Muhammad.

Islamic sources see in the incident with the woman a violation of the Constitution of Medina (دُسْتُور الْمَدِينة) which was drafted by the Prophet shortly after his arrival in 622 (1 AH).

The constitution was created to end the fighting between the rival clans of Banū al-ʾAws (بَنُو الْأَوْس) and Banū Khazraj (بَنُو خَزْرَج), and to maintain peace and cooperation among all local groups. The precise circumstances of the alleged violation of the *Constitution* are not specified in the sources.

In the end, the Jews were expelled for allegedly breaking the treaty known as the Constitution (or Charter) of Medina. Muhammad distributed the property of the Banū Qaynuqāʿ, their arms and tools among his followers.

What made this incident even more complicated was the fact that the marketplace of former Yathrib was located in the Banū Qaynuqāʿ quarters. The Banū Qaynuqāʿ were allied with the local Arab tribe of Khazraj and supported them in their conflicts with the rival Arab tribe of ʾAws.

Muhammad was probably also driven by economic interests when he ousted the Jewish tribe. The market of Medina was controlled previously by the Banū Qaynuqāʿ, but after they were gone, Muhammad could create an Islamic market according to his rules, and thus gained even more power.

66. Muhammad ordered the killing of which Jewish leader?

Answer: Kaʿb ibn al-ʾAshraf (كَعْب بن الْأَشْرَف).

Kaʿb was a Jewish leader in Medina. He was assassinated by Muslims on the order of Muhammad, probably six months after the Battle of Badr (غَزْوة بَدْر).

Kaʿb's father was in fact an Arab who had fled to Yathrib (Medina) after committing a crime. He became an ally of the Banū al-Nadīr (بَنُو النَّضِير), one of the three major Jewish tribes in Medina, and married a Jewish woman, who gave birth to his son, Kaʿb.

Ka'b therefore was Jewish, because in Judaism, it is the mother who passes on the religion to her child. Ka'b was a tall and impressive looking person. He was a well-known poet and was one of the richest men among the Jews. He lived in a big house on the outskirts of Medina where he had extensive palm groves. He was regarded as a Jewish leader of importance throughout the region of Hijāz. He provided means of support and sponsorship to many Jewish rabbis.

Ka'b was openly hostile to Islam. Muslim historians and scholars say that he had often insulted Muslim women. Some claim that he also wrote erotic poetry about Muslim women which Muslims found offensive.

The whole story of Ka'b's assassination is given in the biography of Muhammad by Ibn 'Ishāq (ابن إسحاق) and in some Hadiths. Some minor details are told differently in various sources. However, the main story - which is said to have happened in September 624 (3 AH) - is the same.

After the Quraysh were defeated at Badr, Muhammad had sent 'Abū Qatāda (أَبُو قَتادة) to the southern quarter and another man to the northern quarter to tell the Muslims of Medina about Allah's victory and about the "polytheists who had been killed".

When Ka'b ibn al-'Ashraf heard he news, he said: "Is this true? Did Muhammad actually kill those whom these two men mention? Those are the nobles of the Arabs and kingly men."

When he saw the Muslim army with the prisoners of war [from the Quraysh], he was bitter and furious. He went to Mecca to express his grief and to incite the Quraysh to take further revenge. He also went to other areas, from tribe to tribe, urging people to take up arms against the Prophet.

News of his activities reached the Prophet who said: "O Lord, rid me of the son of 'Ashraf (= Ka'b), however You wish."

Jābir ibn 'Abd Allah (جابِر بن عَبْد الله) narrated that the Messenger of Allah asked: "Who is ready to kill Ka'b ibn al-'Ashraf who has really hurt Allah and His Apostle?"

Muhammad ibn Maslama (مُحَمَّد بن مَسْلَمة الأَنْصاريّ) said: "O Allah's Messenger! Do you like me to kill him?"

He replied in the affirmative.

Muhammad ibn Maslama went to him [i.e. Ka'b] and said: "This person [the Prophet] has put us to task and asked us for charity." Ka'b replied: "By Allah, you will get tired of him." Muhammad ibn Maslama said to him: "We have followed him, so we dislike leaving him until we see the end of his affair."[115]

In this way Muhammad ibn Maslama went on talking to him until he got a chance to kill him. Muhammad ibn Maslama was in fact a nephew of Ka'b by fosterage.

The execution was no easy undertaking. According to one report, Muhammad ibn Maslama went home and stayed for three days without either eating or drinking, just thinking about what he had to do. The Prophet heard of this, called him and asked him why he had not been eating or drinking. He replied: "O Messenger of Allah, I agreed to an undertaking but I do not know whether I can accomplish it or not." – "Your duty is only to try your utmost", the Prophet replied.

In the end, Muhammad ibn Maslama pretended to needing a loan from Ka'b and offered to leave his weapons with him as security. One moonlit night, Muhammad ibn Maslama and four other Muslim men reached Ka'b's house. The Prophet accompanied them for a short distance and is said to have parted with the words: "Go forth in the name of Allah." And he prayed: "O Lord, help them!" Then the Prophet returned home.

They called out to Ka'b. As he got out of bed, his wife held him and warned: "You are a man at war. People at war do not go down at such an hour!" - "It is only my nephew Muhammad ibn Maslama..."

Ka'b came down with his sword drawn. He was heavily scented with the perfume of musk. "I have not smelt such a pleasant scent as today", greeted Muhammad ibn Maslama. "Let me smell your head."

Muhammad ibn Maslama firmly grasped Ka'b's head and called on the others to strike down the enemy of Allah.

---

115 ...أَنَّ النَّبِيَّ قَالَ: "مَنْ لِكَعْبِ بْنِ الْأَشْرَفِ، فَإِنَّهُ قَدْ آذَى اللَّهَ وَرَسُولَهُ." قَالَ مُحَمَّدُ بْنُ مَسْلَمَةَ أَتُحِبُّ أَنْ أَقْتُلَهُ يَا رَسُولَ اللَّهِ قَالَ " نَعَمْ ". قَالَ فَأَتَاهُ فَقَالَ إِنَّ هَذَا يَعْنِي النَّبِيَّ - قَدْ عَنَّانَا وَسَأَلَنَا الصَّدَقَةَ، قَالَ وَأَيْضًا وَاللَّهِ قَالَ فَإِنَّا قَدِ اتَّبَعْنَاهُ فَنَكْرَهُ أَنْ نَدَعَهُ حَتَّى نَنْظُرَ إِلَى مَا يَصِيرُ أَمْرُهُ قَالَ فَلَمْ يَزَلْ يُكَلِّمُهُ حَتَّى اسْتَمْكَنَ مِنْهُ فَقَتَلَهُ. Sahīh al-Bukhārī 3031

67. What happened to the Jewish tribe Banū al-Nadīr?

Answer: They were expelled by the Prophet.

After the assassination of the powerful Jewish leader Kaʻb ibn al-ʼAshraf (كَعْب بن الأَشْرَف), who was from the Banū al-Nadīr tribe (بَنُو النَّضِير), the Jews were terrified. Ibn ʼIshāq (ابن إسحاق) wrote: "There was not a Jew who did not fear for his life."

This changed when half a year later, in March 625, the Muslims were defeated in the second major battle against the Quraysh - at Mount ʼUhud. The Banū al-Nadīr challenged Muhammad's leadership in Medina. Peace was long gone in Medina. Alliances and betrayals were common. The situation became more and more dangerous for the Muslims but also for the other tribes. In July 625, the whole state of affairs escalated when a group of Muslims were attacked. Two Muslims were killed, and two of the assailants' clan were killed in revenge.

Muhammad wanted to settle the dispute. He went to the Banū al-Nadīr and asked them for help in paying the blood money because this was part of the terms of their agreement. The Banū al-Nadīr became hostile to the Muslims since Muhammad had expelled a whole Jewish tribe, the Banū Qaynuqāʻ (بَنُو قَيْنُقاع). For this reason the Banū al-Nadīr were cautious and had established new alliances against the Muslims.

According to Islamic sources, the Banū al-Nadīr wanted to trap Muhammad. They invited him for a discussion. On his way Muhammad received a warning – some say, that it was the Archangel Gabriel, but other sources indicate that it might have been a Muslim convert of the Banū al-Nadīr tribe.

The Prophet chose a special man to deliver his message: Muhammad ibn Maslama (مُحَمَّد بن مَسْلَمة الأَنْصارِئ), the killer of one of their tribe leaders. The tribe had ten days to leave the place, otherwise they would be killed. The Banū al-Nadīr did not accept this and considered it a declaration of war.

Muhammad commanded the Muslims to besiege the fortresses of the Banū al-Nadīr. After the siege had lasted for two weeks, the Jews were forced to surrender when Muhammad ordered the burning and cutting of their palm-trees. On this occasion, the Prophet received a revelation from Allah, sura 59 *The Exile* - in Arabic: al-Hashr (سورة الْحَشْر):

59:5	Whatever you [believers] may have done to [their] palm trees - cutting them down or leaving them on their roots - was done by God's leave, so that He might disgrace those who defied Him.	مَا قَطَعْتُم مِّن لِّينَةٍ أَوْ تَرَكْتُمُوهَا قَائِمَةً عَلَى أُصُولِهَا فَبِإِذْنِ اللَّهِ وَلِيُخْزِيَ الْفَاسِقِينَ.

The Banū al-Nadīr accepted the conditions of surrender. They were allowed to take only with them what they could carry on camels, except for their weapons. The Jews left on 600 camels, some going to Syria and a great number to nearby Khaybar where they found refuge among Jewish tribes – and prepared for revenge.

The Prophet gave their land to his companions who had migrated with him from Mecca.

68. What military strategy saved the Muslims in their third major battle?

Answer: The digging of a trench.

The Battle of the Trench (غَزْوة الْخَنْدَق) was fought two years after the Battle of 'Uhud in 627 (5 AH). It was a 25 or 27-day long siege of Medina by Arab and Jewish tribes. The battle coincided with harsh winter weather of January/February 627.

Many Jews from the Banū al-Nadīr tribe lived in Khaybar after Muhammad had expelled them from Medina. They sought revenge. The same wanted the Quraysh from Mecca. They both wanted to end Muhammad's mission and formed an alliance. They were looking for allies. Their army was strong – around 6,000 to 10,000 soldiers plus 600 horses. They heavily outnumbered the Muslims who had only 3,000 men. The non-Muslim army was led by 'Abū Sufyān (أَبُو سُفْيان).

The battle is also called the Battle of Confederates (غَزْوة الْأَحْزاب). The word al-'Ahzāb (الْأَحْزاب), which means *parties* or *confederates,* is also used in the Qur'an. Sura 33 is named after this term to denote the confederacy of non-Muslims and Jews against Islam.

The plan of the non-Muslims was as follows: They wanted to attack Medina from two sides, encircle it, and eventually finish off the Muslims. However, they didn't expect that a non-Arab Muslim had a much better idea.

Salmān the Persian - in Arabic: Salmān al-Fārisī (سَلْمان الْفارِسِيّ) - suggested that the Muslims should stay in Medina and dig a trench to protect themselves. The trench would prevent the horsemen from crossing into the city. The fact that he was from Persia, saved the Muslims in Medina. Salmān suggested a military tactic which was unknown to the Prophet and the Arabs who were Bedouins. The Persians fought brutal wars against the Byzantines over centuries and had gained knowledge in war techniques and strategies.

The battle was named after this trench, al-Khandaq (الْخَنْدَق), that was dug by the Muslims in preparation for the battle. The word khandaq is the Arabicised form of a Persian word meaning *that which has been dug.*

Let's have a look at the military strategy:

- The Muslims dug a trench at the **north end** of the city. Muhammad is said to have taken part in the work personally, invoking Allah sometimes. They harvested all the crops in every oasis. The idea was to not only have enough food during the siege for themselves, but rather that the enemy would have no access to it.
- The **east and west sides** of the city were rocky and the enemy would not come from those sides.
- The Muslims had a treaty with the Jewish tribe of Banū Qurayza (بَنُو قُرَيْظة) who had a fortress at the **southern** end which helped to protect the city from the south.

The non-Muslim confederates were surprised and did not have enough food for a long siege.

One of the Jews of the Banū al-Nadīr clan spoke to the Jews of Banū Qurayza and tried to convince them to reconsider their agreement with Muhammad, and break their alliance with the Muslims. Eventually, after initial hesitation, the clan chief agreed to revoke the treaty and thus the strategy of the Muslims came apart.

The Muslim army was in real danger now. The confederates had an entry hole and the siege continued. As a first response the Prophet sent one hundred men to the inner city for its protection. The loud voices, in which the Muslim soldiers prayed every night, created the illusion of a large force.

Meanwhile, Muhammad received a visit from a man coming from Mecca, Nuʿaym ibn Masʿud (نُعَيْم بـن مَسْعُود). This man was well-known to all tribes who were besieging Medina. However, none of them knew that Nuʿaym came to Muhammad to announce his conversion to Islam, and he had an idea. He wanted to spread rumours among the Jewish tribe of Qurayza and among the Quraysh. According to Ibn 'Ishāq, Muhammad said to him:"Do what you want to loosen the grip on us; war is deceit!"

Nuʿaym first went to the Banū Qurayza and warned them about the alleged intentions of the leaders of the confederacy. He claimed that if the siege failed, the confederacy would abandon the Jews, leaving them to their fate, and handing them over to Muhammad without protection. The Qurayza should therefore demand that the confederate leaders send some men as hostages – as a guarantee that they would not forsake the Banū Qurayza.

Then Nuʿaym went to 'Abū Sufyān, the leader of the non-Muslim army. He warned him that the Banū Qurayza had defected to Muhammad and that they were in fact Muhammad's allies. He told him that they were going to ask him for hostages as a pledge of their cooperation, but that their real intention was to hand over the men to Muhammad. He suggested that they should not give them a single man. Nuʿaym went to other tribes too with similar messages. The plan worked and the first signs of division and lack of trust became apparent.

Meanwhile, the non-Muslims began to run out of food and, on top of that, the nights were extremely cold. What happened then is a mixture of facts and legends. Since the provisions of the confederate army were running out, their horses and camels were dying out of hunger as well as from wounds. For days the weather had been exceptionally cold and wet. Violent winds blew out the camp fires of the confederate army taking their only source of heat. The Muslim camp, however, was sheltered from such winds wrote Martin Lings in his biography of Muhammad which was published in 1983.

Finally, the troops of the non-Muslims were paralysed and demoralised, and fighters started to leave and retreat to Mecca.

After four weeks the siege was over. However, the story was not finished yet because there was one player left: the Banū Qurayza. They got the ultimate punishment by the Muslims, i.e. death.

69. What happened to the Jewish tribe Banū Qurayza?

Answer: The entire tribe was annihilated by the Muslims. Some western historians call the mass killing a genocide.

This is one of the most difficult and disturbing stories in Islamic history. The Banū Qurayza (بَنُو قُرَيْظَة - in Hebrew: בנו קוריט'ה) was a Jewish tribe which lived near Yathrib (later Medina).

The Banū Qurayza had made an (assistance) agreement with Muhammad. However, in 627 (5 AH) during the Battle of the Trench (غَزْوة الْخَنْدَق), the Banū Qurayza, broke the treaty. Other sources deny this.

Earlier, when Muhammad expelled the Jewish tribe Banū al-Nadīr (بَنُو النَّضِير), who were by the way not friends of the Banū Qurayza, the latter did not rush to help them. After the battle, the Banū Qurayza neighbourhoods were besieged by the Muslims in retaliation for their treachery. The Banū Qurayza unconditionally surrendered and the Muslims seized their possessions.

Several members of the Banū al-'Aws tribe (بَنُو الأَوْس) pleaded for their old Jewish allies and agreed to Muhammad's proposal that one of their chiefs should judge the matter. Muhammad chose Sa'd ibn Mu'ādh (سَعْد بن مُعَاذ) of the Banū al-'Aws as an arbitrator.

This is told in a Hadith narrated by 'Abū Sa'īd al-Khudrī (أَبُو سَعيد الْخُدْرِيّ): "Some people [the Jews of Banū Qurayza] agreed to accept the verdict of Sa'd ibn Mu'ādh, so the Prophet sent for him. He came riding a donkey and when he approached the Mosque, the Prophet said: 'Get up for the best among you.' Or said: 'Get up for your chief.'

The Prophet continued: "O Sa'd! These people have agreed to accept your verdict.' Sa'd said: 'I judge that their warriors should be killed and their children and women should be taken as captives.' The Prophet said: 'You have given a judgement similar to Allah's Judgement (or the King's judgement).'"[116]

How did Sa'd render his decision? Although injured in the Battle of the Trench, he decreed the sentence according to the Torah (Bible):

Deuteronomy 20:10-14: "When you go near a city to fight against it, then proclaim an offer of peace to it. And it shall be that if they accept your offer of peace and open to you, then all the people who are found in it shall be placed under tribute to you, and serve you. Now if the city will not make peace with you, but makes war against you, then you shall besiege it. And when the Lord your God delivers it into your hands, you shall strike every male in it with the edge of the sword. But the women, the little ones, the livestock, and all that is in the city, all its spoil, you shall plunder for yourself; and you shall eat the enemies' plunder which the Lord your God gives you."

This means that according to Sa'd's verdict, the men had to be beheaded while all the women and children had to be taken captive and enslaved. Muhammad approved of this decision and on the next day, the sentence was carried out.

Jābir ibn Abd Allah (جابر بن عَبْد الله) narrated: "On the day of the Battle of the Trench, Sa'd ibn Mu'ādh was struck by an arrow such that the upper vein or lower vein of his forearm was severed. So the Messenger of Allah tried to stop it with fire, but it made his arm bleed profusely so he left it. Then he did it another time but it caused it to bleed profusely. Upon seeing that he said: 'O Allah! Do not allow my soul depart until my eyes are comforted by elimination of Banū Qurayza.' He pressed his vein closed and it did not bleed a drop before they surrendered to the arbitration of Sa'd ibn Mu'ādh. He [the Prophet] sent to him [Sa'd] who judged that their men should be

---

116 ...أَنَّ أُنَاسًا نَزَلُوا عَلَى حُكْمِ سَعْدِ بْنِ مُعَاذٍ، فَأَرْسَلَ إِلَيْهِ فَجَاءَ عَلَى حِمَارٍ، فَلَمَّا بَلَغَ قَرِيبًا مِنَ الْمَسْجِدِ قَالَ النَّبِيُّ: "قُومُوا إِلَى خَيْرِكُمْ أَوْ سَيِّدِكُمْ." فَقَالَ: "يَا سَعْدُ، إِنَّ هَؤُلَاءِ نَزَلُوا عَلَى حُكْمِكَ." قَالَ فَإِنِّي أَحْكُمُ فِيهِمْ أَنْ تُقْتَلَ مُقَاتِلَتُهُمْ وَتُسْبَى ذَرَارِيُّهُمْ. قَالَ: "حَكَمْتَ بِحُكْمِ اللَّهِ، أَوْ بِحُكْمِ الْمَلِكِ."

Sahīh al-Bukhārī 3804

killed, their women should be spared and that the Muslims may share them among themselves. With this, the Messenger of Allah said: 'You have judged according to Allah's judgement for them.' And they were four hundred. Then when he finished killing them, his vein opened up and he died."[117]

Several reports name some of Muhammad's companions as executioners, al-Zubayr ibn al-'Awām (الزُّبَيْر بن الْعَوام) in particular as well as 'Alī ibn 'Abī Tālib (عليّ بن أبي طالب).

Ibn 'Ishāq gave a full account of the killing of the Banū Qurayza in the biography of Muhammad. He stated the number of people at 600 or 700, though some, as Ibn 'Ishāq wrote, put the figure as high as 800 or 900.

"Then the Apostle went out to the market of Medina and dug trenches in it. Then he sent for them and struck off their heads in those trenches as they were brought out to him in batches."[118]

According to Ibn 'Ishāq's biography, a woman who had thrown a millstone from the battlements during the siege and had killed one of the Muslim besiegers, was also beheaded along with the men.

The spoils of battle, including the enslaved women and children of the tribe, were divided up among the Muslims that had participated in the siege.

How do Muslims defend this massacre?

I had several discussions with Muslims and non-Muslims about this story. The most common explanation Muslims point out is that Muhammad was dealing with treachery and that he had taken the maximum punishment against it. Critics say that the alleged treachery is illogical. To have revoked the treaty, the Banū Qurayza must have had joined the confederate forces who attacked the Muslims. If

---

117 ...عَنْ جَابِرٍ، أَنَّهُ قَالَ رُمِيَ يَوْمَ الْأَحْزَابِ سَعْدُ بْنُ مُعَاذٍ فَقَطَعُوا أَكْحَلَهُ أَوْ أَبْجَلَهُ فَحَسَمَهُ رَسُولُ اللَّهِ بِالنَّارِ فَانْتَفَخَتْ يَدُهُ فَتَرَكَهُ فَنَزَفَهُ الدَّمُ فَحَسَمَهُ أُخْرَى فَانْتَفَخَتْ يَدُهُ فَلَمَّا رَأَى ذَلِكَ قَالَ اللَّهُمَّ لَا تُخْرِجْ نَفْسِي حَتَّى تُقِرَّ عَيْنِي مِنْ بَنِي قُرَيْظَةَ. فَاسْتَمْسَكَ عِرْقُهُ فَمَا قَطَرَ قَطْرَةً حَتَّى نَزَلُوا عَلَى حُكْمِ سَعْدِ بْنِ مُعَاذٍ فَأَرْسَلَ إِلَيْهِ فَحَكَمَ أَنْ يُقْتَلَ رِجَالُهُمْ وَيُسْتَحْيَى نِسَاؤُهُمْ يَسْتَعِينُ بِهِنَّ الْمُسْلِمُونَ. فَقَالَ رَسُولُ اللَّهِ: "أَصَبْتَ حُكْمَ اللَّهِ فِيهِمْ." وَكَانُوا أَرْبَعَمِائَةٍ فَلَمَّا فَرَغَ مِنْ قَتْلِهِمْ انْفَتَقَ عِرْقُهُ فَمَاتَ. -Jāmi' al-
Tirmidhī 1582

Ibn 'Ishāq, English translation, p. 464 **118**

that had been the case, the battle would most probably have ended in a fatal defeat of the Muslims.

Another point often brought up by Muslims is that the Banū Qurayza were given a fair choice. Eventually the Jews of Banū Qurayza were massacred because they agreed to accept the verdict of Sa'd ibn Mu'ādh, the arbitrator.

Following Islamic logic, Muhammad is innocent of shedding their blood. However, why did Muhammad applaud Sa'd by saying that his verdict was in accordance with the judgement of Allah? Does this mean he thought it was the right choice?

Some Bible scholars say that the Bible's passage which was used to pronounce the execution of the Banū Qurayza was not appropriate. They claim that the passage in question has nothing to do with "treason" or the treatment of treasonous allies. The Book of Deuteronomy is the fifth book of the Hebrew Bible.

The elimination of an entire tribe was a clear message which was heard across Arabia, i.e. the Prophet does not accept betrayals. In fact, such a situation never occurred again during Muhammad's reign.

70. What was the Treaty of Hudaybīya about?

Answer: A truce between the Muslims and the main non-Muslim tribes of Mecca. It was negotiated in March 628 (6 AH).

Six years after Muhammad and his followers had left Mecca, the Prophet dreamt that he entered Mecca, his head shaved, holding the key to the Ka'ba in his right hand.

He dreamt that he and his followers performed the circumambulation of the Ka'ba, called Tawāf (طواف). His dream was the beginning of the end of the Quraysh.

The Muslims and Meccans had already a history of wars. They had fought several battles against each other: the Battle of Badr, the Battle of 'Uhud, and the Battle of the Trench. And despite winning at least two of the battles (in 'Uhud, they had to retreat), the Muslims were still not strong enough to dare attacking the large Meccan forces.

After his dream, Muhammad decided to go to Mecca with his followers – as pilgrims. He wanted to perform the 'Umra, the lesser pilgrimage. Long before the foundation of Islam, the Ka'ba was a holy sanctuary for Arabian tribes. Visiting the Ka'ba was a legitimate right for centuries.

The Meccan non-Muslim leaders found themselves in a dilemma. They could not ban the Muslims from entering Mecca. However, if they allowed them to enter their city, for sure the Muslims would celebrate this as a victory; it would weaken the position of the Meccan tribe and clan leaders dramatically. They were in a lose-lose situation. Either they would lose their honour by not respecting traditional Arabian rules or they would lose their prestige by granting the Muslims entrance to their city.

The Prophet knew that it was a dangerous plan; nevertheless, he did not anticipate any hostilities because of the Arabian traditions. It was during the lunar month of Dhū al-Qa'da in which he intended to reach Mecca, one of the four sacred months. According to Arabian custom all warfare was forbidden during these months, especially around Mecca.

Muhammad's followers did not carry weapons and started to march. When the Quraysh heard that around 1,400 Muslims were coming this year, they sent Khālid ibn al-Walīd (who would convert to Islam two years later) with 200 fighters to stop them. They saw no other way to defy the centuries-old Arab tradition. The Prophet reacted quickly and changed his route to avoid a confrontation. The Muslims arrived at a place called al-Hudaybīya (الْحُدَيْبِيّة) which is located at the western edge of Mecca.

Although the 1,400 Muslims had no weapons, Muhammad prepared them for war and called his followers to prepare to fight to the bitter end. This alarming news reached the leaders in Mecca, upon which they agreed to negotiate with Muhammad.

The negotiations were not easy, and several attempts were made. Although some Muslims were disappointed about the result, it actually turned out rather favourably for the Muslims. These were the main points according to Ibn 'Ishāq (ابن إسحاق):

- The Muslims were not allowed to perform their pilgrimage in that particular year, but they would be allowed to stay three days in the following year. The following year, when the Prophet returned to perform the 'Umra, there were 2,000 pilgrims with him instead of 1,400 the year before.
- A ten-year truce was negotiated.
- Any Muslim (convert) who left Mecca for Medina would immediately be delivered to the Meccan leaders, whereas anyone who left Medina and went to Mecca would be granted asylum. The latter was actually a legal possibility of getting Muslim "spies" into Mecca.

This treaty is known as the Treaty of Hudaybīya (صُلْح الْحُدَيْبِيّة). It became a turning point in Islamic history. The treaty indirectly showed that the Meccan leaders recognised Muhammad as a leader of the Medina state. When the Prophet returned from Hudaybīya, he received a revelation. Allah called the treaty a *manifest victory* – in Arabic: al-Fath al-Mubīn (الْفَتْح الْمُبِين). This is told in sura 48 *The Triumph* - in Arabic: al-Fath (سُورَة الْفَتْح):

48:1	Truly We have opened up a path to clear triumph for you [Prophet]	إِنَّا فَتَحْنَا لَكَ فَتْحًا مُّبِينًا

In his commentary on the Qur'an, Muhammad Asad wrote that the Treaty of Hudaybīya was of "the greatest importance to the future of Islam". He concluded: "Thus, in fact if not in appearance, the Truce of Hudaybīya ushered in the moral and political victory of Islam over all Arabia."

The treaty ended the hostility of the Quraysh against the Muslims. Moreover, the treaty would become the prelude of the Conquest of Mecca. Soon afterwards the Muslims conquered the Jewish stronghold of Khaybar which made the Muslim army more powerful. Great warriors and arch enemies of Islam realised that the power of the Quraysh was on decline. They changed sides and embraced Islam months before the Conquest of Mecca.

Among them were: Muhammad's uncle 'Abbās ibn Abd al-Muttalib (الْعَبّاس بن عَبْد الْمُطَّلِب); Khālid ibn al-Walīd (خالد بن وَلِيد), a highly respected warrior; 'Amr ibn al 'Ās (عَمْرو بـن الْعـاص), who later

conquered Egypt. Just or after the conquest converted 'Abū Sufyān
(أَبُو سُفْيَان), a highly influential clan chief of the Quraysh, and Wahshī
(وَحْشِيّ بن حَزْب الْحَبَشِيّ), the murderer of Muhammad's uncle Hamza.

Actually, there were no enemies of Islam left in Mecca.

71. In what year was the Battle of Khaybar?

Answer: In late spring 628 (7 AH).

After the truce with the Quraysh at Hudaybīya, the Muslims had
to deal with their other enemies: the Jews which Muhammad had
expelled from Medina. Most of these Jews found refuge in Khaybar,
and sought revenge.

Khaybar was an oasis, located 150 km (93 mi) north from Medina
in the north-western part of the Arabian Peninsula. It was a regional
power with money, weapons, and fortresses. Their leaders were hostile to Islam. They hosted many refugees who had to flee after the
battles with the Muslims. They were mainly Jews belonging to the
three Jewish tribes of Medina which Muhammad either had expelled
or annihilated.

A year after the treaty with the Meccans, Muhammad decided to
attack Khaybar. This war became known as the Battle of Khaybar
(غَزْوة خَيْبَر). He could use his entire force. Since he had negotiated a
truce with Mecca, there was no fear that the Meccans would abuse
the situation of the Muslim forces being occupied in other battles.
The Prophet had his reasons for the battle. The Jews in Khaybar
wanted to unite with other Jewish clans in order to attack Medina.
So, before the Jews were able to unite and execute their plans, the
Muslims needed to attack Khaybar.

According to Islamic sources, the Muslim soldiers attacked the
Jews at night and set up a military camp between two of the Khaybar
fortresses. By doing this, Muhammad could cut off all communica-
tion between the Khaybar people and their allies. The people in
Khaybar barricaded themselves in forts. The Muslims had around
1600 fighters (مُقـاتِلُون) and among them 200 knights (horsemen)
(فارِس). The Jews numbered 10,000.

The Muslims attacked the fortresses one by one and started with the most exposed. The last major fortress was besieged for two weeks. Although the enemy outnumbered the Muslims in terms of fighters and ammunition, the Muslims won.

The Jews of Khaybar finally surrendered and were allowed to live in the oasis on the condition that they would give one-half of their production to the Muslims. Land which belonged to non-Muslims was confiscated and turned into the collective property of the Islamic community. The paying of tribute to the Muslims can be seen as a precursor of the tax known in Islamic law as Jizya (جِزْية).

Jews continued to live in the oasis for several more years until they were eventually expelled by Caliph ʿUmar (عُمَر بن الْخَطّاب).

The Battle of Khaybar was decisive. The Prophet had neutralised his last major enemy.

Now, there was only one left: the Quraysh in Mecca.

72. When was the Conquest of Mecca?

Answer: Most probably: 10th January 630 (20th Ramadan, 8 AH).

Two years prior to the Conquest of Mecca, the Prophet and the Meccan tribes had signed the Treaty of Hudaybīya.

The treaty was meant to secure a truce, but it also allowed Muslims and Meccans to form alliances with other tribes – which both did. The Banū Bakr (بَنُو بَكر) tribe joined the Quraysh in Mecca, and the Banū Khuzāʿa (بَنُو خُزاعة) sided with Muhammad.

Both tribes had a long history of hostility between each other.

From a neutral perspective, it was obvious that this treaty wouldn't last long. Critics of Islam say that the Muslims were even waiting for this moment to happen as they had gained enough military power then to defeat the Quraysh.

Islamic accounts tell how the story continued. Only after twenty-one months (8 AH), the Banū Bakr attacked the Banū Khuzāʿa, and thus broke the treaty. The Banū Bakr wanted to take blood revenge on the Banū Khuzāʿa for something that had happened in the pre-Islamic period. The Quraysh had supported them with men and arms.

Many people were killed. A man of the Banū Khuzāʿa tribe, together with 20 others, headed to Medina and told the Prophet about it.

Muhammad, according to Muslim historians, sent a message to the Quraysh asking them to pay ransom for the persons killed and to terminate their alliance with Banū Bakr. The Quraysh replied that they shall neither pay ransom nor cancel their alliance with Banū Bakr. They told Muhammad that they were ready to abrogate the treaty.

Other historians, mainly critics of Islam, say that the Quraysh tried to maintain the peace. They say that ʾAbū Sufyān ibn Harb (أَبُو سُفْيان بن حَرْب), the leader of the Quraysh, travelled back and forth between Muhammad and Mecca, trying to reach a settlement in order to avoid a war.

Whoever was the good or the bad in this story, Muhammad made a secret plan to surround Mecca with a large force. He concentrated on war preparations without naming the destination. Muslim tribes were commanded to rush to Medina from where they continued to march towards Mecca in January 630 (Ramadan, 8 AH). On the way fighters from allied tribes joined the Muslim army which finally consisted of about 10,000 men. They surrounded the holy city.

The Quraysh were confused by the sudden attack. The Muslims had closed all escape routes. ʾAbū Sufyān, who had negotiated with Muhammad, finally embraced Islam which basically meant that he surrendered. Some days later, the Quraysh gave up their resistance. There were only a few casualties. Muslims like to call this even the *Liberation of Mecca*.

Mecca was the seat of government during the reigns of the first five caliphs.

73. What was the last battle the Prophet fought?

Answer: The Battle of Tabūk (غَـزْوة تَبُـوك), also called Ghazwa(t) al-ʿUsra (غَزْوة الْعُسْرة).

In the year when Muhammad had conquered Mecca, there was another event which changed world history. It was the war between two empires, the Byzantines (Eastern Roman Empire) and the Persians (Sasanian Empire), which came to an end. The final Byzantine-Sasanian war lasted from 602 to 628. The Byzantines won but the war's impact was devastating for both sides. Both empires had exhausted their human and material resources and were in economic trouble. This created room for a new player in the game – the Muslims.

The Byzantine armies realised that and tried to ally with some Arab tribes in order to attack Muhammad, as Islamic historians claim. Otherwise it would be difficult to explain why the Prophet went to war in the month of Rajab (رَجَب), one of the four sacred months of the lunar calendar, during which fighting is strictly forbidden – except in self-defence.

The Battle of Tabūk was in autumn 630 (9 AH). According to Ibn 'Ishāq, Muhammad ordered his companions to prepare to raid the Byzantines at a time when men were facing a hard time. The heat was oppressive and there was a drought. Fruit was ripe and the men wanted to stay in the shade to harvest their crop, and disliked to travel at that season.

The people who did not join Muhammad in the battle were mentioned in sura 9 *The Repentance* – in Arabic al-Tawba (سُورة التَّوبة):

9:81	Those who were left behind were happy to stay behind when God's messenger set out; they hated the thought of striving in God's way with their possessions and their persons. They said to one another, 'Do not go [to war] in this heat.' Say, 'Hellfire is hotter.' If only they understood!	فَرِحَ الْمُخَلَّفُونَ بِمَقْعَدِهِمْ خِلَافَ رَسُولِ اللَّهِ وَكَرِهُوا أَن يُجَاهِدُوا بِأَمْوَالِهِمْ وَأَنفُسِهِمْ فِي سَبِيلِ اللَّهِ وَقَالُوا لَا تَنفِرُوا فِي الْحَرِّ قُلْ نَارُ جَهَنَّمَ أَشَدُّ حَرًّا لَّوْ كَانُوا يَفْقَهُونَ

What were the reasons? Some (mostly western) scholars say they were of economic nature.

Muhammad tried to attack the northern regions to get new bounty as more and more people in the Islamic community grew unsatisfied. Furthermore, this would make the whole of Arabia the *Abode of Islam*, so-called Dar al-Islam (دار الإشلام). It also paved the way for the conquest of al-Shām (الشّام) – which comprises today Jordan, Syria, Lebanon, and Palestine/Israel.

This battle was the start of an ongoing conflict between the Muslims and the Byzantines. The account of these events is based on Byzantine as well as Islamic sources.

Muhammad's army consisted of 30,000 soldiers – a huge army compared to the previous armies of Islam. Muslims had never marched in such great numbers before. The conditions were terrible. Reports say that the number of their camels was so small that many of the men were obliged to walk. There was the unbearable heat of the desert and a severe shortage of water.

When they arrived at Tabūk, the Byzantines were not there. They stayed in Tabūk for a number of days, some say almost three weeks, and scouted the area, but the Byzantines never showed up. Eventually, there was no confrontation – it was a moral victory for the Muslims without shedding blood. It seemed that no tribe was ready for war. Furthermore, there was no sign that the Byzantines were present in that area.

In the end, many Arab tribes abandoned their alliance with the Byzantines and joined the Muslim armies out of fear. Muhammad could thus enlarge his Islamic State. Some scholars and commentators of the Qur'an, for example Ibn Kathīr (ابن كَثِير), claimed that the term Jizya (الْجِزْية), which is a tax for non-Muslim, was revealed during the Battle of Tabūk:

| 9:29 | Fight those of the People of the Book who do not [truly] believe in God and the Last Day, who do not forbid what God and His messenger have forbidden, who do not obey the rule of justice, until they pay the tax and agree to submit. | قَاتِلُوا الَّذِينَ لَا يُؤْمِنُونَ بِاللَّهِ وَلَا بِالْيَوْمِ الْآخِرِ وَلَا يُحَرِّمُونَ مَا حَرَّمَ اللَّهُ وَرَسُولُهُ وَلَا يَدِينُونَ دِينَ الْحَقِّ مِنَ الَّذِينَ أُوتُوا الْكِتَابَ حَتَّى يُعْطُوا الْجِزْيَةَ عَن يَدٍ وَهُمْ صَاغِرُونَ. |

An excursus on the origin of the word al-Shām. It denotes *the northern region, the North*; also *Syria* or *Damascus*. The root of this Arabic word literally denotes *the direction of the left hand* and *to the north*. It describes an area bounded by the Taurus Mountains of Turkey in the north, the Mediterranean Sea in the west, and the northern Arabian Desert and Mesopotamia in the east – the Levant. The opposite term is al-Yaman (الْيَمَن), the Arabic word for Yemen, which literally means *to the right* and therefore *to/in the south*.

74. How many swords did the Prophet possess?

Answer: Some scholars say that he had nine swords. Some say more, but there are no reliable sources.

His most famous sword is Dhū al-Faqār (ذُو الْفَقَار). In the Hadiths, it is mentioned that the handle of this sword was made of silver. It was narrated that 'Anas ibn Mālik (أَنَس بن مالك) said: "The metallic end of the scabbard of the Messenger of Allah was of silver, the pommel of his sword was silver and in between were rings of silver."[119]

This sword was probably taken as booty by Muhammad at the Battle of Badr (غَزْوة بَدْر). This goes back to a Hadith which was narrated by 'Abd Allah ibn 'Abbās (عَبْد الله بن عَبّاس): "The Messenger of Allah acquired his sword Dhū al-Faqār from the spoils of war on the Day of Badr."[120]

It is reported that Muhammad later gave the sword to his cousin and son-in-law, 'Alī ibn 'Abī Tālib (عَليّ بن أَبي طالِب), and also that 'Alī returned from the Battle of 'Uhud covered with blood from his hands to his shoulders, having Dhū al-Faqār with him. Many sources report that this sword remained with 'Alī and his family.

There are rumours and many anecdotes about Muhammad's swords. Especially the Ottoman Sultans were fond of collecting them. However, it is doubtful that they always obtained the original pieces. Anyway, the stories about the swords of Muhammad are interesting.

Let's have a look at the other eight.

Al-'Adb (الْعَضب). The name means *cutting* or *sharp*. This sword was sent to Muhammad by one of his friends just before the Battle of Badr. Muhammad also used this sword at the Battle of 'Uhud and his followers used it to demonstrate their loyalty to him. The sword is said to be stored in the Husayn Mosque (مَسْجِد الإِمام الْحُسَيْن) in Cairo. Some Muslims believe that on the ground of this mosque, the head of Husayn is buried.

---

119 ...قَالَ كَانَ نَعْلُ سَيْفِ رَسُولِ اللَّهِ مِنْ فِضَّةٍ وَقَبِيعَةُ سَيْفِهِ فِضَّةٌ وَمَا بَيْنَ ذَلِكَ حِلَقُ فِضَّةٍ.
Sunan al-Nasā'ī 5374

120 ...أَنَّ رَسُولَ اللَّهِ تَنَفَّلَ سَيْفَهُ ذَا الْفِقَارِ يَوْمَ بَدْرٍ. Sunan ibn Māja 2915; hasan

Al-Ma'thūr (الْمَأْثُوُر) is the sword which was owned by Muhammad before he received his first revelations. He was given this sword after his father had died. When he migrated from Mecca to Medina, the sword remained with him until it was given to 'Alī ibn 'Abī Tālib. Length of blade: 99 cm (39"). The handle is made of gold in the shape of two serpents, encrusted with emeralds and turquoise. Near the handle is an inscription giving the name of Muhammad's father, 'Abd Allah ibn 'Abd al-Muttalib (عَبْد الله بن عَبْد الْمُطَّلِب). This sword is said to be stored in the Topkapı museum in Istanbul.

Al-Rasūb (الرَّسُوب). It has gold circles. Length of the blade: 140 cm (55"), and also preserved in the Topkapı museum.

Al-Battār (الْبَتَّار). This sword was taken by Muhammad as booty from the Banū Qaynuqā' (بَنُو قَيْنُقَاع), the Jewish tribe of Medina which was eradicated by the Muslims. It is called the *sword of the prophets*, because the names of the prophets David, Solomon, Moses, Aaron, Joshua, Zechariah, John, Jesus, and Muhammad were inscribed in it. It also has a drawing showing King David cutting off the head of Goliath. Length of blade: 101 cm (39"). It is said to be in the Topkapı museum. Some people claim that this will be the sword which Jesus will use when he returns to earth to defeat the Anti-Christ, the al-Dajjāl (الدَّجَّال).

Al-Hatf (الْخَتْف). This sword was also taken as booty from the Banū Qaynuqā'. There is a famous legend about this sword. God gave King David the ability to work with iron and make weapons. David also made a sword for himself – al-Hatf. It resembles the al-Battār, but is larger. Length of blade: 112 cm (44"). It is housed in the Topkapı museum.

Al-Qal'ī (الْقَلْعِيُّ). Some scholars say that the word refers to *tin* or *white lead* which was mined in different locations. The name could also refer to a place in Syria or a place in India near China. This sword is one of the three which Muhammad acquired as booty from the Jews of Banū Qaynuqā'. It is stored in the Topkapı museum. Length of blade: 100 cm (39"). The blade of this sword is distinguished from the others because of its wavy design.

Al-Mikhdham (الْمِخْذَم) is reported to have passed from the Prophet to 'Alī ibn 'Abī Ṭālib, and from 'Alī to his sons. Some people claim that 'Alī had taken the sword as booty in a raid he had led in Syria. Length of blade: 97 cm (38"). It is lodged in the Topkapı museum.

Al-Qadib (القَضِيب) is a sword with a narrow blade which resembles a rod (stick) – which is also what the Arabic word basically means. It was a sword of defence or one for the traveller, but not used in battle. The sword has a scabbard of dyed animal hide and is housed in the Topkapı museum.

75. How many times did the Prophet perform the Hajj?

Answer: Only once.

'Abū Qatāda (أَبُو قَتَادة) said: "I asked 'Anas ibn Mālik (أَنَس بن مالِك) about the number of pilgrimages performed by Allah's Messenger and he replied: 'One Hajj and four 'Umras.'"[121]

If we scrutinise the Hadiths[122] and other sources available on this topic[123], we can sum it up as follows:

- **1st 'Umra:** In 6 AH after the Treaty of Hudaybīya (صُلْح الْحُدَيْبِيَة), but the Meccan non-Muslims prevented him from reaching the Ka'ba. Muhammad offered the sacrifice of camels when his way was blocked at Hudaybīya.

  His companions shaved their heads and entered the state of 'Iḥrām (إحْرام). Despite the difficulties almost all scholars count it as an 'Umra.

---

121 ...قَالَ سَأَلْتُ أَنَسًا كَمْ حَجَّ رَسُولُ اللَّهِ قَالَ حَجَّةً وَاحِدَةً وَاعْتَمَرَ أَرْبَعَ عُمَرٍ. ثُمَّ ذَكَرَ بِمِثْلِ حَدِيثِ هَدَّابٍ. Sahīh Muslim 1253.

122 ...سَأَلْتُ أَنَسًا كَمِ اعْتَمَرَ النَّبِيُّ قَالَ أَرْبَعَ عُمَرُ الْحُدَيْبِيَةِ فِي ذِي الْقَعْدَةِ، حَيْثُ صَدَّهُ الْمُشْرِكُونَ، وَعُمْرَةً مِنَ الْعَامِ الْمُقْبِلِ فِي ذِي الْقَعْدَةِ، حَيْثُ صَالَحَهُمْ، وَعُمْرَةُ الْجِعْرَانَةِ إِذْ قَسَمَ غَنِيمَةَ أُرَاهُ حُنَيْنٍ. Sahīh al-Bukhārī 1778

123 ...قَالَ قُلْتُ لِأَنَسِ بْنِ مَالِكٍ كَمْ حَجَّ النَّبِيُّ قَالَ حَجَّةً وَاحِدَةً وَاعْتَمَرَ أَرْبَعَ عُمَرٍ عُمْرَةً فِي ذِي الْقَعْدَةِ وَعُمْرَةُ الْحُدَيْبِيَةِ وَعُمْرَةً مَعَ حَجَّتِهِ وَعُمْرَةُ الْجِعْرَانَةِ إِذْ قَسَمَ غَنِيمَةَ حُنَيْنٍ. Jāmi' al-Tirmidhī 815.

- 2nd 'Umra: In 7 AH since the Treaty of Hudaybīya permitted it. Muhammad entered Mecca and stayed there for three days.

- 3rd 'Umra: In 8 AH after Muhammad's return from the Battle of Hunayn (غَزْوة حُنَيْن). He also distributed the war booty on this occasion. The Muslims fought against the Bedouin tribe of Hawāzin (هَوازِن) and its subsection the Thaqīf (ثَقيف) at a place called Hunayn in a valley near one of the roads between Mecca and al-Tā'if (الطائِف). It was a fight against the tribes who did not accept the Prophet's authority after he had conquered Mecca. The tribes were long-standing enemies of the Meccans and saw in Muhammad just another powerful Quraysh leader.

  The battle ended in a decisive victory for the Muslims who captured tremendous spoils. The Prophet distributed the war booty also to former enemies of Islam, for example to 'Abū Sufyān (أَبُو سُفْيان) who had become Muslim when Muhammad entered Mecca. This was a surprise to the Muslims of Medina, the so-called 'Ansār (الأَنْصار).

  The Prophet knew how important honour and money was, and 'Abū Sufyān was an important new member of the Muslim community. In the end, almost all the booty had been shared out among the Quraysh. Some people from Medina felt that Muhammad was privileging his kin as he himself was from the tribe of the Quraysh.

  Remark: The Battle of Hunayn is one of only two battles mentioned in the Qur'an by name, in sura *The Repentance* – in Arabic: al-Tawba (سُورة التَّوْبة).

- 4th 'Umra: In 10 AH, <u>along with his only Hajj</u>. Mecca had already been conquered, thus the Muslims controlled the Ka'ba.

76. The Prophet did only one pilgrimage together with his companions. What is it called?

Answer: The Farewell Pilgrimage (حِجّة الْوَداع).

The Prophet went for the Hajj from Medina on the 25th of the month Dhū al-Qaʿda (ذُو الْقَعْدة) in 632 (10 AH).

The Farewell Pilgrimage was the only Hajj of Muhammad. He went out with 100,000 male and female Muslims as some sources claim. The Muslims observed every move, every act and every gesture of Muhammad on this occasion, and everything he did would serve as an example for all time.

Before the Conquest of Mecca, Muhammad had lived in Medina for ten years and had not performed Hajj in full, though he had performed the lesser pilgrimage, the so-called ʿUmra (عُمْرة).

The Prophet delivered a sermon during the Farewell Pilgrimage on the Day of Sacrifice at Minā. ʿIkrima ibn Abi Jahl (عِكْرِمة بن أَبي جَهْل) narrated that the Messenger of Allah said on that day: "Verily your blood, your property and your honour are as sacred and inviolable as the sanctity of this day of yours, in this month of yours, and in this town of yours."[124]

Muhammad taught his followers the manners of 'Ihrām (إحْرام), the prescribed state of purity before entering Mecca.

He made Ghusl (غُسْل) - the ritual bath - and then put on the proper attire and prepared himself for Hajj. His 'Ihrām clothes consisted of two pieces of Yemeni unsewn white cotton that became his shroud later on. He did his noon prayers in the Mosque of al-Shajara (مَسْجِد الشَّجَرة), also known as Masjid Dhī al-Halīfa (مَسْجِد ذِي الْحَلِيفة).

Later, Muslims built mosques at some of the places Muhammad stayed or did prayers.

---

124 إِنَّ دِمَاءَكُمْ وَأَمْوَالَكُمْ وَأَعْرَاضَكُمْ عَلَيْكُمْ حَرَامٌ كَحُرْمَةِ يَوْمِكُمْ هَذَا، فِي شَهْرِكُمْ هَذَا، فِي بَلَدِكُمْ هَذَا.

Sahīh al-Bukhārī 1739

77. Where are many companions and members of the Prophet's family buried?

Answer: In the al-Baqīʿ cemetery (مَقْبَرة الْبَقِيع) in Medina. It is next to the Prophet's Mosque - al-Masjid al-Nabawī (الْمَسْجِد النَّبَوِيّ) - where Muhammad's grave is located.

Al-Baqīʿ means literally a *place with tree roots* or simply *tree garden*. In this cemetery, many of Muhammad's relatives and companions are buried. Several Islamic sources indicate that Muhammad prayed there whenever he passed it.

When Muhammad migrated from Mecca in 622 and arrived in Yathrib (Medina), al-Baqīʿ was a land covered with *Lycium shawii* shrubs which is a species of thorny shrub adapted to desert environments, known as *desert thorn* or *Arabian boxthorn*. The thinly leaved bush grows to three metres high with lots of branches and spines.

One of Muhammad's companions, ʾAsʿad ibn Zurāra (أَسْعَد بن زُرَارة), died during the construction of the Prophet's Mosque. This made Muhammad choose the spot for a cemetery, and ʾAsʿad was the first person to be buried in al-Baqīʿ. ʾAsʿad suffered from an illness, similar to diphtheria or meningitis, that entailed a rattling in his throat. Muhammad visited him while he was sick and advised him to be cauterised.[125] It didn't help, and ʾAsʿad died shortly thereafter.

During the Battle of Badr (غَزوة بَدْر), the Muhammad's daughter Ruqayya (رُقَيّة بِنْت مُحَمَّد) fell sick and died in 624. She was the first of his family to be buried there.

Shortly after Muhammad arrived from Badr, ʿUthmān ibn Mazʿūn (عُثْمان بن مَظْعُون) died and was also buried in al-Baqīʿ. He was the first of the so-called Muhājirūn (الْمُهاجِرُون) - the people who migrated with the Prophet from Mecca to Medina - to be buried there.

Most of Muhammad's family (wives, daughters) were buried there. Among them was Hasan, the grandson of Muhammad, the son of his daughter Fātima, and his cousin ʿAlī ibn ʾAbī Tālib (عَلِيّ بن أَبِي طالِب).

The first extension of al-Baqīʿ took place during the reign of the first Umayyad Caliph, Muʿāwiya I (مُعاوية بن أَبِي سُفْيان). His decision had a

---

125 ...أَنَّ النَّبِيَّ كَوَى أَسْعَدَ بْنَ زُرَارَةَ مِنَ الشَّوْكَةِ. Jāmiʿ al-Tirmidhī 2188.

reason. One of his predecessors, Caliph 'Uthmān ibn 'Affān (عُثْمان بن عَفّان), was buried in a neighbouring Jewish graveyard. In order to honour 'Uthmān, Mu'āwiya incorporated the huge Jewish graveyard into the al-Baqī' cemetery.

On 21ˢᵗ April 1926 (1344 AH) the mausoleums in al-Baqī' were destroyed by the Saudi King, Ibn Sa'ūd. In the same year, he also demolished the tombs of several important Islamic figures in the Mu'allā Cemetery (جَنّة الْمُعَلَّى) in Mecca where Muhammad's first wife Khadīja, his grandfather, and other ancestors were buried. This happened despite protests. More graves were destroyed later on by the Saudi regime.

78. Are Muslims allowed to heal with fire (cauterise)?

Answer: Yes and no.

Cauterisation is a medical practice which was common in ancient times. It involves burning a part of the body; mostly to stop severe blood-loss or to close amputations. It was believed that it could prevent infection. The traditions of the Prophet are here contradicting. There are reports that he did it himself, but there are also reports in which he condemns the method.

First, let's check the Hadiths which say that a Muslim may cauterise:

- Jābir ibn 'Abd Allah (جابِر بن عَبْد الله) narrated that Sa'd ibn Mu'ādh (سَعْد بن مُعاذ) was hit by an arrow and bled from a wound in his vein. This happened probably in the Battle of the Trench, also known as the Battle of the Confederates (غَـزْوة الأَحْـزاب). The Prophet cauterised the wound with a rod and when it became swollen, Allah's Messenger did it for the second time.[126]
- 'Abd Allah ibn 'Abbās (عَبْد الله بن عَبّاس) narrated that the Prophet said: "Healing is in three things: A gulp of honey, cupping, and

---

126 ...قَالَ رُمِيَ سَعْدُ بْنُ مُعَاذٍ فِي أَكْحَلِهِ - قَالَ - فَحَسَمَهُ النَّبِيُّ ﷺ بِيَدِهِ بِمِشْقَصٍ ثُمَّ وَرِمَتْ فَحَسَمَهُ الثَّانِيَةَ. Sahīh Muslim 2208.

branding with fire [cauterising]. But I forbid my followers to use branding with fire."[127]

There are also reports that forbid this practise:

'Imrān ibn Husayn (عِمْرَان بن حُصَيْن) recounted: "Verily the Messenger of Allah said: 'Seventy thousand men of my 'Umma would enter Paradise without rendering account. They [the companions] asked: 'Who would be those, Messenger of Allah?' He [the Prophet] answered: 'They would be those who neither practise charm, take omens, nor do they cauterise, but they rest their trust in their Lord.'"[128] The same 'Imrān ibn Husayn narrated: "And I was always blessed until I was branded. I then abandoned branding and the blessing was restored."[129]

When the Islamic Hadd (حَدّ) punishments were announced, a lot of people were cauterised as their hands and feet were chopped of as punishment for thieves or for those who had committed highway (main road) robberies (against travellers). So what do the Islamic scholars make of these contradicting reports? They say that cauterisation is not advisable. It causes pain and for this reason alone, it is disliked (detestable) – so-called makrūh (مَكْرُوه).

Remark: Hijāma (حِجامة) is the Arabic term for (wet) **cupping**, where blood is drawn by vacuum from a small skin incision for therapeutic purposes. This practice was already known to Ancient Greeks and Persians.

79. Why were Mondays important in the Prophet's life?

Answer: Because the most important events in Muhammad's life happened on Mondays (الْإِثْنَيْن).

---

127 ...قَالَ: "الشِّفَاءُ فِي ثَلَاثَةٍ شَرْبَةِ عَسَلٍ، وَشَرْطَةِ مِحْجَمٍ، وَكَيَّةِ نَارٍ، وَأَنْهَى أُمَّتِي عَنِ الْكَيِّ." Saḥīḥ al-Bukhārī 5680

128 ...أَنَّ رَسُولَ اللَّهِ قَالَ: "يَدْخُلُ الْجَنَّةَ مِنْ أُمَّتِي سَبْعُونَ أَلْفًا بِغَيْرِ حِسَابٍ." قَالُوا مَنْ هُمْ يَا رَسُولَ اللَّهِ قَالَ: "هُمُ الَّذِينَ لَا يَسْتَرْقُونَ وَلَا يَتَطَيَّرُونَ وَلَا يَكْتَوُونَ وَعَلَى رَبِّهِمْ يَتَوَكَّلُونَ." Saḥīḥ Muslim 218

129 ...وَقَدْ كَانَ يُسَلَّمُ عَلَيَّ حَتَّى اكْتَوَيْتُ فَتُرِكْتُ ثُمَّ تَرَكْتُ الْكَيَّ فَعَادَ. Saḥīḥ Muslim 1226

The Prophet was born on a Monday, his mission began on a Monday, and he died on a Monday. This was mentioned in several Hadiths. For example, 'Abū Qatāda (أَبُو قَتادة) has reported that the Prophet was asked about fasting on Mondays and he said: "On that day I was born and on that day revelation came to me."[130]

The Islamic scholar Ibn Kathīr (ابن كَثِـير) added that it was on Monday, when Muhammad was taken up to heaven, and it was on Monday when he migrated from Mecca to Medina.

80. How old was Muhammad when he died?

Answer: About 63.

A few months after the Farewell Pilgrimage, Muhammad fell ill and suffered for several days. He had fever, head pain and felt weak.

The Prophet died on Monday, 8th of June 632 (11 AH) or, according to the Islamic calendar, on the 12th of Rabīʿ al-'Awwal (رَبيع الأَوَّل). He died in the morning in Medina and was 62 or 63 years old.

81. What was the Prophet's last advice before he died?

Answer: Probably two things.

There are reports telling Muslims what the Prophet said in his last minutes. Scholars see in them the last pieces of advice which Muhammad gave to his family and his companions:

'Abū 'Ubayda ibn al-Jarrāh (أَبُو عُبَيْدة بن الجَرّاح) narrated that the last words the Prophet said were: "Expel the Jews of the Hijāz and Najrān from the Arabian Peninsula, and know that the most evil of people are those who took [regard] the graves of their prophets as places of worship!"[131]

---

130 ...أَنَّ رَسُولَ اللّهِ سُئِلَ عَنْ صَوْمِ الاِثْنَيْنِ فَقَالَ: "فِيهِ وُلِدْتُ وَفِيهِ أُنْزِلَ عَلَيَّ." Sahih Muslim 1162

131 ...قَالَ: آخِرُ مَا تَكَلَّمَ بِهِ رَسُولُ اللّهِ قَالَ:"أَخْرِجُوا يَهُودَ الحِجَازِ وَأَهْلَ نَجْرَانَ مِنْ جَزِيرَةِ العَرَبِ, وَاعْلَمُوا أَنَّ شَرَّ النَّاسِ الَّذِينَ اتَّخَذُوا قُبُورَهُمْ مَسَاجِدَ." Musnad 'Ahmad ibn Hanbal 1691

Some remarks regarding this quote. The Hijāz (الحِجاز) is a region in the west of present-day Saudi Arabia at the Red Sea. It is bordered by Jordan in the north and Yemen in the south and does not extend very far inland. The main cities are Jidda (جِدّة), Mecca, and Medina. It is basically the region where Muhammad's life took place and therefore the beginning of Islam. There is an authentic Hadith that tells us more about the situation of the Jews in the Hijāz during the time of Muhammad and what happened after his death:

ʿAbd Allah ibn ʿUmar (عَبْد الله بن عُمَر) narrated: "ʿUmar expelled the Jews and the Christians from the Hijāz. When Allah's Messenger had conquered Khaybar, he wanted to expel its Jews as the land became the property of Allah, His Apostle, and of the Muslims. Allah's Messenger intended to expel the Jews but they requested him to let them stay on the condition that they would do the labour and get half of the fruits. Allah's Messenger told them: 'We will let you stay on this condition, as long as we wish.' So, they [i.e. the Jews] kept on living there until ʿUmar forced them to go to [the two villages of] Taymāʾ (تَيْمَاء) and ʾArīhāʾ (أَرِيحَاء).[132]

What else did Muhammad say in his final moments? It is narrated that his cousin and son-in-law, ʿAlī ibn ʾAbī Tālib (عَلِيّ بن أَبِي طالِب), said: "The last words that Allah' Messenger spoke were: 'The prayer, the prayer; and fear Allah for those whom your right hands possess.'"[133]

82. What were the Prophet's last words?

Answer: "(O Allah) with the highest companion."[134]

---

132 ...أَنَّ عُمَرَ بْنَ الْخَطَّابِ أَجْلَى الْيَهُودَ وَالنَّصَارَى مِنْ أَرْضِ الحِجازِ، وَكَانَ رَسُولُ اللهِ لَمَّا ظَهَرَ عَلَى خَيْبَرَ أَرَادَ إِخْرَاجَ الْيَهُودِ مِنْهَا، وَكَانَتِ الأَرْضُ حِينَ ظَهَرَ عَلَيْهَا للهِ وَلِرَسُولِهِ وَلِلْمُسْلِمِينَ، وَأَرَادَ إِخْرَاجَ الْيَهُودِ، مِنْهَا فَسَأَلَتِ الْيَهُودُ رَسُولَ اللهِ لِيُقِرَّهُمْ بِهَا أَنْ يَكْفُوا عَمَلَهَا وَلَهُمْ نِصْفُ الثَّمَرِ، فَقَالَ لَهُمْ رَسُولُ اللهِ: "نُقِرُّكُمْ بِهَا عَلَى ذَلِكَ مَا شِئْنَا." فَقَرُّوا بِهَا حَتَّى أَجْلَاهُمْ عُمَرُ إِلَى تَيْمَاءَ وَأَرِيحَاءَ. -Sahih al-Bukhārī 2338

133 ...قَالَ كَانَ آخِرُ كَلَامِ رَسُولِ اللهِ: "الصَّلَاةَ الصَّلَاةَ اتَّقُوا اللَّهَ فِيمَا مَلَكَتْ أَيْمَانُكُمْ." -Sunan ʾAbī Dāwūd 5156

134 فِي الرَّفِيقِ الأَعْلَى.

There are several authentic reports on the Prophet's last words. However, most Sunni scholars are convinced that only the following Hadith gives information about his final words.

With his head resting on 'Ā'isha's lap, he asked her to dispose of his last worldly goods (seven coins). 'Ā'isha (عائشة بِنْت أَبِي بَكْر) narrated:

"When the Prophet was healthy, he used to say: 'No soul of a prophet is captured until he is shown his place in Paradise and then he is given the option.' When death approached him while his head was on my thigh, he became unconscious and then recovered his consciousness. He then looked at the ceiling of the house and said: 'O Allah! (with) the highest companion.' I said to myself: 'Hence, he is not going to choose us.'

Then I realised that what he had said was the application of the narration which he mentioned to us when he was healthy. The last word he spoke was: 'O Allah! (with) the highest companion.'"[135]

83. In which house did the Prophet die?

Answer: In the house of his wife 'Ā'isha (عائشة بِنْت أَبِي بَكْر).

'Ā'isha narrated that during his fatal illness, Allah's Messenger asked his wives: "Where shall I stay tomorrow? Where shall I stay tomorrow?" He was looking forward to 'Ā'isha's turn. So all his wives allowed him to stay where he wished, and he stayed at 'Ā'isha's house until he died there.[136]

'Ibn 'Abū Mulayka (ابن أَبِي مُلَيْكَة) narrated that 'Ā'isha said: "The Prophet died in my house on the day of my turn while he was lean-

---

135 ...عَائِشَةَ قَالَتْ كَانَ النَّبِيُّ يَقُولُ وَهُوَ صَحِيحٌ: "إِنَّهُ لَمْ يُقْبَضْ نَبِيٌّ حَتَّى يَرَى مَقْعَدَهُ مِنَ الْجَنَّةِ، ثُمَّ يُخَيَّرَ." فَلَمَّا نَزَلَ بِهِ وَرَأْسُهُ عَلَى فَخِذِي غُشِيَ عَلَيْهِ، ثُمَّ أَفَاقَ، فَأَشْخَصَ بَصَرَهُ إِلَى سَقْفِ الْبَيْتِ ثُمَّ قَالَ: "اللَّهُمَّ الرَّفِيقَ الْأَعْلَى." فَقُلْتُ إِذًا لَا يَخْتَارُنَا. وَعَرَفْتُ أَنَّهُ الْحَدِيثُ الَّذِي كَانَ يُحَدِّثُنَا وَهُوَ صَحِيحٌ قَالَتْ فَكَانَتْ آخِرَ كَلِمَةٍ تَكَلَّمَ بِهَا "اللَّهُمَّ الرَّفِيقَ الْأَعْلَى." Sahīh al-Bukhārī 4463

136 ...أَنَّ رَسُولَ اللَّهِ كَانَ يَسْأَلُ فِي مَرَضِهِ الَّذِي مَاتَ فِيهِ: "أَيْنَ أَنَا غَدًا أَيْنَ أَنَا غَدًا؟" يُرِيدُ يَوْمَ عَائِشَةَ، فَأَذِنَ لَهُ أَزْوَاجُهُ يَكُونُ حَيْثُ شَاءَ، فَكَانَ فِي بَيْتِ عَائِشَةَ حَتَّى مَاتَ عِنْدَهَا. Sahīh al-Bukhārī 5217

ing on my chest closer to my neck, and Allah made my saliva mix with his saliva."[137]

'Ā'isha added that "'Abd al-Rahmān came with a Siwāk [a tool to clean the teeth] but the Prophet was too weak to use it, so I took it, chewed it and then gave it to him, and he cleaned his teeth with it."[138]

84. Who said: "Whoever worshipped Muhammad, then Muhammad is dead"?

Answer: 'Abū Bakr al-Siddīq (أَبُو بَكْر الصِّدِّيق).

What we know about Muhammad's last minutes and about the moment he passed away is based mainly on one Hadith which was narrated by 'Ā'isha (عائشة بِنْت أَبِي بَكْر).

When the Prophet died, Muslims gathered in his mosque, al-Masjid al-Nabawī (الْمَسْجِد النَّبَوِيّ). 'Abū Bakr came on a horse from his house in a village where he had been with his new wife.

He dismounted and entered the Prophet's Mosque, but did not speak to anyone until he entered upon 'Ā'isha. He went straight to Muhammad who was covered with a Hibra cloth [a kind of Yemenite cloth]. Then he uncovered Muhammad's face, bowed over him, kissed him and wept, saying: "Let my father and mother be sacrificed for you. By Allah, Allah will never cause you to die twice. As for the death which was written for you, has come upon you."[139]

Then he quoted sura 3:144: "Muhammad is only a messenger before whom many messengers have been and gone."[140]

---

137 ...قَالَتْ عَائِشَةُ: "تُوُفِّيَ النَّبِيُّ فِي بَيْتِي، وَفِي نَوْبَتِي، وَبَيْنَ سَحْرِي وَنَحْرِي، وَجَمَعَ اللَّهُ بَيْنَ رِيقِي وَرِيقِه." Sahīh al-Bukhārī 3100

138 ...قَالَتْ: "دَخَلَ عَبْدُ الرَّحْمَنِ بِسِوَاكٍ، فَضَعُفَ النَّبِيُّ عَنْهُ، فَأَخَذْتُهُ فَمَضَغْتُهُ ثُمَّ سَنَنْتُهُ بِهِ." Sahīh al-Bukhārī 3100

139 ...قَالَ بِأَبِي أَنْتَ وَأُمِّي طِبْتَ حَيًّا وَمَيِّتًا، وَالَّذِي نَفْسِي بِيَدِهِ لَا يُذِيقُكَ اللَّهُ الْمَوْتَتَيْنِ أَبَدًا. Sahīh al-Bukhārī 3667, 3668

140 ...وَمَا مُحَمَّدٌ إِلَّا رَسُولٌ قَدْ خَلَتْ مِن قَبْلِهِ الرُّسُلُ. sura Family of 'Imrān; 3:144

And then 'Abū Bakr said the famous sentence: "Whoever worshipped Muhammad, then Muhammad is dead, but whoever worshipped Allah, then Allah is alive and shall never die."[141]

85. Where is the Prophet buried?

Answer: In Medina. Muhammad was buried where he died: in the house of his wife 'Ā'isha (عائشة بِنْت أَبِي بَكْر), next to the Prophet's Mosque.

Today, the Prophet's grave is inside the mosque which is the second most important mosque in Islam. Over the years it has been gradually enlarged until it incorporated the house in which he died.

86. How big was the number of Muslims at the time of the Prophet's death?

Answer: Probably around 114,000 companions.

In Arabic, a companion of Muhammad is called Sahābī (صحابِيّ). Companionship in Islam - in Arabic: Suhba (صُحْبة) - denotes *close attachment* (المُلازَمة), *accompaniment* (مُرافَقة), as well as *social relationship* (المُعاشَرة).

Muslims must defend the companions of Muhammad when anyone dares to criticise them. Insulting a companion is even considered disbelieve and can be severely punished.

What are the conditions to call somebody a companion? Most scholars say that a person who embraced Islam, saw or met the Prophet and accompanied him - even for only a short time - is a companion. 'Abū Zar'a al-Rāzī (أَبُو زَرْعة الرَّازِيّ), a scholar and historian of the 9th century, stated: "The number of the Prophet's companions at the time of his death reached 114,000 companions."

---

141 ...فَحَمِدَ اللَّهَ أَبُو بَكْرٍ وَأَثْنَى عَلَيْهِ وَقَالَ أَلَا مَنْ كَانَ يَعْبُدُ مُحَمَّدًافَإِنَّ مُحَمَّدًا قَدْ مَاتَ، وَمَنْ كَانَ يَعْبُدُ اللَّهَ فَإِنَّ اللَّهَ حَيٌّ لَا يَمُوتُ. Sahīh al-Bukhārī 3667, 3668.

This number is, for example, encountered in al-Jāmi' (الْجامِع) written by al-Khatīb al-Baghdādī (الْخَطِيب الْبَغْدادِيّ), a Sunni Muslim scholar and historian of the 11ᵗʰ century.

The number, however, might be questioned as nobody had actually counted them.

87. Who was the first person of Muhammad's family to die after the Prophet?

Answer: His youngest daughter, Fātima al-Zahrā' (فاطِمة الزَّهْراء).

Born	~ 604 in Mecca	Died	28ᵗʰ August 632 (11 AH) in Medina

Fātima was Muhammad's youngest daughter. Her mother was Khadīja (خَدِيجة بِنت خُوَيْلِد). She later married the Prophet's cousin, 'Alī ibn 'Abī Tālib (عَلِيّ بن أَبِي طالِب), and became a mother of two sons, al-Hasan (الْحَسَن) and al-Husayn (الْحُسَيْن).

'Abū Sa'īd al-Khudrī (أَبُو سَعِيد الْخُدْرِيّ) has narrated that the Prophet said: "Al-Hasan and al-Husayn are the chiefs of the youth of Paradise."[142]

After her father Muhammad died, Fātima became the centre of a political dispute. Muhammad told his followers about almost every aspect in life – but unfortunately, he did not choose his successor. There are different stories trying to prove who should be the legitimate leader of the Muslims after Muhammad. They all boil down to two people: 'Abū Bakr (أَبُو بَكْر) and 'Alī. The result was the split of the Muslim community, which led to the formation of the two main sects in Islam: Sunni and Shia.

Fātima, her husband 'Alī and her sons played a major role in the split of Islam. Fātima was the only child of Muhammad to have sons who survived childhood. The Fatimids (الْفاطِمِيُّون), the 11ᵗʰ century dynasty which ruled in Egypt at the time of the Crusades, claimed descent from Fātima.

---

142 ...قَالَ رَسُولُ اللَّهِ: "الْحَسَنُ وَالْحُسَيْنُ سَيِّدَا شَبابِ أَهْلِ الْجَنَّةِ. " Jāmi' al-Tirmidhī 4136

According to Sunni historical accounts, Fātima died as a result of the separation from her father Muhammad.

Following the Farewell Pilgrimage, Muhammad summoned Fātima and informed her that he would soon die. He also told her that she would be the next of his family to die.

ʿĀʾisha (عائشة بِنْت أَبِي بَكْر) narrated: "So when the Prophet fell sick and Fātima entered, she bent over and kissed him. Then she lifted her head and cried, then she bent over him and she lifted her head and laughed. So I said: 'I used to think that this was from the most intelligent of our women, but she is really just one of the women.'

So when the Prophet died, I said to her: 'Do you remember when you bent over the Prophet and you lifted your head and cried, then you bent over him, then you lifted your head and laughed. What caused you to do that?' She said: 'Then, I would be the one who spreads the secrets. He told me that he was to die from his illness, so I cried. Then he told me that I would be the quickest of his family to meet up with him. So that is when I laughed."[143]

When Muhammad died, Fātima was grieving. She died a few months later.

Shia Muslims tell a different story: Shia Muslims believe that Muhammad had wanted ʿAlī to succeed him, but that his commands were later ignored. They claim that ʿĀʾisha and her father ʾAbū Bakr conspired to obtain the leadership of the Muslims.

They say that Fātima had talked to her father (the Prophet) emotionally during his last days. They believe that Fātima died as a result of injuries which she sustained when her house was raided by ʿUmar ibn al-Khattāb (عُمَر بن الْخَطَّاب) – who later became the second Caliph after ʾAbū Bakr.

---

143 ...إِذَا دَخَلَتْ عَلَى النَّبِيِّ قَامَ إِلَيْهَا فَقَبَّلَهَا وَأَجْلَسَهَا فِي مَجْلِسِهِ وَكَانَ النَّبِيُّ إِذَا دَخَلَ عَلَيْهَا قَامَتْ مِنْ مَجْلِسِهَا فَقَبَّلَتْهُ وَأَجْلَسَتْهُ فِي مَجْلِسِهَا فَلَمَّا مَرِضَ النَّبِيُّ دَخَلَتْ فَاطِمَةُ فَأَكَبَّتْ عَلَيْهِ فَقَبَّلَتْهُ ثُمَّ رَفَعَتْ رَأْسَهَا فَبَكَتْ ثُمَّ أَكَبَّتْ عَلَيْهِ ثُمَّ رَفَعَتْ رَأْسَهَا فَضَحِكَتْ فَقُلْتُ إِنْ كُنْتُ لَأَظُنُّ أَنَّ هَذِهِ مِنْ أَعْقَلِ نِسَائِنَا فَإِذَا هِيَ مِنَ النِّسَاءِ فَلَمَّا تُوُفِّيَ النَّبِيُّ قُلْتُ لَهَا أَرَأَيْتِ حِينَ أَكْبَبْتِ عَلَى النَّبِيِّ فَرَفَعْتِ رَأْسَكِ فَبَكَيْتِ ثُمَّ أَكْبَبْتِ عَلَيْهِ فَرَفَعْتِ رَأْسَكِ فَضَحِكْتِ مَا حَمَلَكِ عَلَى ذَلِكَ قَالَتْ إِنِّي إِذًا لَبَذِرَةٌ أَخْبَرَنِي أَنَّهُ مَيِّتٌ مِنْ وَجَعِهِ هَذَا فَبَكَيْتُ ثُمَّ أَخْبَرَنِي أَنِّي أَسْرَعُ أَهْلِهِ لُحُوقًا بِهِ فَذَاكَ حِينَ ضَحِكْتُ.

Jāmiʿ al-Tirmidhī 4246

'Umar went to her house to pressure 'Alī and his men to come out and swear allegiance to 'Abū Bakr. The door was supposedly rammed open by one of the assailants, knocking Fātima to the ground. Some say 'Umar threatened her by saying he would set the house on fire. She was pregnant and lost her baby due to the injuries she suffered from the attack.

According to Shia tradition, the Prophet appeared in a dream and informed Fātima that she would die the next day. She told her husband 'Alī about her coming death and asked him not to allow the oppressors to be involved in her funeral. Her resting place is unclear.

However, Sunnis believe that Fātima reconciled her differences with 'Abū Bakr prior to her death.

Note: Do you know the *Church of Fātima?* This has nothing to do with Islam. *Our Lady of Fátima* (Portuguese: Nossa Senhora de Fátima) is a Roman- Catholic title of the *Blessed Virgin Mary* based on visions by three shepherd children at Fátima, Portugal, in 1917.

PART II

On the Qur'an

88. What is the longest word in the Qur'an?

Answer: It is "fa'asqaynākumūhu" (فَأَسْقَيْنَاكُمُوهُ) and means: *so we gave it to you to drink*. Although it looks like a word, it is a sentence!

Arabic is a Semitic language. It works very differently compared to English or French. There is actually only little use in looking for the shortest or longest word because most words have a root consisting of three letters. You can add vowels, pre- and suffixes, and put the root into several patterns. Some people mistakenly refer to فَأَسْقَيْنَاكُمُوهُ as a word – it is actually an entire sentence.

It is worth looking at فَأَسْقَيْنَاكُمُوهُ. It consists of 11 letters and is found in sura 15 *The Rocky Tract* – in Arabic: al-Hijr (سُورة الْحِجْر):

| 15:22 | We send the winds to fertilise, and We bring down water from the sky for you to drink - you do not control its sources. | وَأَرْسَلْنَا الرِّيَاحَ لَوَاقِحَ فَأَنْزَلْنَا مِنَ السَّمَاءِ مَاءً فَأَسْقَيْنَاكُمُوهُ وَمَا أَنْتُمْ لَهُ بِخَازِنِينَ. |

For readers who know Arabic, let's check the components:

so, thus (particle)	فَ	you (1st object)	كُم	
to give to drink (past tense; takes 2 objects!)	أَسْقَى	it (2nd object)	هُ	
we gave to drink	أَسْقَيْنَا			

89. How many words are there in the Qur'an?

Answer: Most scholars say 77,429 words.

It is not clear how to count them. In the Qur'an, at the beginning of some suras, you will find strange combinations of letters which do not have a meaning; at least we don't know them. They are called al-Muqatta'āt (الْمُقَطَّعات).

Let's have a look at some more statistics – please note that some people count several aspects differently, but the order of magnitude is of course the same.

- Number of suras: 114
- Number of verses: 6,236

- Number of dots in Qur'an: 1,015.030
- Number of letters: 323,671
- Most common word: *from* (مِن); it occurs 2,763 times

In the Qur'an are mentioned:

- 16 places, cities or countries
- 15 names of things that can be eaten or drunk
- 7 colours
- 1 month - Ramadan (رَمَضان)
- 1 woman - Maryam (Mary)

90. What is the first number mentioned in the Qur'an?

Answer: The number 7.

The number seven is probably one of the most interesting numbers – maybe not mathematically, but in history, eschatology and theology: There are seven heavens, the rainbow has seven colours, we count seven days.

In Islam, the number seven is of great importance too: Muslims turn around the Ka'ba seven times as well as they pass between the mountains al-Safā (الصَّفا) and al-Marwā (الْمَرْوَى) seven times. They stone the Devil seven times; Islam knows seven great destructive sins which directly lead to Hell; in Heaven there are seven kinds of people which Allah will put under his shade on the Day of Judgement.

This is no coincidence. In Arabic as well as in all the other Semitic languages, the number seven is often synonymous with *several*. The same is true for *seventy* or *seven hundred* – as they can mean *many* or *a very big number*. Let's have a look at the first number in the Qur'an. This is in sura 2 *The Cow* – in Arabic: al-Baqara (سُورَة الْبَقَرة):

| 2:29 | It was He who created all that is on the earth for you, then turned to the sky and made the seven heavens; | هُوَ الَّذِي خَلَقَ لَكُم مَّا فِي الْأَرْضِ جَمِيعًا ثُمَّ اسْتَوَىٰ إِلَى السَّمَاءِ فَسَوَّاهُنَّ سَبْعَ سَمَاوَاتٍ وَهُوَ بِكُلِّ شَيْءٍ عَلِيمٌ؛ |

- Not only that the number of heavens in Islam is seven. If you search the Qur'an for the expression *seven heavens*, there will be seven results.

- The first sura in the Qur'an - al-Fātiha (سُورة الْفَاتِحة) - consists of seven verses.

91. Which sura contains the very first revealed verses?

Answer: Sura 96 *The Clot* – in Arabic: al-ʿAlaq (سُورة الْعَلَق). In English, it is also called *The Germ-Cell* or *The Clinging Form*.

The Arabic word ʿAlaq can denote an embryo as an early stage in the development of a foetus. ʿAlaq can also mean anything that clings: *a clot of blood, a leech, even a lump of mud.* All these meanings involve the basic idea of *clinging* or *sticking*. According to the Islamic scholar Abdel Haleem, whose translations I mostly use in this book, clinging indicates a state of total dependence.

Let's have a look at the very first words Muhammad had received from Allah by the Archangel Gabriel:

96:1	Read! In the name of your Lord who cre-ated:	اقْرَأْ بِاشْمِ رَبِّكَ الَّذِي خَلَقَ:
96:2	He created man from a clinging form.	خَلَقَ الْإِنسَانَ مِنْ عَلَقٍ.
96:3	Read! Your Lord is the Most Bountiful One	اقْرَأْ وَرَبُّكَ الْأَكْرَمُ
96:4	who taught by [means of] the pen	الَّذِي عَلَّمَ بِالْقَلَمِ
96:5	who taught man what he did not know.	عَلَّمَ الْإِنسَانَ مَا لَمْ يَعْلَمْ.

Sura 96 is the earliest sura. It describes the most fundamental concepts of Islam: the oneness of Allah; life after death; ultimate judgement; Paradise and Hell as destination of every human life. In Islam, Paradise and Hell are not seen as arbitrary rewards or punishments.

What happened after this revelation? Most scholars say that there was a break, a period during which the Prophet had not received any revelation. In Arabic, breaks like this are called Fatra al-Wahy (فَتْرة

الْوَحْي). No one knows about the exact duration until the Prophet received another revelation. Scholars disagree and say that it may have been something between six months and three years.

Muhammad Asad wrote in his commentary on the Qur'an that the waiting period after the first revelation was a "time of the deepest distress for the Prophet. The absence of revelation almost led him to believe that his earlier experience in the cave of Mount Hira was an illusion. It was only due to the moral support of his wife Khadīja and her undaunted faith in his prophetic mission that he did not entirely lose his courage and hope. In the end of the intermission the Prophet had a vision of the angel Gabriel, 'sitting between heaven and earth'."

After that vision new verses were revealed, verses of sura 74 *Wrapped in His Cloak* – in Arabic: al-Muddaththir (سُورة الْمُدَّثِّر). After his encounter with Gabriel, the Prophet went home trembling and asked his wife to cover him with his cloak. This is the reason for the name of this sura.

74:1	You, wrapped in your cloak,	يَا أَيُّهَا الْمُدَّثِّرُ
74:2	arise and give warning!	قُمْ فَأَنذِرْ
74:3	Proclaim the greatness of your Lord;	وَرَبَّكَ فَكَبِّرْ
74:4	cleanse yourself;	وَثِيَابَكَ فَطَهِّرْ
74:5	keep away from all filth [from all idolatry];	وَالرُّجْزَ فَاهْجُرْ

After these verses, revelations became intense and continuous.

Jābir ibn 'Abd Allah (جابِر بن عَبْد الله), while talking about the break in revelations, narrated a speech of the Prophet: "While I was walking, all of a sudden I heard a voice from the sky. I looked up and saw the same angel who had visited me at the cave of Hira' sitting on a chair between the sky and the earth. I got afraid of him and came back home and said: 'Wrap me [in blankets].' And then Allah revealed the following holy verses: 'O you [Muhammad]! Wrapped up in garments!'... [sura 74:1-5]. After this the revelation started coming strongly, frequently, and regularly."[144]

---

144 ...قَالَ وَهُوَ يُحَدِّثُ عَنْ فَتْرَةِ الْوَحْيِ، فَقَالَ فِي حَدِيثِهِ: "بَيْنَا أَنَا أَمْشِي، إِذْ سَمِعْتُ صَوْتًا، مِنَ السَّمَاءِ، فَرَفَعْتُ بَصَرِي فَإِذَا الْمَلَكُ الَّذِي جَاءَنِي بِحِرَاءٍ جَالِسٌ عَلَى كُرْسِيٍّ بَيْنَ السَّمَاءِ وَالْأَرْضِ،

What other suras were revealed early?

- 73 *Enfolded* – in Arabic: al-Muzammil (سُورة الْمُزَّمِّل)
- 1 *The Opening* – in Arabic: al-Fātiha (سُورة الْفَاتِحة)
- 81 *Shrouded in Darkness* – in Arabic: al-Takwīr (سُورة التَّكْوِير)
- 87 *The Most High* – in Arabic: al-ʾAʿlā (سُورة الْأَعْلَى)
- 92 *The Night* – in Arabic: al-Layl (سُورة اللَّيْل)
- 89 *Daybreak* – in Arabic: al-Fajr (سُورة الْفَجْر)

92. What is mysterious about the beginning of some suras?

Answer: They start with a combination of letters, so-called *disjointed letters* – in Arabic: al-Muqattaʿāt (الْمُقَطَّعات). Sometimes they are also called *openings* - in Arabic: Fawātih (فَواتِح) – because of their appearance at the beginning of the suras.

How do they look like? Out of the 28 letters of the Arabic alphabet, exactly one half (14 letters) occur in this position, either solo or in different combinations of two, three, four, or five letters. They appear in 29 out of the 114 suras just after the *Basmala*. For example:

- Sura 2:1 *The Cow* – al-Baqara (الْبَقرة): "Alif – Lām - Mīm." (الم)
- Sura 28:1 *The Story* – al-Qasas (الْقَصَص): "Tā - Sīn - Mīm." (طسم)

Four suras are even named after their Muqattaʿāt: Tā - Hā (طه), Yā - Sīn (يس), Sād (ص) and Qāf (ق).

They are always pronounced as a single letter and not as mere sounds: "Alif (أَلِف), Lām (لام), Mīm (مِيم)". And not: "alm" (أ-ل-م).

These mysterious letters have confused commentators and scholars from the very beginning of Islam. The Prophet did not give any explanation; it seems like that none of the companions had ever asked him about it. Nevertheless, most scholars say that these letters are essential to the respective sura – although they can't explain why. Therefore, Muslims have to recite them correctly and with respect.

فَرَعِبْتُ مِنْهُ، فَرَجَعْتُ فَقُلْتُ زَمِّلُونِي. فَأَنْزَلَ اللَّهُ تَعَالَى ﴿يَا أَيُّهَا الْمُدَّثِّر﴾ ■ قُمْ فَأَنْذِرْ﴾ إِلَى قَوْلِهِ ﴿وَالرُّجْزَ فَاهْجُرْ﴾ فَحَمِيَ الْوَحْيُ وَتَتَابَعَ." 4 *Sahīh al-Bukhārī*

So what are the speculations and hypotheses?

- Some Orientalists had the idea that they might have been the initials of the scribes who wrote down the revelations.
- Muhammad Asad wrote in his translation of the Qur'an that some companions, some of their immediate successors, and later Qur'an commentators were convinced that these letters are abbreviations of certain words or even phrases relating to Allah. However, they soon found out that it is rather meaningless as the possible combinations of words are practically unlimited.
- Others have tried to link the Muqatta'āt to the numerological values of the letters of the Arabic alphabet and have derived by this means all kinds of esoteric and mysterious prophecies.
- Famous Islamic scholars and thinkers such as al-Rāzī, Ibn Taymīya, or Ibn Kathīr thought that the Muqatta'āt are meant to illustrate the inimitable nature of the Qur'an. Human kind is not capable of understanding everything what has been revealed in the Qur'an.
- The answer is beyond our understanding. This was the view of the four *Rightly Guided Caliphs*, summarised in the words of 'Abū Bakr (أَبُو بَكْر): "In every divine writ there is [an element of] mystery – and the mystery of the Qur'an is [indicated] in the openings of some suras."[145]

93. Can you name a child after a sura?

Answer: This is not entirely clear. Most say that it is *disliked* (مَكْرُوه).

Traditional scholars say that it is not allowed to name a child after a sura, for example: Ta-Ha, Ya-Sin, Ha-Mim, al-Furqān (*The Differentiator*), however, modern scholars say that it is permitted.

Famous people were named after suras. For example: Taha Husayn (طه حُسَيْن), one of the most influential Egyptian writers and intellectuals of the 20th-century. *Ta Ha* (سُورة طه) is the name of sura 20.

---

145 ...قَالَ أَبُو بَكْرِ الصِّدِّيقِ: فِي كُلِّ كِتَابٍ سِرٌّ وَسِرُّ اللهِ فِي الْقُرْآنِ أَوَائِلُ السُّوَرِ. Ibn Kathīr

Yasin or Yacin (يَس or ياسِين; the latter is easier to grasp when read-ing) is a common name in Turkey and is also encountered in Pakistan and Bosnia. *Ya Sin* (سُورة يس) is the name of sura 36.

Furthermore, traditional scholars suggest that words which are used as synonyms for the Qur'an are also not allowed as baby names.

For example: al-Bayān (الْبَيان) – *the announcement*; or Hudā(n) (هُدًى) which means *right guidance (in a religious sense)*.

However, most Muslims do not follow this strict rule. They have a point here because which authority decides about synonyms for the Qur'an? Some words are rather descriptive. You will find many Muslim women who are named Hudā, also in the early Islam period.

94. Why do Muslims call some suras "Meccan"?

Answer: The suras from Mecca (السُّوَر الْمَكِّيّة) are the ones which were revealed to the Prophet before he migrated to Yathrib (Medina).

This means that they were revealed to Muhammad before June 622 (1 AH), when the Hijra (الْهِجْرة) took place. The Medinan suras (السُّوَر الْمَدَنِيّة) were revealed after the Hijra.

So what is the difference?

Meccan suras. The verses which were revealed to Muhammad in Mecca deal with Allah, his attributes, and the theme of monotheism.

These suras tell the stories of past prophets and what happened to them. In most cases, the people refused to believe in *the One and Only God* and got severely punished if they did. Linguistically speak-ing, regarding structure, rhythm and vocabulary, these verses are brilliant. The people of Mecca at the time of Muhammad were mas-tering classical Arabic.

So the verses had to be in a language by which the Meccan people were impressed. Some historians say that there were even rhetorical and linguistic competitions. People would try to form sentences that would beat sentences from the Qur'an in excellence. That is why, generally speaking, Meccan suras are more difficult to read and understand.

Meccan suras are typically shorter than Medinan suras and mostly come near the end of the Qur'an. As a general rule, the suras of the Qur'an are ordered from longest to shortest.

Medinan suras were the latest 24 suras that were revealed. You will find the Medinan suras mostly at the beginning and in the middle of the Qur'an – although they were the last revealed chronologically. Typically, they are longer and have more verses.

When Muhammad had left Mecca and migrated to Medina, a period of many battles started. Eventually, Islam expanded to other cities and tribes.

This is why you find in Medinan suras topics about marital and family laws, monetary transactions, the prohibition of wine and gambling, the laws of inheritance, order in the community, the relationship of Muslims and non-Muslims as well as information on ethics and morals.

Sura 2 *The Cow* - in Arabic al-Baqara (سُورة الْبَقَرة) - is a good example of a Medinan sura.

How can the type of a sura be identified?

There are some hints: In the Meccan suras, usually, the verses are addressed to Muhammad himself. In contrast, the Medinan verses are mostly addressed to Muhammad's followers and are introduced with: "Oh you who believe!" In Arabic: "Ya 'ayyuhā allathīna 'āmanū" (يَا أَيُّهَا الَّذِينَ آمَنُوا).

Although Muhammad is frequently directly addressed in the Meccan suras, he is normally not the subject of the content of the revelation. This is different in the Medinan suras, where Muhammad and his challenges are often the main subject. For example, Muslims are commanded to salute and follow him; Muslims are not allowed to have more than four wives at the same time.

What is typical for Meccan suras?

- Any sura containing the Arabic word kallā (كَلّ) - *never* - is Meccan and occurs only in the second half of the Qur'an.

- Any sura which has the phrase *O Mankind* (يا أَيُّها النّاس) is Meccan, except for sura 22 *The Pilgrimage* - al-Hajj (الْحَجّ). Sura 22 combines the characteristics of a Meccan and a Medinan sura.
- All suras that start with mysterious, initial letters - al-Hurūf al-Muqatta' (الْحُرُوف الْمُقَطَّعة) - are Meccan, except for suras 2, 3, 13.

What is typical for Medina suras?
- The topic of Jihad (جِهاد)
- The topic of hypocrisy - Nifāq (نِفاق)
- Any verse that starts with *Oh you who believe* (يَأَيُّها اللَّذينَ آمنُوا)

95. What is the shortest sura in the Qur'an?

Answer: Sura 108 *Abundance* – in Arabic: al-Kawthar (سُورة الْكَوْثَر). It has only three verses.

In this sura, Allah tells Muhammad about a river in Paradise which is called *al-Kawthar*. There are Hadiths indicating that this river had been shown to Muhammad when the so-called Mi'rāj (المِعْراج) happened, when the Prophet ascended to heaven during his reign. That's how the sura got its name.

The term kawthar (الْكَوْثَر) is an intensive/exaggerated form (صِيغة الْمُبالَغة) of the Arabic word kathra (كَثْرة) which denotes *multitude* or *abundance*. As an adjective/adverb, it means: *much, abundant*.

This sura features another important theme. Muhammad's first son was al-Qāsim (الْقاسِم). He died at a young age as did his other son 'Abd Allah (عَبْد الله). All his other remaining children were girls. Ibn Kathīr wrote in his commentary on this sura that one of his opponents, al-'Ās ibn Wa'il (الْعاص بن وائل), had said: "His line has come to an end: now he is 'abtār [i.e. cut off from root]." Some Hadiths add that al-'Ās said: "Muhammad is 'abtār (أَبْتَر). He has no son to succeed him.[146] When he dies, his memory will perish and you will be rid of him."

After that, the Prophet received a verse which reassured him:

---

146 إِنَّما مُحَمَّدٌ أَبْتَر، لَيْسَ لَهُ كَما تَرَوْنَ عَقِبٌ.

| 108:3 | it is the one who hates you who has been cut off. | إِنَّ شَانِئَكَ هُوَ الْأَبْتَرُ. |

Remark: Was this sura revealed in Mecca or Medina?

Most of the authorities assign this sura to the early part of the Mecca period. However, Ibn Kathīr (ابن كَثِير) for example considers that it was probably revealed at Medina.

This view is based on a Hadith which was narrated by 'Anas ibn Mālik (أَنَس بن مالك). 'Anas was from Yathrib (Medina) and belonged to the *Helpers*, so-called al-'Ansār (الْأَنْصار), the people who welcomed and helped Muhammad and his followers when they escaped from Mecca and migrated to Medina.

'Anas said: "One day when the Prophet was still among us, he took a nap, then he raised his head, smiling. We said to him: 'Why are you smiling, O Messenger of Allah?' He said: 'Just now this sura was revealed to me: 'In the Name of Allah, the Most Gracious, the Most Merciful (...)' Then he said: 'Do you know what al-Kawthar is?' We replied: 'Allah and His messenger know best.' He said: 'It is a river that my Lord has promised me in Paradise. Its vessels are more than the number of the stars.'"[147]

However, the same 'Anas also recounted that this river of Paradise had been shown to Muhammad on the occasion of al-Mi'rāj (ascension), and it is clear that al-Mi'rāj had taken place at Mecca before the Hijra.

In Islam, it can happen that sources are ambiguous. It is important to keep that in mind when one tries to insist on a certain fact.

96. What is the longest sura in the Qur'an?

Answer: Sura 2 *The Cow* – in Arabic: al-Baqara (سُورة الْبَقَرة).

---

147 ...قَالَ بَيْنَمَا ذَاتَ يَوْمٍ بَيْنَ أَظْهُرِنَا - يُرِيدُ النَّبِيَّ إِذْ أَغْفَى إِغْفَاءَةً ثُمَّ رَفَعَ رَأْسَهُ مُتَبَسِّمًا فَقُلْنَا لَهُ مَا أَضْحَكَكَ يَا رَسُولَ اللَّهِ قَالَ: "نَزَلَتْ عَلَيَّ آنِفًا سُورَةٌ بِسْمِ اللَّهِ الرَّحْمَنِ الرَّحِيمِ. ثُمَّ قَالَ: "هَلْ تَدْرُونَ مَا الْكَوْثَرُ." قُلْنَا اللَّهُ وَرَسُولُهُ أَعْلَمُ. قَالَ: "فَإِنَّهُ نَهْرٌ وَعَدَنِيهِ رَبِّي فِي الْجَنَّةِ آنِيَتُهُ أَكْثَرُ مِنْ عَدَدِ الْكَوَاكِبِ."

Sunan al-Nasā'ī 904

This sura has 286 verses and was revealed in Medina (الْمَدِينة). It is one of the most important suras in the Qur'an and is crucial for a Muslim's faith.

It draws attention to Abraham and his idea of the oneness of Allah. There is also information about the founding of Abraham's Temple, which is, according to Islam, the Ka'ba (الْكَعْبة) in Mecca. Furthermore, this sura gives the reader an idea what it means to be a Muslim, basically a literal translation of the word Muslim: "those who surrender themselves to Allah".

'Abū Mas'ūd al-'Ansārī (أَبُو مَسْعُود الْأَنْصاريّ) had narrated that the Prophet said: "If somebody recites the last two verses of sura al-Baqara at night, that will be sufficient for him."[148]

The titles of suras are sometimes difficult to understand. This sura does not deal with the subject of the cow in general as some might misunderstand. The title is derived from the story of the cow which the Israelites were ordered to slaughter, and which is told in this sura (2:67-73). Let's have a look at one verse:

2:67	Remember when Moses said to his people, 'God commands you to sacrifice a cow.' They said, 'Are you making fun of us?' He answered, 'God forbid that I should be so ignorant.'	وَإِذْ قَالَ مُوسَىٰ لِقَوْمِهِ إِنَّ اللَّهَ يَأْمُرُكُم أَن تَذْبَحُوا بَقَرَةً قَالُوا أَتَتَّخِذُنَا هُزُوًا قَالَ أَعُوذُ بِاللَّهِ أَنْ أَكُونَ مِنَ الْجَاهِلِينَ.

This sura was revealed in Medina, most of it during the first two years after the Hijra. Only verses 275-281 were received during the last months of Muhammad's life. In fact, verse 281 is considered to be probably the very last revelation he received:

2:281	Beware of a Day when you will be re-turned to God: every soul will be paid in full for what it has earned, and one will be wronged.	وَاتَّقُوا يَوْمًا تُرْجَعُونَ فِيهِ إِلَى اللَّهِ ثُمَّ تُوَفَّىٰ كُلُّ نَفْسٍ مَّا كَسَبَتْ وَهُم لَا يُظْلَمُونَ.

---

148 ...قَالَ النَّبِيُّ: "مَنْ قَرَأَ بِالآيَتَيْنِ مِنْ آخِرِ سُورَةِ الْبَقَرَةِ فِي لَيْلَةٍ كَفَتَاهُ." Sahīh al-Bukhārī 5009

97. Which sura equals one third of the Qur'an?

Answer: Sura 112 *Purity (of faith),* in Arabic: al-'Ikhlās (سُورَةُ الإِخْلاص).

Muhammad received this sura in Mecca. It came down very early after the revelation had started. There is something special about it. The title is not mentioned in the body of the sura, which is unusual.

The Arabic word 'Ikhlās (إخْلاص) denotes the meaning of *sincerity in one's religion and total dedication to Allah* – which is one of the most important elements of Islam. Due to the importance of the sura, the Prophet said that this sura, despite its short length of only 4 (!) verses, was equal to one-third of the Qur'an.

'Abū al-Dardā' (أَبُو الدَّرْداء) narrated that Allah's Apostle said: "Is any one of you incapable of reciting a third of the Qur'an in a night? They [the companions] asked: 'How could one recite a third of the Qur'an [in a night]?' Upon this, the Prophet said: 'Say, 'He is God the One...' [sura 112] is equivalent to a third of the Qur'an.'"[149]

Especially the second verse is of great importance for Muslims:

| 112:1 | Say, "He is God the One, | قُلْ هُوَ اللَّهُ أَحَدٌ |
| 112:2 | God the eternal." | اللَّهُ الصَّمَدُ. |

The word Samad (صَمَد) is usually translated as *eternal*, but it is tricky. It could convey the meaning of *self-sufficient* and *sought by all*. The term al-Samad occurs in the Qur'an only once and is applied to Allah alone. Muhammad Asad wrote that "it comprises the idea that everything existing or conceivable goes back to Allah as its source and is therefore, dependent on Allah for its beginning as well as for its continued existence."

98. Why has Allah created human beings and Jinns?

Answer: To worship him.

---

149 ...النَّبِيُّ قَالَ: "أَيَعْجِزُ أَحَدُكُمْ أَنْ يَقْرَأَ فِي لَيْلَةٍ ثُلُثَ الْقُرْآنِ" قَالُوا: "وَكَيْفَ يَقْرَأُ ثُلُثَ الْقُرْآنِ؟" قَالَ: "قُلْ هُوَ اللَّهُ أَحَدٌ تَعْدِلُ ثُلُثَ الْقُرْآنِ." Sahīh Muslim 811

This is stated in the Qur'an in sura 51 *Scattering Winds* - in Arabic: al-Dhāriyāt (سُورة الذّاريات):

51:56	I created Jinn and mankind only to worship Me.	وَمَا خَلَقْتُ الْجِنَّ وَالْإِنسَ إِلَّا لِيَعْبُدُونِ.

Ibn Kathīr (ابن كَثِير), an influential Sunni scholar of the 14th century, explained the meaning of this verse as follows: "I [Allah] have created them so that I may command them to worship Me, not because I have any need of them."[150]

Muhammad Asad, a scholar of the 20th century who had a more metaphysical view on Islam, commented on this verse: "Thus, the innermost purpose of the creation of all rational beings is their cognition – so-called Ma'rifa (مَعْرِفة) of the existence of Allah."

99. What is the epithet for prophet Jonah (Yūnus)?

Answer: *The man with the large fish/whale* – Dhū al-Nūn (ذُو النُّون). Or *the companion of the whale* – Sāhib al-Hūt (صاحِب الْحُوت).

Whales are today classified as mammals and not fish, however, in ancient times, this distinction was unknown.

The expression Dhū al-Nūn is used in sura 21 *The Prophets* - in Arabic: al-ʾAnbiyā' (سُورة الْأَنْبِيـاء). This sura tells the fact that Muhammad was just a human being like earlier prophets.

The Arabic word dhū changes depending on the position in the sentence (cases), so dhū - dhī - dhā all mean the same. For readers who know Arabic: The word Nūn (نُون) does not only denote the letter ن - it can also mean *large fish* or *whale*. Let's now have a look at the expression Dhū al-Nūn:

21:87	And remember the man with the whale, when he went off angrily, thinking We could not restrict him, but then he cried out in the deep darkness, 'There is no god but You, glory be to You, I was wrong.'	وَذَا النُّون إذ ذَّهَبَ مُغَاضِبًا فَظَنَّ أَن لَّن نَّقْدِرَ عَلَيْهِ فَنَادَىٰ فِي الظُّلُمَاتِ أَن لَّا إِلَٰهَ إِلَّا أَنتَ سُبْحَانَكَ إِنِّي كُنتُ مِنَ الظَّالِمِينَ

---

150 ... أَيْ إِنَّمَا خَلَقْتُهُمْ لِآمُرَهُمْ بِعِبَادَتِي لَا لِاحْتِيَاجِي إِلَيْهِمْ. Ibn Kathīr

The other expression Sāhib al-Hūt is found in another sura, in sura
68 *The Pen* – in Arabic: al-Qalam (سُورة الْقَلَم):

| 68:48 | Wait patiently [prophet] for your Lord's judgement: do not be like the man in the whale [the companion of the fish] who called out in distress. | فَاصْبِرْ لِحُكْمِ رَبِّكَ وَلَا تَكُن كَصَاحِبِ الْحُوتِ إِذْ نَادَىٰ وَهُوَ مَكْظُومٌ. |

Sura 68 is an early Meccan sura. It starts dealing with the accusation
that Muhammad was crazy or mad – and not Allah's Messenger:

68:2	Your Lord's grace does not make you [prophet] a madman:	مَا أَنتَ بِنِعْمَةِ رَبِّكَ بِمَجْنُونٍ
68:3	you will have a never-ending reward -	وَإِنَّ لَكَ لَأَجْرًا غَيْرَ مَمْنُونٍ
68:4	truly you have a strong character -	وَإِنَّكَ لَعَلَىٰ خُلُقٍ عَظِيمٍ
68:5	and soon you will see, as will they,	فَسَتُبْصِرُ وَيُبْصِرُونَ
68:6	which of you is afflicted with madness.	بِأَيِّيكُمُ الْمَفْتُونُ.

Who was Yūnus (يُونُس)?

In English, this prophet is called Jonah or Jonas. Yūnus is highly important in Islam as a prophet who was faithful to Allah. The Muslim
tradition follows the Jewish tradition of the Bible, saying that Yūnus'
father was Amitai. Jonah is the only one of the Twelve Minor prophets of the Hebrew Bible to be mentioned by name in the Qur'an.

However, the story of Yūnus in Islam has similarities but also substantial differences to the story in the Hebrew Bible.

Yūnus' message goes back to the 8th century before Jesus Christ
was born. Scholars say that he came after prophet 'Ilyās (إِلْياس). Allah
sent Yūnus to the people of Nineveh (نينوى) who probably lived on
the right bank of the river Tigris (دِجْلة) near Mosul (الْمَوصِل) in
present-day Iraq.

They were worshipping 'Ishtār (عِشْتار), a Mesopotamian East
Semitic (Akkadian, Assyrian, and Babylonian) goddess of sex, love
and beauty at Babylon. 'Ishtār was worshipped from around 3500 BC
until its decline between the 1st and 5th century AD, when Christianity gained popularity.

The Qur'an describes Yūnus as a righteous preacher of the message of Allah – but also as a person who one day fled from his mission because of its overwhelming difficulty.

This is the crucial point when the story with the large fish gets important. The Qur'an says that Yūnus made it onto a ship, but there was a powerful storm with heavy weather. The men on board wanted to find out why this happened. They had an idea. They wanted to cast lots. When the lots were cast three times and Yūnus' name came out each time, he was thrown into the ocean because the people on the ship thought he was guilty.

A huge fish came and swallowed him. Yūnus ended up in the stomach of the fish which didn't stop him from repenting and glorifying Allah. The story is told in the Qur'an in sura 37 *Ranged in Rows* – in Arabic: al-Saffāt (الصَّفَّات):

37:139	Jonah too was one of the messengers.	وَإِنَّ يُونُسَ لَمِنَ الْمُرْسَلِينَ.
37:140	He fled to the overloaded ship.	إِذْ أَبَقَ إِلَى الْفُلْكِ الْمَشْحُونِ.
37:141	They cast lots, he suffered defeat,	فَسَاهَمَ فَكَانَ مِنَ الْمُدْحَضِينَ
37:142	and a great fish swallowed him, for he had committed blameworthy acts.	فَالْتَقَمَهُ الْحُوتُ وَهُوَ مُلِيمٌ.
37:143	If he had not been one of those who glorified God,	فَلَوْلَا أَنَّهُ كَانَ مِنَ الْمُسَبِّحِينَ
37:144	he would have stayed in its belly until the Day when all are raised up,	لَلَبِثَ فِي بَطْنِهِ إِلَى يَوْمِ يُبْعَثُونَ
37:145	but We cast him out, sick, on to a barren shore,	فَنَبَذْنَاهُ بِالْعَرَاءِ وَهُوَ سَقِيمٌ
37:146	and made a gourd tree grow above him.	وَأَنْبَتْنَا عَلَيْهِ شَجَرَةً مِّن يَقْطِينٍ.
37:147	We sent him to a hundred thousand people or more.	وَأَرْسَلْنَاهُ إِلَى مِائَةِ أَلْفٍ أَوْ يَزِيدُونَ.

The big fish cast Yūnus out onto dry land, with Yūnus in a state of sickness. Allah caused a plant to grow where Yūnus was lying to provide shade and comfort for him. After Yūnus got up, fresh and well, Allah told him to go back and preach. 'Abū Hurayra (أَبُو هُرَيْرَة) narrated that the Prophet said: "Whoever says that I am better than Yūnus ibn Mattā is a liar."[151] This is understood by both mainstream Muslims and historians to have been stated by Muhammad to emphasise the notion of equality between all the prophets.

Note: It is interesting that Muhammad said **Ibn Mattā** (مَتَّى). Mattā (مَتَّى) - as some scholars suggest - is the name of Yūnus' <u>mother</u>. Apart from Yūnus (يُونُس بن مَتَّى) there is only one other prophet in the Qur'an who is named after his mother: Jesus (عِيسَى بن مَرْيَم) – literally *Jesus, son of Mary (Maryam)*. All other prophets are named after their fathers.

Christian Arabs call Yūnus usually Yunān ibn 'Amittay (يُونَان بن أُمَّاي) – *Yunan, son of Amitai* (Hebrew: אֲמִתִּי). The Hebrew expression Amitai literally means *my truth*.

100. Which sura has the name of Allah in every verse?

Answer: Sura 58 *The Dispute* – in Arabic: al-Mujādala (سُورة الْمُجَادَلَة).

This sura has 22 verses and was revealed in Medina. The revelation may have happened between the end of 4 AH and the beginning of the year 5 AH.

The title refers to the dispute which is told in a verse. It has to do with divorce. Most classical commentators say that it is about a woman called Khawla (or Khuwayla) bint Tha'laba (خَوْلة بِنْت ثَعْلَبَة) whose husband 'Aws ibn al-Sāmit (أُوس بن الصّامت) divorced her by pronouncing the pre-Islamic oath which was called Zihār (ظهار).

Zihār is the divorce where a man would say to his wife: "You are (henceforth as unlawful) to me as the back (Zahr) of my mother!" The term Zahr (ظهر) has to be interpreted as *body*. By equating his wife with his mother, it is understood that there cannot be any sexual relations between them. This Arab tradition put women at a disadvantage. The man could marry another woman while the woman couldn't marry another man. The woman had to remain forever (!)

---

151 ...النَّبِيُّ قَالَ: "مَنْ قَالَ أَنَا خَيْرٌ مِنْ يُونُسَ بْنِ مَتَّى فَقَدْ كَذَبَ." Sahīh al-Bukhārī 4604

in her former husband's custody but was deprived of all her marital rights. In pre-Islamic Arab society, this type of divorce was considered final. The woman which is mentioned in the sura (without naming her) went to Muhammad and pleaded before him against this divorce. Thereupon the Prophet received a revelation in support of women:

58:1	God has heard the words of the woman who disputed with you [prophet] about her husband and complained to God: God has heard what you both had to say. He is all hearing, all seeing.	قَدْ سَمِعَ اللَّهُ قَوْلَ الَّتِي تُجَادِلُكَ فِي زَوْجِهَا وَتَشْتَكِي إِلَى اللَّهِ وَاللَّهُ يَسْمَعُ تَحَاوُرَكُمَا إِنَّ اللَّهَ سَمِيعٌ بَصِيرٌ.
58:2	Even if any of you say to their wives, 'You are to me like my mother's back, they are not their mothers; their only mothers are those who gave birth to them. What they say is certainly blameworthy and false, but God is pardoning and forgiving.	الَّذِينَ يُظَاهِرُونَ مِنكُم مِّن نِّسَائِهِم مَّا هُنَّ أُمَّهَاتِهِمْ إِنْ أُمَّهَاتُهُمْ إِلَّا اللَّائِي وَلَدْنَهُمْ وَإِنَّهُمْ لَيَقُولُونَ مُنكَرًا مِّنَ الْقَوْلِ وَزُورًا وَإِنَّ اللَّهَ لَعَفُوٌّ غَفُورٌ.
58:3	Those of you who say such a thing to their wives, then go back on what they have said, must free a slave before the couple may touch one another again - this is what you are commanded to do, and God is fully aware of what you do -	وَالَّذِينَ يُظَاهِرُونَ مِن نِّسَائِهِمْ ثُمَّ يَعُودُونَ لِمَا قَالُوا فَتَحْرِيرُ رَقَبَةٍ مِّن قَبْلِ أَن يَتَمَاسَّا ذَلِكُمْ تُوعَظُونَ بِهِ وَاللَّهُ بِمَا تَعْمَلُونَ خَبِيرٌ
58:4	but anyone who does not have the means should fast continuously for two months before they touch each other, and anyone unable to do this should feed sixty needy people. This is so that you may have faith in God and His messenger. These are the bounds set by God: grievous torment awaits those who ignore them.	فَمَن لَّمْ يَجِدْ فَصِيَامُ شَهْرَيْنِ مُتَتَابِعَيْنِ مِن قَبْلِ أَن يَتَمَاسَّا فَمَن لَّمْ يَسْتَطِعْ فَإِطْعَامُ سِتِّينَ مِسْكِينًا ذَلِكَ لِتُؤْمِنُوا بِاللَّهِ وَرَسُولِهِ وَتِلْكَ حُدُودُ اللَّهِ وَلِلْكَافِرِينَ عَذَابٌ أَلِيمٌ.

However, despite the impact which the abolishment of this practice had on Arab society – the remarkable thing about this sura is something else. It is the only sura in which the word *Allah/His Majesty* (الْجَلالة) occurs in every verse.

101. Which companion is mentioned in the Qur'an by name?

Answer: There is only one – Zayd ibn Hāritha (زَيْد بن حارِئة).

Zayd is mentioned by name in sura 33 *The Joint Forces* – in Arabic: al-'Ahzāb (سُورة الأَحْزاب).

Zayd was Muhammad's adopted son. The Prophet married him to Zaynab bint Jahsh (زَيْنَب بِنْت جَحْش), his own cousin and daughter of his paternal aunt. Then the events changed dramatically when Zayd divorced his wife and the Prophet took her as his own wife. See chapter 38 for more details about this story.

Sura 33 shows that the marriage was lawful. The Qur'an states that adoption does not create blood relations that preclude marriage.

33:37	...When Zayd no longer wanted her, We gave her to you in marriage so that there might be no fault in believers marrying the wives of their adopted sons after they no longer wanted them.	...فَلَمَّا قَضَى زَيْدٌ مِّنْهَا وَطَرًا زَوَّجْنَاكَهَا لِكَيْ لَا يَكُونَ عَلَى الْمُؤْمِنِينَ حَرَجٌ فِي أَزْوَاجِ أَدْعِيَائِهِمْ إِذَا قَضَوْا مِنْهُنَّ وَطَرًا.

102. Were parts of the Qur'an translated into other languages during the time of the Prophet?

Answer: Yes.

Although most Muslims claim that the Qur'an cannot, or even should not be translated, it was already done so during Muhammad's reign.

When the Prophet sent a message to Heraclius, the Byzantine emperor, it contained a verse of sura 3 *Family of 'Imrān* – in Arabic: 'Āl 'Imrān (سُورة آل عِمْران). The Messenger of Allah sent that letter to Heraclius in Arabic but Heraclius could not understand Arabic. So the whole message including the following verse from the Qur'an was translated into Greek:

3:64	Say, 'People of the Book, let us arrive at a statement that is common to us all: we	قُلْ يَا أَهْلَ الْكِتَابِ تَعَالَوْا إِلَى كَلِمَةٍ سَوَاءٍ بَيْنَنَا وَبَيْنَكُمْ أَلَّا

worship God alone, we ascribe no part-ner to Him, and none of us takes others beside God as lords.' If they turn away, say, 'Witness our devotion to Him.'	نَعْبُدَ إِلَّا اللَّهَ وَلَا نُشْرِكَ بِهِ شَيْئًا وَلَا يَتَّخِذَ بَعْضُنَا بَعْضًا أَرْبَابًا مِّن دُونِ اللَّهِ فَإِن تَوَلَّوْا فَقُولُوا اشْهَدُوا بِأَنَّا مُسْلِمُونَ.

'Abd Allah ibn 'Abbās (عَبْد الله بن عَبَّاس) narrated: "'Abū Sufyān ibn Harb informed me that Heraclius had sent a messenger to him while he had been accompanying a caravan from the Quraysh. They were merchants doing business in al-Shām [Syria, Palestine, Lebanon, and Jordan] at the time when Allah's Messenger had a truce with 'Abū Sufyān and the Quraysh infidels. So 'Abū Sufyān and his companions went to Heraclius at Ilya (Jerusalem)..."[152]

The long Hadith continues:

"...Heraclius then asked for the letter issued by Allah's Apostle, which was delivered by Dihya al-Kalbī (دِحْية الْكَلْبِي) to the Governor of Busrā, who forwarded it to Heraclius. The content of the letter was as follows: 'In the name of Allah the Beneficent, the Merciful. [This letter is] from Muhammad, the slave of Allah and His Apostle, to Heraclius, the ruler of Byzantine. Peace be upon him, who follows the right path. Furthermore, I invite you to Islam and if you become a Muslim, you will be safe and Allah will double your reward. If you reject this invitation of Islam, you will be committing a sin by mis-guiding your peasants. And I recite to you Allah's statement: ... (sura 3:64)'"[153]

But this was **not the only occasion**: The Muslims who migrated to Abyssinia (Ethiopia) translated verses from sura 19 *Mary* (مَرْيَـم), which contains information about Jesus. They did that in front of the Christian emperor of Abyssinia to show him what Islam is about.

---

152 ...أَنَّ عَبْدَ اللَّهِ بْنَ عَبَّاسٍ، أَخْبَرَهُ أَنَّ أَبَا سُفْيَانَ بْنَ حَرْبٍ أَخْبَرَهُ أَنَّ هِرَقْلَ أَرْسَلَ إِلَيْهِ فِي رَكْبٍ مِنْ قُرَيْشٍ وَكَانُوا تُجَّارًا بِالشَّأْمِ فِي الْمُدَّةِ الَّتِي كَانَ رَسُولُ اللَّهِ مَادَّ فِيهَا أَبَا سُفْيَانَ وَكُفَّارَ قُرَيْشٍ، فَأَتَوْهُ وَهُمْ بِإِيلِيَاءَ فَدَعَاهُمْ فِي مَجْلِسِهِ... Sahīh al-Bukhārī 7

153 ...ثُمَّ دَعَا بِكِتَابِ رَسُولِ اللَّهِ الَّذِي بَعَثَ بِهِ دِحْيَةَ إِلَى عَظِيمِ بُصْرَى، فَدَفَعَهُ إِلَى هِرَقْلَ فَقَرَأَهُ فَإِذَا فِيهِ بِسْمِ اللَّهِ الرَّحْمَنِ الرَّحِيمِ. مِنْ مُحَمَّدٍ عَبْدِ اللَّهِ وَرَسُولِهِ إِلَى هِرَقْلَ عَظِيمِ الرُّومِ. سَلَامٌ عَلَى مَنِ اتَّبَعَ الْهُدَى، أَمَّا بَعْدُ فَإِنِّي أَدْعُوكَ بِدِعَايَةِ الإِسْلَامِ، أَسْلِمْ تَسْلَمْ، يُؤْتِكَ اللَّهُ أَجْرَكَ مَرَّتَيْنِ، فَإِنْ تَوَلَّيْتَ فَإِنَّ عَلَيْكَ إِثْمَ الأَرِيسِيِّينَ وَ{يَا أَهْلَ الْكِتَابِ تَعَالَوْا إِلَى كَلِمَةٍ سَوَاءٍ بَيْنَنَا وَبَيْنَكُمْ أَنْ لَا نَعْبُدَ إِلَّا اللَّهَ وَلَا نُشْرِكَ بِهِ شَيْئًا وَلَا يَتَّخِذَ بَعْضُنَا بَعْضًا أَرْبَابًا مِنْ دُونِ اللَّهِ فَإِنْ تَوَلَّوْا فَقُولُوا اشْهَدُوا بِأَنَّا مُسْلِمُونَ}... Sahīh al-Bukhārī 7

Muslims say the Qur'an contains scientific facts which were only discovered much later. What are they?

165

103. Muslims say the Qur'an contains scientific facts which were only discovered much later. What are they?

Answer: Well, it all depends on interpretation as most of these facts were already known by Egyptians and Greeks long before.

Muslims claim that the Qur'an contains scientific facts which were unknown at the time of the Prophet. They say that this is evidence that the Qur'an originated from Allah. Let's check some of them:

All life originated from water. Muslims find this in sura 21 *The Prophets* – in Arabic: al-'Anbiyā' (سُورة الأَنْبِياء):

| 21:30 | Are the disbelievers not aware that the heavens and the earth used to be joined together and that We ripped them apart, that We made every living thing from water? Will they not believe? | أَوَلَمْ يَرَ الَّذِينَ كَفَرُوا أَنَّ السَّمَاوَاتِ وَالْأَرْضَ كَانَتَا رَتْقًا فَفَتَقْنَاهُمَا وَجَعَلْنَا مِنَ الْمَاءِ كُلَّ شَيْءٍ حَيٍّ أَفَلَا يُؤْمِنُونَ. |

The oxygen content of the air is reduced at higher altitudes. Muslims say that sura 6 *Livestock* - in Arabic: al-'An'am (سُورة الأَنْعام) - is about this fact:

| 6:125 | When God wishes to guide someone, He opens their breast [chest] to Islam; when He wishes to lead them astray, He closes and constricts their breast as if they were climbing up to the skies. That is how God makes the foulness of those who do not believe rebound against them. | فَمَن يُرِدِ اللَّهُ أَن يَهْدِيَهُ يَشْرَحْ صَدْرَهُ لِلْإِسْلَامِ وَمَن يُرِدْ أَن يُضِلَّهُ يَجْعَلْ صَدْرَهُ ضَيِّقًا حَرَجًا كَأَنَّمَا يَصَّعَّدُ فِي السَّمَاءِ كَذَلِكَ يَجْعَلُ اللَّهُ الرِّجْسَ عَلَى الَّذِينَ لَا يُؤْمِنُونَ. |

The embryo in the womb is enclosed by three coverings. Muslims find this in sura 39 *The Throngs* – in Arabic al-Zumar (سُورة الزُّمَر):

| 39:6 | He created you all from a single being, from which He made its mate; He gave you four kinds of livestock in pairs; He creates you in your mothers' wombs, in | خَلَقَكُم مِّن نَّفْسٍ وَاحِدَةٍ ثُمَّ جَعَلَ مِنْهَا زَوْجَهَا وَأَنزَلَ لَكُم مِّنَ الْأَنْعَامِ ثَمَانِيَةَ أَزْوَاجٍ يَخْلُقُكُمْ فِي بُطُونِ |

one stage after another, in threefold depths of darkness. Such is God, your Lord; He holds control, there is no god but Him. How can you turn away?	أُمَّهَاتِكُمْ خَلْقًا مِّن بَعْدِ خَلْقٍ فِي ظُلُمَاتٍ ثَلَاثٍ ذَلِكُمُ اللَّهُ رَبُّكُمْ لَهُ الْمُلْكُ لَا إِلَهَ إِلَّا هُوَ فَأَنَّى تُصْرَفُونَ؟

The fertilisation of certain plants is done by the wind. Muslims learn that from sura 15 *al-Hijr* (سُورَةُ الْحِجْرِ):

15:22	We send the winds to fertilise, and We bring down water from the sky for you to drink - you do not control its sources.	وَأَرْسَلْنَا الرِّيَاحَ لَوَاقِحَ فَأَنزَلْنَا مِنَ السَّمَاءِ مَاءً فَأَسْقَيْنَاكُمُوهُ وَمَا أَنتُمْ لَهُ بِخَازِنِينَ.

Fingerprints are unique. This is said in sura 75 *The Resurrection* – in Arabic: al-Qiyāma (سُورَةُ الْقِيامَةِ):

75:4	In fact, We can reshape his very fingertips.	بَلَى قَادِرِينَ عَلَى أَن نُّسَوِّيَ بَنَانَهُ.

104. In how many days did Allah create the Seven Heavens?

Answer: Two.

The Seven Heavens (سَبْعَ سَماوات) are mentioned in sura 41 *(Verses) Made Distinct (Explained in Detail)* – in Arabic: Fussilat (سُورَةُ فُصِّلَتْ):

41:12	and in two Days He formed seven heavens, and assigned an order to each.	فَقَضَاهُنَّ سَبْعَ سَمَاوَاتٍ فِي يَوْمَيْنِ وَأَوْحَى فِي كُلِّ سَمَاءٍ أَمْرَهَا.

Muhammad Asad wrote about this verse that the term *heaven* or *sky* (سَماء) is applied "to anything that is spread like a canopy above any other thing".

He continued: "And this is the primary meaning of this term in the Qur'an; in a wider sense, it has the connotation of *cosmic system*."

105. Why shouldn't you say: "I buy a Qur'an"?

Answer: Because you can buy a book but not its content.

The root of الْقُرْآن is ق-ر-ء. Many dictionaries say that it is the infinitive noun (مَصْدَرٌ) of the verb *to read* (قَرَأَ / يَقْرَأُ). Hence, قُرْآن denotes the action of to read or to recite.

The origin of the word is not entirely clear. Mainly Western scholars say that the word is borrowed from Aramaic. According to Lane's Lexicon, some scholars had suggested that الْقُرْآن was originally the noun of origin (إِسْمُ الْمَصْدَرِ) of the expression: قَرَأْتُ الشَّيْءَ which means I collected together the thing or of قَرَأْتُ الْكِتَابَ which means I read (or recited) the book or scripture. It was later conventionally applied to signify the Book of God that was revealed to Muhammad.

Precisely speaking, قُرْآن describes all the words that are in the book. So it doesn't make sense to use this term if you want to say that you want a physical copy of the book. Instead, it is better to use the expression al-Mushaf (الْمُصْحَف) which is pronounced: *"al Mus-haf"*. The Arabic word Mushaf means *volume* or *binder*. Hence, al-Mushaf al-Sharīf (الْمُصْحَف الشَّرِيف) means *The Noble Qur'an*.

understandable – poor style	*I bought the Qur'an.*	إِشْتَرَيْتُ الْقُرْآنَ .
better style		إِشْتَرَيْتُ الْمُصْحَفَ الشَّرِيفَ .

106. What should a Muslim say when he starts reading the Qur'an?

Answer: "I seek Allah's refuge from Satan" – in Arabic: "'Aūzu billāhi min ash-Shaytān ir-Rajīm" (أَعُوذُ بِاللهِ مِنَ الشَّيْطَانِ الرَّجِيمِ).

Then a Muslim would continue: "In the name of Allah, the Most Merciful, the Most Compassionate" – in Arabic: "Bismillāhi, ar-Rahmān, ar-Rahīm" (بِسْم اللهِ الرَّحْمَنِ الرَّحِيمِ). This is commanded in the Qur'an, sura 16 *The Bee* – in Arabic: al-Nahl (سُورَة النَّحْل):

16:98	[prophet], when you recite the Qur'an, seek God's protection from the outcast, Satan.	فَإِذَا قَرَأْتَ الْقُرْآنَ فَاسْتَعِذْ بِاللهِ مِنَ الشَّيْطَانِ الرَّجِيمِ.

And what do some Muslims say when they stop reading the Qur'an? They say: "Allah the Almighty has spoken the Truth" – in Arabic: "Sadaqa Allāhu al-'Azīm" (صَدَقَ الله الْعَظِيم).

However, there is nothing recorded in the Hadiths or in the Qur'an itself that tells Muslims to say this.

107. Which sura does not start with: "In the name of Allah..."?

Answer: Sura 9 *The Repentance*. In Arabic: al-Tawba (سُورة التَّوْبة). This sura is also called al-Barrāʾa (الْبَراءة) which means *disavowal*.

Almost all suras start with a so-called Basmala. The Basmala (الْبَسْمَلة) is an artificial word which was derived from the first four pronounced consonants of the Arabic phrase "bismi-llāhi" which means: "In the name of God/Allah".

The Basmala actually stands for: *In the name of Allah, the Most Gracious, the Dispenser of Grace* (or: *The Most Merciful*). In Arabic: "Bismillāhi ar-Rahmān, ar-Rahīm" (بِسْمِ اللهِ الرَّحْمنِ الرَّحِيْم).

The Basmala is of great importance for Muslims and they say it dozens of times every day.

- Muslims should start a task or an action (a speech, starting a car, etc.) by reciting the Basmala. For this reason, you will find the Basmala in books before the preface starts.
- The Basmala is found in most constitutions. In countries where Islam is the official religion, even the constitution is introduced with the Basmala, for example in Egypt, Tunisia, Afghanistan, Bahrain, Bangladesh, Iran, Iraq, and the Maldives. It is usually the first sentence in the preamble.
- In Arabic calligraphy, the Basmala is the most common theme.

For Muslims, it is recommended - mustahabb (مُسْتَحَبّ) - to say the Basmala before reciting a sura. However, reciting the Basmala at the beginning of sura *The Repentance* is *disliked* – makrūh (مَكْرُوه). The reason why has to do with the background of the revelation. Scholars say that it "came with the sword".

The sura *The Repentance* commands Muslims to fight the so-called "unbelievers" and "polytheists" - in Arabic: Mushrikūn (مُشْرِكُون) - and expresses Allah's anger with them. It denounces the so-called "hypocrites". Therefore, the Basmala was not mentioned at the beginning of the sura because it signifies peace and mercy.

Remark: Some scholars say that the suras 8 and 9 are in fact just one sura. Both suras - *Battle Gains* (sura 8) and *The Repentance* (sura 9) - deal with the distinction between Muslims and their enemies, the so-called *unbelievers*. Both deal with the problems of war between the Muslims and the deniers of Islam. Towards the end of sura 8, the Qur'an mentions treaties and that these treaties might be violated by the so-called "unbelievers". Sura 9 begins with this topic.

108. Do "al-Rahmān" and "al-Rahīm" mean the same?

Answer: There is only a minor difference which has to do with the respective object.

The two words al-Rahmān (الرَّحْمَـن) and al-Rahīm (الرَّحِيـم) look almost the same. So what is the difference?

- According to Edward Lane, **al-Rahmān** is <u>more intensive</u>, including in its <u>object the believer and the unbeliever</u>, and may be rendered as *The Compassionate* or *The Most Merciful*.
- The object of **al-Rahīm** includes only the <u>believer</u> and may be rendered as *The Merciful* or *The Most Beneficent [to believers]*.

109. Which sura has the Basmala in the middle of a verse?

Answer: Sura 27 *The Ants* – in Arabic: al-Naml (سُورة النَّمْل).

Almost every sura starts with the Basmala (الْبَسْمَلة) which represents the sentence: "In the name of Allah, the Most Gracious, the Most Merciful" (بِسْم اللّٰهِ الرَّحْمَنِ الرَّحِيم).

There is only one sura in which the Basmala occurs <u>twice</u> at the beginning and in the middle. It is sura 27 *The ants* – in Arabic: al-Naml (سُورة النَّمْل):

27:30	It is from Solomon, and it says, "In the name of God, the Lord of Mercy, the Giver of Mercy",	إِنَّهُ مِن سُلَيْمَانَ وَإِنَّهُ بِسْمِ اللَّهِ الرَّحْمَٰنِ الرَّحِيمِ.

This Meccan sura gets its title from the fact that ants occur in this sura, the story of Solomon (سُلَيْمان):

27:18	and when they came to the Valley of the Ants, one ant said, 'Ants! Go into your homes, in case Solomon and his hosts unwittingly crush you.'	حَتَّىٰ إِذَا أَتَوْا عَلَىٰ وَادِ النَّمْلِ قَالَتْ نَمْلَةٌ يَا أَيُّهَا النَّمْلُ ادْخُلُوا مَسَاكِنَكُمْ لَا يَحْطِمَنَّكُمْ سُلَيْمَانُ وَجُنُودُهُ وَهُمْ لَا يَشْعُرُونَ.

This is typical for the Qur'an. It has good news for Muslims and bad news and warnings for non-Muslims. In the Qur'an, there are various stories of prophets which ended fatally, usually in the destruction of entire communities because they didn't believe in the prophet's message.

Note: The Prophet and several companions called this sura Ta Sin (طس). These are the two letters which precede its first verse.

110. Is a prophet and a messenger the same?

Answer: No, they are not. Islam distinguishes between a *messenger* - Rasūl (رَسُول) - and a *prophet* - Nabī (نَبِيّ).

A *messenger* delivers a new religious law, a so-called Sharīʻa (شَرِيعة), whereas a *prophet* continues an old one. In other words, a *messenger* is one to whom a law is revealed and he is commanded to deliver it, while a *prophet* is the one to whom a law is revealed but he is **not** commanded to convey it.

In general, a *messenger* is one who is sent to a disbelieving people whereas a *prophet* is one who is sent to a believing people, to teach and judge them (by the Sharī'a of the *messenger* who came before him). By the way, all prophets are men.

So what about Muhammad?

Muhammad was both; he was a <u>messenger</u> of Allah and <u>the last prophet</u>. Sura 33 *The Joint Forces* - in Arabic: al-'Aḥzāb (الأَحْزَاب) - notifies:

33:40	Muhammad is not the father of any one of you men; he is God's messenger and the seal of the prophets: God knows everything.	مَّا كَانَ مُحَمَّدٌ أَبَا أَحَدٍ مِّن رِّجَالِكُمْ وَلَٰكِن رَّسُولَ اللَّهِ وَخَاتَمَ النَّبِيِّينَ وَكَانَ اللَّهُ بِكُلِّ شَيْءٍ عَلِيمًا.

Jābir ibn 'Abd Allah (جابر بن عَبْد الله) narrated that the Prophet said to 'Alī ibn 'Abī Ṭālib (عَلِيّ بن أَبِي طالِب): "You are to me in the position that Hārūn was to Mūsā, except that there is no [won't be a] prophet after me."[154]

While all messengers became also prophets, not all prophets were messengers. Even if the divine message ended, there could be another prophet. For this reason, Muhammad said that he was **the last prophet**. The last prophet automatically includes the end of the divine message. This means that both - the divine message <u>and</u> prophethood - has ended. In simple terms, Allah has told mankind everything He wanted them to know. They had enough teachers and His people now have to cope on their own.

111. What is so special about the Arabic word for prophet?

Answer: Its pronunciation.

The word Nabī (نَبِي) is derived from the Arabic root n-b-' (ن-ب-أ). The basic meaning is *to be elevated,* but in different applications, it can also mean *to inform* or *announce.*

Let's dig deeper into the Arabic grammar. In Arabic, the word Nabī follows the grammar pattern Fa'īl (فَعِيل) used in the sense of the

---

154 ...أَنْتَ مِنِّي بِمَنْزِلَةِ هَارُونَ مِنْ مُوسَى إِلاَّ أَنَّهُ لاَ نَبِيَّ بَعْدِي. Jāmi' al-Tirmidhī 4095

measure Fā'il (فاعِل) which means: one who acquaints or informs mankind or who is acquainted or informed, respecting Allah and things unseen. According to other scholars, it is derived from Nabwa (نَبْوة), signifying elevation, in which case it was originally without Hamza (ء).

In Arabic, a glottal stop is called Hamz (هَمْز) or Hamza (هَمْزة). It is a (consonantal) stop sound made by rapidly closing the vocal cords.

The Hamza was frowned upon among many Arab tribes and today most Arabic dialects don't use it. For example, according to several scholars the tribe of Quraysh did not pronounce the Hamza while the tribe of Tamīm probably did.

Now comes the interesting part. Although the Quraysh **did not** pronounce the Hamza, the word Nabī was pronounced with a glottal stop in other tribal dialects. There is an anecdote about that (it only makes sense if you can read Arabic):

A man said to the Prophet: "O Prophet of Allah!" (!يا نَبِيْءَ اللّٰه)

And the Prophet replied: "Don't pronounce my name with Hamz!" (لا تَنْبِزْ باسمي)

Muhammad disapproved pronouncing the word with Hamza, which would be Nabī' (نَبِيء), because it would have suggested that he was not from Mecca since the Quraysh pronounced this word most probably without a Hamza – Nabī (نَبِيّ).

The people of the Hijāz in the time of Muhammad probably gave up the original guttural sound of Hamza in many cases whereas other Arabs still preserved it. The rules of Arabic orthography were mainly fixed by the Qur'an, which was originally written down in the Hijāz in accordance to local pronunciation. William Wright, a British Orientalist and expert on the Arabic language, and who lived in the 19th century, wrote that "this pronunciation did not ultimately prevail over the Arabic area, but the old orthography could not lightly be tampered with, having the character of a sacred tradition." According to Wright, the first scribes wrote in Arabic: جاك, جيت, بوس, because they said: "Bawusa, Jīta, Jāka" (or nearly so). The pronunciation that prevailed, however, was "ba'usa, gi'ta, ga'aka". This was expressed in Arabic, without changing the old consonants, by establishing rules for writing the Hamza: جاءَكَ, جِئتَ, بَؤُس. The spelling rules for the

Hamza - such as: ء ,ئ ,ؤ - are actually rules for preserving the old guttural Hamza (ء) in cases where it was already lost or transformed by the first scribes of the Qur'an.

For readers who know Arabic, there is a humorous anecdote about the Hamza. The pun is only revealed in Arabic. The following question was asked an Arab of the desert: "Do you pronounce the word *mouse* (al-Fa'ra) with Hamza?"[155] And he answered: "The cat squeezes it."[156] The man of the desert understood the question as: *do you squeeze the mouse?*

112. How many prophets are there in Islam?

Answer: There are no exact numbers.

Let's have a look at some estimations:
- Number of prophets/Nabī (نَبِيّ): ~ **124,000** (source: weak Hadith)
- Number messengers - Rasūl (رَسُول): **313**
- Number of messengers mentioned in the Qur'an: 25
- Number of *messengers of strong will* (أُولُو العَزْم): **5** (Nūh, 'Ibrāhīm, Mūsā, 'Īsā, and Muhammad).

113. How many prophets and messengers are mentioned in the Qur'an?

Answer: 25.

Some Islamic prophets are almost identical to a respective biblical figure, while others share some aspects with a biblical figure. However, there are also prophets in Islam, for example Sālih, which have no clear equivalent in the Bible and have very little in common with Biblical figures.

The Biblical names in this table should only give an idea:

155...أَتَهْمِزُ الْفَأْرَةَ؟

156...السِّنَّوْرُ يَهْمِزُها

1	'Ādam	آدَم	Adam
2	Nūh	نُوح	Noah
3	'Idrīs	إِدْرِس	Enoch
4	Sālih	صالح	?
5	'Ibrāhīm	إِبْراهِيم	Abraham
6	Hūd	هُود	Eber
7	Lūt	لُوط	Lot
8	Yūnus	يُونُس	Jonah
9	'Ismā'īl	إِسْماعِيل	Ishmael
10	'Ishāq	إِسْحاق	Isaac
11	Ya'qūb	يَعْقُوب	Jacob
12	Yūsuf	يُوسُف	Joseph
13	'Ayyūb	أَيُّوب	Job
14	Shu'ayb	شُعَيْب	Jethro
15	Mūsā	مُوسى	Moses
16	Hārūn	هارُون	Aaron
17	Alyasa'	الْيَسَع	Elisha
18	Dhūlkifl	ذُو الْكِفْل	Ezekiel
19	Dāwūd	داوُود	David
20	Zakarīyā'	ذَكَرِياء	Zachariah
21	Sulaymān	سُلَيْمان	Solomon
22	'Ilyās	إِلْياس	Elias
23	Yahyā	يَحْيى	John the Baptist
24	'Īsā	عِيسى	Jesus
25	Muhammad	مُحَمَّد	

(probably) equals

114. How many suras are named after Islamic prophets?

Answer: six.

Here is a list of these suras:

sura	Name	
10	Yūnus	يُونُس
11	Hūd	هُود
12	Yūsuf	يُوسُف

sura	Name	
14	’Ibrāhīm	إِبْراهِيم
47	Muhammad	مُحَمَّد
71	Nūh	نُوح

115. How many times is Muhammad mentioned in the Qur'an?

Answer: Four times by name. Some say five.

verse	Name of the sura	Arabic transliteration	Arabic name of the sura
3:144	Family of ‘Imrān	’Āl ’Imrān	سُورة آل عِمْران
33:40	The Joint Forces	al-’Ahzāb	سُورة الأَحْزاب
47:2	Muhammad	Muhammad	سُورة مُحَمَّد
48:29	The Triumph	al-Fath	سُورة الفَتْح

Muhammad is mentioned as ’Ahmad (أَحْمَد) in sura 61 *Solid Lines* - in Arabic: al-Saff (سُورة الصَّفّ) - in verse 6. That is why some Muslims say that Muhammad is mentioned by name five times.

Let's have a look at some other prophets and how many times they are mentioned in the Qur'an:

- Dāwūd (داوُد) - David: 16 times
- Mūsā (مُوسى) - Moses: 136 times
- Yūsuf (يُوسُف) - Joseph: 27 times
- Lūt (لُوط) - Lot: 27 times
- ‘Īsā (عِيسى) - Jesus: 25 times. He is mentioned as Christ or Messiah - in Arabic: al-Masīh (المَسِيح) - another 11 times, and as son of Mary (ابن مَرْيَم) another 23 times.

116. Which of the prophets were married to "unbelievers"?

Answer: According to Islam, the wife of Noah (نُوح) and the wife of Lot (لُوط) were *disbelievers* (كافِرُون).

Let's have a look at the source, sura 66 *The Prohibition* – in Arabic: al-Tahrīm (التّحريم):

66:10	God has given examples of disbelievers: the wives of Noah and Lot who married two of Our righteous servants but betrayed them. Their husbands could not help them against God: it was said, 'Both of you enter the Fire with the others.'	ضَرَبَ اللَّهُ مَثَلًا لِّلَّذِينَ كَفَرُوا امْرَأَتَ نُوحٍ وَامْرَأَتَ لُوطٍ كَانَتَا تَحْتَ عَبْدَيْنِ مِنْ عِبَادِنَا صَالِحَيْنِ فَخَانَتَاهُمَا فَلَمْ يُغْنِيَا عَنْهُمَا مِنَ اللَّهِ شَيْئًا وَقِيلَ ادْخُلَا النَّارَ مَعَ الدَّاخِلِينَ.

This sura was probably revealed in 7 AH, during the second half of the Medina period. It has also been referred to as "The sura of the Prophet". Why is that? The first half of the sura deals with certain aspects of Muhammad's personal and family life. The sura ends by giving examples of believing and disbelieving women.

The story of Lot's wife is mentioned in the Qur'an at several places whereas Noah's wife, and her spiritual betrayal of her husband, is only mentioned once. The Qur'an, according to several scholars, uses the two names for a parable - in Arabic: Mathal (مَثَل). The story should warn Muslims that even the most intimate relationship with a truly righteous person cannot save an unrepentant sinner from the consequences of his/her sin. According to Muhammad Asad, they tell Muslims another lesson, i.e. "that a true believer must cut himself off from any association with those who are bent on denying the truth even if they happen to be those nearest and dearest to him."

117. How many "messengers of strong will" are mentioned in the Qur'an?

Answer: five.

There were five prophets in Islam who had divine books and independent teachings: Muhammad (مُحَمَّد), Abraham (إِبراهِيم), Moses

(مُوسَى), Noah (نُوح), and Jesus (عِيسَى). They are traditionally termed *the messengers of firm resolve* or *strong will* (أُولُو الْعَزْم) for their tenacity in preaching Allah's message. Sometimes they are also called arch-prophets. Let's have a look at sura 46 *The Sand Dunes* – in Arabic: al-'Ahqāf (سُورَة الْأَحْقَاف):

46:35	Be steadfast [Muhammad], like those messengers of firm resolve (strong will).	فَاصْبِرْ كَمَا صَبَرَ أُولُو الْعَزْمِ مِنَ الرُّسُلِ.

Prophets, who came after each of the *messengers of strong will,* invited people to follow the divine religious laws. So what does this mean for Islam? The prophetic mission continued until Allah chose Muhammad to correct and perfect the previous missions and to tell the latest orders of Allah to mankind. This is told in sura 42 *The Consultation* – in Arabic: al-Shūrā (سُورَة الشُّورَى):

42:13	In matters of faith, He has laid down for you [people] the same commandment that He gave Noah, which We have revealed to you [Muhammad] and which We enjoined on Abraham and Moses and Jesus: 'Uphold the faith and do not divide into factions within it' - what you [Prophet] call upon the idolaters to do is hard for them; God chooses whoever He pleases for Himself and guides towards Himself those who turn to Him.	شَرَعَ لَكُم مِّنَ الدِّينِ مَا وَصَّى بِهِ نُوحًا وَالَّذِي أَوْحَيْنَا إِلَيْكَ وَمَا وَصَّيْنَا بِهِ إِبْرَاهِيمَ وَمُوسَى وَعِيسَى أَنْ أَقِيمُوا الدِّينَ وَلَا تَتَفَرَّقُوا فِيهِ كَبُرَ عَلَى الْمُشْرِكِينَ مَا تَدْعُوهُمْ إِلَيْهِ اللَّهُ يَجْتَبِي إِلَيْهِ مَن يَشَاءُ وَيَهْدِي إِلَيْهِ مَن يُنِيبُ.

Muslims see Muhammad as the best of all prophets although he himself did not use this label. Instead, he indicated that he was not better than other prophets by using the name of prophet Yūnus. 'Abū Hurayra (أَبُو هُرَيْرَة) narrated that the Prophet said: "None should say that I am better than Yūnus ibn Matta."[157]

118. What is a Jinn?

Answer: A good or bad demon.

---

157 ...لَا يَنْبَغِي لِعَبْدٍ أَنْ يَقُولَ أَنَا خَيْرٌ مِنْ يُونُسَ بْنِ مَتَّى. Sahīh al-Bukhārī 3416

A Jinn (جِنّ) is a demon. It is an invisible being either harmful or helpful that interferes with the lives of mortals. Let's have a look at the Arabic root from which the word Jinn is derived: j-n-n (ج-ن-ن).

It basically means *to cover, to veil; to be or become dark;* but also *to get madly excited.* From this root, the Arabic word for *garden* (جَنّة) is derived – which is also used for *Paradise.* So don't get confused. This root has several meanings. For example: Sura 6 *Livestock* - in Arabic: al-'An'ām (سُورة الأَنْعام) - speaks of Abraham in a verse. The verb *janna* is rendered as follows:

6:76	When the night overshadowed him with its darkness (grew dark over him)	فَلَمَّا جَنَّ عَلَيْهِ اللَّيْلُ

Since this verb, janna (جَنَّ), can be used in an intransitive sense as well, classical philologists say that the word al-Jinn indicates *intense or confusing darkness;* things that are concealed from our senses. Or, as Muhammad Asad put it: "things, beings, or forces which cannot normally be perceived by man but have, nevertheless, an objective reality, whether concrete or abstract, of their own."

In Islam, there are three kinds or forms of spiritual beings:

*   The good ones: the Angels.
*   The evil ones: the Devils.
*   The middle kind, among whom are good and evil beings: the Jinns.

Jinns were already known in pre-Islamic times. In Arabic folklore, the term Jinn was used to denote all manner of demons. How does the Qur'an use the term Jinn? The Qur'an tells Muslims that Jinns were created out of "the fire of scorching winds"[158] or out of "a confusing flame of fire or from a smokeless flame of fire"[159], or simply "out of fire".[160] Notice: *Out of fire* is referring to 'Iblīs, the Devil. The Qur'an occasionally refers *to the realm which is beyond the reach of human perception* – in Arabic: al-Ghayb (الْغَيْب). Al-Ghayb is the

---

158 ...وَالْجَانَّ خَلَقْنَاهُ مِن قَبْلُ مِن نَّارِ السَّمُومِ؛ 15:27

159 ...وَخَلَقَ الْجَانَّ مِن مَّارِجٍ مِّن نَّارٍ؛ 55:15

160 ...مِن نَّارٍ 7:12 / 38:76

unseen and unknown in reference to Allah. The Qur'an states that mankind is unable to see Allah and his attributes.

What does this mean in practice? Muslims call Allah *the Sustainer of all the <u>worlds</u>* – in Arabic: Rabb al-ʿĀlamīn (رَبّ الْعَالَمِين). This term is used in the Qur'an, but why does the Qur'an use the plural form of world? Some Islamic scholars think that the plural might indicate that apart from the *world* in which we live, there are other *worlds* next to us. In these parallel worlds, there are different forms of life which we haven't seen so far.

Although invisible to human beings, these worlds might interact resulting in what we call strange events, things that our mind cannot grasp. Our imagination has an explanation for such events: ghosts, demons, and the supernatural. Occasionally, the term Jinn is used in the Qur'an for these forces which our senses simply cannot grasp.

119. What is the meaning of the name Gabriel (Jibrīl)?

Answer: In Arabic, Gabriel is called Jibrīl (جِبْرِيل or جِبْرَائِيل) which is an Arabicised version of the Hebrew name. Most scholars state that it means *Man of God.*

The word Gabriel (Hebrew: גַּבְרִיאֵל) consists of two parts:

- The 1ˢᵗ part comes from the Hebrew root g-b-r (גבר) which means *to be mighty* or *to prevail* or *to confirm*. However, the word Geber (גֶּבֶר) - which is derived from this root - simply means *man.*
- The 2ⁿᵈ part is El (אֵל). This is the abbreviated form of Elohim (אֱלוֹהִים) which means *God*. This is often encountered in names.
- Thus, we finally get *Man Of God* or *God's Guy.*

120. What is the role of Angel Gabriel in the Bible?

Answer: Gabriel (Greek: Γαβριήλ; Hebrew: גַּבְרִיאֵל) is one of two named angels in the Bible; Michael is the other one.

In the Bible Michael is an archangel which is an angel of high rank. The word *archangel* itself is usually associated with the Abrahamitic religions. The word is derived from the Greek archaggelos (ἀρχάγγελος), literally *chief angel*.

We do not know if Gabriel is an archangel as well. What we know is that Gabriel is at least a rather important angel. Gabriel explains to Daniel important visions (Daniel 8:16 and 9:21) and more than five centuries later, Gabriel announces to Zechariah and Mary their respective sons: John the Baptist and Jesus Christ (Luke 1:19, 26).

Let's make the difference clear. In the Bible, Gabriel is a divine messenger who was sent to Daniel, Mary, and Zechariah. In Islam, Gabriel was sent to numerous pre-Islamic prophets, including Adam.

A remark about the name Michael: Michael is commonly translated as *Who Is Like God*. This is because in Hebrew the name Michael (מִיכָאֵל) consists of three parts:

- Mi (מִי), a common interrogative pronoun: *who*?
- Ke (כְ), a common particle of comparison: *like, as*
- El (אֵל), the shorter version of Elohim, which means *God*

121. Why do some Jews see Gabriel as an enemy?

Answer: This has historic and theological reasons as explained below.

Some Jews who lived in Medina described Gabriel as "the enemy of the Jews". Why is that?

- If misfortune had befallen the Jews, especially in their early his- tory, Gabriel was the one who had told them. Thus, he became the "harbinger of evil". In the case of Michael, this is different because he is regarded as the bearer of good predictions.

- Some Jews rejected Muhammad's claim that Gabriel revealed him the divine message. For the Jews, Gabriel was an avenging angel. If the Qur'an had been sent by Michael, the Jewish guardi- an angel, they might have believed it.

Even Muslims at the time of the Prophet said that Gabriel was the enemy of the Jews. 'Anas ibn Mālik (أَنَس بن مالك) narrated that the Prophet said: "Just now Gabriel has informed me about that." 'Abd Allah ibn Salām (عَبْد الله بن سَلام) asked: "Gabriel?" The Prophet said: "Yes." 'Abd Allah said: "He, among the angels, is the enemy of the Jews." On that the Prophet recited this verse [related to sura 2:97]: "Whoever is an enemy to Gabriel [let him die in his fury!] for he has brought it [i.e. Qur'an] down to your heart by Allah's permission."[161]

122. Who are the most famous angels in Islam?

Answer: Gabriel, Michael, Azrail, Israfil, Malik, and Ridwan.

Let's have a look at them and their respective function in Islam:

- **Gabriel or Jibrīl** (جِبْرِيل or جِبْرائيل) is the intermediary between Allah and the prophets informing them about His instructions.

- **Michael or Mīkhā'īl** (ميخائيل) is the angel who provides food for bodies and souls. Michael is often portrayed as the archangel of mercy who is responsible for bringing rain and thunder to earth. He is also responsible for the rewards given out to good people in this life. The Qur'an mentions him only once, in sura 2:98, and calls him Mīkāl (مِيكَال).

- **Azrael or 'Azrā'īl** (عَزرائيل) is the *Angel of Death*. He is responsible for parting the soul from the body. He is not mentioned by name in the Qur'an. Instead, the Qur'an calls him the *Angel of Death*, Malik al-Mawt (مَلِك الْمَوْت), in sura 32 *Bowing Down in Worship* – in Arabic: al-Sajda (سُورة السَّجْدة):

32:11	Say, 'The Angel of Death put in charge of you will reclaim you, and then you will be brought back to your Lord.'	قُلْ يَتَوَفَّاكُم مَّلَكُ الْمَوْتِ الَّذِي وُكِّلَ بِكُم ثُمَّ إِلَى رَبِّكُمْ تُرْجَعُونَ.

---

161 ...قَالَ: "أَخْبَرَنِي بِهِنَّ جِبْرِيلُ آنِفًا." قَالَ عَبْدُ الله: "جِبْرِيلُ؟" قَالَ مُحَمَّدٌ: "نَعَمْ." قَالَ ذَاكَ عَدُوُّ الْيَهُودِ مِنَ الْمَلَائِكَةِ. فَقَرَأَ هَذِهِ الآيَةَ {قُلْ مَن كَانَ عَدُوًّا لِّجِبْرِيلَ فَإِنَّهُ نَزَّلَهُ عَلَى قَلْبِكَ بِإِذْنِ اللَّهِ مُصَدِّقًا لِمَا بَيْنَ يَدَيْهِ وَهُدًى وَبُشْرَى لِلْمُؤْمِنِينَ}. Sahīh al-Bukhārī 4480

- **Israfil** or **'Isrāfīl** (إسرافيل) is the angel who will blow the horn on the *Day of Resurrection*. The blowing of the trumpet is described in many places in the Qur'an. Israfil is also mentioned in the Hadiths. It is said that the first blowing will end all life, while the second blowing will bring all human beings back to life again to meet Allah for the final judgement. Some people say there will be three blowings on the Day of Judgement. The first one will cause everyone to be startled. The second will cause everyone to die, and the third blowing will be that of resurrection. Along with Gabriel, Michael and Azrael, he is one of the four Islamic archangels. In Judaism and Christianity, Raphael is the counterpart of Israfil.

- **Mālik** (مَالِك), which literally means *a possessor* or *one in authority*, is the angel in charge of Hell and who is said to superintend the torments of the damned. Some scholars claim that he might be the same as Molekh/Moloch (Hebrew: מֹלֶךְ), the fire-god and deity of the children of Ammon in the Bible.

  The angel is mentioned in the Qur'an in sura 43 *Ornaments of Gold* – in Arabic: al-Zukhruf (سُورة الزُّخْرُف):

43:77	They will cry, 'Malik, if only your Lord would finish us off,' but he will answer, 'No! You are here to stay.'	وَنَادَوْا يَا مَالِكُ لِيَقْضِ عَلَيْنَا رَبُّكَ قَالَ إِنَّكُم مَّاكِثُونَ.

- **Ridwān** (رِضوان) is the *angel in charge of guarding the gates of Paradise*, and is the counterpart of Mālik.

123. Which angels keep notes about a Muslim's actions?

Answer: al-Raqīb (الرَّقِيب) and al-'Atīd (الْعَتِيد).

The recording angel is known to all Abrahamic religions. God assigns the angels to record every event, action and prayer of every human being. In Judaism, Gabriel is the principal recording angel, as shown in Ezekiel 9:3-4.

In Islam, the two recording angels are called al-Raqīb and al-'Atīd. They are also called the Kirāman Kātibīna (كِرامًا كاتِبِينَ) – literally: *honourable scribes*. Raqīb literally means *guardian, observer*. 'Atīd literally means *prepared; forthcoming*. Note: al-Raqīb is also one of the 99 names of Allah.

The Qur'an refers to the recording angels in two places:

In sura 50 *The Letter Qāf* (سُورة ق), verses 50:16-18, and in sura 82 *Torn Apart* – in Arabic: al-'Infitār (الإنفِطار), in verses 82:10-12, in which they are given the name *noble recorders*.

82:10	Over you stand	وَإِنَّ عَلَيْكُمْ لَحَافِظِينَ
82:11	watchers, noble recorders	كِرامًا كاتِبِينَ
82:12	who know what you do	يَعْلَمُونَ مَا تَفْعَلُونَ

The Hadiths are full of stories involving angels. 'Abū Hurayra (أَبُو هُرَيْرة) narrated that the Prophet said: "Every day two angels come down from Heaven and one of them says: 'O Allah! Compensate every person who spends in Your Cause', and the other [angel] says: 'O Allah! Destroy every miser.'"[162]

Remark: Whether a person is sent to Paradise, Janna (جَنّة), or to Hell, Jahannam (جَهَنَّم), is not dependent on whether good deeds outweigh bad deeds. Eventually, Allah will decide.

What about guardian angels?

The concept of the guardian angel in Islam is similar to that of some Jewish and Christian traditions. The Arabic term al-Mu'aqqibāt (مُعَقِّبات) - which means *critic; commentator*, but also *those who follow one behind another* - is a term that occurs in the Qur'an.

Most Islamic commentators suggest that it refers to a class of guardian angels whom Allah has appointed to guard every human being from the front and from behind. When Allah decrees that an accident, a calamity or death befalls a person, the angels withdraw. Sura 13 *The Thunder* - in Arabic: al-Ra'd (سُورة الرَّعْد) - is a sura which

---

162 ..."مَا مِنْ يَوْمٍ يُصْبِحُ الْعِبَادُ فِيهِ إلاَّ مَلَكَانِ يَنْزِلانِ فَيَقُولُ أَحَدُهُمَا اللَّهُمَّ أَعْطِ مُنْفِقًا خَلَفًا. وَيَقُولُ الآخَرُ اللَّهُمَّ أَعْطِ مُمْسِكًا تَلَفًا." Sahīh Muslim 1010

was revealed during Muhammad's time in Medina. It received its title from the thunder that praises Allah in a verse. In a verse of this sura, we find some information about these angels:

13:11	Each person has guardian angels before him and behind, watching over him by God's command.	لَهُ مُعَقِّبَاتٌ مِّن بَيْنِ يَدَيْهِ وَمِنْ خَلْفِهِ يَحْفَظُونَهُ مِنْ أَمْرِ اللَّهِ.

Therefore, these angels are also called al-Hafaza (الْحَفَظَة) which means the *custodians* or *guardian angels*. They protect Muslims from the harm of evil Jinn and Satan (شَيْطان).

124. What does the Qur'an say about the Jewish people?

Answer: The Jews have corrupted God's message and see themselves as *the chosen people*.

In sura 62 *The Day of Congregation* - in Arabic: al-Jum'a (سُورة الْجُمْعة) -, there is additional information about this topic.

62:6	Say [Prophet], 'You who follow the Jewish faith, if you truly claim that out of all people you alone are friends of God, then you should be hoping for death.'	قُلْ يَا أَيُّهَا الَّذِينَ هَادُوا إِن زَعَمْتُمْ أَنَّكُمْ أَوْلِيَاءُ لِلَّهِ مِن دُونِ النَّاسِ فَتَمَنَّوُا الْمَوْتَ إِن كُنتُمْ صَادِقِينَ.

Muslims believe that Allah entrusted the Jews with the task of spreading his message. However, the Jews started to believe that they were "God's chosen people" due to their descent from Abraham, Isaac, and Jacob.

Thus, they started to claim that the divine message was meant for them alone – and not for all human beings. Muslims claim that Muhammad's prophethood was predicted in the Torah, but the Jews reject this idea. They are convinced that a prophet must descend from the children of Israel, else, he cannot be a prophet.

125. Which term does the Qur'an use for Jewish scholars?

Answer: Al-'Aḥbār (الْأَحْبَار).

The single form of this classical Arabic expression is Hibr (جِبْر) or Habr (حَبْر), and denotes a non-Muslim religious authority (عالِم دِينِيّ); *a learned man, scribe; bishop; rabbi.* It comes from the Arabic root *to gladden, make happy; to compose, to write.* The word hibr (جِبْر) itself means *ink; squid.* The expression is found in sura 5 *The Table Spread* – in Arabic: al-Māʾida (سُورَة الْمَائِدَة):

5:63	Why do their rabbis and scholars not forbid them to speak sinfully and consume what is unlawful? How evil their deeds are!	لَوْلَا يَنْهَاهُمُ الرَّبَّانِيُّونَ وَالْأَحْبَارُ عَن قَوْلِهِمُ الْإِثْمَ وَأَكْلِهِمُ السُّحْتَ لَبِئْسَ مَا كَانُوا يَصْنَعُونَ.

Note that according to various scholars, the expression al-Rabbān-iyūn (الرَّبَّانِيُّونَ), which means *men of God*, stands in this context for the spiritual leaders of the Christians, and the expression 'Aḥbār (الْأَحْبَار) for the Jewish scholars (*rabbis*).

126. What are the two most famous mountains in Mecca?

Answer: Al-Ṣafā (الصَّفا) and al-Marwā (الْمَرْوة).

Al-Ṣafā and al-Marwā are actually two small hills in Mecca. The distance between them is 450 m (1470 ft).

In Islamic tradition, Abraham (إِبْرَاهِيم) was commanded by Allah to leave his wife Hāgar (هاجَر) and their infant son alone in the desert between al-Ṣafā and al-Marwā to test their faith. When they ran out of food and water, Hāgar went searching for it, leaving behind her infant son Ishmael (إِسْماعِيل).

She first climbed the nearest hill, al-Ṣafā, to check the surrounding area. When she could not find anything, she went to the other hill, al-Marwā, and looked around. From the top of the two hills, she was able to see Ishmael, so she knew that he was safe.

However, when she was in the valley between the hills, she was unable to see her son. Thus, she tried to hurry in the valley and walk at a normal pace when on the hills. The heat was unbearable, but she travelled back and forth between the hills seven times.

Eventually, she discovered a spring at the spot where the angel Gabriel had hit the ground with his wing. This spring is now known as the *Zamzam Well* (زَمْزَم), and was revealed by Gabriel as a reward for Hāgar's patience.

During the pilgrimages - Hajj (الْحِجّ) and 'Umra (الْعُمْرة) - Muslims travel back and forth between these two hills seven times in order to commemorate Hāgar's search for water and Allah's mercy. This is called al-Saʿy (السَّعْي) which literally means *endeavour; pursuit*.

Al-Safā and al-Marwā are mentioned in the Qur'an, in sura 2 *The Cow* – in Arabic: al-Baqara (الْبَقَرة):

2:158	Safā and Marwā are among the rites of God, so for those who make major or minor pilgrimage to the House it is no offence to circulate between the two. Anyone who does good of his own accord will be rewarded, for God rewards good deeds, and knows everything.	إِنَّ الصَّفَا وَالْمَرْوَةَ مِن شَعَائِرِ اللَّهِ فَمَنْ حَجَّ الْبَيْتَ أَوِ اعْتَمَرَ فَلَا جُنَاحَ عَلَيْهِ أَن يَطَّوَّفَ بِهِمَا وَمَن تَطَوَّعَ خَيْرًا فَإِنَّ اللَّهَ شَاكِرٌ عَلِيمٌ.

127. "If the mountain won't come to Muhammad, Muhammad must go to the mountain." Which mountain is possibly meant?

Answer: Possibly Mount al-Safā (الصَّفا) in Mecca.

In English, there is a famous proverb: "If the mountain will not come to Muhammad, then Muhammad must go to the mountain" – sometimes incorrectly quoted the other way around. In Turkish, the saying exists as well but without the words Muhammad or prophet: "If the mountain won't come to you, you must go to the mountain." (Dağ sana gelmezse, sen dağa gideceksin.)

The first (written) use of this saying in English goes back to Francis Bacon, the English philosopher and scientist. The earliest appearance of the phrase is found in chapter 12 of his Essays, published in 1625: "Mahomet made the people believe that he would call a hill to him, and from the top of it offer up his prayers, for the observers of

"If the mountain won't come to Muhammad, Muhammad must go to the mountain." Which mountain is possibly meant?

187

his law. The people assembled; Mahomet called the hill to come to him, again and again; and when the hill stood still, he was never a whit abashed, but said; If the hill will not come to Mahomet, Mahomet will go to the hill."

Some European scholars tried to trace this saying back to Muhammad, though there is no Arabic source supporting this.

128. Which sura is named after an Islamic principle?

Answer: Sura 22 *The Pilgrimage* – in Arabic: al-Hajj (سُورة الْحَجّ).

This sura consists of 78 verses. Although the name might indicate that it deals with the pilgrimage, it does not. The sura delivers more or less a warning for "polytheists".

The sura begins with the Day of Judgement and condemns those who worship idols describing them as powerless as to create even a fly. Most of the verses were revealed in Medina. Let's look at one of the most famous verses of this sura:

| 22:73 | People, here is an illustration, so listen carefully: those you call on beside God could not, even if they combined all their forces, create a fly, and if a fly took something away from them, they would not be able to retrieve it. How feeble are the petitioners and how feeble are those they petition! | يَا أَيُّهَا النَّاسُ ضُرِبَ مَثَلٌ فَاسْتَمِعُوا لَهُ إِنَّ الَّذِينَ تَدْعُونَ مِن دُونِ اللَّهِ لَن يَخْلُقُوا ذُبَابًا وَلَو اجْتَمَعُوا لَهُ وَإِن يَسْلُبْهُمُ الذُّبَابُ شَيْئًا لَا يَسْتَنقِذُوهُ مِنْهُ ضَعُفَ الطَّالِبُ وَالْمَطْلُوبُ. |

129. Where is Bakka?

Answer: Bakka (بَكّة) is an old name for Mecca (مَكّة).

The name Bakka is found in the Qur'an, for example in sura 3 *Family of 'Imrān* – in Arabic: ʾĀl 'Imrān (سُورة آل عِمْران):

| 3:96 | The first House [of worship] to be established | إِنَّ أَوَّلَ بَيْتٍ وُضِعَ |

for people was the one at Bakka. It is a blessed place; a source of guidance for all people;	لِلنَّاسِ لَلَّذِي بِبَكَّةَ مُبَارَكًا وَهُدًى لِلْعَالَمِينَ

According to the Arabic dictionary *Lisān al-'Arab*, the site of the Ka'ba (الْكَعْبِـة) and its surroundings was called *Bakka* due to the crowding and congestion of people in the area. The Arabic verb bakka (بك) means *to crowd*, like in a bazaar. That is why Bakka (بَكّة) was the ancient name for the area upon which later the Ka'ba in Mecca was built. Some linguists suggest that in the southern parts of Arabia, at the time of Muhammad, the letters *b* and *m* might have been interchangeable.

The Qur'an mentions some alternative names for Mecca:

- 'Umm al-Qurā (أُمِّ الْقُرَى), which literally means *mother of all settlements*.
- Tihāma, also spelled Tihāmah (تهامة), which is another name for the region around Mecca.

130. What is meant by Harf?

Answer: One of the seven different styles or dialects (أَحْرُف سَبْعة) in which the Qur'an was preserved.

The word Harf (حَرْف) can mean a lot, for example: *letter (character); edge; verge*. In the context of the Qur'an, it means *dialect, idiom* or, *mode of expression*.

'Abd Allah ibn 'Abbās (عَبْد الله بن عَبَّاس) reported that Allah's Messenger said: "Gabriel taught me to recite in one style. I replied to him and kept asking him to give more [styles], until he reached seven modes [of recitation/expression]."[163]

So, what is meant by that? Most scholars say that there are seven ways of reciting the Qur'an. The wording may differ but the meaning stays the same. Some say that what is meant by "seven ways" are in fact seven dialects.

---

163 ...أَنَّ رَسُولَ اللّه قَالَ: "أَقْرَأَنِي جِبْرِيلُ عَلَى حَرْفٍ فَرَاجَعْتُهُ فَلَمْ أَزَلْ أَسْتَزِيدُهُ فَيَزِيدُنِي حَتَّى انْتَهَى إِلَى سَبْعَةِ أَحْرُفٍ." قَالَ ابْنُ شِهَابٍ بَلَغَنِي أَنَّ تِلْكَ السَّبْعَةَ الْأَحْرُفَ إِنَّمَا هِيَ فِي الْأَمْرِ الَّذِي يَكُونُ وَاحِدًا لاَ يَخْتَلِفُ فِي حَلاَلٍ وَلاَ حَرَامٍ. Sahīh Muslim 819.

This was indicated in a Hadith. 'Umar ibn al-Khattāb (عُمَر بن الخَطَّاب) said: "I heard Hishām ibn Hakīm ibn Hizām reciting sura al-Furqān in a style different from that in which I used to recite it, and in which Allah's Messenger had taught me to recite it. I was about to dispute with him [on this style] but I delayed until he had finished it.

Then I caught hold of his cloak and brought him to the Messenger of Allah and said: 'Messenger of Allah, I heard this man reciting sura al-Furqān in a style different from the one in which you taught me to recite.' Upon this the Messenger of Allah told [me] to let him [Hishām] go and asked him to recite.

The Messenger of Allah then said: 'Thus, it was sent down.' He then asked me to recite and I did, and he said: 'Thus, it was sent down. The Qur'an was sent down in seven dialects. So recite you are most comfortable with.'"[164]

Ibn Mas'ūd (ابن مَسْعُود) said that he heard the first reading of the Qur'an. However, he commented on the different styles: "It is like one of you saying 'halumma' (هَلُمَّ) or 'ta'āl' (تَعَالَ)."[165] Both, halumma and ta'āl, are different ways of expressing *come here!*

Since many Muslims claim that the Qur'an cannot be translated without changing its pure meaning, they run into difficulties defending that as there were different, synonymous versions. From a linguistic point of view, there is a difference between halumma and ta'āl. Every word has a different connotation, history, etc.

If it is all about meaning, it would be possible to interpret the entire Qur'an, but this is rejected by traditional scholars – although they follow the rule that the seven different readings all mean the same. This is an unresolved dilemma among traditional Muslims. This is in addition to the fact that the Qur'an initially was written

164 ...قَالَ سَمِعْتُ عُمَرَ بْنَ الْخَطَّابِ، يَقُولُ سَمِعْتُ هِشَامَ بْنِ، حَكِيمِ بْنِ جِزَامٍ يَقْرَأُ سُورَةَ الْفُرْقَانِ عَلَى غَيْرِ مَا أَقْرَوُهَا وَكَانَ رَسُولُ اللَّهِ أَقْرَأَنِيهَا فَكِدْتُ أَنْ أَعْجَلَ عَلَيْهِ ثُمَّ أَمْهَلْتُهُ حَتَّى انْصَرَفَ ثُمَّ لَبَّبْتُهُ بِرِدَائِهِ فَجِئْتُ بِهِ رَسُولَ اللَّهِ فَقُلْتُ يَا رَسُولَ اللَّهِ إِنِّي سَمِعْتُ هَذَا يَقْرَأُ سُورَةَ الْفُرْقَانِ عَلَى غَيْرِ مَا أَقْرَأْتَنِيهَا. فَقَالَ رَسُولُ اللَّهِ: "أَرْسِلْهُ اقْرَأْ." فَقَرَأَ الْقِرَاءَةَ الَّتِي سَمِعْتُهُ يَقْرَأُ فَقَالَ رَسُولُ اللَّهِ: "هَكَذَا أُنْزِلَتْ." ثُمَّ قَالَ لِي: "اقْرَأْ." فَقَرَأْتُ فَقَالَ: "هَكَذَا أُنْزِلَتْ إِنَّ هَذَا الْقُرْآنَ أُنْزِلَ عَلَى سَبْعَةِ أَحْرُفٍ فَاقْرَءُوا مَا تَيَسَّرَ مِنْهُ." Sahīh Muslim 818

165 ...إِنِّي قَدْ سَمِعْتُ أُولَى الْقُرَّاءِ، فَوَجَدْتُهُمْ مُتَقَارِبِينَ، فَاقْرَءُوهُ كَمَا عُلِّمْتُمْ، وَإِيَّاكُمْ وَالتَّنَطُّعَ وَالِاخْتِلَافَ، إِنَّمَا هُوَ كَقَوْلِ أَحَدِكُمْ: "هَلُمَّ وَتَعَالَ." Ibn 'Abī Shayba 127/6.

without dots (which are essential for some letters) and without vowel markers. In Arabic, a single vowel can change the meaning of a word dramatically. The seven versions were eventually reduced to one: that of the Quraysh. This happened during the reign of Caliph 'Uthmān ibn 'Affān and all the methods of recitation are now based on this version. What about **dots and vowel markers**? They were added later, mainly by 'Abū al-'Aswad al-Du'alī (أَبُو الأَسْوَد الدُّؤَلِيّ) who died in 688 (69 AH).

Note: The **seven styles/versions** have nothing to do with the different **ways of reading** the Qur'an – which are basically different methods of pronunciation used in recitations.

131. Which Caliph standardised the Qur'an?

Answer: Caliph 'Uthmān ibn 'Affān (عُثْمان بن عَفّان).

When the Prophet died in June 632, Muslims faced difficult times. More and more people who had memorised the Qur'an died in battles, e.g. in the Battle of Yamāma (مَعْرَكة الْيَمامة) in December 632.

'Abū Bakr, the first Caliph after Muhammad's death, had started the *Apostate Wars,* so-called Ridda wars (حُرُوب الرِّدّة), against rebellious Arabian tribes. The rebels insisted that they had submitted to Muhammad, but owed nothing to 'Abū Bakr. In response to that, 'Abū Bakr launched bloody wars in order to crush the resistance.

Since a lot of Muslims were killed in these battles, there was suddenly great danger that the divine message might get lost. Therefore, 'Abū Bakr instructed Zayd ibn Thābit (زَيْد بن ثابِت الأَنْصارِيّ) to collect the Qur'an from various written material and from the memories of people. He should then compile a complete text.

Later on, the collection was given to 'Umar, and then to his daughter Hafsa, who was one of Muhammad's wives. It was the third Caliph 'Uthmān who reduced the Qur'an's content to one style. During 'Uthmān's rule, disputes had arisen among Muslims in the vast Muslim empire about the correct manner of reciting the Qur'an. The Syrians followed the teachings of 'Ubayy ibn Ka'b, the Kufans followed 'Abd Allah ibn Mas'ūd, the people of Hims followed al-

Miqdād, and the people of Basra followed 'Abū Mūsā – all of them using different styles/versions. Therefore, 'Uthmān decided to unite the community behind one, standardised text.

'Uthmān borrowed the scripts from Hafsa and ordered four companions, among them Zayd ibn Thābit, to rewrite the Qur'anic script in perfect copies. Then, 'Uthmān sent a perfect copy to the main centres of the Islamic world to replace the copies that were in circulation. This version of the Qur'an has remained to this day.

132. Which men memorised the revelation at the beginning of Islam?

Answer: There were many.

Let's look at the most important ones:
- 'Abū Bakr (أَبُو بَكْر الصِّدِّيق)
- 'Umar ibn al-Khattāb (عُمَر بن الْخَطّاب)
- 'Uthmān ibn 'Affān (عُثْمان بن عَفّان)
- 'Alī ibn 'Abī Tālib (عَليّ بن أَبي طالِب)
- 'Abd Allah ibn Mas'ūd (عَبْد الله بن مَسْعُود)
- 'Abd Allah ibn 'Abbās (عَبْد الله بن عَبّاس)
- 'Abd Allah ibn 'Amr ibn al-'Ās (عَبْد الله بن عَمْرُو بن الْعاص)
- 'Abū Hurayra (أَبُو هُرَيْرة)

133. Which women memorised the revelation at the beginning of Islam?

Answer: At least three wives of Muhammad.

'Ā'isha (عائشة بِنْت أَبي بَكْر). She did not only memorise the Qur'an, she was also one of the most important sources for the Hadiths.

Hafsa bint 'Umar (حَفْصة بِنْت عُمَر), a daughter of 'Umar ibn al-Khattāb (عُمَر بن الْخَطّاب). She became a widow during the Battle of

Badr (غَزْوة بَدْر) when her husband Khunays ibn Hudhayfa (بن خُنَيْس حُذَيْفة) was killed. Arabs preferred to marry their daughters off at an early age. If they became a widow, they could get married again quickly. One day, ʿUmar ibn al-Khaṭṭāb walked to the house of ʾAbū Bakr and offered him his daughter. ʾAbū Bakr remained silent and did not say a word. He then went to ʿUthmān, but he also didn't want to marry her. Eventually, Muhammad married her in 625 (3 AH). Some sources say that Hafsa was then perhaps 21 years old.

Hind bint ʾAbī ʾUmayya (هِنْد بِنْت أَبِي أُمَيّة), better known as **ʾUmm Salama** (أُمّ سَلَمة). Her husband, ʾAbū Salama, a Muslim and cousin of Muhammad, died of his wounds in the Battle of ʾUhud (غَزْوة أُحُد) in 625 (3 AH). ʾUmm Salama was already quite old for getting remarried - possibly 29 -, but Muhammad said that he too was of old age – around 52 years - and that her family was like his family. She married him and became his sixth wife.

ʾUmm Salama was one of the most influential wives of Muhammad and played an important role in Shia history as well. She narrated numerous Hadiths. She died in 683 (64 AH).

134. Which companions had memorised the Qur'an and discussed it with the Prophet before his death?

Answer: There were at least three.

ʾUbayy ibn Kaʿb (أُبَيّ بن كَعْب). He was one of the first to accept Islam and pledge allegiance to Muhammad at al-ʿAqaba. He worked as a scribe of Muhammad, writing letters for him. ʾUbayy was one of the few who put the suras into writing.

Muʾāz ibn Jabal (مُعاذ بن جَبَل). He was one of the early Islamic scholars and a companion of Muhammad. His epithet (لَقَب) was *Imam of the Scholars* - in Arabic: Imām al-ʿUlamāʾ (إِمام الْعُلَماء). The Prophet said about him that he was "the most knowledgeable of what is lawful and unlawful".[166] He died of the plague in Jordan during the Syrian expedition in 639 (18 AH).

---

166 ...أَعْلَمُهُمْ بِالْحَلالِ وَالْحَرامِ مُعاذُ بْنُ جَبَلٍ. Sunan ibn Māja 149.

Zayd ibn Thābit (زَيْد بن ثابِت). He too was a personal scribe of the Prophet and was from the Helpers of Medina, the so-called al-'Ansār. After Muhammad's death, Zayd was assigned the role of authenticating and collecting the oral and written revelations into a single bounded volume (الْمُصْحَف). Muhammad said about him that he was "the most knowledgeable of the rules of inheritance".[167] He died around 665 (45 AH).

135. What is a Juz'?

Answer: A Juz' (جُزْء) is one of the 30 parts the Qur'an can be divided in.

The word Juz' in Arabic means *part*. In medieval times, when it was too costly for most Muslims to purchase a manuscript, copies of the Qur'an were held in mosques in order to make them accessible to people. These copies took the form of a series of thirty parts of equal length into which the Qur'an can be divided.

The 30 parts are useful for Muslims who want to read through the Qur'an in one month, i.e. one Juz' a day. Some of these parts are known by names which are usually the first words by which the Juz' starts. However, most of them are not known by special names because the Juz' usually begins in the middle of a sura.

A Juz' is sometimes further subdivided into two Hizb (جِزْب). This means that the Qur'an consists of 60 Hizb.

The division of the Qur'an into thirty parts was not practiced during the time of the Prophet. This system started in Iraq and was implemented during the reign of al-Hajjāj ibn Yūsuf (الْحَجّاج بن يُوسُف), who died in 714 (110 AH).

The most commonly memorised Juz' is called Juz' 'Amma (جُزْء عَمّ) which is the 30th Juz' containing most of the shortest suras of the Qur'an, namely sura 78 to 114. Juz' 'Amma is named after the first word in this Juz', which is sura 78 *The Announcement* - al-Naba' (سُورة النَّبَأ). The word 'Amma literally means *about what* (عَمّ).

---

167 ...أَفْرَضُهُم زَيْدُ بْنُ ثَابِتٍ. Sunan ibn Māja 159.

Another famous Juz' is called Juz' Tabāraka (جُزْء تَبَارَك). This Juz' is named after the first word of sura 67 *Control* or *Sovereignty* - in Arabic: al-Mulk (سُورة الْمُلْك) - which is the verb *Tabāraka* (تَبَارَك). It means *to be blessed*.

Juz' 29 Tabāraka (جُزْء تَبَارَك):
- Hizb 57 consisting of (67:1) - (71:28)
- Hizb 58 consisting of (72:1) - (77:50)

Juz' 30: 'Amma (جُزْء عَمّ):
- Hizb 59 consisting of (78:1) - (86:17)
- Hizb 60 consisting of (87:1) - (114:6)

136. When was the current version of the Qur'an printed for the first time?

Answer: In 1924 (1342 AH) in Cairo, Egypt.

The Qur'anic text in printed form, which Muslims generally use worldwide, is the so-called Egyptian edition. This is also known as the King Fu'ād edition, since it was introduced in Egypt under King Fu'ād. This edition is based on the reading of Hafs 'an ʿAsim (حَفْص عَن عَاصِم). The year 1924 might sound surprising as it was so late. Why was the Islamic world so reluctant in adopting the printing press?

There were already printed copies of the Qur'an before this, in the so-called block-print form. Woodblock printings of extracts from the Qur'an were found as early as the 10th century. However, printed copies of the Qur'an clashed with the teachings of traditional Islamic scholars from the very beginning. Printing was against the traditional way of transmitting knowledge, i.e. by conversation.

In Islam, the chain of narration has always been of great importance. Muhammad transmitted the message of Allah orally to his followers. When they were later written down, they were still transmitted orally. The writings were just an aid. This is also the reason why Muslims should memorise the Qur'an. The written form is only a tool, an aid, but it is the oral transmission which counts and has value. The Egyptian edition has had a huge impact because the only printed versions of the Qur'an available before were published by non-Muslims.

Johannes Gutenberg (~ 1398 - 1468) was a German craftsman who introduced the printing press to Europe in the 15th century. One of the major faults of the Muslims was that they were reluctant in adopting the invention of the letterpress. Instead, they copied by hand because writing was a craft and art in Islam. Printed books were not used in the Islamic world until the 19th century, four centuries after it had been established in the Christian world.

It wasn't that Muslims did not know about printing presses. As early as 1493, Jewish refugees from Spain set up printing presses in Istanbul, printing Bibles and secular books. Jewish and Christian communities continued to use printing presses in various parts of the Muslim world. The problem was not the Arabic alphabet. As early as the 15th century the Qur'an was printed in Arabic in Italy, and in the 16th century, Christians were using the press for Arabic printing in Syria.

The first Qur'an printed with movable type was produced in Venice in 1537/1538 for the Ottoman market by Pagani Paganini and Alessandro Paganini. Later on, the German protestant theologian and pastor Abraham Hinckelmann published an edition in Hamburg in 1694. This copy was full of mistakes compared to the near flawlessness of the *Gutenberg Bible*. Therefore, Muslims thought that it could have been only Satan himself who could have produced such a bad and faulty version of the Qur'an.

Between 1483 and 1726 printing anything in Arabic was prohibited in the Ottoman Empire – punished, initially, by the death penalty. The Ottoman ban on printing in Arabic script was lifted in 1726, but only for non-religious texts. Islamic scholars of al-'Azhar in Cairo issued Fatwas declaring that printing religious books is forbidden. Only when the Islamic world was in decline military and economically, did they start to use the printing press as a weapon or as a rescue tool in defence of Islam.

The German Orientalist Gustav Leberecht Flügel published an edition of the Qur'an in 1834 in Leipzig, which remained authoritative for almost a century until the al-'Azhar University in Cairo rethought the traditional Islamic view and published an edition in 1924. This edition became the standard version of the Qur'an which is used until today. Some remarks:

- Writing the Qur'an has always been a noble craft. A person who copied the Qur'an by hand was called Nāsikh (ناسِخ) or Warrāq (وَرَّاق). In the 18th century in Istanbul, the number of such writers was estimated to be between 20,000 and 90,000.

- Hafs ʿan ʿAsim (mentioned at the beginning) is an important figure in the art of Qur'an reading (قِراءات). ʿĀsim ibn Abī al-Najūd died around 796 ʿCE (180 AH). The majority of Muslims use his method; so, most copies of the Qur'an sold today follow his reading – except for those in North Africa and West Africa which use the recitation transmitted by Warsh (وَرْش).

137. Which are the most important Qur'an commentaries?

Answer: There are several. The Arabic word for *explanation* or *exegesis*, simply for *commentary*, is Tafsīr (تَفْسِير).

Let's have a look at some classical works:

Tafsīr al-Tabarī (تَفْسِير الطَّبَرِيّ). This commentary was written by the Persian scholar Muhammad ibn Jarīr al-Tabarī (مُحَمَّد بن جَرِير الطّبَرِيّ). He was born in 838 (224 AH) and died in 923 (310 AH).

It is the earliest major commentary which has survived in its original form. Al-Tabarī had lived in Iraq and travelled to Egypt and Syria. His work is mainly based on reports from the Prophet and his companions. Almost every commentator after him referred to this extensive work (30 volumes).

Tafsīr ibn Kathīr (تَفْسِير ابن كَثِير). This popular commentary focuses on the soundness of reports. ʾIsmāʿīl ibn ʿUmar ibn Kathīr (إِسماعِيل بن عُمَر بن كَثِير) was born around 1300 (701 AH) and died in 1373 (774 AH). He was a scholar of the Sunni Shāfiʿī School during the Mamluk Rule of Syria.

His work is more or less a summary of the Tafsīr by al-Tabarī. The reason for its popularity is Ibn Kathīr's method. He mostly used the Hadiths to explain the verses of the Qur'an and gave the reader hints where he could find additional information in the Hadiths. Today, the Tafsīr of Ibn Kathīr is the most widely used commentary (not only in the Arab world).

There are also several modern approaches. Most translators of the Qur'an have extended their work with a commentary. Muhammad Asad's exegesis, which has been frequently used in this book, is a good example of a more flexible approach to reading the Qur'an. It was written in the 20th century.

Some works gained popularity in particular regions. In Asia, for example, **Tafhīm al-Qur'an** (تَفْهِيم الْقُرْآن) became rather influential. It was written by ʼAbū al-ʼAʻlā Mawdūdī (أَبُو أَلْأَعْلَى مَوْدُودِيّ). He was an Indian-Pakistani Islamic scholar who died in 1979 at the age of 75. His work, written in Urdu, was completed in 1973. It has been translated into several, mostly Asian, languages.

It is a combination of traditional and modern views. The author was the founder of the *Jamaat-e-Islami*, one of the most important political Islamic organisations in Asia.

138. How do you pronounce "Allah" correctly?

Answer: You have to focus on the second "l" (ل) in Allah (الله).

What I mean here by correctly is the reading of the Qur'an according to the rules of Tajwīd (تَجْوِيد). The word Tajwīd is derived from the triliteral root j-w-d (ج-و-د). Tajwīd literally means *to make better; to ameliorate*. It is the way of reciting the Qur'an according to well-established rules of pronunciation and intonation.

Tajwīd is a religious duty, a so-called Fard (فَرْض), whenever a Muslim recites the Qur'an. A Muslim must try to read the Qur'an according to certain rules as good as he can and knows.

There are two important rules which bring us closer to the correct pronunciation of the word *Allah*:

1. The emphatic Arabic consonants ق غ ظ ط ض ص خ - known as Mufakhkham (مُفَخَّم) - are pronounced with a **heavy accentuation**, so-called Tafkhīm (تَفْخِيم). To produce this sound, the

tongue elevates towards the roof of the mouth in order to force a thick and heavy sound that fills the mouth. This can be achieved either by pharyngealisation (pronounced while squeezing one's voicebox) or by velarisation. The voicebox (larynx) is the part of the breathing tract which contains the vocal cords. Velarisation means that the tongue is drawn far up and back in the mouth towards the soft palate (velum).

2. The remaining letters - known as Muraqqaq (مُرَقَّق) - have a **light accentuation**, so-called Tarqīq (تَرْقِـيـق). They are pronounced normally, without pharyngealisation (except ع, which is often considered a pharyngeal sound). To produce this sound, the back of the tongue lowers, so that a flat sound is produced.

There are two letters which are special:

- The Rā' (ر) is pronounced with a <u>heavy</u> accentuation when accompanied by the vowel *a* (فَتْحة) or vowel *u* (ضَمّة). The rā' is <u>light</u> when it is accompanied by the vowel *i* (كَسرة).

- The Lām (ل) in general is a Tarqīq-letter. However, this is not the case in the word *Allah*. The Lām in the word *Allah* can be pronounced as a thick (Tafkhīm) or thin (Tarqīq) letter depending on the vowel before. The rules are similar to the ones mentioned above for the letter Rā'.

Let's check the Arabic word for *God*, *Allah* (الله), in detail. Scholars refer to this word as the *Grand Word* – in Arabic: Lafz al-Jalāla (لَفظ الجَلالة).

Allah is a special word in Arabic. It has a distinct appearance and is written with two Lām (ل) along with a Shadda (شَدّة). The word Shadda literally means *strengthening* and is marked by a small *w* on top (ّ) in the Arabic script. It indicates a doubling/gemination of a consonant. This is found over the <u>second</u> Lām: الله. This is because Allah literally means *the God*; the first Lām is part of the definite article: *al* (ال).

Now let's check the pronunciation.

- When the word *Allah* is preceded by the vowel *a* (فَتْحة) or the vowel *u* (ضَمّة), then the Lām is pronounced in a distinct heavy manner – with Tafkhīm. This heavy Lām is thus articulated with the entire body of the tongue rather than its tip alone.

Let's take for example the term Hezbollah (حِزْبُ اللهِ), literally *Party of Allah,* which is the name of a Shia Islamist group and political party based in Lebanon. Or a part of the verse 58:22: "man haddaAllah" (مَنْ حَادَّ اللهَ) which means: *those who oppose Allah.*

- If, however, the preceding vowel is *i* (كَسْرة), then the Lām in Allah is light, such as in the Basmala: *Bismillahi...* (بِسْمِ اللهِ الرَّحْمٰنِ الرَّحِيـمِ). So if a Muslim says "Bismillahi", he should not pronounce the Lām with a heavy emphasis – instead, just with the tip of the tongue.

139. Who was probably the worst "disbeliever" ever?

Answer: The Pharaoh (فِرْعَوْن).

In the Qur'an there are many stories about people who did not follow Allah's prophets or messengers. There is one leader whose story and fate is told in detail, and this is the story of the Pharaoh. However, we don't know which particular Pharaoh the story is about.

His words, his bad deeds and wrongdoings, as well as his brutal tyranny are all mentioned in the Qur'an. His (and his people's) fate is told in sura 40 *The Forgiver* – in Arabic: Ghāfir (سُورة غافِر):

40:46	(A terrible punishment engulfed Pharaoh's people;) they will be brought before the Fire morning and evening. On the Day the Hour comes, it will be said, 'Throw Pharaoh's people into the worst torment.'	(وَحَاقَ بِآلِ فِرْعَوْنَ سُوءُ الْعَذَابِ) النَّارُ يُعْرَضُونَ عَلَيْهَا غُدُوًّا وَعَشِيًّا وَيَوْمَ تَقُومُ السَّاعَةُ أَدْخِلُوا آلَ فِرْعَوْنَ أَشَدَّ الْعَذَابِ.
40:47	In the Fire they will quarrel with one another: the weak will say to the haughty, 'We were your followers, so can you now relieve us from some share of the Fire?'	وَإِذْ يَتَحَاجُّونَ فِي النَّارِ فَيَقُولُ الضُّعَفَاءُ لِلَّذِينَ اسْتَكْبَرُوا إِنَّا كُنَّا لَكُمْ تَبَعًا فَهَلْ أَنتُم مُّغْنُونَ عَنَّا نَصِيبًا مِّنَ النَّارِ.
40:48	but they will say, 'We are all in this to-	قَالَ الَّذِينَ اسْتَكْبَرُوا إِنَّا

| | gether. God has judged between His creatures.¹ | كُلٌّ فِيهَا إِنَّ اللَّهَ قَدْ حَكَمَ بَيْنَ الْعِبَادِ. |

Why was the Pharaoh the worst? Muslims believe that all the other enemies (of the true Divine Message) had caused less harm to the believers than the Pharaoh(s). The reason for this is that the other enemies' disbelief was not of such large extent as was the disbelief of the Pharaoh(s).

Remark: In Egypt, someone told me that the three pyramids in Giza are for Muslims what the concentration camp *Auschwitz* is for German people: a symbol of a time that must never return! It is a strange comparison. However, I have met several Egyptians who had never visited the pyramids. They told me that they were afraid that the pyramids would mislead them in faith.

140. Which prophet was sent to the Pharaohs?

Answer: Mūsā (مُوسَى) – Moses.

This is found in sura 11 Hūd (هُود):

11:59	These were the 'Ād: they rejected their Lord's signs, disobeyed His messengers, and followed the command of every obstinate tyrant.	وَتِلْكَ عَادٌ جَحَدُوا بِآيَاتِ رَبِّهِمْ وَعَصَوْا رُسُلَهُ وَاتَّبَعُوا أَمْرَ كُلِّ جَبَّارٍ عَنِيدٍ.
11:96	We also sent Moses, with Our signs and clear authority,	وَلَقَدْ أَرْسَلْنَا مُوسَى بِآيَاتِنَا وَسُلْطَانٍ مُبِينٍ
11:97	to Pharaoh and his supporters, but they followed Pharaoh's orders, and Pharaoh's orders were misguided.	إِلَى فِرْعَوْنَ وَمَلَئِهِ فَاتَّبَعُوا أَمْرَ فِرْعَوْنَ وَمَا أَمْرُ فِرْعَوْنَ بِرَشِيدٍ.

Only a short passage deals with Mūsā and the Pharaoh. Muhammad Asad mentioned in his exegesis "that it connects and amplifies the reference to the tribe of 'Ād (عاد) who, as stated in verse 59 of this sura, followed the command of every obstinate tyrant". Islamic scholars see in this passage the problem of leadership; the relationship between an evil leader and his followers. According to the Qur'an, the leader and the led are equally guilty. There is no escape by saying that one was blindly following orders of the leader. Muhammad Asad pointed out that "this is an indirect allusion to man's relative free will, i.e., his freedom of choice between right and wrong".

However, in certain situations, Islam also commands to follow a (bad) leader – as long as he fears and obeys Allah. This led to a discussion among Muslims during the Egyptian Revolution in 2011 when traditional Salafists refused to participate in the uprising against the dictatorship of Hosni Mubarak. See chapter 389.

141. Which sura is named after a weekday?

Answer: Sura 62 *Friday* (or: *The Day of Congregation*) - in Arabic: al-Juma (سُورة الجُمْعة).

On Friday, the congregational prayer at noon is obligatory for Muslim men. This sura, which was revealed to Muhammad in Medina, takes its title from the command that Muslim men have to obey the call to the Friday prayer at the mosque.

Muslim women may pray at home. Tāriq ibn Shihāb (طارق بن شهاب) narrated that the Prophet said: "The Friday prayer in congregation is a necessary duty for every Muslim, with four exceptions; a slave, a woman, a boy, and a sick person."[168]

142. In which sura does every verse end with the letter Dāl?

Answer: Sura 112 *Purity (of faith)*. In Arabic: al-'Ikhlās (سُورة الإخْلاص).

This sura was revealed in Mecca (مَكِّيّة) and has only four verses. It talks exclusively about the unity of Allah, the so-called Tawhīd (تَوْحيد), which means that God does not have a son, He does not give birth, and He does not have any equivalent. Let's check the verses:

---

168 ...عَن النَّبِيِّ قَالَ: "الْجُمُعَةُ حَقٌّ وَاجِبٌ عَلَى كُلِّ مُسْلِمٍ فِي جَمَاعَةٍ إِلَّا أَرْبَعَةً عَبْدٌ مَمْلُوكٌ أَوِ امْرَأَةٌ أَوْ صَبِيٌّ أَوْ مَريضٌ." Sunan 'Abī Dāwūd 1067 (1062)

112:1	Say, 'He is God the One,	قُلْ هُوَ اللَّهُ أَحَدٌ
112:2	God the eternal.	اللَّهُ الصَّمَدُ
112:3	He begot no one nor was He begotten.	وَلَمْ يَكُن لَّهُ كُفُوًا أَحَدٌ
112:4	No one is comparable to Him.	لَمْ يَلِدْ وَلَمْ يُولَدْ

The Arabic letter Dāl (د) is marked in grey to show that every verse ends with it. This is unique in the entire Qur'an. Furthermore, it is also the only sura which is not named after a word that appears in its verses. In other words, the term al-'Ikhlās does not occur in sura 112. The name was chosen in view of its meaning and subject. Muslims say that whoever understands this sura will be able to get rid of polytheism (شِرْك).

143. Which sura ends with the name of two prophets?

Answer: Sura 87 *The Most High* – in Arabic: al-'A'lā (سُورَة الْأَعْلَى).

Let's have a look at the ending:

| 87:18 | All this is in the earlier scriptures, | إِنَّ هَٰذَا لَفِي الصُّحُفِ الْأُولَىٰ |
| 87:19 | the scriptures of Abraham and Moses. | صُحُفِ إِبْرَاهِيمَ وَمُوسَىٰ. |

Abraham (إِبْرَاهِيم) and Moses (مُوسَى) in this context should perhaps be understood as examples of earlier prophetic revelations.

The interesting point in this sura is actually that Allah tells Muslims about the temporary nature of this world. The Qur'an uses a metaphor for this, i.e. the short life of a green pasture.

| 87:4 | who (Allah) brought out the green pasture | وَالَّذِي أَخْرَجَ الْمَرْعَىٰ |
| 87:5 | then made it dark debris. | فَجَعَلَهُ غُثَاءً أَحْوَىٰ. |

144. Which sura is named after a woman?

Answer: Sura 19 *Mary* – in Arabic: Maryam (سُورَة مَرْيَم).

In Islam, Mary is called Maryam bint 'Imrān (مَرْيَم بِنت عِمْران). She is believed to be the mother of 'Īsā (عِيسَى) – Jesus.

The sura was revealed in Mecca perhaps about seven or eight years before the Hijra (الْهِجْرة). The title is based on the story of Mary and Jesus, which (together with the story of Zechariah) fills about one-third of the entire sura.

'Imrān (عِمْران) is the Arabic word for the biblical figure Amram (Hebrew: עַמְרָם), the father of Moses and Aaron. Muslims see in him the ancestor of Mary and Jesus through his son Aaron. However, in Islam the Christian Joachim has been attributed the name 'Imrān (عِمْران) as well. Muslims distinguish between the two different individuals by adding the Arabic word for *family* (آل) if they refer to the father of Mary:

- 'Imrān (عِمْران), Amram, the ancestor of Mary
- 'Imrān (آل عِمْران), Joachim, the father of Mary

This sura was important for the Islamic history. The companions of Muhammad who migrated from Mecca to Abyssinia (Ethiopia) already knew this sura.

The Prophet's cousin Ja'far ibn 'Abī Tālib (جَعْفَر بن أَبِي طالِب) - who was also the elder brother of 'Alī ibn 'Abī Tālib (عَلِيّ بن أَبِي طالِب) - recited it before the Negus of Abyssinia (نَجاشِي) in order to explain how Islam treats Jesus. The word Negus was the epithet for the King of Abyssinia (لَقَبُ مَلِكِ الْحَبَشة).

145. Prophet Abraham was ordered to slaughter whom?

Answer: Most Islamic scholars say it was Ishmael – 'Ismā'īl (إِسْماعِيل).

The story of Abraham, who is called 'Ibrāhīm in Islam, is crucial if you want to understand the differences between Islam, Judaism and Christianity. Let us first look at the party they have in common:

- Abraham's wife was Sarah.
- Hāgar was their maiden or slave.
- 'Ismā'īl/Ishmael was Abraham's first son, whose mother was Hāgar.

- 'Ishāq/Isaac was Abraham's son from his wife Sarah. Ishmael and Isaac are thus half-brothers.

According to the Bible, Hāgar was the Egyptian handmaiden of Sarah. Sarah was already relatively old for becoming a mother, so she offered Hāgar to Abraham "to be his wife" (Genesis 16:1-3) – i.e. to make her pregnant. When Hāgar was pregnant, Sarah became jealous and mistreated her upon which she fled from Abraham's house (Genesis 16:4-6) into the desert.

An angel appeared instructing Hāgar to return and bear a child who "shall be a wild man; His hand shall be against every man, and every man's hand against him. And he shall dwell in the presence of all his brethren." (Genesis 16:12). Then she was told to call her son Ishmael. Fourteen years later, Sarah gave birth to Isaac – and the relationship between the two women escalated.

Also in Islam says, Hāgar was the Egyptian handmaiden of Abraham's first wife Sarah. After a revelation, Abraham married Hāgar because Sarah could not become pregnant. During a journey in southern Arabia, Hāgar gave birth to Ishmael. When they arrived at Mecca, Abraham was told by Allah to leave Hāgar and Ishmael back at this place – which would eventually become the holiest place on earth (for people who believe in Allah). Abraham fulfils Allah's command and leaves his wife and son behind.

Neither Sarah nor Hāgar is mentioned by name in the Qur'an. However, Hāgar is mentioned quite often in the Hadiths.

Muslims consider Ishmael ('Ismāʿīl) a prophet. Muslims believe that Muhammad is a descendant of Abraham through Ishmael.

Now let's get to the crucial difference:

Christians and Jews believe that Abraham had to sacrifice his son Isaac while most Muslims believe that Abraham was told to sacrifice his son Ishmael, though the Qur'an does not name the son. The Hadiths contradict each other about which son had to be sacrificed – some say Isaac, others Ishmael. So why do Muslims believe it was Ishmael? Let us have a look at some important points:

- Ishmael - as all three Abrahamitic religions agree - was older than Isaac. The first son is usually dearer to a parent than other children, so the command to sacrifice him is a more challenging test. So it must have been Ishmael according to Islam.

- Shortly after Allah told Abraham to sacrifice his son, Abraham was told of the coming of Isaac's birth. Therefore, it must have been Ishmael, because Isaac had not been born yet.

- Early Islamic scholars claimed that rhe reason Jews insisted it was Isaac to be sacrified, was because they were jealous as Ishmael was actually the ancestor of the Arabs, and also because the horns of the ram, which was sacrificed instead, were afterwards placed in the Ka'ba in Mecca. Legend has it that the ram's horns survived until 683, when the Ummayads destroyed the holy place.

Did Abraham kill Ishmael?

The Bible says that when Abraham was about to sacrifice his son Isaac, God sent an angel and Abraham found behind him a "ram caught in a thicket by his horns" which he sacrificed instead of his son. And what does the Qur'an say? The answer is found in sura 37 *Ranged in Rows* – in Arabic: al-Saffāt (الصَّفَّات):

37:102	When the boy was old enough to work with his father, Abraham said, 'My son, I have seen myself sacrificing you in a dream. What do you think?' He said, 'Father, do as you are commanded and, God willing, you will find me steadfast.'	فَلَمَّا بَلَغَ مَعَهُ السَّعْيَ قَالَ يَا بُنَيَّ إِنِّي أَرَى فِي الْمَنَامِ أَنِّي أَذْبَحُكَ فَانظُرْ مَاذَا تَرَى قَالَ يَا أَبَتِ افْعَلْ مَا تُؤْمَرُ سَتَجِدُنِي إِن شَاءَ اللَّهُ مِنَ الصَّابِرِينَ.
37:103	When they had both submitted to God, and he had laid his son down on the side of his face,	فَلَمَّا أَسْلَمَا وَتَلَّهُ لِلْجَبِينِ
37:104	We called out to him, 'Abraham,	وَنَادَيْنَاهُ أَن يَا إِبْرَاهِيمُ
37:105	you have fulfilled the dream.' This is how We reward those who do good -	قَدْ صَدَّقْتَ الرُّؤْيَا إِنَّا كَذَلِكَ نَجْزِي الْمُحْسِنِينَ
37:106	it was a test to prove (their true characters)	إِنَّ هَذَا لَهُوَ الْبَلَاءُ الْمُبِينُ

Abraham, as Islam tells it, was instrumental in cleansing the civilisation of idolatry in Arabia and Canaan. It was said that he wanted to slaughter his son from behind so that he would not see his face. Abraham passed the knife over the boy's throat but it did not cut him. The Islamic scholar Ibn Kathīr reported about this event that a sheet of copper was placed between the knife and the boy's throat.[169]

Allah told Abraham that he had fulfilled His command. In contrast to the Bible, there is no mention of an animal which replaced the son. Nevertheless, legend has it that there the ram's horn was placed in the Ka'ba. Once a year on 'Īd al-'Adhā (عيد الأضحى), which means *sacrifice feast*, Muslims around the world slaughter an animal to commemorate Abraham's will to sacrifice.

A remark on verse 37:103 and the verb **'aslama** (أَسْلَمَ) which is in the table above marked in grey. This verb is nowadays used if someone converts to Islam. It signifies that someone *surrendered himself to Allah* or *to Allah's will*. Since the Arabic dual form 'aslamā (أَسْلَمَا) is used in the respective verse, it probably means that both of them surrendered to Allah's will – or to what they thought to be His will.

146. When and why do Muslims slaughter animals annually?

Answer: On 'Īd al-'Adhā (عيد الأضحى) which is the tenth day of Dhū al-Hijja, the last month of the Hijri calendar during which the annual pilgrimage to Mecca takes place. This day is also known as the Day of Immolation.

For Muslims, it is the greatest day of the year. 'Abd Allah ibn Qurt (عَبْدُ الله بن قُرْط) narrated that the Prophet said: "The greatest day in Allah's sight is the Day of Sacrifice and next the Day of Resting [the succeeding day]."[170]

---

169 ...وَذَكَرَ السُّدِّيّ وَغَيْره أَنَّهُ أَمَرَّ السِّكِّين عَلَى رَقَبته فَلَمْ تَقْطَع شَيْئًا بَلْ حَالَ بَيْنهَا وَبَيْنه صَفْحَة مِنْ نُحَاس. Tafsīr Ibn Kathīr, 37:104.

170 ...النَّبِيُّ قَالَ: "إِنَّ أَعْظَم الأَيَّام عِنْدَ اللَّهِ تَبَارَكَ وَتَعَالَى يَوْمُ النَّحْرِ ثُمَّ يَوْمُ الْقَرِّ." Sunan 'Abī Dāwūd 1765 (1761)

The *Day of Immolation* has several names:

- **ʿĪd al-ʾAdhā** (عيد الأَضحَى) literally means *feast of blood sacrifice.*
- **Yawm al-Nahr** (يَوْم النَّحْر), which literally means *day of killing, slaughtering, butchering.*
- **al-ʿĪd al-Kabīr** (عيد الكَبِير), which means *the big/great feast.* It is used to distinguish this from the other important feast, the ʿĪd al-Fitr, which is sometimes called *the small feast.* Traditional Muslims, however, don't like these two terms.

The offer of a sacrifice combined with the special ʿĪd prayers honour the willingness of Abraham to sacrifice his son as an act of submission to Allah's command. The Arabic word for *sacrifice* is ʾUdhīya (أُضحِيّة).

In Islam, any animal of grazing livestock, ʾAnʿām (أنعام), can be sacrificed, camel, cow, sheep, or goat. The sacrifice is seen as an act of worship which should bring a Muslim closer to Allah. The tradition goes back to Muhammad himself.

ʾAnas ibn Mālik (أنَس بن مالك) narrated that the Prophet offered as sacrifice two horned rams, black and white in colour. He slaughtered them with his own hands and mentioned Allah's Name over them, said the Takbīr ["Allāhu ʾakbar!"], and put his foot on their sides.[171]

The same ʾAnas ibn Mālik narrated also that the Prophet said: "Whoever slaughtered the sacrifice before the prayer, he just slaughtered it for himself, and whoever slaughtered it after the prayer, he slaughtered it at the right time and followed the tradition of the Muslims."[172]

Remark: The day which follows the Day of Sacrifice is called Yawm al-Qarr (يَوْم القَرّ) and means *resting day.* On this day, the pilgrims stay in Minā (مِنى).

---

171 ...قَالَ ضَحَّى النَّبِيُّ بِكَبْشَيْنِ أَمْلَحَيْنِ أَقْرَنَيْنِ، ذَبَحَهُمَا بِيَدِهِ، وَسَمَّى وَكَبَّرَ وَوَضَعَ رِجْلَهُ عَلَى صِفَاحِهِمَا. Sahīh al-Bukhārī 5565.

172 ...قَالَ النَّبِيُّ: "مَنْ ذَبَحَ قَبْلَ الصَّلاةِ فَإِنَّمَا ذَبَحَ لِنَفْسِهِ، وَمَنْ ذَبَحَ بَعْدَ الصَّلاةِ فَقَدْ تَمَّ نُسُكُهُ، وَأَصَابَ سُنَّةَ الْمُسْلِمِينَ." Sahīh al-Bukhārī 5546.

147. At which mountain did Noah's ark set anchor?

Answer: Mount Judi. In Arabic: Jabal al-Jūdī (جَبَل الْجُودِيّ).

It is the location where the Ark came to rest after the Great Flood. The name of this mountain is found in sura 11 *Hūd* (هُود):

| 11:44 | Then it was said, 'Earth, swallow up your water, and sky, hold back', and the water subsided, the command was fulfilled. The Ark settled on Mount Judi, and it was said, 'Gone are those evildoing people!' | وَقِيلَ يَا أَرْضُ ابْلَعِي مَاءَكِ وَيَا سَمَاءُ أَقْلِعِي وَغِيضَ الْمَاءُ وَقُضِيَ الْأَمْرُ وَاسْتَوَتْ عَلَى الْجُودِيِّ وَقِيلَ بُعْدًا لِّلْقَوْمِ الظَّالِمِينَ |

In the sura, the word mount(ain) is not mentioned. Islamic scholars think that since the word was used with the definite article *al* (ال), the definite place could be understood implicitly.

But where is this mountain located? According to Islamic scholars, this mountain was known in ancient Syriac as Qardu. It is situated in eastern Anatolia near the border between Syria and Turkey in the region of Lake Van around 40 km (25 mi) north-east of the town *Jazīra(t) ibn ʿUmar* (جَزِيرَة ابن عُمَر). This place is now known as Cizre, a Kurdish town and district of the Şırnak Province in the south-eastern Anatolia Region of Turkey. The mountain range (in Turkish: Cudi) reaches as high as 2,089 m (6,854 ft).

Why do Christians believe that the Ark stranded at the much higher Mount Ararat (5,137 m; 16,854 ft)?

Mount Ararat is a volcanic massif on the border between Turkey and Armenia, known in Turkish as Ağrı Dağı. This information is found in Genesis 8:4 in which it is said that Noah's Ark landed on the "mountains of Ararat" (Hebrew: הָרֵי אֲרָרָט): "and on the seventeenth day of the seventh month the ark came to rest on the mountains of Ararat."

However, most Bible scholars think that Ararat is the Hebrew name (Urartu) for the region which is now Armenia. Ararat could be understood as a wider region and not as the mountain which is currently known as Ararat.

148. Did Noah's son join him in the Ark?

Answer: No.

The people at Noah's time worshipped idols. So Allah decided to charge Noah, who is called Nūh (نُوح) in Islam, with a mission. He should call the people to worship Allah alone and warn them of severe punishment if they did not.

Nevertheless, only a few followed Noah's message while most of his people did not worship Allah alone. Therefore, Noah asked Allah to get rid of them. This is told in sura 71 *Nūh* (سُورة نُوح):

71:26	And Noah said, 'Lord, do not leave any of the disbelievers on the earth	وَقَالَ نُوحٌ رَّبِّ لَا تَذَرْ عَلَى الْأَرْضِ مِنَ الْكَافِرِينَ دَيَّارًا

Allah ordered a huge flood and the sky sent heavy rains. The waves were as high as mountains. Noah was commanded to build an Ark. He took each kind of bird and animal with him; a male and female. But he had to leave his family behind. His wife had disobeyed Allah and was left behind. Noah asked his son to believe in Allah and to join him, but also his son disobeyed and said that he would be saved by going to the top of a mountain. But the waves overwhelmed Noah's son. This is all told in sura 11 *Hūd* (سُورة هُود):

11:40	When Our command came, and water gushed up out of the earth, We said, 'Place on board this Ark a pair of each species, and your own family - except those against whom the sentence has already been passed - and those who have believed', though only a few believed with him.	حَتَّى إِذَا جَاءَ أَمْرُنَا وَفَارَ التَّنُّورُ قُلْنَا احْمِلْ فِيهَا مِن كُلٍّ زَوْجَيْنِ اثْنَيْنِ وَأَهْلَكَ إِلَّا مَن سَبَقَ عَلَيْهِ الْقَوْلُ وَمَنْ آمَنَ وَمَا آمَنَ مَعَهُ إِلَّا قَلِيلٌ.
11:41	He said, 'Board the Ark. In the name of God it shall sail and anchor. My God is most forgiving and merciful.'	وَقَالَ ارْكَبُوا فِيهَا بِسْمِ اللَّهِ مَجْرَاهَا وَمُرْسَاهَا إِنَّ رَبِّي لَغَفُورٌ رَّحِيمٌ.
11:42	It sailed with them on waves like moun-tains, and Noah called out to his son, who stayed behind, 'Come aboard with us, my son, do not stay with the disbelievers.'	وَهِيَ تَجْرِي بِهِمْ فِي مَوْجٍ كَالْجِبَالِ وَنَادَى نُوحٌ ابْنَهُ وَكَانَ فِي مَعْزِلٍ يَا بُنَيَّ ارْكَب مَّعَنَا وَلَا تَكُن مَّعَ الْكَافِرِينَ.

| 11:43 | But he replied, 'I will seek refuge on a mountain to save me from the water.' Noah said, 'Today there is no refuge from God's command, except for those on whom He has mercy.' The waves cut them off from each other and he was among the drowned. | قَالَ سَآوِي إِلَىٰ جَبَلٍ يَعْصِمُنِي مِنَ الْمَاءِ قَالَ لَا عَاصِمَ الْيَوْمَ مِنْ أَمْرِ اللَّهِ إِلَّا مَن رَّحِمَ وَحَالَ بَيْنَهُمَا الْمَوْجُ فَكَانَ مِنَ الْمُغْرَقِينَ. |

149. To whom was prophet Sālih sent?

Answer: To the Thamūd (ثَمُود), an ancient people living in a land between Arabia and Syria.

Sālih is mentioned nine times in the Qur'an, but he is not particularly known to Christians or Jews.

Historical references to the Thamūd indicate that they were probably the greatest and most powerful Arab tribe of their time. They were known from the 1st millennium BC to near the time of Muhammad. Thamūd people are believed to have been the successors to the ancient tribe of 'Ād (عاد). For this reason the Thamūd people are often referred to as *the Second 'Ād* in pre-Islamic poetry.

Sālih is believed to have been the second prophet, after Hūd, sent to the Arabs. Sālih's message to the tribe of Thamūd is identical to that of Solomon to the Queen of Sheba. The reason why Allah sent Sālih to Thamūd is found in sura 27 *The Ants* – al-Naml (سُورة النَّمل):

| 27:45 | To the people of Thamūd We sent their brother, Sālih, saying, 'Worship God alone', but they split into two rival factions. | وَلَقَدْ أَرْسَلْنَا إِلَىٰ ثَمُودَ أَخَاهُمْ صَالِحًا أَنِ اعْبُدُوا اللَّهَ فَإِذَا هُمْ فَرِيقَانِ يَخْتَصِمُونَ |

As a sign of prophecy, Allah gave Sālih (صالح) a she-camel. This is mentioned in sura 7 *The Heights* – in Arabic: al-'A'rāf (سُورة الأَعْراف):

| 7:73 | To the people of Thamūd We sent their brother, Sālih. He said, 'My people, serve God: you have no god other than Him. A clear sign has come to you now from your | وَإِلَىٰ ثَمُودَ أَخَاهُمْ صَالِحًا قَالَ يَا قَوْمِ اعْبُدُوا اللَّهَ مَا لَكُم مِّنْ إِلَٰهٍ غَيْرُهُ قَدْ جَاءَتْكُم بَيِّنَةٌ مِّن رَّبِّكُمْ |

	Lord: this is God's she-camel - a sign for you - so let her graze in God's land and do not harm her in any way, or you will be struck by a painful torment.	هَٰذِهِ نَاقَةُ اللَّهِ لَكُمْ آيَةً فَذَرُوهَا تَأْكُلْ فِي أَرْضِ اللَّهِ وَلَا تَمَسُّوهَا بِسُوءٍ فَيَأْخُذَكُمْ عَذَابٌ أَلِيمٌ.

Pasture was considered a gift of Allah, and the camel would be a trial to see if the greedy would let the camel graze there. However, the camel was slaughtered. This is indicated in sura 11 Hūd (هُود سُورَة):

11:66	this warning will not prove false.' And so, when Our command was fulfilled, by Our mercy We saved Sālih and his fellow believers from the disgrace of that day. [Prophet], it is your Lord who is the Strong, the Mighty One.	فَلَمَّا جَاءَ أَمْرُنَا نَجَّيْنَا صَالِحًا وَالَّذِينَ آمَنُوا مَعَهُ بِرَحْمَةٍ مِّنَّا وَمِنْ خِزْيِ يَوْمِئِذٍ إِنَّ رَبَّكَ هُوَ الْقَوِيُّ الْعَزِيزُ.
11:67	The blast struck the evildoers and they lay dead in their homes,	وَأَخَذَ الَّذِينَ ظَلَمُوا الصَّيْحَةُ فَأَصْبَحُوا فِي دِيَارِهِمْ جَاثِمِينَ
11:68	as though they had never lived and flourished there. Yes, the Thamūd denied their Lord – so away with the Thamūd!	كَأَن لَّمْ يَغْنَوْا فِيهَا أَلَا إِنَّ ثَمُودَ كَفَرُوا رَبَّهُمْ أَلَا بُعْدًا لِّثَمُودَ

Eventually, a terrible earthquake came by night on the third day, preceded by a mighty blast in the sky. It is possible that an earthquake accompanied by a volcanic eruption destroyed the historical dwellings of the Thamūd tribe. In the northern Hijāz there are black lavafields, so-called Harra (الْحَرَّة), which are occasionally mentioned in the Hadiths.

Muhammad Asad mentioned in his exegesis that "there is some historical evidence of the name and the people of Thamūd. Thus, the inscription of the Assyrian King Sargon of the year 715 BC mentions the Thamūd among the people of eastern and central Arabia subjected by the Assyrians."

At the time of which the Qur'an speaks, the Thamūd were perhaps settled in the northernmost Hijāz. The Thamūd carved out dwellings in the cliffs west of al-Hijr, in northern Hijāz. These rock-dwellings are called *The Towns of Sālih*.

150. Which sura talks about an insect?

Answer: Sura 27 *The Ants* – in Arabic: al-Naml (سُورة النَّمْل).

The insect is the ant, al-Naml (النَّمْل), from which the sura received its name. The ants are mentioned in the story of Solomon (سُلَيْمان). This sura was revealed to Muhammad in Mecca:

27:18	and when they came to the Valley of the Ants, one ant said, 'Ants! Go into your homes, in case Solomon and his hosts unwittingly crush you.'	حَتَّى إِذَا أَتَوْا عَلَى وَادِ النَّمْل قَالَتْ نَمْلَةٌ يَا أَيُّهَا النَّمْلُ ادْخُلُوا مَسَاكِنَكُمْ لَا يَحْطِمَنَّكُمْ سُلَيْمَانُ وَجُنُودُهُ وَهُمْ لَا يَشْعُرُونَ.
27:19	Solomon smiled broadly at her words and said, 'Lord, inspire me to be thankful for the blessings You have granted me and my parents, and to do good deeds that please You; admit me by Your grace into the ranks of Your righteous servants.'	فَتَبَسَّمَ ضَاحِكًا مِّن قَوْلِهَا وَقَالَ رَبِّ أَوْزِعْنِي أَنْ أَشْكُرَ نِعْمَتَكَ الَّتِي أَنْعَمْتَ عَلَيَّ وَعَلَى وَالِدَيَّ وَأَنْ أَعْمَلَ صَالِحًا تَرْضَاهُ وَأَدْخِلْنِي بِرَحْمَتِكَ فِي عِبَادِكَ الصَّالِحِينَ.

Note: Because of this story, ants have a special place in Islam. 'Abd Allah ibn 'Abbās (عَبْد الله بن عَبَّاس) narrated that the Prophet prohibited to kill four creatures: ants, bees, hoopoes and sparrow-hawks.[173]

151. Which bird can speak in the Qur'an?

Answer: The hoopoe (*Upupa epops*). In Arabic: al-Hudhud (الْهُدْهُد).

The hoopoe is a medium-sized, colourful bird with a distinctive crown of feathers. The bird is found across Afro-Eurasia. It probably received its name due to its call which sounds like "oop-oop-oop".

Another explanation for his English and scientific name says that its name is derived from the French name for the bird, *Huppée*, which means *crested*. Let's have a look at the story in the Qur'an, sura 27 *The Ants* – in Arabic: al-Naml (سُورة النَّمْل):

---

173 ...قَالَ إِنَّ النَّبِيَّ نَهَى عَنْ قَتْلِ أَرْبَعٍ مِنَ الدَّوَابِّ النَّمْلَةُ وَالنَّحْلَةُ وَالْهُدْهُدُ وَالصُّرَدُ. Sunan 'Abī Dāwūd 5267 (5247)

27:20	Solomon inspected the birds and said, "Why do I not see the hoopoe? Is he absent?	وَتَفَقَّدَ الطَّيْرَ فَقَالَ مَا لِيَ لَا أَرَى الْهُدْهُدَ أَمْ كَانَ مِنَ الْغَائِبِينَ؟
27:21	I will punish him severely, or kill him, unless he brings me a convincing excuse for his absence."	لَأُعَذِّبَنَّهُ عَذَابًا شَدِيدًا أَوْ لَأَذْبَحَنَّهُ أَوْ لَيَأْتِيَنِّي بِسُلْطَانٍ مُّبِينٍ.
27:22	But the hoopoe did not stay away long: he came and said, "I have learned something you did not know: I come to you from Sheba with firm news."	فَمَكَثَ غَيْرَ بَعِيدٍ فَقَالَ أَحَطتُ بِمَا لَمْ تُحِطْ بِهِ وَجِئْتُكَ مِن سَبَإٍ بِنَبَإٍ يَقِينٍ.

The information brought by the Hoopoe is the first link between the kingdoms of Sheba (سَبَإ) and Solomon (سُلَيْمان). The information revealed that the Sabaeans were worshipping the sun besides Allah.

For this reason Allah sends Solomon to the people of Sheba: to abandon this blasphemy and to accept Allah's law and unity.

152. Which prophet celebrated with mountains and birds?

Answer: David – in Arabic: Dāwūd (دَاوُود).

Muslims read in sura 21 *The Prophets* - in Arabic: al-'Anbiyā' (سُورة الْأَنْبِيَاء) - that prophet David celebrated with mountains and birds. Muhammad learnt this sura during his time in Mecca. It received its name from a list of prophets which were mentioned therein:

21:79	...and made Solomon understand the case [better], though We gave sound judgement and knowledge to both of them. We made the mountains and the birds celebrate Our praises with David - We did all these things -	...فَفَهَّمْنَاهَا سُلَيْمَانَ وَكُلًّا آتَيْنَا حُكْمًا وَعِلْمًا وَسَخَّرْنَا مَعَ دَاوُودَ الْجِبَالَ يُسَبِّحْنَ وَالطَّيْرَ وَكُنَّا فَاعِلِينَ

But why did they celebrate? The metaphorical theme - inhuman and inanimate objects praising Allah - is encountered several times in the Qur'an. Here are two of them:

17:44	The seven heavens and the earth and every-one in them glorify Him. There is not a single thing that does not celebrate His praise, though you do not understand their praise: He is most forbearing, most forgiving.	تُسَبِّحُ لَهُ السَّمَاوَاتُ السَّبْعُ وَالْأَرْضُ وَمَن فِيهِنَّ وَإِن مِّن شَيْءٍ إِلَّا يُسَبِّحُ بِحَمْدِهِ وَلَكِن لَّا تَفْقَهُونَ تَسْبِيحَهُمْ إِنَّهُ كَانَ حَلِيمًا غَفُورًا
34:10	We graced David with Our favour. We said, 'You mountains, echo God's praises together with him, and you birds, too.' We softened iron for him,	وَلَقَدْ آتَيْنَا دَاوُودَ مِنَّا فَضْلًا يَا جِبَالُ أَوِّبِي مَعَهُ وَالطَّيْرَ وَأَلَنَّا لَهُ الْحَدِيدَ

Let us look at the story of David and his son Solomon who is called Sulaymān (سُلَيْمَان) in Arabic. Neither the Qur'an nor the Hadiths tell his story, however, there is a legend:

A flock of sheep strayed into a neighbouring field and destroyed the crop of a man. David decided that the owner of the sheep should give the whole flock as compensation to the man who lost his crop – as the value of the sheep equalled the amount of damage.

David's son, Solomon, criticised his father's judgement. His point was that the sheep represented the entire capital of their owner whereas the damage done to the field was of a transitory nature as in the following year there would be another harvest. Solomon suggested that the owner of the field should have the temporary possession of the sheep and could use their products such as their milk, wool, and new-born lambs. The owner of the sheep on the other hand should tend the damaged field until it was restored to its former productivity. David agreed – and Allah, in the words of the Qur'an, "witnessed their judgement":

21:78	And remember David and Solomon, when they gave judgement regarding the field into which sheep strayed by night and grazed. We witnessed their judgement.	وَدَاوُودَ وَسُلَيْمَانَ إِذْ يَحْكُمَانِ فِي الْحَرْثِ إِذْ نَفَشَتْ فِيهِ غَنَمُ الْقَوْمِ وَكُنَّا لِحُكْمِهِمْ شَاهِدِينَ.

Excursus: What is Solomon's story in the Bible about?

The most famous is *The Judgement of Solomon* (Kings 3:16-28): Two women claiming to be the mother of the same child. Solomon easily cut through the dispute by commanding the child to be cut in half and shared between the two.

One woman promptly gave up her claim – which showed that she would rather give up the child than see it killed. Solomon declared the woman, who showed compassion, to be the true mother – and entitled to the whole child.

From this story, several sayings and proverbs were derived indicating a wise but also stunning verdict: For example *Salomonisches Urteil* in German. In English, you might hear *splitting the baby* for describing the action of making an unreasonable judgement in an attempt to flush out the truth.

However, David (دَاوُودَ) is more famous for another story, i.e. his fight against **Goliath**. Goliath - in Arabic: Jālūt (جَالُوت) - appears in sura 2 *The Cow* - in Arabic: al-Baqara (سُورة الْبَقَرة). Goliath's mention in the Qur'an is brief, and it is encountered in the story of David and Saul's battle against the Philistines:

2:250	And when they met Goliath and his warriors, they said, 'Our Lord, pour patience on us, make us stand firm, and help us against the disbelievers',	وَلَمَّا بَرَزُوا لِجَالُوتَ وَجُنُودِهِ قَالُوا رَبَّنَا أَفْرِغْ عَلَيْنَا صَبْرًا وَثَبِّتْ أَقْدَامَنَا وَانصُرْنَا عَلَى الْقَوْمِ الْكَافِرِينَ
2:251	and so with God's permission they defeated them. David killed Goliath, and God gave him sovereignty and wisdom and taught him what He pleased. If God did not drive some back by means of others the earth would be completely corrupt, but God is bountiful to all.	فَهَزَمُوهُم بِإِذْنِ اللَّهِ وَقَتَلَ دَاوُودُ جَالُوتَ وَآتَاهُ اللَّهُ الْمُلْكَ وَالْحِكْمَةَ وَعَلَّمَهُ مِمَّا يَشَاءُ وَلَوْلَا دَفْعُ اللَّهِ النَّاسَ بَعْضَهُم بِبَعْضٍ لَفَسَدَتِ الْأَرْضُ وَلَكِنَّ اللَّهَ ذُو فَضْلٍ عَلَى الْعَالَمِينَ.

Scholars have tried to trace Goliath's origins to the Amalekites, in Arabic: al-ʿAmālīq (الْعَمالِيق) which means huge, gigantic, super.

In the Old Testament, the Amalekites were a nomadic people who inhabited the Sinai Peninsula and parts of the Negev Desert. They are considered to be Amalek's (Hebrew: עֲמָלֵק) descendants through the genealogy of Esau (Hebrew: עֵשָׂו) who, according to the Bible, is the elder son of Isaac. The Amalekites were the first of the nations to launch an attack, near Mount Sinai, on the Israelites after their Exodus, in which they were defeated. God thus decreed the final extinction for the Amalekites (Num. 24:20; Exod. 17:8-16; Deut. 25:17-19). Later on, the term Amalekites was sometimes used for *enemies of Israel.*

153. What is a Kāfir?

Answer: An *unbeliever* or *infidel.*

The Arabic term Kāfir (كافِر) is probably the most controversial and dangerous word in Islam. It is the opposite of *believer* – in Arabic: Mu'min (مُؤْمِن). A sura (109) is even named *The Disbelievers* – in Arabic: al-Kāfirūn (سُورة الْكافِرُون).

The so-called "disbelievers" are the enemies of the Muslims and they will be punished heavily by Allah. Sadly enough, some Muslims think that they are obliged to carry out Allah's work in this life. Most victims are Christians living in Islamic countries, minorities like the Yazīdi people in Iraq and Syria, but also Shia Muslims living in Sunni dominated countries. They are all denounced as *unbelievers.*

The Arabic root k-f-r (كَفَر) is tricky. It helps us to get closer to the Islamic concept of *disbelieve.* Of this root, 17 forms occur 510 (!) times in the Qur'an.

The root has several meanings and most of them have to do with: *to veil* or *to cover.* It is an old Semitic root that is found in Hebrew as well, some say also in Nabataean.

Let us look at some examples of how the root is used:

He covered the sown seed with earth.	كَفَرَ الْبَذْرَ الْمَبْذُورَ
The clouds covered the sky.	كَفَرَ السُّحابُ السَّماءَ
A dark night. ("lail kāfir" is a classical Arabic term.)	لَيْل كافِ
Mukaffar is the passive participle of كَفَّر and used to describe a *bird covered with feathers.*	مُكَفَّر

Since its original meaning is *to cover*, the term Kāfir (كافِر), in pre-Islamic times, was also used to denote a *sower* or a *tiller of the ground* – because he covers the seed with earth.

This is important when Muslims want to fully understand the Qur'an. Sadly enough, many Muslims, also native Arabic speakers, think that the word Kāfir only means *unbeliever*, and therefore could misinterpret several verses in the Qur'an.

Let's have a look at a verse of sura 57 *The Iron* - in Arabic: al-Hadīd (سُورة الْحَدِيد) - in which Kāfir does not mean *unbeliever*, but *tiller/ sower*:

| 57:20 | Bear in mind that the present life is just a game, a diversion, an attraction, a cause of boasting among you, of rivalry in wealth and children. It is like plants that spring up after the rain: their growth at first delights the sowers, but then you see them wither away, turn yellow, and become stubble. There is terrible punishment in the next life as well as forgiveness and approval from God; the life of this world is only an illusory pleasure. | اعْلَمُوا أَنَّمَا الْحَيَاةُ الدُّنْيَا لَعِبٌ وَلَهْوٌ وَزِينَةٌ وَتَفَاخُرٌ بَيْنَكُمْ وَتَكَاثُرٌ فِي الْأَمْوَالِ وَالْأَوْلَادِ كَمَثَلِ غَيْثٍ أَعْجَبَ الْكُفَّارَ نَبَاتُهُ ثُمَّ يَهِيجُ فَتَرَاهُ مُصْفَرًّا ثُمَّ يَكُونُ حُطَامًا وَفِي الْآخِرَةِ عَذَابٌ شَدِيدٌ وَمَغْفِرَةٌ مِّنَ اللَّهِ وَرِضْوَانٌ وَمَا الْحَيَاةُ الدُّنْيَا إِلَّا مَتَاعُ الْغُرُورِ. |

The root can also express *to be ungrateful*, that someone is *ungrateful for the benefits which he received*. This too is found in the Qur'an. Let's look at sura 16 *The Bee* – in Arabic: al-Nahl (سُورة النَّحْل):

| 16:72 | And it is God who has given you spouses from among yourselves and through them He has given you children and grandchildren and provided you with good things. How can they believe in falsehood and deny God's blessings? | وَاللَّهُ جَعَلَ لَكُم مِّنْ أَنفُسِكُمْ أَزْوَاجًا وَجَعَلَ لَكُم مِّنْ أَزْوَاجِكُم بَنِينَ وَحَفَدَةً وَرَزَقَكُم مِّنَ الطَّيِّبَاتِ أَفَبِالْبَاطِلِ يُؤْمِنُونَ وَبِنِعْمَتِ اللَّهِ هُمْ يَكْفُرُونَ |

So how can *to cover* also mean *to disbelieve*?

The sentence *he disbelieved in Allah* (كَفَرَ بِاللَّهِ) can be interpreted as follows: Someone disbelieves because *he conceals* or *covers* the truth of Allah. Even in the Qur'an, a metaphorical meaning of *to cover* in the sense of *to disbelieve* is found.

It is a verse in sura 5 *The Feast/The Table Spread* - in Arabic: *al-Māʾida* (سُورة الْمائدة) - which talks about the Christians. Christians belong to the *People of the Book* - in Arabic: ʾAhl al-Kitāb (أَهْل الْكِتاب). Muslims use this term for Jews and Christians. From an Islamic perspective, Christians literally *cover* the knowledge that a prophet (i.e. Muhammad) will come after Jesus. Let's look at the verse:

5:17	Those who say, 'God is the Messiah, the son of Mary', are defying the truth (= have disbelieved).	لَّقَدْ كَفَرَ الَّذِينَ قَالُوا إِنَّ اللَّهَ هُوَ الْمَسِيحُ ابْنُ مَرْيَمَ

Some more remarks:

- The Arabic word Kafr (كَفْر) can also mean *village*. It is a Syrian word and mostly used in Syria and Egypt.
- The English word *Kaffir* has Arabic roots. Kaffir (Kaffer in Afrikaans) is an insulting term for a black African used in South Africa. The history of this word most probably goes back to the Islamic conquest of East Africa. Some native peoples there believed in several gods, and therefore the Muslims called them Kāfir. English missionaries picked it up to denounce the Bantu people in South Africa. This happened possibly in the middle of the 18th century. Later, the expression was used in English and Dutch (Afrikaans) for *South African blacks*. It is a racist term.

154. Do Kuffār and Kāfirūn mean the same?

Answer: Yes.

However, most Islamic preachers prefer Kuffār (كُفّار) over Kāfirūn (كافِرُون) in their speeches because the doubling of the consonant *f*, especially when combined with foreign languages - English or German - gives the word a special accentuation.

Let's look at the various forms: First of all, a Kāfir (كافِر) is a male person who denies or does not acknowledge the favours or benefits of Allah. Kāfira (كافِرة) is the female form. Both forms are the active participle of the verb kafara (كَفَر).

There are three possibilities to form the plural of Kāfir (كافِر):

1. Masculine plural: Kāfirūn (كافِرُون) or Kuffār (كُفّار)
2. Feminine plural: Kawāfir (كَوافِر) or Kāfirāt (كافِرات)
3. Masculine OR feminine plural (same form!): Kafara (كَفَرة)

According to some scholars, the first two plural forms describe a *disbeliever* or *someone who denies Allah* – whereas the last form (3) is used in the sense of being *ungrateful* to Allah.

There are forms which look almost the same and have only one different vowel – but have a slightly different, mostly **intensifying** meaning. In Arabic grammar, the following two words are called an exaggerated form (صِيغة مُبالَغة):

A **Kafūr** (كَفُور) is an intensive epithet which expresses *very ungrateful* or *unthankful to Allah*. It is found, for example, in a verse of sura 11 *Hūd* (سُورة هُود):

11:9	How desperate and ungrateful man becomes when We let him taste Our mercy and then withhold it!	وَلَئِنْ أَذَقْنَا الْإِنسَانَ مِنَّا رَحْمَةً ثُمَّ نَزَعْنَاهَا مِنْهُ إِنَّهُ لَيَئُوسٌ كَفُورٌ .

Note that Kafūr (كَفُور) can be feminine or masculine because they have the same form in both genders. Its plural form is Kufur (كُفُر) for both masculine and feminine.

The word **Kaffār** (كَفّار) - notice the vowel *a* at the beginning - has a more intensive signification than Kafūr (كَفُور) and expresses *habitually ungrateful*. It is used in sura 14 *'Ibrāhīm* (سُورة إِبْراهِيم):

14:34	and given you some of everything you asked Him for. If you tried to count God's favours you could never calculate them: man is truly unjust and ungrateful (= most unjust and ungrateful).	وَآتَاكُم مِّن كُلِّ مَا سَأَلْتُمُوهُ وَإِن تَعُدُّوا نِعْمَتَ اللَّهِ لَا تُحْصُوهَا إِنَّ الْإِنسَانَ لَظَلُومٌ كَفّارٌ .

155. How many types of disbelieve are there in Islam?

Answer: Numerous.

Disbelieve in Islam - Kufr (كُفْر) - is the denial or unacceptance of the oneness of Allah, of his prophets or of Allah's law. Basically there are two main types:

- **Kufr Ibtidā'** (كُفْر إِبْتِداء). This applies to people who are <u>non-Muslims;</u> a Muslim should strive that Islam reaches them. The word Ibtidā' means *beginning, start*.

- **Kufr Ridda** (كُفْر رِدّة) or Kufr Irtidād (كُفْر إِرْتِداد). This applies to a <u>Muslim</u> who denies a principle of Islam (رُكْن) or does not accept Islamic law. From this root, the word Murtadd (مُرْتَدّ) is derived which means *ex-Muslim, apostate*.

Let's dig deeper now and identify the nuances of Kufr (كُفْر) in Islam:

1. **Kufr 'Inkār** (كُفْر إِنْكار). This describes the denial of Allah with the heart and the tongue despite having knowledge of what is told about Allah. 'Inkār (إِنْكار) means *disavowal, refusal*.

2. **Kufr Juhūd** (كُفْر جُحُود). The heart acknowledges Allah but the tongue has not confessed. The word Juhūd (جُحُود) means *denial, rejection*.

3. **Kufr al-Mu'ānada** (كُفْر الْمُعانَدة). The person acknowledges Allah with the heart and confesses with the tongue, but refuses to accept Islam's message. Mu'ānada literally means: *resistance, stubbornness*.

4. **Kufr al-Nifāq** (كُفْر النِّفاق). This is the confession with the tongue, but with disbelief in the heart. Nifāq (نِفاق) means *hypocrisy*. Therefore, a Munāfiq (مُنافِق) is someone who pretends to be a Muslim, but isn't. This is considered to be the <u>worst category</u>.

Watch out: Sometimes, people mix up the word **Kāfir** (كافِر) - *unbeliever* - and **Mushrik** (مُشرِك) which means *polytheist*. The Kāfir is the one who denies and conceals Islam (Muslims say: the truth) or rejects it. However, a Mushrik (مُشرِك) may also believe in Allah but worships other deities.

The basic meaning of the Arabic word Kufr (كُفْر) is *concealment*. On the other hand, Shirk (شِرْك) means *devoting worship to anyone or anything other than Allah*.

156. What is a Mulhid?

Answer: An *atheist*; an *apostate*. An *impugner of religion*.

The Arabic word Mulhid (مُلْحِد) comes from the root l-h-d (ل-ح-د). It is the active participle of the Arabic IV-verb 'alhada (أَلْحَدَ). Both - the root and the derived IV-verb - mean *to dig a grave, to dig a niche in an older tomb and bury the dead in it*; *to deviate from the right course, to apostatise*; *to become a heretic*. But it can also mean *to allude to, to refer to; to insinuate*.

According to Edward Lane, the term al-Mulhidūn (الْمُلْحِدُون), which is the masculine plural of Mulhid, has been applied in particular to the Bátinees, al-Bātinīya (الْبَاطِنِيّة) in Arabic. Al-Batiniya is the name of a school of thought in Islam. Followers of this doctrine assert that the Qur'an has an outward (ظاهِر) and an inward sense (باطِن). It is especially common in Shia sects. On the other hand, Sunni Muslims have used the term al-Bātinīya pejoratively throughout history, especially for the followers of the Ismā'īlī Shia branches.

Remark: The word Mulhid – which is the active participle of the (present tense) verb yulhid (يُلْحِد) - does not appear in the Qur'an. However, the verb itself, yulhid, is found six times in total. But you have to be careful as the meaning is mostly *to allude to; to refer to*. Let's have a look at a verse of sura 16 *The Bee* – in Arabic: al-Nahl (سُورة النَّحْل):

16:103	We know very well that they say, 'It is a man who teaches him', but the language of the person they allude to is foreign, while this revelation is in clear Arabic.	وَلَقَدْ نَعْلَمُ أَنَّهُمْ يَقُولُونَ إِنَّمَا يُعَلِّمُهُ بَشَرٌ لِّسَانُ الَّذِي يُلْحِدُونَ إِلَيْهِ أَعْجَمِيٌّ وَهَذَا لِسَانٌ عَرَبِيٌّ مُّبِينٌ.

An excursus: Do you know how to say "secular" in Arabic? It is the word 'ilmānī (عِلْمانِيّ). Pronunciation is crucial here because the word for *German* in Arabic is 'almānī (أَلْمانِيّ).

157. What is an 'Ilj?

Answer: A certain kind of *unbeliever.*

The word 'Ilj (عِلْج) - plural: 'ulūj (عُلُوج) - is an old word which was used in the beginning of Islam's expansion. It means a *Persian unbeliever.*

'Ilj, in its original meaning, describes *a strong or sturdy, big man; a strong and big* or *bulky unbeliever; a fat and strong wild ass; an ugly donkey.* According to old, classical dictionaries, the Arabs called the Persian "unbelievers" (non-Muslims) as if that was due to the thickness, bigness, or coarseness of their build. Nowadays it is very rarely used, but when it is, it could mean *infidel; uncouth fellow; lout.*

The Arabs and Persians share a difficult history, not only because most people in Iran nowadays are Shia Muslims while most Arabs are Sunni. Persians, who were at one point ruling a big part of the world and who were famous for their poetry and arts, always have looked down on the Bedouins of Arabia.

Remark: To understand the relationship between the Persians and the Arabs (from the Arabic point of view), it helps to have a look at the Arabic expressions that were and are still used to describe Persia.

Persians were called 'Ajam (عَجَم), a collective noun which denotes *barbarians, non-Arabs, those who don't speak Arabic,* or *other foreigners.* Words that are not of Arabic origin are called 'Ajamī (عَجَمِي) in Arabic. The Arabic X-verb ista'jama (اسْتَعْجَم) means *to become un-Arabic,* also *to be unable to speak.* The word 'A'jam (أَعْجَم) was used to express that *someone is speaking incorrect Arabic.* It can also mean *dumb, speechless, barbarian,* or simply *non-Arab* or *foreigner.*

158. In which sura does Allah threaten the "unbelievers" by: "Woe, on that Day, to those who denied the truth!"?

Answer: In sura 77 *Winds Sent Forth (The Emissaries)* – in Arabic: al-Mursalāt (سُورة الْمُرْسَلات).

This sura was probably revealed in the fourth year of Muhammad's mission; hence in Mecca. The sura has 50 verses and describes the

Day of Judgement, i.e. its inevitability, arguments for its coming. The expression *"Woe, on that Day, to those who denied the truth!"* (وَيْلٌ يَوْمَئِذٍ لِّلْمُكَذِّبِينَ) is repeated **10 (!) times** in this sura.

The tone of this warning and its many repetitions is meant to scare the reader – in particular those who do not believe in the Day of Judgement.

159. Who are the Sabians?

Answer: The Sabians - in Arabic: Sābi'ūn (الصَّابِئون) – were members of a religious pre-Islamic sect.

The religious sect itself is called al-Sābi'a (مَذْهَب الصَّابِئَة); a single member is Sābi' (صابِئ). The masculine plural is al-Sābi'ūn (الصَّابِئون) or, if used in a different (grammatical) inflection, Sābi'īn (الصَّابِئِين).

It is not entirely clear what the Qur'an meant by the Sabians. There were various religious sects in parts of Arabia and nearby countries. Muhammad Asad suggested that "the Sabians seem to be a monotheistic religious group, intermediate between Judaism and Christianity". He argued that their name was probably derived from the Aramaic verb tseeba which means: *he immersed himself (in water)*.

This would indicate that they were followers of John the Baptist, in which case they could be identified with the Madaean, a community in Iraq which still exists to this day.

However, the name Sabians was applied to other sects and religions as well, and some of these might have been referring to the same people. There is just not enough information available. Let's have a look at some of the hypotheses.

The name Sabians was possibly referring to:

- star-worshipping people living in Iraq. Al-Baydāwī (الْبَيْضاوِئ), a Muslim scholar who lived in the 13th century, said that some Sabians declared that they were worshippers of angels.

- a faith that was a mixture of Judaism, Christianity, and Zoroastrianism. They are variously described as followers of the religion of Noah. Some said that they are thus called the S*on of Lāmak* (or لامَك) because Lāmak is Noah's father. This sect is also called the religion of Sābi, the son of Sheyt (Seth) who was the third son of Adam and Eve. Sabis view him as a righteous son, a gift for Adam after the death of Abel. Although Seth is not mentioned in the Qur'an, Islam regards him as a prophet, like his father, because he continued teaching Allah's message after Adam had died.

- a people who lived near Mosul (الْمَوصِل) in present-day Iraq and believed in one God, but didn't possess a law or a divine book.

- a people who lived somewhere in Iraq. They had a special system of praying and fasting and believed in the prophets of God. Some say they possessed revealed scripture. Some say that their religion resembled Christianity – except that they prayed towards the place whence blows southerly wind or the place from where blows the northerly wind at midday.

Watch out and don't get confused:

The word **Sabians** (الصَّابِئون) should not be confused with the **Sabaeans** (قَوْم سَبَأ) who too are mentioned in the Qur'an. The Sabaeans are an ancient Semitic people who ruled Saba in southwestern Arabia from the 7th to the 5th century BC. Their capital was Ma'rib (مَأرِب) in northeastern Yemen. Sheba was a queen from Saba and she is also mentioned in the Bible as a visitor of Salomo. In Assyrian texts of the 8th/7th century BC, the Sabaeans delivered incense and spices, as is also mentioned in the Bible.

In several translations of the Qur'an, both words, Sabians and Sabaeans, are unfortunately mixed up. So let's see them both in verses:

| 2:62 | The [Muslim] believers, the Jews, the Christians and the Sabians – all those who believe in God and the Last Day and do good - will have their rewards with their Lord. fear for them, nor will they grieve. | إِنَّ الَّذِينَ آمَنُوا وَالَّذِينَ هَادُوا وَالنَّصَارَىٰ وَالصَّابِئِينَ مَنْ آمَنَ بِاللَّهِ وَالْيَوْمِ الْآخِرِ وَعَمِلَ صَالِحًا فَلَهُمْ أَجْرُهُمْ عِندَ رَبِّهِمْ وَلَا خَوْفٌ عَلَيْهِمْ وَلَا هُمْ يَحْزَنُونَ |

| 34:15 | There was a sign for the people of Sheba (the tribe of Saba'), too, in their dwelling place: two gardens, one on the right, one on the left: 'Eat from what your Lord has provided for you and give Him thanks, for your land is good, and your Lord most forgiving.' | لَقَدْ كَانَ لِسَبَإٍ فِي مَسْكَنِهِمْ آيَةٌ جَنَّتَانِ عَن يَمِينٍ وَشِمَالٍ كُلُوا مِن رِّزْقِ رَبِّكُمْ وَاشْكُرُوا لَهُ بَلْدَةٌ طَيِّبَةٌ وَرَبٌّ غَفُورٌ |

Note that the **Sabians** should also not be confused with the so-called *Sabians of Harran*, which are a gnostic sect that still existed in the early centuries of Islam and which may have deliberately adopted the name *Sabians*. Why did they do that? Maybe to get the advantages which Muslims gave to followers of a monotheistic faith (since they are mentioned in the Qur'an along with Jews and Christians).

160. Before which prophet should the angels bow down?

Answer: Adam (آدَم).

This is told in sura 2 *The Cow* – in Arabic: al-Baqara (سُورَةُ الْبَقَرَة):

| 2:34 | When We told the angels, 'Bow down before Adam', they all bowed. But not 'Iblīs, who refused and was arrogant: he was one of the disobedient. | وَإِذْ قُلْنَا لِلْمَلَائِكَةِ اسْجُدُوا لِآدَمَ فَسَجَدُوا إِلَّا إِبْلِيسَ أَبَى وَاسْتَكْبَرَ وَكَانَ مِنَ الْكَافِرِينَ. |

'Iblīs - the Devil - was a Jinn (demon) whose high rank allowed him to worship Allah together with the angels. The Devil is believed to be descended from the evil Jinn. Some say that he was originally named 'Azāzīl (عَزَازِيل or عزازل). Legend has it that he had the authority over the animal and spiritual kingdom.

However, when Allah created Adam and commanded the angels to bow down before Adam, the Devil refused to prostrate (as is told in the Qur'an). The Devil was created of fire while Adam was created of clay, and because of this, the Devil felt superior.

For this act of disobedience, Allah cursed him to Hell (جَهَنَّم) for eternity, but gave him respite until the Day of Judgement, when he would be destroyed. 'Iblīs had requested this respite. Thus, he was called Shaytān (شَيْطَان): Satan. This is told in sura 7 *The Heights* – al-'A'rāf (سُورة الْأَعْرَاف):

7:12	God said, 'What prevented you from bowing down as I commanded you?' and he said, 'I am better than him: You created me from fire and him from clay.'	قَالَ مَا مَنَعَكَ أَلَّا تَسْجُدَ إِذْ أَمَرْتُكَ قَالَ أَنَا خَيْرٌ مِّنْهُ خَلَقْتَنِي مِن نَّارٍ وَخَلَقْتَهُ مِن طِينٍ.
7:13	God said, 'Get down from here! This is no place for your arrogance. Get out! You are contemptible!'	قَالَ فَاهْبِطْ مِنْهَا فَمَا يَكُونُ لَكَ أَن تَتَكَبَّرَ فِيهَا فَاخْرُجْ إِنَّكَ مِنَ الصَّاغِرِينَ!
7:14	but 'Iblīs said, 'Give me respite until the Day people are raised from the dead',	قَالَ أَنظِرْنِي إِلَى يَوْمِ يُبْعَثُونَ
7:15	and God replied, 'You have respite.'	قَالَ إِنَّكَ مِنَ الْمُنظَرِينَ.
7:16	And then 'Iblīs said, 'Because You have put me in the wrong, I will lie in wait for them all on Your straight path:	قَالَ فَبِمَا أَغْوَيْتَنِي لَأَقْعُدَنَّ لَهُمْ صِرَاطَكَ الْمُسْتَقِيمَ
7:17	I will come at them - from their front and their back, from their right and their left - and You will find that most of them are ungrateful.'	ثُمَّ لَآتِيَنَّهُم مِّن بَيْنِ أَيْدِيهِمْ وَمِنْ خَلْفِهِمْ وَعَنْ أَيْمَانِهِمْ وَعَن شَمَائِلِهِمْ وَلَا تَجِدُ أَكْثَرَهُمْ شَاكِرِينَ.
7:18	God said, 'Get out! You are disgraced and banished! I swear I shall fill Hell with you and all who follow you!	قَالَ اخْرُجْ مِنْهَا مَذْءُومًا مَّدْحُورًا لَّمَن تَبِعَكَ مِنْهُمْ لَأَمْلَأَنَّ جَهَنَّمَ مِنكُمْ أَجْمَعِينَ!
7:19	But you and your wife, Adam, live in the Garden. Both of you eat whatever you like, but do not go near this tree or you will become wrongdoers.'	وَيَا آدَمُ اسْكُنْ أَنتَ وَزَوْجُكَ الْجَنَّةَ فَكُلَا مِنْ حَيْثُ شِئْتُمَا وَلَا تَقْرَبَا هَٰذِهِ الشَّجَرَةَ فَتَكُونَا مِنَ الظَّالِمِينَ.

In Christianity, Satan is the opposite of God. In Islam, 'Iblīs is "just" one of the enemies of the humans and the Jinns. The term Shaytān (شَيْطَان) has the same origin as the Hebrew term Satan (שָׂטָן) which is the source of the English *Satan*. In popular Islamic culture, Shaytān is often simply translated as *The Devil*, but the term can also refer to any Jinn who disobeys Allah and follows 'Iblīs. In Islamic theology, Shaytān and his minions are *whisperers* who whisper into the hearts of humans and Jinns urging them to sin.

161. Is there a difference between Satan and the Devil?

Answer: Yes. The Devil refers to a singularity (person or demon) while Satan can refer to many different demons. We say "the Devil" but never "the Satan".

Shaytān (شَيْطان) is a word which refers to any Jinn (demon) that does not believe and obey Allah. 'Iblīs (إِبلِيس) is the name of the **first Shaytān** who disobeyed Allah's order to prostrate for Adam. In the Qur'an, the word Shaytān can refer to the group of all Shaytāns in general as well as to 'Iblīs only.

The term Shaytān is derived from the root sh-t-n (ش-ط-ن) which, according to Edward Lane's dictionary, means: *he was* or *became remote (from all good and true)*. The term Shaytān (شَيْطان) is of the Arabic measure fay'āl (فَيعال) signifying that *he was or became distant or remote (from the truth and from the mercy of God)*.

'Anas ibn Mālik (أَنَس بن مالِك) reported that the Messenger of Allah said: "Satan flows in a man like his blood."[174]

The term Shaytān is often used in a broader sense – as a metaphor for every human impulse that is immoral. Satan, as some scholars have put it, fulfils a definite function in Allah's plan. He is the eternal tempter who enables man to exercise his God given freedom of choice between good and evil, and thus to become a being endowed with a moral free will.

Excursus: The evil in the English language

Satan, Devil, Lucifer, Beelzebub – there are several expressions which basically describe the evil. The Devil as a conceptual figure is found in many cultures but especially in the three Abrahamitic religions.

In Christianity there are many words for Satan. The most common English synonym for Satan is **Devil**, which descends from Middle English *devel*, from Old English *dēofol* – which derives from a Germanic borrowing from the Latin diabolus. This in turn was borrowed from the Greek word diábolos (διάβολος) which means *accuser*.

In the New Testament, *Satan* occurs more than thirty times alongside *slanderer*, etc, which refer to the same person or thing as Satan.

---

174 ...قَالَ رَسُولُ اللَّهِ: "إِنَّ الشَّيْطَانَ يَجْرِي مِن ابْنِ آدَمَ مَجْرَى الدَّمِ." Sunan 'Abī Dāwūd 4719

Beelzebub, meaning *Lord of Flies*, is the scornful name given in the Hebrew Bible and in the New Testament to a Philistine God whose original name has been reconstructed as probably *Ba'al Zabul* - meaning *Baal the Prince*. This wordplay was later used to refer to Satan.

The Book of Revelation refers to the **great dragon:** "So the great dragon was cast out, that serpent of old, called the Devil and Satan, who deceives the whole world; he was cast to the earth, and his angels were cast out with him" (Revelation 12:9). The Book of Revelation refers also to **the deceiver**.

There is one more important word which is used in Christianity for describing the evil: **Lucifer**. Lucifer literally means *Light bringer, Light bearer, Bringer of Dawn, Shining One or Morning Star*. It goes probably back to the Hebrew word Heylel (הילל) which is found one time in the Hebrew Bible. The Septuagint - the oldest continuous translation of the Hebrew-Aramaic Bible into the classical (old) Greek language - renders Heylel in Greek as heōsphoros (ἑωσφόρος) – which literally means *bringer of dawn, the morning star*. This was latinised as Lucifer.

Let's look at the only Bible passage (Isaiah 14:12) that mentions Lucifer: "How you are fallen from heaven, O Lucifer, son of the morning! How you are cut down to the ground, You who weakened the nations!"

Historically and astronomically, the term *Morning Star* has always been applied to the planet Venus. The image of a morning star fallen from the sky has some parallels in Canaanite mythology as scholars found out. The Bible does not state that Lucifer is Satan. It was Pope Gregory the Great (540-604) who applied this term to Satan and put Lucifer on the same level with Satan. The Christian theologians connected this term with a saying of Jesus in the gospels of Luke 10:18: "And He said to them: "I saw Satan fall like lightning from heaven."

How about Judaism? Lucifer, which in Christianity equates with Satan, does not exist in Judaism.

Remark: In Dutch, the word *lucifer* means *match* (the wooden stick used to spark a fire).

162. Is 'Iblīs an angel or a Jinn?

Answer: He is probably a Jinn (demon).

'Iblīs, as most scholars suggest, is a Jinn. Ibn Kathīr, in his commentary, quoted al-Hasan al-Basrī (الْحَسَن الْبَصْرِيّ): "'Iblīs was not one of the angels, not even for a single moment."[175]

Muslims believe that 'Iblīs is still among humans until the Day of Judgement, and because of that, the present tense is generally used when talking about him.

Let's look at the Islamic sources and check why 'Iblīs is a Jinn. According to Islam, angels never disobey Allah when he commands them to do something. Since 'Iblīs is not one of the angels, he is not forced to obey Allah. He enjoys freedom of will like human beings.

Furthermore, one of the attributes of angels is that they were created from light whereas Jinns were created from fire. The Qur'an says that 'Iblīs was created from fire. In the view of the Devil, fire is superior to the clay out of which man has been created.

'Iblīs himself said so in a verse when Allah asked him why he refused to prostrate before Adam when Allah ordered him to do so.

This is told in sura 7 *The Heights* – in Arabic: al-'A‘rāf (سورة الْأَعْراف):

7:12	God said, 'What prevented you from bowing down as I commanded you?' and he said, 'I am better than him: You created me from fire and him from clay.'	قَالَ مَا مَنَعَكَ أَلَّا تَسْجُدَ إِذْ أَمَرْتُكَ قَالَ أَنَا خَيْرٌ مِّنْهُ خَلَقْتَنِي مِن نَّارٍ وَخَلَقْتَهُ مِن طِينٍ

An authentic Hadith supports what the Qur'an says about Jinns.

'Ā'isha (عائشة بِنْت أَبِي بَكْر) reported that Allah's Messenger said: "The Angels were born out of light and the Jinns were born out of the spark of fire and Adam was born as he has been defined [in the Qur'an] for you [i.e. he is fashioned out of clay]."[176]

---

175 ...مَا كَانَ إِبْلِيس مِنَ الْمَلَائِكَة طَرْفَة عَيْن قَطُّ وَإِنَّهُ لَأَصْل الْجِنّ كَمَا أَنَّ آدَم أَصْل الْبَشَر. al-Tabarī 89/3

176 ...قَالَ رَسُولُ اللَّهِ: "خُلِقَتِ الْمَلَائِكَةُ مِنْ نُورٍ وَخُلِقَ الْجَانُّ مِنْ مَارِجٍ مِنْ نَارٍ وَخُلِقَ آدَمُ مِمَّا وُصِفَ لَكُمْ." Sahīh Muslim 2996

Contrary to this, some scholars interpret the episode of the Qur'an differently. 'Iblīs' refused to obey; this perhaps indicates that at the time of the command, 'Iblīs was indeed one of the heavenly hosts, an angle. This is for example the view of Muhammad Asad. He suggests that 'Iblīs is a *Fallen Angel*. 'Iblīs' rebellion, as Muhammad Asad concluded, "has a purely symbolic significance and is, in reality, the outcome of a specific function assigned to him by God."

A *Fallen Angel* is a rebellious angel that has been kicked out of Paradise. The term *Fallen Angel* is used in religious contexts although the term itself is not used in the Bible or in the Qur'an. In Christianity, Satan is often described as the leader of the Fallen Angels.

However, most Muslims prefer the view of Ibn Kathīr who wrote that 'Iblīs could not have been an angel. They find proof for this in sura 16 *The Bee* – in Arabic: al-Nahl (سُورة النَّحْل):

16:49	It is to God that everything in the heavens and earth submits, every beast that moves, even the angels - they are free from arrogance:	وَلِلَّهِ يَسْجُدُ مَا فِي السَّمَاوَاتِ وَمَا فِي الْأَرْضِ مِن دَابَّةٍ وَالْمَلَائِكَةُ وَهُمْ لَا يَسْتَكْبِرُونَ:
16:50	they fear their Lord above them, and they do as they are commanded.	يَخَافُونَ رَبَّهُم مِّن فَوْقِهِمْ وَيَفْعَلُونَ مَا يُؤْمَرُونَ ۩

163. What does the word 'Iblīs mean?

Answer: The literal meaning is not entirely clear, but he is the Devil.

Western scholars have suggested that the word 'Iblīs (إِبْلِيس) maybe have its root in the Greek term diabolos.

Some Arabic linguists have another hypothesis. They say it is perhaps the other way round, that the Greek word diabolos is a Hellenised form of the Arabic name 'Iblīs. As proof for this, they take the Arabic root b-l-s (بَلَسَ) which means *to be expelled, be dismissed, be driven out*. In the Arabic IV-form, the verb 'ablasa (أَبْلَسَ) means *he despaired* or *became broken in spirit*.

Let's dig a bit deeper. 'Iblīs' former name is ʿAzāzīl (عَزازيل or عَزازِل) which is a Hebrew word (עֲזָאזֵל). ʿAzāzīl is *the Devil* in Judaism and

Christianity. In some narrations, 'Azāzīl is also the name for a *Fallen Angel*; in the Bible, 'Azāzīl is associated with the scapegoat rite. His epithet is 'Abū Kurdūs (أَبُو كُرْدُوس); Kurdūs means *squadron of horsemen*.

164. Is Satan ruling in Hell?

Answer: No, it is Allah himself who will punish the unbelievers.

Islam teaches that Hell is a real place prepared by Allah for those who do not believe in Him, for those who rebel against His rules, and for all those who reject His messengers.

The Qur'an tells a lot about the torture, pain and punishments in Hell. Muslims believe that these are real but different to all worldly pain we know. In short, we could say that Hell is the place of ultimate disgrace, humiliation, and suffering.

There is a major question: **Will Satan be in Hell?** And can Allah punish him since Satan was born out of fire?

Traditional scholars say that although 'Iblīs, as well as the other Jinns (demons), was created from fire, this does not automatically mean that he is fire now. Man was created from dust, as told in the Qur'an, but he is not dust now (at least not the ones alive). Muslims believe anyhow that Allah is capable of everything.

Muslims don't know for sure why Allah let 'Iblīs (the first of the Devils) "live" until the Day of Judgement, especially because Allah disapproves totally of what 'Iblīs constantly does and enjoys, i.e. leading human beings astray. It is thus not entirely clear what will happen to Satan after the Final Day.

An Excursus: How is it in Christianity?

Also in Christianity there is a common misconception that Satan is in charge of Hell. In fact, Satan will be one of the tortured people in the *Lake of Fire* – and not the tormentor. The universal punishment for all who reject Jesus Christ as Saviour is to be "cast into the Lake of Fire". This is shown in the Bible, *Revelation* 20:10: "The Devil, who deceived them, was cast into the Lake of Fire and brimstone,

where the beast and the false prophet are. And they will be tormented day and night forever and ever."

This shows that in Christianity too, Satan is not the ruler of Hell. It
is God who is in charge. God alone has the power to throw a person
into Hell. Jesus says in Luke 12:4-5: "I tell you, my friends, do not be
afraid of those who kill the body and after that can do more. But I
will show you whom you should fear: Fear him who, after your body
has been killed, has authority to throw you into Hell. Yes, I tell you,
fear him." Most Christian theologians agree that Jesus is referring to
God here.

The Bible does not say that Satan has been to Hell yet; instead,
"eternal fire" is awaiting him. Most Christians believe that Hell was
originally created to punish Satan and the demons, and not to give
them a kingdom to rule. This information is given in Matthew 25:41:
"Then He will also say to those on the left hand, 'Depart from Me,
you cursed, into the everlasting fire prepared for the Devil and his
angels'."

Until Satan is thrown into the Lake of Fire, he spends his time
between heaven (Job 1:6–12) and earth: "Be sober, be vigilant;
because your adversary the Devil walks about like a roaring lion,
seeking whom he may devour." (1 Peter 5:8).

165. What is the Tree of Hell called?

Answer: Al-Zaqqūm (شَجَرة الزَّقُّوم).

This demonic tree was mentioned in the Qur'an. The fruits were
described as extremely bitter; they are the food for the people in Hell.
Linguists say that the word Zaqqūm denotes any *deadly food.*

According to the Qur'an, Zaqqūm is a tree that *springs out of the
bottom of Hellfire.* Its fruits look like devils' heads. Some scholars
claim that the fruit tears bodies apart and releases bodily fluids. Others say that the fruits churn like burning oil in the stomach.

However, Zaqqūm is also the Arabic expression for *fresh butter
with dates* or some other certain foods of the Arabs in old times.
When sura 37 *Ranged in Rows* - in Arabic: al-Saffāt (سورة الصَّفّات) -
was revealed in which the tree is mentioned, one of Muhammad's

fiercest enemies, 'Abū Jahl (أَبُو جَهْل), said: "Dates and fresh butter; we will swallow it leisurely!"[177]

37:62	Is this the better welcome, or the tree of Zaqqūm,	أَذَٰلِكَ خَيْرٌ نُّزُلًا أَمْ شَجَرَةُ الزَّقُّومِ
37:63	which we have made a test for the evil-doers?	إِنَّا جَعَلْنَاهَا فِتْنَةً لِّلظَّالِمِينَ
37:64	This tree grows in the heart of the blazing Fire,	إِنَّهَا شَجَرَةٌ تَخْرُجُ فِي أَصْلِ الْجَحِيمِ
37:65	and its fruits are like devils' heads.	طَلْعُهَا كَأَنَّهُ رُءُوسُ الشَّيَاطِينِ

The tree is mentioned in other suras as well. In sura 17:60 it is named the *cursed tree* (الشَّجَرَةَ الْمَلْعُونة).

Remark: Several cultures use the name Zaqqūm for real tree species. It has been applied to *Euphorbia abyssinica* by the Beja people in eastern Sudan. In Jordan, it is applied to the species *Balanites aegyptiaca*, and in Turkey, Zaqqūm (zakkum) refers to *Nerium oleander*.

166. How many gates does Hell have?

Answer: Seven.

This information is found in sura 15 *al-Hijr* (سُورة الْحِجْر):

15:43	Hell is the promised place for them all.	وَإِنَّ جَهَنَّمَ لَمَوْعِدُهُمْ أَجْمَعِينَ.
15:44	It has seven gates, each gate having its allotted share of them.	لَهَا سَبْعَةُ أَبْوَابٍ لِّكُلِّ بَابٍ مِّنْهُمْ جُزْءٌ مَّقْسُومٌ.

This sura was revealed during the last year before the Hijra (الْهِجْرة). The title is the name of an Arabian region or place known as al-Hijr. An ancient township of that name is mentioned by the Greek-Egyptian writer Ptolemy as *Hegra*. Some translators rendered the name al-Hijr to *rocky tract* or *forbidden tract*, however, since it is most likely the name of a place, it is better to leave it untranslated.

---

177 ...قَالَ أَبُو جَهْل لَعَنَهُ اللّه إِنَّمَا الزَّقُّوم التَّمْر وَالزُّبْد أَتَزَقَّمُهُ. Tafsīr Ibn Kathīr.

There are no authentic Hadiths which give further details on the number of Hell gates. Some companions shared information which was recorded by the Islamic scholar al-Qurtubī (الْقُرْطُبِيّ) in his commentary on the above-mentioned verses. However, the authenticity is questionable. Anyway, al-Qurtubī quoted ʿAlī ibn ʾAbī Ṭālib (عليّ بن أبي طالب) saying that the Gates of Hell are one above the other. ʿAlī then put one of his hands above the other, saying that the Gates of Paradise are horizontal but the ones of Hell are vertical.[178]

Furthermore, al-Qurtubī mentioned that each gate is 70 times hotter than the gate above it.[179]

167. What are the Islamic names of Hell and Hellfire?

Answer: There are several; most of them are found in the Qur'an.

Some Islamic sources for the stages or types of Hell are contradicting. ʿAlī ibn ʾAbī Ṭālib (عَلِيّ بن أَبِي طالب) said that the levels of Hell are ranked according to the degree of torture in descending order. Let's look at the most important terms:

Jahannam	جَهَنَّم	Generally used for *Hell* or *Hellfire*
Jahannam is mentioned in the Qur'an 77 times and is usually translated as *Hell* or *Hellfire*. A name of the fire with which Allah will punish in the life to come all disobedient, unbelieving slaves. Some linguists suggest that it was originally a Persian word. Others say that it originates from the Hebrew word Gehinnom (Old Hebrew: גהנום/גהנם), derived from a place outside ancient Jerusalem known in the Hebrew Bible as the Valley of the Son of Hinnom (Hebrew: גיא בן-הינום or גֵיא בֶן-הִנֹם, Gai Ben-Hinnom). At this place some kings sacrificed their children by fire to the idol Moloch.		
50:24 "Hurl/throw every obstinate disbeliever into Hell."[180] Note: The verb here is in the dual (a special grammatical form in Arabic) and the addressee is either the two recording angels or two angels who guard Hell.		

---

178 ...سَمِعْتُ عَلِيًّا, يَقُولُ: "هَلْ تَدْرُونَ كَيْفَ أَبْوَابُ جَهَنَّمَ؟ قَالَ: "قُلْنَا: "هِيَ مِثْلُ أَبْوَابِنَا هَذِهِ",
قَالَ:"لَا, هِيَ هَكَذَا بَعْضُهَا فَوْقَ بَعْض." Tafsīr al-Qurtubī

179 ...كُلّ بابٍ أَشَدُّ حَرًّا مِن الَّذِي يَلِيهِ سَبْعِينَ مَرَّة. Tafsīr al-Qurtubī.

180 ...أَلْقِيَا فِي جَهَنَّمَ كُلَّ كَفَّارٍ عَنِيدٍ.

| **Hutama** | الْحُطَمة | *crusher* (which smashes or breaks into pieces) |

A vehement fire that breaks into pieces everything that is cast into it. Some say it is the fourth stage of Hell, some say it is a gate of Hell.

104:4 "He will surely be thrown into the Crusher."[181]

| **Saqar** | سَقَر | scorching fire |

The verb saqara (سَقَرَ) means *to injure by heat, burn* (e.g. the sun). Therefore Hell is called saqar because of the intensity of its heat. Notice: The word saqar (سَقَر) is feminine in Arabic! For Arabic speaker: it is a diptote which suggests that it is of foreign origin.

54:48: "Taste the touch of Saqar."[182]

| **Jahīm** | جَحِيم | *Hellfire; the fierce fire* |

Al-Jahīm (الْجَحِيم) appears 26 times in the Qur'an. It is from the Arabic root j-h-m (ج-ح-م) and describes a burning fire, a fiercely, blazed or flamed fire. Thus the word Jahīm describes a fire burning or blazing or flaming vehemently or having many live coals and is flaming much.

26:91: "and the Fire is placed in full view of the misguided."[183]

| **Hāwiya** | هَاوِية | *abyss/the pit* |

Hell is called Hāwiya because the one who is thrown into it is thrown from top to bottom.

101:9 "His refuge will be an abyss [bottomless pit]."[184]

| **Sa'īr** | سَعِير | *blaze; the burning fire* |

It is called Sa'īr because it is kindled and ignited. This is also what the Arabic root of the term means.

---

181 كَلَّا لَيُنبَذَنَّ فِي الْحُطَمَةِ.

182 ذُوقُوا مَسَّ سَقَرَ.

183 وَبُرِّزَتِ الْجَحِيمُ لِلْغَاوِينَ.

184 فَأُمُّهُ هَاوِيَةٌ.

42:7: "And warn about the Day of Gathering, of which there is no doubt, when some shall be in the Garden and some in the blazing Flame."[185]

Lazā	لَظَى	fierce blaze
70:15: "But no! There is a raging flame."[186]		

168. Who is the keeper of Hell?

Answer: Mighty and strict angels who never disobey Allah stand over Hell. Angels, per Islamic definition, always do precisely as ordered. The chief angel who guards over Hell is called Mālik (مالك).

Mālik literally means *reigning, ruling; owner* or *master*. It is also the name of the chief angel guarding over Hell. This was stated in sura 43 *Ornaments of Gold* – in Arabic: al-Zukhruf (سُورة الزُّخْرُف):

43:74	But the evildoers will remain in Hell's punishment,	إِنَّ الْمُجْرِمِينَ فِي عَذَابِ جَهَنَّمَ خَالِدُونَ
43:75	from which there is no relief: they will remain in utter despair.	لَا يُفَتَّرُ عَنْهُمْ وَهُمْ فِيهِ مُبْلِسُونَ
43:76	We never wronged them; they were the ones who did wrong.	وَمَا ظَلَمْنَاهُمْ وَلَكِن كَانُوا هُمُ الظَّالِمِينَ.
43:77	They will cry, 'Mālik, if only your Lord would finish us off', but he will answer, 'No! You are here to stay.'	وَنَادَوْا يَا مَالِكُ لِيَقْضِ عَلَيْنَا رَبُّكَ قَالَ إِنَّكُم مَّاكِثُونَ
43:78	We have brought you the Truth but most of you despise it.	لَقَدْ جِئْنَاكُم بِالْحَقِّ وَلَكِنَّ أَكْثَرَكُمْ لِلْحَقِّ كَارِهُونَ.

In sura 66 *The Prohibition* - in Arabic: al-Tahrīm (سُورة التَّحْرِيم) - it is told that angels guard Hell:

---

185 وَتُنذِرَ يَوْمَ الْجَمْعِ لَا رَيْبَ فِيهِ فَرِيقٌ فِي الْجَنَّةِ وَفَرِيقٌ فِي السَّعِيرِ.
186 كَلَّا إِنَّهَا لَظَى.

| 66:6 | Believers, guard yourselves and your families against a Fire fuelled by people and stones, over which stand angels, stern and strong; angels who never disobey God's commands to them, but do as they are ordered: | يَا أَيُّهَا الَّذِينَ آمَنُوا قُوا أَنفُسَكُمْ وَأَهْلِيكُمْ نَارًا وَقُودُهَا النَّاسُ وَالْحِجَارَةُ عَلَيْهَا مَلَائِكَةٌ غِلَاظٌ شِدَادٌ لَّا يَعْصُونَ اللَّهَ مَا أَمَرَهُمْ وَيَفْعَلُونَ مَا يُؤْمَرُونَ |

There are 19 keepers of Hell as the Qur'an states in sura 74 Wrapped in His Cloak – in Arabic: al-Muddaththir (سُورَةُ الْمُدَّثِّرِ):

74:26	I will throw him into the scorching Fire	سَأُصْلِيهِ سَقَرَ
74:27	What will explain to you what the scorching Fire is?	وَمَا أَدْرَاكَ مَا سَقَرُ
74:28	It spares nothing and leaves nothing;	لَا تُبْقِي وَلَا تَذَرُ
74:29	it scorches the flesh of humans;	لَوَّاحَةٌ لِّلْبَشَرِ
74:30	there are nineteen in charge of it -	عَلَيْهَا تِسْعَةَ عَشَرَ
74:31	none other than angels appointed by Us to guard Hellfire - and We have made their number a test for the disbelievers. So those who have been given the Scripture will be certain and those who believe will have their faith increased: neither those who have been given the Scripture nor the believers will have any doubts, but the sick at heart and the disbelievers will say, 'What could God mean by this description?' God leaves whoever He will to stray and guides whoever He will - no one knows your Lord's forces except Him - this [description] is a warning to mortals.	وَمَا جَعَلْنَا أَصْحَابَ النَّارِ إِلَّا مَلَائِكَةً وَمَا جَعَلْنَا عِدَّتَهُمْ إِلَّا فِتْنَةً لِّلَّذِينَ كَفَرُوا لِيَسْتَيْقِنَ الَّذِينَ أُوتُوا الْكِتَابَ وَيَزْدَادَ الَّذِينَ آمَنُوا إِيمَانًا وَلَا يَرْتَابَ الَّذِينَ أُوتُوا الْكِتَابَ وَالْمُؤْمِنُونَ وَلِيَقُولَ الَّذِينَ فِي قُلُوبِهِم مَّرَضٌ وَالْكَافِرُونَ مَاذَا أَرَادَ اللَّهُ بِهَٰذَا مَثَلًا كَذَٰلِكَ يُضِلُّ اللَّهُ مَن يَشَاءُ وَيَهْدِي مَن يَشَاءُ وَمَا يَعْلَمُ جُنُودَ رَبِّكَ إِلَّا هُوَ وَمَا هِيَ إِلَّا ذِكْرَىٰ لِلْبَشَرِ

If you might think that nineteen keepers of Hell will easily be defeated by the inconceivably huge number of people in Hell - well, it is said that each of them has the strength to crush all humanity. They do not know any form of mercy as stated in sura 40 *The Forgiver* – in Arabic: Ghāfir (سُورَةُ غَافِرٍ):

40:49	Those in the Fire will say to the keepers of Hell, 'Ask your Lord to lessen our suffering for one day',	وَقَالَ الَّذِينَ فِي النَّارِ لِخَزَنَةِ جَهَنَّمَ ادْعُوا رَبَّكُمْ يُخَفِّفْ عَنَّا يَوْمًا مِّنَ الْعَذَابِ
40:50	but they will say, 'Did your messengers not come to you with clear evidence of the truth?' They will say, 'Yes they did', and the keeper will say, 'You can plead, then, but the pleas of disbelievers will always be in vain.'	قَالُوا أَوَلَمْ تَكُ تَأْتِيكُمْ رُسُلُكُم بِالْبَيِّنَاتِ قَالُوا بَلَىٰ قَالُوا فَادْعُوا وَمَا دُعَاءُ الْكَافِرِينَ إِلَّا فِي ضَلَالٍ.

169. What is the *evil eye*?

Answer: It expresses that someone envies you for a blessing or a cause of happiness.

The *evil eye* usually comes from people who are jealous or envious. The Arabic word for *envy* is Hasad (حَسَد). Envy implies the wish that a blessing or a cause of happiness may depart from its possessor. The root h-s-d (ح-س-د) means that a person dislikes that you should possess it and wishes that it might depart from you (and be transferred to himself). The Arabic term for *evil eye* is al-'Ayn (الْعَيْن) which literally means: *the eye*. Another term is *Lamma* (لامَّة). The father of 'Abd Allah ibn 'Āmir ibn Rabī'a (عَبْد الله بن عامِر بن رَبيعة) narrated that the Prophet said: "The evil eye is real."[187]

So what is the evil eye all about? It begins when you like something that doesn't belong to you. Your evil soul dwells on the matter and by continually looking at the person who has the thing of which you feel jealous, you direct your venom towards the person.

'Abd Allah ibn 'Abbās (عَبْد الله بن عَبّاس) narrated that the Prophet used to seek refuge with Allah for al-Hasan and al-Husayn [his grandchildren] and say: "Your forefather [i.e. Abraham] used to seek refuge with Allah for Ishmael and Isaac by reciting the following: 'O Allah! I seek refuge with Your Perfect Words from every devil and from poisonous pests and from every evil, harmful, envious eye.'"[188]

---

187 ...عَنِ النَّبِيِّ قَالَ: "الْعَيْنُ حَقٌّ." Sunan ibn Māja 3635 (3506)

188 ...قَالَ كَانَ النَّبِيُّ يُعَوِّذُ الْحَسَنَ وَالْحُسَيْنَ وَيَقُولُ: "إِنَّ أَبَاكُمَا كَانَ يُعَوِّذُ بِهَا إِسْمَاعِيلَ وَإِسْحَاقَ، أَعُوذُ بِكَلِمَاتِ اللهِ التَّامَّةِ مِنْ كُلِّ شَيْطَانٍ وَهَامَّةٍ، وَمِنْ كُلِّ عَيْنٍ لَامَّةٍ." Sahīh al-Bukhārī 3371

In Arabic, the saying is a rhyme as it contains the words "hamma" (هَامَّة) which denotes lethally poisonous animals and "lamma" (لامَّة). What is meant here by lamma is every disease or harm that a person may suffer such as insanity or mental disturbance.

What can a Muslim do about it? 'Abd Allah ibn 'Abbās reported that Allah's Messenger said: "The influence of an evil eye is a fact; if anything would precede the destiny it would be the influence of an evil eye and when you are asked to take a bath [as a cure] from the influence of an evil eye, you should bath."[189]

- 'Anas ibn Mālik (أَنَس بن مالِك) narrated that the Messenger of Allah granted him sanction to use incantation [as a cure] for the influence of an evil eye, the sting of the scorpion and al-Namla [small pustules].[190]

- 'Ā'isha (عائشة بِنْت أَبِي بَكْر), Muhammad's wife, narrated: "Allah's Messenger commanded me that I should make use of incantation for curing the influence of an evil eye."[191]

What is meant by incantation? It is the Islamic concept of al-Ruqiya (الرُّقْية) which means *spell; charm; incantation; magic.* 'Ā'isha narrated that when any of the members of the household fell ill, Allah's Messenger used to blow over him by reciting [the suras called] al-Mu'awwidhatān (الْمُعَوِّذَتانِ), and when he suffered from an illness of which he died, I used to blow over him and rubbed his body with his hand for his hand had greater healing power than my hand.[192]

To seek protection, Muslims usually recite sura 1 *The Opening* - al-Fātiha (سُورة الْفَاتِحة) - or as indicated in the Hadith above the last two suras which are also called al-Mu'awwidhatān – *the two protectors.*

Remark: There is debate going on among scholars whether a Muslim can take precautions against the evil eye or not. Traditional

---

189 ...عَنِ النَّبِيِّ قَالَ: "الْعَيْنُ حَقٌّ وَلَوْ كَانَ شَيْءٌ سَابَقَ الْقَدَرَ سَبَقَتْهُ الْعَيْنُ وَإِذَا اسْتُغْسِلْتُمْ فَاغْسِلُوا." Sahīh Muslim 2188

190 ...قَالَ رَخَّصَ رَسُولُ اللَّهِ فِي الرُّقْيَةِ مِنَ الْعَيْنِ وَالْحُمَةِ وَالنَّمْلَةِ. Sahīh Muslim 2196

191 ...قَالَتْ كَانَ رَسُولُ اللَّهِ يَأْمُرُنِي أَنْ أَسْتَرْقِيَ مِنَ الْعَيْنِ. Sahīh Muslim 2195

192 ...قَالَتْ كَانَ رَسُولُ اللَّهِ إِذَا مَرِضَ أَحَدٌ مِنْ أَهْلِهِ نَفَثَ عَلَيْهِ بِالْمُعَوِّذَاتِ فَلَمَّا مَرِضَ مَرَضَهُ الَّذِي مَاتَ فِيهِ جَعَلْتُ أَنْفُثُ عَلَيْهِ وَأَمْسَحُهُ بِيَدِ نَفْسِهِ لِأَنَّهَا كَانَتْ أَعْظَمَ بَرَكَةً مِنْ يَدِي. Sahīh Muslim 2192

scholars say that taking precautions against the evil eye before it happens contradicts with the idea of al-Tawakkul (تَوَكُّل) - putting one's trust in Allah - as Allah, by definition, knows what he is doing.

170. What do people say to not harm anyone by the evil eye?

Answer: By blessing Allah (and not showing any kind of envy).

When Muslims like something, for example, if they got a new car; or if a woman delivered a baby; or if someone got a new house, then Muslims don't say "congratulations!" because that could be interpreted as envy. Instead, Muslims praise Allah and thank him for the blessing someone got.

Imam Mālik narrated the following Hadith: "My father, Sahl ibn Hunayf (سَهْل بن حُنَيْف), did a ritual bath (Ghusl) at al-Kharrār. He removed his garment, so-called Jubba (جُبَّة), while 'Āmir ibn Rabī'a was watching. Sahl was a man with a beautiful white skin. 'Āmir said to him: 'I have never seen anything like what I have seen today, not even the skin of a virgin.'

Sahl fell ill on the spot and his condition grew worse. Somebody went to the Messenger of Allah and told him that Sahl was ill and could not go with him. The Messenger of Allah came to him, and Sahl told him what had happened with 'Āmir.

The Messenger of Allah said: 'Why does one of you kill his brother? Why did you not say: May Allah bless you?' The evil eye is true. Do Wudū' [ritual ablution] from it.'

'Āmir did Wudū' and Sahl went with the Messenger of Allah, and there was nothing wrong with him."[193]

So what is the solution? If a Muslim sees something beautiful or something he admires, he should follow the advice of the Prophet

---

193 ...يَقُولُ اغْتَسَلَ أَبِي سَهْلُ بْنُ حُنَيْفٍ بِالْخَرَّارِ فَنَزَعَ جُبَّةً كَانَتْ عَلَيْهِ وَعَامِرُ بْنُ رَبِيعَةَ يَنْظُرُ قَالَ وَكَانَ سَهْلٌ رَجُلاً أَبْيَضَ حَسَنَ الْجِلْدِ - قَالَ - فَقَالَ لَهُ عَامِرُ بْنُ رَبِيعَةَ مَا رَأَيْتُ كَالْيَوْمِ وَلاَ جِلْدَ عَذْرَاءَ. قَالَ فَوُعِكَ سَهْلٌ مَكَانَهُ وَاشْتَدَّ وَعْكُهُ فَأُتِيَ رَسُولُ اللَّهِ فَأُخْبِرَ أَنَّ سَهْلاً وُعِكَ وَأَنَّهُ غَيْرُ رَائِحٍ مَعَكَ يَا رَسُولَ اللَّهِ فَأَتَاهُ رَسُولُ اللَّهِ فَأَخْبَرَهُ سَهْلٌ بِالَّذِي كَانَ مِنْ شَأْنِ عَامِرٍ فَقَالَ رَسُولُ اللَّهِ: "عَلاَمَ يَقْتُلُ أَحَدُكُمْ أَخَاهُ أَلاَّ بَرَّكْتَ إِنَّ الْعَيْنَ حَقٌّ تَوَضَّأْ لَهُ." فَتَوَضَّأَ لَهُ عَامِرٌ فَرَاحَ سَهْلٌ مَعَ رَسُولِ اللَّهِ لَيْسَ بِهِ بَأْسٌ. Muwatta' Mālik 1714 (1811).

who commanded Muslims to say: "*May Allah bless you.*" Here are some possible phrases that are used by Muslims:

- Directly said to a Person: "BārakAllahu fīka/fīkum" (بارَكَ الله فيكَ) – *may Allah bless you.*
- Directly said to a woman: "BārakAllahu fīki" (بارَكَ الله فيكِ) – *may Allah bless you.*
- Said about a man: "Allahumma Bārik lahu" (اللّٰهُمَّ بارِكْ لَهُ) – *may Allah bless him.*
- Said about a woman: "Allahumma Bārik laha" (اللّٰهُمَّ بارِكْ لَها) – *may Allah bless her.*
- Said about/to an object such as a car, etc: "BārakAllahu laka fīha" (بارَكَ الله لَكَ فيها) – *may Allah bless it.*

Muslims, for example in Turkey and in the Maghreb, use different phrases which traditional Islamic scholars don't like, simply because the Prophet didn't teach them that way. Anyway, what probably counts in the end is the intention. Here are some examples:

- *Whatever Allah wills/intends* – in Arabic: "Mā shā' Allah" (ما شاء الله). This is also used as an exclamation of surprise, meaning: *Amazing! Good! Bravo!*
- You might also hear *May Allah bless you* – in Arabic: "tubāriku Allah ʿalayka" (تُبارِكُ الله عَلَيْكَ).
- Muslims also say: *This is Allah's will. There is no power not [given] by Allah.* In Arabic: "La Quwwa 'illā bi Allāh" (لَا قُوَّة إِلَّا بِاللَّهِ). Muslims take this sentence from sura 18 *The Cave* – in Arabic: al-Kahf (سُورة الْكَهْف). However, the subject of this verse is not particularly about envy. Allah actually destroyed a person's garden because of his <u>disbelieve</u>:

18:39	If only, when you entered your garden, you had said, "This is God's will. There is no power not [given] by God." Although you see I have less wealth and offspring than you,	وَلَوْلَا إِذْ دَخَلْتَ جَنَّتَكَ قُلْتَ مَا شَاءَ اللَّهُ لَا قُوَّةَ إِلَّا بِاللَّهِ إِن تَرَنِ أَنَا أَقَلَّ مِنكَ مَالًا وَوَلَدًا
18:40	my Lord may well give me something better than your garden, and send thunderbolts	فَعَسَىٰ رَبِّي أَن يُؤْتِيَنِ خَيْرًا مِّن جَنَّتِكَ وَيُرْسِلَ

	on your garden from the sky, so that it becomes a heap of barren dust;	عَلَيْهَا حُسْبَانًا مِّنَ السَّمَاءِ فَتُصْبِحَ صَعِيدًا زَلَقًا؛
18:41	or its water may sink so deep into the ground that you will never be able to reach it again.'	أَوْ يُصْبِحَ مَاؤُهَا غَوْرًا فَلَن تَسْتَطِيعَ لَهُ طَلَبًا.
18:42	And so it was: his fruit **was completely destroyed**, and there he was, wringing his hands over what he had invested in it, as it drooped on its trellises, and saying, 'I wish I had not set up any partner to my Lord.'	وَأُحِيطَ بِثَمَرِهِ فَأَصْبَحَ يُقَلِّبُ كَفَّيْهِ عَلَىٰ مَا أَنفَقَ فِيهَا وَهِيَ خَاوِيَةٌ عَلَىٰ عُرُوشِهَا وَيَقُولُ يَا لَيْتَنِي لَمْ أُشْرِكْ بِرَبِّي أَحَدًا.

How about amulets?

There are several Hadiths, though most of them are *weak*, which condemn the use of amulets. There is one Hadith classified as authentic by al-ʾAlbānī (الْأَلْبَانِيّ). It was narrated from ʿUqba ibn ʿĀmir al-Juhanī (عُقْبَةَ بن عَامِر الْجُهَنِيّ) that people came to the Messenger of Allah and he accepted the oath of allegiance from nine of them but not from one man. They said: "O Messenger of Allah, you accepted the allegiance of nine and not from one." He [the Prophet] said: "He is wearing an amulet." So he put his hand in [his garment] and broke it, then he [the Prophet] accepted his oath of allegiance and said: "Whoever wears an amulet has associated others with Allah."[194]

The *Khamsa* (خَمْسة) - a palm-shaped amulet - or the *Nazar* (Turkish: nazar boncuğu) - an eye-shaped, blue amulet - are rejected by most scholars. The amulet could indicate that protection is coming from the object rather than from Allah. Scholars disagree if Muslims are allowed to use amulets on which verses of the Qur'an are printed.

171. Which sura is used to protect oneself from the evil eye?

Answer: Sura 113 *The Daybreak* – in Arabic: al-Falaq (الْفَلَق).

---

194 ...أَقْبَلَ إِلَيْهِ رَهْطٌ فَبَايَعَ تِسْعَةً وَأَمْسَكَ عَنْ وَاحِدٍ، فَقَالُوا: "يَا رَسُولَ اللَّهِ، بَايَعْتَ تِسْعَةً وَتَرَكْتَ هَذَا." قَالَ: "إِنَّ عَلَيْهِ تَمِيمَةً، فَأَدْخَلَ يَدَهُ فَقَطَعَهَا فَبَايَعَهُ، وَقَالَ: "مَنْ عَلَّقَ تَمِيمَةً فَقَدْ أَشْرَكَ."
ʾAhmad 16781

Let's look at the verse in question:

113:5	(Say: I seek refuge in the Lord of daybreak from) *"the harm in the envier when he envies."*	وَمِن شَرِّ حَاسِدٍ إِذَا حَسَدَ.

This saying, as Muslims believe, protects a person from the bad effect which another person's envy may have on one's life. But it also prevents a person from succumbing to envy.

Zamakhshari (زمخشري) quoted 'Umar ibn 'Abd al-'Azīz (عُمَر بن عَبْد العزيز), better known as Caliph 'Umar II. The quote was heard by al-'Asma'ī (الأَصْمَعِيّ): "I cannot think of any wrongdoer who is more likely to be the wronged one than he who envies another."[195]

172. Which two suras are nicknamed "the two protectors"?

Answer: Sura 113 *The Daybreak* - in Arabic: al-Falaq (الفَلَق) - and sura 114 *The People* – in Arabic: al-Nās (سُورة الناس).

These two suras are the last two suras of the Qur'an. They are called al-Mu'awwidhatān (الْمُعَوِّذَتانِ) - *the two protectors* - and were revealed to seek protection from evil. Sura 113 is particularly used against witchcraft and spells. Both are Meccan suras and start with "Say [Prophet]: I seek refuge".[196] Let's look at the two verses:

113:5	Say [Prophet], 'I seek refuge with the Lord of daybreak	قُلْ أَعُوذُ بِرَبِّ الفَلَقِ
114:1	Say, 'I seek refuge with the Lord of people,	قُلْ أَعُوذُ بِرَبِّ النَّاسِ

'Ā'isha (عائشة بِنْت أَبِي بَكْر) narrated that whenever the Prophet went to bed, he would blow into his hands, recite al-Mu'awwidhatān, then wipe his hands over his body.[197]

'Ā'isha narrated that "whenever Allah's Messenger became sick, he would recite al-Mu'awwidhatān and then blow his breath over his

---

195 ...مَا رَأَيْتُ ظَالِمًا أَشْبَهَ بِمَظْلُومٍ مِنَ الْحَاسِدِ.

196 قُلْ أَعُوذُ بِ

197 ...أَنَّ النَّبِيَّ كَانَ إِذَا أَخَذَ مَضْجَعَهُ نَفَثَ فِي يَدَيْهِ وَقَرَأَ بِالْمُعَوِّذَتَيْنِ وَمَسَحَ بِهِمَا جَسَدَهُ. Sunan ibn
Māja 3875

body. When he became seriously ill [in Muhammad's last days], I used to recite [these two suras] and rub his hands over his body hoping for its blessings."[198]

Let's look again at the word al-Mu'awwidhatān. It is derived from the same root as the word in the two suras which is used for *to seek refuge with*: Aūdhu (أَعُوذُ). The root is '-w-dh (ع - و - ذ) and means *to seek the protection*. There is a famous phrase which Muslims quote many times each day: "I seek protection in Allah from the accursed Devil." In Arabic: "Aūdhu billāhi min ash-Shaytān-ir-Rajīm".[199]

Muslim scholars think that it was in sura *The People* that the term Jinn (الجِنّة – synonymous with الْجِنّ) was mentioned in the Qur'an for the first time. It also includes all kinds of mysterious things to which a Muslim is exposed.

173. What is al-Taqīya?

Answer: An Islamic concept that allows Muslims to hide their religion in certain situations.

The term al-Taqīya (التَّقِيّة) means *fear, caution, prudence*. In a figurative sense, it goes along with an Arabic proverb: *Save a thief from the gallows and he'll cut your throat*. This literally means: "You should beware of those who you were good to."[200]

The basis for hiding one's religion is found in the Qur'an, in sura 16 *The Bee* – in Arabic: al-Nahl (سورة النَّحْل):

| 16:106 | With the exception of those who are forced to say they do not believe, although their hearts remain firm in faith, those who reject God after believing in Him and open their hearts to disbelief will have the wrath of God upon them and a grievous punishment awaiting them. | مَن كَفَرَ بِاللَّهِ مِن بَعْدِ إِيمَانِهِ إِلَّا مَنْ أُكْرِهَ وَقَلْبُهُ مُطْمَئِنٌّ بِالْإِيمَانِ وَلَٰكِن مَّن شَرَحَ بِالْكُفْرِ صَدْرًا فَعَلَيْهِمْ غَضَبٌ مِّنَ اللَّهِ وَلَهُمْ عَذَابٌ عَظِيمٌ. |

---

198 ...أَنَّ رَسُولَ اللَّهِ كَانَ إِذَا اشْتَكَى يَقْرَأُ عَلَى نَفْسِهِ بِالْمُعَوِّذَاتِ وَيَنْفُثُ، فَلَمَّا اشْتَدَّ وَجَعُهُ كُنْتُ أَقْرَأُ عَلَيْهِ وَأَمْسَحُ بِيَدِهِ رَجَاءَ بَرَكَتِهَا. Sahīh al-Bukhārī 5016.

199 أَعُوذُ بِاللَّهِ مِنَ الشَّيْطَنِ الرَّجِيمِ

200 اتَّقِ شَرَّ مَنْ أَحْسَنْتَ إِلَيْهِ.

According to this verse, fear of persecution is a legitimate excuse for a Muslim to hide his faith. A Muslim can therefore verbally renounce his faith, provided that he still is a believer in his heart.

This verse contradicts several passages in the Qur'an where it is said that martyrdom in the cause of Islam is honourable and worthy. However, Allah says in sura 2:233: "No one should be burdened with more than they can bear."[201]

Sura 40:28 tells Muslims about a man among the people of the Pharaoh who believed in the prophet Moses but hid his true faith and allegiance. Only when the Pharaoh threatened to kill Moses, the man declared his true faith and his support for Moses.

The principle of Taqīya is accepted by Sunni scholars, though they tend to restrict it to dealing with non-Muslims and when under compulsion – while Shia scholars allow it even in interactions with Muslims and in all necessary matters. Shia Muslims have always been a minority in the Islamic world.

The practice of Taqīya is particularly emphasised in Shia Islam. It is permissible in situations where there is immediate and great danger. The Shia Muslims have used it in a broader spectrum, especially during the Umayyad and Abbasid Caliphate to protect themselves against other Muslims, namely the Sunni rulers.

Sunnis call the act of protecting one's religion in dangerous and extreme circumstances Idtirār (اِضْطِرار) which translates as emergency; *being forced* or *being coerced*. This concept is not limited to hiding one's religion. Idtirār can be used to legally allow the consumption of prohibited food in order to avoid starving to death.

After the Muslim leaders in the Iberian Peninsula (Spain) had been defeated in 1492, Muslims and Jews were persecuted by the Roman-Catholic rulers. Taqīya allowed Muslims to "convert" officially to Christianity while remaining Muslims in their hearts and practising Islam secretly.

The Qur'an approves this in sura 3 *Family of 'Imrān* – in Arabic: 'Āl 'Imrān (سُورة آل عِمْران):

---

201 لَا تُكَلَّفُ نَفْسٌ إِلَّا وُسْعَهَا; 2:233

3:28	The believers should not make the disbelievers their allies rather than other believers - anyone who does such a thing will isolate himself completely from God - except when you need to protect yourselves from them. God warns you to beware of Him: the Final Return is to God.	لَّا يَتَّخِذِ الْمُؤْمِنُونَ الْكَافِرِينَ أَوْلِيَاءَ مِن دُونِ الْمُؤْمِنِينَ وَمَن يَفْعَلْ ذَٰلِكَ فَلَيْسَ مِنَ اللَّهِ فِي شَيْءٍ إِلَّا أَن تَتَّقُوا مِنْهُمْ تُقَاةً وَيُحَذِّرُكُمُ اللَّهُ نَفْسَهُ وَإِلَى اللَّهِ الْمَصِيرُ.

Muslims in danger are allowed to show friendship to non-Muslims outwardly – but never inwardly. In his commentary on this sura, Ibn Kathīr recorded that ʾAbū al-Dardāʾ (أَبُو الدَّرْداء), one of Muhammad's companions, said: "We smile in the face of some people although our hearts curse them.'"[202]

However, in contrast, if a <u>non-Muslim</u> pretends to be a Muslim outwardly, he is considered to be the worst form of a human being.

Excursus: The concept of al-Taqīya is connected to the history of basically all religions in times of persecution. The Jews had to hide their religion throughout their history. The first Christians used this concept in the era of the Roman emperor Diocletian (284 to 305), although Christianity, strictly speaking, does not approve of hiding one's faith. Christians have to sacrifice their life for their religion; there is no lying about their religion. This is clearly stated by the Gospels of Matthew, the Apostle:

16:24	Then Jesus said to His disciples, "If anyone desires to come after Me, let him deny himself, and take up his cross, and follow Me.
16:25	For whoever desires to save his life will lose it, but whoever loses his life for My sake will find it."

174. Which famous dam is mentioned in the Qur'an?

Answer: The Great Dam of Maʿrib.

Let's have a look at sura 34 *Sheba* – in Arabic: Sabaʾ (سُورة سَبَأ):

---

202 ...إِنَّا لَنَكْشِرُ فِي وُجُوهِ أَقْوَامٍ وَقُلُوبُنَا تَلْعَنُهُمْ. Ibn Kathīr.

34:16	But they paid no heed, so We let loose on them a flood from the dam and replaced their two gardens with others that yielded bitter fruit, tamarisk bushes, and a few lote trees.	فَأَعْرَضُوا فَأَرْسَلْنَا عَلَيْهِمْ سَيْلَ الْعَرِمِ وَبَدَّلْنَاهُم بِجَنَّتَيْهِمْ جَنَّتَيْنِ ذَوَاتَيْ أُكُلٍ خَمْطٍ وَأَثْلٍ وَشَيْءٍ مِّن سِدْرٍ قَلِيلٍ.

The dam is perhaps the Ma'rib Dam (سَدّ مَأْرِب), which was built to regulate the waters of the Wādī Saba' (وادي سباء) in antiquity. The ancient dam, perhaps about 550 metres (1,800 ft) long, irrigated more than 1,600 hectares (4,000 acres).

It was located in the kingdom of Sheba (سَبَإ), an empire in south-western Arabia. At the time of its greatest prosperity, in the first millennium BC, it included Yemen, a large part of Hadramawt and the Mahrah country and probably a large part of present-day Ethiopia. Over the centuries the Sabaeans had built a remarkable system of dams, dikes, and locks in the proximity of its capital Ma'rib.

The Great Dam was breached and rebuilt several times. One inscription says that it required 20,000 men and more than 14,000 camels to repair it. The dam broke and was repaired in ~ 450 AD and again several times in the sixth century. According to early Muslim historians, the dam broke again in the year 570. Its final destruction, perhaps by an earthquake or volcanic eruption, took place probably in the 7th century. The Qur'an, in verse 24:16, speaks of the *Flood of 'Arim* (سَيْلُ الْعَرِمِ), sometimes translated as *the flood or bursting of the dike*. It is a popular topic in Islamic myth and legend. The Qur'an refers to the collapse of the Ma'rib Dam as a punishment for the Sabaeans because they had rejected Allah.

Remark: At present, the region is one of the poorest and driest in the world. The people whose ancestors once fed a large part of the Middle East now have to import much of their food; the town of Ma'rib is largely in ruins. In June 2015, during the war between Saudi Arabia and the Houthis in Yemen - in Arabic: al-Hūthīyūn (الْحُوثِيُّون), the remains of the ancient dam were damaged in an air strike conducted by Saudi Arabia, according to local news reports and archaeological experts.

175. What happened to the People of 'Ād?

Answer: The People of 'Ād (قَوم عاد) were destroyed by a fierce wind which Allah caused to blow against them for 7 nights and 8 days.

The annihilation of the People of 'Ād is told in sura 69 *The Inevitable Hour/The Reality* – in Arabic: al-Hāqqa (سُورة الحاقّة):

69:6	'Ād was destroyed by a furious wind	وَأَمَّا عَادٌ فَأُهْلِكُوا بِرِيحٍ صَرْصَرٍ عَاتِيَةٍ
69:7	that God let loose against them for seven consecutive nights, eight consecutive days, so that you could have seen its people lying dead like hollow palm-trunks.	سَخَّرَهَا عَلَيْهِمْ سَبْعَ لَيَالٍ وَثَمَانِيَةَ أَيَّامٍ حُسُومًا فَتَرَى الْقَوْمَ فِيهَا صَرْعَىٰ كَأَنَّهُمْ أَعْجَازُ نَخْلٍ خَاوِيَةٍ.

So who was 'Ād? 'Ād was an ancient tribe mentioned frequently in the Qur'an. They probably lived in the south of the Arabian Peninsula, in a location called al-'Ahqāf (الأَحْقاف) - *the Sand Dunes* - a large desert region between present-day Oman and Hadramawt (حَضْرَمَوْت) in Yemen.

The members of the tribe - sometimes called 'Ādites - had founded a community that prospered and was well-off. After having rejected the divine message preached by prophet Hūd (هُود), Allah decided to extinguish them. 'Ād is regarded as one of the original Arab tribes, sometimes also called "the lost Arabs".

Remark: Hūd, according to Muhammad Asad, is said to have been the first Arabian prophet. He may be identical with the Biblical Eber (עֵבֶר), the ancestor of the Hebrews who, like most Semitic tribes, had probably originated in southern Arabia. The ancient name Hūd is still reflected in that of Jacob's son Judah/Judas - Yahudah (יהודה) in Hebrew -, which is the origin of the word *Jews*.

176. How did Allah punish the People of Madyan?

Answer: The People of Madyan (قَوْم مَدْيَن) were destroyed by a terrible earthquake. Only prophet Shu'ayb (شُعَيْب) and his followers survived.

Shuʿayb told the People of Madyan to worship exclusively Allah. He warned them of a fate similar to that of the people of Noah, Hūd or Sālih. However, the People of Madyan rejected the warning, scorned and threatened that they would drive Shuʿayb and his few followers out of Madyan. Sura 29 *The Spider* - in Arabic: al-ʿAnkabūt (سُورة الْعَنْكَبُوت) - tells what happened to the People of Madyan:

29:36	To the people of Midian (Madyan) We sent their brother Shuʿayb. He said, 'My people, serve God and think ahead to the Last Day. Do not commit evil and spread corruption in the land.'	وَإِلَى مَدْيَنَ أَخَاهُمْ شُعَيْبًا فَقَالَ يَا قَوْمِ اعْبُدُوا اللَّهَ وَارْجُوا الْيَوْمَ الْآخِرَ وَلَا تَعْثَوْا فِي الْأَرْضِ مُفْسِدِينَ.
29:37	They rejected him and so the earthquake overtook them. When morning came, they were lying dead in their homes.	فَكَذَّبُوهُ فَأَخَذَتْهُمُ الرَّجْفَةُ فَأَصْبَحُوا فِي دَارِهِمْ جَاثِمِينَ.

Sura 11 *Hūd* (سُورة هُود) gives more details:

11:94	When what We had ordained came about, in Our mercy We saved Shuʿayb and his fellow believers, but a mighty blast struck the wrongdoers. By morning they lay dead in their homes,	وَلَمَّا جَاءَ أَمْرُنَا نَجَّيْنَا شُعَيْبًا وَالَّذِينَ آمَنُوا مَعَهُ بِرَحْمَةٍ مِّنَّا وَأَخَذَتِ الَّذِينَ ظَلَمُوا الصَّيْحَةُ فَأَصْبَحُوا فِي دِيَارِهِمْ جَاثِمِينَ
11:95	as if they had never lived and flourished there. Yes, away with the People of Midian, just like the Thamūd!	كَأَن لَّمْ يَغْنَوْا فِيهَا أَلَا بُعْدًا لِّمَدْيَنَ كَمَا بَعِدَتْ ثَمُودُ.

In the Bible, the People of Madyan are called Midian (Hebrew: מִדְיָן). The region of Madyan (the Biblical Midian) extended from the present-day Gulf of Aqaba westwards into the Sinai Peninsula and to the mountains of Moab east of the Dead Sea. Some scholars say that the People of Madyan could either have been annihilated by an earthquake or/and by a volcanic eruption. The neighbouring region of Madyan shows evidence of volcanic eruptions and earthquakes – similar to those found in the Harra (الْحَرّة) which was once inhabited by the Thamūd (ثَمُود) tribe.

Note: The People of Madyan are occasionally called *The Forest-Dweller* – in Arabic: ʾAshāb al-ʾAyka (أصحاب الأَيْكَة) because they used to worship a large tree. Most historians think that the Forest Dwellers and the People of Madyan were the same people. The Arabic word al-'Ayka means a place with many trees standing close together, a forest. It could have been used to refer to the land near Madyan because it had enough water and many trees.

177. Does Islam know the Christian concept of *original sin*?

Answer: No, Islam doesn't.

In Christianity, every human being is burdened from birth with the original or ancestral sin. This results from the fall of man. When Adam and Eve rebelled in Eden and ignored all warnings, disobeyed God, and ate from the tree of the knowledge of good and evil. Islam does not know this doctrine. This is stated in the Qur'an, sura 53 *The Star/The Unfolding* – in Arabic: al-Najm (سُورة النَّجْم).

| 53:38 | that no soul shall bear the burden of another | أَلَّا تَزِرُ وَازِرَةٌ وِزْرَ أُخْرَىٰ |

This verse is crucial to understand the differences between Islam and Christianity. It refutes the idea that a person's sins could be atoned for by the self-sacrifice of Jesus. And there is a clear refutation of the Roman-Catholic Sacrament of Penance (confession), for which a Roman-Catholic believer needs a priest, because Islam does not know any mediation between the sinner and Allah.

178. What is the name for Jesus in Arabic?

Answer: There is an Islamic and a Christian Arabic version.

- 'Īsā (عِيسَى) is used by Muslims.
- Yasū' or Yasūa (يَسُوع) is used by Arabic speaking Christians who want to stress that the Christian Jesus is different from the Islamic Jesus. The word Yasū' came from Aramaic into Hebrew, and from there it entered Arabic. It is a combined name of two words and means *God saves*.

The English word *Jesus* is similar to the Arabic Yasūʿ. The name Jesus is derived from the Latin Iesus, a transliteration of the Greek Iesous (Ἰησοῦς). The Greek form is a rendering of the Hebrew Yeshua (יֵשׁוּעַ), a variant of the earlier name Yehoshua (יְהוֹשֻׁעַ) – in English Joshua.

The name Yeshua appears to have been in use in Judea at the time of the birth of Jesus. Since Greek had no equivalent to the Semitic letter shin (שׁ), it was replaced with a sigma (σ), and a masculine singular ending (-s) was added in the nominative case, in order to allow the name to be inflected for case in Greek.

Christians call Jesus normally Jesus Christ. The word Christ is taken from the Greek Christos (Χριστός) which is a translation of the Hebrew Mashiach (Hebrew: מָשִׁיחַ) – *the anointed*. The English transliteration is *Messiah*.

In Arabic, an epithet for Jesus is al-Masīh (الْمَسِيح), which is similar to the Hebrew word. The Arabic root likewise means *to wipe out; to anoint*. Christians believe that Jesus is the awaited Messiah.

179. Why does Jesus say in the Qur'an that there will be "a messenger to come after me, whose name is ʾAhmad"?

Answer: ʾAhmad (أَحْمَد) and Muhammad (مُحَمَّد) can be treated as synonyms.

Muhammad literally means *praised; commendable, laudable* (for his good character)

ʾAhmad literally means *more laudable, more commendable*. But practically, we could say that they both mean the same.

Let us check sura 61 *Solid Lines* – in Arabic: al-Saff (سُورة الصَّف):

61:6	Jesus, son of Mary, said, 'Children of Israel, I am sent to you by God, confirming the Torah that came before me and bringing good news of a messenger to follow me whose name will be Ahmad.	وَإِذْ قَالَ عِيسَى ابْنُ مَرْيَمَ يَا بَنِي إِسْرَائِيلَ إِنِّي رَسُولُ اللَّهِ إِلَيْكُم مُّصَدِّقًا لِّمَا بَيْنَ يَدَيَّ مِنَ التَّوْرَاةِ وَمُبَشِّرًا بِرَسُولٍ يَأْتِي مِن بَعْدِي اسْمُهُ أَحْمَدُ فَلَمَّا جَاءَهُم بِالْبَيِّنَاتِ قَالُوا هَٰذَا سِحْرٌ مُّبِينٌ.

180. Was Jesus crucified?

Answer: No, the Qur'an denies that.

The Qur'an has its own view about what had happened to Jesus. This is found in sura 4 *Women* – in Arabic: al-Nisā' (سُورَة النِّساء). The sura was revealed during Muhammad's time in Medina and received its title from various references to women, mostly in the context of legal issues such as rules of inheritance or marriage.

4:157	and [they] said, 'We have killed the Messiah, Jesus, son of Mary, the Messenger of God.' They did not kill him, nor did they crucify him, though it was made to appear like that to them; those that disagreed about him are full of doubt, with no knowledge to follow, only supposition: they certainly did not kill him.	وَقَوْلِهِمْ إِنَّا قَتَلْنَا الْمَسِيحَ عِيسَى ابْنَ مَرْيَمَ رَسُولَ اللَّهِ وَمَا قَتَلُوهُ وَمَا صَلَبُوهُ وَلَكِن شُبِّهَ لَهُمْ وَإِنَّ الَّذِينَ اخْتَلَفُوا فِيهِ لَفِي شَكٍّ مِّنْهُ مَا لَهُم بِهِ مِنْ عِلْمٍ إِلَّا اتِّبَاعَ الظَّنِّ وَمَا قَتَلُوهُ يَقِينًا.
4:158	God raised him up to Himself. God is almighty and wise.	بَل رَّفَعَهُ اللَّهُ إِلَيْهِ وَكَانَ اللَّهُ عَزِيزًا حَكِيمًا.

There are several stories circulating among Muslims about the fate of Jesus. Some say that Allah replaced Jesus with a person closely resembling him (according to some accounts, that person was Judas) who was crucified in his place. However, neither one of these legends is based on the Qur'an or on authentic Hadiths.

In the end, it all comes down to the phrase which is marked in grey in the above table: "wa-lākin shubbiha lahum" (وَلَكِن شُبِّهَ لَهُمْ) which means: *but it only appeared to them as if it had been so*. This is a reference to the Christians who say that Jesus was crucified in order to atone for the original sin.

181. Did Jesus rise to heaven?

Answer: It depends whom you ask. The Qur'an denies that.

The Qur'an states that Jesus was a prophet and that he died. But what happened to Jesus' body after his death?

Christians believe that Jesus rose to heaven. They claim that he was resurrected and that his grave was empty. Islam rejects this. In sura 3 *Family of ʿImrān* - in Arabic: ʾĀl ʿImrān (سُورة آل عِمْران) - Allah talks to Jesus:

| 3:55 | God said, 'Jesus, I will take you back and raise you up to Me: I will purify you of the disbelievers. To the Day of Resurrection, I will make those who follow you superior to those who disbelieved. Then you will all return to Me and I will judge between you regarding your differences. | إِذْ قَالَ اللَّهُ يَا عِيسَى إِنِّي مُتَوَفِّيكَ وَرَافِعُكَ إِلَيَّ وَمُطَهِّرُكَ مِنَ الَّذِينَ كَفَرُوا وَجَاعِلُ الَّذِينَ اتَّبَعُوكَ فَوْقَ الَّذِينَ كَفَرُوا إِلَى يَوْمِ الْقِيَامَةِ ثُمَّ إِلَيَّ مَرْجِعُكُمْ فَأَحْكُمُ بَيْنَكُمْ فِيمَا كُنتُمْ فِيهِ تَخْتَلِفُونَ. |

The crucial expression here is: (*Allah) raises* (رافِع). Muhammad Asad wrote that whenever the Qur'an talks about the act of elevating (رَفْع) a human being by Allah, the meaning is more of *honouring* or *exalting*. Nowhere in the Qur'an is there any warrant for the Christian belief that God has *taken up* Jesus bodily, in his lifetime, into heaven. The expression Allah *exalted him/raised him up unto Himself* means that Jesus entered the realm of Allah's special grace – a blessing all prophets received, as said in the Qur'an, sura 19 *Mary* (سُورة مَرْيَم):

| 19:56 | Mention too, in the Qur'an, the story of ʾIdrīs. He was a man of truth, a prophet. | وَاذْكُرْ فِي الْكِتَابِ إِدْرِيسَ إِنَّهُ كَانَ صِدِّيقًا نَبِيًّا. |
| 19:57 | We raised him to a high position. | وَرَفَعْنَاهُ مَكَانًا عَلِيًّا. |

In these verses the Qur'an talks about prophet ʾIdrīs. Again, the Qur'an uses the verb rafaʿa (رَفَعَ) in the meaning of: *We exalted him*. This has a big impact on Muslims. Muslims like to tell that Allah has exalted Jesus unto Himself and did not finish his life by granting him a shameful death at the cross because at the time of Jesus, crucifixion was a punishment for criminals of mostly lower classes.

182. Was Jesus the son of God?

Answer: No, the Qur'an denies that.

This is one of the most discussed topics as Muslims insist that Jesus was just a prophet, which Christians, by definition, reject totally.

Since Christians claim that Jesus was the son of God, Allah instructed Muhammad to correct this view. This is what Muslims believe. In Islam, it is one of the reasons to justify why Allah has sent Muhammad the Qur'an because Muhammad's main mission was to fix the messages of his predecessors. Muslims believe that these messages were corrupted mainly by the Jews and the Christians.

Let's see what the Qur'an tells Muslims in sura 3 *Family of 'Imrān* – in Arabic: 'Āl 'Imrān (سُورة آل عِمْران). Most scholars think that the verses of this sura, which deal with the topic of Jesus, were revealed in the year 10 AH, when Muhammad had a disagreement with some Christians of Najrān (نجران), a city in south-western (present-day) Saudi Arabia near the border with Yemen.

3:59	In God's eyes Jesus is just like Adam: He created him from dust, said to him, 'Be', and he was.	إِنَّ مَثَلَ عِيسَىٰ عِندَ اللَّهِ كَمَثَلِ آدَمَ خَلَقَهُ مِن تُرَابٍ ثُمَّ قَالَ لَهُ كُن فَيَكُونُ

This verse was used to reject the Christian doctrine that Jesus embodied God. Every religion claims for oneself the absolute truth. Islam, Christianity and Judaism are somehow interconnected. However, there is a hierarchy simply based on the fact that the religions were founded one after another.

This means that Christianity updated and upgraded Judaism, and that Islam updated and upgraded both of them. Therefore, a dialogue between the three Abrahamitic religions is difficult. Judaism neither mentions Christianity nor Islam. However, Islam sees itself above them and as the seal of all religions.

This is not something Muslims claim; it is stated in the Qur'an, in sura 5 *The Feast* – in Arabic: al-Māʾida (سُورة الْمائدة):

5:48	We sent to you [Muhammad] the Scripture with the truth, confirming the Scriptures that came before it, and with final authority over them: so judge between them according to what God has sent down.	وَأَنزَلْنَا إِلَيْكَ الْكِتَابَ بِالْحَقِّ مُصَدِّقًا لِّمَا بَيْنَ يَدَيْهِ مِنَ الْكِتَابِ وَمُهَيْمِنًا عَلَيْهِ فَاحْكُم بَيْنَهُم بِمَا أَنزَلَ اللَّهُ

183. Why do some Muslims call Jews and Christians infidels?

Answer: There are several reasons.

Regarding Christianity, the main reason why some Muslims denounce Christians as unbelievers is the trinity of God (God, his son Jesus and the Holy Spirit) which some Muslims interpret as three Gods. The Qur'an says that Jesus was not the son of God, but just a servant of Allah:

4:172	The Messiah would never disdain to be a servant of God, nor would the angels who are close to Him. He will gather before Him all those who disdain His worship and are arrogant:	لَّن يَسْتَنكِفَ الْمَسِيحُ أَن يَكُونَ عَبْدًا لِّلَّهِ وَلَا الْمَلَائِكَةُ الْمُقَرَّبُونَ وَمَن يَسْتَنكِفْ عَنْ عِبَادَتِهِ وَيَسْتَكْبِرْ فَسَيَحْشُرُهُمْ إِلَيْهِ جَمِيعًا:

The following verses of sura 5 *The Feast* - in Arabic: al-Māʾida (سورة المائدة) - are specifically about Christians:

5:72	Those who say, 'God is the Messiah, son of Mary,' have defied God. The Messiah himself said, 'Children of Israel, worship God, my Lord and your Lord.' If anyone associates others with God, God will forbid him from the Garden, and Hell will be his home. No one will help such evildoers.	لَقَدْ كَفَرَ الَّذِينَ قَالُوا إِنَّ اللَّهَ هُوَ الْمَسِيحُ ابْنُ مَرْيَمَ وَقَالَ الْمَسِيحُ يَا بَنِي إِسْرَائِيلَ اعْبُدُوا اللَّهَ رَبِّي وَرَبَّكُمْ إِنَّهُ مَن يُشْرِكْ بِاللَّهِ فَقَدْ حَرَّمَ اللَّهُ عَلَيْهِ الْجَنَّةَ وَمَأْوَاهُ النَّارُ وَمَا لِلظَّالِمِينَ مِنْ أَنصَارٍ
5:73	Those people who say that God is the third of three are defying [the truth]: there is only One God. If they persist in what they are saying, a painful punishment will afflict those of them who persist.	لَقَدْ كَفَرَ الَّذِينَ قَالُوا إِنَّ اللَّهَ ثَالِثُ ثَلَاثَةٍ وَمَا مِنْ إِلَهٍ إِلَّا إِلَهٌ وَاحِدٌ وَإِن لَّمْ يَنتَهُوا عَمَّا يَقُولُونَ لَيَمَسَّنَّ الَّذِينَ كَفَرُوا مِنْهُمْ عَذَابٌ أَلِيمٌ

Muslims are convinced that Christians and Jews deny the Islamic truth on purpose even though they know the truth. They find evidence for this in sura 3 *Family of ʿImrān* – in Arabic: ʾĀl ʿImrān (سورة آل عِمران). The people referred to in this verse are Jews and Christians. Muslims believe that the Bible predicts the coming of the prophet Muhammad:

| 3:86 | Why would God guide people who deny the truth, after they have believed and acknowledged that the Messenger is true, and after they have been shown clear proof? God does not guide evildoers. | كَيْفَ يَهْدِي اللَّهُ قَوْمًا كَفَرُوا بَعْدَ إِيمَانِهِمْ وَشَهِدُوا أَنَّ الرَّسُولَ حَقٌّ وَجَاءَهُمُ الْبَيِّنَاتُ وَاللَّهُ لَا يَهْدِي الْقَوْمَ الظَّالِمِينَ. |

In sura 5 *The Feast,* Muslims are warned that they should not take Jews and Christians as allies:

| 5:51 | You who believe, do not take the Jews and Christians as allies: they are allies only to each other. Anyone who takes them as an ally becomes one of them - God does not guide such wrongdoers. | يَا أَيُّهَا الَّذِينَ آمَنُوا لَا تَتَّخِذُوا الْيَهُودَ وَالنَّصَارَى أَوْلِيَاءَ بَعْضُهُمْ أَوْلِيَاءُ بَعْضٍ وَمَن يَتَوَلَّهُم مِّنكُمْ فَإِنَّهُ مِنْهُمْ إِنَّ اللَّهَ لَا يَهْدِي الْقَوْمَ الظَّالِمِينَ. |

Muhammad Asad claimed in his exegesis that this verse should be read (also) in the moral sense of the word: "that is, not to imitate their way of life and their social concepts at the expense of the principles of Islam." This warning, wrote Muhammad Asad, "is necessitated by the fact, repeatedly stressed in this sura, that both the Jews and the Christians have abandoned and corrupted the truths conveyed to them by their prophets, and thus no longer adhere to the genuine, original message of the Bible".

Islam commands to believe in Allah and <u>all</u> his prophets. Jews and Christians don't do that according to the Qur'an:

4:150	As for those who ignore God and His messengers and want to make a distinction between them, saying, 'We believe in some but not in others,' seeking a middle way,	إِنَّ الَّذِينَ يَكْفُرُونَ بِاللَّهِ وَرُسُلِهِ وَيُرِيدُونَ أَن يُفَرِّقُوا بَيْنَ اللَّهِ وَرُسُلِهِ وَيَقُولُونَ نُؤْمِنُ بِبَعْضٍ وَنَكْفُرُ بِبَعْضٍ وَيُرِيدُونَ أَن يَتَّخِذُوا بَيْنَ ذَلِكَ سَبِيلًا.
4:151	they are really disbelievers: We have prepared a humiliating punishment for those who disbelieve.	أُولَئِكَ هُمُ الْكَافِرُونَ حَقًّا وَأَعْتَدْنَا لِلْكَافِرِينَ عَذَابًا مُّهِينًا.
4:152	But God will give [due] rewards to those who believe in Him and His messengers and make no distinction between any of them. God is most for-	وَالَّذِينَ آمَنُوا بِاللَّهِ وَرُسُلِهِ وَلَمْ يُفَرِّقُوا بَيْنَ أَحَدٍ مِّنْهُمْ أُولَئِكَ سَوْفَ يُؤْتِيهِمْ أُجُورَهُمْ وَكَانَ اللَّهُ غَفُورًا رَّحِيمًا.

	giving and merciful.	

These verses refute the possibility of believing in God without believing in His prophets. The Jews, however, deny the prophethood not only of Muhammad but also of Jesus. But there are further reasons why some Muslims denounce Jews as unbelievers. This has to do with the Jewish history. The Qur'an states that when Allah made a covenant with (the children of) Israel through Moses, the people responded by saying that they will not obey. Sura 2 *The Cow* - in Arabic: al-Baqara (سُورَة الْبَقَرة) - condemns them:

2:92	Moses brought you clear signs, but then, while he was away, you chose to worship the calf - you did wrong.'	وَلَقَدْ جَاءَكُم مُّوسَىٰ بِالْبَيِّنَاتِ ثُمَّ اتَّخَذْتُمُ الْعِجْلَ مِن بَعْدِهِ وَأَنتُمْ ظَالِمُونَ.
2:93	Remember when We took your pledge, making the mountain tower above you, and said, 'Hold on firmly to what We have given you, and listen to [what We say].' They said, 'We hear and we <u>disobey</u>', and through their disbelief they were made to drink [the love of] the calf deep into their hearts.	وَإِذْ أَخَذْنَا مِيثَاقَكُمْ وَرَفَعْنَا فَوْقَكُمُ الطُّورَ خُذُوا مَا آتَيْنَاكُم بِقُوَّةٍ وَاسْمَعُوا قَالُوا سَمِعْنَا وَعَصَيْنَا وَأُشْرِبُوا فِي قُلُوبِهِمُ الْعِجْلَ بِكُفْرِهِمْ قُلْ بِئْسَمَا يَأْمُرُكُم بِهِ إِيمَانُكُمْ إِن كُنتُم مُّؤْمِنِينَ.

Muslims say that one should not be like the *Children of Israel*. On the contrary, a Muslim has to accept even those things for which Allah has not given a reason. The Muslim says: "We hear and we *obey*." This, too, was stated in sura *The Cow*:

2:285	The Messenger believes in what has been sent down to him from his Lord, as do the faithful. They all believe in God, His angels, His scriptures, and His messengers. 'We make no distinction between any of His messengers,' they say, 'We hear and <u>obey</u>. Grant us Your forgiveness, our Lord. To You we all return!'	آمَنَ الرَّسُولُ بِمَا أُنزِلَ إِلَيْهِ مِن رَّبِّهِ وَالْمُؤْمِنُونَ كُلٌّ آمَنَ بِاللَّهِ وَمَلَائِكَتِهِ وَكُتُبِهِ وَرُسُلِهِ لَا نُفَرِّقُ بَيْنَ أَحَدٍ مِّن رُّسُلِهِ وَقَالُوا سَمِعْنَا وَأَطَعْنَا غُفْرَانَكَ رَبَّنَا وَإِلَيْكَ الْمَصِيرُ!

The following verses of sura 5 *The Feast* are specifically about Jews:

5:70	We took a pledge from the Children of Israel, and sent messengers to them. Whenever a messenger brought them anything they did not like, they accused some of lying and put others to death;	لَقَدْ أَخَذْنَا مِيثَاقَ بَنِي إِسْرَائِيلَ وَأَرْسَلْنَا إِلَيْهِم رُسُلًا كُلَّمَا جَاءَهُمْ رَسُولٌ بِمَا لَا تَهْوَى أَنفُسُهُمْ فَرِيقًا كَذَّبُوا وَفَرِيقًا يَقْتُلُونَ
5:71	they thought no harm could come to them and so became blind and deaf [to God]. God turned to them in mercy but many of them again became blind and deaf: God is fully aware of their actions.	وَحَسِبُوا أَلَّا تَكُونَ فِتْنَةٌ فَعَمُوا وَصَمُّوا ثُمَّ تَابَ اللَّهُ عَلَيْهِمْ ثُمَّ عَمُوا وَصَمُّوا كَثِيرٌ مِّنْهُمْ وَاللَّهُ بَصِيرٌ بِمَا يَعْمَلُونَ.

184. Why does the Sheikh of al-'Azhar attend the feast of Coptic Christmas but not that of Coptic Easter?

Answer: Because he accepts the idea that Jesus was born, but rejects the idea that Jesus was the son of God who was crucified and rose to heaven (Easter) to sit next to God.

The Sheikh of al-'Azhar, which is a famous Egyptian Islamic institution, is one of the most important religious leaders in (Sunni) Islam. He usually attends the festival of Christmas in order to show respect to the Christian minority in Egypt, but he would never do so on Easter, the most important Christian festival celebrating the resurrection of Jesus from the dead.

Muslims accept Jesus as a prophet, but they reject the Christian doctrine that claims he is the son of God. Furthermore, Muslims reject the idea that Jesus was crucified and rose to heaven.

185. Which sura has to be said in every prayer?

Answer: Sura 1 *The Opening* - in Arabic: al-Fātiha (سُورة الْفَاتِحة).

The sura was revealed to Muhammad in Mecca and has only seven verses. Although it is the first sura in the Qur'an, it was most probably not the first the Prophet had received.

It is said that ʿAlī ibn ʾAbī Ṭālib (عَلِيّ بن أَبِي طالِب), Muhammad's cousin and son-in-law, thought that this was the very first revelation. However, both (Sunni) authorities on the Hadiths, al-Bukhārī and al-Muslim, claim that it was sura 96 *The Clinging Form* - in Arabic: al-ʿAlaq (سُورة الْعَلَق) - which marks the beginning of revelation.

Nevertheless, there is something remarkable about this sura which could explain ʿAlī 's view. Sura 1 *The Opening* was the first sura which was revealed to Muhammad completely at one time! The verses of most other suras were revealed step-by-step with sometimes considerably big lapses of time in between the revelations.

ʿUbāda ibn al-Sāmit (عُبادة بن الصَّامِت) narrated that Allah's Messenger said: "Whoever does not recite al-Fātiha in his prayer, his prayer is invalid."[203]

Therefore, this sura has to be said in every Rakʿa (رَكْعة) during a Muslim's prayer. A Rakʿa is the bending of the torso from an upright position, followed by prostrations. The sura *The Opening* is recited at least 17 times in a Muslim's daily prayers. There are several other common names for this sura:

- *The Opening of the (divine) Book* – in Arabic called: Fātiha(t) al-Kitāb (فاتِحة الْكِتاب).
- *The Essence of the Divine Writ* – in Arabic: ʾUmm al-Kitāb (أُمّ الْكِتـاب). According to al-Bukhārī, this was how Muhammad referred to this sura.
- *The Sura of Praise* – in Arabic: sura(t) al-Hamd (سُورة الْحَمْد).
- *The Foundation of the Qurʾan* – in Arabic: ʾAsās al-Qurʾan (أَساس الْقُرْآن).
- *The Seven Oft-Repeated (Verses)* – in Arabic: al-Sabʿa al-Mathānī (السَّبْع الْمَثانِي). This name is related to the fact that a Muslim has to recite these verses in each of his daily prayers.

This sura can be seen as a summary of the message of the Qurʾan:

1:1	In the name of God, the Lord of Mercy, the Giver of Mercy!	بِسْمِ اللَّهِ الرَّحْمَنِ الرَّحِيمِ!
1:2	Praise belongs to God, Lord of the Worlds,	الْحَمْدُ لِلَّهِ رَبِّ الْعَالَمِينَ

---

203 ...أَنَّ رَسُولَ اللَّهِ قَالَ: "لاَ صَلاَةَ لِمَنْ لَمْ يَقْرَأْ بِفَاتِحَةِ الْكِتَابِ." Ṣaḥīḥ al-Bukhārī 756

1:3	the Lord of Mercy, the Giver of Mercy,	الرَّحْمَنِ الرَّحِيمِ
1:4	Master of the Day of Judgement.	مَالِكِ يَوْمِ الدِّينِ.
1:5	It is You we worship; it is You we ask for help.	إِيَّاكَ نَعْبُدُ وَإِيَّاكَ نَسْتَعِينُ.
1:6	Guide us to the straight path:	اهْدِنَا الصِّرَاطَ الْمُسْتَقِيمَ:
1:7	the path of those You have blessed, those who incur no anger and who have not gone astray.	صِرَاطَ الَّذِينَ أَنْعَمْتَ عَلَيْهِمْ غَيْرِ الْمَغْضُوبِ عَلَيْهِمْ وَلَا الضَّالِّينَ.

186. In which sura is Allah talking about Dhū al-Qarnayn?

Answer: Sura 18 *The Cave* – in Arabic: al-Kahf (سُورَة الْكَهْف).

This sura contains 110 verses and was revealed in the last year of Muhammad's stay in Mecca, before he migrated with his followers to Yathrib (Medina).

Dhū al-Qarnayn (ذُو الْقَرْنَيْنِ) is the name of a benevolent king who moved around the world from the east to the west, to help people and invite them to believe in Allah.

The meaning of the epithet Dhū al-Qarnayn (ذُو الْقَرْنَيْـنِ) is not entirely clear. It could mean *The Two-Horned One* as well as *He of the Two Epochs* because the Arabic word qarn (قَرْن) can denote *horn* as well as *generation, epoch,* or *century.*

Most classical commentators preferred *The Two-Horned.* A possible explanation could be that the ancient Middle-Eastern symbol of *horns* was used to describe power and greatness. The Qur'an does not give any hint if this is the correct interpretation of the name. Instead, the Qur'an even complicates the matter because the word qarn is used in the Qur'an twenty times and exclusively in the meaning of *generation,* i.e. people who lived in a particular epoch.

The allegory of *The Two-Horned One* tells Muslims that worldly life and power need not conflict with religion. As long as the ruler follows the rules of Allah, everything is fine. The Qur'an tries to illustrate the qualities of a powerful and just ruler in sura 18 *The Cave:*

| 18:110 | Anyone who fears to meet his Lord should do good deeds and give no one a share in the worship due to his Lord. | فَمَن كَانَ يَرْجُو لِقَاءَ رَبِّهِ فَلْيَعْمَلْ عَمَلًا صَالِحًا وَلَا يُشْرِكْ بِعِبَادَةِ رَبِّهِ أَحَدًا. |

Muhammad Asad wrote that within the context of the Qur'anic allegory, the *two horns* may be taken to denote the two sources of power with which Dhū al-Qarnayn is said to have been endowed: "namely, the worldly might and prestige of kingship as well as the spiritual strength resulting from his faith in Allah".

This last point is important because in earlier times, some commentators thought that Dhū al-Qarnayn could have been identified as Alexander the Great, because he was represented on some coins with two horns on his head. Others thought it could have been one of the pre-Islamic Himyaritic kings of Yemen.

However, most pre-Islamic kings as well as Alexander the Great were pagans and worshipped a variety of deities. In the Qur'an, king Dhū al-Qarnayn is portrayed as a strong believer in Allah.

Muhammad Asad concludes that Dhū al-Qarnayn had most probably nothing to do with history or legend. The verse is merely a parable discussing faith and ethics in relation to the problems of worldly power.

187. What does al-Walā' wa al-Barā' mean?

Answer: *Loyalty and disavowal* (الوَلاء البَراء).

The word Barā' (بَراءة) means *freedom* or *release from an obligation, exemption, abrogation*. In pre-Islamic Arabia, the word also meant *to exempt* or *expel* (a rebellious, unruly) member from a tribe. The word Barā' is derived from the verb bari'a (بَرِئَ) which means *to become free (of something)* or *quit of having any part (in something)*. According to Edward Lane, it describes in particular the declaration of being freed of any bond with a person. If it is referring to Allah or Muhammad, translators usually render it as *disavowal*.

The term is used in the Qur'an in sura 9 *The Repentance* – in Arabic: al-Tawba or al-Barā' (سُورة التَّوبة or البَراءة). This is the only sura of the Qur'an which does not start with the Basmala ("In the name of

Allah…"; see chapter 107). Let's not forget the circumstances, because this sura was revealed during a time of war. The events which are discussed in this sura took place after the Treaty of Hudaybīya (صُلْح الْحُدَيْبِيّة).

The Muslim forces were already a big player as one-third of Arabia had come under the power of Islam. For this reason, the first two verses of this sura describe the separation of Muslims and non-Muslims:

9:1	[This is a declaration of] disassociation, from Allah and His Messenger, to those with whom you had made a treaty among the polytheists.	بَرَاءَةٌ مِّنَ اللَّهِ وَرَسُولِهِ إِلَى الَّذِينَ عَاهَدتُّم مِّنَ الْمُشْرِكِينَ.
9:2	you [idolaters] may move freely about the land for four months, but you should bear in mind both that you will not escape God, and that God will disgrace those who defy [Him].	فَسِيحُوا فِي الْأَرْضِ أَرْبَعَةَ أَشْهُرٍ وَاعْلَمُوا أَنَّكُمْ غَيْرُ مُعْجِزِي اللَّهِ وَأَنَّ اللَّهَ مُخْزِي الْكَافِرِينَ.

The four months which are mentioned in the verse above are probably the four sacred months of Islam during which fighting and wars are forbidden.

Why did the expression "loyalty and disavowal" become popular?

Al-Walā' wa al-Barā' (الـوَلاء البَـراء) means *loyalty and disavowal*. It describes a person who strives to do all that pleases Allah and quits and opposes all things which Allah does not like.

This doctrine is popular with strict, traditional Muslims. They are convinced, for example, that a Muslim should only have Muslim friends and should not go near non-Muslims. There are some suras which are indicating this command:

3:28	The believers should not make the disbelievers their allies rather than other believers - anyone who does such a thing will isolate himself completely from God - except when you need to protect yourselves from them. God warns you to beware of Him: the Final Return is to God.	لَّا يَتَّخِذِ الْمُؤْمِنُونَ الْكَافِرِينَ أَوْلِيَاءَ مِن دُونِ الْمُؤْمِنِينَ وَمَن يَفْعَلْ ذَٰلِكَ فَلَيْسَ مِنَ اللَّهِ فِي شَيْءٍ إِلَّا أَن تَتَّقُوا مِنْهُمْ تُقَاةً وَيُحَذِّرُكُمُ اللَّهُ نَفْسَهُ وَإِلَى اللَّهِ الْمَصِيرُ.

4:89	They would dearly like you to reject faith, as they themselves have done, to be like them. So do not take them as allies until they migrate [to Medina] for God's cause. If they turn [on you], then seize and kill them wherever you encounter them. Take none of them as an ally or supporter.	وَدُّوا لَوْ تَكْفُرُونَ كَمَا كَفَرُوا فَتَكُونُونَ سَوَاءً فَلَا تَتَّخِذُوا مِنْهُمْ أَوْلِيَاءَ حَتَّىٰ يُهَاجِرُوا فِي سَبِيلِ اللَّهِ فَإِن تَوَلَّوْا فَخُذُوهُمْ وَاقْتُلُوهُمْ حَيْثُ وَجَدتُّمُوهُمْ وَلَا تَتَّخِذُوا مِنْهُمْ وَلِيًّا وَلَا نَصِيرًا.
5:51	You who believe, do not take the Jews and Christians as allies: they are allies only to each other. Anyone who takes them as an ally becomes one of them - God does not guide such wrongdoers.	يَا أَيُّهَا الَّذِينَ آمَنُوا لَا تَتَّخِذُوا الْيَهُودَ وَالنَّصَارَىٰ أَوْلِيَاءَ بَعْضُهُمْ أَوْلِيَاءُ بَعْضٍ وَمَن يَتَوَلَّهُم مِّنكُمْ فَإِنَّهُ مِنْهُمْ إِنَّ اللَّهَ لَا يَهْدِي الْقَوْمَ الظَّالِمِينَ.

188. Which sura mentions the blind son of ’Umm Maktūm?

Answer: Sura 80 *He Frowned* – in Arabic: ‘Abasa (سُورة عَبَسَ).

This sura has 42 verses and was revealed during a rather early stage of the Prophet's mission in Mecca. In this sura, Muhammad is speaking to a group of influential non-Muslims (chieftains) in Mecca. He wants them to embrace Islam.

Suddenly, one of his followers, the blind ‘Abd Allah ibn ’Umm Maktūm (عَبْد الله بن أُمّ مَكْتُوم), approached him asking to recite some verses of the Qur'an. However, the Prophet was annoyed by this interruption. He regarded his mission - to convert the Meccans - more important, so Muhammad “frowned and turned away” from the blind man.

Let's look at a Hadith which tells more about this incident. The Hadith was reported by Hishām ibn ‘Urwa (هشام بن عُروة) who heard his father say that when ‘Abasa (sura 80) was revealed, it was about ‘Abd Allah ibn ’Umm Maktūm [the blind man]:

“He [‘Abd Allah] came to the Prophet and began to say: 'O Muhammad, show me a place near you [where I can sit]', whilst one of the leading men of the idol worshippers was in audience with the Prophet.

The Prophet began to turn away from him ['Abd Allah] giving attention to the other man. He said: "Father of so-and-so, do you see any harm in what I am saying?", and he replied: 'No, by the blood [of our sacrifices], I see no harm in what you are saying.' And 'Abasa - 'He frowned and turned away when the blind man came' - was sent down."[204]

Upon that, Muhammad received the first ten verses of this sura in which the Prophet is told to not concern himself with the non-Muslims. The first two verses are special because the Qur'an uses the third-person in verses 1 and 2 to underline the rebuke.

| 80:1 | He [Muhammad] frowned and turned away | عَبَسَ وَتَوَلَّىٰ |
| 80:2 | when the blind man came to him | أَن جَاءَهُ الْأَعْمَىٰ |

Some sources indicate that later on, Muhammad occasionally greeted the blind man saying: "Welcome unto him on whose account my Sustainer has rebuked me!"

The Arabic word maktūm (مَكْتُوم) means *hidden; concealed*. His mother was called 'Umm Maktūm (أُمّ مَكْتُوم) - literally *mother of the concealed one* - because she gave birth to a blind child. Various schol-ars claim that 'Abd Allah was a cousin of Khadīja (خَدِيجَة بِنت خُوَيْلِد), Muhammad's first wife. According to Hadiths, the blind 'Abd Allah was not only a companion, but also a muezzin. 'Abd Allah ibn 'Umar (عَبْد الله بِن عُمَر) reported that the Messenger of Allah had two muezzins: Bilāl and 'Abd Allah ibn 'Umm Maktūm, who was blind.[205]

Remark: In the beginning of Islam, the muezzins were standing on roofs calling upon Muslims to come to pray. From an elevated posi-tion, however, they could have violated other people's privacy because it was possible to see into other houses from above. Jonathan M. Bloom, a professor of Islamic Art, said that in the earlier years of Islam, blind men were often selected as muezzin, for the simple reason that they could not violate other people's privacy.

---

204 ... أَنَّهُ قَالَ أُنْزِلَتْ {عَبَسَ وَتَوَلَّى} فِي عَبْدِ اللَّهِ بْنِ أُمِّ مَكْتُومٍ جَاءَ إِلَى رَسُولِ اللَّهِ فَجَعَلَ يَقُولُ يَا مُحَمَّدُ اسْتَدْنِينِي وَعِنْدَ النَّبِيِّ رَجُلٌ مِنْ عُظَمَاءِ الْمُشْرِكِينَ فَجَعَلَ النَّبِيُّ يُعْرِضُ عَنْهُ وَيُقْبِلُ عَلَى الْآخَرِ وَيَقُولُ: "يَا أَبَا فُلَانٍ هَلْ تَرَى بِمَا أَقُولُ بَأْسًا." فَيَقُولُ لَا وَالدِّمَاءِ مَا أَرَى بِمَا تَقُولُ بَأْسًا. فَأُنْزِلَتْ {عَبَسَ وَتَوَلَّى أَنْ جَاءَهُ الْأَعْمَى}. Muwatta' Mālik 480.

205 ...قَالَ كَانَ لِرَسُولِ اللَّهِ مُؤَذِّنَانِ بِلَالٌ وَابْنُ أُمِّ مَكْتُومٍ الْأَعْمَى. Sahīh Muslim 380.

189. What does "the evil of the blowers upon knots" mean?

Answer: It is said that "blowing upon knots" was a means of practising witchcraft and casting spells.

This saying goes back to pre-Islamic Arabia. It is an idiomatic phrase to describe occult incantations. The expression is found in sura 113 *The Daybreak* – in Arabic: al-Falaq (سُورة الْفَلَق):

113:4	the harm in witches when they blow on knots	وَمِن شَرِّ النَّفَّاثَاتِ فِي الْعُقَدِ

The word al-Naffāthāt (النَّفَّاثَات), which is used in the Qur'an, is the female sound plural of the word Naffātha (نَفَّاثة). In its basic form this word denotes *an enchanter; a* (woman) *who blows or casts a spell*.

The word Naffātha comes from the root n-f-th (ن-ف-ث) which basically means *to exhale, puff out* (e.g. smoke); also *to spit* or *blow without spitting*. It can even mean *to inject venom* (by a snake). Thus, a Naffātha is a woman who practises Arabian witchcraft by tying knots in a cord and blow upon them with a curse – according to Edward Lane, they most probably did not spit. The knots are tied in a thread or string. The term Nafth al-Shaytān (نَفْث الشَّيْطان) is used to express *erotic verses*.

In Islam, a Muslim is commanded to seek refuge with Allah from such practices. Any attempt at influencing the course of events by means of supernatural power is forbidden in Islam and seen as an offence against Allah.

190. How does the Qur'an call the day of the Battle of Badr?

Answer: Yawm al-Furqān (يَوْم الْفُرْقان).

This expression is found in sura 8 *Battle Gains/The Spoils of War* – in Arabic: al-'Anfāl (سُورة الْأَنْفال). This sura also gives information about how the spoils of war should be distributed.

8:41	Know that one-fifth of your battle gains belongs to God and the Messenger, to close relatives and orphans, to the needy	وَاعْلَمُوا أَنَّمَا غَنِمْتُم مِّن شَيْءٍ فَأَنَّ لِلَّهِ خُمُسَهُ وَلِلرَّسُولِ وَلِذِي الْقُرْبَى

and travellers, if you believe in God and the revelation We sent down to Our servant on the day of the decision, the day when the two forces met in battle. God has power over all things.	وَالْيَتَامَى وَالْمَسَاكِين وَابْن السَّبِيل إِن كُنتُم آمَنتُم بِاللَّه وَمَا أَنزَلْنَا عَلَى عَبْدِنَا يَوْمَ الْفُرْقَان يَوْمَ الْتَقَى الْجَمْعَان وَاللَّهُ عَلَى كُلِّ شَيْءٍ قَدِيرٌ.

The Arabic word Furqān (فُرْقان) means *proof, evidence*. But note that if it is used with the definite article, i.e. al-Furqān (الْفُرْقان), then it simply means *The Qur'an*. Why is that? Al-Furqān basically describes the criterion for distinguishing right and wrong, good and evil. In a broader sense, al-Furqān could thus be applied to any sacred book or religious text.

The main part of sura 8 is about the Battle of Badr (غَزْوة بَدْر), the first major fight between the Muslims and their enemies in Mecca, two years after the migration to Medina. The Battle of Badr is described in this verse as "the day when the true was distinguished from the false", in Arabic: Yawm al-Furqān (يَوْم الْفُرْقان).

The Muslims were outnumbered more than three times, but they nevertheless won.

The sura reminds Muslims that it was Allah who brought the victory. This is said in verse 12 to 14:

8:12	Your Lord revealed to the angels: 'I am with you: give the believers firmness; I shall put terror into the hearts of the disbelievers - strike above their necks and strike all their fingertips.'	إِذْ يُوحِي رَبُّكَ إِلَى الْمَلَائِكَةِ أَنِّي مَعَكُمْ فَثَبِّتُوا الَّذِينَ آمَنُوا سَأُلْقِي فِي قُلُوبِ الَّذِينَ كَفَرُوا الرُّعْبَ فَاضْرِبُوا فَوْقَ الْأَعْنَاقِ وَاضْرِبُوا مِنْهُمْ كُلَّ بَنَانٍ.
8:13	That was because they opposed God and His Messenger, and if anyone opposes God and His Messenger, God punishes them severely -	ذَلِكَ بِأَنَّهُمْ شَاقُّوا اللَّهَ وَرَسُولَهُ وَمَن يُشَاقِقِ اللَّهَ وَرَسُولَهُ فَإِنَّ اللَّهَ شَدِيدُ الْعِقَابِ
8:14	'That is what you get! Taste that!' - and the torment of the Fire awaits the disbelievers.	ذَلِكُمْ فَذُوقُوهُ وَأَنَّ لِلْكَافِرِينَ عَذَابَ النَّارِ.

191. Which sura pardoned Muhammad's wife 'Ā'isha in *The Incident of Slander*?

Answer: Sura 24 *The Light* – in Arabic: al-Nūr (سُورة النُّور).

The *Incident of Slander* or *Incident of Ifk* (حادِثة الإفْك) is one of the most discussed stories in Islam. The Arabic word 'Ifk (إفك) means *lie, untruth,* or *falsehood.* Let's look at the whole story:

'Ā'isha (عائشة بِنت أبي بَكر), the Prophet's wife, had left her camel litter (Howdah) and was looking for a dropped necklace. However, the slaves thought that she was inside the camel litter when they started to leave camp and set off with her camel. Thus, they left the place without her.

'Ā'isha thus had to stay overnight by herself. She remained at the camp until the next morning. The "official" Islamic version tells that Safwān ibn al-Mu'attal (صَفْوان بن المُعَطِّل), a nomad, companion and member of Muhammad's army, found her and brought her back to the Prophet at the army's next camp. This left a lot of questions unanswered. What had happened during the night? Where had 'Ā'isha been? And where had Safwān been? Rumours started to spread that she might have had sex with Safwān. This put the Prophet into a very difficult situation.

'Ā'isha herself - which makes it easy for critics to doubt it – tells the following story in an authentic Hadith:

"Whenever Allah's Messenger intended to go on a journey, he would draw lots among his wives and would take with him the one upon whom the lot fell. During a battle of his, he drew lots among us and the lot fell upon me, and I proceeded with him after Allah had decreed the use of the veil by women." [206]

She continued: "I was carried in a Howdah [on the camel] which was dismounted while I stayed in it. When Allah's Messenger was through with his battle and returning home, we approached the city of Medina. Allah's Messenger ordered us to proceed at night. When the order of setting off was given, I walked until I was past the army

---

206 ...كَانَ رَسُولُ اللَّه إِذَا أَرَادَ أَنْ يَخْرُجَ سَفَرًا أَقْرَعَ بَيْنَ أَزْوَاجِه، فَأَيَّتُهُنَّ خَرَجَ سَهْمُهَا خَرَجَ بِهَا مَعَهُ، فَأَقْرَعَ بَيْنَنَا فِي غَزَاةٍ غَزَاهَا فَخَرَجَ مَعَهُ سَهْمِي، فَخَرَجْتُ مَعَهُ بَعْدَ مَا أُنْزِلَ الْحِجَابُ. Sahīh al-Bukhārī.
2661

to answer the call of nature."[207] She continued: "After finishing I returned [to the camp] to depart [with the others] and suddenly realised that my necklace over my chest was missing. So, I returned to look for it and was delayed because of that."[208]

She continued: "The people who used to carry me on the camel, came to my Howdah and put it on the back of the camel, thinking that I was in it, as, at that time, women were light in weight and thin and lean, and were not used to eat much. So, those people did not notice the difference in the weight of the Howdah while lifting it, and they put it over the camel. At that time I was a young lady. They set the camel moving and proceeded on."[209]

She continued: "I found my necklace after the army had gone and came to their camp to find nobody. So, I went to the place where I used to stay, thinking that they would discover my absence and come back in my search. While in that state, I felt sleepy and slept. Safwān ibn al-Muʿatta was behind the army and reached my abode in the morning. When he saw a sleeping person, he came to me. He used to see me before veiling. So, I got up when I heard him saying: 'We are for Allah, and we will return to Him.'

He made his camel kneel down. He got down from his camel and put his leg on the front legs of the camel, and then I rode and sat over it. Safwān set out walking, leading the camel by the rope until we reached the army who had halted to take rest at midday.[210]

---

207 ...فَأَنَا أُحْمَلُ فِي هَوْدَجٍ وَأُنْزَلُ فِيهِ، فَسِرْنَا حَتَّى إِذَا فَرَغَ رَسُولُ اللَّهِ مِنْ غَزْوَتِهِ تِلْكَ، وَقَفَلَ وَدَنَوْنَا مِنَ الْمَدِينَةِ، آذَنَ لَيْلَةً بِالرَّحِيلِ، فَقُمْتُ حِينَ آذَنُوا بِالرَّحِيلِ، فَمَشَيْتُ حَتَّى جَاوَزْتُ الْجَيْشَ، فَلَمَّا قَضَيْتُ شَأْنِي أَقْبَلْتُ إِلَى الرَّحْلِ، فَلَمَسْتُ صَدْرِي. Sahīh al-Bukhārī 2661.

208 ...فَإِذَا عِقْدٌ لِي مِنْ جَزْعِ أَظْفَارٍ قَدِ انْقَطَعَ، فَرَجَعْتُ فَالْتَمَسْتُ عِقْدِي، فَحَبَسَنِي ابْتِغَاؤُهُ، فَأَقْبَلَ الَّذِينَ يَرْحَلُونَ لِي. Sahīh al-Bukhārī 2661.

209 ...فَأَقْبَلَ الَّذِينَ يَرْحَلُونَ لِي، فَاحْتَمَلُوا هَوْدَجِي فَرَحَلُوهُ عَلَى بَعِيرِي الَّذِي كُنْتُ أَرْكَبُ، وَهُمْ يَحْسِبُونَ أَنِّي فِيهِ، وَكَانَ النِّسَاءُ إِذْ ذَاكَ خِفَافًا لَمْ يُثْقِلْنَ وَلَمْ يَغْشَهُنَّ اللَّحْمُ، وَإِنَّمَا يَأْكُلْنَ الْعُلْقَةَ مِنَ الطَّعَامِ، فَلَمْ يَسْتَنْكِرِ الْقَوْمُ حِينَ رَفَعُوهُ ثِقَلَ الْهَوْدَجِ فَاحْتَمَلُوهُ وَكُنْتُ جَارِيَةً حَدِيثَةَ السِّنِّ، فَبَعَثُوا الْجَمَلَ وَسَارُوا.. Sahīh al-Bukhārī 2661.

210 ...فَوَجَدْتُ عِقْدِي بَعْدَ مَا اسْتَمَرَّ الْجَيْشُ، فَجِئْتُ مَنْزِلَهُمْ وَلَيْسَ فِيهِ أَحَدٌ، فَأَمَمْتُ مَنْزِلِي الَّذِي كُنْتُ بِهِ فَظَنَنْتُ أَنَّهُمْ سَيَفْقِدُونِي فَيَرْجِعُونَ إِلَيَّ، فَبَيْنَا أَنَا جَالِسَةٌ غَلَبَتْنِي عَيْنَاىَ فَنِمْتُ، وَكَانَ صَفْوَانُ بْنُ الْمُعَطَّلِ السُّلَمِيُّ ثُمَّ الذَّكْوَانِيُّ مِنْ وَرَاءِ الْجَيْشِ، فَأَصْبَحَ عِنْدَ مَنْزِلِي فَرَأَى سَوَادَ إِنْسَانٍ نَائِمٍ فَأَتَانِي، وَكَانَ يَرَانِي قَبْلَ الْحِجَابِ فَاسْتَيْقَظْتُ بِاسْتِرْجَاعِهِ حِينَ أَنَاخَ رَاحِلَتَهُ، فَوَطِئَ يَدَهَا فَرَكِبْتُهَا فَانْطَلَقَ يَقُودُ بِي الرَّاحِلَةَ، حَتَّى أَتَيْنَا الْجَيْشَ بَعْدَ مَا نَزَلُوا مُعَرِّسِينَ فِي نَحْرِ الظَّهِيرَةِ، فَهَلَكَ مَنْ هَلَكَ. Sahīh al- Bukhārī 2661

She continued: "Then whoever was meant for destruction, fell into destruction, [some people accused me falsely] and the leader of the false accusers was 'Abd Allah ibn 'Ubayy ibn Salūl (عَبْد الله بن أُبَيّ بن سَلُول). After that we returned to Medina and I became ill for one month while the people were spreading the forged statements of the false accusers. During my ailment I was feeling as if I were not receiving the usual kindness from the Prophet which I used to receive from him when I was sick. But he would come, greet and say: 'How is that (girl)?'"[211]

She continued: Allah's Messenger also asked Zaynab bint Jahsh [one of the other Prophet's wives] about me saying: 'What do you know and what did you see?' She replied: 'O Allah's Messenger! I refrain to claim hearing or seeing what I have not heard or seen. By Allah, I know nothing except goodness about 'Ā'isha.'"[212]

The rumours had a great impact. The situation became more and more difficult for the Prophet as well as for 'Ā'isha. Adultery was a major crime.

'Alī ibn 'Abī Tālib (عَلِيّ بن أَبِي طَالِب), as some sources indicate, suggested that Muhammad should divorce her. This made 'Ā'isha's father 'Abū Bakr (أَبُو بَكْر) angry. 'Ā'isha and 'Abū Bakr never forgave 'Alī for this. Until today, Sunni and Shia Muslims remember this episode and use it to justify why the other is wrong or bad.

Eventually, Muhammad came to speak directly to 'Ā'isha about the rumours. He was still sitting in her house when he announced that he had received a revelation from Allah which confirmed 'Ā'isha's innocence; verses of sura 24 *The Light* – in Arabic: al-Nūr (سُورة النُّور):

| 24:11 | It was a group from among you that concocted the lie - do not consider it a bad thing for you [people]; it was a good thing - and every one of them will be | إِنَّ الَّذِينَ جَاءُوا بِالإِفْكِ عُصْبَةٌ مِّنكُمْ لَا تَحْسَبُوهُ شَرًّا لَّكُم بَلْ هُوَ خَيْرٌ لَّكُمْ لِكُلِّ امْرِئٍ مِّنْهُم مَّا اكْتَسَبَ مِنَ |

---

211 ...وَكَانَ الَّذِي تَوَلَّى الإِفْكَ عَبْدُ اللَّهِ بْنُ أُبَيٍّ ابْنُ سَلُولَ، فَقَدِمْنَا الْمَدِينَةَ فَاشْتَكَيْتُ بِهَا شَهْرًا، يُفِيضُونَ مِنْ قَوْلِ أَصْحَابِ الإِفْكِ، وَيَرِيبُنِي فِي وَجَعِي أَنِّي لَا أَرَى مِنَ النَّبِيِّ اللُّطْفَ الَّذِي كُنْتُ أَرَى مِنْهُ حِينَ أَمْرَضُ، إِنَّمَا يَدْخُلُ فَيُسَلِّمُ ثُمَّ يَقُولُ: "كَيْفَ تِيكُمْ." Sahīh al-Bukhārī 2661

212 ...وَكَانَ رَسُولُ اللَّهِ يَسْأَلُ زَيْنَبَ بِنْتَ جَحْشٍ عَنْ أَمْرِي، فَقَالَ: "يَا زَيْنَبُ، مَا عَلِمْتِ مَا رَأَيْتِ." فَقَالَتْ يَا رَسُولَ اللَّهِ، أَحْمِي سَمْعِي وَبَصَرِي، وَاللَّهِ مَا عَلِمْتُ عَلَيْهَا إِلاَّ خَيْرًا. Sahīh al-Bukhārī 2661

		charged with the sin he has earned. He who took the greatest part in it will have a painful punishment.	الْإِثْمِ وَالَّذِي تَوَلَّى كِبْرَهُ مِنْهُمْ لَهُ عَذَابٌ عَظِيمٌ.
	24:12	When you heard the lie, why did believing men and women not think well of their own people and declare, 'This is obviously a lie'?	لَّوْلَا إِذْ سَمِعْتُمُوهُ ظَنَّ الْمُؤْمِنُونَ وَالْمُؤْمِنَاتُ بِأَنفُسِهِمْ خَيْرًا وَقَالُوا هَٰذَا إِفْكٌ مُّبِينٌ؟
	24:13	And why did the accusers not bring four witnesses to it? If they cannot produce such witnesses, they are the liars in God's eyes.	لَّوْلَا جَاءُوا عَلَيْهِ بِأَرْبَعَةِ شُهَدَاءَ فَإِذْ لَمْ يَأْتُوا بِالشُّهَدَاءِ فَأُولَٰئِكَ عِندَ اللَّهِ هُمُ الْكَاذِبُونَ.

This sura was revealed at the end of the fifth or at the beginning of the sixth year after the Prophet had migrated from Mecca to Medina. The Incident of Slander might have happened some time after Muhammad's battle against the tribe of al-Mustaliq (بَنُو الْمُصْطَلِق).

The sura is of great importance. Not only does Allah state in these verses that 'A'isha was innocent. These verses also tell Muslims how to deal with people who accuse someone of adultery.

In Islam, the Arabic word **Zina'** (زناء or الزِّنَى) is used for consensual sexual intercourse between a man and a woman who are not married to one another. Islam does not differentiate between the Western concepts of *adultery* (sexual intercourse of a married man or married woman other than the respective partner) and *fornication* (sexual intercourse between two unmarried persons).

Islam requires four (!) witnesses in these cases. This was told in the Qur'an, sura 24:13, and is in stark contrast to other crimes for which two witnesses are usually sufficient.

What is meant by "witness" considering adultery or fornication? The evidence of the four witnesses must be direct and not circumstantial. In other words, it is not sufficient for them to have witnessed a situation which made it evident that sexual intercourse had taken place. They must have witnessed the sexual act as such.

This is, of course, almost impossible.

That is why Islam prohibits strongly the spread of rumours or the accusation of Zina' which is all based on the case of 'A'isha. In fact, it is treated as a Hadd crime. The punishment is 80 lashes if the accuser cannot present four eyewitnesses.

Let's see what happened in the case of 'Ā'isha:

- 'Ā'isha's accusers were subjected to punishments of 80 lashes.
- Safwān was killed in the year 640 (19 AH) during a battle in Armenia (مَعْرَكة أُرْمِينِيّة).

192. Is stoning mentioned in the Qur'an?

Answer: No, stoning, in Arabic called Rajm (رَجْم), is not explicitly mentioned in the Qur'an, but it is mentioned in the Hadiths.

However, some people claim that the verses in the Qur'an about stoning were lost. Therefore these verses were abrogated in recitation, but not in ruling. Many non-Muslims in the Western world connect Islam with stoning since the practice is nowadays mostly found in Islamic countries such as Iran, Somalia or Sudan. Let's see what might have happened to the holy verses:

'Abd Allah ibn 'Abbās (عَبْد الله بن عَبَّاس) reported that 'Umar ibn al-Khattāb (عُمَر بن الْخَطَّاب) sat on the pulpit of Allah's Messenger and said: "Verily, Allah sent Muhammad with truth and He sent down the Book upon him, and the verse of stoning was included in what was sent down to him. We recited it, retained it in our memory, and understood it. Allah's Messenger awarded the punishment of stoning to death [to the married adulterer and adulteress]. After him, we also awarded the punishment of stoning.

I am afraid that with the lapse of time, the people [may forget it] and may say: 'We do not find the punishment of stoning in the Book of Allah, and thus go astray by abandoning this duty prescribed by Allah.' Stoning is a duty laid down in Allah's Book for married men and women who commit adultery when proof is established or if there is pregnancy or a confession."[213]

---

213 ...قَالَ عُمَرُ بْنُ الْخَطَّابِ وَهُوَ جَالِسٌ عَلَى مِنْبَرِ رَسُولِ اللَّهِ إِنَّ اللَّهَ قَدْ بَعَثَ مُحَمَّدًا بِالْحَقِّ وَأَنْزَلَ عَلَيْهِ الْكِتَابَ فَكَانَ مِمَّا أُنْزِلَ عَلَيْهِ آيَةُ الرَّجْمِ قَرَأْنَاهَا وَوَعَيْنَاهَا وَعَقَلْنَاهَا فَرَجَمَ رَسُولُ اللَّهِ وَرَجَمْنَا بَعْدَهُ فَأَخْشَى إِنْ طَالَ بِالنَّاسِ زَمَانٌ أَنْ يَقُولَ قَائِلٌ مَا نَجِدُ الرَّجْمَ فِي كِتَابِ اللَّهِ فَيَضِلُّوا بِتَرْكِ فَرِيضَةٍ أَنْزَلَهَا اللَّهُ وَإِنَّ الرَّجْمَ فِي كِتَابِ اللَّهِ حَقٌّ عَلَى مَنْ زَنَى إِذَا أَحْصَنَ مِنَ الرِّجَالِ وَالنِّسَاءِ إِذَا قَامَتِ الْبَيِّنَةُ أَوْ كَانَ

So why is the verse not in the Qur'an?

According to a Hadith, the verses were perhaps eaten by a sheep!

It was narrated that 'Ā'isha (عائشة بِنْت أَبِي بَكْر) said: "The verse of stoning [and of breastfeeding an adult ten times] was revealed, and the paper was with me under my pillow. When the Messenger of Allah died, we were preoccupied with his death and a tame sheep came in and ate it."[214]

It is not clear whether it was a sheep or maybe a goat. In the Arabic text, it just says Dājin (دَاجِن) which literally means *domesticated, tame sheep* – a sheep that people feed in their homes. However, this is only the minor problem. The main problem of this Hadith is the chain of narration which is hasan (حَسَن):

'Ā'isha -> 'Amra (عَمْرة) -> 'Abd Allah ibn 'Abī Bakr (عَبْد الله بن أَبِي بَكْر) -> Muhammad ibn 'Ishāq (مُحَمَّد بن إِسْحَاق).

Some scholars say (especially with regard to Muhammad ibn 'Ishāq who wrote the first and most accepted biography of Muhammad) that this chain might contain narrators charged with dishonesty when disclosing their sources. On the other hand, critics of Islam see in this Hadith proof that the Qur'an is incomplete.

Nevertheless, the stoning as a penalty is found in the Hadiths too. Let's look at the most important narrations:

The following Hadith shows that Muhammad approved stoning in the case of adultery. 'Abd Allah ibn 'Umar (عَبْد الله بن عُمَر) narrated: "The Jews came to Allah's Messenger and mentioned to him that a man and a lady among them had committed illegal sexual intercourse. Allah's Messenger said to them: 'What do you find in the Torah regarding stoning?'[215]

They replied: 'We only disgrace and flog them with lashes. 'Abd Allah ibn Salam said to them: 'You have told a lie; the penalty of stoning is in the Torah.' They brought the Torah and opened it. One

---

الْحَبَلُ أَوْ الإِعْتِرَافُ. Sahīh Muslim 1691.

214 ...عَائِشَةَ قَالَتْ لَقَدْ نَزَلَتْ آيَةُ الرَّجْمِ وَرَضَاعَةُ الْكَبِيرِ عَشْرًا وَلَقَدْ كَانَ فِي صَحِيفَةٍ تَحْتَ سَرِيرِي فَلَمَّا مَاتَ رَسُولُ اللَّهِ وَتَشَاغَلْنَا بِمَوْتِهِ دَخَلَ دَاجِنٌ فَأَكَلَهَا. Sunan ibn Māja 2020; hasan.

215 ...قَالَ إِنَّ الْيَهُودَ جَاءُوا إِلَى رَسُولِ اللَّهِ فَذَكَرُوا لَهُ أَنَّ رَجُلًا مِنْهُمْ وَامْرَأَةً زَنَيَا فَقَالَ لَهُمْ رَسُولُ اللَّهِ: "مَا تَجِدُونَ فِي التَّوْرَاةِ فِي شَأْنِ الرَّجْمِ؟" Sahīh al-Bukhārī 6841

of them put his hand over the verse of stoning and read what was preceding and following it. 'Abd Allah ibn Salam said to him: 'Lift up your hand.' Where he lifted it there appeared the verse of stoning. So they said: "O Muhammad! He has said the truth, the verse of stoning is in it [the Torah]."[216]

Then Allah's Messenger ordered that the two persons [guilty of illegal sexual intercourse] be stoned to death, and so they were stoned and I saw the man bending over the woman so as to protect her from the stones."[217]

Let's turn to another authentic Hadith which was narrated by 'Abū Hurayra (أَبُو هُرَيْرة) and Zayd ibn Khālid al-Juhanī (زَيْد بن خَالِد الْجُهَنيِّ). It shows that Muhammad commanded to stone a woman to death after having her found guilty of committing adultery:

A Bedouin came and said: "O Allah's Messenger! Judge between us according to Allah's Book." His opponent stood up and said: "He has said the truth, so judge between us according to Allah's Laws." The Bedouin said: "My son was a labourer for this man and committed illegal sexual intercourse with his wife. The people said to me: 'Your son is to be stoned to death', so I ransomed my son for one hundred sheep and a slave girl. Then I asked the religious learned men and they said to me: 'Your son has to receive one hundred lashes plus one year of exile.'

The Prophet said: "I shall judge between you according to Allah's Book! As for the slave girl and the sheep, it shall be returned to you and your son shall receive one hundred lashes and be exiled for one year." The Prophet addressed a man: "O you, 'Unays (أُنَيْس)! Go in the morning to the wife of this man and stone her to death!" So 'Unays went to her the next morning and stoned her to death.[218]

---

216 ...فَقَالُوا نَفْضَحُهُمْ وَيُجْلَدُونَ. قَالَ عَبْدُ اللَّهِ بْنُ سَلامٍ إِنَّ فِيهِمْ كَذَبْتُمْ فِيهَا الرَّجْمَ. فَأَتَوْا بِالتَّوْرَاةِ فَنَشَرُوهَا، فَوَضَعَ أَحَدُهُمْ يَدَهُ عَلَى آيَةِ الرَّجْمِ فَقَرَأَ مَا قَبْلَهَا وَمَا بَعْدَهَا. فَقَالَ لَهُ عَبْدُ اللَّهِ بْنُ سَلامٍ ارْفَعْ يَدَكَ. فَرَفَعَ يَدَهُ فَإِذَا فِيهَا آيَةُ الرَّجْمِ. قَالُوا صَدَقَ يَا مُحَمَّدُ فِيهَا آيَةُ الرَّجْمِ. Sahīh al-Bukhārī 6841.

217 ...فَأَمَرَ بِهِمَا رَسُولُ اللَّهِ فَرُجِمَا، فَرَأَيْتُ الرَّجُلَ يَحْنِي عَلَى الْمَرْأَةِ يَقِيهَا الْحِجَارَةَ. Sahīh al-Bukhārī 6841

218 ...قَالا جَاءَ أَعْرَابِيٌّ فَقَالَ يَا رَسُولَ اللَّهِ اقْضِ بَيْنَنَا بِكِتَابِ اللَّهِ فَقَامَ خَصْمُهُ فَقَالَ صَدَقَ فَاقْضِ بَيْنَنَا بِكِتَابِ اللَّهِ. فَقَالَ الأَعْرَابِيُّ إِنَّ ابْنِي كَانَ عَسِيفًا عَلَى هَذَا فَزَنَى بِامْرَأَتِهِ، فَقَالُوا لِي عَلَى ابْنِكَ الرَّجْمُ. فَفَدَيْتُ ابْنِي مِنْهُ بِمائَةٍ مِنَ الْغَنَمِ وَوَلِيدَةٍ، ثُمَّ سَأَلْتُ أَهْلَ الْعِلْمِ فَقَالُوا إِنَّمَا عَلَى ابْنِكَ جَلْدُ مائَةٍ

Traditional scholars use this Hadith as proof that stoning should not be replaced by other methods of killing due to its severity. They say that adultery, Zinā' (زِناء), is the most dreadful sin after believing in other Gods and after killing a person whom Allah didn't allow to kill.

193. What does the Qur'an mean by "protected eggs"?

Answer: Beautiful women.

The term *protected eggs* (بَيْضٌ مَكْنُونٌ) is found in sura 37 *Ranged in Rows* – in Arabic: al-Saffāt (سورة الصَّفّات). The sura was revealed in Mecca.

37:48	With them will be spouses - modest of gaze and beautiful of eye -	وَعِندَهُمْ قَاصِرَاتُ الطَّرْفِ عِينٌ
37:49	like protected eggs.	كَأَنَّهُنَّ بَيْضٌ مَّكْنُونٌ.

So how can it be that the Qur'an compares beautiful women to eggs? Well, this is an ancient Arabic saying. Arabs described beautiful women as being as precious as the ostrich eggs being protected from the dust with feathers. It was derived from the habit of the female ostrich which buries its eggs in the sand for protection.

The expression *egg of an ostrich* is a metaphor in Arabic sayings. When said in **dispraise**, it may mean that a person is like the egg of the ostrich from which the young bird has come forth, and which the male ostrich has cast away, so that men and camels tread upon it. When said in **praise**, it may mean that a person is like the ostrich's egg in which is the young bird, because the male ostrich protects it.

وَتَغْرِيبُ عَامٍ. فَقَالَ النَّبِيُّ: "لَأَقْضِيَنَّ بَيْنَكُمَا بِكِتَابِ اللَّهِ، أَمَّا الْوَلِيدَةُ وَالْغَنَمُ فَرَدٌّ عَلَيْكَ، وَعَلَى ابْنِكَ جَلْدُ مِائَةٍ وَتَغْرِيبُ عَامٍ، وَأَمَّا أَنْتَ يَا أُنَيْسُ لِرَجُلٍ فَاغْدُ عَلَى امْرَأَةِ هَذَا فَارْجُمْهَا." فَغَدَا عَلَيْهَا أُنَيْسُ فَرَجَمَهَا.

Sahīh al-Bukhārī 7193, 7194

194. What does the name Tāriq mean?

Answer: The Night-Comer.

Tāriq (طارق) - *The Night-Comer* - is the name of sura 86. The sura was revealed in Mecca and has as the predominant topic the resurrection from the grave on the Day of Judgement.

Tāriq is derived from the Arabic verb *taraqa* (طَرَق) which primarily means *he beat* (something) or *knocked* (at something); e.g., taraqa al-Bāb (طَرَقَ الْبَابَ), which means *he knocked at the door.*

In general the word Tāriq signifies *anything that comes in the night,* because a person who comes to a house at night is expected to knock at the door. In a metaphorical meaning, the word Tāriq is used in the Qur'an to show that even in the deepest darkness there will be light.

Some commentators suggest that what is described as al-Tāriq, meaning *that which comes in the night,* is the morning-star because it appears towards the end of the night. Others, like Zamakhshari, claim that it is a star in a generic sense.

195. What is so special about the sura *The Forceful Chargers*?

Answer: The first five verses are very difficult to explain.

Sura 79 *The Forceful Chargers* - in Arabic: al-Nāzi'āt (سُورة النّازِعات) - is a late Meccan sura. Among other things, it tells the story of Moses and the Pharaoh.

However, from a linguistic perspective the most interesting part are the first five verses which are a challenge for translators. Let's look at the various translations of them and discuss why they are so strange and difficult to understand:

79:1	"Wannāzi'āti gharqa(n)"	وَالنَّازِعَاتِ غَرْقًا

- By the forceful chargers – *Abdel Haleem*
- Consider those (stars) that rise only to set – *Muhammad Asad*
- By those (angels) who extract with violence – *Sahīh International*
- By those who drag forth to destruction – *Pickthall*

- By the (angels) who tear out (the souls of the wicked) with violence – *Yūsuf 'Alī*
- I swear by the angels who violently pull out the souls of the wicked – *Shakir*
- By the angels who violently tear-out the souls of the disbelievers from their bodies – *Muhammad Sarwar*
- By those (angels) who pull out (the souls of the disbelievers and the wicked) with great violence – *Mohsin Khan*
- By those that pluck out vehemently – *Arberry*

79:2	"Wannāshitāti nashta(n)"	وَالنَّاشِطَاتِ نَشْطًا

- Raring to go – *Abdel Haleem*
- And move (in their orbits) with steady motion – *Muhammad* Asad
- And (by) those who remove with ease – *Sahīh International*
- By the meteors rushing – *Pickthall*
- By those who gently draw out (the souls of the blessed) – *Yūsuf 'Alī*
- And by those who gently draw out the souls of the blessed – *Shakir*
- By the angels who gently release the souls of the believers – *Muhammad Sarwar*
- By those (angels) who gently take out (the souls of the believers) – *Mohsin Khan*
- And those that draw out violently – *Arberry*

79:3	"Wassābihāti sabha(n)"	وَالسَّابِحَاتِ سَبْحًا

- Sweeping ahead at full stretch – *Abdel Haleem*
- And float (through space) with floating serene – *Muhammad Asad*
- And (by) those who glide (as if) swimming – *Sahīh International*
- By the lone stars floating – *Pickthall*
- And by those who glide along (on errands of mercy) – *Yūsuf 'Alī*
- And by those who float in space – *Shakir*
- By the angels who float (in the heavens by the will of God) – *Muhammad Sarwar*
- And by those that swim along (i.e. angels or planets in their orbits) – *Mohsin Khan*

- By those that swim serenely – *Arberry*

79:4	"Fassābiqāti sabqa(n)"	فَالسَّابِقَاتِ سَبْقًا

- Overtaking swiftly – *Abdel Haleem*
- And yet overtake (one another) with swift overtaking – *M. Asad*
- And those who race each other in a race – *Sahīh International*
- By the angels hastening – *Pickthall*
- Then press forward as in a race – *Yūsuf 'Alī*
- Then those who are foremost going ahead – *Shakir*
- By the angels who hasten along – *Muhammad Sarwar*
- And by those that press forward as in a race (i.e. the angels or stars or the horses, etc.) – *Mohsin Khan*
- And those that outstrip suddenly – *Arberry*

79:5	"Falmudabbirati amra"	فَالْمُدَبِّرَاتِ أَمْرًا

- To bring the matter to an end – *Abdel Haleem*
- And thus they fulfil the (Creator's) behest! – *Muhammad Asad*
- And those who arrange (each) matter – *Sahīh International*
- And those who govern the event – *Pickthall*
- Then arrange to do (the Commands of their Lord) – *Yūsuf 'Alī*
- Then those who regulate the affair – *Shakir*
- And by the angels who regulate the affairs, (you will certainly be resurrected) – *Muhammad Sarwar*
- And by those angels who arrange to do the Commands of their Lord, (so verily, you disbelievers will be called to account) – *Mohsin Khan*
- By those that direct an affair! – *Arberry*

As you can see, the early commentators differ widely in their explanations of these verses.

The most popular interpretation is that these verses refer to angels and their activities with regard to the souls of the dying. This is based on the view that the Arabic words al-Nāzi'āt (النَّازِعَات), al-Nāshitāt (النَّاشِطَات), al-Sābihāt (السَّابِحَات), al-Sābiqāt (السَّابِقَات), and al-Mudabbirāt (الْمُدَبِّرَات) could refer to descriptions of angels.

However, this is categorically rejected by some scholars who pointed out that in the Qur'an angels are never referred to in the female gender – as is the case in the above five words. Other translators tried to connect these words to human souls; some even to warriors in the Jihād.

Muhammad Asad claimed in his commentary that "the clearest and simplest interpretation is that what is meant in this passage are the stars, including the sun and the moon, and their movements in space. This interpretation is fully in tune with many other passages in the Qur'an in which the harmony of these celestial bodies in their multiform orbits and graded speeds is cited as an evidence of Allah's planning and creativeness."

In the end, we don't know for sure what these five verses really mean, as is obvious from the interpreters' different approaches.

196. Do Muslims worship the Ka'ba?

Answer: No. However, when non-Muslims look at the way Muslims glorify the cube in Mecca, one could assume that they do worship it.

Muslims have to pray facing the direction of Mecca, precisely the Ka'ba. In Mecca, they prostrate in front of the Ka'ba. A picture of the Ka'ba is found in many Muslim homes, and one could easily assume that Muslims worship this cube. However, Islam clearly states that a Muslim is only allowed to worship Allah. It also states that Muslims are commanded to destroy and dismantle anything that people worship besides Allah.

The reason why Muslims don't worship the Ka'ba is simple: The Ka'ba is actually a mosque. It serves as a unifying direction for prayer. It houses the Black Stone (الْحَجَر الْأَسْوَد) in its eastern corner.

'Abd Allah ibn 'Abbās (عَبْد الله بن عَبَّاس) narrated that the Messenger of Allah said: "The Black Stone descended from Paradise and was whiter than milk, then it was blackened by the sins of the children of Adam."[219]

---

219 ...قَالَ رَسُولُ اللَّهِ: "نَزَلَ الْحَجَرُ الْأَسْوَدُ مِنَ الْجَنَّةِ وَهُوَ أَشَدُّ بَيَاضًا مِنَ اللَّبَنِ فَسَوَّدَتْهُ خَطَايَا بَنِي آدَمَ". Jāmi' al-Tirmidhī 877

One is not allowed to use this stone as an object of worship. Although it looks like that Muslims adore this cube, they deny that and say that they only follow a tradition of the Prophet.

There is a narration of 'Umar ibn al-Khattāb (عُمَر بن الْخَطَّاب) who later became the second Caliph. According to the Hadith, 'Umar came near the Black Stone, kissed it and said: "No doubt, I know that you are a stone and can neither benefit anyone nor harm anyone. Had I not seen Allah's Messenger kissing you I would not have kissed you."[220]

197. What is Zamzam?

Answer: A water well in Mecca.

Zamzam (زَمْزَم) is the name of a well located within the biggest and most important mosque (complex) worldwide, the Grand Mosque in Mecca, called al-Masjid al-Harām (الْمَسْجِد الْحَرَام). The well is located around 20 m (66 ft) east of the holiest place in Islam, the Ka'ba. Millions of pilgrims visit the well each year while performing the Hajj or 'Umra pilgrimages.

According to Islam, it is a miraculous source of water which was found thousands of years ago when Abraham's infant son Ishmael was thirsty. His mother Hāgar (هاجَر) was searching desperately for water and ran seven times back and forth in the sweltering heat between the two hills called al-Safā (الصَّفا) and al-Marwā (الْمَرْوة).

Muslims believe that Allah sent the angel Gabriel who scraped the ground (with his wings), upon which suddenly a spring appeared. Hāgar was afraid that it might run out of water, thus, she enclosed it with stones and sand.

Arab historians claim that the Zamzam well, except for a few periods when it dried up or was buried under sand, has been in use for around 4000 years. The origin of its name is not clear. Some say that the well is called Zamzam because its water is somewhat brackish (which is an old, classical meaning of the word Zamzam), while oth-

---

220 ...أَنَّهُ [عُمَر] جَاءَ إِلَى الْحَجَرِ الْأَسْوَدِ فَقَبَّلَهُ، فَقَالَ إِنِّي أَعْلَمُ أَنَّكَ حَجَرٌ لَا تَضُرُّ وَلَا تَنْفَعُ، وَلَوْلَا أَنِّي رَأَيْتُ النَّبِيَّ يُقَبِّلُكَ مَا قَبَّلْتُكَ. Sahīh al-Bukhārī 1597.

ers suggest that the name is related to the copiousness of its water. According to *The Saudi Geological Survey* the name originates from the phrase *Zomë Zomë* (زُم زُم), which means *stop flowing* – a command repeated by Hāgar (possibly in Egyptian) during her attempt to contain the spring water. The area around the spring, which was later converted to a well, became a resting place for caravans.

198. What is a Tāghūt?

Answer: Tāghūt (طاغُوت) is an Arabic term that is specifically used to denounce everything that is worshipped instead or besides Allah.

The Arabic term Tāghūt (الطَّاغُوت) can refer to idols, a tyrant, an oracle, or an enemy of Muhammad. Tāghūt means "one who has crossed the limits", in plain language: *a rebel*. It is any power or being that rebels against Allah and demands loyalty and obedience. In a broader sense, it stands for everything that may direct a Muslim into evil things. In Arabic, the term can be interpreted as singular or plural. It is therefore commonly translated as *the powers of evil*.

Remark: This expression was used in Tunisia by Moncef Marzouki, a Tunisian politician who was the president of Tunisia from 2011 to 2014. He defamed his rival party, *Nidaa Tounes* (نداء تُونس), using this term, which caused him a lot of criticism.

The term is mentioned in the Qur'an, for example in sura 2 *The Cow* – in Arabic: al-Baqara (سُورة الْبَقَرة); or in sura 4 *Women* – in Arabic: al-Nisā' (سُورة النِّساء):

| 4:60 | Do you [Prophet] not see those who claim to believe in what has been sent down to you, and in what was sent down before you, yet still want to turn to unjust tyrants for judgement, although they have been ordered to reject them? Satan wants to lead them far astray. | أَلَمْ تَرَ إِلَى الَّذِينَ يَزْعُمُونَ أَنَّهُمْ آمَنُوا بِمَا أُنزِلَ إِلَيْكَ وَمَا أُنزِلَ مِن قَبْلِكَ يُرِيدُونَ أَن يَتَحَاكَمُوا إِلَى الطَّاغُوتِ وَقَدْ أُمِرُوا أَن يَكْفُرُوا بِهِ وَيُرِيدُ الشَّيْطَانُ أَن يُضِلَّهُمْ ضَلَالًا بَعِيدًا. |

199. What does Jihād literally mean?

Answer: In principal it means *to struggle against difficulties*, but also *to strive, to endeavour, to contend with,* or *to fight* (in particular against the enemies of Islam).

The word Jihād (جهاد) is one of the most misunderstood and misused words in Islam. It is derived from the Arabic root j-h-d (ج-ه-د) which means *to be diligent* or *to exert oneself.*

Jihād denotes *a contending, a striving, a going forth to fight* (in the Holy War). Jihād is the verbal (infinitive) noun of the Arabic III-verb jāhada (جاهَدَ). The active participle of this verb is Mujāhid (مُجاهد). A Mujāhid is *one who strives, goes forth to fight in the cause of Islam.*

In Edward Lane's dictionary, we find the following description of Jihād which shows the full spectrum: "The using or exerting one's utmost power, efforts, endeavours, or ability in contending with an object of disapprobation; and this is of three kinds, namely, a visible enemy, the Devil, and one's self."

It is difficult to translate Jihād because one word is simply not enough. It is important to understand the full spectrum of the word – from striving to killing. Sura 22 *The Pilgrimage* - in Arabic: al-Hajj (سورة الْحَجّ) - was revealed after the migration from Mecca to Medina, the so-called Hijra. The sura condemns those who prevent the Muslims from access to the Kaʿba and gives the Muslims the permission to fight when they are being attacked. The following verse comes close to the overall meaning of Jihād:

| 22:78 | Strive hard ("*jahidu*") for God as is His due: He has chosen you and placed no hardship in your religion, the faith of your forefather Abraham. God has called you Muslims - both in the past and in this [message] - so that the Messenger can bear witness about you and so that you can bear witness about other people. So keep up the prayer, give the prescribed alms, and seek refuge in God: He is your protector - an excellent protector and an excellent helper. | وَجَاهِدُوا فِي اللَّهِ حَقَّ جِهَادِهِ هُوَ اجْتَبَاكُمْ وَمَا جَعَلَ عَلَيْكُمْ فِي الدِّينِ مِنْ حَرَجٍ مِّلَّةَ أَبِيكُمْ إِبْرَاهِيمَ هُوَ سَمَّاكُمُ الْمُسْلِمِينَ مِن قَبْلُ وَفِي هَٰذَا لِيَكُونَ الرَّسُولُ شَهِيدًا عَلَيْكُمْ وَتَكُونُوا شُهَدَاءَ عَلَى النَّاسِ فَأَقِيمُوا الصَّلَاةَ وَآتُوا الزَّكَاةَ وَاعْتَصِمُوا بِاللَّهِ هُوَ مَوْلَاكُمْ فَنِعْمَ الْمَوْلَىٰ وَنِعْمَ النَّصِيرُ. |

200. What is the so-called "sword verse"?

Answer: Allah's command to kill idolaters (polytheists).

The name *sword verse* is neither found in the Qur'an nor in the Hadiths. In fact, several commentators of the Qur'an had started to use this expression in the early period of Islam.

The *sword verse* is called 'Āya(t) al-Sayf (آيَةُ السَّيْفِ) in Arabic, which more or less means exactly the same as the English translation.

The verse itself is found in sura 9 *The Repentance* – in Arabic: al-Tawba (سُورة التَّوْبة):

| 9:5 | When the [four] forbidden months are over, wherever you encounter the idolaters, kill them, seize them, besiege them, wait for them at every lookout post; but if they turn [to God], maintain the prayer, and pay the prescribed alms, let them go on their way, for God is most forgiving and merciful. | فَإِذَا انسَلَخَ الْأَشْهُرُ الْحُرُمُ فَاقْتُلُوا الْمُشْرِكِينَ حَيْثُ وَجَدتُّمُوهُمْ وَخُذُوهُمْ وَاحْصُرُوهُمْ وَاقْعُدُوا لَهُمْ كُلَّ مَرْصَدٍ فَإِن تَابُوا وَأَقَامُوا الصَّلَاةَ وَآتَوُا الزَّكَاةَ فَخَلُّوا سَبِيلَهُمْ إِنَّ اللَّهَ غَفُورٌ رَّحِيمٌ. |

These few lines stirred a lot of controversies, especially when a part of the verse was isolated: *"wherever you encounter the idolaters, kill them"*.

Fanatical Muslims see in this verse a command and justification for killing non-Muslims. For some Muslims, this is even the main reason for Jihād. Although there are several verses in the Qur'an telling Muslims how to live together with non-Muslims, this verse, with its clear and severe command, is standing above them, as some classical scholars argued. Islam's critics use these lines to prove that Islam is barbaric and that it promotes violence against non-Muslims, mainly idolaters – the so-called Mushrikūn (مُشْرِكُون). Furthermore, critics claim that these verses show that Christians and Jews are only safe and accepted if they pay the special tax called Jizya.

Why did Allah command this?

Let's look at the historical background. Mainstream scholars say that this verse is linked to a specific event in Islamic history, namely that when Arabian non-Muslims ("pagans" or "idolaters") violated a treaty with the Muslims. The verses immediately preceding and following the verse 9:5 indicate that perhaps only the "idolaters" who broke the covenant were to be killed. Furthermore, as some liberal commentators say, any non-Muslim ("idolater") who respected the treaty as well as those who converted to Islam were to be spared.

Further on, the sura deals with the preparations and recruitment for the Battle of Tabūk (غَزْوة تَبُوك), which took place in 631 (9 AH). It was one of the most difficult times for the Muslims. This is the only sura which does not start with the Basmala: "In the name of Allah...", perhaps signifying that its topic is war and not peace.

The crucial point is that if you say that the sword verse has to be read in a historical context, then this should be true for the entire text in the Qur'an. However, this clashes with the assumption that the Qur'an is timeless, i.e. valid forever. So, is the Qur'an just a historic text and should it be understood like that? The majority of Muslims rejects this idea. However, in this case, they will have to find a solution for how to deal with the sword verse today. This is a dilemma for many Muslims.

Muhammad Asad suggested that every verse of the Qur'an must be read and interpreted against the background of the Qur'an as a whole. However, this complicates the whole matter even more. Let's have a look at an example. The Qur'an states:

| 2:256 | There is no compulsion in religion. | لَا إِكْرَاهَ فِي الدِّينِ. |

According to Muhammad Asad, "this verse lays down categorically that any attempt at a forcible conversion of unbelievers is prohibited – which precludes the possibility of the Muslims' demanding or expecting that a defeated enemy should embrace Islam as the price of immunity." However, this would directly contradict a verse in the very same sura:

| 2:190 | Fight in God's cause against those who fight you, but do not overstep the limits: God does not love those who overstep the limits. | وَقَاتِلُوا فِي سَبِيلِ اللَّهِ الَّذِينَ يُقَاتِلُونَكُمْ وَلَا تَعْتَدُوا إِنَّ اللَّهَ لَا يُحِبُّ الْمُعْتَدِينَ. |

Most traditional scholars deny that the Qur'an is a historic document. They claim that the rules and commands are valid forever. This debate will continue among Muslims.

201. What is the Islamic name of the Final Day?

Answer: There are several (see below).

Islam teaches that there will be a Day of Judgement when all humans will be divided between the eternal destinations of Paradise and Hell. On this Last Day the world will be destroyed and Allah will raise all people and Jinns from the graves to be judged.

Until the Day of Judgement, deceased souls remain in their graves awaiting the resurrection. However, they will get a taste of their future destiny. Those who are checked-in for Hell will suffer in their graves, while those bound for heaven will be in peace during this waiting period. The resurrection is physical and Muslims believe that Allah will recreate the decayed body.

The Day of Judgement has many names in Islam. Let's check the names in the Qur'an, their meaning and how often they occur (last column):

Transliteration	Arabic	Meaning	
Yawm al-Qiyāma	يَوْم الْقِيامة	Day of Resurrection	70
al-Yawm al-'Ākhir	الْيَوْم الآخِر	The Last Day	26
al-'Ākhira	الآخِرة	The Hereafter	111
al-Dār al-'Ākhira	الدّار الآخِرة	The Abode of The Hereafter	9
al-Sā'a	السّاعة	The Hour	39
Yawm al-Ba'th	يَوْم الْبَعْث	The Day of Resurrection	2
Yawm al-Khurūj	يَوْم الْخُرُوج	The Day of Emergence	1
al-Qāri'a	الْقارِعة	The Striking Calamity	4
Yawm al-Fasl	يَوْم الْفَصْل	The Day of Decision, Sorting out	6
Yawm al-Dīn	يَوْم الدِّين	The Day of Recompense	10
al-Sākhkha	الصّاخّة	The Deafening Blast	1
al-Tāmma al-Kubrā	الطّامّة الْكُبْرَى	The Greatest Catastrophe, The Greatest Overwhelming Calamity	1
Yawm al-Hasra	يَوْم الْحَسْرة	The Day of Regret	1
al-Ghāshiya	الْغاشِية	The Overwhelming [Event]	1

al-Wāqiʿa	الْواقِعة	The Great Event	2
Yawm al-Hisāb	يَوْم الْحِساب	The Day of Account	4
Yawm al-Waʿīd	يَوْم الْوَعِيد	The Day of [carrying out] the Threat; the Day whereof warning had been given.	1
Yawm al-’Āzifa	يَوْم الآزِفة	The Approaching Day	1
Yawm al-Jamʿ	يَوْم الْجَمْع	The Day of Assembly	3
al-Hāqqa	الْحَاقَّة	The Sure Reality	3
Yawm al-Tanād	يَوْم التَّناد	The Day of Calling	1
Yawm al-Talāq	يَوْم التَّلَاق	The Day of Meeting	1
Yawm al-Taghābun	يَوْم التَّغَابُن	The Day of Mutual Loss and Gain	1
Yawm al-Khulūd	يَوْم الْخُلُود	The Day of Eternity	1

202. What is the Islamic name for Paradise?

Answer: There are many (see below).

Let us focus on the names which are used in the Qur'an as most of them are used in the Hadiths as well:

al-Firdaws	الْفِرْدَوْس	The Highest Gardens of the Paradise	18:107
		Meaning: a garden. Although some Islamic scholars deny it, the word is most probably derived from Greek (parádeisos - παράδεισος). Mostly, it was understood as a place with grape vines.	
Dar al-Maqāma	دَار الْمُقَامة	The (everlasting) Home	35:35
Dar al-Salām	دار السَّلام	Home of Peace	6:127
al-Dar al-’Ākhira	الدَّار الآخِرة	Final Home	33:29
Dar al-Muttaqīn	دَار الْمُتَّقِين	Home of the Righteous	16:30
al-Janna	الْجَنّة	Garden	13:35

	This is the most common term in the Qur'an and Hadiths. The word comes from the Arabic word for *garden*. The root j-n-n (ن-ن-ج-) has several meanings, but its basic meaning is *to cover; to conceal*. Thus, Janna (جَنّة) can mean *a single act of veiling* or *concealing*. If it is used with the definite article *al-* (ال), it means *Paradise* – because the nice things for the people in Paradise are *concealed* in this world.		
Janna(t) al-'Adn	جَنّات عَدْن	Gardens of Everlasting Bliss	38:50
	Notice that in English or German, there is the expression: Garden of Eden. The Arabic root 'a-d-n (ن-د-ع) expresses that someone remains, dwells, or resides in it, namely a place. It is applied to Paradise, meaning: Garden of (perpetual) residence.		
Janna(t) al-Khuld	جَنّة الْخُلْد	Garden of Eternity; The Lasting Garden	25:15
Janna(t) al-Ma'wā	جَنّة الْمَأْوَى	Garden of Abode/Restfulness	53:15
Janna(t) al-Na'īm	جَنّة النَّعِيم	Garden of Pleasure; Garden of Bliss; The Gardens of Delight	26:85
al-Ghurfa	الْغُرْفة	The Chamber	25:75

203. What is the Qur'anic view of the life to come?

Answer: It does exist.

If there was no life after death, the permanent striving of a Muslim for the sake of pleasing Allah would be useless. Else, why would Allah have created man when he does not care about him in the end?

What are the reasons for Muslims to believe in life after death?

- All prophets of Allah told their people about it and commanded them to believe in it.

- Muslims fear Allah. Islamic history includes a lot of examples of people who had rejected Allah's message, were warned, and finally punished or obliterated by Allah.

- If there is no life after death, several things which happen in our life would become even more difficult to understand.

Muslims are convinced that without Islam, the world would turn into an evil place. Their fear is based on life in pre-Islamic times, when people were drinking alcohol, were addicted to gambling, and followed brutal traditions. Muslims say that once these people had accepted Islam and its rules, their life became disciplined and much better. Let's now look what the Qur'an says about the afterlife.

Sura 45 *Kneeling* - in Arabic: al-Jāthiya (سُورة الْجَاثِية) was revealed during Muhammad's time in Mecca. The title is no coincidence, because on the Day of Judgement all human beings will have to kneel down. This sura tells Muslims that there will be something after death.

The Day of Judgement is believed to be the final assessment of humanity by Allah, consisting of the annihilation of all life, the resurrection, followed by Allah's final verdict.

45:26	[Prophet], say, 'It is God who gives you life, then causes you to die, and then He gathers you all to the Day of Resurrection of which there is no doubt, though most people do not comprehend.'	قُلِ اللَّهُ يُحْيِيكُمْ ثُمَّ يُمِيتُكُمْ ثُمَّ يَجْمَعُكُمْ إِلَى يَوْمِ الْقِيَامَةِ لَا رَيْبَ فِيهِ وَلَٰكِنَّ أَكْثَرَ النَّاسِ لَا يَعْلَمُونَ.
45:27	Control of everything in the heavens and the earth belongs to God. When the Hour [The Day of Judgement] comes, those who follow falsehood will be the losers on that Day.	وَلِلَّهِ مُلْكُ السَّمَاوَاتِ وَالْأَرْضِ وَيَوْمَ تَقُومُ السَّاعَةُ يَوْمَئِذٍ يَخْسَرُ الْمُبْطِلُونَ.

Sura 78 *The Announcement* (*Of the Resurrection and Judgement*) - in Arabic: al-Naba' (سُورة النَّبَأ) states, as the title suggests, that life won't end with (physical) death.

78:1	What are they asking about?	عَمَّ يَتَسَاءَلُونَ؟
78:2	The momentous announcement [of resurrection]	عَنِ النَّبَإِ الْعَظِيمِ
78:3	about which they [so utterly] differ.	الَّذِي هُمْ فِيهِ مُخْتَلِفُونَ.
78:4	They will find out.	كَلَّا سَيَعْلَمُونَ.

78:5	In the end they will find out.	ثُمَّ كَلَّا سَيَعْلَمُونَ.

How does life after death look like? People have always tried to find answers to the three main questions: Where do I come from? Why am I here? What will happen after death?

They are the main reason for the establishment of religions; all religions primarily deal with these questions.

There are several possible answers:

- Non-religious people think that death ends all life. Period.
- Some people believe in the impermanence of life and rebirth – for example Buddhists. The spirit of a person will still remain, but in a new body and with a new life. Every person will be reborn in one of six realms: heaven, human beings, Asura, hungry ghost, animal, or hell. It all depends on the past, on the balance sheet of positive and negative actions. The resultant karma (cause and effect) is a result of past actions.
- Some people believe that only the soul continues to live after death, without a body.

And what about Islam? Muslims believe in the survival of the individual personality and consciousness. Muslims are sure that the entire human body and personality will be recreated in whatever form.

204. Is there any Muslim believer in Paradise now?

Answer: After Islam was founded, no one has (physically) entered Paradise so far.

I have met many non-Muslims who thought that a Muslim martyr is automatically in Paradise. This is not true. A deceased Muslim, no matter if he is seen as a martyr or not, has to wait until the Day of Judgement. However, there is something special about martyrs.

Let's see what the Qur'an tells about the status of a martyr. Sura 3 *Family of 'Imrān* – in Arabic: ʾĀl ʿImrān (سُورة آل عِمْران):

3:169	[Prophet], do not think of those who have	وَلَا تَحْسَبَنَّ الَّذِينَ قُتِلُوا

been killed in Allah's way as dead. They are alive with their Lord, well provided for,	فِي سَبِيلِ اللَّهِ أَمْوَاتًا بَلْ أَحْيَاءٌ عِندَ رَبِّهِمْ يُرْزَقُونَ

Muslims at the time of Muhammad were curious and asked the Prophet what this verse means. This is found in a Hadith which was narrated on the authority of Masrūq (مَسْرُوق):

"We asked the meaning of the verse [from the Prophet] who said: "The souls of the martyrs live in the bodies of green birds that have their nests in chandeliers hung from the throne of the Almighty. They eat the fruits of Paradise from wherever they like and then nestle in these chandeliers."[221]

So what do Muslims learn from that?

Prior to the Day of Judgement, Paradise can be entered only spiritually, which means in the form of the soul. This is true for prophets, martyrs, and foetuses (after four months). However, regarding entering Paradise in both forms - body and soul -, this will only happen on the Day of Judgement, also called the Day of Resurrection.

The only exception to this is Adam who was in Paradise before he came down to this earth, as was mentioned by various Islamic scholars, for example Ibn al-Qayyim (ابن الْقَيِّم).

When The Hour comes, the final decision - Paradise or Hell - will be taken by Allah and Muhammad will be the first to enter Paradise in the full and real sense.

'Anas ibn Mālik (أَنَس بن مالك) reported that the Messenger of Allah said: "I will come to the gate of Paradise on the Day of Resurrection. and would seek its opening and the keeper would say: 'Who are you?' I would say: 'Muhammad.' He would then say: 'It is for you that I have been ordered and not to open it for anyone before you.'"[222]

---

221 ...قَالَ أَمَا إِنَّا قَدْ سَأَلْنَا عَنْ ذَلِكَ فَقَالَ: "أَرْوَاحُهُمْ فِي جَوْفِ طَيْرٍ خُضْرٍ لَهَا قَنَادِيلُ مُعَلَّقَةٌ بِالْعَرْشِ تَسْرَحُ مِنَ الْجَنَّةِ حَيْثُ شَاءَتْ ثُمَّ تَأْوِي إِلَى تِلْكَ الْقَنَادِيلِ. Sahīh Muslim 1887.

222 ...قَالَ رَسُولُ اللَّهِ: "آتِي بَابَ الْجَنَّةِ يَوْمَ الْقِيَامَةِ فَأَسْتَفْتِحُ فَيَقُولُ الْخَازِنُ مَنْ أَنْتَ فَأَقُولُ مُحَمَّدٌ. فَيَقُولُ بِكَ أُمِرْتُ لَا أَفْتَحُ لِأَحَدٍ قَبْلَكَ." Sahīh Muslim 197.

205. Can a foetus enter Paradise?

Answer: Yes.

First of all, at what age do Muslims think that a foetus is a human being with a soul? Answer: four months.

Scholars derived this from the Qur'an and Hadiths.

'Abd Allah ibn Mas'ūd (عَبْد الله بن مَسْعُود) narrated that Allah's Messenger said: "[The matter of the creation of] a human being is put together in the womb of the mother in forty days, and then he becomes a clot of thick blood for a similar period, and then a piece of flesh for a similar period. Then Allah sends an angel who is ordered to write down four things. He is ordered to write down his [the new creature] deeds, his livelihood, his [time of] death, and whether he will be blessed or wretched [in religion]. Then the soul is breathed into him."[223]

But when will this happen? Sura 23 *The Believers* - in Arabic: al-Mu'minūn (سُورة الْمُؤْمِنُون) – tells more:

23:12	We created man from an essence of clay,	وَلَقَدْ خَلَقْنَا الإِنسَانَ مِن سُلَالَةٍ مِّن طِينٍ
23:13	then We placed him as a drop of fluid in a safe place,	ثُمَّ جَعَلْنَاهُ نُطْفَةً فِي قَرَارٍ مَّكِينٍ
23:14	then We made that drop into a clinging form, and We made that form into a lump of flesh, and We made that lump into bones, and We clothed those bones with flesh, and later We made him into other forms - glory be to God, the best of creators!	ثُمَّ خَلَقْنَا النُّطْفَةَ عَلَقَةً فَخَلَقْنَا الْعَلَقَةَ مُضْغَةً فَخَلَقْنَا الْمُضْغَةَ عِظَامًا فَكَسَوْنَا الْعِظَامَ لَحْمًا ثُمَّ أَنشَأْنَاهُ خَلْقًا آخَرَ فَتَبَارَكَ اللَّهُ أَحْسَنُ الْخَالِقِينَ

Most scholars derive from these verses that when the age of the unborn child reaches 120 days (4 months), it no longer remains a lifeless object, but rather becomes a living human being.

Therefore, a foetus that died after four months of age should be given a name, washed, shrouded, and buried with other Muslims.

---

223 ...حَدَّثَنَا رَسُولُ اللَّهِ قَالَ: "إِنَّ أَحَدَكُمْ يُجْمَعُ خَلْقُهُ فِي بَطْنِ أُمِّهِ أَرْبَعِينَ يَوْمًا، ثُمَّ يَكُونُ عَلَقَةً مِثْلَ ذَلِكَ، ثُمَّ يَكُونُ مُضْغَةً مِثْلَ ذَلِكَ، ثُمَّ يَبْعَثُ اللَّهُ مَلَكًا، فَيُؤْمَرُ بِأَرْبَعِ كَلِمَاتٍ، وَيُقَالُ لَهُ اكْتُبْ عَمَلَهُ وَرِزْقَهُ وَأَجَلَهُ وَشَقِيٌّ أَوْ سَعِيدٌ. ثُمَّ يُنْفَخُ فِيهِ الرُّوحُ." Saḥīḥ al-Bukhārī 3208

Even the 'Aqīqa (عَقِيقة) - the sacrifice of an animal - should be offered.

Younger than 4 months, a foetus has no soul according to Islam, therefore, the foetus could be buried anywhere, and neither should it be named nor should a funeral prayer be offered.

Al-Mughīra ibn Shu'ba (الْمُغِيرة بن شُعْبة) narrated that the Prophet said: "Prayer should be offered for an abortion, and forgiveness and mercy supplicated for its parents."[224]

Let's now focus on an important question for Muslims: Will a foetus be in Paradise? When a foetus dies, he or she will enter the stage of al-Barzakh (الْبَرْزَخ). Immediately after that, his or her soul will enter Paradise where prophet Abraham takes care of them.

'Abd Allah ibn Mas'ūd narrated: "The souls of the children of the believers are in the crops of birds which go wherever they want in Paradise and return to lamps hanging from the Throne."[225]

On the Day of Resurrection, people will be raised from their graves and the children will also be raised in the state of childhood and youth at which they died and they will intercede for their parents and admit them to Paradise. Samura ibn Jundab (سَمُرة بن جُنْدب) narrated that whenever the Prophet finished the morning prayer, "he would face us and ask: 'Who amongst you had a dream last night?' So if anyone had seen a dream he would narrate it.[226]

One day, he asked us whether anyone of us had seen a dream. We replied in the negative. The Prophet said: 'But I had seen (a dream) last night that two men came to me, caught hold of my hands, and took me to the Sacred Land (Jerusalem)...'"[227]

[He mentioned things that he had seen...] "We reached a garden of deep green dense vegetation, having all sorts of spring colours. In the midst of the garden there was a very tall man and I could hardly see

---

224 ...قَالَ النَّبِيُّ: "وَالسِّقْط يُصَلَّى عَلَيْه." Sunan 'Abī Dāwūd 3180 (3174)

225 ...وَإِنَّ أَرْوَاحَ وِلْدَانِ الْمُؤْمِنِينَ فِي أَجْوَافِ عَصَافِيرَ تَسْرَحُ فِي الْجَنَّةِ حَيْثُ شَاءَتْ، فَتَأْوِي إِلَى قَنَادِيلَ مُعَلَّقَةٍ فِي الْعَرْشِ. Abū Hātim 6569

226 ...قَالَ كَانَ النَّبِيُّ إِذَا صَلَّى صَلَاةً أَقْبَلَ عَلَيْنَا بِوَجْهِهِ فَقَالَ: "مَنْ رَأَى مِنْكُم اللَّيْلَةَ رُؤْيَا." قَالَ فَإِنْ رَأَى أَحَدٌ قَصَّهَا، فَيَقُولُ مَا شَاءَ اللَّهُ. Sahīh al-Bukhārī 1386

227 ...فَسَأَلَنَا يَوْمًا، فَقَالَ: " هَلْ رَأَى مِنْكُمْ أَحَدٌ رُؤْيَا ". قُلْنَا لَا. قَالَ: " لَكِنِّي رَأَيْتُ اللَّيْلَةَ رَجُلَيْنِ أَتَيَانِي فَأَخَذَا بِيَدِي، فَأَخْرَجَانِي إِلَى الْأَرْضِ الْمُقَدَّسَةِ... Sahīh al-Bukhārī 1386

his head because of his great height, and around him there were children in such a large number as I have never seen."[228]

In the end, Muhammad was told by two angels what he saw. They explained to him: "...and the tall man, which you saw in the garden, is Abraham and the surrounding children are those children who died with al-Fitra (the Islamic Faith)." The narrator added: "Some Muslims asked the Prophet: 'Oh, Allah's Messenger! What about the children of pagans?' He replied: 'And also the children of pagans.'"[229]

There is another interesting Hadith which gives Muslims some details about unborn babies. ʾAbū Hassān (أَبُو حَسّان) reported: "I told ʾAbū Hurayra (أَبُو هُرَيْرَة) that my two children had died. 'Would you narrate to me anything from Allah's Messenger, which would soothe our hearts in our bereavements?'

He said: 'Yes. Small children are the fowls of Paradise. If one of them meets his father (or he said his parents), he would take hold of his cloth (or he said with his hand) as I take hold of them of your cloth (with my hand). And he [the child] would not take off [his hand] from it until Allah causes his father to enter Paradise.'"[230]

An uncommon Arabic word is used in this Hadith: Dʾāmīs (دَعَامِيص). This is the plural of Daʿmūs (دَعْمُوص), which, according to Edward Lane, is a very small animal that lives in water.

When the word is used together with *children*, especially in the expression - al-ʾAtfāl Dʾāmīs al-Janna (الأَطْفَال دَعَامِيص الجَنّة) - which means *[infants will be] roamers in Paradise*; it means that the children will not be barred from any dwelling. So they can go anywhere in Paradise and can enter any place.

---

228 ...فَانْطَلَقْنَا فَأَتَيْنَا عَلَى رَوْضَةٍ مُعْتَمَّةٍ فِيهَا مِنْ كُلِّ نَوْرِ الرَّبِيعِ، وَإِذَا بَيْنَ ظَهْرَيِ الرَّوْضَةِ رَجُلٌ طَوِيلٌ لاَ أَكَادُ أَرَى رَأْسَهُ طُولاً فِي السَّمَاءِ، وَإِذَا حَوْلَ الرَّجُلِ مِنْ أَكْثَرِ وِلْدَانٍ رَأَيْتُهُمْ قَطُّ... Sahīh al-Bukhārī 7047

229 ...وَأَمَّا الرَّجُلُ الطَّوِيلُ الَّذِي فِي الرَّوْضَةِ فَإِنَّهُ إِبْرَاهِيمُ وَأَمَّا الْوِلْدَانُ الَّذِينَ حَوْلَهُ فَكُلُّ مَوْلُودٍ مَاتَ عَلَى الْفِطْرَةِ." قَالَ فَقَالَ بَعْضُ الْمُسْلِمِينَ يَا رَسُولَ اللَّهِ وَأَوْلاَدُ الْمُشْرِكِينَ فَقَالَ رَسُولُ اللَّهِ: "وَأَوْلاَدُ الْمُشْرِكِينَ. Sahīh al-Bukhārī 7047.

230 ...قَالَ قُلْتُ لأَبِي هُرَيْرَةَ إِنَّهُ قَدْ مَاتَ لِي ابْنَانِ فَمَا أَنْتَ مُحَدِّثِي عَنْ رَسُولِ اللَّهِ بِحَدِيثٍ تُطَيِّبُ بِهِ أَنْفُسَنَا عَنْ مَوْتَانَا قَالَ قَالَ نَعَمْ: "صِغَارُهُمْ دَعَامِيصُ الْجَنَّةِ يَتَلَقَّى أَحَدُهُمْ أَبَاهُ - أَوْ قَالَ أَبَوَيْهِ - فَيَأْخُذُ بِثَوْبِهِ - أَوْ قَالَ بِيَدِهِ - كَمَا آخُذُ أَنَا بِصَنِفَةِ ثَوْبِكَ هَذَا فَلاَ يَتَنَاهَى - أَوْ قَالَ فَلاَ يَنْتَهِي - حَتَّى يُدْخِلَهُ اللَّهُ وَأَبَاهُ الْجَنَّةَ." Sahīh Muslim 2635.

In Arabic, the word Da'mūs usually denotes an embryo in the belly of a mare when not older than 40 days. After that, its make becomes apparent and it is called Dūda (دُودة) until an age of about three months, after which it is called Salīl (سَليل).

Muslims learn from all these sources that the children will remain as children at the time of resurrection, recompense, and reckoning, and even the miscarried foetus, into whom the soul had been breathed, will remain as he was on the day he was miscarried from his mother's womb.

206. Are there 72 virgins waiting in Paradise?

Answer: Most probably not.

This misconception is widespread especially among desperate Muslim men. So why do Muslim men think that there will be 72 virgins waiting for each martyr?

First of all, the Qur'an says that all Muslims, who will be permitted to enter Paradise, will receive more than one *Houri* - in Arabic: al-Hūr al-'Ayn (الْحُور الْعِيْن) -, which is explicitly mentioned in the plural.

But is a *Houri* a young, female virgin? Well, let's have a look. We find some information about that in sura 56 *That Which is Coming* – in Arabic: al-Wāqi'a (سُورة الْواقِعة).

Since none of us has ever seen a Houri and since we cannot know how they look like or what kind of creatures they are, I'll give several examples of translations to show how difficult the whole matter is:

56:22	*"Wahūr(un) 'Ayn(un)"*	وَحُورٌ عِينٌ
	and beautiful companions	*Abdel Haleem*
	And [with them will be their] companions pure, most beautiful of eye	*Muhammad Asad*
	And [for them are] fair women with large, [beautiful] eyes,	*Sahīh International*
	And (there are) fair ones with wide, lovely eyes,	*Pickthall*

	And (there will be) Companions with beautiful, big, and lustrous eyes,	*Yūsuf ʿAlī*
	And pure, beautiful ones,	*Shakir*

Most translators rendered the word Houri as *companions*.

The Arabic noun *Hūr* (حُور) is a plural form of both the masculine ʾAhwar (أَحْوَر) and the feminine Hawrāʾ (حَوْراءُ).

The word is an *adjective resembling an active participle* (صِـفة مُشَبَّهة). It describes a person distinguished by Hawar (حَـوَر). This Arabic word describes the *intense whiteness of the eyeballs and lustrous black of the iris*. In a broader sense, the word can mean *whiteness* or *pureness*. In Hebrew, the corresponding adjective *hiwer* (חִיוֵר) has the same root and means *pale, whitish*.

In the following verses, we will see how the Houris look like:

56:23	like hidden pearls:	كَأَمْثَالِ اللُّؤْلُؤِ الْمَكْنُونِ
56:24	a reward for what they used to do.	جَزَاءً بِمَا كَانُوا يَعْمَلُونَ
56:25	They will hear no idle or sinful talk there,	لَا يَسْمَعُونَ فِيهَا لَغْوًا وَلَا تَأْثِيمًا

The next verse is even more difficult to translate. It could indicate that Houris are women which would perhaps be a disappointment for all Muslim women. Let's see:

78:33	"Wakawāʿiba ʾatrab(an)"	وَكَوَاعِبَ أَتْرَابًا
	nubile, well-matched companions,	Abdel Haleem
	and splendid companions well matched	Muhammad Asad
	And full-breasted [companions] of equal age	Sahīh International
	And voluptuous women of equal age;	Pickthall
	And voluptuous women of equal age;	*Yūsuf ʿAlī*
	And voluptuous women of equal age;	*Shakir*

Most sources in Islam are written from a pure male perspective.

All prophets in Islam were men. All important companions of Muhammad were men, except for his wives and daughters.

Not only that; all influential translators and commentators of the Qur'an were men which means that their interpretations of verses were usually written from a male perspective. And, in addition to this all, every Sheikh and Imam in the world is a man. Islam is clearly a man's world.

The problem with the translation of the verses in question is the perspective – the male perspective. This becomes evident in one verse as most women, I assume, may not like to have *large-breasted companions*. In the end, there is no solution, simply because Muslims have no more information than what is given in the Qur'an. Furthermore, nobody knows for certain what the word Houri meant in the 7th century when the Qur'an was revealed to Muhammad.

Let's have a closer look at *the large-breasted companions.*

The word Kawā'ib (كَوَاعِب) is the plural of *Kā'ib* (كاعِب) and means *well-developed, full and round, swelling* (bosom); *having swelling breasts,* buxom (girls). According to the dictionary of Hans Wehr (Modern Standard Arabic), the plural explicitly means *buxom girls.*

Edward Lane said that the root and some of its derivatives, for example the word Ta'kīb (تَفْكِيب), means *the girl's breast swelled* or *became prominent or protuberant and round.* It can be applied to the successive stages of growth of the breast.

Ibn Kathīr (ابن كَثِير) writes in his exegesis that the adjective means *round breasts.* He goes on stating that it is "meant by this that the breasts of these girls will be fully rounded and not sagging, because they will be virgins, equal in age."

Muhammad Asad, on the other hand, renders Kawā'ib as *splendid companions,* because one of the meanings of the root is also *prominence, eminence,* or *glory* (Lisān al-'Arab).

So, let's summarise how Houris might look like. They are "restraining in their glances", with "modest gazes", "wide and beautiful/lovely eyes", "eyes like pearls", "splendid" and "physically prominent" – some say "large-breasted".

Still, we have no information about their alleged virginity. This, however, is found in sura 56 in which, by the way, the feminine gender - the Arabic suffix *...hunna* (هُنَّ) - is explicitly used:

56:35	We have specially created -	إِنَّا أَنشَأْنَاهُنَّ إِنشَاءً
56:36	virginal	فَجَعَلْنَاهُنَّ أَبْكَارًا
56:37	loving (devoted to their husbands), of matching age -	عُرُبًا أَتْرَابًا
56:38	for those on the Right,	لِّأَصْحَابِ الْيَمِينِ

The word Bikr (بِكْر) and its plural ʾAbkār (أَبْكار) can mean *first-born, unprecedented* – but also: *virgin, virginal*. Almost every translator does stick to the meaning of *being a virgin* or *untouched*. There is a broad consensus on this. It is only a matter of wording: "made them virgins", "made them virgin, pure and undefiled" or "virginal".

Ibn Kathīr (ابن كثير) is more precise and even says that the Houris "are delightful virgins of comparable age who never had sexual intercourse with anyone, whether from mankind or Jinns, before their husbands."[231]

So what about women? What will all the women receive?

It is difficult for some female Muslims that by reading Islamic, holy texts one could assume that only men get this kind of reward in Paradise.

The Qur'an, on the other hand, does not indicate that only men would be granted the company of Houris. Furthermore, all adjectives used in the Qur'an to describe the Houris can be applied to both females and males, for example: splendid, pure, companions, modest, wide-eyed, and gazelle-eyed – <u>except for large-breasted</u>.

---

231 ...أَيْ بَلْ هُنَّ أَبْكَار عُرُب أَتْرَاب لَمْ يَطَأْهُنَّ أَحَد قَبْل أَزْوَاجِهِنَّ مِنَ الْإِنْس وَالْجِنّ.

Now, what about the mysterious number 72?

This goes back to several Hadiths with good (حَسَن) and weak (ضَعِيف) chains of narrators.

Al-Miqdām ibn Maʻd Yakrib (الْمِقْدَام بن مَعْد يَكْرِب) narrated that the Messenger of Allah said: "There are six things for the martyr. He is forgiven with the first flow of blood he suffers, he is shown his place in Paradise, he is protected from punishment in the grave, secured from the greatest terror, the crown of dignity is placed upon his head - and its gems are better than the world and what is in it -, he is married to seventy two wives along al-Hūr al-ʻAyn of Paradise, and he may intercede for seventy of his close relatives."[232]

There is an authentic Hadith that talks about two Houris "only".

'Abū Hurayra (أَبُو هُرَيْرَة) narrated that the Prophet said: "The first batch [of people] who will enter Paradise will be [glittering] like the full moon, and the batch next to them will be [glittering] like the most brilliant star in the sky. Their hearts will be as the heart of a single man, for they will have neither enmity nor jealousy among themselves; everyone will have two wives from the Houris, [who will be so beautiful, pure and transparent that] the marrow of the bones of their legs will be seen through the bones and the flesh."[233]

Remark: A German scholar, writing under the pseudonym Christoph Luxenberg, even claims that the word Hūr in Syro-Aramaic was a poetic word to describe *wine grapes*. He therefore claims that the Qur'an uses the Christian view of the Paradise.

---

232 ...قَالَ رَسُولُ اللَّهِ: "لِلشَّهِيدِ عِنْدَ اللَّهِ سِتُّ خِصَالٍ يُغْفَرُ لَهُ فِي أَوَّلِ دَفْعَةٍ وَيَرَى مَقْعَدَهُ مِنَ الْجَنَّةِ وَيُجَارُ مِنْ عَذَابِ الْقَبْرِ وَيَأْمَنُ مِنَ الْفَزَعِ الأَكْبَرِ وَيُوضَعُ عَلَى رَأْسِهِ تَاجُ الْوَقَارِ الْيَاقُوتَةُ مِنْهَا خَيْرٌ مِنَ الدُّنْيَا وَمَا فِيهَا وَيُزَوَّجُ اثْنَتَيْنِ وَسَبْعِينَ زَوْجَةً مِنَ الْحُورِ الْعِينِ وَيُشَفَّعُ فِي سَبْعِينَ مِنْ أَقَارِبِهِ." hasan;
Jāmiʻ al-Tirmidhī 1663

233 ...قَالَ النَّبِيُّ: "أَوَّلُ زُمْرَةٍ تَدْخُلُ الْجَنَّةَ عَلَى صُورَةِ الْقَمَرِ لَيْلَةَ الْبَدْرِ، وَالَّذِينَ عَلَى آثَارِهِمْ كَأَحْسَنِ كَوْكَبٍ دُرِّيٍّ فِي السَّمَاءِ إِضَاءَةً، قُلُوبُهُمْ عَلَى قَلْبِ رَجُلٍ وَاحِدٍ، لاَ تَبَاغُضَ بَيْنَهُمْ وَلاَ تَحَاسُدَ، لِكُلِّ امْرِئٍ زَوْجَتَانِ مِنَ الْحُورِ الْعِينِ، يُرَى مُخُّ سُوقِهِنَّ مِنْ وَرَاءِ الْعَظْمِ وَاللَّحْمِ." Sahīh al-Bukhārī 3254

207. Do men have sex in Paradise?

Answer: Probably yes.

Ibn Kathīr wrote in his works that Muhammad had confirmed that there would be sexual intercourse in Paradise.

There is even information about the potency of men in Paradise. 'Anas ibn Mālik (أَنَس بن مالك) narrated that the Prophet said: "The believer shall be given in Paradise such and such strength in intercourse." It was said: "O Messenger of Allah! And will he able to do that?" He said: "He will be given the **strength of a hundred.**"[234]

A man will have intercourse in Paradise with his wives from among the Houris and his wives from among the people of this world (if they enter Paradise).

Thumāma Ibn 'Uqba (ثُمَامة بن عُقْبة) narrated that the Prophet said: "A man among the people of Paradise will be given the strength of a hundred men for eating, drinking, desire and sexual intercourse. A man among the Jews said: 'The one who eats or drinks needs to excrete!' The Messenger of Allah told him: 'The excretion of any one of them will be in the form of sweat which comes out through his skin, then his stomach will reduce in size again.'"[235]

Remark: To express that one has sexual intercourse, Muslims prefer to use the Arabic III-verb yujāmi' (يُجامِع) or the verbal noun Jimā' (جِماع). It comes from the root *to unite, to put together.*

Scholars are not sure whether children would be born as a result of having sex. Some claim that there would be children if the man wants them, but a pregnancy and birth would take just one hour. The Prophet told his followers only about men; there is no information about women. 'Abū Sa'īd al-Khudrī narrated that the Prophet said: "If the believer wants a child in Paradise, the pregnancy and delivery will take only an hour, then the child will be the age that the <u>man</u> wants."[236]

234... النَّبِيُّ قَالَ: "يُعْطَى الْمُؤْمِنُ فِي الْجَنَّةِ قُوَّةَ كَذَا وَكَذَا مِنَ الْجِمَاعِ." قِيلَ يَا رَسُولَ اللَّهِ أَوَيُطِيقُ ذَلِكَ قَالَ " يُعْطَى قُوَّةَ مِائَةٍ." .Jāmi' al-Tirmidhī 2732; hasan

235 ...إِنَّ الرَّجُلَ مِنْ أَهْلِ الْجَنَّةِ يُعْطَى قُوَّةَ مِائَةِ رَجُلٍ فِي الْأَكْلِ وَالشُّرْبِ وَالشَّهْوَةِ وَالْجِمَاعِ. فَقَالَ رَجُلٌ مِنَ الْيَهُودِ: فَإِنَّ الَّذِي يَأْكُلُ وَيَشْرَبُ تَكُونُ لَهُ الْحَاجَةُ ؟ قَالَ فَقَالَ لَهُ رَسُولُ اللَّهِ: حَاجَةُ أَحَدِهِمْ عَرَقٌ يَفِيضُ مِنْ جِلْدِهِ فَإِذَا بَطْنُهُ قَدْ ضَمَرَ." Ahmad 18509

208. What was the last revealed sura/verse?

Answer: It is not clear.

There are several possibilities and each of them is based on an authentic (صَحِيح) Hadith. This is not untypical for Islam. A Muslim can find several authentic sources which contradict each other. Although religions should strive to give a believer only one truth, Islam sometimes does not. This is the most difficult thing for a Muslim, i.e. finding his own answers to his questions. Islam does not always give a Muslim just one choice. Let's look what could have been the last revelation:

- **Sura 110** *Help* – in Arabic: al-Nasr (سورة النَّصر)

  This is stated in a Hadith narrated by ʿUbayd Allah ibn ʿAbd Allah ibn ʿUtba (عُبَيْد الله بن عَبْد الله بن عُتْبة). He told that Ibn ʿAbbās said to him: "Do you know the last sura which was revealed in the Qurʾan as a whole?" I said: "Yes, sura 110." Thereupon, he said: "You have told the truth."[237]

- **Sura 9** *The Repentance* – in Arabic: al-Tawba (سورة التَّوْبة) or al-Barāʾ (سورة البَراء)

  Al-Barāʾ ibn ʿĀzib (البَراء بن عازب) narrated that the last sura which was revealed in full was sura 9 *The Repentance*. [238] [239]

- **Sura 5** *The Feast* – in Arabic: al-Māʾida (سورة المائدة)

  It was narrated by Jubayr ibn Nufayr (جُبَيْر بن نُفَيْر): "I entered upon ʿĀisha (عائشة بِنْت أَبي بَكْر) and she said: 'Did you read sura al-Māʾida?' I said: 'Yes.' She said: 'It is the last sura to be revealed, so whatever you find in it of halāl, accept it as halāl, and whatever you find in it of harām, accept it as harām.'"[240]

---

236 ...إِنَّ الْمُؤْمِنَ إِذَا اشْتَهَى الْوَلَدَ فِي الْجَنَّةِ كَانَ حَمْلُهُ وَوَضْعُهُ وَسِنُّهُ فِي سَاعَةٍ كَمَا اشْتَهَى. Jāmiʿ al-Tirmidhī 2762

237 ...قَالَ لِي ابْنُ عَبَّاسٍ تَعْلَمُ آخِرَ سُورَةٍ نَزَلَتْ مِنَ الْقُرْآنِ نَزَلَتْ جَمِيعًا؟ قُلْتُ نَعَمْ. {إِذَا جَاءَ نَصْرُ اللَّهِ وَالْفَتْحُ} قَالَ صَدَقْتَ. Sahīh Muslim 3024

238 ...قَالَ آخِرُ سُورَةٍ نَزَلَتْ كَامِلَةً بَرَاءَةٌ، وَآخِرُ سُورَةٍ نَزَلَتْ خَاتِمَةَ سُورَةِ النِّسَاءِ {يَسْتَفْتُونَكَ قُلِ اللَّهُ يُفْتِيكُمْ فِي الْكَلَالَةِ}. Sahīh al-Bukhārī 4364

239 يَقُولُ آخِرُ آيَةٍ أُنْزِلَتْ آيَةُ الْكَلَالَةِ وَآخِرُ سُورَةٍ أُنْزِلَتْ بَرَاءَةُ. Sahīh Muslim 1618

240 ...قَالَ: دَخَلْتُ عَلَى عَائِشَةَ، فَقَالَتْ: "هَلْ تَقْرَأُ سُورَةَ الْمَائِدَةِ ؟" قَالَ: قُلْتُ: نَعَمْ، قَالَتْ: "فَإِنَّهَا آخِرُ سُورَةٍ نَزَلَتْ، فَمَا وَجَدْتُمْ فِيهَا مِنْ حَلَالٍ ،فَاسْتَحِلُّوهُ، وَمَا وَجَدْتُمْ فِيهَا مِنْ حَرَامٍ، فَحَرِّمُوهُ."

If ʿĀʾisha was right, the following verse would possibly be the last revealed verse to Muhammad. It contains one of the most famous lines of the Qurʾan:

5:3	You are forbidden to eat carrion; blood; pig's meat; any animal over which any name other than God's has been invoked; any animal strangled, or victim of a violent blow or a fall, or gored or savaged by a beast of prey, unless you still slaughter it [in the correct manner]; or anything sacrificed on idolatrous altars. You are also forbidden to allot shares [of meat] by drawing marked arrows - a heinous practice - today the disbelievers have lost all hope that you will give up your religion. Do not fear them: fear Me. Today I have perfected your religion for you, completed My blessing upon you, and chosen as your religion Islam: [total devotion to God]; but if any of you is forced by hunger to eat forbidden food, with no intention of doing wrong, then God is most forgiving and merciful.	حُرِّمَتْ عَلَيْكُمُ الْمَيْتَةُ وَالدَّمُ وَلَحْمُ الْخِنزِيرِ وَمَا أُهِلَّ لِغَيْرِ اللَّهِ بِهِ وَالْمُنْخَنِقَةُ وَالْمَوْقُوذَةُ وَالْمُتَرَدِّيَةُ وَالنَّطِيحَةُ وَمَا أَكَلَ السَّبُعُ إِلَّا مَا ذَكَّيْتُمْ وَمَا ذُبِحَ عَلَى النُّصُبِ وَأَن تَسْتَقْسِمُوا بِالْأَزْلَامِ ذَلِكُمْ فِسْقٌ الْيَوْمَ يَئِسَ الَّذِينَ كَفَرُوا مِن دِينِكُمْ فَلَا تَخْشَوْهُمْ وَاخْشَوْنِ الْيَوْمَ أَكْمَلْتُ لَكُمْ دِينَكُمْ وَأَتْمَمْتُ عَلَيْكُمْ نِعْمَتِي وَرَضِيتُ لَكُمُ الْإِسْلَامَ دِينًا فَمَنِ اضْطُرَّ فِي مَخْمَصَةٍ غَيْرَ مُتَجَانِفٍ لِّإِثْمٍ فَإِنَّ اللَّهَ غَفُورٌ رَّحِيمٌ

Some scholars claim that Muhammad died less than three months after this revelation.

The Prophet passed away on Monday, June 8, 632 (11 AH).

Ahmad ibn Hanbal 24977

PART III

On the Hadiths

209. How can you categorise a Hadith?

Answer: There are several ways (see below).

If you want to check the reliability of a Hadith, you should mainly ask yourself two things:

- Who reported it? -> Chain of narrators, so-called **'Isnād** (إسناد). Every Hadith starts with the chain of authorities going back to the original narrator and finally to the Prophet. This process is called 'Isnād – *the ascription of an Islamic tradition.*
- What is the content about? -> so-called **Matn** (مَتْن).

I have created a diagram which helps to roughly evaluate a Hadith:

مُتَواتِر consecutive	مُتَّفِق عَلَيْهِ agreed upon	مَشْهُور famous	عَزِيز rare 2 narrators	غَرِيب strange 1 narrator	حَسَن good
مُتَّصِل continuous	صَحِيح ↑ ↑ considered correct; **authentic** ↑ ↑				مُنْكَر denounced
مُسْنَد supported	مِن حَيْثُ السَّنَد ← ← according to the chain of narrators	حديث		مِن حَيْثُ المَتْن → → according to the content	مَتْرُوك abandoned
آحاد isolated	ضَعِيف ↓ ↓ considered **weak** ↓ ↓				مُدْرَج interpolated
مُنْقَطِع interrupted	مُضْطَرِب shaky	مُدَلَّس forged	مَوْقُوف stopped	مُنْقَطِع broken	مَوْضُوع fabricated

Let's look closer to the most important terms that are used to evaluate the quality of a Hadith:

1. According to the reference to a particular authority:

- Qudsī (قُدْسِيّ) – *divine*: a revelation from Allah that was directly sent to Muhammad who passed it on to his followers himself.

- Marfū' (مَرْفُوع) – *elevated*: a revelation with a high status in Islam as the content was said by Muhammad and was directly heard by his companions. e.g., "I heard the Prophet say..."
- Mawqūf (مَوْقُوف) – *stopped*: a narration from a companion only, e.g., "we were commanded to..." Usually, this is a command which was directly given by Muhammad to his followers.
- Maqtū' (مَقْطُوع) – *severed*: a narration from a successor.

2. According to the chain of narrators ('Isnād):

- Musnad (مُسْنَد) – *Having been related or attributed to; supported.* A narration whose chain of narrators reaches a companion of the Prophet who in turn reports from the Prophet. This means that the Hadith is actually *marfū'* and that the chain is *muttasil*.
- Muttasil (مُتَّصِل) – *continuous*. A Hadith with an uninterrupted 'Isnād.
- Munqati' (مُنْقَطِع) – *interrupted/broken*. A Hadith with a missing link before it reaches the successor of the actual narrator.

3. According to the number of reporters:

- Mutawātir (مُتَواتِر) – *consecutive*. A Hadith reported by such numerous companions that it is agreed upon as authentic.
- 'Āhād (آحاد) – *isolated*. A Hadith which was narrated by a countable number of people (very few).
- Mashhūr (مَشْهُور) – *famous*. A Hadith which was reported by more than two individuals.
- 'Azīz (عَزيز) – *rare yet strong*. A Hadith having only two reporters (in its 'Isnād).
- Gharib (غَريب) – *strange*. Only one narrator (in its 'Isnād).

4. According to nature of the Matn (content) and the 'Isnād:

- Munkar (مُنْكَر) – *denounced; disapproved*. A Hadith which was related by a weak reporter.
- Mudraj (مُدْرَج) – *interpolated*. A Hadith which had some words added by its narrator.

5. According to the authenticity of the correspondents:

- Sahīh (صَحِيح) – *sound*. A Hadith which was reported by people known for their truthfulness, knowledge, and their correct way of narrating. This is the best quality – it is considered *authentic*.

- Hasan (حَسَن) – *good*. A Hadith whose reporters were known and trustworthy, and the content is in line with the teachings of Muhammad and Islam. However, some narrators or minor details of the content possibly have a (small) defect.

- Da'īf (ضَعِيف) – *weak*. In this Hadith there is some defect – in the chain of transmission, in the proper understanding of one of the transmitters, or in the content itself.

- Mawdū' (مَوْضُوع) – *fabricated*. A Hadith containing a lie according to Muslims. It relates to things which contradict the teachings and traditions of Muhammad. This is the worst type of a weak Hadith.

210. Which collection of Hadiths do Sunni Muslims use?

Answer: The al-Kutub al-Sitta (الْكُتُب السِّتة), literally *the six books*.

Sunni Muslims use the six (originally five) books that contain the sayings and acts of Muhammad compiled by six Sunni Muslim scholars (starting) in the ninth century. They are also referred to as al-Sihāh al-Sitta (الصِّحاح السِّتة), literally *The Authentic Six*.

Since the 11th century they are accepted as a major part of (Sunni) Islam. Note that all collectors of the Sunni authentic Hadiths, except one, were of Persian origin.

Let's look at the books:

1. **Sahīh al-Bukhārī** (صحيح الْبُخاريّ), collected by Muhammad ibn 'Ismā'īl Bukhārī (مُحَمَّد بن إسماعِيل الْبُخاريّ), a Persian scholar who died in 870 (256 AH). It includes 7,275 Hadiths.

2. **Sahīh Muslim** (صحيح مُسلِم), collected by Imam Muslim ibn al-Hajjāj (مُسلِم بن الْحَجّاج), a Persian scholar who died in 875 (261 AH). It includes 9,200 Hadiths.

3. **Sunan 'Abī Dāwūd** (سُنَن أَبِي داوُد), collected by 'Abū Dāwūd (أَبُو داوُد), a Persian scholar who died in 888 (275 AH). It includes 4,800 Hadiths.

4. **Jāmiʿ al-Tirmidhī** (جامِع التِّرمِذِيّ), collected by Muhammad ibn ʿĪsā ibn Saura al-Sulamī at-Tirmidhī (التِّرمِذِيّ), a Persian scholar who died in 892 (279 AH). It includes 3,956 Hadiths.

5. **al-Sunan al-Sughra** (السُّنَن الصُّغرَى), collected by 'Ahmad ibn Shuʿayb al-Nasāʾī (أَحمَد بن شُعَيب النَّسائِيّ), a Persian scholar who died in 915 (303 AH). It includes 5,270 Hadiths.

There is a dispute over the sixth book – a debate between these two:

- **Sunan ibn Māja** (سُنَن ابن ماجَة), collected by Ibn Majah (ابن ماجه), a Persian scholar who died in 887 (273 AH). It includes over 4,000 Hadiths.

- **Muwatta' Mālik** (المُوَطَّأ), a work by Imam Mālik ibn 'Anas (مالك بن أَنَس), an Arab scholar from Medina who died in 795 (179 AH). The word Muwatta' literally means *smoothened; something that was made accessible.* Al-Muwatta' was the first legal work to incorporate and join Hadiths and Fiqh (Islamic jurisprudence) together. It is a kind of law book. Mālik is said to have been working on it for forty years. It includes 1,720 Hadiths.

What is the discussion about? Not all Sunni Muslim jurisprudence scholars agree on the addition of Sunan ibn Māja. In fact, it contains many Hadiths which do not fit the other five collections, whereas all the Hadiths in the Muwatta' go well with the other sahīh books. Nevertheless, some Hadiths included in Sunan ibn Māja are of great importance to Islamic rules.

211. Which collection of Hadiths do Shia Muslims use?

Answer: They have their own Hadiths literature (see below).

Shia Muslims do not use the six major Hadith collections of Sunni Muslims. They have their own collections: *The Four Books* - in Arabic: al-Kutub al-'Arba'a (الكُتُب الأَربَعة) - which were compiled by three authors who are known as the *Three Muhammads.*

Sunni and Shia Muslims consider the reliability of some narrators and transmitters of the Hadiths differently. In general, Shia Muslims see as unreliable all narrators who took side with 'Abū Bakr (أَبُو بَكْر) and 'Umar ibn al-Khattāb (عُمَر بن الْخَطَّاب) in the disputes over the leadership after Muhammad's death. Instead, Shia Muslims prefer narrations that go back to the Prophet's cousin and son-in-law, 'Alī ibn 'Abī Tālib (عَلِيّ بن أَبِي طالِب), and his supporters.

On the other hand, Sunni scholars put trust in narrators such as 'Ā'isha (عائشة بِنْت أَبِي بَكْر), whom Shia Muslims mostly reject, because 'Ā'isha was not only Muhammad's wife but also the daughter of 'Abū Bakr who opposed 'Alī. The Four Books Shia Muslims use are:

1. **Kitāb al-Kāfī** (الْكافِي) – *The Sufficient* by <u>Muhammad</u> ibn Ya'qūb Kulaynī (مُحَمَّد بن يَعْقُوب كُلَيْنِي). He was a Persian scholar who died died in 941 (329 AH). The book contains 16,199 Hadiths.

2. **Man lā yahduruhu al-Faqīh** (مَن لا يَحْضُرُهُ الْفَقِيه) - literally: *For him not in the Presence of a Jurisprudent* (some translate it as: *Every man his own lawyer*) - by 'Abū Ja'far <u>Muhammad</u> ibn 'Alī ibn Bābawayh (أَبُو جَعْفَر مُحَمَّد بن عَلِيّ ابن بابَوَيْه), a Persian scholar who died in 991 (380 AH). The book includes 9,044 Hadiths.

3. **Tahdhīb al-'Ahkām** (تَهْذِيب الأَحْكام) – *confirmation of decision*. It includes 13,590 Hadiths.

4. **Al-'Istibsār** (الإِسْتِبْصار) – *The Insight*. It includes 5,511 Hadiths.

5. Both number 3 and 4 were written by 'Abū Ja'far <u>Muhammad</u> ibn Hasan Tūsī (Persian: ابوجعفر محمد بن حسن طوسى), a Persian scholar, who is commonly known as al-Tūsī (الطُّوسِي) or al-Ta'ifa (الطّائفة). He died in the year 1067 (460 AH).

212. Who collected most of the Prophet's sayings and actions?

Answer: More or less five people, according to Sunni Muslims.

Here is a list of them:

- 'Abū Hurayra (أَبُو هُرَيْرة), who was a companion, who collected 5374 Hadiths. He died in about 676 (57 AH).

- 'Abd Allah ibn 'Umar (عَبْد الله بن عُمَر), the son of the second Caliph 'Umar and brother-in-law of Muhammad, who collected 2630 Hadiths. He died in 693 (73 AH).
- 'Anas ibn Mālik (أَنَس بن مالك), Muhammad's servant, who collected 2286 Hadiths. He died in about 712 (93 AH).
- 'Ā'isha bint 'Abī Bakr (عائشة بِنْت أَبِي بَكْر), Muhammad's wife, who collected 2210 Hadiths. She died in 678 (58 AH).
- 'Abd Allah ibn 'Abbās (عَبْد الله بن عَبّاس), Muhammad's cousin, who collected 1660 Hadiths. He died in about 687 (68 AH).

213. When did the compiling of the Hadiths start?

Answer: In the year 720 (101 AH).

It was the second Caliph, 'Umar ibn 'Abd al-'Azīz (عُمَر بن عَبْد الْعَزِيز), who instructed Islamic scholars to compile the Prophet's sayings and traditions. This was quite a complicated task.

The scholars first had to set up rules in order to evaluate the sources of the traditions and the biographical data of the narrators. The main criteria were the character and honesty of the narrator as well as the content of the tradition.

214. Who authored the most authentic book after the Qur'an?

Answer: Al-Bukhārī (الإمام الْبُخارِيّ) – according to Sunni Muslims. He collected more than 7,000 Hadiths of Muhammad.

Born	810 (194 AH) in Buxoro, (present-day Uzbekistan)	Died	870 (256 AH) in Samarqand (Uzbekistan)

Al-Bukhārī was from Bukhara/Buxoro (Persian: بخارا), former Persia, which is now Uzbekistan. Bukhārī (بُخارِيّ) is a common surname in central and western Asia and literally means *from Bukhara*.

Muhammad al-Bukhārī came from a wealthy family. He travelled throughout the Abbasid Caliphate (الْخِلافة الْعَبّاسِيّة) and made the pilgrimage to Mecca. He visited the most important centres of Islamic teaching of his time, talked to scholars, and exchanged information on Hadiths. It is said that he talked to over a thousand men and learned over 600,000 traditions.

After he had spent sixteen years abroad in research, he returned to Bukhara. He examined over 60,000 Hadiths and finally compiled a collection of 7,275 (or even more) traditions, arranged in chapters. If repetitions and different versions of the same report are deducted, the number of Hadiths would be reduced to 2,602, some scholars say.

His collection consists of 97 books and is usually referred to as Sahīh al-Bukhārī (صَحِيح الْبُخَارِي) or al-Jāmi' al-Sahīh (الْجامِع الصَّحِيح). The Arabic word sahīh (صَحِيح) means *authentic* or *correct*. Sahīh al-Bukhārī covers almost all aspects of life, for example manners, supporting the family, divorce, medicine, and trade.

Al-Bukhārī paid great attention to the chain of narrators. He used two criteria:

1. The lifetime of a narrator should overlap with the lifetime of the authority from whom he relates.
2. It should be verifiable that narrators have met with their source in person.

215. Who is the author of the second-most authentic Hadith collection?

Answer: Imam Muslim (إمام مُسْلِم).

Born	after 815 (206 AH) in Nishapur (present-day Iran)	Died	875 (261 AH), buried in Nasarabad (Iran)

Muslim ibn al-Hajjāj (مُسْلِم بن الْحَجّاج), commonly known as Imam Muslim, was a Persian Islamic scholar.

His collection of Hadiths, known as Sahīh Muslim (صَحِيح مُسْلِم), is one of the six major Hadith collections in Sunni Islam and is regarded as one of the two most authentic collections.

He is said to have compiled his work within 15 years. He examined approximately 300,000 Hadiths. Imam Muslim arranged the Hadiths almost scientifically and put all known variations of the narrated text or the chain of narration together, which makes it easy to compare and identify the nuances. Finally, he compiled 43 books containing around 3,000 Hadiths; some even say 12,000 depending on how duplicate versions are counted.

The collection touches all aspects of life, e.g. *The Book of Menstruation* (كِتاب الْحَيْض), *The Book of Marriage* (كِتاب النِّكاح) or *The Book of Destiny* (كِتاب الْقَدْر).

Imam Muslim recorded only narratives which were recounted by two reliable narrators, successors (تابِعُون), who heard the same story from two (different) companions. Similar to al-Bukhārī, his collection contains only *authentic* - sahīh (صَحيح) - Hadiths. Because of that, both al-Bukhārī and Muslim are referred to as the *Two Sahīhs*.

Note: Both authors of the (for Sunni Muslims) most important collections of the sayings and traditions of Muhammad, al-Bukhārī and Muslim, were non-Arabs and Persian native speakers.

216. What does "muttafaq alayhi" mean?

Answer: The expression *muttafaq 'alayhi* (مُتَّفَق عَلَيْهِ) means *agreed upon*. It marks a Hadith which was accepted and agreed upon by both Imams, al-Bukhārī and Muslim.

Basically, it is a seal of quality. If a Muslim sees this, he knows that there is nothing better regarding the quality of the narration. Furthermore, *muttafaq 'alayhi* indicates that the Hadith is related by Imam al-Bukhārī and Imam Muslim on the authority of the (same) companion who narrated the Hadith from the Prophet, and that both Imams al-Bukhārī and Muslim agreed on the authenticity of the Hadith.

A Hadith of this type has the same content and the same chain of narration, and is considered to have the best quality and authenticity. There are around 2000 Hadiths of this type.

Note: The narrator of the Hadith is crucial. If, for example, al-Bukhārī derives the content of a Hadith from 'Abū Hurayra and while Imam Muslim from 'Anas ibn Mālik, then it is not called *muttafaq 'alayhi*.

217. Which of Muhammad's companions was the most prolific narrator of Hadiths?

Answer: 'Abū Hurayra (أَبُو هُرَيْرة) – according to Sunni Muslims.

Born	599 (19 BH) in Yemen		Died	676 (57 AH) in Medina; buried at al-Baqī'

'Abū Hurayra's name literally means *father of the kitten*. Some accounts indicate that he had a cat which he deeply loved. When he herded his people's goats, he kept this kitten to play with. His real name is not entirely certain, but most people think it was 'Abd al-Rahmān ibn Sakhr (عَبْد الرَّحْمَن بن صَخْر). 'Abū Hurayra was born in Baha, Yemen, and belonged to a tribe from the Red Sea coast. His father died when 'Abū Hurayra was still young.

'Abū Hurayra probably did not spend a lot of time in the company of Muhammad, some claimed only around two years.

He accepted Islam less than three years before Muhammad died. In 628, right before the Battle of Khaybar (غَزْوة خَيْبَر), 'Abū Hurayra moved to Medina where he embraced Islam. He belonged to the so-called 'Ahl al-Suffa (أَهْل الصُّفَّة) or 'Ashāb al-Suffa (أَصْحاب الصُّفَّة) – the *Suffa Companions*.

Suffa denotes a (stone) moulding; ledge; a building for shade and shelter with a long roof or ceiling.

The Suffa adjacent to the Prophet's Mosque (الْمَسْجِد النَّبَوِيّ) in Medina was a shelter built from palm leaves next to the northern wall of the Prophet's Mosque. The Muslims which stayed there were companions who neither had a house, tribe, nor relatives in Medina.

It is not clear how many Hadiths 'Abū Hurayra has narrated. Some say, they were more than 3,300, while others claim he narrated 5,374 Hadiths.

Critics argue that most of his Hadiths were witnessed by only a few people or even a single person. The term for this is 'Āhād (آحاد), which literally means *isolated*.

'Abū Hurayra responded to the claims himself: "The people used to say: ''Abū Hurayra narrates too many narrations.' In fact, I used to keep close to Allah's Messenger and was satisfied with what filled my stomach. I ate no leavened bread and did not wear stripe-decorated clothes, and never did a man or a woman serve me, and I often used to press my belly against gravel because of hunger, and I used to ask a man to recite a Qur'anic verse to me although I knew it, so that he would take me to his home and feed me."[241]

Sunni Muslims are convinced that 'Abū Hurayra had an exceptional, unfailing memory. They portray him as a man who lived an ascetic life, sought knowledge, and was a pious believer.

By contrast, Shia Muslims reject the authenticity of 'Abū Hurayra's Hadiths. They accept his narrations only if there exists a similar Hadith which was narrated by a member of Muhammad's family, who are considered reliable by Shia Islam. Shia Muslims consider him an enemy of 'Alī and his children, Hasan and Husayn, because 'Abū Hurayra took side with Mu'āwiya I (مُعاوِيّة بن أَبِي سُفْيان), according to Shia sources.

Mu'āwiya I established the Umayyad <u>dynasty</u> and was the second Caliph from the Umayyad <u>clan</u>. He fought in the Battle of Siffin against 'Alī ibn 'Abī Tālib (عَلِيّ بن أَبِي طالِب), Muhammad's (true and only) successor according to Shia Muslims. Shia Muslims are convinced that Mu'āwiya is responsible for the death of 'Alī's son Hasan by bribing his wife to poison him.

Remark: Mu'āwiya (مُعاوِيَة) literally means: *bitch (in heat) that howls at the dogs.*

---

241 ...أَنَّ النَّاسَ، كانُوا يَقُولُونَ أَكْثَرَ أَبُو هُرَيْرَةَ. وَإِنِّي كُنْتُ أَلْزَمُ رَسُولَ اللَّهِ بِشِبَعِ بَطْنِي، حَتَّى لا آكُلُ الخَمِيرَ، وَلا أَلْبَسُ الحَبِيرَ، وَلاَ يَخْدُمُنِي فُلانٌ وَلاَ فُلانَةُ، وَكُنْتُ أَلْصِقُ بَطْنِي بِالحَصْباءِ مِنَ الجُوعِ، وَإِنْ كُنْتُ لأَسْتَقْرِئُ الرَّجُلَ الآيَةَ هِيَ مَعِي كَيْ يَنْقَلِبَ بِي فَيُطْعِمَنِي. Sahīh al-Bukhārī 3708

218. What is the best chain of narration?

Answer: Mālik, who narrated from Nāfiʿ, who narrated from Ibn ʿUmar, who narrated from the Prophet (مَالِك عَنْ نَافِع عَنْ ابن عُمَر).

Imam al-Bukhārī (الْبُخَارِيّ) said that this is the soundest of all chains of Hadiths.[242] Some Sunnis call it the *Golden Chain* (أحَادِيث السَّلْسِلة الذَّهَبِيّة). Let's have a look at these three people:

- **Mālik ibn ʾAnas** (مَالِك بن أَنَس), who died in 795 (179 AH), is known as Imam Mālik. He is one of the most highly respected scholars of Islamic jurisprudence - Fiqh (الْفِقْه) - in Sunni Islam. The Mālikī rite, named after Mālik, is one of the four schools of jurisprudence that are followed by Sunni Muslims to this day. His nickname was *Imam of the Abode of Emigration* – in Arabic: Imam Dār al-Hijra (إمام دار الْهِجْرة).

- **Nāfiʿ Mawlā ibn ʿUmar** (نافِع مَوْلَى ابن عُمَر), who died in 726 (117 AH), is a key person in the Golden Chain. He was a freed slave of ʿAbd Allah ibn ʿUmar and stayed with ʿAbd Allah ibn ʿUmar even after he had been freed. He was one of the best narrators of the Qur'an and it is said that he spent most of the time in the mosque teaching others. He received most of the Hadiths from ʿAbd Allah ibn ʿUmar, but some others also from ʿĀʾisha (عائشة بِنْت أَبِي بَكْر), ʾUmm Salama (أُمّ سَلَمة), and ʾAbū Hurayra (أَبُو هُرَيْرة). He was an uncle and first teacher of Mālik ibn ʾAnas.

- **ʿAbd Allah ibn ʿUmar** (عَبْد الله بن عُمَر بن الْخَطّاب), who died in the year 693 (73 AH), was the son of the second Caliph ʿUmar ibn al-Khattāb (عُمَر بن الْخَطّاب) and a brother-in-law of the Prophet. His sister Hafsa married Muhammad in 625. ʿAbd Allah ibn ʿUmar was the second most prolific narrator of Hadiths with a total of 2,630 narrations.

Watch out and don't get confused with the term *Golden Chain*:

Shia Muslims recognise a very similar term, i.e. *the narration of the chain of gold* – in Arabic: Hadith Silsila(t) al-Dhahab (حَدِيث سِلْسِلة الذَّهَب). It refers to a Hadith narrated from ʿAlī al-Ridā (إمام رضا), the

---

242 ...أَصَحُّ الأَسَانِيدِ كُلِّهَا: مَالِكٌ عَنْ نَافِعٍ عَنِ ابْنِ عُمَرَ.

eighth Imam of Shia Islam, and traces back to Muhammad, ʿAlī ibn ʾAbī Ṭālib (عليّ بن أبي طالب), and the (Shia) Imams.

219. How many names does Allah have?

Answer: At least 99 names.

Although some Muslims claim to know the 99 names, there is no reliable source which identifies these 99 names. Scholars even suggest that the number may not be limited to 99.

Muhammad had told his followers only about the number. ʾAbū Hurayra (أَبُو هُرَيْرة) narrated that the Messenger of Allah said: "There are ninety-nine names of Allah; he who commits them to memory would get into Paradise. Verily, Allah is Odd [He is one, and this is an odd number] and He loves odd numbers."[243]

Various scholars have tried to derive the names of Allah from the Qurʾan and the Hadiths. These names are of great importance to Muslims. Most Muslim names are a combination of *slave/servant* - in Arabic: ʿAbd (عَبْد) - plus one of the 99 attributes.

Therefore, if you see names like ʿAbd al-ʿAzīz (عَبْد الْعَزيز) - *Slave of the Almighty* - or ʿAbd al-Fattāh (عَبْد الْفَتّاح) - *Slave of He who opens all things* -, you can be sure that he is a Muslim (man). There is a Hadith which gives the 99 names of Allah. It was transmitted by al-Tirmidhī, however, its chain of narration is weak (ضَعيف).

Nevertheless, most Muslims I know stick to the names listed in this Hadith. ʾAbū Hurayra (أَبُو هُرَيْرة) narrated that the Messenger of Allah said: "Indeed, Allah has 99 names, one hundred less one, whoever recounts them shall enter Paradise. He is Allah, the one whom there is none worthy of worship except for Him, the Most Merciful (al-Rahmān), the Most Beneficent (al-Rahīm), the King (al-Malik), the Free of Deficiencies (al-Quddūs), the Granter of Safety (al-Salām), the Granter of Security (al-Muʾmin), the Watcher (al-Muhaymin), the Mighty (al-ʿAzīz), the Compeller (al-Jabbār), the Supreme (al-Mutakabbir), the Creator (al-Khāliq), the Originator (al-Bāriʾ),

---

243 ...عَنِ النَّبِيِّ قَالَ: "لِلّهِ تِسْعَةٌ وَتِسْعُونَ اسْمًا مَنْ حَفِظَهَا دَخَلَ الْجَنَّةَ وَإِنَّ اللَّهَ وِتْرٌ يُحِبُّ الْوِتْرَ."
Sahīh Muslim 2677

the Fashioner (al-Musawwir), the Pardoner (al-Ghaffār), the Over-whelming (al-Qahhār), the Giving (al-Wahhāb), the Provider (al-Razzāq), the Opener (al-Fattāh), the Knowing (al-'Alīm), the Taker (al-Qābid), the Giver (al-Bāsit), the Abaser (al-Khāfid), the Exalter (al-Rāfi'), the One who grants honour (al-Mu'izz), the One who humiliates (al-Mudhill), the Hearing (al-Samī'), the Seeing (al-Basīr), the Judge (al-Hakam), the Just (al-'Adl), the Kind (al-Latīf), the Aware (al-Khabīr), the Forbearing (al-Halīm), the Magnificent (al-'Azīm), the Oft-Forgiving (al-Ghafūr), the Grateful (al-Shakūr), the Most High (al-'Alīy), the Great (al-Kabīr), the Guardian (al-Hafīz), the Powerful (al-Muqīt), the Reckoner (al-Hasīb), the Glori-ous (al-Jalīl), the Generous (al-Karīm), the Watcher (al-Raqīb), the Responder (al-Mujīb), the Liberal Giver (al-Wāsi'), the Wise (al-Hakīm), the Loving (al-Wadūd), the Majestic (al-Majīd), the Reviver (al-Bā'ith), the Witness (al-Shahīd), the Truth (al-Haqq), the Guar-antor (al-Wakīl), the Strong (al-Qawīy), the Firm (al-Matīn), the One who aids (al-Walīy), the Praiseworthy (al-Hamīd), the Encompasser (al-Muhsī), the One who begins things (al-Mubdi'), the One who brings back things (al-Mu'īd), the One who gives life (al-Muhyi), the One who causes death (al-Mumīt), the Living (al-Hayyu), the Self-Sufficient (al-Qayyūm), the One who brings into existence (al-Wājid), the Illustrious (al-Mājid), the One (al-Wāhid), the Master (al-Samad), the Able (al-Qādir), the Powerful (al-Muqtadir), the One who hastens (al-Muqaddim), the One who delays (al-Mu'akhkhir), the First (al-'Awwal), the Last (al-'Ākhir), the Apparent (al-Zāhir), the Inner (al-Bātin), the Owner (al-Wālī), the Exalted (al-Muta'ālī), the Doer of Good (al-Barr), the Acceptor of repentance (alt-Tawwāb), the Avenger (al-Muntaqim), the Pardoning (al-'Afuww), the Kind (al-Ra'ūf), the Owner of Dominion (Mālik al-Mulk), the Possessor of Glory and Generosity (Dhū al-Jalāli wal 'Ikrām), the One who does justice (al-Muqsit), the Gatherer (al-Jāmi'), the Rich (al-Ghanīy), the Enricher (al-Mughni), the Preventer (al-Māni'), the Harmer (al-Dārr), the One who benefits (al-Nāfi'), the Light (al-Nūr), the Guide (al-Hādī), the Originator (al-Badī'), the Lasting (al-Bāqī), the Inheritor (al-Wārith), the Guide (al-Rashīd), and the Tol-erant (al-Sabūr)."[244]

---

244 ...قَالَ رَسُولُ اللَّهِ: "إِنَّ لِلَّهِ تَعَالَى تِسْعَةً وَتِسْعِينَ اسْمًا مِائَةً غَيْرَ وَاحِدَةٍ مَنْ أَحْصَاهَا دَخَلَ الْجَنَّةَ هُوَ اللَّهُ الَّذِي لاَ إِلَهَ إِلاَّ هُوَ الرَّحْمَنُ الرَّحِيمُ الْمَلِكُ الْقُدُّوسُ السَّلاَمُ الْمُؤْمِنُ الْمُهَيْمِنُ الْعَزِيزُ الْجَبَّارُ

220. How did Khadīja find out that the Prophet verily saw Gabriel?

Answer: She seduced Muhammad and undressed herself tempting Gabriel to watch, but since he vanished, they both thought that he must have been an angel. If Gabriel had been the Devil, he would have had no shame to watch.

'Ā'isha (عائشة بِنت أَبي بَكر) said that the Messenger of Allah was sitting with Khadīja (خَدِيجة) shortly after the first revelation. Ibn 'Ishāq told in his biography of Muhammad that when the "spirit" (Gabriel) came another time, Khadīja tested him:

Khadīja said to the apostle of Allah: "O son of my uncle, are you able to tell me about your visitant, when he comes to you?" He replied that he could. So when Gabriel came to him, as he was used to, the apostle said to Khadīja: "This is Gabriel who has just come to me." – "Get up, O son of my uncle", she said, "and sit by my left thigh." The apostle did so, and she asked: "Can you see him?"

"Yes", he replied. She said: "Then turn around and sit on my right thigh." He did so, and she asked: "Can you see him?" When he said that he could, she asked him to move and sit in her lap.

When he had done this, she again asked if he could see him and when he said yes, she disclosed her form and cast aside her veil while Muhammad was sitting in her lap. Then she asked: "Can you see him?" And he replied: "No."

She said: "O son of my uncle, rejoice and be of good heart, by God he is an angel and not a Satan."[245]

الْمُتَكَبِّرُ الْخَالِقُ الْبَارِئُ الْمُصَوِّرُ الْغَفَّارُ الْقَهَّارُ الْوَهَّابُ الرَّزَّاقُ الْفَتَّاحُ الْعَلِيمُ الْقَابِضُ الْخَافِضُ الرَّافِعُ الْمُعِزُّ الْمُذِلُّ السَّمِيعُ الْبَصِيرُ الْحَكَمُ الْعَدْلُ اللَّطِيفُ الْخَبِيرُ الْحَلِيمُ الْعَظِيمُ الْغَفُورُ الشَّكُورُ الْعَلِيُّ الْكَبِيرُ الْحَفِيظُ الْمُقِيتُ الْحَسِيبُ الْجَلِيلُ الْكَرِيمُ الرَّقِيبُ الْمُجِيبُ الْوَاسِعُ الْحَكِيمُ الْوَدُودُ الْمَجِيدُ الْبَاعِثُ الشَّهِيدُ الْحَقُّ الْوَكِيلُ الْقَوِيُّ الْمَتِينُ الْوَلِيُّ الْحَمِيدُ الْمُحْصِي الْمُبْدِئُ الْمُعِيدُ الْمُحْيِي الْمُمِيتُ الْحَيُّ الْقَيُّومُ الْوَاجِدُ الْمَاجِدُ الْوَاحِدُ الصَّمَدُ الْقَادِرُ الْمُقْتَدِرُ الْمُقَدِّمُ الْمُؤَخِّرُ الأَوَّلُ الآخِرُ الظَّاهِرُ الْبَاطِنُ الْوَالِي الْمُتَعَالِي الْبَرُّ التَّوَّابُ الْمُنْتَقِمُ الْعَفُوُّ الرَّءُوفُ مَالِكُ الْمُلْكِ ذُو الْجَلَالِ وَالإِكْرَامِ الْمُقْسِطُ الْجَامِعُ الْغَنِيُّ الْمُغْنِي الْمَانِعُ الضَّارُّ النَّافِعُ النُّورُ الْهَادِي الْبَدِيعُ الْبَاقِي الْوَارِثُ الرَّشِيدُ الصَّبُورُ." -Jāmi' al-Tirmidhī 3507; weak

245 ...قَالَ ابْنُ إِسْحَاقَ: وَحَدَّثَنِي إِسْمَاعِيلُ بْنُ أَبِي حَكِيمٍ مَوْلَى آلِ الزُّبَيْرِ: أَنَّهُ حُدِّثَ عَنْ خَدِيجَةَ أَنَّهَا قَالَتْ لِرَسُولِ اللَّهِ أَيْ ابْنَ عَمِّ أَتَسْتَطِيعُ أَنْ تُخْبِرَنِي بِصَاحِبِكَ هَذَا الَّذِي يَأْتِيكَ إِذَا جَاءَكَ؟ قَالَ نَعَمْ. قَالَتْ فَإِذَا جَاءَكَ فَأَخْبِرْنِي بِهِ. فَجَاءَهُ جِبْرِيلُ كَمَا كَانَ يَصْنَعُ فَقَالَ رَسُولُ اللَّهِ لِخَدِيجَةَ يَا خَدِيجَةُ هَذَا جِبْرِيلُ قَدْ جَاءَنِي، قَالَتْ قُمْ يَا ابْنَ عَمِّ فَاجْلِسْ عَلَى فَخِذِي الْيُسْرَى؛ قَالَ فَقَامَ رَسُولُ اللَّهِ فَجَلَسَ

Khadīja was sure that the Devil would have had no shame to stay on and watch.

Note: This attempt of testing the Devil was probably an old method of testing spirits. In Chinese culture, however, it is the opposite! Demons and devils are the ones afraid of female nude appearances; the exact opposite of Khadīja's test.

221. What is the so-called Hadith of Gabriel?

Answer: In Sunni Islam, the *Hadith of Gabriel* (حَدِيث جِبْرِيل) is the single most important Hadith.

This Hadith contains a summary of Islam. It mentions the **five pillars of Islam, the six articles of Faith, and 'Ihsān** (perfection; excellence; doing what is beautiful).

It is one of those very rare Hadiths in which the Archangel Gabriel appeared in a human form, not only before the Prophet, but also before his companions (which is unique). This Hadith is found in both authentic collections, Sahīh al-Bukhārī and Sahīh Muslim.

It was narrated on the authority of Yahyā ibn Ya'mar (يَحْيَى بن يَعْمَر): "One day we were sitting in the company of Allah's Apostle when there appeared before us a man dressed in pure white clothes, his hair extraordinarily black. There were no signs of travel on him. None among us recognised him. At last, he sat with the Apostle. He knelt before him, placed his palms on his thighs and said: 'Muhammad, inform me about **Islam**.'

The Messenger of Allah said: 'Islam implies that you testify that there is no god but Allah and that Muhammad is the Messenger of Allah, and you establish prayer, pay Zakā, observe the fast of Ramadan, and perform the pilgrimage [to the Ka'ba] if you are solvent enough [to bear the expense of] the journey.'

عَلَيْهَا، قَالَتْ هَلْ تَرَاهُ؟ قَالَ نَعَمْ قَالَتْ فَتَحَوَّلْ فَاجْلِسْ عَلَى فَخِذِي الْيُمْنَى؛ قَالَتْ فَتَحَوَّلَ رَسُولُ اللّهِ فَجَلَسَ عَلَى فَخِذِهَا الْيُمْنَى، فَقَالَتْ هَلْ تَرَاهُ؟ قَالَ نَعَمْ. قَالَتْ فَتَحَوَّلْ فَاجْلِسْ فِي حِجْرِي، قَالَتْ فَتَحَوَّلَ رَسُولُ اللّهِ فَجَلَسَ فِي حِجْرِهَا. قَالَتْ هَلْ تَرَاهُ؟ قَالَ نَعَمْ قَالَ فَتَحَسَّرَتْ وَأَلْقَتْ خِمَارَهَا وَرَسُولُ اللّهِ جَالِسٌ فِي حِجْرِهَا، ثُمَّ قَالَتْ لَهُ هَلْ تَرَاهُ؟ قَالَ لَا، قَالَتْ يَا ابْنَ عَمِّ اثْبُتْ وَأَبْشِرْ فَوَاللّهِ إِنَّهُ لَمَلَكٌ وَمَا هَذَا بِشَيْطَانٍ. Ibn 'Ishāq.

He [the inquirer] said: 'You have told the truth.' He [one of the narrators, 'Umar ibn al-Khattāb] said: 'It amazed us that he would put the question and then he would himself verify the truth.'

He [the inquirer] said: 'Inform me about **'Imān** (faith).'

He [the Prophet] replied: 'That you affirm your faith in Allah, in His Angels, in His Books, in His Apostles, in the Day of Judgement, and you affirm your faith in the Divine Decree about good and evil.' He [the inquirer] said: 'You have told the truth.'

He [the inquirer] again said: 'Inform me about **al-'Ihsān** [performance of good deeds].'

He [the Prophet] said: 'That you worship Allah as if you are seeing Him, for though you don't see Him, He, verily, sees you.'[246]

He [one of the narrators, 'Umar ibn al-Khattāb] said: 'Then he [the inquirer] went on his way but I stayed with him [the Prophet] for a long while.' He then, said to me: ''Umar, do you know who this inquirer was?' I replied: 'Allah and His Apostle knows best.'

He (the Prophet) remarked: 'He was Gabriel [the angel]. He came to you in order to instruct you in matters of religion.'"[247]

222. What is a Sā'?

Answer: A Sā' (صاع) is an ancient measure of volume used in the Hadiths.

Various scholars have struggled to interpret this ancient measurement. One Sā' is a cubic measure of varying magnitude. According to Edward Lane's dictionary, it was originally used for measuring

---

246 ... ثُمَّ قَالَ حَدَّثَنِي أَبِي عُمَرُ بْنُ الْخَطَّابِ قَالَ بَيْنَمَا نَحْنُ عِنْدَ رَسُولِ اللَّهِ ذَاتَ يَوْمٍ إِذْ طَلَعَ عَلَيْنَا رَجُلٌ شَدِيدُ بَيَاضِ الثِّيَابِ شَدِيدُ سَوَادِ الشَّعَرِ لاَ يُرَى عَلَيْهِ أَثَرُ السَّفَرِ وَلاَ يَعْرِفُهُ مِنَّا أَحَدٌ حَتَّى جَلَسَ إِلَى النَّبِيِّ فَأَسْنَدَ رُكْبَتَيْهِ إِلَى رُكْبَتَيْهِ وَوَضَعَ كَفَّيْهِ عَلَى فَخِذَيْهِ وَقَالَ يَا مُحَمَّدُ أَخْبِرْنِي عَنِ الإِسْلاَمِ. فَقَالَ رَسُولُ اللَّهِ: "الإِسْلاَمُ أَنْ تَشْهَدَ أَنْ لاَ إِلَهَ إِلاَّ اللَّهُ وَأَنَّ مُحَمَّدًا رَسُولُ اللَّهِ وَتُقِيمَ الصَّلاَةَ وَتُؤْتِيَ الزَّكَاةَ وَتَصُومَ رَمَضَانَ وَتَحُجَّ الْبَيْتَ إِنِ اسْتَطَعْتَ إِلَيْهِ سَبِيلاً. قَالَ صَدَقْتَ. قَالَ فَعَجِبْنَا لَهُ يَسْأَلُهُ وَيُصَدِّقُهُ. قَالَ فَأَخْبِرْنِي عَنِ الإِيمَانِ. قَالَ: "أَنْ تُؤْمِنَ بِاللَّهِ وَمَلاَئِكَتِهِ وَكُتُبِهِ وَرُسُلِهِ وَالْيَوْمِ الآخِرِ وَتُؤْمِنَ بِالْقَدَرِ خَيْرِهِ وَشَرِّهِ." قَالَ صَدَقْتَ. قَالَ فَأَخْبِرْنِي عَنِ الإِحْسَانِ. قَالَ: "أَنْ تَعْبُدَ اللَّهَ كَأَنَّكَ تَرَاهُ فَإِنْ لَمْ تَكُنْ تَرَاهُ فَإِنَّهُ يَرَاكَ". Sahīh Muslim 8

247 ...قَالَ لِي: "يَا عُمَرُ أَتَدْرِي مَنِ السَّائِلُ." قُلْتُ اللَّهُ وَرَسُولُهُ أَعْلَمَ. قَالَ: "فَإِنَّهُ جِبْرِيلُ أَتَاكُمْ يُعَلِّمُكُمْ دِينَكُمْ". Sahīh Muslim 8

grains. So how much is it? The problem with this measurement is that it varies from region to region, and it has also changed in the course of centuries. Some scholars say that it is four times the quantity (of wheat) that would fill two hands, neither large nor small, of a man. It could also be five pints (أَرْطال) and a third, and in some other regions also eight pints.

For Muslims, it is important to know how much one Sā' was at the time of Muhammad, because this measurement is used in several rules, e.g.: Zakā al-Fitr (زَكاة الْفِطر) and al-Fidya (الْفِدْية) which is the compensation for not fasting.

For this reason, scholars have tried to fix the Sā' at the time of the Prophet (الصّاع النَّبَوِيّ) and finally concluded:

One Sā' is 4 Mudd (الْمُدّ), and one Mudd equals roughly 650 grams. Therefore, one Sā' is approximately **2.6 kilograms (5.7 lbs) of wheat**. Some also say that **one Sā' equals 1.5 litres**.

223. What is the first deed a Muslim will be called to account for on the Day of Resurrection?

Answer: The prayer (الصَّلاة).

It was narrated from 'Abū Hurayra (أَبُو هُرَيْرة) that the Prophet said: "The first thing for which a person will be brought to account on the Day of Resurrection will be his prayer."[248]

Jābir ibn 'Abd Allah (جابِر بن عَبْد الله) reported that the Messenger of Allah said: "The five daily prayers are like a great river running by your door in which you take a bath five times a day."[249]

It was narrated that 'Abd Allah ibn Mas'ūd (عَبْد الله بن مَسْعُود) said: "I asked the Messenger of Allah which action is most beloved to Allah? He said: 'Establishing prayer on time, honouring one's parents, and Jihād in the cause of Allah.'"[250]

---

248 ...أَنَّ النَّبِيَّ قَالَ: "إِنَّ أَوَّلَ مَا يُحَاسَبُ بِهِ الْعَبْدُ يَوْمَ الْقِيَامَةِ صَلَاتُهُ." Sunan al-Nasā'ī 466

249 قَالَ رَسُولُ الله: "مَثَلُ الصَّلَوَاتِ الْخَمْسِ كَمَثَلِ نَهَرٍ جَارٍ غَمْرٍ عَلَى بَابِ أَحَدِكُمْ يَغْتَسِلُ مِنْهُ كُلَّ يَوْمٍ خَمْسَ مَرَّاتٍ." Sahīh Muslim 668

250 ...قَالَ سَأَلْتُ رَسُولَ الله أَيُّ الْعَمَلِ أَحَبُّ إِلَى الله عَزَّ وَجَلَّ قَالَ: "إِقَامُ الصَّلَاةِ لِوَقْتِهَا وَبِرُّ الْوَالِدَيْنِ وَالْجِهَادُ فِي سَبِيلِ الله عَزَّ وَجَلَّ." Sunan al-Nasā'ī 618

224. How does a Muslim get the reward of fasting for an entire year?

Answer: If a Muslim fasts the entire month of Ramadan and on six days of Shawwāl (شَوّال), the succeeding month.

This goes back to a Hadith. ʾAbū Ayyūb al-ʾAnsārī (أَبُو أَيُّوب الأَنْصاريّ) reported that Allah's Messenger said: "He who observed the fast of Ramadan and then followed it with six (fasts) of Shawwāl, it would be as if he fasted perpetually."[251]

Shawwāl (شَوّال) is the tenth month of the lunar Islamic calendar and comes after the month of Ramadan (شَهْر رَمَضان). Shawwāl means *to lift* or *carry*, which is no coincidence. When the names were set for the first time, this month happened to be the time of the year when a female camel normally would be carrying a foetus.

The first day of Shawwāl is ʿĪd al-Fitr (عيد الفِطْر), which marks the end of Ramadan. Some Muslims observe six days of fasting during Shawwāl beginning the day after ʿĪd al-Fitr since fasting is prohibited on this day.

The reasoning behind this tradition is that a good deed in Islam is rewarded ten times, hence fasting thirty days during Ramadan and six days during Shawwāl is equivalent to fasting the whole year. In numbers: $(30+6)*10=\mathbf{360}$.

Notice: For Shia Muslims, it is not important if the six days are consecutive, but Sunnis, especially followers of the Shāfiʿī (شافِعيّ) rite, pay great attention that fasting is observed on six consecutive days.

---

251 ...أَنَّ رَسُولَ اللَّهِ قَالَ: "مَنْ صَامَ رَمَضَانَ ثُمَّ أَتْبَعَهُ سِتًّا مِنْ شَوَّالٍ كَانَ كَصِيَامِ الدَّهْرِ." Sahīh
Muslim 1164

225. What is the reward for fasting on the Day of 'Arafa?

Answer: It compensates for the sins of the year before and for the year after. Hence, fasting on the Day of 'Arafa (يَوْم عَرَفة) is expiation for two years.

The Day of 'Arafa is the ninth day in the Islamic month of Dhū al-Hijja (ذُو الْحِجّة). 'Arafa is the name of a mountain, actually more of a hill, which is 70 m (230 ft) high. The mountain is called 'Arafa (جَبَل عَرَفة) or 'Arafāt (جَبَـل عَرَفات) and is the place where Muhammad delivered his Farewell Sermon to his followers who had accompanied him. It was the Prophet's one and only pilgrimage, only months before he died. It was narrated from 'Abū Qatāda (أَبُو قَتَادة) that the Messenger of Allah said: "Fasting on the Day of 'Arafa, I hope from Allah, expiates for the sins of the year before and the year after."[252]

Note: This fasting is only recommended for those who are **not undertaking the pilgrimage** (الْحَـجّ). Pilgrims should refrain from fasting on the Day of 'Arafa because the Prophet did not fast on this day when he was there. His wife, Maymūna (مَيْمُونة), narrated: "The people doubted whether the Prophet was fasting on the Day of 'Arafa or not, so I sent milk while he was standing at 'Arafa, he drank it and the people were looking at him."[253]

'Uqba ibn 'Āmir (عُقْبة بن عَامِر) narrated that the Prophet said: "The Day of 'Arafa, the Day of Sacrifice, the Days of Tashrīq are [the days of] our festival, O people of Islam. These are the days of eating and drinking."[254]

Remark: The origin of the word Tashrīq (تَشْرِيق) is not entirely clear. Tashrīq is the verbal noun/infinitive of the Arabic II-verb sharraqa (شَرَّقَ) which can mean *to cut the flesh/meat into strips and dry it in the sun*; simply *to cut meat into pieces*. That is why the word al-Tashrīq denotes the three days following the Day of Sacrifice (which is the 'Īd al-'Adhā). According to Edward Lane's dictionary, these

---

252 ...قَالَ رَسُولُ اللّهِ: "صِيَامُ يَوْمِ عَرَفَةَ إِنِّي أَحْتَسِبُ عَلَى اللّهِ أَنْ يُكَفِّرَ السَّنَةَ الَّتِي قَبْلَهُ وَالَّتِي بَعْدَهُ." Sunan ibn Māja 1802

253 ...أَنَّ النَّاسَ، شَكُّوا فِي صِيَامِ النَّبِيِّ يَوْمَ عَرَفَةَ، فَأَرْسَلَتْ إِلَيْهِ بِحِلَابٍ وَهُوَ وَاقِفٌ فِي الْمَوْقِفِ، فَشَرِبَ مِنْهُ، وَالنَّاسُ يَنْظُرُونَ. Sahīh al-Bukhārī 1989

254 ...قَالَ رَسُولُ اللّهِ: "يَوْمُ عَرَفَةَ وَيَوْمُ النَّحْرِ وَأَيَّامُ التَّشْرِيقِ عِيدُنَا أَهْلَ الإِسْلَامِ وَهِيَ أَيَّامُ أَكْلٍ وَشُرْبٍ." Sunan 'Abī Dāwūd 2419

days were named Tashrīq because the flesh of the victims - they were not sacrificed until the sun rose - was then cut into strips and dried in the sun. The tradition of drying fresh meat in the sun is still kept alive in several Islamic countries. My neighbour in Tunis, after he had slaughtered a sheep, hung several stripes of fresh meat on the clothesline on our roof to let it dry in the sun for days. The meat is called Qadīd (قَدِيد) and is used in a traditional Couscous dish.

Note: In the US, beef jerky is very common by American Indians. And in Africa, it is called *biltong*.

226. A Muslim comes closest to Allah by doing what?

Answer: To prostrate (in adoration).

'Abū Hurayra reported (أَبُو هُرَيْرة) that the Messenger of Allah said: "The nearest a servant comes to his Lord is when he is prostrating himself, so make supplication [in this state]."[255]

Even a whole sura is named *Bowing Down in Worship* – in Arabic: al-Sajda (سُورة السَّجْدة). It is sura 32.

The command to prostrate oneself - to degrade, bow and throw oneself down - before Allah is essential for the understanding of Islam, especially for the concept of the Devil ('Iblīs). Let's check the crucial verse of sura 2 *The Cow* – in Arabic: al-Baqara (سُورة البَقَرة):

2:34	When We told the angels, 'Bow down before Adam', they all bowed. But not 'Iblīs, who refused and was arrogant: he was one of the disobedient.	وَإِذْ قُلْنَا لِلْمَلَائِكَةِ اسْجُدُوا لِآدَمَ فَسَجَدُوا إِلَّا إِبْلِيسَ أَبَى وَاسْتَكْبَرَ وَكَانَ مِنَ الْكَافِرِينَ.

The Arabic root s-j-d (سَجَدَ) is used to denote the act of prostrating oneself which is called Sujūd (سُجُود). The root means *submission; worship; to prostrate oneself or bow down in humility; to prostrate oneself as a part of the prayers; to submit and accept the Faith*. From this the Arabic word for mosque is derived: masjid (مَسْجِد) which denotes the place where a person bows down and prostrates.

---

255 ...أَنَّ رَسُولَ اللَّهِ قَالَ: "أَقْرَبُ مَا يَكُونُ الْعَبْدُ مِنْ رَبِّهِ وَهُوَ سَاجِدٌ فَأَكْثِرُوا الدُّعَاءَ." Saḥīḥ Muslim

Excursus: It is a duty for Muslims to make a special Sujūd during the recitation of some verses of the Qur'an for the one who recites, the one who is actively listening, and the one who just happens to hear the recitation. This special act of prostrating oneself is called Sujūd al-Tilāwa (سُجُود التِّلاوة).

The word Tilāwa (تِلاوة) means *recitation*. The word Sujūd (سُجُود) describes the position in the Muslim's prayer with head, hands, knees and toes on the **ground**. There are 14 positions in the Qur'an. In most copies, there is a sign (for example: ۩) that tells the reader/reciter to prostrate. I will only give four examples. Normally, these verses contain the word *bow down, prostrate*:

7:206	[even] those who live in the presence of your Lord are not too proud to worship Him: they glorify Him and bow down before Him.	إِنَّ الَّذِينَ عِندَ رَبِّكَ لَا يَسْتَكْبِرُونَ عَنْ عِبَادَتِهِ وَيُسَبِّحُونَهُ وَلَهُ يَسْجُدُونَ ۩
13:15	All that are in heaven and earth prostrate [submit] to God alone, willingly or unwillingly, as do their shadows in the mornings and in the evenings.	وَلِلَّهِ يَسْجُدُ مَن فِي السَّمَاوَاتِ وَالْأَرْضِ طَوْعًا وَكَرْهًا وَظِلَالُهُم بِالْغُدُوِّ وَالْآصَالِ ۩
84:21	Why, when the Qur'an is read to them, do they not prostrate themselves [to God]	وَإِذَا قُرِئَ عَلَيْهِمُ الْقُرْآنُ لَا يَسْجُدُونَ ۩
96:19	No! Do not obey him [Prophet]: bow down in worship and draw close.	كَلَّا لَا تُطِعْهُ وَاسْجُدْ وَاقْتَرِب ۩

The main components of the prostration during the recitation of the Qur'an are:

- The intention (النِّيَّة): This means that by doing this action, praying, a Muslim is seeking Allah and nothing else.
- Say: "Allāhu 'akbar" (الله أَكْبَر).
- Prostrating – so-called Sujūd.
- A moment of serenity – so-called Tama'na (طَمْأنة).
- Sitting after the prostration – so-called Julūs (جُلُوس).
- Say: "al-Salāmu 'alaykum" (السَّلام عَلَيْكُم).
- Doing all this in the above order.

227. How many mortal sins doom a Muslim to Hell?

Answer: Seven.

In Islam, the seven mortal (great destructive) sins are called al-Sabʿ al-Mūbiqāt (السَّبْع الْمُوبِقـات). The seven sins which, according to Islamic doctrine, doom a Muslim to Hell are recorded in a Hadith which was narrated by ʾAbū Hurayra (أَبُو هُرَيْرة)[256]:

1. **Associating anything or anyone with Allah** (الشِّرْكُ بِاللَّهِ); i.e. worshipping other deities. This is the utmost sin for a Muslim; several scholars claim that this is even more sinful than murder.

2. **To practice sorcery/magic** (السِّحْرُ). The second Caliph in Islam, ʿUmar ibn al-Khattāb (عُمَر بن الْخَطّاب), instructed his governors to execute any male or female practitioner of witchcraft.

3. **To kill life except for a just cause** according to Islamic law (قَتْلُ النَّفْس الَّتِي حَرَّمَ اللهُ إلاَّ بِالْحَقّ). This does not mean that a Muslim is not allowed to kill. Islamic law commands the execution in several cases: execution of an adulterer by stoning; execution of certain criminals (such as banditry); the execution of a murderer is possible under certain conditions as well as the execution of an apostate. Killing for the sake of Allah if Islam is attacked (Jihād) is lawful too.

4. To practice **usury** (interest at unreasonably high rates). The so-called Ribā (أَكْلُ الرِّبَا) in Arabic.

5. Wrongfully **consuming property of an orphan** (أَكْل مَال الْيَتِيم)

6. **Retreating when the army advances** (التَّوَلِّي يَوْمَ الزَّحْفِ), i.e. to turn one's back on the enemy and fleeing from the battle-field. Note: The terrorist network ISIL killed dozens of their own fighters when they tried to escape or defect during a battle, justifying it by using this Islamic source.

7. **To slander chaste women** (قَذْفُ الْمُحْصَنَاتِ الْمُؤْمِنَاتِ الْغَافِلَاتِ). The punishment for this is 80 lashes.

---

256 ...النَّبِيُّ قَالَ: "اجْتَنِبُوا السَّبْعَ الْمُوبِقَاتِ ." قَالُوا يَا رَسُولَ اللَّهِ وَمَا هُنَّ قَالَ: "الشِّرْكُ بِاللَّهِ، وَالسِّحْرُ، وَقَتْلُ النَّفْسِ الَّتِي حَرَّمَ اللَّهُ إلاَّ بِالْحَقِّ، وَأَكْلُ الرِّبَا، وَأَكْلُ مَالِ الْيَتِيمِ، وَالتَّوَلِّي يَوْمَ الزَّحْفِ، وَقَذْفُ الْمُحْصَنَاتِ الْمُؤْمِنَاتِ الْغَافِلَاتِ." Sahīh al-Bukhārī 6857

228. What is Waswasa?

Answer: The whispering of the Devil.

The Arabic term Waswasa (وَشوَسة) - plural Wasawis (وَساوِس) - means *inspiring* or *suggesting*.

It is derived from the quadriliteral root w-s-w-s (وسوس). The verb وَشوَس means *to speak under one's breath, to whisper; to tempt somebody with wicked suggestions*. Therefore, the term Waswasa is used to describe a devilish temptation. However, it can also describe the *whisper of leaves, tombs – or of Jinns* (demons).

'Abū Hurayra (أَبُو هُرَيْرة) narrated that the Prophet said: "When any human being is born, Satan touches him at both sides of the body with his two fingers, except Jesus, the son of Mary, whom Satan tried to touch but failed, for he touched the placenta-cover instead."[257]

The Arabic expression "Waswasa(t) al-Shaytān" (وَشوَسةُ الشَّيْطانِ) describes that somebody is talking evil and that there is nothing good in it. The expression al-Waswās (الْوَشوَاس) - with the definite article *al* - denotes *the Tempter, Satan,* or *the Devil*.

229. How long does it take for a stone to reach Hell?

Answer: 70 years.

'Abū Hurayra (أَبُو هُرَيْرة) reported: "We were in the company of Allah's Messenger when we heard a terrible sound. Thereupon Allah's Apostle said: 'Do you know what [sound] this is?' We replied: 'Allah and His Messenger know best.' Thereupon he said: 'That is a stone which was thrown seventy years before in Hell and it has been constantly sliding down, and now it has reached its base.'"[258]

Note: The number seven occasionally signifies *many*. Seventy years could be just a symbol for "a very long time".

---

257 ...قَالَ النَّبِيُّ: "كُلُّ بَنِي آدَمَ يَطْعُنُ الشَّيْطَانُ فِي جَنْبَيْهِ بِإِصْبَعِهِ حِينَ يُولَدُ، غَيْرَ عِيسَى بْنِ مَرْيَمَ، ذَهَبَ يَطْعُنُ فَطَعَنَ فِي الْحِجَابِ." Sahīh al-Bukhārī 3286

258 ...قَالَ كُنَّا مَعَ رَسُولِ اللَّهِ إِذْ سَمِعَ وَجْبَةً فَقَالَ النَّبِيُّ: "تَدْرُونَ مَا هَذَا." قَالَ قُلْنَا اللَّهُ وَرَسُولُهُ أَعْلَمُ. قَالَ: "هَذَا حَجَرٌ رُمِيَ بِهِ فِي النَّارِ مُنْذُ سَبْعِينَ خَرِيفًا فَهُوَ يَهْوِي فِي النَّارِ الآنَ حَتَّى انْتَهَى إِلَى قَعْرِهَا."
Sahīh Muslim 2844

230. What is the least punishment in Hell?

Answer: Coals under the feet.

This information is found in a Hadith. It was narrated by Al-Nuʿmān ibn Bashīr (النُّعْمَان بن بَشِير) that he heard the Prophet say: "The least punished person of the people in Hell on the Day of Resurrection will be a man under whose (arches of the) feet will be placed two smouldering embers. His brain will boil just like a boiling Mirjal [copper vessel] or a Qum-qum [narrow-necked vessel]."[259]

The Qur'an and the Hadiths mention by name some people who will definitely be in Hell: ʾAbū Lahab (أَبُو لَهَب) and his wife as well as ʾAbū Tālib (أَبُو طالِب) and ʿAmr ibn Luhaī (عَمْرُو بن لُحَيّ).

Muhammad's uncle ʾAbū Tālib played an important role in protecting the Prophet in the beginning. Nevertheless, he never embraced Islam according to Sunni Muslims. Shia Muslims say that he was a Muslim at heart at least. Both believe that because of ʾAbū Tālib's efforts to protect Islam in the beginning, Allah will reduce his punishment in Hell.

ʿAbd Allah ibn ʿAbbās (عَبْد الله بن عَبّاس) reported that the Prophet said: "Among the inhabitants of the Fire, ʾAbū Tālib would have the least suffering, and he would be wearing two shoes [of Fire] which would boil his brain."[260]

231. For how long can a Muslim abandon a fellow Muslim?

Answer: Not more than three nights.

The concept of brotherhood - in Arabic: ʾIkhwān (إِخْوان) - is significant for Islam.

ʾAnas ibn Mālik (أَنَس بْن مَالِك) narrated that Allah's Messenger said: "Do not hate one another, nor be jealous of one another; and do not desert one another, but O Allah's worshippers! Be Brothers! And it is

---

259 ...قَالَ سَمِعْتُ النَّبِيَّ يَقُولُ: "إِنَّ أَهْوَنَ أَهْلِ النَّارِ عَذَابًا يَوْمَ الْقِيَامَةِ رَجُلٌ عَلَى أَخْمَصِ قَدَمَيْهِ جَمْرَتَانِ يَغْلِي مِنْهُمَا دِمَاغُهُ، كَمَا يَغْلِي الْمِرْجَلُ وَالْقُمْقُمُ." Sahīh al-Bukhārī 6562

260 ...أَنَّ رَسُولَ اللَّهِ قَالَ: "أَهْوَنُ أَهْلِ النَّارِ عَذَابًا أَبُو طَالِبٍ وَهُوَ مُنْتَعِلٌ بِنَعْلَيْنِ يَغْلِي مِنْهُمَا دِمَاغُهُ."
Sahīh Muslim 212

unlawful for a Muslim to desert his brother Muslim [and not talk to him] for more than three nights."[261]

'Abū Ayyub (أَبُو أَيُّوب) reported that the Messenger of Allah said: "It is not permissible for a Muslim to have estranged relations with his brother beyond three nights, the one turning one way and the other turning the other way when they meet; the better of the two is the one who is the first to give a greeting."[262]

This applies in particular when the person is a relative, because in such cases desertion is an even greater sin.

Remark: It is no coincidence that the Egyptian political Islamic group *The Muslim Brotherhood* - in Arabic: al-'Ikhwān al-Muslimūn (الْإِخْوان الْمُسْلِمُونَ) - chose its name. The Muslim Brotherhood won the elections in 2012 after the Egyptian revolution which sacked Hosni Mubarak. Just one year later, after the Egyptian military took over in June 2013, the political movement was banned and its members hunted by the police.

232. On which day does Allah free people from Hellfire more than on any other day?

Answer: On the Day of ʿArafa (يَوْم عَرَفة).

ʿĀʾisha (عائشة بِنْت أَبِي بَكْر) reported that the Messenger of Allah said: "There is no day when Allah sets free more servants from Hell than on the Day of ʿArafa."[263]

The pilgrimage - in Arabic: al-Hajj (الْحَجّ) - reaches its climax on the Day of ʿArafa, the 9th of the Islamic month of Dhū al-Hijja (ذُو الْحِجّة). The pilgrims' stop at ʿArafa is the major pillar of the Hajj because Muhammad said: "Hajj is ʿArafa."

---

261 ...أَنَّ رَسُولَ اللَّهِ قَالَ: "لاَ تَبَاغَضُوا، وَلاَ تَحَاسَدُوا، وَلاَ تَدَابَرُوا، وَكُونُوا عِبَادَ اللَّهِ إِخْوَانًا، وَلاَ يَحِلُّ لِمُسْلِمٍ أَنْ يَهْجُرَ أَخَاهُ فَوْقَ ثَلاَثِ لَيَالٍ." Sahīh al-Bukhārī 6076

262 ...أَنَّ رَسُولَ اللَّهِ قَالَ: "لاَ يَحِلُّ لِمُسْلِمٍ أَنْ يَهْجُرَ أَخَاهُ فَوْقَ ثَلاَثِ لَيَالٍ يَلْتَقِيان فَيُعْرِضُ هَذَا وَيُعْرِضُ هَذَا وَخَيْرُهُمَا الَّذِي يَبْدَأُ بِالسَّلاَمِ." Sahīh Muslim 2560

263 ...قَالَتْ عَائِشَةُ إِنَّ رَسُولَ اللَّهِ قَالَ: "مَا مِنْ يَوْمٍ أَكْثَرَ مِنْ أَنْ يُعْتِقَ اللَّهُ فِيهِ عَبْدًا مِنَ النَّارِ مِنْ يَوْمِ عَرَفَةَ وَإِنَّهُ لَيَدْنُو ثُمَّ يُبَاهِي بِهِمُ الْمَلاَئِكَةَ فَيَقُولُ مَا أَرَادَ هَؤُلاَءِ." Sahīh Muslim 1348

This is found in a Hadith which was narrated by 'Abd al-Raḥmān ibn Ya'mar (عَبْد الرَّحْمٰن بن يَعْمَر). According to the report the Messenger of Allah said: "The Hajj is 'Arafa, the Hajj is 'Arafa, the Hajj is 'Arafa. The days of Minā are three, but whoever hastens to leave in two days, there is no sin on him, and whoever stays on, there is no sin on him. And whoever sees [attends] the 'Arafa before the rising of Fajr, then he has performed the Hajj."[264]

Why is this day so important? Islam was perfected on the Day of 'Arafa. This information is found in a Hadith which refers to a verse in sura 5 *The Feast* – in Arabic: al-Māʾida (سورة الْمَائِدة):

5:3	Today I have perfected your religion for you, completed My blessing upon you, and chosen as your religion Islam: [total devotion to God]	الْيَوْمَ أَكْمَلْتُ لَكُمْ دِينَكُمْ وَأَتْمَمْتُ عَلَيْكُمْ نِعْمَتِي وَرَضِيتُ لَكُمُ الْإِسْلَامَ دِينًا.

A Hadith tells Muslims that this day was the Day of 'Arafa. Ṭāriq ibn Shihāb (طارق بن شهاب) narrated: "A Jew said to 'Umar: 'O Chief of the Believers, if this verse [5:3] had been revealed upon us, we would have taken that day as a feast day ('Īd).'

'Umar replied: 'I know definitely on what day this verse was revealed; it was revealed on the Day of 'Arafa, on a Friday.'"[265]

233. Which person should be treated with a Muslim's best companionship?

Answer: The mother (الْأُمّ).

'Abū Hurayra (أَبُو هُرَيْرَة) reported of a man who came to Allah's Messenger and asked: "O Messenger of Allah! Who is most entitled to be treated with the best companionship by me?"

---

264 ...قَالَ رَسُولُ اللَّهِ: "الْحَجُّ عَرَفَاتٌ الْحَجُّ عَرَفَاتٌ الْحَجُّ عَرَفَاتٌ أَيَّامُ مِنًى ثَلَاثٌ : فَمَنْ تَعَجَّلَ فِي يَوْمَيْنِ فَلَا إِثْمَ عَلَيْهِ وَمَنْ تَأَخَّرَ فَلَا إِثْمَ عَلَيْهِ وَمَنْ أَدْرَكَ عَرَفَةَ قَبْلَ أَنْ يَطْلُعَ الْفَجْرُ فَقَدْ أَدْرَكَ الْحَجَّ.
Jāmiʿ al-Tirmidhī 3241

265 ...قَالَ رَجُلٌ مِنَ الْيَهُودِ لِعُمَرَ يَا أَمِيرَ الْمُؤْمِنِينَ لَوْ أَنَّ عَلَيْنَا نَزَلَتْ هَذِهِ الآيَةُ {5:3} لَاتَّخَذْنَا ذَلِكَ الْيَوْمَ عِيدًا. فَقَالَ عُمَرُ إِنِّي لَأَعْلَمُ أَيَّ يَوْمٍ نَزَلَتْ هَذِهِ الآيَةُ، نَزَلَتْ يَوْمَ عَرَفَةَ فِي يَوْمِ جُمُعَةٍ.   Sahīh al-Bukhārī 7268

The Prophet answered: "Your mother."

The man asked: "Who is next?" The Prophet said: "Your mother." The man again asked: "Who is next?" The Prophet said: "Your mother." The man asked for the fourth time: "Who is next?" The Prophet said: "Your father."[266]

234. What do Muslims wish someone who wears new clothes?

Answer: "May you wear new clothes, live a good life, and die a martyr." In Arabic, this is a rhyme: "'Ilbas jadīdan, wa'ish hamīdan, wamut shahīdan!"[267]

You will occasionally hear this saying in the Arab world. It traces back to a Hadith which is, however, considered by most scholars to be weak (ضَعِيف). It was narrated from 'Abd Allah ibn 'Umar (عَبْد الله بن عُمَر) that the Messenger of Allah saw him wearing a white shirt whereupon the Prophet asked: "Is this garment of yours washed or a new one?" He answered: "Rather it has been washed." The Prophet said: "May you wear new clothes, live a good life, and die a martyr!"[268]

Muhammad was very fond of new clothes which is mentioned in several authentic Hadiths. Let's look at two of them:

'Abū Saʿīd al-Khudrī (أَبُو سَعيد الخُدْرِيّ) narrated that when the Messenger of Allah put on a new garment, he mentioned it by name, turban or shirt, and would then say: "O Allah! For You is the praise, You have clothed me, I ask You for its good and the good for which it was made, and I seek refuge in You from its evil and the evil for which it was made."[269]

---

266 ...جَاءَ رَجُلٌ إِلَى رَسُولِ اللهِ فَقَالَ يَا رَسُولَ اللهِ مَنْ أَحَقُّ بِحُسْنِ صَحَابَتِي قَالَ: "أُمَّكَ." قَالَ ثُمَّ مَنْ قَالَ: "أُمَّكَ." قَالَ ثُمَّ مَنْ قَالَ: "أُمَّكَ." قَالَ ثُمَّ مَنْ قَالَ: "ثُمَّ أَبُوكَ." Sahīh al-Bukhārī 5971

267 اِلْبَسْ جَدِيدًا وَعِشْ حَمِيدًا وَمُتْ شَهِيدًا

268 ...أَنَّ رَسُولَ اللهِ رَأَى عَلَى عُمَرَ قَمِيصًا أَبْيَضَ فَقَالَ: "ثَوْبُكَ هَذَا غَسِيلٌ أَمْ جَدِيدٌ." قَالَ لَا بَلْ غَسِيلٌ. قَالَ: "اِلْبَسْ جَدِيدًا وَعِشْ حَمِيدًا وَمُتْ شَهِيدًا." Sunan ibn Māja 3687 (3558)

269 ...قَالَ كَانَ رَسُولُ اللهِ إِذَا اسْتَجَدَّ ثَوْبًا سَمَّاهُ بِاسْمِهِ إِمَّا قَمِيصًا أَوْ عِمَامَةً ثُمَّ يَقُولُ: "اللَّهُمَّ لَكَ الْحَمْدُ أَنْتَ كَسَوْتَنِيهِ أَسْأَلُكَ مِنْ خَيْرِهِ وَخَيْرِ مَا صُنِعَ لَهُ وَأَعُوذُ بِكَ مِنْ شَرِّهِ وَشَرِّ مَا صُنِعَ لَهُ." Sunan 'Abī Dāwūd 4020

'Abū Nadra (أَبُو نَضْرة) recounted that when any of the companions of the Prophet put on a new garment, he was told: "May you wear it out and may Allah give you another in its place."[270]

235. Why don't most Muslim men wear their hair long?

Answer: Because the Prophet said so.

There are several Hadiths which tell Muslims what Muhammad thought about hairstyle. 'Atā' ibn Yasār (عَطَاء بن يَسَار) narrated that the Messenger of Allah was in the mosque when a man came in with dishevelled hair and beard. The Messenger of Allah motioned with his hand that he should be sent out to groom his hair and beard. The man did so and then returned. The Messenger of Allah said: "Isn't this better than that one of you should come with his head dishevelled, as if he were a Shaytān (a devil)?"[271]

Keeping the hair trimmed is better than growing it long – simply because the Prophet considered it "better". This was narrated in a Hadith which was about a man, Wā'il ibn Hujr (وَائِل بن حُجْر), who approached the Prophet with his hair and beard dishevelled. The man said: "I came to the Prophet and I had long hair. He said: 'It is not good.' I thought he meant me, so I went and cut my hair. [After that, the Prophet] said: 'I did not mean you, but this is better.'"[272]

On the other hand, a Muslim should not give too much attention to his hairstyle. 'Abd Allah ibn Mughaffal (عَبْد الله بن مُغَفَّل) narrated that the Messenger of Allah forbade combing one's hair except every second day.[273]

It was narrated that 'Abd Allah ibn Shaqīq (عَبْد الله بن شَقيق) said: "One of the companions was a governor in Egypt, and one of his

---

270 ...قَالَ أَبُو نَضْرَة فَكَانَ إِذَا أَصْحَابُ النَّبِيِّ إِذَا لَبِسَ أَحَدُهُمْ ثَوْبًا جَديدًا قِيلَ لَهُ تُبْلِي وَيُخْلِفُ اللَّهُ تَعَالَى.

Sunan 'Abī Dāwūd 4020

271 ...كَانَ رَسُولُ اللَّهِ فِي الْمَسْجِدِ فَدَخَلَ رَجُلٌ ثَائِرَ الرَّأْسِ وَاللِّحْيَةِ فَأَشَارَ إِلَيْهِ رَسُولُ اللَّهِ بِيَدِهِ أَنِ اخْرُجْ كَأَنَّهُ يَعْنِي إِصْلَاحَ شَعَرِ رَأْسِهِ وَلِحْيَتِهِ فَفَعَلَ الرَّجُلُ ثُمَّ رَجَعَ فَقَالَ رَسُولُ اللَّهِ: "أَلَيْسَ هَذَا خَيْرًا مِنْ أَنْ يَأْتِيَ أَحَدُكُمْ ثَائِرَ الرَّأْسِ كَأَنَّهُ شَيْطَانٌ." *Muwatta' Mālik 1739*

272 ...قَالَ أَتَيْتُ النَّبِيَّ وَلِي جُمَّةٌ قَالَ:"ذُبَابٌ." وَظَنَنْتُ أَنَّهُ يَعْنِينِي فَانْطَلَقْتُ فَأَخَذْتُ مِنْ شَعْرِي فَقَالَ:"إِنِّي لَمْ أَعْنِكَ وَهَذَا أَحْسَنُ." *Sunan al-Nasā'ī 5066*

273 ...قَالَ نَهَى رَسُولُ اللَّهِ عَنِ التَّرَجُّلِ إِلاَّ غِبًّا. *Sunan 'Abī Dāwūd 4159*

companions came to him and found him with unkempt, wild hair and asked: 'How come I see you with wild hair when you are a governor?' He replied: 'The Prophet of Allah forbade us from al-'Irfāh'. So we asked: 'What is al-'Irfāh?' He replied: 'To comb your hair every day.'"[274]

A remark on the expression al-'Irfāh: This verbal noun/infinitive is derived from the Arabic IV-verb 'arfaha (أَرْفَهَ) which means *to live in luxury; to live near water (cattle); to comb or anoint hair every day*[275].

According to Edward Lane's dictionary, the root r-f-h (رَفَهَ) is used to describe a life that is ample in its means or circumstances or plentiful. In another form of the verb, it can mean *to keep continually or constantly to the eating of dainty food and indulge oneself largely in eating and drinking*. This is said to be meant in the Hadith in which al-'Irfāh (الإِرْفَاه) is forbidden, because it is one of the practices of the foreigners and of worldly people.

And what about women?

In general women should pay great attention to their hair, mostly for their husbands. Jābir ibn 'Abd Allah (جَابِر بن عَبْد الله) narrated that the Prophet said: "If you enter [your town] at night [after coming from a journey], do not enter upon your family until the wife [the woman whose husband was absent from the house] shaves her pubic hair and the woman with unkempt hair, combs her hair."[276]

236. What is al-Fitra?

Answer: The word al-Fitra (الْفِطْرة) is difficult to translate, but is often interpreted *the innate character*.

---

274 ...قَالَ كَانَ رَجُلٌ مِنْ أَصْحَابِ النَّبِيِّ عَامِلاً بِمِصْرَ فَأَتَاهُ رَجُلٌ مِنْ أَصْحَابِهِ فَإِذَا هُوَ شَعِثُ الرَّأْسِ مُشْعَانٌّ قَالَ مَا لِي أَرَاكَ مُشْعَانًّا وَأَنْتَ أَمِيرٌ قَالَ كَانَ نَبِيُّ اللَّهِ يَنْهَانَا عَنِ الإِرْفَاهِ. قُلْنَا وَمَا الإِرْفَاهُ قَالَ التَّرَجُّلُ كُلَّ يَوْمٍ. Sunan al-Nasā'ī 5058.

275 ...أَرْفَهَ: رَجَّلَ شَعره وادَّهَنَ كُلَّ يَوْمٍ.

276 ...النَّبِيُّ قَالَ: "إِذَا دَخَلْتَ لَيْلاً فَلاَ تَدْخُلْ عَلَى أَهْلِكَ حَتَّى تَسْتَحِدَّ الْمُغِيبَةُ وَتَمْتَشِطَ الشَّعِثَةُ." Sahīh al-Bukhārī 5246

Al-Fitra denotes the *original unadulterated nature of things; the natural disposition*. It can also mean: *the natural constitution with which a child is created in his mother's womb*.

This Islamic concept is important for explaining several things the Prophet commanded; for example that a Muslim has to shave his body hair.

237. Why do Muslims shave their body hair?

Answer: Islam places a lot of attention on cleanliness. Muslims try hard to not get in contact with urine or excrements. Hair should therefore be removed so that they do not get contaminated with any impurity when relieving oneself.

'Abū Hurayra (أَبُو هُرَيْرة) narrated that he heard the Prophet say: "Five practices are characteristics of al-Fitra (الْفِطرة): circumcision, shaving of pubic hair, keeping moustaches short, clipping of nails, and the removal of armpit hair."[277]

The rulings on the removal of pubic hair are the same for men as for women. The removal of "dirty" hair should be understood in a broader sense: Muslim men should remove the hair on testicles and around the anus eliminating the possibility of impurities - in Arabic: Najāsa (نجاسة) - getting attached to it.

However, there is no explanation, neither in the Qur'an nor in the Hadiths, why Allah, who is by definition absolutely perfect in all matters, had created mankind with pubic hair in the first place – when he later commands Muslims to remove it.

Muhammad told his followers even of a deadline; the maximum number of days after which they have to shave. It was narrated that 'Anas ibn Mālik (أَنَس بن مالك) said: "The Messenger of Allah fixed the time for us to pare a moustache, trim fingernails, shave pubic hairs, and pluck underarm hairs: that we not leave it for more than **forty days**."[278]

---

277 ...النَّبِيُّ يَقُولُ: "الْفِطْرَةُ خَمْسٌ الْخِتَانُ، وَالإسْتِحْدَادُ، وَقَصُّ الشَّارِبِ، وَتَقْلِيمُ الأَظْفَارِ، وَنَتْفُ الآبَاطِ". *Sahīh al-Bukhārī 5891*

In another Hadith, it is recorded that ʿAbd Allah ibn ʿUmar (عَبْدُ الله بْن عُمَر), the son of the second Caliph ʿUmar and brother-in-law of Muhammad, used to trim his nails every fifteen days and shave his pubic hair every month.[279]

Note: The pubic hair was used to distinguish whether a boy was still a child or a man – and with dramatic consequences. If a boy was captured during a battle and had grown pubic hair, then Muslims at the time of Muhammad were allowed to kill him.

It was narrated that ʿAtiya al-Qurāzī (عَطِيّة الْقُرَظِي) said: "On the day that Saʿd ibn Muʿādh (سَعْد بن مُعاذ) passed judgement on the [Jewish] tribe Banū Qurayza (بَنُو قُرَيْظة), I was a young boy and they were not sure about me, but did not find any pubic hair, so they let me live, and here I am among you."[280]

238. What is so special about dates (fruit) in Islam?

Answer: Muhammad used to break his fast with dates.

It was narrated by ʾAnas ibn Mālik (أَنَس بن مالك) that the Messenger of Allah used to break his fast before praying with some fresh dates, but if there were no fresh dates, he would have a few dry dates, and if there were no dry dates, he would take some mouthfuls of water.[281]

Saʿd ibn Muʿādh (سَعْد بن مُعاذ) narrated: "I heard Allah's Messenger say: 'Whoever takes seven ʿAjwa dates in the morning will not be affected by magic or poison on that day.'"[282]

---

278 ...قَالَ وَقَّتَ لَنَا رَسُولُ اللّهِ فِي قَصِّ الشَّارِبِ وَتَقْلِيمِ الأَظْفَارِ وَحَلْقِ الْعَانَةِ وَنَتْفِ الإِبْطِ أَنْ لاَ نَتْرُكَ أَكْثَرَ مِنْ أَرْبَعِينَ يَوْمًا. (2759) Jāmiʿ al-Tirmidhī 2984.

279 ... أَنَّ ابْنَ عُمَرَ كَانَ يُقَلِّمُ أَظَافِيرَهُ فِي كُلِّ خَمْسَ عَشْرَةَ لَيْلَةً، وَيَسْتَحِدُّ فِي كُلِّ شَهْرٍ. -al-ʾAdab al-Mufrad 1258; sahīh mawqūf

280 ...قَالَ كُنْتُ يَوْمَ حُكْمِ سَعْدٍ فِي بَنِي قُرَيْظَةَ غُلاَمًا فَشَكُّوا فِيَّ فَلَمْ يَجِدُونِي أَنْبَتُّ فَاسْتُبْقِيتُ فَهَا أَنَا ذَا بَيْنَ أَظْهُرِكُمْ. Sunan al-Nasāʾī 3430.

281 ...يَقُولُ كَانَ رَسُولُ اللّهِ يُفْطِرُ عَلَى رُطَبَاتٍ قَبْلَ أَنْ يُصَلِّيَ فَإِنْ لَمْ تَكُنْ رُطَبَاتٌ فَعَلَى تَمَرَاتٍ فَإِنْ لَمْ تَكُنْ حَسَا حَسَوَاتٍ مِنْ مَاءٍ. Sunan ʾAbī Dāwūd 2356; hasan sahīh.

282 ...سَمِعْتُ رَسُولَ اللّهِ يَقُولُ: "مَنِ اصْطَبَحَ بِسَبْعِ تَمَرَاتٍ عَجْوَةٍ لَمْ يَضُرَّهُ ذَلِكَ الْيَوْمَ سَمٌّ وَلاَ سِحْرٌ." Sahīh al-Bukhārī 5779.

ʿAjwa (عَجْوة), according to Edward Lane, is a kind of date from Medina. They are among the best kinds and therefore termed *The Mother of Dates* (أُمُّ التَّمْر).

One of the many physical benefits of breaking the fast with dates is that the body benefits from the date's high level of natural sugars.

239. Which tree is like a Muslim according to the Prophet?

Answer: The date palm tree.

The date palm is a special tree in Islam, not only because of its fruits, the dates. It was the Prophet himself who compared this tree to a Muslim.

It was narrated by ʿAbd Allah ibn ʿUmar (عَبْد الله بن عُمَر) that the Prophet said [to his followers]: "Among the trees, there is a tree, the leaves of which do not fall, [a tree] that is like a Muslim. Tell me the name of that tree."

Everybody started thinking about the trees of the desert areas. And I [the narrator] thought of the date palm tree. The others asked: "Please inform us what is that tree, O Messenger of Allah?"

He [the Prophet] replied: "It is the date palm tree."[283]

240. What is the connection between a Muslim and citron, date, basil and colocynth?

Answer: They are symbols for the types of believers according to Muhammad.

It was narrated by ʾAnas ibn Mālik (أَنَس بن مالك) that the Prophet said: "A believer who recites the Qurʾan is like a **citron** [*citrus medica* (الأُتْرُجَّة)] whose fragrance is sweet and whose taste is sweet,

---

283 ...النَّبِيُّ قَالَ: "إِنَّ مِنَ الشَّجَرِ شَجَرَةً لاَ يَسْقُطُ وَرَقُهَا، وَإِنَّهَا مَثَلُ الْمُسْلِمِ، حَدِّثُونِي مَا هِيَ." قَالَ فَوَقَعَ النَّاسُ فِي شَجَرِ الْبَوَادِي. قَالَ عَبْدُ اللهِ فَوَقَعَ فِي نَفْسِي أَنَّهَا النَّخْلَةُ، ثُمَّ قَالُوا حَدِّثْنَا مَا هِيَ يَا.

- a believer who does not recite the Qur'an is like a **dried date** (التَّمْرة) which has no fragrance but has sweet taste,

- a profligate (الْفَاجِر) who recites the Qur'an is like **sweet basil** [*Ocimum basilicum* (الرَّيْحَانـة)] whose fragrance is sweet but whose taste is bitter,

- and the profligate who does not recite the Qur'an is like the **colocynth** [*Citrullus colocynthis* (الْحَنْظَلـة)] which has a bitter taste and no fragrance."[284]

The Hadith continues: "A good companion is like a man who has musk; if nothing of it goes to you, its fragrance will get to you; and a bad companion is like a man who has the bellows; if the soot does not get to you, the smoke [certainly] will."[285]

What is colocynth? *Citrullus colocynthis* has many common names: *bitter apple, apple of the Devil, bitter cucumber, desert gourd, vine of Sodom,* or *wild gourd.*

The colocynth is a desert plant native to the Mediterranean and Asia. It is found from North Africa to India. It resembles a common watermelon vine but bears small, hard, extremely bitter fruits. It has been widely used in folk medicine for centuries. It is said that when cooked in olive-oil, the oil could then be dropped into the ear to heal tinnitus (ringing in the ears). It was prepared by boiling in water or added to beer for relieving menses. Some pregnant women even used it to induce an abortion.

There is a saying: *The camel became sick from eating colocynth.* If a human being takes too many of the seeds, it can become toxic and cause internal bleeding. A deadly dose is about 3 grams.

The term *wild gourd* is mentioned in the Bible (2 Kings 4:39-40). Bible scholars suggest that it could be colocynth.

---

284 ...مَثَلُ الْمُؤْمِنِ الَّذِي يَقْرَأُ الْقُرْآنَ مَثَلُ الأُتْرُجَّةِ رِيحُهَا طَيِّبٌ وَطَعْمُهَا طَيِّبٌ وَمَثَلُ الْمُؤْمِنِ الَّذِي لاَ يَقْرَأُ الْقُرْآنَ كَمَثَلِ التَّمْرَةِ طَعْمُهَا طَيِّبٌ وَلاَ رِيحَ لَهَا وَمَثَلُ الْفَاجِرِ الَّذِي يَقْرَأُ الْقُرْآنَ كَمَثَلِ الرَّيْحَانَةِ رِيحُهَا طَيِّبٌ وَطَعْمُهَا مُرٌّ وَمَثَلُ الْفَاجِرِ الَّذِي لاَ يَقْرَأُ الْقُرْآنَ كَمَثَلِ الْحَنْظَلَةِ طَعْمُهَا مُرٌّ وَلاَ رِيحَ لَهَا. Sunan 'Abī Dāwūd 4829

285 ...وَمَثَلُ الْجَلِيسِ الصَّالِحِ كَمَثَلِ صَاحِبِ الْمِسْكِ إِنْ لَمْ يُصِبْكَ مِنْهُ شَيْءٌ أَصَابَكَ مِنْ رِيحِهِ وَمَثَلُ جَلِيسِ السُّوءِ كَمَثَلِ صَاحِبِ الْكِيرِ إِنْ لَمْ يُصِبْكَ مِنْ سَوَادِهِ أَصَابَكَ مِنْ دُخَانِهِ. Sunan 'Abī Dāwūd 4829

241. What is Allah's position on yawning?

Answer: Allah does not like it.

It was revealed in a Hadith which was narrated by 'Abū Hurayra (أَبُو هُرَيْرة) that the Prophet took a clear position here.

"Allah loves sneezing but hates yawning. When one of you sneezes and praises Allah, it is a duty for every Muslim who hears that to say: 'May Allah have mercy on you.' Yawning comes from the Devil. When one of you yawns, you should control it as much as possible. When a man says 'Aawh!', the Devil laughs at him."[286]

It was narrated that 'Abd Allah ibn 'Abbās (عَبْد الله بن عَبّاس) had said: "When someone yawns, he should place his hand over his mouth. Yawning comes from the Devil."[287]

242. What does a Muslim say to a fellow Muslim who sneezes?

Answer: "May Allah bestow His mercy on you." In Arabic: "Yar-hamuka-llāh."[288]

It was narrated by 'Abū Hurayra (أَبُو هُرَيْرة) that the Prophet said: "If anyone of you sneezes, he should say: 'Praise be to Allah' (al-Hamdu lillāh), and his [Muslim] brother or companion should say to him: 'May Allah bestow his Mercy on you' (Yarhamuka-llāh). When the latter says that, the former should say: 'May Allah give you guidance and improve your condition!' (Yahdīkumul-lāh wa yuslih bālakum).[289]

It was reported by 'Abū Burda (أَبُو بُرْدة) that the Messenger of Allah said: "When one of you sneezes and praises Allah [al-Hamdu lillāh],

---

286 ...النَّبِيُّ قَالَ: إِنَّ اللَّهَ يُحِبُّ الْعُطَاسَ، وَيَكْرَهُ التَّثَاؤُبَ، فَإِذَا عَطَسَ فَحَمِدَ اللَّهَ فَحَقٌّ عَلَى كُلِّ مُسْلِمٍ سَمِعَهُ أَنْ يُشَمِّتَهُ، وَأَمَّا التَّثَاؤُبُ فَإِنَّمَا هُوَ مِنَ الشَّيْطَانِ، فَلْيَرُدَّهُ مَا اسْتَطَاعَ، فَإِذَا قَالَ: هَاهْ، ضَحِكَ مِنْهُ الشَّيْطَانُ. al-'Adab al-Mufrad 919

287 ابْنُ عَبَّاسٍ قَالَ: إِذَا تَثَاءَبَ فَلْيَضَعْ يَدَهُ عَلَى فِيهِ، فَإِنَّمَا هُوَ مِنَ الشَّيْطَانِ. al-'Adab al-Mufrad 950; sahīh mawqūf

288 يَرْحَمُكَ اللَّهُ.

289 ...النَّبِيُّ قَالَ:"إِذَا عَطَسَ أَحَدُكُمْ فَلْيَقُلِ الْحَمْدُ لِلَّهِ. وَلْيَقُلْ لَهُ أَخُوهُ أَوْ صَاحِبُهُ يَرْحَمُكَ اللَّهُ. فَإِذَا قَالَ لَهُ يَرْحَمُكَ اللَّهُ. فَلْيَقُلْ يَهْدِيكُمُ اللَّهُ وَيُصْلِحُ بَالَكُمْ." Sahīh al-Bukhārī 6224

you should invoke Allah's mercy upon him [i.e., to say Yarhamuka Allāh]; but if he does not praise Allah, you should not respond."[290]

243. What does a Muslim say when he goes to sleep?

Answer: There are several possibilities, but a common one is: "With Your name, O Allah, I die and I live." In Arabic: "Bismika Allahumma ʾamūtu wa ʾahyā."

This invocation - Duʿāʾ (دُعاء) - traces back to a Hadith reported by Hudhayfa ibn al-Yamān (حُذَيْفة بن الْيَمَان). He narrated that whenever the Prophet went to bed, he would say: "With Your name, O Allah, I die and I live."[291]

Some remarks on the importance of the night for the Arabs and in Islam. In Arabic, you don't wish *good night;* instead, the parting word at night is *may you be well tomorrow morning* – in Arabic: "Tusbih ʿala Khayr" (تُصْبِح عَلَى خَيْر).

In Medieval times in Europe, the night was a time of danger whereas for the people of Arabia, it was, despite its dangers, mostly a time for conversation and enjoyment.

There are special verbs in Arabic that are related to the night: *to pass the night awake* (سَهِرَ) or *to travel by night* (أَشرَى). From the latter verb, the word *a night traveller* (سارٍ) is derived. In Islam, there is the extra night prayer performed in Ramadan, which is called al-Tarāwīh (التَراوِيح).

Night and moon belong together. If you miss somebody, you may say in Arabic *I am like a night without a moon* – in Arabic: "Ana ka laylatin bilā qamar" (أَنا كَلَيْلةٍ بِلا قَمَر). We should not forget that it is the moon which determines the Islamic calendar.

Asleep, a human being is powerless. Let's look at sura 39 *The Throngs* - in Arabic: al-Zumar (سُورة الزُّمَر) - to understand what is happening during sleep:

---

290 ...سَمِعْتُ رَسُولَ اللَّهِ وسلم يَقُولُ: "إِذَا عَطَسَ أَحَدُكُم فَحَمِدَ اللَّهَ فَشَمِّتُوهُ فَإِنْ لَمْ يَحْمَدِ اللَّهَ فَلَا
تُشَمِّتُوهُ." Sahīh Muslim 2992

291 ...كَانَ النَّبِيُّ إِذَا أَوَى إِلَى فِرَاشِهِ، قَالَ: اللَّهُمَّ بِاسْمِكَ أَمُوتُ وَأَحْيَا. Sahīh al-Bukhārī 6324

39:42	God takes the souls of the dead and the souls of the living while they sleep - He keeps hold of those whose death He has ordained and sends the others back until their appointed time - there truly are signs in this for those who reflect.	اللَّهُ يَتَوَفَّى الْأَنْفُسَ حِينَ مَوْتِهَا وَالَّتِي لَمْ تَمُتْ فِي مَنَامِهَا فَيُمْسِكُ الَّتِي قَضَى عَلَيْهَا الْمَوْتَ وَيُرْسِلُ الْأُخْرَى إِلَى أَجَلٍ مُسَمًّى إِنَّ فِي ذَلِكَ لَآيَاتٍ لَقَوْمٍ يَتَفَكَّرُونَ.

An Egyptian friend once told me that "in the West, people think that they can control and understand everything. They fly to the moon but fail to understand a simple thing like sleeping. When we sleep, our consciousness fades and we are no longer in charge of our own selves. When you sleep, you lose control; you are half dead. And then, in the morning, you miraculously wake up."

Islamic scholars put it like this: When people are awake, during the day, their face is turned towards this world, but when asleep, it is turned inwards in an incomprehensible mode of existence. Muhammad Asad said that in sleep "we may have flashes and glimpses of other levels - of a realm in which traits, tendencies, and knowledge can take on forms and shapes independent of the physical matter of this world (much as desires, fears, anxieties, etc. can take on symbolic forms and images in dreams)."

This is maybe one of the reasons why Muslims say that sleep has a likeness of death - it can provide a glimpse into another mode of existence. This idea is found in sura 6 *Livestock* – in Arabic: al-'An'ām (سُورة الْأَنْعام):

6:60	It is He who calls your souls back by night, knowing what you have done by day, then raises you up again in the daytime until your fixed term is fulfilled. It is to Him that you will return in the end, and He will tell you what you have done.	وَهُوَ الَّذِي يَتَوَفَّاكُم بِاللَّيْلِ وَيَعْلَمُ مَا جَرَحْتُم بِالنَّهَارِ ثُمَّ يَبْعَثُكُمْ فِيهِ لِيُقْضَى أَجَلٌ مُسَمًّى ثُمَّ إِلَيْهِ مَرْجِعُكُمْ ثُمَّ يُنَبِّئُكُم بِمَا كُنتُمْ تَعْمَلُونَ.

Remark: What does a Muslim say when he wakes up?

There are again several possibilities, but a common phrase is: "All the praises are for Allah Who has made us alive after He made us die [sleep] and unto Him is the resurrection." In Arabic: "al-Hamdu lillāh alladhī 'ahyāna ba'da mā 'amātana; wa 'ilayhi an-Nushūr."

This invocation, Du'ā' (دُعاء), traces back to a Hadith reported by Hudhayfa ibn al-Yamān (حُذَيْفة بن الْيَمَان). He narrated: "And when he [the Prophet] woke up from his sleep, he would say: 'All the praises are for Allah who has made us alive after He made us die [sleep] and unto Him is the resurrection.'"[292]

244. How should a Muslim behave towards others?

Answer: In a nutshell: Make it easy, make it pleasant, and don't frighten people.

It was narrated by 'Anas ibn Mālik (أَنَس بن مالك) that the Messenger of Allah said: "Facilitate things to people [concerning religious matters] and do not make it hard for them and give them good tidings, and do not make them run away [from Islam]."[293]

In Arabic, this is a famous rhyme: "Yassirū walā Tu'assirū wa Bash-shirū walā Tunaffirū!"[294]

245. What are the signs of a hypocrite according to Islam?

Answer: There are three signs (see below).

'Abū Hurayra (أَبُو هُرَيْرة) reported that the Messenger of Allah said: "Three are the signs of a hypocrite, i.e. when he speaks, he tells a lie; when he makes a promise, he acts treacherously against it; and when he is trusted, he betrays."[295]

In Arabic, a *hypocrite* is called Munāfiq (مُنافِق).

---

292 ...وَإِذَا اسْتَيْقَظَ مِنْ مَنَامِهِ قَالَ الْحَمْدُ لِلَّهِ الَّذِي أَحْيَانَا بَعْدَ مَا أَمَاتَنَا وَإِلَيْهِ النُّشُورُ. -Sahīh al-Bukhārī 6324

293 ...النَّبِيُّ قَالَ: "يَسِّرُوا وَلَا تُعَسِّرُوا، وَبَشِّرُوا وَلَا تُنَفِّرُوا." Sahīh al-Bukhārī 69

294 ...يَسِّرُوا وَلَا تُعَسِّرُوا، وَبَشِّرُوا وَلَا تُنَفِّرُوا!

295 ...أَنَّ رَسُولَ اللَّهِ قَالَ: "آيَةُ الْمُنَافِقِ ثَلَاثٌ إِذَا حَدَّثَ كَذَبَ، وَإِذَا وَعَدَ أَخْلَفَ، وَإِذَا اؤْتُمِنَ خَانَ." Sahīh al-Bukhārī 6095

The root n-f-q (ن-ف-ق) denotes a *desert rat's tunnel; to go into a tunnel entrance* and *come out of another;* also: *to die; to become depleted; to spend, to donate for a good cause, to support one's family.* The Arabic III-verb nāfaqa (نافَقَ) means: *to be a hypocrite in religion, professing to believe first one thing and then another.* The word Nifāq (نِفاق) means *hypocrisy.* The word *Munāfiqūn* (مُنافِقُون) is found 27 times in the Qur'an. It is the plural of Munāfiq and means: *hypocrites.*

Hypocrisy is considered a "sickness" and a serious crime in Islam. It means making an outward display of Islam whilst concealing inward disbelief – kufr (كُفر). Hypocrisy is even more dangerous than kufr itself and the punishment for it is more severe because its harmful effects are greater according to Islamic doctrine. Hence, Allah will put the hypocrites in the worst level of Hell as Muslims learn from sura 4 called *Women* – in Arabic: al-Nisā' (سُورة النِّساء):

4:145	The hypocrites will be in the lowest depths of Hell, and you will find no one to help them.	إِنَّ الْمُنَافِقِينَ فِي الدَّرْكِ الْأَسْفَلِ مِنَ النَّارِ وَلَن تَجِدَ لَهُمْ نَصِيرًا.

246. Is a Muslim allowed to travel in order to visit a mosque?

Answer: Strictly speaking, no, but the three main mosques are excepted.

It was narrated by 'Abū Hurayra (أَبُو هُرَيْرة) that the Prophet said: "Do not set out on a journey except for three Mosques: al-Masjid al-Harām [in Mecca], the Prophet's Mosque [in Medina], and the Mosque of al-'Aqsā [in Jerusalem]."[296]

However, most Muslims don't really care about this command. Several scholars even agree that if a person visits a mosque other than his own and his purpose is to seek knowledge or to call people to Islam, then this can be done anywhere.

---

296 ...النَّبِيُّ قَالَ: "لَا تُشَدُّ الرِّحَالُ إِلاَّ إِلَى ثَلَاثَةِ مَسَاجِدَ الْمَسْجِدِ الْحَرَامِ، وَمَسْجِدِ الرَّسُولِ وَمَسْجِدِ الْأَقْصَى." Saḥīḥ al-Bukhārī 1189

247. Who killed "the best" and "the worst" of men?

Answer: Wahshī ibn Harb (وَحْشِيّ بن حَرْب الْحَبَشِيّ), an Ethiopian slave.

Let's start with the "best of men" who was killed by Wahshī. It was Muhammad's uncle Hamza ibn ʿAbd al-Muttalib (حَمْزة بن عَبْد الْمُطَّلِب).

One story that is widespread among Muslims is that Wahshī had been appointed by Hind bint ʿUtba (هِنْد بِنْت عُتْبة) to kill one of the three following persons: either the Prophet, ʿAlī ibn ʾAbī Tālib (عَلِيّ بن أَبِي طالب), or Hamza ibn ʿAbd al-Muttalib (حَمْزة بن عَبْد الْمُطَّلِب), so that she might avenge the death of her father, her uncle, as well as her brother, who all were killed in the Battle of Badr (غَزْوة بَدْر).

However, Muslims find a different story in a Hadith. It was narrated by Jaʿfar ibn ʿAmr ibn ʾUmayya (جَعْفَر بن عَمْرو بن أُمَيّة) that he went out to see Wahshī and asked: "Will you tell us [the story of] the killing of Hamza?" Wahshī replied: "Yes, Hamza killed Tuʿayma (طُعَيْمة) at the Battle of Badr, so my master, Jubayr ibn Mutʿim (جُبَيْر بن مُطْعِم) told me: 'If you kill Hamza in revenge for my uncle, then you will be set free.'"[297]

The Hadith goes on: "I hid myself behind a rock and when he [i.e. Hamza] came near, I threw my spear at him, driving it into his navel so that it came out through his buttocks, causing him to die."[298]

Now let's turn to the "worst of men".

According to historians Wahshī himself said: "I killed the best of men in a time of ignorance [before Islam; i.e. Hamza ibn ʿAbd al-Muttalib] and the worst man in the time of Islam."[299] This was mentioned by Ibn al-ʾAthīr (إِبْن الْأَثِير), a historian and biographer of the 12th century, in his book "The Lions of the Forest and the knowledge about the Companions".[300]

So who was **the worst of men**?

---

297 ...ثُمَّ قَالَ أَلَا تُخْبِرُنَا بِقَتْلِ حَمْزَة قَالَ نَعَمْ، إِنَّ حَمْزَة قَتَلَ طُعَيْمَةَ بْنَ عَدِيِّ بْنِ الْجِيَارِ بِبَدْرٍ، فَقَالَ لِي مَوْلَاىَ جُبَيْرُ بْنُ مُطْعِمٍ إِنْ قَتَلْتَ حَمْزَةَ بِعَمِّي فَأَنْتَ حُرٌّ. Sahīh al-Bukhārī 4072.

298 ...وَكَمَنْتُ لِحَمْزَةَ تَحْتَ صَخْرَةٍ فَلَمَّا دَنَا مِنِّي رَمَيْتُهُ بِحَرْبَتِي، فَأَضَعُهَا فِي ثُنَّتِهِ حَتَّى خَرَجَتْ مِنْ بَيْنِ وَرِكَيْهِ قَالَ فَكَانَ ذَاكَ الْعَهْدَ بِهِ. Sahīh al-Bukhārī 4072.

299 ...قَتَلْتُ خَيْرُ النَّاسِ فِي الْجَاهِلِيّةِ وَشَرَّ النَّاسِ فِي الْإِسْلَامِ.

300 ...أُسَد الْغَابة فِي مَعْرِفة الصَّحابة.

It was Musaylima (مُسَيْلِمة), the leader of a non-Muslim army, who was probably killed in 633 (12 AH) in the Battle of Yamāma (مَعْرَكة الْيَمامة) during the Apostate Wars.

Musaylima (مُسَيْلِمة) was one of the persons who claimed proph-ethood. He is considered by Muslims to be a false prophet and is occasionally referred to as *Musaylima the Liar* – in Arabic: al-Kad-hdhāb (الكذّاب). Note: The name Musaylima is the (insulting) dimin-utive of Maslama (مَسْلَمة).

The killing is told in the second part of the Hadith narrated by Ja'far ibn 'Amr ibn 'Umayya in which Wahshī told about murdering Hamza: "About the killing of Musaylima... I said: 'I will go out to Musaylima so that I may kill him and make amends for killing Hamza. So I went out with the people [to fight Musaylima and his followers] and then famous events took place concerning that battle.

Suddenly I saw a man [i.e. Musaylima] standing near a gap in a wall. He looked like an ash-coloured camel and his hair was dishevelled. So I threw my spear at him, driving it into his chest in between his breasts until it passed out through his shoulders, and then a man from the Helpers (al-'Ansār) attacked him and struck him on the head with a sword."[301]

However, the legend that Wahshī killed Musaylima is something which he had claimed himself. There are no other sources. Islam crit-ics say that Wahshī's life deteriorated in his last years and that he was caught drinking alcohol.

Wahshī died in Homs (now Syria) and is buried there.

---

301 ...قُلْتُ لَأَخْرُجَنَّ إِلَى مُسَيْلِمَةَ لَعَلِّي أَقْتُلُهُ فَأُكَافِئَ بِهِ حَمْزَةَ قَالَ فَخَرَجْتُ مَعَ النَّاسِ، فَكَانَ مِنْ أَمْرِهِ مَا كَانَ قَالَ فَإِذَا رَجُلٌ قَائِمٌ فِي ثَلْمَةِ جِدَارٍ، كَأَنَّهُ جَمَلٌ أَوْرَقُ ثَائِرُ الرَّأْسِ قَالَ فَرَمَيْتُهُ بِحَرْبَتِي، فَأَضَعُهَا بَيْنَ ثَدْيَيْهِ حَتَّى خَرَجَتْ مِنْ بَيْنِ كَتِفَيْهِ قَالَ وَوَثَبَ إِلَيْهِ رَجُلٌ مِنَ الْأَنْصَارِ، فَضَرَبَهُ بِالسَّيْفِ عَلَى هَامَتِهِ. Saḥīḥ al-Bukhārī 4072.

248. What are the Mukhannathūn?

Answer: People with two genders, according to various scholars.

The Arabic (plural) word Mukhannathūn (مُخَنَّثُون) means *effeminate ones; men who resemble women.* The classical Arabic term is used for people who would now perhaps be called *transgender,* although the Western categories of LGTB don't really fit here. Later on, they were associated with music and entertainment.

The root kh-n-th (خ-ن-ث) basically means *to be soft, effeminate, to bend.* The word Mukhannath (مُخَنَّث) is the passive participle of the Arabic II-verb of this root. Mukhannath denotes *effeminate; powerless, impotent, weak.* It is very much related to the term Khunthā (خُنْثى) which means *hermaphrodite.* In biology, a hermaphrodite is an organism that has reproductive organs normally associated with both the male and female sex. Edward Lane describes a Khunthā as "one who has what is proper to the male and what is proper to the female." It is a person who has, by creation, the genitals of a man and that of a woman. In the language of lawyers: one who has what is proper to both sexes.

However, it is not clear how they looked like and how they were distinguished from homosexuals. It seems that the Mukhannathūn were common during the time of the Prophet because they are mentioned various times in the Hadiths, which suggests that also *eunuchs* were perhaps included in this term. The word *eunuch* is used for castrated men to guard a harem. It's from Greek meaning *bedroom guard.* To castrate a man/slave is easier to accomplish then to search the population for the one in a thousand hermaphrodite. Plus, castrated men usually have no sex drive while this is not the case with hermaphrodites. There was certainly a need for these men: A Mukhannath was not attracted to women. The Mukhannath played therefore a significant role as matchmaker between unmarried men and secluded women, because they were allowed into the women's living quarters. They were allowed to see unveiled women, thus, they were used as domestic servants.

There are Hadiths which report that at least one Muhkannath was present in the house of Muhammad. However, at a later point, the Prophet didn't like to have them around. It was narrated by ʿĀ'isha (عائشة بِنْت أَبِي بَكْر) that "a Mukhannath used to enter upon the

Prophet's wives. They [the people] counted him among those who were free of physical needs. One day the Prophet entered upon us when he [the Mukhannath] was with one of his wives and was describing the qualities of a woman, saying: 'When she comes in, she advances with four [folds in her stomach], and when she retreats, she goes with eight [folds in her stomach].' The Prophet said: 'Do I not see that this man knows who is here?' Then the wives veiled before him. [And he was kept away after that]."[302] In another narration, Muhammad expelled a Mukhannath to a region near Medina, but forbade the people to kill him. 'Abd Allah ibn 'Abbās (عَبْد الله ابن عَبَّاس) narrated: "The Prophet cursed effeminate men [Mukhannath] and those women who assume the manners of men, and he said: 'Throw them out of your houses!' The Prophet threw out such-and-such man, and 'Umar threw out such-and-such woman."[303]

So what about the **punishment** for a Mukhannath? There is a Hadith which is common to justify the punishment of (transgender, bisexual, gay, etc.) people, however, it is considered weak (ضَعِيف). It was narrated from 'Abd Allah ibn 'Abbās that the Prophet said: "If one man says to another: 'O effeminate one!', give him twenty lashes. And if one man says to another: 'O homosexual!', give him twenty lashes."[304] During the Umayyad dynasty, a Caliph, most probably Sulaymān ibn 'Abd al-Malik (سُلَيْمان بن عَبْد الْمَلِك), ordered that all so-called Mukhannathūn should be castrated.

249. To whom will Allah give shade on the Day "when there will be no shade but His"?

Answer: Seven kinds of people – according to Muhammad.

---

302 ...قَالَتْ كَانَ يَدْخُلُ عَلَى أَزْوَاج النَّبِيِّ مُخَنَّثٌ فَكَانُوا يَعُدُّونَهُ مِنْ غَيْرِ أُولِي الْإِرْبَةِ فَدَخَلَ عَلَيْنَا النَّبِيُّ يَوْمًا وَهُوَ عِنْدَ بَعْضِ نِسَائِهِ وَهُوَ يَنْعَتُ امْرَأَةً فَقَالَ إِنَّهَا إِذَا أَقْبَلَتْ أَقْبَلَتْ بِأَرْبَع وَإِذَا أَدْبَرَتْ أَدْبَرَتْ بِثَمَانٍ. فَقَالَ النَّبِيُّ:"أَلَا أَرَى هَذَا يَعْلَمُ مَا هَا هُنَا لَا يَدْخُلَنَّ عَلَيْكُنَّ هَذَا." Sunan 'Abī Dāwūd 4107

303 ...قَالَ لَعَنَ النَّبِيُّ الْمُخَنَّثِينَ مِنَ الرِّجَالِ، وَالْمُتَرَجِّلَاتِ مِنَ النِّسَاءِ وَقَالَ: "أَخْرِجُوهُمْ مِنْ بُيُوتِكُمْ." قَالَ فَأَخْرَجَ النَّبِيُّ فُلَانًا، وَأَخْرَجَ عُمَرُ فُلَانًا. Sahīh al-Bukhārī 5886

304 ...النَّبِيُّ قَالَ: "إِذَا قَالَ الرَّجُلُ لِلرَّجُلِ يَا مُخَنَّثُ فَاجْلِدُوهُ عِشْرِينَ وَإِذَا قَالَ الرَّجُلُ لِلرَّجُلِ يَا لُوطِيُّ فَاجْلِدُوهُ عِشْرِينَ." Sunan ibn Māja 2665 (2568)

According to Islam, Allah has promised to protect seven kinds of people from the heat of the sun on Doom's Day by being under Allah's shade. 'Abū Hurayra (أَبُو هُرَيْرَة) reported that the Messenger of Allah said: "Allah will give shade, to seven, on the Day when there will be no shade but His."

They are:

- a just ruler;
- a youth who grew up worshipping Allah;
- a person whose heart is attached to the mosques;
- two men who love and meet each other and separte from each other for the sake of Allah;
- a man who was seduced by a beautiful woman (for an illicit relation), but who (rejects this offer and) says: 'I fear Allah';
- a man who gives to charity and conceals it (to such an extent) that the left hand does not know what the right has given;
- and a man who in solitude remembers Allah and his eyes become tearful".[305]

Al-Miqdād ibn al-'Aswad (الْمِقْدَاد بن الأَسْوَد) reported that he heard the Messenger of Allah say: "On the Day of Resurrection, the sun will come so close to people that there would be left only a distance of one Mīl."[306] Sulaym ibn 'Āmir (سُلَيْم بن عامِر) added: "By Allah, I do not know whether he meant by *Mīl* the mile of the distance measure or the stick used for applying antimony powder to the eye."[307]

The above mentioned Hadith continues. The Messenger of Allah said: "The people will stand in deep perspiration according to their deeds, some up to the knees, some up to the waist, and some will

---

305 ...النَّبِيُّ قَالَ: "سَبْعَةٌ يُظِلُّهُمُ اللَّهُ فِي ظِلِّهِ يَوْمَ لاَ ظِلَّ إِلاَّ ظِلُّهُ الإِمَامُ الْعَادِلُ، وَشَابٌّ نَشَأَ فِي عِبَادَةِ رَبِّهِ، وَرَجُلٌ قَلْبُهُ مُعَلَّقٌ فِي الْمَسَاجِدِ، وَرَجُلاَنِ تَحَابًّا فِي اللَّهِ اجْتَمَعَا عَلَيْهِ وَتَفَرَّقَا عَلَيْهِ، وَرَجُلٌ طَلَبَتْهُ امْرَأَةٌ ذَاتُ مَنْصِبٍ وَجَمَالٍ فَقَالَ إِنِّي أَخَافُ اللَّهَ، وَرَجُلٌ تَصَدَّقَ أَخْفَى حَتَّى لاَ تَعْلَمَ شِمَالُهُ مَا تُنْفِقُ يَمِينُهُ، وَرَجُلٌ ذَكَرَ اللَّهَ خَالِيًا فَفَاضَتْ عَيْنَاهُ." Sahīh al-Bukhārī 660

306 ...قَالَ سَمِعْتُ رَسُولَ اللَّهِ يَقُولُ: "تُدْنَى الشَّمْسُ يَوْمَ الْقِيَامَةِ مِنَ الْخَلْقِ حَتَّى تَكُونَ مِنْهُمْ كَمِقْدَارِ مِيلٍ." Sahīh Muslim 2864

307 ...قَالَ سُلَيْمُ بْنُ عَامِرٍ فَوَاللَّهِ مَا أَدْرِي مَا يَعْنِي بِالْمِيلِ أَمَسَافَةَ الأَرْضِ أَمِ الْمِيلَ الَّذِي تُكْتَحَلُ بِهِ الْعَيْنُ. Sahīh Muslim 2864

have this level of perspiration, and while saying this, Allah's Apostle held his hand at mouth level."[308]

Note: In Edward Lane's dictionary, a *Mīl* (ميل), as used by the Arabs, was the distance to which the eye reaches along land. And that was, according to ancient astronomers, 3,000 cubits; according to modern astronomers, 4,000 cubits. The cubit is an ancient unit based on the forearm length, measured from middle finger tip to elbow.

But the difference is merely verbal for they all agree that its extent is 96,000 digits; (about 5166 English ft). The digit or finger is an ancient unit of measurement of length: each digit is the total length of six barley grains, each placed with its belly next to another (about the breadth of a human finger.) However, the ancient astronomers say that the cubit is 32 digits, which makes the *Mīl* 3,000 cubits.

250. What did the Prophet say about women?

Answer: He ordered to treat them, and described them, as "captives in a man's hand".

There is a famous Hadith narrated by Sulaymān ibn 'Amr ibn al-'Ahwas (سُلَيْمان بن الأَحْوَص). According to this narration, Sulaymān's father heard the Prophet say: "Treat women kindly, they are like captives in your hands; you do not owe anything else to them."[309]

The Hadith continues: "In case they are guilty of open indecency, then do not share their beds and beat them lightly, and if they return to obedience, do not have anything else against them. You have rights over your wives and they have their rights over you. Your right is that they shall not permit anyone you dislike entering your home, and their right is that you should treat them well in the matter of food and clothing".[310]

---

308. ...قَالَ: "فَيَكُونُ النَّاسُ عَلَى قَدْرِ أَعْمَالِهِمْ فِي الْعَرَقِ فَمِنْهُمْ مَنْ يَكُونُ إِلَى كَعْبَيْهِ وَمِنْهُمْ مَنْ يَكُونُ إِلَى رُكْبَتَيْهِ وَمِنْهُمْ مَنْ يَكُونُ إِلَى حَقْوَيْهِ وَمِنْهُمْ مَنْ يُلْجِمُهُ الْعَرَقُ إِلْجَامًا." قَالَ وَأَشَارَ رَسُولُ اللَّهِ بِيَدِهِ إِلَى فِيهِ. Sahīh Muslim 2864.

309. ...قَالَ النَّبِيُّ: "أَلَا وَاسْتَوْصُوا بِالنِّسَاءِ خَيْرًا فَإِنَّمَا هُنَّ عَوَانٌ عِنْدَكُمْ لَيْسَ تَمْلِكُونَ مِنْهُنَّ شَيْئًا غَيْرَ ذَلِكَ ". Jāmi' al-Tirmidhī 1163.

251. What is the dearest deed to Allah after observing prayers?

Answer: To be good and dutiful to your parents (بِرّ الْوَالِدَيْن).

'Abd Allah ibn Mas'ūd (عَبْد الله بن مَسْعُود) narrated that he asked the Prophet: "Which deed is the dearest to Allah?" He replied: "To offer the prayers at their early stated fixed times." I asked: "What is the next (in goodness)?" He replied: "To be good and dutiful to your parents." I again asked: "What is the next (in goodness)?" He replied: "To participate in Jihād in Allah's cause."

'Abd Allah added: "I asked only that much and if I had asked more, the Prophet would have told me more."[311]

Honouring one's parents is very important in Islam. This is manifested too in sura 31 *Luqmān* (سُورة لُقمان):

31:14	We have commanded people to be good to their parents: their mothers carried them, with strain upon strain, and it takes two years to wean them. Give thanks to Me and to your parents - all will return to Me.	وَوَصَّيْنَا الْإِنْسَانَ بِوَالِدَيْهِ حَمَلَتْهُ أُمُّهُ وَهْنًا عَلَى وَهْنٍ وَفِصَالُهُ فِي عَامَيْنِ أَنِ اشْكُرْ لِي وَلِوَالِدَيْكَ إِلَيَّ الْمَصِيرُ.

I once had a discussion with a Muslim woman in Alexandria. I asked her what she would do if her father would have molested her, and she answered: "I have to honour him. The punishment is up to Allah."

'Abd Allah ibn 'Amr (عَبْد الله بن عَمْرو) narrated that Allah's Messenger said: "It is one of the greatest sins should a man curse his parents."[312]

For a child one of the most important acts of worship is to obey its parents. A child has to do whatever they demand. A child must refrain from whatever they tell it not to do. Honouring the mother is

---

310 ...إلاّ أَنْ يَأْتِينَ بِفَاحِشَةٍ مُبَيِّنَةٍ فَإِنْ فَعَلْنَ فَاهْجُرُوهُنَّ فِي الْمَضَاجِعِ وَاضْرِبُوهُنَّ ضَرْبًا غَيْرَ مُبَرِّح فَإِنْ أَطَعْنَكُمْ فَلَا تَبْغُوا عَلَيْهِنَّ سَبِيلاً أَلَا إِنَّ لَكُمْ عَلَى نِسَائِكُمْ حَقًّا وَلِنِسَائِكُمْ عَلَيْكُمْ حَقًّا فَأَمَّا حَقُّكُمْ عَلَى نِسَائِكُمْ فَلَا يُوطِئْنَ فُرُشَكُمْ مَنْ تَكْرَهُونَ وَلَا يَأْذَنَّ فِي بُيُوتِكُمْ لِمَنْ تَكْرَهُونَ أَلَا وَحَقُّهُنَّ عَلَيْكُمْ أَنْ تُحْسِنُوا إِلَيْهِنَّ فِي كِسْوَتِهِنَّ وَطَعَامِهِنَّ. Jāmi' al-Tirmidhī 1163

311 ...قَالَ سَأَلْتُ النَّبِيَّ أَيُّ الْعَمَلِ أَحَبُّ إِلَى اللَّهِ قَالَ: "الصَّلَاةُ عَلَى وَقْتِهَا." قَالَ ثُمَّ أَيٌّ قَالَ: "ثُمَّ بِرُّ الْوَالِدَيْنِ." قَالَ ثُمَّ أَيٌّ قَالَ: "الْجِهَادُ فِي سَبِيلِ اللَّهِ." قَالَ حَدَّثَنِي بِهِنَّ وَلَوِ اسْتَزَدْتُهُ لَزَادَنِي. -Sahīh al-Bukhārī 527

312 ...قَالَ رَسُولُ اللَّهِ: "إِنَّ مِنْ أَكْبَرِ الْكَبَائِرِ أَنْ يَلْعَنَ الرَّجُلُ وَالِدَيْهِ." Sahīh al-Bukhārī 5973

even emphasised more because of her suffering during pregnancy and birth. This idea is found in sura 17 *The Night Journey* - in Arabic: al-’Isrā’ (سُورة الإِسْراء):

17:23	Your Lord has commanded that you should worship none but Him, and that you be kind to your parents. If either or both of them reach old age with you, say no word that shows impatience with them, and do not be harsh with them, but speak to them respectfully	وَقَضَىٰ رَبُّكَ أَلَّا تَعْبُدُوا إِلَّا إِيَّاهُ وَبِالْوَالِدَيْنِ إِحْسَانًا إِمَّا يَبْلُغَنَّ عِندَكَ الْكِبَرَ أَحَدُهُمَا أَوْ كِلَاهُمَا فَلَا تَقُل لَّهُمَا أُفٍّ وَلَا تَنْهَرْهُمَا وَقُل لَّهُمَا قَوْلًا كَرِيمًا
17:24	and lower your wing in humility towards them in kindness and say, 'Lord, have mercy on them, just as they cared for me when I was little.'	وَاخْفِضْ لَهُمَا جَنَاحَ الذُّلِّ مِنَ الرَّحْمَةِ وَقُل رَّبِّ ارْحَمْهُمَا كَمَا رَبَّيَانِي صَغِيرًا.

Islam emphasises treating parents kindly, especially when they are old. Muhammad Asad puts it like this: "Whereas God is the real, ultimate cause of man's coming to life, his parents are its outward, immediate cause: and so the preceding call to God is followed by the injunction to honour and cherish one's parents."

This goes even further: It is advisable for Muslims to treat friends of the father with kindness. Muslims know the story of 'Abd Allah, the son of 'Umar al-Khattāb (عُمَر بن الْخَطَّاب):

'Abd Allah ibn 'Umar met a Bedouin on his way to Mecca, he greeted him, offered him to mount the donkey he was riding and gave him the turban he wore on his head. When a companion asked him why he did that, 'Abd Allah said that the father of this man was one of 'Umar's friends whom he loved best and that he heard the Messenger of Allah say: "The finest act of goodness is the kind treatment of a person who was a loved one of his father after his death."[313]

Notice that in Arab countries, every child bears the name of his father – which is the <u>second</u> name. The third name is usually the name of the grandfather. Even in more "liberal" Islamic countries

---

313 ...إِنِّي سَمِعْتُ رَسُولَ اللَّهِ يَقُولُ: "إِنَّ مِنْ أَبَرِّ الْبِرِّ صِلَةَ الرَّجُلِ أَهْلَ وُدِّ أَبِيهِ بَعْدَ أَنْ يُوَلِّيَ." Sahīh
Muslim 2552

such as Tunisia, if a mother does not know the name of the baby's father, it is extremely difficult (nearly impossible) to get her child officially registered.

How is the situation if the parents of a Muslim are non-Muslims?

Even in this case, Islam forbids a Muslim to be disrespectful to his ("disbelieving") parents. This does not change even if they were putting pressure on a Muslim to give up Islam. In this case, the Muslim must keep his faith, he should treat them well but he should not obey his parents – as it is told in sura 31 *Luqmān*:

| 31:15 | If they strive to make you associate with Me anything about which you have knowledge, then do not obey them. Yet keep their company in this life according to what is right, and follow the path of those who turn to Me. You will all return to Me in the end, and I will tell you everything that you have done. | وَإِن جَاهَدَاكَ عَلَى أَن تُشْرِكَ بِي مَا لَيْسَ لَكَ بِهِ عِلْمٌ فَلَا تُطِعْهُمَا وَصَاحِبْهُمَا فِي الدُّنْيَا مَعْرُوفًا وَاتَّبِعْ سَبِيلَ مَنْ أَنَابَ إِلَيَّ ثُمَّ إِلَيَّ مَرْجِعُكُمْ فَأُنَبِّئُكُم بِمَا كُنتُمْ تَعْمَلُونَ. |

Excursus: Sura Luqmān (سُورة لُقْمان) was revealed in Mecca.

It derives its title from *Luqmān the Wise* (popularly associated with Aesop). The Qur'an does not state whether Luqmān was a prophet. Most scholars say that he was a wise man, but probably not a prophet. Before Islam, Luqmān played a huge role in legends and parables about wisdom and spiritual maturity.

There is a similar mythical figure in the Qur'an. It is called al-Khidr (الخِضْر) – literally, *The Green One*.

Al-Khidr is mentioned e.g. in sura 18. Al-Khidr is described as a righteous servant of Allah and who is very wise. The *Green One*, as most scholars view it, is an epithet and not a name. It should express that his wisdom was ever-fresh (or "green").

Who is Muhammad's companion in Paradise (being like fore finger and middle finger together)?

349

252. Who is Muhammad's companion in Paradise (being like fore finger and middle finger together)?

Answer: The one who takes care of an orphan (كافِل الْيَتِيم).

It was reported by 'Abū Hurayra (أَبُو هُرَيْرَة) that the Messenger of Allah said: "He who takes care of an orphan, whether he is his relative or a stranger, will be in Paradise with me like these two." The narrator, Mālik ibn 'Anas (مالِك بن أَنَس) raised his forefinger and middle finger for illustration.[314]

This brings us to an interesting question: Is adoption allowed in Islam? It depends what you understand by *adoption*. The type of adoption which is banned in Islam is that which makes a boy or girl a member of the family – with all the rights of inheritance and with all the rights to mix freely with other members of the household.

There is another type of adoption, however, which is allowed in Islam. The Islamic way of adopting a child is like taking care of someone. When a man brings home an orphan to educate and to treat him or her as his own child – meaning he protects, feeds, clothes, and teaches the child. But this child is not attributed to the family. Islam does not give the "adopted" child the same rights that a fathered child would have, for example in regard to inheritance, etc.

If a Muslim takes care of an orphan, he will be rewarded later by being admitted to Paradise.

253. When a person dies, his deeds are discontinued – except for which?

Answer: Three deeds.

They are:

1. Continuing charity (صَدَقة جَارِية).

---

314 ...قَالَ رَسُولُ اللَّهِ: "كَافِلُ الْيَتِيمِ لَهُ أَوْ لِغَيْرِهِ أَنَا وَهُوَ كَهَاتَيْنِ فِي الْجَنَّةِ." وَأَشَارَ مَالِكٌ بِالسَّبَّابَةِ وَالْوُسْطَى. Sahīh Muslim 2983.

2. Knowledge from which people benefit (عِلْم يُنْتَفَع بِه).

3. A righteous son who prays for the deceased (وَلَد صَالِح يَدْعُو لَهُ).

This information is given in a Hadith. ʾAbū Hurayra (أَبُو هُرَيْرة) repor-ted that Allah's Messenger said: "When a man dies, his acts come to an end – except for three: recurring charity; knowledge [from which people] benefit; and a pious son who prays for him [for the deceased]."[315]

Remark: That's why some Muslims claim that one should write a book, because this knowledge will survive him.

254. How can a Muslim's prayer be 27 times better?

Answer: By praying in congregation.

It was narrated by ʿAbd Allah ibn ʿUmar (عَبْد الله بن عُمَر) that the Messenger of Allah said: "Praying in congregation is twenty-seven times better than praying alone."[316]

It is obligatory for a Muslim to pray in the mosque in congregation as it is commanded in a Hadith reported by ʾAbū Hurayra (أَبُو هُرَيْرة). This narration is about the son of ʾUmm Maktūm (أُم مَكْتُوم), who was a blind man. "There came to the Messenger of Allah a blind man and said: 'Messenger of Allah, I have no one to guide me to the mosque.'

Therefore, he asked Allah's Messenger to permit him to say the prayer in his house. The Prophet granted him permission. But then, when the man turned away, he called him and said: 'Do you hear the call to prayer?' He replied: 'Yes.' He [the Prophet] said: 'Respond to it!'"[317]

---

315 ...أَنَّ رَسُولَ اللَّهِ قَالَ: "إِذَا مَاتَ الإِنْسَانُ انْقَطَعَ عَنْهُ عَمَلُهُ إِلاَّ مِنْ ثَلاَثَةٍ إِلاَّ مِنْ صَدَقَةٍ جَارِيَةٍ أَوْ عِلْم يُنْتَفَع بِه أَوْ وَلَدٍ صَالِح يَدْعُو لَهُ." Sahīh Muslim 1631.

316 ...أَنَّ رَسُولَ اللَّهِ قَالَ: "صَلاَةُ الْجَمَاعَةِ تَفْضُلُ صَلاَةَ الْفَذِّ بِسَبْعٍ وَعِشْرِينَ دَرَجَةً." Sahīh al-Bukhārī 645

317 ...قَالَ أَتَى النَّبِيَّ رَجُلٌ أَعْمَى فَقَالَ يَا رَسُولَ اللَّهِ إِنَّهُ لَيْسَ لِي قَائِدٌ يَقُودُنِي إِلَى الْمَسْجِد. فَسَأَلَ رَسُولَ اللَّهِ أَنْ يُرَخِّصَ لَهُ فَيُصَلِّيَ فِي بَيْتِهِ فَرَخَّصَ لَهُ فَلَمَّا وَلَّى دَعَاهُ فَقَالَ: "هَلْ تَسْمَعُ النِّدَاءَ بِالصَّلاَةِ." فَقَالَ نَعَمْ. قَالَ: "فَأَجِبْ." Sahīh Muslim 653

In a similar narration, the Prophet also responded: "I do not find any permission for you."[318]

This means that if there is no concession for a blind man who had no one to lead him, most scholars conclude, that then there should be no concession for other Muslims.

Two people are enough to pray in congregation, whether that is in the house or elsewhere. It was narrated that Mālik ibn al-Huwayrith (مَالِك بن الْحُوَيْرِث) said: "The Messenger of Allah told me and one of my companions: 'When the time for prayer comes, let the two of you call for the prayer ['Adhān] then the two of you say the 'Iqāma [second call to prayer; immediately before the prayer begins], then let one of you lead the prayer.'"[319]

255. The Prophet thought that Gabriel would order him to make which people his heirs?

Answer: The neighbour (الْجَار).

The neighbour is an important person in a Muslim's life. He has a social function. A neighbour is a hidden control organ, he watches and intervenes. He shares food with other Muslims and is there when a Muslim needs him.

Muslims should try to have a very good relationship with their neighbours. If a Muslim gets too close to someone, or if he observes people too much, then there is a danger of a backlash. It also means that people know a lot about other people. In Egypt, I witnessed the phenomenon of rumours spreading in the streets. I had the impression that people were more eager to judge other people's life and so forgot about their own.

The daily life status of a neighbour is a big part of Arab culture and has as such also entered the Arabic language. There are several proverbs and sayings, for example: "Buy the neighbour before the house!" This is a rhyme in Arabic: "'Ishtari al-Jār qabl al-Dār" (إشْتَرِ

---

318 ...قَالَ: "لاَ أَجِدُ لَكَ رُخْصَةً." Sunan 'Abī Dāwūd 552

319 ...قَالَ لِي رَسُولُ اللَّهِ وَلِصَاحِبٍ لِي: "إِذَا حَضَرَتِ الصَّلاَةُ فَأَذِّنَا ثُمَّ أَقِيمَا ثُمَّ لِيَؤُمَّكُمَا أَحَدُكُمَا."
Sunan al-Nasā'ī 677

الْجار قَبْل الدَّار). Meaning that you have to choose your neighbours before you choose your house. In other words, a good neighbour is more important than a good house.

There are plenty of Hadiths that tell Muslims how they should treat their neighbours. Let's look at some of them:

- 'Abd Allah ibn 'Umar (عَبْد الله بن عُمَر) narrated that Allah's Messenger said: "Gabriel kept on recommending me to treat the neighbours in a kind and polite manner, so much so that I thought that he would order [me] to make them [my] heirs."[320]

- 'Abū Dharr (أَبُو ذَرّ) reported that Allah's Messenger commanded him: "Whenever you prepare a broth, put plenty of water in it and give some of it to your neighbours."[321]

- 'Abd Allah ibn 'Abbās (عَبْد الله بن عَبّاس) narrated that he heard the Prophet say: "A man is not a believer who fills his stomach while his neighbour is hungry."[322]

- 'Abū Hurayra (أَبُو هُرَيْرة) narrated that the Messenger of Allah said: "O Muslim women! None of you should look down upon the gift sent by your female neighbour even if it were the trotters [meatless feet] of the sheep."[323] This Hadith means that neighbours - rich and poor - should present gifts to each other, according to their means. A poor Muslim, as stated in the Hadith, should not be judged. Furthermore, the poor Muslim should not think that his gift to the (rich) neighbour is not worthy. It is the act of giving that counts in the view of Allah.

- It was narrated by 'Abū Hurayra that the Messenger of Allah said: "He will not enter Paradise whose neighbour is not secure from his wrongful conduct."[324] This Hadith shows that hurting or troubling a neighbour is a serious offence.

---

320 ...قَالَ رَسُولُ اللَّهِ: "مَا زَالَ جِبْرِيلُ يُوصِينِي بِالْجَارِ حَتَّى ظَنَنْتُ أَنَّهُ سَيُوَرِّثُهُ." Sahīh al-Bukhārī 6015

321 ...قَالَ إِنَّ خَلِيلِي أَوْصَانِي: "إِذَا طَبَخْتَ مَرَقًا فَأَكْثِرْ مَاءَهُ ثُمَّ انْظُرْ أَهْلَ بَيْتٍ مِنْ جِيرَانِكَ فَأَصِبْهُمْ مِنْهَا بِمَعْرُوفٍ." Sahīh Muslim 2625

322 ...النَّبِيُّ يَقُولُ: لَيْسَ الْمُؤْمِنُ الَّذِي يَشْبَعُ وَجَارُهُ جَائِعٌ. al-'Adab al-Mufrad 112

323 ...النَّبِيُّ قَالَ: "يَا نِسَاءَ الْمُسْلِمَاتِ لَا تَحْقِرَنَّ جَارَةٌ لِجَارَتِهَا، وَلَوْ فِرْسِنَ شَاةٍ." Sahīh al-Bukhārī 2566

324 ...أَنَّ رَسُولَ اللَّهِ قَالَ: "لَا يَدْخُلُ الْجَنَّةَ مَنْ لَا يَأْمَنُ جَارُهُ بَوَائِقَهُ." Sahīh Muslim 46

256. How should Muslims treat old people?

Answer: A Muslim should honour them.

'Abū Hurayra (أَبُو هُرَيْرَة) reported that the Prophet said: "Anyone who does not show mercy to our children or does not acknowledge the right of our old people is not one of us."[325]

Muslims pay great attention to older people. They help them in the streets and use a formal, respectful form of address when talking to them.

The Prophet said: "I dreamt that I was cleaning my teeth with a Siwāk [a natural toothbrush] and two persons came to me. One of them was older than the other and I gave the Siwāk to the younger. I was told that I should give it to the older and so I did."[326]

257. What is better before Allah than the fragrance of musk?

Answer: The breath of the observer of fast.

It was reported by 'Abū Hurayra (أَبُو هُرَيْرَة) and 'Abū Sa'īd al-Khudrī (أَبُو سَعِيد الْجُدْرِيّ) that Allah's Messenger had said: "There are two [occasions] of joy for the observer of fast: He feels joy when he breaks the fast, and he is happy when he meets Allah. By Allah, in whose hand is the life of Muhammad, the breath of the observer of fast is sweeter to Allah than the fragrance of musk."[327]

To show the value of fasting, consider the following comparison. 'Abū Sa'īd al-Khudrī narrated that the Messenger of Allah said: "The best scent is the perfume of musk."[328]

---

325 ...النَّبِيُّ قَالَ: مَنْ لَمْ يَرْحَمْ صَغِيرَنَا، وَيَعْرِفْ حَقَّ كَبِيرِنَا، فَلَيْسَ مِنَّا. al-'Adab al-Mufrad 353.

326 ...أَنَّ النَّبِيَّ قَالَ: "أَرَانِي أَتَسَوَّكُ بِسِوَاكِي، فَجَاءَنِي رَجُلَانِ أَحَدُهُمَا أَكْبَرُ مِنَ الآخَرِ، فَنَاوَلْتُ السِّوَاكَ الأَصْغَرَ مِنْهُمَا، فَقِيلَ لِي الأَكْبَرَ. فَدَفَعْتُهُ إِلَى الأَكْبَرِ مِنْهُمَا." Sahīh al-Bukhārī 246.

327 ...قَالَ رَسُولُ اللَّهِ: "إِنَّ اللَّهَ عَزَّ وَجَلَّ يَقُولُ إِنَّ الصَّوْمَ لِي وَأَنَا أَجْزِي بِهِ إِنَّ لِلصَّائِمِ فَرْحَتَيْنِ إِذَا أَفْطَرَ فَرِحَ وَإِذَا لَقِيَ اللَّهَ فَرِحَ. وَالَّذِي نَفْسُ مُحَمَّدٍ بِيَدِهِ لَخُلُوفُ فَمِ الصَّائِمِ أَطْيَبُ عِنْدَ اللَّهِ مِنْ رِيحِ الْمِسْكِ." Sahīh Muslim 1151

328 ...أَنَّ رَسُولَ اللَّهِ ذَكَرَ: "الْمِسْكُ أَطْيَبُ الطِّيبِ." Sahīh Muslim 2252

258. What is the invocation when entering a mosque?

Answer: "O Allah, open to me the gates of your mercy."[329]

An invocation is called Du'ā' (دُعاء) in Islam. It was narrated that 'Abd al-Malik ibn Sa'īd (عَبْد الْمَلِك بن سَعِيد) heard 'Abū Humayd (أَبُو حُمَيْد) and 'Abū 'Usayd (أَبُو أُسَيْد) say that the Messenger of Allah said: "When any one of you enters the mosque, let him say: O Allah, open to me the gates of your mercy!"[330]

And what is the invocation when leaving a mosque?

Answer: " O Allah, I ask You of Your bounty!"[331]

It was narrated that 'Abd al-Malik ibn Sa'īd heard 'Abū Humayd and 'Abū 'Usayd recount that the Messenger of Allah said: "...and when he leaves [the mosque] let him say: 'O Allah, I ask You of Your bounty!'"[332]

259. Which form of greeting did Muhammad teach Muslims?

Answer: "Peace be upon you, and the mercy and blessings of Allah." In Arabic: "As-Salāmu 'alaykum wa Rahmatullāhi wa Barakātuh".[333]

It was narrated by 'Abū Tamīma al-Hujaymī (أَبُو تَمِيمة الْهُجَيْمِي) that a man among his people said: "I went looking for the Prophet but I was not able to find him. So I sat down and saw a group of people, and he was among them but I did not recognise him.

He was settling some matter between them so when he was finished, some of them stood up with him and they said: 'O Messenger of Allah.' When I saw that, I said: '*Upon you be peace* ('Alayk as-Salām) O Messenger of Allah! [3 times]'[334]

---

329 ...افْتَحْ لِي أَبْوَابَ رَحْمَتِكَ!

330 قَالَ رَسُولُ اللَّهِ: "إِذَا دَخَلَ أَحَدُكُمُ الْمَسْجِدَ فَلْيَقُلِ اللَّهُمَّ افْتَحْ لِي أَبْوَابَ رَحْمَتِكَ." Saḥīḥ Muslim 713

331 ...اللَّهُمَّ إِنِّي أَسْأَلُكَ مِنْ فَضْلِكَ!

332 ...وَإِذَا خَرَجَ فَلْيَقُلِ اللَّهُمَّ إِنِّي أَسْأَلُكَ مِنْ فَضْلِكَ." Saḥīḥ Muslim 713

333 ...السَّلَامُ عَلَيْكُمْ وَرَحْمَةُ اللَّهِ وَبَرَكَاتُهُ.

The Prophet replied: "'Indeed, *Upon you be peace* ('Alayk as-Salām) is the greeting for the dead!"[335]

Then the Prophet came toward me and said: 'When a man meets his Muslim brother, then he should say: '*Peace be upon you, and the mercy and blessings of Allah!*'" (As-Salāmu 'alaykum wa Rahmatullāhi wa Barakātuh)."[336]

Then the Prophet responded to my greeting, and he said: '*And upon you, Allah's mercy!* (Wa 'Alayka wa Rahma(tu) Allāh) [3 times]."[337]

When a non-Muslim greets a Muslim with "As-Salāmu 'alaykum", the scholars differ whether the Muslim has to return the greeting. The majority of scholars agree that Muslims should return the greeting.

260. Should a Muslim greet a Jew or Christian first or last?

Answer: Last.

'Abū Hurayra (أَبُو هُرَيْرَة) reported that the Messenger of Allah said: "Do not greet the Jews and the Christians before they greet you; and when you meet any one of them on the road, force him to go to the narrowest part of it."[338]

What is meant by narrowest part? Scholars say that it generally means that Muslims should not give them (Jew or Christian) a position of authority (among Muslims).

---

334 ...قَالَ طَلَبْتُ النَّبِيَّ فَلَمْ أَقْدِرْ عَلَيْهِ فَجَلَسْتُ فَإِذَا نَفَرٌ هُوَ فِيهِمْ وَلاَ أَعْرِفُهُ وَهُوَ يُصْلِحُ بَيْنَهُمْ فَلَمَّا فَرَغَ قَامَ مَعَهُ بَعْضُهُمْ فَقَالُوا يَا رَسُولَ اللَّهِ. فَلَمَّا رَأَيْتُ ذَلِكَ قُلْتُ عَلَيْكَ السَّلاَمُ يَا رَسُولَ اللَّهِ عَلَيْكَ السَّلاَمُ يَا رَسُولَ اللَّهِ عَلَيْكَ السَّلاَمُ يَا رَسُولَ اللَّهِ. Jāmi' al-Tirmidhī 2721

335 ...قَالَ: "إِنَّ عَلَيْكَ السَّلاَمَ تَحِيَّةُ الْمَيِّتِ إِنَّ عَلَيْكَ السَّلاَمَ تَحِيَّةُ الْمَيِّتِ." Jāmi' al-Tirmidhī 2721

336 ...ثُمَّ أَقْبَلَ عَلَيَّ فَقَالَ: "إِذَا لَقِيَ الرَّجُلُ أَخَاهُ الْمُسْلِمَ فَلْيَقُلِ السَّلاَمُ عَلَيْكُمْ وَرَحْمَةُ اللَّهِ." -Jāmi' al-Tirmidhī 2721

337 ...ثُمَّ رَدَّ عَلَيَّ النَّبِيُّ قَالَ: "وَعَلَيْكَ وَرَحْمَةُ اللَّهِ وَعَلَيْكَ وَرَحْمَةُ اللَّهِ وَعَلَيْكَ وَرَحْمَةُ اللَّهِ." -Jāmi' al-Tirmidhī 2721

338 ...أَنَّ رَسُولَ اللَّهِ قَالَ: "لاَ تَبْدَءُوا الْيَهُودَ وَلاَ النَّصَارَى بِالسَّلاَمِ فَإِذَا لَقِيتُمْ أَحَدَهُمْ فِي طَرِيقٍ فَاضْطَرُّوهُ إِلَى أَضْيَقِهِ." Sahīh Muslim 2167

But also among Muslims, there is a hierarchy. 'Abū Hurayra reported that Allah's Messenger said: "The rider should first greet the pedestrian, and the pedestrian the one who is seated and a small group should greet a larger group [with as-Salāmu 'alaykum]."[339]

261. How did Jews greet Muslims at the time of the Prophet?

Answer: "Death be upon you!" – in Arabic: "Sām(un) 'alayka!"[340]

'Abd Allah ibn 'Umar (عَبْد الله بن عُمَر) narrated that Allah's Messenger said: "When the Jews greet anyone of you, they say: Sām 'alayka [death be upon you]; so you should reply: 'Wa 'alayka [and upon you]."[341]

The word Sām (سَامّ), in this application, means *death*. It comes from the root s-w-m (س-و-م) which denotes *to injure, to savage; to impose a hard task* or *punishment upon*. Some suppose that this word may be derived from another Arabic root, wasama (وَسَمَ), because it could have the meaning of *sign, mark*. Some claim that it might even be of Greek origin through Persian.

262. What object is called a "lavatory for the mouth and a gratification for Allah"?

Answer: Al-Miswāk (الْمِسْواك).

A Siwāk (سِواك) or Miswāk (مِسْواك) is a small stick, the tip of which is softened by chewing or beating, used for cleaning and polishing the teeth. But why is this "toothbrush" called a "lavatory for the mouth" and a "gratification for Allah"? Because 'Ā'isha (عائِشة بِنْت

---

339 ...قَالَ رَسُولُ اللَّهِ: "يُسَلِّمُ الرَّاكِبُ عَلَى الْمَاشِي وَالْمَاشِي عَلَى الْقَاعِدِ وَالْقَلِيلُ عَلَى الْكَثِيرِ."
Ṣaḥīḥ Muslim 2160

340 ...سَامٌّ عَلَيْكَ!

341 ...قَالَ رَسُولُ اللَّهِ: "إِنَّ الْيَهُودَ إِذَا سَلَّمُوا عَلَى أَحَدِكُمْ إِنَّمَا يَقُولُونَ سَامٌّ عَلَيْكَ. فَقُلْ عَلَيْكَ."
Ṣaḥīḥ al-Bukhārī 6928

أَبِي بَكْر) heard the Prophet say: "The Miswak [tooth stick] cleanses and purifies the mouth and pleases the Lord."[342]

'Abū Hurayra (أَبُو هُرَيْرة) reported that the Apostle said: "Were it not that I might overburden the believers, I would have ordered them to use a Siwāk[tooth stick] at every time of prayer."[343]

It was narrated that Shaqīq ibn Salama (شَقِيق بن سَلَمة) said: "We were commanded, when we got up to pray at night, to clean our mouths with the Siwāk."[344]

What is it exactly made of? It is made from a branch of the so-called *toothbrush tree,* an evergreen bush from tropical Africa and Asia. The tree is called: *Salvadora persica* (toothbrush tree; mustard tree). Sticks of it have been used for a long time as a natural toothbrush; it is known to reduce tooth decay, plaque, and gum diseases.

The fresh leaves are edible and used in traditional medicine to soothe cough, asthma, rheumatism, and other diseases. The flowers are small and fragrant and used as a stimulant. The berries are small and barely noticeable; they are edible either fresh or dried.

How do you use the Siwāk? First you have to chew off the bark of the stick, at least for one 1 cm (~ 1/2 inch) at the tip. Then chew on the exposed end until the twig forms bristles – that's your brush. You don't need toothpaste. After some days of use, cut off the exposed bristles and repeat the same procedure.

Remark: In Arabic grammar the word Miswāk is the so-called noun of tool (إِسم آلة) of the root s-w-k (س-و-ك). The Arabic root basically means *to rub, to scrub.* The II-verb means *to clean* and *polish, to brush clean* (e.g. the teeth).

---

342 ...سَمِعْتُ عَائِشَةَ، عَنِ النَّبِيِّ قَالَ: "السِّوَاكُ مَظْهَرَةٌ لِلْفَمِ مَرْضَاةٌ لِلرَّبِّ." Sunan al-Nasā'ī 5

343 ...قَالَ النَّبِيُّ: "لَوْلَا أَنْ أَشُقَّ عَلَى الْمُؤْمِنِينَ - وَفِي حَدِيثِ زُهَيْرٍ عَلَى أُمَّتِي - لَأَمَرْتُهُمْ بِالسِّوَاكِ عِنْدَ كُلِّ صَلَاةٍ." Sahīh Muslim 252

344 ...قَالَ كُنَّا نُؤْمَرُ إِذَا قُمْنَا مِنَ اللَّيْلِ أَنْ نَشُوصَ أَفْوَاهَنَا بِالسِّوَاكِ. Sunan al-Nasā'ī 1624

263. What should Muslims do when they see a solar or lunar eclipse?

Answer: Pray.

It might sound strange that the Prophet ordered his followers to pray when they see the eclipse of the sun or the moon as this could be interpreted as worshipping stars and planets – which is absolutely forbidden in Islam.

However, he did it himself, so Muslims must do it too.

'Abū Mūsā (أَبُو مُوسَى) told that when sun eclipsed, the Prophet became afraid that it might be The Hour (Day of Judgement). He went to the Mosque and offered the prayer with the longest Qiyām [part of the prayer], and more bowing and prostrating than that I had ever seen him doing.

Then he [the Prophet] said: "These signs which Allah sends do not occur because of the life or death of somebody, but Allah scares His worshippers with them. So when you see anything thereof, proceed to remember Allah, invoke Him and ask for His forgiveness."[345]

'Abū Masʿūd (أَبُو مَسْعُود الْأَنْصَارِيّ) narrated that Allah's Messenger said: "The sun and the moon do not eclipse because of someone's death or life but they are two signs among the signs of Allah, so pray whenever you see them."[346]

264. What is the nature of the soul in Islam?

Answer: Immaterial, immortal, and transcending.

Allah created Adam and breathed the soul into him; this is stated in the Qur'an and in the Hadiths.

---

345 ...قَالَ خَسَفَتِ الشَّمْسُ، فَقَامَ النَّبِيُّ فَزِعًا، يَخْشَى أَنْ تَكُونَ السَّاعَةُ، فَأَتَى الْمَسْجِدَ، فَصَلَّى بِأَطْوَلِ قِيَامٍ وَرُكُوعٍ وَسُجُودٍ رَأَيْتُهُ قَطُّ يَفْعَلُهُ وَقَالَ: "هَذِهِ الآيَاتُ الَّتِي يُرْسِلُ اللَّهُ لاَ تَكُونُ لِمَوْتِ أَحَدٍ وَلاَ لِحَيَاتِهِ، وَلَكِنْ يُخَوِّفُ اللَّهُ بِهِ عِبَادَهُ، فَإِذَا رَأَيْتُمْ شَيْئًا مِنْ ذَلِكَ فَافْزَعُوا إِلَى ذِكْرِهِ وَدُعَائِهِ وَاسْتِغْفَارِهِ."
Sahīh al-Bukhārī 1059

346 ...قَالَ رَسُولُ اللَّهِ: "الشَّمْسُ وَالْقَمَرُ لاَ يَنْكَسِفَانِ لِمَوْتِ أَحَدٍ وَلاَ لِحَيَاتِهِ، وَلَكِنَّهُمَا آيَتَانِ مِنْ آيَاتِ اللَّهِ، فَإِذَا رَأَيْتُمُوهُمَا فَصَلُّوا." Sahīh al-Bukhārī 1057

'Abū Hurayra (أَبُو هُرَيْرة) narrated that the Messenger of Allah said: "When Allah created Adam, He breathed the soul into him, then he [Adam] sneezed and said: 'All praise is due to Allah.' So he praised Allah by His permission. Then His Lord told him: 'May Allah have mercy upon you, O Adam. Go to those angels, to that gathering where they are sitting, and say: "al-Salāmu 'alaykum." They replied: "wa 'alayka al-Salām wa Rahma(tu) Allah."[347]

The soul of the deceased is taken from the ends of the toes towards the top of the body, the eyes glaze over and roll upwards. It was narrated that 'Umm Salama (أُمّ سَلَمة) said: "The Messenger of Allah entered upon 'Abū Salama [after he had died] and his eyes were wide open. He closed his eyes, then he said: 'When the soul is taken, the sight follows it.'"[348]

Have some people already been brought to account and admitted to Paradise or Hell? As for Paradise and Hell, no one will enter them fully (body and soul) until after the second stage of the reckoning, which is the reckoning in the Hereafter following the Day of Judgement. However, the soul - not the body! - may enter Paradise before the Day of Resurrection. Some souls may also be exposed to the Fire and feel some of its heat and torment.

When people sleep (and sleep, in Islam, is referred to as the "lesser death"), the soul is taken, but not completely, as the sleeper is still alive. This idea is found in sura 39 *The Throngs* – in Arabic: al-Zumar (سُورة الزُّمَر):

| 39:42 | God takes the souls of the dead and the souls of the living while they sleep - He keeps hold of those whose death He has ordained and sends the others back until their appointed time - there truly are signs in this for those who reflect. | اللَّهُ يَتَوَفَّى الْأَنْفُسَ حِينَ مَوْتِهَا وَالَّتِي لَمْ تَمُتْ فِي مَنَامِهَا فَيُمْسِكُ الَّتِي قَضَى عَلَيْهَا الْمَوْتَ وَيُرْسِلُ الْأُخْرَى إِلَى أَجَلٍ مُسَمًّى إِنَّ فِي ذَلِكَ لَآيَاتٍ لِقَوْمٍ يَتَفَكَّرُونَ |

---

347 ...قَالَ رَسُولُ اللَّهِ: "لَمَّا خَلَقَ اللَّهُ آدَمَ وَنَفَخَ فِيهِ الرُّوحَ عَطَسَ فَقَالَ الْحَمْدُ لِلَّهِ فَحَمِدَ اللَّهَ بِإِذْنِهِ فَقَالَ لَهُ رَبُّهُ يَرْحَمُكَ اللَّهُ يَا آدَمُ اذْهَبْ إِلَى أُولَئِكَ الْمَلَائِكَةِ إِلَى مَلَإٍ مِنْهُمْ جُلُوسٍ فَقُلِ: "السَّلَامُ عَلَيْكُمْ." قَالُوا: "وَعَلَيْكَ السَّلَامُ وَرَحْمَةُ اللَّهِ." Jāmi' al-Tirmidhī 3694 (3367); hasan.

348 ...قَالَتْ دَخَلَ رَسُولُ اللَّهِ عَلَى أَبِي سَلَمَةَ وَقَدْ شَقَّ بَصَرُهُ فَأَغْمَضَهُ ثُمَّ قَالَ: "إِنَّ الرُّوحَ إِذَا قُبِضَ تَبِعَهُ الْبَصَرُ." Sunan ibn Māja 1521 (1454).

Notice the verb in this verse which is marked in grey: yatawaffā (يَتَوَفَّى). It comes from the root w-f-a (وَفَى) which means *to be perfect, integral; to satisfy; to serve; to fulfil; to compensate fully.* The meaning of the Arabic V-verb is *to exact fully; to take one's full share of; to receive in full.*

In Arabic this verb is used when someone has died. There is some-thing special about it. The <u>active form</u> of the verb tawaffā (تَوَفَّى) can only be used if Allah is the <u>subject</u>. For example: Allah has taken him unto Him (تَوَفَّاهُ اللهُ). This expression has the meaning of Allah taking his soul or Allah causing the death of somebody. In Islam, only Allah knows and decides when death will happen. That's why you should use the active form of the verb only with Allah as a subject.

This verb is therefore almost exclusively used in the passive form expressing that somebody *has died*: tuwuffiya (تُوُفِّيَ). The passive verb is translated into English with: *to die; to pass away.*

265. What happens when a Muslim dies?

Answer: He will pass on to stage two out of three stages in total.

A Muslim's life is divided into three sections:

1. The life of this world – which ends with death.
2. The life in al-Barzakh (الْبَرْزَخ) – which starts after death and ends when The Hour begins.
3. The life of the Hereafter – which begins after the people are raised from their graves. The final destination is either Paradise or Hell.

First of all, although it might sound strange, death is the most important part of a Muslim's life. A Muslim's only goal in this life is to strive so hard that he will finally get admission to Paradise.

Sa'd ibn Hishām (سَعْد بن هِشام) narrated that 'Ā'isha (عائِشة بِنْت أَبي بَكْر) mentioned that the Messenger of Allah said: "Whoever loves to meet Allah, then Allah loves to meet him. And whoever dislikes meeting Allah, then Allah dislikes meeting him."

She continued: "O Messenger of Allah! All of us dislike death."

The Prophet replied: "It is not like that. But when the believer is given the good news of Allah's mercy, His pleasure and His Paradise, then he loves to meet Allah and Allah loves to meet him.

Whereas when the disbeliever is given the news of Allah's punishment and His wrath, he dislikes meeting Allah, and Allah dislikes meeting him."[349]

Only Allah knows when death will happen, which is stated in sura 50 *The Letter Qāf* (سورة ق) and in sura 16 *The Bee* – al-Nahl (سورة النَّحْل):

50:19	The trance of death will bring the Truth with it: 'This is what you tried to escape.'	وَجَاءَتْ سَكْرَةُ الْمَوْتِ بِالْحَقِّ ذَلِكَ مَا كُنتَ مِنْهُ تَحِيدُ.
50:20	The Trumpet will be sounded: 'This is the Day [you were] warned of.'	وَنُفِخَ فِي الصُّورِ ذَلِكَ يَوْمُ الْوَعِيدِ.
50:21	Each person [every soul] will arrive attended by an [angel] to drive him on and another to bear witness.	وَجَاءَتْ كُلُّ نَفْسٍ مَّعَهَا سَائِقٌ وَشَهِيدٌ.
16:61	If Allah took people to task for the evil they do, He would not leave one living creature on earth, but He reprieves them until an appointed time: when their time comes they cannot delay it for a moment nor can they bring it forward.	وَلَوْ يُؤَاخِذُ اللَّهُ النَّاسَ بِظُلْمِهِم مَّا تَرَكَ عَلَيْهَا مِن دَابَّةٍ وَلَكِن يُؤَخِّرُهُمْ إِلَى أَجَلٍ مُّسَمًّى فَإِذَا جَاءَ أَجَلُهُمْ لَا يَسْتَأْخِرُونَ سَاعَةً وَلَا يَسْتَقْدِمُونَ

The sentence: "**Every soul will taste death**" (كُلُّ نَفْسٍ ذَائِقَةُ الْمَوْتِ) is often found in Islamic graveyards and on tombstones. It is a sentence taken from the Qur'an where it is mentioned three times, e.g. in sura 3 *Family of 'Imrān* – in Arabic: 'Āl 'Imrān (سورة آل عِمْران):

3:185	Every soul will taste death and you will be paid in full only on the Day of Resurrection. Whoever is kept away from the Fire	كُلُّ نَفْسٍ ذَائِقَةُ الْمَوْتِ وَإِنَّمَا تُوَفَّوْنَ أُجُورَكُمْ يَوْمَ الْقِيَامَةِ فَمَن زُحْزِحَ عَنِ

349 ...أَنَّهَا ذَكَرَتْ أَنَّ رَسُولَ اللَّهِ قَالَ: "مَنْ أَحَبَّ لِقَاءَ اللَّهِ أَحَبَّ اللَّهُ لِقَاءَهُ وَمَنْ كَرِهَ لِقَاءَ اللَّهِ كَرِهَ اللَّهُ لِقَاءَهُ". قَالَتْ فَقُلْتُ يَا رَسُولَ اللَّهِ كُلُّنَا نَكْرَهُ الْمَوْتَ. قَالَ: "لَيْسَ ذَلِكَ وَلَكِنَّ الْمُؤْمِنَ إِذَا بُشِّرَ بِرَحْمَةِ اللَّهِ وَرِضْوَانِهِ وَجَنَّتِهِ أَحَبَّ لِقَاءَ اللَّهِ وَأَحَبَّ اللَّهُ لِقَاءَهُ وَإِنَّ الْكَافِرَ إِذَا بُشِّرَ بِعَذَابِ اللَّهِ وَسَخَطِهِ كَرِهَ لِقَاءَ اللَّهِ وَكَرِهَ اللَّهُ لِقَاءَهُ". Jāmi' al-Tirmidhī 1067

and admitted to the Garden will have triumphed. The present world is only an illusory pleasure.	النَّارِ وَأُدْخِلَ الْجَنَّةَ فَقَدْ فَازَ وَمَا الْحَيَاةُ الدُّنْيَا إِلَّا مَتَاعُ الْغُرُورِ.

Let's see what will happen when a Muslim is buried.

The first trial will happen right after death, in the grave. That is when two angels come and ask him about his Lord, his religion, and his Prophet, as is mentioned in the following Hadith.

ʾAbū Hurayra (أَبُو هُرَيْرة) narrated that the Messenger of Allāh said: "When the deceased - or he said: when one of you - is buried, two angels, black and blue eyed, come to him. One of them is called al-Munkar and the other al-Nakīr.

They ask: 'What did you use to say about this man [Muhammad]?' So he says what he was saying [before death]: 'He is Allah's slave and His messenger. I testify that none has the right to be worshipped but Allah and that Muhammad is His slave and His messenger.' So they reply: 'We knew that you would say this.'

Then his grave is expanded to seventy by seventy cubits, and it is illuminated for him. Then they tell him: 'Sleep!' Upon which he asks: 'Can I return to my family to inform them?' They reply: 'Sleep as a newly-wed whom none awakens but the dearest of his family until Allah resurrects him from his resting place.'

If he was a hypocrite, he would say: 'I heard people saying something, so I said the same; I do not know.' So they reply: 'We knew you would say that.' Then the earth is told: 'Constrict him!' So it constricts around him, squeezing his ribs together. He continues being punished like that until Allah resurrects him from his resting place."[350]

---

350 ...قَالَ رَسُولُ اللَّهِ :"إِذَا قُبِرَ الْمَيِّتُ - أَوْ قَالَ أَحَدُكُمْ أَتَاهُ مَلَكَانِ أَسْوَدَانِ أَزْرَقَانِ يُقَالُ لِأَحَدِهِمَا الْمُنْكَرُ وَالْآخَرُ النَّكِيرُ فَيَقُولَانِ مَا كُنْتَ تَقُولُ فِي هَذَا الرَّجُلِ فَيَقُولُ مَا كَانَ يَقُولُ هُوَ عَبْدُ اللَّهِ وَرَسُولُهُ أَشْهَدُ أَنْ لَا إِلَهَ إِلَّا اللَّهُ وَأَنَّ مُحَمَّدًا عَبْدُهُ وَرَسُولُهُ. فَيَقُولَانِ قَدْ كُنَّا نَعْلَمُ أَنَّكَ تَقُولُ هَذَا. ثُمَّ يُفْسَحُ لَهُ فِي قَبْرِهِ سَبْعُونَ ذِرَاعًا فِي سَبْعِينَ ثُمَّ يُنَوَّرُ لَهُ فِيهِ ثُمَّ يُقَالُ لَهُ نَمْ. فَيَقُولُ أَرْجِعُ إِلَى أَهْلِي فَأُخْبِرُهُمْ فَيَقُولَانِ نَمْ كَنَوْمَةِ الْعَرُوسِ الَّذِي لَا يُوقِظُهُ إِلَّا أَحَبُّ أَهْلِهِ إِلَيْهِ. حَتَّى يَبْعَثَهُ اللَّهُ مِنْ مَضْجَعِهِ ذَلِكَ. وَإِنْ كَانَ مُنَافِقًا قَالَ سَمِعْتُ النَّاسَ يَقُولُونَ فَقُلْتُ مِثْلَهُ لَا أَدْرِي. فَيَقُولَانِ قَدْ كُنَّا نَعْلَمُ أَنَّكَ تَقُولُ ذَلِكَ. فَيُقَالُ لِلْأَرْضِ الْتَئِمِي عَلَيْهِ. فَتَلْتَئِمُ عَلَيْهِ. فَتَخْتَلِفُ فِيهَا أَضْلَاعُهُ فَلَا يَزَالُ فِيهَا مُعَذَّبًا حَتَّى يَبْعَثَهُ اللَّهُ مِنْ مَضْجَعِهِ ذَلِكَ." Jāmiʿ al-Tirmidhī 1071; hasan.

266. What remains of a Muslim's body in the grave?

Answer: According to Islam the body disintegrates and vanishes apart from the tailbone which is a bone at the base of the spine (*coccyx*).

When the Resurrection begins, on the Day of Judgement, Allah will cause the bodies to grow using rain from the earth, which will make these bones grow until each person's body is restored to the way it was before the person died.

'Abū Hurayra (أَضبُو هُرَيْرَة) narrated that the Prophet said: "Between the two times blowing of the trumpet there will be forty."

'Abū Hurayra further reported that the people asked him: "O 'Abū Hurayra! Forty days?" 'Abū Hurayra said: "I refused to reply." The people asked: "Forty years?" – "I refused to reply and added: Everything of the human body will decay except the *coccyx* and from that bone, Allah will reconstruct the body."[351]

267. What is al-Barzakh?

Answer: It is basically stage two out of three, i.e. the period between a person's death and his resurrection on the Day of Resurrection.

The Arabic word Barzakh (بَرْزَخ), and plural Barāzikh (بَرازِخ), literally means *barrier; dividing place*. Edward Lane describes it as a thing that intervenes between any two other things. The word is used in the Qur'an in the meaning of **the period of death until the resurrection** upon which he who dies enters. This is found in sura 23 *The Believers* – in Arabic: al-Mu'minūn (سُورة الْمُؤْمِنُون):

23:99	When death comes to one of them, he cries, 'My Lord, let me return	حَتَّى إِذَا جَاءَ أَحَدَهُمُ الْمَوْتُ قَالَ رَبِّ ارْجِعُونِ
23:100	so as to make amends for the things I neglected.' Never! This will not go beyond	لَعَلِّي أَعْمَلُ صَالِحًا فِيمَا تَرَكْتُ كَلَّا إِنَّها كَلِمَةٌ هُوَ

---

351 ...قَالَ سَمِعْتُ أَبَا هُرَيْرَةَ، عَنِ النَّبِيِّ قَالَ: "بَيْنَ النَّفْخَتَيْنِ أَرْبَعُونَ". قَالُوا يَا أَبَا هُرَيْرَةَ أَرْبَعُونَ يَوْمًا قَالَ أَبَيْتُ. قَالَ أَرْبَعُونَ سَنَةً قَالَ أَبَيْتُ. قَالَ أَرْبَعُونَ شَهْرًا. قَالَ أَبَيْتُ، وَيَبْلَى كُلُّ شَيْءٍ مِنَ الْإِنْسَانِ إِلاَّ عَجْبَ ذَنَبِهِ، فِيهِ يُرَكَّبُ الْخَلْقُ. Ṣaḥīḥ al-Bukhārī 4814.

	his words: a barrier stands behind such people until the very Day they are resurrected.	قَائِلُهَا وَمِن وَرَائِهِم بَرْزَخٌ إِلَى يَوْمِ يُبْعَثُونَ.
23:101	On that Day when the Trumpet is blown, the ties between them will be as nothing and they will not ask about each other:	فَإِذَا نُفِخَ فِي الصُّورِ فَلَا أَنسَابَ بَيْنَهُمْ يَوْمَئِذٍ وَلَا يَتَسَاءَلُونَ:
23:102	those whose good deeds weigh heavy will be successful,	فَمَن ثَقُلَتْ مَوَازِينُهُ فَأُولَئِكَ هُمُ الْمُفْلِحُونَ
23:103	but those whose balance is light will have lost their souls forever and will stay in Hell	وَمَنْ خَفَّتْ مَوَازِينُهُ فَأُولَئِكَ الَّذِينَ خَسِرُوا أَنفُسَهُمْ فِي جَهَنَّمَ خَالِدُونَ
23:104	the Fire will scorch their faces and their lips will be twisted in pain.	تَلْفَحُ وُجُوهَهُمُ النَّارُ وَهُمْ فِيهَا كَالِحُونَ.

What happens during this period – in al-Barzakh?

Whoever dies as a Muslim and has obeyed Allah, will be okay. The so-called "unbeliever" will be punished. Muslims believe that there will be punishment already during this intermediate stage. The torments vary according to the sins.

'Abū 'Ayyūb (أَبُو أَيُّوب) narrated: "Once the Prophet went out after sunset, he heard a dreadful sound and said: 'The Jews are being punished in their graves.'"[352]

But they were not only the Jews as Muhammad found out himself. 'Ā'isha reported: "The Prophet entered my house when a Jewish woman was with me and who said: 'Do you know that you would be put to trial in the grave?' The Messenger of Allah trembled and said: 'It is the Jews only who would be put to trial.'

'Ā'isha continued: 'We passed some nights and then the Messenger of Allah said: 'Do you know that it has been revealed to me that you would be put to trial in the grave?' 'Ā'isha said: 'I heard the Messenger of Allah seeking refuge from the torment of the grave after this.'"[353]

---

352 ...قَالَ خَرَجَ النَّبِيُّ وَقَدْ وَجَبَتِ الشَّمْسُ، فَسَمِعَ صَوْتًا فَقَالَ: "يَهُودُ تُعَذَّبُ فِي قُبُورِهَا." Ṣaḥīḥ
al-Bukhārī 1375

353 ...أَنَّ عَائِشَةَ، قَالَتْ، دَخَلَ عَلَيَّ رَسُولُ اللَّهِ وَعِنْدِي امْرَأَةٌ مِنَ الْيَهُودِ وَهِيَ تَقُولُ هَلْ شَعَرْتِ أَنَّكُمْ تُفْتَنُونَ فِي الْقُبُورِ قَالَتْ فَارْتَاعَ رَسُولُ اللَّهِ وَقَالَ: "إِنَّمَا تُفْتَنُ يَهُودُ." قَالَتْ عَائِشَةُ فَلَبِثْنَا لَيَالِيَ ثُمَّ قَالَ

Muslims find some more information in a long, authentic Hadith. In this narration, the torments which will happen during the period of al-Barzakh are described – for all those who committed major sins.

Samura ibn Jundab (سَمُرة بن جُنْدَب) narrated that Allah's Messenger often used to ask his companions: "Did anyone of you see a dream?" So dreams would be narrated to him by those whom Allah wished to tell.

One morning the Prophet said: "Last night two persons came to me [in a dream] and woke me up and told me: 'Proceed!' I set out with them and we came across a man lying down, and behold, another man was standing over his head, holding a big rock. Behold, he was **throwing the rock at the man's head**, injuring him. The rock rolled away and the thrower followed it and retrieved it. By the time he reached the man, his head had returned to the normal state. The thrower then did the same as he had done before. I said to my two companions: 'Subhāna Allah! Who are these two persons?' They replied: 'Proceed!'[354]

So we proceeded and came to a man lying flat on his back and another man standing over his head with an iron hook, and behold, he would **put the hook in one side of the man's mouth and tear off that side of his face to the back [of the neck] and similarly tear his nose from front to back and his eye from front to back**. Then he turned to the other side of the man's face and did just as he had done with the previous side. He hardly completed this side when the previous side returned to its normal state. Then he returned to it to repeat what he had done before. I asked my two companions: 'Subhāna Allah! Who are these two persons?' They told me: 'Proceed!'[355]

رَسُولُ اللَّهِ: "هَلْ شَعَرْتِ أَنَّهُ أُوحِيَ إِلَيَّ أَنَّكُمْ تُفْتَنُونَ فِي الْقُبُورِ." قَالَتْ فَسَمِعْتُ رَسُولَ اللَّهِ بَعْدُ يَسْتَعِيذُ مِنْ عَذَابِ الْقَبْرِ. Sahīh Muslim 584.

354 ...قَالَ كَانَ رَسُولُ اللَّهِ مِمَّا يُكْثِرُ أَنْ يَقُولَ لِأَصْحَابِهِ: "هَلْ رَأَى أَحَدٌ مِنْكُمْ مِنْ رُؤْيَا؟" قَالَ فَيَقُصُّ عَلَيْهِ مَنْ شَاءَ اللَّهُ أَنْ يَقُصَّ، وَإِنَّهُ قَالَ ذَاتَ غَدَاةٍ: "إِنَّهُ أَتَانِي اللَّيْلَةَ آتِيَانِ، وَإِنَّهُمَا ابْتَعَثَانِي، وَإِنَّهُمَا قَالَا لِي انْطَلِقْ. وَإِنِّي انْطَلَقْتُ مَعَهُمَا، وَإِنَّا أَتَيْنَا عَلَى رَجُلٍ مُضْطَجِعٍ، وَإِذَا آخَرُ قَائِمٌ عَلَيْهِ بِصَخْرَةٍ، وَإِذَا هُوَ يَهْوِي بِالصَّخْرَةِ لِرَأْسِهِ، فَيَثْلَغُ رَأْسَهُ فَيَتَهَدْهَدُ الْحَجَرُ هَا هُنَا، فَيَتْبَعُ الْحَجَرَ فَيَأْخُذُهُ، فَلَا يَرْجِعُ إِلَيْهِ حَتَّى يَصِحَّ رَأْسُهُ كَمَا كَانَ، ثُمَّ يَعُودُ عَلَيْهِ، فَيَفْعَلُ بِهِ مِثْلَ مَا فَعَلَ الْمَرَّةَ الْأُولَى. قَالَ قُلْتُ لَهُمَا سُبْحَانَ اللَّهِ مَا هَذَانِ قَالَ قَالَا لِي انْطَلِقْ! Sahīh al-Bukhārī 7047

355 ...فَانْطَلَقْنَا فَأَتَيْنَا عَلَى رَجُلٍ مُسْتَلْقٍ لِقَفَاهُ، وَإِذَا آخَرُ قَائِمٌ عَلَيْهِ بِكَلُّوبٍ مِنْ حَدِيدٍ، وَإِذَا هُوَ يَأْتِي أَحَدَ شِقَّيْ وَجْهِهِ فَيُشَرْشِرُ شِدْقَهُ إِلَى قَفَاهُ، وَمَنْخِرَهُ إِلَى قَفَاهُ وَعَيْنَهُ إِلَى قَفَاهُ قَالَ وَرُبَّمَا قَالَ أَبُو رَجَاءٍ فَيُشَقُّ قَالَ ثُمَّ يَتَحَوَّلُ إِلَى الْجَانِبِ الْآخَرِ، فَيَفْعَلُ بِهِ مِثْلَ مَا فَعَلَ بِالْجَانِبِ الْأَوَّلِ، فَمَا يَفْرُغُ مِنْ ذَلِكَ

So we proceeded and came across something like a Tannūr [a kind of baking oven, a pit usually clay-lined for baking bread]." [The narrator remarks: I think the Prophet said that 'In that oven there was much noise and many voices.']

We looked into it and found **naked men and women, and behold, a flame of fire was reaching to them from underneath, and when it reached them, they cried loudly**. I asked them: 'Who are these?' They told me: 'Proceed! Proceed!'[356]

And so we proceeded and came across a river. [The narrator adds: I think he said, '...red like blood.']

And behold, in the river **there was a man swimming**, and on the bank there was a man who had collected many stones. Behold, while the other man was swimming, he went near him. The former **opened his mouth and the latter [on the bank] threw a stone into his mouth whereupon he went swimming again**. He returned and every time the performance was repeated. I asked my two companions: 'Who are these persons?' They replied: 'Proceed! Proceed!'[357]

And we proceeded until we came to a **man with a repulsive appearance**, the most repulsive appearance, you ever saw a man having! Beside him there was a fire and he was kindling it and running around it. I asked my companions: 'Who is this man?' They replied: 'Proceed! Proceed!'

So we proceeded until we reached a garden of deep green dense vegetation, having all sorts of spring colours. In the midst of the garden there was a very tall man and I could hardly see his head because of his great height, and around him there were children in

---

الْجَانِبِ حَتَّى يَصِحَّ ذَلِكَ الْجَانِبُ كَمَا كَانَ، ثُمَّ يَعُودُ عَلَيْهِ فَيَفْعَلُ مِثْلَ مَا فَعَلَ الْمَرَّةَ الْأُولَى. قَالَ قُلْتُ سُبْحَانَ اللَّهِ مَا هَذَانِ قَالَ قَالَا لِي انْطَلِقْ! Sahīh al-Bukhārī 7047

356 ...فَانْطَلَقْنَا فَأَتَيْنَا عَلَى مِثْلِ التَّنُّورِ قَالَ فَأَحْسِبُ أَنَّهُ كَانَ يَقُولُ فَإِذَا فِيهِ لَغَطٌ وَأَصْوَاتٌ قَالَ فَاطَّلَعْنَا فِيهِ، فَإِذَا فِيهِ رِجَالٌ وَنِسَاءٌ عُرَاةٌ، وَإِذَا هُمْ يَأْتِيهِمْ لَهَبٌ مِنْ أَسْفَلَ مِنْهُمْ، فَإِذَا أَتَاهُمْ ذَلِكَ اللَّهَبُ ضَوْضَوْا قَالَ قُلْتُ لَهُمَا مَا هَؤُلَاءِ قَالَ قَالَا لِي انْطَلِقِ انْطَلِقْ! Sahīh al-Bukhārī 7047

357 ...فَانْطَلَقْنَا فَأَتَيْنَا عَلَى نَهَرٍ حَسِبْتُ أَنَّهُ كَانَ يَقُولُ أَحْمَرَ مِثْلِ الدَّمِ، وَإِذَا فِي النَّهَرِ رَجُلٌ سَابِحٌ يَسْبَحُ، وَإِذَا عَلَى شَطِّ النَّهَرِ رَجُلٌ قَدْ جَمَعَ عِنْدَهُ حِجَارَةً كَثِيرَةً، وَإِذَا ذَلِكَ السَّابِحُ يَسْبَحُ مَا يَسْبَحُ، ثُمَّ يَأْتِي ذَلِكَ الَّذِي قَدْ جَمَعَ عِنْدَهُ الْحِجَارَةَ فَيَفْغَرُ لَهُ فَاهُ فَيُلْقِمُهُ حَجَرًا فَيَنْطَلِقُ يَسْبَحُ، ثُمَّ يَرْجِعُ إِلَيْهِ، كُلَّمَا رَجَعَ إِلَيْهِ فَغَرَ لَهُ فَاهُ فَأَلْقَمَهُ حَجَرًا قَالَ قُلْتُ لَهُمَا مَا هَذَانِ قَالَ قَالَا لِي انْطَلِقْ! -Sahīh al Bukhārī 7047

such a large number as I have never seen. I asked my companions: 'Who is this?' They replied: 'Proceed! Proceed!'[358]

So we proceeded until we came to a majestic huge garden, greater and better than I have ever seen! My two companions told me: 'Go up', and I went up. So we ascended until we reached a city built of gold and silver bricks and we went to its gate and asked [the gate-keeper] to open the gate, and it was opened and we entered the city and found in it, men with one side of their bodies as handsome as the handsomest person you have ever seen, and the other side as ugly as the ugliest person you have ever seen. My two companions ordered those men to throw themselves into the river. Behold, there was a river flowing across [the city], and its water was like milk in whiteness. Those men went and threw themselves in it and then returned to us after the ugliness [of their bodies] had disappeared and they became in the best shape.

My two companions [angels] told me: 'This place is the Eden Paradise, and that is your place.' I raised up my sight, and behold, there I saw a palace like a white cloud! My two companions said to me: 'That [palace] is your place.' I said to them: 'May Allah bless you both! Let me enter it.' They replied: 'As for now, you will not enter it, but you shall enter it (one day).'[359]

I told them: 'I have seen many wonders tonight. **What does all that mean which I have seen?'**

They replied: 'We will inform you: As for the **first man** you came upon whose head was being smashed with the rock, he is the **symbol**

---

358 ...فَانْطَلَقْنَا فَأَتَيْنَا عَلَى رَجُلٍ كَرِيهِ الْمَرْآةِ كَأَكْرَهِ مَا أَنْتَ رَاءٍ رَجُلاً مَرْآةً، وَإِذَا عِنْدَهُ نَارٌ يَحُشُّهَا وَيَسْعَى حَوْلَهَا قَالَ قُلْتُ لَهُمَا مَا هَذَا قَالَ قَالَا لِي انْطَلِقِ انْطَلِقْ. فَانْطَلَقْنَا فَأَتَيْنَا عَلَى رَوْضَةٍ مُعْتَمَّةٍ فِيهَا مِنْ كُلِّ نَوْرِ الرَّبِيعِ، وَإِذَا بَيْنَ ظَهْرَيِ الرَّوْضَةِ رَجُلٌ طَوِيلٌ لاَ أَكَادُ أَرَى رَأْسَهُ طُولاً فِي السَّمَاءِ، وَإِذَا حَوْلَ الرَّجُلِ مِنْ أَكْثَرِ وِلْدَانٍ رَأَيْتُهُمْ قَطُّ قَالَ لَهُمَا مَا هَذَا مَا هَؤُلاَءِ قَالَ قَالَا لِي انْطَلِقِ انْطَلِقْ. Sahīh al-Bukhārī 7047

359 ...فَانْطَلَقْنَا فَانْتَهَيْنَا إِلَى رَوْضَةٍ عَظِيمَةٍ لَمْ أَرَ رَوْضَةً قَطُّ أَعْظَمَ مِنْهَا وَلاَ أَحْسَنَ. قَالَ قَالَا لِي ارْقَ فِيهَا. قَالَ فَارْتَقَيْنَا فِيهَا فَانْتَهَيْنَا إِلَى مَدِينَةٍ مَبْنِيَّةٍ بِلَبِنِ ذَهَبٍ وَلَبِنِ فِضَّةٍ، فَأَتَيْنَا بَابَ الْمَدِينَةِ فَاسْتَفْتَحْنَا فَفُتِحَ لَنَا، فَدَخَلْنَاهَا فَتَلَقَّانَا فِيهَا رِجَالٌ شَطْرٌ مِنْ خَلْقِهِمْ كَأَحْسَنِ مَا أَنْتَ رَاءٍ، وَشَطْرٌ كَأَقْبَحِ مَا أَنْتَ رَاءٍ قَالَ قَالَ لَهُمُ اذْهَبُوا فَقَعُوا فِي ذَلِكَ النَّهَرِ. قَالَ وَإِذَا نَهَرٌ مُعْتَرِضٌ يَجْرِي كَأَنَّ مَاءَهُ الْمَحْضُ فِي الْبَيَاضِ، فَذَهَبُوا فَوَقَعُوا فِيهِ، ثُمَّ رَجَعُوا إِلَيْنَا قَدْ ذَهَبَ ذَلِكَ السُّوءُ عَنْهُمْ، فَصَارُوا فِي أَحْسَنِ صُورَةٍ قَالَ قَالَا لِي هَذِهِ جَنَّةُ عَدْنٍ، وَهَذَاكَ مَنْزِلُكَ. قَالَ فَسَمَا بَصَرِي صُعُدًا، فَإِذَا قَصْرٌ مِثْلُ الرَّبَابَةِ الْبَيْضَاءِ قَالَ قَالَا هَذَاكَ مَنْزِلُكَ. قَالَ قُلْتُ لَهُمَا بَارَكَ اللَّهُ فِيكُمَا، ذَرَانِي فَأَدْخُلَهُ. قَالَا أَمَّا الآنَ فَلاَ وَأَنْتَ دَاخِلُهُ. Sahīh al-Bukhārī 7047.

of the one who studies the Qur'an and then neither recites it nor acts on its orders, and sleeps, neglecting the enjoined prayers.

As for the man you came upon whose sides of mouth, nostrils and eyes were torn off from front to back, he is the **symbol of the man who goes out of his house in the morning and tells so many lies** that it spreads all over the world.

And those naked men and women whom you saw in a construction resembling an oven, they are the **adulterers and the adulteresses.**

And the man whom you saw swimming in the river and given a stone to swallow, he is the **eater of usury.**

And the bad looking man whom you saw near the fire kindling it and going round it, he is **Mālik, the Gatekeeper of Hell.**

And the **tall man whom you saw in the garden**, is Abraham and the surrounding children are those children who died with al-Fitra [with the Islamic faith].[360]

The narrator added that some Muslims asked the Prophet: "O Allah's Messenger! What about the children of pagans?" The Prophet replied: "and also the children of pagans."

The Prophet continued: "My two companions added that 'the men you saw half handsome and half ugly were those persons who had mixed an act that was good with another that was bad, but Allah forgave them.'"[361]

The reasons why a Muslim is getting punished in a grave can be because of minor things.

---

360 ...قَالَ قُلْتُ لَهُمَا فَإِنِّي قَدْ رَأَيْتُ مُنْذُ اللَّيْلَةِ عَجَبًا، فَمَا هَذَا الَّذِي رَأَيْتُ قَالَ قَالاَ لِي أَمَا إِنَّا سَنُخْبِرُكَ، أَمَّا الرَّجُلُ الأَوَّلُ الَّذِي أَتَيْتَ عَلَيْهِ يُثْلَغُ رَأْسُهُ بِالْحَجَرِ، فَإِنَّهُ الرَّجُلُ يَأْخُذُ الْقُرْآنَ فَيَرْفُضُهُ وَيَنَامُ عَنِ الصَّلاَةِ الْمَكْتُوبَةِ، وَأَمَّا الرَّجُلُ الَّذِي أَتَيْتَ عَلَيْهِ يُشَرْشَرُ شِدْقُهُ إِلَى قَفَاهُ، وَمَنْخِرُهُ إِلَى قَفَاهُ، وَعَيْنُهُ إِلَى قَفَاهُ، فَإِنَّهُ الرَّجُلُ يَغْدُو مِنْ بَيْتِهِ فَيَكْذِبُ الْكَذْبَةَ تَبْلُغُ الآفَاقَ، وَأَمَّا الرِّجَالُ وَالنِّسَاءُ الْعُرَاةُ الَّذِينَ فِي مِثْلِ بِنَاءِ التَّنُّورِ فَإِنَّهُمُ الزُّنَاةُ وَالزَّوَانِي. وَأَمَّا الرَّجُلُ الَّذِي أَتَيْتَ عَلَيْهِ يَسْبَحُ فِي النَّهَرِ وَيُلْقَمُ الْحَجَرَ، فَإِنَّهُ آكِلُ الرِّبَا، وَأَمَّا الرَّجُلُ الْكَرِيهُ الْمَرْآةِ الَّذِي عِنْدَ النَّارِ يَحُشُّهَا وَيَسْعَى حَوْلَهَا، فَإِنَّهُ مَالِكٌ خَازِنُ جَهَنَّمَ، وَأَمَّا الرَّجُلُ الطَّوِيلُ الَّذِي فِي الرَّوْضَةِ فَإِنَّهُ إِبْرَاهِيمُ وَأَمَّا الْوِلْدَانُ الَّذِينَ حَوْلَهُ فَكُلُّ مَوْلُودٍ مَاتَ عَلَى الْفِطْرَةِ."
Saḥīḥ al-Bukhārī 7047

361 ...قَالَ فَقَالَ بَعْضُ الْمُسْلِمِينَ يَا رَسُولَ اللَّهِ وَأَوْلاَدُ الْمُشْرِكِينَ فَقَالَ رَسُولُ اللَّهِ: "وَأَوْلاَدُ الْمُشْرِكِينَ. وَأَمَّا الْقَوْمُ الَّذِينَ كَانُوا شَطْرٌ مِنْهُمْ حَسَنًا وَشَطْرٌ مِنْهُمْ قَبِيحًا، فَإِنَّهُمْ قَوْمٌ خَلَطُوا عَمَلاً صَالِحًا وَآخَرَ سَيِّئًا، تَجَاوَزَ اللَّهُ عَنْهُمْ."
Saḥīḥ al-Bukhārī 7047

'Abd Allah ibn 'Abbās (عَبْد الله بن عَبَّاس) narrated that the Prophet once passed by two graves and said: "These two persons are being tortured not for a major sin. One of them never prevented himself from being soiled with his urine, while the other used to go about with calumnies [slanderers]."

The Prophet then took a green leaf of a date palm tree, split it into pieces and placed a piece on each grave. They asked: "O Allah's Apostle! Why have you done so?" He replied: "I hope that their punishment might be lessened until these [the pieces of the leaf] become dry."[362]

In fact, according to the Prophet, urine is one of the major causes for torment in the grave. 'Abū Hurayra (أَبُو هُرَيْرَة) narrated that the Messenger of Allah said: "Beware of [smearing yourselves with] urine, because it is the main cause of punishment in the grave."[363]

Note: The period of al-Barzakh lasts from the moment a person dies until he is resurrected, whether he is buried in a grave or not, whether he is burned or eaten by wild animals. Somehow, a buried person can still follow what is going on in the worldly life. Muslims find evidence for that in a Hadith.

'Anas ibn Mālik (أَنَس بن مالِك) narrated that the Prophet said: "When a human being is laid in his grave and his companions return, he can even hear their footsteps..."[364]

'Abd Allah ibn 'Umar (عَبْد الله بن عُمَر) narrated that the Messenger of Allah said: "When anyone of you dies, he will be shown his destination both in the morning and in the evening, and if he belongs to the people of Paradise, he will be shown his place in Paradise, and if he is from the people of Hell, he will be shown his place in Hell."[365]

---

362 ...قَالَ مَرَّ النَّبِيُّ بِقَبْرَيْنِ فَقَالَ: "إِنَّهُمَا لَيُعَذَّبَانِ، وَمَا يُعَذَّبَانِ فِي كَبِيرٍ أَمَّا أَحَدُهُمَا لاَ يَسْتَتِرُ مِنَ الْبَوْلِ، وَأَمَّا الآخَرُ فَكَانَ يَمْشِي بِالنَّمِيمَةِ." ثُمَّ أَخَذَ جَرِيدَةً رَطْبَةً، فَشَقَّهَا نِصْفَيْنِ، فَغَرَزَ فِي كُلِّ قَبْرٍ وَاحِدَةً. قَالُوا يَا رَسُولَ اللَّهِ، لِمَ فَعَلْتَ هَذَا قَالَ: "لَعَلَّهُ يُخَفَّفُ عَنْهُمَا مَا لَمْ يَيْبَسَا." Saḥīḥ al-Bukhārī 218

363 ...قَالَ رَسُولُ اللَّهِ: "اِسْتَنْزِهُوا مِنْ اَلْبَوْلِ, فَإِنَّ عَامَّةَ عَذَابِ اَلْقَبْرِ مِنْهُ." Bulūgh al-Marām 103 (109)

364 ...عَنِ النَّبِيِّ قَالَ: "الْعَبْدُ إِذَا وُضِعَ فِي قَبْرِهِ، وَتُوُلِّيَ وَذَهَبَ أَصْحَابُهُ حَتَّى إِنَّهُ لَيَسْمَعُ قَرْعَ نِعَالِهِمْ."... Saḥīḥ al-Bukhārī 1338

365 قَالَ رَسُولُ اللَّهِ: "إِذَا مَاتَ أَحَدُكُمْ فَإِنَّهُ يُعْرَضُ عَلَيْهِ مَقْعَدُهُ بِالْغَدَاةِ وَالْعَشِيِّ، فَإِنْ كَانَ مِنْ أَهْلِ الْجَنَّةِ فَمِنْ أَهْلِ الْجَنَّةِ، وَإِنْ كَانَ مِنْ أَهْلِ النَّارِ فَمِنْ أَهْلِ النَّارِ." Saḥīḥ al-Bukhārī 3240

268. How will a Muslim look like when he enters Paradise?

Answer: Everyone who enters Paradise will be in the form of (prophet) Adam.

Before the Day of Judgement, in the grave, only the soul is punished. This is important for understanding the torment. When someone died by drowning, was crushed in an accident, eaten by animals, or was burned – all these souls too will have their share of torment or blessing.

So, what happens on the Day of Resurrection? The people of Paradise will enter Paradise in the most perfect and beautiful form, i.e. in the form of their father Adam, whom Allah created with His own hand and perfected his form and made his shape beautiful.

’Abū Hurayra (أَبُو هُرَيْرة) narrated that Allah's Messenger said: "The first group of people who will enter Paradise will be glittering like the full moon and those who will follow them will glitter like the most brilliant star in the sky. They will not urinate, excrete, spit, nor have any nasal secretions. Their combs will be of gold and their sweat will smell like musk. In their censors, the aloe wood will be used [*note: in our world an aloe is a succulent and has no wood worth burning*]. Their wives will be Houris. All of them will look alike and will resemble their father Adam (in stature), sixty cubits tall."[366]

’Abū Hurayra further reported that the Prophet said: "Allah created Adam in His likeness, sixty cubits (about 30 metres) in height. When He created him, He said (to him): 'Go and greet that group of angels sitting there and listen to what they will say in reply to you, for that will be your greeting and the greeting of your offspring.'[367]

However, it is not clear if women will look like Adam as well. Regarding their ages and their shape, there is a Hadith narrated from Mu’āz ibn Jabal (مُعَاذ بن جَبَل) in which more information about that is given. The Prophet said: "The people of Paradise shall enter Paradise

---

366 ...قَالَ رَسُولُ اللَّهِ: "إِنَّ أَوَّلَ زُمْرَةٍ يَدْخُلُونَ الْجَنَّةَ عَلَى صُورَةِ الْقَمَرِ لَيْلَةَ الْبَدْرِ, ثُمَّ الَّذِينَ يَلُونَهُمْ عَلَى أَشَدِّ كَوْكَبٍ دُرِّيٍّ فِي السَّمَاءِ إِضَاءَةً، لاَ يَبُولُونَ وَلاَ يَتَغَوَّطُونَ وَلاَ يَتْفِلُونَ وَلاَ يَمْتَخِطُونَ، أَمْشَاطُهُمُ الذَّهَبُ، وَرَشْحُهُمُ الْمِسْكُ، وَمَجَامِرُهُمُ الأَلُوَّةُ الأَنْجُوجُ عُودُ الطِّيبِ، وَأَزْوَاجُهُمُ الْحُورُ الْعِينُ، عَلَى خَلْقِ رَجُلٍ وَاحِدٍ عَلَى صُورَةِ أَبِيهِمْ آدَمَ، سِتُّونَ ذِرَاعًا فِي السَّمَاءِ." Sahīh al-Bukhārī 3327

367 ...عَنِ النَّبِيِّ قَالَ: "خَلَقَ اللَّهُ آدَمَ عَلَى صُورَتِهِ، طُولُهُ سِتُّونَ ذِرَاعًا، فَلَمَّا خَلَقَهُ قَالَ اذْهَبْ فَسَلِّمْ عَلَى أُولَئِكَ النَّفَرِ مِنَ الْمَلاَئِكَةِ جُلُوسٌ، فَاسْتَمِعْ مَا يُحَيُّونَكَ، فَإِنَّهَا تَحِيَّتُكَ وَتَحِيَّةُ ذُرِّيَّتِكَ." Sahīh al-Bukhārī 6227

without body hair, without beard, with Kuhl in their eyes, thirty years of age or thirty-three years."[368]

Why 33? All this is speculation; maybe just because it is a figure consisting of identical digits. Some also speculate that this is the age when a man is at the height of his physical strength.

Do people grow older in Paradise?

Answer: Most probably not, according to Islamic doctrine. 'Abū Hurayra narrated that the Messenger of Allah said: "Their [the people in Paradise] youth does not come to an end and their clothes do not wear out."[369]

Some scholars suggest that all Muslims will be aged 33 in Paradise, and they will not grow older.

Remark: Christians believe that Jesus was probably 33 years of age when he died and rose to Heaven.

And what about children? In a dream about Paradise, Muhammad had seen small children around Abraham. Most Muslims believe that Allah will make children grow older and old men grow younger until they are all the same age, i.e. 33.

Other scholars refer to the Qur'an and interpret a verse in such a way that children, who die young, will be the servants of the people in Paradise. They refer to two suras: 56 *That Which is Coming* – in Arabic: al-Wāqiʿa (سُورة الْواقِعة) and sura 76 *Man* – in Arabic: al-'Insān (سُورة الإِنْسان). Similar to other questions, the Qur'an does not say anything about female babies or children:

56:17	everlasting youths [literally: immortal boys] will go round among them	يَطُوفُ عَلَيْهِمْ وِلْدَانٌ مُّخَلَّدُونَ
56:18	with glasses, flagons, and cups of a pure drink	بِأَكْوَابٍ وَأَبَارِيقَ وَكَأْسٍ مِّن مَّعِينٍ
76:19	Everlasting youths [literally: young boys made	وَيَطُوفُ عَلَيْهِمْ وِلْدَانٌ

---

368 ...أَنَّ النَّبِيَّ قَالَ: يَدْخُلُ أَهْلُ الْجَنَّةِ الْجَنَّةَ جُرْدًا مُرْدًا مُكَحَّلِينَ أَبْنَاءَ ثَلَاثِينَ أَوْ ثَلَاثٍ وَثَلَاثِينَ سَنَةً. "
Jāmiʿ al-Tirmidhī 2545

369 ...قَالَ رَسُولُ اللَّهِ: "[أَهْلُ الْجَنَّةِ] لَا يَفْنَى شَبَابُهُمْ وَلَا تَبْلَى ثِيَابُهُمْ. "; Jāmiʿ al-Tirmidhī 2539
hasan

eternal] will attend them if you could see them, you would think they were scattered pearls	مُّخَلَّدُونَ إِذَا رَأَيْتَهُمْ حَسِبْتَهُمْ لُؤْلُؤًا مَّنثُورًا

However, the majority of scholars have a different view. The young boys, who are mentioned in the verses above, are not the children of Muslims who had died in <u>this</u> world. These children who will serve the people of Paradise are slaves who are created especially for Paradise, like the Houris (حُور عَيْن) are.

269. How many gates does Paradise have?

Answer: Eight.

Sahl ibn Saʿd (سَهْل بن سَعْد) narrated that the Prophet said: "Paradise has eight gates, and one of them is called al-Rayyān through which none will enter but those who observe fasting."[370]

270. What are the names of the gates of Paradise?

Answer: The names of the eight gates are not entirely clear. Some of them are mentioned in Hadiths, some are deduced from other texts.

Let's look at some names of the Gates of Paradise which were deduced from various authentic Hadiths:

1. The *prayer gate* – in Arabic: Bāb al-Salā (الصَّلاة). For those who were accurate in observing their prayers.
2. The *holy war gate* – in Arabic: Bāb al-Jihād (الجِهاد). For those who participated in Jihād.
3. The *charity gate* – in Arabic Bāb al-Sadaqa (الصَّدَقة). For those who gave alms on a regular basis.
4. The *fasting gate* – in Arabic: Bāb al-Rayyān (باب الرَّيَّان), literally: *well irrigated; verdant*. For those who have regularly fasted.

---

370 ...النَّبِيُّ قَالَ: "فِي الْجَنَّةِ ثَمَانِيَةُ أَبْوَابٍ، فِيهَا باب يُسَمَّى الرَّيَّانَ لاَ يَدْخُلُهُ إِلاَّ الصَّائِمُونَ." Ṣaḥīḥ al-Bukhārī 3257

5. The *anger-suppression gate* – in Arabic: Bāb al-Kāthimīn al-Ghayth (باب الْكَاظِمِين الْفَيْظ). This door is reserved for those who have suppressed their anger and pardon others.

The following names are less common. They are deduced from various Islamic texts. For this reason we get more than 8 names in total:

6. The *repentance gate* – in Arabic: Bāb al-Tawba (باب التَّوْبة)
7. The *mentioning-Allah gate* – in Arabic: Bāb al-Dhikr (باب الذِّكْر)
8. The *knowledge gate* – in Arabic: Bāb al-'Ilm (باب الْعِلْم)
9. The *those who are content-gate* – in Arabic: Bāb al-Rādhīn (باب الرَّاضِين)
10. The *pilgrimage gate* – in Arabic: Bāb al-Hajj (باب الْحَجّ)
11. The *righteous gate* – in Arabic: Bāb al-'Ayman (باب الأَيْمَن)

271. What counts as if it was for the whole night?

Answer: Morning prayer in congregation.

'Abd al-Rahmān ibn 'Abī 'Amra (عَبْد الرَّحْمَن بن أَبِي عَمْرة) reported that 'Uthmān ibn 'Affān (عُثْمان بن عَفّان) had heard the Messenger of Allah say: "One who performs 'Ishā' [night time] prayer in congregation, it is as if he has performed praying for half of the night. And one who performs the Fajr [first morning] prayer in congregation, it is as if he has prayed the whole night."[371]

272. Which day of the week will be Judgement Day?

Answer: Friday (يَوْم الْجُمْعة).

'Abū Hurayra (أَبُو هُرَيْرة) reported that the Messenger of Allah said: "The best day on which the sun has risen is Friday; on it Adam was created. On it he was made to enter Paradise, on it he was expelled

---

371 ...سَمِعْتُ رَسُولَ اللَّهِ يَقُولُ: "مَنْ صَلَّى الْعِشَاءَ فِي جَمَاعَةٍ فَكَأَنَّمَا قَامَ نِصْفَ اللَّيْلِ وَمَنْ صَلَّى الصُّبْحَ فِي جَمَاعَةٍ فَكَأَنَّمَا صَلَّى اللَّيْلَ كُلَّهُ." Sahīh Muslim 656.

from it. And the Last Hour [The Day of Judgement] will take place on no other day than Friday."[372]

Friday is a special day in Islam. 'Abū Hurayra reported that Allah's Messenger, when talking about Friday, said: "There is an hour [a time] on Friday and if a Muslim gets it while praying and asking something from Allah, then Allah will definitely meet his demand." And the Prophet pointed out the shortness of that time with his hands.[373]

'Abū Hurayra further narrated that the Messenger of Allah said: "It was Friday from which Allah diverted those who were before us. For the Jews [the day set aside for prayer] was Sabt [Saturday] and for the Christians it was Sunday. And Allah turned towards us and guided us to Friday [as the day of prayer]."

The Prophet continued: "In fact, Allah made Friday, Saturday and Sunday [as days of prayer]. In this order they [Jews and Christians] would come after us on the Day of Resurrection. We are the last among the people in this world and the first among the created to be judged on the Day of Resurrection."[374]

273. Is there an "Anti-Christ" in Islam?

Answer: Yes.

He is called al-Masīh al-Dajjāl (الْمَسِيح الدَّجَّال) – the *False Christ* or *Anti-Christ*. He is an evil figure in Islamic eschatology.

---

372 ...أَنَّ النَّبِيَّ قَالَ: "خَيْرُ يَوْمٍ طَلَعَتْ عَلَيْهِ الشَّمْسُ يَوْمُ الْجُمُعَةِ فِيهِ خُلِقَ آدَمُ وَفِيهِ أُدْخِلَ الْجَنَّةَ وَفِيهِ أُخْرِجَ مِنْهَا وَلاَ تَقُومُ السَّاعَةُ إلاَّ فِي يَوْمِ الْجُمُعَةِ." Sahīh Muslim 854

373 ...أَنَّ رَسُولَ اللَّهِ ذَكَرَ يَوْمَ الْجُمُعَةِ فَقَالَ: "فِيهِ سَاعَةٌ لاَ يُوَافِقُهَا عَبْدٌ مُسْلِمٌ، وَهْوَ قَائِمٌ يُصَلِّي، يَسْأَلُ اللَّهَ تَعَالَى شَيْئًا إلاَّ أَعْطَاهُ إيَّاهُ." وَأَشَارَ بِيَدِهِ يُقَلِّلُهَا. Sahīh al-Bukhārī 935.

374 ...قَالَ رَسُولُ اللَّهِ: "أَضَلَّ اللَّهُ عَنِ الْجُمُعَةِ مَنْ كَانَ قَبْلَنَا فَكَانَ لِلْيَهُودِ يَوْمُ السَّبْتِ وَكَانَ لِلنَّصَارَى يَوْمُ الأَحَدِ فَجَاءَ اللَّهُ بِنَا فَهَدَانَا اللَّهُ لِيَوْمِ الْجُمُعَةِ فَجَعَلَ الْجُمُعَةَ وَالسَّبْتَ وَالأَحَدَ وَكَذَلِكَ هُمْ تَبَعٌ لَنَا يَوْمَ الْقِيَامَةِ نَحْنُ الآخِرُونَ مِنْ أَهْلِ الدُّنْيَا وَالأَوَّلُونَ يَوْمَ الْقِيَامَةِ الْمَقْضِيُّ لَهُمْ قَبْلَ الْخَلَائِقِ." Sahīh Muslim 856

The word Dajjāl means *swindler, charlatan*. It comes from the root d-j-l (د-ج-ل) which means *to deceive, to be a swindler*; in classical Arabic it was also used in the meaning of *to cover*.

The Dajjāl will appear before the Day of Resurrection – in Arabic: Yawm al-Qiyāmā (يَوْم الْقِيامة). He will pretend to be the Messiah. The Dajjāl is comparable to the Antichrist in Christian eschatology and to Armilus in medieval Jewish eschatology. The Dajjāl will be a man from among the sons of Adam. He will have many attributes which were described in the Hadiths. So when he comes, the Muslims will know him and shall not be misled by him; they shall know his features because the Prophet has told Muslims about them:

- He will be a young man with a ruddy skin colour; short, with thick curly hair, a wide forehead and broad upper chest. He will have a blind or defective (mamsūh) right eye. This eye will be neither prominent nor sunken and will look like a floating grape. His left eye will be covered with a thick piece of flesh growing from the edge of his eye.

- He will be dressed in robes of green coloured satin.

- Between his eyes, three separate Arabic letters will be written: "K-F-R" (ك-ف-ر) or "Kāfir" (كافر) with the letters joined. This will be understood by every Muslim, literate or illiterate. It means: disbelieve or disbeliever.

- The Dajjāl will be sterile; he will not have children.

Let's look at some Hadiths:
- ʿAbd Allah ibn ʿUmar (عَبْد الله بن عُمَر) narrated that the Dajjāl was mentioned in the presence of the Prophet who said: "Allah is not hidden from you; He is not one-eyed", and pointed with his hand towards his eye, adding: "While al-Masīh al-Dajjāl is blind in the right eye and his eye looks like a protruding grape."[375]

- ʾAnas ibn Mālik (أَنَس بن مالك) reported that Allah's Messenger said: "The Dajjāl is blind of one eye and there is written between

---

375 ...قَالَ ذُكِرَ الدَّجَّالُ عِنْدَ النَّبِيِّ فَقَالَ: "إِنَّ اللَّهَ لاَ يَخْفَى عَلَيْكُمْ، إِنَّ اللَّهَ لَيْسَ بِأَعْوَرَ وَأَشَارَ بِيَدِهِ إِلَى عَيْنِهِ وَإِنَّ الْمَسِيحَ الدَّجَّالَ أَعْوَرُ الْعَيْنِ الْيُمْنَى كَأَنَّ عَيْنَهُ عِنَبَةٌ طَافِيَةٌ." Ṣaḥīḥ al-Bukhārī 7407

his eyes the word Kāfir." He then spelled the word as k. f. r., which every Muslim would be able to read.[376]

- 'Anas ibn Mālik further reported that the Messenger of Allah said: "The Dajjāl will be followed by seventy thousand Jews of Isfahan and will be dressed in robes of green-coloured satin."[377]

- 'Anas ibn Mālik narrated that the Prophet said: "The Dajjāl will come to Medina and find the angels guarding it. So Allah willing, neither the Dajjāl, nor plague will be able to come near it."[378]

- 'Umm Sharīk (أُمّ شَرِيك) reported that she heard Allah's Messenger say: "The people would run away from the Dajjāl seeking shelter in the mountains." She asked: "Where would the Arabs be then on that day?" The Prophet replied: "They would be small in number."[379]

- 'Abū Saʿīd (أَبُو سَعِيد) recounted that one day Allah's Messenger told to them a long narration about the Dajjāl: "The Dajjāl will come and he will be forbidden to enter the mountain passes of Medina. He will encamp in one of the salt areas neighbouring Medina and there will appear to him a man who will be the best or one of the best of the people.

He will say: 'I testify that you are the Dajjāl whose story Allah's Messenger has told us.' The Dajjāl will respond [to his audience]: 'Look, if I kill this man and then give him life, will you have any doubt about my claim?' They will reply: 'No!' Then, the Dajjāl will kill that man and then make him alive. The man will say: 'By Allah, now I recognise you more than ever!' The Dajjāl

---

376 ...قَالَ رَسُولُ اللَّهِ: "الدَّجَّالُ مَمْسُوحُ الْعَيْنِ مَكْتُوبٌ بَيْنَ عَيْنَيْهِ كَافِرٌ." ثُمَّ تَهَجَّاهَا ك ف ر. يَقْرَؤُهُ كُلُّ مُسْلِمٍ." Sahīh Muslim 2933

377 ...أَنَّ رَسُولَ اللَّهِ قَالَ: "يَتْبَعُ الدَّجَّالَ مِنْ يَهُودِ أَصْبَهَانَ سَبْعُونَ أَلْفًا عَلَيْهِمِ الطَّيَالِسَةُ." Sahīh Muslim 2944

378 ...عَنِ النَّبِيِّ قَالَ: "الْمَدِينَةُ يَأْتِيهَا الدَّجَّالُ، فَيَجِدُ الْمَلَائِكَةَ يَحْرُسُونَهَا، فَلَا يَقْرَبُهَا الدَّجَّالُ قَالَ وَلَا الطَّاعُونُ، إِنْ شَاءَ اللَّهُ." Sahīh al-Bukhārī 7134

379 ...أَنَّهَا سَمِعَتِ النَّبِيَّ يَقُولُ: "لَيَفِرَّنَّ النَّاسُ مِنَ الدَّجَّالِ فِي الْجِبَالِ." قَالَتْ أُمُّ شَرِيكٍ يَا رَسُولَ اللَّهِ فَأَيْنَ الْعَرَبُ يَوْمَئِذٍ قَالَ: "هُمْ قَلِيلٌ." Sahīh Muslim 2945

will then try to kill him [again] but he will not be given the power to do so."[380]

- It was narrated from Nāfiʿ ibn ʿUtba ibn ʾAbī Waqqāṣ (نافِعِ بن عُتْبة بن أَبِي وَقّاص) that the Prophet said: "You will fight the Arabian Peninsula and victory will be granted by Allah. Then you will fight the Romans and victory will be granted (by Allah). Then you will fight the Dajjāl and victory will be granted."[381]

Why is he called the Dajjāl? There are some hypotheses:

- The Dajjāl received this name because of the classical meaning of the underlying Arabic root: he will cover the earth (with his followers) like the tarp covers the body of the mangy camel. Or because he will envelop mankind with this infidelity.

- The Arabic root d-j-l (د-ج-ل) can also mean *to mix*. The Dajjāl is the one who acts in vagaries, who tells many lies and deceives many people – one who deliberately confuses matters.

- The word Dajjāl became a title given to the lying, one-eyed, false Messiah. The Dajjāl is called so because he conceals his disbelieve from people by lying to them, deceiving them, and confusing them. Scholars suggested that the reason why the Dajjāl is called (False) Messiah is because one of his eyes is *smooth* or *abraded*; he is blind or defective in one eye. In Arabic this is called mamsūḥ (مَمْسُوحُ), which comes from the same root as Masīh (الْمَسِيح) – the Arabic word for Messiah.

---

380 ...قَالَ حَدَّثَنَا رَسُولُ اللَّهِ يَوْمًا حَدِيثًا طَوِيلاً عَنِ الدَّجَّالِ، فَكَانَ فِيمَا يُحَدِّثُنَا بِهِ قَالَ: "يَأْتِي الدَّجَّالُ وَهُوَ مُحَرَّمٌ عَلَيْهِ أَنْ يَدْخُلَ نِقَابَ الْمَدِينَةِ، فَيَنْزِلُ بَعْضَ السِّبَاخِ الَّتِي تَلِي الْمَدِينَةِ، فَيَخْرُجُ إِلَيْهِ يَوْمَئِذٍ رَجُلٌ وَهُوَ خَيْرُ النَّاسِ أَوْ مِنْ خِيَارِ النَّاسِ، فَيَقُولُ أَشْهَدُ أَنَّكَ الدَّجَّالُ الَّذِي حَدَّثَنَا رَسُولُ اللَّهِ حَدِيثَهُ، فَيَقُولُ الدَّجَّالُ أَرَأَيْتُمْ إِنْ قَتَلْتُ هَذَا ثُمَّ أَحْيَيْتُهُ، هَلْ تَشُكُّونَ فِي الأَمْرِ فَيَقُولُونَ لاَ. فَيَقْتُلُهُ ثُمَّ يُحْيِيهِ فَيَقُولُ وَاللَّهِ مَا كُنْتُ فِيكَ أَشَدَّ بَصِيرَةً مِنِّي الْيَوْمَ. فَيُرِيدُ الدَّجَّالُ أَنْ يَقْتُلَهُ فَلاَ يُسَلَّطُ عَلَيْهِ."

Ṣaḥīḥ al-Bukhārī 7132

381 ...عَنِ النَّبِيِّ قَالَ: "سَتُقَاتِلُونَ جَزِيرَةَ الْعَرَبِ فَيَفْتَحُهَا اللَّهُ ثُمَّ تُقَاتِلُونَ الرُّومَ فَيَفْتَحُهَا اللَّهُ ثُمَّ تُقَاتِلُونَ الدَّجَّالَ فَيَفْتَحُهَا اللَّهُ."

Sunan ibn Māja 4091

274. Who are Gog and Magog?

Answer: They will be one of the signs indicating the end of times.

In the Bible, the two names are first mentioned in the *Book of Ezekiel*. Gog is an individual and Magog is his land: In *Revelation*, Gog and Magog together signify the hostile nations of the world.

In Islam, this is similar but with a few differences. Gog is also called Ya'jūj (يَأْجُوج). Magog is referred to as Ma'jūj (مَأْجُوج). They represent two tribes of Allah's creatures; two nations; or two tribes of the children of Japheth, son of Noah. Some Islamic scholars claim that they represent people of the Turks or people beyond the Deylem, the historic name of a mountainous region near the Caspian Sea. Muslim geographers identified them as Turkic tribes from Central Asia and later as Mongols.

Muslims find information in the Hadiths about how Gog and Magog look like. 'Abū Hurayra (أَبُو هُرَيْرَة) reported that the Prophet said: "The Last Hour will not come before you fight with a people whose sandals are of hair and the Last Hour will not come before you fight with a people who have small eyes, short noses, and whose faces look as if they were shields covered with skin."[382]

Gog and Magog are mentioned in the Qur'an several times, mainly in sura 18 *The Cave* – in Arabic: al-Kahf (سُورة الْكَهْف). The Islamic story goes like this: Dhū al-Qarnayn (ذُو الْقَرْنَيْن) - *he of the two horns* - is a figure in the Qur'an who conquered land.

He went on until he reached the shore where he found "the sun setting into a muddy spring"[383], perhaps the Black Sea, and then he turned to the east and conquered and subdued vast territories – perhaps the land between the Black Sea and the Caspian Sea. There, Gog and Magog made great inroads, so Dhū al-Qarnayn built an iron wall/barrier to stop them.

When the time comes (Last Hour), Allah will remove the barrier and Gog and Magog will swarm throughout.

---

382 ...أَنَّ النَّبِيَّ قَالَ: "لاَ تَقُومُ السَّاعَةُ حَتَّى تُقَاتِلُوا قَوْمًا نِعَالُهُمُ الشَّعْرُ وَلاَ تَقُومُ السَّاعَةُ حَتَّى تُقَاتِلُوا قَوْمًا صِغَارَ الأَعْيُنِ ذُلْفَ الآنُفِ كَأَنَّ وُجُوهَهُمُ الْمَجَانُّ الْمُطْرَقَةُ." Sunan 'Abī Dāwud 4304 (4290)

383 ...حَتَّى إِذَا بَلَغَ مَغْرِبَ الشَّمْسِ وَجَدَهَا تَغْرُبُ فِي عَيْنٍ حَمِئَةٍ وَوَجَدَ عِندَهَا قَوْمًا قُلْنَا يَا ذَا الْقَرْنَيْنِ إِمَّا أَن تُعَذِّبَ وَإِمَّا أَن تَتَّخِذَ فِيهِمْ حُسْنًا؛ Qur'an 18:86

| 18:94 | They said, Dhu l-Qarnayn, Gog and Magog are ruining this land. Will you build a barrier between them and us if we pay you a tribute?' | قَالُوا يَا ذَا الْقَرْنَيْنِ إِنَّ يَأْجُوجَ وَمَأْجُوجَ مُفْسِدُونَ فِي الْأَرْضِ فَهَلْ نَجْعَلُ لَكَ خَرْجًا عَلَى أَن تَجْعَلَ بَيْنَنَا وَبَيْنَهُمْ سَدًّا؟ |
| 18:98 | and he said, 'This is a mercy from my Lord. But when my Lord's promise is fulfilled, He will raze this barrier to the ground: my Lord's promise always comes true.' | قَالَ هَذَا رَحْمَةٌ مِّن رَّبِّي فَإِذَا جَاءَ وَعْدُ رَبِّي جَعَلَهُ دَكَّاءَ وَكَانَ وَعْدُ رَبِّي حَقًّا. |

Most of the post-classical commentators identify these tribes as the Mongols and Tatars. That is also the reason why some commentators of the Qur'an see in 18:98 a prediction of a historic event: the Mongol invasion in the 13th century which destroyed the Abbasid Empire and thus the political power of the Arabs. Others claim it was earlier, when the Turks threatened northern Iran.

Muslims find proof for this in several authentic Hadiths which describe that the Messenger of Allah had a prophetic dream.

Zaynab bint Jahsh (زَيْنَب بِنْت جَحْش) narrated that one day, Allah's Messenger entered upon her in a state of fear and said: "None has the right to be worshipped but Allah! Woe to the Arabs from the Great Evil that has approached [them]. Today, a hole has been opened in the Gog and Magog dam like this."

The Prophet made a circle with his index finger and thumb. Zaynab bint Jahsh continued: "I said, 'O Allah's Apostle! Shall we be destroyed though there will be righteous people among us?' The Prophet said: 'Yes, if the [number] of evil [persons] increased.'"[384]

Some see in this Hadith a prophetic vision and even see in it the possibility that Gog and Magog invaded with the permission of Allah. Others suggested that it should be understood metaphorically: that the gates of evil and turmoil were opened, thus ever bringing disaster and misfortune as a trial to mankind.

---

384 ...أَنَّ رَسُولَ اللَّهِ دَخَلَ عَلَيْهَا يَوْمًا فَزِعًا يَقُولُ: "لاَ إِلَهَ إِلاَّ اللَّهُ، وَيْلٌ لِلْعَرَب مِنْ شَرٍّ قَدِ اقْتَرَبَ، فُتِحَ الْيَوْمَ مِنْ رَدْمِ يَأْجُوجَ وَمَأْجُوجَ مِثْلُ هَذِهِ". وَحَلَّقَ بِإِصْبَعَيْهِ الإِبْهَامِ وَالَّتِي تَلِيهَا. قَالَتْ زَيْنَبُ ابْنَةُ جَحْشٍ فَقُلْتُ يَا رَسُولَ اللَّهِ أَفَنَهْلِكُ وَفِينَا الصَّالِحُونَ قَالَ: "نَعَمْ إِذَا كَثُرَ الْخُبْثُ". Sahīh al-Bukhārī 7135

Muhammad Asad wrote in his commentary of the Qur'an that "it is most logical to assume that the terms Gog and Magog are purely allegorical, applying not to any specific tribes or beings but to a series of social catastrophes which would cause a complete destruction of man's civilisation before the coming of the Last Hour."

There are several early accounts which indicate that some Muslims claim to have seen the dam or the barrier which prevent Gog and Magog from entering "our" civilisation. Historians have tried to identify the dam or barrier.

Here are two possibilities:
- The Great Wall of China
- A wall in Central Asia called *The Gates of Alexander*, also known as the *Caspian Gate*. It was a legendary barrier supposedly built by Alexander the Great in the Caucasus to keep the barbarians of the north from invading his land to the south. There are two possible locations, i.e. the Pass of Derbent (Dagestan, Russia) or the Pass of Dariel (Caspian Sea).

  Some scholars even claim that Dhū al-Qarnayn, who is mentioned by name in the Qur'an, could have been Alexander the Great. However, there is very little evidence for this, and some scholars even totally reject this idea.

What will happen in the Last Hour?

The Final Days will be a fight between several figures: the Anti-Christ Dajjāl (الدَّجَّال), the (Islamic) saviour al-Mahdī (الْمَهْدِي), Jesus (عِيسَى), and Gog and Magog will appear.

Al-Nawwās ibn Samʿān (النَّوَّاس بن سَمْعان) reported that the Prophet was asked about the Dajjāl and the Last Hour, and he heard what Allah's Messenger said:

"And then Allah would send Gog and Magog and they would swarm down from every slope. The first of them would pass along Lake Tiberias and drink out of it. And when the last of them would pass, he would say: 'There was once water here.'

Jesus and his companions would then be besieged here [at Tur], and they would be so much hard pressed that the head of an oxen would be dearer to them than one hundred dinars, and Allah's Apostle, Jesus, and his companions would supplicate Allah, Who would send to them insects [which would attack their necks] and in the morning they would perish like a single person.

Allah's Apostle, Jesus, and his companions would then come down to earth and they would not find in the earth as much space as a single span that is not filled with their putrefaction and stench. Allah's Apostle, Jesus, and his companions would then again beseech Allah, Who would send birds whose necks would be like those of Bactrian camels and they would carry them and throw them where God would will.

Then, Allah would send rain which no house of clay or [the tent of] camel's hair would keep out and it would wash away the earth until it would appear as a mirror.

Then the earth would be told to bring forth its fruit and restore its blessing and, as a result thereof, there would grow [such a big] pomegranate that would be able to feed a group of persons and they could seek shelter under its skin, and a cow would give so much milk that a whole party would be able to drink from it.

And the camel would give such [a large quantity of] milk that the whole tribe would be able to drink from that and the sheep would give so much milk that the whole family would be able to drink from that, and at that time Allah would send a pleasant wind which would soothe [people] even under their armpits, and would take the life of every Muslim."[385]

---

385 ...وَيَبْعَثُ اللَّهُ يَأْجُوجَ وَمَأْجُوجَ وَهُمْ مِنْ كُلِّ حَدَبٍ يَنْسِلُونَ فَيَمُرُّ أَوَائِلُهُمْ عَلَى بُحَيْرَةِ طَبَرِيَّةَ فَيَشْرَبُونَ مَا فِيهَا وَيَمُرُّ آخِرُهُمْ فَيَقُولُونَ لَقَدْ كَانَ بِهَذِهِ مَرَّةً مَاءٌ. وَيُحْصَرُ نَبِيُّ اللَّهِ عِيسَى وَأَصْحَابُهُ حَتَّى يَكُونَ رَأْسُ الثَّوْرِ لِأَحَدِهِمْ خَيْرًا مِنْ مِائَةِ دِينَارٍ لِأَحَدِكُمُ الْيَوْمَ فَيَرْغَبُ نَبِيُّ اللَّهِ عِيسَى وَأَصْحَابُهُ فَيُرْسِلُ اللَّهُ عَلَيْهِمُ النَّغَفَ فِي رِقَابِهِمْ فَيُصْبِحُونَ كَمَوْتِ نَفْسٍ وَاحِدَةٍ ثُمَّ يَهْبِطُ نَبِيُّ اللَّهِ عِيسَى وَأَصْحَابُهُ إِلَى الْأَرْضِ فَلَا يَجِدُونَ فِي الْأَرْضِ مَوْضِعَ شِبْرٍ إِلاَّ مَلَأَهُ زَهَمُهُمْ وَنَتْنُهُمْ فَيَرْغَبُ نَبِيُّ اللَّهِ عِيسَى وَأَصْحَابُهُ إِلَى اللَّهِ فَيُرْسِلُ اللَّهُ طَيْرًا كَأَعْنَاقِ الْبُخْتِ فَتَحْمِلُهُمْ فَتَطْرَحُهُمْ حَيْثُ شَاءَ اللَّهُ ثُمَّ يُرْسِلُ اللَّهُ مَطَرًا لَا يَكُنُّ مِنْهُ بَيْتُ مَدَرٍ وَلاَ وَبَرٍ فَيَغْسِلُ الْأَرْضَ حَتَّى يَتْرُكَهَا كَالزَّلَفَةِ ثُمَّ يُقَالُ لِلْأَرْضِ أَنْبِتِي ثَمَرَتَكِ وَرُدِّي بَرَكَتَكِ. فَيَوْمَئِذٍ تَأْكُلُ الْعِصَابَةُ مِنَ الرُّمَّانَةِ وَيَسْتَظِلُّونَ بِقِحْفِهَا وَيُبَارَكُ فِي الرِّسْلِ حَتَّى أَنَّ اللِّقْحَةَ مِنَ الْإِبِلِ لَتَكْفِي الْفِئَامَ مِنَ النَّاسِ وَاللِّقْحَةَ مِنَ الْبَقَرِ لَتَكْفِي الْقَبِيلَةَ مِنَ النَّاسِ وَاللِّقْحَةَ مِنَ الْغَنَمِ لَتَكْفِي الْفَخِذَ مِنَ النَّاسِ فَبَيْنَمَا هُمْ كَذَلِكَ إِذْ بَعَثَ اللَّهُ رِيحًا طَيِّبَةً فَتَأْخُذُهُمْ تَحْتَ آبَاطِهِمْ فَتَقْبِضُ رُوحَ كُلِّ مُؤْمِنٍ وَكُلِّ مُسْلِمٍ وَيَبْقَى شِرَارُ النَّاسِ يَتَهَارَجُونَ فِيهَا تَهَارُجَ الْحُمُرِ فَعَلَيْهِمْ تَقُومُ السَّاعَةُ." Sahīh Muslim 2937

Will Gog and Magog eventually survive?

Not according to the Prophet. This is also reported in a Hadith. 'Abū Hurayra (أَبُو هُرَيْرة) narrated that the Messenger of Allah said: "Gog and Magog people dig every day until they can almost see the rays of the sun, and when the one in charge of them says: 'Go back and we will continue digging tomorrow.'

Then Allah puts it [the barrier] back, stronger than it was before. This will continue until their time has come, and Allah wants to send them against His people. They will dig until they can almost see the rays of the sun, then the one who is in charge of them will say: 'Go back, and we will dig it tomorrow if Allah wills.' So they will respond: 'If Allah wills.'

Then they will return. So they will dig and will come out to the people, and they will drink all the water. The people will fortify themselves against them in their fortresses. They will shoot their arrows towards the sky and they will come back with blood on them, and they will say: 'We have defeated the people of earth and dominated the people of heaven.'

Then Allah will send a worm in the napes of their necks and will thereby kill them.'"

The Messenger of Allah said: "By the One in Whose Hand is my soul, the beasts of the earth will grow fat on their flesh."[386]

Remark: Gog and Magog (Hebrew: גּוֹג וּמָגוֹג) in the Hebrew Bible can represent individuals, peoples, or lands. According to Genesis, Gog and Magog descended from Japheth, son of Noah. According to the Book of Ezekiel, they are a prophesied enemy nation of God's people.

---

386 ...قَالَ رَسُولُ اللَّهِ: "إِنَّ يَأْجُوجَ وَمَأْجُوجَ يَحْفِرُونَ كُلَّ يَوْمٍ حَتَّى إِذَا كَادُوا يَرَوْنَ شُعَاعَ الشَّمْسِ قَالَ الَّذِي عَلَيْهِمُ ارْجِعُوا فَسَنَحْفِرُهُ غَدًا. فَيُعِيدُهُ اللَّهُ أَشَدَّ مَا كَانَ حَتَّى إِذَا بَلَغَتْ مُدَّتُهُمْ وَأَرَادَ اللَّهُ أَنْ يَبْعَثَهُمْ عَلَى النَّاسِ حَفَرُوا حَتَّى إِذَا كَادُوا يَرَوْنَ شُعَاعَ الشَّمْسِ قَالَ الَّذِي عَلَيْهِمُ ارْجِعُوا فَسَتَحْفِرُونَهُ غَدًا إِنْ شَاءَ اللَّهُ تَعَالَى وَاسْتَثْنَوْا فَيَعُودُونَ إِلَيْهِ وَهُوَ كَهَيْئَتِهِ حِينَ تَرَكُوهُ فَيَحْفِرُونَهُ وَيَخْرُجُونَ عَلَى النَّاسِ فَيَنْشِفُونَ الْمَاءَ وَيَتَحَصَّنُ النَّاسُ مِنْهُمْ فِي حُصُونِهِمْ فَيَرْمُونَ بِسِهَامِهِمْ إِلَى السَّمَاءِ فَتَرْجِعُ عَلَيْهَا الدَّمُ الَّذِي اجْفَظَّ فَيَقُولُونَ قَهَرْنَا أَهْلَ الْأَرْضِ وَعَلَوْنَا أَهْلَ السَّمَاءِ فَيَبْعَثُ اللَّهُ نَغَفًا فِي أَقْفَائِهِمْ فَيَقْتُلُهُمْ بِهَا." قَالَ رَسُولُ اللَّهِ: "وَالَّذِي نَفْسِي بِيَدِهِ إِنَّ دَوَابَّ الْأَرْضِ لَتَسْمَنُ وَتَشْكَرُ شَكَرًا مِنْ لُحُومِهِمْ."

Sunan ibn Māja 4080

Jewish eschatology views Gog and Magog as enemies to be defeated by Messiah ben Joseph, which will usher in the age of the true Messiah.

The interpretation in Christianity is more apocalyptic: Gog and Magog are allies of Satan against God at the end of the millennium, as can be read in the *Book of Revelation*.

275. Why does Allah want the majority of people to enter Hell?

Answer: According to Islam, Allah wants to punish the disbelievers. So far most of the people on earth aren't Muslims. According to Islam, they were created by Allah – nevertheless, they will enter Hell.

There is nothing to debate: Allah does not approve of people's disbelief. He demands the affirmation of the Oneness of Allah.

Islam clearly states that anyone who does not believe in Allah will enter Hell.

It might sound strange that eventually, after the Day of Judgement, most of the people will end up in Hell. In sura *39 The Throngs* - in Arabic: al-Zumar (سُورة الزُّمَر) -, it is mentioned that Allah has neither interest, nor need in people who don't worship him:

| 39:7 | **If you are ungrateful, remember God has no need of you,** yet He is not pleased by ingratitude in His servants; if you are grateful, He is pleased [to see] it in you. No soul will bear another's burden. You will return to your Lord in the end and He will inform you of what you have done: He knows well what is in the depths of [your] hearts. | إن تَكْفُرُوا فَإِنَّ اللَّهَ غَنِيٌّ عَنكُم وَلَا يَرْضَى لِعِبَادِهِ الْكُفْرَ وَإِن تَشْكُرُوا يَرْضَهُ لَكُم وَلَا تَزِرُ وَازِرَةٌ وِزْرَ أُخْرَى ثُمَّ إِلَى رَبِّكُم مَّرْجِعُكُم فَيُنَبِّئُكُم بِمَا كُنتُم تَعْمَلُونَ إِنَّهُ عَلِيمٌ بِذَاتِ الصُّدُورِ |

PART IV

On the history
of Islam

276. Who invented the lunar calendar?

Answer: Unknown, but certainly not the Arabs.

The oldest known lunar calendar was found in Scotland at a place called Warren Field. It dates back to around 8,000 BC.

The Arabs used the lunar calendar prior to the foundation of Islam. The calendar consisted of twelve months which were determined by the sighting of the new moon from one month to the next.

Islamic historians usually relate this story: There was a meeting in the year 412, around 150 years before Muhammad received his revelation. It took place in Mecca and was attended by Kulāb (or Kilāb) ibn Murra (كُلاب بن مُرّة) who was the Prophet's fifth grandfather in ascending order. The meeting's participants set new names for the months, and all Arab tribes accepted them. These names were the same which the Muslims used later on for the Islamic Hijri calendar. Among these were four sacred months (الأَشْهُر الْحَرَم) during which the people should refrain from fighting.

The Arabs before Islam used a so-called lunisolar calendar. The months were lunar, but years were solar. In order to adjust the calendar (a lunar calendar year is about 11 days shorter than a solar year), people added a separate month every third year. This type of calendar was used in the early civilisations of the Middle East, except for Egypt and Greece. The Arabs in the 5th century did not have a system in place to date important events. They would rather link them to historical events, for example the destruction of the Great Dam of Ma'rib.

But why does the Muslim calendar start in the year 622?

This decision was taken by Muhammad's <u>companions</u> after his death – and not by the Prophet himself. Scholars say that the Hijri calendar was set during Caliph 'Umar's reign (between 16 and 18 AH). Sahl ibn Sa'd (سَهْل بن سَعْد) narrated that "the Prophet's companions did not take as a starting date for the Muslim calendar the day when the Prophet had been sent as an Apostle or the day of his death, but the day of his arrival at Medina."[387]

---

387 ...قَالَ مَا عَدُّوا مِنْ مَبْعَثِ النَّبِيِّ وَلاَ مِنْ وَفَاتِهِ، مَا عَدُّوا إِلاَّ مِنْ مَقْدِمِهِ الْمَدِينَةَ. -Sahīh al
Bukhārī 3934

Let's have a look at the Islamic calendar (التَّقْويم الهِجْرِيّ الْقَمَـرِيّ). There are five months whose names describe the seasonal condition of that month at the time when their names were set:

3 – Rabī' al-'Awwal (رَبِيع الأَوَّل) – literally, the First Rabī'

4 – Rabī' al-'Ākhir (رَبِيع الْآخِر) – literally, the Last Rabī'

The word Rabī' comes from the root r-b-' (ر-ب-ع) and means *spring*. Why Rabī'? When the months received these names, herbage was produced during that particular time of year. Some say it was called Rabī' because the first rain, al-Wasmī (الْوَسْمِيّ), fell therein.

This means that in 412 AD, al-Rabī' al-'Awwal was *the season in which the truffles and the blossoms appear,* and al-Rabī' al-Thānī (or al-'Ākhir) was *the season in which fruits ripen*. The word month (شَهْر) is necessarily added in order to distinguish between the *months* and the *season* (spring). Note that the Arabs, before they had a calendar, called *autumn* Rabī' (spring) because it was the first rain after a hot summer, thus fruits and vegetables started to grow.

5 – Jumādā al-'Ūlā (جُمادَى الأُوَلَى) – literally, the First Jumādā

6 – Jumādā al-'Ākhira (جُمادَى الْآخِرة) – literally, the Last Jumādā

The Arabic root j-m-d (ج-م-د) denotes a *dry* or *frozen state*. How is that possible after spring? This is not entirely clear. Some scholars say that the Arabs used the word *spring* (the first rain after summer) actually for *autumn*. When the months were named, these two months fell in the season when water froze. However, according to Edward Lane, this "seems to have been invented when the two months thus named had fallen back into, or beyond, winter".

Edward Lane held the opinion that "they [the months] were thus called because falling in a period when the earth had become dry and hard by reason of paucity of rain". From the word Jamād (جَماد), an epithet applied to *land upon which rain has not fallen*, or from the word Jumādā (جُمادَى), an epithet applied to *an eye that sheds few tears*. During these two months, at the time when they received these names, people were satisfied; there was no urgent need of water, the pastures were green.

9 – Ramadān (رَمَضـان): The name Ramadan was taken from the Arabic word ramdā' (رَمْضاء), which means *sun-baked ground, very hot* – simply because when the name was given, the month coincided with summer. Note: The revelation of the Quran began on the *Night of the Decree* - Layla(t) al-Qadr (لَيْلة القَدْر) - in Ramadan.

The other seven months were named according to the condition of the society and social cycle at that time:

1 – Muharram (مُحَـرَّم): This name comes from the Arabic word haram (حَرَم) which means *holy*, since this month is one of the four holy months. Remark: The word haram (حَرَم) can also mean *forbidden, taboo*.

2 – Safar (صَفَر): This name was taken from the Arabic word Sifr (صِفْر) which means *zero*. The people used to procure their provision of wheat from the places at which it was collected. The month might have been called like that because of the scarcity of provisions as their granaries had become empty - Sifr (صِفْر) - in the season in which it fell when it was first named (as it then fell in winter). Another hypothesis: It was so named because in this month many houses were empty because the occupants had left to go to war.

7 – Rajab (رَجَب): The Arabic root r-j-b (ر-ج-ب) denotes that *a man was frightened*. Before Islam, people glorified this month and sacrificed animals. Edward Lane claimed that this month was thus named "because of the honour in which it was held in the *Time of Ignorance* [before Islam], inasmuch as war or fighting during it was held unlawful." It is the only sacred month that is not preceded nor followed by another sacred month. During Rajab war was strictly forbidden.

8 – Sha'bān (شَعْبان): The Arabic V-verb tasha"ab (تَشَعَّب) means *it became separated*. Edward Lane suggested that this month received this name because of "predatory expeditions" after having been restrained thereof during the preceding month of Rajab. Some scholars said that, long before Islam, Arabs used this name because during this month they used to disperse themselves in search of water (when the months were regulated by the solar year).

10 – Shawwāl (شَوّال): The name goes back to the root sh-w-l (ش-و-ل) which means *to rise, to elevate, to carry* – because this was the time when the she-camels (being 7 or 8 months gone with young) raised their tails (indicating to stallions that they have conceived). Camels generally mate in winter. Or, as Edward Lane wrote, "because of their milk becoming then withdrawn, such being the case with the camels in the time of vehement heat and of the coming to an end of the juicy fresh herbage."

The Arabs considered the making of marriage-contracts in this month a bad idea, because the woman then married would resist the man who married her – in similar fashion like the she-camel resists the stallion by raising her tail. The Prophet, however, abolished these traditions when he married 'Ā'isha (عائشة بِنْت أَبِي بَكْر) in this month.

11 – Dhū al-Qaʿda (ذُو الْقَعْدَة): The name was taken from the root q-ʿ-d (قَعَدَ), which means *to sit, to rest*. It was chosen because the Arabs (when their year was solar) then abstained from journeys and plundering expeditions as they prepared themselves for the pilgrimage in the following month.

12 – Dhū al-Hijja (ذُو الحِجَّة): This name is derived from the act of worshipping that traditionally took place in this month, i.e. the pilgrimage to the house of Allah, the Kaʿba. This was already common practice prior to Islam.

Some remarks:

- Previously the Arabs mentioned all months without the word shahr (شَهر) - the Arabic word for *month* - except for the two months of Rabīʿ and the month of Ramadan (رَمَضان).
- The Muslim calendar has 354.367 days on average.

277. How many months are sacred in Islam?

Answer: Four.

These months should give people a break from battles and wars. They could hold their markets, go on pilgrimage to the Kaʿba in

Mecca, and they would be safe from raids and banditry on the road as well as at home. The number of sacred months is given in sura 9 *The Repentance* – in Arabic: al-Tawba (سُورة التَّوْبة):

9:36	God decrees that there are 12 months - ordained in God's Book on the Day when He created the heavens and earth - **4 months of which are sacred**: this is the correct calculation. Do not wrong your souls in these months – though you may fight the idolaters at any time, if they first fight you – remember God is with those who are mindful of Him.	إِنَّ عِدَّةَ الشُّهُورِ عِندَ اللَّهِ اثْنَا عَشَرَ شَهْرًا فِي كِتَابِ اللَّهِ يَوْمَ خَلَقَ السَّمَاوَاتِ وَالْأَرْضَ مِنْهَا أَرْبَعَةٌ حُرُمٌ ذَٰلِكَ الدِّينُ الْقَيِّمُ فَلَا تَظْلِمُوا فِيهِنَّ أَنفُسَكُمْ وَقَاتِلُوا الْمُشْرِكِينَ كَافَّةً كَمَا يُقَاتِلُونَكُمْ كَافَّةً وَاعْلَمُوا أَنَّ اللَّهَ مَعَ الْمُتَّقِينَ.

The sacred months (الْأَشْهُر الْحَرَم) in the Islamic calendar are: Dhū al-Qaʿda (ذُو الْقَعْدة), Dhū al-Hijja (ذُو الْحِجّة), al-Muharram (الْمُحَرَّم), and Rajab (رَجَب). Fighting was not allowed during these months (except in self-defence). Ibn Kathīr (ابن كَثِير) reasoned in his commentary on the Qur'an why these four months are sacred. He argued that the four sacred months were made four, three in succession and one alone, so that the Hajj and ʿUmra could be performed with ease.

- **Dhū al-Qaʿda,** the month before the Hajj month, was made sacred because the people should refrain from fighting and prepare for the pilgrimage.

- **Dhū al-Hijja,** the succeeding month, was made sacred because it is the month of Hajj during which the people underdook the pilgrimage.

- **Muharram,** which follows, was made sacred so that the people would be able to return to their areas in safety after the Hajj.

- **Rajab,** in the middle of the lunar year, was made sacred so that those coming from the farthest corners of Arabia would be able to perform the ʿUmra, and then safely return to their areas.

278. What (Gregorian) year is 1435 Hijri?

Answer: 2014.

The name Hijra (هِجْرَة) denotes the migration of Muhammad and his followers from Mecca to Medina in June 622. This date marks the beginning of the Islamic Hijri calendar.

The Muslim calendar is a lunar calendar and doesn't follow a solar system like the Gregorian or Persian calendar. Normally, in Arabic, it is marked by the letter ه, which is written in the form it has at the beginning of a word (ه) – and not as the stand-alone form (ه).

Let us return to our question: What (Gregorian) year is 1435 Hijri? First of all, one lunar year has about 354 days and we thus need to convert it. The most effective way is to use a corrective factor, i.e. 354 divided by 365 which is about 0.97.

This brings us to the following calculation:

1. If you want to convert a Hijri date to a Gregorian date, you need to multiply the Hijri year by 0.97 and then add 622:
2. Year Gregorian ≈ Year Hijri × 0.97 + 622
3. If you want to convert a Gregorian date to a Hijri date, you have to subtract 622 from the year and multiply it by 1.03:
4. Year Hijri ≈ (Year Gregorian– 622) × 1.03
5. In our example, the result is: 1435 x 0.97 + 622 = 2013.95
6. It is the year 2014.

279. Who was the first man to convert to Islam?

Answer: This is not entirely clear.

According to the Muslim historian Ibn 'Ishāq (مُحَمَّد بن إسحاق) and some other scholars, 'Alī ibn 'Abī Tālib (عَلِيّ بن أبي طالِب) was the first male person to embrace Islam. 'Alī was Muhammad's cousin and son-in-law. However, some scholars say that 'Alī was a child (maybe 10 y. old) when this happened. For this reason, they argue, his conversion is not worthy enough to consider him the first male Muslim.

Another early Islamic historian, al-Tabarī (الطَّبَرِيّ), claimed that either Zayd ibn Hāritha (زَيْد بن حارِثة) - a freed slave who became Muhammad's adopted son - was the first Muslim, or 'Abū Bakr al-Siddīq (أَبُو بَكْر الصِّدِّيق).

The answer to this question (the first male Muslim convert) is not trivial. It is essential for the debate who should have taken the leadership of the Muslim community after Muhammad's death.

'Alī's followers, the Shia Muslims, are convinced that the Prophet indicated that he wanted 'Alī as the successor. Other Muslims, on the other hand, were in favour of 'Abū Bakr, who eventually became the first Caliph.

What is the answer? **Who was the first Muslim?**

- For Shia Muslims, it was clearly 'Alī.
- Sunni Muslims see it differently: They, for the most part, agree that 'Alī was the **first child** to convert to Islam – and that 'Abū Bakr was the **first adult** male convert. However, they do not argue who was first because this is not important to them.

So, there is no correct answer and it is not clear whether 'Abū Bakr or 'Alī was the very first male Muslim convert.

280. Was Jesus a Muslim?

Answer: Muslims would say: yes.

I had a teacher in Egypt who insisted that Jesus was a Muslim and he tried to prove this to non-Muslim students in a 2-hour presentation. In fact, the Qur'an claims that all believers were essentially Muslims. My teacher basically used a verse of sura 22 *The Pilgrimage* - in Arabic: al-Hajj (سورة الحَجّ) - for his argumentation:

| 22:78 | Strive hard for God as is His due: He has chosen you and placed no hardship in your religion, the faith of your forefather Abraham. God has called you Muslims - both in the past and in this [message] - so that the Messenger can bear witness about you and so that you can bear witness about other people. | وَجَاهِدُوا فِي اللَّهِ حَقَّ جِهَادِهِ هُوَ اجْتَبَاكُمْ وَمَا جَعَلَ عَلَيْكُمْ فِى الدِّين مِنْ حَرَج مِّلَّةَ أَبِيكُمْ إِبْرَاهِيمَ هُوَ سَمَّاكُمُ الْمُسْلِمِينَ مِن قَبْلُ وَفِي هَذَا لِيَكُونَ الرَّسُولُ شَهِيدًا عَلَيْكُمْ وَتَكُونُوا شُهَدَاءَ عَلَى النَّاسِ. |

If we follow the Qur'an, then all Abrahamitic prophets were indeed Muslims as well as all believers. This would make Adam the first believer, and thus the first Muslim. According to Islamic logic, Jesus would therefore have been a Muslim too. Muslims claim that the Christians later on corrupted the divine message of Jesus.

It is a theoretical discussion. Other religions which were founded prior to Islam would instantly reject all this. The claim that all believers were Muslims is only true if you follow Islamic sources only, and only then it sounds totally logic. Muslims claim that the (one and only correct) religion had already existed prior to Islam, but that the message of the prophets had been corrupted, which had caused Allah to send a last messenger: Muhammad.

281. Who was the first woman to embrace Islam?

Answer: Khadīja bint Khuwaylid (خَدِيجة بِنْت خُوَيْلِد).

Born	~ 556 (68 BH) in Mecca	Died	619 (3 BH) in Mecca

Khadīja was the first wife of Muhammad. She had been married twice before and had children from all her marriages.

282. Who was the first of the 'Ansār to convert to Islam?

Answer: 'As'ad ibn Zurāra (أَشْعَد بن زُرارة), also called 'Abū Umāma (أَبُو أُمامة).

Born	unknown	Died	623 1 (AH)

'As'ad was from the tribe Banū al-Khazraj (بَنُو الْخَزْرَج) and was the tribe's representative in the *Pledges of al-'Aqaba*.

In 623 'As'ad suffered from an illness, probably diphtheria or meningitis. Muhammad advised cauterising 'As'ad, and the Prophet did it himself.

'Anas ibn Mālik (أَنَس بن مالِك) later confirmed this: "The Prophet cauterised 'As'ad ibn Zurāra."[388] According to some sources, 'As'ad was burned twice in the arm and twice on his throat. It did not help; As'ad died within days.

As'ad was known for his hatred towards Jews which is related in a Hadith. 'Usāma ibn Zayd (أُسامة بن زَيْد) narrated that the Messenger of Allah went out to visit 'Abd Allah ibn 'Ubayy (عَبْد الله بن أُبَيّ) when he was ill. When the Prophet came upon him, he realised that death was close. He said: "I used to forbid you from the love of Jews." He ['Abd Allah] replied: "'As'ad ibn Zurāra hated them."[389]

283. Who was the first Persian man to convert to Islam?

Answer: Salmān al-Fārisī (سَلْمان الْفارِسِيّ).

Born	probably in ~ 568, Isfahan Province (Persia)	Died	656 (36 AH), aged ~88, buried in al-Madā'in (present-day Iraq)

His name literally means *Salmān the Persian*. He was a companion of Muhammad and the first Persian who converted to Islam.

Salmān al-Fārisī is a popular figure in Islamic myths and a national hero in Iran. He is the role-model of a Persian man, who embraced Islam. According to popular Shia tradition, Muhammad considered Salmān as part of his household ('Ahl al-Bayt). He became a follower of 'Alī ibn 'Abī Tālib (عَلِيّ بن أَبي طالِب) after the death of the Prophet.

His biography is very colourful and it is not entirely clear what part is legend and what is historical fact. This is what is told about him: In his youth, Salmān studied hard to become a Zoroastrian priest (a so-called *magus*) which would have made him the guardian of a fire temple, which was then a well-respected job.

---

388 ...أَنَّ النَّبِيَّ كَوَى أَسْعَدَ بْنَ زُرَارَةَ مِنَ الشَّوْكَةِ. Jāmi' al-Tirmidhī 2188

389 ...قَالَ خَرَجَ رَسُولُ اللَّهِ يَعُودُ عَبْدَ اللَّهِ بْنَ أُبَيٍّ فِي مَرَضِهِ الَّذِي مَاتَ فِيهِ فَلَمَّا دَخَلَ عَلَيْهِ عَرَفَ فِيهِ الْمَوْتَ قَالَ: "قَدْ كُنْتُ أَنْهَاكَ عَنْ حُبِّ يَهُودَ." قَالَ فَقَدْ أَبْغَضَهُمْ أَسْعَدُ بْنُ زُرَارَةَ. Sunan 'Abī Dāwūd 3094

Later on, still in his youth, he converted to Christianity. Salmān began to travel the Middle East and discussed his ideas with priests, theologians and scholars in his quest to find the truth.

While he was in Syria, he heard of Muhammad whose coming had been predicted by Salmān's last Christian teacher on his deathbed. During his travels, Salmān got into some troubles and was sold to a Jew in Medina. In Medina, he met Muhammad personally and got free. When he recognised the signs which his former teacher (the monk) had told him about, he converted to Islam.

The most important event linked to Salmān is the Battle of the Trench (غَزْوةُ الْخَنْدَق) in 627 (5 AH). According to Islamic sources, when Muhammad was besieged in Medina, it was Salmān who suggested that a trench should be dug around Medina. This was an innovation in Arabian warfare and was decisive in Muhammad's successful defence.

ʿAlī is said to have referred to him as Luqmān al-Hakīm (لُقْمان الْحَكِيـم) which means: *Luqmān the Wise*. Maybe this was because Salmān had, as ʿAlī stated, "read the First Book and the Last Book"[390] – namely, the Bible and the Qur'an. Therefore, ʾAbū Hurayra (أَبُو هُرَيْرة) called him ʾAbū al-Kitābayn (أَبُو الْكِتابَيْن) which means: *The father of the two books*. According to some accounts, Salmān translated parts of the Qur'an into Persian, thus being probably the first person to interpret and translate the Qur'an into Persian.

Remark: Some Hadiths indicate that Salmān became governor of a city in present-day Iraq. Salmān Pāk (سَلْمان باك), a city approximately 15 miles south of Baghdad, is named after Salmān the Persian, who is said to be buried there.

284. Were there self-acclaimed prophets besides Muhammad?

Answer: There were at least three of them.

It is interesting that Muhammad had some "competitors".

---

390 ...قَرَأَ الْكِتَابَ الأَوَّلَ, وَالْكِتَابَ الآخَرَ

They all believed to be a prophet and claimed to have had received a divine message. Let's look at them.

- **Maslama** (مَسْلَمة بن حَبِيب الْحَنَفِيّ). Most Muslims prefer to use the scornful diminutive form Musaylima (مُسَيْلِمة). Maslama fought and was killed in the Battle of Yamāma (مَعْرَكة الْيَمامة) by the former Ethiopian slave Wahshī ibn Harb (وَحْشِيّ بن حَرْب) – the same man who killed Muhammad's uncle Hamza (حَمْزة بن عَبْد الْمُطَّلِب) in the Battle of 'Uhud (غَزْوة أُحُد) before his conversion to Islam (see chapter 247). Remark: In the film *The Message* (1976), there is a scene which shows how Wahshī killed Hamza.

- **Sajāh** (سَجاح بِنْت الْحارِث) declared that <u>she</u> was a prophetess after learning that Musaylima and Tulayha had declared prophethood. Sajāh had a reputation as a soothsayer. Her plan to attack Medina was called off after she learned that the army of Khālid ibn al-Walīd (خالِد بن الْوَلِيد) had defeated Tulayha. Thereafter, she sought cooperation with Musaylima to fight Khālid ibn al-Walīd. Sajāh then married Musaylima and accepted his self-declared prophethood. After the Battle of Yamāma, in which Musaylima was killed, Sajāh converted to Islam.

- **Tulayha** (طُلَيْحة) embraced Islam in 630. However, in 631, he rebelled against Muhammad and claimed to be a prophet himself. 'Abū Bakr raised an army against him and his followers. Thereafter, Khālid ibn al-Walīd was commanded to crush him and his people. Tulayha escaped and sought refuge in Syria. When Syria was conquered by the Muslims, Tulayha embraced Islam.

285. Which catastrophes happened after Muhammad's death?

Answer: The Black Death/bubonic plague (in Syria) and famine (in Saudi Arabia).

The famine. The year 639 (18 AH) was called *the year of grey* (عام الرَّمادة). The landscape had become ash-coloured because it had not rained for nine months. Especially the northern half of the Arabian Peninsula suffered from the drought. People were desperate and fled to Medina. Caliph 'Umar sent a letter to 'Abū Mūsā al-'Ash'arī (أَبُو مُوسَى الْأَشْعَرِيّ) in Basra (present-day Iraq) and sent a caravan to him. The caravan, consisting of 4,000 camels, eventually brought food and water to the Muslims.

The Black Death or bubonic plague. It was an outbreak of plague, possibly the bubonic plague, which occurred in 639 in Emmaus (Imwas) (عِمْواس) in Judea/Palestine shortly after the Muslims had conquered the town. It quickly spread north.

It is not entirely clear why this epidemic broke out. Perhaps it had to do with the fact that thousands of killed Byzantine soldiers had not been buried by the Muslims – which may have turned out to be a fatal mistake. The epidemic is infamous in Islamic history due to the death of many famous companions of Muhammad. It is estimated that 25,000 people died in this outbreak. Among the victims were 'Abū 'Ubayda ibn al-Jarrāh (أَبُو عُبَيْدة بن الْجَرَّاح) and Yazīd ibn 'Abū Sufyān (يَزِيد بن أَبِي سُفْيان).

286. Who was the first muezzin in Islam?

Answer: Bilāl ibn Rabāh (بِلال بن رَباح).

Born	between 578 and 582 in Ethiopia (الْحَبَشة)	Died	~ 640 (~19 AH) in Damascus

Bilāl was one of the slaves of the Quraysh and later became an important companion of the Prophet. He is said to have been tortured by his master 'Umayya ibn Khalf (أُمَيّة بن خَلْف). 'Abū Bakr (أَبُو بَكْر الصَّدِّيق) bought and manumitted (freed) him.

In the movie *The Message* (1976), Bilāl was played by Johnny Sekka, an actor who was born in Dakar, Senegal. However, according to the movie database *IMDB*, the famous boxer Muhammad Ali expressed interest in playing the role of Bilāl – but the producer, Moustapha Akkad, refused his offer.

He was afraid that such casting "would smack of commercialism".

287. Did the first mosques have minarets?

Answer: Probably not.

The very first Muslims came to pray without answering a specific call. When Islam was revealed in the early 7th century, Jews called the faithful to prayer with the shofar (Hebrew: שׁוֹפָר) - a ram's horn -, and Christians used a bell, a wooden gong, or a clacker. The sound of a bell from a distant monastery was a frequent image in pre Islamic poetry. When Muslims became aware of that, they wanted something equivalent.

One of the companions suggested using the human voice. It is not entirely clear who had the idea of a call to prayer, the so-called al-'Adhān (الأَذان). There is a Hadith telling the story of 'Abd Allah ibn Zayd (عَبْد الله بن زَيْد). One of the Prophet's companions narrated that when the Messenger of Allah ordered a bell to be made so that it might be struck to gather the people for prayer, a man carrying a bell in his hand appeared to him in a dream while 'Abd Allah was asleep. 'Abd Allah said: "Will you sell the bell?" The man asked: "What will you do with it?" 'Abd Allah replied: "We shall use it to call the people to prayer." The man said: "Should I not suggest you something better than that?" 'Abd Allah replied: "Certainly." Then he told 'Abd Allah to call: "Allah is most great, Allah is most great... I testify that..."[391]

When the morning came, 'Abd Allah went to the Messenger of Allah and informed him of what he had seen in his dream. He [the Prophet] said: "It is a genuine vision and he then should use it to call people to prayer, for he has a louder voice than you have."

So I got up along with Bilāl and began to teach him, and he used it in calling to prayer.[392]

---

391 ...قَالَ لَمَّا أَمَرَ رَسُولُ اللَّهِ بِالنَّاقُوسِ يُعْمَلُ لِيُضْرَبَ بِهِ لِلنَّاسِ لِجَمْعِ الصَّلَاةِ طَافَ بِي وَأَنَا نَائِمٌ رَجُلٌ يَحْمِلُ نَاقُوسًا فِي يَدِهِ فَقُلْتُ يَا عَبْدَ اللَّهِ أَتَبِيعُ النَّاقُوسَ قَالَ وَمَا تَصْنَعُ بِهِ فَقُلْتُ نَدْعُو بِهِ إِلَى الصَّلَاةِ. قَالَ أَفَلَا أَدُلُّكَ عَلَى مَا هُوَ خَيْرٌ مِنْ ذَلِكَ فَقُلْتُ لَهُ بَلَى. قَالَ فَقَالَ تَقُولُ اللَّهُ أَكْبَرُ اللَّهُ أَكْبَرُ...

Sunan 'Abī Dāwūd 499

392 ...فَلَمَّا أَصْبَحْتُ أَتَيْتُ رَسُولَ اللَّهِ فَأَخْبَرْتُهُ بِمَا رَأَيْتُ فَقَالَ " إِنَّهَا لَرُؤْيَا حَقٌّ إِنْ شَاءَ اللَّهُ فَقُمْ مَعَ بِلَالٍ فَأَلْقِ عَلَيْهِ مَا رَأَيْتَ فَلْيُؤَذِّنْ بِهِ فَإِنَّهُ أَنْدَى صَوْتًا مِنْكَ ". فَقُمْتُ مَعَ بِلَالٍ فَجَعَلْتُ أُلْقِيهِ عَلَيْهِ وَيُؤَذِّنُ بِهِ. Sunan 'Abī Dāwūd 499

In the film *The Message* (1976), which was approved by several Muslim historians and scholars, Bilāl went up to the roof to make the very first call to prayer in Islam. The earliest mosques most probably lacked minarets. According to Islamic tradition, Bilāl and his early successors gave the call to prayer from a high or public place, such as the doorway or roof of a mosque, an elevated neighbouring structure or even the city wall, but never from a tall tower. The idea of a min-aret first arose under the Umayyad Caliphate (الْخِلَافة الأُمَوِيَّة) in Syria where Muslims came in contact with Syrian church towers. They converted the churches into mosques and adapted the towers.

In 673, four towers were erected on the roof of the mosque in al-Fustāt (الْفُسْطاط) by the Umayyad governor of Egypt. Al-Fustāt was the first capital of Egypt under Islamic rule and was located close to Cairo (which, by the way, had not been established yet). The English architectural historian Cameron Creswell identified them as the first minarets built as such in Islam.

The minaret is certainly a later invention, coming after the call to prayer. Jonathan M. Bloom, a professor of Islamic and Asian Art, gave in his book *The Minaret* (2013) interesting facts about the genesis of the Islamic minaret. It is said that ʿAlī ibn ʾAbī Tālib (عليّ بن أبي طالب), the Prophet's cousin, son-in-law and fourth Caliph, ordered a tall place from which the call to prayer was given to be dismantled because its height enabled the muezzin (مُؤَذِّن) to see into the homes around the mosque. The call to prayer, ʿAlī believed, should not be given from any place higher than the roof of the mosque. "It is for the same reason that, in later years, blind men have often been selec-ted and trained as muezzins, for they are unable to inadvertently violate the privacy of other people's homes", Bloom wrote.

Scholars tried to trace minarets back to various traditions of tower building in the pre-Islamic cultures of Eurasia. Over a century ago, for example, A. J. Butler, the British historian of Roman Egypt, spec-ulated that the multi storied form of the typical Cairene minaret of the Mamluk period might have been derived from the Pharos (light-house) of Alexandria, one of the wonders of the ancient world.

The German archaeologist Hermann Thiersch (1874-1939) thought that square minarets, such as those found in Syria, North Africa, and Spain, were derived from church towers. Bloom noticed that this church tower theory was strengthened by the survival of the Arabic term al-Sawma'a (الصَّوْمَعة), meaning *hermitage*, which had been used in medieval North Africa and Spain to refer to minarets. Thiersch believed that cylindrical minarets, like those common in Iran, Afghanistan, and Central Asia, were derived from Roman and Byzantine monumental victory columns. Bloom suggested that this explanation would support Thiersch's view that minarets were "erected principally as symbols of Islam's triumph over other religions".

European scholars sought the origins of the minaret in the ancient nomadic cultures of Central Asia and India. The Austrian art historian Josef Strzygowski (1862-1941) compared the round brick minarets of Iran and Central Asia to early medieval round towers in Ireland. He set up the hypothesis that all these towers derived from a common source in the folk arts of the steppe nomads of Asia who had migrated to western Europe in the early Middle Ages.

A remark on the word for *minaret* in Arabic: In classical Arabic, the word for *minaret* is Mi'dhana (مِئْذَنة). This noun is describing a tool or instrument derived from the verb *to call to prayer*. In Arabic grammar, this is a so-called *noun of instrument* (اسم آلة). In dialects, nowadays, people usually say Ma'dhana (مَأْذَنة) – which would be the place or time, where the act of *calling to prayer* is carried out. This indicates that early sources probably saw in the *minaret* not a place, but rather a tool or instrument.

288. Who was the first martyr in Islam?

Answer: A woman – Sumayya bint al-Khayyāt (سُمَيّة بِنْت الْخَيّاط).

Born	~ 550 in Ethiopia		Died	~ 615 in Mecca

She was the first Muslim (not only regarding women!) to become a martyr – in Arabic: Shahīd (شَهِيد) or Shahīda (شَهِيدة) for women.

Sumayya later married Yāsir ibn 'Āmir (ياسِر بن عامِر). They had a son, 'Ammār (عَمّار بن ياسِر). That is why Sumayya is better known under the epithet 'Umm 'Ammār (أُمّ عَمّار). All three were among the earliest converts to Islam, some claim they were "the first family" to embrace Islam. In 615 Muhammad began to preach publicly in Mecca, which resulted in the persecution of the small Muslim community. The first to be targeted were those who did not have any tribal protection. Sumayya, who had been a slave before converting to Islam, was one of the many Muslims who had no position or rank that would protect her. So, she (along with her husband and son) were among the many newly converted Muslims who were beaten.

Sumayya was stabbed by 'Amr ibn Hishām (عَمْرُو بن هِشام), who was better known as 'Abū Jahl (أَبُو جَهْل). The Meccan leader killed her when she refused to forswear her faith – thus making her the first martyr of Islam. The first male (and second) martyr in Islam was her husband who was also killed. Most scholars suggest that his wife was killed before him.

Some remarks:

- Sumayya's son, 'Ammār, became one of the Prophet's companions; he died during the first war between Muslims, in the Battle of Siffin (وَقْعة صِفِّين), the First Fitna (فِتْنة). 'Ammār is one of the so-called *Four Pillars of the Sahaba* (الْأَرْكان الْأَرْبعة). This is a Shia term referring to the four companions who stayed most loyal to 'Alī after Muhammad's death. The other three are: 'Abū Dharr al-Ghifārī (أَبُو ذَرّ الْغِفاريّ), Miqdād ibn al-'Aswad (مُقْداد بن الأَسْوَد), and Salmān the Persian (سَلْمان الْفارِسيّ).
- On 11th March 2013, Sunni extremist groups such as al-Nusra Front (جَبْهة النُّصرة) were blamed for the bombing of the shrine of 'Ammār, which is located in al-Raqqa (الرَّقّة) in Syria.

289. Which of Muhammad's companions was described as "the most knowledgeable in halāl and harām"?

Answer: Mu'ādh ibn Jabal (مُعاذ بن جَبَل).

Born	~ 607-602 in Yathrib	Died	639 (18 AH) in the Jordan Valley

Mu'ādh was among those people from Yathrib (Medina) who met with Muhammad at al-'Aqaba in 621 (1 BH) – one year before the al-

Hijra. There, the famous (second) pledge was made at which the new Muslims of Yathrib, including some women, swore to support and defend the Prophet at any cost.

Mu'ādh converted to Islam when he was a young man (perhaps eighteen years old). Wherever Mu'ādh went, people would consult him for legal judgements, because he was brought up in the school of Muhammad himself and had learnt as much as he could from him. Mu'ādh belonged to the group of six who collected the Qur'an during the lifetime of the Prophet.

Muhammad himself praised the knowledge of Mu'ādh. It was narrated from 'Anas ibn Mālik (أَنَس بن مالِك) that the Messenger of Allah said: "The most knowledgeable of what is lawful [halāl] and unlawful [harām] is Mu'ādh ibn Jabal."[393]

After the Conquest of Mecca in 630 (8 AH), when more and more people became Muslim, Muhammad saw the need for teachers to instruct them in the fundamentals of Islam. He appointed 'Attāb ibn 'Asīd (عَتّاب بن أَسِيد) as his deputy in Mecca. 'Attāb was not only the first governor, but also the first permanent civil appointment made in Islam. Muhammad asked Mu'ādh to stay with 'Attāb in order to teach people the Qur'an.

The Prophet also sent Mu'ādh as the head of a group of missionaries to Yemen. The Prophet himself bade farewell to this mission and walked for some distance alongside Mu'ādh. Finally, he told him: "O Mu'ādh, perhaps you shall not meet me again after this year. Perhaps when you return, you shall only see my mosque and my grave."[394]

Muhammad died before Mu'ādh returned from Yemen. When he came back, 'Abū Bakr was already Caliph. Mu'ādh joined the Muslim forces to Syria and died from the plague.

Note: The college for the study of Sharī'a Law at Mosul University - while it was occupied by the terrorist network ISIL (Islamic State of Iraq and the Levant) - was named after Mu'āz ibn Jabal.

---

393 ... أَنَّ رَسُولَ اللَّهِ قَالَ: "أَعْلَمُهُمْ بِالْحَلَالِ وَالْحَرَامِ مُعَاذُ بْنُ جَبَلٍ." Sunan ibn Māja 159 (154)

394 ... يَا مُعَاذُ! إِنَّكَ عَسَى أَلا تَلْقَانِي بَعْدَ عَامِي هَذَا, وَلَعَلَّكَ أَنْ تَمُرَّ بِمَسْجِدِي وَقَبْرِي. Ahmad ibn Hanbal' 21548

290. Which of the companions had the nickname "the learned man of this 'Umma"?

Answer: ʿAbd Allah ibn ʿAbbās (عَبْد الله بن عبّاس).

Born	~ 618 in Mecca		Died	687 in al-Ṭāʾif

ʿAbd Allah was one of Muhammad's cousins and one of the early Qurʾan scholars. He was the son of a wealthy merchant. After he was born, his mother took him to Muhammad who put some of his saliva on the baby's tongue, even before he began to suckle. This was the beginning of the close and intimate tie between ʿAbd Allah and Muhammad.

ʿAbd Allah observed very closely whatever Muhammad did and said. He would run to fetch water for him when he wanted to make the ritual washing – Wuḍūʾ (وُضوء). During prayers, he would stand behind Muhammad. He also followed him closely during battles. It was said that ʿAbd Allah became like the Prophet's shadow.

ʿAbd Allah not only became probably the most learned companion of the Prophet. He also collected Muhammad's words, about 1,660 authentic sayings of the Prophet which are recorded and authenticated in the collections of Imam al-Bukhārī and Imam Muslim. For this reason, ʿAbd Allah became known as "the learned man of this 'Umma" (حَبْر هذِهِ الأُمّة).

291. In the presence of which Prophet's companion did angels feel embarrassed?

Answer: ʿUthmān ibn ʿAffān (عُثْمان بن عَفّان).

Born	576 (47 BH) in al-Ṭāʾif, (present-day Saudi Arabia)		Died	656 (35 AH), aged 79, in Medina.

ʿUthmān was one of the earliest converts to Islam. He was the son of a wealthy man and later became a successful trader and cloth merchant. He belonged to the Umayyad clan. The Umayyads were the most influential branch of the Quraysh tribe. It was said that they were the strongest and wealthiest. 'Uthmān could read and write, which was unusual at that time.

His nickname is *the possessor of two lights* (ذُو النُّورَيْنِ) because he had been married to two daughters of Muhammad: Ruqayya (رُقَيّة) and, after she had passed away, he married 'Umm Kulthūm (أُمّ كُلْثُوم). Muslims say that no other man had ever been married to two daughters of a prophet.

The saying that angels had shown modesty to this man goes back to a story which 'Ā'isha (عائشة بِنْت أَبِي بَكْر) recounted: "The Prophet was lying down in my room with his thigh uncovered when 'Abū Bakr [her father] asked for permission to enter. The Prophet gave him permission to enter, remaining as he was. Then 'Umar asked for permission to come in and the Prophet gave him permission, remaining as he was. Then 'Uthmān asked for permission to enter and the Prophet sat up and arranged his garment, and then he came in and spoke. When he left, I said: 'Messenger of Allah, 'Abū Bakr came in and you did not exert yourself nor concern yourself with him. Then 'Umar came in and you did not exert yourself nor concern yourself with him. Then 'Uthmān came in and you sat up and arranged your garment.' He replied: 'Should I not show modesty to a man whom even the angels show modesty?'"[395]

When 'Uthmān was almost 70 year old, about twelve years after the Prophet's death, 'Uthmān became the new leader of the Muslims: the Caliph. This was in 644 AD (23 AH). He was the third *Rightly Guided Caliph* (الْخُلَفَاء الرَّاشِدُونَ) - as the Sunni doctrine calls the first four Caliphs - and ruled for around twelve years.

Like his predecessor, 'Uthmān was assassinated. Rebels were upset and accused him of appointing his kin, the clan of the Banū 'Umayya (بَنُو أُمَيّة), to key positions. His house became under siege and was set on fire, while some attackers were able to jump into the back of his house where they found 'Uthmān reading the Qur'an. They stabbed him to death.

---

395 ...قَالَتْ كَانَ رَسُولُ اللَّهِ مُضْطَجِعًا فِي بَيْتِي كَاشِفًا عَنْ فَخِذَيْهِ أَوْ سَاقَيْهِ فَاسْتَأْذَنَ أَبُو بَكْرٍ فَأَذِنَ لَهُ وَهُوَ عَلَى تِلْكَ الْحَالِ فَتَحَدَّثَ ثُمَّ اسْتَأْذَنَ عُمَرُ فَأَذِنَ لَهُ وَهُوَ كَذَلِكَ فَتَحَدَّثَ ثُمَّ اسْتَأْذَنَ عُثْمَانُ فَجَلَسَ رَسُولُ اللَّهِ وَسَوَّى ثِيَابَهُ - قَالَ مُحَمَّدٌ وَلاَ أَقُولُ ذَلِكَ فِي يَوْمٍ وَاحِدٍ - فَدَخَلَ فَتَحَدَّثَ فَلَمَّا خَرَجَ قَالَتْ عَائِشَةُ دَخَلَ أَبُو بَكْرٍ فَلَمْ تَهْتَشَّ لَهُ وَلَمْ تُبَالِهِ ثُمَّ دَخَلَ عُمَرُ فَلَمْ تَهْتَشَّ لَهُ وَلَمْ تُبَالِهِ ثُمَّ دَخَلَ عُثْمَانُ فَجَلَسْتَ وَسَوَّيْتَ ثِيَابَكَ فَقَالَ: "أَلاَ أَسْتَحِي مِنْ رَجُلٍ تَسْتَحِي مِنْهُ الْمَلاَئِكَةُ." Sahīh Muslim
2401

At the time, 'Uthmān's death had a polarising effect in the Muslim world. It started the first Islamic civil war, also called the First Fitna.

'Uthmān is one of "the ten (who were) promised Paradise" – so-called al-'Ashra al-Mubashsharūn bi al-Janna (الْعَشرة الْمُبشَّرون بالْجنّة). Muhammad - in a Hadith accepted by Sunni Muslims but rejected by Shia Muslims - named ten of his companions who were promised Paradise.[396]

Although the names are not entirely certain, they could be the fol-lowing: 'Abū Bakr (أَبُو بَكْر), 'Umar ibn al-Khattāb (عُمَر بن الْخطّاب), 'Uth-mān ibn 'Affān (عُثمان بن عَفّان), 'Alī ibn 'Abī Tālib (عَلِيّ بن أَبي طالِب), Talha ibn 'Ubayd Allah (طَلْحة بن عُبَيد لله), al-Zubayr (الزُّبَير), 'Abd al-Rahmān ibn 'Awf (عَبْد الرَّحْمن بن عَوْف), Sa'd ibn 'Abī Waqqās (سَعْد بن أَبِي وَقّاص), Saīd ibn Zayd (سَعِيد بن زَيْد), and 'Abū 'Ubayda ibn al-Jarrāh (أَبُو عُبَيْدة بن الْجَرّاح).

292. Who was called the "leader of the hypocrites"?

Answer: 'Abd Allah ibn 'Ubayy (عَبْد الله بن أُبَيّ).

Born	unknown	Died	631 (9 AH)

'Abd Allah ibn 'Ubayy had several conflicts with the Prophet. Islamic sources therefore refer to him as *Munāfiq* (hypocrite). He was labelled as the *leader of the hypocrites* (رَأْس الْمُنافِقِين).

Before Muhammad had started his Islamic mission, 'Abd Allah was the most outstanding leader of the people of Medina (then known as Yathrib). 'Abd Allah had never forgiven the Prophet for outshining him.

When the attacks on the Prophet and his followers in Mecca con-centrated, Muhammad decided to escape to Yathrib. The followers who migrated with him are called the Muhājirūn. According to some Islamic sources, 'Abd Allah ibn 'Ubayy tried to persuade the people

---

396 ...أَنَّهُ كَانَ في الْمَسْجِدِ فَذَكَرَ رَجُلٌ عَلِيًّا فَقَامَ سَعِيدُ بْنُ زَيْدٍ فَقَالَ أَشْهَدُ عَلَى رَسُولِ اللَّهِ أَنِّي
سَمِعْتُهُ وَهُوَ يَقُولُ: "عَشْرَةٌ في الْجَنَّةِ النَّبِيُّ في الْجَنَّةِ وَأَبُو بَكْرٍ في الْجَنَّةِ وَعُمَرُ في الْجَنَّةِ وَعُثْمَانُ في
الْجَنَّةِ وَعَلِيٌّ في الْجَنَّةِ وَطَلْحَةُ في الْجَنَّةِ وَالزُّبَيْرُ بْنُ الْعَوَّام في الْجَنَّةِ وَسَعْدُ بْنُ مَالِكٍ في الْجَنَّةِ وَعَبْدُ
الرَّحْمَن بْنُ عَوْفٍ في الْجَنَّةِ." Sunan 'Abi Dāwūd 4649

of Yathrib to withdraw their material support for the Prophet and his followers.

This would have forced the Muhājirūn to leave Medina again because most of them were very poor. However, the Prophet's supporters in Medina - the 'Ansār (الْأَنْصار) - rejected this.

It is not clear how 'Abd Allah reacted to that though some sources claim that he converted to Islam, but this is questionable. There are stories indicating that he was still opposing the Prophet and that he played a rather furtive game. A verse in sura 63 *The Hypocrites* - in Arabic: al-Munāfiqūn (سُورة الْمُنافِقُونَ) - is related to 'Abd Allah:

63:8	They say, 'Once we return to Medina the powerful will drive out the weak', but power belongs to God, to His Messenger, and to the believers, though the hypocrites do not know this.	يَقُولُونَ لَئِن رَّجَعْنَا إِلَى الْمَدِينَةِ لَيُخْرِجَنَّ الْأَعَزُّ مِنْهَا الْأَذَلَّ وَلِلَّهِ الْعِزَّةُ وَلِرَسُولِهِ وَلِلْمُؤْمِنِينَ وَلَكِنَّ الْمُنَافِقِينَ لَا يَعْلَمُونَ.

Let's look at sura 4 *Women* - in Arabic: al-Nisā' (سُورة النِّساء) - which also deals with the so-called *hypocrites*:

4:61	When they are told, 'Turn to God's revelations and the Messenger [for judgement]', you see the hypocrites turn right away from you [Prophet].	وَإِذَا قِيلَ لَهُمْ تَعَالَوْا إِلَى مَا أَنزَلَ اللَّهُ وَإِلَى الرَّسُولِ رَأَيْتَ الْمُنَافِقِينَ يَصُدُّونَ عَنكَ صُدُودًا.

The classical commentators see in this verse a reference to the hypocrites of Medina who pretended to be Muhammad's followers, but did not really believe in his teachings.

The second major battle between the Muslims in Medina and their enemies in Mecca, the Battle of 'Uhud (غَزْوة أُحُد), convinced the Muslims that there were hypocrites among them, especially among their allies in Medina. For this important battle, Muhammad's army consisted of less than one thousand men. On the way to Mount 'Uhud, this number was further reduced, caused by the defection of some three hundred men – who were led by 'Abd Allah ibn 'Ubayy.

Furthermore, 'Abd Allah played a role in the fight between Muhammad and the Jewish tribe Banū al-Nadīr in 625 (4 AH). The

Prophet had been informed that some members of the Banū al-Nadīr planned to assassinate him. The Prophet then sent a message to the Jewish clans and tribes telling them to leave Medina. However, the Banū al-Nadīr resisted Muhammad.

The Muslim historian Ibn 'Ishāq claimed that 'Abd Allah had promised the Jewish clan leaders two thousand warriors in case they decided to remain in their fortified settlements on the outskirts of Medina. The Banū al-Nadīr followed his advice and put up resistance against the Prophet. The Muslims besieged their fortresses for more than two weeks, but when the promised warriors of 'Abd Allah ibn 'Ubayy's did not show up, the Banū al-Nadīr eventually surrendered. Muhammad then expelled the entire tribe. Most of them migrated to Syria in a caravan of about six hundred camels; some families chose to settle in the oasis of Khaybar, while a few individuals went as far as lower Mesopotamia. Most of their fields and plantations were confiscated by the Muslims.

In addition, there are claims that 'Abd Allah ibn 'Ubayy was among the people who spread the rumours about 'Ā'isha (عائشة بِنْت أَبِي بَكْر), Muhammad's wife, in the so-called *Incident of Slander/Ifk*.

'Abd Allah ibn 'Ubayy died in 631 (9 AH).

There is a famous Hadith about his death which was narrated by 'Abd Allah ibn 'Abbās (عَبْد الله بن عَبّاس): "When 'Abd Allah ibn 'Ubayy died, his son ['Abd Allah ibn 'Abd Allah] came to Allah's Messenger and asked him for his shirt so that he could shroud his father in it. He gave it to him, and then the son asked the Prophet if he could offer the funeral prayer for his father. Allah's Messenger got up to offer the funeral prayer, but 'Umar stood up too and grabbed the garment of Allah's Messenger and said: 'O Allah's Messenger, will you offer the funeral prayer for him ['Abd Allah] though your Lord forbade you to pray for him?'

Allah's Messenger replied: 'But Allah has given me the choice by saying: 'It makes no difference whether you ask forgiveness for them or not: Allah will not forgive them even if you ask seventy times, because they reject Allah and His Messenger. Allah does not guide those who rebel against Him.' [sura 9:80][397] So I will ask more than seventy times.' 'Umar said: 'But he ['Abd Allah ibn 'Ubayy] is a hypocrite!' However, Allah's Messenger did offer the funeral prayer whereupon Allah revealed [sura 9:84][398]: 'Do not hold prayers for any of them when they die, and do not stand by their graves: they disbelieved in Allah and His Messenger and died rebellious.'"[399]

The last part of this Hadith is difficult to understand. Should Muhammad have rejected the request to offer a funeral prayer for 'Abd Allah? Some scholars use this Hadith to say that Allah was mad at Muhammad and therefore revealed the verse 9:84 upon this event.

Other scholars, however, refuse this idea. Muhammad Asad claimed in his commentary on verse 9:84 that the verse is not about 'Abd Allah ibn 'Ubayy. In his view, 'Abd Allah died some time after the Prophet's return from the Battle of Tabūk; however, most parts of sura 84 were revealed during the Battle of Tabūk which took place in October 630 (9 AH). This shows, according to Muhammad Asad, that "the prohibition expressed in this verse relates only to unrepentant sinners."

293. Who was nicknamed "she of the two belts"?

Answer: ʾAsmāʾ bint ʾAbī Bakr (أَسْماء بِنْت أَبِي بَكْر).

Born	ca. 595 CE (27 BH) in Mecca, Arabia	Died	ca. 692 CE (73 AH), aged 97, in Mecca

---

397 ...اسْتَغْفِرْ لَهُمْ أَوْ لَا تَسْتَغْفِرْ لَهُمْ إِن تَسْتَغْفِرْ لَهُمْ سَبْعِينَ مَرَّةً فَلَن يَغْفِرَ اللَّهُ لَهُمْ ذَلِكَ بِأَنَّهُمْ كَفَرُوا بِاللَّهِ وَرَسُولِهِ وَاللَّهُ لَا يَهْدِي الْقَوْمَ الْفَاسِقِينَ. sura 9:80

398 ...وَلَا تُصَلِّ عَلَى أَحَدٍ مِّنْهُم مَّاتَ أَبَدًا وَلَا تَقُمْ عَلَى قَبْرِهِ إِنَّهُمْ كَفَرُوا بِاللَّهِ وَرَسُولِهِ وَمَاتُوا وَهُمْ فَاسِقُونَ. sura 9:84

399 ...قَالَ لَمَّا تُوُفِّيَ عَبْدُ اللَّهِ جَاءَ ابْنُهُ عَبْدُ اللَّهِ بْنُ عَبْدِ اللَّهِ إِلَى رَسُولِ اللَّهِ فَسَأَلَهُ أَنْ يُعْطِيَهُ قَمِيصَهُ يُكَفِّنُ فِيهِ أَبَاهُ فَأَعْطَاهُ، ثُمَّ سَأَلَهُ أَنْ يُصَلِّيَ عَلَيْهِ، فَقَامَ رَسُولُ اللَّهِ لِيُصَلِّيَ فَقَامَ عُمَرُ فَأَخَذَ بِثَوْبِ رَسُولِ اللَّهِ فَقَالَ يَا رَسُولَ اللَّهِ تُصَلِّي عَلَيْهِ وَقَدْ نَهَاكَ رَبُّكَ أَنْ تُصَلِّيَ عَلَيْهِ فَقَالَ رَسُولُ اللَّهِ: "إِنَّمَا خَيَّرَنِي اللَّهُ فَقَالَ {اسْتَغْفِرْ لَهُمْ أَوْ لَا تَسْتَغْفِرْ لَهُمْ إِن تَسْتَغْفِرْ لَهُمْ سَبْعِينَ مَرَّةً} وَسَأَزِيدُهُ عَلَى السَّبْعِينَ." قَالَ إِنَّهُ مُنَافِقٌ. قَالَ فَصَلَّى عَلَيْهِ رَسُولُ اللَّهِ فَأَنْزَلَ اللَّهُ {وَلَا تُصَلِّ عَلَى أَحَدٍ مِنْهُم مَاتَ أَبَدًا وَلَا تَقُمْ عَلَى قَبْرِهِ}. Sahīh al-Bukhārī 4670

'Asmā' was not only 'Abū Bakr's daughter, but also one of Muhammad's companions.

'Asmā' was the half sister of 'Ā'isha (عائشة بِنْت أَبِي بَكْر), who was ten years younger and one of Muhammad's wives.

It was in 622, when Muhammad and 'Abū Bakr sought refuge in the cave of Thawr - Mount Bull (جَبَل ثَوْر) - outside of Mecca while migrating to Medina (Yathrib). 'Asmā' provided them with food and water. So how come that she was named *she of the two belts/owner of the two belts* – in Arabic: Dhāt al-Nitāqayn (ذَات النِّطَاقَيْن)?

'Asmā' herself narrated in a Hadith how this happened: "I prepared the journey food for the Prophet and 'Abū Bakr when they wanted [to migrate to] Medina. I said to my father ['Abū Bakr]: 'I do not have anything to tie the container of the journey food with except my waist belt.' He said: 'Divide it lengthwise into two.'

I did so; and for this reason I was named Dhāt al-Nitāqayn [i.e. *the owner of two belts*].[400]

294. What is the nickname of Hamza ibn 'Abd al-Muttalib?

Answer: Chief of the Martyrs. In Arabic: Sayyid al-Shuhadā' (سَيِّد الشُّهَداء).

Born	ca. 568 CE (54 BH) in Mecca	Died	ca. 625 CE (3 AH), aged 57, in the mountains of 'Uhud

Hamza ibn 'Abd al-Muttalib (حَمْزة بن عَبد الْمُطَّلِب) was a paternal uncle of the Prophet who later became a companion. Hamza was also Muhammad's foster brother, because they had both been suckled by the same slave: Thuwayba (ثُوَيْبة).

If this is true, Muhammad and Hamza should have been almost of the same age. Some scholars say that Hamza was four years older, others say two. 'Abd Allah ibn 'Abbās (عَبْد الله بن عَبّاس) narrated that the Prophet said the following about Hamza's daughter: "I am not legally permitted to marry her, as foster relations are treated like

---

400 ...صَنَعْتُ سُفْرَةً لِلنَّبِيّ وَأَبِي بَكْرٍ حِينَ أَرَادَا الْمَدِينَةَ، فَقُلْتُ لِأَبِي مَا أَجِدُ شَيْئًا أَرْبُطُهُ إِلاَّ نِطَاقِي. قَالَ فَشُقِّيه. فَفَعَلْتُ، فَسُمِّيتُ ذَاتَ النِّطَاقَيْن. Sahīh al-Bukhārī 3907

blood relations [in marital affairs]. She is the daughter of my foster brother."[401]

Hamza was skilled in wrestling, archery and swordsmanship. Muslims like to describe him as the "strongest man of the Quraysh" and see in him one of the greatest fighters and warriors of the Muslims. Hamza was therefore nicknamed "Lion of Allah" – 'Asad Allah (أَسَد الله). When he was fighting in battles, he had an ostrich feather in his turban.

Hamza was killed in the Battle of 'Uhud in 625 (3 AH) at the age of 57. In this battle, he killed a standard-bearer of the Muslim's enemy. When he was fighting his way through the enemy, he was hit by a javelin hurled by Wahshī, an Abyssinian slave. Wahshī later said that he had "killed the best of men".

Muhammad said about Hamza: "The master of martyrs on the Day of Resurrection is Hamza ibn 'Abd al-Muttalib."[402]

295. The body of which Prophet's companion was embodied by Archangel Gabriel?

Answer: Dihya al-Kalbī (دِحْية الْكَلْبِي).

Born	year unknown		Died	died ~ 50 (AH)

Dihya al-Kalbī was the envoy - a sort of ambassador or early Muslim diplomat - of Muhammad to the Roman Emperor Heraclius, and Dihya was thus the man who delivered the Prophet's messages. There is not much known about him. In Islamic sources, Dihya is described as a handsome man among the companions of Muhammad. Dihya is rarely mentioned in the Hadiths, and when he is, rarely plays an important role.

'Anas ibn Mālik (أَنَس بن مالك) narrated that the Messenger of Allah offered the morning prayer when it was still dark, then he rode and said: "Allāhu 'akbar! Khaybar is ruined. When we approach closely a

---

401 ...قَالَ النَّبِيُّ في بِنْتِ حَمْزَةَ: "لاَ تَحِلُّ لِي، يَحْرُمُ مِنَ الرَّضَاعِ مَا يَحْرُمُ مِنَ النَّسَبِ، هِيَ بِنْتُ أَخِي مِنَ الرَّضَاعَةِ." Sahīh al-Bukhārī 2645.

402 ...سَيِّدُ الشُّهَدَاءِ يَوْمَ الْقِيَامَةِ حَمْزَةُ بْنُ عَبْدِ الْمُطَّلِبِ. Mustadrak al-Hakim (3/215) no. 4884.

nation, most unfortunate is the morning of those who have been warned."

The Hadith continues: The people came out into the streets saying: "Muhammad and his army!" Allah's Messenger vanquished them by force and their warriors were killed, while the children and women were taken as captives. Safīya bint Huyayy (صَفِيّة بِنْت حُيَيّ) was taken by Dihya al-Kalbī – and later she belonged to Allah's Apostle who married her, and her Mahr (مَهْر) was her manumission [amount to free a slave]."[403]

Note: When talking about marriage, a Mahr is similar to a dowry. A Mahr is a mandatory payment in the form of money or possessions paid or promised to pay by the groom or by the groom's father to the bride at the time of marriage; this then legally becomes her property.

So what has the Archangel Gabriel to do with Dihya? Angels are created from light and don't have a human body. According to some accounts, Muhammad saw Gabriel twice in the form that Gabriel was created – and on other occasions as a man resembling Dihya al-Kalbī. This is mentioned in a Hadith:

'Abū 'Uthmān al-Nahdī (أبو عثمان النَّهدي) narrated: "I received the news that Gabriel came to the Prophet while 'Umm Salama was present. Gabriel started talking [to the Prophet] and then left. The Prophet asked 'Umm Salama: 'Do you know who it was?' [or a similar question]. She answered: 'It was Dihya.'"[404]

Note: There is a village that is named after Dihya. It is called el-Dahi, also spelled ad-Dahi (الدَّحِي) or Dahi (דחי) in Hebrew. It is an Arab village in north eastern Israel.

---

403 ...أَنَّ رَسُولَ اللَّهِ صَلَّى اللَّهُ الصُّبْحَ بِغَلَسٍ ثُمَّ رَكِبَ فَقَالَ: "اللَّهُ أَكْبَرُ خَرِبَتْ خَيْبَرُ، إِنَّا إِذَا نَزَلْنَا بِسَاحَةِ قَوْمٍ فَسَاءَ صَبَاحُ الْمُنْذَرِينَ." فَخَرَجُوا يَسْعَوْنَ فِي السِّكَكِ وَيَقُولُونَ مُحَمَّدٌ وَالْخَمِيسُ قَالَ وَالْخَمِيسُ الْجَيْشُ فَظَهَرَ عَلَيْهِمْ رَسُولُ اللَّهِ فَقَتَلَ الْمُقَاتِلَةَ وَسَبَى الذَّرَارِيَّ، فَصَارَتْ صَفِيَّةُ لِدِحْيَةَ الْكَلْبِيِّ، وَصَارَتْ لِرَسُولِ اللَّهِ ثُمَّ تَزَوَّجَهَا وَجَعَلَ صَدَاقَهَا عِتْقَهَا. فَقَالَ عَبْدُ الْعَزِيزِ لِثَابِتٍ يَا أَبَا مُحَمَّدٍ، أَنْتَ سَأَلْتَ أَنَسًا مَا أَمْهَرَهَا قَالَ أَمْهَرَهَا نَفْسَهَا. فَتَبَسَّمَ. Sahīh al-Bukhārī 947.

404 ...قَالَ أُنْبِئْتُ أَنَّ جِبْرِيلَ أَتَى النَّبِيَّ وَعِنْدَهُ أُمُّ سَلَمَةَ، فَجَعَلَ يُحَدِّثُ ثُمَّ قَامَ، فَقَالَ النَّبِيُّ لِأُمِّ سَلَمَةَ: "مَنْ هَذَا؟" أَوْ كَمَا قَالَ. قَالَ قَالَتْ هَذَا دِحْيَةُ. قَالَتْ أُمُّ سَلَمَةَ ايْمُ اللَّهِ مَا حَسِبْتُهُ إِلَّا إِيَّاهُ حَتَّى سَمِعْتُ خُطْبَةَ نَبِيِّ اللَّهِ يُخْبِرُ جِبْرِيلَ. Sahīh al-Bukhārī 3634.

296. The body of which companion was washed by angels after his martyrdom at 'Uhud?

Answer: Hanzala ibn 'Abī 'Āmir (حَنْظَلة بن أَبي عامِر).

Born	date unknown; in Yathrib	Died	625 (3 AH) in the mountains of 'Uhud

Hanzala was killed in the Battle of 'Uhud (غَزْوة أُحُد), the second major battle between the Muslims and their enemies in Mecca, when he was about 24 years old. He married during the Battle of 'Uhud and asked the Prophet if he was allowed to spend the wedding night with his wife – and Muhammad said yes.

The next morning, Hanzala rushed to the battlefield, without having performed the so-called Ghusl (غُسل), the ritual cleansing of impurities from his body. Hanzala was a foot soldier and managed to assault the mount of the enemy's leader, 'Abū Sufyān ibn Harb (أَبو سُفيان بن حَرْب), in order to kill him, but Hanzala got killed first.

What is important here is the fact that a martyr, according to Islam, does not need a ritual washing of the whole body; he is clean anyhow. However, when Muhammad asked Hanzala's family, he was informed that Hanzala did not have a chance for the ritual washing of the body after the wedding night. Such ablution (a Ghusl) after sex is mandatory in Islam.

Muslims call the condition after sexual intercourse or seminal discharge (masturbation) Janāba (جَنابة). In Islamic law, this condition is a major impurity, and the person, therefore, is junub (جُنُب), i.e. *impure*. In such a case, according to Islamic rules, a person needs to clean the body entirely. Otherwise, you are not allowed to offer your daily prayers or enter a mosque.

The Arabic term junub is derived from the verb janaba (جَنَب) which means: *he made (a thing) remote*. We could thus say that it signifies one's remoteness from prayer because of the immersion in sexual passion.

'Ā'isha (عائشة بِنْت أَبي بَكْر) narrated: "I used to wash the traces of Janāba [semen] from the clothes of the Prophet and he used to go for prayers while traces of water were still on it [water spots were still visible]."[405]

So what happened to Hanzala? Although he was a martyr and automatically clean according to Islam, his dead body was washed – and this makes Hanzala special. Because of this honour, Muslims call Hanzala *the one cleansed by the angels* – in Arabic: Ghasīl al-Malā'ika (غَسِيل الْمَلائكة).

'Abd Allah ibn 'Abbās (عَبْد الله بن عَبّاس) narrated that the Messenger of Allah said [about Hanzala]: "The Angels washed your companion. He went out of the house and was in a state of Junb." The Prophet said: "That is why the angels washed him."[406]

Note: It is said that Hanzala's wife became pregnant in the wedding night. Her son was called 'Abd Allah.

Many years later, in 683, 'Abd Allah became the main leader of the resistance in Medina in the Battle of al-Harra (وَقْعَة الْحَرّة) against Caliph Yazīd ibn Mu'āwiya (يَزيد بن مُعاوية) – commonly known as Yazīd I. Yazīd was the second Caliph of the Umayyad Caliphate in Damascus and the first one through inheritance. He was a military commander but had only little experience in governance. Some claim that he drank alcohol and was extremely brutal. He had the reputation of an unjust ruler.

During his reign (680 - 683), cruel and crucial events took place. It was a period of instability and wars:

- The killing of Husayn ibn 'Alī (who refused to pledge allegiance to Yazīd) in the Battle of Karbalā' in October 680 (61 AH). Husayn is a very important figure for Shia Muslims.
- The Battle of al-Harra (at Medina) in summer 683 (63 AH), in which one of Yazīd's generals assaulted and plundered Medina. The people of Medina rebelled against the Caliph and refused to

---

405 ...قَالَتْ كُنْتُ أَغْسِلُ الْجَنَابَةَ مِنْ ثَوْبِ النَّبِيِّ، فَيَخْرُجُ إِلَى الصَّلاةِ، وَإِنَّ بُقَعَ الْمَاءِ في ثَوْبِهِ. Sahīh al-Bukhārī 229

406 ...أَنَّ رَسُولَ اللَّهِ قَالَ: "إِنَّ صَاحِبَكُمْ تَغْسِلُهُ الْمَلائِكَةُ، يَعْنِي حَنْظَلَةَ، فَاسْأَلُوا أَهْلَهُ مَا شَأْنُهُ، فَسُئِلَتْ صَاحِبَتُهُ، فَقَالَتْ: خَرَجَ وَهُوَ جُنُبٌ حِينَ سَمِعَ الْهَائِعَةَ، فَقَالَ رَسُولُ اللَّهِ: لِذَلِكَ غَسَّلَتْهُ الْمَلائِكَةُ". al-Sunan al-Kubrā li al-Bahayqī 6296 or al-Mustadrak 4905

pledge allegiance. A popular uprising followed, and people were fed up with the Caliph's politics. The rebelling people had no political programme, nor a plan.

When the Caliph sent his troops from Syria and attacked Medina, the people in Medina tried to imitate the Prophet's military tactics. They dug trenches as the Prophet did in the Battle of the Trench (غَزوة الْخَنْدَق) in 627 (5 AH). Their leaders called upon fighting until death (as the companions of the Prophet did). It didn't work out. The battle ended in a massacre; several companions of Muhammad were killed. The assault on Medina and its destruction is one of the darkest chapters in Islamic history.

- The burning of the Ka'ba during the Siege of Mecca in September 683 (64 AH). The assault was blamed on one of the commanders of Yazīd I. The people of Mecca rebelled against the Caliph too, for similar reasons like the people of Medina. Their leader was 'Abd Allah ibn al-Zubayr (عَبْد الله بن الزُّبَيْر). The battles (of Medina and Mecca) were among the first tragic events of the second Islamic civil war.

Yazīd ruled as Caliph only for three years. He died in November 683 at the age of 36. It is said that his own horse killed him when Yazīd lost control over it.

297. Allah's throne shook at the death of which of Muhammad's companions?

Answer: Sa'd ibn Mu'ādh (سَعْد بن مُعَاذ).

Born	unknown; maybe in 32 BH in Yathrib	Died	627 (5 AH), possibly aged 36, at Medina

Sa'd was the chief of the Banū al-'Aws (بَنُو الْأَوْس) tribe, one of the two main Arab tribes of Medina - the other major tribe was the Banū Khazraj (بَنُو خَزْرَج) in Medina - and became an important companion of Muhammad in the early Medina days.

Saʻd became Muslim in 622 (1 AH) after the arrival of Muhammad in Yathrib which then became Medina. Saʻd became one of the leading persons among the ʾAnsār (الْأَنْصار).

What happened then?

Muhammad had expelled the Jewish tribe Banū al-Nadīr (بَنُو النَّضِير). They then wanted to take vengeance and attack together with other tribes the Prophet in Medina. Following this, some Arabian tribes formed a confederacy in an effort to finish off Islam. In January 627 (5 AH), a force of over 10,000 men of the Quraysh and their allies approached Medina. The Medina defenders (the Muslims) numbered 3,000. The Prophet ordered to dig a trench around the town which made the enemy's cavalry useless. This fight, a 27-day long siege of Medina, became known as the *Battle of the Trench* (غَزْوة الخَنْدَق), also called the *Battle of Confederates* (غَزْوة الْأَحْزاب). A stalemate was the result.

So what about Saʻd?

Saʻd had been wounded in earlier battles. He was known as a fierce fighter and one of the few companions who remained on the battlefield of the second major fight, the Battle of ʾUhud.

During the Battle of the Trench, Saʻd ibn Muʻādh was struck by an arrow which severed a vein in his forearm. The Prophet tried to help him cauterising the wounds, but Saʻd died of his wounds a month later. Jābir ibn ʻAbd Allah (جابِر بن عَبد الله) narrated that he heard the Prophet say: "The Throne [of Allah] shook at the death of Saʻd ibn Muʻādh."[407]

Weeks before he died, Saʻd ibn Muʻādh played a major role in the extinction of the Jewish tribe Banū Qurayza (بَنُو قُرَيْظة). Although he was injured in the Battle of the Trench, he functioned as an arbitrator in the dispute between the Prophet and the Jewish tribe. When the non-Muslims attacked Medina, the Jews of this tribe - who had a pact with Muhammad – instead conspired with the enemy. The final verdict was the obliteration of this tribe.

---

407 ...سَمِعتُ النَّبِيَّ يَقُولُ: "اهْتَزَّ الْعَرْشُ لِمَوْتِ سَعدِ بْنِ مُعَاذٍ." Sahīh al-Bukhārī 3803

'Anas ibn Mālik (أَنَس بن مالك) narrated: "When the funeral of Sa'd ibn Mu'ādh took place, the hypocrites said: 'How light [simple] his funeral is.' And this was due to his judgement concerning Banū Qurayza. So this reached the Prophet and he said: 'Indeed, the angels were carrying him.'"[408]

How do Muslims view the "shaking"?

It is not entirely clear what the "shaking of the throne" means. Could it be the joy of Allah [=The Throne] because one of his slaves was coming? Such is indicated in a Hadith. 'Abū Mūsā (أَبُو مُوسَى) narrated that the Prophet said: "Whoever loves the meeting with Allah, Allah too loves the meeting with him; and whoever hates the meeting with Allah, Allah too hates the meeting with him."[409] However, the "shaking" should have happened many times then.

Even after Sa'd's death, Muhammad made a reference to him. Al-Barā' ibn 'Āzib (الْبَراء بن عازب) narrated that a silken cloth was given to the Prophet as a present. His companions touched it and admired its softness. The Prophet said: "Are you admiring its softness? The handkerchiefs of Sa'd ibn Mu'ādh [in Paradise] are better and softer than it."[410]

Note: There is a famous misquote.

In some books and internet forums, the following quote is mistakenly attributed to Sa'd: "Messenger of Allah, you want us [to speak]. By God in whose control is my life, if you order us to plunge our horses into the sea, we would do so. If you order us to goad our horses to the most distant place like Bark al-Ghimād, we would do so."[411]

---

408 ...قَالَ لَمَّا حُمِلَتْ جَنَازَةُ سَعْدِ بْنِ مُعَاذٍ قَالَ الْمُنَافِقُونَ مَا أَخَفَّ جَنَازَتَهُ. وَذَلِكَ لِحُكْمِهِ فِي بَنِي قُرْظَةَ فَبَلَغَ ذَلِكَ النَّبِيَّ فَقَالَ: "إِنَّ الْمَلَائِكَةَ كَانَتْ تَحْمِلُهُ." Jāmi' al-Tirmidhī 4220 (3849)

409 ...النَّبِيُّ قَالَ: "مَنْ أَحَبَّ لِقَاءَ اللَّهِ أَحَبَّ اللَّهُ لِقَاءَهُ، وَمَنْ كَرِهَ لِقَاءَ اللَّهِ كَرِهَ اللَّهُ لِقَاءَهُ." Sahīh al-Bukhārī 6508

410 ...يَقُولُ أُهْدِيَتْ لِلنَّبِيِّ حُلَّةُ حَرِيرٍ، فَجَعَلَ أَصْحَابُهُ يَمَسُّونَهَا وَيَعْجَبُونَ مِنْ لِينِهَا فَقَالَ: "أَتَعْجَبُونَ مِنْ لِينِ هَذِهِ لَمَنَادِيلُ سَعْدِ بْنِ مُعَاذٍ خَيْرٌ مِنْهَا." Sahīh al-Bukhārī 3802

411 ...إِيَّانَا تُرِيدُ يَا رَسُولَ اللَّهِ وَالَّذِي نَفْسِي بِيَدِهِ لَوْ أَمَرْتَنَا أَنْ نُخِيضَهَا الْبَحْرَ لَأَخَضْنَاهَا وَلَوْ أَمَرْتَنَا أَنْ نَضْرِبَ أَكْبَادَهَا إِلَى بَرْكِ الْغِمَادِ لَفَعَلْنَا. Sahīh Muslim 1779

In fact this was Sa'd ibn 'Ubāda (سَعْد بن عُبادة) who was the leader of another Arab tribe, the Banū Khazraj (بَنُو خَزْرَج).

298. Which Prophet's companion is called "custodian of the 'Umma"?

Answer: ʾAbū ʿUbayda ibn al-Jarrāḥ (أَبُو عُبَيْدة بن الْجَرَّاح).

Born	584 (40 BH) in Mecca	Died	639 (18 AH) in the Jordan Valley due to the Plague of Emmaus

ʾAbū ʿUbayda was the son of a merchant. He became one of Muhammad's companions and is said to have embraced Islam just a day after ʾAbū Bakr did in the year 611 (11 BH).

In the year 624, ʾAbū ʿUbayda participated in the first major battle between the Muslims in Medina and their enemies in Mecca, in the Battle of Badr (غَزْوة بَدْر). In this fight, he was attacked by his father 'Abd Allah who was fighting alongside the army of the Quraysh. ʾAbū ʿUbayda avoided fighting him, but his father eventually succeeded in blocking ʾAbū ʿUbayda's path. ʾAbū ʿUbayda attacked and killed his father.

It is difficult and disturbing when a man kills his own father. Most Muslims I talked to justified it by saying that in a way it could be argued that ʾAbū ʿUbayda did not kill his father, but that he merely killed the polytheism personified by his father.

How did ʾAbū ʿUbayda get his nickname Custodian of the 'Umma – in Arabic: ʾAmīn al-ʾUmma (أَمِين الْأُمَّة)? This is found in a Hadith. ʾAnas ibn Mālik (أَنَس بن مالك) narrated that the Prophet said: "Every nation has an ʾAmīn [i.e. the most honest man], and the ʾAmīn of this nation is ʾAbū ʿUbayda ibn al-Jarrāḥ."[412]

ʾAbū ʾUbayda is famous for his principles. Shortly after the Prophet had died, during the reign of Caliph 'Umar ibn al-Khattāb (عُمَر بن الْخَطَّاب), the Plague broke out in Syria and western Iraq. When the

---

412 ...النَّبِيُّ قَالَ: "لِكُلِّ أُمَّةٍ أَمِينٌ، وَأَمِينُ هَذِهِ الْأُمَّةِ أَبُو عُبَيْدَةَ بْنُ الْجَرَّاح." Sahīh al-Bukhārī 4382

news of the Plague reached him, 'Abū 'Ubayda was in the region while he was engaged in wars with the Byzantine (Roman) Empire.

The Muslims had fought on the southern borders of the Byzantine Empire, even prior to Muhammad's death, in the Battle of Mu'ta in 629 (غَزْوة مُؤْتة), but the real invasion began in 634 under the Prophet's successors, the caliphs 'Abū Bakr and 'Umar.

After exhausting wars with Persia, the Byzantine Empire was on the verge of collapse. After the recapture of Syria from the Persians (Sassanians), Byzantine Emperor Heraclius had to deal with a new enemy which he had perhaps underestimated: the Muslims. Most of the Byzantine army had remained in northern Syria preventing any Persian attack, and the Muslims could take advantage of this when the Islamic troops emerged from the desert in the south.

Although the Muslims had less military experience and weaponry, they literally overran the Byzantine soldiers. The Muslim army conquered Syria, Iraq, Lebanon and Palestine in no time. It is not clear why the Plague finally broke out, but some historians claim that the Muslims did not bury the slain Byzantine soldiers or at least did not bury them properly.

When Caliph 'Umar wanted to make 'Abū 'Ubayda his successor, he didn't want him to remain in the epidemic region. 'Umar therefore dispatched a courier to 'Abū 'Ubayda with a message saying that he urges him to leave: "I am in urgent need of you. If my letter reaches you at night, I strongly urge you to leave before dawn. If this letter reaches you during the day, I strongly urge you to leave before evening and hasten to me."[413]

When 'Abū 'Ubayda received the letter, he wrote back to 'Umar: "I know that you need me. But I am with an army of Muslims, and I have the desire to save myself from what is afflicting them. I do not want to separate from them until Allah wills. So, when this letter reaches you, release me from the command and permit me to stay on."[414]

---

413 ...إِنِّي بَدَتْ لِي إِلَيْكَ حاجةٌ، لا غِنى لي عنك فيها، فَإِنْ أتاكَ كِتابي هذا، إِنْ أتاكَ لَيْلاً فإني أعْزِمُ
عليك ألاَّ تُصْبِحُ حتى تَرْكَبَ إلَيَّ، وإنْ أتاكَ كِتابي نهاراً فإني أعْزِمُ عليك ألاَّ تُمْسي حتى تَرْكَبَ إلَيَّ.
Ibn Kathīr, al-Bidāya wa al-Nihāya

When Caliph 'Umar read this letter, tears filled his eyes and those who were with him asked: "Has 'Abū 'Ubayda died?" He replied: "No, but death is near to him."[415] Caliph 'Umar sent another courier with the message that if he is not coming back, he should at least move to any highland with a less humid environment, and 'Abū 'Ubayda complied. Nevertheless, he became afflicted with the Plague and died soon thereafter.

Note: Another possible reason why 'Abū 'Ubayda did not leave Syria is because Muhammad once ordered that if a state is being hit by a plague, none from the state should escape and none from outside the state shall enter it. This is also the reason why 'Umar, on his way to Syria, returned when he heard about the Plague.

299. Which of Muhammad's companions was "the drawn sword of Allah"?

Answer: Khālid ibn al-Walīd (خالد بن الْوَليد).

Born	592 in Mecca	Died	642 (21 AH) in Homs (present-day Syria)

During his childhood Khālid ibn al-Walīd suffered a mild attack of smallpox which he survived, but it left some pockmarks on his left cheek. Khālid was from the Meccan Quraysh, a tribe that initially opposed Muhammad, and he played a vital role in victories over the Muslims. His last battle against the Muslims was in 627 (Battle of the Trench). He embraced Islam shortly after the Treaty of Hudaybīya (صُلْح الْحُدَيْبِيّة) in 629 (7 AH).

After his conversion to Islam, Khālid became the military commander of the Muslims due to his strategic and fighting skills.

'Abū Hurayra (أَبُو هُرَيْرة) narrated: "We camped with the Messenger of Allah at a place and the people were passing by. The Messenger of Allah would ask: 'Who is this, O 'Abū Hurayra?' So I would say: 'So-

---

414 ...يا أَمِيرَ الْمُؤْمِنِينَ، إِنِّي قَدْ عَرَفْتُ حَاجَتَكَ إِلَيَّ، إِنِّي في جُنْدٍ مِن الْمُسْلِمِينَ وَلا أَجِدُ بِنَفْسِي رَغْبَةً عَن الَّذِي يُصِيبُهُم. Ibn Kathīr, al-Bidāya wa al-Nihāya.

415 ...أَمات أبو عُبَيْدة؟ قال: لا، وَلكِنَّ الْمَوْتَ قَرِيبٌ مِنه. Ibn Kathīr, al-Bidāya wa al-Nihāya.

and-so.' So the Prophet would say: 'What an excellent slave of Allah this is.' And he would say: 'Who is this?' So I would answer: 'So-and-so.' Then the Prophet would say: 'What a bad slave of Allah this is.'

Until Khālid ibn al-Walīd passed, and he asked: 'Who is this?' So I replied: 'This is Khālid ibn al-Walīd.' Then he [the Prophet] said: 'What an excellent slave of Allah is Khālid ibn al-Walīd, **a sword from among the swords of Allah.**'"[416]

During his military career Khālid is said to have fought around one hundred battles, both major battles and minor skirmishes as well as single duels. Khālid was the mastermind of almost every major tactic that Muslims used during early Islamic conquests.

He developed a form of psychological warfare. Much of Khālid's strategic and tactical genius lies in his use of extreme methods of blood and fear. His warriors were highly trained and skilled swordsmen, whom Khālid utilised effectively to slay as many enemy officers as possible, giving a psychological blow to the enemy's morale.

It was narrated from Sālim ibn 'Abd Allah (سالم بن عَبْد الله) that his father said: "The Prophet sent Khālid ibn al-Walīd to Banū Jadhīma (بَنُو جَذِيمة) [an Arabian tribe]. He called them to Islam, but they could not say 'Aslamna ["we submitted", i.e. we became Muslim] so they started to say Saba'na ["we changed our religion"].

Khālid started killing and taking prisoners, and he gave a prisoner to each [of his] man. The next day Khālid issued orders that each man among us kill his prisoner. 'Abd Allah ibn 'Umar said: 'By Allah, I will not kill my prisoner and no one [among my companions] will kill his prisoner.' We came to the Prophet and he was told of what Khālid had done. The Prophet said: 'I disavow what Khālid has done.'" [he said this twice].[417]

---

416 ...قَالَ نَزَلْنَا مَعَ رَسُولِ اللَّهِ مَنْزِلاً فَجَعَلَ النَّاسُ يَمُرُّونَ فَيَقُولُ رَسُولُ اللَّهِ: "مَنْ هَذَا يَا أَبَا هُرَيْرَةَ" فَأَقُولُ فُلَانٌ. فَيَقُولُ: "نِعْمَ عَبْدُ اللَّهِ هَذَا." وَيَقُولُ: "مَنْ هَذَا؟" فَأَقُولُ فُلَانٌ. فَيَقُولُ: "بِئْسَ عَبْدُ اللَّهِ هَذَا." حَتَّى مَرَّ خَالِدُ بْنُ الْوَلِيدِ فَقَالَ: "مَنْ هَذَا؟" فَقُلْتُ هَذَا خَالِدُ بْنُ الْوَلِيدِ. فَقَالَ: "نِعْمَ عَبْدُ اللَّهِ خَالِدُ بْنُ الْوَلِيدِ سَيْفٌ مِنْ سُيُوفِ اللَّهِ." Jāmi' al-Tirmidhī 4217 (3846); hasan

417 ...قَالَ بَعَثَ النَّبِيُّ خَالِدَ بْنَ الْوَلِيدِ إِلَى بَنِي جَذِيمَةَ فَدَعَاهُمْ إِلَى الإِسْلامِ فَلَمْ يُحْسِنُوا أَنْ يَقُولُوا أَسْلَمْنَا فَجَعَلُوا يَقُولُونَ صَبَأْنَا صَبَأْنَا وَجَعَلَ خَالِدٌ قَتْلاً وَأَسْرًا - قَالَ - فَدَفَعَ إِلَى كُلِّ رَجُلٍ مِنَّا أَسِيرَهُ حَتَّى إِذَا أَصْبَحَ يَوْمُنَا أَمَرَ خَالِدُ بْنُ الْوَلِيدِ أَنْ يَقْتُلَ كُلُّ رَجُلٍ مِنَّا أَسِيرَهُ. قَالَ ابْنُ عُمَرَ فَقُلْتُ وَاللَّهِ لاَ أَقْتُلُ أَسِيرِي وَلاَ يَقْتُلُ أَحَدٌ - وَقَالَ بِشْرٌ - مِنْ أَصْحَابِي أَسِيرَهُ - قَالَ - فَقَدِمْنَا عَلَى النَّبِيِّ فَذُكِرَ لَهُ صُنْعُ خَالِدٍ فَقَالَ النَّبِيُّ

Khālid was one of the main leaders in the first battle between the Romans and the Muslims. The Battle of Mu'ta (غَزْوة مُؤْتة) was fought in September 629 (8 AH), near a village east of the Jordan River. Khālid was able to maintain his heavily outnumbered army of 3,000 men against an army of 10,000 soldiers of the Byzantine Empire, but many important companions were killed in the battle.

It was narrated by 'Anas ibn Mālik (أَنَس بن مالك) that the Prophet had informed the people about the death of Zayd, Ja'far and Ibn Rawāha [during the Battle of Mu'ta] before the news of their death had reached them. He said with his eyes flowing with tears, "Zayd took the flag and was martyred; then Ja'far took the flag and was martyred, and then Ibn Rawāha took the flag and was martyred. Finally, the flag was taken by one of *Allah's Swords* [i.e. Khālid ibn al-Walīd] and Allah gave them [the Muslims] victory."[418]

Khālid is said to have fought fanatically at the Battle of Mu'ta and to have broken nine swords during the battle. He himself told that: "On the day of Mu'ta, nine swords were broken in my hand and only a Yemenite sword of mine remained in my hand."[419]

Because of his fighting (and killing) spirit, Muslims called him *the drawn sword of Allah* (سَيْف الله الْمَسْلُول).

Note 1: On July 2013, the shrine of Khālid ibn al-Walīd in Homs in Syria was destroyed by a bomb from the Syrian army.

At the site there was a stone in which his alleged famous last words were engraved. It is said that he had wanted to die as a martyr in a battle. He was disappointed when he knew that he would die in his bed at home.

Legend has it that Khālid expressed his sadness in his last words: "I've fought in so many battles seeking martyrdom that there is no spot in my body left without a scar or a wound made by a spear or

---

وَرَفَعَ يَدَيْهِ: "اللَّهُمَّ إِنِّي أَبْرَأُ إِلَيْكَ مِمَّا صَنَعَ خَالِدٌ." قَالَ زَكَرِيَّا فِي حَدِيثِهِ فَذُكِرَ وَفِي حَدِيثِ بِشْرٍ فَقَالَ: "اللَّهُمَّ إِنِّي أَبْرَأُ إِلَيْكَ مِمَّا صَنَعَ خَالِدٌ." مَرَّتَيْنِ. (5407) Sunan al-Nasā'ī 5404

418 ...أَنَّ النَّبِيَّ نَعَى زَيْدًا وَجَعْفَرًا وَابْنَ رَوَاحَةَ لِلنَّاسِ قَبْلَ أَنْ يَأْتِيَهُمْ خَبَرُهُمْ، فَقَالَ: "أَخَذَ الرَّايَةَ زَيْدٌ فَأُصِيبَ، ثُمَّ أَخَذَ جَعْفَرٌ فَأُصِيبَ، ثُمَّ أَخَذَ ابْنُ رَوَاحَةَ فَأُصِيبَ وَعَيْنَاهُ تَذْرِفَانِ حَتَّى أَخَذَ سَيْفٌ مِنْ سُيُوفِ اللَّهِ حَتَّى فَتَحَ اللَّهُ عَلَيْهِمْ." Sahīh al-Bukhārī 3757

419 ...يَقُولُ لَقَدْ دُقَّ فِي يَدِي يَوْمَ مُوتَةَ تِسْعَةُ أَسْيَافٍ، وَصَبَرَتْ فِي يَدِي صَفِيحَةً لِي يَمَانِيَةٌ. Sahīh al-Bukhārī 4266

sword. And yet here I am, dying on my bed like an old camel. May the eyes of the cowards never rest."[420]

Many Islamic countries like to name weapons after Khālid:

- The Pakistan Army's main battle tank (MBT), "al-Khālid", is named after Khālid ibn al-Walīd.
- A submarine of Pakistan's Navy is called "PNS/M Khālid (S137)".
- A frigate of Bangladesh's Navy is called "BNS Khālid Ibni Walid".
- The troops sent by Pakistan's military during the Gulf War in the "Operation Desert Storm" was named "Khālid Bin Walīd Independent Armoured Brigade Group".

Note 2: Khālid was one of 'Abū Bakr's main advisers and the architect of the strategic planning of the first inner Islamic war, the so-called Ridda Wars (حُرُوب الرِّدة). Shia Muslims do not respect him because they believe that he helped 'Abū Bakr in suppressing the supporters of 'Alī ibn 'Abī Tālib (عَليّ بن أَبي طالِب), who, according to Shia Muslims, was appointed by Muhammad as his successor.

300. Who dismantled the Arabian Goddess al-'Uzzā?

Answer: Khālid ibn al-Walīd (خالِد بن الوَليد).

After the Conquest of Mecca the Prophet cleansed his hometown by dismantling and demolishing 360 sculptures around the Ka'ba. Furthermore, Muhammad commanded Khālid in 630 (8 AH) to a place called Nakhla (نَخْلة) and ordered him to destroy the statue of al-'Uzzā (الْعُزَّى). The Arabs believed in the goddess al-'Uzzā and her statue was perhaps the largest of a deity in the region.

There were at least three deities and all of them, by the way, were female. They were called al-Lāt (اللّات), Manā (مَنـاة), and al-'Uzzā

---

420 ...لَقَد شَهدتُ مائَةَ زَحفٍ أو زُهاءَها، وما في بَدَني مَوضِعُ شِبرٍ إلا وفيهِ ضَربةٌ بِسَيفٍ أو رَميةٌ بِسَهمٍ أو طَعنةٌ بِرُمحٍ. وها أَنذا أَموتُ على فِراشي حَتفَ أَنفي، فَلا نامت أَعينُ الجُبَناء

(الْعُزَّى). These three goddesses were regarded as "God's daughters", side by side with the angels who were also female.

They were worshipped in most of pre-Islamic Arabia and had several shrines in the Hijāz and in Najd. The worship of al-Lāt was particularly ancient and almost certainly of southern Arabian origin. She may have been the prototype of the Greek semi-goddess Leto, one of the wives of Zeus and mother of Apollo and Artemis. All three goddesses are mentioned in the Qur'an, in sura 53 *The Star* – in Arabic: al-Najm (سُورَةُ النَّجْمِ):

53:19	[Disbelievers], consider al-Lāt and al-'Uzzā,	أَفَرَأَيْتُمُ اللَّاتَ وَالْعُزَّى
53:20	and the third one, Mana(t)	وَمَنَاةَ الثَّالِثَةَ الْأُخْرَى
53:21	are you to have the male and He the female?	أَلَكُمُ الذَّكَرُ وَلَهُ الْأُنثَى
53:22	That would be a most unjust distribution!	تِلْكَ إِذًا قِسْمَةٌ ضِيزَى
53:23	these are nothing but names you have invented yourselves, you and your forefathers. God has sent no authority for them. These people merely follow guesswork and the whims of their souls, even though guidance has come.	إِنْ هِيَ إِلَّا أَسْمَاءٌ سَمَّيْتُمُوهَا أَنتُمْ وَآبَاؤُكُم مَّا أَنزَلَ اللَّهُ بِهَا مِن سُلْطَانٍ إِن يَتَّبِعُونَ إِلَّا الظَّنَّ وَمَا تَهْوَى الْأَنفُسُ وَلَقَدْ جَاءَهُم مِّن رَّبِّهِمُ الْهُدَى.

'Abū Hurayra (أَبُو هُرَيْرَة) narrated that the Messenger of Allah said: "Whoever takes an oath in which he mentions al-Lāt and al-'Uzzā [forgetfully], should say: None has the right to be worshipped but Allah."[421]

It is interesting that the Arabs before the time of the Prophet worshipped a female deity – as the Arabs regarded (and some still regard) a daughter as a humiliation. The Qur'an argues that it was particularly illogical of the disbelievers to attribute daughters to God.

The Prophet ordered Khālid to destroy the idol of al-'Uzzā. Ibn 'Ishāq wrote that Khālid set out with thirty horsemen to destroy the

---

421 ...قَالَ رَسُولُ اللَّهِ: "مَنْ حَلَفَ فَقَالَ فِي حَلِفِهِ وَاللَّاتِ وَالْعُزَّى. فَلْيَقُلْ لاَ إِلَهَ إِلاَّ اللَّهُ." Sahīh al-Bukhārī 4860

shrine. Other Muslim scholars indicated that there were perhaps two idols of al-ʿUzzā: one original and one copy.

Khālid first had located the fake statue and had destroyed it upon which he returned to the Prophet to report that he had fulfilled his mission. "Did you see anything unusual?", asked the Prophet. "No", replied Khālid. "Then you have not destroyed al-ʿUzzā", replied the Prophet. "Go again!"

Khālid went back and found the temple. When he entered the temple, he was faced by a naked, dark-skinned woman who stood in his way and wailed. Khālid did not stop to decide whether this woman might be there to seduce him or to protect the idol, so he drew his sword in the name of Allah and cut the women in two. He then dismantled the idol, returned to Mecca, and asked Muhammad again. Then the Prophet said: "Yes, that was al-ʿUzzā; and never again shall she be worshipped in your land."[422]

301. Who was the first to shed blood in the name of Islam?

Answer: Saʿd ibn ʾAbī Waqqās (سَعْد بن أَبِي وَقَّاص).

Born	595 23 (BH) in Mecca	Died	674 55 (AH), buried in Medina at al-Baqīʿ (البَقِيع)

Before he accepted Islam, Saʿd ibn ʾAbī Waqqās worked as a crafts-man who trimmed arrows and shaped bows. He was one of the very first to accept Islam, probably in 610/611, at the age of 17. He himself narrated: "No one embraced Islam, except on the day I embraced it. And for seven days I was one of the three persons who were Muslims [one-third of Islam]."[423]

ʾAbū Bakr (أَبُو بِكْر الصِّدِّيق) and ʿAlī ibn ʾAbī Tālib (عَلِيّ بن أَبِي طالِب) probably embraced Islam prior to Saʿd.

Saʿd was one of the most important companions who later became a guard of Muhammad (حارِس الرَّسُول). People describe him as short,

---

422 ...نَعَمْ تِلْكَ الْعُزَّى وَقَدْ يَئِسَتْ أَنْ تُعْبَدَ بِبِلَادِكُمْ أَبَدًا. Ibn Hishām.

423 ...سَعْدَ بْنَ أَبِي وَقَّاصٍ يَقُولُ مَا أَسْلَمَ أَحَدٌ إِلاَّ فِي الْيَوْمِ الَّذِي أَسْلَمْتُ فِيهِ، وَلَقَدْ مَكَثْتُ سَبْعَةَ أَيَّامٍ وَإِنِّي لَثُلُثُ الْإِسْلَامِ. Sahīh al-Bukhārī 3858.

corpulent and tight. Sunni Muslims regard Sa'd as one of the ten to whom Paradise had been promised (الْعَشَرة الْمُبشَّرون). Sa'd has out-lived all of the other (nine) blessed companions.

How about first blood?[424]

This is recorded in the biography of Muhammad by Ibn 'Ishāq: "When the Apostle's companions prayed, they went to the glens [narrow valleys] so that their people could not see them praying. When Sa'd ibn 'Abī Waqqās was with a number of the Prophet's companions in one of the glens of Mecca, a band of polytheists came upon them while they were praying and rudely interrupted them.

They blamed them for what they were doing until they came to blows, and it was on that occasion that Sa'd smote a polytheist with the jawbone of a camel and wounded him. This was **the first blood to be shed in Islam.**"[425]

It is not entirely clear when this incident happened. It was probably in 613 or 614 when Muhammad started to preach publicly. Some also say it could have been earlier, for example in 610.

Sa'd also shot **the first arrow in the name of Islam.**[426]

In April 623 (1 AH), Muhammad sent 'Ubayda ibn al-Hārith (عَبَيْدة بن الْحارِث) with sixty to eighty armed Muhājirūn (مُهاجِرُون) to the valley of Ghadīr Khumm (غَدِير خُم), half-way between Mecca and Medina.

This mission became famous as *The Expedition of 'Ubayda* – in Arabic: Sarīya(t) 'Ubayda Ibn al-Hārith (سَرِيَّة عُبَيْدة بن الْحارِث). It is also known as the Expedition to Rābigh (سَرِيّة رابغ).

There are contradicting reports whether 'Ubayda was sent out to deal with 'Abū Sufyān ibn Harb (أبُو سُفيَان بن حَرب) and his men, or whether he was sent to intercept a caravan of the Quraysh that was returning from Syria under the protection of 'Abū Sufyān. The Muslims travelled as far as the wells at Thanya(t) al-Murra (ثَنْية الْمُرّة),

---

424 ...أَوَّل مَن أُراق دَمًا فِي سَبِيل الله

Ibn 'Ishāq, 166 (p. 118). English translation 425

426 ...أَوَّل مَن رَمَى سَهْمًا فِي سَبِيل الله

a watering place in the Hijāz where they encountered numerous men of the Quraysh, some say around 200 armed men.

No fighting took place except that Sa'd ibn 'Abī Waqqās shot an arrow at the Quraysh on that day. This is known as the **first arrow** shot for the cause of Islam.

Sa'd fought in all major battles in the beginning of Islam. In the Battle of 'Uhud, Sa'd was fighting as an archer and was among those who fought in defence of Muhammad after some other Muslims had deserted their positions. Muhammad honoured him by declaring him one of the best archers of that time. During the battle, Muhammad gathered some arrows for him.

Sa'd ibn 'Abī Waqqās narrated: "The Prophet took out a quiver [of arrows] for me on the day of [the battle of] 'Uhud and said: 'Throw [arrows]! Let my father and mother be sacrificed for you!'"[427]

In another version of the incident, 'Alī ibn 'Abī Tālib (علي بن أبي طالب) narrated: "I never heard the Prophet mentioning both of his parents being ransomed for anyone except for Sa'd. On the Day of 'Uhud, I heard him say: 'Shoot, Sa'd, may my father and mother be ransomed for you!'"[428]

Some say that 'Ubayda ibn al-Hārith (عُبَيْدة بن الحارث) was the first to whom Muhammad gave a banner on a military expedition; others say that Hamza was the first.

Later, Sa'd became known for his military leadership in the conquest of Persia in 636. In addition, he has also been credited by Chinese Muslims with introducing Islam to China in 650, during the reign of Emperor Gaozong of Tang.

---

427 ...يَقُولُ نَثَلَ لِي النَّبِيُّ كِنَانَتَهُ يَوْمَ أُحُدٍ فَقَالَ: "ارْمِ فِدَاكَ أَبِي وَأُمِّي." Sahīh al-Bukhārī 4055

428 ...قَالَ مَا سَمِعْتُ النَّبِيَّ يُفَدِّي أَحَدًا بِأَبَوَيْهِ إِلاَّ لِسَعْدٍ فَإِنِّي سَمِعْتُهُ يَقُولُ يَوْمَ أُحُدٍ: "ارْمِ سَعْدٌ فِدَاكَ أَبِي وَأُمِّي." Jāmi' al-Tirmidhī 4121 (3755)

302. Who was nicknamed "the deserter of the sedition"?

Answer: Muhammad ibn Maslama (مُحَمَّد بن مَسلَمة).

Born	~ 589 (34 BH)	Died	666 (43 AH) in Medina

Muhammad ibn Maslama was one of the strongest warriors and loyal fighters of Islam during the time of Muhammad.

The only battle in which he did not fight was Tabūk (Muhammad had appointed him as the governor of Medina at the time). In 628 (7 AH) in the Battle of Khaybar (غَزْوة خَيْبَر) he avenged the killing of his brother. He slashed Marhab's [the murderer's] thighs and felled him. He shouted: "Taste death, just as my brother Mahmūd tasted it!" But before he could strike the death-blow, 'Alī ibn 'Abī Tālib (عَليّ بن أَبي طالِب) passed by and cut off Marhab's head.

This entitled 'Alī to take the booty, but Muhammad ibn Maslama challenged him and after they referred their dispute to the Prophet, Muhammad granted Marhab's sword, shield, cap and helmet to Muhammad ibn Maslama.

After the Prophet's death, Muhammad ibn Maslama fought on and was at the beginning loyal to the Caliphs. He also faithfully served 'Umar's successor, 'Uthmān ibn 'Affān. However, when the latter was killed and a civil war broke out among the Muslims – the so-called al-Fitna (الفِتْنة) -, Muhammad ibn Maslama did not participate.

He remembered what the Prophet had told him. This is described in a Hadith which was narrated by 'Abū Burda (أَبو بُرْدة) who said: "I entered upon Muhammad ibn Maslama and he said that the Messenger of Allah had said: 'There will be tribulation, division and dissension. When that comes, take your sword to 'Uhud and strike it until it breaks, then sit in your house until there comes to you the hand of the evildoer [to kill you] or a predestined [natural] death.' And that came to pass, and I did as the Messenger of Allah said.'"[429]

---

429 ...قَالَ إِنَّ رَسُولَ اللَّهِ قَالَ: "إِنَّهَا سَتَكُونُ فِتْنَةٌ وَفُرْقَةٌ وَاخْتِلَافٌ فَإِذَا كَانَ كَذَلِكَ فَأْتِ بِسَيْفِكَ أُحُدًا فَاضْرِبْهُ حَتَّى يَنْقَطِعَ ثُمَّ اجْلِسْ فِي بَيْتِكَ حَتَّى تَأْتِيَكَ يَدٌ خَاطِئَةٌ أَوْ مَنِيَّةٌ قَاضِيَةٌ." فَقَدْ وَقَعَتْ وَفَعَلْتُ مَا قَالَ رَسُولُ اللَّهِ. Sunan ibn Māja 3962; hasan.

One of the greatest warriors of early Islam withdrew. He is therefore called *The Deserter/Runaway of the Sedition* – in Arabic: al-Hārib min al-Fitan (الْهَارِبُ مِنَ الْفِتَن). Muhammad ibn Maslama broke his sword and made a sword from wood. He placed it in a scabbard and hung it inside his house. When he was asked about it, he would say: "I simply hung it there to terrify people."

Muhammad ibn Maslama died in Medina in the year 666 (43 AH). He was nearly 80 years old.

Note: At the time of the Prophet, Muhammad ibn Maslama was called *Knight of Allah's Messenger* (فَارِس رَسُول الله).

However, there were several people in Islam who were called *Knight of Islam* or *Knight of the Messenger of Allah*, for example: Khālid ibn al-Walīd (خَالِد بن الْوَلِيد) or 'Abu Qatāda (أَبُو قَتَادة).

303. Who was the last of Muhammad's companions to die?

Answer: 'Abū al-Tufayl 'Āmir ibn Wāthila (أَبُو الطُّفَيْل عامِر بن وائِلة).

Born	3 (AH)		Died	between 100 (AH) and 110 (AH)

Most scholars agree that 'Abū al-Tufayl was the last person to die who had seen Muhammad in person. However, there is some disagreement about his age and the year of death. Some scholars say he was more than 80 years old and might have been blind in the end. He might have died in Mecca.

'Abū al-Tufayl had seen the Prophet during his Hajj – the Farewell Pilgrimage (حِجّة الْوِداع).

304. What do the kings of Jordan and Morocco have in common?

Answer: King 'Abd Allah II of Jordan (عَبْد الله الثّانِي بن الْحُسَيْن) and King Muhammad VI of Morocco (مُحَمّد السّادِس بن الْحَسَن) both claim to be direct descendants of the Prophet.

428 What do the kings of Jordan and Morocco have in common?

The Prophet's clan was the Banū Hāshim (بَنُو هاشِم). His great-grandfather was Hāshim ibn ʿAbd Mānaf (هاشِم بن عَبْد مَناف) – after whom the tribe was named, i.e., al-Hāshimīyūn (الْهاشِمِيُّون), in English the *Hashemites*.

The founder's real name was ʿAmr al-ʿUlā (عَمْرو الْعُلا) but he was given the nickname Hāshim which means *pulveriser* or *crusher*. The root of the word basically denotes *to break, especially anything dry or hollow*. There are many legends about the reasons for giving him the name Hāshim. He might have received this name because he initiated the practice of providing crumbled bread in broth for the pilgrims to the Kaʿba in Mecca.

The Hashemites belonged to the Quraysh (قُرَيْش) who claimed to be descendants of the prophet ʾIsmāʿīl (إسْماعيل), himself the son of prophet Abraham (إِبْراهيم). The Quraysh first came to Mecca during the second century AD. Six generations later, Qusayy ibn Kilāb (قُصَيّ ابن كِلاب) became the leader of Mecca in the year 480 AD. His grandson was Hāshim ibn ʿAbd Mānaf, the man from whom the Hashemites got their name. Thus, the Hashemites today claim to be the direct descendants of the Prophet through his daughter Fātima and her husband ʿAlī ibn ʾAbī Tālib (عَليّ بن أَبي طالِب), who was also Muhammad's paternal first cousin and later the fourth Caliph.

Descent in Islam is patrilineal. ʿAlī and Fātima had two sons: al-Hasan (الْحَسَن) and al-Husayn (الْحُسَيْن). The direct descendants of their eldest son, Hasan, are known as *Sharifs* (شَريف) - literally, *noble, high-born* -, while the descendants of Husayn are called *Sayyids* (سَيِّد), literally *lord, mister*.

There are no reliable statistics about the total number of descendants. However, estimates put the number of Sayyids and Sharifs in the tens of millions.

The country of Jordan today is officially called the *Hashemite Kingdom of Jordan*. The royal family of Jordan claim to be descendants through the *Sharif*-branch of lineage.

The first king of Jordan (Emirate of Transjordan), ʿAbd Allah, was born in 1882 in Mecca. His father Husayn allied the Arabs with British forces in 1916, leading to a revolt that liberated the Levant from Ottoman control. Husayn was the last leader of the Hashemites in Mecca.

And what about Morocco?

The al-ʿAlawīyūn (الْعَلَوِيُّونَ) - in English also spelled *Alaouites* or Alawites - are a clan from the Moroccan oasis of Tafilalt (تفيلالة) near the medieval, historic city of Sijilmasa (سجلماسة) at the northern edge of the Sahara Desert in Morocco.

The *Alaouites* are said to have entered Morocco at the end of the 13th century and gained control of most of Morocco in 1664. The current Moroccan royal family are descendants of this dynasty.

The *Alaouite* family claims descent from the Prophet through his daughter Fātima and her husband ʿAlī ibn ʾAbī Tālib. The name Alaouite is derived from ʿAlī ibn ʾAbī Tālib, whose descendant *Sharif ibn ʿAlī* became Prince of Tafilalt in 1631. His son Mulay al-Rashīd (1664–1672) was able to unite the tribes and pacify the country.

305. How many "Rightly Guided Caliphs" are there in Islam?

Answer: Four – according to Sunni Muslims.

- ʾAbū Bakr al-Siddīq (أَبُو بَكْر الصَّدِّيق), who ruled 2 years
- ʿUmar ibn al-Khattāb (عُمَر بن الْخَطّاب), who ruled 10 years
- ʿUthmān ibn ʿAffān (عُثْمان بن عَفّان), who ruled 12 years
- ʿAlī ibn ʾAbī Tālib (عَلِيّ بن أَبي طالِب), who ruled 5 years

The *Rightly Guided Caliphs* - al-Khulafāʾ al-Rāshidūn (الْخُلَفاء الرّاشِدُون) - is a term used by Sunni Muslims to refer to the 29-year ruling of the first four Caliphs - successors - following the death of Muhammad. Unfortunately, the Prophet had not named a successor. For Shia Muslims, the first three of the four Caliphs were usurpers.

Right after the establishment of the Caliphate of the Rāshidūn in 632, the *Wars of Apostasy* - in Arabic: Hurūb al-Ridda (حُرُوب الرِّدة) - followed. They were a series of military campaigns launched by the first Caliph ʾAbū Bakr against rebellious Arab tribes just after Muhammad had died. The rebels' position was that they had submitted to Muhammad as the Prophet of Allah, but owed nothing to ʾAbū Bakr. The Caliphate of the Rāshidūn ended disastrously with the first Muslim civil war - al-Fitna (الْفِتنة) - which lasted from 656 to 661.

The 29-year rule of the Rāshidūn was Islam's first experience without the leadership of Muhammad. The Rāshidūn assumed all of Muhammad's duties except the prophetic. They led the congregation in prayer in the mosques. They delivered the Friday sermons and commanded the army.

The Islamic empire grew extraordinarily during that period, and Iraq, Syria, Palestine, Egypt, Iran and Armenia were conquered.

The successors of the four Rāshidūn Caliphs were the Umayyads.

306. What happened to three of the first four Caliphs?

Answer: They were assassinated.

Sunni tradition refers to the first four Caliphs as *The Rightly Guided* – in Arabic: al-Khulafā' al-Rāshidūn (الْخُلَفاء الرَّاشِدُون). They ruled from 632 to 661 (11 AH - 41 AH). Let's see what happened to the first four Caliphs.

The **first, Caliph 'Abū Bakr** (أَبُو بَكْر), whose daughter 'Ā'isha (عائشة بِنْت أَبي بَكْر) was married to Muhammad, ruled for two years. He was the only one of the four Caliphs who died from natural causes in 634 (13 AH) after he had developed high fever and did not recover due to his old age (~ 61).

The **second, Caliph 'Umar** (عُمَر بن الْخَطّاب), was assassinated in 644 (23 H) by Persians in response to the Muslim conquest of Persia. He was stabbed while praying in the Prophet's Mosque (الْمَسْجِد النَّبوِيّ) in Medina and died three days later.

The murderer was a Sasanian soldier, Piruz Nahavandi (Farsi: پيروز نهاوندى), known in Arabic as 'Abū Lu'lu'a (أَبُو لُؤْلُؤَة), literally *father of the pearl*. The Sasanian Empire was the last Persian empire before the rise of Islam. When the Muslim army of 'Umar defeated the Sasanians, Piruz was captured and sold as a slave to the tribe of al-Mughīra ibn Shu'ba (الْمُغِيرة بن شُعْبة).

There is a lot of contradictory information about the religion of the murderer. The Persian historian al-Tabarī (الطَّبَـرِيّ) described Nahavandi as a Christian, while others claim that he was an infidel especially because Nahavandi had been referred to with the epithet al-Majūsī (الْمَجُوسِيّ), indicating Zoroastrian beliefs. The Arabic word Majūs (مَجُوس) means Zoroastrianism (Mazdaism).

Sunni Muslims claim that he was a Shia Muslim. This led to rumours that Nahavandi was buried in Kashan (Persian: کاشان) in the province of Isfahan where he had fled to after the assassination of the Caliph. According to other sources, however, Nahavandi is buried in Medina.

The **third, Caliph ʿUthmān** (عُثْمان بن عَفّان), was assassinated twelve years later in 656 (35 AH) in his home in Medina by a group of Egyptians, who accused him of nepotism. After his assassination, a civil war erupted. Muslims fought against Muslims over who should be the next leader. The unresolved conflict between Sunni and Shia came to a head.

Also his successor, the **fourth, Caliph ʿAlī ibn ʾAbī Tālib** (عَلِيّ بن أبي طالب), was assassinated. The reign of ʿAlī, from 656 until his death in 661, was very tumultuous. A rebellious Islamic sect decided to kill several Muslim leaders: Caliph ʿAlī, Muʿāwiya, and ʿAmr ibn al-ʿĀs.

Although the latter two escaped, ʿAlī did not. On Ramadan 19, 661, he was struck in the back of his head with a poisoned sword while praying in the mosque of al-Kūfa (الْكُوفة), which currently is in Iraq. He died two days later and was buried in al-Najaf (النَّجَف), a city in central Iraq about 160 km (100 miles) south of Baghdad.

The killer was identified as ʿAbd al-Rahmān ibn Muljam (عَبْد الرَّحْمَن بن مُلْجَم), a Kharijite. He was decapitated three days later by ʿAlī's son, Hasan ibn ʿAlī (الْحَسَن بن عَلِيّ بن أبي طالب).

307. What is the real name of ʾAbū Bakr?

Answer: ʾAbd Allah ibn ʿUthmān (عَبْد الله بن عُثْمان بن عامِر).

Born	574 (50 BH) in Mecca	Died	634 (13 AH), aged 61, in Medina

ʾAbū Bakr was the first Caliph after Muhammad's death. For Sunni Muslims, he was the first of the four *Rightly Guided Caliphs* (الْخُلَفاء الرّاشِدُون).

His father, ʿUthmān, was nicknamed ʾAbū Quhāfa (أَبُو قُحافة).

308. What does 'Abū Bakr literally mean?

Answer: Father of the camel's calf.

'Abū Bakr al-Siddīq (أَبُو بَكْرِ الصّدّيق) spent his childhood among
Bedouins. He developed a particular fondness for camels. In his early
years, he played with the camel calves and with goats. He was thus
nicknamed 'Abū Bakr – which literally means: *father of the camel's
calf*. The Arabic word Bakr (بَكْر) means *young camel*.

Like the other children of the rich Meccan merchant families, 'Abū
Bakr was literate and liked poetry. He regularly attended the annual
fair at the famous market of 'Ukāz (عُكاظ) near Mecca. He is said to
have had a remarkable memory and good knowledge of the genealogy of Arab tribes.

'Abū Bakr had other nicknames too. The most famous one is probably 'Atīq (عَتِيق). This term was originally used for a horse that runs
in front of other horses giving it a safe and secure position. Therefore, the word - besides other meanings such as *old* or *matured* - can
mean *freed* or *secure* which let some scholars assume that his nickname means *free from Hellfire*.

This is narrated in a (weak) Hadith from Abu Bakr's daughter
'Ā'isha (عائشة بِنْت أَبِي بَكْر). According to the story, 'Abū Bakr entered
upon Muhammad, and the Prophet said: "You are Allah's *'Atīq* from
Hellfire." From that day on he was called 'Atīq.[430]

309. Who decided to collect the verses of the Qur'an?

Answer: 'Abū Bakr al-Siddīq (أَبُو بَكْرِ الصّدّيق).

Shortly after the Prophet had died, the Muslim community was
driven into chaos. During the *Apostate Wars* - al-Ridda (حُرُوب الرّدّة) -,
a lot of the companions, who had memorised the Qur'an, were killed.
Therefore, Caliph 'Abū Bakr feared that the Qur'an could vanish and
consulted senior companions to collect the Qur'an entirely in a single
book – to protect the divine message from being lost.

---

430 ...أَنَّ أَبَا بَكْرٍ، دَخَلَ عَلَى رَسُولِ اللَّهِ فَقَالَ: "أَنْتَ عَتِيقُ اللَّهِ مِنَ النَّارِ." فَيَوْمَئِذٍ سُمِّيَ عَتِيقًا. Jāmi'
al-Tirmidhī 4043 (3679); weak

Who said: "We are a nation whom Allah has honoured with Islam, if we seek the honour in other than it, Allah will humiliate us (again)."

433

310. Who said: "We are a nation whom Allah has honoured with Islam, if we seek the honour in other than it, Allah will humiliate us (again)."

Answer: ʿUmar ibn al-Khattāb (عُمَر بن الْخَطَّاب).

Born	between 583 and 590 (~ 35 BH) in Mecca	Died	644 (23 AH) in Medina

ʿUmar was the second Caliph of the *Rightly Guided Caliphs*, the so-called al-Rāshidūn (الرَّاشِدُون). He was the first to introduce the Hijri calendar and the first who awarded prizes for memorising the Qur'an. He was taught wrestling and horsemanship. ʿUmar was a trader at the market of ʿUkāz (عُكاظ) not far from Mecca. He was one of the richest men in Mecca. In the summer he would travel north - in Arabic: al-Shām (الشّام) - and in the winter, he would go to Yemen.

Like many others in Mecca, ʿUmar initially opposed Islam and even threatened to kill the Prophet. Eventually he went to Muhammad with the same sword with which he intended to kill him, and accepted Islam at the age of 39. This was in the year 616 (6 BH). It was narrated by ʿUqba ibn ʿĀmir (عُقْبة بن عامِر) that the Prophet said: "If there were to be a prophet after me, then it would have been ʿUmar ibn al-Khattāb."[431]

His most famous sword was named Dhū al-Wishāh (ذُو الْوِشاح). The word al-Wishāh means *strings of pearls and jewels*.

After the Battle of Badr (غَزوة بَدْر) people noticed that ʿUmar became harsher. The Islamic scholar al-Tabarīy (الطَّبَرِيّ) reported that when the captives were brought to the most important companions, the Prophet asked: "What do you say concerning these captives?"

'Abū Bakr responded: "O Messenger of Allah, they are your people and your family. Spare them and give them time. Perhaps Allah will relent against them." ʿUmar replied: "O Messenger of Allah, they

---

431 ...قَالَ رَسُولُ اللَّهِ: لَوْ كَانَ بَعْدِي نَبِيٌّ لَكَانَ عُمَرُ بْنَ الْخَطَّابِ.; Jāmiʿ al-Tirmidhī 4050 (3686);
hasan; AND: 'Ahmad ibn Hanbal (17405)

have called you a liar and driven you out. Bring them forward and cut off their heads."[432]

The answers given by 'Abū Bakr and especially 'Umar are famous among Muslims; however, most scholars say that this Hadith is weak (ضَعِيف). According to Sunni Muslims, 'Umar is the second greatest of the companions after 'Abū Bakr.

He defeated the Sasanians, the rulers over Persia. This victory made it possible to conquer Persia in fewer than two years. The Sasanian imperial dynasty was the last Persian Empire before the rise of Islam, ruled by and named after the Sasanian dynasty which lasted from 224 to 651. The Sasanian Empire was a leading world power along with its rival, the Roman-Byzantine Empire, for more than 400 years. At its peak, the Empire stretched from Egypt, Yemen, the Caucasus, all the way to Central Asia (today's Afghanistan). Most people in Persia believed in Zoroastrianism.

Furthermore, Jerusalem and the al-Aqsā-mosque – known as *The Third of the Two Sanctuaries,* Thālith al-Haramayn (ثالِث الْحَرَمَيْن) in Arabic - came under Islamic rule for the first time during 'Umar's reign.

Let's return to our question, which is a famous quote. 'Umar was on the way to Syria and was accompanied by 'Abū 'Ubayda (أَبُو عُبَيْدة), a companion of Muhammad. When they arrived at a creek 'Umar dismounted from his camel, took off his sandals and placed them over his shoulder, and then led the camel through the creek.

'Abū 'Ubayda asked: "O commander of the faithful, are you [really] doing this? You have taken off your sandals and placed them on your back and you led the camel through the creek yourself. I do not think it will be easy for me to get the people of this country to honour you."

'Umar said: "If only someone else had said this, O 'Abū 'Ubayda! I have made this a deterrent for the nation of Muhammad. Verily, we were a disgraceful people and Allah honoured us with Islam, so if we seek honour from other than Islam, then Allah will humiliate us

---

432 ...قَالَ رَسُولُ اللَّهِ: "مَا يَقُولُونَ فِي هَؤُلَاءِ الْأَسْرَى؟" فَقَالَ أَبُو بَكْرٍ: قَوْمُكَ أَهْلُكَ اسْتَبْقِهِمْ وَاسْتَأْنِ بِهِمْ, لَعَلَّ اللَّهَ عَزَّ وَجَلَّ أَنْ يَتُوبَ عَلَيْهِمْ, وَقَالَ عُمَرُ كَذَّبُوكَ وَأَخْرَجُوكَ فَقَدِّمْهُمْ فَاضْرِبْ أَعْنَاقَهُمْ. weak; Jāmi' al-Tirmidhī, 3084.

Who said: "We are a nation whom Allah has honoured with Islam, if we seek the honour in other than it, Allah will humiliate us (again)."

435

(again)."[433] Note: Historians sometimes refer to him as 'Umar I because another Caliph, ruling much later in the Umayyad dynasty, i.e. 'Umar II, bore the same name.

311. Which Caliph was nicknamed "the one who distinguishes between truth and falsehood" (al-Fārūq)?

Answer: 'Umar ibn al-Khattāb (عُمَر بن الْخَطَّاب).

His nickname (لَقَب) was al-Fārūq (الْفَارُوق) which means the *one who distinguishes the truth* (حَقّ) *from falsehood* (باطِل).

'Umar was the founder of Fiqh (فِقْه), the Islamic jurisprudence. Sunni Muslims regard him as one of the greatest experts on Islamic law. 'Umar, in fact, started the process of codifying it.

Furthermore, he established a special department for the investigation of complaints against officers of the Islamic State. He forbade any of his governors from working in any sort of business whilst being in a position of power.

Note: One of 'Umar's epithets (كُنْية) was 'Abū Hafs (أَبُو حَفْص). The Arabic word Hafs (حَفْص) means *cub of a lion*.

312. Which Caliph was nicknamed "the 5ᵗʰ Righteous Caliph"?

Answer: 'Umar ibn 'Abd al-'Azīz (عُمَر بن عَبْد الْعَزِيز).

Born	682/683 (61 AH), most say in Medina, some say in Egypt where he spent his first years	Died	720 (101 AH), at Sim'ān convent (دير سِمْعان), near Aleppo (حَلَب), Syria

'Umar's father was the governor of Egypt; some say he was a de facto viceroy of the country. 'Umar grew up and lived there until the death of his father, after which he was summoned to Damascus.

---

433 ...نَحْنُ قَوْم أَعَزَّنا اللَّه بِالإِسلام فَإِنْ إِنْتَغَيْنا الْعِزّة بِغَيْرِه أَذَلّنا اللَّه. -al-Mustadrak 'ala al-Sahīhayn 214

Later, he became the eighth Caliph of the Umayyad dynasty. His time as a Caliph lasted for 65 months and 4 days. His nickname was 'Umar II He became a symbol for justice and asceticism in Islam. Islamic scholars describe him as a person who longed for a modest life and preferred to live in a tent.

'Umar II is credited with having ordered the first official collection of Hadiths, fearing that the narrations might get lost.

He thus ordered 'Abū Bakr ibn Muhammad ibn Hazm (أَبُو بَكْر بن مُحَمَّد بن حَزْم), before he died in 737 (120 AH), to write them down.

Among Muslims 'Umar II is known as al-Khalīfa al-Sālih (الْخَلِيفة الصّـالِح) which means *the pious Caliph* and also as al-Khalīfa al-Khāmis (الْخَلِيفة الْخامِس) which means: *the fifth Rightly Guided Caliph*.

How did he die? He was poisoned by a slave of the Caliph who was bribed to give the deadly poison. When the Caliph felt the effect of the poison, he detained the slave and questioned him. The slave said that he was given one thousand dinars for the task.

Islamic accounts indicate that the Caliph deposited the said amount in the public treasury, acquitted the slave and advised him to leave immediately or else he might get killed by people.

313. About which Caliph did the Prophet say: "He loves Allah and His messenger, and Allah and His messenger love him."

Answer: 'Alī ibn 'Abī Tālib (عَلِي بن أَبِي طالِب).

Born	601 (21 BH) in Mecca	Died	661 (40 AH), in Kufa (Iraq)

'Alī's father was Muhammad's uncle 'Abū Tālib (أَبُو طالِب). 'Alī's mother was Abū Tālib's cousin, Fātima bint 'Asad (فاطِمة بِنْت أَسَد). As many, in particular Shia sources claim, 'Alī was the only person born in the sacred sanctuary of the Ka'ba in Mecca, the holiest place in Islam. According to some sources, 'Alī was the first young male who converted to Islam. He was Muhammad's cousin (son of his paternal uncle) and his son-in-law.

After migrating to Medina, 'Alī married Muhammad's daughter Fātima (فاطِمة بِنْت مُحَمَّد). He then became father of two sons, al-Husayn (الْحَسَن بن عَلِيّ بن أَبِي طالِب) and al-Hasan (الْحُسَيْن بن عَلِيّ بن أَبِي طالِب). 'Alī had a third son, Muhsin (مُحْسِين بن عَلِيّ), but he died at a very young age; some mention that Muhsin was a stillborn infant.

Shia Muslims claim that he was a miscarried child of Fātima. They say that she lost her baby when 'Umar and 'Abū Bakr attacked Fātima in 'Alī's house in order to force 'Alī into submission (accepting them as successors). Sunni Muslims reject this claim and insist that Muhsin died in infancy from natural causes.

'Alī took part in the early raids on caravans from Mecca and later in almost all the battles fought by the Muslims. He was appointed as the Caliph - the forth *Rightly Guided Caliph* (الرّاشِدُون) as Sunni Muslims say - by Muhammad's companions in 656, after Caliph 'Uthmān ibn 'Affān (عُثْمان بن عَفّان) was assassinated.

'Alī's reign saw civil unrest and in 661 (40 AH), he was attacked and assassinated while praying in the Great Mosque of Kufa, dying from his injuries two days later.

While Sunnis consider 'Alī as the fourth and last of the *Rightly Guided Caliphs*, Shia Muslims regard 'Alī as the first Imam (religious leader) after Muhammad. Shias believe furthermore that 'Alī and the other Shia Imams - all of whom are members of Muhammad's household, so-called 'Ahl al-Bayt (أَهْل الْبَيْت) - are the Prophet's rightful successors. This disagreement split the Muslim community, the so-called 'Umma (أُمّة), into the Sunni and Shia branches.

Now let's return to our question, the quote: "He loves Allah and His messenger, and Allah and His messenger love him".

Sahl ibn Sa'd (سَهْل بن سَعْد) reported the following: "On the day [of the Battle] of Khaybar, the Prophet said: 'Tomorrow I will give the flag to somebody who will be given victory [by Allah] and who loves Allah and His Apostle and is loved by Allah and His Apostle.'

So, the people wondered all that night who would receive the flag and in the morning everyone hoped that he would be that person. Allah's Messenger asked: 'Where is 'Alī?' He was told that 'Alī was suffering from eye-trouble, so he applied saliva to his eyes and invoked Allah to cure him. He at once was cured as if he had no ailment. The Prophet gave him the flag. 'Alī asked: 'Should I fight them until they become like us [i.e. Muslims]?'

The Prophet said: 'Go to them patiently and calmly until you enter the land. Then, invite them to Islam and inform them what is enjoined upon them, for, by Allah, if Allah gives guidance to somebody through you, it is better for you than possessing red camels.'"[434]

Note: 'Alī's mother is called Fātima bint 'Asad. Don't confuse her with 'Alī wife who too is called Fātima (فَاطِمَة بِنْت مُحَمَّد) but is Muhammad's daughter and 'Alī's wife!

314. What does the name of 'Alī's sword "Zulfiqar" mean?

Answer: Not entirely clear.

The legendary sword of 'Alī ibn 'Abī Tālib (عَلِيّ بن أَبِي طالب) is called Zulfiqar in transliteration – in Arabic Dhū al-Faqār (ذُو الْفَقَار).

The Prophet, as most Muslim historians say, gave this sword to 'Alī, his cousin and son-in-law, during the Battle of 'Uhud (غَزْوَة أُحُد). It is not clear how Muhammad had obtained this sword which had also appeared in his dreams. A Hadith gives some more information:

'Abd Allah ibn 'Abbās (عَبْد الله بن عَبّاس) narrated that the Messenger of Allah acquired the sword Dhū al-Faqār from the spoils of war on the Day of Badr.[435]

The sword has often been depicted on Muslim flags as a scissor-like double bladed sword. It is commonly shown in Shia depictions of 'Alī and serves as talismans, for example in the form of jewellery as a scimitar terminating in two tips.

---

434 ...قَالَ النَّبِيُّ يَوْمَ خَيْبَرَ: "لَأُعْطِيَنَّ الرَّايَةَ غَدًا رَجُلًا يُفْتَحُ عَلَى يَدَيْهِ، يُحِبُّ اللهَ وَرَسُولَهُ، وَيُحِبُّهُ اللهُ وَرَسُولُهُ." فَبَاتَ النَّاسُ لَيْلَتَهُمْ أَيُّهُمْ يُعْطَى فَغَدَوْا كُلُّهُمْ يَرْجُوهُ فَقَالَ: "أَيْنَ عَلِيٌّ؟" فَقِيلَ يَشْتَكِي عَيْنَيْهِ، فَبَصَقَ فِي عَيْنَيْهِ وَدَعَا لَهُ، فَبَرَأَ كَأَنْ لَمْ يَكُنْ بِهِ وَجَعٌ، فَأَعْطَاهُ فَقَالَ أُقَاتِلُهُمْ حَتَّى يَكُونُوا مِثْلَنَا. فَقَالَ: "انْفُذْ عَلَى رِسْلِكَ حَتَّى تَنْزِلَ بِسَاحَتِهِمْ، ثُمَّ ادْعُهُمْ إِلَى الإِسْلامِ، وَأَخْبِرْهُمْ بِمَا يَجِبُ عَلَيْهِمْ، فَوَاللهِ لَأَنْ يَهْدِيَ اللهُ بِكَ رَجُلًا خَيْرٌ لَكَ مِنْ أَنْ يَكُونَ لَكَ حُمْرُ النَّعَمِ." Sahīh al-Bukhārī 3009

435 ...أَنَّ رَسُولَ اللهِ تَنَفَّلَ سَيْفَهُ ذَا الْفِقَارِ يَوْمَ بَدْرٍ. Sunan ibn Māja 2915 (2808); hasan

Let's now focus on the meaning of the sword's name: Dhū al-Faqār.

The Arabic word dhū (ذُ) denotes ownership. It is therefore usually translated as *master* or *owner of*.

The meaning of Faqār or Fiqār (فَقار), on the other hand, is unclear. Edward Lane cites authorities preferring Faqār and rejecting Fiqār as "vulgar", but the vocalisation Fiqār is still more common. It is a strange word and linguists are not sure about the meaning. Let's look at some possibilities:

- One meaning of the word Faqār is *the bones of the spine*; so the sword could be interpreted as *the spine-splitter*.

- It could refer to the stars in the Belt of Orion, emphasising the celestial provenance of the sword.

- Some scholars have interpreted Faqār as an unfamiliar plural of Fuqra (فُقْرة) which means *notch, groove,* or *indentation*. Therefore, it could be a reference to a kind of decoration of regularly spaced notches or dents on the sword. The sword had fine and beautiful engravings on it – in Arabic, engravings can be called Fiqra (فِقْرة). Sunni Muslims favour this interpretation.

- Others refer to a *notch* formed by the sword's supposed termination in two points. This interpretation is the most common among Shia Muslims and gives rise to the popular depiction of the sword as a double-bladed scimitar in Shia iconography.

There is a famous saying which goes like this: "There is no sword like Dhū al-Faqār. There is no juvenile like 'Alī".[436] In Arabic, it reads: "Lā Sayfa illā Dhū al-Faqār wa lā Fatā illā 'Alī". The famous quote is found on talismans used by Shia Muslims.

Shia Muslims believe that this sentence was said by the Prophet. Muhammad allegedly said it during the Battle of 'Uhud (غَزْوة أُحُد) in praise of 'Alī's achievement of splitting the shield and helmet of the strongest Meccan warrior, shattering his own sword in the same stroke. Others claim that the exclamation was uttered by a soldier on the battlefield. Legend has it that the Prophet gave his own sword - Dhū al-Faqār - to 'Alī to replace his broken sword.

---

436 ...لا سَيْفَ إلّا ذُو الْفِقار وَلا فَتَى إلاّ عَلِيّ

Some say that the famous Shia saying goes back to a poem by Hassān ibn Thābit (حَسّان بن ثابِت) who was one of the 'Ansār (الأَنْصار). According to an Islamic legend, Hassān had lived for 120 years, the first half of it he spent as a non-Muslim, and the second sixty years he spent as a Muslim.

It is most likely that after 'Alī's death his children inherited the sword. There is no proof that the sword still exists. 'Alī had many swords. One is said to be kept at the Topkapı museum in Istanbul, Turkey.

According to the Twelver Shia, Dhū al-Faqār is currently in the possession of the "hidden" Imam Muhammad ibn al-Hasan al-Mahdī (مُحَمَّد بن الْحَسَن الْمَهْدِي). He is believed to be the Mahdī – which is an ultimate saviour of mankind and the final Imam of the Twelve Imams who will emerge with Jesus in order to fulfil their mission of bringing peace to the world.

Note:

- An Iranian battle tank is named after the sword: *Zulfiqār.*
- During the Bosnian War, a special force of the Muslims was named *Zulfikar.*

315. What does the word *Sunni* mean?

Answer: One who follows the institutes or ways of the Prophet.

The word Sunnī (سُنِّيّ) is a derived adjective from the noun Sunna (سُنَّة). In Arabic grammar, a word like this is called Nisba (نِسبة). The word Sunna basically means *a way, course, rule, mode or manner of acting/conduct/life; habitual practice.*

When used with the definite article - al-Sunna (السُّنة) -, the word only denotes what Muhammad has commanded and what has been handed down from him by tradition. In other words, what Muhammad has invited his followers to do by word or deed, mainly things that are not mentioned in the Qur'an.

Muslims therefore say that Islam is made of the Book (الْكِتاب) and the Sunna (السُّنّة) – the Qur'an and the Hadiths.

Nowadays the word Sunnī denotes a follower of Sunni Islam. Sunni Muslims are called ʾAhl al-Sunna (أَهْل السُّنَّة) which translates as *traditional Muslims* as they are following only what is written in the Qurʾan and what was said and practised by Muhammad.

316. What does the word *Shia* literally mean?

Answer: Faction or party.

The word Shīʿa (شيعة) is the short form of Shīʿa(t) ʿAlī (شيعة عليّ) – *followers of ʿAlī; faction of ʿAlī.* In English, Shiite as well as Shia is used to denote members of Shia Islam. The word comes from the Arabic root sh-y-ʿ (ش-ي-ع) which has the meaning of *to spread, to be divulged, to become known, to become public*

If used with the definite article - al-Shīʿa (الشِّيعة) -, it has the meaning of the *Shiites* and denotes those Muslims who recognise ʿAlī ibn ʾAbī Tālib (عَلِيّ بن أَبِي طالب), the Prophet's cousin and son-in-law, as Muhammad's rightful successor.

Shia Islam has different branches. The Shia belief throughout its history split over the issue of the Imamate. The largest branch are the *Twelvers*, followed by the *Zaydi* (*Fivers*) and *Ismāʿīlī*. All three groups follow a different line of Imamate.

In general, Shia Islam is divided into these groups:

- **Twelver** (اِثْنا عَشَرِيَّة) or Imamīya (إمامِيَّة): The largest branch of Shia Islam; the term Shia Muslim often refers to the Twelvers by default. The term Twelver refers to its followers' belief in twelve Imams, divinely appointed, known as the Twelve Imams, and to their belief that the last Imam, Muhammad al-Mahdī, will re-appear as the promised Mahdī (المَهْدِي). Twelvers believe that the Twelve Imams are the spiritual and political successors of Muhammad. Twelvers constitute the majority of the population in Iran (90%), Azerbaijan (85%), Bahrain (70%), Iraq (65%), Lebanon (65% of the Muslims).

- **Zaydī (Fiver)**: Zaydism (الزَّيْدِيَّة) is the second largest branch of Shia Islam. It emerged in the 8ᵗʰ century and is named after Zayd Ibn ʿAlī (زَيْد بن عَلِيّ بن الْحُسَيْن), the grandson of ʿAlī ibn ʾAbī Tālib's son Husayn. Followers are called Zaydis or occasionally Fivers as they follow only five (divinely appointed) Imams. Zaydis constitute roughly 40% of the population in Yemen. Zaydis are probably the closest to Sunni Islam.

The most well-known Zaydi movement nowadays is the Houthi (حُوثِيُّون) movement in Yemen. In 2014 Houthis took over the government in Yemen's capital Sana'a, which led to the fall of the Saudi Arabian-backed government of 'Abd Rabbihi Mansūr Hādī (عَبْد رَبِّه مَنْصُور هادِي). Because Saudi Arabia was afraid of the new Shia rulers, their army, together with some allies, attacked Yemen which resulted in a bloody war.

- **Ismāʿīlī (Sevener)**: Ismailis (الْإِسْماعِيلِيّة) got their name from their acceptance of Ismāʿīl ibn Jaʿfar (إِسماعِيل بن جَعْفَر) as the divinely appointed successor (Imam) to Jaʿfar al-Sādiq (جَعْفَر الصّادِق) - whereas the Twelvers accept Mūsā al-Kāzim (مُوسَى بن جَعْفَر الْكاظِم), the younger brother of 'Ismāʿīl, as the true Imam. The most important groups are: Nizari, Alavi, Dawoodi, Sulaymāni, and Aga Khan followers.

  During the Fatimid Caliphate (10th to 12th century) in Egypt this was the largest sect of Shia Islam.

- **Ghulā (غُلاة)**: Minorities who don't fit into mainstream Shia sects. The most important groups are: Alawites, Hurufsim, Bektashi Order, and Qizilbash.

- **Druzes (دُرُوز)**.

Twelvers refer to the Ja'farite School of jurisprudence (جَعْفَرِيّة), which is named after Ja'far ibn Muhammad al-Sādiq (جَعْفَر بن مُحَمَّد الصادِق), the 6th Shia Imam. This school of jurisprudence is followed by Twelvers, Alevis and Ismailis, as well as a small minority of Zaydis.

Remark: The *Hazara* (Persian: هزاره) is not a sect. They are a Persian-speaking people who mainly live in central Afghanistan and in some parts of Pakistan. They are overwhelmingly Twelver Shia Muslims and make up the third largest ethnic group in Afghanistan.

317. Why do Sunnis and Shias quarrel about 'Alī?

Answer: This is related to the question of who had the right to follow Muhammad after his death. In other words, who should have been the leader of the Muslims after Muhammad?

The main person in this dispute is 'Alī ibn 'Abī Tālib (عَلِيّ بن أَبِي طالِب), cousin and son-in-law of Muhammad, and like him a descendant of the tribe Banū Hāshim (بَنُو هاشِم).

The (political) beginning of Shia Islam dates back to the death of Muhammad in 632 (11 AH). 'Alī was about to turn 31 when the Prophet died. Some argue that mostly because of his relatively young age, he did not succeed him. 'Alī was passed over for leadership (Caliph) three times after Muhammad's death.

Nevertheless, according to Shia sources, 'Alī recognised the Caliph's authority and even ordered his sons to protect Caliph 'Uthmān's house when the (third) Caliph was attacked. When 'Uthmān died, 'Alī was then in his fifties. He was finally chosen as the new and fourth Caliph.

'Alī moved his capital to Kufa in present-day Iraq. After some turbulent and bloody years of what is termed the first Muslim civil war, a group of puritanical Muslims called Kharijites (خارِجِيّ), who at the beginning were following 'Alī, decided to assassinate him.

While praying in the mosque of Kufa on the 19th of Ramadan in the year 661, he was stabbed to death. At his own request his burial place was kept secret; though many Muslims think that it is in the *Mosque of 'Alī* in al-Najaf in present-day Iraq.

This event closed the door on the period of the *Rightly Guided Caliphs* as it is known in Sunni tradition. Shia Islam only accepts 'Alī and his successors as the legitimate successors of Muhammad.

The dispute between Sunni and Shia Muslims escalated and culminated, when 'Alī's son al-Husayn (الْحُسَيْن بن عَلِيّ) was killed in the Battle of Karbalā' (مَعْرَكة كَرْبَلاء) in 680 (61 AH). The battle took place between a group of supporters of Muhammad's grandson Husayn and a larger military detachment of the forces of Yazīd I, the Umayyad Caliph.

Husayn was beheaded along with most of his family and companions. This marked the definitive separation of Sunni and Shia
Muslims.

318. What happened in Ghadīr Khumm?

Answer: The appointment of 'Alī ibn 'Abī Tālib (عَلِيّ بن أَبِي طالِب) by
Muhammad as his successor (according to Shia Muslims).

The place called Ghadīr Khumm is located between Mecca and
Medina. It was perhaps a well or watering place.

Ghadīr (غَدِير) in Arabic means *small stream, creek*. The place itself
was called *Khumm* (خُم) and is close to al-Juhfa (الجُحْفة) in present-
day Saudi Arabia.

What happened there? When Muhammad returned from the
Farewell Pilgrimage (حِجّة الوُداع), he stopped in Ghadīr Khumm. The
events which took place there have been differently interpreted by
the two main branches of Islam:

- Shia Muslims claim that Muhammad then appointed 'Alī as his
  heir and successor.
- Sunni Muslims, on the other hand, do not deny Muhammad's
  declaration about 'Alī at Ghadīr Khumm, but they insist that he
  was simply urging the audience to hold his cousin and son-in-
  law in high esteem and affection. Sunni Muslims do not believe
  that there was any appointment of a successor by Muhammad in
  Ghadīr Khumm (or elsewhere).

The Hadith of Ghadīr Khumm is an account of a speech given by the
Prophet possibly on Sunday, 15th March 632 (18th of Dhū al-Hijja, 10
AH). Yazīd ibn Hayyān (يَزِيد بن حَيَّان) reported that he went along with
Husayn ibn Sabra (حُسَيْن بن صَبْرة) and 'Umar ibn Muslim (عُمَر بن
مُسْلِم) to Zayd ibn 'Arqam (زَيْد بن أَرْقَم) and, as they sat by his side,
Husayn asked Zayd to tell them what he had heard from the Prophet.
Zayd recounted: "...one day Allah's Messenger stood up to deliver the
sermon at a watering place known as Khumm situated between

Mecca and Medina. He praised Allah, extolled Him and delivered the sermon and exhorted [us] and said: 'Now to our purpose. O people, I am a human being. I am about to receive a messenger [the Angel of Death] from my Lord and I, in response to Allah's call, [would bid good-bye to you], but I am leaving among you two weighty things: the one being the Book of Allah in which there is right guidance and light, so hold fast to the Book of Allah and adhere to it.' He exhorted [us] to hold fast to the Book of Allah and then said: 'The second are the members of my household I remind you [of your duties] to the members of my family.'

He [Husayn ibn Sabra] asked Zayd: 'Who are the members of his household? Aren't his wives the members of his family?' Thereupon Zayd said: 'His wives are the members of his family [but here] the members of his family are those for whom acceptance of Zakā is forbidden.' And he [Husayn] asked: **'Who are they?'** Thereupon he **[Zayd] said: "Alī and the offspring of 'Alī,** 'Aqīl and the offspring of 'Aqīl and the offspring of Ja'far and the offspring of 'Abbās.' Husayn said: 'These are those for whom the acceptance of Zakā is forbidden.' Zayd said: 'Yes.'"[437]

Who are the other persons mentioned in this Hadith?

- **'Aqīl:** He was 'Aqīl ibn 'Abī Tālib (عقيل بن أبي طالب), born around the year 578 (44 BH); he was the second son of 'Abū Tālib (أَبُو طالِب) and Fātima (فاطِمة بِنْت أَسَد) – hence he was a brother of 'Alī. He died in 679 (60 AH).

- **Ja'far:** He was Ja'far ibn 'Abī Tālib (جَعْفَر بن أَبي طالِب). He was the third son of 'Abū Tālib and Fātima, and an older brother of 'Alī (and a cousin of Muhammad). He was born ~ 590 (~ 33/34 BH) and died in 629 (8 AH) in the Battle of Mu'ta (غَزْوة مُؤْتة).

---

437 ...ثُمَّ قَالَ قَامَ رَسُولُ اللَّهِ يَوْمًا فِينَا خَطِيبًا بِمَاءٍ يُدْعَى خُمًّا بَيْنَ مَكَّةَ وَالْمَدِينَةِ فَحَمِدَ اللَّهَ وَأَثْنَى عَلَيْهِ وَوَعَظَ وَذَكَّرَ ثُمَّ قَالَ: "أَمَّا بَعْدُ أَلَا أَيُّهَا النَّاسُ فَإِنَّمَا أَنَا بَشَرٌ يُوشِكُ أَنْ يَأْتِيَ رَسُولُ رَبِّي فَأُجِيبَ وَأَنَا تَارِكٌ فِيكُمْ ثَقَلَيْنِ أَوَّلُهُمَا كِتَابُ اللَّهِ فِيهِ الْهُدَى وَالنُّورُ فَخُذُوا بِكِتَابِ اللَّهِ وَاسْتَمْسِكُوا بِهِ." فَحَثَّ عَلَى كِتَابِ اللَّهِ وَرَغَّبَ فِيهِ ثُمَّ قَالَ: "وَأَهْلُ بَيْتِي أُذَكِّرُكُمُ اللَّهَ فِي أَهْلِ بَيْتِي أُذَكِّرُكُمُ اللَّهَ فِي أَهْلِ بَيْتِي أُذَكِّرُكُمُ اللَّهَ فِي أَهْلِ بَيْتِي." فَقَالَ لَهُ حُصَيْنٌ وَمَنْ أَهْلُ بَيْتِهِ يَا زَيْدُ أَلَيْسَ نِسَاؤُهُ مِنْ أَهْلِ بَيْتِهِ قَالَ نِسَاؤُهُ مِنْ أَهْلِ بَيْتِهِ وَلَكِنْ أَهْلُ بَيْتِهِ مَنْ حُرِمَ الصَّدَقَةَ بَعْدَهُ. قَالَ وَمَنْ هُمْ قَالَ هُمْ آلُ عَلِيٍّ وَآلُ عَقِيلٍ وَآلُ جَعْفَرٍ وَآلُ عَبَّاسٍ. قَالَ كُلُّ هَؤُلَاءِ حُرِمَ الصَّدَقَةَ قَالَ نَعَم. Sahīh Muslim 2408.

- **'Abbās:** His full name was al-'Abbās ibn 'Abd al-Muttalib (الْعَبّاس بن عَبْد الْمُطَّلِب), he was a paternal uncle of Muhammad and a wealthy spice-merchant in Mecca. He was born ~ 565 (56 BH) and died ~ 653 (32 AH), perhaps at the age of 88 years. His descendants founded the Abbasid Caliphate in 750 (132 AH),

'Ahl al-Bayt means *people of the house or family of the house*. It is not entirely clear who belongs to it. Muslims agree that it is Muhammad himself, his wives and daughters which includes Fātima – 'Alī' wife. All other people are a matter of discussion, especially between Sunni and Shia Muslims.

'Īd al-Ghadīr (عيد الْغَدِير) is an important feast and holiday in Shia Islam. It is held on Dhū al-Hijja 18. Shias celebrate this day with various customs, e.g. fasting, ritual bath, and with visiting relatives.

319. What marks the Battle of the Camel?

Answer: A battle that resulted in a civil war among Muslims. The *Battle of the Camel* (مَوْقِعـة الْجَمَـل) took place at Basra (الْبَصـرة) in present-day Iraq on 7th November 656 (36 H).

Let us first look at the precursors to the war: The third Caliph 'Uthmān (عَثْمان بن عَفّان), a member of the Umayyad family (الْأُمَويُّون) had disappointed a lot of people because he favoured his own Meccan family in official appointments.

People in Egypt, Kufa, and Basra were angry. They started a rebellion and marched towards Medina. When Egyptian rebels gathered there, 'Uthmān asked two of his men to talk to them: 'Alī ibn 'Abī Tālib (عَلي بن أَبِي طالِب) who represented the Muhājirūn (مُهـاجِرُون) which are the Muslims who once migrated with Muhammad from Mecca to Medina, and Muhammad ibn Maslama (مُحَمَّد بن مَسْلَمة) who represented the 'Ansār (الْأَنْصار), *the Helpers*, people from Yathrib (Medina) who welcomed and helped Muhammad when he migrated from Mecca in 622 (الْهِجْرة).

Both tried to persuade the Egyptians by promising that the Caliph will fulfil their demands. It worked and the Egyptian rebels returned to Egypt. However, on their way back home they were overtaken by a courier from Medina. He had a letter with the official seal from the office of Caliph 'Uthmān. The letter instructed the Egyptian governor to kill the rebels once they returned home. Historians are not sure if Caliph 'Uthmān issued the letter by himself. Whoever it was, the Egyptian rebels immediately turned around and went back to Medina where they began the siege of the Caliph's house – which ultimately ended in the Caliph's assassination.

The murder of the third Caliph sets the beginning of the first Islamic civil war which is called the First Fitna (فِتْنَة مَقْتَل عُثْمان). The details of the events are still debated as the two sects of Islam, Sunni and Shia, which eventually emerged from this battle, have different views. Let's look at both versions.

The major role in the upcoming fight - the Battle of the Camel - play two important and most famous people in Islam: 'Alī, Muhammad's cousin and son-in-law, who became Caliph after 'Uthmān's assassination. And 'Ā'isha (عائشة بِنْت أَبِي بَكْر), the daughter of the first Caliph 'Abū Bakr, and who was left a childless widow of 18 when Muhammad died.

'Ā'isha had been returning to Medina from Mecca after her pilgrimage, when she heard the news that Caliph 'Uthmān was assassinated. But what she angered even more was the accession of 'Alī to the Caliphate. 'Ā'isha managed to get the clan of Banū 'Umayya (the Umayyads), to whom 'Uthmān had belonged, on her side. Her two brothers-in-law were two senior companions: Talha (طَلْحة بن عُبَيْد الله) and al-Zubayr (الزُّبَيْر بن الْعَوام). They had also arrived in Mecca. Talha - as indicated in some accounts - only wanted to get rid of 'Alī to became Caliph himself.

'Ā'isha claimed that 'Alī had been unsuccessful in finding 'Uthmān's murderer and called for retaliation – Qisās (قصاص) in Arabic. 'Alī argued that 'Ā'isha was not related to 'Uthmān and therefore could not demand revenge – according to Islamic law. Shia Muslims say that 'Alī wanted to wait until the Fitna calmed down.

'Ā'isha is said to have delivered a fiery speech in the mosque of Mecca calling for vengeance against 'Alī. Together with Talha and Zubayr she rode on a camel from Mecca leading 1,000 men. More and more people joined them on their way and the number of fighters soon was 3,000 and was increasing quickly.

Talha, Zubayr, and 'Ā'isha wanted to reach present-day Iraq to challenge 'Alī. According to Shia sources a strange event then happened to 'Ā'isha. It had to do with the *Dogs of Haw'ab* (كِلَاب حَوْأَب) – these dogs play an important role in Shia Islam. Shia Muslims say that Muhammad had warned 'Ā'isha that one day, she would pass a place called Haw'ab where she would hear dogs barking – the signal that she was heading to make a huge mistake and that she should stop and go back.[438]

On their way to Basra to fight against Caliph 'Alī, 'Ā'isha, Talha, and Zubayr came across a place where dogs were barking. When she asked Talha about the name of the place, he answered: Haw'ab. 'Ā'isha remembered the words of the Prophet, but Zubayr assured her that the place is not called Haw'ab: "Whoever said this was Haw'ab was lying." And they all moved on. Shia Muslims calls these dogs the "dogs of sin".

Meanwhile, 'Alī had gathered fighters from all over. It came to a showdown at Basra in November 656. An estimated 18,000 soldiers (13,000 of 'Ā'isha's troops and 5,000 of 'Alī's) were killed, and among them were Talha and Zubayr. It was a civil war driven by hate. 'Ā'isha's brother, Muhammad, fought against her on the side of 'Alī. Zubayr, who was 'Alī's cousin, was on 'Ā'isha's side. Eventually 'Alī's troops won.

The Battle of the Camel secured 'Alī's position, but only temporarily. 'Ā'isha went back to Mecca, performed the 'Umra (lesser Pilgrimage), and retired in Medina — she was 45 years old. She never again attempted to interfere with the affairs of the Islamic state.

The Battle derived its name from the fierce fighting that centred around the camel, in particular the iron camel litter, the so-called Hawdaj (هَـوْدَج), upon which 'Ā'isha was mounted. The forces of 'Ā'isha, Zubayr, and Talha are referred to as the *companions of the camel* – in Arabic: 'Ashāb al-Jamal (أَصْحاب الْجَمَل).

---

438 ...قَالَ: لَمَّا أَقْبَلَتْ عَائِشَةُ، مَرَّتْ بِبَعْضِ مِيَاهِ بَنِي عَامِرٍ طَرَقَتْهُمْ لَيْلا ، فَسَمِعَتْ نُبَاحَ الْكِلابِ،
فَقَالَتْ: أَيُّ مَاءٍ هَذَا؟ قَالُوا: مَاءُ الْحَوْءَبِ، قَالَتْ: مَا أَظُنُّنِي إلا رَاجِعَةٌ، قَالُوا: مَهْلا يَرْحَمُكِ اللَّهُ، تَقْدَمِينَ
فَيَرَاكِ الْمُسْلِمُونَ، فَيُصْلِحُ اللَّهُ بِكِ، قَالَتْ: مَا أَظُنُّنِي إلا رَاجِعَةٌ، إِنِّي سَمِعْتُ رَسُولَ اللَّهِ، يَقُولُ:
"كَيْفَ بِإِحْدَاكُنَّ تَنْبَحُ عَلَيْهَا كِلابُ الْحَوْءَبِ."

Sahīh Ibn Hibbān 6887

Note 1: Some scholars say that this was not the first Islamic civil war. They say that it was the first Caliph, 'Abū Bakr, who waged war right after Muhammad's death against apostates or dissident Muslims – the so-called Ridda Wars.

Note 2: There is another Battle of the Camel in Arab history. It took place only a few years ago, during the Egyptian Revolution on 2nd February 2011 when the dictatorship of Hosni Mubarak sent out people on camels to beat and frighten the protestors in Tahrīr Square in Cairo.

320. What is a Fitna?

Answer: Fitna (فِتْنة) is a tricky word which means: *trial, enticement,* or *discord.*

In Islam, Fitna has been used in the sense of *revolt* or *civil war* that causes separatism and breeds schism. The assassination of the third Caliph, 'Uthmān (عُثْمان بن عَفّان), marks the *First Fitna* (فِتْنة مَقْتَل عُثْمان), i.e. the first Islamic civil war. The term Fitna was later applied to any period of disturbance in Muslim history: The *Second Fitna* (680-692), the *Third Fitna* (744-747), the *Fourth Fitna* (809-827) and the *Fitna of al-'Andalus* (1009-1031).

Edward Lane suggested that the primary meaning of the root is *to burn.* The verb came to be applied to the *smelting of gold and silver.* It was extended to mean *causing one to enter into fire and into a state of punishment or affliction*; in general, when some good or evil quality is put to the test.

Fitna can therefore be translated variously as *a trial, a probation, affliction, distress,* or *hardship.* If we take all this together, we could say that the sum of its meaning in the language of the Arabs is *an affliction whereby one is tried* or *tested.*

Note: *Fitna* was also the title of an Anti-Islam-film by the Dutch right-wing politician Geert Wilders.

321. What is the oldest Islamic sect?

Answer: The Khawārij or Kharijites (خارِجيّ ; plural: خَوارِج).

The Arabic word Khāriji literally means *dissidents, backsliders,* or *rebels.* The word comes from the Arabic root kh-r-j (خ-ر-ج) which means *to go out, come out, leave, separate,* or *secede.* The earliest Islamic sect traces its beginning to a controversy over the Caliphate. It all goes back to the governor of Syria, Mu'āwiya (مُعاوِيّة), who - like 'Ā'isha - sought to avenge the killing of 'Uthmān (عُثْمان بن عَفّان), the third Caliph.

'Alī ibn 'Abī Ṭālib (عَلِيّ بن أَبي طالِب), who succeeded Uthmān, had strong support in Iraq, particularly in the city of Kufa, where his supporters were angry about Mu'āwiya's refusal to pledge allegiance. Eventually, it came to war. In the summer of 657 (37 AH), only months after the Battle of the Camel, the armies of 'Alī and Mu'āwiya met near al-Raqqa (الرَّقّة) in Syria in the Battle of Siffin (وَقْعَة صِفّين).

Mu'āwiya's forces were close to losing, but then he employed a tactical trick. Mu'āwiya's men fixed copies of the Qur'an to their spears and cried out that Allah should decide. Some of 'Alī's soldiers - there were claims that they had been bought by Mu'āwiya earlier - put their swords down and stopped fighting. 'Alī was thus forced to a settlement (arbitration) and agreed to Mu'āwiya's proposal.

'Amr ibn al-'Āṣ (عَمْرو بن الْعاص), the arbiter of Mu'āwiya, convinced the arbiter of 'Alī that the solution should be as follows: They should deprive both 'Alī and Mu'āwiya of the Caliphate, and give the Muslims the right to elect the Caliph. 'Alī refused as he did not want to step down and hold an election. This weakened his position drastically and Mu'āwiya's forces moved into other areas and eventually overpowered Egypt and Yemen.

'Alī's decision had fatal consequences. It led to the formation of the Kharijites who previously were followers of 'Alī, but eventually killed him. The Kharijites initially followed 'Alī but later rejected his leadership after he had agreed to arbitration with Mu'āwiya rather than combat to decide the succession of the Caliphate.

They found prove for their position in a verse of sura 6 *Livestock* – in Arabic: al-'An'ām (سُورة الأَنْعام):

| 6:57 | Say, 'I stand on clear proof from my Lord, though you deny it. What you seek to hasten is not within my power. Judgement is for God alone: He tells the truth, and He is the best of judges.' | قُل إِنِّي عَلَى بَيِّنَةٍ مِّن رَّبِّي وَكَذَّبْتُم بِهِ مَا عِندِى مَا تَسْتَعْجِلُونَ بِهِ إِنِ الْحُكْمُ إِلَّا لِلَّهِ يَقُصُّ الْحَقَّ وَهُوَ خَيْرُ الْفَاصِلِينَ. |

They also believed that arbitration would be a rejection of the Islamic rule stated in sura 49 *The Private Rooms* – in Arabic: al-Hujurāt (سُورة الْحُجُرات):

| 49:9 | If two groups of the believers fight, you [believers] should try to reconcile them; if one of them is [clearly] oppressing the other, fight the oppressors until they submit to God's command, then make a just and even-handed reconciliation between the two of them: God loves those who are even-handed. | وَإِن طَائِفَتَانِ مِنَ الْمُؤْمِنِينَ اقْتَتَلُوا فَأَصْلِحُوا بَيْنَهُمَا فَإِن بَغَتْ إِحْدَاهُمَا عَلَى الْأُخْرَى فَقَاتِلُوا الَّتِي تَبْغِي حَتَّى تَفِيءَ إِلَى أَمْرِ اللَّهِ فَإِن فَاءَتْ فَأَصْلِحُوا بَيْنَهُمَا بِالْعَدْلِ وَأَقْسِطُوا إِنَّ اللَّهَ يُحِبُّ الْمُقْسِطِينَ. |

They thus started a revolt against 'Alī. The Kharijites claimed that 'Alī had lost legitimacy by submitting himself to arbitration.

It came to a showdown between the Caliph and the Kharijites in the Battle of Nahrawān (مَعْرَكة النَّهْرَوان) in 659. Prior to that, 'Alī had received the news that the Kharijites had slaughtered the Governor of Nahrawān. Nahrawān is located near Baghdad. The Kharijites were heavily outnumbered as some sources say that they had 2,800 fighters whereas the army of 'Alī consisted of nearly 80,000 men.

Although 'Alī won the battle, the bloody conflict was actually just about to begin. 'Alī was assassinated by a Kharijite partisan in 661.

The Kharijites thought that the successor of Muhammad should be the most dignified Muslim regardless if he was a relative of Muhammad or not. They said that Allah's judgement could only be expressed through the free choice of the entire Muslim community.

They insisted that anyone, even a black slave, could be elected Caliph. The Kharijites thus set themselves against the legitimate claims of the tribe of Quraysh (among the Sunnis) and of 'Alī's descendants (among the Shia). Besides their democratic theory of the Caliphate, the Kharijites were known for their puritanism and fanaticism. Any Muslim who committed a major sin was considered an apostate. Literal interpretation of the Qur'an was insisted upon. The al-'Ibādīya (الإباضيّة) - named after 'Abd Allah ibn 'Ibād (عَبْد الله بن إباض) - are a moderate Kharijite sect that started in the 7th century. The sect has survived until today in North Africa (Tunisia, Island of Djerba), Oman, and Zanzibar and has about half a million followers.

Although it is not entirely clear whom Muhammad had in mind in the following Hadith, fanatical Muslims refer to this Hadith to denounce Muslims by calling them Kharijites. It was narrated that Ibn 'Abī 'Awfa (ابن أبي أوفَى) said: "The Messenger of Allah said: 'The Khawārij are the dogs of Hell.'"[439]

322. Who was the last Shia Caliph?

Answer: 'Alī's son, Hasan.

After 'Alī's death in 661, his son Hasan became Caliph, which was not accepted by Mu'āwiya (مُعاويّة), the influential and successful member of the Umayyad dynasty. Mu'āwiya had already rejected 'Alī as Caliph.

Six months later in the same year (661) Hasan made a peace treaty with Mu'āwiya. In the Hasan-Mu'āwiya treaty, power was handed over to Mu'āwiya on the condition that he would be just to the people and would not appoint someone from this family. Hasan was also the last Imam of the Shia Muslims to be Caliph.

Later, Mu'āwiya broke the conditions of the agreement and founded the Umayyad dynasty with its capital in Damascus. He became Caliph in 661 and was the second Caliph from the Umayyad clan, the first being 'Uthmān ibn 'Affān.

One of Mu'āwiya's most controversial decisions was the appointment of his son Yazīd as his successor. Yazīd ruled for three years from 680 until his death in 683. He was killed in his thirties, by his own horse after he lost control.

---

439 ... قَالَ رَسُولُ اللَّهِ: "الْخَوَارِجُ كِلَابُ النَّارِ." (173) Sunan ibn Māja 178

Shia Muslims reject Mu'āwiya. They claim that he broke the treaty he had made with Hasan because he appointed his son as his successor. Furthermore, Shia Muslims claim that he was responsible for the killing of Hasan by bribing Hasan's wife to poison him.

Mu'āwiya died in 680 at a high age of almost 80. After his death, a conflict over succession broke out again in a civil war which became known as the *Second Fitna*.

During the Umayyad dynasty, Arabic became the official language in the empire. The dynasty also kept control of the caravan trade between Syria and Yemen. For this reason, Mu'āwiya had chosen to stay in Damascus, the provincial capital.

The financial administration of the empire was reorganised, with Arabs replacing Persian and Greek officials; and a new Arabic coinage replaced the former imitations of Byzantine and Persian coins. The Umayyads were lax Muslims. There are claims that some of Mu'āwiya's descendants were drinking alcohol and there were rumours of sexual exploitation.

Major revolts started when the empire became more and more multicultural. Syria remained the base of Umayyad power until the end of the dynasty. The last Umayyad Caliph, Marwān II (reigned 744-750), was defeated at the Battle of the Zāb River (مَعْرَكة الزّاب) in 750. Members of the Umayyad were hunted down and killed, but one of the survivors, 'Abd al-Rahmān (عَبْد الرَّحْمٰن), escaped and established himself as a Muslim ruler in Spain (756), where he founded a Umayyad dynasty in Córdoba (قُرْطُبة).

In Córdoba (al-'Andalus, i.e. present-day Portugal and Spain) the dynasty was reborn in the form of an independent Emirate and a Caliphate following the Umayyad conquest of Hispania in 711 to 718. The rulers of this province established their capital in Córdoba.

When the Umayyads had lost their ruling position in Damascus to the Abbasids in 750, al-'Andalus continued as an independent emirate.

323. What is the *Greek Fire*?

Answer: A weapon employed by the Byzantines to stop the Muslims.

Within a generation Syria, Palestine, and Egypt had fallen to the Arabs who, in 672, set out to conquer Constantinople (now Istanbul). The Caliphs Sulaymān and 'Umar II started the Islamic Expansion into Europe in 717-718. The Byzantines were weakened by the long wars with Sassanid Persia, but Emperor Leo III could stop the Muslims – with a newly invented weapon.

The so-called *Greek fire* was as an incendiary weapon (working with fire) developed around 672. It provided a technological advantage and was the key to many Byzantine victories. The *Greek fire* was used against the Muslim fleet, and was successful in repelling the Muslims in the first two Arab sieges of Constantinople.

It is not clear how the *Greek fire* worked, especially what the flammable liquids consisted of. Most probably it was made of various substances including pine resin, naphtha, quicklime, calcium phosphide, sulphur, or nitre.

Although the term *Greek fire* has been used in English since the Crusades, original Byzantine sources called the substance a variety of names, for example: *sea fire* (ancient Greek: πῦρ θαλάσσιον; pŷr thalássion), *Roman fire*, *war fire*, or *manufactured fire*.

324. What happened to the Colossus of Rhodes?

Answer: At first it was destroyed by an earthquake. Then, as legend has it, Islamic conquerors sold the ruins.

Rhodes is a Greek island north-east of Crete, just off the Anatolian coast of Turkey. The island was already inhabited in the Neolithic period and was later overtaken by the Mycenaean Greeks, the Dorians, the Persians, and then the Romans. Today, around 120,000 people live there. Historically, Rhodes was famous for the Colossus of Rhodes, one of the Seven Wonders of the Ancient World.

The Colossus was a statue of Helios, the Greek titan-god of the sun, and was built in 280 BC. It was 30 m (98 ft) tall making it one of the tallest statues of the ancient world. It was constructed to celebrate

Rhodes' victory over Cyprus which unsuccessfully besieged Rhodes in 305 BC.

In 226 BC, however, an earthquake struck Rhodes. Most of the island was destroyed and the statue collapsed.

Ptolemy III (of Egypt) offered to pay for the reconstruction of the statue, but the oracle of Delphi warned the Rhodians from rebuilding it because they had offended Helios. According to Greek historians the remains of the statue had been laying on the ground for over 800 years. Even broken up they were impressive. Gaius Plinius Secundus (Pliny the Elder), a Roman author and natural philosopher, wrote that few people could wrap their arms around the fallen thumb and that each of its fingers was larger than most statues. When I lived in Egypt, Muslims told me that the Colossus was "the biggest idol in the world at that time".

Rhodes was occupied by the Islamic forces of the Umayyad Caliph Muʿāwiya I (مُعاوِيّة بن أَبي سُفْيان) in 653/654 (31 AH). It was Christian at that time. There is a rumour that Muʿāwiya pillaged the remains of the Colossus of Rhodes.

Legend has it that the Arabs disassembled the remains of the broken Colossus and shipped them to Asia Minor. According to *The Chronicle* of Theophanes the Confessor, a monk and chronicler of the 7th century, the bronze parts of the statue were melted and sold to a Jewish merchant of Edessa who loaded the bronze on 900 camels. Edessa is the ancient name of Şanlıurfa in Turkey. Some sources, however, say the Jew was from Emesa which would be Homs in present-day Syria.

In 715 the Byzantine fleet launched a rebellion at Rhodes.

325. During the reign of which "commander of the faithful" has Tunisia been conquered?

Answer: ʿUthmān ibn ʿAffān (عُثْمان بن عَفّان).

Born	~ 576 (47 BH) in al-Ṭāʾif or Mecca	Died	656 (35 AH) in Medina

'Uthmān was a companion of the Prophet and the third of the *Rightly Guided Caliphs* – in Arabic: al-Rāshidūn (الرّاشِدُون). 'Uthmān was born into the rich and powerful Umayyad clan of Mecca (بَنُو أُمَيّة). He became a wealthy merchant. In the beginning, he had opposed Muhammad as did the entire Umayyad clan, but approximately five years after the Prophet had started his mission, 'Uthmān embraced Islam. He was the first convert of high social and economic standing. When the second Caliph, 'Umar ibn al-Khattāb (عُمَر بن الْخَطّاب), was assassinated in 644 (23 AH) by a Persian slave, 'Uthmān was elected as his successor after some tactical manoeuvres. His rival was 'Alī ibn 'Abī Tālib (عَلي بن أَبي طالِب).

It was 'Uthmān who established an official version of the Qur'an for the first time. 'Uthmān also centralised the administration of the Caliphate. During his 12-year rule, 'Uthmān had continued the military expeditions which had increased the size of the Islamic Empire dramatically. However, the victories now came at a greater cost and brought less booty in return.

The first invasion of North Africa, respectively the Maghreb, started in 647 (26/27 AH) when 20,000 Arabs marched from Medina in Arabia, another 20,000 joined them in Memphis in Egypt. The Byzantine army was defeated in the Battle of Sbeitla, a city 150 miles south of Carthage (which is in present-day Tunisia).

326. Who are the al-'Abādila?

Answer: The four companions with the name 'Abd Allah.

Among the most important Muslim warriors who conquered North Africa (Maghreb) were men who had the name 'Abd Allah. For this reason, the term al-'Abādila (الْعَبادِلة) came up. It is probably related to the fact that all these warriors were named 'Abd Allah.

The four most important Muslim fighters in North Africa were:

- 'Abd Allah ibn 'Umar (عَبْد الله بن عُمَر)
- 'Abd Allah ibn 'Abbās (عَبْد الله بن عَبّاس)
- 'Abd Allah ibn al-Zubayr (عَبْد الله بن الزُّبَيْر)
- 'Abd Allah ibn 'Amr ibn al-'Ās (عَبْد الله بن عَمْرُو بن الْعاص)

Note: Some Muslims, mostly followers of the Hanafi School of juris-prudence (الْحَنَفِيّة), claim that 'Abd Allah ibn Mas'ūd (عَبْد الله بن مَسْعُود) should belong to this group, and not 'Abd Allah ibn 'Amr ibn al-'Ās.

327. Who established the first mosque in Africa?

Answer: 'Amr ibn al-'Ās (عَمْرُو بن الْعاص).

Born	between 573 and 583 in Mecca	Died	664 (42 AH) in al-Fustāt, Egypt

In 639 Caliph 'Umar ibn al-Khattāb (عُمَر بن الْخَطّاب) dispatched an army of initially 4,000 men to Egypt under the command of 'Amr ibn al-'Ās.

In 640 his army defeated the Byzantine soldiers in the Battle of Heliopolis in Egypt – a decisive blow which initiated the decline of the Byzantine power in Egypt. 'Amr moved on to Alexandria which was surrendered to him by the Byzantine Empire in November 641.

In 642/643 (22 AH) 'Amr built the first mosque in Africa in al-Fustāt (الْفُسْطاط), the Muslim capital at that time of Egypt, south of present-day Cairo.

328. Why do some Muslims regard the Tunisian city of Kairouan holy?

Answer: Because of its connection to Mecca.

Today, the city of Kairouan (الْقَيْرُوان) in Tunisia is a UNESCO World Heritage site. In 2014 the city had about 190,000 inhabitants. It is a dry and hot place in summer. It was said that it was once the city with the highest density of mosques in the world.

In 670 the city of Kairouan, approximately 160 km (80 mi) south of Tunis, was established as a refuge and base for military operations of the Muslims. According to a legend, one of the soldiers of 'Uqba ibn Nāfi' (عُقْبة بن نافِع) - the founder of Kairouan - stumbled across a golden goblet buried in the sands. It was recognised as one that had disappeared from Mecca years before and when it was dug out of the sand a spring appeared, with waters said to come from the same source as those of the sacred Zamzam Well (زَمْزَم) in Mecca.

Kairouan became a place of pilgrimage. Some Muslims even call it "the Mecca of the Maghreb". It is perhaps the most important Islamic place in the Maghreb. ʿUqba ibn Nāfiʿ established the first Tunisian mosque in Kairouan. Tunisia was called 'Ifrīqiyā (إِفْرِيقِيا) at the time.

329. Which army leader conquered al-'Andalus?

Answer: Tāriq ibn Ziyād (طارِق بن زِياد).

Born	~ 679-670 (57-57 AH) probably in Algeria	Died	720 (101 AH) in Damascus

Tāriq was a Berber general which most Arabs don't like to hear as they consider themselves superior to the Berber tribes. He led the Muslim conquest of Spain and conquered al-'Andalus (الْأَنْدَلُس) which is called Andalusia in English. The name denotes those parts of Spain which were Arabised in the Middle Ages.

In May 711 Tāriq landed on Gibraltar with an army of 7,000 men, consisting mostly of Berbers, Syrians and Yemenites. Gibraltar became known as Jabal Tāriq (جَبَل طارِق) – lit: *Mount of Tāriq*. From this Arabic name, the Anglicised form *Gibraltar* became popular.

Spain at that time was under Visigothic rule but was dragged into a civil war. The rulers asked the Muslims for help, and they quickly responded to this request. The Muslims wanted to conquer Spain. The Visigoth king, Roderic, responded to the Muslim intrusion and organised an army of 100,000 soldiers. The two armies met in July 711 at the Guadalete River near the southern tip of the Iberian pen-insula. The Muslims were outnumbered as they had only 12,000 men – but they won nevertheless. 3,000 Muslim soldiers died.

King Roderic fled the battle, and Tāriq moved on and conquered Toledo, Seville, Jaen and Cordoba. The then appointed ruler of Morocco, Mūsā ibn Nusayr (مُوسَى بن نُصَيْر), also entered the Iberian

Peninsula with 18,000 soldiers in the following year. He conquered Seville, Mareda and Lisbon. Together, the two generals occupied more than two-thirds of the Iberian Peninsula. However, in 714, both Mūsā and Tāriq were summoned by the Caliph to Damascus. When they reached the capital, the Caliph was on his death bed, but he honoured them lavishly. When Caliph Sulaymān (سُلَيْمان بن عَبْد الْمَلِك) succeeded his brother, al-Walīd I (الْوَلِيد بن عَبْد الْمَلِك), in 715, he turned against the two commanders. He deprived them of all amenities. Tāriq died in Damascus in 720 in anonymity.

Remark: Gibraltar had been under the rule of Phoenicians, Carthaginians, Romans, and Visigoths but remained uninhabited until the Islamic invasion in 711. The Spaniards captured Gibraltar from the Moors in 1462 and retained it until 1704. In that year, it was surrendered to an Anglo Dutch force during the war of the Spanish Succession, and has since remained in British hands.

330. What did Tāriq ibn Ziyād do to motivate his warriors when he arrived at Gibraltar?

Answer: He (allegedly) burnt his own fleet.

This legend is based mainly on Western sources, but it is nevertheless very popular among Arabs.

After his warriors set foot on Iberian soil, Tāriq burnt his ships to further motivate his soldiers. He left them with only two choices: to either conquer Spain or to die in honour. His army consisted of around 12,000 soldiers, and most of them were infantry.

Tāriq became famous for the following quote:

"Oh my warriors, whither would you flee? Behind you is the sea, before you the enemy. You have left now only the hope of your courage and your constancy."[440]

From an Islamic point of view, this legend has some inconsistencies:

---

440 ...أَيُّها النّاس، أَيْنَ المَفَرُّ؟ الْبَحْرُ مِن وَرائِكُم، والْعَدُوُّ أَمامَكُم وَلَيْسَ لَكُم وَاللَّهِ إلّا الصِّدْقُ والصَّبْرُ.

- According to Sharī'a Law burning is unacceptable in Islam and a pious and god-fearing man like Tāriq ibn Ziyād would probably not have done such a thing.
- Most of his ships were borrowed from the ruler of Ceuta (Morocco).
- In Jihād (جِهاد) Muslims are not allowed to flee. Tāriq either did not know about this rule, or he just didn't want to give his soldiers a chance to decide.
- Tāriq's brinkmanship seems to be at odds with his previous strategies.
- Furthermore, this legend is only found in Western sources. There is only one Arabic source, a book written by Muhammad al-'Idrīsī (مُحَمَّد الإدْرِيسِيّ) with the title *The Pleasure Excursion of One Who Is Eager to Traverse the Regions of the World*. In Arabic: Nuzha al-Mushtāqq fī 'Ikhtirāq al-'Āfāq (نُزهة المَشْتاقّ فِي إخْتِراق الآفاق). The author was a Muslim geographer and Egyptologist who lived in Palermo (Sicily). He published his work almost five centuries after Tāriq's conquest.

331. What is the Islamic "Golden Age"?

Answer: A period during which the Islamic world experienced scientific, economic and cultural flourishing.

The *Golden Age of Islam* (العَصر الذَّهَبِيّ) refers to the period in the history of Islam, traditionally dated from the 8th century to the 13th century, when Muslim scientists and scholars took a lead in mathematics, physics, astronomy, architecture, and medicine.

This period is understood to have begun during the reign of the Abbasid Caliph Hārūn al-Rashīd (هارُون الرَّشِيد) with the opening of the House of Wisdom (بَيْت الحِكْمة) in Baghdad where scholars from various parts of the world gathered and translated the world's classical knowledge (e.g. Greek) into Arabic.

The Crusades put the Islamic world under pressure in the 11th and 12th centuries. However, the far greater threat was coming from the east during the 13th century. In 1206 Genghis Khan had established a powerful dynasty among the Mongols of Central Asia. At the time of his death the Mongol Empire stretched from the Caspian Sea to the Sea of Japan. The empire's expansion continued after Genghis's death in 1227.

The invasion of Baghdad in 1258 - which had been the seat of the Caliphate since 751 - is considered to mark the end of the Islamic Golden Age during which the Caliphs had extended their rule from the Iberian Peninsula to Sindh (province of today's Pakistan).

The Mongols looted mosques, palaces, libraries and hospitals. The Grand Library of Baghdad was destroyed. Survivors reported that the waters of the Tigris ran black with ink from the enormous quantities of books thrown into the river and red from the blood of the scientists and philosophers killed.

The Mongol destruction of Baghdad was a psychological blow from which the Islamic Empire never recovered.

332. What does al-Mu'tazila mean?

Answer: It is an Islamic school of thought often described as the *Tationalists of Islam*. The literal translation of the Arabic word Mu'tazila (الْمُعْتَزِلة) means: *Those who withdraw* or *stand apart*.

In English, they are usually called Mu'tazilites. This school was formed in the 8th century and flourished in Basra and Baghdad (until the 10th century). The followers of al-Mu'tazila believed in the free will and in the supremacy of reasoned faith against faith which was adopted from other earlier authorities. They favoured a reasonable approach - in Arabic: 'aqlī (عَقْلِيّ) - over a traditional approach – in Arabic: naqlī (نَقْلِيّ).

A follower of this school is called Mu'tazilī (مُعْتَزِلِيّ). It is derived from the root '-z-l (ع-ز-ل) which basically means *to separate, to segregate*. In a reflexive meaning the term Mu'tazilī could be translated as *one who separates (oneself); withdraws from*.

Mu'tazila theology started when Wāsil ibn 'Atā' (واصل بن عطاء) had a religious dispute with his teacher in Basra in the 8th century. Wāsil asked about the legal state of a sinner: Is a person who has committed a serious sin a believer or an unbeliever?

His teacher replied that they remain a Muslim, i.e. a believer.

Wāsil disagreed and suggested that one who commits one of the greater sins in Islam, such as drinking alcohol or adultery, could be classed neither as *believer* - a Mu'min (مُؤْمِن) - nor as an *unbeliever* - Kāfir (كافِر). Instead, he would be in an intermediate position.

Wāsil's description became famous as "a position between two positions" – in Arabic referred to as al-Manzila bayna Manzilatayn (الْمَنْزِلة بَيْنَ مَنْزِلَتَيْنِ). Since his colleagues claimed that "Wāsil has withdrawn from us", this is said to be the origin of the movement's name. Therefore, he and his followers were labelled Mu'tazilī.

What are their most important demands and positions?

- Mu'tazilites rely on the freedom of will.
- Mu'tazilites deny the status of the Qur'an as co-eternal with Allah.
- Mu'tazilites say that good and evil were not determined by the divine books, but that they can be understood by reason instead. Reason, they claim, is the final arbiter to distinguish right from wrong.

Mu'tazila beliefs were usually denounced by Sunni Muslims. Shia Muslims, on the other hand, occasionally accepted their views. After the 10th century, the movement declined.

When the Sunni Seljuks came to power in the middle of the 11th century, the Mu'tazila school in Iraq lost its official support and gradually vanished.

Traditional Muslims and fanatics use the term Mu'tazila to denounce Muslim opponents. Thoughtful scholars like Muhammad Asad (L. Weiß), whose ideas are occasionally cited in this book, were denounced as being a follower of the school of al-Mu'tazila.

333. Who is the most famous Abbasid Caliph?

Answer: Hārūn al-Rashīd (هارُون الرَّشيد).

Born	766 (149 AH) in Rey, Abbasid Caliphate, present-day Iran	Died	809 (193 AH), aged 43, in Tus, Khorasan (Iran)

The Abbasid Caliphate (الْخِلافة الْعَبّاسِيّة) is often described as the *Golden Age of Islamic Culture.* The dynasty ruled the Caliphate from 750 to 1258, making it one of the longest and most influential Islamic dynasties. For most of its early history it was the largest empire in the world and this meant that it had contact with distant neighbours such as the Chinese and Indians in the east and the Byzantines in the west.

The Abbasid dynasty overthrew the preceding Umayyad dynasty in Damascus, Syria. The Umayyads had become increasingly unpopular, especially in the eastern territories of the Caliphate. The early Muslim conquest of Persia was coupled with an anti-Persian Arabisation policy which led to much discontent. The Umayyads favoured Arabs over other Muslims and treated newly converted Muslims as second-class citizens.

The Battle of the Zāb (مَعْركة الزّاب) took place on the banks of the Great Zāb River in present-day Iraq in the winter of 750. It marked the end of the Umayyad Caliphate and the rise of the Abbasid dynasty. The Abbasid dynasty claimed to be members of the family of the Prophet, descendants of Muhammad's uncle al-'Abbās (الْعَبّاس بن عَبْد الْمُطَّلِب), whom they are also named after. The end of the Umayyad dynasty changed the character of the Islamic empire drastically: It marked the end of the Arab empire and the beginning of a more inclusive, multi-ethnic state in the Middle East. It reoriented the focus of the Muslim world to the east.

Hārūn al-Rashīd was the son of the third Abbasid Caliph (ruled 775–785) and a former slave girl from Yemen. Later Hārūn became the 5th Caliph in the reign of the Abbasid dynasty. His Caliphate (786-809) is considered the Golden Age of the Abbasid reign.

His military expedition brought him to the Bosporus, opposite Constantinople, and peace was concluded on terms favourable to the Muslims in 782. For this achievement, Hārūn was honoured with the honorific title of al-Rashīd (الرَّشيد) – literally *the one following the right path.*

Despite the revolts and rebellions in his empire (especially in Egypt, Syria, and Yemen) it remained more or less peaceful. This led to a great development of industries, such as textiles, metal goods, paper, and to an expansion of trade.

However, Caliph Hārūn did not live the life of a modest Muslim. He ruled Islam at the zenith of its empire with a luxury in Baghdad memorialised in *One Thousand and One Nights* (The Arabian Nights), a collection of folk tales and stories. The fabulous descriptions of Hārūn and his court in *The Thousand and One Nights* are idealised and romanticised; there is, however, some truth in it. His wife drank and ate only from vessels of gold and silver (which the Prophet strictly prohibited). Hārūn's palace was an extraordinary place with numerous eunuchs, concubines, singing girls, and with male and female servants. Hārūn loved music and poetry and gave generous gifts to musicians and poets.

Hārūn was not a great ruler; instead he became famous for his love of arts and luxury. Hārūn ruled for 21 years. In autumn of 808 he fell sick on his way to Khorasan (Iran) where he wanted to settle a revolt. Months later, in 809, he died at the age of about 46.

334. Who was 'Abū al-'Abbās?

Answer: An Asian elephant. It was a gift from the Abbasid Caliph Hārūn al-Rashīd (هارُون الرَّشِيد) to the Carolingian emperor Charlemagne (Charles the Great; in German: Karl der Große).

The elephant was called 'Abū al-'Abbās (أَبُو الْعَبَّاس). The elephant's name and adventures are recorded in the Carolingian *Annales regni Francorum* and in Einhard's Vita Karoli Magni. However, references to the gift or to interactions with Charlemagne in general are only found in Abbasid records.

'Abū al-'Abbās was taken from Baghdad, the capital city of the Abbasid empire, by a Frankish Jew named Isaac. Researchers have tried to retrace Isaac's route and came to the following possible course: from the Egyptian coast, he went to Tunisia and set sail probably from the port of Carthage. What is known for certain is that they arrived in Porto Venere (near Genoa) in October 801. Isaac and the elephant spent the winter in Vercelli, and in spring they started the march across the Alps to the Emperor's residence in Aachen (Germany), arriving on 20th July 802.

Charlemagne used the elephant in battles. 'Abū al-'Abbās suffered from rheumatism when he had accompanied Charlemagne across the Rhine heading into Friesland. According to various sources, in a spell of "cool rainy weather", 'Abū al-'Abbās developed pneumonia.

He died in the year 810, probably at an age above forty. His death was officially announced.

335. Who built the Ka'ba?

Answer: Probably Abraham – in Islam called 'Ibrāhīm (إِبْراهِيم).

The Ka'ba (الْكَعْبة) is 14 metres high (46 ft) from the eastern side, around 12 m (39,7 ft) from the western and southern sides, and roughly 11 m (36 ft) from the northern side. The door of the Ka'ba is made of wood and covered with 280 kg (617 lb) of pure gold.

The word Ka'ba literally means *cube* or *cubic structure*. It denotes any square (or cubic) house or chamber. The Ka'ba is also called al-Bayt (الْبَيْت). Normally, the Arabic word Bayt is used for *house*, but here it denotes *The Temple*. The Qur'an names the Ka'ba also *The Ancient Temple* (الْبَيْت الْعَتيق) as well as *The Inviolable House of Worship* (الْمَسْجِد الْحَرام).

Some Muslims suggest that it were angels who set the foundation of the Ka'ba, some say it was Adam (آدَم). The majority of Muslims are convinced that it was Abraham ('Ibrāhīm). The Black Stone (الْحَجَر الْأَسْوَد) and the stone, on which Abraham stood for height while building the structure, are the only remnants of the original structure according to Islamic sources.

In fact the Ka'ba was never worshipped prior to Muhammad's prophethood. The building contained idols of worship but the building itself was never an object of worship. Over the centuries local tribes who lived around the water well of Zamzam started to worship idols which were placed inside the Ka'ba.

Thirty years after Muhammad was born (but still some years before he received his first revelation), there was a big fire in the Ka'ba. A woman had set it on fire, and the building became fragile. This was not the only incident that destroyed the Ka'ba; it had happened many times.

In fact the Ka'ba has been rebuilt at least 12 times and among the people who reconstructed it were probably: Abraham, Ishmael, Qusayy ibn Kilāb (قُصَي بن كِلاب), 'Abd Allah ibn al-Zubayr (عَبْد الله بن الزُّبَيْر) in 685 (65 AH), al-Hajjāj ibn Yūsuf (الْحَجّاج بن يُوسُف) in 693 (74 AH), and Sultan Murad IV (السُّلْطان مُراد الرّابِع) in 1631 (1040 AH).

There is some information in the Hadiths that the Black Stone was once dazzling white but that had turned black because of the sins it has absorbed over the years. 'Abd Allah ibn 'Abbās (عَبْد الله بن عَبّاس) narrated that the Messenger of Allah said: "The Black Stone descended from Paradise and it was whiter than milk, then it was blackened by the sins of Adam's children."[441] Another Hadith mentions that it was *whiter than snow/ice* (الثَّلْج).

336. Who stole the Black Stone from the Ka'ba?

Answer: 'Abū Tāhir (أَبُو طاهِر); his full name is 'Abū Tāhir Sulaymān al-Jannābī (أَبُو طاهِر سُلَيْمان الْجَنّابِيّ).

Born	906 (293 AH) in Bahrain (historical region)	Died	944 (333 AH)

The Black Stone (الْحَجَر الأَسْوَد) has suffered significant damage over the course of time. It is said to have been struck and smashed to pieces by a rock shot from a catapult during the Umayyad siege of Mecca in 683 (64 AH). Afterwards the pieces were put together by 'Abd Allah ibn al-Zubayr (عَبْد الله بن الزُّبَيْر) using a silver ligament.

'Abū Tāhir was a ruler of the Qarmatian state (a Shia sect) in (historical) Bahrain. Note that Eastern Arabia was historically known as Bahrain (الْبَحْرَيْن) - which literally means *the two seas* - until the 18th century and stretched from south of Basra along the Persian Gulf coast and included the regions of Bahrain, Kuwait, Qatif, United Arab Emirates, Qatar, southern Iraq and northern Oman.

---

441 ...قَالَ رَسُولُ اللَّهِ: " نَزَلَ الْحَجَرُ الْأَسْوَدُ مِنَ الْجَنَّةِ وَهُوَ أَشَدُّ بَيَاضًا مِنَ اللَّبَنِ فَسَوَّدَتْهُ خَطَايَا بَنِي آدَمَ ". *Jāmi' al-Tirmidhī 877; hasan*

The Qarmatians were a religious sect that combined elements of Ismāʿīlī Shia Islam with Persian mysticism. They tried to establish a religious utopian republic in 899 in al-'Ahsā' (الأَحْساء), a traditional oasis region in present-day eastern Saudi Arabia. Historically, they became known for their revolt against the Abbasid Caliphate.

In 930 (317 AH), 'Abū Tāhir attacked Mecca during the Hajj pilgrimage season. Thousands of pilgrims were slaughtered. Reports claim that many dead bodies were thrown into the streets and even into the well of Zamzam, and were left to rot.

The Ka'ba was looted. 'Abū Tāhir stole the Black Stone and brought it to al-'Ahsā'. The Ottoman historian Qutb al-Dīn wrote centuries later that 'Abū Tāhir set the Black Stone up in his own mosque with the idea to redirect the pilgrims away from Mecca.

According to historian al-Juwaynī (الجُوَيْنِي), the Stone was returned 23 years later in 952. The Qarmatians held the Black Stone for ransom and forced the Abbasids to pay a huge sum for its return. It was wrapped in a bag and thrown into the *Friday Mosque* at Kūfa, together with a note that said: "By command we took it and by command we have brought it back."

Some reports claim that the abduction and removal of the stone caused further damage, breaking it into seven pieces. 'Abū Tāhir is said to have met a terrible fate. The Ottoman historian Qutb al-Dīn claimed that "the filthy 'Abū Tāhir was afflicted with a gangrenous sore, his flesh eaten away by worms, and that he died a most terrible death."

337. Who has the keys to the Ka'ba?

Answer: The Banū Shayba tribe (بَنُو شَيْبة).

The word for custodian or gatekeeper in Arabic is Sidāna (سدانة). The Sidāna(t) al-Ka'ba (سدانة الْكَعْبة) - gatekeeper of the Ka'ba - is a very old profession. It basically means taking care of the Ka'ba, open and close its doors, clean and wash it, repair and be responsible for the Kiswa (كِسْوة), the Ka'ba's cover.

For more than 16 centuries, starting before the founding of Islam, the descendants of Qusayy ibn Kilāb (قُصَيّ بن كلاب) have this job.

Quasyy is the great-great-great-grandfather of the Prophet. So, he was the great-grandfather of Shayba ibn Hāshim (شَيْبة بن هاشِم), who is better known as 'Abd al-Muttalib (عَبْد الْمُطَّلِـب), Muhammad's grand-father. Thus, the clan's name - Banū Shayba (بَنُو شَيْبة) - derives from Muhammad's great-grandfather.

Qusayy ruled as a king. He reconstructed the Ka'ba from a state of decay and made the Arab people build their houses around it. He is known to have built the first "town hall" in the Arabian Peninsula, a spacious domicile where leaders of different clans met to discuss their social, commercial, cultural, and political problems.

The Ka'ba is opened twice a year for cleaning, when it is washed with a mixture made from Zamzam water, al-Tā'if rosewater, and expensive Oud oil (agarwood) that is traditionally used in Arabian perfumes.

The cleaning takes place twice a year, on the 15th of Sha'bān (the month preceding Ramadan) and in mid-Muharram (the month after Dhū al-Hijja when Muslims perform Hajj). Sometimes influential people and foreign diplomats are invited to the ceremony.

338. Which of Muhammad's companions publicly recited the Qur'an for the first time at the Ka'ba (after the Prophet)?

Answer: 'Abd Allah ibn Mas'ūd (عَبْد الله بن مَشعُود).

Born	~ 594 (~31 BH) in Mecca	Died	~ 652 (32 AH)

'Abd Allah's parents were slaves and his family was of low status. He was one of the first people who embraced Islam. According to a Hadith, he was a physically weak person.

'Umm Mūsā (أُمّ مُوسَى) said: "I heard 'Alī say that the Prophet commanded 'Abd Allah ibn Mas'ūd to climb a tree and bring him something from it. His companions looked at 'Abd Allah's thigh and laughed at its thinness. The Messenger of Allah said: 'Why are you laughing? 'Abd Allah's foot is heavier in the balance than the mountain of 'Uhud.'"[442]

Let's now focus on the recitation (جَهْر بِالْقُرْآن) at the Ka'ba. This event is mentioned in the biography of Muhammad by Ibn 'Ishāq.

Ibn 'Ishāq reported that the companions came together one day: "The Quraysh had never heard the Qur'an distinctly read to them and who was there who would make them listen to it?" When 'Abd Allah answered that he would do so, the other companions replied that they were afraid of his status and that they wanted a man from a good family, who could protect him if he would be attacked.

He replied: "Let me alone, for Allah will protect me."[443] In the morning 'Abd Allah went to the Ka'ba and recited the Basmala ("In the name of Allah..."), raising his voice as he did so, "the compassionate who taught the Qur'an."

Then he turned towards them [the Quraysh] so that they noticed him, and they said: "What on earth is this son of a slave woman saying?" And when they realised that he was reading some of what Muhammad prayed [preached], they got up and began to hit him in the face.

Then he went to his companions with the marks of the blows on his face. They said: "This is just what we feared would happen to you."[444] He said: "Allah's enemies were never more contemptible in my sight than they are now and if you like, I will go and do the same thing before them tomorrow."[445]

Note: 'Abd Allah ibn Mas'ūd said that, according to the writings of Ibn 'Ishāq, "we [Muslims] could not pray at the Ka'ba until 'Umar became a Muslim and then, he fought the Quraysh until he could pray there, and we prayed with him."

---

442 ...أُمِّ مُوسَى قَالَتْ:... أَمَرَ النَّبِيُّ عَبْدَ اللهِ بْنَ مَسْعُودٍ أَنْ يَصْعَدَ شَجَرَةً فَيَأْتِيَهُ مِنْهَا بِشَيْءٍ، فَنَظَرَ أَصْحَابُهُ إِلَى سَاقِ عَبْدِ اللهِ فَضَحِكُوا مِنْ حُمُوشَةِ سَاقَيْهِ، فَقَالَ رَسُولُ اللهِ: مَا تَضْحَكُونَ؟ لَرِجْلُ عَبْدِ اللهِ أَثْقَلُ فِي الْمِيزَانِ مِنْ أُحُدٍ. al-'Adab al-Mufrad 237.

443 ...دَعُونِي فَإِنَّ اللهَ سَيَمْنَعُنِي. Ibn 'Ishāq.

444 ...هَذَا الَّذِي خَشِينَا عَلَيْكَ. Ibn Hishām/'Ishāq or al-Mustadrak 3:215.

445 ...كَانَ أَعْدَاءُ اللهِ أَهْوَنَ عَلَيَّ مِنهم الآنَ، ولئِنْ شِئتم لأُغَادِيَنَّهُمْ بِمِثلِها غَدًا. Ibn Hishām/'Ishāq or al-Mustadrak 3:215

339. Which famous battles were fought during Ramadan?

Answer: The Battle of Badr (غَزْوة بَدْر) in 624 (2 AH) and the Conquest of Mecca (غَزوة فَتْح مَكّة) in 630 (8 AH).

It is a widespread misconception, especially among non-Muslims, that Muslims are not allowed to fight in the month of Ramadan. Instead, if we look at the history of Islam, Ramadan was one of the bloodiest months. In addition to that, Ramadan was also used to train for wars.

For Muslims, Ramadan is a time of great trials and crucial events. Muslims in Egypt and Tunisia told me that Ramadan is the month of Jihād. This perception goes back to a Hadith. ʾAbū Hurayra (أَبُو هُرَيْرة) narrated that the Messenger of Allah said: "When Ramadan begins, the gates of Paradise are opened, the gates of Hell are closed, and the devils are chained up."[446]

During Ramadan, in addition to fasting, Muslims are instructed to refrain from sinful behaviour – such as lies, insults, but also fighting. However, Ramadan is also the month of heroism and victory in Islam. Such was the month of Ramadan in the time of the Prophet.

After the migration from Mecca to Medina the Prophet and his companions passed through approximately nine Ramadans together. It was this specific month which, over the years, was filled with decisive events.

Here are some decisive battles that took place during Ramadan:

- 624 – Battle of Badr (غَزْوة بَدْر). This was the first major battle between the Muslims and their enemies in Mecca.

- 627 – Battle of the Trench (غَزْوة الْخَنْدَق). Muslims trained for this battle during Ramadan, though it was most probably fought in the succeeding month (Shawwāl).

- 630 – Conquest of Mecca (غَزوة فَتْح مَكّة) by the Muslims.

- 653 – Conquest of Rhodes.

---

446 ...قَالَ رَسُولُ اللَّهِ: "إِذَا دَخَلَ رَمَضَانُ فُتِّحَتْ أَبْوَابُ الْجَنَّةِ وَغُلِّقَتْ أَبْوَابُ جَهَنَّمَ وَسُلْسِلَتِ الشَّيَاطِينُ." Sunan al-Nasāʾī 2099

- 710 – Muslims led by Tāriq ibn Ziyād (طارق بن زياد) invaded the Spanish southern frontier defeating King Roderick. The Muslims stayed for around eight hundred years.

- 1099 – Battle of Ascalon. It took place during Ramadan shortly after the Crusaders had captured Jerusalem from the Fatimid Caliphate. It is considered the last action of the First Crusade defeating the Muslims.

- 1260 – Battle of 'Ayn Jālūt (مَعْرَكة عَيْن جالُوت), literally *the Spring of Goliath*. Muslim Mamluks fought against the Mongols in south-eastern Galilee. For the first time, a Mongol advance was stopped.

- 1973 – October War (حَرْب أُكْتُوبَر), also known as the Yom Kippur War. The fighting took place in the Sinai and Golan Heights, territories that had been occupied by Israel since the Six-Day War of 1967. The war started when the Arab coalition launched a joint surprise attack on Israeli occupied territories on Yom Kippur, the holiest day in Judaism, which occurred in that particular year in the month of Ramadan. Eventually, Israel won.

- 1981 – Iran rejected Iraqi offers for a Ramadan ceasefire.

- 1982 – Iran launched an attack on Iraq near Basra which they explicitly called "Operation Ramadan". It was one of the largest land battles since World War II.

- 2000 – Kashmir Conflict, the territorial conflict between India and Pakistan. India offered a cease-fire in Ramadan. However, fighting continued between Indian forces and guerrilla fighters of Jammu and Kashmir which are mainly inhabited by Muslims.

340. What happened in the Muslim world in 1492?

Answer: The fall of Andalusia – in Arabic: al-'Andalus (الأَنْدَلُس).

In the West most people connect the year 1492 with Christopher Columbus and the discovery of the New World (America). In the Arab world, most people connect it with the end of the golden period of al-'Andalus (Muslim Spain). If you mention the word al-'Andalus, most Muslims in the Arab world feel proud and enthusiastic. The Islamic forces conquered most parts of the Iberian Peninsula (Spain and Portugal) in 710.

Instead of expelling all non-Muslims, Jews and Christians were forced to pay a tax, the so-called Jizya (جِزْية). And if they paid the tax, then they lived more or less in freedom. It was a relatively stable and peaceful atmosphere. Later, Córdoba became one of the leading cultural and economic centres of Europe where sciences flourished. Even today, Muslims use al-'Andalus as proof of their claim that an Islamic State or an Islamic Emirate would work well in reality.

However, the Christian forces in Europe did everything to regain their land. The so-called **Reconquista** (literally, *the reconquest*), a series of bloody wars, lasted for 770 years until the last Muslim state in Iberia at Granada was conquered in 1492. Not only the Muslims, but also the Jews had to leave, some of them escaped to North Africa.

So we could say that the year 1492 marks two things:

- The **end** of the good times in the eyes of many Muslims.
- The **start** of the good times in the eyes of many Europeans.

341. Was Cairo once a Shia city?

Answer: Yes. It was founded in the 10th century by a Shia dynasty.

Some people think that Cairo (القاهرة) is an ancient city with a tremendously old history. Well, it is actually not like that.

Egypt became Islamic in the middle of the 7th century, and after that, the Umayyad and Abbasid dynasty ruled there. Both were Sunni Muslims. Then a new power emerged: the Fatimids (الْفاطِمِيُّون), a Shia dynasty who claimed descent from the Prophet's daughter – Fātima bint Muhammad (فاطِمة بنت مُحَمَّد).

The Fatimids' aim was to overthrow the existing religious and political order in the Islamic world. They did not recognise the Abbasid Caliphs. Instead, the Fatimids were convinced that they were the rightful Caliphs – by descent and by divine choice. They were already strong in the Maghreb and finally achieved to conquer Egypt in 969 (358 AH). There they founded the city of Cairo. In

Arabic, Cairo is called al-Qāhira (القاهِرة). It means *the vanquisher* or *the conqueror.* The Fatimids established al-'Azhar (الْأَزْهَـر) which became the most prestigious place of Islamic learning.

One of their rulers, 'Abū Mansūr (أَبُو مَنْصُور), known as al-Hākim bi 'Amr Allah (الْحاكِم بِأَمْر الله), literally *the ruler by Allah's command,* was only eleven years old when he became Caliph. His reign was characterised by utmost cruelty and bloodshed. He ordered to destroy the Church of the Holy Sepulchre in Jerusalem which some historians see as the cause for the Crusades.

His successors were not much better. In addition to a lack of good leadership, natural disasters and famines, and the attacks of the crusaders weakened the Fatimid Empire dramatically.

In 1171 the last Caliph died. The Fatimid Caliphate (909 - 1171) was formally abolished when Saladin (صَلاح الدِّين الْأَيُّوبِيّ) became Sultan of Egypt and returned the country to the roots of the Sunni Muslim Abbasid Caliphate (الْخِلافة الْعَبّاسِيّة).

The impression that Shia Islam is imported or alien to Egypt is wrong. Today, up to two million Shia Muslims live in Egypt. According to the *CIA World Factbook* the total population in 2016 was about 94 million.

There are still some shrines and mosques dedicated to Husayn, Hasan, Zaynab, 'Alī, and other Shia Imams. Many of the Fatimids' traditions are still practised, such as celebrating the Prophet's birthday - in Arabic: Mawlid al-Nabī (مَولِد النَّبِي) -, the commemorating of al-Husayn's death - in Arabic: 'Āshūrā' (عاشُوراء) -, and even the usage of lanterns during Ramadan - called Fānūs (فانُوس) - is common in Egypt. The word *Fānūs* is a term of Greek origin. It means *light* or *lantern.* It was historically used in its meaning of *the light of the world* and is a symbol of hope (*light in the darkness*).

Ultra-conservative Salafis despise Shia Muslims as heretics. When I was in Egypt right after the revolution in 2011, Salafis were distributing leaflets saying: "Shia Muslims – they are more dangerous than the Jews and your biggest enemy".

342. Who founded the famous al-'Azhar university?

Answer: The Fatimid dynasty, a Shia sect.

This might sound strange at first. The al-'Azhar (الأَزْهَر) is a university in Cairo and is renowned as Sunni Islam's most prestigious university. Nowadays, al-'Azhar represents the four schools of Sunni Islamic jurisprudence (Hanafī, Mālikī, Shāfi'ī and Hanbalī) and the seven main Sufi orders.

That is also the reason why it is a hot topic when talking about Shia Islam in Egypt. Shia Islam has a long pedigree in Egypt. Fātima, the daughter of the Prophet and wife of 'Alī ibn 'Abī Tālib (عَلِيّ بن أَبِي طالِب) was called al-Zahrā' (الزَّهْرة) which means: *the luminous*. The university al-'Azhar was named in her honour.

In Egypt most people are afraid that one day Shia Muslims from Iran might take over al-'Azhar. In May 2012 al-'Azhar Grand Imam, 'Ahmad al-Tayyib, held a meeting with scholars, Muslim Brotherhood members, and Salafis at which they declared their total rejection of "attempts to spread Shia Islam in Egypt".

343. Who are the Druze?

Answer: A religious sect originating from a Shia Ismā'īlī sect.

The Druze people (دروز) reside primarily in Syria, Lebanon, Israel, and Jordan. It is <u>impossible</u> to convert to (or from) the Druze faith. The Druze faith originated in Egypt in the early 11th century as an offshoot of Ismā'īlī Shia during the reign of the 6th Fatimid Caliph, al-Hākim bi 'Amr Allah (الْحاكِم بِأَمْر الله), who ruled from 996 to 1021.

Some Ismā'īlī theologians began to organise a movement proclaiming al-Hākim a divine figure. Although the idea might have been encouraged by al-Hākim himself, it was condemned as heresy by the Fatimid religious establishment, which claimed that al-Hākim and his predecessors were divinely appointed but not themselves divine. In 1017 the doctrine was publicly preached for the first time, causing riots in Cairo.

Although the Druze religion began as a movement in Ismā'īlī Islam, it was later influenced by Greek philosophy and Gnosticism.

The name Druze is derived from Muhammad ibn 'Ismā'īl Nash-takin al-Darazi who was an early preacher. Although the Druze consider al-Darazi a heretic, the name stuck to identify them.

344. Whom is the district Sayyida Zaynab in Cairo named after?

Answer: This working-class quarter is one of the city's oldest. It was named after a mosque there: the Mosque of Sayyida Zaynab.

Zaynab (زَيْنَب بِنْت عَلِيّ) was one of the daughters of 'Alī ibn 'Abī Tālib (عَلِي بن أَبِي طالِب) and his (first) wife Fātima, the daughter of the Prophet. She was therefore a member of the household of Muhammad, so-called 'Ahl al-Bayt (أَهْل الْبَيْت).

Especially among Shia Muslims, she is revered as a symbol of sacrifice, strength, and piety. When her brother al-Husayn (بن الْحُسَيْن عَلِيّ) confronted the Umayyad Caliph Yazīd I (يَزِيد بن مُعاوِيّة) in 680 CE (61 AH) at Karbala, Zaynab played a central role in the aftermath by preserving his legacy and bearing witness to the tragedy. Shia Muslims honor her memory by naming her the *Hero of Karbalā'*.

The exact date and place of her death is not clear but she probably died in the year 681/682 (62 AH). Her shrine is located in Damascus, Syria. Some Sunni Muslims believe, however, that her grave can be found in a different mosque bearing the same name: the *Sayyida Zaynab Mosque* in Cairo. There is some historical evidence suggesting that Zaynab lived in Cairo near the end of her life.

Remark: When you hear that a girl is named after Zaynab, in many cases, it is likely that she is a Shia Muslim and not a Sunni.

345. Which Islamic hero was of Kurdish origin?

Answer: Saladin. In Arabic: Salāh al-Dīn al-'Ayyūbī (صَلاح الـدِّين الأَيُّوبِيّ).

Born	1138 (AH 532) in Tikrit (present-day Iraq)	Died	1193 (589 AH) in Damascus

His real name was Yūsuf ibn 'Ayyūb (يُوسُف بن أَيُّوب). The name Salāh al-Dīn is a so-called laqab (لَقَـب), a descriptive epithet. It means: *Righteousness of the Faith*. In English, he is called Saladin.

Saladin was born in 1138 (some say: 1137) in Tikrit in present-day Iraq (Upper Mesopotamia; Abbasid Caliphate). He was a Sunni Muslim of Kurdish origin. He is the founder of the Ayyubid dynasty (الأَيُّوبِيُّون), a Muslim sultanate, and Saladin thus became their first Sultan of Egypt and Syria.

Saladin led the Muslim military campaigns against the Crusaders. Under Saladin's command the Ayyubid army defeated the Crusaders at the decisive Battle of Hattīn in 1187. Saladin died in March 1193 (aged 55) in Damascus. He is buried in a mausoleum adjacent to the Umayyad Mosque.

346. Which Islamic leader retook the al-Aqsā Mosque in 1187?

Answer: Saladin. Arabic name: Salāh al-Dīn al-'Ayyūbī (صَلاح الدِّين الأَيُّوبيّ).

Muslims see the Crusades as one of the darkest chapters of Western history. The Siege of Jerusalem took place from June 7 to July 15, 1099, during the First Crusade. The Crusaders eventually seized Jerusalem from the Fatimid Caliphate.

However, a Muslim general managed to take it back almost 90 years later. Several Islamic scholars claim that the army of Saladin entered Jerusalem in 1187 (583 AH) shouting: "Allāhu 'akbar… Allāhu 'akbar!" as a sign of victory. After a siege, Jerusalem capitulated on Friday, 2nd October 1187.

The Battle of Hattīn and the Fall of Jerusalem prompted the Third Crusade (1189–1192), also known as *The Kings' Crusade*. It was an attempt by European leaders to recapture the Holy Land from Saladin. It was a bloody war. In Acre (present-day Akko in Israel), around 3,000 Muslim prisoners were executed, some say also including women and children. Saladin managed to defeat any attempt by *Richard the Lionheart* to retake Jerusalem. Richard had roughly 8,000-9,000 soldiers to use in battle. With such a small force, he could not expect or hope to take Jerusalem.

Saladin's relationship with Richard was complicated despite their military rivalry. The two men probably never met face to face, but they respected each other. At Arsuf, when Richard lost his horse, Saladin sent him two replacements. Richard proposed that his sister (and Queen of Sicily), Joan of England, should marry Saladin's brother and that Jerusalem could be their wedding gift. As leaders of their respective factions, the two men came to an agreement in 1192 (Treaty of Jaffa): Jerusalem would remain in Muslim hands but Christians would be allowed to do their pilgrimage.

Nevertheless, the wars continued until 1291, when the Crusades finally came to an end.

347. Where is Hattīn?

Answer: In Palestine.

Hattīn (حَطّين) was a Palestinian village located 8 km (5 mi) west of Tiberias in present-day Israel. The Battle of Hattīn took place there in 1187 and it was decisive. Saladin (صَلاح الدِّين) conquered most of Palestine from the Crusaders. Hattīn later became an Arab national-ist symbol.

Thereafter, the Muslims seized control of Palestine from the Cru-saders who had captured the area 88 years earlier. The defeat at Hat-tīn marked a turning point in the conflict with the Muslims.

The village Hattīn was later ruled by the Ottoman Empire, from the 16th century until the end of World War I, when Palestine became part of the British Mandate. In the 1948 Arab-Israeli war the village was depopulated.

Note: Hattīn has a mythical meaning for Islamic extremists and ter-rorists who claim to kill in Allah's name. There is a book called *Man-agement of Savagery* - in Arabic: 'Idāra(t) al-Tawahhush (إدارة التَّوَحُّش) - published in 2004 in Arabic by an author who calls himself 'Abū Bakr Nājī (أَبُو بَكْر ناجِي); his real identity is not entirely clear. The author writes that the defeat of the crusaders in the past "was only achieved by small battles that are hardly mentioned in history". Thus, it was a process of exhaustion and depletion. The author calls it "the power of vexation and exhaustion". He argues that the Muslim victory in the Battle of Hattīn was only possible because of previous small-scale skirmishes in several locations. "They were the primary reason for the achievement of the final, major victory."

He concluded: "Although the blow of the rod may only strike a (single) Crusader head, its spread and escalation will have an effect for a long period of time."

348. Where does the word *assassin* come from?

Answer: Probably from Arabic.

During the 16th century it entered the English language via Anglo-Latin and French. The word comes probably from the Arabic word Hashshāshīyūn (حَشّاشِيُّون) which literally means *hashish consumers.*

The Hashshāshīyūn were a fanatical Muslim sect at the time of the Crusades, with a reputation for murdering opposing leaders after intoxicating themselves by hashish. Modern scholars suggest this narrative was maybe propagated by rivals or later embellishments.

The word *assassin* is often believed to have derived from the word Hashshāshīyūn and shares its etymological roots with hashish (حَشِيش) which, in Arabic, literally means *grass.*

The story of the *Assassins (or Hashshāshīyūn)* goes back to 1090 (483 AH) when they stormed the mountain fortress of Alamut (Persian: الموت, perhaps meaning *Eagle's Nest*), located in the Alamut district of the South Caspian region, ca. 100 km (60 mi) from present-day Tehran. The leader of the assassins was Hasan al-Sabbāh (حَسَن الصَّباح), a Persian Nizārī Ismāʿīlī missionary. The Nizārīya (النّزاريّة) constitute the largest subgroup within Ismāʿīlī Shia Islam – which is the second-largest branch of Shia Islam. The group carried out targeted assassinations against key figures in the Seljuq, Abbasid as well as some Christian Crusader leaders, mainly for religious but also for political reasons. The Hashshāshīyūn even tried to kill Saladin (صَلاح الدِّين). The primary destruction of the Nizārī Ismāʿīlī state in Persia occurred when the Mongol invasion under Hulagu Khan culminated in the capture of Alamut in 1256; later, remnants of the Assassin network in Syria were subdued by the Mamluks.

Although it is commonly believed that the Assassins were under the influence of *hashish* during their killings or during their indoctrination, most scholars nowadays think that drug-use was perhaps not the key feature behind the name. In Arabic texts the term Hashshāshīyūn has been used without any further explanations.

Later, in Europe, Marco Polo described them as a sect consuming hashish, celebrating orgies, and killing important people with poison or dagger. He did not give sources, so it was more or less based on what he had been told. The earliest known literary use of the word *assassination* is in Macbeth by William Shakespeare (1605).

349. What does Sufism mean?

Answer: Sufism (تَصَوُّف) is a mystic and ascetic movement which originated in the Golden Age of Islam, in the 9ᵗʰ and 10ᵗʰ century.

Sufism denotes mystical Islamic belief and practice in which Muslims seek to find the truth of divine love and knowledge through direct personal experience of Allah.

Islamic mysticism is called Tasawwuf (تَصَوُّف) which means: *to dress in wool.* In English it is called Sufism since the early 19ᵗʰ century. The Arabic word Tasawwuf derives from the term sūf (صُوف), *wool*, probably a reference to the woollen garment of early Islamic ascetics.

The Sufis are also generally known as *the poor* - in Arabic: Fuqarā' (فُقَراء), which is the plural of the Arabic word faqīr (فَقير) -, and in Persian *darvish* (درويش), from which the English words *fakir* and *dervish* are derived.

The movement grew out of the desire and demand for Islamic asceticism in the early Umayyad period (661-749). Later, foreign elements from Europe and India entered the mystical theology and practices. Mystical trends grew then everywhere in the Islamic world, partly through an exchange of ideas with Christian hermits.

A number of mystics of the early generations had concentrated their efforts upon Tawakkul (تَوَكُّل), i.e. absolute trust in Allah, which became a central concept of Sufism.

Since they are constantly meditating the words in the Qur'an about Judgement Day, the ascetics became known as *those who always weep* and those who considered this world *a hut of sorrows.*

Remark: The city of Konya in Turkey is a centre for Sufism and Dervish-dancers. In the 13th century, the Persian Sufi mystic Rumi moved from Balkh (present-day Afghanistan) to Konya in Anatolia.

His name was Jalāl al-Dīn Muhammad Rūmī (Persian: جلال‌الدین محمد رومی). *Mevlana* (Turkish for مَوْلَانَا - *our master*) is a common epithet for Rumi. مَوْلَوِي typically refers to a follower of the Mevlevi Sufi order or the order itself, not directly as an alternative name for Rumi in the same way Mevlana is used. His poems, originally written in Persian, have been translated into many languages.

350. Who was the (first) Sufi woman?

Answer: Rābi'a al-'Adawīya al-Qaysīya (رابعة الْعَدَوِيّة الْقَيْسِيّة).

Born	~ 714 or 718 (96 or 100 AH) in al-Basra (الْبَصْرة)	Died	801 (185 AH) in Jerusalem; some say Basra

Rābi'a was a female Sufi mystic. She is known in some parts of the world as Rābi'a Basrī.

She was the fourth daughter of a poor but respected family and therefore named Rābi'a which is the Arabic word for *fourth.*

After the death of her father a famine overtook the city of Basra and Rābi'a had to leave her sisters. Legend has it that she was accompanying a caravan which fell into the hands of robbers. The chief of the robbers took Rābi'a captive and sold her in the market as a slave.

After she had finished her tasks in the house of her master, she would pass the whole night in prayer. She spent many of her days fasting. One day her master got up in the middle of the night and was attracted by Rābi'a's voice and overheard her praying: "Lord! You know well that my keen desire is to carry out Your commandments and to serve You with all my heart, O light of my eyes. If I were free, I would spend the whole day and night praying to You. But what should I do when You have made me a slave of a human being?"

In the morning, the master summoned her and said that if she wanted to leave the house he would be willing to set her free. She agreed and left. Rābi'a went into the desert and became an ascetic. She is also known as the *queen of saintly women*.

She thus became not only the first but probably also the most famous and influential Sufi woman in Islamic history.

351. Why did Iran (Persia) become a Shia country?

Answer: This is related to the Safavid dynasty.

The Islamic conquest of Persia (637-651) led to the end of the Sasanian Empire and the decline of the Zoroastrian religion in Persia. By the late 11th century the majority of Persians had embraced Islam. Nevertheless, the Persians had always tried to protect and revive their language and culture over the centuries.

Today Iran is a stronghold of Shia Islam. Until the early 16th century, both Iran and the Azerbaijan region were predominantly Sunni.

This all changed in 1501 when 'Ismā'īl I, a Shia Muslim, became the ruler (Shah) of a region which more or less corresponds with present-day Azerbaijan. 'Ismā'īl I (1487-1524) - in Persian: Shah 'Ismā'īl I (شاه اسماعیل) - was the founder of the Safavid dynasty (Persian: صفویان) which lasted until 1736. He was born in Ardabil, an ancient city near the border with the Republic of Azerbaijan at the Caspian Sea in present-day Iran. During his early reign he managed to conquer Iran and the neighbouring region: Iraq, Dagestan, Eastern Anatolia, and Armenia. Sunni Muslims that lived in these conquered territories were forced to adopt Shia Islam; it is said that some were even killed when they refused to do so.

By the mid-17th century most people in present-day Iran and the Republic of Azerbaijan had become Shia Muslims.

The Safavids were a so-called Twelver Shia religious sect. The Safavid dynasty ruled for over two centuries. It was a vast empire which would comprise today's Iran, Azerbaijan, Armenia, most of Georgia, the North Caucasus, Iraq, Kuwait, Afghanistan, parts of present-day Syria, Turkey, Pakistan, Uzbekistan, and Turkmenistan. Shia Islam became state religion in all these territories. This put a lot of pressure on the Ottoman Sultan Selim I who was a Sunni Muslim. He attacked 'Ismā'īl's forces in 1514 at Chaldiran (present-day Turkey) and won. It was the beginning of a long and bloody conflict. The Safavids lost Kurdistan, Diyarbakır, and Baghdad. Due to military setbacks and administrative challenges, Shah 'Abbās I eventually relocated the Safavid capital – moving it from Qazvin to the culturally and strategically significant city of Isfahan.

Many mosques and monuments were built in Isfahan, which is now a UNESCO world heritage site. The Naghsh-e Jahan Square is one of the largest city squares in the world and a remarkable example of Islamic architecture.

During his reign, Shah 'Abbās the Great managed to regain much of the lost territory, including the recapture of Baghdad in 1624, with the aid of military reforms and foreign expertise. 'Abbās I was aided by an Englishman, Sir Robert Shirley, who modernised and improved his military forces and introduced new weapons. In 1722 the Safavid dynasty came to its end. Isfahan fell to the Ghilzai Afghans of Kandahar (Pashto: کندهار, Persian: قندهار) in 1722.

Note: Shah is the Persian word for *king*, and *Schach* is the German word for *chess*. The German term *Schachmatt* (checkmate) is widely believed to derive from the compound expression *shah mat*. In this phrase, while the Arabic word *māta* (ماتَ) means *he died*, the Persian adjective *māt* (مات) more accurately means *helpless* or *stunned*. In other words, *shah mat* can be understood to mean *the king is left helpless* – a notion that later evolved into the checkmate concept in chess. Many linguists contend that this interpretation, rather than the idea that the king has died, captures the original idea better.

352. On which day do Iranians celebrate Mother's Day?

Answer: On the birthday of the Prophet's daughter Fātima (فاطِمة بِنْت مُحَمَّد).

Fātima was the wife of 'Alī ibn 'Abī Tālib (عَلِيّ بـن أَبِي طالِب), Muhammad's cousin. 'Alī later became the fourth (rightly guided) Caliph according to Sunni Islam. Shia Muslims treat him as the first Imam of Shia Islam. Fātima, especially among Shias, is referred to as a role model for all Muslim women. Mother's Day was originally observed on 16ᵗʰ December but the date was changed after the Iranian Revolution in 1979. Mother's Day in Iran is now celebrated on 20ᵗʰ Jumādā al-'Ākhira (جُمادَى الآخِرة) - the 6th month in the Islamic calendar - which coincided with 30ᵗʰ March 30 in 2016.

The celebration is both Women's Day (replacing International Women's Day) and Mother's Day. Note that since the Islamic calendar is a lunar calendar, there is no fixed equivalent date in the Gregorian calendar used in the West.

353. What does Dābiq mean?

Answer: It is a town in Syria where - according to Islamic eschatology - one of the *Final Battles* will take place.

Dābiq (دابِق) is a small town in northern Syria, about 40 km (25 mi) north-east of Aleppo and around 10 km (6 mi) south of Syria's border with Turkey. Before the civil war in Syria, there were around 3,300 people living there. The town was the location of the Battle of Marj Dābiq in 1516 in which the Ottoman Empire decisively defeated the Mamluk Sultanate.

However, Dābiq is supposedly also the location for one of the *Final Battles* according to Islamic myths about the apocalypse, when the Mahdī (الْهُدي) and (the Islamic version of) Jesus will bring victory over those who opposed Islam.

The source for this apocalyptic view is an authentic Hadith.

'Abū Hurayra (أَبُو هُرَيْرة) reported that Allah's Messenger has said: "The Last Hour would not come until the Romans would land at al-'Aʿmāq or in Dābiq. An army consisting of the best [soldiers] of the people of the earth at that time will come from Medina [to counteract them]. When they will arrange themselves in ranks, the Romans would say: 'Do not stand between us and those [Muslims] who took prisoners from among us. Let us fight with them'; and the Muslims would say: 'Nay, by Allah, we would never get aside from you and from our brethren that you may fight them.' They will then fight and a third [part] of the army would run away, whom Allah will never forgive. A third [part of the army], which would be constituted of excellent martyrs in Allah's eye, would be killed and the third, who would never be put to trial, would win and they would be conquerors of Constantinople [present-day Istanbul]. And as they would be busy in distributing the spoils of war [among themselves] after hanging their swords by the olive trees, the Satan would cry: The Dajjāl has taken your place among your family.

They would then come out, but it would be of no avail. And when they would come to Syria, he would come out while they would be still preparing themselves for battle drawing up the ranks. Certainly, the time of prayer shall come and then Jesus, son of Mary, would descend and would lead them in prayer.

When the enemy of Allah would see him, it would [disappear] just as the salt dissolves itself in water and if he [Jesus] were not to confront them at all, even then it would dissolve completely, but Allah would kill them by his hand and he would show them their blood on his lance [the lance of Jesus Christ]."[447]

It is probably no coincidence that the terrorist network ISIL (*Islamic State of Iraq and the Levant*) chose **Dābiq** as the name for its propaganda magazine. It was first published in July 2014 in a number of different languages, including English. Furthermore, ISIL's self-proclaimed "news agency" is called **al-'A'māq**.

Scholars and Hadith commentators suggest that the word *Romans* refers to Christians in general. The Hadith further relates the subsequent Muslim victory, followed by the (peaceful) takeover of Constantinople with invocations of "Allāhu 'akbar"- takbir (تَكْبِير) - and "Subhana Allah" - tasbih (تَسْبِيح), and finally the defeat of the Anti-Christ - in Islam called al-Dajjāl (الدَّجَال) - following the return and descent of Jesus Christ.

---

447 ...أَنَّ رَسُولَ اللَّهِ قَالَ: "لاَ تَقُومُ السَّاعَةُ حَتَّى يَنْزِلَ الرُّومُ بِالأَعْمَاقِ أَوْ بِدَابِقَ فَيَخْرُجُ إِلَيْهِمْ جَيْشٌ مِنَ الْمَدِينَةِ مِنْ خِيَارِ أَهْلِ الأَرْضِ يَوْمَئِذٍ فَإِذَا تَصَافُّوا قَالَتِ الرُّومُ خَلُّوا بَيْنَنَا وَبَيْنَ الَّذِينَ سَبَوْا مِنَّا نُقَاتِلْهُمْ. فَيَقُولُ الْمُسْلِمُونَ لاَ وَاللَّهِ لاَ نُخَلِّي بَيْنَكُمْ وَبَيْنَ إِخْوَانِنَا. فَيُقَاتِلُونَهُمْ فَيَنْهَزِمُ ثُلُثٌ لاَ يَتُوبُ اللَّهُ عَلَيْهِمْ أَبَدًا وَيُقْتَلُ ثُلُثُهُمْ أَفْضَلُ الشُّهَدَاءِ عِنْدَ اللَّهِ وَيَفْتَتِحُ الثُّلُثُ لاَ يُفْتَنُونَ أَبَدًا فَيَفْتَتِحُونَ قُسْطَنْطِينِيَّةَ فَبَيْنَمَا هُمْ يَقْتَسِمُونَ الْغَنَائِمَ قَدْ عَلَّقُوا سُيُوفَهُمْ بِالزَّيْتُونِ إِذْ صَاحَ فِيهِمُ الشَّيْطَانُ إِنَّ الْمَسِيحَ قَدْ خَلَفَكُمْ فِي أَهْلِيكُمْ. فَيَخْرُجُونَ وَذَلِكَ بَاطِلٌ فَإِذَا جَاءُوا الشَّأْمَ خَرَجَ فَبَيْنَمَا هُمْ يُعِدُّونَ لِلْقِتَالِ يُسَوُّونَ الصُّفُوفَ إِذْ أُقِيمَتِ الصَّلاَةُ فَيَنْزِلُ عِيسَى ابْنُ مَرْيَمَ فَأَمَّهُمْ فَإِذَا رَآهُ عَدُوُّ اللَّهِ ذَابَ كَمَا يَذُوبُ الْمِلْحُ فِي الْمَاءِ فَلَوْ تَرَكَهُ لاَنْذَابَ حَتَّى يَهْلِكَ وَلَكِنْ يَقْتُلُهُ اللَّهُ بِيَدِهِ فَيُرِيهِمْ دَمَهُ فِي حَرْبَتِهِ."

Sahīh Muslim 2897

354. Where is Kāfiristan ("the land of the infidel")?

Answer: in Afghanistan.

Kafiristan (Persian: کافرستان) is the old name for a region around Nuristan, a province in the north east of Afghanistan. Kafiristan or Kafirstan literally means *Land of the Unbelievers*. The suffix *-stan* in Farsi (Persian Language) means *land* or *place of*, whereas the name Kāfir is Arabic and means *unbeliever*. Kafiristan was inhabited by people who followed a form of an indigenous pre-Islamic pagan (some say: ancient Hinduism) until the end of the 19th century although for centuries Islam had been prevalent in almost all other areas of what is now Afghanistan.

These people had probably lived in the lower plains of Afghanistan before they were driven back into the mountains when Islamic forces conquered their land at the beginning of the 8th century. However, starting in 1890 their hideouts in the mountains were finally conquered by the Islamic Emir of Afghanistan, 'Abd al-Rahmān Khān (عَبْد الرَّحْمن خان). His nickname was *Iron Emir* due to his vehemence and brutality in crushing rebellions.

When the people in Kāfiristan were forced to convert to Islam in the 1890s, the Muslims changed the name from Kafiristan - the *Land of the Infidels* - to Nuristan, which means *Land of Light*. Today the inhabitants are called Nuristani.

During the 1980s Soviet war in Afghanistan, the region of Nuristan was the location for some of the heaviest guerrilla fights. Nuristan is nowadays one of the poorest and most remote provinces of Afghanistan.

An excursus: How did Afghanistan became Islamic?

The religion Zoroastrianism is believed by some to have originated between 1800 and 800 BC in what is Afghanistan today. Its founder, Zoroaster, is thought to have lived and died in Balkh, an ancient city in present-day northern Afghanistan. Before Islam was introduced, people of the region were mostly Buddhists and Zoroastrians.

The Islamic conquest of Afghanistan (642-870) began very early in the history of Islam. It started in the middle of the 7th century after the conquest of Persia was completed and when the Muslim Arabs began to move towards the regions east of Persia. In 652, they conquered Herat (هرات) which is located in West Afghanistan.

Almost all Afghans, except for those of Kafiristan, had converted to Islam during the period of the Ghaznavids in the 10th and 11th century. The Ghaznavids (Persian: غزنویان) were of Turkic origin and ruled large parts of Iran, much of Transoxiana, and North India from 977 to 1186.

355. In which Islamic country is Shia Islam illegal?

Answer: In Malaysia.

This south-eastern Asian country is a federal constitutional monarchy. Islam was established in the 15th century by traders from Arabia, China, and India. Today around 30 million people live in Malaysia, around two third of whom are Muslims. They predominately follow the Shāfiʿī School of jurisprudence of Sunni Islam. Malaysia has two parallel legal systems: traditional common law, that applies to everyone, and Sharīʿa Law, applied only to Muslims.

In 1996 the *Fatwā Committee for Religious Affairs* issued a Fatwā (Islamic ruling) that denounced Shia Islam as "deviant". The decree prohibited Shia Muslims from spreading their beliefs, banning also the distributing of electronic or printed Shia propaganda.

Malaysia follows a federal system which means that every individual state or territory had to adopt the decree – eventually, a huge majority of states implemented the Fatwā.

This has lead to several persecutions. In 2011, for example, Malaysian religious police raided a multi-story house and detained more than one hundred Shia Muslims. They had gathered to mark the death of the Prophet's grandson Husayn, who was killed in the Battle of Karbalāʾ (مَعْرَكة كَرْبَلاء) in 680.

In addition, prior to the elections in 2013, the Saudi-Arabian royal family had transferred 680 million US$ to the Malaysian prime minister's private bank account prior. "A personal donation", as the Saudi royal family called it. Prime Minister Najib Razak, who had been in office since 2009, is widely known for his crackdown on Shia minorities in Malaysia. Malaysia was one of the first non-Arab countries to join a Saudi led coalition which carried out air strikes against (Shia) Houthi rebels in Yemen, causing a humanitarian catastrophe.

356. Who was the Egyptian woman who stopped wearing the veil in 1923 and became famous for that?

Answer: Hudā Shaʻrāwī (هُدَى شَعْراوِيّ).

Born	1879 in al-Minya (Egypt)		Died	1947 in Cairo

Hudā Shaʻrāwī was an Egyptian feminist and nationalist who established numerous organisations dedicated to women's rights and is considered the founder of the women's movement in Egypt (Egyptian Feminist Union).

Hudā was born into a prosperous family in the southern Egyptian city of al-Minya and was raised in Cairo. Her father, a landowner, was active in Egyptian national politics. Hudā grew up in the *harem system*, in which women were confined to secluded apartments within the home and wore face veils when going outside. Since she came from an upper-class family, she learned French, but also memorised the Qur'an in Arabic. When she was 13 years old, she was married to her older cousin who was already in his late forties.

After her husband died in 1922, Huda Shaʻrāwī's life took a decisive turn. In 1923, following her attendance at a women's conference in Rome, she returned to Egypt. As she disembarked from the train at Cairo's station, she boldly removed her veil in front of the gathered crowd. It is said that some women joined her and removed their veils as well. It caused an outcry.

Later that year she founded the *Egyptian Feminist Union* which demanded reforms regarding personal status laws.

In the following decades only very conservative women wore veils, most went without. In films and pictures Egyptian women were sunbathing on the beach, some just wearing a bikini.

This changed dramatically in the 1990s when the big majority of Egyptian Muslim women chose to wear the Hijāb again and the trend of the Niqāb - the full face veil - emerged. The idea of the

Niqāb was mainly brought back by Egyptians working in Saudi Arabia and in other Arabian Gulf countries.

357. How did Saudi Arabia get its name?

Answer: It was named after an Arabian tribe, the *House of Saʿūd* (آل سَعُود).

A friend in Egypt told me that he "cannot not take a country seriously which is named after a person". He meant Saudi Arabia, which is officially called Kingdom of Saudi Arabia (الْمَمْلَكة الْعَرَبِيّة السَّعُودِيّة).

How did Saudi Arabia get its name? Let's go back to the year 1703 when in a small oasis village, Muhammad ibn ʿAbd al-Wahhāb (مُحَمَّد بن عَبْد الْوَهّاب) was born. His family was from a line of scholars of the Hanbalī School of jurisprudence, the most rigid and traditional of all Sunni schools.

Later he became a religious scholar himself and saw his mission in the purification of Islam by returning to the teachings of the first three generations of Muslims. He ordered the cutting down of sacred trees – some say, he cut them even himself – because "holy trees" were against the teachings of Islam. It is said that he even organised the stoning of a woman who had committed adultery. For some tribes in this region, he went too far. They opposed his teachings and actions. Eventually ʿAbd al-Wahhab was forced to leave. He found refuge in al-Dirʿīya (الدِّرْعِيّة), 65 km away from his birth-place where he was granted protection by the local tribe leader, Muhammad ibn Saʿūd (مُحَمَّد بن سَعُود).

Muhammad ibn ʿAbd al-Wahhāb and Muhammad ibn Saʿūd came to an agreement in 1744 (1157 AH) to take the Arabs of the peninsula back to the true principles of Islam. Some claim to have recorded a dialogue between the two. I quote the version which is given in the book *A History of Saudi Arabia* by Madawi al-Rasheed, a Saudi-Arabian professor of social anthropology.

The following dialogue is typical in illustrating the split of power between religious and political leaders.

Muhammad ibn Saʿūd said: "This oasis is yours, do not fear your enemies. By the name of Allah, if all al-Najd [a central region in present-day Saudi Arabia] was summoned to throw you out, we will never agree to expel you."

Muhammad ibn ʿAbd al-Wahhāb replied: "You are the settlement's chief and a wise man. I want you to grant me an oath that you will perform Jihād against the unbelievers. **In return you will be Imam, leader of the Muslim community, and I will be leader in religious matters.**"

In the same year, 1744, they called out the Emirate of Dirʿīya which was the first Saudi state. Muhammad ibn ʿAbd al-Wahhāb and Muhammad ibn Saʿūd formed an alliance to establish a new religious sect: *Wahhabism* (الْوَهَّابِيّة). And they did what dynasties usually do, they started with intermarriage. Muhammad ibn Saʿūd's son ʿAbd al-ʿAzīz married the daughter of Muhammad ibn ʿAbd al-Wahhāb. This pact lasts until today.

ʿAbd al-ʿAzīz captured Riyadh (الرِّياض), Saudi Arabia's current capital, in 1765. In 1802 he conquered the Shia city of Karbalāʾ (كَرْبَلاء) in present-day Iraq. During the raid his warriors destroyed monuments, graves of Shia saints and killed more than 5,000 civilians. This incident is one of the numerous reasons why the Iranian regime and the regime in Saudi Arabia are antagonists.

In 1803 the Saudi-Wahhabi army marched towards the two holy cities of Islam - Mecca and Medina - and captured them. However, after that the Saudis suffered some serious setbacks. The Shia Muslims had sought revenge for the attack on Karbalāʾ and assassinated ʿAbd al-ʿAzīz. Ten years later, in 1814, the Ottoman Sultan ordered his Viceroy of Egypt, Muhammad ʿAlī (مُحَمَّد عَلِيّ), to reconquer the Hijāz region. He succeeded and executed ʿAbd al-ʿAzīz's successor.

In 1902 it was the turn of another ʿAbd al-ʿAzīz from the Saʿūd-clan to shape the future of the Arabian Gulf: ʿAbd al-ʿAzīz ibn ʿAbd al-Rahmān ʾĀl Saʿūd (عَبْد الْعَزِيز بن عَبْد الرَّحْمٰن آل سَعُود) who later became known in the West as *Ibn Saʿūd* (1875-1953), the founder and first king of Saudi Arabia. ʿAbd al-ʿAzīz is said to have fathered 45 sons, among them the subsequent kings of Saudi Arabia.

He was 27 years old when he stormed Riyadh and captured it, which led to a decisive turn of events. This victory marked the beginning of the conquest of major parts of Arabia. Then World War I erupted. The old rules were overthrown. The Ottoman Sultans sided with Germany and Austria-Hungary. The Sultan called upon all Muslims to rise up against the Allied Powers of Britain, France, and Russia – the so-called *Triple Entente*. It was a call for Jihād.

The British government established diplomatic relations with Ibn Saʿūd. They negotiated a treaty in December 1915 which made the lands of the House of Saʿūd a British protectorate and attempted to define the boundaries of the developing Saudi state. Later, after the war, Ibn Saʿūd received further support from the British empire in form of weapons which he needed for his wars across the Arabian Peninsula. Ibn Saʿūd agreed to recognise British territories along the Persian Gulf coast and in Iraq.

Meanwhile, the tradition of the *Grand Sharīf of Mecca* (شَرِيف مَكّة) - the Sharifate - came to an end. The Sharīf was the leader of Mecca. The two sons of the last Sharīf - Faysal and ʿAbd Allah - were given control over Iraq (King Faysal I) and Transjordan (King ʿAbd Allah I) by the British. In 1925, Ibn Saʿūd conquered the Hijāz, expelled the whole family of the Grand Sharīf (who were Hashemites) and took control over the two holy cities, Mecca and Medina. This is the situation till today.

In 1926 Ibn Saʿūd became *King of the Hijāz* and *Sultan of Najd*. After three decades of conquests, he managed to rule over nearly all of central Arabia. Present-day Saudi Arabia once consisted of four (classical) regions: Hijāz, Najd, parts of eastern Arabia – so-called al-ʾAhsāʾ (الأَحْساء) - and southern Arabia - so-called ʿAsīr (عَسِير). In 1932 he united the four regions into a single state: The Kingdom of Saudi Arabia. Riyadh became its capital, the ancestral home of his family, the House of Saʿūd. The official title of the king is *Custodian of the Two Holy Mosques* (خادِم الْحَرَمَيْن الشَّرِيفَيْن). One of Ibn Saʿūd's male descendants rules the country until today, as required by the law.

The year 1938 marked a turning point because oil had been discovered. This made the country rich but also stirred a lot of internal troubles – especially, as the major oil reserves are located in the eastern province which is inhabited mainly by Shia Muslims.

358. Who were the 'Ikhwān?

Answer: A Sunni religious militia in (Saudi) Arabia.

The 'Ikhwān (الْإِخْوان) - *the brethren/the brothers* - was a religious militia in the 20th century (1912-1930) during the reign of 'Abd al-'Azīz ibn 'Abd al-Raḥmān 'Āl Sa'ūd (عَبْد الْعَزيز بن عَبْد الرَّحْمْن آل سَعُود), better known in the West as *Ibn Sa'ūd*.

Ibn Sa'ūd started the 'Ikhwān in 1912. They were his military forces and played an important role in establishing him as the ruler of major parts of the Arabian Peninsula – which is today known as Saudi Arabia. In 1924, they conquered al-Ṭā'if; a year later, Mecca surrendered. The 'Ikhwān destroyed everything in Mecca which was not "Islamic" according to their interpretation, mainly graves. Not only that Ibn Sa'ūd could not stop them, he also lost more and more control. The 'Ikhwān became stricter and more fanatical. They attacked Ibn Sa'ūd for introducing telephones or cars and for sending his son to a country of "unbelievers" (Egypt). They became a threat to Ibn Sa'ūd.

The 'Ikhwān demanded from Ibn Sa'ūd to follow the pure doctrine of *Wahhabism* (الْوَهّابِيّة) – whereas Ibn Sa'ūd opted for a more flexible approach taking local circumstances into consideration. Ibn Sa'ūd, for example, tolerated Shia Muslims whereas the 'Ikhwān wanted to force them to convert to their very strict Sunni doctrine.

The British Empire, who had close links to Ibn Sa'ūd, was not pleased with the 'Ikhwān. Ibn Sa'ūd had negotiated border agreements with his neighbours, the British protectorates of Transjordan, Iraq, and Kuwait. Some 'Ikhwān leaders wanted to continue the expansion of the Wahhabi realm into these states – and launched raids in 1927. This was a declaration of war. Ibn Sa'ūd had only two options. Either he stopped the 'Ikhwān to calm down the British forces, or the British forces would attack him too.

Ibn Sa'ūd went for the first option. He helped the British forces to stop the militia he once had created himself. A bloody war started at the end of 1928. The largest confrontation between the House of Sa'ūd and the 'Ikhwān happened in March 1929 in the Battle of al-Sabilla (مَعْرَكة السَّبِلّة). The leaders of the 'Ikhwān were massacred. This battle was the last major war in which camel cavalries fought. The 'Ikhwān had no chance against the modern machine-guns of Ibn

Saʿūd's army which they had received from British forces. Ibn Saʿūd was also supported by four British planes (flown by British pilots) and a fleet of 200 military vehicles. The 'Ikhwān surrendered on the Saudi-Kuwaiti border in January 1930.

Traditional Salafis condemn Ibn Saʿūd as a traitor. Although the House of Saʿūd and the Wahhabis were initially allied, Ibn Saʿūd eventually allowed the British to crush the 'Ikhwān. This is one of the reasons why there were terrorist attacks in the name of the terrorist networks ISIL and al-Qāʿida in Saudi Arabia – targeting the House of Ibn Saʿūd.

359. Which European country is predominantly Muslim?

Answer: Albania.

Since there is no official membership registration for Muslims, there is no data about the percentage of Muslims in any country.

Albania is a country with 2.8 million people in south-eastern Europe, bordered by Montenegro, the Republic of Macedonia and Greece. Of the approximately three million inhabitants, an estimated 56% are Muslim. In April 2011 Albania's first private Islamic university (Bedër University) opened in the country's capital, Tirana.

Most of the Albanian Muslims are Sunni. There is, however, also a minority who follows the teachings of the Bektashi Order. This is a dervish order named after the 13th century Alevi Wali Haji Bektash Verli from Khorasan (a historical region in north-eastern Persia). Poetry plays an important role in their spirituality. Telling jokes and humorous tales are part of Bektashi culture. During the Ottoman Empire many famous poets were Bektashis – for example the Turkish poet and Sufy mystic Yunus Emre (1238-1320), who greatly influenced Turkish culture.

Albania is a secular country according to its constitution, and declared its independence from the Ottoman Empire in 1912. During the Second World War Albania was conquered by Italy in 1939 and was occupied by Germany in 1943. Communist partisans took over the country in 1944. Albania allied itself first with the Soviet Union (until 1960) and then with China (to 1978).

Enver Hoxha - pronounced "Hoja" in English - was the communist leader of Albania from 1944 until his death in 1985. During the dictator's 40-year period of rule, he eliminated political opponents and relocated their families to remote villages. Enver Hoxha excessively used the death penalty. The secret police (Sigurimi) watched and hunted down everybody who was not in line with the leader.

Enver Hoxha declared Albania an atheist state in 1967. It was the first and only constitutionally atheist state in the world. Religion was thus forbidden by law. Article 37 of the Albanian Constitution of 1976 read: "The State recognises no religion and supports atheistic propaganda in order to implant a scientific materialistic world outlook in the people".

In 1967 the Albanian regime began a violent campaign trying to eliminate religious life in Albania. Religious institutions were forced to give up their houses of worships, i.e. more than two thousand churches, mosques, and shrines in Albania. Many of them were destroyed while others were converted into cultural centres for young people. During Ramadan, when the Muslims were fasting, the authorities distributed pork in schools and factories. They promoted the consumption of alcohol.

In the early 1990s the communist regime in Albania collapsed. Albania is currently considered the poorest country in Europe.

360. In which European country is an Arabic dialect spoken although its population is almost entirely Roman-Catholic?

Answer: Malta.

Malta is an island in the Mediterranean Sea, south of Sicily (Italy), with 410,000 inhabitants, 90% of which are Roman-Catholic.

Maltese (*Malti*) is the national language of Malta (alongside English). This makes it an official language of the European Union. Furthermore, this Arabic dialect is the only Semitic language in the EU. The origins of the Maltese language can be traced back to the Arab period in Malta and Sicily. When the North-African Aghlabids began their conquest of Sicily in 827, Arab influence spread to Malta, and the local population adopted a dialect of Arabic—specifically a variety later known as Siculo-Arabic—that evolved over the centuries into modern Maltese. Although earlier texts were sometimes written in a modified Arabic script, modern Maltese is now written using the Latin alphabet.

Malta returned to Christian rule in 1091 when the Normans—a people of Scandinavian origin who had settled in Normandy (France) and embraced Roman Catholicism—conquered the island. Although the political Muslim presence gradually vanished by the mid-thirteenth century (with the last remnants being expelled around 1249), the Arab cultural and linguistic legacy endured. This is in contrast to Sicily, where Siculo-Arabic eventually became extinct. Furthermore, the legacy of Islamic influence in Malta is evident not only in the language but also in many place names, as well as in the introduction of advanced irrigation techniques and the cultivation of crops such as citrus, figs, almonds, and cotton.

361. Where is the southernmost mosque in continental Europe?

Answer: In Gibraltar.

The mosque is located at the so-called *Europa Point* (Spanish: Punta de Europa or Punta Europa) which is Gibraltar's the southernmost point. On a clear day you can see North Africa, the Rif Mountains of Morocco.

The mosque is one of the largest mosques in a predominantly non-Muslim country. The minaret is 71 m (233 ft) high, crowned by a 6 metre (20 ft) high crescent made of brass. Around four hundred people find place in the main prayer hall.

The mosque is called *The Mosque of the Custodian of the Holy Mosques*. This is no coincidence. The building (cost: 5 million British Pounds; 6.5 million Euros) was a gift from King Fahd of Saudi Arabia. It is said that this is possibly the most expensive mosque in Europe per square metre. It was officially inaugurated in August 1997 with hundreds of guests who arrived in more than sixty limousines.

Gibraltar is a peninsula connected to southern Spain and a British overseas territory. It is inhabited by 30,000 people. The religion practised in Gibraltar is mainly Roman Catholicism (78%) – Muslims amount to about 4%. The official language in Gibraltar is English. Many Internet gambling companies moved offshore to Gibraltar because of its low taxes.

362. Where was the first mosque in the United States built?

Answer: It was in Ross, in a remote part of North Dakota.

Around one hundred people - twenty families - live in Ross. The village was founded in 1902. The first mosque of the United States was established there in 1929.

The community that built the mosque were Syrian-Lebanese immigrants who took advantage of the Homestead Act and settled in the region starting in the late 19th century. The Homestead Act was a federal law that made public lands available to settlers and gave an applicant ownership of land, typically called a *homestead*, at little or no cost.

There are rough winters in North Dakota. Therefore, the mosque was constructed as a sub-basement (partly underground) to shelter it from wind and cold. It was small - about 111 square metres (1200 square feet) - and contained a coal stove, benches, and a floor cover.

Later, after the Great Depression, many Muslims left Ross while others died and were buried in the Muslim cemetery near the mosque. The building became dilapidated and was finally dismantled in the 1970s. However, in 2005, the mosque was rebuilt by one of the last remaining Muslim families in the area.

Islam is the fastest-growing religion in the United States. According to the Pew Forum on Religion & Public Life, there are currently almost 1,900 mosques in the United States. The majority of Muslims live in major metropolitan areas, especially in New York and in California.

Note: The *Mother Mosque of America* - once known as *The Rose of Fraternity Lodge* or *Moslem Temple* - in Cedar Rapids, Iowa, is the longest standing mosque in North America. Built in 1934, it is the second oldest after the mosque built in Ross, North Dakota. Since the one in Ross had been dismantled earlier, the *Mother Mosque* became the oldest standing.

363. Which town in the USA is named after an Islamic hero?

Answer: Elkader in Iowa. It is named after ʿAbd al-Qādir ibn Muhī al-Dīn (عَبْد الْقَادِر بن مُحْيِي الدِّين).

Born	1808 (1223 AH) in Guetna (القيطنة), Ottoman Empire (present-day Algeria)	Died	1883 (1300 AH) in Damascus, Ottoman Empire

He is also known as Emir Abdelkader or ʿAbd al-Qādir al-Djazāʾirī (عَبْد الْقَادِر الْجَزَائِرِيّ) – al-Djazāʾirī literally means *the Algerian*.

ʿAbd al-Qādir was an Algerian religious and military leader who led a resistance against the French colonial invasion in the mid-19th century. The name ʿAbd al-Qādir means *servant of the Powerful (Allah)*. The town of Elkader - the Anglicised equivalent of ʿAbd al-Qādir - in Iowa in the US has about 1,250 inhabitants. The town's founders - Timothy Davis, John Thompson, and Chester Sage - were impressed by ʿAbd al-Qādir's fight against French colonial power and decided to choose his name for their new settlement in 1846.

When France occupied Algeria in 1830, Muhyī al-Dīn, the leader of one of the Islamic brotherhoods and director of a religious school near Mascara, was asked to lead the fight against the French troops in Oran (وَهْران). In November 1832 his son ʿAbd al-Qādir took over and attacked Oran with 5,000 men. He succeeded in controlling the city. ʿAbd al-Qādir was henceforth called *commander of the believers*. In only two years, he had organised a state. He established juridical equality and imposed equal taxes on all citizens. Mascara (مُعَسْكَر) in north-western Algeria was the capital city of Emir ʿAbd al-Qādir.

In 1847, after the French had chased him to Morocco, ʿAbd al-Qādir returned to Algeria and turned himself in to the French rulers. He is a not only a national hero in Algeria but also in the entire Maghreb.

364. Why was the Hollywood film *The Message* rarely shown in cinemas in Europe or in the US?

Answer: Because there were death threats by Islamic extremists if they would.

The film *The Message* (الرّسالة), originally known as *Mohammad, Messenger of God*, is a 1976 epic historical drama film directed by Moustapha al-Akkad and portrays the life of the Prophet.

Muhammad is neither shown nor heard in the entire film. At the beginning of the film, the following disclaimer is displayed: "The makers of this film honour the Islamic tradition which holds that the impersonation of the Prophet offends against the spirituality of his message. Therefore, the person of Mohammad will not be shown (or heard)."

Whenever the Prophet was present or close by in the film, his presence was indicated by light organ music. His words were "repeated" by a famous companion. When a scene called for him to be present, the action was filmed from his point of view.

His wives and daughters, his sons-in-law as well as the first Caliphs ('Abū Bakr, 'Umar, 'Uthmān, and 'Alī) were not shown either. The main character in the film was Muhammad's uncle Hamza ibn 'Abd al-Muttalib (حَمْزة بن عَبْد الْمُطَّلِب), who was played by Anthony Quinn. The Battles of Badr and 'Uhud are major parts of the film. Originally these battles were led by Muhammad himself, but in the film Hamza was in nominal command.

This film was made twice with two different casts for the English and the Arabic version. *The Message* was nominated for *Best Original Score* in the 50th *Academy Awards*, composed by Maurice Jarre, but eventually didn't get the Oscar. In the *Internet Movie Database* (IMDB), the film is holding a high rating of around 8.5/10.

Muslims in Egypt told me, that the film has never been showed in European theatres due to fears that people might convert to Islam after watching it, but that was not the main reason.

In July 1976, days before the film started in London, the cinemas received bomb threats because the name of the Prophet was used in the title. They demanded a change of the film's title. Instead of

Mohammad, Messenger of God it should be *The Message.* Arabs demonstrated in London demanding the same. There are rumours that the director consulted the embassies of Kuwait and Libya. He eventually changed the title, which allegedly costed £50,000 (€ 65,000).

The worst things were yet to come. In March 1977 twelve Muslim gunmen seized three buildings in Washington, D.C., and took 149 hostages. The attack was led by a former secretary of the *Nation of Islam.* One of their demands was a ban of the film. The attackers thought that Anthony Quinn played Muhammad in the film. They didn't know that the Prophet was not shown. *Time* magazine wrote that a "concern over the film was thought to have triggered the attack". The siege lasted for 39 hours. Two people died. The *New York Times* wrote that "the film's American box office prospects never recovered from the unfortunate controversy."

Similar things happened in Germany. Muslim Turks took to the streets - 400 in Berlin, 500 in Hamburg - to boycott the film. Cinemas received bomb threats. The police checked bags and used German Shepherd dogs to detect bombs. In the end only very few cinemas eventually showed the film.

It was the same story in the Middle East and North Africa. There were protests; Saudi Arabia rejected the film and several Islamic governments came under pressure. It all became political.

Nowadays, *The Message* is regularly shown in the Arab world during Islamic holidays.

365. What happened to the film director of *The Message*?

Answer: He was unintentionally killed by al-Qāʿida in a hotel bombing in Amman, Jordan.

Moustapha al-Akkad (مُصْطَفَى الْعَقَّاد) was a Muslim film producer and director. He is best known for the *Halloween* films and directing *The Message* and *Lion of the Desert.* He was born in Aleppo (Syria) in 1930. Legend has it that he arrived in Los Angeles in the 1950s to study film making with only two things his father had given him: a copy of the Qur'an and 200 US$.

On November 9, 2005, Moustapha, 75, and his daughter Rima, 34, were killed in Amman. They were both at the *Grand Hyatt* hotel when a bomb exploded in the lobby; his daughter died instantly; Akkad died two days later in a hospital.

The bombing was part of a series of coordinated bomb attacks on three hotel lobbies in Amman on the same day: *Grand Hyatt, Radisson SAS,* and *Days Inn.* 60 people were killed. Al-Qāʻida in Iraq claimed responsibility for the attacks.

Al-Akkad was not only famous in the Middle East and North Africa for *The Message*. In 1980, he had directed *Lion of the Desert*, starring Anthony Quinn, Irene Papas, and Oliver Reed. The film was about ʻUmar al-Mukhtār (عُمَر الْمُخْتَار) who fought Benito Mussolini's Italian troops in the desert of Libya. Muammar Gaddafi financed the film with 35 million US$. Italy was upset and banned the film in 1982.

When Gaddafi visited Italy in June 2009, the film was shown there on TV for the first time.

366. Which name did the Egyptian army choose for their attack on Israel in 1973?

Answer: Operation Badr (عَمَلِيَّة بَدْر).

Operation Badr was the code name for the Egyptian military operation against Israel on October 6, 1973. This attack was in conjunction with a Syrian assault on the Golan Heights. Both marked the start of the *Yom Kippur War*.

October 6 was chosen for several reasons. It was full moon and the speed of the water current and tide were optimal. It was also the day of Yom Kippur, the Jewish Day of Atonement. Jews fast on that day and abstain from using fire or electricity.

October in 1973 coincided with the month of Ramadan. It was also in Ramadan in the year 624 (2 AH) when the Muslims won their first major victory in the *Battle of Badr* (غَزْوة بَدْر). Furthermore, the Arabic word Badr means *full moon*.

367. What happened in 1979 in Mecca?

Answer: Several hundreds, maybe thousands of people were killed when the Grand Mosque was besieged by Muslim extremists.

November 20th 1979 was the first day of the year 1400 AH according to the Islamic calendar. On this day, in the early morning hours, 400 to 500 armed men stormed and seized the Grand Mosque in Mecca – in Arabic: al-Masjid al-Harām (الْمَسْجِد الْحَرام). Shots were fired; the attackers closed all gates and killed two policemen who were only armed with wooden clubs. The attackers placed snipers on the minarets. Around 50,000 Muslim pilgrims were trapped inside the holy compound.

Over the loudspeakers, a man called upon all Muslims to follow Muhammad ibn 'Abd Allah al-Qahtānī (مُحَمَّد بن عَبْد الله الْقَحْطانِيّ), who, as the speaker claimed, was the al-Mahdī (الْمَهْدِي), the prophesied saviour of Islam who will clean the world from all evil.

Who was the man on the loudspeaker?

It was Juhaymān ibn Muhammad ibn Sayf al-'Utaybī (جُهَيْمان بن مُحَمَّد بن سَيْف الْعُتَيْبِيّ), a member of an influential tribe in Najd (نَجْد), the geographical centre of Saudi Arabia. People from there used to be called the "dominant minority" in Saudi Arabia. The alleged al-Mahdī was his brother-in-law.

Juhaymān, born 1936, was a member of a local group of Salafis called al-Jāmi'a al-Salafīya al-Muhtasiba (الْجَماعة السَّلَفِيّة الْمُحْتَسِبة) – JSM. This group was founded and became popular in the poorer neighbourhoods of Medina in 1966. Their aim was to oppose the rapid modernisation and urbanisation as a result of the oil boom. They opposed the presence of the American oil company *Aramco* on Saudi soil as well as soccer players in shorts, TV sets, the integration of women into the workforce and Saudi Arabia's currency because it showed a picture of the Saudi king. Later, Juhaymān moved to Mecca and lived in a makeshift shelter about a half-hour's walk from the Prophet's Mosque.

What were their demands when they seized the holy place?

They wanted to overthrow the Saudi regime and demanded the immediate stop of oil exports to the USA. For the first time in history, militant Muslims were opposing the House of Ibn Sa'ūd – the clan which had ruled Saudi Arabia in its current form since 1932. The attackers claimed that the Qur'an does not accept a king or a dynasty.

What happened then?

Saudi Arabia tried to censor the attack. The regime instantly cut international phone communications and closed the borders. A media blackout was imposed. However, the news went viral. The US State Department accused Ayatollah Khomeini (he had declared Iran an Islamic Republic months earlier). In a radio speech, however, Ayatollah Khomeini, accused the Americans and the Jews ("the Zionists"). Within hours, a mob tried to storm the US embassy in Islamabad (Pakistan) and burnt it down; a number of American and Pakistani personnel died. Throughout the Muslim world, there were demonstrations with some of them becoming violent.

According to several accounts the Saudi Arabian Ministry of Interior gave orders to recapture the holy mosque, but they failed leaving dozens of people dead. The Saudis had no emergency plan. The only idea they had come up with was to starve the attackers.

There was another problem because severe violence at the Ka'ba is strictly forbidden. The Saudi regime therefore asked religious leaders for their opinion. The resulting decree (Fatwā) was not issued for another two days and the Saudi authorities had to wait. Since the legitimacy of their ruling was at stake, the royal family needed an Islamic permission to storm the holy site. The Fatwā, issued on Friday, November 23rd, stated: "The 'Ulamā' [religious authorities] unanimously agreed that fighting inside the mosque had become permissible... If they fight you, then you must kill them because this is the punishment for non-believers."

According to several reports the Saudi regime asked France for help. French security forces were thus sent to Mecca to direct the operation, because the Saudi forces were not trained for this. The French government also sent large amounts of tear gas and ammunition. On December 4th, 1979, Saudi authorities regained control of the mosque. The militants were captured and paraded on Saudi state television for two consecutive nights.

The Saudis tried to hide that the attack had in fact ended in a tragedy, as around 300 people were killed – and this is only the official num-

ber. A cable from the US-embassy noted that hospital figures indic-
ated that both casualties and injuries were much higher. At dawn on
January 9, 1980, 63 culprits were decapitated in eight Saudi Arabian
cities. This was the largest mass execution in Saudi Arabian history.
The list of those executed included 41 Saudis, 10 Egyptians, 7
Yemenis, 3 Kuwaitis, 1 Iraqi, and 1 Sudanese.

Excursus: Several Western historians claimed that **Osama bin Laden**
(أُسامة بن لادن), who was in his twenties at the time and later became
the leader of the terrorist network al-Qāʿida, had been inspired by
the attack. Some even say that this was the first operation of global
Jihād.

I believe, however, that the events leading to al-Qāʿida were somewhat different, but it is true that the siege of Mecca inspired militant
Islamic groups all over the world. And it had definitely influenced
the policy of Saudi Arabia. The demand for oil from the West flushed
a lot of money into Saudi Arabia. The regime had learned from the
attack that their Islamic legitimacy was being questioned. In order to
get rid of all possible threats, the Saudi regime tried to "export" all
"radical elements" - fighters - to foreign countries.

Osama bin Laden for example went to Afghanistan to fight against
the non-Muslim Soviets. In this way one could say that the siege of
1979 was precursor to the terrorist network of al-Qāʿida (القاعِدة),
which literally means *the base*.

Many Muslims in Saudi Arabia were upset about the Soviet invasion of Afghanistan. Therefore, the Saudi leaders directed, via different paths, millions of oil dollars towards the Jihād movement against
the Soviets in Afghanistan in the 1980s. This should show fanatical
Muslims in Saudi Arabia that the regime cared about Islam. And it
was perfectly fine for their Western allies as well, since it was the
USA who supported the so-called *Mujahideen* (Muslim Afghan warriors) in the first place. In the 1990s, the Saudis continued their plan
– and supported Jihād elements in Bosnia during the civil war. But
the Saudi plan was not thought out well. They had not thought about
the backlash when these fanatics would return from Afghanistan or
Bosnia – some of them being traumatised or even more radicalised.

Note: There is a difference between the ideology of groups like al-
Qāʿida and that of the attackers in 1979 in Mecca: It is related to the

concept of Takfīr (تَكْفِير), which means denouncing others as *unbelievers*, as non-Muslims.

The leader of the 1979 siege - Juhaymān ibn Muhammad ibn Sayf al-'Utaybī - said that declaring the rulers (i.e. the individuals) as *unbelievers* (كافِر) was forbidden as long as they continue to call themselves Muslims. He made the important distinction between the position and the people who were holding this position, in other words between an illegitimate regime and individual Muslims.

And what about al-Qā'ida? Osama bin Laden ignored this distinction. He justified violent attacks on both: individuals and governments by applying the concept of Takfīr which means: declaring them as unbelievers.

368. What does the crash of an Egypt Air plane in 1999 have to do with Islam?

Answer: The last words of the first officer.

Egypt-Air flight 990 was a flight from Los Angeles to Cairo with a stop at JFK airport in New York. On October 31, 1999, the airplane - a Boeing 767-366ER named *Tuthmosis III* - crashed into the Atlantic Ocean, about 100 km (60 mi) south of Nantucket Island, Massachusetts. All 217 people on board died.

According to the voice recorder, the captain excused himself to go to the lavatory. Thirty seconds later the first officer said in Egyptian Arabic: "I put my trust in Allah" (تَوَكَّلْتُ عَلَى اللهِ).

A minute later the autopilot was turned-off and immediately after that both engines were reduced to idle. The first officer repeated: "I put my trust in Allah" ten more times before the captain (who had returned) shouted repeatedly: "What's happening, what's happening?" (Notice: This was before 9/11 when it was possible to enter the cockpit from outside.)

The last words of the captain according to the voice recorder are: "What is this? What is this? Did you shut the engine(s)? Pull! Pull with me! Pull with me! Pull with me!"

The reason for the crash is still unclear. The US investigators claimed that the expression "I put my trust in Allah" ("I rely on Allah") indicated that the first officer wanted to commit suicide and may have intentionally caused the crash. US officials concluded that the "probable cause" for the crash was deliberate action by the first officer.

The Egyptians offered several control failure scenarios. Some Egyptians claimed that the flight data recorder was manipulated to help the US company *Boeing* to cover technical failures. Others said that the Israeli Secret Service (Mossad) took down the plane because there were 33 Egyptian army officers on board.

The phrase "Tawakkaltu 'ala Allāh" (تَوَكَّلْتُ عَلَى الله) - "I put my trust in Allah" or "I rely on Allah" - is very common in the Muslim world. Bumper stickers on cars bear the phrase, especially on the rear windows of taxis or pick-ups. Egyptian soldiers in the 1973 war against Israel uttered this phrase while they crossed the Suez-Canal.

The Arabic root w-k-l (و-ك-ل) means *to entrust, to put in charge*. The Arabic V-verb tawakkala (تَوَكَّلَ) means to place one's confidence in. For example, *I put my trust in Allah* (إِنِّي تَوَكَّلْتُ عَلَى الله). The verb is normally used in the past tense but it denotes the meaning of the present or even future tense.

There are Hadiths that mention this prayer. 'Anas ibn Mālik (أَنَس بن مالِك) narrated that the Prophet said: "When a man goes out of his house and says: 'In the name of Allah, I trust in Allah; there is no might and no power but in Allah', the following will be said to him at that time: 'You are guided, defended, and protected.' The devils will go far from him and another devil will say: 'How can you deal with a man who has been guided, defended and protected?'"[448]

---

448 ...أَنَّ النَّبِيَّ قَالَ: "إِذَا خَرَجَ الرَّجُلُ مِنْ بَيْتِهِ فَقَالَ بِسْمِ اللَّهِ تَوَكَّلْتُ عَلَى اللَّهِ لاَ حَوْلَ وَلاَ قُوَّةَ إِلاَّ بِاللَّهِ." قَالَ: "يُقَالُ حِينَئِذٍ هُدِيتَ وَكُفِيتَ وَوُقِيتَ فَتَتَنَحَّى لَهُ الشَّيَاطِينُ فَيَقُولُ لَهُ شَيْطَانٌ آخَرُ كَيْفَ لَكَ بِرَجُلٍ قَدْ هُدِيَ وَكُفِيَ وَوُقِيَ." Sunan 'Abī Dāwūd 5095

369. Whose star on the *Walk of Fame* in Hollywood is not embedded in the side walk?

Answer: The star of Muhammad Ali (مُحَمَّد عَلِيّ), the boxer.

Born	January 17, 1942, Louisville, Kentucky, USA	Died	June 3, 2016; Louisville, Kentucky

When Cassius Clay converted to Islam he became a member of *Nation of Islam*, also known as *Black Muslims*. Initially, however, they refused him because of his boxing career – traditional Muslims claim that boxing is forbidden in Islam.

After Cassius Clay had won the heavyweight title in 1964, the *Nation of Islam* agreed to announce his membership. Shortly afterwards, Cassius Clay changed his name to Muhammad Ali. He made the pilgrimage to Mecca in 1972 and later, in 1975, he converted from the *Nation of Islam* to mainstream Sunni Islam.

The Hollywood Chamber of Commerce honoured Muhammad Ali with a star on Hollywood's *Walk of Fame*. Ali's star was placed in front of the Kodak Theatre in 2002. There is something special about it. The star was mounted on the wall making Muhammad Ali the only celebrity whose star is placed vertically. All other stars are embedded in the pavement.

The boxer said that he did not want his name to be walked on by "people who have no respect for me". The champion initially rejected the star stating: "I bear the name of our beloved Prophet Muhammad and it is impossible that I allow people to trample over his name", news channel CBC reported.

370. Who said "I went to the West and saw Islam, but no Muslims. I got back to the East and saw Muslims, but not Islam"?

Answer: Muhammad 'Abduh (مُحَمَّد عَبْدُه).

Born	1849 (1266 AH) in Nile Delta, Egypt	Died	1905 (1323 AH) in Alexandria, Egypt

Muhammad 'Abduh was an Egyptian religious scholar and liberal reformer of the 19ᵗʰ century. His family belonged to the Egyptian elite. He was one of the most important figures of a movement that tried to modernise Islam. Sometimes, this movement is called Neo-Mu'tazilism. Al-Mu'tazila (الْمُعْتَزِلَة) was a medieval Islamic school which was based on rationalism.

Muhammad 'Abduh attended al-'Azhar University in Cairo and studied Islamic mysticism, philosophy and logic. Later he became a student of Jamāl al-Dīn al-Afghānī, a philosopher and Muslim religious reformer who promoted Pan-Islamism as a tool to resist European colonialism.

After he returned from France in 1888, Muhammad 'Abduh allegedly said: "I went to the West and saw Islam, but no Muslims; I got back to the East and saw Muslims, but not Islam."[449]

In Egypt, even in the Maghreb, I came across this quote occasionally. Muslims use it to express their frustration with the Islamic world nowadays. The core values of Western societies are freedom, human rights and justice. These values should be universal for human kind. Most Muslims are convinced that these values do not conflict with Islam, hence they are disappointed with the living conditions in their countries as almost every Islamic country lacks human rights and freedom.

Muhammad 'Abduh said that Muslims should stop using texts which were written by medieval clerics. He propagated the use of reason to keep up with the problems and challenges of modern times. He was convinced that man was given intelligence so that he could be guided by knowledge, and not by a bridle like a horse. He believed that the emergence of Western civilisation in Europe was based on two principles: freedom of will and freedom of thought and opinion. Traditional Muslims called (and still call) him an infidel.

Note: Some Western scholars link Muhammad 'Abduh to the Salafi movement. In Hans Wehr's dictionary, which is commonly referred to in the West, the term al-Salafīya (السَّلَفِيّة) is explained as an

---

449 ذَهَبْتُ لِلْغَرْبِ فَوَجَدْتُ إِسْلامًا وَلَمْ أَجِدْ مُسْلِمِينَ وَلَمَّا عُدْتُ لِلشَّرْقِ وَجَدْتُ مُسْلِمِينَ وَلكِن... لَمْ أَجِدْ إِسْلامًا.

Who said "I went to the West and saw Islam, but no Mus-lims. I got back to the East and saw Muslims, but not Islam"?

507

"Islamic reform movement in Egypt, founded by Muhammad 'Abduh".

This is not wrong, but it can be terribly misleading. Islam is becoming more and more political nowadays. Europe is constantly discussing Islamic symbols. Nowadays the concept of Salafism is regarded as the most backward, stupid and violent movement in Islam, mainly because of videos and comments from religious preachers who claim to be Salafis.

So what has Salafism to do with a reformer and liberal thinker like Muhammad 'Abduh?

Well, it is true that Muhammad 'Abduh founded a school called al-Salafiya. He also claimed that Islam had not been properly under-stood by anyone since the Prophet. His idea was to return to the religion's roots.

However, when we talk about Muhammad 'Abduh and Salafism, we should understand it like this: Muhammad 'Abduh called for a revival of the spirit of the ancestors of Islam in order to find appro-priate solutions for our modern times.

This type of Salafism is occasionally called al-Salafīya al-Ijtihādīya (السَّلَفِيّة الْإِجْتِهادِيّة). It basically means that Muslims should stick to independent legal judgement and reject strict adherence to one of the fours schools of Islamic jurisprudence.

But he certainly did not mean to restore the conditions and way of life of the Islamic ancestors in the 7th and 8th century.

PART V

On Fiqh (jurisprudence) and daily Muslim life

371. What does Islam actually mean?

Answer: Total submission to Allah.

It is irrelevant for a Muslim what his or her mind suggests or desires, what his or her partner prefers, what family or friends recommend, or what the ancestors used to do. A Muslim has to follow the Qur'an and the Hadiths. Islam means that Allah's rules must be carried out at all times, day and night.

Muhammad has a special role in Islam. Muslims believe that there won't be a prophet after him, that he corrected the mistakes in the scripts which mainly Jews and Christians had corrupted, and that by his revelation he sealed the Message of Allah.

For all these reasons, Allah warns Muslims that if someone does not embrace Islam, he will be in Hell. This warning is issued in sura 3 *Family of 'Imrān* – in Arabic: 'Āl-'Imrān (سُورة آل عِمْران):

| 3:85 | If anyone seeks a religion other than complete devotion to Allah [Islam], it will not be accepted from him: he will be one of the losers in the Hereafter. | وَمَن يَبْتَغِ غَيْرَ الْإِسْلَامِ دِينًا فَلَن يُقْبَلَ مِنْهُ وَهُوَ فِي الْآخِرَةِ مِنَ الْخَاسِرِينَ. |

Muhammad's teachings are of utmost importance in Islam. In the Qur'an, Allah says that whoever disobeys the Prophet will be doomed to eternal Hell. Muslims can read that in sura 24 *The Light* – in Arabic: al-Nūr (سُورة النُّور):

| 24:63 | [People], do not regard the Messenger's summons to you like one of you summoning another - God is well aware of those of you who steal away surreptitiously - and those who go against his order should beware lest a trial afflict them or they receive a painful punishment. | لَّا تَجْعَلُوا دُعَاءَ الرَّسُولِ بَيْنَكُمْ كَدُعَاءِ بَعْضِكُم بَعْضًا قَدْ يَعْلَمُ اللَّهُ الَّذِينَ يَتَسَلَّلُونَ مِنكُمْ لِوَاذًا فَلْيَحْذَرِ الَّذِينَ يُخَالِفُونَ عَنْ أَمْرِهِ أَن تُصِيبَهُمْ فِتْنَةٌ أَوْ يُصِيبَهُمْ عَذَابٌ أَلِيمٌ. |

Generally speaking the Arabic root s-l-m (س-ل-م) means *to be safe and sound; to be certain; to be free* or *unharmed*. From this root, the word *peace* or *safety* - Salām (سلام) - is derived.

The word *Muslim* (مُسْلِم) is the active participle of the Arabic IV-verb 'aslama (أَسْلَمَ) which means *to forsake; to hand over, to resign to the will of Allah*. The verb *'aslama* is also used to express that someone has become a Muslim or converted to Islam.

Should Muslims obey the traditions of the (first) Caliphs?

Answer: Yes, according to an authentic Hadith.

The following was narrated by Al-ʿIrbād ibn Sāriya (الْعِرْبَاض بن سَارِية): "A man said: Messenger of Allah! It seems as if it were a farewell exhortation, so what injunction do you give us? He [the Prophet] replied: 'I enjoin you to fear Allah and to hear and obey even if it was an Abyssinian slave, for those of you who live after me will see great disagreement. You must then follow my traditions [the Sunna] and that of the Rightly Guided Caliphs. Hold to it and stick fast to it. Avoid novelties, for every novelty is an innovation, and every innovation is an error.'"[450]

Muhammad's command that Muslims have to follow the *Rightly Guided Caliphs* led to disturbances, in particular when considering that two of them burnt people alive as a way of punishment, which was clearly against the teachings of Muhammad. The Caliphs justified their punishment by saying that they did use excessive violence for reasons of deterrence.

372. How does a person convert to Islam?

Answer: By saying the Declaration of Faith. In Arabic, this act is called Tashahhud (تَشَهُّد).

The first step when someone wants to become a Muslim is the proclamation of the Shahāda (الشهادة) – that there is no god but Allah and that Muhammad is His messenger. Then, the new Muslim should purify himself by taking a (ritual) bath - Ghusl (غُسل) - for purification. To ensure complete cleanliness a new Muslim should shave pubic and under-arm hair, and a man should be circumcised. After that a Muslim can start to pray.

---

450 ...قَالَ قَائِلٌ يَا رَسُولَ اللَّهِ كَأَنَّ هَذِهِ مَوْعِظَةُ مُوَدِّعٍ فَمَاذَا تَعْهَدُ إِلَيْنَا فَقَالَ: "أُوصِيكُمْ بِتَقْوَى اللَّهِ وَالسَّمْعِ وَالطَّاعَةِ وَإِنْ عَبْدًا حَبَشِيًّا فَإِنَّهُ مَنْ يَعِشْ مِنْكُمْ بَعْدِي فَسَيَرَى اخْتِلَافًا كَثِيرًا فَعَلَيْكُمْ بِسُنَّتِي وَسُنَّةِ الْخُلَفَاءِ الْمَهْدِيِّينَ الرَّاشِدِينَ تَمَسَّكُوا بِهَا وَعَضُّوا عَلَيْهَا بِالنَّوَاجِذِ وَإِيَّاكُمْ وَمُحْدَثَاتِ الأُمُورِ فَإِنَّ كُلَّ مُحْدَثَةٍ بِدْعَةٌ وَكُلَّ بِدْعَةٍ ضَلَالَةٌ". Sunan ʾAbī Dāwūd 4607

Note: A conversion to Islam wipes out all previous sins. Ibn Shumāsa (ابن شُماسة) reported that the Messenger of Allah said: "Are you not aware of the fact that [embracing] Islam wipes out all that has gone before it [previous misdeeds]?"[451]

In the same Hadith, two other occasions are mentioned that will erase all previous sins: "Verily migration [al-Hijra] wipes out all the previous [misdeeds], and verily the pilgrimage [al-Hajj] erases all the [previous] misdeeds."[452]

373. Can you apply the Islamic laws fully to any Muslim?

Answer: Only if he lives in an Islamic state.

Although many Westerners, but also Muslims, think that the laws of Islam have to be applied to any Muslim, this is strictly speaking not possible – due to the system of Islam.

Punishments in Islam are only enforced by the authority of an Islamic state. If nowadays a country does not have an Islamic ruler nor the Sharī'a in its constitution, it is not possible to apply the Sharī'a Law by individual Muslims. This is sometimes misunderstood by (extremist) Muslims in the West who are convinced that they are entitled to apply Sharī'a Law. Some even think they can apply the Laws of Sharī'a also to Western non-Muslims, which is impossible in Islam.

In general punishments in Islam are only implemented by a Muslim **leader** – and not by ordinary Muslims living in the country. For the full application of Sharī'a Law, Muslims need to be in an Islamic state. In an Islamic state a Muslim ruler guides Muslims; there is an Islamic court with appointed Muslim (male) judges who pronounce verdicts. And only through their verdicts the punishments of Sharī'a Law can be enforced.

Several classical scholars shared this view, al-Qurtubī, for example, who wrote in his commentary on the Qur'an: "There is no dispute among the scholars that retaliatory punishments [Qisās], such as

---

451 ...قَالَ: "أَمَا عَلِمْتَ أَنَّ الإِسلاَمَ يَهْدِمُ مَا كَانَ قَبْلَهُ ؟" Sahīh Muslim 121

452 ...وَأَنَّ الْهِجْرَةَ تَهْدِمُ مَا كَانَ قَبْلَهَا وَأَنَّ الْحَجَّ يَهْدِمُ مَا كَانَ قَبْلَهُ. Sahīh Muslim 121

execution, cannot be carried out except by those in authority who are obliged to carry out these punishments and carry out Hadd punishments [for major crimes against Allah], because Allah has addressed the command regarding Qiṣās to all the Muslims, and it is not possible for all the Muslims to get together to carry out the Qiṣās, which is why they appointed a leader who may represent them in carrying out the Qiṣās and Hadd punishments."[453]

This means that an individual, ordinary Muslim is only allowed to enforce Sharī'a Law if he gets the permission from the Islamic ruler. There is a reason why only educated and knowledgeable Islamic scholars are allowed to judge in legal matters. Otherwise, there would be chaos based on vigilantism and barbarity. Islam pays great attention that all people are equal before the law and that the Islamic rules have to be applied carefully and thoroughly.

This also means that any Muslim who apostatises in a non-Muslim country doesn't come under the Islamic punishment of apostasy, until he or she moves to an Islamic state. In other words, Muslims who have left Islam and live in a non-Muslim (Western) country are not subject to Sharī'a Law.

Nowadays many predominantly Muslim countries have incorporated parts of Islamic law into their legal systems and have stated in their constitution that Islam is their state religion, however, they do not apply pure Sharī'a Law in their courts.

Egypt, for example, likes to call itself Islamic, but in reality, the country lies somewhere in between a Western and an Islamic country. Several Muslim countries have been colonised. The French colonialists usually implemented the *Code Civile* (Code Napoléon) which had a great impact. In Egypt the current civil law is widely based on Western views. The first version of the Egyptian Civil Code was written in 1949. The Egyptian author received help from the University of Lille in France. The 1949 civil code therefore mainly followed the French model.

---

453 ...لا خِلاف أَنَّ الْقِصاص فِي الْقَتْل لا يقيمه إِلّا أُولُو الْأَمْر الَّذِينَ فُرِضَ عَلَيْهِم النهوض بِالْقِصاص وَإِقامة الْحُدُود وَغَيْر ذَلِك لِأَنّ الله سُبْحانه خاطب جَمِيع الْمُؤْمِنِين بِالْقِصاص ثُمّ لا يتهيأ لِلْمُؤْمِنِين جَمِيعًا أَنْ يَجْتَمِعُوا عَلَى الْقِصاص فأقاموا السُّلطان مقام أَنْفُسهم فِي إِقامة الْقِصاص وَغَيْره مِن الْحُدُود ". Tafsīr al-Qurṭubī, 2/245, 246

Most Arab countries have civil codes which are fully or partly based on that of Egypt. This means that the civil laws that predominate throughout the Middle East are mostly of French origin.

374. Is Islam limited to certain regions?

Answer: No.

The Prophet told his followers that Islam would reach all corners of the earth. It was narrated that Tamīm al-Dārī (تميم الدَّارِئ) said: "I heard the Messenger of Allah say: 'This matter [Islam] will certainly reach everywhere that night and day reach and Allah will not leave any house or tent, but Allah will cause this religion to enter it and some people will be honoured because of it and others will be humiliated because of it [for refusing to embrace it], and they will be ruled by the Muslims, an honour which Allah will bestow on Islam and a humiliation which He will inflict on disbelief."[454]

So much for the theory.

Most teachings and rules of Islam fit perfectly the desert region of Arabia. Like all other religions, Islam, too, was founded at a certain time and in a certain place. The Qur'an mostly relates to problems which Muhammad faced in Mecca and in Medina in the early 7th century. The Prophet, on the other hand, gave advice to his companions who mainly had problems related to the environment and cultural traditions of the Arab tribes.

The Prophet did not give advice to people who were living in northern Europe, Russia, Alaska, or South America. The date palm and the olive tree - two very important things in Islam - were not known in several parts of the world until international trade was established. There are rules in Islam which are difficult to follow in certain parts of the world. For example, fasting during Ramadan when Ramadan falls into June or July is sheer impossible in the very northern latitudes. In these regions, there is the phenomenon of *white nights,* i.e. days in summer on which the sun almost never sets.

---

454 ...سَمِعْتُ رَسُولَ اللّٰهِ يَقُولُ: "لَيَبْلُغَنَّ هَذَا الدِّينُ مَا بَلَغَ اللَّيْلُ وَالنَّهَارُ، وَلَا يَتْرُكُ اللَّهُ عَزَّ وَجَلَّ بَيْتَ مَدَرٍ وَلَا وَبَرٍ إلا أَدْخَلَهُ اللَّهُ هَذَا الدِّينَ، بِعِزِّ عَزِيزٍ أَوْ بِذُلِّ ذَلِيلٍ، عِزًّ يُعِزُّ اللَّهُ عَزَّ وَجَلَّ بِهِ الإِسْلامَ، أَوْ ذُلٍّ يُذِلُّ بِهِ الْكُفْرَ." Musnad 'Ahmad ibn Hanbal 16509

The Islamic rules for fasting are thus not suitable; people would starve to death as they would have to fast for almost 24 hours per day!

For problems like this, Islamic scholars issue Fatwas - religious decrees - which should provide Muslims with a plausible solution. In the case of *white nights*, people who observe fasting could follow the time of Mecca during Ramadan.

Since the Qur'an fits to Arab life and since the language of the Qur'an is Arabic, a lot of Arabs think that Islam is "their" religion. Muslim converts with pale skin or Asian Muslims for example are not considered to be real and equal Muslims by many Arabs, which is totally unacceptable according to Islam.

375. Should a Muslim living in a non-Islamic country take up the local customs?

Answer: No.

'Abd Allah ibn 'Umar (عَبْد اللهِ بن عُمَر) narrated that the Messenger of Allah said: "He who imitates any people [in their actions] is considered to be one of them."[455]

This Hadith indicates that a Muslim must not imitate non-Muslims. In other words, he must not follow their customs, use their style (clothes, food), etc. The crucial point in this Hadith is that it indicates that the other people are *disbelievers*. This goes along with a verse in sura 5 *The Table Spread* - in Arabic: al-Māʾida (سُورة الْمَائِدة):

| 5:51 | You who believe, do not take the Jews and Christians as allies [friends, helpers, ...]: they are allies only to each other. Anyone who takes them as an ally becomes one of them - God does not guide such wrongdoers | يَا أَيُّهَا الَّذِينَ آمَنُوا لَا تَتَّخِذُوا الْيَهُودَ وَالنَّصَارَىٰ أَوْلِيَاءَ بَعْضُهُمْ أَوْلِيَاءُ بَعْضٍ وَمَن يَتَوَلَّهُم مِّنكُمْ فَإِنَّهُ مِنْهُمْ إِنَّ اللَّهَ لَا يَهْدِي الْقَوْمَ الظَّالِمِينَ. |

---

455 ...قَالَ رَسُولُ اللَّهِ: "مَنْ تَشَبَّهَ بِقَوْمٍ، فَهُوَ مِنْهُمْ." Sunan ʾAbī Dāwūd 4031

When I lived in Egypt, some of my friends from the USA and Europe made a disturbing experience. They were hanging out with young Egyptians, students from the Nile Delta with a conservative background. After some time, most of them cut off contact because their Imam saw them with the Western people (he presumed they were non-Muslims). The Imam told them that this was dangerous for them and not allowed in Islam.

The Islamic sources which the Imam had quoted were authentic and supported his decision. Let's look at one of these critical Hadiths. 'Ā'isha (عائشة بِنْت أَبِي بَكْر) narrated that the Messenger of Allah set out for [the Battle of] Badr. When he reached Harra al-Wabara [a place near Medina], he met a man who was known for his valour and courage. The companions of the Messenger of Allah were pleased to see him. The man said: "I have come so that I may follow you and get a share from the booty."

The Messenger of Allah asked him: "Do you believe in Allah and His Apostle?" The man replied: "No." The Messenger of Allah said: "Go back, I will not seek help from a polytheist [Mushrik]!"

The man went on until we [the Muslims] reached al-Shajara, where the man met him [the Prophet] again. The Prophet asked him the same questions and the man gave him the same answer. The Prophet said: "Go back. I will not seek help from a Mushrik!"

The man backed off but met the Prophet again at al-Baydā'. The Prophet asked the same questions which he had previously asked: "Do you believe in Allah and His Apostle?"

The man answered: "Yes."

The Messenger of Allah told him: "Then come along with us!"[456]

Traditional scholars use this Hadith to justify why Muslims, for example in companies, should avoid working under non-Muslim bosses – as they could humiliate the Muslims, and by doing this, humiliate Islam. Furthermore, they could prevent them from prac-

---

456 ...أَنَّهَا قَالَتْ خَرَجَ رَسُولُ اللَّهِ قِبَلَ بَدْرٍ فَلَمَّا كَانَ بِحَرَّةِ الْوَبَرَةِ أَدْرَكَهُ رَجُلٌ قَدْ كَانَ يُذْكَرُ مِنْهُ جُرْأَةٌ وَنَجْدَةٌ فَفَرِحَ أَصْحَابُ رَسُولِ اللَّهِ حِينَ رَأَوْهُ فَلَمَّا أَدْرَكَهُ قَالَ لِرَسُولِ اللَّهِ جِئْتُ لِأَتَّبِعَكَ وَأُصِيبَ مَعَكَ قَالَ لَهُ رَسُولُ اللَّهِ " تُؤْمِنُ بِاللَّهِ وَرَسُولِهِ." قَالَ لاَ قَالَ " فَارْجِعْ فَلَنْ أَسْتَعِينَ بِمُشْرِكٍ." قَالَتْ ثُمَّ مَضَى حَتَّى إِذَا كُنَّا بِالشَّجَرَةِ أَدْرَكَهُ الرَّجُلُ فَقَالَ لَهُ كَمَا قَالَ أَوَّلَ مَرَّةٍ فَقَالَ لَهُ النَّبِيُّ كَمَا قَالَ أَوَّلَ مَرَّةٍ قَالَ: "فَارْجِعْ فَلَنْ أَسْتَعِينَ بِمُشْرِكٍ." قَالَ ثُمَّ رَجَعَ فَأَدْرَكَهُ بِالْبَيْدَاءِ فَقَالَ لَهُ كَمَا قَالَ أَوَّلَ مَرَّةٍ: "تُؤْمِنُ بِاللَّهِ وَرَسُولِهِ." قَالَ نَعَمْ. فَقَالَ لَهُ رَسُولُ اللَّهِ "فَانْطَلِقْ!" Sahīh Muslim 1817

tising Islam. Traditional scholars therefore demand from Muslim parents to not send their children to non-Muslim nurseries or schools, or make them live with non-Muslim families.

ʾAbū Saʿīd al-Khudrī (أَبُو سَعيد الْخُدْرِيّ) narrated that the Prophet said: "Associate only with a believer and let only a God-fearing man eat your meals."[457]

Another Hadith tells indirectly about the hierarchy between Muslims and non-Muslims. ʾAbū Hurayra (أَبُو هُرَيْرة) reported that Allah's Messenger said: "Do not greet the Jews and the Christians before they greet you and when you meet any one of them on the roads force him to go to the narrowest part of it."[458]

376. Is a Muslim allowed to live in a non-Islamic country?

Answer: Only under certain conditions, such as when a Muslim is oppressed in his own Muslim country or sets out to a non-Muslim country with the aim of spreading Islam.

This is a difficult question as many Muslims from poor Islamic countries leave their homeland seeking a better life. However, this contradicts with the teachings of Islam.

Jarīr ibn ʿAbd Allah (جَرِير بن عَبْد اللّٰه) narrated: "The Messenger of Allah sent a detachment of troops to [the clan of] Khathʿam. Some people of Khathʿam sought to protect themselves by prostrating [to demonstrate that they were in fact Muslims], but [nevertheless] they were quickly killed. News of this reached the Prophet upon which he commanded that they be given half of the ʿAql [blood money], and he said: "I am not responsible for any Muslim who stays among polytheists."

They answered: "O Messenger of Allah: How is that?" He replied: "They should not see each other's camp fires."[459]

---

457 ...النَّبِيُّ قَالَ: "لاَ تُصَاحِبْ إلاَّ مُؤْمِنًا وَلاَ يَأْكُلْ طَعَامَكَ إلاَّ تَقِيٌّ." ;Jāmiʿ al-Tirmidhī 2395
hasan

458 ...أَنَّ رَسُولَ اللّٰهِ قَالَ: "لاَ تَبْدَءُوا الْيَهُودَ وَلاَ النَّصَارَى بِالسَّلاَمِ فَإِذَا لَقِيتُمْ أَحَدَهُمْ فِي طَرِيقٍ فَاضْطَرُّوهُ إلَى أَضْيَقِهِ." Saḥīḥ Muslim 2167

Islamic scholars use this Hadith to show that it is forbidden for a Muslim to live among non-Muslims when there is no need to do so. Only in case of danger or for medical reasons, it is allowed for a Muslim to go to a non-Muslim country temporarily.

This is also true if a Muslim wants to do business as some companions of Muhammad had done that. If there is no need any more for a Muslim to live in a non-Islamic country, he is obliged to return to the Islamic world.

Hijra (migration), from an Islamic point of view, means to leave a non-Muslim region - so-called Dār al-Harb (دار الْحَرْب) - in order to go to a Muslim region - so-called Dār al-Islam (دار الْإِسلام). The term Dār al-Harb literally means *house of war*. It is used for countries in which non-Islamic customs and rules prevail.

Muslims are therefore even advised to leave non-Muslim countries and move to predominately Islamic ones. However, nowadays, it is usually the other way around which is - strictly speaking - against the teachings of the Prophet.

However, it is possible to migrate from a non-Muslim country to another non-Muslim country – if the situation there is better for Muslims. This was shown by the early Muslims, when some of them migrated from Mecca (which was pagan) to Abyssinia (which was Christian).

377. "Allāhu 'akbar!" Does it mean "God is great" or "God is greater" or "God is the Greatest"?

Answer: There is no clear answer.

---

459 ...قَالَ بَعَثَ رَسُولُ اللَّهِ سَرِيَّةً إِلَى خَثْعَمَ فَاعْتَصَمَ نَاسٌ مِنْهُمْ بِالسُّجُودِ فَأَسْرَعَ فِيهِمُ الْقَتْلُ فَبَلَغَ ذَلِكَ النَّبِيَّ فَأَمَرَ لَهُمْ بِنِصْفِ الْعَقْلِ وَقَالَ: أَنَا بَرِيءٌ مِنْ كُلِّ مُسْلِمٍ يُقِيمُ بَيْنَ أَظْهُرِ الْمُشْرِكِينَ. " قَالُوا يَا رَسُولَ اللَّهِ لِمَ قَالَ " لاَ تَرَاءَى نَارَاهُمَا. " قَالَ أَبُو دَاوُدَ رَوَاهُ هُشَيْمٌ وَمُعْتَمِرٌ وَخَالِدٌ الْوَاسِطِيُّ وَجَمَاعَةٌ لَمْ يَذْكُرُوا جَرِيرًا. Sunan 'Abī Dāwūd 2645.

Notice: Al-'Albānī said that this narration is authentic - sahīh - but only without the sentence that Muhammad ordered to give them half of the blood money.

Although Muslims say this sentence every day many times, it is not easy to translate "Allāhu 'akbar!" (اللهُ أَكْبَر). Let's see why.

The word 'akbar (أَكْبَر) is a comparative and superlative form in Arabic. Thus, it means *greater* or *greatest*. Here comes the problem: If you want to say *Allah is great*, you cannot use a comparative; but 'akbar is grammatically speaking a comparative.

If you want to say: *Allah is the greatest*, you need a definite article in Arabic which means it should be: Allāhu al-'Akbar (اللهُ الأَكْبَر). Note that the word *Allah* is definite in Arabic and already means *the God*.

Some scholars suggested that 'akbar (أَكْبَر) has the meaning of the Arabic word kabīr (كَبِير) which means *great*. Thus, the sentence Allāhu 'akbar could mean: *Allah is great*. Edward Lane said that this explanation is of weak authority.

According to the majority of scholars, the phrase Allāhu 'akbar is **elliptical** and means: *God is the greatest great (being)*. Or: *Allah is greater than every other great (being)*. Or: *Greater than such as that one knows the measure of His majesty*. Thus, it may be rendered *Allah is most great*, meaning: greater than any other being.

It is considered as elliptical because it is necessary that 'akbar should have the definite article al (ال) in Arabic. If it is used without the definite article, it must be followed by:

- a noun in the genitive (مَجْرُور) case - so-called 'Idāfa (إضافة) meaning: *Allah is the Greatest of...* Some Muslims, on the other hand, came to the conclusion that the second part is elided on purpose. The blank spot stands for *everything*. In the meaning of Allah is the greatest of... the biggest of... the wisest of...

- or by the Arabic preposition min (مِن): Allāhu 'akbaru min (اللهُ أَكْبَرُ مِن) - which would express a comparative meaning: *God is greater than...*

So what is the solution?

- In English, most non-Muslims will say *Allah is great*. Also newspapers like The Guardian or The New York Times usually write "God is great".

- This isn't wrong, but Muslims will say that it is "greater than just great". English readers, however, will find it difficult to read "Allah is greater" as they ask – okay, but greater than what?
- *Allah is the greatest* could be a solution, but the newspaper might receive some letters from linguists saying that this doesn't really work grammatically.
- For Muslims, there is no problem. Muslims will stick to the Arabic version "Allāhu 'akbar" anyway – in any language.

Note: There is another saying in Islam which deals with similar grammatical problems: "Allāhu 'a'lam" (اللهُ أَعْلَم). 'A'lam means *more* or *most knowing*. It is usually applied to Allah. It may often be rendered as *supreme in knowledge*.

Therefore, Allāhu 'a'lam (اللهُ أَعْلَم) virtually means *Allah knows best*. Or *Allah knows all things*, or sometimes simply: *Allah knows*.

This phrase is usually found at the end of an explanation of an Islamic problem. It means that Muslims strive to find the correct answer, but in the end, it is only Allah who knows best.

378. What does "786" in some countries mean?

Answer: It is an abbreviation for the Basmala (بَسْمَلَة), i.e. "In the name of Allah, ..."

Why is that? 786 is the total numeric value of the Arabic letters of "Bismillāhi ar-Rahmān, ar-Rahīm" (بِسْم اللهِ الرَّحْمنِ الرَّحِيْم) – the so-called Basmala: *In the name of Allah, the Most Gracious, the Dispenser of Grace* (or: *Most Merciful*).

In Arabic, there are two methods of arranging letters in the alphabet: 'Abjad and Hijā'ī.

- The so-called **'Abjad** order (أَبْجَدِيّ) is derived **from the order of the Phoenician alphabet**. Each letter can be given a <u>numeric value</u>. The so-called 'Abjad numerals are a decimal numeral system in which the 28 letters of the Arabic alphabet are assigned numerical values. This arrangement was most probably set up in

the 3rd century after the Hijra (الْهِجْرة) during the Abbasid period
(الْخِلافة الْعَبّاسِيّة).

- The **Hijā'ī** (هِجائي) or **Alifbā'ī** (أَلِفْبائي) order is used for lists, in
  which words are sorted, for example phone books, classroom
  lists and Arabic dictionaries. This system groups letters by <u>simil-
  arity of shape</u>. The letters in the Hijā'ī order don't have a numerical value.

Let's take the first four letters of each system to check the difference
(don't forget to read the Arabic letters from right to left):

- 'Abjad: د - ج - ب - أ
- Hijā'ī: ث - ت- ب - أ

So how do the numbers work? For the first nine letters, the numbers
from 1 to 9 are used. For the succeeding nine letters, successive intervals of ten are used: 10, 20, 30, 40 until 90. Then, successive intervals
of hundred are used: 100, 200, 300, 400 until 1000. This makes it in
total 28 different numbers for 28 letters.

Some examples:

The first letter of the Arabic alphabet, Alif (أ) can be described by
the number 1; the second letter, Ba' (ب), by the number 2. For Yā' (ي)
the number 10 is used; for Qāf (ق) the 100. The last letter, Ghayn (غ),
gets the number 1000.

On the Indian subcontinent, the 'Abjad numerals became quite
popular. Some people, mostly in India and Pakistan, use 786 in Internet chats as a substitute for the Basmala.

If you take the numeric values of all the letters of the Basmala,
according to the 'Abjad order, the total will be **786**.

Let's count:

- 2 + 60 + 40 + 1 + 30 + 30 + 5 + 1 + 30 + 200 + 8 + 40 + 50 + 1 +
  30 + 200 + 8 + 10 + 40 = **786**.
- The name Allah (الله) has the value 66: **1 + 30 + 30 + 5.**

379. What does it mean when a Muslim raises the index-finger?

Answer: Expressing the unity (oneness) of Allah.

In Arabic, the *index* or *fore finger* is called Musabbiha (مُسَبِّحة), mostly used with the definite article: al-Musabbiha (الْمُسَبِّحة). Sometimes also al-Sabbāha (السَّبّاحة) is used.

This finger, when a Muslim raises it, symbolises the unity of Allah.

Let's dig deeper. You might know the Arabic word Subhāna (سُبْحانَ). The Arabic expression "Subhāna Allah" (سُبْحانَ الله) states an exclamation of surprise or admiration. It is used often in a Muslim's daily life. We could translate it as: *Praise Allah!* Or: *Allah be praised!*

Let's look at another Arabic word derived from the same root:

A rosary is called Misbaha (مِسْبَحة) or Subha (سُبْحة). It consists of beads on a string, 99 in number, and having a mark after each set of 33 beads where a Muslim performs the act called al-Tasbīh (التَّسْبِيح), meaning the repetition of the praises of Allah.

Usually Muslims repeat the expressions *Subhana Allah* and *Allāhu 'akbar*.

380. How many pillars (principles) are there in Islam?

Answer: Five.

A pillar is called Rukn (رُكْن); the plural is Arkan (أَرْكان). It is narrated on the authority of 'Abd Allah ibn 'Umar (عَبْد الله بن عُمَر) that the Messenger of Allah said: "[The superstructure of] Islam is raised on five (pillars):[460]

These principles are:

1. To testify that none has the right to be worshipped except Allah and Muhammad

2. To offer the (compulsory congregational) prayers (إقَام الصَّلاة)

3. To pay Zakā, the obligatory charity (إيتَاء الزَّكاة)

---

460 ...قَالَ رَسُولُ اللَّهِ: "بُنِيَ الإِسْلامُ عَلَى خَمْسٍ شَهَادَةِ أَنْ لاَ إِلَهَ إِلاَّ اللَّهُ وَأَنَّ مُحَمَّدًا عَبْدُهُ وَرَسُولُهُ وَإِقَامِ الصَّلاَةِ وَإِيتَاءِ الزَّكَاةِ وَحَجِّ الْبَيْتِ وَصَوْمِ رَمَضَانَ." Sahīh Muslim 16

4. To perform Hajj, the pilgrimage to Mecca (الْحَجّ)
5. To observe fast during the month of Ramadan (صَوْم رَمَضان)

381. What does a Muslim have to testify?

Answer: The two Shahadas (الشَّهادَتان).

A Muslim must testify that none has the right to be worshipped except Allah and that Muhammad is Allah's Messenger. The declaration - in principle - goes as follows: "There is no god but Allah (and) Muhammad is the Messenger of Allah." In Arabic: "La 'Ilāha 'illa-llāhu wa Muhammadun Rasūlu-llāh."[461] The act of saying this declaration is called Tashahhud (تَشَهُّد).

A Muslim has to worship Allah alone; furthermore, he has to obey the commands of the Prophet, believe his words, practise his teachings, and avoid what he has forbidden. Muslims believe that the teachings of Muhammad were in fact revelations and inspirations conveyed to him by Allah.

Giving false testimony - in Arabic called Shahāda(t) al-Zūr (شَهادة الزُّور) - is among the most serious of sins. 'Abū Bakra (أَبُو بَكْرة) narrated that the Prophet asked three times: "Should I inform you about the greatest of the great sins?"

His followers replied: "Yes, O Allah's Messenger!"

The Prophet said: "To associate others in worship of Allah and to be disobedient to one's parents."

The Prophet sat up after he had been reclining [on a pillow] and said: "And I warn you against giving a false witness!" 'Abū Bakra said that "the Prophet kept on saying this warning until we thought he would not stop."[462]

---

461 لَا إِلَهَ إِلَّا الله مُحَمَّدٌ رَسُولُ الله.

462 ...قَالَ النَّبِيُّ: "أَلَا أُنَبِّئُكُمْ بِأَكْبَرِ الْكَبَائِرِ؟" ثَلَاثًا. قَالُوا بَلَى يَا رَسُولَ اللَّهِ! قَالَ: "الْإِشْرَاكُ بِاللَّهِ، وَعُقُوقُ الْوَالِدَيْنِ." وَجَلَسَ مُتَّكِئًا فَقَالَ: "أَلَا وَقَوْلُ الزُّورِ." قَالَ فَمَا زَالَ يُكَرِّرُهَا حَتَّى قُلْنَا لَيْتَهُ سَكَتَ. Sahīh al-Bukhārī 2654.

382. What is 'Ihsān?

Answer: A term used in the Hadiths for sincere worship of Allah. It means to perform an act in perfect manner.

Al-'Ihsān (الإِحْسان) is an Arabic term which can be translated as *perfection* or *excellence; to do beautiful things*. In Islam, 'Ihsān is the Muslim's responsibility to reach perfection or excellence in worship. The active participle of the corresponding word is a common Arabic male name: Muhsin (مُحْسِن) - one who does what is beautiful.

Islam, when we look at it as an "operating system" for life, has three dimensions, and all of them are interconnected:

1. **Islam** means *submission* to Allah and fulfilling the five pillars. Traditionally, Islamic <u>jurists</u> have concentrated on this layer.

2. **Al-'Imān** (الإِيمان) means *faith* and in turn includes 'Ihsān. It means the belief in the six articles of faith of Islam based on the *Hadith of Gabriel* which we will have a look at later in this chapter. Traditionally, Islamic <u>theologians</u> have concentrated on this layer.

3. **Al-'Ihsān** (الإِحْسان) means the deployment of righteousness on earth, doing good things to people. For example: A Muslim should honour his parents, help the poor, and strive for the sake of Allah. Traditionally, <u>Sufis</u> have focused on this layer.

A description of all this is found in the so-called *Hadith of Gabriel*. This Hadith was reported by 'Abū Hurayra (أَبُو هُرَيْرة) and is one of the most important narrations.

Here is why.

The Messenger of Allah said: "Ask me [about matters pertaining to religion]!"

However, they [the companions] were too much overawed. Out of respect, they did not dare to ask him [anything].

Meanwhile, a man came and sat near his [the Prophet's] knees and asked: "Messenger of Allah, what is al-Islam?" To which he [the Prophet] replied: "You must not associate anything with Allah, and establish prayer, pay the poor-rate [Zakā] and observe [the fasts of] Ramadan." He said: "You have told the truth."[463]

He [again] asked: "Messenger of Allah, what is al-'Imān [the faith]?" He [the Prophet] replied: "That you affirm your faith in Allah, His angels, His Books, His meeting, His Apostles, and that you believe in Resurrection and that you believe in Qadr [Divine Decree] in all its entirety." He [the inquirer] said: "You have told the truth."[464]

He [again] asked: "Messenger of Allah, what is al-'Ihsān?" Upon this he [the Prophet] answered: "Al-'Ihsān implies that you fear Allah as if you are seeing Him, and though you see Him not, verily He is seeing you." He [the inquirer] said: "You have told the truth."[465]

He [the inquirer] asked: "When would be The Hour of Doom?" Upon this, the Prophet replied: "The one who is being asked about it is no better informed than the inquirer himself. I, however, narrate some of its signs [and they are]: when you see a slave [woman] giving birth to her master – that is one of the signs of Doom; when you see barefooted, naked, deaf and dumb [ignorant and foolish persons] as rulers of the earth – that is one of the signs of Doom. And when you see the shepherds of black camels exult in buildings – that is one of the signs of Doom. The Doom is one of the five things [wrapped] in the unseen. No one knows them except Allah."[466]

Then the Prophet recited the following verse: "Verily Allah! With Him alone is the knowledge of The Hour and He it is who sends down the rain and knows that which is in the wombs and no person knows whatsoever he shall earn tomorrow and a person knows not in whatsoever land he shall die. Verily, Allah knows, is aware."[467]

---

463 ...قَالَ رَسُولُ اللَّهِ: "سَلُونِي!" فَهَابُوهُ أَنْ يَسْأَلُوهُ. فَجَاءَ رَجُلٌ فَجَلَسَ عِنْدَ رُكْبَتَيْهِ. فَقَالَ يَا رَسُولَ اللَّهِ مَا الإِسْلاَمُ قَالَ: "لاَ تُشْرِكُ بِاللَّهِ شَيْئًا وَتُقِيمُ الصَّلاَةَ وَتُؤْتِي الزَّكَاةَ وَتَصُومُ رَمَضَانَ." قَالَ صَدَقْتَ.
Sahīh Muslim 10

464 ...قَالَ يَا رَسُولَ اللَّهِ مَا الإِيمَانُ قَالَ: "أَنْ تُؤْمِنَ بِاللَّهِ وَمَلاَئِكَتِهِ وَكِتَابِهِ وَلِقَائِهِ وَرُسُلِهِ وَتُؤْمِنَ بِالْبَعْثِ وَتُؤْمِنَ بِالْقَدَرِ كُلِّهِ." قَالَ صَدَقْتَ. Sahīh Muslim 10

465 ...قَالَ يَا رَسُولَ اللَّهِ مَا الإِحْسَانُ قَالَ: "أَنْ تَخْشَى اللَّهَ كَأَنَّكَ تَرَاهُ فَإِنَّكَ إِنْ لاَ تَكُنْ تَرَاهُ فَإِنَّهُ يَرَاكَ." قَالَ صَدَقْتَ. Sahīh Muslim 10

466 ...قَالَ يَا رَسُولَ اللَّهِ مَتَى تَقُومُ السَّاعَةُ قَالَ: "مَا الْمَسْؤُولُ عَنْهَا بِأَعْلَمَ مِنَ السَّائِلِ وَسَأُحَدِّثُكَ عَنْ أَشْرَاطِهَا إِذَا رَأَيْتَ الْمَرْأَةَ تَلِدُ رَبَّهَا فَذَاكَ مِنْ أَشْرَاطِهَا وَإِذَا رَأَيْتَ الْحُفَاةَ الْعُرَاةَ الصُّمَّ الْبُكْمَ مُلُوكَ الأَرْضِ فَذَاكَ مِنْ أَشْرَاطِهَا وَإِذَا رَأَيْتَ رِعَاءَ الْبَهْمِ يَتَطَاوَلُونَ فِي الْبُنْيَانِ فَذَاكَ مِنْ أَشْرَاطِهَا فِي خَمْسٍ مِنَ الْغَيْبِ لاَ يَعْلَمُهُنَّ إِلاَّ اللَّهُ." Sahīh Muslim 10

He [the narrator, 'Abū Hurayra] continued: Then the person stood up and made his way. The Prophet said: "Bring him back to me!"

They searched for him, but the companions could not find him. The Messenger of Allah thereupon said: "This was Gabriel and he wanted to teach you [things pertaining to religion] when you did not ask [them yourselves].[468]

The concept of 'Ihsān is important for the daily life of a Muslim. It means that a Muslim should not deal in half-measures. It was narrated from Shaddād ibn 'Aws (شَدّاد بن أَوْس) that the Messenger of Allah said: "Allah has prescribed al-'Ihsān [proficiency] in all things. So if you kill, then kill well; and if you slaughter, then slaughter well. Let one of you sharpen his blade and spare suffering to the animal he slaughters."[469]

383. What is Dhikr?

Answer: Dhikr (ذِكْر) means *remembrance*. It comprises all devotional acts in Islam in which short phrases or prayers are repeatedly recited silently or aloud.

These are the most common phrases:

- "Allah is great; greater; or the greatest" – in Arabic: "Allāhu 'akbar" (اللهُ أَكْبَر)
- "Glory be to Allah" or "Exalted be Allah" – in Arabic: "Subhāna Allāh" (سُبحان الله)
- "All praise is due to Allah", an expression of gratitude – in Arabic: "al-Hamd(u) lillāh" (الْحَمْدُ لِلَّه)

---

467 ...ثُمَّ قَرَأَ {إِنَّ اللَّهَ عِنْدَهُ عِلْمُ السَّاعَةِ وَيُنَزِّلُ الْغَيْثَ وَيَعْلَمُ مَا فِي الْأَرْحَامِ وَمَا تَدْرِي نَفْسٌ مَاذَا تَكْسِبُ غَدًا وَمَا تَدْرِي نَفْسٌ بِأَيِّ أَرْضٍ تَمُوتُ إِنَّ اللَّهَ عَلِيمٌ خَبِيرٌ} Sahīh Muslim 10

468 ...قَالَ ثُمَّ قَامَ الرَّجُلُ فَقَالَ رَسُولُ اللَّهِ: "رُدُّوهُ عَلَيَّ!" فَالْتُمِسَ فَلَمْ يَجِدُوهُ فَقَالَ رَسُولُ اللَّهِ: "هَذَا جِبْرِيلُ أَرَادَ أَنْ تَعَلَّمُوا إِذْ لَمْ تَسْأَلُوا." Sahīh Muslim 10

469 ...رَسُولُ اللَّهِ قَالَ: "إِنَّ اللَّهَ كَتَبَ الإِحْسَانَ عَلَى كُلِّ شَيْءٍ فَإِذَا قَتَلْتُمْ فَأَحْسِنُوا الْقِتْلَةَ وَإِذَا ذَبَحْتُمْ فَأَحْسِنُوا الذَّبْحَ وَلْيُحِدَّ أَحَدُكُمْ شَفْرَتَهُ فَلْيُرِحْ ذَبِيحَتَهُ." Sahīh Muslim 1955

- "There is no god but Allah" – in Arabic: "La 'ilāha illā Allāh" (لا إله إلّا الله)
- "There is no power or strength except with Allah" – in Arabic: "La Hawla wa lā Quwwa(ta) illā bi Allāh" (لا حَوْلَ وَلَا قُوّةَ إِلّا بِاللَّه)
- "In the name of God, The Gracious, The Merciful" – in Arabic: Bismillāhi al-Rahmān al-Rahīm (بِسْم اللَّه الرَّحْمَنِ الرَّحِيم). This is said before anything of spiritual significance; e.g. eating, ritual ablution, praying, going to sleep, waking up, before work, etc.

Ka'b ibn 'Ujra (كَعْب بن عُجْرة) narrated that Allah's Messenger said: "There are certain exclamations, and the performance of these after every prescribed prayer will never cause disappointment: 'Glory be to Allah' thirty-three times. 'Praise be to Allah' thirty-three times, and 'Allah is most Great' thirty-four times."[470]

Especially older Muslim men like to use prayer beads - so-called Tasbīh (تَسْبِيح) or Misbaha (مِسْبَحة) - to perform Dhikr. The beads are on a string, usually 99 in number, which correspond to the 99 names of Allah in Islam. The Tasbīh makes counting easier and helps a Muslim to keep track of the number of recitations for the Dhikr.

384. How many categories does the Sharī'a Law know to classify if something is lawful or not?

Answer: Five.

Every act of a Muslim can be classified on a scale from 1 to 5, ranging from compulsory to sinful. The Islamic term for these five evaluation criteria is al-'Ahkam al-Khamsa (الْأَحْكَام الْخَمْسَة). Let's look at them:

| 1 | compulsory, obligatory | wājib/fard | واجِب / فَرْض |
| 2 | recommended | mustahabb/mandūb | مُسْتَحَبّ / مَنْدُوب |

---

470 ...عَنْ رَسُولِ اللَّه قَالَ: "مُعَقِّبَاتٌ لاَ يَخِيبُ قَائِلُهُنَّ - أَوْ فَاعِلُهُنَّ - دُبُرَ كُلِّ صَلاةٍ مَكْتُوبَةٍ ثَلاَثٌ وَثَلاَثُونَ تَسْبِيحَةً وَثَلاَثٌ وَثَلاَثُونَ تَحْمِيدَةً وَأَرْبَعٌ وَثَلاَثُونَ تَكْبِيرَةً." Sahīh Muslim 596

3	permitted	halāl/mubāh	حَلال / مُباح
4	disliked; abstaining is recommended and will be rewarded	makrūh	مَكْرُوه
5	sinful; abstaining is obligatory	harām	حَرام

Here are some examples:

1	obligatory	performing the daily prayers; paying Zakā
2	recommended	the lesser pilgrimage called 'Umra (عُمْرة)
3	permitted	eating honey or rice, drinking milk
4	disliked	eating fresh garlic
5	sinful	eating pork

385. Does harām mean *forbidden* or *sacred*?

Answer: It can mean both. The Arabic word harām (حَرام) means *forbidden for Muslims*. In some situations it has the meaning of *sacred* (see below).

There are two interpretations of this word. Harām can refer to something *sacred*. Only people in the state of purity are allowed to enter or touch it. For example: The Grand Mosque of Mecca, in Arabic called al-Masjid al-Harām (الْمَسْجِد الْحَرام).

However, in most cases, harām denotes an evil thing, a sinful action that is forbidden for Muslims. For example: gambling, drinking alcohol, eating pork. The Arabic word Harīm (حَرِيم) is derived from the same root. It entered the English language too: *harem*. It literally means *sacred* but is usually used to refer to the female members of the family.

The concept of harām brings us to an important question in Islam: Do good intentions make something that was *harām* acceptable?

Clearly, no. Islam does not support the principle that the end justifies the means. For example, if a Muslims wants to build a mosque with money he won in a lottery, then this worthy ambition is still harām. The same is true for money made by selling alcohol.

Therefore, Muslims who work in tourism are in a dilemma. On the one hand, they make good money in hotels. But since most hotels are serving alcohol, the money they earn is actually harām.

386. What is Takfīr?

Answer: To declare Muslims as *disbelievers* (non-Muslims).

Takfīr (تَكْفِير) is derived from the Arabic root k-f-r (ك-ف-ر) which means *to be an infidel; to not believe (in God); to blaspheme God.* The active participle of the verb is one of the most emotive words in Islam: Kāfir (كافِر), which means *infidel* or *unbeliever.* The plural of Kāfir is Kāfirūn (كافِرُون) or Kuffār (كُفّار).

The Arabic II-verb of this root - kaffara (كَفَّرَ) - describes the process of *to make someone an infidel; to seduce someone to unbelief; to accuse of infidelity.* Takfīr is the verbal noun/infinitive of this action.

The concept of Takfīr goes back as far as the beginning of Islam. The fourth Caliph, ʿAlī ibn ʾAbī Tālib (عَلِيّ بن أبي طالِب), was engaged in a battle with Muʿāwiya (مُعاوِيَة بن أَبي سُفْيان) who later established the Umayyad Dynasty of the caliphate. There was a group (mostly desert Bedouin raiders) which first sided with ʿAlī. However, when ʿAlī agreed to solve the conflict by arbitration, the group said that this was against Islam, and left. The people seceded from ʿAlī's camp and became known as the Kharijis/Kharijites (الْخَوارِج) meaning *those who left.* They denounced ʿAlī as a non-Muslim.

The Kharijis went even further. They argued that sins itself were a form of Kufr (disbelief). Following their logic, if a Muslim commits a sin, he is a disbeliever in Allah and thus could be fought and killed – even if he was a companion of Muhammad or a Caliph. Furthermore, again following their logic, if a Muslim disagreed with their mantra that sins are disbelief, he was a disbeliever too and could be fought and killed.

However, most Islamic scholars say that the only thing that invalidates someone's status as a Muslim is the open declaration that he does not believe in Islam, i.e. that there is no god but Allah and that Muhammad is His messenger.

Takfir became a major part of the ideology of so-called *Islamists*, the adherents of political Islam and extremism. For example: Sayyid Qutb (سَيِّد قُطب), who was a leading member of the Egyptian Muslim Brotherhood in the 1950s and 1960s. In his book *Milestones* - in Arabic: Ma'ālim fī al-Tarīq (مَعالِم في الطَّريق) - he develops and justifies a radical plan to getting rid of the Western culture which he calls *Jāhilīya* with the goal of re-establishing an Islamic world on the basis of the Qur'an and the teachings of Muhammad and his followers. In 1966 he was executed in Egypt by hanging.

Or examples are Hasan Nasr Allah (حَسَن نَصر الله), the leader of the Lebanese political party and militant group Hezbollah (حِزْب الله), who calls the Sunni Muslims that are fighting in Syria "Takfiris", or the members of the terrorist network ISIL who basically denounce all Muslims around the world as unbelievers, because they do not follow their ideology.

387. What is a Salafi?

Answer: This term is used to identify the earliest Muslims.

Followers of Salafism view the first generation of Muslims as an eternal model for the true Islamic life in regard to belief, manners, moral, piety, and to reading the divine sources.

For traditional Islamic scholars, the word Salafī (سَلَفِي), or *early Muslim*, denotes someone who died within the first four hundred years after the Prophet, including the founders of the Islamic schools of jurisprudence. Anyone else is a *latter-day Muslim*, also called khalaf (خَلَف) which literally means *successor*.

The Arabic root s-l-f (س-ل-ف) means *to be over; to be past*; from this root, the word Salaf (سَلَف) is derived which means *predecessors, ancestors, forefathers*. A Salafī (سَلَفِي) is someone who tries to follow the founding fathers of Islam. It is a rather modern term as the dictionary of Edward Lane (1863) doesn't know the term Salafiya. Actually, it was the Egyptian liberal reformer Muhammad 'Abduh (مُحَمَّد عَبْدُه) who introduced this term in the 19th century.

The whole concept of the first Muslims being the best is based on a saying of the Prophet. It was narrated by Zahdam ibn Mudarrib (زَهْدَم بن مُضَرِّب) that 'Imrān ibn Husayn (عِمْران بن حُصَيْن) heard that the Prophet said: "The best of you [people] are my generation, and the second best will be those who will follow them, and then those who will follow the second generation." 'Imrān added: "I do not remember whether he mentioned two or three [generations] after his generation."

He [the Prophet] continued: "Then will come some people who will make vows but will not fulfil them; and they will be dishonest and will not be trustworthy, and they will give their witness without being asked to give their witness, and fatness will appear among them."[471]

Note: Most Sunni Salafis are following the Hanbalī School of jurisprudence which is the most conservative and strict interpretation of Islam. In fact, Salafism has nothing to do with Islamic jurisprudence. Salafis (today) follow any of the four Sunni schools, which are: Hanafi, Mālikī, Shāfi'ī and Hanbalī. Muhammad 'Abduh, who branded Salafism, even rejected these schools and thought that Muslims are capable enough to judge themselves without following fixed rules.

Today, Salafis have nothing in common with the Salafism movement of Muhammad 'Abduh. Most Salafis insist that Salafism existed from the very beginning of Islam, but was just not labelled as such.

Pay attention to the differences:

- The term al-Salaf al-Muqaddam (السَّلَف الْمُقَدَّم) is applied to the Prophet (Muhammad).

- The term al-Salaf (السَّلَف) is understood by Sunni scholars to be applied to Muhammad's wife 'Ā'isha (عائشة بِنْت أَبِي بَكْر), the three *Rightly Guided Caliphs* 'Abū Bakr, 'Umar and 'Uthmān. In addition to Talha ibn 'Ubayd Allah (طَلْحة بن عُبَيْد الله), al-Zubayr ibn al-'Awām (الزُّبَيْر بن الْعَوام), Caliph Mu'āwiya (مُعاوية), and to 'Amr

---

471 ..النَّبِيُّ قَالَ: "خَيْرُكُمْ قَرْنِي، ثُمَّ الَّذِينَ يَلُونَهُمْ، ثُمَّ الَّذِينَ يَلُونَهُمْ قَالَ عِمْرانُ لاَ أَدْرِي ذَكَرَ يْنَتَيْنِ أَوْ ثَلاَثًا بَعْدَ قَرْنِه ثُمَّ يَجِيءُ قَوْمٌ يَنْذُرُونَ وَلاَ يَفُونَ، وَيَخُونُونَ وَلاَ يُؤْتَمَنُونَ، وَيَشْهَدُونَ وَلاَ يُسْتَشْهَدُونَ، وَيَظْهَرُ فِيهِم السَّمَنُ." Sahīh al-Bukhārī 6695

ibn al-ʿĀs (عَمْرو بـن الْعـاص). Shia Muslims, however, see this entirely different and reject this definition.

- The term al-Salaf al-Sālih (السَّلَف الصّالِح) according to Sunni Muslims denotes: 1) the Prophet, 2) his companions, 3) his followers, so-called al-Tābiʾūn (التّابِعُون), which is the generation of Muslims who were born after Muhammad's death but who were contemporaries of his companions, and 4) the followers of the followers (تابِع التّابِعِين), which is the generation after the followers in Islam.

388. What is an Islamist?

Answer: This term originated in the Western world and has no universal definition.

For most Westerners, an Islamist is a follower of the so-called *Political Islam* which means a Muslim who wants to force Islam onto public life. The term is mostly used for political movements such as the Muslim Brotherhood in Egypt or al-Nahda (النَّهْضة) in Tunisia.

Islamism is like populism. Their leaders have simple solutions for complex questions. Every Islamist movement picks the same topic by asking Muslims to accept that Islam is the best system and the best religion for human mankind for eternity.

Let's try to define Islamists by the one thing they all have in common: Every Islamist movement starts by proclaiming that no one has properly understood Islam except the Prophet, the very early Muslims, and our movement.

Islamists denounce all other Muslims, especially other Muslim rivals, as misguided. This is a dilemma in the Islamic world as there is simply no monopoly on the one and only true Islam. After almost 1400 years following the foundation of Islam, it is useless to debate the correct form of Islam that which was practised by the Prophet. We simply don't know.

We don't even know about the correct meaning of words as languages constantly develop.

389. Why had most Salafis not participated in the Egyptian revolution in 2011?

Answer: Because they were following a Hadith which commands Muslims to follow their leader without questioning his authority.

In January 2011, I was present during the uprising in Alexandria – Egypt's, probably even the world's, capital of Salafism. In Egypt Salafis equal around one third of the population. However, most of them did not attend the protests – which angered many Egyptians.

Let's check why they did that. It all originates from a quote of Muhammad:

'Abd Allah ibn Mas'ūd (عَبْد الله بن مَسْعُود) narrated that the Prophet said: "A Muslim has to listen to and obey [the orders of his ruler] whether he likes it or not, as long as his orders does not involve disobedience [to Allah], but if an act of disobedience [to Allah] is imposed, one should not listen to it or obey it."[472]

The Prophet, as evident in many Hadiths, forbade Muslims to rebel against the rulers – as long as they pray and allow Islam to be practised. The traditional view is that violence could lead to civil war which is likely to result in a much worse situation. While an unjust ruler is an evil in itself, the violence required to overthrow him is regarded as being even worse.

Hudhayfa ibn al-Yamān (حُذَيْفة بن الْيَمَان) narrated that he told the Prophet: "Messenger of Allah, no doubt, we had an evil time [i.e. the days of Jāhilīya; before Islam] and Allah brought us a good time [i.e. the Islamic period] through which we are now living. Will there be a bad time after this good time?"

He [the Prophet] said: "Yes." Hudhayfa asked: "Will there be a good time after this bad time?" He [the Prophet] answered: "Yes." Hudhayfa asked: "Will there be a bad time after good time?" He [the Prophet] replied: "Yes." Hudhayfa asked: "How?" Whereupon the Prophet said: "There will be leaders who will not be led by my guidance and who will not adopt my ways. There will be among them men who will have the hearts of devils in the bodies of human beings." Hudhayfa asked: "What should I do, Messenger of Allah, if I

---

472 ...عَنِ النَّبِيِّ قَالَ: "السَّمْعُ والطَّاعَةُ عَلَى الْمَرْءِ الْمُسْلِمِ، فِيمَا أَحَبَّ وَكَرِهَ، مَا لَمْ يُؤْمَرْ بِمَعْصِيَةٍ،
فَإِذَا أُمِرَ بِمَعْصِيَةٍ فَلَا سَمْعَ وَلَا طَاعَةَ." Sahīh al-Bukhārī 7144.

[happen] to live in that time?" The Prophet answered: "You will listen to the 'Amīr [the leader] and carry out his orders; even if your back is flogged and your wealth is snatched, you should listen and obey."[473]

'Ahmad ibn Hanbal (أَحْمَد بن حَنْبَل), an Islamic scholar and theologian who is considered the founder of the very conservative Hanbalī School of Islamic jurisprudence, proclaimed: "Do not confront the ruler, for his sword is unsheathed."[474]

390. Why do Shia Muslims pray with their heads on a pebble or clay tablet?

Answer: It symbolises earth.

A Turba (تُرْبة) - in Persian: mohr (مهـر) - is a small piece of hardened soil, often a clay tablet, which is used during prayers to symbolise earth. The Arabic word Turba (تُرْبة) means *dust, earth*.

The most favoured soil is that from Karbalā' in present-day Iraq where Husayn (الْحُسَيْن بن عَلِيّ), the son of 'Alī ibn 'Abī Tālib (عَلِيّ بن أَبِي طالِب) and grandson of the Prophet, was killed. Since Muslims are spread all over the world, Shia Muslims have created small clay tablets from the mud of Karbalā'. However, soil from anywhere may be used.

The Turba is compulsory in most Shia sects. Shias see as enough evidence for the tradition in a Hadith by 'Abū Sa'īd al-Khudrī (أَبُو سَعِيد الْخُدْرِيّ), who narrated: "I saw Allah's Messenger prostrating in mud and water and saw the mark of mud on his forehead."[475]

There is another Hadith indicating that the early Muslims touched earth with their forehead while praying. 'Anas ibn Mālik (أنَس بن

---

473 ...قُلْتُ يَا رَسُولَ اللَّهِ إِنَّا كُنَّا بِشَرٍّ فَجَاءَ اللَّهُ بِخَيْرٍ فَنَحْنُ فِيهِ فَهَلْ مِنْ وَرَاءِ هَذَا الْخَيْرِ شَرٌّ قَالَ نَعَمْ. قُلْتُ هَلْ وَرَاءَ ذَلِكَ الشَّرِّ خَيْرٌ قَالَ: "نَعَمْ." قُلْتُ فَهَلْ وَرَاءَ ذَلِكَ الْخَيْرِ شَرٌّ قَالَ: "نَعَمْ." قُلْتُ كَيْفَ قَالَ: "يَكُونُ بَعْدِي أَئِمَّةٌ لاَ يَهْتَدُونَ بِهُدَايَ وَلاَ يَسْتَنُّونَ بِسُنَّتِي وَسَيَقُومُ فِيهِمْ رِجَالٌ قُلُوبُهُمْ قُلُوبُ الشَّيَاطِينِ فِى جُثْمَانِ إِنْسٍ." قَالَ قُلْتُ كَيْفَ أَصْنَعُ يَا رَسُولَ اللَّهِ إِنْ أَدْرَكْتُ ذَلِكَ قَالَ: "تَسْمَعُ وَتُطِيعُ لِلأَمِيرِ وَإِنْ ضُرِبَ ظَهْرُكَ وَأُخِذَ مَالُكَ فَاسْمَعْ وَأَطِعْ." Sahīh Muslim 1847

474 ...لاَ يُتَعَرَّضُ بِالسُّلْطَانِ فَإِنَّ سَيْفَهُ مَسْلُولٌ. Jāmi' al-'Ulūm wa al-Hikam

475 ...رَأَيْتُ رَسُولَ يَسْجُدُ فِي الْمَاءِ وَالطِّينِ حَتَّى رَأَيْتُ أَثَرَ الطِّينِ فِي جَبْهَتِهِ. Sahīh al-Bukhārī

مالِك) narrated: "We used to pray with the Prophet in scorching heat and if someone of us could not put his face on the earth [because of the heat] then he would spread his clothes and prostrate over them."[476]

According to the Shia Jaʿfarī School of jurisprudence (جَعْفَرِئ) - which is one of the five main schools of law in Shia Islam - prostration must be performed on pure earth or what grows on it, provided that it is not eaten or worn. If there is no suitable soil available, plants or items made from plants may be used. Thus, prostration on paper is allowed because it is made of a material which grows in soil. This means that cloth or carpets are not allowed.

How about Sunnis? There is nothing wrong with prostration on soil. However, traditional Sunnis reject the use of Turba. They say that neither the Prophet nor his companions ever <u>carried</u> a clay tablet which they used for praying. So praying on soil is fine; carrying something that symbolises earth not.

Traditional Sunni Muslims reject the Turba for another reason, i.e. sometimes the Turba used by Shia have inscribed invocations to their revered figures, e.g. "Ya Husayn" (O Husayn) or "Ya Zahrāʾ" (name for Fātima, the wife of ʿAlī and mother of Husayn). For traditional Sunni Muslims a Muslim is only allowed to ask Allah for help.

391. When and why do Shia Muslims hit themselves?

Answer: They do it on the day called ʿĀshūrāʾ to commemorate the death of Muhammad's grandson, al-Husayn (الْحُسَيْن بن عَلِيّ).

ʿĀshūrāʾ (عاشُوراء) falls on the 10th day of the Islamic month Muharram. On that day in 680 (61 AH), Husayn was killed in the Battle of Karbalāʾ (مَعْرَكة كَرْبَلاء) which is in present-day Iraq. The word ʿĀshūrāʾ is derived from the word *ten* (عَشرة).

The battle took place between a small group of supporters and relatives of Muhammad's grandson Husayn and a larger group of the

---

476 ...قَالَ كُنَّا نُصَلِّي مَعَ النَّبِيِّ فِي شِدَّةِ الْحَرِّ، فَإِذَا لَمْ يَسْتَطِعْ أَحَدُنَا أَنْ يُمَكِّنَ وَجْهَهُ مِنَ الأَرْضِ بَسَطَ ثَوْبَهُ فَسَجَدَ عَلَيْهِ. Sahīh al-Bukhārī 1208.

forces of Yazīd I (يَزِيد بن مُعاوِيّة) who became the Umayyad Caliph after the death of his father Muʾāwiya (the founder of the Umayyad Dynasty of the caliphate).

Husayn did not pledge allegiance to Yazīd. Husayn and Yazīd's father, Muʾāwiya, had signed a treaty in which it was stated that Caliph Muʾāwiya would not name a successor during his reign. However, Muʾāwiya did just that, thus breaching the treaty.

When Husayn travelled towards Kūfa (الْكُوفة) his caravan was intercepted by Yazīd's soldiers at a place called Karbalāʾ. Husayn was beheaded.

Husayn's martyrdom is widely interpreted by Shia as a symbol for the struggle against injustice, tyranny, and oppression. Shia Muslims worldwide cut themselves with chains, knives, or even swords to mourn the death of the Prophet's grandson. Nowadays in some countries, it is officially banned.

During the Battle of Karbalāʾ Husayn's son, al-ʿAbbās, tried to get water from the Euphrates River for children who were nearly dying of thirst. He didn't succeed. Legend has it that he had lost both arms in a fight and therefore could not carry water to the camp. He died in the year 680, on Muharram 10, 61 AH, the same day as his father.

392. Who is the Mahdī?

Answer: The guided one.

In Islamic eschatology the Mahdī (الْمَهْدِي) is the prophesied redeemer of Islam who will rule for five, seven, nine or nineteen years (according to alternative interpretations) before the Day of Judgement and will free the world of evil.

The Islamic term Mahdī does not occur in the Qurʾan, but it does in the Hadiths. The word is derived from the Arabic root h-d-y (ه-د-ى), which means: *to lead on the right way; to guide.* The term al-Mahdī was used from the beginning of Islam, but mainly as an honorific epithet, without any messianic implication.

This changed during the Second Fitna, some call it the second Islamic civil war (680-692), which started after the death of the

Umayyad Caliph Muʿāwiya (مُعاوية). The term Mahdī - mainly due to Shia influence - was then used for a ruler who would restore Islam to its perfect form and restore justice after oppression.

Islamic eschatology states that the Mahdī will coincide with the second coming of Jesus Christ (عيسى) who will help the Mahdī fight against the *False Messiah* or *Antichrist* - in Arabic called Masīh al-Dajjāl (مَسيح الدَّجَّال).

Sunni Muslims view the Mahdī as the successor of Muhammad, but do not believe the Mahdī has already been born. The Mahdī is expected to arrive to rule the world and to re-establish righteousness.

For most Shia Muslims the Mahdī was born but has disappeared and will remain hidden from humanity until he reappears to bring justice to the world.

What kind of person will the al-Mahdī be? Muslims find some information about that in the Hadiths. ʼUmm Salama (أُمّ سَلَمة) narrated that the Prophet said: "The Mahdī will be of my family, of the descendants of Fātima."[477]

ʼAbū Saʿīd al-Khudrī (أَبُو سَعيد الْخُدْري) narrated that the Prophet said: "The Mahdī will be of my stock and will have a broad forehead and a prominent nose. He will fill the earth with equity and justice as it was filled with oppression and tyranny, and he will rule for seven years."[478]

393. Are Turkish Alevites Muslims?

Answer: It depends on whom you ask.

The word *Muslim* (مُسْلِم) is the active participle of the Arabic IV-verb ʼaslama (أَسْلَمَ) which means *to commit to the will of Allah*. A Muslim is thus a person who submits to the will of Allah. Generally speaking, anyone who willingly submits to the will of Allah and

---

477 ...قَالَتْ سَمِعْتُ رَسُولَ يَقُولُ: "الْمَهْدِيُّ مِنْ عِتْرَتي مِنْ وَلَدِ فَاطِمَةَ." Sunan ʼAbī Dāwūd 4284

478 ...قَالَ رَسُولُ اللَّهِ: "الْمَهْدِيُّ مِنِّي أَجْلَى الْجَبْهَةِ أَقْنَى الأَنْفِ يَمْلأُ الأَرْضَ قِسْطًا وَعَدْلاً كَمَا مُلِئَتْ جَوْرًا وَظُلْمًا يَمْلِكُ سَبْعَ سِنينَ." Sunan ʼAbī Dāwūd 4285

accepts Muhammad as His messenger is a Muslim. However, being a Muslim also means to follow the Qur'an and the teachings of the Prophet. Here is the crucial point. In order to get closer to an answer, let us check the **most common types of non-Muslims** (and unbelievers) in Islam:

1. **Munāfiq** (مُنافِق): One who verbally claims to be a Muslim, but is not so in his heart.

2. **Murtad** (مُرْتَدّ): an apostate – a Muslim who quit Islam.

3. **Mushrik** (مُشْرِك): a polytheist. One who subscribes to or believes in more than one Divine Being.

4. **Kitābī** (كِتابِيّ): Jews and Christians. The term is derived from the Arabic word for *book* (كِتاب), thus relating to the revealed Scriptures (Qur'an, Bible, Torah). It is similar to the term Dhimmī (ذِمِّي) which refers to a non-Muslim who has to pay taxes in an Islamic State.

5. **Dahrīya** (دَهْرِيّة): One who believes in the eternity of time and credits creation to time (= evolution). This term is also used to describe materialism.

6. **Muaʻttil** (مُعَطِّل): One who denies the existence of Allah and denies Allah all attributes. It is the active participle of the Arabic II-verb ʻattala (عَطَّلَ) which means *to leave without care, to neglect, to discontinue,* or *to annul.*

There is one left which brings us closer to the answer:

7. **Zindīq** (زِنْديق): freethinker, one who deviates from the right religion; unbeliever. Zindīq is originally a Persian word. Traditional Muslims have used this term wholesale to denounce Manichaeans, Mandaeans, Mazdakites, Zoroastrians, Buddhists, Christians – **and "self-proclaimed", "free thinking", "spiritual" Muslims.** Alevites belong to this category.

Traditional (Sunni) Muslims denounce followers of certain Islamic sects as *unbelievers* because these sects have adopted elements of folk culture, science, or modernity. The followers of these self-proclaimed Islamic sects believe in Allah, acknowledge the prophethood of

Muhammad, and follow Islamic ceremonies and rites like praying or the pilgrimage to Mecca or Hajj. But they also practice beliefs which are considered heretic by traditional (mostly Sunni) Islamic scholars. The followers of Alevi Islam, which is one of the biggest Islamic sects in Turkey, don't pray in mosques but in a so-called *Cemevi*. Turkish Alevites do not pray towards the direction of the Ka'ba; they do not follow compulsory prayers anyway.

Alevi women are usually not veiled. Some Alevites even eat pork and drink alcohol. They use candles and music in rituals, the classical four elements (earth, air, fire, water) - similar to Zoroastrians - are very important. Alevi Islam is way more spiritual and mystical than Sunni Islam. Turkish Alevis do not mind interpreting the holy Islamic scripts and adopt them to modern life. In short, Alevi Islam is less strict and pretty flexible.

But are Alevis Muslims? The Turkish Alevis say that they believe in Allah and His messenger which is the most important thing in Islam, and therefore they are Muslims. However, strictly following the teachings and commands of the Qur'an and the Prophet are of great importance as well. Turkish Alevis are certainly not doing this. Here, traditional (Sunni) scholars have a point. But is this enough to denounce them as non-Muslims? Who is entitled to call a person a Muslim? Liberal Muslims hold the view that it should be up to Allah (on the Day of Judgement) to decide that.

There are many Islamic sects everywhere in the world. Most of them combine the core of Islam with other elements, for example the Alevis (mainly in Turkey) or the Ahmadīya (worldwide).

There are also Islamic sects that are more political, for example the *Nation of Islam* (mainly in the USA). Other Islamic sects are rather dubious – for example the movement of Rashad Khalifa which later became known as *United Submitters International*. Rashad Khalifa was an Egyptian-American biochemist who proclaimed that the Archangel Gabriel told him that verse 3 in sura 36 in the Qur'an referred to him. His followers referred to him as God's messenger of the Covenant. He rejected the Hadiths as fabrications attributed to Muhammad by later scholars.

Rashad Khalifa was found stabbed to death in a mosque in Tucson, Arizona, on January 31, 1990.

394. What does Ayatollah mean?

Answer: A title given to high-ranked Twelver Shia clerics.

Ayatollah is a Shia religious title. The word Ayatollah (Persian: آیت الله) is derived from the Arabic expression 'Āya(t) Allah (آية الله), which means *Sign of Allah*. Those who carry the title are experts in Islamic studies und jurisprudence. The term was not commonly used as a title until the early twentieth century.

395. What is a Mawlā?

Answer: It depends on the context, but in Islam it mostly denotes a patron of new converts who are of non-Arab origin.

Mawlā (مَوْلًى) is an Arabic word with many meanings depending on the context and the time in history: *inheritor; a freed slave; kin-folk; ally, friend; master, protector, patron*. The root w-l-y (و-ل-ي) is tricky. Basically, it means *to be very near to any one*, either through kinship or as a neighbour. In the Qur'an and Hadiths the word Mawlā is used in many senses, such as *helper* or *protector*, but it can even refer to Allah:

47:11	That is because God protects the believers while the disbelievers have no one to protect them.	ذَٰلِكَ بِأَنَّ اللَّهَ مَوْلَى الَّذِينَ آمَنُوا وَأَنَّ الْكَافِرِينَ لَا مَوْلَى لَهُمْ.

The concept of Mawlā changed throughout history. When Islam spread, the institution of Mawlā was used to incorporate new converts to Islam into the Arab-Muslim society through patronage. During the Umayyad Caliphate, when the Arabs conquered more and more non-Arab lands, Persians, Africans, Turks, and Kurds converted to Islam.

Although Islam does not know racism, the Arab society did and still does. In the early years of Islam the Arab society was strongly based on tribal structures. This was indicated by the name which showed how powerful, rich, and influential a person was. Moreover, the name also indicated under whose (tribal) protection a person was. Therefore, newly converted non-Arab Muslims got an Arab patron – a Mawlā. However, the converts were mostly treated as second-class citizens by the Arabs.

The term Mawlā, during the Umayyad Caliphate, was gradually used to denounce non-Arab Muslims. Most non-Arab converts were excluded from higher positions in the government and military. There was a special tax implemented for non-Arab converts, similar to the tax for Christians and Jews, despite the fact they were Muslims.

In 750 (132 AH) the Abbasids put an end to the political and social privileges held by the Arabs, even though they were Arabs themselves. Nevertheless, they made Islam more open and brought it closer to Persia. Islam became more "multicultural". They moved their capital first to Kūfa and later to Baghdad.

396. What does a Muslim have to do once in a lifetime?

Answer: A pilgrimage to Mecca – the so-called al-Hajj (الْحَجّ).

’Abū Hurayra (أَبُو هُرَيْرة) reported that Allah's Messenger said: "O people, Allah has made Hajj obligatory for you; so perform Hajj."

Thereupon a person asked: "Messenger of Allah, is it to be performed every year?" He [the Prophet] kept quiet until the person repeated these words thrice, whereupon Allah's Messenger said: "If I were to say yes, it would become obligatory for you to perform it every year and you would not be able to do it."[479]

The pilgrimage takes place once a year, in the month of Dhū al-Hijja (ذُو الْحِجّة). It is compulsory for every Muslim who can afford it.

397. What is the first principle during the Hajj?

Answer: Al-’Iḥrām (الْإِحْرام) – the state of ritual dedication, which is typically symbolised by a special garment.

---

479 ...قَالَ خَطَبَنَا رَسُولُ اللَّهِ فَقَالَ: "أَيُّهَا النَّاسُ قَدْ فَرَضَ اللَّهُ عَلَيْكُمُ الْحَجَّ فَحُجُّوا." فَقَالَ رَجُلٌ أَكُلَّ عَامٍ يَا رَسُولَ اللَّهِ فَسَكَتَ حَتَّى قَالَهَا ثَلَاثًا فَقَالَ رَسُولُ اللَّهِ: "لَوْ قُلْتُ نَعَمْ لَوَجَبَتْ وَلَمَا اسْتَطَعْتُمْ.

Saḥīḥ Muslim 1337

'Ihrām in Islam is a sacred state which a Muslim must enter in order to perform the major pilgrimage (Hajj) or the minor pilgrimage ('Umra). A pilgrim must enter into this state before crossing the pilgrimage boundary, known as Mīqāt, by performing the cleansing rituals and wearing the proper clothes. Therefore, Ihrām is the intention (نِيّة) to enter the pilgrimage ceremonies.

A male Muslim in the state of Ihrām is not allowed to use any scents on the body. He is not allowed to tie any knots or wear any stitched clothes. Sandals must not be stitched either and should allow the ankle and back of foot to be exposed.

Female Muslims must have their faces <u>un</u>covered. Women are forbidden to wear the Burquʻ (بُرْقُع) or Niqāb (نقاب), but the veil - the so-called Hijāb (حجاب) - is okay.

'Abd Allah ibn 'Umar (عَبْد الله بن عُمَر) narrated: "A person stood up and asked: 'O Allah's Apostle! What clothes may be worn in the state of Ihrām?' The Prophet replied: 'Do not wear a shirt or trousers or any headgear [e.g. a turban], or a hooded cloak; but if somebody has no shoes he can wear leather stockings provided they are cut short off the ankles, and also, do not wear anything perfumed with saffron, and the Muhrima [a woman in the state of Ihrām] should not cover her face or wear gloves.'"[480]

Unlike in mosques, men and women pray together, not just in the same area but also on the same prayer line. This is to remind everyone that on the Day of Judgement, men and women will be standing together, side by side, in the same rows.

After having entered the state of 'Ihrām, Muslims begin saying the Talbiya (التَّلْبِية). This means, they have to say: "I am at Your service, O Allah, I am at Your service. You have no partner. I am at Your service. Praise and blessings belong to You and the Kingdom. You have no partner." This is all found in a Hadith narrated by Imam Mālik.

In Arabic: "Labbayka, Allahumma labbayka, la Sharīka laka labbayk. Inna'l-Hamda wa'n-niʻmata laka wa'l-mulka, la Sharīka lak."[481]

---

480 ...قَالَ قَامَ رَجُلٌ فَقَالَ يَا رَسُولَ اللهِ مَاذَا تَأْمُرُنَا أَنْ نَلْبَسَ مِنَ الثِّيَابِ فِي الإِحْرَامِ فَقَالَ النَّبِيُّ: "لاَ تَلْبَسُوا الْقَمِيصَ وَلاَ السَّرَاوِيلاَتِ وَلاَ الْعَمَائِمَ، وَلاَ الْبَرَانِسَ إِلاَّ أَنْ يَكُونَ أَحَدٌ لَيْسَتْ لَهُ نَعْلاَنِ، فَلْيَلْبَسِ الْخُفَّيْنِ، وَلْيَقْطَعْ أَسْفَلَ مِنَ الْكَعْبَيْنِ، وَلاَ تَلْبَسُوا شَيْئًا مَسَّهُ زَعْفَرَانٌ، وَلاَ الْوَرْسُ، وَلاَ تَنْتَقِبِ الْمَرْأَةُ الْمُحْرِمَةُ وَلاَ تَلْبَسِ الْقُفَّازَيْنِ ". Sahīh al-Bukhārī 1838

If you watch the Hajj pilgrimage on TV, you will hear "Labbayka" continuously.

398. What is al-Tawāf?

Answer: Tawāf (طواف) means *circling*. If it is used with the definite article, al-Tawāf, it describes one of the Hajj rituals.

During the Hajj and ‘Umra, Muslims must circumambulate, in a counter-clockwise direction, the Ka‘ba seven times. This is called al-Tawāf. The circling is believed to demonstrate the unity of the believing Muslims while supplicating to Allah.

It is interesting that a number of rituals that are related to life and death are done counter-clockwise. For example: When a Christian priest moves in an anti-clockwise direction around the altar, he symbolises that human life is not finite, that life does not end on earth.

399. When does a pilgrim have to put on special garments?

Answer: When he crosses a Mīqāt (ميقات).

In Saudi Arabia Mīqāts are special places on the way to Mecca, which Muslim pilgrims cannot cross without being in the state of ’Ihrām (الإحْرام).

This basically means that the pilgrims - during Hajj or ‘Umra - have to wear the prescribed garment when they go beyond the Mīqāt. If one ignores this rule, a Muslim shall have to sacrifice a sheep in Mecca; its meat must be distributed to the poor.

Mīqāts were set for all directions. The information is given in a Hadith. ’Abū al-Zubayr (أَبُو الزُّبَيْرِ) heard that Jābir ibn ‘Abd Allah (جَابِر بن عَبْد الله) was asked about the place for entering into the state of ’Ihrām. He replied that he heard the Messenger of Allah say: "For the people of Medina, Dhū al-Hulayfa is the place for entering into the

---

481 ...لَبَّيْكَ اللَّهُمَّ لَبَّيْكَ لَبَّيْكَ لاَ شَرِيكَ لَكَ لَبَّيْكَ إِنَّ الْحَمْدَ وَالنِّعْمَةَ لَكَ وَالْمُلْكَ لاَ شَرِيكَ لَكَ.
Muwatta’ Mālik, Book 20, Hadith 736

state of 'Iḥrām, and for the people coming through the other way [i.e. Syria], it is al-Juḥfa; for the people of Iraq, it is Dhāt ʿIrq; for the people of Najd, it is Qarn [al-Manāzil] and for the people of Yemen, it is Yalamlam."[482]

Let's have a closer look:

- First of all, if a Muslim lives between the Mīqāt and Mecca, he enters 'Iḥrām from where he is.

- For pilgrims coming from Medina, it is Dhū al-Ḥulayfa (ذُو الْحُلَيْفة). This is a place in the north, commonly known as Masjid al-Shajara (مَسْجِد الشَّجَرة). Pilgrims who first go to Medina use this Mīqāt. It is about 7 km outside the city of Medina and around 450 km (281 mi) away from Mecca.

- For pilgrims coming from Syria, it is al-Juḥfa (الْجُحْفة) which is around 180 km (112 mi) north-west of Mecca.

- For pilgrims coming from Najd (نَجْد), the central region of present-day Saudi Arabia, it is Qarn al-Manāzil (قَرن الْمَنَازِل). This place is about 90 km (56 mi) east of Mecca.

- For pilgrims coming from Yemen, it is Yalamlam (يَلَمْلَم), which is a small city around 100 km (62 mi) south-west of Mecca.

- For pilgrims coming from Iraq and Iran, it is Dhāt ʿIrq (ذَاتِ عِرْق), a place about 85 km (53 mi) north-east of Mecca.

What about a Muslim who does not travel by land?

Generally speaking, if there is a Mīqāt on a person's route, he should enter 'Iḥrām when he comes in line with the nearest place to it. Usually the pilot gives an announcement to the passengers when the plane approaches a Mīqāt. It is crucial for a Muslim to not cross a Mīqāt – not even in an air plane. In order to be on the safe side there is nothing wrong with entering 'Iḥrām a little before that.

Many Muslim pilgrims wear the proper garments already when boarding the plane. That is why you occasionally see pilgrims at the airport in Istanbul, Turkey, wearing the white garments for the Hajj.

---

482 ...النَّبِيُّ قَالَ: "مُهَلُّ أَهْلِ الْمَدِينةِ مِنْ ذِي الْحُلَيْفةِ وَالطَّرِيقِ الآخَرُ الْجُحْفةُ وَمُهَلُّ أَهْلِ الْعِراقِ مِنْ ذَاتِ عِرْقٍ وَمُهَلُّ أَهْلِ نَجْدٍ مِنْ قَرْنٍ وَمُهَلُّ أَهْلِ الْيَمَنِ مِنْ يَلَمْلَمَ." Saḥīḥ Muslim 1183

400. What is the 'Umra?

Answer: The lesser pilgrimage. A pious visit.

The 'Umra (عُمْرة) is a pilgrimage to Mecca that can be done at any time of the year. The Hajj, on the other hand, has to be performed in the month of Dhū al-Hijja (ذُو الْحِجّة).

In Arabic, the root '-m-r (ع-م-ر) - from which the word 'Umra is derived - means *to thrive, to prosper; to be populated; to fill with life.*

The 'Umra is sometimes called the *minor pilgrimage* or *lesser pilgrimage,* in contrast to the Hajj which is the *major pilgrimage.* The 'Umra is not compulsory for Muslims. It is recommended, so-called mustahabb (مُسْتَحَبّ). According to Islam, if a Muslim does it, he will be rewarded from Allah, but if he doesn't, there won't be any punishment. There are differences to the Hajj regarding the rites.

What they share:

- During both pilgrimages, pilgrims are required to walk seven times around the Ka'ba and seven times between the hills al-Safā and al-Marwā.

Where they differ:

- During the 'Umra, pilgrims do not go to Minā (مِنَى) where the Hajj pilgrims usually stay overnight.
- Furthermore, they don't go to Mount 'Arafāt (جَبَل عَرَفات or جَبَل عَرَفـة) – the place which is thought to be the hill where Muhammad stood while delivering the *Farewell Sermon* to the Muslims who had accompanied him for the Hajj towards the end of his life.
- 'Umra pilgrims don't go to Muzdalifa (مُزْدَلِفة) – an open area near Mecca.
- 'Umra pilgrims don't throw stones and do not sacrifice an animal.

401. Can Muslims have pets?

Answer: Yes.

It was narrated by 'Anas ibn Mālik (أَنَس بن مالك) that the Messenger of Allah used to come visiting them. 'Anas had a younger brother who had a nughar (a small bird like a sparrow or a nightingale). The bird died, and the Prophet saw him looking sad, so he joked with him and said things which scholars interpreted as an approval of keeping birds.

'Anas went on saying: "I had a younger brother who was called 'Abū 'Umayr. He had a sparrow with which he played, but it died. So one day the Prophet came to see him and saw him grieved. The Prophet asked: 'What is the matter with him?' The people replied: 'His sparrow has died.' He [the Prophet] then said: 'O 'Abū 'Umayr! What has happened to the little sparrow?'" [Note: This is rhymes in Arabic: "O 'Abū Umayr, what happened to the nughayr?"][483]

Scholars derived from this Hadith that a Muslim can have a bird at home. But there is more about this topic: 'Abd Allah ibn 'Umar (عَبْد الله بن عُمَر) narrated that the Prophet had said: "A woman went to (Hell) Fire because of a cat which she had kept, neither giving it food nor setting it free to eat from the vermin of the earth."[484]

From this Hadith it may be understood that if the woman had fed it, she would have been saved from that threat. This means that she would have been allowed to keep the cat as a pet at home.

Note: Pets can be a complicated matter for strict Muslims. Traditional scholars say that listening to birds is an idle action and Muslims should better read in the Qur'an instead. Therefore, they conclude that it is better to avoid pets.

---

483 ...قَالَ كَانَ رَسُولُ اللّهِ يَدْخُلُ عَلَيْنَا وَلِي أَخٌ صَغِيرٌ يُكْنَى أَبَا عُمَيْرٍ وَكَانَ لَهُ نُغَرٌ يَلْعَبُ بِهِ فَمَاتَ فَدَخَلَ عَلَيْهِ النَّبِيُّ ذَاتَ يَوْمٍ فَرَآهُ حَزِينًا فَقَالَ: "مَا شَأْنُهُ." قَالُوا مَاتَ نُغَرُهُ فَقَالَ: "يَا أَبَا عُمَيْرٍ مَا فَعَلَ النُّغَيْرُ." Sunan 'Abī Dāwūd 4969 (4951)

484 ...عَنِ النَّبِيِّ قَالَ: "دَخَلَتِ امْرَأَةٌ النَّارَ فِي هِرَّةٍ رَبَطَتْهَا، فَلَمْ تُطْعِمْهَا، وَلَمْ تَدَعْهَا تَأْكُلُ مِنْ خِشَاشِ الْأَرْضِ." Sahīh al-Bukhārī 3318

402. Which kind of meat is permissible for Muslims?

Answer: This is a complicated matter.

There are several rules for Muslims regarding animals living on land:

- A Muslim is not allowed to eat any wild animal that has canine teeth or any bird that has talons. For example lion, wolf, hawk, or eagle. 'Abd Allah ibn 'Abbās (عَبْد الله بن عَبّاس) reported: "The Messenger of Allah prohibited the eating of any beast of prey that has fangs and any bird that has talons."[485]

- A Muslim is not allowed to eat the flesh of any animal which died naturally.

- Pork is strictly forbidden.

- A Muslim is not allowed to drink blood (which means that meat should not contain blood)

- The slaughtering process is important, i.e. animals must not be killed by venom or electric shock. They must be killed by cutting the throat with a sharp knife.

- Muslims may eat food which was prepared by Christians or Jews. Some scholars, however, claim that it is questionable whether a Muslim is allowed to eat food which was prepared by Hindus or Buddhists.

So much for theory. In general, Muslims do not necessarily have to inquire about things they haven't seen since they cannot know for sure anyway. They shouldn't panic if they don't know whether the butcher has uttered "in the name of Allah" when he killed the animal or not. They shouldn't be bothered too much whether the butcher was a Muslim or not.

Instead, they should follow the rule of the Prophet and say the Basmala ("in the name of Allah") before eating. This is the most important part when it comes to food because it is the last step before a Muslim's body gets in contact with food.

Note: The Basmala does not suspend the Islamic rules for forbidden meat. A Muslim must avoid pork at all times.

---

485 ...قَالَ نَهَى رَسُولُ اللَّهِ عَنْ أَكْلِ كُلِّ ذِي نَابٍ مِنَ السَّبُعِ وَعَنْ كُلِّ ذِي مِخْلَبٍ مِنَ الطَّيْرِ. Sunan
'Abī Dāwūd 3803

403. What is so special about fish?

Answer: Muslims are allowed to eat any marine animal; they are halāl (خلال).

With marine animals are meant animals which cannot live outside the water. Allah gave Muslims carte blanche to consume marine animals. It does not matter whether it is fish, a marine mammal, or a plant. It doesn't matter either whether it was caught by a Muslim or a non-Muslim; whether it was taken out of the water alive, dead or in pieces. Muslims are even allowed to eat fish which were found dead in the water – something which is strictly forbidden regarding land animals. Furthermore, Muslims are not required to slaughter the marine animal according to the Islamic rule (bleeding).

However, meat of crocodiles, otters, and turtles is not allowed because these animals live and hunt on land as well. Frogs are forbidden as well, because the Prophet forbade their killing.

In sura 35 *The Creator* - in Arabic: al-Fātir (سورة الفاطِر) -, the Qur'an says that fresh and salt water fish is fine:

| 35:12 | The two bodies of water are not alike - one is palatable, sweet, and pleasant to drink, the other salty and bitter - yet from each you eat fresh fish and extract ornaments to wear, and in each you see the ships ploughing their course so that you may seek God's bounty and be grateful. | وَمَا يَسْتَوِي الْبَحْرَانِ هَٰذَا عَذْبٌ فُرَاتٌ سَائِغٌ شَرَابُهُ وَهَٰذَا مِلْحٌ أُجَاجٌ وَمِن كُلٍّ تَأْكُلُونَ لَحْمًا طَرِيًّا وَتَسْتَخْرِجُونَ حِلْيَةً تَلْبَسُونَهَا وَتَرَى الْفُلْكَ فِيهِ مَوَاخِرَ لِتَبْتَغُوا مِن فَضْلِهِ وَلَعَلَّكُمْ تَشْكُرُونَ. |

All kinds of food from the sea are permissible as sura 5 *The Feast* - in Arabic: al-Māʾida (سورة الْمائدة) - tells Muslims:

| 5:96 | It is permitted for you to catch and eat seafood - an enjoyment for you and the traveller - but hunting game is forbidden while you are in the state of consecration [for pilgrimage]. Be mindful of God to whom you will be gathered. | أُحِلَّ لَكُمْ صَيْدُ الْبَحْرِ وَطَعَامُهُ مَتَاعًا لَّكُمْ وَلِلسَّيَّارَةِ وَحُرِّمَ عَلَيْكُمْ صَيْدُ الْبَرِّ مَا دُمْتُمْ حُرُمًا وَاتَّقُوا اللَّهَ الَّذِي إِلَيْهِ تُحْشَرُونَ. |

Eating shrimp and crab is okay according to the verse above. However, Shia Muslims claim that fish which do not have scales must not be eaten, so sharks and eel are forbidden. Some Sunni Muslims follow this rule as well, although neither the Qur'an, nor any Hadith state anything like this.

Let's have a closer look to the special rule that the meat of a fish that was found dead is permissible. Muslims find this information in a Hadith which was narrated by Abū Hurayra (أَبُو هُرَيْرَة). The Messenger of Allah said: "Its water is a means of purification and its dead meat is permissible. [i.e. the fish found dead in the sea.]"[486]

Jābir ibn ʿAbd Allah (جَابِر بن عَبْد الله) narrated: "We set out with the army of al-Khabt and ʾAbū ʿUbayda was the commander of the troops. We were struck with severe hunger and the sea threw out a dead fish the likes of which we had never seen before, and it was called al-ʿAnbar [probably a whale]. We ate of it for half a month. ʾAbū ʿUbayda took [and mounted] one of its bones and a rider passed underneath [without touching it]. ʾAbū ʿUbayda said [to us]: 'Eat [of that fish]!'

When we arrived at Medina, we informed the Prophet about that and he said: 'Eat, for it is food Allah has brought out for you, and feed us if you have some of it.' So some of them gave him [of that fish], and he ate it."[487]

404. Are Muslims allowed to eat lizards?

Answer: Yes, but Muhammad did not like them.

It was narrated by Saʿīd ibn Jubayr (سَعِيد بن جُبَيْر) that he had heard ʿAbd Allah ibn ʿAbbās (عَبْد الله بن عَبَّاس) say: "The sister of my mother [ʾUmm Hufayd] presented to the Messenger of Allah clarified butter

---

486 ...فَقَالَ رَسُولُ اللَّهِ: "هُوَ الطَّهُورُ مَاؤُهُ الْحِلُّ مَيْتَتُهُ." Sunan ibn Māja 417 (386)

487 أَنَّهُ سَمِعَ جَابِرًا يَقُولُ غَزَوْنَا جَيْشَ الْخَبَطِ وَأُمِّرَ أَبُو عُبَيْدَةَ، فَجُعْنَا جُوعًا شَدِيدًا فَأَلْقَى الْبَحْرُ حُوتًا مَيِّتًا، لَم نَرَ مِثْلَهُ، يُقَالُ لَهُ الْعَنْبَرُ، فَأَكَلْنَا مِنْهُ نِصْف شَهْرٍ، فَأَخَذَ أَبُو عُبَيْدَةَ عَظمًا مِنْ عِظَامِهِ فَمَرَّ الرَّاكِبُ تَحْتَهُ. فَأَخْبَرَنِي أَبُو الزُّبَيْرِ أَنَّهُ سَمِعَ جَابِرًا يَقُولُ قَالَ أَبُو عُبَيْدَةَ كُلُوا. فَلَمَّا قَدِمْنَا الْمَدِينَةَ ذَكَرْنَا ذَلِكَ لِلنَّبِيِّ فَقَالَ: "كُلُوا رِزْقًا أَخْرَجَهُ اللَّهُ، أَطْعِمُونَا إِنْ كَانَ مَعَكُمْ." فَأَتَاهُ بَعْضُهُمْ {بِعُضْوٍ} فَأَكَلَهُ. Sahīh al-Bukhārī 4362

[ghee], cheese, and some lizards. He ate from the clarified butter and cheese, but left the lizard finding no liking for it. But it was eaten on the table of Allah's Messenger. Had it been forbidden [harām], it would not have been eaten on the table of Allah's Messenger."[488]

It is interesting that Muhammad hesitated about a verdict on the question of eating lizards when his companions wanted a yes or no answer. He indicated vaguely that the lizards might have been transformed once and that they belonged to the tribe of Banū Isrā'īl (بَنُو إِسْرائِيل), also spelled Banū Israel.

It was narrated by 'Abū Sa'īd (أَبُو سَعِيد) that an Arab of the desert came to Allah's Messenger and said: "I live in a low land abounding in lizards and these are the common diet of my family", but he [the Prophet] did not reply. We told him: "Repeat it [your problem]!", and so he repeated it, but he [the Prophet] did not give any reply. [His question was repeated thrice].

Then Allah's Messenger called him out after the third time saying: "O man of the desert, verily Allah cursed [or showed wrath to] a tribe of Banū Isrā'īl and distorted them to beasts which move on the earth. I do not know, perhaps this [lizard] may be one of them. So I do not eat it, nor do I prohibit the eating of it."[489]

Are Muslims allowed to eat locusts?

Answer: yes.

Ibn 'Abū 'Awfā (ابن أَبِي أَوْفَى) reported: "We went on seven expeditions with Allah's Messenger and ate locusts."[490]

---

488 ...يَقُولُ أَهْدَتْ خَالَتِي أُمُّ حُفَيْدٍ إِلَى رَسُولِ اللَّهِ سَمْنًا وَأَقِطًا وَأَضُبًّا فَأَكَلَ مِنَ السَّمْنِ وَالْأَقِطِ وَتَرَكَ الضَّبَّ تَقَذُّرًا وَأُكِلَ عَلَى مَائِدَةِ رَسُولِ اللَّهِ وَلَوْ كَانَ حَرَامًا مَا أُكِلَ عَلَى مَائِدَةِ رَسُولِ اللَّهِ. Sahīh Muslim 1947

489 ...أَنَّ أَعْرَابِيًّا، أَتَى رَسُولَ اللَّهِ فَقَالَ إِنِّي فِي غَائِطٍ مَضَبَّةٍ وَإِنَّهُ عَامَّةُ طَعَامِ أَهْلِي - قَالَ - فَلَمْ يُجِبْهُ فَقُلْنَا عَاوِدْهُ. فَعَاوَدَهُ فَلَمْ يُجِبْهُ ثَلَاثًا ثُمَّ نَادَاهُ رَسُولُ اللَّهِ فِي الثَّالِثَةِ فَقَالَ: "يَا أَعْرَابِيُّ إِنَّ اللَّهَ لَعَنَ أَوْ غَضِبَ عَلَى سِبْطٍ مِنْ بَنِي إِسْرَائِيلَ فَمَسَخَهُمْ دَوَابَّ يَدِبُّونَ فِي الْأَرْضِ فَلَا أَدْرِي لَعَلَّ هَذَا مِنْهَا فَلَسْتُ آكُلُهَا وَلَا أَنْهَى عَنْهَا." Sahīh Muslim 1951

490 ...أَبِي أَوْفَى قَالَ غَزَوْنَا مَعَ رَسُولِ اللَّهِ سَبْعَ غَزَوَاتٍ نَأْكُلُ الْجَرَادَ. Sahīh Muslim 1952

405. May a Muslim woman marry a non-Muslim?

Answer: This is a difficult question.

Most Muslims claim that a Muslim woman must marry a Muslim man and that she is not allowed to marry a Christian or Jew. However, there is nothing in the Qur'an or Hadiths that tells this.

The Prophet had not said anything about the religion of a Muslim woman's husband as it was simply not important when Islam emerged. The Qur'an only says that a Muslim woman is not allowed to marry a <u>polytheist</u> – in Arabic: al-Mushrikūn (الْمُشْرِكُون) – however, Jews and Christians are considered *People of the Book* and not Mushrikūn.

This occurs in sura 2 *The Cow* – in Arabic: al-Baqara (سُورة الْبَقَرة):

| 2:221 | Do not marry idolatresses until they believe: a believing slave woman is certainly better than an idolatress, even though she may please you. And do not give your women in marriage to idolaters until they believe: a believing slave is certainly better than an idolater, even though he may please you. Such people call [you] to the Fire, while God calls [you] to the Garden and forgiveness by His leave. He makes His messages clear to people, so that they may bear them in mind. | وَلَا تَنكِحُوا الْمُشْرِكَاتِ حَتَّىٰ يُؤْمِنَّ وَلَأَمَةٌ مُّؤْمِنَةٌ خَيْرٌ مِّن مُّشْرِكَةٍ وَلَوْ أَعْجَبَتْكُمْ وَلَا تُنكِحُوا الْمُشْرِكِينَ حَتَّىٰ يُؤْمِنُوا وَلَعَبْدٌ مُّؤْمِنٌ خَيْرٌ مِّن مُّشْرِكٍ وَلَوْ أَعْجَبَكُمْ أُولَٰئِكَ يَدْعُونَ إِلَى النَّارِ وَاللَّهُ يَدْعُو إِلَى الْجَنَّةِ وَالْمَغْفِرَةِ بِإِذْنِهِ وَيُبَيِّنُ آيَاتِهِ لِلنَّاسِ لَعَلَّهُمْ يَتَذَكَّرُونَ. |

Nevertheless, over the centuries, scholars have derived that Muslim women are prohibited from marrying a non-Muslim in general. They did that by claiming that the man has authority over his wife and that for this reason, it is not possible that a non-Muslim man (hence, not only a polytheist) has authority over a Muslim woman.

Yūsuf al-Qaradāwī, an Egyptian conservative theologian and preacher, confirms in his book *The Lawful and the Prohibited in Islam* that a Muslim woman must marry a Muslim.

However, he does not cite a Hadith or a sura which commands such. In fact, the only explanation he gives is that "no text exists which makes exception for the People of the Book; hence, on the basis of the Qur'anic verse (2:221), there is consensus among Muslims concerning this prohibition."

We should keep in mind that husband and wife have different roles in Islam. The Muslim husband has to earn the money for the family and has the authority over his wife; while his Muslim wife is in charge of the household and the children. Non-Muslims, especially in Western countries, are likely to reject this concept of marriage.

Furthermore, the whole concept of marriage is different. In the Arab world, most marriages are pre-arranged. Dating is difficult since unmarried women are not allowed to meet with men in public. In Islam, marriage is often not based on love, but it is seen as an institution. My Egyptian Bawwāb (gatekeeper) told me that love is not important for marriage. There is only one love in life, he told me: "You love Allah!"

'Abū Hurayra (أَبُـو هُرَيْـرة) reported that the Prophet had said: "Women may be married for four reasons: for her property, her status, her beauty, and for her religiosity. So get the one who is religious and prosper [lit. may your hands cleave to the dust]."[491]

But what will happen if a Muslim woman marries a non-Muslim?

According to the majority of Islamic scholars, she would be a Zān-iya (زانية) which means a *whore, harlot,* or *adulteress.* The punishment in Islam is therefore the punishment for adultery.

Adultery belongs to the so-called Hadd or Hudūd (حُدُود) crimes which literally means *limit* or *restriction.* The punishment for adultery is lashes. However, if the woman was ignorant of the ruling then she is excused, but the couple must be separated. There is need for a divorce because the marriage is null and void in the first place.

406. Who is born a Muslim?

Answer: A baby whose father is a Muslim.

---

491 ...النَّبِيُّ قَالَ: "تُنْكَحُ الْمَرْأَةُ لأَرْبَعٍ لِمَالِهَا وَلِحَسَبِهَا وَلِجَمَالِهَا وَلِدِينِهَا فَاظْفَرْ بِذَاتِ الدِّينِ تَرِبَتْ يَدَاكَ". Sahīh Muslim 1466

First of all, there are no clear rules for this. Neither the Qur'an nor the Hadiths give Muslims a clear answer to this question. Over the centuries Islamic scholars have tried to derive some rules and they could agree on two things: A child who is born to two Muslim parents is automatically a Muslim, and secondly, if the father is a Muslim, the child is a Muslim as well.

It is extremely rare that only the child's mother is a Muslim because almost all Muslims claim that a Muslim woman must always marry a Muslim man.

However, centuries ago, the scholars did think about this case. The 13th century scholar Ibn Taymīya (ابن تَيْمِيّة), a very conservative and rigid theologian, said that if the parents of a child are both Muslims, then the child is a Muslim too, which is the consensus among Muslims. The same applies if the child's mother is Muslim – according to the majority of scholars such as 'Abū Ḥanīfa, al-Shāfi'ī and 'Aḥmad.[492]

Note: The child, nevertheless, needs to pronounce the Shahāda before reaching puberty. If the boy or girl rejects that, he or she will be treated as an apostate.

407. Why do some Muslims say that Barack Obama is a Muslim?

Answer: Because his father, Barack Hussein, was born a Muslim.

I was in Egypt when Barack Obama was a presidential candidate in 2008. When Egyptians found out about his middle name - Hussein (حُسَيْن) -, a discussion about his religion emerged. There is consensus among Muslim scholars that if your father is a Muslim the son is Muslim too. However, it was Obama's grandfather who had converted to Islam and adopted the name Hussein; his father had converted to Anglicanism at a very young age, many years before Barack Obama was born. Some (Salafi) Muslims claimed that

---

492 ..."الطِّفْل إذا كانَ أَبْواهُ مُسْلِمِينَ كان مُسْلِمًا تَبعًا لأَبويه بِاتِّفاق الْمُسْلِمِين، وَكَذَلِكَ إذا كانَتْ أُمُّهُ مُسْلِمة عَنْد جُمْهُور الْعُلَماء كأَبِي حَنِيفة والشافِعِيّ وأَحْمَد." Majmūʿ al-Fatāwā 10/437

Obama's father was Muslim and said that Obama had to be re-invited to Islam; if he would reject such re-invitation, he would have to be killed which is the verdict for apostates in Islam.

Obama was asked about his religion at a town hall meeting in Albuquerque in 2010. According to several media reports, he responded : "I'm a Christian by choice. My family didn't - frankly, they weren't folks who went to church every week."

408. Why are so many Muslim men called 'Abd Allah?

Answer: Because the belief is that Allah likes this name best.

Have you ever wondered why most Muslims are called Muhammad or 'Abd Allah? Muslims believe that their name will be used in this world and in the Hereafter. A personal name is a kind of tag, and for Muslims: it not only indicates to which family one belongs but also to which religion.

In Egypt, for example, people will always ask you about your name mostly to identify whether you are Muslim or not. If the first name is not clearly a Muslim name, they will ask you about your father's and grandfather's name especially as older generations did not use non-Muslim names. This can be difficult for people who were brought up in secular countries. Whether they like it or not, if their parents were Muslims, they will be treated as a Muslim too.

Furthermore, in Islam, the child must be named after his/her father ("son/daughter of") even if the father is deceased or divorced, even if he does not take care of the child. In Islam, it is forbidden to name a child after anyone other than his father, except in one case: When the child is born as a result of adultery. In this case, the child should be named after the mother. However, there is hardly any mother who follows this Islamic rule as her child, as well as the mother, would be stigmatised.

A convert to Islam should change his or her name. There are several stories about men whose names were changed by the Prophet himself. Let's look at an example. The companion 'Abd al-Rahmān ibn 'Awf (عَبْد الرَّحْمٰن بن عَوْف) once said: "My name was 'Abd 'Amr [lit. slave of 'Amr] – or, according to one source, 'Abd al-Ka'ba [slave of the Ka'ba] - and when I became Muslim, the Messenger of Allah called me 'Abd al-Rahmān [slave of the (most) Merciful]."[493]

But what names are best?

It was narrated from 'Abd Allah ibn 'Umar (عَبْد الله بن عُمَر) that the Prophet had said: "The most beloved of names to Allah are 'Abd Allah and 'Abd al-Rahmān."[494] These are male names. The Prophet did not inform his followers about female names, at least there has nothing been recorded on that.

Which names are disliked or not even allowed for Muslims?

The Arabic word 'Abd (عَبْد) means *slave* or *servant*. A Muslim cannot enslave himself except to Allah. In Islam any other enslavement is forbidden, including enslavement to prophets and angels. For example, Muslims are not allowed to use the name *Slave of the Messenger* (عَبْد الرَّسُول).

Also forbidden are names (attributes) which only Allah can have. For example: al-Khāliq (الخالِق) – *the Creator*; al-Rāziq (الرَّازِق) – *the Provider*; and al-Rabb (الرَّبّ) – *the Lord.*

Names that belong exclusively to non-Muslims, mainly Jews and Christians, are also not allowed. For example: 'Abd al-Masīh (عَبْد المَسيح) – *Slave of the Messiah*; Butrus (بُطْرُس) – *Peter*; Girgis or Jurjus (جُرْجُس) – *George.*

Traditional scholars say that Muslims should avoid using names of angels or names of Qur'anic Suras, such as Ta-Ha and Ya-Sin. Nevertheless, the name Yacin (Turkish for Ya-Sin) is rather popular in Turkey. Traditional scholars also reject the idea of adding words to the Arabic word for *religion* al-Dīn (الدِّين) or *Islam* (الإسلام).

However, these names are common in Islam, for example Nūr al-Dīn (نُور الدِّين) – *light of the religion;* or Muhī al-Dīn (مُحي الدِّين) – *reviver of the religion.* Traditional scholars claim that these names give a person more than the person deserves.

---

493 ...كَانَ اسْمِي عَبْدَ عَمْرٍو فَلَمَّا أَسْلَمْتُ سَمَّانِي رَسُولُ اللَّهِ عَبْدَ الرَّحْمَنِ. al-Hakim 3/306

494 ...النَّبِيُّ قَالَ: "أَحَبُّ الأَسْمَاءِ إِلَى اللَّهِ عَزَّ وَجَلَّ عَبْدُ اللَّهِ وَعَبْدُ الرَّحْمَنِ." Sunan ibn Māja 3728

So let's sum it up:

1. The best names are ʿAbd Allah (عَبْد الله) and ʿAbd al-Rahmān (عَبْد الرَّحْمٰن).

2. The second best are names which express enslavement to Allah, which means that they start with ʿAbd (عَبْد). For example: ʿAbd al-ʿAzīz (عَبْد الْعَزِيز) – *Servant of the Mighty.*

3. Names of Islamic prophets and messengers are a good choice for Muslims. That is also the reason why so many Muslims are called after Muhammad, ʾIbrāhīm or Yūsuf.

   By the way, there are several other names which all mean Muhammad, e.g. ʾAhmad (أَحْمَد) or Mustapha (مُصْطَفى) which is an epithet for Muhammad.

4. A Muslim may name his child after one of Muhammad's companions.

What about Shia Muslims?

The same rules as stated above apply for Shia Muslims as well. However, they have some preferences:

- Shia Muslims are very fond of the name ʿAlī (عَلِيّ), the name of Muhammad's son-in-law and cousin ʿAlī ibn ʾAbī Tālib (عَلِيّ بن أَبِي طالِب).

- They also like to name their male children after ʿAlī's children: Hasan (حَسَن) or Husayn (حُسَيْن).

- For girls, they like to use the name of Muhammad's daughter Fātima (فاطِمة) who became ʿAlī's wife.

- Also very common is one of Fātima's epithets, for example: al-Zahrāʾ (الزَّهْراء) meaning: *the shining.*

- Another common name for Shia girls is Zaynab (زَيْنَب), the name of ʿAlī and Fātima's daughter.

- However, you will hardly come across a female Shia Muslim who is named after Muhammad's wife ʿĀʾisha (عائشة بِنْت أَبِي بَكْر). After the Prophet's death, she became one of ʿAlī's opponents.

Note: The name Zahrāʾ (زَهْراء) is often mistaken for Sarah (سارة). There is a German left-wing politician called Sahra (Zahrāʾ) Wagenknecht who is the daughter of an Iranian father, but almost every German calls her: Sarah. She once told the story that when her parents chose the name Sahra (the German transliteration for: Zahrā'), a German official said: "Sahra with an h in the middle does not exist. It is Sarah."

Years later, she changed it to Sahra – but the Germans still call her "Sarah" as the position of the *h* doesn't really matter in the pronunciation. In Arabic and Persian, however, Sahra and Sarah are two different names: Sarah was the wife of prophet Abraham and Zahrā' (Sahra) was the epithet of Muhammad's daughter Fātima.

409. Which materials are prohibited in the clothes of men?

Answer: Gold (الذَّهَب) and silk (الْحَرِير).

It was narrated from 'Abū Mūsā (أَبُو مُوسَى) that the Messenger of Allah had said: "Allah has permitted silk and gold to the females of my 'Umma and has forbidden them to the males."[495]

Traditional scholars say that Islam is the religion of strengths. They claim that it doesn't suit a man to wear clothes made of fine material.

Moreover, Muhammad forbade men <u>and</u> women to use gold and silver utensils. Hudhayfa (حُذَيْفة) stated that the Prophet forbade Muslims to drink out of gold and silver vessels or to eat out of them.[496] 'Umm Salama (أُمّ سَلَمة) reported that Allah's Messenger said: "He who drinks from a silver utensil is only filling his abdomen/ stomach with Hellfire."[497]

Islam sees in the excessive use of luxury goods a sign of social injustice. In reality rich Arabs like to show off their wealth. They like to buy expensive watches, cars, mobile phones, etc. This is against the teachings of Islam.

---

495 ...أَنَّ رَسُولَ اللَّهِ قَالَ: "إِنَّ اللَّهَ عَزَّ وَجَلَّ أَحَلَّ لإِنَاثِ أُمَّتِي الْحَرِيرَ وَالذَّهبَ وَحَرَّمَهُ عَلَى ذُكُورِها."

Sunan al-Nasā'ī 5265 (5267)

496 ...قَالَ نَهَانَا النَّبِيُّ أَنْ نَشْرَبَ فِي آنِيَةِ الذَّهَبِ وَالْفِضَّةِ، وَأَنْ نَأْكُلَ فِيهَا. Sahīh al-Bukhārī 5837

497 ...قَالَ رَسُولُ اللَّهِ: "الَّذِي يَشْرَبُ فِي إِنَاءِ الْفِضَّةِ إِنَّمَا يُجَرْجِرُ فِي بَطْنِهِ نَارَ جَهَنَّمَ." Sahīh al-

Bukhārī 5634

In sura 17 *The Night Journey* - in Arabic: al-'Isrā' (سُورة الإِشراء) - there is a warning for all those who seek money and wealth:

17:16	When We decide to destroy a town, We command those corrupted by wealth [to reform], but they [persist in their] disobedience; Our sentence is passed, and We destroy them utterly.	وَإِذَا أَرَدْنَا أَن نُّهْلِكَ قَرْيَةً أَمَرْنَا مُتْرَفِيهَا فَفَسَقُوا فِيهَا فَحَقَّ عَلَيْهَا الْقَوْلُ فَدَمَّرْنَاهَا تَدْمِيرًا

Historians suggest that it may also have been economic reasons that were behind the prohibition. Gold was a universal medium of exchange. It was more or less used as a currency. Household tools or ornaments made of gold or silver would have been a waste of money.

Islam underlines what Muslims call the feminine nature of women. For this reason they are allowed to wear jewellery and ornaments – but only at home.

Is there an exception?

Yes, Muhammad said that men are allowed to wear silver rings. 'Abd Allah ibn 'Umar (عَبْد الله بن عُمَر) narrated: "Allah's Messenger wore a gold ring or a silver ring and placed its stone towards the palm of his hand and had the name 'Muhammad, the Messenger of Allah' engraved on it. The people also started wearing gold rings like it, but when the Prophet saw them wearing such rings, he threw away his own ring and said: 'I will never wear it', and then he wore a silver ring, whereupon the people, too, started wearing silver rings."

Ibn 'Umar added: "After the Prophet [died], 'Abū Bakr wore this ring and then 'Umar, and then 'Uthmān wore it – until it fell in the well of 'Arīs (أَرِيس)."[498]

---

498 ...أَنَّ رَسُولَ اللَّهِ اتَّخَذَ خَاتَمًا مِنْ ذَهَبٍ أَوْ فِضَّةٍ، وَجَعَلَ فَصَّهُ مِمَّا يَلِي كَفَّهُ، وَنَقَشَ فِيهِ مُحَمَّدٌ رَسُولُ اللَّهِ. فَاتَّخَذَ النَّاسُ مِثْلَهُ، فَلَمَّا رَآهُمْ قَدِ اتَّخَذُوهَا رَمَى بِهِ، وَقَالَ: "لاَ أَلْبَسُهُ أَبَدًا." ثُمَّ اتَّخَذَ خَاتَمًا مِنْ فِضَّةٍ، فَاتَّخَذَ النَّاسُ خَوَاتِيمَ الْفِضَّةِ. قَالَ ابْنُ عُمَرَ فَلَبِسَ الْخَاتَمَ بَعْدَ النَّبِيِّ أَبُو بَكْرٍ ثُمَّ عُمَرُ ثُمَّ عُثْمَانُ، حَتَّى وَقَعَ مِنْ عُثْمَانَ فِي بِئْرِ أَرِيسَ. Sahīh al-Bukhārī 5866.

410. Are tattoos allowed in Islam?

Answer: No.

A tattoo is made by piercing the skin with a needle and injecting a coloured dye. This is forbidden in Islam. Muslims see in that the "changing" of Allah's creation. The Prophet cursed the one who does tattoos as well as the receiver of the tattoo. 'Abd Allah ibn 'Umar (عَبْد الله بن عُمَر) narrated that Allah's Messenger had said: "Allah has cursed such a lady who lengthens [her or someone else's] hair artificially or gets it lengthened and also a lady who tattoos [herself or someone else] or gets herself tattooed."[499]

When a Muslim feels guilty about it, he can remove a tattoo. This is possible in Islam. 'Abū Mus'ab al-Zarqāwī (أَبُو مُصْعَب الزَّرْقاوِيّ), who was a leader of the terrorist network al-Qā'ida in Iraq which later became ISIL, had many tattoos. He had so many tattoos that friends in his neighbourhood in Jordan called him "The Green Man". He later went to Afghanistan to join the Mujahideen who were fighting the invading Soviet troops. When he returned, he was arrested. In jail, he became more religious and learned that his tattoos were viewed as sinful. He managed to smuggle a razor blade into his prison cell. Al-Zarqāwī used the razor blade to cut off his skin, until his tattoos were gone.

However, temporary adornment such as Kuhl (كُحْل) is acceptable. This is also true for Henna tattoos as they are not permanent.

Similarly, the Prophet banned the widening of the space between the teeth. 'Abd Allah ibn Mas'ūd (عَبْد الله بن مَسْعُود) said: "The Messenger of Allah cursed the women who do tattoos and the women who have them done, women who remove hair from their faces, and the women who have their teeth separated for the sake of beauty, those who change (the creation of Allah.)"[500]

How about braces for children? It depends. If there is a medical indication, it is permitted, else it is not allowed. However, there is no clear distinction between enhancing beauty and correcting a fault.

---

499 ...أَنَّ رَسُولَ اللَّهِ قَالَ: "لَعَنَ اللَّهُ الْوَاصِلَةَ وَالْمُسْتَوْصِلَةَ، وَالْوَاشِمَةَ وَالْمُسْتَوْشِمَةَ." Sahīh al-Bukhārī 5937

500 ...قَالَ لَعَنَ رَسُولُ اللَّهِ الْوَاشِمَاتِ وَالْمُوتَشِمَاتِ وَالْمُتَنَمِّصَاتِ وَالْمُتَفَلِّجَاتِ لِلْحُسْنِ الْمُغَيِّرَاتِ. Sunan al-Nasā'ī 5099 (5102)

411. How should a Muslim drink?

Answer: There are several rules concerning proper conduct while drinking.

Let's look at the most important rules:

- A Muslim should drink using his right hand.
- A Muslim should say "In the name of Allah" (Basmala) before he drinks.
- A Muslim should take at least three sips and never drink all at once.
- A Muslim should sit down while drinking (if possible).
- A Muslim who passes along his bottle or glass should start on his right hand side when doing so.
- A Muslim who gives his bottle/glass to others should drink last.
- However, no one in the group should drink from the bottle or glass, but should pour some of the liquid (e.g. water) into a dish or cup and then drink it.
- A Muslim must not drink from gold or silver cups.
- A Muslim should praise Allah after he has finished drinking.

Let's look at some sources for the above rules:

Sitting while drinking. 'Abū Hurayra reported that Allah's Messenger had said: "None of you should drink while standing; and if anyone forgets, he must vomit."[501]

This strict rule, according to some narrations, was violated by the Prophet himself. That is why scholars consider sitting while drinking only as a recommendation - mustahabb (مُسْتَحَبّ). Al-Nazzāl (النَّزَّال) narrated: 'Alī came to the gate of the courtyard [of the Mosque] and drank [water] while he was standing and said: "Some people dislike to drink while standing, but I saw the Prophet doing [drinking water] as you have seen me doing now."[502] **At least three sips.** 'Anas ibn Mālik (أَنَس بن مالك) reported that Allah's Messenger used to

---

501 ...قَالَ رَسُولُ اللَّهِ: "لاَ يَشْرَبَنَّ أَحَدٌ مِنْكُمْ قَائِمًا فَمَنْ نَسِيَ فَلْيَسْتَقِئْ." Saḥīḥ Muslim 2026

502 ...قَالَ أَتَى عَلِيٌّ عَلَى باب الرَّحَبَةِ، فَشَرِبَ قَائِمًا فَقَالَ إِنَّ نَاسًا يَكْرَهُ أَحَدُهُمْ أَنْ يَشْرَبَ وَهُوَ قَائِمٌ، وَإِنِّي رَأَيْتُ النَّبِيَّ فَعَلَ كَمَا رَأَيْتُمُونِي فَعَلْتُ. Saḥīḥ al-Bukhārī 5615

breathe three times in the course of a drink [he used to drink in three gulps] and declared: "It is more thirst-quenching, healthier and more wholesome. 'Anas added: "So I also breathe three times in the course of a drink."[503]

Saying the Basmala. One of my teachers in Tunis whispered the Basmala ("In the name of Allah") every time she took a sip of water from her bottle. There is a source for this rule. It was narrated that Muhammad ibn 'Abd al-Rahmān ibn 'Abū Bakr (مُحَمَّد بن عَبْد الرَّحْمٰن بن أَبِي بَكْر) said: "I was sitting with Ibn 'Abbās and when a man came to him, he asked: 'Where have you come from?' The man replied: 'From Zamzam.' He then asked: 'Did you drink from it as you should?' The man answered: 'How is that?' He said: 'When you drink from it, turn to face the Qibla [facing the direction of Mecca] and mention the name of Allah, drink three draughts and drink your fill of it. When you have finished, then praise Allah.' The Messenger of Allah has said: 'The sign [that differentiates] between us and the hypocrites is that they do not drink their fill from Zamzam.'"[504]

How about eating?

It was narrated that 'Ā'isha (عائشة بِنْت أَبِي بَكْر) said: "The Messenger of Allah was eating food with six of his companions when a Bedouin came and ate it all in two bites.

The Messenger of Allah said: 'If he had said 'In the name of Allah' [the Basmala], it would have sufficed you [all]. When anyone of you eats food, let him say the Basmala and if he forgets to say the Basmala at the beginning, let him say: 'In the Name of Allah at the beginning and at the end'."[505]

---

503 ...قَالَ كَانَ رَسُولُ اللَّهِ يَتَنَفَّسُ فِي الشَّرَابِ ثَلَاثًا وَيَقُولُ: "إِنَّهُ أَرْوَى وَأَبْرَأُ وَأَمْرَأُ." قَالَ أَنَسٌ فَأَنَا أَتَنَفَّسُ فِي الشَّرَابِ ثَلَاثًا. Ṣaḥīḥ Muslim 2028.

504 ...قَالَ كُنْتُ عِنْدَ ابْنِ عَبَّاسٍ جَالِسًا فَجَاءَهُ رَجُلٌ فَقَالَ مِنْ أَيْنَ جِئْتَ قَالَ مِنْ زَمْزَمَ. قَالَ فَشَرِبْتَ مِنْهَا كَمَا يَنْبَغِي قَالَ وَكَيْفَ قَالَ إِذَا شَرِبْتَ مِنْهَا فَاسْتَقْبِلِ الْكَعْبَةَ وَاذْكُرِ اسْمَ اللَّهِ وَتَنَفَّسْ ثَلَاثًا وَتَضَلَّعْ مِنْهَا فَإِذَا فَرَغْتَ فَاحْمَدِ اللَّهَ عَزَّ وَجَلَّ فَإِنَّ رَسُولَ اللَّهِ قَالَ: "إِنَّ آيَةَ مَا بَيْنَنَا وَبَيْنَ الْمُنَافِقِينَ أَنَّهُمْ لاَ يَتَضَلَّعُونَ مِنْ زَمْزَمَ." Sunan ibn Māja 3177 (3061); hasan

505 ...قَالَتْ كَانَ رَسُولُ اللَّهِ يَأْكُلُ طَعَامًا فِي سِتَّةِ نَفَرٍ مِنْ أَصْحَابِهِ فَجَاءَ أَعْرَابِيٌّ فَأَكَلَهُ بِلُقْمَتَيْنِ فَقَالَ رَسُولُ اللَّهِ: "أَمَا أَنَّهُ لَوْ كَانَ قَالَ بِسْمِ اللَّهِ لَكَفَاكُمْ فَإِذَا أَكَلَ أَحَدُكُمْ طَعَامًا فَلْيَقُلْ بِسْمِ اللَّهِ فَإِنْ نَسِيَ أَنْ يَقُولَ بِسْمِ اللَّهِ فِي أَوَّلِهِ فَلْيَقُلْ بِسْمِ اللَّهِ فِي أَوَّلِهِ وَآخِرِهِ." Sunan ibn Māja 3388 (3264)

412. Why do many Muslim men let their beards grow?

Answer: They don't want to be mixed up with men of other religions.

The growing of beards is related to the topic of dyeing the hair. ʿAbd Allah ibn ʿUmar (عَبْد الله بن عُمَر) reported that the Messenger of Allah said: "Act against the polytheists, trim closely the moustache and let the beard grow."[506]

The "polytheists", that the Prophet was referring to, were most probably Zoroastrians, the worshippers of light and dark, whose practice was either to clip or shave their beards.

Islam has a lot of rules which command Muslims to behave and appear in another way than Jews, Christians, and so-called "polytheists" used to do. Ibn Taymīya (اْبن تَيْمِيّة) - a scholar from the 13th century who was a follower of Ibn Hanbal (أَحْمَد بن حَنْبَل), the founder of the strictest school in Sunni Islam - argues that the Qur'an and the Sunna teach Muslims to be distinct from other believers. Traditional scholars are convinced that if a Muslim imitates the appearance of the non-Muslims, their "immoral behaviour" will just be a step away. Furthermore, traditional scholars say that a man who shaves his beard acts against his masculine nature. They claim that a man has to grow a beard simply because a woman cannot grow one.

However, letting a beard grow does not mean letting it grow wild or very long. One should certainly trim it in both length and breadth. Nāfiʿ ibn ʿUmar (نافِع بن عُمَر) narrated: "Whenever ʿAbd Allah ibn ʿUmar performed the Hajj or ʿUmra, he used to hold his beard with his hand and cut whatever remained outside his hold."[507]

So, are all Muslims - including Muslim leaders like the Egyptian president al-Sisi or the Turkish president Erdoğan - imitating the polytheists because they don't have a beard?

It depends. There are different opinions on this topic. Traditional scholars follow the opinion of Ibn Taymīya (ابن تَيْمِيّة) and say it is forbidden to shave. Modern scholars say that it is okay to shave because shaving alone does not mean that a Muslim imitates unbelievers.

---

506 ...قَالَ رَسُولُ اللَّهِ: "خَالِفُوا الْمُشْرِكِينَ أَحْفُوا الشَّوَارِبَ وَأَوْفُوا اللِّحَى." Sahīh Muslim 259

507 ...وَكَانَ ابْنُ عُمَرَ إِذَا حَجَّ أَوِ اعْتَمَرَ قَبَضَ عَلَى لِحْيَتِهِ، فَمَا فَضَلَ أَخَذَهُ. Sahīh al-Bukhārī 5892

413. Why do older Muslims sometimes dye their beard red?

Answer: They don't want to be confused with Jews or Christians.

Muhammad advised his followers to be noticeable, to be different from the others. His followers should therefore refrain from imitating mainly Jews or Christians. Instead, Muslims should develop their own distinctive style.

Jews and Christians (men) did not dye their hair during the time of the Prophet. They thought that this would be against piety and simply would not fit to rabbis or priests. It was narrated that 'Abū Hurayra (أَبُو هُرَيْرَة) reported that the Messenger of Allah had said: "The Jews and the Christians do not dye their hair, so be different from them and dye your hair."[508]

That is why traditional (Salafi) Muslims sometimes have a red coloured beard. Important companions of the Prophet, for example 'Abū Bakr (أَبُو بَكْر) and ʿUmar (عُمَر بن الْخَطَّاب), used to dye their hair. However, others, for example: 'Alī (عليّ بن أَبِي طالِب), 'Ubayy ibn Kaʿb (أُبَي بن كَعْب), and 'Anas ibn Mālik (أَنَس بن مالِك), did not. Most scholars make from this that the dyeing of the beard is not a command but rather a recommendation. For this reason, only few, very religious Muslims dye their beard. They are almost exclusively Sunni Muslims. Shias usually don't do that, because, first of all, they don't like 'Abū Bakr, and secondly, Alī didn't dye his beard.

In Egypt and Tunisia, I only saw very few old men with coloured beards. Actually, it has now become more a fashion among political Salafi preachers. They even dye their beards when they have no grey hair yet. The Prophet himself cannot be used as an example. Thābit ibn 'Aslam al-Banānī (ثابِت بن أَسْلَم الْبَنانِيّ) narrated that 'Anas ibn Mālik was asked whether the Prophet used a hair dye or not. 'Anas replied: "The Prophet did not have enough grey hair to dye."[509]

---

508 ...قَالَ رَسُولُ اللَّهِ: "إِنَّ الْيَهُودَ وَالنَّصَارَى لاَ تَصْبُغُ فَخَالِفُوا عَلَيْهِمْ فَاصْبُغُوا." Sunan al-Nasāʾī 5071 (5074)

509 ...قَالَ سُئِلَ أَنَسٌ عَنْ خِضَابِ النَّبِيِّ، فَقَالَ إِنَّهُ لَمْ يَبْلُغْ مَا يَخْضِبُ، لَوْ شِئْتُ أَنْ أَعُدَّ شَمَطَاتِهِ فِي لِحْيَتِهِ. شاها شمظلآعناشقه Sahīh al-Bukhārī 5895.

Let's look at two other Hadiths. 'Abū Dharr (أَبُو ذَرّ) narrated that the Prophet said: "The best things with which grey hair are changed are Henna and Katam."[510]

'Anas ibn Mālik said: "When the Prophet arrived at Medina, the eldest among his companions was 'Abū Bakr. He dyed his hair with Henna and Katam until it became of dark red colour."[511] This is also the **source for using a red colour.** In any case Muslims should avoid black. On the day of the Conquest of Mecca (فَتْح مَكّة), 'Abū Bakr brought his aged father, 'Abū Quhāfa (أَبُو قُحافة), carrying him until he had him seated in front of the Prophet. Jābir ibn 'Abd Allah (جَابِر بن عَبْد الله) narrated: "'Abū Quhāfa was brought on the day of the Conquest of Mecca [to the audience of the Prophet] and his hair and beard were white like the Thaghamah. The Messenger of Allah said: 'Change this with something, but avoid black.'"[512]

Note: Thaghama (*Artemisia;* in Persian: درمنه) is a kind of plant, generally found in the mountains, having a green stem, which becomes white when it dries and to which hoariness is likened. It has a white blossom and fruit. **So what should a Muslim use to dye his beard (hair) with?** The Prophet mentioned two things (as mentioned in the Hadith above):

Henna (حِنّاء) - *Lawsonia inermis* or *Egyptian privet* - has been used as a cosmetic hair dye for more than 6,000 years.

Henna is a tall shrub or small tree, standing 1.8 to 7.6 m tall (6 to 25 ft). Historically, Henna was used in the Arabian Peninsula, South Asia, Carthage and other parts of North Africa and in the Horn of Africa. Henna is used for dyeing the extremities, i.e. the hands and feet and head as well as fabrics including silk, wool and leather. Henna does not change the colour of the skin; the colour vanishes after a while.

---

510 قَالَ رَسُولُ اللَّهِ: "إِنَّ أَحْسَنَ مَا غُيِّرَ بِهِ هَذَا الشَّيْبُ الْجِنَّاءُ وَالْكَتَمُ." Sunan 'Abī Dāwūd 4205 (4193)

511 ...قَالَ قَدِمَ النَّبِيُّ الْمَدِينَةَ، فَكَانَ أَسَنَّ أَصْحَابِهِ أَبُو بَكْرٍ، فَخَلَفَهَا بِالْجِنَّاءِ وَالْكَتَمِ حَتَّى قَنَأَ لَوْنُهَا. Sahīh al-Bukhārī 3920

512 ...قَالَ أُتِيَ بِأَبِي قُحَافَةَ يَوْمَ فَتْحِ مَكَّةَ وَرَأْسُهُ وَلِحْيَتُهُ كَالثَّغَامَةِ بَيَاضًا فَقَالَ رَسُولُ اللَّهِ: "غَيِّرُوا هَذَا بِشَيْءٍ وَاجْتَنِبُوا السَّوَادَ." Sahīh Muslim 2102

Bridal henna nights remain an important custom in many Islamic (Arab) countries. The henna party (usually a week before the wedding) is smaller than the actual wedding, and only close friends and family members are invited.

Katam (كَتَم) is a plant from Yemen, a species of boxwood (*Myrsine africana L.*), which produces a reddish-black dye.

It somewhat resembles Myrtle (الآس). The fruits look similar to pepper (الْفُلْفُل). Katam should not to be used by itself because it produces a pure, coal-black colour. Henna produces a red dye, so when both are mixed, they create a colour that is between black and red. Katam has also been used for ink in old times.

How about dyeing nails?

According to a Hadith, women are encouraged to dye their nails to demonstrate femininity and distinguish their hands from those of men.

'Ā'isha (عائشة بِنْت أَبِي بَكْر) narrated that once a woman made a sign from behind a curtain indicating that she had a letter for the Messenger of Allah. The Prophet closed his hand: "I do not know if this is a man's or a woman's hand." She said: "No, [of] a woman." He said: "If you were a woman, you would make a difference to your nails!" [i.e. with henna][513]

414. Is a Muslim allowed to commit suicide?

Answer: No. A Muslim, who killed himself, won't enter Paradise in any case. Furthermore, he will be punished in Hell with exactly the same method he had used to commit suicide with.

Jundub ibn 'Abd Allah (جُنْدُب بن عَبْد الله) narrated that the Messenger of Allah had said the following: "Among the nations before you, there was a man who got a wound and grew impatient [with its pain], so he took a knife and cut his hand with it and the blood did

---

513 ...قَالَتْ أَوْمَتِ امْرَأَةٌ مِنْ وَرَاء سِتْرٍ بِيَدِهَا كِتَابٌ إِلَى رَسُولِ اللَّهِ فَقَبَضَ النَّبِيُّ يَدَهُ فَقَالَ: "مَا أَدْرِي أَيَدُ رَجُلٍ أَمْ يَدُ امْرَأَةٍ." قَالَتْ بَل امْرَأَةٌ. قَالَ: "لَوْ كُنْتِ امْرَأَةً لَغَيَّرْتِ أَظْفَارَكِ." يَعْنِي بِالْحِنَّاء . Sunan
'Abī Dāwūd 4166; hasan

not stop until he died. Allah said: 'My slave hurried to bring death upon himself so I have forbidden him [to enter] Paradise.'"[514]

Thābit ibn al-Daḥḥāk (ثَابِت بن الضَّحَّاك) narrated that Allah's Messenger said: "If somebody commits suicide with anything in this world, he will be tortured with that very thing on the Day of Resurrection."[515]

The Prophet gave some examples.

'Abū Hurayra (أَبُو هُرَيْرَة) narrated that the Prophet said: "Whoever purposely throws from a mountain and kills himself will be in Hellfire falling down into it and remaining therein forever; and whoever drinks poison and kills himself with it, he will be carrying his poison in his hand and will be drinking it in Hellfire wherein he will abide eternally; and whoever kills himself with an iron weapon will be carrying that weapon in his hand and stabbing his abdomen with it in Hellfire wherein he will abide eternally."[516]

Furthermore, Muslims are not allowed to offer the funeral prayer for someone who has committed suicide.

Jābir ibn Samura (جَابِر بم سَمُرَة) reported that when [the dead body] of a person, who had killed himself with a broad-headed arrow, was brought to the Messenger of Allah, he did not offer prayers for him.[517]

---

514 ...قَالَ رَسُولُ اللَّهِ: "كَانَ فِيمَنْ كَانَ قَبْلَكُمْ رَجُلٌ بِهِ جُرْحٌ، فَجَزِعَ فَأَخَذَ سِكِّينًا فَحَزَّ بِهَا يَدَهُ، فَمَا رَقَأَ الدَّمُ حَتَّى مَاتَ، قَالَ اللَّهُ تَعَالَى بَادَرَنِي عَبْدِي بِنَفْسِهِ، حَرَّمْتُ عَلَيْهِ الْجَنَّةَ." Saḥīḥ al-Bukhārī 3463

515 ...أَنَّ رَسُولَ اللَّهِ قَالَ: "وَمَنْ قَتَلَ نَفْسَهُ بِشَيْءٍ فِي الدُّنْيَا عُذِّبَ بِهِ يَوْمَ الْقِيَامَةِ." Saḥīḥ al-Bukhārī 6047

516 ...عَنِ النَّبِيِّ قَالَ: "مَنْ تَرَدَّى مِنْ جَبَلٍ فَقَتَلَ نَفْسَهُ، فَهُوَ فِي نَارِ جَهَنَّمَ، يَتَرَدَّى فِيهِ خَالِدًا مُخَلَّدًا فِيهَا أَبَدًا، وَمَنْ تَحَسَّى سَمًّا فَقَتَلَ نَفْسَهُ، فَسَمُّهُ فِي يَدِهِ، يَتَحَسَّاهُ فِي نَارِ جَهَنَّمَ خَالِدًا مُخَلَّدًا فِيهَا أَبَدًا، وَمَنْ قَتَلَ نَفْسَهُ بِحَدِيدَةٍ، فَحَدِيدَتُهُ فِي يَدِهِ، يَجَأُ بِهَا فِي بَطْنِهِ فِي نَارِ جَهَنَّمَ خَالِدًا مُخَلَّدًا فِيهَا أَبَدًا." Saḥīḥ al-Bukhārī 5778

517 ...قَالَ أُتِيَ النَّبِيُّ بِرَجُلٍ قَتَلَ نَفْسَهُ بِمَشَاقِصَ فَلَمْ يُصَلِّ عَلَيْهِ. Saḥīḥ Muslim 978

415. Should Muslims sacrifice a sheep when a baby is born?

Answer: Yes, Muslim parents should do that.

The Islamic tradition of sacrificing an animal when a child is born is usually called ʿAqīqa (عَقيقة). Traditional Sunni Muslims slaughter **one** sheep for a baby girl and **two** sheep for a baby boy. Some Muslims believe that after performing ʿAqīqa their children will be protected from harm.

It was narrated that ʿAbd Allah ibn ʿAbbās (عَبد الله بن عَبّاس) said: "The Messenger of Allah offered ʿAqīqa for al-Hasan and al-Husayn [his two grandsons], two rams for each."[518]

Salmān ibn ʿĀmir (سَلمان بن عامِر) narrated that the Messenger of Allah had said: "For a boy, there is an ʿAqīqa. So spill blood for him and remove harm from him."[519]

Most Hadiths only talk about a sacrifice for a boy. However, there are few telling about a sacrifice for a girl. ʾUmm Kurz (أُمّ كُرز) narrated that she asked the Messenger of Allah about the ʿAqīqa. He said: "For the **boy is two sheep** [of equal age], and **for the girl is one**."[520] In another variation, the Prophet also added: "it will not harm you if they [i.e. the sheep] are male or female."[521]

The word ʿAqīqa has several meanings. It can be the prepuce of a boy, but it is usually associated with the hair of a recently born baby, which grew on his head in his mother's belly. The word refers to the hair of a recently-born infant. On the seventh day after birth the infant's hair is shaved; sheep or goats are sacrificed on that occasion, and therefore the word is also applied to the sacrificed animals.

This goes back to a Hadith. Samura ibn Jundub (سَمُرة بن جُنْدُب) nar-rated that the Messenger of Allah said: "The boy is mortgaged by his

---

518 ...قَالَ عَقَّ رَسُولُ اللَّهِ عَنِ الْحَسَنِ وَالْحُسَيْنِ بِكَبْشَيْنِ. (4224) 4219 Sunan al-Nasāʾī

519 ...قَالَ رَسُولُ اللَّهِ: "مَعَ الْغُلَامِ عَقِيقَةٌ فَأَهْرِيقُوا عَنْهُ دَمًا وَأَميطُوا عَنْهُ الْأَذَى." -Jāmiʿ al-Tirmidhī 1515

520 ...أَنَّ رَسُولَ اللَّهِ قَالَ: "فِي الْغُلَامِ شَاتَانِ مُكَافَأَتَانِ وَفِي الْجَارِيَةِ شَاةٌ." (4220) -Sunan al-Nasāʾī 4215

521 ...قَالَتْ أَتَيْتُ النَّبِيَّ بِالْحُدَيْبِيَةِ أَسْأَلُهُ عَنْ لُحُومِ الْهَدْيِ فَسَمِعْتُهُ يَقُولُ: "عَلَى الْغُلَامِ شَاتَانِ وَعَلَى الْجَارِيَةِ شَاةٌ لَا يَضُرُّكُمْ ذُكْرَانًا كُنَّ أَمْ إِنَاثًا." Sunan al-Nasāʾī 4217; hasan

'Aqīqa; slaughtering should be done for him on the seventh day, he should be given a name, and his head should be shaved."[522]

The limbs of the sacrificed animal are divided and cooked with water and salt and given to the poor to eat. The 'Aqīqa of an infant (i.e. hair) should be weighed and its weight in silver should be given to the poor. It is interesting that Herodotus mentioned a similar custom already at the time of the ancient Egyptians.

The Prophet didn't like the word 'Aqīqa very much. The Arabic root '-q-q (ق-ق-ع) from which the word 'Aqīqa is derived, can also mean *to be disobedient* or *disrespectful to one's parents or father*. For this reason the Prophet is said to have preferred the Arabic word Nasīka (نسيكة) which means *sacrifice*. It is derived from the root n-s-k (ن-س-ك) which means *to lead to a devout life; to live the life of an ascetic*.

'Amr ibn Shu'ayb (عَمرو بن شُعَيْب) - on his father's authority - said that his grandfather said that the Messenger of Allah was asked about the 'Aqīqa. The messenger replied: "Allah does not like the breaking of ties [Uqūq], as though he disliked the name [word]."[523]

In classical Arabic texts, the word 'Aqīqa had the meaning of *lightning which one sees in the midst of the clouds, resembling a drawn sword*. Furthermore, in pre-Islamic times, it was associated with an Arab tradition. People would shoot an arrow towards the sky, and that arrow was called 'Aqīqa. According to Edward Lane such was "the arrow of self-excuse". People did that to determine a blood-revenge.

If the arrow returned smeared with blood, it meant retaliation "by blood" – and not money.

If it returned clean, they would stroke their beards and reconcile on the terms of the bloodwit – they would take the money.

---

522 ...قَالَ رَسُولُ اللَّهِ: "الْغُلَامُ مُرْتَهَنٌ بِعَقِيقَتِهِ يُذْبَحُ عَنْهُ يَوْمَ السَّابِعِ وَيُسَمَّى وَيُحْلَقُ رَأْسُهُ." Jāmi'
al-Tirmidhī 1522

523 ...قَالَ سُئِلَ رَسُولُ اللَّهِ نِ الْعَقِيقَةِ فَقَالَ: "لاَ يُحِبُّ اللَّهُ الْعُقُوقَ." كَأَنَّهُ كَرِهَ الإِسمَ. Sunan 'Abī
Dāwūd 2842 (2836)

416. Are Muslims allowed to shave their head?

Answer: In some cases, yes.

In Islam, shaving one's head as an act of worship is allowed and recommended. For Muslims, this is a way of getting closer to Allah.

However, this should only be done in the following four situations:

1. The Pilgrimage – Hajj (الْحَجّ)

2. The lesser pilgrimage – 'Umra (عُمْرة). Shaving the head belongs to the final rites of pilgrimage. This is commanded in sura 48 *The Triumph* – in Arabic: al-Fath (سُورة الْفَتْح):

48:27	God has truly fulfilled His Messenger's vision: 'God willing, you will most certainly enter the Sacred Mosque in safety, shavenheaded or with cropped hair, without fear!' - God knew what you did not - and He has granted you a speedy triumph.	لَقَدْ صَدَقَ اللَّهُ رَسُولَهُ الرُّؤْيَا بِالْحَقِّ لَتَدْخُلُنَّ الْمَسْجِدَ الْحَرَامَ إِن شَاءَ اللَّهُ آمِنِينَ مُحَلِّقِينَ رُءُوسَكُمْ وَمُقَصِّرِينَ لَا تَخَافُونَ فَعَلِمَ مَا لَمْ تَعْلَمُوا فَجَعَلَ مِن دُونِ ذَٰلِكَ فَتْحًا قَرِيبًا.

3. Shaving the baby's head on the seventh day after birth. Samura ibn Jundub (سَمُرة بن جُنْدُب) narrated that the Messenger of Allah had said: "Slaughtering should be done for him [the newborn] on the seventh day, he should be given a name, and his head should be shaved."[524]

4. Conversion to Islam. The non-Muslim (man), when he becomes a Muslim, should shave his head. 'Uthaym ibn Kulayb (عُثَيْم بن كُلَيْب) reported that the Prophet had told a man [who became a Muslim]: "Shave off the hair of disbelief (kufr) and get circumcised!"[525]

---

524 ...قَالَ رَسُولُ اللَّهِ: "الْغُلَامُ مُرْتَهَنٌ بِعَقِيقَتِهِ يُذْبَحُ عَنْهُ يَوْمَ السَّابِعِ وَيُسَمَّى وَيُحْلَقُ رَأْسُهُ." Jāmi' al-Tirmidhī 1522

525 ...أَنَّهُ جَاءَ إِلَى النَّبِيِّ فَقَالَ قَدْ أَسْلَمْتُ. فَقَالَ لَهُ النَّبِيُّ: "أَلْقِ عَنْكَ شَعْرَ الْكُفْرِ." Sunan 'Abī Dāwūd 356; hasan

417. Is boxing allowed in Islam?

Answer: No; most scholars regard boxing as forbidden.

The famous boxer Muhammad Ali (Cassius Clay) converted to Islam in 1960. He wanted to join the *Nation of Islam* (also called *Black Muslims*), but they didn't want him – due to his boxing career. However, after he won the championship from Sonny Liston in 1964, the *Nation of Islam* suddenly agreed and even publicly announced his conversion.

It is interesting that some influential Salafi preachers were boxers, for example Pierre Vogel in Germany. Vogel is also said to have quit boxing when he became a Muslim in 2001 because it was not compatible with his new religion. Boxing involves attacking the face. Blows to the face earn more points than blows to any other part of the body, but this goes against the teachings of the Prophet.

’Abū Hurayra (أَبُو هُرَيْرة) reported that the Messenger of Allah said: "When any one of you fights with his brother, he should avoid the face."[526]

Furthermore, boxing might involve uncovering the 'Awra (عَوْرة) – the part of a man's body from the navel to the knee which he is not allowed to show. However, especially recently, a number of young (self-proclaimed) Salafi Muslims are taking up boxing. They justify it by claiming that they need the skill for Jihād.

418. What should a Muslim father teach his son?

Answer: Most Muslims would say swimming, shooting and riding a horse.

In Egypt, many Muslims told me that the Prophet had said that a Muslim should teach his children to swim, to ride a horse and to shoot (a bow and arrow/archery).

However, there is no authentic Hadith indicating that the Prophet gave such advice, but by digging deeper into the Hadiths, it is possible to find sources justifying the popular saying.

---

526 ...أَنَّ رَسُولَ اللَّهِ قَالَ: "إِذَا قَاتَلَ أَحَدُكُمْ أَخَاهُ فَلْيَجْتَنِبِ الْوَجْهَ." Sahīh Muslim 2612

About shooting. It has been narrated on the authority of 'Uqba ibn 'Āmir (عُقْبة بن عامِر) who said: "I heard Allah's Messenger say: 'Beware, strength is [comes from] shooting (archery)!'"[527]

About horse-riding. 'Urwa al-Bāriqī (عُرْوة البارِقيّ) narrated that the Prophet said: "Good will remain in the foreheads of horses [for Jihād] until the Day of Resurrection, for they bring about either a reward [in the Hereafter] or [war] booty [in this world]."[528]

'Abd Allah ibn 'Abd al-Rahmān ibn 'Abū Husayn (عَبْد الله بن عَبْد الرَّحْمٰن بن أبي حُسَيْن) narrated that the Messenger of Allah said: "All idle pastimes that the Muslim man engages in, are falsehoods, except for the shooting of his bow, the training of his horse and the playing with his family [wife], for they are from truth."[529]

About swimming. There is no Hadith indicating that Muhammad practised swimming. However, there are several Hadiths in which Muhammad saw a man swimming, and he did not say anything about it. The Islamic scholars concluded from this that swimming is permitted.

There is, however, a Hadith in which Muhammad mentioned that swimming is beneficial. 'Atā' ibn 'Abī Rabāh (عَطاء بن أبي رَباح) narrated that when he saw Jābir ibn 'Abd Allah and Jābir ibn 'Umayr, one of them said that he had heard the Prophet say: "Any act devoid of the remembrance of Allah is void except four: a man playing with his wife, a man's training of his horse, shooting, and a man learning to swim."[530]

Notice that this Hadith only talks about men. From this narration, Muslims have derived what they should teach their sons.

---

527 ...يَقُولُ سَمِعْتُ رَسُولَ اللَّهِ وَهُوَ عَلَى الْمِنْبَرِ يَقُولُ: "وَأَعِدُّوا لَهُمْ مَا اسْتَطَعْتُمْ مِنْ قُوَّةٍ أَلَا إِنَّ الْقُوَّةَ الرَّمْىُ." Sahīh Muslim 1917

528 ...أَنَّ النَّبِيَّ قَالَ: "الْخَيْلُ مَعْقُودٌ فِي نَوَاصِيهَا الْخَيْرُ إِلَى يَوْمِ الْقِيَامَةِ الْأَجْرُ وَالْمَغْنَمُ." Sahīh al-Bukhārī 2852

529 ...أَنَّ رَسُولَ اللَّهِ قَالَ: "ارْمُوا وَارْكَبُوا وَلأَنْ تَرْمُوا أَحَبُّ إِلَيَّ مِنْ أَنْ تَرْكَبُوا كُلُّ مَا يَلْهُو بِهِ الرَّجُلُ الْمُسْلِمُ بَاطِلٌ إِلاَّ رَمْيَهُ بِقَوْسِهِ وَتَأْدِيبَهُ فَرَسَهُ وَمُلاَعَبَتَهُ أَهْلَهُ فَإِنَّهُنَّ مِنَ الْحَقِّ." Jāmi' al-Tirmidhī 1637

530 ...قَالَ النَّبِيُّ: "كُلُّ شَيْءٍ لَيْسَ فِيهِ ذِكْرُ اللَّهِ، فَهُوَ لَهْوٌ وَلَعِبٌ، إلا أَرْبَعَ: مُلاعَبَةُ الرَّجُلِ امْرَأَتَهُ، وَتَأْدِيبُ الرَّجُلِ فَرَسَهُ، وَمَشْيُهُ بَيْنَ الْغَرَضَيْنِ، وَتَعْلِيمُ الرَّجُلِ السِّبَاحَةَ." Sunan al-Nasā'ī ; al-Sunan al-Kubra 8889

What other activities are possible?

- **Foot racing:** While she was on a journey along with the Messenger of Allah, 'Ā'isha (عَائِشة بِنْت أَبِي بَكْر) reported: "I had a race with him [the Prophet] and I outstripped him on my feet. When I became fleshy [put on some weight], I had a race with him [the Prophet] and he outstripped me.' He said: 'This is for that outstripping.'"[531] Note: The Prophet must have been older than 50 years when that happened.

- **Wrestling:** There are some Hadiths - although most of them are weak (ضَعِيف) - indicating that Muhammad had occasionally wrestled. He is said to have wrestled with Rukāna (رُكَانة).[532]

- **Spear play:** 'Urwa (عُرْوة) narrated that 'Ā'isha said: "I remember Allah's Messenger standing on the door of my flat screening me with his mantle enabling me to see the sport of the Abyssinians [Ethiopians] as they played with their daggers [spears] in the mosque of the Messenger of Allah. He [the Prophet] kept standing for my sake until I was satiated and then I went back; and thus you can well imagine how long entertained a girl tender of age who is fond of sports [could have watched it]."[533]

419. Which prayer do you hear in an *Egypt Air* plane before take-off?

Answer: The supplication of travelling, the so-called: Du'ā' al-Safar (دُعاء السَّفَر).

Egypt Air always broadcasts a prayer over the TV devices and loudspeakers before take-off. It is an extract of a Hadith. It goes as

531 ...أَنَّهَا كَانَتْ مَعَ النَّبِيِّ فِي سَفَرٍ قَالَتْ فَسَابَقْتُهُ فَسَبَقْتُهُ عَلَى رِجْلَيَّ فَلَمَّا حَمَلْتُ اللَّحْمَ سَابَقْتُهُ فَسَبَقَنِي فَقَالَ: "هَذِهِ بِتِلْكَ السَّبْقَةِ". Sunan 'Abī Dāwūd 2578

532 ...أَنَّ رُكَانَةَ، صَارَعَ النَّبِيَّ فَصَرَعَهُ النَّبِيُّ قَالَ رُكَانَةُ وَسَمِعْتُ النَّبِيَّ يَقُولُ: "فَرْقُ مَا بَيْنَنَا وَبَيْنَ الْمُشْرِكِينَ الْعَمَائِمُ عَلَى الْقَلَانِسِ". Sunan 'Abī Dāwūd 4078 (4067); weak

533 ...قَالَتْ عَائِشَةُ وَاللَّهِ لَقَدْ رَأَيْتُ رَسُولَ اللَّهِ يَقُومُ عَلَى بَابِ حُجْرَتِي - وَالْحَبَشَةُ يَلْعَبُونَ بِحِرَابِهِمْ فِي مَسْجِدِ رَسُولِ اللَّهِ - يَسْتُرُنِي بِرِدَائِهِ لِكَنْ أَنْظُرَ إِلَى لَعِبِهِمْ ثُمَّ يَقُومُ مِنْ أَجْلِي حَتَّى أَكُونَ أَنَا الَّتِي أَنْصَرِفُ. فَاقْدُرُوا قَدْرَ الْجَارِيَةِ الْحَدِيثَةِ السِّنِّ حَرِيصَةً عَلَى اللَّهْوِ. Sahīh Muslim 892

follows: "O Allah, I seek refuge with You from the hardships of the journey, gloominess of the sights, and finding of evil changes in property and family on return. And he [the Prophet] uttered [these words] and made this addition to them: 'We are returning, repentant, worshipping our Lord and praising Him.'"[534]

Let's look for the source of this prayer.

'Abd Alla ibn 'Umar (عَبْد الله بن عُمَر) reported that whenever Allah's Messenger mounted his camel while setting out on a journey, he glorified Allah [he said: "Allāhu 'Akbar"] thrice and then said: "Hallowed is He Who subdued for us this [ride] and we were not ourselves powerful enough to use it as a ride and we are going to return to our Lord. O Allah, we seek virtue and piety from You in this journey of ours and the act which pleases You. O Allah, lighten this journey of ours and make its distance easy for us. O Allah, You are [our] companion during the journey and guardian of [our] family. O Allah, I seek refuge with You from hardships of the journey, gloominess of the sights and finding of evil changes in property and family on return. And he [the Prophet] uttered [these words] and made this addition to them: 'We are returning, repentant, worshipping our Lord and praising Him.'"[535]

420. What does a Muslim have to say when entering a toilet?

Answer: "In the name of Allah. O Allah, I take refuge with You from all male and female devils."[536]

This is the supplication when entering a toilet (دُعاء دُخُول بَيْت الْخَلاء).
It goes back to a Hadith which was reported by 'Anas ibn Mālik (أنَس

---

534 ...إِنِّي أَعُوذُ بِكَ مِنْ وَعْثَاءِ السَّفَرِ وَكَآبَةِ الْمَنْظَرِ وَسُوءِ الْمُنْقَلَبِ فِي الْمَالِ وَالأَهْلِ. وَإِذَا رَجَعَ قَالَهُنَّ. وَزَادَ فِيهِنَّ: "آيِبُونَ تَائِبُونَ عَابِدُونَ لِرَبِّنَا حَامِدُونَ." Sahīh Muslim 1342

535 ...أَنَّ رَسُولَ اللَّهِ كَانَ إِذَا اسْتَوَى عَلَى بَعِيرِهِ خَارِجًا إِلَى سَفَرٍ كَبَّرَ ثَلاثًا ثُمَّ قَالَ: "سُبْحَانَ الَّذِي سَخَّرَ لَنَا هَذَا وَمَا كُنَّا لَهُ مُقْرِنِينَ وَإِنَّا إِلَى رَبِّنَا لَمُنْقَلِبُونَ اللَّهُمَّ إِنَّا نَسْأَلُكَ فِي سَفَرِنَا هَذَا الْبِرَّ وَالتَّقْوَى وَمِنَ الْعَمَلِ مَا تَرْضَى اللَّهُمَّ هَوِّنْ عَلَيْنَا سَفَرَنَا هَذَا وَاطْوِ عَنَّا بُعْدَهُ اللَّهُمَّ أَنْتَ الصَّاحِبُ فِي السَّفَرِ وَالْخَلِيفَةُ فِي الأَهْلِ اللَّهُمَّ إِنِّي أَعُوذُ بِكَ مِنْ وَعْثَاءِ السَّفَرِ وَكَآبَةِ الْمَنْظَرِ وَسُوءِ الْمُنْقَلَبِ فِي الْمَالِ وَالأَهْلِ." وَإِذَا رَجَعَ قَالَهُنَّ. وَزَادَ فِيهِنَّ " آيِبُونَ تَائِبُونَ عَابِدُونَ لِرَبِّنَا حَامِدُونَ." Sahīh Muslim 1342

536 بِسْمِ اللهِ، اللَّهُمَّ إِنِّي أَعُوذُ بِكَ مِنَ الْخُبْثِ وَالْخَبَائِثِ

بن مالك): "Whenever the Prophet went to answer the call of nature, he used to say: 'O Allah, I seek refuge with You from all offensive and wicked things [evil deeds and evil spirits, from all male and female devils]!'" In Arabic: "Allahumma 'inni 'a'udhu bika min al-Khubuthi wa al-Khabā'ith!"[537]

Zayd ibn 'Arqam (زَيْد بن أَرْقَم) narrated that the Messenger of Allah once said: "These privies/waste areas [i.e. toilets] are frequented by the Jinns and devils."[538]

'Anas ibn Mālik reported: "Whenever Allah's Messenger went to answer the call of nature, I, along with another boy, used to carry a tumbler full of water [for cleaning the private parts] and a short spear [or stick]."[539]

Muhammad even told his followers how to urinate:

- 'Abū Qatāda (أَبُو قَتَادَة) reported from his father's authority that the Messenger of Allah said: "None of you should hold his penis with his right hand while urinating, or wipe himself with his right hand in privy and should not breathe into the vessel [from which he drinks]."[540]

- A Muslim <u>must not</u> urinate towards the direction of Mecca. 'Abd Allah ibn Umar (عَبْد الله بن عُمَر) stated: "One day I climbed on Hafsa's house and saw the Prophet relieving himself while facing al-Shām [Syria], with his back toward the Ka'ba."[541]

---

537 ...قَالَ كَانَ النَّبِيُّ إِذَا دَخَلَ الْخَلَاءَ قَالَ: "اللَّهُمَّ إِنِّي أَعُوذُ بِكَ مِنَ الْخُبُثِ وَالْخَبَائِثِ." -Sahīh al-Bukhārī 6322

538 ...عَنْ رَسُولِ اللَّهِ قَالَ: "إِنَّ هَذِهِ الْحُشُوشَ مُحْتَضَرَةٌ فَإِذَا أَتَى أَحَدُكُمُ الْخَلَاءَ فَلْيَقُلْ أَعُوذُ بِاللَّهِ مِنَ الْخُبُثِ وَالْخَبَائِثِ." Sunan 'Abī Dāwūd 6

539 ...سَمِعَ أَنَسَ بْنَ مَالِكٍ، يَقُولُ كَانَ رَسُولُ اللَّهِ يَدْخُلُ الْخَلَاءَ، فَأَحْمِلُ أَنَا وَغُلَامٌ إِدَاوَةً مِنْ مَاءٍ، وَعَنَزَةً، يَسْتَنْجِي بِالْمَاءِ. تَابَعَهُ النَّضْرُ وَشَاذَانُ عَنْ شُعْبَةَ. الْعَنَزَةُ عَصًا عَلَيْهِ زُجٌّ. Sahīh al-Bukhārī 152

540 ...قَالَ رَسُولُ اللَّهِ: "لاَ يُمْسِكَنَّ أَحَدُكُمْ ذَكَرَهُ بِيَمِينِهِ وَهُوَ يَبُولُ وَلاَ يَتَمَسَّحْ مِنَ الْخَلَاءِ بِيَمِينِهِ وَلاَ يَتَنَفَّسْ فِي الإِنَاءِ." Sahīh Muslim 267

541 ...قَالَ رَقِيتُ يَوْمًا عَلَى بَيْتِ حَفْصَةَ فَرَأَيْتُ النَّبِيَّ عَلَى حَاجَتِهِ مُسْتَقْبِلَ الشَّأْمِ مُسْتَدْبِرَ الْكَعْبَةِ. Jāmi' al-Tirmidhī 11

- ʾAbū Hurayra (أَبُو هُرَيْرة) said: "When anyone amongst you squats for answering the call of nature, he should neither turn his face towards the Qibla [Mecca] nor turn his back towards it."[542]

- Note: When a Muslim enters a toilet or bathroom, he enters with the left foot first and leaves with the right one. On the other hand, a Muslim should enter a mosque with the right foot first and step out with the left one. This was derived from the tradition of the Prophet to start important and good things from the right side.

And what does a Muslim have to say when leaving the toilet?

Answer: "Grant me Your forgiveness" - "Ghufrānaka!" (غُفْرَانَكَ).

ʿĀʾisha (عائشة بِنْت أَبِي بَكْر) has narrated: "When the Prophet left the privy, he used to say: 'Grant me Your forgiveness!'"[543]

Muslims believe that if one repeats this prayer regularly, one will not be faced with any urinary or intestinal diseases. Such illnesses have a great impact on the validity of the prayers.

Some Muslims also say: "O Allah, I seek your forgiveness. All praises are due to Allah who has taken away from me the discomfort and granted me comfort." This was narrated by ʾAnas ibn Mālik in a Hadith, however, the chain of narration is weak (ضَعِيف)[544]

421. Are Muslim girls allowed to play with dolls?

Answer: Yes.

This question is anything but trivial since Muslims are not allowed to produce images of human beings and animals. So should children be allowed to play with toys in the shape of humans or animals?

---

542 ...عَنْ رَسُولِ اللَّهِ قَالَ: "إِذَا جَلَسَ أَحَدُكُمْ عَلَى حَاجَتِهِ فَلَا يَسْتَقْبِلِ الْقِبْلَةَ وَلَا يَسْتَدْبِرْهَا." Sahīh Muslim 265

543 ...أَنَّ النَّبِيَّ كَانَ إِذَا خَرَجَ مِنَ الْغَائِطِ قَالَ: "غُفْرَانَكَ." Sunan ʾAbī Dāwūd 30

544 قَالَ كَانَ النَّبِيُّ إِذَا خَرَجَ مِنَ الْخَلَاءِ قَالَ: "الْحَمْدُ لِلَّهِ الَّذِي أَذْهَبَ عَنِّي الْأَذَى وَعَافَانِي." Sunan ibn Māja 320 (301); weak

Muslims learn from a Hadith that the angels do not enter a house where pictures of living things [humans or animals] are displayed. 'Abū Sālim (أبو سالم) narrated: "Once Gabriel promised to visit the Prophet but he delayed and the Prophet got worried about that. At last, he came out and found Gabriel and complained to him of his grief [for his delay]. Gabriel said to him: 'We do not enter a place in which there is a picture or a dog.'"[545]

The Prophet himself became pretty angry when his people did not follow this rule. 'Ā'isha (عائشة بِنْت أبي بَكْر) reported a situation, in which the Messenger of Allah entered her home: "I had hung [on the door of the building] a thin curtain having pictures on it. The colour of his face underwent a change. He [the Prophet] then took hold of that curtain, tore it and then said: 'The most grievous torment for the people on the Day of Resurrection would be for those who try to imitate Allah in the act of creation.'"[546]

'Ā'isha added: "We tore it into pieces and made a cushion or two cushions out of that."[547]

What about dolls then?

This is an exception because 'Ā'isha was allowed to play with dolls (when she was a little girl and had not yet reached the age of puberty). This information is found in a Hadith narrated by 'Ā'isha herself: "I used to play with the dolls in the presence of the Prophet and my girl friends also played with me. When Allah's Messenger would enter [my dwelling place] they would first hide themselves, but the Prophet would call them to join and play with me."[548]

Note: If a child plays with a toy that doesn't have a face, it is certainly not a problem according to the Islamic rules.

---

545 ...قَالَ وَعَدَ النَّبِيَّ جِبْرِيلُ فَرَاثَ عَلَيْهِ حَتَّى اشْتَدَّ عَلَى النَّبِيِّ فَخَرَجَ النَّبِيُّ فَلَقِيَهُ، فَشَكَا إِلَيْهِ مَا وَجَدَ، فَقَالَ لَهُ: "إِنَّا لاَ نَدْخُلُ بَيْتًا فِيهِ صُورَةٌ وَلاَ كَلْبٌ." Sahīh al-Bukhārī 5960.

546 ...قَالَتْ دَخَلَ عَلَيَّ رَسُولُ اللَّهِ وَأَنَا مُتَسَتِّرَةٌ بِقِرَامٍ فِيهِ صُورَةٌ فَتَلَوَّنَ وَجْهُهُ ثُمَّ تَنَاوَلَ السِّتْرَ فَهَتَكَهُ ثُمَّ قَالَ: "إِنَّ مِنْ أَشَدِّ النَّاسِ عَذَابًا يَوْمَ الْقِيَامَةِ الَّذِينَ يُشَبِّهُونَ بِخَلْقِ اللَّهِ." Sahīh Muslim 2107.

547 ...قَالَتْ عَائِشَةُ فَقَطَعْنَاهُ فَجَعَلْنَا مِنْهُ وِسَادَةً أَوْ وِسَادَتَيْنِ. Sahīh Muslim 2107.

548 قَالَتْ كُنْتُ أَلْعَبُ بِالْبَنَاتِ عِنْدَ النَّبِيِّ وَكَانَ لِي صَوَاحِبُ يَلْعَبْنَ مَعِي، فَكَانَ رَسُولُ اللَّهِ إِذَا دَخَلَ يَتَقَمَّعْنَ مِنْهُ، فَيُسَرِّبُهُنَّ إِلَيَّ فَيَلْعَبْنَ مَعِي. Sahīh al-Bukhārī 6130.

422. Should a Muslim interfere in the life of others?

Answer: Yes, he has to.

It was narrated that 'Abū Sa'īd (أَبُو سَعِيد) heard the Messenger of Allah say: "Whoever among you sees an evil action and is able to change it with his hand, then change it with his hand [by taking action]; if he cannot [do that], then with his tongue [by speaking out]; and if he cannot [do that], then with his heart [by hating it and feeling that it is wrong], and that is the weakest of faith."[549]

This means that every Muslim is entitled and commanded to prevent other Muslims from committing sins. This is different from the Western culture, especially in big cities where the society is more or less based on anonymity. In Islam, neighbours will approach you when they see you drinking alcohol, having female visitors, etc.

423. Are men and women equal in Islam?

Answer: They are equivalent (German: *gleichwertig*), but don't have equal rights (German: *gleichberechtigt*).

In Islam, men and women have different roles in life. Muslims believe that Allah has given men and women different qualities. The Prophet spoke of *twin halves* or *counterpart of men* - in Arabic: Shaqā'iq al-Rijāl (شَقَائِق الرِّجَال) - as quoted in a Hadith which was narrated by 'Ā'isha (عائشة بِنْت أَبِي بَكْر)[550].

There are some people who speak of *equality* in gender in Islam, but this is actually not true. Equality signifies that there is no difference between the two. For this reason several Muslims told me that they prefer the word *justice*.

Muslims usually don't say that Islam is a religion of equality. In fact, there are several suras in the Qur'an which traditional Muslims use to justify that the (Western) concept of equality is alien to Islam.

---

549 ...سَمِعْتُ رَسُولَ اللَّهِ يَقُولُ: "مَنْ رَأَى مُنْكَرًا فَاسْتَطَاعَ أَنْ يُغَيِّرَهُ بِيَدِهِ فَلْيُغَيِّرْهُ بِيَدِهِ فَإِنْ لَمْ يَسْتَطِعْ فَبِلِسَانِهِ فَإِنْ لَمْ يَسْتَطِعْ بِلِسَانِهِ فَبِقَلْبِهِ وَذَلِكَ أَضْعَفُ الإِيمَانِ." Sunan ibn Māja 1334
(1275)

550 ...قَالَ: "نَعَمْ إِنَّمَا النِّسَاءُ شَقَائِقُ الرِّجَالِ." Sunan 'Abī Dāwūd 236

Let's look at a verse of sura 13 *The Thunder* – in Arabic: al-Ra'd (سُورةُ الرَّعْد):

| 13:16 | Say [Prophet], 'Are the blind equal to those who can see? And are the depths of darkness equal to the light?' | قُلْ هَلْ يَسْتَوِي الْأَعْمَى وَالْبَصِيرُ أَمْ هَلْ تَسْتَوِي الظُّلُمَاتُ وَالنُّورُ؟ |

Islam distinguishes between men and women a lot. If they were equal, there would be no need for these rules. Let's have a look at some of them:

Different roles:

A man, as traditional scholars argue, is inherently better than a woman, he is superior to her – because he spends money on her. The Qur'an gives a clear description about the hierarchy between men and women in sura 4 *Women* – in Arabic: al-Nisā' (سُورةُ النِّساء):

| 4:34 | Husbands should take good care of their wives, with [the bounties] God has given to some more than others and with what they spend out of their own money. Righteous wives are devout and guard what God would have them guard in their husbands' absence. If you fear high-handedness from your wives, remind them [of the teachings of God], then ignore them when you go to bed, then hit them. If they obey you, you have no right to act against them: God is most high and great. | الرِّجَالُ قَوَّامُونَ عَلَى النِّسَاءِ بِمَا فَضَّلَ اللَّهُ بَعْضَهُمْ عَلَى بَعْضٍ وَبِمَا أَنْفَقُوا مِنْ أَمْوَالِهِمْ فَالصَّالِحَاتُ قَانِتَاتٌ حَافِظَاتٌ لِّلْغَيْبِ بِمَا حَفِظَ اللَّهُ وَاللَّاتِي تَخَافُونَ نُشُوزَهُنَّ فَعِظُوهُنَّ وَاهْجُرُوهُنَّ فِي الْمَضَاجِعِ وَاضْرِبُوهُنَّ فَإِنْ أَطَعْنَكُمْ فَلَا تَبْغُوا عَلَيْهِنَّ سَبِيلًا إِنَّ اللَّهَ كَانَ عَلِيًّا كَبِيرًا. |

In Egypt I met a woman who had converted to Islam. She was from a European country and was around forty when I met her. She was married to a Muslim. When I asked her about her job, she said: "I am retired." She told me that she used to work in a restaurant in Europe.

Now, her Muslim husband has to earn the money. She is cooking and cleaning at home and looks after their child. She told me that she prefers this lifestyle and the fixed rules.

Leadership

All prophets were men, all Caliphs were men. There are no female Imams. Female judges, female rulers or high-ranked female politicians are the exception in Islamic countries.

It was narrated that 'Abū Bakra (أَبُو بَكْرة) once said: "Allah protected me with something that I heard from the Messenger of Allah. When Kisrā died, he asked: 'Whom have they appointed as his successor?' They said: 'His daughter.' He said: 'No people will ever prosper who entrust their leadership to a woman.'"[551]

Note: The Prophet perhaps referred to Boran (590-628 or 631), the daughter of Khosrow II (Kisrā). She was the first and one of only two women to ever rule the Sasanian (Persian) Empire.

Testimony or bearing witness

The Qur'an says that the testimony of one man is equivalent to the testimony of two women. This is found in sura 2 *The Cow* – in Arabic: al-Baqara (سُورة الْبَقَرة):

| 2:282 | Call in two men as witnesses. If two men are not there, then call one man and two women out of those you approve as witnesses, so that if one of the two women should err [some translate it as: forget] the other can remind her. | وَاسْتَشْهِدُوا شَهِيدَيْنِ مِن رِّجَالِكُمْ فَإِن لَّمْ يَكُونَا رَجُلَيْنِ فَرَجُلٌ وَامْرَأَتَانِ مِمَّن تَرْضَوْنَ مِنَ الشُّهَدَاءِ أَن تَضِلَّ إِحْدَاهُمَا فَتُذَكِّرَ إِحْدَاهُمَا الْأُخْرَىٰ. |

Inheritance

A woman inherits half of what a man inherits. This is said in sura 4 *Women* – in Arabic: al-Nisā' (سُورة النِّساء):

| 4:11 | Concerning your children, God commands you that a son should have the equivalent share of two daughters. | يُوصِيكُمُ اللَّهُ فِي أَوْلَادِكُمْ لِلذَّكَرِ مِثْلُ حَظِّ الْأُنثَيَيْنِ. |

---

551 ...قَالَ عَصَمَنِي اللَّهُ بِشَيْءٍ سَمِعْتُهُ مِنْ رَسُولِ اللَّهِ لَمَّا هَلَكَ كِسْرَى قَالَ: "مَنِ اسْتَخْلَفُوا." قَالُوا بِنْتَهُ. قَالَ: "لَنْ يُفْلِحَ قَوْمٌ وَلَّوْا أَمْرَهُمُ امْرَأَةً." Sunan al-Nasā'ī 5388 (5390)

Most Islamic countries, for example Tunisia, have incorporated this rule in their respective laws.

Style and amount of clothing

A woman may wear silk and gold, but a man must not wear them. The amount of "skin" which men and women are allowed to show differs greatly. The Islamic term for this is 'Awra (عَوْرة).

A woman's 'Awra basically includes her entire body. According to Islam, a woman should not show anything except for her face and hands; some say only her eyes can be uncovered – whereas the 'Awra of a man is the area from the navel to the knees. This means: Men can go swimming wearing swimming trunks. Women have to be fully clothed.

Marriage

A man could marry four women, but a woman can only have one husband. This is said in sura 4 *Women* – in Arabic: al-Nisa' (سورة النِّساء):

4:3	If you fear that you will not deal fairly with orphan girls, you may marry whichever [other] women seem good to you, two, three or four. If you fear that you cannot be equitable [to them], then marry only one, or your slave(s): that is more likely to make you avoid bias.	وَإِنْ خِفْتُمْ أَلَّا تُقْسِطُوا فِي الْيَتَامَىٰ فَانكِحُوا مَا طَابَ لَكُم مِّنَ النِّسَاء مَثْنَىٰ وَثُلَاثَ وَرُبَاعَ فَإِنْ خِفْتُمْ أَلَّا تَعْدِلُوا فَوَاحِدَةً أَوْ مَا مَلَكَتْ أَيْمَانُكُمْ ذَٰلِكَ أَدْنَىٰ أَلَّا تَعُولُوا.

Divorce

A man has the right to divorce his wife.

However, a woman - generally speaking - is not allowed to ask for a divorce. If she dislikes her husband, she is not permitted by Islamic law to ask for a divorce. Only if he maltreats her badly, she is allowed to do so.

It was narrated from Thawbān (ثوبان) that the Messenger of Allah had said: "Any woman who asks her husband for a divorce when it is not absolutely necessary, the fragrance of Paradise will be forbidden to her."[552]

Note: A wife is not allowed to punish her husband by refusing having sex with him. 'Abū Hurayra (أَبُو هُرَيْرَة) narrated that Allah's Messenger once said: "If a husband calls his wife to his bed [i.e. to have sex] and she refuses and causes him to sleep in anger, the angels will curse her until morning."[553]

Travelling

A man can travel alone. But a woman, following Islamic rules, is not allowed to travel – unless she is accompanied by her husband or a so-called Mahram (مَحْرَم), i.e. a person of her family which she is not allowed to marry according to Islam.

Worship

Most acts of worship are performed in the same way for example the ritual washing, so-called Wudū' (وُضوء), or the ritual bath, so-called Ghusl (غُسْل). Women observe fast as men do and pray as men do, except when they are menstruating or bleeding following childbirth.

424. Why do more men than women go to the mosque?

Answer: Because Muhammad said that it is better for a woman to pray at home.

Prayer in the mosque is obligatory for men, but not for women. 'Abd Allah ibn 'Umar (عَبْد الله بن عُمَر) narrated that the Messenger of Allah said: "Do not prevent your women from visiting the mosque; but their houses are better for them [for praying]."[554]

---

552 ...قَالَ رَسُولُ اللَّهِ: "أَيُّمَا امْرَأَةٍ سَأَلَتْ زَوْجَهَا الطَّلاَقَ فِي غَيْرِ مَا بَأْسٍ فَحَرَامٌ عَلَيْهَا رَائِحَةُ الْجَنَّةِ."
Sunan ibn Māja 2133 (2055)

553 ...قَالَ رَسُولُ اللَّهِ: "إِذَا دَعَا الرَّجُلُ امْرَأَتَهُ إِلَى فِرَاشِهِ فَأَبَتْ، فَبَاتَ غَضْبَانَ عَلَيْهَا، لَعَنَتْهَا الْمَلاَئِكَةُ حَتَّى تُصْبِحَ."
Sahīh al-Bukhārī 3237

554 ...قَالَ رَسُولُ اللَّهِ: "لاَ تَمْنَعُوا نِسَاءَكُمُ الْمَسَاجِدَ وَبُيُوتُهُنَّ خَيْرٌ لَهُنَّ." Sunan 'Abī Dāwūd 567

It goes even further: 'Abd Allah ibn Mas'ūd (عَبْد الله بن مَسْعُود) narrated that the Prophet said: "A woman's prayer in her house is better than her prayer in her courtyard [central part of the house to which all doors open], and her prayer in her bedroom is better than her prayer in her house."[555]

Note: This is also true for the Friday prayer – see chapter 141.

425. May a menstruating woman touch the Qur'an?

Answer: No (most probably).

Sura 56 *That Which is Coming/The Inevitable* - in Arabic: al-Wāqi'a (سُورة الْوَاقِعة) - describes the status of the Qur'an in Islam:

56:77	that this is truly a noble Qur'an,	إِنَّهُ لَقُرْآنٌ كَرِيمٌ
56:78	in a protected Record	فِي كِتَابٍ مَّكْنُونٍ
56:79	that only the purified can touch,	لَّا يَمَسُّهُ إِلَّا الْمُطَهَّرُونَ
56:80	sent down from the Lord of all being.	تَنزِيلٌ مِّن رَّبِّ الْعَالَمِينَ.

The scholars are not sure what is meant by the expression: *that only the purified can touch.* Some people even suggested that Allah might have referred to the angels because they are free from all sins unlike humans. But most scholars agree that this verse of the Qur'an is referring to someone who is free from impurity. This means that when a woman is menstruating, she cannot touch the book of the Qur'an – unless she is wearing gloves.

Some remarks on the topic of *menstruation*:

In Islam there are many rules regarding the menses. In Sahih Muslim - one of the biggest and most important collections of Hadiths - a chapter is named *The Book of Menstruation* (كِتاب الْحَيْض).

From a modern-day Western perspective, it is difficult to accept that women are weak and unclean during menstruation. In Islam,

555 ...قَالَ رَسُولُ اللَّهِ: "صَلَاةُ الْمَرْأَةِ فِي بَيْتِهَا أَفْضَلُ مِنْ صَلَاتِهَا فِي حُجْرَتِهَا وَصَلَاتُهَا فِي مَخْدَعِهَا
أَفْضَلُ مِنْ صَلَاتِهَا فِي بَيْتِهَا." Sunan 'Abī Dāwūd 570

this is an important concept which is part of daily culture. Muslims are convinced that Allah prefers to be worshipped only by a pure - tāhir (طاهر) - person and a menstruating woman is *not clean* according to Islam.

Let's look at the main rulings:

- It is forbidden for a menstruating woman to pray; if she does it anyway, her prayers are invalid.

  'Umm Salama (أُم سَلَمة) narrated about a woman asking the Prophet: "I suffer from persistent bleeding and I never become pure; should I stop praying?" He said: "No. Stop praying for the number of days and nights that you used to menstruate, then perform Ghusl, wrap a cloth around yourself and pray."[556]

- It is forbidden for a menstruating woman to stay in the mosque.

  'Umm 'Atīya (أُم عَطِيّة) narrated that the Messenger of Allah said: "Bring out the women who have attained puberty and those who are in seclusion so that they may attend the 'Īd prayer and (join in) the supplication of the Muslims. But let the women who are menstruating avoid the prayer place."[557]

- It is forbidden for a menstruating woman to fast.

  Mu'ādha (مُعَاذة) narrated that she asked 'Ā'isha (عائشة بِنْت أَبِي بَكْر): "What is the reason that a menstruating woman completes the fasts [that she abandons during menses] but she does not complete the prayers?" She ['Ā'isha] asked: "Are you one of the Harūrīya [from a town in present-day Iraq; it is a place associated with a group of the Khawārij]?" I said: "I am not a Harūrīya, but I simply want to inquire." 'Ā'isha said: "We passed through this [period of menstruation] and then we were ordered to complete the fasts, but were not ordered to complete the prayers."[558]

556 ...قَالَتْ سَأَلَتِ امْرَأَةُ النَّبِيَّ قَالَتْ إِنِّي أُسْتَحَاضُ فَلاَ أَطْهُرُ أَفَأَدَعُ الصَّلاَةَ قَالَ: "لاَ وَلَكِنْ دَعِي قَدْرَ تِلْكَ الأَيَّامِ وَاللَّيَالِي الَّتِي كُنْتِ تَحِيضِينَ فِيهَا ثُمَّ اغْتَسِلِي وَاسْتَثْفِرِي وَصَلِّي." Sunan al-Nasā'ī 354

557 ...قَالَ رَسُولُ اللَّهِ: "أَخْرِجُوا الْعَوَاتِقَ وَذَوَاتِ الْخُدُورِ لِيَشْهَدْنَ الْعِيدَ وَدَعْوَةَ الْمُسْلِمِينَ. وَلِيَجْتَنِبْنَّ الْحُيَّضُ مُصَلَّى النَّاسِ." Sunan ibn Māja 1368 (1308)

558 ...قَالَتْ سَأَلْتُ عَائِشَةَ فَقُلْتُ مَا بَالُ الْحَائِضِ تَقْضِي الصَّوْمَ وَلاَ تَقْضِي الصَّلاَةَ فَقَالَتْ أَحَرُورِيَّةٌ أَنْتِ قُلْتُ لَسْتُ بِحَرُورِيَّةٍ وَلَكِنِّي أَسْأَلُ. قَالَتْ كَانَ يُصِيبُنَا ذَلِكَ فَنُؤْمَرُ بِقَضَاءِ الصَّوْمِ وَلاَ نُؤْمَرُ بِقَضَاءِ

- It is forbidden for her husband to have sex with her during this period. This is found in sura 2 *The Cow* – in Arabic: al-Baqara (سُورَة الْبَقَرَة). This verse is generally used to justify why women are "different" during their menses:

2:222	They ask you [Prophet] about menstruation. Say, 'Menstruation is a painful condition, so keep away from women during it. Do not approach them until they are cleansed; when they are cleansed, you may approach them as God has ordained. God loves those who turn to Him, and He loves those who keep themselves clean.	وَيَسْأَلُونَكَ عَنِ الْمَحِيضِ قُلْ هُوَ أَذًى فَاعْتَزِلُوا النِّسَاءَ فِي الْمَحِيضِ وَلَا تَقْرَبُوهُنَّ حَتَّى يَطْهُرْنَ فَإِذَا تَطَهَّرْنَ فَأْتُوهُنَّ مِنْ حَيْثُ أَمَرَكُمُ اللَّهُ إِنَّ اللَّهَ يُحِبُّ التَّوَّابِينَ وَيُحِبُّ الْمُتَطَهِّرِينَ.

Note: The Qur'an scholar and translator Abdel Haleem wrote that the Arabic expressions used in this verse "are clear euphemisms for *do not have sexual intercourse with them.*"

- It is forbidden for a husband to divorce a woman during her menses.

  'Abd Allah ibn 'Umar (عَبْد الله بن عُمَر) reported that he divorced his wife during her menstrual period. 'Umar asked the Messenger of Allah about that and the Prophet said: "Order him, he must take her back and retain her until she is purified, then has another menstrual period and is purified. Thereafter, if he desires, he may divorce her before having intercourse with her, for that is the period of waiting which Allah has commanded for the divorce of women."[559]

- It is forbidden for a menstruating woman to circumambulate the Ka'ba.

  'Ā'isha narrated: "When we came to a place called Sarif, I menstruated and the Prophet told me: 'You should perform all that a

---

559...أَنَّهُ طَلَّقَ امْرَأَتَهُ وَهِيَ حَائِضٌ عَلَى عَهْد رَسُولِ اللَّهِ فَسَأَلَ عُمَرُ بْنُ الْخَطَّابِ رَسُولَ اللَّهِ عَنْ ذَلِكَ فَقَالَ رَسُولُ اللَّهِ: "مُرْهُ فَلْيُرَاجِعْهَا ثُمَّ لِيُمْسِكْهَا حَتَّى تَطْهُرَ ثُمَّ تَحِيضَ ثُمَّ تَطْهُرَ ثُمَّ إِنْ شَاءَ أَمْسَكَ بَعْدَ ذَلِكَ وَإِنْ شَاءَ طَلَّقَ قَبْلَ أَنْ يَمَسَّ فَتِلْكَ الْعِدَّةُ الَّتِي أَمَرَ اللَّهُ سُبْحَانَهُ أَنْ تُطَلَّقَ لَهَا النِّسَاءُ." Sunan 'Abī Dāwūd 2179 (2174)

pilgrim would do, except circumambulation until you are pure [i.e. performed Ghusl]'.[560]

- When the menstrual period ends, a woman must do a bath - Ghusl (غُسل) - to purify her entire body.

However, it is permissible for a menstruating woman to wash her husband's head and even comb his hair.

- 'Ā'isha narrated: "While in menses, I used to comb the hair of Allah's Messenger."[561]
- 'Ā'isha further reported: "The Messenger of Allah would recline in my lap when I was menstruating and recite the Qur'an."[562]
- 'Umm Salama reported: "While I was laying with the Prophet under a single woollen sheet, I got the menses. I slipped away and put on the clothes for menses." He [the Prophet] asked: "Have you got the menses?" I replied: "Yes." He then called me and made me lie with him under the same sheet.[563]

Traditional scholars use the topic of menstruation to justify why women should not be appointed as judges. During menses, as these men claim, a woman's body and her understanding of things is "weaker" than usual.

But there are other reasons as well.

A (female) judge has to mix with (male) disputants and witnesses and may need to be alone with them. According to Islam, a woman is not allowed to do that unless she has a guardian, so-called Mahram (مَحْرَم).

Can a woman offer her prayers in the clothes in which she had her menses? Yes, that is possible.

---

560 ...لَمَّا جِئْنَا سَرِفَ حِضْتُ، فَقَالَ النَّبِيُّ: "افْعَلِي مَا يَفْعَلُ الْحَاجُّ، غَيْرَ أَنْ لَا تَطُوفِي بِالْبَيْتِ حَتَّى تَطْهُرِي." Sahīh Muslim 1211.

561 ...قَالَتْ كُنْتُ أُرَجِّلُ رَأْسَ رَسُولِ اللَّهِ وَأَنَا حَائِضٌ. Sahīh al-Bukhārī 295.

562 ...أَنَّهَا قَالَتْ كَانَ رَسُولُ يَتَّكِئُ فِي حِجْرِي وَأَنَا حَائِضٌ فَيَقْرَأُ الْقُرْآنَ. Sahīh Muslim 301.

563 ...أَنَا مَعَ النَّبِيِّ، مُضْطَجِعَةٌ فِي خَمِيصَةٍ إِذْ حِضْتُ، فَانْسَلَلْتُ فَأَخَذْتُ ثِيَابَ حِيضَتِي قَالَ: "أَنَفِسْتِ." قُلْتُ نَعَمْ. فَدَعَانِي فَاضْطَجَعْتُ مَعَهُ فِي الْخَمِيلَةِ. Sahīh al-Bukhārī 298.

'Asmā' (أَسماء), daughter of 'Abū Bakr, reported that a woman came to the Messenger of Allah and asked: "What should one do if the blood of menses smears the garment of one of us?" He (the Prophet) replied: "She should scrape it, then rub it with water, then pour water over it and then offer prayer in it."[564]

During the time of Muhammad, life was different. 'Ā'isha narrated: "None of us had more than a single garment and we used to have our menses while wearing it. Whenever it got soiled with blood of the menses, we would apply saliva to the bloody spot and rub off the blood with our nails."[565]

426. May a Muslim beat his wife?

Answer: Yes.

Sura 4 *Women* - in Arabic: al-Nisā' (سُورة النِّساء) - tells Muslims more about the relationship between husband and wife:

| 4:34 | Husbands should take good care of their wives, with [the bounties] God has given to some more than others and with what they spend out of their own money. Righteous wives are devout and guard what God would have them guard in their husbands' absence. If you fear high-handedness from your wives, remind them [of the teachings of God], then ignore them when you go to bed, then hit them. If they obey you, you have no right to act against them: God is most high and great. | الرِّجَالُ قَوَّامُونَ عَلَى النِّسَاء بِمَا فَضَّلَ اللّهُ بَعْضَهُمْ عَلَى بَعْضٍ وَبِمَا أَنفَقُوا مِنْ أَمْوَالِهِمْ فَالصَّالِحَاتُ قَانِتَاتٌ حَافِظَاتٌ لِّلْغَيْبِ بِمَا حَفِظَ اللّهُ وَاللاَّتِي تَخَافُونَ نُشُوزَهُنَّ فَعِظُوهُنَّ وَاهْجُرُوهُنَّ فِي الْمَضَاجِعِ وَاضْرِبُوهُنَّ فَإِنْ أَطَعْنَكُمْ فَلاَ تَبْغُوا عَلَيْهِنَّ سَبِيلاً إِنَّ اللّهَ كَانَ عَلِيًّا كَبِيرًا. |

---

564 ...قَالَتْ جَاءَتْ امْرَأَةٌ النَّبِيَّ فَقَالَتْ أَرَأَيْتَ إِحْدَانَا تَحِيضُ فِي الثَّوْبِ كَيْفَ تَصْنَعُ قَالَ: "تَحُتُّهُ، ثُمَّ تَقْرُصُهُ بِالْمَاءِ، وَتَنْضَحُهُ وَتُصَلِّي فِيهِ." Sahīh al-Bukhārī 227

565 ...قَالَتْ عَائِشَةُ مَا كَانَ لإِحْدَانَا إِلاَّ ثَوْبٌ وَاحِدٌ تَحِيضُ فِيهِ، فَإِذَا أَصَابَهُ شَيْءٌ مِنْ دَمٍ، قَالَتْ بِرِيقِهَا فَقَصَعَتْهُ بِظُفُرِهَا. Sahīh al-Bukhārī 312

Hitting is subject to the condition that it should not be harsh or cause injury. Most scholars agree that this means that it should not cause pain. The hitting should mainly show the wife that the husband has the right to set her straight and discipline her.

Al-Tabarī related in his exegesis of the Qur'an a story from 'Attā' ibn 'Abī Rabāh (عَطّاء بن أَبِي رَباح), a scholar and student of 'Abd Allah ibn 'Abbās and 'Abd Allah ibn 'Umar, who said: "I asked Ibn 'Abbās, what is the kind of hitting that is not harsh?" He said: "Hitting with a Siwāk [Islamic toothbrush] and the like."[566]

The beating of women is also found in several Hadiths:

- 'Umar ibn al-Khattāb (عُمَر بن الْخَطّاب) reported that the Prophet once said: "A man will not be asked why he beat his wife."[567] This Hadith is considered weak (ضَعِيف) by most scholars, but it is widespread among Muslims and used to justify the beating of one's wife.

- It is indicated in the Hadiths that Muslims at the time of the Prophet beat their slave-girls and probably their wives too. Laqīt ibn Sabira (لَقِيط بن صَبِرة) narrated: "I said: 'Messenger of Allah, I have a wife who has something [wrong] in her tongue [i.e. she is insolent].' The Prophet said: 'Then divorce her.'

  I said: 'Messenger of Allah, she had company with me and I have children from her.' He [the Prophet] said: 'Then ask her [to obey you]. If there is something good in her, she will do so [obey]; and do not beat your wife as you beat your slave-girl.'"[568]

The Qur'an states that a woman has rights over her husband, just as her husband has rights over her. A wife has rights over her husband regarding living expenses: her husband has to earn the money for the whole family. In return, she must obey and respect her husband. This is found in sura *The Cow* – in Arabic: al-Baqara (سُورة الْبَقَرة):

---

566 ...قَالَ عَطَاء: قُلْت لِابْنِ عَبّاس مَا الضَّرْبُ غَيْرُ الْمُبَرِّحِ؟ قال: بِالسِّوَاكِ ونَحْوِه. Tafsīr al-Tabarī.

567 ...النَّبِيُّ قَالَ: "لاَ يُسْأَلُ الرَّجُلُ فِيمَا ضَرَبَ امْرَأَتَهُ". Sunan 'Abī Dāwūd 2147 (2142); weak.

568 ...قُلْتُ يَا رَسُولَ اللَّهِ إِنَّ لِي امْرَأَةً وَإِنَّ فِي لِسانِها شَيْئًا يَعْنِي الْبَذاءَ. قَالَ: "فَطَلِّقْهَا إِذًا." قَالَ قُلْتُ يَا رَسُولَ اللَّهِ إِنَّ لَهَا صُحْبَةً وَلِي مِنْها وَلَدٌ. قَالَ: "فَمُرْهَا - يَقُولُ عِظْهَا - فَإِنْ يَكُ فِيهَا خَيْرٌ فَسَتَفْعَلُ وَلاَ تَضْرِبْ ظَعِينَتَكَ كَضَرْبِكَ أُمَيَّتَكَ". Sunan 'Abī Dāwūd 142.

| 2:228 | Wives have [rights] similar to their [obligations], according to what is reasonable. But the men have a degree over them [in responsibility and authority]. And Allah is Exalted in Might and Wise. | ‫...وَلَهُنَّ مِثْلُ الَّذِي عَلَيْهِنَّ بِالْمَعْرُوفِ وَلِلرِّجَالِ عَلَيْهِنَّ دَرَجَةٌ وَاللَّهُ عَزِيزٌ حَكِيمٌ.‬ |

This verse indicates that the man has additional rights, corresponding with his role as protector and maintainer and his responsibility of providing living expenses (for his wife).

427. What is the 'Awra?

Answer: The 'Awra (عَوْرة) denotes the private body parts of a person.

Islam uses the Arabic term 'Awra to denote those parts of a body which must not be exposed to anybody except one's wife or husband, or, in case of emergency or illness, to a doctor. Furthermore, the whole topic is not only about showing these body parts to any other person, but also about looking at them if a person exposes them, which is forbidden for Muslims.

The word 'Awra is derived from the root '-r-w (ع-و-ر) which means *to be blind in one eye*. In a broader sense, it can express *weakness*, *badness*, or *disgrace*, but also *a thing having no keeper or guardian*.

In Islam, the word 'Awra denotes a body's *pudenda*, the *external genitals*, or simply *a weak spot*. So what are these private parts?

- **'Awra of a man**: from the navel to the knees. That is why you occasionally see Muslim soccer players taking a shower in their shorts after the game (in the locker room).

- **'Awra of a woman**: her entire body except for her face and hands.

428. Does a Muslim woman have to be veiled?

Answer: Most sources are indicating yes.

Several Arabic and English words are used in discussions about this topic: headscarf, veil, Hijāb, Khimār, Niqāb, Burqu' (Burqa), etc. These words are actually pretty useless in discussions between Muslims and non-Muslims – simply because the most important Islamic sources only give a qualitative description and don't use these words.

Let's look at an example: "The Qur'an doesn't command women to wear the Burqa." This sentence is true – simply, because the Qur'an doesn't use the word Burqu' (Burqa). These tricks ("not mentioned in the Qur'an") are often used in debates in Europe, but are totally mis-leading. Furthermore, these names may have a cultural background and don't mean the same in every Islamic country.

Let's check what the Qur'an and the Hadiths say about this topic.

The Qur'an does not use the word **Hijāb** (حجاب) in the way it is used today – meaning a veil (headscarf) covering the hair and the neck of a woman. In Arabic, the word Hijāb is a very vague word. It denotes anything that intervenes as an obstacle between things; it conceals, shelters, or protects the one from the other. This means that a Hijāb is the name of something that is used to cover. Moreover, a Hijāb can be anything that comes between two things/objects.

This can be everything such as curtains, door keepers or garments. Therefore Hijāb can be translated as *curtain, obstacle, partition – or veil*. The Qur'an uses the word Hijāb for a specific situation: that the wife should not be visible to other men at home. Sura 33 *The Joint Forces* - in Arabic: al-'Ahzāb (سورة الأَحْزاب) - commands people to approach the Prophet's wives only "from behind a screen" or "cur-tain". Most of the companions took this verse literally.

| 33:53 | Believers, do not enter the Prophet's apartments for a meal unless you are given permission to do so; do not linger until [a meal] is ready. When you are invited, go in; then, when you have taken your meal, leave. Do not stay on and | يَا أَيُّهَا الَّذِينَ آمَنُوا لَا تَدْخُلُوا بُيُوتَ النَّبِيِّ إِلَّا أَن يُؤْذَنَ لَكُمْ إِلَى طَعَامٍ غَيْرَ نَاظِرِينَ إِنَاهُ وَلَكِنْ إِذَا دُعِيتُمْ فَادْخُلُوا فَإِذَا طَعِمْتُمْ فَانتَشِرُوا وَلَا مُسْتَأْنِسِينَ لِحَدِيثٍ إِنَّ |

talk, for that would offend the Prophet, though he would shrink from asking you to leave. God does not shrink from the truth. When you ask his wives for something, do so from behind a screen: this is purer both for your hearts and for theirs. It is not right for you to offend God's Messenger, just as you should never marry his wives after him: that would be grievous in God's eyes.	ذَلِكُمْ كَانَ يُؤْذِي النَّبِيَّ فَيَسْتَحْيِي مِنكُمْ وَاللَّهُ لَا يَسْتَحْيِي مِنَ الْحَقِّ وَإِذَا سَأَلْتُمُوهُنَّ مَتَاعًا فَاسْأَلُوهُنَّ مِن وَرَاءِ حِجَابٍ ذَلِكُمْ أَطْهَرُ لِقُلُوبِكُمْ وَقُلُوبِهِنَّ وَمَا كَانَ لَكُمْ أَن تُؤْذُوا رَسُولَ اللَّهِ وَلَا أَن تَنكِحُوا أَزْوَاجَهُ مِن بَعْدِهِ أَبَدًا إِنَّ ذَلِكُمْ كَانَ عِندَ اللَّهِ عَظِيمًا.

The word Hijāb in this verse does not mean a piece of cloth that covers a woman's hair and neck. Instead, the meaning of *screen* or *barrier* is meant. A Hadith informs Muslims in which situation the Prophet received this verse which Muslims call *the verses of al-Hijāb*.

The following was narrated by 'Anas ibn Mālik (أَنَس بن مالك): "I was ten years old when Allah's Messenger arrived in Medina. My mother and aunts urged me to serve the Prophet regularly, and I served him for ten years. When the Prophet died I was twenty years old, and I knew about the order of al-Hijāb [veiling of women] more than any other person, when it was revealed.

It was revealed for the first time when Allah's Messenger had consummated his marriage with Zaynab bint Jahsh. When the day dawned, the Prophet was a bridegroom and he invited the people to a banquet, so they came, ate, and then all left except for a few who remained with the Prophet for a long time. The Prophet got up and went out and I too went out with him so that those people might leave too. The Prophet proceeded, and so did I, until he came to the threshold of 'Ā'isha's dwelling.

Then, thinking that the people had left, he returned and so did I along with him until he entered upon Zaynab and behold, they [the people] were still sitting and had not gone.

So the Prophet again went away, and I went along with him. When we reached the threshold of 'Ā'isha's place, he thought that they had left, and so he returned and I too, returned along with him and found that those people had left.

Then the Prophet pulled a curtain between me and him, and the verses of al-Hijāb were revealed.[569]

However, this verse does not say that a woman should cover her hair or face. But does this mean that a Muslim woman should not cover her hair or face ?

No, it doesn't either.

It is only half of the story. There are other sources which tell Muslim women why they should probably cover themselves when they leave the house. Let's have a look at a Hadith.

ʿĀʾisha (عائشة بِنْت أَبِي بَكْر) narrated that the wives of the Prophet used to go to al-Manāsiʿ, a vast open place [near al-Baqīʿ in Medina], to answer the call of nature at night.

ʿUmar ibn al-Khattāb used to tell the Prophet: "Let your wives be veiled!", but Allah's Apostle did not do so. One night Sawda bint Zamʿa, one of the Prophet's wives, went out at ʿIshāʾ time [when it was getting dark]. She was a tall lady.

ʿUmar addressed her and said: "I have recognised you, O Sawda!" He said so, as he desired eagerly that the verses of al-Hijāb [the observing of veils by the Muslim women] may be revealed. So Allah revealed the verses of al-Hijāb [Traditional scholars have added: A complete body cover excluding the eyes].[570]

This Hadith was discussed a lot. It seems that ʿUmar ibn al-Khattāb was the driving force behind the veiling of women. It mentions

569 ...أَنَّهُ كَانَ ابْنَ عَشْرِ سِنِينَ مَقْدَمَ رَسُولِ اللَّهِ الْمَدِينَةَ، فَكَانَ أُمَّهَاتِي يُوَاظِبْنَنِي عَلَى خِدْمَةِ النَّبِيِّ فَخَدَمْتُهُ عَشْرَ سِنِينَ، وَتُوُفِّيَ النَّبِيُّ وَأَنَا ابْنُ عِشْرِينَ سَنَةً، فَكُنْتُ أَعْلَمَ النَّاسِ بِشَأْنِ الْحِجَابِ حِينَ أُنْزِلَ، وَكَانَ أَوَّلَ مَا أُنْزِلَ فِي مُبْتَنَى رَسُولِ اللَّهِ بِزَيْنَبَ ابْنَةِ جَحْشٍ، أَصْبَحَ النَّبِيُّ بِهَا عَرُوسًا، فَدَعَا الْقَوْمَ فَأَصَابُوا مِنَ الطَّعَامِ، ثُمَّ خَرَجُوا وَبَقِيَ رَهْطٌ مِنْهُمْ عِنْدَ النَّبِيِّ فَأَطَالُوا الْمُكْثَ، فَقَامَ النَّبِيُّ فَخَرَجَ وَخَرَجْتُ مَعَهُ لِكَىْ يَخْرُجُوا، فَمَشَى النَّبِيُّ وَمَشَيْتُ، حَتَّى جَاءَ عَتَبَةَ حُجْرَةِ عَائِشَةَ، ثُمَّ ظَنَّ أَنَّهُمْ خَرَجُوا فَرَجَعَ وَرَجَعْتُ مَعَهُ، حَتَّى إِذَا دَخَلَ عَلَى زَيْنَبَ فَإِذَا هُمْ جُلُوسٌ لَمْ يَقُومُوا، فَرَجَعَ النَّبِيُّ وَرَجَعْتُ مَعَهُ، حَتَّى إِذَا بَلَغَ عَتَبَةَ حُجْرَةِ عَائِشَةَ، وَظَنَّ أَنَّهُمْ خَرَجُوا، فَرَجَعَ وَرَجَعْتُ مَعَهُ فَإِذَا هُمْ قَدْ خَرَجُوا فَضَرَبَ النَّبِيُّ بَيْنِي وَبَيْنَهُ بِالسَّتْرِ، وَأُنْزِلَ الْحِجَابُ. Sahīh al-Bukhārī 5166

570 ...أَنَّ أَزْوَاجَ النَّبِيِّ كُنَّ يَخْرُجْنَ بِاللَّيْلِ إِذَا تَبَرَّزْنَ إِلَى الْمَنَاصِعِ وَهُوَ صَعِيدٌ أَفْيَحُ فَكَانَ عُمَرُ يَقُولُ لِلنَّبِيِّ احْجُبْ نِسَاءَكَ. فَلَمْ يَكُنْ رَسُولُ اللَّهِ يَفْعَلُ. فَخَرَجَتْ سَوْدَةُ بِنْتُ زَمْعَةَ زَوْجُ النَّبِيِّ لَيْلَةً مِنَ اللَّيَالِي عِشَاءً، وَكَانَتِ امْرَأَةً طَوِيلَةً، فَنَادَاهَا عُمَرُ أَلَا قَدْ عَرَفْنَاكِ يَا سَوْدَةُ. حِرْصًا عَلَى أَنْ يَنْزِلَ الْحِجَابُ، فَأَنْزَلَ اللَّهُ آيَةَ الْحِجَابِ. Sahīh al-Bukhārī 146.

that 'Umar had asked the Prophet several times about the veiling of his wives. 'Umar had spied on one of the Prophet's wives when she went to the toilet and exposed and harassed her. Only after that the Prophet received some information from Allah about the veiling of women.

Although the veil nowadays has become such a big and controversial topic in Islam, it seems that Muhammad himself, when we look at the Islamic sources, did not pay too much attention to it. In the above mentioned Hadith, we again encountered the expression "verses of al-Hijāb". This expression, however, is probably derived from another sura – than to the verses which are nowadays used to justify the veil of a woman. The expression is found in sura 24 *The Light* – in Arabic: al-Nūr (سُورة النُّور). In the following verse, we will encounter two words which are crucial in the whole debate about covering hair and face: the Arabic word juyūbihinna (جُيُوب) and the Arabic word Khumur (خُمُر). Let's check the verse:

| 24:31 | And tell believing women that they should lower their glances, guard their private parts, and not display their charms beyond what [it is acceptable] to reveal; they should let their head-scarves fall to cover their necklines and not reveal their charms except to their husbands, their fathers, their husbands' fathers, their sons, their husbands' sons, their brothers, their brothers' sons, their sisters' sons, their womenfolk, their slaves, such men as attend them who have no sexual desire, or children who are not yet aware of women's nakedness; they should not stamp their feet so as to draw attention to any hidden. | وَقُل لِّلْمُؤْمِنَاتِ يَغْضُضْنَ مِنْ أَبْصَارِهِنَّ وَيَحْفَظْنَ فُرُوجَهُنَّ وَلَا يُبْدِينَ زِينَتَهُنَّ إِلَّا مَا ظَهَرَ مِنْهَا وَلْيَضْرِبْنَ بِخُمُرِهِنَّ عَلَى جُيُوبِهِنَّ وَلَا يُبْدِينَ زِينَتَهُنَّ إِلَّا لِبُعُولَتِهِنَّ أَوْ آبَائِهِنَّ أَوْ آبَاءِ بُعُولَتِهِنَّ أَوْ أَبْنَائِهِنَّ أَوْ أَبْنَاءِ بُعُولَتِهِنَّ أَوْ إِخْوَانِهِنَّ أَوْ بَنِي إِخْوَانِهِنَّ أَوْ بَنِي أَخَوَاتِهِنَّ أَوْ نِسَائِهِنَّ أَوْ مَا مَلَكَتْ أَيْمَانُهُنَّ أَوِ التَّابِعِينَ غَيْرِ أُولِي الْإِرْبَةِ مِنَ الرِّجَالِ أَوِ الطِّفْلِ الَّذِينَ لَمْ يَظْهَرُوا عَلَى عَوْرَاتِ النِّسَاءِ وَلَا يَضْرِبْنَ بِأَرْجُلِهِنَّ لِيُعْلَمَ مَا يُخْفِينَ مِن زِينَتِهِنَّ وَتُوبُوا إِلَى اللَّهِ جَمِيعًا أَيُّهَ الْمُؤْمِنُونَ لَعَلَّكُمْ تُفْلِحُونَ. |

In the translation, it says *head-scarf*. So is the word head-scarf found in the Qur'an and what is the Arabic word for it? It is not that easy. In the translation of Abdel Haleem, the word *head-scarf* is used.

However, the word in question is not *Hijāb* – it is *Khumur* (خُمُر),
marked in grey in the table. How did other translators render Khumur? Let's have a look:

should let their **head-scarves** fall to cover their neck-lines	*Abdel Haleem*
hence, let them draw their **head-coverings** over their bosoms	*Muhammad Asad*
should draw their **veils** over their bosoms and not display their beauty	*Yūsuf ʿAlī*
wrap their **headcovers** over their chests and not expose their adornment	*Sahīh International*
draw their **veils** over their bosoms, and not to reveal their adornment	*Pickthall*
draw their veils all over "**Juyūbihinna**" (i.e. their bodies, faces, necks and bosoms, etc.) and not to reveal their adornment	*Muhsin Khan*

Let's focus again on the word (also marked in grey in verse 24:31)
which is often misinterpreted: **Khumur**. It is the plural form of
Khimār (خِمار). Khimār comes from the root kh-m-r (خ-م-ر) which has
the basic meaning of *to cover* or *to conceal*. Everything that covers
something is called a Khimār.

The same root is even used to derive one of the several words for
alcohol. The word Khamr (خَمْر) means *something that intoxicates,
alcohol in general,* or *wine* – because it *clouds, obscures, covers* and
conceals the intellect.

Khimār, despite its vague meaning, became the name for a certain
piece of cloth. Edward Lane (1863) gave the following description of
Khimār: "A woman's muffler or veil with which she covers her head
and the lower part of their face, leaving exposed only the eyes and
part or the whole of the nose. Such is the Khimār worn in the present
day".

Besides, Edward Lanes mentioned that the word Khumr (خُمْر) is a
man's turban. A man covers his head in a similar manner as a
woman covers hers with the Khimār. "When he disposes it in the

Arab manner, he turns a part of it under the jaws nearly in the same manner in which a woman disposes her Khimār."

The word **Juyūb** (جُيُوب) is the plural form of Jayb (جَيْب) which means: *The opening at the neck and bosom of a shirt; neckline* or *décolleté*. In other words, it is the opening at the top and front of the dress that allows the head to fit through. However, the expression *beyond what [is acceptable] to show* does not really help to decide what a Muslim woman has to do. It is ambiguous in Arabic. In pre-Islamic times, Arabs used to carry things inside (a pocket in) the bosom of the shirt.

There is nothing more in the Qur'an about the veiling of a woman. This brings us to the next important question: **How much is a woman allowed to show? And what are the sources for such rules?**

There is no clear answer either. Most Islamic scholars say that in pre-Islamic times women already covered their hair. However, by letting the ends of their Khimār hang down behind their back, their ears, neck and chest were exposed. The Qur'an is more precise on this because the Khimār should "cover their **Juyūb**." This means that women - when Islam started - had to cover their previously exposed areas, i.e. ears, neck and chest. Therefore, most Islamic scholars agree that a woman must not show her hair and neck. But how about the face? Traditional scholars say that women are only allowed to show their eyes.

The Hadiths don't really help if a Muslim wants to find an answer because they can be interpreted in both ways, and are actually used by people who claim that the face has to be veiled as well as by people who insist that the face can be shown.

- 'Ā'isha narrated that 'Asmā', her half-sister, entered upon the Messenger of Allah wearing thin clothes. The Messenger of Allah turned away from her. He said: "O 'Asmā', when a woman reaches the age of menstruation, it does not suit her that she displays her parts of body except this and this and he pointed to his face and hands."[571]

- Safya bint Shayba (صَفْية بِنْت شَيْبة) narrated that 'Ā'isha had said: "When the verse [24:31] was revealed, the women cut their waist sheets at the edges and covered their heads and faces with those cut pieces of cloth."[572]

- 'Alqama ibn 'Abī 'Alqama (عَلْقَمة بن أَبِي عَلْقَمة) narrated that his mother said: "Hafsa bint 'Abd al-Rahmān visited 'Ā'isha, a wife of the Prophet, and Hafsa was wearing a long thin head scarf. 'Ā'isha tore it in two and made a thick one for her."[573]

  This is used by conservative Muslims to justify that it is not permissible to show more than the eyes and that it is not permissible to make the Khimār so thin that it shows the face.

- 'Abd Allah ibn 'Umar (عَبْد الله بن عُمَر) reported about a person who once stood up and asked Muhammad the following: "O Allah's Apostle! What clothes may be worn in the state of 'Ihrām [during the Hajj]?" The Prophet replied: "...the Muhrima [a woman in the state of 'Ihrām] should not cover her face or wear gloves."[574]

  Traditional scholars use this as a proof that women at the time of the Prophet had veiled their face. Otherwise, there would have been no need for the Prophet to forbid women in 'Ihrām to wear a face veil (during the pilgrimage in Mecca).

- 'Abd Allah ibn 'Umar said that he had heard the Apostle of Allah prohibit women in the sacred state ['Ihrām] to wear gloves, veil [their faces] and to wear clothes with dye of Wars [name of a plant] or saffron on them.[575]

---

571 ...أَنَّ أَسْمَاءَ بِنْتَ أَبِي بَكْرٍ، دَخَلَتْ عَلَى رَسُولِ اللَّهِ وَعَلَيْهَا ثِيَابٌ رِقَاقٌ فَأَعْرَضَ عَنْهَا رَسُولُ اللَّهِ وَقَالَ: "يَا أَسْمَاءُ إِنَّ الْمَرْأَةَ إِذَا بَلَغَتِ الْمَحِيضَ لَمْ تَصْلُحْ أَنْ يُرَى مِنْهَا إِلاَّ هَذَا وَهَذَا". وَأَشَارَ إِلَى وَجْهِهِ وَكَفَّيْهِ. Sunan 'Abī Dāwūd 4104 (4092).

572 ...أَنَّ عَائِشَةَ كَانَتْ تَقُولُ لَمَّا نَزَلَتْ هَذِهِ الآيَةُ {وَلْيَضْرِبْنَ بِخُمُرِهِنَّ عَلَى جُيُوبِهِنَّ} أَخَذْنَ أُزْرَهُنَّ فَشَقَّقْنَهَا مِنْ قِبَلِ الْحَوَاشِي فَاخْتَمَرْنَ بِهَا. Sahīh al-Bukhārī 4759.

573 ...أَنَّهَا قَالَتْ دَخَلَتْ حَفْصَةُ بِنْتُ عَبْدِ الرَّحْمَنِ عَلَى عَائِشَةَ زَوْجِ النَّبِيِّ وَعَلَى حَفْصَةَ خِمَارٌ رَقِيقٌ فَشَقَّتْهُ عَائِشَةُ وَكَسَتْهَا خِمَارًا كَثِيفًا. al-Muwatta' (1660).

574 ...قَالَ قَامَ رَجُلٌ فَقَالَ يَا رَسُولَ اللَّهِ مَاذَا تَأْمُرُنَا أَنْ نَلْبَسَ مِنَ الثِّيَابِ فِي الإِحْرَامِ فَقَالَ النَّبِيُّ: "... وَلاَ تَنْتَقِبِ الْمَرْأَةُ الْمُحْرِمَةُ وَلاَ تَلْبَسِ الْقُفَّازَيْنِ." Sahīh al-Bukhārī 1838.

In the two narrations of 'Abd Allah ibn 'Umar, in the Arabic source, we come across another Arabic word which is controversial nowadays: **Niqāb** (نقاب), or when used as a verb, Intaqaba (اِنْتَقَبَ) – both words are marked in grey in the Arabic original of the Hadith (see footnotes). So what is the relevance of these words?

The Arabic root n-q-b (ن-ق-ب) means: *to perforate, to pierce, to make a hole through* or *in* or *into something*. The Arabic VIII-verb Intaqaba (اِنْتَقَبَ) is only used in the female form: Intaqabat (اِنْتَقَبَتْ), because it means: *She (a woman) veiled her face with a Niqāb.* The Niqāb is a face veil that only exposes a woman's eyes.

There is another controversial word: the **Burqa**, in Arabic mostly pronounced Burqu' (بُرْقُع). Edward Lane (1863) wrote that it is "a small piece of cloth or rag, pierced for the eyes, worn by horses or similar beasts and by the women of the Arabs of the desert." Its colour was black, blue, or white, concealing the whole of the woman's face, except her eyes, and reaching nearly to the feet.

What about the colour of the veil? Muhammad did not say anything about that (and neither does the Qur'an). Most women, who fully cover their body, wear black because they think it is the farthest removed from being an adornment.

What about accessories? Strictly speaking, they are not allowed Some Muslim women in the West go to court to get their right to wear the Hijāb, but at the same time, they like to use make-up and perfume, and wear fashion clothes and sunglasses. From a religious point of view, this perverts the idea of the veil as an object hiding all possible female temptations, and thus making it nothing but a political symbol. Make-up is meant to attract men, traditional Muslim scholars say, the same is true for perfume which the Prophet only liked at home. Outside the house a woman using perfume receives the worst verdict:

It was narrated that 'Abū Mūsā al-'Ash'arī (أَبُو مُوسَى الأَشْعَرِي) said that the Messenger of Allah said: "Any woman who puts on perfume

---

575 ...أَنَّ رَسُولَ اللَّهِ نَهَى النِّسَاءَ فِي إِحْرَامِهِنَّ عَنِ الْقُفَّازَيْنِ وَالنِّقَابِ وَمَا مَسَّ الْوَرْسُ وَالزَّعْفَرَانُ مِنَ الثِّيَابِ. Sunan 'Abī Dāwūd 1827

then passes by people so that they can smell her fragrance then she is an adulteress."[576]

What about the style of clothes (used to "veil" the body)? If a Muslim woman wears a head-scarf, she must not wear tight clothes. She is not allowed to wear clothes which reveal the colour of the skin and the size and shape of her body. Traditional Muslim scholars are convinced that such would create a lifelike image in men's minds. Therefore, the clothes must be wide.

This is derived from a Hadith which was recorded by Imam Mālik who stated that 'Abū Hurayra had said: "Women who are naked even though they are wearing clothes, go astray and make others go astray, and they will not enter the Garden and they will not find its scent, and its scent is experienced from as far as the distance travelled in five hundred years."[577]

Let's take a moment to summarise what a pious Muslim woman is demanded to do. She should...

- lower her gaze
- guard her private parts
- use her Khimār and cover at least her chest, neck and head
- not expose her body except to her husband(s) and father.

Every Muslim woman has to decide what this means to her.

Will women be veiled in Paradise? There is no answer. Some traditional scholars use a Hadith to say yes, but there is little evidence.

'Anas ibn Mālik narrated that the Prophet said: "A single endeavour [of fighting] in Allah's cause in the afternoon or in the forenoon is better than the entire world and whatever is in it. A place in Paradise as small as the bow or lash of one of you is better than all the world and whatever is in it. And if a Houri from Paradise appeared to the people of the earth, she would fill the space between Heaven

---

576 ...قَالَ رَسُولُ اللَّهِ: "أَيُّمَا امْرَأَةٍ اسْتَعْطَرَتْ فَمَرَّتْ عَلَى قَوْمٍ لِيَجِدُوا مِنْ رِيحِهَا فَهِيَ زَانِيَةٌ." Sunan al-Nasā'ī 5126 (5129); hasan

577 ...عَنْ أَبِي هُرَيْرَةَ أَنَّهُ قَالَ نِسَاءٌ كَاسِيَاتٌ عَارِيَاتٌ مَائِلَاتٌ مُمِيلَاتٌ لَا يَدْخُلْنَ الْجَنَّةَ وَلَا يَجِدْنَ رِيحَهَا وَرِيحُهَا يُوجَدُ مِنْ مَسِيرَةِ خَمْسِمِائَةِ سَنَةٍ. Muwatta' Mālik 1661

and the Earth with light and pleasant scent and her head cover would be better than the world and whatever is in it."[578]

In the Arabic version, the word Nasīf (نَصِيف) is used (grey highlighted). Edward Lane (1863) said that it has the same meaning as Khimār (خِمَار) – *a woman's muffler*. I talked to traditional scholars about that. They told me that Muslims wouldn't know enough about Paradise. They said that it could be interpreted as a kerchief, a kind of band(ana) that women wrap around the head, which might not even cover the head and something that is just used for adornment.

429. Who is allowed to see a Muslim woman unveiled?

Answer: Twelve types of people, basically her closest family, slaves and young children.

The Qur'an says that women are prohibited to show their *charms* to men. This includes basically all her skin except for her eyes and her hands in the most conservative interpretation. Only men whom she is not allowed to marry are exempted from this rule. This is stated in sura 24 *The Light* – in Arabic: al-Nūr (سُورَة النُّور):

| 24:31 | ...and not reveal their charms except to their husbands, their fathers, their husbands' fathers, their sons, their husbands' sons, their brothers, their brothers' sons, their sisters' sons, their womenfolk, their slaves, such men as attend them who have no sexual desire, or children who are not yet aware of women's nakedness; they should not stamp their feet so as to draw attention to any hidden. | ...وَلَا يُبْدِينَ زِينَتَهُنَّ إِلَّا لِبُعُولَتِهِنَّ أَوْ آبَائِهِنَّ أَوْ آبَاءِ بُعُولَتِهِنَّ أَوْ أَبْنَائِهِنَّ أَوْ أَبْنَاءِ بُعُولَتِهِنَّ أَوْ إِخْوَانِهِنَّ أَوْ بَنِي إِخْوَانِهِنَّ أَوْ بَنِي أَخَوَاتِهِنَّ أَوْ نِسَائِهِنَّ أَوْ مَا مَلَكَتْ أَيْمَانُهُنَّ أَوِ التَّابِعِينَ غَيْرِ أُولِي الْإِرْبَةِ مِنَ الرِّجَالِ أَوِ الطِّفْلِ الَّذِينَ لَمْ يَظْهَرُوا عَلَى عَوْرَاتِ النِّسَاءِ وَلَا يَضْرِبْنَ بِأَرْجُلِهِنَّ لِيُعْلَمَ مَا يُخْفِينَ مِن زِينَتِهِنَّ وَتُوبُوا إِلَى اللَّهِ جَمِيعًا أَيُّهَ الْمُؤْمِنُونَ لَعَلَّكُمْ تُفْلِحُونَ. |

---

578 ...قَالَ رَسُولُ اللَّهِ: "لَرَوْحَةٌ فِي سَبِيلِ اللَّهِ أَوْ غَدْوَةٌ خَيْرٌ مِنَ الدُّنْيَا وَمَا فِيهَا، وَلَقَابُ قَوْسِ أَحَدِكُمْ مِنَ الْجَنَّةِ أَوْ مَوْضِعُ قِيدٍ يَعْنِي سَوْطَهُ خَيْرٌ مِنَ الدُّنْيَا وَمَا فِيهَا، وَلَوْ أَنَّ امْرَأَةً مِنْ أَهْلِ الْجَنَّةِ اطَّلَعَتْ إِلَى أَهْلِ الْأَرْضِ لَأَضَاءَتْ مَا بَيْنَهُمَا وَلَمَلَأَتْهُ رِيحًا، وَلَنَصِيفُهَا عَلَى رَأْسِهَا خَيْرٌ مِنَ الدُّنْيَا وَمَا فِيهَا. Sahīh al-Bukhārī 2796

But this is not only limited to the *appearance* of the woman. Alone and unescorted she is not allowed to be together with someone she could marry (and who has sexual desires), even if she is properly veiled.

ʿAbd Allah ibn ʿAbbās (عَبْد الله بن عَبّاس) reported: "I heard Allah's Messenger deliver a sermon and make the following statement: '**No person should be alone with a woman except when there is a Mahram with her, and the woman should not undertake a journey except with a Mahram.'**"

A person stood up and said: 'O Allah's Messenger, my wife has set out for pilgrimage whereas I am enlisted to fight in such and such battle', whereupon he [the Prophet] said: 'You go and perform Hajj with your wife.'"[579]

In Islam, a Mahram (مَحْرَم) is a man whom she cannot marry; a close relative. Let's have a closer look at the Mahram relatives of a woman:

1. Her **husband**: husband and wife can see whatever they want (of each other).

2. Her **father**, including the **grandfathers** from both mother's and father's sides.

3. Her **husband's father** – because he is regarded as a father to a woman.

4. Her sons and **grandsons** (from both sons and daughters).

5. Her husband's sons (**stepsons**) – because the woman is regarded as their mother.

6. Her **brothers**, including half- and step-brothers.

7. Her **brothers' sons**, since marriage is permanently prohibited between a man and his paternal aunt.

8. Her **sisters' sons**, since marriage is permanently prohibited between a man and his maternal aunt.

9. Female relatives and **other Muslim women**. Watch out: Most scholars say that this isn't valid for <u>non</u>-Muslim female relatives. A non-Muslim woman is not allowed to see a Muslim woman

---

579 ...يَقُولُ سَمِعْتُ النَّبِيَّ يَخْطُبُ يَقُولُ: "لاَ يَخْلُوَنَّ رَجُلٌ بِامْرَأَةٍ إلاَّ وَمَعَها ذُو مَحْرَمٍ وَلاَ تُسَافِرُ الْمَرْأَةُ إلاَّ مَعَ ذِي مَحْرَمٍ." فَقَامَ رَجُلٌ فَقَالَ يَا رَسُولَ اللَّهِ إنَّ امْرَأَتِي خَرَجَتْ حَاجَّةً وَإِنِّي اكْتُتِبْتُ فِي غَزْوَةِ كَذَا وَكَذَا. قَالَ: "انْطَلِقْ فَحُجَّ مَعَ امْرَأَتِكَ." Ṣaḥīḥ Muslim 1341

naked. She is only allowed to see what non-Mahram men may see.

10. Those whom their right hands possess – which refers to **bond-servants** (slaves) because in Islam they are considered members of the family. Some scholars restrict this permission to female bond-servants.

11. **Male servants who lack sexual desire.** This refers to household servants who don't feel sexual desire because of physical or mental conditions.

12. **Small children** who have not developed yet a consciousness of sex.

Note: The Qur'an does neither mention maternal nor paternal uncles – because, according to Islam, they have the same status as the father. 'Abū Hurayra (أَبُو هُرَيْرَة) narrated that the Messenger of Allah had said to 'Umar ibn al-Khattāb: "Bear this in mind, the uncle of a person is like his father."[580]

430. What is the purpose of circumcision?

Answer: Being pure for praying and showing that one is a Muslim.

Circumcision (in the case of men) means that the skin at the tip of the penis (the foreskin) is removed so that the entire glans becomes visible. Muslims say that if the foreskin remains, it might collect urine and this might cause an infection. Furthermore, these drops of urine cause impurity – so-called: Najāsa (نَجَاسَة). In Islam, such impurities make prayers invalid.

Let's look at the most important Islamic terms concerning this topic: The circumciser is called **al-Khātin** (الْخَاتِن). Al-**Khitān** (الْخِتَان) is a noun describing the action of the circumciser, i.e. the circumcision. It can also denote the banquet at a wedding or at a circumcision. The latter is also called **'I'dhār** (إِعْذَار) – which is the feast for a child's circumcision.

---

580 ...قَالَ: "يَا عُمَرُ أَمَا شَعَرْتَ أَنَّ عَمَّ الرَّجُلِ صِنْوُ أَبِيهِ." Sahīh Muslim 983

Edward Lane (1863) mentioned in his dictionary that the Arabic root kh-t-n (خ-ت-ن) primarily means *to circumcise a boy - or a girl*.

However, some scholars say, that the word Khatn (خَتْن) relates to men/boys only and that **Khafd** (خَفْض) relates to women/girls. Literally, the word Khafd denotes *a state of abatement, freedom from trouble; quietness* or *pleasant life*. A Khāfida (خافِضة) is a woman who circumcises a girl.

A person who is uncircumcised is called 'aghlaf (أَغْلَف) which literally means: *covered*. In the case of a woman, the Arabic term 'aqlaf (أَقْلَف) is mostly used. The word Qulfa (قُلْفة) is the woman's prepuce (the fold of skin surrounding the clitoris), a piece of flesh between the **Shughrān** (شُغْران) - *labia minora* - which is cut off in circumcision. The root sh-gh-r (ش-غ-ر) in Arabic means that a *woman raised her leg* or *legs for the purpose of copulation*. When used for a dog, it means *to lift the leg to make water*.

When should the circumcision be done?

There is no exact time. The duties of the Islamic law - Sharī'a (شَريعة) - are not obligatory until a person has reached puberty. However, the Prophet said that fathers should tell their children to pray at the age of seven and if a child doesn't want to pray, he can hit it when it is ten. Most scholars agree that it should be done at the latest when a person reaches puberty.

Sa'īd ibn Jubayr (سَعِيد بن جُبَيْر) narrated that 'Abd Allah ibn 'Abbās was asked: "How old were you when the Prophet died?" He replied: "At that time I had been circumcised." At that time, he continued, people did not circumcise the boys until they attained the age of puberty.[581]

Why is circumcision necessary when Allah is perfect?

This is a difficult question for Muslims. If Allah was perfect as Muslims believe, why did he create a man with a penis (with foreskin) that is not perfect according to Islamic rules? Since Muslims consider every human being as a perfect creation of Allah and since

---

581 ...قَالَ سُئِلَ ابْنُ عَبَّاسٍ مِثْلَ مَنْ أَنْتَ حِينَ قُبِضَ النَّبِيُّ قَالَ أَنَا يَوْمَئِذٍ مَخْتُونٌ. قَالَ وَكَانُوا لاَ يَخْتِنُونَ الرَّجُلَ حَتَّى يُدْرِكَ. Sahīh al-Bukhārī 6299.

Allah commanded his followers that they must not change anything in His creation, a Muslim gets into trouble finding an answer why he should change Allah's creation.

According to a Hadith, the Prophet said that a Muslim - when he will be resurrected after death - will be <u>un</u>circumcised. 'Abd Allah ibn 'Abbās (عَبْد الله بن عَبّاس) narrated that the Messenger of Allah said: "You will be resurrected [and assembled] bare-footed, naked and uncircumcised."[582]

So when a Muslim man is born <u>un</u>circumcised and he will be <u>un</u>circumcised in the afterlife, what is the point of being circumcised in his present life? If it was for health reasons only, why didn't Allah create men without a foreskin at the first place?

Muslim scholars don't have an answer to this. They only say that a Muslim cannot understand the wisdom of Allah, but he must obey the rules and believe that Allah has His reasons. Allah, as Muslims are convinced, does not command anything – unless it is good for his followers, the Muslims.

431. Should Muslim women be circumcised?

Answer: Not entirely clear. Some Muslims say no, but others refer to a tradition of the Prophet to justify female circumcision.

Traditional scholars claim that in the case of women, the circumcision serves a special purpose – to reduce desire.

There is a controversial Hadith which sparked the whole discussion. Some scholars say that its chain of narration is weak (ضَعِيف), others consider it hasan (حَسَن) and the scholar al-'Albānī came to the conclusion that this Hadith is even authentic (صَحِيح). Some Muslims take from this Hadith that women were circumcised at the time of the Prophet and - what is more important - that he approved it.

The following was narrated by 'Umm 'Atīya (أُمّ عَطِيّة الأنْصارِيّة): "A woman used to perform circumcision in Medina. The Prophet said

---

to her: 'Do not cut severely as that is better for a woman and more desirable for a husband.'"[583]

This is not the only source. There are authentic Hadiths which command Muslims what they have to do after the "circumcised **parts have touched/met each other**" – the plural in these narrations indicate that men and women were circumcised.

'Abū Hurayra reported the Prophet said: "When anyone sits between the four parts of a woman and the parts [of the male and female], which are circumcised, join together, then bath becomes obligatory."[584]

What is perhaps meant here: When a man sits between a woman's legs and their circumcised genitalia touch each other, they both need a bath. Or: When a man is embraced by a woman and their...

Furthermore, Imam Mālik in his Muwatta' Mālik (863) speaks of "the meeting of the two circumcised parts" (الْتِقَاءُ الْخِتَانَيْنِ) to describe having sex.

What do traditional scholars make of all of that?

Their view is that circumcision is obligatory for men as it is one of the symbols of Islam. Circumcision of women is not obligatory, which also means, however, that it is not forbidden. The centuries-old practice involves the partial or full removal of the external sex organs (mainly the clitoris), usually with a knife or razor blade. The cutting can lead to urinary infections, menstrual problems, infertility and death.

According to the *World Health Organisation*, Egypt has some of the highest rates of FGM (female genital mutilation), together with Somalia, Djibouti and Sierra Leone. A UNICEF study in 2013 found that as many as 27.2 million women in Egypt have been circumcised.

---

583 ...أَنَّ امْرَأَةً، كَانَتْ تَخْتِنُ بِالْمَدِينَةِ فَقَالَ لَهَا النَّبِيُّ: "لاَ تُنْهِكِي فَإِنَّ ذَلِكَ أَحْظَى لِلْمَرْأَةِ وَأَحَبُّ إِلَى الْبَعْلِ." Sunan 'Abī Dāwud 5271 (5251)

584 ...أَنَّ النَّبِيَّ قَالَ: "إِذَا قَعَدَ بَيْنَ شُعَبِهَا الأَرْبَعِ وَأَلْزَقَ الْخِتَانَ بِالْخِتَانِ فَقَدْ وَجَبَ الْغُسْلُ." Sunan 'Abī Dāwud 216

432. What are the two official holidays in Islam?

Answer: 'Īd al-Fitr (عيد الْفِطر) and 'Īd al-'Adhā (عيد الأضحى).

A feast is called 'Īd (عيد) in Arabic. There are <u>only</u> two official holidays in Islam: 'Īd al-Fitr and 'Īd al-'Adhā.

'Anas ibn Mālik (أَنَس بن مالك) narrated: "When the Messenger of Allah came to Medina, the people had two days during which they engaged in games. He asked: 'What are these two days [what is their significance]?' They replied: 'We entertained ourselves on these days before Islam.' The Messenger of Allah said: 'Allah has substituted them for something better, the Day of Sacrifice and the Day of the Breaking of the Fast.'"[585]

- **'Īd al-Fitr** is celebrated at the end of Ramadan. It is the Feast of Breaking the Ramadan Fast, also called Lesser Bayram. It is celebrated on the 1st of the Hijri month Shawwāl (شَوّال).
- **'Īd al-'Adhā** is celebrated on the 10th day of Dhū al-Hijja (ذُو الْحِجَّة) and lasts for four days during which Muslims sacrifice a sheep, cut and divide its meat into three parts and share it with the family, friends, and the poor.

On both Islamic holidays, people give presents to their family members, especially children, which can be toys, candies or money. This is called: al-'Īdīya (الْعيدِيَّة).

433. What is a Musaharātī?

Answer: A person who wakes up people in the night during Ramadan so that they can eat their pre-dawn meal.

The pre-dawn meal - the final meal before another round of fasting begins - is called Sahūr (سحُور). The meal is eaten before the first prayer. The word Sahar (سحَر) denotes dawn, the time before daybreak or early morning. The Musaharātī (الْمُسْحِر or الْمُسَحْراتيّ) - in dialects also Mesaharaty - is a person who wakens people for the

---

585 ...قَدِمَ رَسُولُ اللَّهِ الْمَدِينَةَ وَلَهُمْ يَوْمَانِ يَلْعَبُونَ فِيهِمَا فَقَالَ:" مَا هَذَانِ الْيَوْمَانِ؟" قَالُوا كُنَّا نَلْعَبُ فِيهِمَا فِي الْجَاهِلِيَّةِ. فَقَالَ رَسُولُ اللَّهِ: "إِنَّ اللَّهَ قَدْ أَبْدَلَكُمْ بِهِمَا خَيْرًا مِنْهُمَا يَوْمَ الأَضْحَى وَيَوْمَ الْفِطْرِ."

Sunan 'Abī Dāwūd 1134 (1130)

Sahūr meal and dawn prayer during Ramadan. According to some historic accounts, Bilāl ibn Rabāh al-Habashī (بِلال بن رَباح الْحَبَشيّ) was the first Musaharātī in Islamic history.

In Egypt, in the early days of Islam, the Mesaharaty called from the mosques. Later on, he walked across the streets and used a drum to replace his voice, but some were also chanting traditional songs. Nowadays, this tradition is very rarely performed and only found in rural areas.

434. Who is entitled to receive alms (Zakā)?

Answer: There is no clear definition, but basically the poor and the needy. Some claim that they have to be Muslim.

In Islamic law, Zakā (الزَّكاة) denotes an obligatory tax Muslims have to pay. It is meant to purify a person's capital and income from traces of selfishness and greed. The root z-k-w (ز-ك-و) means *to thrive*, but also: *to be pure in heart, to be just*.

The word Zakā (زَكاة) literally means *purity, justness,* or *justification*. Let's see who is entitled to receive *alms* – in Arabic: Sadaqa (صَدَقة). This information is given in sura 9 *Repentance* – in Arabic: al-Tawba (سُورة التَّوْبة):

9:60	Alms are meant only for the poor, the needy, those who administer them, those whose hearts need winning over, to free slaves and help those in debt, for God's cause, and for travellers in need. This is ordained by God; God is all knowing and wise.	إِنَّمَا الصَّدَقَاتُ لِلْفُقَرَاءِ وَالْمَسَاكِينِ وَالْعَامِلِينَ عَلَيْهَا وَالْمُؤَلَّفَةِ قُلُوبُهُمْ وَفِي الرِّقَابِ وَالْغَارِمِينَ وَفِي سَبِيلِ اللَّهِ وَابْنِ السَّبِيلِ فَرِيضَةً مِّنَ اللَّهِ وَاللَّهُ عَلِيمٌ حَكِيمٌ.

Note: In the above mentioned verse, the Qur'an uses the term Sadaqāt (الصَّدَقَات) for *alms* and not Zakā. The word Sadaqa denotes *rightfulness* – but can be used in the meaning of *charity*. In the Qur'an and in the Hadiths, these two words are mostly used synonymously. However, with the development of Islam, scholars started to define the two words:

- If a Muslim helps a needy person, who is not hostile towards Islam, it is usually called *charity* – Sadaqa.
- Most scholars agree that Zakā is only for Muslims and must not be given to non-Muslims – unless they are very close to embrace Islam. In that case, the Zakā could be seen as an "incentive", as some scholars say. However, the Qur'an does not say that Zakā is only for Muslims.
- There are Muslims who say that if a Muslim gives more than the obliged Zakā, then this is called Sadaqa.

Furthermore, sura 9 tells Muslims that those who pray and pay alms are a Muslim's brothers:

9:11	If they turn to God, keep up the prayer, and pay the prescribed alms, then they are your brothers in faith: We make the messages clear for people who are willing to learn.	فَإِن تَابُوا وَأَقَامُوا الصَّلَاةَ وَآتَوُا الزَّكَاةَ فَإِخْوَانُكُمْ فِي الدِّينِ وَنُفَصِّلُ الْآيَاتِ لِقَوْمٍ يَعْلَمُونَ.

435. Should a Muslim help a non-Muslim beggar?

Answer: Generally speaking, yes.

First of all, although some Muslims say that begging is not allowed in Islam, the Qur'an states that a Muslim should not repel a needy person. This is stated in sura 93 *The Morning Brightness* – in Arabic: al-Duhā (سُورَة الضُّحَى), an early sura revealed in Mecca. When Muhammad had not received any revelation for some time, this Sura told him that Allah had not forsaken him.

93:10	and do not chide the one who asks for help; (Alternative translation: And as for the beggar, do not repel [him].)	وَأَمَّا السَّائِلَ فَلَا تَنْهَرْ

But does this command include non-Muslims, the so-called "unbelievers"? The answer is, in principle, yes. Islamic scholars derive this from sura 76 *Man* – in Arabic: al-'Insān (سُورَة الإِنْسَان):

76:8	they give food to the poor, the orphan, and the captive, though they love it themselves,	وَيُطْعِمُونَ الطَّعَامَ عَلَىٰ حُبِّهِ مِسْكِينًا وَيَتِيمًا وَأَسِيرًا

In this verse, the Qur'an does not say anything about unbelievers. So, how did the scholars come to this conclusion? Even very traditional scholars like Ibn Qudāma (ابن قُدامة), a Ḥanbalī ascetic and theologian of the 12th century, suggested that at the very beginning of Islam, when this verse was revealed, *captives* - which are mentioned in the verse - could only have been *unbelievers*.

However, there are conditions for begging: The person asking for help must be in need and not be able to earn a living. Otherwise, begging is (as most Muslims claim) *forbidden* – harām (حَرام).

It was narrated that Qabīṣa ibn Mukhāriq (قَبيصة بن مُخارِق) said: "I undertook a financial responsibility, then I came to the Prophet and asked him [for help] concerning that. The Prophet said: 'Hold on, O Qabīṣa! When we get some charity we will give you some.'

Then the Messenger of Allah said: 'O Qabīṣa, charity is not permissible except for one of three: **A man who undertakes a financial responsibility** [in order to reconcile between two parties], so it is permissible for him to be given charity until he finds means to make him independent and to suffice him; **a man who was stricken by calamity and his wealth was destroyed**, so it is permissible for him to ask for help until he has enough to keep him going, then he should refrain from asking; and **a man who is stricken with poverty and three wise men from among his own people testify that** so-and-so is in desperate need, then it is permissible for him to ask for help until he finds means to make him independent and to suffice him. Asking for help in cases other than these, Qabīṣa, is unlawful, and the one who takes it, is consuming it unlawfully.'"[586]

---

586 ...قَالَ تَحَمَّلْتُ حَمَالَةً فَأَتَيْتُ رَسُولَ اللَّهِ أَسْأَلُهُ فِيهَا فَقَالَ: "أَقِمْ يَا قَبِيصَةُ حَتَّى تَأْتِيَنَا الصَّدَقَةُ فَنَأْمُرَ لَكَ." قَالَ ثُمَّ قَالَ رَسُولُ اللَّهِ: "يَا قَبِيصَةُ إِنَّ الصَّدَقَةَ لاَ تَحِلُّ إِلاَّ لِأَحَدِ ثَلاَثَةٍ رَجُلٍ تَحَمَّلَ حَمَالَةً فَحَلَّتْ لَهُ الْمَسْأَلَةُ حَتَّى يُصِيبَ قِوَامًا مِنْ عَيْشٍ أَوْ سِدَادًا مِنْ عَيْشٍ وَرَجُلٍ أَصَابَتْهُ جَائِحَةٌ فَاجْتَاحَتْ مَالَهُ فَحَلَّتْ لَهُ الْمَسْأَلَةُ حَتَّى يُصِيبَهَا ثُمَّ يُمْسِكُ وَرَجُلٍ أَصَابَتْهُ فَاقَةٌ حَتَّى يَشْهَدَ ثَلاَثَةٌ مِنْ ذَوِي الْحِجَا مِنْ قَوْمِهِ قَدْ أَصَابَتْ فُلاَنًا فَاقَةٌ فَحَلَّتْ لَهُ الْمَسْأَلَةُ حَتَّى يُصِيبَ قِوَامًا مِنْ عَيْشٍ أَوْ سِدَادًا مِنْ عَيْشٍ فَمَا سِوَى هَذَا مِنَ الْمَسْأَلَةِ يَا قَبِيصَةُ سُحْتٌ يَأْكُلُهَا صَاحِبُهَا سُحْتًا." Sunan al-Nasā'ī 2580

Most scholars say that Muslims should first and foremost give their charity to their Muslim fellows. However, the narrations of the Prophet prove that it is all right for a Muslim to give away money or food to people – even if the Muslim doesn't know them. In addition, a Muslim will have the reward for that act of charity even if it turns out later that the beggar had not been in need.

'Abū Hurayra (أَبُو هُرَيْرَة) narrated that Allah's Messenger said: "A man said that he would give a charitable donation. He went out with his object of charity and unknowingly gave it to a thief.

Next morning the people said that he had given his object of charity/donation to a thief. [On hearing that] he said: 'O Allah! All the praises are for you. I will give alms again.' And so he again went out with his alms and [unknowingly] gave it to an adulteress.

Next morning the people said that he had given his alms to an adulteress last night. The man said: 'O Allah! All the praises are for you. [I gave my alms] to an adulteress. I will give alms again.' So he went out with his alms again and gave it to a rich person. Next morning the people said that he had given his alms to a wealthy person. He said: 'O Allah! All the praises are for you. I had given alms to a thief, to an adulteress, and to a wealthy man.' Then someone came and said: 'The alms which you gave to the thief, might make him abstain from stealing and that given to the adulteress might make her abstain from illegal sexual intercourse, and that given to the wealthy man might make him take a lesson from it and spend his wealth which Allah has given him, in Allah's cause.'"[587]

436. What is the work that extinguishes Allah's anger?

Answer: Charity, alms (الصَّدَقة).

---

587 ...أَنَّ رَسُولَ اللَّهِ قَالَ: "قَالَ رَجُلٌ لَأَتَصَدَّقَنَّ بِصَدَقَةٍ. فَخَرَجَ بِصَدَقَتِهِ فَوَضَعَهَا فِي يَدِ سَارِقٍ فَأَصْبَحُوا يَتَحَدَّثُونَ تُصُدِّقَ عَلَى سَارِقٍ. فَقَالَ اللَّهُمَّ لَكَ الْحَمْدُ لَأَتَصَدَّقَنَّ بِصَدَقَةٍ. فَخَرَجَ بِصَدَقَتِهِ فَوَضَعَهَا فِي يَدَيْ زَانِيَةٍ، فَأَصْبَحُوا يَتَحَدَّثُونَ تُصُدِّقَ اللَّيْلَةَ عَلَى زَانِيَةٍ. فَقَالَ اللَّهُمَّ لَكَ الْحَمْدُ عَلَى زَانِيَةٍ، لَأَتَصَدَّقَنَّ بِصَدَقَةٍ. فَخَرَجَ بِصَدَقَتِهِ فَوَضَعَهَا فِي يَدَيْ غَنِيٍّ فَأَصْبَحُوا يَتَحَدَّثُونَ تُصُدِّقَ عَلَى غَنِيٍّ فَقَالَ اللَّهُمَّ لَكَ الْحَمْدُ، عَلَى سَارِقٍ وَعَلَى زَانِيَةٍ وَعَلَى غَنِيٍّ. فَأُتِيَ فَقِيلَ لَهُ أَمَّا صَدَقَتُكَ عَلَى سَارِقٍ فَلَعَلَّهُ أَنْ يَسْتَعِفَّ عَنْ سَرِقَتِهِ، وَأَمَّا الزَّانِيَةُ فَلَعَلَّهَا أَنْ تَسْتَعِفَّ عَنْ زِنَاهَا، وَأَمَّا الْغَنِيُّ فَلَعَلَّهُ يَعْتَبِرُ فَيُنْفِقُ مِمَّا أَعْطَاهُ اللَّهُ." *Ṣaḥīḥ al-Bukhārī* 1421

It was narrated by a companion of Muhammad, Ka'b ibn 'Ajra (كَعْب بن عُجرة), that the Messenger of Allah had told him: "Charity extinguishes sin as water extinguishes fire."[588]

But how much should a Muslim donate? Definitely not all he or she owns. Information about this is given in a Hadith.

Ka'b ibn 'Mālik (كَعْب بن مَالك) from the 'Ansār did not participate in the Battle of Tabūk (غَزْوة تَبُوك) and therefore had not joined the Prophet in the fight, for which he wanted to show repentance. Ka'b said: "O Allah's Messenger! For the acceptance of my repentance I wish to give all my property in charity for Allah's sake through His Apostle." The Prophet said: "It is better for you to keep some property for yourself."[589]

If a Muslim donates money or whatever, he should keep it secret as told in sura 2 *The Cow* – in Arabic: al-Baqara (سُورة الْبَقَرة) :

2:271	If you give charity openly, it is good, but if you keep it secret and give to the needy in private, that is better for you, and it will atone for some of your bad deeds: God is well aware of all that you do.	إِن تُبْدُوا الصَّدَقَاتِ فَنِعِمَّا هِيَ وَإِن تُخْفُوهَا وَتُؤْتُوهَا الْفُقَرَاءَ فَهُوَ خَيْرٌ لَّكُمْ وَيُكَفِّرُ عَنكُم مِّن سَيِّئَاتِكُمْ وَاللَّهُ بِمَا تَعْمَلُونَ خَبِيرٌ.

437. How much does a Muslim have to pay as alms (Zakā)?

Answer: It is a matter of calculation.

Two terms are important for the calculation of the Zakā (زَكاة): al-Nisāb (النِّصاب) and al-Hawl (الْحَوْل).

1. Al-Nisāb (النِّصاب). The Arabic word Nisāb literally means *origin, minimum amount* or *quorum*. In Islamic law, it is the minimum amount of a fortune or capital which imposes the duty of paying the Zakā. In other words: Nisāb is the exemption limit for the payment

---

588 ...قَالَ لِي رَسُولُ اللَّهِ: "الصَّدَقَةُ تُطْفِئُ الْخَطِيئَةَ كَمَا يُطْفِئُ الْمَاءُ النَّارَ." ;Jāmi' al-Tirmidhī 614
hasan

589 ...قُلْتُ يَا رَسُولَ اللَّهِ، إِنَّ مِنْ تَوْبَتِي أَنْ أَنْخَلِعَ مِنْ مَالِي صَدَقَةً إِلَى اللَّهِ وَإِلَى رَسُولِهِ . قَالَ: "أَمْسِكْ عَلَيْكَ بَعْضَ مَالِكَ فَهُوَ خَيْرٌ لَكَ." Sahīh al-Bukhārī 2757

of Zakā. If a Muslim's net yearly savings fall below this amount, he or she is exempt from paying Zakā.

The Nisāb is equivalent to the value of 3 ounces of gold – which equals 85 grams of gold or also 595 grams of silver. The original measurement was 20 Mithqālan (1 Mithqāl = 4.25 grams). Nisāb for silver and currencies made from silver is 200 dirhams (1 dirham = 2.975 grams).

2. Al-Hawl (الْحَوْل). The wealth on which Zakā should be paid must have been held for at least one full year. This period is called Hawl. It is one lunar year. Therefore, the word Hawl is also used to denote an entire year (سَنة كامِلة).

So how much does a Muslim have to pay?

ʿAlī ibn ʾAbū Tālib (عَلِيّ بن أَبِي طالِب) narrated that the Prophet said: "When you possess two hundred dirhams and one year passes on them, five dirhams are payable. Nothing is incumbent on you, that is, on gold, until it reaches twenty dinars. When you possess twenty dinars and one year passes on them, then half a dinar is payable. Whatever exceeds, that will be reckoned properly. No Zakā is payable on property until a year passes on it."[590]

From this Hadith, Muslims derive that the percentage of **Zakā is 2.5% of the net savings.** The net savings are the total maintained wealth one possesses (for at least one lunar year) above the Nisāb.

What is the Nisāb value in 2016?

Muslim scholars and organisations try to calculate the Nisāb for every year. For 2016, the Nisāb using the value of 3 ounces of gold is around 4,000 US dollars. For silver (595 grams), however, it is only 595 US dollars. These two figures are the Nisāb thresholds. If a Muslim's yearly net-savings are below that line, he or she is exempted from paying Zakā, else, he or she has to pay 2.5%.

---

590 ...النَّبِيُّ قالَ: "فَإِذَا كَانَتْ لَكَ مِائَتَا دِرْهَمٍ وَحَالَ عَلَيْهَا الْحَوْلُ فَفِيهَا خَمْسَةُ دَرَاهِمَ وَلَيْسَ عَلَيْكَ شَيْءٌ - يَعْنِي فِي الذَّهَبِ - حَتَّى يَكُونَ لَكَ عِشْرُونَ دِينَارًا فَإِذَا كَانَ لَكَ عِشْرُونَ دِينَارًا وَحَالَ عَلَيْهَا الْحَوْلُ فَفِيهَا نِصْفُ دِينَارٍ فَمَا زَادَ فَبِحِسَابِ ذَلِكَ." قَالَ فَلَا أَدْرِي أَعَلِيٌّ يَقُولُ فَبِحِسَابِ ذَلِكَ. أَوْ رَفَعَهُ إِلَى النَّبِيِّ: "وَلَيْسَ فِي مَالٍ زَكَاةٌ حَتَّى يَحُولَ عَلَيْهِ الْحَوْلُ." Sunan ʾAbī Dāwūd 1573

There is a huge gap between the two values. The Nisāb calculated with the help of silver is significantly lower than its gold counterpart. This shows that the value for silver against gold has dropped dramatically since the time of the Prophet.

Most scholars say that it is better to use the silver Nisāb since it will increase the amount of charity while others maintain that the gold Nisāb is closer to that applied at the time of the Prophet.

There is another problem, because 4,000 US$ are a relatively low amount in the USA or in certain European countries, but in Egypt it is a fortune and most people would not be obliged to pay Zakā.

Is this fair?

This is a difficult question. I met several Muslims in Egypt and Tunisia who had difficulties to explain that the old measurements are just and fair. The measurements were set in the 7th century, but despite the tremendous gap in today's standard of living in rich and poor countries, they are still applied in the same way without any adjustment, as this is strictly prohibited in Islam.

For example, according to Islamic laws, a Muslim millionaire or billionaire - which probably did not exist during the time of Muhammad - only has to pay 2.5% from his net assets although he could pay many times more.

Muslims told me that we simply don't know why Allah has put some people into a desperate situation, for example, the poor people in Egypt or Bangladesh – whereas people elsewhere have lots of money. Allah's plan must not be questioned.

In Egypt, I have met many Muslims who told beggars: "Allah will make it easier for you!"[591] Or: "Allah will provide"[592] or "Allah will give you".

For a non-Muslim, this sounds cynical, but for a Muslim, it is faith.

---

591 سَهِّل اللّه عَلَيْكَ!

592 رَزَقَهُ اللّه! or اللّه هُوَ الرَّزَّاقُ!

438. How many days may a woman travel alone?

Answer: Three days.

'Abd Allah ibn 'Umar (عَبْد الله بن عُمَر) narrated that the Prophet said: "A woman should not travel for more than three days except with a Mahram [i.e. a male whom she cannot marry, e.g. her brother, father, grandfather] or her own husband."[593]

The Prophet was stricter when a woman wanted to travel at night. 'Abū Hurayra (أَبُو هُرَيْرة) reported that Allah's Messenger said: "It is not lawful for a Muslim woman to travel a night's journey except when there is a Mahram with her."[594]

It is not only the limit (three days) but mainly the fact that women are not allowed to travel without a male guardian at all.

At the time of the Prophet, travelling was not safe. Modern Islamic scholars claimed that the Hadith was for the purpose of safety only and concluded that travelling by women today should be fine. Traditional Muslims reject this since they see no evidence for this in the Islamic sources.

This is a major field of tension among Muslims. The rules of Allah were revealed to the Prophet under the condition that they are valid forever and must not be changed.

439. Who was the first judge in Islam?

Answer: 'Umar ibn al-Khattāb (عُمَر بن الْخَطّاب).

The Qādī (الْقاضِي) is a Muslim judge who decides according to the Sharī'a, the derived law of Islam. It is debatable if the Prophet himself counts when we talk about the first Qādī, because Muhammad, of course, also acted as a judge.

The first Caliph after Muhammad's death, 'Abū Bakr (أَبُو بَكْر), had put 'Umar ibn al-Khattāb in charge of the judiciary and appointed him as Qādī. However, 'Abū Bakr still supervised the jurisprudence.

---

593 ...قَالَ النَّبِيُّ: "لاَ تُسَافِرِ الْمَرْأَةُ ثَلاَثَةَ أَيَّامٍ إِلاَّ مَعَ ذِي مَحْرَمٍ." Sahīh al-Bukhārī 1086

594 ...قَالَ رَسُولُ اللَّهِ: "لاَ يَحِلُّ لِامْرَأَةٍ مُسْلِمَةٍ تُسَافِرُ مَسِيرَةَ لَيْلَةٍ إِلاَّ وَمَعَهَا رَجُلٌ ذُو حُرْمَةٍ مِنْها."
Sahīh Muslim 1339

Only when 'Umar himself became Caliph, jurisprudence was form-ally integrated into the Islamic state. 'Umar did not want to person-ally judge every dispute. On several occasions in Islamic history, the Caliph himself appeared before the judge to defend himself in a dis-pute.

'Umar was also the first Caliph to fix salaries for judges (which were high). He founded the first "police force" in Islamic history and separated them from the judiciary. 'Umar bought five houses in Mecca and used them as prisons. Punishment by exile was intro-duced by 'Umar for the first time. It is said that he exiled a man to an island – as punishment for drinking alcohol.

Since 'Umar was very familiar with the Islamic laws, he occasionally also pronounced the verdict. Imam Mālik recorded the following Hadith: 'Umar ibn al-Khattāb came out to the people. He said: "I have found the smell of wine on so-and-so, and he claimed that it was the drink of boiled fruit juice, and I am inquiring about what he has drunk. If it intoxicates, I will flog him."

'Umar then flogged the accused person with the Hadd punishment [most probably 80 lashes].[595]

It is not clear if the man, who was punished by the Caliph, as legend has it, was 'Umar's own son 'Abū Shahma (أَبُو شَحْمة). There are a lot of stories indicating that 'Umar punished his son for drinking alcohol with 80 lashes. The lashes were so severe that he died.

Muslims like to use this story as evidence that the first Muslims did not favour anybody – they just ruled according to Islamic laws.

Remark: What sources does an Islamic judge use?

It was narrated from Shurayh ibn al-Hārith (شُرَيْح بن الحارِث) that he had written to 'Umar asking him [a question], and 'Umar wrote back telling him: "Judge according to what is in the Book of Allah. If it is not [mentioned] in the Book of Allah, then [judge] according to the Sunna of the Messenger of Allah. If it is not (mentioned) in the Book of Allah or in the Sunna of the Messenger of Allah, then pass judge-

---

595 ...وَحَدَّثَنِي عَنْ مَالِكٍ، عَنِ ابْنِ شِهَابٍ، عَنِ السَّائِبِ بْنِ يَزِيدَ، أَنَّهُ أَخْبَرَهُ أَنَّ عُمَرَ بْنَ الْخَطَّابِ خَرَجَ عَلَيْهِمْ فَقَالَ إِنِّي وَجَدْتُ مِنْ فُلَانٍ رِيحَ شَرَابٍ فَزَعَمَ أَنَّهُ شَرَابُ الطَّلَاءِ وَأَنَا سَائِلٌ عَمَّا شَرِبَ فَإِنْ كَانَ يُسْكِرُ جَلَدْتُهُ. فَجَلَدَهُ عُمَرُ الْحَدَّ تَامًّا. Muwatta' Mālik 1540.

ment according to the way the righteous passed judgement. If it is not [mentioned] in the Book of Allah or the Sunna of the Messenger of Allah, and the righteous did not pass judgement concerning it, then, if you wish, go ahead [and try to work it out by yourself], or if you wish, leave it. And I think that leaving it is better for you. And peace be upon you."[596]

440. What kinds of Muslims cannot be held accountable?

Answer: Three kinds of people, i.e. a lunatic, someone asleep until awakened, and a boy until he reaches puberty.

ʿAbd Allah ibn ʿAbbās (عَبْد الله بن عَبَّاس) narrated that a lunatic woman who had committed adultery was brought to ʿUmar ibn al-Khattāb (عُمَر بن الْخطاب). He consulted the people and ordered that she should be stoned.

ʿAlī ibn ʾAbī Tālib (عليّ بن أَبِي طالِب) passed by and asked: "What is the matter with this woman?" They replied: "This is a lunatic woman belonging to a certain family. She has committed adultery. ʿUmar has given orders that she should be stoned."

He [ʿAlī] shouted: "Take her back!" He then went to ʿUmar and declared: "Commander of the Faithful, do you not know that there are three [kinds of] people whose actions are not recorded: a lunatic until he is restored to reason, a sleeper until he awakes, and a boy until he reaches puberty?"

He replied: "Yes." ʿAlī then asked: "Why is it that this woman is being stoned?"

ʿUmar answered: "There is nothing." ʿAlī then said: "Let her go."

ʿUmar let her go and uttered: "Allah is most great!"[597]

---

596 ...أَنَّهُ كَتَبَ إِلَى عُمَرَ يَسْأَلُهُ فَكَتَبَ إِلَيْهِ أَنِ اقْضِ بِمَا فِي كِتَابِ اللَّهِ فَإِنْ لَمْ يَكُنْ فِي كِتَابِ اللَّهِ فَبِسُنَّةِ رَسُولِ اللَّهِ فَإِنْ لَمْ يَكُنْ فِي كِتَابِ اللَّهِ وَلاَ فِي سُنَّةِ رَسُولِ اللَّهِ فَاقْضِ بِمَا قَضَى بِهِ الصَّالِحُونَ فَإِنْ لَمْ يَكُنْ فِي كِتَابِ اللَّهِ وَلاَ فِي سُنَّةِ رَسُولِ اللَّهِ وَلَمْ يَقْضِ بِهِ الصَّالِحُونَ فَإِنْ شِئْتَ فَتَقَدَّمْ وَإِنْ شِئْتَ فَتَأَخَّرْ وَلاَ أَرَى التَّأَخُّرَ إِلاَّ خَيْرًا لَكَ وَالسَّلاَمُ عَلَيْكُمْ. (5401) Sunan al-Nasāʾī 5399

597 ...قَالَ أُتِيَ عُمَرُ بِمَجْنُونَةٍ قَدْ زَنَتْ فَاسْتَشَارَ فِيهَا أُنَاسًا فَأَمَرَ بِهَا عُمَرُ أَنْ تُرْجَمَ فَمُرَّ بِهَا عَلَى عَلِيِّ بْنِ أَبِي طَالِبٍ رِضْوَانُ اللَّهِ عَلَيْهِ فَقَالَ مَا شَأْنُ هَذِهِ قَالُوا مَجْنُونَةُ بَنِي فُلاَنٍ زَنَتْ فَأَمَرَ بِهَا عُمَرُ أَنْ تُرْجَمَ. قَالَ فَقَالَ ارْجِعُوا بِهَا ثُمَّ أَتَاهُ فَقَالَ يَا أَمِيرَ الْمُؤْمِنِينَ أَمَا عَلِمْتَ أَنَّ الْقَلَمَ قَدْ رُفِعَ عَنْ ثَلاَثَةٍ عَنْ

441. When does a child enter adulthood in Islam?

Answer: At the age of 15.

'Abd Allah ibn 'Umar (عَبْد الله بن عُمَر) narrated: "Allah's Messenger called me to present myself in front of him on the eve of the Battle of 'Uhud, when I was fourteen years old at that time, and he did not allow me to take part in that battle. But he called me in front of him on the eve of the Battle of the Trench when I was fifteen years old, and he allowed me [to join the battle]."

Nāfi' Mawlā ibn 'Umar (نافِع مَوْلَى بن عُمَر) said: "I went to 'Umar ibn 'Abd al-'Azīz who was Caliph at that time and related the above narration to him. He said: "This age [fifteen] is the limit between childhood and manhood" – and wrote to his governors to give salaries to those who reached the age of fifteen.[598]

Another criterion (especially for boys) is pubic hair.

Abd al-Malik ibn 'Umayr (عَبْد الْمَلِك بن عُمَيْر) heard 'Atīya al-Qurazī say: "We were presented to the Messenger of Allah on the Day of Qurayza [when the Jewish tribe Banū Qurayza was extinguished by the Muslims]. Those whose pubic hair had grown were killed, and those whose pubic hair had not yet grown were let go. I was one of those whose pubic hair had not yet grown, so I was let go."[599]

For girls, it is the beginning of menstruation. 'Ā'isha (عائِشة بِنْت أَبِي بَكْر) narrated that Allah's Messenger said: "The prayer of a woman who has reached the age of menstruation is not accepted without a Khimār [veil]".[600]

الْمَجْنُونِ حَتَّى يَبْرَأَ وَعَنِ النَّائِمِ حَتَّى يَسْتَيْقِظَ وَعَنِ الصَّبِيِّ حَتَّى يَعْقِلَ قَالَ بَلَى. قَالَ فَمَا بَالُ هَذِهِ تُرْجَمُ قَالَ لَا شَيْءَ. قَالَ فَأَرْسِلْهَا. قَالَ فَجَعَلَ يُكَبِّرُ. Sunan 'Abī Dāwūd 4399 (4385)

598 ...أَنَّ رَسُولَ اللَّهِ عَرَضَهُ يَوْمَ أُحُدٍ وَهُوَ ابْنُ أَرْبَعَ عَشْرَةَ سَنَةً، فَلَمْ يُجِزْنِي، ثُمَّ عَرَضَنِي يَوْمَ الْخَنْدَقِ وَأَنَا ابْنُ خَمْسَ عَشْرَةَ فَأَجَازَنِي. قَالَ نَافِعٌ فَقَدِمْتُ عَلَى عُمَرَ بْنِ عَبْدِ الْعَزِيزِ وَهُوَ خَلِيفَةٌ، فَحَدَّثْتُهُ هَذَا الْحَدِيثَ، فَقَالَ إِنَّ هَذَا لَحَدٌّ بَيْنَ الصَّغِيرِ وَالْكَبِيرِ. وَكَتَبَ إِلَى عُمَّالِهِ أَنْ يَفْرِضُوا لِمَنْ بَلَغَ خَمْسَ عَشْرَةَ. Sahīh al-Bukhārī 2664

599 ...قَالَ سَمِعْتُ عَطِيَّةَ الْقُرَظِيَّ، يَقُولُ عُرِضْنَا عَلَى رَسُولِ اللَّهِ يَوْمَ قُرَيْظَةَ فَكَانَ مَنْ أَنْبَتَ قُتِلَ وَمَنْ لَمْ يُنْبِتْ خُلِّيَ سَبِيلُهُ فَكُنْتُ فِيمَنْ لَمْ يُنْبِتْ فَخُلِّيَ سَبِيلِي. Sunan ibn Māja 2638 (2541)

600 ...قَالَتْ قَالَ رَسُولُ اللَّهِ: "لَا تُقْبَلُ صَلَاةُ الْحَائِضِ إِلَّا بِخِمَارٍ." قَالَ وَفِي الْبَابِ عَنْ عَبْدِ اللَّهِ بْنِ عَمْرٍو. وَقَوْلُهُ: "الْحَائِضُ." يَعْنِي الْمَرْأَةَ الْبَالِغَ يَعْنِي إِذَا حَاضَتْ. Jāmi' al-Tirmidhī 377

442. What is a Fāsiq?

Answer: A Muslim who habitually commits a grave sin, therefore also called: *evildoer.*

Fāsiq (فاسِق), generally speaking, is an Arabic term referring to someone who violates Islamic law. A Fāsiq is considered unreliable, thus, his testimony is not accepted in Islamic courts.

The root f-s-q (ف-س-ق) means *to stray from the right course, to act unlawfully, sinfully, immorally,* and also *to disobey Allah's command.* Fāsiq is the active participle of respective the verb. Thus, a Fāsiq is a *sinner, trespasser, adulterer;* or, in Islamic law, *a person not meeting the legal requirements of righteousness.*

Note: In the late 1970s, when politics became heated in Iran lead-ing up to the 1979 Islamic Revolution, Ayatollah Khomeini (آية الله خمينى) denounced two people by the word Fāsiq: the Shah of Iran and Saddām Husayn (صدّام حُسَيْن).

443. What is the name of the tax which Christians and Jews have to pay in an Islamic State?

Answer: The Jizya (جِزْيَة).

Christian and Jews, who live in an Islamic State and pay a special tax, are called ʾAhl al-Dhimma (أَهْل الذِّمَة) which literally means: pro-tected *or covenanted people.* The justification for this tax is found in sura 9 *The Repentance* – in Arabic: al-Tawba (سُورَة التَّوْبة):

| 9:29 | Fight those of the People of the Book who do not [truly] believe in God and the Last Day, who do not forbid what God and His Messenger have forbidden, who do not obey the rule of justice, until they pay the tax and agree to submit (**while they are humbled**). | قَاتِلُوا الَّذِينَ لَا يُؤْمِنُونَ بِاللَّهِ وَلَا بِالْيَوْمِ الْآخِرِ وَلَا يُحَرِّمُونَ مَا حَرَّمَ اللَّهُ وَرَسُولُهُ وَلَا يَدِينُونَ دِينَ الْحَقِّ مِنَ الَّذِينَ أُوتُوا الْكِتَابَ حَتَّى يُعْطُوا الْجِزْيَةَ عَن يَدٍ وَهُمْ صَاغِرُونَ. |

Before we move on, a remark on the expressions *while they are humbled* in the above verse: Classical commentators generally understood that the Arabic expression "wa hum sāghirūn" (وَهُمْ صَاغِرُونَ) means that *they should be humiliated when paying*.

However, other scholars suggested that the Jews and Christians (as understood from the verse) were unwilling to pay, and the expression simply means that they should be submitted to paying this tax. The word sāghir (صاغِر) literally means *contemptible; dejected*.

The Arabic term Jizya occurs in the Qur'an only once. It basically means *payment in return*. The root j-z-a (ج-ز-ى) denotes to *requite, to recompense; to compensate*.

Therefore, Islamic scholars interpret the meaning of Jizya like an amount of money which is paid to receive the protection by the Islamic State. In return, the Jews and Christians get religious freedom, equal treatment before a judge and protection of their civic rights. Furthermore, it is seen as a monetary compensation for the exemption from military service (Jihād) and from the paying of the Zakā (زَكاة), the religious duty of giving alms. This "unequal distribution of civic burdens" - as Muslims like to call it - is equalled by the Jizya.

The following people do <u>not</u> have to pay the Jizya:
(a) all women, (b) males who have not yet reached full maturity, (c) old men, (d) all sick or crippled men, (e) priests and monks.

How much is the rate of the Jizya? Neither the Prophet, nor the Qur'an gave Muslims specific information about that. However, Islamic scholars have derived the rate from various sources and examples of the first Caliphs:

- Imam Mālik (إمام مالك) related the following story. 'Umar ibn al-Khattāb (عُمَر بن الْخَطّاب) imposed a Jizya tax of four dinars on those living where gold was the currency and forty dirhams on those living where silver was the currency. In addition, they had to provide for the Muslims and host them as guests for three days.[601]
- Notice that there is no differentiation between rich and poor.

---

601 ...أَنَّ عُمَرَ بْنَ الْخَطّابِ، ضَرَبَ الْجِزْيَةَ عَلَى أَهْلِ الذَّهَبِ أَرْبَعَةَ دَنَانِيرَ وَعَلَى أَهْلِ الْوَرِقِ أَرْبَعِينَ دِرْهَمًا مَعَ ذَلِكَ أَرْزَاقُ الْمُسْلِمِينَ وَضِيَافَةُ ثَلاَثَةِ أَيَّامٍ. Muwatta' Mālik 620

- 1 dirham = 2.975 grams of silver. In the year 2016, 40 dirhams would be worth 76 US$.

- Others have calculated that the wealthy man should pay forty-eight dirhams per year, the average man should pay twenty-four dirhams, and that the poor man who is able to work should pay twelve dirhams.

- Other Scholars concluded that it should be considerably lower than the Zakā (زَكاة) which Muslims are obliged to pay.

Note: Although most Muslims say that the Jizya is only applied to the People of the Book (Jews and Christians), the Prophet himself did not stick to this rule:

The Prophet accepted the tax for non-Muslims - Jizya (جِزْية) - also from the Zoroastrians of Hajar. Bajāla al-Tamīmī (بَجالة التَّميمي) narrated that 'Umar would not take the Jizya from the Zoroastrians until 'Abd al-Rahmān ibn 'Awf (عَبْد الرَّحْمَن بن عَوْف) informed him that the Prophet took the Jizya from the Zoroastrians of Hajar.[602]

444. What are the six crimes against Allah?

Answer: Adultery, making unproven accusation of illicit sex, apostasy, consuming intoxicants, highway (main road) robbery (against travellers) and theft.

The Islamic law knows two major kinds of offences: those against Allah and those against humans. Offences against Allah violate Allah's *boundaries*. This is also the reason why they are called Hudūd (حُدُود), as its singular form Hadd (حَدّ) in Arabic means *the end, limit, restriction,* or *boundary.*

The Hadd or Hudūd punishments should protect the limits which Allah has forbidden Muslims to transgress. Practically speaking, in Islamic law, Hudūd denotes all *legal punishments* which were told and specified explicitly in the Qur'an (or Hadiths). Therefore, the

---

602 ...أَنَّ عُمَرَ، كَانَ لاَ يَأْخُذُ الْجِزْيَةَ مِنَ الْمَجُوسِ حَتَّى أَخْبَرَهُ عَبْدُ الرَّحْمَنِ بْنُ عَوْفٍ أَنَّ النَّبِيَّ أَخَذَ الْجِزْيَةَ مِنْ مَجُوسِ هَجَرَ. Jāmi' al-Tirmidhī 1587.

Hudūd crimes are special in the way that the punishments are mandated and fixed by Allah. Let's look at the six types:

	offence	Arabic	punishment
1	Adultery/illicit sexual relations	الزِّنَاء or اللِّوَاط	Death by stoning or one hundred lashes.
2	Making unproven accusations of illicit sex and failing to present four male Muslim eyewitnesses	القَذْف	Eighty lashes.
3	Consuming intoxicants, for example alcohol	شُرْب الْخَمْر	Eighty lashes. Some say: giving more than forty lashes is left to the decision of the Muslim leader. Liberal scholars do not consider it a Hadd crime.
4	Apostasy	الرِّدة	Death by crucifixion or banishment. Scholars' opinions vary on this crime.
5	Highway robbery	الْجِرابة or قَطْعُ الطَّريق	With homicide: death by crucifixion. Without homicide: amputation of feet.
6	Robbery and theft	السَّرِقة	Amputation of hands. The hand should be cut off from the wrist joint.

Notice that even a minor incident may lead to the severest punishment. 'Abū Hurayra (أَبُو هُرَيْرَة) narrated that the Prophet said: "Allah curses the thief who steals an egg [or a helmet] for which his hand is to be cut off, or steals a rope, for which his hand is to be cut off."[603]

---

603 ...قَالَ رَسُولُ اللَّهِ: "لَعَنَ اللَّهُ السَّارِقَ، يَسرِقُ الْبَيْضَةَ فَتُقْطَعُ يَدُهُ، وَيَسرِقُ الْحَبْلَ فَتُقْطَعُ يَدُهُ."
Sahīh al-Bukhārī 6799

'Ā'isha (عائشة بِنْت أَبِي بَكْر) narrated that the hand of a thief was not cut off during the lifetime of the Prophet except when stealing something equal to a shield in value.[604]

How much was the value of a shield? 'Abd Allah ibn 'Umar (عَبْد الله بن عُمَر) narrated that Allah's Messenger cut off the hand of a thief for stealing a shield that was worth three dirhams.[605]

Three dirhams then equals around US$ 5.80 today (1 dirham = 2.975 grams of silver) But note that although very traditional scholars would certainly use this amount for their judgement, we should bear in mind that the relative value of silver was probably rather different at the time of Muhammad.

Nevertheless, there is no further information in the Islamic sources. We don't know anything about the purchasing power parity, but consider the following comparison: Around thirty years after Muhammad's, Caliph Mu'āwiya I imposed a tax on non-Muslims, and they had to pay 40 dirhams (perhaps per year).

By the way, the Prophet cut off hands himself. 'Ā'isha narrated: "The Prophet cut off the hand of a lady and that lady used to come to me, and I used to convey her message to the Prophet and she repented, and her repentance was sincere."[606]

Note: Hudūd offences are overturned by the slightest of doubts, and for this reason, such punishments were relatively rarely applied throughout the history of Islam.

Such crimes cannot be pardoned by the victim or by the state, and the punishments must be carried out in public.

Most of the Hudūd punishments were issued to protect the Muslim community at the very beginning of Islam. This becomes evident in the severe penalty for highway robbery in order to protect the wealth of the travelling Muslims.

---

604 ...أَنَّ يَدَ السَّارِقِ، لَمْ تُقْطَعْ عَلَى عَهْدِ النَّبِيِّ إلاَّ فِي ثَمَنِ مِجَنٍّ حَجَفَةٍ أَوْ تُرْسٍ. Sahīh al-Bukhārī 6792

605 ...أَنَّ رَسُولَ اللَّهِ قَطَعَ فِي مِجَنٍّ ثَمَنُهُ ثَلاَثَةُ دَرَاهِمَ. Sahīh al-Bukhārī 6795.

606 ...أَنَّ النَّبِيَّ قَطَعَ يَدَ امْرَأَةٍ. قَالَتْ عَائِشَةُ وَكَانَتْ تَأْتِي بَعْدَ ذَلِكَ، فَأَرْفَعُ حَاجَتَهَا إِلَى النَّبِيِّ فَتَابَتْ وَحَسُنَتْ تَوْبَتُهَا. Sahīh al-Bukhārī 6800.

Hudūd punishments are not the only form of punishments in Islamic jurisprudence. There are two others:

- Qisās (قصاص) – retaliation as a punishment; used for private disputes between parties.
- Ta'zīr (تَعْزِير) – the punishment is left to an Islamic judge's discretion.

Note that these crimes are different from the *seven deadly sins* (seven capital vices or cardinal sins) in Christianity, which are hubris, greed, lust, malicious envy, gluttony, inordinate anger, and sloth.

445. Does a murderer in Islam receive the death penalty?

Answer: It depends.

Murder is <u>not</u> among the so-called Hudūd (حُدُود) crimes. They fall into another category of Islamic punishments. Murder (as opposed to **murder during highway robbery**) is treated as a private dispute between the murderer and the victim's heirs.

The heirs of the victim may be granted:

- the right to forgive the murderer
- demand compensation
- demand the death of the murderer

This form of Islamic punishment is called: Qisās (قصاص). Qisās is an Islamic term meaning *retaliation in kind* or *revenge*, "*eye for an eye*", or *retributive justice*. Qisās is an ancient word which originally meant *to track down*; but also *making a thing equal (to another thing)*. Qisās in an old, classical meaning also denoted *tracking the footsteps of an enemy*.

It is a category of crimes in Islamic jurisprudence in which the Laws of Sharī'a allow equal retaliation for punishment. Qisās is applied **when a Muslim is murdered, suffers bodily injury, or suffers property damage**.

In the case of murder, Qiṣāṣ means the right of a victim's nearest relative or legal guardian to take the life of the killer, provided that the court approves. This principle was revealed in sura 2 *The Cow* – in Arabic: al-Baqara (الْبَقَرة):

| 2:178 | You who believe, fair retribution is pre-scribed for you in cases of murder: the free man for the free man, the slave for the slave, the female for the female. But if the culprit is pardoned by his aggrieved brother, this shall be adhered to fairly, and the culprit shall pay what is due in a good way. This is an alleviation from your Lord and an act of mercy. If anyone then exceeds these limits, grievous suffering awaits him. | يَا أَيُّهَا الَّذِينَ آمَنُوا كُتِبَ عَلَيْكُمُ الْقِصَاصُ فِي الْقَتْلَى الْحُرُّ بِالْحُرِّ وَالْعَبْدُ بِالْعَبْدِ وَالْأُنثَى بِالْأُنثَى فَمَنْ عُفِيَ لَهُ مِنْ أَخِيهِ شَيْءٌ فَاتِّبَاعٌ بِالْمَعْرُوفِ وَأَدَاءٌ إِلَيْهِ بِإِحْسَانٍ ذَلِكَ تَخْفِيفٌ مِّن رَّبِّكُمْ وَرَحْمَةٌ فَمَنِ اعْتَدَى بَعْدَ ذَلِكَ فَلَهُ عَذَابٌ أَلِيمٌ. |

In his exegesis, Abdel Haleem remarked on this verse that "before Islam, the Arabs did not observe equality in retribution, but a stronger tribe would demand more, e.g. a man for a woman, a free man for a slave, or several men for one man, likewise for financial compensation. The intention of this verse is to insist on equality."

446. In which cases is the death penalty allowed in Islam?

Answer: At least in three cases: apostasy, murder, and adultery.

ʿAbd Allah ibn Masʿūd (عَبْد الله بن مَسْعُود) reported that the Messenger of Allah said: "It is not permissible to spill the blood of a Muslim except in three [instances]: the married person who commits adultery, a life for a life [i.e. a murderer], and the one who forsakes his religion and separates from the community."[607]

---

607 ...قَالَ رَسُولُ اللَّهِ: "لاَ يَحِلُّ دَمُ امْرِئٍ مُسْلِمٍ يَشْهَدُ أَنْ لاَ إِلَهَ إِلاَّ اللَّهُ وَأَنِّي رَسُولُ اللَّهِ إِلاَّ بِإِحْدَى ثَلاَثٍ الثَّيِّبُ الزَّانِي وَالنَّفْسُ بِالنَّفْسِ وَالتَّارِكُ لِدِينِهِ الْمُفَارِقُ لِلْجَمَاعَةِ." Sahīh Muslim 1676

447. What is the punishment for apostasy?

Answer: The apostate has to be killed (according to the Prophet).

Let's start with the term *apostate*. In Arabic, an apostate is called Murtadd (مُرْتَدّ). Islam is very easy to join, because there are no special rituals demanding weeks or months of preparation; you don't need to prove any blood line; you don't need to organise a priest who baptises you, etc.

You basically just have to say the profession of faith, the so-called Shahāda (شهادة). However, at the same time, Islam does not provide a way out. Actually, it is merely impossible to leave this religion.

But what happens if a Muslim still wants to leave Islam to become an apostate? Let's look at the Islamic sources.

First of all the Qur'an does not say anything about the punishment in this life and basically hands it over to the hereafter which is indicated in sura 16 *The Bee* – in Arabic: al-Nahl (سُورَة النَّحْل):

16:106	With the exception of those who are forced to say they do not believe, although their hearts remain firm in faith, those who reject God after believing in Him and open their hearts to disbelief will have the wrath of God upon them and a grievous punishment awaiting them.	مَن كَفَرَ بِاللَّهِ مِن بَعْدِ إِيمَانِهِ إِلَّا مَنْ أُكْرِهَ وَقَلْبُهُ مُطْمَئِنٌّ بِالْإِيمَانِ وَلَٰكِن مَّن شَرَحَ بِالْكُفْرِ صَدْرًا فَعَلَيْهِمْ غَضَبٌ مِّنَ اللَّهِ وَلَهُمْ عَذَابٌ عَظِيمٌ.

Sura 2 *The Cow* - in Arabic: al-Baqara (سُورَة الْبَقَرَة) - even says that there is no compulsion in religion. This sentence is usually quoted by Muslims when defending Islam against accusations of not accepting other religions.

2:256	There is no compulsion in religion: true guidance has become distinct from error, so whoever rejects false gods and believes in God has grasped the firmest hand-hold, one that will never break. God is all hearing and all knowing.	لَا إِكْرَاهَ فِي الدِّينِ قَد تَّبَيَّنَ الرُّشْدُ مِنَ الْغَيِّ فَمَن يَكْفُرْ بِالطَّاغُوتِ وَيُؤْمِن بِاللَّهِ فَقَدِ اسْتَمْسَكَ بِالْعُرْوَةِ الْوُثْقَىٰ لَا انفِصَامَ لَهَا وَاللَّهُ سَمِيعٌ عَلِيمٌ.

This is one of the **most discussed and debated verses in the Qur'an**. What do Muslims and non-Muslims make out of this verse? Classical scholars have suggested that this verse only talks about people from whom the tax called Jizya may be taken, which means that nobody has to become Muslim, as long as they pay. Others suggested that this verse was only true in the beginning of Islam because it was gradually abrogated by other commands of Allah, for example by the *sword verse* and by several traditions of the Prophet.

The classical commentator Ibn Kathīr (ابن كَثِير) suggested that this verse shows that a Muslim doesn't need force to make people converting to Islam. They will do it anyway because the teachings of Islam are so clear and self-evident. Ibn Kathīr stated: "Do not force anyone to become Muslim, for Islam is plain and clear, and its proofs and evidence are plain and clear. Therefore, there is no need to force anyone to embrace Islam. Rather, whoever Allah directs to Islam, opens his heart for it and enlightens his mind, and will embrace Islam with certainty. Whoever Allah blinds his heart and seals his hearing and sight, then he will not benefit from being forced to embrace Islam."[608]

Ibn Kathīr gives an explanation on which occasion this verse might have been revealed. In a Hadith (Sunan ʾAbī Dāwūd 2676), ʿAbd Allah ibn ʿAbbās (عَبْد الله بن عَبَّاس) indicated that the ʾAnsār in Medina were the reason behind revealing this verse. Prior to Islam, when a Jewish woman could not bear children who would live, she would vow that if she gives birth to a child [boy] who remains alive, she would raise him as a Jew. When the Jewish tribe Banū al-Nadīr was expelled from Medina, some of the children of the ʾAnsār were being raised among them and the ʾAnsār said: "We will not abandon our children." After this, Allah revealed the verse.[609]

Modern scholars, for example Muhammad Asad, use this verse to show that Islam does indeed accept other religions. Muhammad

---

608 ...أي لَا تُكْرِهُوا أَحَدًا عَلَى الدُّخُولِ فِي دِينِ الْإِسْلَامِ فَإِنَّهُ بَيِّنٌ وَاضِحٌ جَلِيٌّ دَلَائِلُهُ وَبَرَاهِينُهُ لَا يَحْتَاجُ إِلَى أَنْ يُكْرَهَ أَحَدٌ عَلَى الدُّخُولِ فِيهِ، بَلْ مَنْ هَدَاهُ اللَّهُ لِلْإِسْلَامِ وَشَرَحَ صَدْرَهُ وَنَوَّرَ بَصِيرَتَهُ دَخَلَ فِيهِ عَلَى بَيِّنَةٍ، وَمَنْ أَعْمَى اللَّهُ قَلْبَهُ وَخَتَمَ عَلَى سَمْعِهِ وَبَصَرِهِ فَإِنَّهُ لَا يُفِيدُهُ الدُّخُولُ فِي الدِّينِ مُكْرَهًا مَقْسُورًا.

Tafsīr Ibn Kathīr

609 ... ابن عبّاس قال: انَتِ الْمَرْأَةُ تَكُونُ مِقْلَاتًا فَتَجْعَلُ عَلَى نَفْسِهَا إِنْ عَاشَ لَهَا وَلَدٌ أَنْ تُهَوِّدَهُ، فَلَمَّا أُجْلِيَتْ بَنُو النَّضِيرِ كَانَ فِيهِمْ مِنْ أَبْنَاءِ الْأَنْصَارِ فَقَالُوا لَا نَدَعُ أَبْنَاءَنَا فَأَنْزَلَ اللَّهُ عَزَّ وَجَلَّ { لَا إِكْرَاهَ فِي الدِّينِ قَدْ تَبَيَّنَ الرُّشْدُ مِنَ الْغَيِّ }. Tafsīr Ibn Kathīr

Asad stated: "That forcible conversion is under all circumstances null and void, and that any attempt at coercing a non-believer [non-Muslim] to accept the faith of Islam is a grievous sin: a verdict which disposes of the widespread fallacy that Islam places before the unbelievers the alternative of 'conversion or the sword'."

In general the Qur'an condemns people who don't believe in Islam, but regarding their punishment on earth, it is very vague. However, there are several Hadiths that contain further advice for Muslims. There are more than a dozen authentic Hadiths reporting that the Messenger of Allah commanded that apostates should be executed. For example: 'Abd Allah ibn 'Abbās narrated that the Messenger of Allah said: "Whoever changes his religion, kill him."[610]

'Abū Hurayra (أَبُو هُرَيْرَة) narrated that Allah's Apostle said: "I have been commanded to fight the people until they say 'Lā Ilāha illAllāh' [There is no god but Allah], and whoever says it, his life and his wealth are safe from me; except for a right that is due, and his reckoning will be with Allah."[611]

If a Muslim apostatises and meets the conditions of apostasy - namely when he is of sound mind, an adult, and does it of his own free will - then his blood may be shed by other Muslims. He or she is to be executed by the Islamic ruler or by his deputy – for example by an Islamic judge. The body of the deceased must not be washed, the funeral prayer is not to be offered, and he must not to be buried with other Muslims.

However, some Muslims apply the command to kill apostates also to other people (non-Muslims). In fact, the sources are not really clear and do not always distinguish between a Muslim who has left Islam and a non-Muslim who does not want to convert to Islam.

'Ikrima Mawlā ibn 'Abbās (عِكْرِمة مَوْلَى بن عَبّاس) narrated that some Zanādiqa were brought to 'Alī, and that he burnt them. The news of this event reached 'Abd Allah ibn 'Abbās who said: "If I had been in his place, I would not have burnt them because Allah's Messenger forbade it, saying: 'Do not punish anybody with Allah's punishment

---

610 ...قَالَ رَسُولُ اللَّهِ: "مَنْ بَدَّلَ دِينَهُ فَاقْتُلُوهُ." Sunan al-Nasā'ī 4059

611 ...أَنَّ رَسُولَ اللَّهِ قَالَ: "أُمِرْتُ أَنْ أُقَاتِلَ النَّاسَ حَتَّى يَقُولُوا لاَ إِلَهَ إِلاَّ اللَّهُ فَمَنْ قَالَهَا فَقَدْ عَصَمَ مِنِّي نَفْسَهُ وَمَالَهُ إِلاَّ بِحَقِّهِ وَحِسَابُهُ عَلَى اللَّهِ." Sahīh al-Bukhārī 2946

[= fire].' I would have killed them according to the statement of Allah's Messenger: 'Whoever changed his Islamic religion, kill him.'"[612]

A remark on the term Zanādiqa (زَنادِقة):

This is the plural of Zindīq (زِنْدِيق) which means *unbeliever, free-thinker, atheist*. The term Zandaqa (زَنْدَقة) in general denotes *atheism*.

In ancient times, the word was used to denote a person who asserts his belief in the two principles of Light and Darkness; or one who does not believe in the world to come, nor in the unity of the Creator. The word is originally Persian, from al-Zand (الزَّنْد), i.e. the book of Zoroaster. Zoroaster was also known as Zarathustra who was the founder of Zoroastrianism – the most common religion of Persia from 600 BC until the Islamic conquest.

There are several hypotheses about the origin of the word Zanādiqa . Some say that it is related to the Zand (زَنْد) - which means *explanation* – i.e. the explanation of the book of Zarádusht or Zoroaster the Persian. An Arab of the desert, according to Edward Lane, is said to have explained it as meaning one who looks much into things or affairs – which is the reason why the term Zindiq can also mean *freethinker*.

Another term for atheist is Mulhid (مُلْحِد) which is a person who has deviated from the "right religion" [as seen by Muslims]; or an impugner of religions, one who does not hold any religion and who asserts his belief in the endlessness of time.

The thing about being Muslim and not being able to leave the religion is especially difficult for people who have a Muslim father, but were raised in the West and are not interested in Islam.

They don't consider themselves Muslims. They will be re-invited to return to Islam and if they refuse, theoretically, they have to be killed. Nowadays only very few Islamic countries apply these strict laws. Many Islamic scholars consider apostasy as one of the Hudūd crimes, as one of the major crimes against Allah. Under traditional Islamic law, an apostate may be given a waiting period while in con-

---

612 ...قَالَ أُتِيَ عَلِيٌّ بِزَنَادِقَةٍ فَأَحْرَقَهُمْ فَبَلَغَ ذَلِكَ ابْنَ عَبَّاسٍ فَقَالَ لَوْ كُنْتُ أَنَا لَمْ أُحْرِقْهُمْ لِنَهْيِ رَسُولِ اللَّهِ وَلَقَتَلْتُهُمْ لِقَوْلِ رَسُولِ اللَّهِ: "مَنْ بَدَّلَ دِينَهُ فَاقْتُلُوهُ." Sahīh al-Bukhārī 6922

finement to repent and return to Islam. If the apostate rejects, he or she is to be killed without any reservations. Let's now look at the different approaches of the Islamic schools of jurisprudence:

- Hanafi (حَنَفِيّ): Three days of imprisonment to allow the Muslim apostate to repent although the delay before killing the Muslim apostate is not mandatory. Male apostates must be killed if they reject the offer. Female apostates have to be kept in a solitary confinement and beaten (lashes) every three days until they repent, renounce and return to Islam – or die in custody.

- Māliki (مالِكِيّ): Apostates are given up to ten days for repentance; after that the apostate must be killed. Both men and women apostates should be executed.

- Shāfi'ī (شافِعِيّ): Apostates have three days to repent and return to Islam. After that, the execution is recommended (for both genders).

- Hanbalī (حَنْبَلِيّ). A waiting period may be granted, but it is not necessary before the execution of an apostate (male or female).

- Ja'farī (جَعْفَرِيّ). A waiting period is not necessary, but may be granted according to this Shia school of jurisprudence. Male apostates must be executed. A female apostate must be kept in solitary confinement until she repents and returns to Islam. This is very similar to the Hanafi School.

The main problem, however, is the question about who is eligible to be punished.

The Sharī'a, as most Muslims agree, can only be applied to people who are Muslims. And even being a Muslim has some nuances. At the beginning of the Islamic jurisprudence, it was differentiated if somebody was born Muslim. Then, he or she had to be killed immediately without trying to change opinion or forcing his reconversion. However, the convert, before being executed, was asked for repentance.

Remark: If a Muslim insults Muhammad (سَبّ), it is considered apostasy (رِدّة).

This is also true for other actions, for example if a Muslim declares forbidden things such as alcohol or sex before marriage as permissible – halāl (حلال). Theoretically, as traditional scholars claim, he could be given a death sentence. This logic could even be applied if a Muslim does not pray on purpose – this could be considered as apostasy too.

In Iran, Muslims who change their religion receive a lifetime imprisonment, in rare cases the death penalty. In Libya, under the dictatorship of Muammar Gaddafi, apostasy was punished by withdrawing the apostate's citizenship.

In Sudan, apostasy is punishable by death. In May 2014 a heavily pregnant young Sudanese woman had been sentenced to death by a court in Khartoum for renouncing Islam and marrying a Christian man. She was given three days to convert, but refused. After international protests she was released and took refuge in the US embassy in Sudan. Later, she was allowed to board a plane to Italy.

448. What happens if a person insults Islam (blasphemy)?

Answer: Similar to apostasy the person will receive the death penalty.

First of all, the Qur'an does not explicitly mention any worldly punishment for blasphemy which in Arabic is called sabb (سَبّ). The traditions of the Prophet indicate that people (Muslims and non-Muslims) who insulted Muhammad were killed.

Jābir ibn 'Abd Allah (جابِر بن عَبْد الله) narrated that Allah's Messenger said: "Who is willing to kill Ka'b ibn al-'Ashraf who has hurt Allah and His Apostle?" Thereupon Muhammad ibn Maslama got up and said: "O Allah's Messenger! Would you like that I kill him?" The Prophet replied: "Yes."[613]

'Abd Allah ibn 'Abbās (عَبْد الله بن عبّاس) narrated: "A blind man had a slave-mother who used to abuse the Prophet and disparage him. He forbade her, but she did not stop. He rebuked her, but she did not give up her habit. One night she [again] began to slander and abuse the Prophet. So he took a dagger, placed it on her belly, pushed it,

---

613 ...قَالَ رَسُولُ اللَّهِ: "مَنْ لِكَعْبِ بْنِ الأَشْرَفِ فَإِنَّهُ قَدْ آذَى اللَّهَ وَرَسُولَهُ." فَقَامَ مُحَمَّدُ بْنُ مَسْلَمَةَ فَقَالَ يَا رَسُولَ اللَّهِ أَتُحِبُّ أَنْ أَقْتُلَهُ قَالَ: "نَعَمْ." Sahīh al-Bukhārī 4037

and killed her. A child who came between her legs became smeared with the blood that was there.

When the morning came, the Prophet was informed about it. He assembled the people and proclaimed: 'I adjure by Allah the man who has done this action and I adjure him by my right to him that he should stand up.' Jumping over the necks of the people and trembling, the man stood up. He sat before the Prophet and said: 'Messenger of Allah! I am her master. She used to abuse you and disparage you. I forbade her, but she did not stop and I rebuked her, but she did not abandon her habit. I have two sons like pearls from her, and she was my companion. Last night, she began to abuse and disparage you. So I took a dagger, put it on her belly and pushed it until I killed her.' Thereupon the Prophet said: 'Oh be witness, no retaliation is payable for her blood.'"[614] This Hadith shows that Muhammad did not imprison the man for killing the mother of his two children.

However, there is also an authentic Hadith which says that people who insult the Prophet will be punished in Hell. 'Alī ibn 'Abī Tālib (عَلِيّ بن أَبِي طالِب) narrated that the Prophet said: "Do not tell a lie against me for whoever tells a lie against me [intentionally], then he will surely enter the Hell-fire."[615]

Based on the Hadiths Islamic jurists derived the Islamic law that if someone abuses or insults the Prophet, it is considered a serious crime that could be punished by the death penalty.

In Islam, this transgression is called: Sabb al-Nabī (سَبّ النَّبِيّ). This also means that if someone insults the Prophet, the Muslim community is obliged to avenge the insult because after Muhammad's death, the possibility of forgiveness has disappeared. Let's now look

---

614 ...أَنَّ أَعْمَى، كَانَتْ لَهُ أُمُّ وَلَدٍ تَشْتُمُ النَّبِيَّ وَتَقَعُ فِيهِ فَيَنْهَاهَا فَلَا تَنْتَهِي وَيَزْجُرُهَا فَلَا تَنْزَجِرُ - قَالَ - فَلَمَّا كَانَتْ ذَاتَ لَيْلَةٍ جَعَلَتْ تَقَعُ فِي النَّبِيِّ وَتَشْتِمُهُ فَأَخَذَ الْمِغْوَلَ فَوَضَعَهُ فِي بَطْنِهَا وَاتَّكَأَ عَلَيْهَا فَقَتَلَهَا فَوَقَعَ بَيْنَ رِجْلَيْهَا طِفْلٌ فَلَطَخَتْ مَا هُنَاكَ بِالدَّمِ فَلَمَّا أَصْبَحَ ذُكِرَ ذَلِكَ لِرَسُولِ اللَّهِ فَجَمَعَ النَّاسَ فَقَالَ: "أَنْشُدُ اللَّهَ رَجُلاً فَعَلَ مَا فَعَلَ لِي عَلَيْهِ حَقٌّ إلاَّ قَامَ." فَقَامَ الأَعْمَى يَتَخَطَّى النَّاسَ وَهُوَ يَتَزَلْزَلُ حَتَّى قَعَدَ بَيْنَ يَدَىِ النَّبِيِّ فَقَالَ يَا رَسُولَ اللَّهِ أَنَا صَاحِبُهَا كَانَتْ تَشْتِمُكَ وَتَقَعُ فِيكَ فَأَنْهَاهَا فَلَا تَنْتَهِي وَأَزْجُرُهَا فَلَا تَنْزَجِرُ وَلِي مِنْهَا ابْنَانِ مِثْلُ اللُّؤْلُؤَتَيْنِ وَكَانَتْ بِي رَفِيقَةً فَلَمَّا كَانَتِ الْبَارِحَةَ جَعَلَتْ تَشْتِمُكَ وَتَقَعُ فِيكَ فَأَخَذْتُ الْمِغْوَلَ فَوَضَعْتُهُ فِي بَطْنِهَا وَاتَّكَأْتُ عَلَيْهَا حَتَّى قَتَلْتُهَا. فَقَالَ النَّبِيُّ: "أَلاَ اشْهَدُوا أَنَّ دَمَهَا هَدَرٌ". Sunan 'Abī Dāwūd 4361

615 ...قَالَ النَّبِيُّ: "لاَ تَكْذِبُوا عَلَىَّ، فَإِنَّهُ مَنْ كَذَبَ عَلَىَّ فَلْيَلِجِ النَّارَ." Sahīh al-Bukhārī 106

at the Sunni and Shia schools of jurisprudence and their treatment of blasphemy:

- Hanafī (حَنَفِيّ): This Sunni school views blasphemy as synonymous with apostasy. The blasphemer can show repentance. A man who refuses to repent, receives the death penalty. A woman must be imprisoned and beaten until she repents. If a non-Muslim living in an Islamic State commits blasphemy, his punishment is up to the judge. It varies from a discretionary to an arrest, caning, or to a death sentence.

- Mālikī (مالِكِيّ): This Sunni school sees in blasphemy an even more serious offence than apostasy, though the punishments are similar. Men are sentenced to death; women are arrested and beaten until they repent or die in custody. A non-Muslim who commits blasphemy against Islam must be punished; however, the blasphemer can escape punishment by converting to Islam.

- Hanbalī (حَنْبَلِيّ): This Sunni school shares the view that blasphemy is an offence more severe than apostasy. Death is mandatory for men and women; repentance is not accepted.

- Shāfiʿī (شافِعِيّ): This Sunni school recognises blasphemy as a separate offence from apostasy but accepts the repentance of the blasphemer (man or woman). If the blasphemer rejects the offer, he or she must be executed.

- Jaʿfarī (جَعْفَرِيّ): This Shia school says that blasphemy is punishable by death. If the blasphemer is a non-Muslim, he is given an invitation to convert to Islam. If he rejects, he has to be killed.

In 2005, the Danish newspaper Jyllands-Posten published some cartoons most of which depicted Muhammad. It caused an outrage in several Islamic countries. If a Muslim had done it, it would have been clear. But can Muslims punish a non-Muslim? Well, it mainly depends on if the non-Muslim lives in an Islamic State or not.

A non-Muslim, who lives **inside an Islamic State** under the treaty with the Muslims, is called a Dhimmī (ذِمِّيّ). These non-Muslims (mainly Christians and Jews) have to pay a tax, the so-called Jizya

(جِزْية) which is part of the treaty. A Dhimmī is secure for his property – and his blood.

In medieval Islamic societies the Islamic judge usually could not interfere in the matters of non-Muslims unless the parties voluntarily chose to be judged according to Islamic laws. This shows that the Dhimmī communities in an Islamic State usually had their own laws and did not apply the Laws of Sharī'a. The Jews even had their own rabbinical courts, but these courts did not deal with cases involving other religious groups or capital offences such as blasphemy.

If a Dhimmī insults Muhammad, it is considered a violation of the treaty which means that he must be executed, but also that it should be left to the Islamic authorities and not to the Muslims on the street.

If the non-Muslim lives in a **non-Islamic state**, let's say in Europe, the situation is different. The Laws of Sharī'a do not apply to non-Muslims. There is no Islamic authority to punish the non-Muslim, and there is no Islamic judge who can pronounce the verdict which is a must in Islam in order to apply Sharī'a Law.

So what can a Muslim do if he hears a Christian or anyone else in a non-Islamic country defame and insult the Prophet? The majority of scholars say that the Muslim has to denounce the person in strong terms. It is also permissible to insult such person.

449. What is al-Ta'zīr?

Answer: Ta'zīr (التَّعْزِير) refers to offences mentioned in the Qur'an or in the Hadiths. However, neither the Qur'an nor the Hadiths specify a punishment for these crimes.

Instead, the form of punishment is up to the Islamic ruler or a judge on behalf of the ruler. Usually these offences were committed by an individual who violated the behaviour prescribed in the Qur'an and the Hadiths.

Punishments vary with the nature of the crime and include prison, whipping, a (monetary) fine, banishment, and seizure of property.

Execution is allowed too, for example for habitual homosexuality or espionage on behalf of an enemy of the Islamic state.

450. How does a Muslim call a religious duty?

Answer: A duty in Islam is called Fard (فَرْض).

The duties of Muslims are divided into two groups:

- The **individual obligation,** so-called Fard al-ʿAyn (فَرْض الْعَيْن). Every Muslim must perform such duties. For example prayer, charity, fasting, and pilgrimage.

- The **communal obligation,** so-called Fard al-Kifāya (فَرْض كفاية). If a sufficient number of people of the Islamic community do it, the rest won't have to, for example Jihād.

451. How many prayers per day should a Muslim perform?

Answer: Five.

In Islam, the rules for praying are derived from several verses of the Qur'an as well as from several Hadiths.

First of all, praying is essential in Islam. In sura 4 *Women* - in Arabic: al-Nisā' (سُورة النّساء) - it is told:

| 4:103 | After performing the ritual prayer, continue to remember God - standing, sitting, and lying on your sides - and once you are safe, keep up regular prayer, for prayer is obligatory for the believers at prescribed times. | فَإِذَا قَضَيْتُمُ الصَّلَاةَ فَاذْكُرُوا اللَّهَ قِيَامًا وَقُعُودًا وَعَلَىٰ جُنُوبِكُمْ فَإِذَا اطْمَأْنَنتُمْ فَأَقِيمُوا الصَّلَاةَ إِنَّ الصَّلَاةَ كَانَتْ عَلَى الْمُؤْمِنِينَ كِتَابًا مَّوْقُوتًا. |

Praying is so essential in Islam that when I lived in Egypt, I felt like people have nothing else to do but pray. Muslims in the Arab World don't have a problem praying in public but such is rarely seen in Western countries. Taxi drivers in Egypt would stop their cars, get their little carpets (prayer mat) and just pray beside the car. On Fridays, streets are filled with carpets in most Muslim countries.

It is narrated on the authority of ʾAbū al-Zubayr (أَبُو الزُّبَيْرِ) that he heard Jābir ibn ʿAbd Allah (جابِر بن عَبْد الله) say: "I heard the Messenger of Allah observing this: 'Between man and polytheism and unbelief is the abandonment of prayer.'"[616]

Sura 30 *The Byzantines* - in Arabic: al-Rūm (سُورة الرُّوم) - tells more about the prayer times.

30:17	So celebrate God's glory in the evening, in the morning -	فَسُبْحَانَ اللَّهِ حِينَ تُمْسُونَ وَحِينَ تُصْبِحُونَ
30:18	praise is due to Him in the heavens and the earth - in the late afternoon, and at midday.	وَلَهُ الْحَمْدُ فِي السَّمَاوَاتِ وَالأَرْضِ وَعَشِيًّا وَحِينَ تُظْهِرُونَ.

The verb which is used in sura 30:17 - tumsūna (تُمْسُونَ) - means to spend the evening and indicates the prayer after sunset - so-called al-Maghrib (صلاة الْمَغْرِب) as well as that after nightfall – al-ʿIshāʾ (صَلاة الْعِشاء). Some commentators noticed that this verse only mentions four of the prayers and claim that the nightfall-prayer is not included. In sura 11 Hūd (سُورة هُود), there is more information about that last prayer:

11:114	[Prophet], keep up the prayer at both ends of the day, and during parts of the night, for good things drive bad away - this is a reminder for those who are aware.	وَأَقِمِ الصَّلَاةَ طَرَفَيِ النَّهَارِ وَزُلَفًا مِّنَ اللَّيْلِ إِنَّ الْحَسَنَاتِ يُذْهِبْنَ السَّيِّئَاتِ ذَلِكَ ذِكْرَىٰ لِلذَّاكِرِينَ.

The time for the respective prayers was fixed in several Hadiths. ʿAbd Allah ibn ʿAmr ibn al-ʿĀs (عَبْد الله بن عَمْرو بن الْعاص) reported that the Messenger of Allah was asked about the prayer times. The Prophet said: "The time for the morning prayer [lasts] as long as the first visible part of the rising sun does not appear. The time of the noon prayer is when the sun declines from the zenith and there is

---

616 ...يَقُولُ سَمِعْتُ رَسُولَ اللَّهِ يَقُولُ: "بَيْنَ الرَّجُلِ وَبَيْنَ الشِّرْكِ وَالْكُفْرِ تَرْكُ الصَّلاةِ." Sahīh Muslim 82

not a time for the afternoon prayer. The time for the afternoon prayer is so long as the sun does not become pale and its first visible part does not set. The time for the evening prayer is that when the sun disappears and [it lasts] until the twilight is no more. The time for the night prayer is up to midnight."[617]

In short:

1. At dawn – al-Fajr (الْفَجْر)
2. Shortly after mid-day – al-Zuhr (الظُّهْر)
3. In the afternoon – al-ʿAsr (الْعَصْر)
4. Immediately after sunset – al-Maghrib (الْمَغْرِب)
5. In the first part of the night – al-ʿIshāʾ (الْعِشَاء)

ʾAbū Hurayra (أَبُو هُرَيْرَة) narrated that the Prophet had said: "No prayer is heavier upon the hypocrites than the al-Fajr and the al-ʿIshāʾ prayers, and if they knew what is in them [in reward], they would have attended them, even crawling."[618]

Note: The Imam and the Muslim who is praying with (behind) him should recite the second prayer (al-Zuhr) and the third (al-ʿAsr) silently.

452. What is the sign indicating the timing of the noon prayer?

Answer: When a man's shadow has the same length as his height.

The Salā(t) al-Zuhr (صَلاة الظُّهْر) is the (after) midday prayer. ʿAbd ʿAbd Allah ibn ʿAmr (عَبْد الله بن عَمْرُو) reported that the Messenger of Allah said: "The time of the noon prayer is when the sun passes the meridian and a man's shadow is the same (length) as his height, (and it lasts) as long as the time for the afternoon prayer has not come."[619]

---

617 ...نَّهُ قَالَ سُئِلَ رَسُولُ اللَّهِ عَنْ وَقْتِ الصَّلَوَاتِ فَقَالَ: "وَقْتُ صَلاةِ الْفَجْرِ مَا لَمْ يَطْلُعْ قَرْنُ الشَّمْسِ الأَوَّلُ وَوَقْتُ صَلاةِ الظُّهْرِ إِذَا زَالَتِ الشَّمْسُ عَنْ بَطْنِ السَّمَاءِ مَا لَمْ يَحْضُرِ الْعَصْرُ وَوَقْتُ صَلاةِ الْعَصْرِ مَا لَمْ تَصْفَرَّ الشَّمْسُ وَيَسْقُطْ قَرْنُهَا الأَوَّلُ وَوَقْتُ صَلاةِ الْمَغْرِبِ إِذَا غَابَتِ الشَّمْسُ مَا لَمْ يَسْقُطِ الشَّفَقُ وَوَقْتُ صَلاةِ الْعِشَاءِ إِلَى نِصْفِ اللَّيْلِ." Sahīh Muslim 612

618 ...قَالَ النَّبِيُّ: "لَيْسَ صَلاةٌ أَثْقَلَ عَلَى الْمُنَافِقِينَ مِنَ الْفَجْرِ وَالْعِشَاءِ، وَلَوْ يَعْلَمُونَ مَا فِيهِمَا لأَتَوْهُمَا وَلَوْ حَبْوًا." Sahīh al-Bukhārī 657

Remark: Mecca is further south than the tropic of cancer which means that several months of the year the sun is 90° overhead. Before the sun casts a shadow of a man's length at that time it should be about 3 pm, i.e. not shortly after noon.

453. How are Muslims told that a compulsory prayer is due?

Answer: By the call to prayer - al-’Azān (الأذان) - of the muezzin.

’Abū Mahdhūra (أَبُو مَحْذُورَة) reported that the Messenger of Allah had taught him the call to prayer verbatim.[620] This is what Muhammad had told him:

4x	Allah is most great	"Allāhu ’akbar"	اللهُ أَكْبَرُ
2x	I testify that there is no god but Allah	"’Ashhadu ’an la Ilāha ’illallāh"	أَشْهَدُ أَنْ لَا إِلَهَ إِلاَّ اللهُ
2x	I testify that Muhammad is the Messenger of Allah	"Ashhadu ’anna Muhammadan Rasūlallāh"	أَشْهَدُ أَنَّ مُحَمَّدًا رَسُولُ اللهِ
2x	I testify that there is no god but Allah.	"Ashhadu ’an la Ilāha il-lallāh"	أَشْهَدُ أَنْ لَا إِلَهَ إِلاَّ اللهُ
2x	I testify that Muhammad is the Messenger of Allah	"Ashhadu ’anna Muhammadan Rasūlallāh"	أَشْهَدُ أَنَّ مُحَمَّدًا رَسُولُ اللهِ
2x	come to prayer	"Hayya ’alās-Salā"	حَيَّ عَلَى الصَّلَاةِ
2x	come to salvation	"Hayya ’alāl-Falāh"	حَيَّ عَلَى الْفَلَاحِ
2x	Allah is most great	"Allāhu ’akbar"	اللهُ أَكْبَرُ
1x	there is no god but Allah	"La ilāha ’ill-Allāh"	لَا إِلَهَ إِلاَّ اللهُ

---

619 ...أَنَّ رَسُولَ اللَّهِ قَالَ: "وَقْتُ الظُّهْرِ إِذَا زَالَتِ الشَّمْسُ وَكَانَ ظِلُّ الرَّجُلِ كَطُولِهِ مَا لَمْ يَحْضُرِ الْعَصْرُ. Sahīh Muslim 612.

620 ...يَذْكُرُ أَنَّهُ سَمِعَ أَبَا مَحْذُورَةَ، يَقُولُ أَلْقَى عَلَيَّ رَسُولُ اللَّهِ الأَذَانَ حَرْفًا حَرْفًا. Sunan ’Abī Dāwūd.

Note: In the first prayer of the day at dawn, al-Fajr (الْفَجْر), a Sunni muezzin would add: "Prayer is better than sleep". In Arabic: al-Salātu khayrun min al-Nawm (الصَّلاة خَيْرٌ مِن النَّوْم).

What do Muslims recite during the call to prayer? While listening to the muezzin's call, Muslims repeat his words silently – except for when he says "Hayya 'alās-Salā" or "Hayya 'alāl-Falāh".

Then, they silently say: "There is no strength or power except from Allah". In Arabic: "La Hawla wa la Quwwata 'illā billāh" (لا حَوْلَ وَلا قُوَّةَ إِلَّا بِاللَّه). This is a famous sentence that you see quite often written on taxis, minibuses, or trucks.

454. What is a Khumra?

Answer: A Khumra (خُمْرَة) is a small mat sufficient just for the face and the hands while prostrating during prayers.

It was narrated by 'Abd Allah ibn Shaddād (عَبْد الله بن شَدّاد) that Muhammad's wife Maymūna (مَيْمُونة) said: "Allah's Messenger was praying while I was in my menses, sitting beside him, and sometimes his clothes would touch me during his prostration."

Maymūna added: "He prayed on a Khumra."[621]

The Khumra was usually made of palm-leaves tied with threads or strings. Its name derives from the fact that it covers the ground and protects the face of the person praying on it, or, alternatively, from the fact that its threads or strings were often hidden.

Note: The correct pronunciation of the vowels in Khmura is crucial because they change the meaning dramatically:

- Khimra (خِمْرة): a mode/manner of doing something (technique)
- Khamra (خَمْرة): wine/alcohol (pressed juice of fermented fruits)
- Khumra (خُمْرة): ferment of dough or perfume
- Khamar (خَمَرة): nice smell; odour of perfume

---

621 ...قَالَتْ كَانَ رَسُولُ اللَّهِ يُصَلِّي وَأَنَا حِذَاءَهُ وَأَنَا حَائِضٌ وَرُبَّمَا أَصَابَنِي ثَوْبُهُ إِذَا سَجَدَ. قَالَتْ وَكَانَ يُصَلِّي عَلَى الْخُمْرَةِ. Sahīh al-Bukhārī 379.

455. Are there times at which a Muslim is not allowed to pray?

Answer: Yes.

ʿAbd Allah ibn ʿAmr (عَبْد الله بن عَمْرو) narrated: "When the (upper) edge of the sun emerges [in the morning], don't perform a prayer until the sun appears in full and when the lower edge of the sun sets, don't perform a prayer until it is set completely. And you should not seek to pray at sunrise or sunset for the sun rises between two sides of the head of the Devil."[622]

To make it clear: It is forbidden for a Muslim to pray after the first prayer - al-Fajr (صَلاة الْفَجْر) - until the sun has risen above the horizon to the height of a spear, and furthermore, at noon when the sun is at its zenith, and after the afternoon prayer - al-ʿAsr (صَلاة الْعَصْر) - until the sun is fully set.

This rule is also true for funerals. ʿUqba ibn ʿĀmir (عُقْبة بن عامِر) said: "There were three times at which Allah's Messenger forbade us to pray or **bury our dead**: When the sun begins to rise until it is fully up, when the sun is at its height at midday until it passes over the meridian and when the sun draws near to setting until it sets."[623]

Why is that? Most probably to avoid Muslims (accidentally) prostrating to the sun which is strictly forbidden in Islam. Let's see what Muhammad else said about it.

ʿAmr ibn ʿAbasa (عَمْرو بن عَبَسة) once asked the Prophet: "O Messenger of Allah, is there any moment which brings one closer to Allah than another, or any moment that should be sought out for remembering Allah?" The Prophet replied: "Yes, the closest that the Lord is to His slave is in the last part of the night, so if you can be among those who remember Allah at that time, then do so because the prayer is attended and witnessed [by the angels] until the sun rises; then, it rises between the two horns of Satan which is the time when the disbelievers pray, so do not pray until the sun had risen to the

---

622 ...قَالَ رَسُولُ اللَّهِ: "إِذَا طَلَعَ حَاجِبُ الشَّمْسِ فَدَعُوا الصَّلَاةَ حَتَّى تَبْرُزَ، وَإِذَا غَابَ حَاجِبُ الشَّمْسِ فَدَعُوا الصَّلَاةَ حَتَّى تَغِيبَ." "وَلَا تَحَيَّنُوا بِصَلَاتِكُمْ طُلُوعَ الشَّمْسِ وَلَا غُرُوبَهَا، فَإِنَّهَا تَطْلُعُ بَيْنَ قَرْنَيْ شَيْطَانٍ أَوِ الشَّيْطَانِ." Sahīh al-Bukhārī 3273, 3273

623 ...يَقُولُ ثَلَاثُ سَاعَاتٍ كَانَ رَسُولُ اللَّهِ يَنْهَانَا أَنْ نُصَلِّيَ فِيهِنَّ أَوْ أَنْ نَقْبُرَ فِيهِنَّ مَوْتَانَا حِينَ تَطْلُعُ الشَّمْسُ بَازِغَةً حَتَّى تَرْتَفِعَ وَحِينَ يَقُومُ قَائِمُ الظَّهِيرَةِ حَتَّى تَمِيلَ الشَّمْسُ وَحِينَ تَضَيَّفُ الشَّمْسُ لِلْغُرُوبِ حَتَّى تَغْرُبَ. Sahīh Muslim 831

height of a spear and its rays have disappeared. After that the prayer is attended and witnessed [by the angels] until **the sun is directly overhead at midday, which is the time when the gates of Hell are opened and its fires are stoked up. So, do not pray until the shadows appear.** After that prayer is [again] attended and witnessed [by angels] until the sun sets and it sets between the horns of Satan, and that is the time when the disbelievers pray."[624]

456. What did the Prophet order on cold and rainy nights?

Answer: To pray at home.

Nāfi' Mawlā ibn 'Umar (نافِع مَوْلَى بن عُمَر) narrated that once on a very cold and stormy night, Ibn 'Umar pronounced the call for the prayer and then said: "Pray in your homes!" He (Ibn 'Umar) added: "On very cold and rainy nights Allah's Messenger used to order the muezzin to say: 'Pray in your homes.'"[625]

457. What are major (ritual) impurities?

Answer: Major impurities are caused by sexual intercourse, discharging semen (جَنابة), menstruation (حَيْض) and childbirth (نِفاس).

How does a Muslim clean him- or herself from a major impurity? When a bath of the whole body becomes obligatory for a man or a woman, the state is called al-Hadath al-'Akbar (الْحَدَث الْأَكْبَر) which is

---

624 ...يَقُولُ سَمِعْتُ عَمْرَو بْنَ عَبَسَةَ، يَقُولُ قُلْتُ يَا رَسُولَ اللَّهِ هَلْ مِنْ سَاعَةٍ أَقْرَبُ مِنَ الْأُخْرَى أَوْ هَلْ مِنْ سَاعَةٍ يُبْتَغَى ذِكْرُهَا قَالَ: "نَعَمْ إِنَّ أَقْرَبَ مَا يَكُونُ الرَّبُّ عَزَّ وَجَلَّ مِنَ الْعَبْدِ جَوْفُ اللَّيْلِ الْآخِرِ فَإِنِ اسْتَطَعْتَ أَنْ تَكُونَ مِمَّنْ يَذْكُرُ اللَّهَ عَزَّ وَجَلَّ فِي تِلْكَ السَّاعَةِ فَكُنْ فَإِنَّ الصَّلَاةَ مَحْضُورَةٌ مَشْهُودَةٌ إِلَى طُلُوعِ الشَّمْسِ فَإِنَّهَا تَطْلُعُ بَيْنَ قَرْنَيِ الشَّيْطَانِ وَهِيَ سَاعَةُ صَلَاةِ الْكُفَّارِ فَدَعِ الصَّلَاةَ حَتَّى تَرْتَفِعَ قِيدَ رُمْحٍ وَيَذْهَبَ شُعَاعُهَا ثُمَّ الصَّلَاةُ مَحْضُورَةٌ مَشْهُودَةٌ حَتَّى تَعْتَدِلَ الشَّمْسُ اعْتِدَالَ الرُّمْحِ بِنِصْفِ النَّهَارِ فَإِنَّهَا سَاعَةٌ تُفْتَحُ فِيهَا أَبْوَابُ جَهَنَّمَ وَتُسْجَرُ فَدَعِ الصَّلَاةَ حَتَّى يَفِيءَ الْفَيْءُ ثُمَّ الصَّلَاةُ مَحْضُورَةٌ مَشْهُودَةٌ حَتَّى تَغِيبَ الشَّمْسُ فَإِنَّهَا تَغِيبُ بَيْنَ قَرْنَيْ شَيْطَانٍ وَهِيَ صَلَاةُ الْكُفَّارِ." Sunan al-Nasā'ī 579 (573)

625 ...أَنَّ ابْنَ عُمَرَ، أَذَّنَ بِالصَّلَاةِ فِي لَيْلَةٍ ذَاتِ بَرْدٍ وَرِيحٍ ثُمَّ قَالَ أَلَا صَلُّوا فِي الرِّحَالِ. ثُمَّ قَالَ إِنَّ رَسُولَ اللَّهِ كَانَ يَأْمُرُ الْمُؤَذِّنَ إِذَا كَانَتْ لَيْلَةٌ ذَاتُ بَرْدٍ وَمَطَرٍ يَقُولُ أَلَا صَلُّوا فِي الرِّحَالِ. Sahīh al-Bukhārī

often meaning-wise translated as *major ritual impurity*. The bath is called Ghusl (غُسْل) or Ightisāl (إغْتِسال). This is commanded in sura 5 *The Feast* – in Arabic: al-Māʾida (سُورة الْمائِدة):

5:6	if required (if you are in *Janāba*, i.e. ritual impurity), wash your whole body	وَإِن كُنتُمْ جُنُبًا فَاطَّهَّرُوا

Remark: The al-Hadath al-ʾAsghar (الْحَدَث الْأَصْغَر) denotes a minor impurity, cause for example by passing wind, excrement or urine.

458. Which body parts must a Muslim clean before praying?

Answer: Many of them; see below.

A Muslim must wash certain parts of his body before praying. The ritual ablution is called Wudūʾ (وُضوء) and is normally done in preparation for the prayers. In fact without the ablution, the prayer is most probably not valid. The full ablution is called Ghusl (غُسْل) and means the cleaning (washing) of the entire body – basically, it means taking a bath. After a Muslim had sex, he needs a Ghusl.

Theoretically, a Muslim is "clean" until he does certain acts, for example urination or vomiting, that make him "unclean".

Let's look what body parts have to be washed for Wudūʾ:

- Hands, up to the wrists: 3 times
- Mouth, including gargling with water: 3 times
- Nose; the left hand is used to remove the water from the nose: 3 times.
- Face, from the hairline to the jawbone and chin and from ear to ear: 3 times.
- Arms; right then left, from the fingertips (including the nails) to the lower part of the upper arm up to the elbow: 3 times.
- A Muslim should wipe his head and ears once with fresh water.
- Feet, right then left foot up to the ankles (until the bones at the bottom of the leg) and between the toes: 3 times.

'Amr ibn Yaḥyā (عَمْرو بن يَحْيَى) narrated the following on the authority of his father: "My uncle used to perform ablution extravagantly. Once he asked 'Abd Allah ibn Zayd to tell him how he had seen the Prophet performing ablution. He asked for an earthenware pot containing water and poured water from it on his hands and washed them thrice and then put his hand in the earthenware pot and rinsed his mouth and washed his nose by putting water in it and then blowing it out thrice with one handful of water; he again put his hand in the water and took a handful of water and washed his face thrice, then washed his hands up to the elbows twice and took water with his hand and passed it over his head from front to back and then from back to front and then washed his feet [up to the ankles] and said: 'I saw the Prophet performing ablution in that way.'"[626]

459. What kind of water is suitable for the ritual ablution?

Answer: Water that did not change its taste (طَعْم), colour (لَوْن) or smell (رائحة).

In Islam water from several sources can be considered as pure (ظهارة) and thus suitable (صالح) for ritual ablution: rain (ماء الْمَطَر), snow or ice (الثَّلْج), hail (الْبَرْد), sea water (الْبَحْر), spring water (الْعَيْن), and well water (الآبَار).

Let's look in some more detail regarding **rain, snow/ice and hail** – i.e. water that falls from the sky. A verse in sura 8 *Battle Gains* - in Arabic: al-'Anfāl (سُورة الأَنْفال) - tells us more about it:

| 8:11 | Remember when He gave you sleep as a reassurance from Him, and sent down water from the sky to cleanse you, to remove Satan's pollution from you, to make your hearts strong and your feet firm. | إِذْ يُغَشِّيكُمُ النُّعَاسَ أَمَنَةً مِّنْهُ وَيُنَزِّلُ عَلَيْكُم مِّنَ السَّمَاءِ مَاءً لِّيُطَهِّرَكُم بِهِ وَيُذْهِبَ عَنكُمْ رِجْزَ الشَّيْطَانِ وَلِيَرْبِطَ عَلَى قُلُوبِكُمْ وَيُثَبِّتَ |

---

626 ...قَالَ كَانَ عَمِّي يُكْثِرُ مِنَ الْوُضُوءِ، قَالَ لِعَبْدِ اللَّهِ بْنِ زَيْدٍ أَخْبِرْنِي كَيْفَ رَأَيْتَ النَّبِيَّ يَتَوَضَّأُ فَدَعَا بِتَوْرٍ مِنْ مَاءٍ، فَكَفَأَ عَلَى يَدَيْهِ فَغَسَلَهُمَا ثَلَاثَ مِرَارٍ، ثُمَّ أَدْخَلَ يَدَهُ فِي التَّوْرِ، فَمَضْمَضَ وَاسْتَنْثَرَ ثَلَاثَ مَرَّاتٍ مِنْ غَرْفَةٍ وَاحِدَةٍ، ثُمَّ أَدْخَلَ يَدَهُ فَاغْتَرَفَ بِهَا فَغَسَلَ وَجْهَهُ ثَلَاثَ مَرَّاتٍ، ثُمَّ غَسَلَ يَدَيْهِ إِلَى الْمِرْفَقَيْنِ مَرَّتَيْنِ مَرَّتَيْنِ، ثُمَّ أَخَذَ بِيَدِهِ مَاءً، فَمَسَحَ رَأْسَهُ، فَأَدْبَرَ بِيَدَيْهِ وَأَقْبَلَ ثُمَّ غَسَلَ رِجْلَيْهِ، فَقَالَ هَكَذَا رَأَيْتُ النَّبِيَّ يَتَوَضَّأُ. Ṣaḥīḥ al-Bukhārī 199.

		بِهِ الْأَقْدَامَ.

Furthermore, a verse in sura 25 *The Differentiator* - in Arabic: al-Furqān (سُورة الْفُرْقان) - confirms all this:

25:48	It is He who sends the winds as heralds of good news before His Mercy. We send down pure water from the sky	وَهُوَ الَّذِي أَرْسَلَ الرِّيَاحَ بُشْرًا بَيْنَ يَدَيْ رَحْمَتِهِ وَأَنزَلْنَا مِنَ السَّمَاءِ مَاءً طَهُورًا

Sea water's purity is based on the following Hadith: 'Abū Hurayra (أَبُو هُرَيْرَة) said: "A man asked the Prophet: 'O Messenger of Allah, we travel by sea and we take a little water with us, but if we use it for Wuḍū', we will go thirsty. Can we perform Wuḍū' with seawater?' The Messenger of Allah said: 'Its water is a means of purification and its meat [even if the animal is already dead] is permissible.'"[627]

460. What can a Muslim do if he can't find water for ablution?

Answer: He can use sand instead.

This is found in sura 4 *Women* – in Arabic: al-Nisā' (سُورة النِّساء):

4:43	You who believe, do not come anywhere near the prayer if you are intoxicated, not until you know what you are saying; nor if you are in a state of major ritual impurity - though you may pass through the mosque - not until you have bathed; if you are ill, on a journey, have relieved yourselves, or had intercourse, and cannot find any water, then find some clean sand and wipe your faces and hands with it. God is always ready to pardon and forgive.	يَا أَيُّهَا الَّذِينَ آمَنُوا لَا تَقْرَبُوا الصَّلَاةَ وَأَنتُمْ سُكَارَى حَتَّى تَعْلَمُوا مَا تَقُولُونَ وَلَا جُنُبًا إِلَّا عَابِرِي سَبِيلٍ حَتَّى تَغْتَسِلُوا وَإِن كُنتُم مَّرْضَى أَوْ عَلَى سَفَرٍ أَوْ جَاءَ أَحَدٌ مِّنكُم مِّنَ الْغَائِطِ أَوْ لَامَسْتُمُ النِّسَاءَ فَلَمْ تَجِدُوا مَاءً فَتَيَمَّمُوا صَعِيدًا طَيِّبًا فَامْسَحُوا بِوُجُوهِكُمْ وَأَيْدِيكُمْ إِنَّ اللَّهَ كَانَ عَفُوًّا غَفُورًا.

---

627 ...سَأَلَ رَجُلٌ رَسُولَ اللَّهِ فَقَالَ يَا رَسُولَ اللَّهِ إِنَّا نَرْكَبُ الْبَحْرَ وَنَحْمِلُ مَعَنَا الْقَلِيلَ مِنَ الْمَاءِ فَإِنْ تَوَضَّأْنَا بِهِ عَطِشْنَا أَفَنَتَوَضَّأُ مِنْ مَاءِ الْبَحْرِ فَقَالَ رَسُولُ اللَّهِ: "هُوَ الطَّهُورُ مَاؤُهُ الْحِلُّ مَيْتَتُهُ." Sunan
al-Nasā'ī 322 (333)

The Qur'an uses the term Saʿīd (ﺻﻌﻴﺪ) which means *dust, earth, soil* or *sand*. In a classical meaning, it may denote *elevated land*. Notice that the southern part of Egypt (Upper Egypt) is called al-Saʿīd (ﺍﻟﺼّﻌﻴﺪ) in Arabic. Regarding the verse in the sura, most scholars say that the word means *earth containing dust*.

This symbolic ablution, so-called Tayammum (ﺗَﻴَﻤُّﻢ), works as follows: A Muslim touches the earth or anything supposed to contain dust with the palms of the hands and then passes them lightly over face and hands. The sand substitutes both, i.e. the total ablution/bath, Ghusl (ﻏُﺴْﻞ), and the partial ablution before prayers - Wudūʾ (ﻭُﺿُﻮﺀ).

Note: Arabic has even a special verb for this: yammama (ﻳَﻤَّﻢ) or yatammama (ﺗَﻴَﻤَّﻢ). Both mean *to intend; to perform one's ablutions with sand.*

461. What does a Muslim actually do when he prays?

Answer: This is a pretty complicated ritual; see below.

In Islam praying does not mean that you talk to Allah. There are several (strict) rules you have to follow and if a Muslim misses one step, the prayer might be invalid.

Each school of jurisprudence has some nuances. Furthermore, the steps differ depending on the type of prayer, the timing, or the circumstances. For example, a Muslim is allowed to shorten the prayers when he is fighting (a war; Jihād) or travelling. For this reason, I only mention the main parts of a prayer and explain what a Muslim does and says when he or she prays. Note that this is a simplified version which should show the outline of a prayer to non-Muslims.

Let's have a look:

- At first the Muslim has to stand correctly, which means that the feet must be a four finger-width apart from each other.

- Then he makes (pronounced) the intention to pray – so-called Nīya (ﻧِﻴّﺔ) by saying for example: "I intend to perform the Friday Prayer."

- The Muslim pronounces the Takbīr (تَكْبِير) by saying "Allāhu 'akbar" ("Allah is great") and raising both hands. The tips of the thumbs touch the earlobes and the hands (palms) must be turned towards Mecca. Then the Muslim says again: "Allāhu 'akbar".

- While standing, the Muslim changes the position of the hands by placing the right hand on top of the left hand on one's chest/navel. He then says: "I seek Allah's shelter from Satan, the condemned."

- Then the Muslim recites the first sura of the Qur'an – *The Opening;* in Arabic: al-Fātiha (الْفاتِحة):

  "*1* In the name of God, the Lord of Mercy, the Giver of Mercy! *2* Praise belongs to God, Lord of the Worlds, *3* the Lord of Mercy, the Giver of Mercy, *4* Master of the Day of Judgement. *5* It is You we worship; it is You we ask for help. *6* Guide us to the straight path: *7* the path of those You have blessed, those who incur no anger and who have not gone astray."

- When a Muslim has finished this sura, any other passage from the Qur'an is recited. Muslims usually recite sura 112 *Purity of Faith* - in Arabic: (سُورة الْإِخْلاص) - which goes as follows: "*1* Say, He is God the One, *2* God the eternal. *3* He begot no one nor was He begotten. *4* No one is comparable to Him."

- Then a Muslim says again: "Allāhu 'akbar" (3 times) and bows down. A Muslim's back and head should be in a 90 degree angle with his legs. The following prayer has to be said three times: "Glory be to my Lord, the Almighty."

- While going back to the standing position, the first prayer is said: "Allah hears those who praise Him"; "Our Lord, praise be to You."

- Then, a Muslim again says "Allāhu 'akbar" and prostrates to express complete submission and humility before Allah. This is the most important part of the prayer.

  A Muslim places his forehead on the ground. According to the teachings of Islam, at this moment of humility, the worshipper is closest to Allah. While prostrating Muslims glorify Allah:

"Glory be to my Lord, the most High." This is also the moment when a Muslim asks Allah for forgiveness, mercy, or blessings.

- After that, a Muslim again says "Allāhu 'akbar" and sits for a moment, again he says "Allāhu 'akbar" and prostrates one more time before he stands up again.

- Depending on the type of prayer, Muslims repeat this cycle once, twice, or three times in each prayer.

- In the end [and sometimes also in the middle], a Muslim sits on his knees. At this point he testifies that "there is no god but Allah and that Muhammad is His messenger."

  A Muslim also asks Allah to send His peace and blessings on His Messenger Muhammad as He did on Prophet Abraham. He says: "All service is for Allah and all acts of worship and good deeds are for Him. Peace and the mercy and blessings of Allah be upon you, O Prophet. Peace be upon us and all of Allah's righteous slaves. I bear witness that none has the right to be worshipped except Allah and I bear witness that Muhammad is His Messenger. O Allah, exalt Muhammad and the followers of Muhammad, just as you exalted Abraham and the followers of Abraham. Verily you are full of praise and majesty. O Allah, send blessings on Muhammad and the family of Muhammad, just as you sent blessings on Abraham and upon the followers of Abraham. Verily you are full of praise and majesty."

- He turns his face to the right and says to his fellow Muslim: "May the Peace and mercy of Allah be upon you." The, he turns his face to the left and says again: "May peace and mercy of Allah be upon you."

- With this greeting, the obligatory prayer is completed.

What is forbidden during praying?

- Laughing makes the prayer invalid.
- A Muslim should not look towards the sky while praying. He should look down and forward.
- If prayer and a meal time are close, the person should eat first.
- A Muslim can open or close his eyes while praying.

Muslims have to watch out which symbol they might form with their hands. It was narrated that Ziyād ibn Subayḥ (زياد بن صُبَيح) once said: "I prayed beside 'Abd Allah ibn 'Umar (عَبْد الله بن عُمَر) and put my hand on my waist and he did this to me [meaning: he knocked it with his hand]. When I had finished praying I asked a man: 'Who is this?'" He answered: "'Abd Allah ibn 'Umar." I said: "O 'Abū 'Abd al-Rahmān [= 'Abd Allah ibn 'Umar], why are you angry with me?" He said: "This is the **posture of crucifixion**, and the Messenger of Allah forbade us to do this."[628]

462. How many body parts should touch the ground in a prayer?

Answer: Seven.

During a prayer, seven parts of a Muslim's body should touch the ground:

1	the forehead (nose included)
2 + 3	both hands
4 + 5	both knees
6 + 7	ends (toes) of the feet

This was stated in a Hadith. 'Abd Allah ibn 'Abbās (عَبْد الله بن عَبَّاس) narrated that the Messenger of Allah said: "I have been commanded to prostrate myself on seven bones: forehead, and then pointed with his hand towards his nose, hands, feet, and the extremities of the feet. And we were forbidden to fold back clothing and hair."[629]

Note: If a Muslim omits one of these parts, then his prayer is not valid.

---

628 ...قَالَ صَلَّيْتُ إِلَى جَنْبِ ابْنِ عُمَرَ فَوَضَعْتُ يَدِي عَلَى خَصْرِي فَقَالَ لِي هَكَذَا ضَرْبَةً بِيَدِهِ فَلَمَّا صَلَّيْتُ قُلْتُ لِرَجُلٍ مَنْ هَذَا قَالَ عَبْدُ اللَّهِ بْنُ عُمَرَ. قُلْتُ يَا أَبَا عَبْدِ الرَّحْمَنِ مَا رَابَكَ مِنِّي قَالَ إِنَّ هَذَا الصُّلْبُ وَإِنَّ رَسُولَ اللَّهِ نَهَانَا عَنْهُ. Sunan al-Nasā'ī 891

629 ...أَنَّ رَسُولَ اللَّهِ قَالَ: "أُمِرْتُ أَنْ أَسْجُدَ عَلَى سَبْعَةِ أَعْظُمٍ الْجَبْهَةِ - وَأَشَارَ بِيَدِهِ عَلَى أَنْفِهِ - وَالْيَدَيْنِ وَالرِّجْلَيْنِ وَأَطْرَافِ الْقَدَمَيْنِ وَلاَ نَكْفِتَ الثِّيَابَ وَلاَ الشَّعْرَ." Sahīh Muslim 490

463. When should Muslim parents tell their children to pray?

Answer: At the age of 7.

'Abd Allah ibn 'Amr (عَبْد الله بن عَمْرو) narrated that the Messenger of Allah once said: "Command your children to pray when they become 7 years old. And beat them if they do not do so when they become 10 years old. And arrange their beds [to sleep] separately."[630]

464. Which night is "better than a thousand months"?

Answer: The *Night of Power* – in Arabic: Layla(t) al-Qadr (لَيْلَة الْقَدْر).

Even a sura - number 97 - is named after this night which has several names in English: *The Night of Power; The Night of Glory; The Night of Decree.* In Arabic it is called al-Qadr (سُورة الْقَدْر). It received its name from the following verse:

97:3	The Night of Glory is better than a thousand months;	لَيْلَةُ الْقَدْرِ خَيْرٌ مِّنْ أَلْفِ شَهْرٍ؛

What is so special about this night? The Night of Power is the night when the Prophet received his first revelation. Many Muslims try to pray in this night because they believe that all their sins will be forgiven. 'Abū Hurayra (أَبُو هُرَيْرة) narrated that the Prophet once said: "Whoever fasted the month of Ramadan out of sincere faith and hoping for a reward from Allah, then all his past sins will be forgiven, and whoever stood for the prayers in the Night of Qadr out of sincere faith and hoping for a reward from Allah, then all his previous sins will be forgiven."[631]

When is this night?

Neither the Qur'an nor the Hadiths give sound information about the exact date of this night. Some Hadiths - although all of them are

---

630 ...قَالَ رَسُولُ اللَّهِ: "مُرُوا أَوْلَادَكُمْ بِالصَّلَاةِ وَهُمْ أَبْنَاءُ سَبْعِ سِنِينَ وَاضْرِبُوهُمْ عَلَيْهَا وَهُمْ أَبْنَاءُ عَشْرِ سِنِينَ وَفَرِّقُوا بَيْنَهُمْ فِي الْمَضَاجِعِ." Sunan 'Abī Dāwūd 495; hasan sahīh.

631 ...النَّبِيُّ قَالَ: "مَنْ صَامَ رَمَضَانَ إِيمَانًا وَاحْتِسَابًا غُفِرَ لَهُ مَا تَقَدَّمَ مِنْ ذَنْبِهِ، وَمَنْ قَامَ لَيْلَةَ الْقَدْرِ إِيمَانًا وَاحْتِسَابًا غُفِرَ لَهُ مَا تَقَدَّمَ مِنْ ذَنْبِهِ." Sahīh al-Bukhārī 2014.

authentic - contradict each other, but they all indicate that the night is in the last five odd nights (21st, 23rd, 25th, 27th or 29th) of the final ten days of Ramadan.

It has been narrated by 'Ubāda ibn al-Sāmit (عُبادة بن الصّامِت) that Allah's Messenger went out to inform the people about the [date of the] night of decree [al-Qadr] but there was a quarrel between two Muslim men. The Prophet said: "I came out to inform you about [the date of] the night of al-Qadr, but as so and so and so and so quarrelled, its knowledge was taken away [I forgot it] and maybe it was better for you. Now look for it in the 7th, the 9th and the 5th [of the last 10 nights of the month of Ramadan]."[632]

Most Sunni Muslims observe Layla(t) al-Qadr on the night before the 27th of Ramadan. It was narrated by Mu'āwiya ibn 'Abī Sufyān (مُعاوِية بن أَبي سُفيان) that the Prophet had said: "Layla(t) al-Qadr is the twenty-seventh night [of Ramadan]."[633]

Note: Shia Muslims normally observe Layla(t) al-Qadr on the 23rd night of Ramadan. The 19th, according to Shias, coincides with the night when 'Alī ibn 'Abī Tālib (عَلِيّ بن أَبِس طالِب) was attacked in the Great Mosque of Kufa and died on the 21st of Ramadan. Shia Muslims regard these three nights (19th, 21st, and 23rd) as greatly rewarding.

465. What is meant by the "white days"?

Answer: The 13th, 14th and 15th of each lunar month.

It was narrated from Jarīr ibn 'Abd Allah (جَرِير بن عَبْد الله) that the Prophet had said: "Fasting three days of each month is fasting for a lifetime and the shining days of *al-Bīd*, the thirteenth, fourteenth, and fifteenth."[634]

---

٦٣٢ ...أَنَّ رَسُولَ اللَّهِ خَرَجَ يُخْبِرُ بِلَيْلَةِ الْقَدْرِ، فَتَلَاحَى رَجُلَانِ مِنَ الْمُسْلِمِينَ فَقَالَ: "إِنِّي خَرَجْتُ لِأُخْبِرَكُمْ بِلَيْلَةِ الْقَدْرِ، وَإِنَّهُ تَلَاحَى فُلَانٌ وَفُلَانٌ فَرُفِعَتْ وَعَسَى أَنْ يَكُونَ خَيْرًا لَكُمُ الْتَمِسُوهَا فِي السَّبْعِ وَالتَّسْعِ وَالْخَمْسِ." Sahīh al-Bukhārī 49

٦٣٣ ...النَّبِيُّ فِي لَيْلَةِ الْقَدْرِ قَالَ: "لَيْلَةُ الْقَدْرِ لَيْلَةُ سَبْعٍ وَعِشْرِينَ." Sunan 'Abī Dāwūd 1386

٦٣٤ ...النَّبِيِّ قَالَ: "صِيَامُ ثَلَاثَةِ أَيَّامٍ مِنْ كُلِّ شَهْرٍ صِيَامُ الدَّهْرِ وَأَيَّامُ الْبِيضِ صَبِيحَةَ ثَلَاثَ عَشْرَةَ وَأَرْبَعَ عَشْرَةَ وَخَمْسَ عَشْرَةَ." Sunan al-Nasā'ī 2420 (2422)

They are called *White Nights* - 'Ayyām al-Bīd (أَيَّام الْبِيض) - because those are the three days in which the moon is full and the nights are bright. The term *Bīd* is the plural form of the colour *white* in Arabic (for masculine and feminine).

466. Why do some Muslims stay in the mosque voluntarily?

Answer: To get closer to Allah. It is called al-I'tikāf (اِعْتِكاف).

The meaning of I'tikāf is *sticking and adhering to something*. In an Islamic context it means *to confine oneself in a mosque for prayers and invocations, leaving the worldly activities for a limited number of days*.

Any day on which fasting is allowed is appropriate for I'tikāf. However, the best times to perform it are the *White Days* - which are the 13th, 14th and 15th of every lunar month - as well as the last ten days of Ramadan. Note: A Muslim can not perform I'tikāf on the day of 'Īd al-'Adhā or 'Īd al-Fitra because it is forbidden to fast on these days.

'Abū Hurayra (أَبُو هُرَيْرَة) reported that the Prophet used to perform I'tikāf every year in the month of Ramadan for ten days, and when it was the year of his death, he stayed in I'tikāf for twenty days.[635]

'Ā'isha (عائِشة بِنْت أَبِي بَكْر) narrated: "When the Messenger of Allah observed I'tikāf, he would put his head near me and I would comb his hair. He entered the house only to fulfil human needs [i.e. to relieve himself]."[636]

Note that the mosque was adjacent to the Prophet's house.

635 ...قَالَ كَانَ النَّبِيُّ يَعْتَكِفُ فِي كُلِّ رَمَضَانَ عَشْرَةَ أَيَّامٍ، فَلَمَّا كَانَ الْعَامُ الَّذِي قُبِضَ فِيهِ اعْتَكَفَ عِشْرِينَ يَوْمًا. Sahīh al-Bukhārī 2044.

636 ...قَالَتْ كَانَ رَسُولُ اللَّهِ إِذَا اعْتَكَفَ يُدْنِي إِلَيَّ رَأْسَهُ فَأُرَجِّلُهُ وَكَانَ لاَ يَدْخُلُ الْبَيْتَ إِلاَّ لِحَاجَةِ الإِنْسَانِ. Sunan 'Abī Dāwūd 2467.

467. What is the name of the voluntary prayer which is performed through the entire night in the nights of Ramadan?

Answer: Salā(t) al-Tarāwīh (صَلاة التَّراويح).

In Islam, the term al-Tarāwīh (تَراويح) is used for the extra prayers performed by Sunni Muslims at night in the month of Ramadan. It is a voluntary prayer (صَلاة الْقِيام النَّافِلة). It can be recited any time after the night prayer (الْعِشاء) and before dawn.

It was reported by 'Abū Hurayra (أَبُو هُرَيْرة) that the Messenger of Allah used to exhort [his Companions] to pray [at night] during Ramadan without commanding them to observe it as an obligatory act. The Prophet had said: "He who observed the night prayer in Ramadan because of faith and seeking his reward [from Allah], all his previous sins will be forgiven."

When Allah's Messenger died, this was the practice and it continued thus during 'Abū Bakr's Caliphate and the early part of 'Umar's Caliphate.[637]

At the time of the Prophet the word al-Tarāwīh had never been used. In the Hadiths, the Tarāwīh prayer was called *Standing of the Night (Prayer)* – in Arabic: Qiyam al-Layl (صَلاة قِيام اللَّيل فِي رَمَضان). The word Tarāwīh is derived from the Arabic root r-w-h (ح-و-ر) which has several meanings, in some applications it means: *to rest* or *to relax*. The word Tarāwīh is the plural of Tarwīha (تَرْويحة) which translates as: *a (single) rest*. According to Edward Lane (1863), this prayer received its name because the reciter rests after a certain time.

How about Shia Muslims? Most of them see the Tarāwīh prayer as something that was introduced after the death of Muhammad, so they treat it as an *invention* – Bid'a (بِدْعة).

---

637 ...قَالَ كَانَ رَسُولُ اللَّهِ يُرَغِّبُ فِي قِيَامِ رَمَضَانَ مِنْ غَيْرِ أَنْ يَأْمُرَهُمْ فِيهِ بِعَزِيمَةٍ فَيَقُولُ: "مَنْ قَامَ رَمَضَانَ إِيمَانًا وَاحْتِسَابًا غُفِرَ لَهُ مَا تَقَدَّمَ مِنْ ذَنْبِهِ." فَتُوُفِّيَ رَسُولُ اللَّهِ وَالأَمْرُ عَلَى ذَلِكَ ثُمَّ كَانَ الأَمْرُ عَلَى ذَلِكَ فِي خِلَافَةِ أَبِي بَكْرٍ وَصَدْرًا مِنْ خِلَافَةِ عُمَرَ عَلَى ذَلِكَ. Sahīh Muslim 759

468. When a Muslim opens a business, what does he pray for?

Answer: Salā(t) al-Istikhāra (صلاة الاستخارة) which means: *to get the right decision.* In Islam it means: *to ask Allah for proper guidance.*

You will hear this prayer pretty often in the Muslim world.

It goes back to a Hadith which was narrated by Jābir ibn 'Abd Allah (جَابِر بن عَبْد الله السَّلمِيّ): "The Prophet used to teach us the Istikhāra for each and every matter as he used to teach us the suras from the Qur'an. He used to say: 'If anyone of you intends to do something, he should offer a two Rakaʿāt prayer [Rakaʿa is a single unit of Islamic prayer] other than the obligatory prayer and then say:[638]

O Allah! I consult You, as You have all knowledge, and appeal to You to support me with Your Power and ask for Your Bounty, for You are able to do things while I am not, and You know while I do not; and You are the Knower of the Unseen. O Allah If You know it, this matter [the Muslim should name the matter now] is good for me both at present and in the future, [or in my religion], in my this life and in the Hereafter, then fulfil it for me and make it easy for me, and then bestow Your Blessings on me in that matter.

O Allah! If You know that this matter is not good for me in my religion, in my present life and in my coming Hereafter [or at present or in the future], then divert me from it and choose for me what is good wherever it may be and make me be pleased with it.'" [Then he should mention his matter or need.][639]

---

638 ...قَالَ كَانَ رَسُولُ اللَّهِ يُعَلِّمُ أَصْحَابَهُ الإِسْتِخَارَةَ فِي الأُمُورِ كُلِّهَا، كَمَا يُعَلِّمُ السُّورَةَ مِنَ الْقُرْآنِ يَقُولُ: "إِذَا هَمَّ أَحَدُكُم بِالأَمْرِ فَلْيَرْكَعْ رَكْعَتَيْنِ مِنْ غَيْرِ الْفَرِيضَةِ ثُمَّ لِيَقُلْ." Sahīh al-Bukhārī 7390

639 ...اللَّهُمَّ إِنِّي أَسْتَخِيرُكَ بِعِلْمِكَ، وَأَسْتَقْدِرُكَ بِقُدْرَتِكَ، وَأَسْأَلُكَ مِنْ فَضْلِكَ، فَإِنَّكَ تَقْدِرُ وَلاَ أَقْدِرُ، وَتَعْلَمُ وَلاَ أَعْلَمُ، وَأَنْتَ عَلاَّمُ الْغُيُوبِ، اللَّهُمَّ فَإِنْ كُنْتَ تَعْلَمُ هَذَا الأَمْرَ ثُمَّ تُسَمِّيهِ بِعَيْنِهِ خَيْرًا لِي فِي عَاجِلِ أَمْرِي وَآجِلِهِ قَالَ أَوْ فِي دِينِي وَمَعَاشِي وَعَاقِبَةِ أَمْرِي فَاقْدُرْهُ لِي، وَيَسِّرْهُ لِي، ثُمَّ بَارِكْ لِي فِيهِ، اللَّهُمَّ وَإِنْ كُنْتَ تَعْلَمُ أَنَّهُ شَرٌّ لِي فِي دِينِي وَمَعَاشِي وَعَاقِبَةِ أَمْرِي أَوْ قَالَ فِي عَاجِلِ أَمْرِي وَآجِلِهِ فَاصْرِفْنِي عَنْهُ، وَاقْدُرْ لِيَ الْخَيْرَ حَيْثُ كَانَ، ثُمَّ رَضِّنِي بِهِ. Sahīh al-Bukhārī 7390

469. What is Wakīra?

Answer: Food that is prepared on account of the completion of a building.

Muslims like to prepare food and invite people, especially their neighbours, as they see this as a way of showing gratitude to Allah. When a Muslim has finished a building or has bought property, he wants to repel evil things. He tries to achieve this by giving out food to people.

Such an event is called Wakīra (وَكِيرة). Muslims are not obliged by this, but it is recommended in Islam. The root w-k-r (و-ك-ر) means that *(a bird) comes to his nest*. Or *(the bird) prepared for himself a nest*. The Arabic word Wakr (وَكْر) denotes a *nest, abode,* or *retreat*. The term Wakīra is also used for food prepared by a woman as a requisite for a bride's preparation or for a traveller.

470. What does a Muslim recite when he gets a new house?

Answer: He reads sura 2 *The Cow* – in Arabic: al-Baqara (سُورة الْبَقَرة).

'Abū Hurayra (أَبُو هُرَيْرة) reported that Allah's Messenger had said: "Do not turn your houses into graveyards. Satan runs away from a house in which sura al-Baqara is recited."[640]

It doesn't matter if the (Muslim) owner recites the sura or turns on the TV or the internet to play the sura. What counts is that the whole sura - which is by the way the longest sura in the Qur'an - is recited entirely. Muslims believe what Muhammad has said, namely that the Devil will flee instantly from their house.

Note: Muslims must remember Allah every time they enter their house. Jābir ibn 'Abd Allah (جابِر بن عَبْد الله) narrated that he had heard the Prophet say: "When a man enters his house and remembers Allah, Satan would say [addressing himself]: 'You have <u>no</u> place to stay and <u>no</u> supper!' If he enters his house and does not remember Allah upon entering, Satan would say [addressing himself]: 'You

---

640 ...أَنَّ رَسُولَ اللَّهِ قَالَ: "لاَ تَجْعَلُوا بُيُوتَكُمْ مَقَابِرَ إِنَّ الشَّيْطَانَ يَنْفِرُ مِنَ الْبَيْتِ الَّذِي تُقْرَأُ فِيهِ سُورَةُ الْبَقَرَة." Sahīh Muslim 780

have found a place to stay!' And if he does not remember Allah when he eats, Satan would say [addressing himself]: 'You have found a place to stay and supper.'"[641]

471. What does a Muslim have to do after a dog has licked something?

Answer: The Muslim has to wash the spot seven times and then rub it once with earth/dust.

When I was in Egypt, every once in a while, reports came out about wild dogs that were killed in the streets, mostly by poison. People justified the killing by saying that such is commanded in Islam. In fact, this isn't entirely fiction.

- It was narrated from 'Abd Allah ibn 'Umar (عَبْد الله بن عُمَر) that the Messenger of Allah commanded that all dogs have to be killed, except dogs used for hunting or herding livestock.[642]

- 'Abd Allah ibn 'Umar reported that the Messenger of Allah ordered the killing of dogs and that he had sent [men] to the corners of Medina so that they should kill.[643]

- 'Abū al-Zubayr (أَبُو الزُّبَيْر) had heard Jābir ibn 'Abd Allah (جابِر بن عَبْد الله) as saying: "Allah's Messenger ordered us to kill dogs and we carried out this order so much so that we also killed the dog accompanying a woman from the desert. Then Allah's Apostle forbade their killing. He [the Prophet] said: 'Confine yourselves to the type jet-black [dog] which has two spots [on the eyes], for it is a devil.'"[644]

641 ... أَنَّهُ سَمِعَ النَّبِيَّ يَقُولُ: "إِذَا دَخَلَ الرَّجُلُ بَيْتَهُ فَذَكَرَ اللَّهَ عِنْدَ دُخُولِهِ وَعِنْدَ طَعَامِهِ قَالَ الشَّيْطَانُ لاَ مَبِيتَ لَكُمْ وَلاَ عَشَاءَ. وَإِذَا دَخَلَ وَلَمْ يَذْكُرِ اللَّهَ عِنْدَ دُخُولِهِ قَالَ الشَّيْطَانُ أَدْرَكْتُمُ الْمَبِيتَ. فَإِذَا لَمْ يَذْكُرِ اللَّهَ عِنْدَ طَعَامِهِ قَالَ أَدْرَكْتُمُ الْمَبِيتَ وَالْعَشَاءَ." Sunan ibn Māja 3887

642 ...أَنَّ رَسُولَ اللَّهِ أَمَرَ بِقَتْلِ الْكِلاَبِ إِلاَّ كَلْبَ صَيْدٍ أَوْ كَلْبَ مَاشِيَةٍ. Sunan al-Nasā'ī 4279

643 ...قَالَ أَمَرَ رَسُولُ اللَّهِ بِقَتْلِ الْكِلاَبِ فَأَرْسَلَ فِي أَقْطَارِ الْمَدِينَةِ أَنْ تُقْتَلَ. Sahīh Muslim 1570

644 ...يَقُولُ أَمَرَنَا رَسُولُ اللَّهِ بِقَتْلِ الْكِلاَبِ حَتَّى إِنَّ الْمَرْأَةَ تَقْدَمُ مِنَ الْبَادِيَةِ بِكَلْبِهَا فَنَقْتُلُهُ ثُمَّ نَهَى النَّبِيُّ عَنْ قَتْلِهَا وَقَالَ: "عَلَيْكُمْ بِالأَسْوَدِ الْبَهِيمِ ذِي النُّقْطَتَيْنِ فَإِنَّهُ شَيْطَانٌ." Sahīh Muslim 1572

There is a Hadith which gives Muslims an idea why Muhammad came to the conclusion that Muslims should avoid dogs and why he perhaps gave the order to kill them. In short: angels do not enter a house in which there is a dog or a picture, or statue.

Maymūna (مَيْمُونة بِنْت الْحارِث), one of Muhammad's wives, reported that one morning Allah's Messenger was silent with grief. Maymūna said: "O Messenger of Allah, I find a change in your mood today." The Prophet said: "Gabriel had promised me that he would meet me tonight, but he did not meet me. By Allah, he never broke his prom- ises." Allah's Messenger spent the day in this sad mood.

Then it occurred to him that there had been a puppy under their cot. He commanded to have it removed. He then took some water in his hand and sprinkled it at that place.

When it was evening, Gabriel met him and he [the Prophet] said to him: "You promised me that you would meet me the previous night."

Gabriel answered: "Yes, but we do not enter a house in which there is a dog or a picture."

Then, on that very morning, the Prophet commanded the killing of the dogs until he announced that the dog kept for the orchards should also be killed, but he spared the dog meant for the protection of extensive fields [or big gardens].[645]

In Islamic countries, you hardly see dogs held as pets. In recent years, however, rich Muslim families especially in Egypt and Tunisia started to have watchdogs. If a Muslim keeps a dog at home, he will receive a punishment. ʿAbd Allah ibn ʿUmar narrated that the Prophet had said: "Whoever keeps a dog [pet] which is neither a watch dog nor a hunting dog, will get a daily deduction of two Qīrāt from his good deeds."[646]

---

645 ...أَنَّ رَسُولَ اللَّهِ أَصْبَحَ يَوْمًا وَاجِمًا فَقَالَتْ مَيْمُونَةُ يَا رَسُولَ اللَّهِ لَقَدِ اسْتَنْكَرْتُ هَيْئَتَكَ مُنْذُ الْيَوْمِ. قَالَ رَسُولُ اللَّهِ " إِنَّ جِبْرِيلَ كَانَ وَعَدَنِي أَنْ يَلْقَانِي اللَّيْلَةَ فَلَمْ يَلْقَنِي أَمَ وَاللَّهِ مَا أَخْلَفَنِي ". قَالَ فَظَلَّ رَسُولُ اللَّهِ يَوْمَهُ ذَلِكَ عَلَى ذَلِكَ ثُمَّ وَقَعَ فِي نَفْسِهِ جِرْوُ كَلْبٍ تَحْتَ فُسْطَاطٍ لَنَا فَأَمَرَ بِهِ فَأُخْرِجَ ثُمَّ أَخَذَ بِيَدِهِ مَاءً فَنَضَحَ مَكَانَهُ فَلَمَّا أَمْسَى لَقِيَهُ جِبْرِيلُ فَقَالَ لَهُ " قَدْ كُنْتَ وَعَدْتَنِي أَنْ تَلْقَانِي الْبَارِحَةَ ". قَالَ أَجَلْ وَلَكِنَّا لاَ نَدْخُلُ بَيْتًا فِيهِ كَلْبٌ وَلاَ صُورَةٌ. فَأَصْبَحَ رَسُولُ اللَّهِ يَوْمَئِذٍ فَأَمَرَ بِقَتْلِ الْكِلاَبِ حَتَّى إِنَّهُ يَأْمُرُ بِقَتْلِ كَلْبِ الْحَائِطِ الصَّغِيرِ وَيَتْرُكُ كَلْبَ الْحَائِطِ الْكَبِيرِ. Sahīh Muslim 2105

646 ...النَّبِيُّ قَالَ: "مَنِ اقْتَنَى كَلْبًا لَيْسَ بِكَلْبِ مَاشِيَةٍ أَوْ ضَارِيَةٍ، نَقَصَ كُلَّ يَوْمٍ مِنْ عَمَلِهِ قِيرَاطَانِ."
Sahīh al-Bukhārī 5480

Excursus: What is a Qīrāt (قيراط)? According to the dictionary of the German scholar Hans Wehr, Qīrāt in modern-standard Arabic generally describes a measurement, for example: *inch, a dry measure,* or *a square measure.* Or it means: *carat* (fineness of a gold alloy).

In the Ancient Greek language, the word signifies a seed of the carob tree and also the weight thereof; a carat - which is: four grains. According to Edward Lane, in Mecca, a Qīrāt was the twenty-fourth part of a dinar. In most other countries, it was the twentieth part of a dinar.

There is no information in the Hadiths what Muhammad meant when he said Qīrāt. In some narrations, the term Qīrāt is either used as a measurement for small scales or metaphorically. In a Hadith narrated by Thawbān (ثَوْبان مَوْلَى رَسُّول الله), a freed slave of the Messenger of Allah, it is reported that Allah's Messenger once said: "He who offered prayers for the dead, for him is the reward of one Qīrāt, and he who attended the burial, he would have two Qīrāt as his reward. And Qīrāt is equivalent to 'Uhud."[647] The meaning here is that two Qīrāt is a very great reward.

However, Muslims who love dogs use another story to show fellow Muslims that dogs were not always bad. In sura 18 *The Cave* - in Arabic: al-Kahf (سُورة الْكَهْف) -, the story is told of the *Seven Sleepers*, in Islam known as the *men of the cave* – 'Ashāb al-Kahf (أَصْحاب الْكَهْف).

This legend is found in Christianity and Judaism as well. Islamic sources claim that the Jews tried to challenge the Prophet by asking him to explain the story of the Sleepers. The Prophet promised to do it "tomorrow" as quoted in verse 18:23, but he did not receive a revelation for some days. Eventually the information came down.

Legend has it that at a time when Christians were persecuted, some young Christians (perhaps from Ephesus in present-day Turkey) withdrew into a secluded cave. **In the Islamic version, these so-called *Sleepers* had a dog with them.** The dog was also asleep, but when someone would approach the cave, the dog woold look as if it was watching the entrance, making any intruder afraid and leave.

---

647 ...النَّبِيُّ قَالَ: "مَنْ صَلَّى عَلَى جَنَازَةٍ فَلَهُ قِيرَاطٌ وَمَنِ اتَّبَعَهَا حَتَّى تُوضَعَ فِي الْقَبْرِ فَقِيرَاطَانِ." قَالَ
قُلْتُ يَا أَبَا هُرَيْرَةَ وَمَا الْقِيرَاطُ قَالَ: "مِثْلُ أُحُدٍ." Sahīh Muslim 945

The young men miraculously slept for about three centuries. When they awoke, one of them tried to get some food in town and discovered that the situation had changed completely: Christians were no longer persecuted and furthermore, Christianity had become the official religion of the Roman Empire.

Classical Islamic commentators mainly used this Christian legend to explain the Qur'anic verses about the *Men of the Cave*. However, modern scholars such as Muhammad Asad suggest that "the Christian formulation of this theme is a later development of a much older oral tradition – a tradition which, in fact, goes back to pre-Christian, Jewish sources."

Let's go back to our topic: What if a cat licks something?

This is a minor problem. 'Abū Hurayra (أَبُو هُرَيْرَة) narrated that the Prophet had said: "And when the cat drinks out of it, wash it once."[648]

What other animals did the Prophet order to kill?

Mainly snakes.

'Abd Allah ibn 'Umar reported: "I heard Allah's Messenger commanding the killing of dogs and the killing of the striped and the short-tailed snakes, for both of them affect the eyesight adversely and cause miscarriage."

'Abd Allah ibn 'Umar added: "I did not spare any snake. I rather killed everyone that I saw. One day when I was pursuing a snake from among the snakes of the house, Zayd ibn al-Khattāb (زَيْد بن الْخَطَّاب) or 'Abū Lubāba (أَبُو لُبَابة) happened to pass by me and found me pursuing it.

He said: "O 'Abd Allah, wait!" I replied: "Allah's Messenger commanded [us] to kill them, whereupon he said that Allah's Messenger forbade the killing of snakes found in the houses [except the short-tailed snakes and those having streaks upon them]."[649]

---

648 ...قَالَ النَّبِيُّ: "إِذَا وَلَغَتْ فِيه الْهِرَّةُ غُسِلَ مَرَّةً." Jāmiʿ al-Tirmidhī 91

649 ...قَالَ سَمِعْتُ رَسُولَ اللَّهِ يَأْمُرُ بِقَتْلِ الْكِلَابِ يَقُولُ: "اقْتُلُوا الْحَيَّاتِ وَالْكِلَابَ وَاقْتُلُوا ذَا الطُّفْيَتَيْنِ وَالْأَبْتَرَ فَإِنَّهُمَا يَلْتَمِسَانِ الْبَصَرَ وَيَسْتَسْقِطَانِ الْحَبَالَى." قَالَ سَالِمٌ قَالَ عَبْدُ اللَّهِ بْنُ عُمَرَ فَلَبِثْتُ لَا أَتْرُكُ حَيَّةً أَرَاهَا إِلَّا قَتَلْتُهَا فَبَيْنَمَا أَنَا أُطَارِدُ حَيَّةً يَوْمًا مِنْ ذَوَاتِ الْبُيُوتِ مَرَّ بِي زَيْدُ بْنُ الْخَطَّابِ أَوْ أَبُو لُبَابَةَ وَأَنَا أُطَارِدُهَا فَقَالَ مَهْلًا يَا عَبْدَ اللَّهِ. فَقُلْتُ إِنَّ رَسُولَ اللَّهِ أَمَرَ بِقَتْلِهِنَّ. قَالَ إِنَّ رَسُولَ اللَّهِ قَدْ نَهَى عَنْ ذَوَاتِ الْبُيُوتِ. Sahīh Muslim 2233

472. Should Muslims kill geckos?

Answer: Yes.

It was narrated by 'Ā'isha (عائشة بِنْت أَبِي بَكْر) that the Prophet had said: "Geckos are vermin."[650]

Muhammad even commanded Muslims to kill geckos. 'Āmir ibn Sa'd (عامِر بن سَعْد) reported on the authority of his father that Allah's Apostle commanded the killing of geckos and he called them little noxious creatures.[651]

'Abū Hurayra (أَبُو هُرَيْرة) narrated that the Messenger of Allah had said: "He who killed a gecko with the first stroke for him is such and such a reward, and he who killed it with a second stroke for him is such and such reward less than the first one, and he who killed it with the third stroke for him is such and such a reward [less than the second one]."[652]

It was narrated from Sa'īd ibn al-Musayyab (سَعِيد بن الْمُسَيَّب) that a woman once entered upon 'Ā'isha. In 'Ā'isha's hand was an iron-footed stick. She [the woman] asked: "What is this?" She ['Ā'isha] answered: "It is for these geckos because the Prophet told us that there was nothing that did not try to extinguish the fire for Abraham [who was thrown into the fire] except for this animal [which kept it burning], so he told us to kill it."[653]

The story of Abraham and the gecko - as mentioned in the Hadith - is well-known in Islamic mythology. After Abraham had built the Ka'ba and had destroyed all other symbols of belief, the people wanted to burn him. When the fire was burning, the <u>frog</u> tried to help Abraham, by taking water in its mouth and spitting it in the fire. However, the <u>gecko</u> did the opposite as it blew into the fire so that

650 ...أَنَّ رَسُولَ اللَّهِ قَالَ: "الْوَزَغُ الْفُوَيْسِقُ." Sunan al-Nasā'ī 2886

651 ...أَنَّ النَّبِيَّ أَمَرَ بِقَتْلِ الْوَزَغِ وَسَمَّاهُ فُوَيْسِقًا. Sahīh Muslim 2238

652 ...قَالَ رَسُولُ اللَّهِ: "مَنْ قَتَلَ وَزَغَةً فِي أَوَّلِ ضَرْبَةٍ فَلَهُ كَذَا وَكَذَا حَسَنَةً وَمَنْ قَتَلَهَا فِي الضَّرْبَةِ الثَّانِيَةِ فَلَهُ كَذَا وَكَذَا حَسَنَةً لِدُونِ الأُولَى وَإِنْ قَتَلَهَا فِي الضَّرْبَةِ الثَّالِثَةِ فَلَهُ كَذَا وَكَذَا حَسَنَةً لِدُونِ الثَّانِيَةِ". Sahīh Muslim 2240

653 ...أَنَّ امْرَأَةً، دَخَلَتْ عَلَى عَائِشَةَ وَبِيَدِهَا عُكَّازٌ فَقَالَتْ مَا هَذَا فَقَالَتْ لِهَذِهِ الْوَزَغِ لأَنَّ نَبِيَّ اللَّهِ حَدَّثَنَا: "أَنَّهُ لَمْ يَكُنْ شَيْءٌ إِلاَّ يُطْفِئُ عَلَى إِبْرَاهِيمَ إِلاَّ هَذِهِ الدَّابَّةُ." فَأَمَرَنَا بِقَتْلِهَا وَنَهَى عَنْ قَتْلِ الْجِنَّانِ إِلاَّ ذَا الطُّفْيَتَيْنِ وَالأَبْتَرَ فَإِنَّهُمَا يُطْمِسَانِ الْبَصَرَ وَيُسْقِطَانِ مَا فِي بُطُونِ النِّسَاءِ. Sunan al-Nasā'ī 2831 (2834)

the flames would get higher. From that time one the gecko became a symbol for unbelievers in Islam.

It is not clear which type of gecko the Prophet meant, but very likely a species that was common inside the house.

In the Hadiths the Arabic word Wazagha (وَزَغة) is used. Although this word is today used for geckos (or certain types of lizards), the word Wazagha denoted perhaps a special type: perhaps the common Baluch Rock Gecko (*Bunopus tuberculatus*) which is commonly found in homes in Saudi Arabia. Because of its mottled skin, resembling that of a leper, it is also called Burs (بُرَص). In Arabic, Baras (بَرَص) is the word for leprosy. Some even claimed that the gecko caused leprosy, a disease which was widespread at the time of the Prophet, and which perhaps has led to his command to exterminate them.

Excursus: Are Muslims allowed to kill frogs?

Answer: No. The Arabic word for frog is Difda' (ضِفْضَع). 'Abd al-Rahmān ibn 'Uthmān (عَبْد الرَّحْمن بن عُثْمان) narrated: "When a physician consulted the Prophet about using frogs in medicine, he forbade him to kill them."[654]

In Islam the frog is seen as a good animal because it helped to extinguish the fire which was meant to kill Abraham. Furthermore, Muslims are not allowed to eat frogs (mainly for reasons of cleanliness). As a general rule we could say that animals which Muslims are forbidden to kill should not be eaten.

654... أَنَّ طَبِيبًا، سَأَلَ النَّبِيَّ عَنْ ضِفْدَعٍ يَجْعَلُهَا في دَوَاءٍ فَنَهَاهُ النَّبِيُّ عَنْ قَتْلِهَا. Sunan 'Abī Dāwūd.
5269

473. Why is pork forbidden in Islam?

Answer: Because it is written in the Qur'an and the Prophet has said so.

Muslims have difficulties explaining why pork is forbidden. Some name health risks. Devout Muslims, however, told me that neither the Prophet nor the Qur'an gave any reason why pork is forbidden.

When Muslims struggle to explain a particular command of Allah, the Qur'an offers them a way out. They can cite two verses which basically say whether the reason behind a duty or a prohibition is clear or not, a Muslim has to obey and should not think about it too much.

33:36	When God and His Messenger have decided on a matter that concerns them, it is not fitting for any believing man or woman to claim freedom of choice in that matter: whoever disobeys God and His Messenger is far astray.	وَمَا كَانَ لِمُؤْمِنٍ وَلَا مُؤْمِنَةٍ إِذَا قَضَى اللَّهُ وَرَسُولُهُ أَمْرًا أَن يَكُونَ لَهُمُ الْخِيَرَةُ مِنْ أَمْرِهِمْ وَمَن يَعْصِ اللَّهَ وَرَسُولَهُ فَقَدْ ضَلَّ ضَلَالًا مُّبِينًا.
4:65	By your Lord, they will not be true believers until they let you decide between them in all matters of dispute, and find no resistance in their souls to your decisions, accepting them totally.	فَلَا وَرَبِّكَ لَا يُؤْمِنُونَ حَتَّى يُحَكِّمُوكَ فِيمَا شَجَرَ بَيْنَهُمْ ثُمَّ لَا يَجِدُوا فِي أَنفُسِهِمْ حَرَجًا مِّمَّا قَضَيْتَ وَيُسَلِّمُوا تَسْلِيمًا.

Now let's look what the Qur'an says about pork. Sura 2 *The Cow* - al-Baqara (سورة الْبَقَرة) - states that pork is forbidden for Muslims:

2:173	He has only forbidden you carrion, blood, pig's meat [pork], and animals over which any name other than God's has been invoked. But if anyone is forced to eat such things by hunger, rather than desire or excess, he commits no sin: God is most merciful and forgiving.	إِنَّمَا حَرَّمَ عَلَيْكُمُ الْمَيْتَةَ وَالدَّمَ وَلَحْمَ الْخِنزِيرِ وَمَا أُهِلَّ بِهِ لِغَيْرِ اللَّهِ فَمَنِ اضْطُرَّ غَيْرَ بَاغٍ وَلَا عَادٍ فَلَا إِثْمَ عَلَيْهِ إِنَّ اللَّهَ غَفُورٌ رَّحِيمٌ.

This means that only if there is no other food available and when a Muslim is starving to such an extent that he is on the edge of dying, he can eat pork. As a general rule in Islam, in cases of danger or necessity, forbidden things may be permitted.

May a Muslim sell pork (for example in a restaurant or shop)?

Clearly, no. Traditional scholars even say a Muslim is not allowed to work as a dishwasher in a pizzeria which sells Pizza Prosciutto simply because a Muslim should not support things that are against the teachings of Islam. This means that selling pork is forbidden under any circumstance.

This is based on an important Hadith which states: When Allah forbids something, Allah also forbids its price. This means that a Muslim shall not sell or trade it. It was narrated by 'Abū Hurayra (أَبُو هُرَيْرَة) that the Messenger of Allah had said: "Allah forbade wine and the price paid for it, and forbade dead meat and the price paid for it, and forbade swine and the price paid for it."[655]

Other Hadiths, however, indicate that pork was eaten and used variously at the time of the Prophet. It was reported by 'Urwa ibn al-Zubayr (عُرْوة بن الزُّبَيْر) that 'Abd Allah ibn al-Zubayr (عَبْد الله بن الزُّبَيْر), during a speech delivered in Mecca, came across the topic of al-Mut'a (الْمُتْعة) [*which is the temporary marriage; an ancient Islamic practice that unites man and woman as husband and wife for a limited time. Historically it was used so that a man could have a wife for a short while when travelling long distances.*]. Ibn 'Abū 'Amra al-'Ansārī commented on this: "It was permitted in the early days of Islam, [for one] who was driven to it under the stress of necessity just as [the eating of] carrion and the blood and **flesh of swine.** Then Allah intensified [the commands of] His religion and prohibited it [altogether]."[656]

The pig became more and more a symbol for bad things in Islam starting at the time of Muhammad. Sulaymān ibn Burayda (سُلَيْمان بن بُرَيْدة) reported, on the authority of his father, that Allah's Apostle had said: "He who played Nardashīr (نَرْدَشِير) [a game similar to backgam-

---

655 ...أَنَّ رَسُولَ اللَّهِ قَالَ: "إِنَّ اللَّهَ حَرَّمَ الْخَمْرَ وَثَمَنَهَا وَحَرَّمَ الْمَيْتَةَ وَثَمَنَهَا وَحَرَّمَ الْجِنْزِيرَ وَثَمَنَهُ."
Sunan 'Abī Dāwūd 3485 (3478)

656 ...قَالَ ابْنُ أَبِي عَمْرَةَ إِنَّهَا كَانَتْ رُخْصَةً فِي أَوَّلِ الإِسْلامِ لِمَنِ اضْطُرَّ إِلَيْهَا كَالْمَيْتَةِ وَالدَّمِ وَلَحْمِ الْجِنْزِيرِ ثُمَّ أَحْكَمَ اللَّهُ الدِّينَ وَنَهَى عَنْهَا. Sahīh Muslim 1406

mon] is like one who dyed his hand with the flesh and blood of swine."[657]

What should a Muslim do if someone cooked pork in his pot?

Some Muslims use the narrations about dogs (when the dog has licked something; see chapter 471) and apply it to the pig. This means that they wash such pots seven times with water and one time with earth/dust.

There is no Islamic source which states that dogs and pigs are interlinked regarding prohibitions. Actually there is no need for a Muslim to wash things excessively after a pig has touched them – one time thoroughly should be enough. This is supported by the Hadiths.

'Abū Tha'laba al-Khushanī (أَبُو ثَعْلَبَة الْخُشَنِيّ) recounted that he had asked Allah's Messenger: "We live in the neighbourhood of the People of the Book and they cook in their pots [the flesh of] swine and drink wine in their vessels." The Messenger of Allah said: "If you find any other pots, then eat and drink from them. But if you do not find any others, then wash them with water and eat and drink [from them]."[658]

Excursus: What about the Jews and Christians?

Religious restrictions on the consumption of pork had already been a tradition in the ancient Near East. Jews until today are not allowed to eat pork because it is written in their holy scripts, for example in *Deuteronomy* 14:8: "Also the swine is unclean for you, because it has cloven hooves, yet does not chew the cud; you shall not eat their flesh or touch their dead carcasses."

Most Christian sects, however, permit pork. They justify eating pork by Saint Peter's vision. According to the *Acts of the Apostles*, chapter 10, Peter had a vision of a sheet full of animals being lowered from heaven. A voice from heaven told Peter to kill and eat, but since the sheet contained unclean animals, Peter declined. The command

---

657 ...أَنَّ النَّبِيَّ قَالَ: "مَنْ لَعِبَ بِالنَّرْدَشِيرِ فَكَأَنَّمَا صَبَغَ يَدَهُ فِي لَحْم خِنْزِيرٍ وَدَمِهِ." Ṣaḥīḥ Muslim 2260

658 ...أَنَّهُ سَأَلَ رَسُولَ اللَّهِ قَالَ إِنَّا نُجَاوِرُ أَهْلَ الْكِتَابِ وَهُمْ يَطْبُخُونَ فِي قُدُورِهِمُ الْخِنْزِيرَ وَيَشْرَبُونَ فِي آنِيَتِهِمُ الْخَمْرَ. فَقَالَ رَسُولُ اللَّهِ: "إِنْ وَجَدْتُمْ غَيْرَهَا فَكُلُوا فِيهَا وَاشْرَبُوا وَإِنْ لَمْ تَجِدُوا غَيْرَهَا فَارْحَضُوهَا بِالْمَاءِ وَكُلُوا وَاشْرَبُوا." Sunan 'Abī Dāwūd 3839

was repeated two more times, along with the voice saying: "This was done three times. And the object was taken up into heaven again. And a voice spoke to him again the second time, 'What God has cleansed you shall not call common (profane).'" (Acts 10:15-16).

How did the pig get such a bad reputation?

The simplest explanation Muslims told me is that the pig is a filthy animal and people might have thought that the meat is bad too because of this.

Several Muslims told me that it had to do with the parasitic disease *Trichinosis*, which is caused by roundworms and can be present in pork. However, if the meat - ccooked or grilled - reaches an internal temperature of at least 74 °C (165 °F) for at least 15 seconds, it should be safe. Raw meat in general is a health risk, so why should only pork be forbidden?

In the Middle East archaeologists found pig remains related to ritual pig slaughtering indicating that the pig was not a "bad" animal in the pre-Bronze Age. Marvin Harris, a US anthropologist who died in 2001, suggested that the main reason for prohibiting the consumption of pork could have been "ecological-economical". Pigs require water and shady woods with seed plants. Those conditions are scarce in the Middle East. Two thousand years BC, the woods became scarce because people started farming and smelting copper ore for which a lot of firewood was needed. Through the deforestation the living space of the pigs changed dramatically. Pigs used to live and find food in oak and beech woods.

Pigs cannot sweat - they do not have sweat glands - so they need water/mud to cool down. Since they could not find enough open water, they started to wallow in their excrements for cooling purposes. The shrinking forests forced the pigs to find space and food elsewhere and they started to eat the grains in the fields. Harris concluded in his book *The Abominable Pig* (1985) that "raising pigs in the Middle East therefore was and still is a lot costlier than raising ruminants, because pigs must be provided with artificial shade, extra water for wallowing and their diet must be supplemented with grains and other plant foods that humans themselves can eat".

The pig had been domesticated for one purpose only, namely to supply meat. People used to breed cows, sheep, and goats – ruminants that eat plants that are high in cellulose content and unfit for human consumption. Harris suggested that it was perhaps at that time, when the prohibition of pig meat started. In the Middle East, as ecological conditions became unfavourable for raising pigs, the creature became not only useless, but worse than that: it became detrimental to the well-being of humans.

In the Qur'an, pork is specifically prohibited while camel flesh is specifically allowed. Harris wrote: "The whole way of life of Muhammad's desert-dwelling, pastoral Bedouin followers was based on the camel. The camel was their main source of transport and their main source of animal food, primarily in the form of camel milk." He concluded: "An Islam that banned camel flesh would never have become a great world religion. It would have been unable to conquer the Arabian heartlands, to launch its attack against the Byzantine and Persian empires and to cross the Sahara to the Sahel and West Africa."

Marvin Harris had an interesting hypothesis why Islam failed to conquer some countries – and the main reason was because of pigs.

In his book *The Abominable Pig*, Harris wrote: "Wherever Islam has penetrated to regions in which pig raising was a mainstay of the traditional farming systems, it has failed to win over substantial portions of the population.

Regions such as Malaysia, Indonesia, the Philippines and Africa south of the Sahara, parts of which are ecologically well suited for pig raising, constitute the outer limits of the active spread of Islam. All along this frontier, the resistance of pig-eating Christians has prevented Islam from becoming the dominant religion."

He continued: "In China, one of the world centres of pig production, Islam has made small inroads and is confined largely to the arid and semiarid western provinces. Islam, in other words, to this very day has a geographical limit which coincides with the ecological zones of transition between forested regions well suited for pig husbandry and regions where too much sun and dry heat make pig husbandry a risky and expensive practice."

474. Are Muslims allowed to eat gummy bears?

Answer: If they were produced in Europe, most probably not.

Around 80 per cent of the edible gelatine produced in Europe is pure **pig-skin** gelatine which is the main ingredient of gummy bears.

In Islam, the prohibition of pork is not limited to the consumption of the pig's meat; the use of any body part of a pig is forbidden.

Jābir ibn 'Abd Allah (جابر بن عَبْد الله) reported that Allah's Messenger, while he was in Mecca, said in the year of the Conquest of Mecca: "Verily Allah and His Messenger have forbidden the sale of wine, carcass, swine, and idols." The people said: "Allah's Messenger, you see that the fat of the carcass is used for coating the boats and varnishing the hides and people use it for lighting purposes." Whereupon he [Muhammad] said: "No, it is forbidden!"[659]

Allah's Messenger further said: "May Allah the Exalted and Majestic destroy the Jews! When Allah forbade the use of fat of the carcass for them, they melted it and then sold it and made use of its price [profited from it]."[660]

475. Muslims are only allowed to swear by whom?

Answer: By Allah.

In Arabic countries, you will hear the expression "Wallāhi!" (وَاللَّهِ) all the time. It literally means: "By Allah!"

'Abd Allah ibn 'Umar (عَبْد الله بن عُمَر) reported that Allah's Messenger once found 'Umar ibn al-Khattāb among the riders and he was taking an oath by his father. Allah's Messenger called them [saying]: "Our Allah, the Exalted and Majestic, has forbidden that you take an oath by your father. He who need to take an oath, he must take it by Allah or keep quiet."[661]

---

659 ...سَمِعَ رَسُولَ اللَّهِ يَقُولُ عَامَ الْفَتْحِ وَهُوَ بِمَكَّةَ: "إِنَّ اللَّهَ وَرَسُولَهُ حَرَّمَ بَيْعَ الْخَمْرِ وَالْمَيْتَةِ وَالْجِنْزِيرِ وَالْأَصْنَامِ." فَقِيلَ يَا رَسُولَ اللَّهِ أَرَأَيْتَ شُحُومَ الْمَيْتَةِ فَإِنَّهُ يُطْلَى بِهَا السُّفُنُ وَيُدْهَنُ بِهَا الْجُلُودُ وَيَسْتَصْبِحُ بِهَا النَّاسُ فَقَالَ: "لَا هُوَ حَرَامٌ." Sahīh Muslim 1581

660 ...ثُمَّ قَالَ رَسُولُ اللَّهِ عِنْدَ ذَلِكَ: "قَاتَلَ اللَّهُ الْيَهُودَ إِنَّ اللَّهَ عَزَّ وَجَلَّ لَمَّا حَرَّمَ عَلَيْهِمْ شُحُومَهَا أَجْمَلُوهُ ثُمَّ بَاعُوهُ فَأَكَلُوا ثَمَنَهُ." Sahīh Muslim 1581

661 ...أَدْرَكَ عُمَرَ بْنَ الْخَطَّابِ فِي رَكْبٍ وَعُمَرُ يَحْلِفُ بِأَبِيهِ فَنَادَاهُمْ رَسُولُ اللَّهِ: "أَلَا إِنَّ اللَّهَ عَزَّ وَجَلَّ يَنْهَاكُمْ أَنْ تَحْلِفُوا بِآبَائِكُمْ فَمَنْ كَانَ حَالِفًا فَلْيَحْلِفْ بِاللَّهِ أَوْ لِيَصْمُتْ." Sahīh Muslim 1646

An oath is not binding unless it is sworn by Allah, one of the names of Allah or by one of Allah's attributes. Swearing by the Qur'an is swearing by the word of Allah which is seen as one of Allah's attributes. Traditional scholars say that it is better not to swear by the Qur'an. Since it is a printed book, it contains paper and ink which should not be sworn by.

Saʿd ibn ʿUbayda (سَعْد بن عُبَيْدة) narrated that ʿAbd Allah ibn ʿUmar heard a man say: "By the Kaʿba!" So Ibn ʿUmar said: "Nothing is sworn by other than Allah, for I heard the Messenger of Allah say: 'Whoever swears by other than Allah, he has committed disbelief or shirk [sin of polytheism].'"[662]

476. Why do some Muslims call Jews *apes and swine*?

Answer: They refer to parts in the Qur'an and in the Hadiths.

In the Qur'an it is written that Allah transformed some of the *Children of Israel* into monkeys. Allah was angry and punished them for their disobedience. This is told in sura 2 *The Cow* – in Arabic: al-Baqara (سُورة الْبَقَرة):

2:65	You know about those of you who broke the Sabbath [i.e. Saturday], and so We said to them, 'Be like apes! Be outcasts!'	وَلَقَدْ عَلِمْتُمُ الَّذِينَ اعْتَدَوْا مِنكُمْ فِي السَّبْتِ فَقُلْنَا لَهُمْ كُونُوا قِرَدَةً خَاسِئِينَ!

Some translators interpret this as a metaphor. Abdel Haleem - whose translation of the verse is used here - writes that "this is understood by some as 'physically turn into apes' but in fact it is a figure of speech - the structure 'be apes' is like 'be stones/iron' in [verse] 17: 50. Just as the Qur'an describes the disbelievers as blind, deaf, and dumb, here the transgressors are apes."

The Hadiths indicate that the Prophet was serious about this and did not regard this as a figure of speech. The Prophet told his followers that these transformed apes (later he mentions also swine) did not have offspring. ʿAbd Allah ibn Masʿūd (عَبْد الله بن مَسْعُود) narrated

---

662 ...سَمِعَ رَجُلًا، يَقُولُ لاَ وَالْكَعْبَةِ. فَقَالَ ابْنُ عُمَرَ لاَ يُحْلَفُ بِغَيْرِ اللَّهِ فَإِنِّي سَمِعْتُ رَسُولَ اللَّهِ يَقُولُ: "مَنْ حَلَفَ بِغَيْرِ اللَّهِ فَقَدْ كَفَرَ أَوْ أَشْرَكَ." Jāmiʿ al-Tirmidhī 1535

that 'Umm Habība (أُمّ حَبِيبة) said: "A person asked: Allah's Messenger, what about those apes and swine which suffered metamorphosis?" Thereupon Allah's Apostle said: "Verily, Allah, the Exalted and Glorious, did not destroy a people or did not torment a people, and let their race grow. **Apes and swine** had been even before that [when the deniers of truth were tormented and suffered metamorphosis]."[663]

This punishment was not exclusively for the Children of Israel. The Prophet told his followers that the Day of Judgement will not begin until such transformation happens among his followers - his 'Umma - too. It was narrated from 'Abū Mālik al-'Ash'arī (أَبُو مالِك الْأَشْعَرِيّ) that the Messenger of Allah had said: "People among my nation ['Umma] will drink wine, calling it by another name, and musical instruments will be played for them and singing girls [will sing for them]. Allah will cause the earth to swallow them up and will turn them into **monkeys and pigs**."[664]

The *Book of Bloody Fights* - in Arabic: Kitāb al-Malāhim (كِتاب الْمَلاحِم) - is the name of a chapter in the Hadith collection *Sunan 'Abī Dāwūd* (سُنَن أَبِي داوُد). Therein are some obscure narrations of the Prophet about future wars, for example against Rome and Constantinople, about battles with the Turks, and about strange descriptions of cities. One is about a place called al-Basra or al-Busayra.

'Anas ibn Mālik (أَنَس بن مالِك) narrated that the Prophet said: "The people will establish cities, 'Anas, and one of them will be called al-Basra or al-Busayra. If you should pass by it or enter it, avoid its salt-marshes, its pastures, its market and the gate of its commanders, and keep to its surroundings, for the earth will swallow some people up, pelting rain will fall and earthquakes will take place in it, and there will be people who will spend the night in it and become **apes and swine** in the morning."[665]

---

663 ...فَقَالَ رَجُلٌ يَا رَسُولَ اللَّهِ الْقِرَدَةُ وَالْخَنَازِيرُ هِيَ مِمَّا مُسِخَ فَقَالَ النَّبِيُّ: "إِنَّ اللَّهَ عَزَّ وَجَلَّ لَمْ يُهْلِكْ قَوْمًا أَوْ يُعَذِّبْ قَوْمًا فَيَجْعَلَ لَهُمْ نَسْلاً وَإِنَّ الْقِرَدَةَ وَالْخَنَازِيرَ كَانُوا قَبْلَ ذَلِكَ." Sahīh Muslim 2663

664 ...قَالَ رَسُولُ اللَّهِ: "لَيَشْرَبَنَّ نَاسٌ مِنْ أُمَّتِي الْخَمْرَ يُسَمُّونَهَا بِغَيْرِ اسْمِهَا يُعْزَفُ عَلَى رُءُوسِهِمْ بِالْمَعَازِفِ وَالْمُغَنِّيَاتِ يَخْسِفُ اللَّهُ بِهِمُ الْأَرْضَ وَيَجْعَلُ مِنْهُمُ الْقِرَدَةَ وَالْخَنَازِيرَ." Sunan ibn Māja 4020; hasan

665 ....أَنَّ رَسُولَ اللَّهِ قَالَ لَهُ: "يَا أَنَسُ إِنَّ النَّاسَ يُمَصِّرُونَ أَمْصَارًا وَإِنَّ مِصْرًا مِنْهَا يُقَالُ لَهُ الْبَصْرَةُ أَوِ الْبُصَيْرَةُ فَإِنْ أَنْتَ مَرَرْتَ بِهَا أَوْ دَخَلْتَهَا فَإِيَّاكَ وَسِبَاخَهَا وَكِلاَءَهَا وَسُوقَهَا وَبَابَ أُمَرَائِهَا وَعَلَيْكَ

The swine will play a role in the *Day of Judgement* - Allah's final verdict. 'Abū Hurayra (أَبُو هُرَيْرة) narrated that the Messenger of Allah said: "I swear by Allah that the son of Mary will certainly descend as a just judge and he would definitely break the cross and **kill swine** and abolish Jizya and would leave the young she-camel and no one would endeavour to [collect Zakā on it]. Spite, mutual hatred and jealousy against one another will certainly disappear and when he summons people to accept wealth, not even one would do so."[666]

Note: In a TV interview in 2010, Muhammad Mursi, a leading figure of the Muslim Brotherhood in Egypt and who later became president of Egypt, described Jews ("Zionists") as "descendants of apes and pigs". This stirred an outcry in the West when it was discovered during Mursi's presidency.

Western media and politicians accused him of anti-Semitism. The office of the US-president (Barack Obama) strongly condemned the saying. The president's spokesperson said: "We completely reject these statements [apes and pigs], as we do any language that espouses religious hatred. This kind of discourse has been acceptable in the region for far too long, and is counter to the goal of peace."

477. What is a Zabība?

Answer: Zabība (زَبِيبة) is an Egyptian term for a prayer bump.

A Zabība is a mark on the forehead of Muslim men, apparently due to the friction generated by repeated contact of the forehead with the prayer mat. Although Muslim women pray as well, the mark is almost exclusively found among men. This has to do with the politicisation of Islam. 'Anwar al-Sādāt, the Egyptian president who made peace with Israel in the 1970s, was the first Egyptian president with a slightly visible Zabība. After Sādāt was assassinated by mem-

---

بِضَوَاجِيهَا فَإِنَّهُ يَكُونُ بِهَا خَسْفٌ وَقَذْفٌ وَرَجْفٌ وَقَوْمٌ يَبِيتُونَ يُصْبِحُونَ قِرَدَةً وَخَنَازِيرَ." Sunan 'Abī Dāwūd 4307 (4293)

666 ...قَالَ رَسُولُ اللَّهِ: "وَاللَّهِ لَيَنْزِلَنَّ ابْنُ مَرْيَمَ حَكَمًا عَادِلاً فَلَيَكْسِرَنَّ الصَّلِيبَ وَلَيَقْتُلَنَّ الْخِنْزِيرَ وَلَيَضَعَنَّ الْجِزْيَةَ وَلَتُتْرَكَنَّ الْقِلاَصُ فَلاَ يُسْعَى عَلَيْهَا وَلَتَذْهَبَنَّ الشَّحْنَاءُ وَالتَّبَاغُضُ وَالتَّحَاسُدُ وَلَيَدْعُوَنَّ إِلَى الْمَالِ فَلاَ يَقْبَلُهُ أَحَدٌ." Sahīh Muslim 155

bers of a militant Islamic group, Hosni Mubarak, a military general, succeeded him. He oppressed any kind of freedom. At the same time, poor Egyptians from the countryside started to work in Saudi Arabia and other Gulf countries and "imported" a very conservative view of Islam. Women started to wear the veil, some also the Niqāb. And what did Egyptian men do to show that they are very pious Muslims? They got a Zabība.

Pious Muslims were treated with respect in a country that did not respect its people. Islam, furthermore, was the only free space the regime could not take from the people. The Zabība became an Islam- ic symbol. It became popular among the members of the Muslim Brotherhood – for example two of their most important figures, Muhammad al-Biltāgī (الْبِلْتَاجِيّ) and Saʿd al-Katātnī (الْكَتَاتْنِيّ) had huge prayer bumps. And it was popular among Salafi Muslims as well. A huge Zabība is on the forehead of Yāssir Burhāmī (ياسِر بُرْهامِي), an influential Salafi preacher in Alexandria. It almost covers his whole forehead in the form of an oval ring.

The Zabība is so widespread in Egypt that it is now almost easier to find a man with a Zabība than without it. Even the current Egyp- tian ruler, ʿAbd al-Fattāh al-Sisī, has a slight spot on his forehead. The Zabība has spread to neighbouring countries as well.

Now let's look at the origin of the Zabība. There is a verse in the Qur'an which can be interpreted as a source for the Zabība, sura 48 *The Triumph* – in Arabic: al-Fath (سُورة الْفَتْح):

| 48:29 | Muhammad is the Messenger of God. Those who follow him are harsh towards the disbelievers and compassionate to- wards each other. You see them kneeling and prostrating, seeking God's bounty and His good pleasure: on their faces they bear the marks of their prostrations. | مُحَمَّدٌ رَّسُولُ اللَّهِ وَالَّذِينَ مَعَهُ أَشِدَّاءُ عَلَى الْكُفَّارِ رُحَمَاءُ بَيْنَهُمْ تَرَاهُمْ رُكَّعًا سُجَّدًا يَبْتَغُونَ فَضْلًا مِّنَ اللَّهِ وَرِضْوَانًا سِيمَاهُمْ فِي وُجُوهِهِم مِّنْ أَثَرِ السُّجُودِ ۚ |

The expression that the face bears the mark of the prostrations was commonly interpreted as a spot on the forehead.

The Arabic word Zabība (زبيبة) can mean (*one piece of*) *raisin* or *a small purulent swelling* or *pustule* that comes forth upon the hand (*abscess in the hand*). Originally, the word Zabība was used for animals. In the Hadiths, Zabība is used in the meaning of *the poison gland in the mouth of a serpent.*

'Abū Hurayra (أَبُو هُرَيْرة) has narrated that Allah's Messenger said: "Anyone whom Allah has given wealth but who does not pay the Zakā, then, on the Day of Resurrection, his wealth will be presented to him in the shape of a bald-headed poisonous male snake with two poisonous glands in its mouth and it will encircle itself round his neck and bite him over his cheeks and say: 'I am your wealth! I am your treasure!'"[667]

478. Why is it tricky to find the direction to Mecca in New York?

Answer: Because the earth is not flat.

The so-called Qibla (قِبْلة) is the prayer direction in Islam. Muslims around the world have to turn their faces in the direction of Mecca in Saudi Arabia while praying.

Some people think that the direction to Mecca from North America is south-east, while others say it is north-east. Those who favour south-east, however, are misled by looking at the flat map.

If you want to find the shortest distance to Mecca, take a globe and stretch a thread from Alaska to Mecca, you will see that the thread passes through the North Pole (or close by). So, the correct prayer direction from Alaska will be towards the north – whereas on a flat map, Mecca appears to be south-east from Alaska.

There are two distinct schools of thought for determining the Qibla: the *great circle* method and the less common *rhumb-line* method. A straight line is called a rhumb line (a line that cuts equal angles across all lines of longitude). Most Internet prayer direction compasses are based on the *great circle* method.

The shortest rhumb line from most points in North America to Mecca will point toward the south-east, but the distance to Mecca along this route on the actual surface of the earth is (about 20 per-

---

667 ...قَالَ رَسُولُ اللَّهِ: "مَنْ آتَاهُ اللَّهُ مَالاً فَلَمْ يُؤَدِّ زَكَاتَهُ، مُثِّلَ لَهُ مَالُهُ شُجَاعًا أَقْرَعَ، لَهُ زَبِيبَتَانِ يُطَوَّقُهُ يَوْمَ الْقِيَامَةِ، يَأْخُذُ بِلِهْزِمَتَيْهِ يَعْنِي بِشِدْقَيْهِ يَقُولُ أَنَا مَالُكَ أَنَا كَنْزُكَ!" Sahīh al-Bukhārī 4565

cent) longer than the *great circle* route. Therefore, the Qibla - the shortest distance to Mecca - from North America is generally north-east, except from Alaska and California where it is close to north.

However, in the USA, only some mosques have used the correct Qibla, for example the Islamic Center of Washington, D.C., built in 1953. Most of the early mosques were oriented towards the south-east. At the end of the 1970s, Muslims started to realise the "mistake".

Muslims, as the Qur'an tells them, have to turn towards the **direction** of the Ka'ba and not towards the Ka'ba itself as they must not worship the cube. This is commanded in sura 2 *The Cow* – in Arabic: al-Baqara (سُورة الْبَقَرة):

| 2:150 | wherever you may have started out, turn your face in the direction of the Sacred Mosque; wherever any of you may be, turn your faces towards it, so that people may have no argument against you – except for the wrongdoers among them: do not fear them; fear Me - and so that I may perfect My favour on you and you may be guided, | وَمِنْ حَيْثُ خَرَجْتَ فَوَلِّ وَجْهَكَ شَطْرَ الْمَسْجِدِ الْحَرَامِ وَحَيْثُ مَا كُنتُمْ فَوَلُّوا وُجُوهَكُمْ شَطْرَهُ لِئَلَّا يَكُونَ لِلنَّاسِ عَلَيْكُمْ حُجَّةٌ إِلَّا الَّذِينَ ظَلَمُوا مِنْهُمْ فَلَا تَخْشَوْهُمْ وَاخْشَوْنِي وَلِأُتِمَّ نِعْمَتِي عَلَيْكُمْ وَلَعَلَّكُمْ تَهْتَدُونَ، |

So how can Muslims solve this task mathematically?

Our planet has a spherical shape. The direction between two points on a sphere is along the shortest path that connects the two points on the surface of the sphere. Such a path lies on the arc of a circle that passes through the two points and is centred at the centre of the sphere. Finally, we can derive the following formula:

$$q = \arctan\left(\frac{\sin(\lambda - \lambda M)}{\cos\varphi \times \tan\varphi M - \sin\varphi \times \cos(\lambda - \lambda M)}\right)$$

In this formula, (φ, λ) is the latitude and longitude of your location and $(\varphi M, \lambda M = 21.42, 39.83)$ is the (fixed) latitude and longitude of the Ka'ba in Mecca. The returned value q specifies the angle of the Qibla clockwise from north. The result of this formula should have a (+) sign for the eastern regions and (-) sign for the western regions.

In case of opposite results, the angle of the Qibla is easily found by adding (+ 180°) or (-180°).

For example: Istanbul's longitude is λ=29 and its latitude is φ=41.

$$q = \arctan\left(\frac{\sin(29 - 39.83)}{\cos 41 \times \tan 21.42 - \sin 41 \times \cos(29 - 39.83)}\right)$$

We finally get q=0.492579771 which equals: **+28° 21'**.

479. In what direction does a Muslim pray on the Samoan Islands?

Answer: He can use any direction.

The Samoan Islands are an archipelago in the central south Pacific, forming a part of Polynesia and the wider region of Oceania. The antipode of the Ka'ba is somewhere near the Samoan Islands. When a Muslim passes this spot, on a boat for example, all directions would be equidistant and he can choose any.

480. The dilemma of a Muslim astronaut: How can he pray towards Mecca from space?

Answer: If a Muslim would land on the moon, he will not be able to face the Ka'ba on earth in a correct manner due to the earth's rotation; nor will he be able to adhere to the correct prayer times following the sun's rising, passing of the meridian, and its setting.

Malaysia's first astronaut, Sheikh Muszaphar Shukor, a devout Muslim, flew in a Russian Soyuz spacecraft to the ISS (International Space Station) on October 10, 2007. This was during the month of Ramadan. From the ISS, orbiting 250 km (220 mi) above the surface of the earth, the Qibla - the direction to Mecca - changes in a blink of an eye. Furthermore, ISS travels at 17,400 miles per hour and orbits the earth 16 times a day. Would that mean that a Muslim has to pray 80 times in 24 hours?

Malaysia's space agency (MNSA) held a conference with 150 Islamic scientists and scholars to find a solution. The resulting document was called *"A Guideline of Performing Ibadah (worship) at the International Space Station (ISS)"* and was finally approved by Malaysia's National Fatwa Council.

They concluded that daily prayer in space is not linked to sunrises and sunsets, but to a 24-hour cycle based on the home time zone of Baikonur, the Russian-leased launch site in Kazakhstan. The astronaut has to pray towards the earth, as much as possible to Mecca. But how does that work in space? Mathematically, an astronaut would need to place both ISS and Mecca on the same imaginary sphere. The Fatwa Council proclaimed that he should do this by projecting the Ka'ba into space.

There was another problem: praying towards the earth is not trivial in space, but nevertheless of high importance. What happens if he accidentally prays towards other planets or stars? In sura 41 *(Verses) Made Distinct* - in Arabic: Fussilat (سُورة فُصِّلَتْ) -, there is a clear command:

41:37	The night, the day, the sun, the moon, are only a few of His signs. Do not bow down in worship to the sun or the moon, but bow down to God who created them, if it is truly Him that you worship.	وَمِنْ آيَاتِهِ اللَّيْلُ وَالنَّهَارُ وَالشَّمْسُ وَالْقَمَرُ لَا تَسْجُدُوا لِلشَّمْسِ وَلَا لِلْقَمَرِ وَاسْجُدُوا لِلَّهِ الَّذِي خَلَقَهُنَّ إِن كُنتُمْ إِيَّاهُ تَعْبُدُونَ.

But it appeared that not only the correct direction for praying was a challenge. How should a Muslim be able to perform all the necessary movements and positions for a valid prayer? In zero gravity, the sequence of the praying postures - standing, bowing, kneeling, and prostrating - is almost impossible.

Malaysian Islamic authorities held the opinion that the astronaut should preferably stand and if he can't stand, he should sit. And if he can't sit, he should lie down. And if he can't do any of them, he is allowed to symbolically indicate the postures "with his eyelids" or to simply imagine them, according to the MNSA booklet.

There was still one problem left: the ritual washing. Water on the ISS is so precious that even sweat and urine are recycled. Therefore, a

Muslim astronaut is permitted "dry ablution". In desert areas on earth, Muslims may use dirt and sand for the ritual ablution. The astronaut will strike his palms on a wall or mirror.

This question is not as theoretical and rare as it might look like. In a plane or a train, Muslims also have to deal with a constantly changing Qibla. Thus it is best for a Muslim to start in the correct direction and continue like that, no matter whether the Qibla has changed or not.

481. Can the direction to Mecca be determined by the sun?

Answer: Yes, on two special days.

Twice a year, the sun passes exactly above Mecca at around noon. On approximately May 28 (9:18 UTC or Greenwich Mean Time) and July 16 (9:27 GMT).

A Muslim has to convert the GMT to his local time and just look at the sun to determine the direction of Mecca. Why is that? If there was a minaret in Mecca reaching up to the sky, then you would see it just like you are seeing the sun at exactly this time.

For most places on earth, this works pretty well. Some examples:

- If you are in Istanbul (GMT +2, which means plus 2 hours difference from Greenwich), the local time to observe the sun would be 11:18 am on May 28 and 11:27 am on July 16.
- If you are in Karachi (GMT +5), the local time to observe the sun would be 2:18 pm on May 28 and 2:27 pm on July 16.
- If you are in Brasil (GMT -2), the local time to observe the sun would be 7:18 am on May 28 and 7:27 am on July 16.

But what can you do if you cannot see the sun at that moment? For example in places, where it is night at this time? Well, then we can make it the other way round.

There are two other days when the sun stands vertically above the place which is directly opposite to the Ka'ba in Mecca on the other side of the earth – the correct term for this is the antipodes of Mecca. This happens approximately on November 28 (at 21:09 GMT) and

January 13 (at 21:29 GMT). Note: The direction to Mecca is then the direct opposite of the direction in which the sun is at that time, so a Muslim should turn his back to the sun. The direction which is in front of him is the direction towards Mecca.

482. What is Bidʿa?

Answer: (Improper) innovation in Islamic religious matters.

Linguistically the term Bidʿa (بِدْعة) means *innovation, novelty*. In Islam, it refers to *innovation in religious matters*. Bidʿa describes a novelty in Islamic theology and jurisprudence that has no roots in the traditional practice of the Muslim community.

Bidʿa only refers to the doctrine of Islam. It has nothing to do with people accepting material inventions that came after Muhammad such as cars, mobile phones, air planes, etc. In general, Bidʿa is strictly forbidden.

Sura 5 *The Feast* - in Arabic: al-Māʾida (سورة المائدة) - tells Muslims that their religion Islam was perfected in the 7th century and must not be changed. However, in the same verse the Qurʾan gives Muslims a loophole, namely that a Muslim can always claim that he did this or that without knowing or without having the intention of doing it wrong.

5:3	Today I have perfected your religion for you, completed My blessing upon you, and chosen as your religion Islam [total submission to God]...	الْيَوْمَ يَئِسَ الَّذِينَ كَفَرُوا مِن دِينِكُمْ فَلَا تَخْشَوْهُمْ وَاخْشَوْنِ الْيَوْمَ أَكْمَلْتُ لَكُمْ دِينَكُمْ وَأَتْمَمْتُ عَلَيْكُمْ نِعْمَتِي وَرَضِيتُ لَكُمُ الْإِسْلَامَ دِينًا
	...but if any of you is forced by hunger to eat forbidden food, with no intention of doing wrong, then God is most forgiving and merciful.	...فَمَنِ اضْطُرَّ فِي مَخْمَصَةٍ غَيْرَ مُتَجَانِفٍ لِّإِثْمٍ فَإِنَّ اللَّهَ غَفُورٌ رَّحِيمٌ.

The prohibition of innovation [some also say: interpretation] of the Islamic foundations is also stated in the Hadiths.

Jābir ibn ʿAbd Allah (جابِر بن عَبْد الله) said: "In his Khutba [Friday sermon] the Messenger of Allah praised Allah as He deserves to be praised, then he said: 'Whomsoever Allah guides, none can lead him astray, and whomsoever Allah sends astray, none can guide. The truest of word is the Book of Allah and the best of guidance is the guidance of Muhammad. The worst of things are those that are newly invented; every newly-invented thing is an innovation, and every innovation is going astray and every going astray is in the Fire.'

Then he said: 'The Hour and I have been sent like these two.' Whenever the Prophet mentioned the Hour, his cheeks would turn red, and he would raise his voice and become angry, as if he were warning of an approaching army and saying: 'An army is coming to attack you in the morning or in the evening!'"[668]

Where does Bid'a start and where does it stop? This is debatable. For example, some Muslims like to use the Arabic pronoun for *He* - Huwa (هُوَ) - as a reference to Allah. Traditional scholars say that this is an innovation because the Prophet did not do so. Another example: Shia Muslims consider the voluntary prayers during Ramadan - so-called al-Tarāwīh (التَّوارِيح) - a Bid'a.

In a broader sense, some Muslims even characterise Judaism and Christianity as Bid'a because Muslims claim that both of them had contained the true message of Allah (= Islam) but were changed and corrupted over the centuries. For this reason, Allah had sent Gabriel to Muhammad in order to correct Allah's message.

The topic may sound trivial but the consequences can be severe because an "innovation" may be equal to *disbelieve* - kufr (كُفْر) - in some cases.

---

668 ...قَالَ كَانَ رَسُولُ اللَّهِ يَقُولُ فِي خُطْبَتِهِ يَحْمَدُ اللَّهَ وَيُثْنِي عَلَيْهِ بِمَا هُوَ أَهْلُهُ ثُمَّ يَقُولُ: "مَنْ يَهْدِهِ اللَّهُ فَلاَ مُضِلَّ لَهُ وَمَنْ يُضْلِلْهُ فَلاَ هَادِيَ لَهُ إِنَّ أَصْدَقَ الْحَدِيثِ كِتَابُ اللَّهِ وَأَحْسَنَ الْهَدْيِ هَدْيُ مُحَمَّدٍ وَشَرَّ الأُمُورِ مُحْدَثَاتُهَا وَكُلَّ مُحْدَثَةٍ بِدْعَةٌ وَكُلَّ بِدْعَةٍ ضَلاَلَةٌ وَكُلَّ ضَلاَلَةٍ فِي النَّارِ." ثُمَّ يَقُولُ: "بُعِثْتُ أَنَا وَالسَّاعَةَ كَهَاتَيْنِ." وَكَانَ إِذَا ذَكَرَ السَّاعَةَ احْمَرَّتْ وَجْنَتَاهُ وَعَلاَ صَوْتُهُ وَاشْتَدَّ غَضَبُهُ كَأَنَّهُ نَذِيرُ جَيْشٍ يَقُولُ: "صَبَّحَكُمْ مَسَّاكُمْ." Sunan al-Nasā'ī 1578

483. When does the fasting of a Muslim start and end?

Answer: He must fast from approaching dawn (طُلُوع الْفَجْر) until sunset (غُروب الشَّمْس).

This time period is called Mudda(t) al-'Imsāk (مُدّة الْإِمْساك). The word 'Imsāk denotes the start of the (daily) Ramadan fast; it literally means *restraint*. The exact duration of fasting is commanded in sura 2 *The Cow* – in Arabic: al-Baqara (الْبَقَرة):

2:187	eat and drink until the white thread of dawn becomes distinct from the black. Then fast until nightfall.	وَكُلُوا وَاشْرَبُوا حَتَّى يَتَبَيَّنَ لَكُمُ الْخَيْطُ الْأَبْيَضُ مِنَ الْخَيْطِ الْأَسْوَدِ مِنَ الْفَجْرِ ثُمَّ أَتِمُّوا الصِّيَامَ إِلَى اللَّيْلِ﴾

Note: This verse is occasionally slightly mistranslated. I bought a copy of the Qur'an in Cairo which was printed in Syria. It contained several documents which approved the correctness of the translation.

However, translation had some inaccuracies. The verse was given in English as "to distinguish between a white and a black thread" - which is often claimed by Muslims, but you should be able to distinguish "the white line of dawn from the black line of night".

According to all Arab philologists, the *black line* - in Arabic: al-Khayt al-'Aswad (الْخَيْط الْأَسْوَد) - signifies the *blackness of night*; and the expression *the two lines* or *streaks* - in Arabic: al-Khaytān (الْخَيْطان) - denotes *day and night* as explained in the dictionary Lisān al-'Arab.

484. Is punishment with fire allowed in Islam?

Answer: No, but some Caliphs did it anyway.

The whole topic came up recently when the terror organisation ISIL burnt a Jordanian pilot alive. According to the traditions of Muhammad, such is strictly forbidden.

'Abū Hurayra (أَبُو هُرَيْرة) narrated: "Allah's Messenger sent us on military expedition telling us: 'If you find such and such persons [he named two men from Quraysh], burn them with fire.'

Then we came to bid him farewell when we wanted to set out. He [the Prophet] said: 'Previously, I ordered you to burn so-and-so and so-and-so with fire, but punishment with fire is done by none except by Allah. If you capture them, kill' them [instead].'"[669]

However, there are reports that 'Abū Bakr (أَبُو بَكْر), the first Caliph of Islam, burnt a homosexual man alive and that 'Alī ibn 'Abī Tālib (عَلِيّ بن أَبِي طالِب) burnt a man who had left Islam.

It was narrated from 'Ikrima (عِكْرِمة): "Some people apostatised after accepting Islam, and 'Alī burned them with fire."

'Abd Allah ibn 'Abbās (عَبْد الله بن عَبّاس) said: "If it had been me, I would not have burned them. The Messenger of Allah said: 'No one should be punished with the punishment of Allah.' If it had been me, I would have killed them. The Messenger of Allah said: 'Whoever changes his religion, kill him.'"[670]

485. How does Islam view homosexuality?

Answer: It is punished by the death penalty.

Let's first look at the words that are used for homosexuals:

* Mithlī (مِثْلِيّ), literally meaning: *alike*. It is the (politically) correct Arabic term for a *homosexual*. Homosexuality means al-Jinsīya al-Mithlīya (الْجِنْسِيّة الْمِثْلِسّة). The old meaning of the Arabic root m-th-l (م-ث-ل) was *to mutilate somebody* or *to castrate somebody*; namely a sheep or a goat. Nowadays the root means: *to be alike, to resemble,* or *to make one similar to the other.*

---

669 ...أَنَّهُ قَالَ بَعَثَنَا رَسُولُ اللَّهِ فِي بَعْثٍ، وَقَالَ لَنَا: "إِنْ لَقِيتُمْ فُلَانًا وَفُلَانًا." لِرَجُلَيْنِ مِنْ قُرَيْشٍ سَمَّاهُمَا فَحَرِّقُوهُمَا بِالنَّارِ. قَالَ ثُمَّ أَتَيْنَاهُ نُوَدِّعُهُ حِينَ أَرَدْنَا الْخُرُوجَ فَقَالَ: "إِنِّي كُنْتُ أَمَرْتُكُمْ أَنْ تُحَرِّقُوا فُلَانًا وَفُلَانًا بِالنَّارِ، وَإِنَّ النَّارَ لَا يُعَذِّبُ بِهَا إِلَّا اللَّهُ، فَإِنْ أَخَذْتُمُوهُمَا فَاقْتُلُوهُمَا." Sahīh al-Bukhārī 2954

670 ...أَنَّ نَاسًا، ارْتَدُّوا عَنِ الْإِسْلَامِ، فَحَرَّقَهُمْ عَلِيٌّ بِالنَّارِ قَالَ ابْنُ عَبَّاسٍ لَوْ كُنْتُ أَنَا لَمْ، أُحَرِّقْهُمْ قَالَ رَسُولُ اللَّهِ:" لَا تُعَذِّبُوا بِعَذَابِ اللَّهِ أَحَدًا." وَلَوْ كُنْتُ أَنَا لَقَتَلْتُهُمْ قَالَ رَسُولُ اللَّهِ: "مَنْ بَدَّلَ دِينَهُ فَاقْتُلُوهُ." Sunan al-Nasā'ī 4060 (4065)

- However, in daily conversations, many Arabs use the word shād-hdh (شاذّ), pronounced "shaazz", which literally means: *(sexually) abnormal, anomalous, deviant,* or *pervert.*
- The Islamic term is Lūtī (لُوطِيّ) which means *homosexual* or *sodomite.* Liwāt (لِواط) means *sodomy, pederasty,* or *homosexuality.* The general meaning of both expressions is: *he commits the act of the people of Lūt.* Both words are derived from the story of the People of Lot (لُوط) who were destroyed by Allah because they engaged in "lustful" acts between men.

Let's look at the story of Lot (لُوط) which is similar to the one told in the Bible. Lot, a son of Abraham's brother, lived east of the river Jordan, close to the Dead Sea. That is why some Arabs still call the Dead Sea also "Lot's Sea" – in Arabic: *Buhayra(t) Lot* (بُحَيْرة لُوط).

Lot was commanded by Allah to go to the land of the two twin cities Sodom and Gomorrah. He should tell the people there to only worship one God and he should stop them from their sexual habits, namely sodomy and homosexuality. The people did not listen to Lot, instead, they threatened him.

Then two angels in the disguise of handsome young boys came to Lot who did not know that they were angels. The people overjoyed at the news of fresh young boys in the village. They went to Lot to snatch them (the boys). Lot tried to convince them to abstain from their sexual desires – and offered his own daughters to them in return for the boys' release. However, the people rejected his offer and said that they have no need for girls.

Lot failed to protect the boys.

All of a sudden, the boys told Lot that they were angels and that Allah had sent them to punish the people for their sins. They advised Lot to leave the place during the night and to not look back.

They informed Lot that his wife would be left behind. Lot's wife did not believe in his message and was condemned to Hell. Note that at this point the Qur'an contradicts the Bible. In the *Book of Genesis,* Lot's wife turned into a pillar of salt after she - despite God's warning - looked back at Sodom.

When morning came Allah destroyed the cities. He turned them "upside down", according to sura 11 Hūd (سُورة هُود):

11:81	They [the messengers] said, 'Lot, we are your Lord's messengers. They will not reach you. Leave with your household in the dead of night, and let none of you turn back. Only your wife will suffer the fate that befalls the others. Their appointed time is the morning: is the morning not near?'	قَالُوا يَا لُوطُ إِنَّا رُسُلُ رَبِّكَ لَن يَصِلُوا إِلَيْكَ فَأَسْرِ بِأَهْلِكَ بِقِطْعٍ مِّنَ اللَّيْلِ وَلَا يَلْتَفِتْ مِنكُمْ أَحَدٌ إِلَّا امْرَأَتَكَ إِنَّهُ مُصِيبُهَا مَا أَصَابَهُمْ إِنَّ مَوْعِدَهُمُ الصُّبْحُ أَلَيْسَ الصُّبْحُ بِقَرِيبٍ؟
11:82	And so when what We had ordained came about, We turned their town upside down and rained down stones of baked clay on it, layer upon layer.	فَلَمَّا جَاءَ أَمْرُنَا جَعَلْنَا عَالِيَهَا سَافِلَهَا وَأَمْطَرْنَا عَلَيْهَا حِجَارَةً مِّن سِجِّيلٍ مَّنضُودٍ

What is the punishment for homosexuality in Islam?

'Abd Allah ibn 'Abbās (عَبْد الله بن عَبَّاس) narrated that the Prophet said: "Whoever you find doing as the people of Lot did [i.e. homosexuality], kill the one who does it and the one to whom it is done, and if you find anyone having sexual intercourse with animals [buggery], kill him and kill the animal."[671]

There are various opinions and examples of how the death penalty should be carried out. The companions agreed on the execution of homosexuals, but they were not sure how the homosexuals should be executed. Some of them said that homosexuals should be burned with fire, which was the (initial) view of 'Alī ibn 'Abī Tālib (عَلِيّ بن أَبِي طالِب) and 'Abū Bakr (أَبُو بَكْر).

Khālid ibn al-Walīd (خالِد بن الْوَلِيد) narrated that he found a man among one of the Arab tribes with whom men would have intercourse as with a woman. He wrote about it to 'Abū Bakr, who consulted the companions. 'Alī ibn 'Abī Tālib had the strongest opinion and said: "No one did that but one of the nations [Sodom and Gomorrah], and you know what Allah did to them. I think that he

---

671 ...أَنَّ اَلنَّبِيَّ قَالَ: "مَنْ وَجَدْتُمُوهُ يَعْمَلُ عَمَلَ قَوْمِ لُوطٍ، فَاقْتُلُوا اَلْفَاعِلَ وَالْمَفْعُولَ بِهِ، وَمَنْ وَجَدْتُمُوهُ وَقَعَ عَلَى بَهِيمَةٍ، فَاقْتُلُوهُ وَاقْتُلُوا اَلْبَهِيمَةَ". Bulūgh al-Marām (1216); hasan sahīh

should be burned with fire." So 'Abū Bakr wrote to Khālid and he had him burned.[672]

Others thought that homosexuals should be thrown down from a high place and then have stones thrown at them. This was the view of 'Abd Allah ibn 'Abbās, one of Muhammad's cousins and an early Qur'an scholar. 'Abd Allah ibn 'Abbās had said: "The highest point in the town should be found and the homosexual should be thrown head first from it, then stones should be thrown at him."[673]

The punishment with stones is derived from the verse in the above mentioned sura in the Qur'an: "We turned their town upside down and **rained down stones of baked clay on it**". The terrorist network ISIL issued videos in which they executed several men exactly in this manner.

However, according to modern scholars, Muslims found guilty of homosexuality should repent rather than confess.

In some Muslim countries such as Egypt - for example in Luxor or Aswan - young men prostitute themselves for money. Almost all of these young men play **the passive part** and never the active. There are reasons for this. Generally speaking, the one to whom it is done is like the one who does it, because they both took part in the sin. So both are to be punished by execution.

However, according to scholars two exceptions can be made to that:

- The Hadd (حَدّ) punishment is not pronounced if the one **who was penetrated** (the passive part), was forced into it. A Muslim can always claim that he was threatened.

- If the passive part is a minor and has not yet reached the age of puberty, there is no Hadd punishment. The child should be disciplined and punished in a way that he won't do it again.

---

672 ...عَنْ خَالِد بن الْوَلِيد - أَنَّهُ وُجِدَ فِي بَعْضِ ضَوَاحِي الْعَرَبِ رَجُلٌ يُنْكَحُ كَمَا تُنْكَحُ الْمَرْأَةَ، فَكَتَبَ إِلَى أَبِي بَكْرٍ، فَاسْتَشَارَ أَبُو بَكْرٍ الصَّحَابَةَ فِيهِ، فَكَانَ عَلِيٌّ أَشَدَّهُمْ قَوْلًا فِيهِ فَقَالَ: مَا فَعَلَ هَذَا إِلَّا أُمَّةٌ مِنْ الْأُمَمِ وَاحِدَةٌ، وَقَدْ عَلِمْتُمْ مَا فَعَلَ اللَّهُ بِهَا، أَرَى أَنْ يُحْرَقَ بِالنَّارِ، فَكَتَبَ أَبُو بَكْرٍ إِلَى خَالِد بِذلك، فَحَرَّقه.

673 ...يُرْمَى بِه مِن أَعْلَى شاهِقٍ، وَيُتْبَعُ بِالْحَجَارَةِ.

486. Is anal sex allowed in Islam?

Answer: No, it is strictly forbidden.

Anal sex is strictly forbidden, even between heterosexual, married couples. This question is not trivial. Anal sex is a huge topic in the Middle East and North Africa since premarital sex between men and women is almost impossible. If you are not married, you cannot get a hotel room in most Arab countries. You cannot rent a flat unless you are rich and move to the upper-class parts of a city (and bribe the gatekeeper).

A woman's virginity is a big topic in most Islamic countries. If the husband finds out in the wedding night that his wife is not a virgin, she will be in big trouble. Premarital sex is very rare among women in conservative, Islamic countries. Women who don't want to lose their virginity before marriage but also don't want to live without sex until marriage can only practice oral or anal sex with their boy friends.

In Egypt, men need to own a flat in order to get married. Since real estate prices are skyrocketing, men are usually in their thirties when they touch a woman for the first time. Sexual harassment in the streets is a plague. Furthermore, anal sex among men is not as rare as one might think. "If you can't have sex with a girl, you take what you get", an Egyptian young man told me. Another said: "My father told me: 'Do whatever you like, but don't be the active part!'" Thus, many young Arabs make their first sexual experiences with anal sex because they cannot have (premarital) sexual relations.

What are the Islamic sources for the prohibition of anal sex?

- Khuzayma ibn Thābit (خُزَيْمة بن ثابت) narrated that the Prophet said: "Allah is not too shy to tell the truth! [three times] Do not have intercourse with women in their buttocks!"[674]
- 'Abū Hurayra (أَبُو هُرَيْرة) narrated that the Prophet said: "He who has intercourse with his wife through her anus is accursed."[675]

---

674 ...قَالَ رَسُولُ اللَّهِ: "إِنَّ اللَّهَ لاَ يَسْتَحْيِي مِنَ الْحَقِّ." ثَلاَثَ مَرَّاتٍ لاَ تَأْتُوا النِّسَاءَ فِي أَدْبَارِهِنَّ."
Sunan ibn Māja 1999 (1924)

675 ...قَالَ رَسُولُ اللَّهِ: "مَلْعُونٌ مَنْ أَتَى امْرَأَتَهُ فِي دُبُرِهَا." ;(2157) Sunan 'Abī Dāwūd 2162
hasan

487. What will happen to a Muslim who builds a mosque?

Answer: He will get a similar house in Paradise.

Mahmūd ibn Labīd (مَحْمُود بـن لَبِيـد) reported that 'Uthmān ibn 'Affān (عُثْمان بن عَفّان) once decided to rebuild the mosque of Allah's Messenger in Medina, but the people did not like this idea and they wished that it should be preserved in the same [old] form. Thereupon 'Uthmān said: "I heard Allah's Messenger say: 'He who builds a mosque for Allah, Allah will build for him [a house] in Paradise like it.[676]

488. How many causes of death are eligible for martyrdom?

Answer: In principle there are five causes. Scholars say that all of these deaths should involve hardship.

'Abū Hurayra (أَبُو هُرَيْرة) narrated that Allah's Messenger said: "Five are regarded as martyrs: They are those who die because of plague, abdominal/stomach disease [for example: diarrhoea/cholera], drowning or of being crushed [buried alive by a falling building], and one who dies while fighting for the cause of Allah [Jihād]."[677]

Some Hadiths indicate that a woman who dies in childbirth is also a martyr. It was narrated from the father of 'Abd Allah ibn 'Abd Allah ibn Jabr (عَبْد الله بن عَبْد الله بن جَبْر) that the Messenger of Allah paid a visit to Jabr [when he was sick]. When he entered [the house], he heard women cry. They said: "We thought that one's death would come when fighting in the cause of Allah."

The Prophet said: "You think that martyrdom only comes when one is killed in the cause of Allah. In that case, the martyrs would be few. Being killed in the cause of Allah is martyrdom, dying of an abdominal complaint is martyrdom, being burnt to death is martyrdom, being drowned is martyrdom, being crushed beneath a falling

---

676 ...أَنَّ عُثْمَانَ بْنَ عَفَّانَ، أَرَادَ بِنَاءَ الْمَسْجِدِ فَكَرِهَ النَّاسُ ذَلِكَ وَأَحَبُّوا أَنْ يَدَعَهُ عَلَى هَيْئَتِهِ فَقَالَ سَمِعْتُ رَسُولَ اللَّهِ يَقُولُ: "مَنْ بَنَى مَسْجِدًا لِلَّهِ بَنَى اللَّهُ لَهُ فِي الْجَنَّةِ مِثْلَهُ." Sahīh Muslim 533

677 ...أَنَّ رَسُولَ اللَّهِ قَالَ: "الشُّهَدَاءُ خَمْسَةٌ الْمَطْعُونُ، وَالْمَبْطُونُ، وَالْغَرِقُ وَصَاحِبُ الْهَدْمِ، وَالشَّهِيدُ فِي سَبِيلِ اللَّهِ." Sahīh al-Bukhārī 2829

wall is martyrdom, dying of pleurisy is martyrdom, and the woman who dies along with her foetus is a martyr."[678]

A Muslim who died drowning is, according to Islam, a martyr. This gives at least some emotional support to relatives of Muslim refugees who tried to make their way across the Mediterranean to Europe but sadly died at sea.

In February 2006, when I was in Egypt, a passenger ferry sunk in the Red Sea leaving more than a thousand people dead. The *MS al-Salam Boccaccio 98* was en route from Saudi Arabia to Safaga in southern Egypt. The ship was carrying about 1400 passengers and crew, most of them were Egyptians working in Saudi Arabia and pilgrims from Mecca. Only 388 people were rescued. After this tragedy, many people told me that the victims were martyrs.

489. May a Muslim join the Jihād without asking for his parent's permission?

Answer: No.

The following was told by 'Abū Sa'īd al-Khudrī (أَبُو سَعِيد الْخُدْرِيّ): "A man migrated from Yemen to join the Messenger of Allah. The Prophet asked him: 'Do you have anyone [of your relatives] in Yemen?' He replied: 'My parents.' He [the Messenger of Allah] asked: 'Did they permit that?' He replied: 'No'. The Prophet said: 'Go back to them and ask for their permission. If they permit you to fight, then fight [in the path of Allah], otherwise be devoted to them.'"[679]

Pleasing one's parents is considered so important in Islam that the son is forbidden to fight in the Jihād without his parent's permission.

---

678 ...أَنَّ رَسُولَ اللَّهِ عَادَ جَبْرًا فَلَمَّا دَخَلَ سَمِعَ النِّسَاءَ يَبْكِينَ وَيَقُلْنَ كُنَّا نَحْسُبُ وَفَاتَكَ قَتْلاً فِي سَبِيلِ اللَّهِ. فَقَالَ: "وَمَا تَعُدُّونَ الشَّهَادَةَ إِلاَّ مَنْ قُتِلَ فِي سَبِيلِ اللَّهِ إِنَّ شُهَدَاءَكُمْ إِذًا لَقَلِيلٌ الْقَتْلُ فِي سَبِيلِ اللَّهِ شَهَادَةٌ وَالْبَطْنُ شَهَادَةٌ وَالْحَرَقُ شَهَادَةٌ وَالْغَرَقُ شَهَادَةٌ وَالْمَغْمُومُ - يَعْنِي الْهَدِمَ - شَهَادَةٌ وَالْمَجْنُوبُ شَهَادَةٌ وَالْمَرْأَةُ تَمُوتُ بِجُمْعٍ شَهِيدَةٌ." Sunan al-Nasā'ī 3194

679 ...أَنَّ رَجُلاً، هَاجَرَ إِلَى رَسُولِ اللَّهِ مِنَ الْيَمَنِ، فَقَالَ: "هَلْ لَكَ أَحَدٌ بِالْيَمَنِ." قَالَ: أَبَوَايَ. قَالَ: "أَذِنَا لَكَ." قَالَ: لَا. قَالَ: "ارْجِعْ إِلَيْهِمَا فَاسْتَأْذِنْهُمَا، فَإِنْ أَذِنَا لَكَ فَجَاهِدْ، وَإِلاَّ فَبِرَّهُمَا." Sunan 'Abī Dāwūd 2530

490. Can women join the Jihād?

Answer: No.

Generally, there are 7 requirements a Muslim has to meet in order to join the Jihād. A fighter in Jihād - a Mujāhid (مُجاهد) – has to be:

1	Muslim		5	mentally stable
2	male		6	physically sound
3	adult		7	should be able to afford it
4	free			

It is difficult to say who is an adult. Muslims don't accept what is written in civil laws. Instead, they prefer using a narration of 'Abd Allah ibn 'Umar (عَبْد الله بن عُمَر) who said: "I was presented to the Messenger of Allah on the day of the Battle of 'Uhud when I was fourteen years old, but he did not permit me [to fight]. I was presented to him on the day of the Battle of the Trench when I was fifteen years old and he permitted me [to fight]."[680]

Are only men allowed to join Jihād? The Prophet didn't want women to fight. 'Ā'isha (عائشة بِنْت أبي بَكْر) narrated: "O Allah's Messenger! We consider Jihād as the best deed. Should we [the women] not fight in Allah's Cause?" The Prophet said: "The best Jihād [for women] is Hajj."[681]

Another authentic Hadith confirms that the pilgrimages Hajj and 'Umra are Jihād for women. It was narrated that 'Ā'isha said: 'O Messenger of Allah, is Jihād obligatory for women?' He said: "Yes. For them is a Jihād in which there is no fighting: al-Hajj and al-'Umra."[682]

Muslims think that a woman does not have the physical abilities for fighting. They say there is proof for this in a Hadith narrated by

---

680 ...قَالَ عُرِضْتُ عَلَى رَسُولِ اللَّهِ يَوْمَ أُحُدٍ وَأَنَا ابْنُ أَرْبَعَ عَشْرَةَ سَنَةً فَلَمْ يُجِزْنِي وَعُرِضْتُ عَلَيْهِ يَوْمَ الْخَنْدَقِ وَأَنَا ابْنُ خَمْسَ عَشْرَةَ سَنَةً فَأَجَازَنِي. (2543) 2640 Sunan ibn Māja

681 ...أَنَّهَا قَالَتْ يَا رَسُولَ اللَّهِ تُرَى الْجِهَادَ أَفْضَلَ الْعَمَلِ، أَفَلَا نُجَاهِدُ قَالَ: "لَكِنَّ أَفْضَلَ الْجِهَادِ حَجٌّ مَبْرُورٌ." Sahīh al-Bukhārī 2784

682 ...قُلْتُ يَا رَسُولَ اللَّهِ عَلَى النِّسَاءِ جِهَادٌ قَالَ: "نَعَمْ عَلَيْهِنَّ جِهَادٌ لَا قِتَالَ فِيهِ الْحَجُّ وَالْعُمْرَةُ." Sunan ibn Māja 3013 (2901)

'Abū al-Zinād (أَبُو الزِّناد): When Muhammad saw the body of a woman slain in the battlefield, he said: "This one was not a fighter".[683]

In Europe, a number of newspapers recently reported that Muslim women were "joining the Jihād in Syria". According to most Islamic scholars, however, this is not possible for women.

491. If a person dies in Jihād, should his body be washed?

Answer: No.

Most scholars say that if a so-called Islamic martyr dies in a battle, he should not be washed and shrouded. There are several Hadiths indicating this. Jābir ibn 'Abd Allah (جابِر بن عَبْد الله) narrated that the Prophet said: "Bury them [i.e. the martyrs] with their blood." That was on the day of the Battle of 'Uhud (غَزْوة أُحُد). He did not get them washed.[684]

This shows that the traces of martyrdom should be left on the body. 'Abd Allah ibn Tha'laba (عَبْد الله بن نَعْلَبة) narrated what the Prophet had said about those who had been slain in the Battle of 'Uhud: "Wrap them up in their clothes that are stained with blood, for there is a wound that was sustained for the sake of Allah, but it will bleed again on the Day of Resurrection. Its colour will be the colour of blood, but its scent will be the fragrance of musk."[685]

'Abū Hurayra (أَبُو هُرَيْرة) confirmed this and narrated that Allah's Messenger had said: "By Him in Whose Hands my soul is! Whoever is wounded in Allah's cause - and Allah knows well who gets wounded in His cause - will come on the Day of Resurrection with his wound having the colour of blood but the scent of musk."[686]

---

683 ...فَانْفَرَجُوا عن الْمَرْأَةِ, فَوَقَفَ عَلَيْهَا رَسُولُ اللَّهِ ثُمَّ قَالَ: "هَاهْ مَا كَانَتْ هَذِهِ تُقَاتِلُ." Musnad 'Ahmad ibn Hanbal 15562

684 ...قَالَ النَّبِيُّ: "ادْفِنُوهُمْ فِي دِمَائِهِمْ." يَعْنِي يَوْمَ أُحُد وَلَمْ يُغَسِّلْهُمْ. Sahīh al-Bukhārī 1346.

685 ...قَالَ رَسُولُ اللَّهِ لِقَتْلَى أُحُد: "زَمِّلُوهُمْ بِدِمَائِهِمْ, فَإِنَّهُ لَيْسَ كَلْمٌ يُكْلَمُ فِي اللَّهِ إلاَّ يَأْتِي يَوْمَ الْقِيَامَةِ يَدْمَى, لَوْنُهُ لَوْنُ الدَّمِ وَرِيحُهُ رِيحُ الْمِسْكِ." Sunan al-Nasā'ī 2002 (2004)

686 ...أَنَّ رَسُولَ اللَّهِ قَالَ: "وَالَّذِي نَفْسِي بِيَدِهِ لاَ يُكْلَمُ أَحَدٌ فِي سَبِيلِ اللَّهِ وَاللَّهُ أَعْلَمُ بِمَنْ يُكْلَمُ فِي سَبِيلِهِ إلاَّ جَاءَ يَوْمَ الْقِيَامَةِ وَاللَّوْنُ لَوْنُ الدَّمِ وَالرِّيحُ رِيحُ الْمِسْكِ." Sahīh al-Bukhārī 2803

However, in the history of Islam, there are some well-known exceptions to this rule. ‘Abd Allah ibn Hanzala (عَبْد الله بن حَنْزَلة) was washed by angels – because after he had sex with his newly-wed wife, he did not perform the ritual washing as commanded. Instead, he immediately ran to the battlefield – and got killed. Islamic scholars say that the rulings for human beings cannot be compared to those for angels. They say that this was a way of honouring Hanzala.

What is the procedure for all other deceased?

Apart from a martyr killed in battle, any other deceased body must be washed – Ghusl (غُسْل). ’Umm ‘Atīya (أُم عَطِيّة) reported that when the Prophet's daughter Zaynab died, Muhammad told them: “Wash her an odd number of times, i.e. three or five times, and put camphor or something like camphor at the fifth time, and after you have washed her inform me.” So they informed him and he gave them his under-garment, saying: “Put it next to her body.”[687]

‘Abd Allah ibn ‘Abbās (عَبْد الله بن عَبَّاس) narrated that while a man was standing with the Prophet near [the region of] ‘Arafāt, he fell from his mount and broke his neck. The Prophet said: “Wash the deceased with water and Sidr [Lotus tree] and shroud him in two pieces of cloth, and neither perfume him nor cover his head, for Allah will resurrect him on the Day of Resurrection and he will say: 'I am here at your service' [Talbiya].”[688]

---

687 ...قَالَتْ لَمَّا مَاتَتْ زَيْنَبُ بِنْتُ رَسُولِ اللَّهِ قَالَ لَنَا رَسُولُ اللَّهِ: "اغْسِلْنَهَا وِتْرًا ثَلاَثًا أَوْ خَمْسًا وَاجْعَلْنَ فِي الْخَامِسَةِ كَافُورًا أَوْ شَيْئًا مِنْ كَافُورٍ فَإِذَا غَسَلْتُنَّهَا فَأَعْلِمْنَنِي." قَالَتْ فَأَعْلَمْنَاهُ. فَأَعْطَانَا حِقْوَهُ وَقَالَ: "أَشْعِرْنَهَا إِيَّاهُ." Sahīh Muslim 939

688 ...قَالَ بَيْنَا رَجُلٌ وَاقِفٌ مَعَ النَّبِيِّ بِعَرَفَةَ إِذْ وَقَعَ عَنْ رَاحِلَتِهِ، فَوَقَصَتْهُ أَوْ قَالَ فَأَقْعَصَتْهُ فَقَالَ النَّبِيُّ:" اغْسِلُوهُ بِمَاءٍ وَسِدْرٍ، وَكَفِّنُوهُ فِي ثَوْبَيْنِ أَوْ قَالَ ثَوْبَيْهِ وَلاَ تُحَنِّطُوهُ وَلاَ تُخَمِّرُوا رَأْسَهُ، فَإِنَّ اللَّهَ يَبْعَثُهُ يَوْمَ الْقِيَامَةِ يُلَبِّي." Sahīh al-Bukhārī 1849

492. Was it "Islamic" to bury Osama bin Laden at sea?

Answer: Probably not. Burials at sea for Muslims are only permissible under extraordinary circumstances.

US Special Forces killed Osama bin Laden (أُسامة بن لادن), the leader of the terrorist network al-Qāʿida (تَنْظِيم الْقاعِدة), in Pakistan in May 2011.

People in Egypt had told me again and again that Osama bin Laden was no longer a Muslim each time his terror organisation had committed a brutal crime. Nevertheless, when US forces killed Bin Laden a lot of people got upset about his burial at sea – because it was against the rules of Islam. But was it really?

"Finding a country willing to accept the remains of the world's most wanted terrorist would have been difficult", a US official explained. "So the US decided to bury him at sea."

In a classified e-mail, which found its way to the press, an admiral described how Osama bin Laden was buried: "The deceased's body was washed [ablution] and then wrapped in a white sheet. The body was then placed in a weighted bag. A military officer read prepared religious remarks, which were translated into Arabic by a native speaker. After the words were said, the body was placed on a flat board, tipped up, whereupon the body slid into the sea.."

So what are the Islamic rules?

There is nothing in the Hadiths that indicates that a companion of Muhammad was moved to a place other than the graveyard of the country or (nearby) city in which he had died. The general rule is that martyrs should be buried where they died.

Scholars say that the body of a deceased should only be moved if there are fears that his or her grave might be desecrated. Muslim families who once migrated from Islamic countries to Europe usually want to take the deceased's body back to the "homeland". There is no report in the Hadiths which commands this, but most scholars permit it.

Because of all this, Osama bin Laden should have been buried in Pakistan in the graveyard of Abbottabad in Pakistan where he was killed. However, there were concerns that his grave would be demolished. Thus, it was okay to move his body. Muslims who criticise the

US government say that his body should have been handed over to his family.

Now, let's move on to the crucial part of the question: **Can you bury a Muslim at sea?** Generally speaking, no.

First of all, the head of a deceased Muslim must be arranged to face Mecca. This is not possible at sea.

If a Muslim dies on a ship while travelling at sea, the people on the ship should try to reach an island or beach (a place to bury him). But this must happen within a day or two and only if they are sure that the body will not decay in the meantime.

However, if the body poses a health risk to the passengers or if there is no possibility to find land within a certain period, the passengers should wash and shroud the body, then pray the funeral prayer. Finally, they should tie something heavy to the body and drop it in the water – which is exactly what the US officials did.

Followers of Osama bin Laden meanwhile were upset that the Americans washed the body. In their view, Osama bin Laden died as a martyr and in Islam, the blood of a martyr should not be washed off the deceased.

493. Are Muslims allowed to take captives?

Answer: Yes, but only under certain circumstances.

In general, a Muslim is not allowed to take captives unless Muslims are in a state of war (Jihād). This is told in sura 8 *Battle Gains* – in Arabic: al-'Anfāl (سُورة الْأَنْفال):

| 8:67 | It is not right for a prophet to take captives before he has conquered the battlefield. You [people] desire the transient goods of this world, but God desires the Hereafter [for you] - God is mighty and wise. | مَا كَانَ لِنَبِيٍّ أَنْ يَكُونَ لَهُ أَسْرَى حَتَّى يُثْخِنَ فِي الْأَرْضِ تُرِيدُونَ عَرَضَ الدُّنْيَا وَاللَّهُ يُرِيدُ الْآخِرَةَ وَاللَّهُ عَزِيزٌ حَكِيمٌ. |

In the Qur'an, most orders were given to Muhammad personally and not to Muslims in general. However, as soon as Muhammad did something, it became binding for all of his fellow Muslims. This means that none can be taken into captivity unless he was taken prisoner in Jihād (جهاد). This is a clear command in the Qur'an which is somehow repeated in sura 47 *Muhammad* (سُورة مُحَمَّد):

| 47:4 | When you meet the disbelievers in battle, strike them in the neck, and once they are defeated, bind any captives firmly - later you can release them by grace or by ransom - until the toils of war have ended. That [is the way]. God could have defeated them Himself if He had willed, but His purpose is to test some of you by means of others. He will not let the deeds of those who are killed for His cause come to nothing; | فَإِذَا لَقِيتُمُ الَّذِينَ كَفَرُوا فَضَرْبَ الرِّقَابِ حَتَّى إِذَا أَثْخَنتُمُوهُمْ فَشُدُّوا الْوَثَاقَ فَإِمَّا مَنًّا بَعْدُ وَإِمَّا فِدَاءً حَتَّى تَضَعَ الْحَرْبُ أَوْزَارَهَا ذَلِكَ وَلَوْ يَشَاءُ اللَّهُ لَانتَصَرَ مِنْهُمْ وَلَكِن لِّيَبْلُوَ بَعْضَكُم بِبَعْضٍ وَالَّذِينَ قُتِلُوا فِي سَبِيلِ اللَّهِ فَلَن يُضِلَّ أَعْمَالَهُمْ; |

Note: Since the word *grace* is mentioned first, most commentators agree that this is the recommended action. So, prisoners should be set free after the war (if possible).

494. Are Muslims allowed to have sex with female captives?

Answer: Most scholars say yes.

This is a difficult topic, especially as members of the terrorist-network ISIL raped dozens of female captives. However, there are several Hadiths which indicate that such is allowed.

Two of the most important collectors of Hadiths - al-Bukhārī and al-Muslim - mentioned such a situation when they recalled what 'Abū Sa'īd al-Khudrī (أَبُو سَعِيد الْخُدْرِيّ) narrated: "We went out with Allah's Messenger on the Battle of Banū Mustaliq (غَزْوة بَنُو الْمُصْطَلِق) and took captive some excellent Arab women; and we desired them, for we were suffering from the absence of our wives, [but at the same time] we also desired ransom for them.

So we decided to have sexual intercourse with them but by observing 'Azl (عَزْل) [which means: withdrawing the penis before emission of semen to avoid-conception]. But we said: 'We are doing an act whereas Allah's Messenger is among us; why not ask him?' So we asked Allah's Messenger and he said: 'It does not matter if you do it or not because every soul that is to be born up to the Day of Resurrection will be born.'"[689]

In other words, they could have sex with them as the Prophet did not forbid it. The reason why Muslims were asking about a *coitus interruptus* has to do with the legal, Islamic consequences. They did not want the women to become pregnant because they wanted to be able to sell them – and if a captive/slave woman was pregnant, she could not be sold.

495. For how many days do Muslim women mourn?

Answer: Three days for any dead person and four months plus ten days for their deceased husband.

Zaynab bint 'Abī Salama (زَيْنَب بِنْت أَبِي سَلَمَة) narrated that she went to 'Umm Habība, one of the Prophet's wives, who said: "I heard the Prophet say: 'It is not legal for a woman who believes in Allah and the Last Day to mourn for any dead person for more than three days except for her husband, [for whom she should mourn] for four months and ten days.'"[690]

'Umm 'Atīya (أُمّ عَطِيَّة) narrated that the Messenger of Allah said: "[A woman who mourns] should not wear dyed clothes, except for a garment of 'Asb [a plain dress from Yemen], and she should not wear Kuhl on her eyes or perfume, except at the beginning of her purity [after finishing her menstruation], when she may apply a little Qust and 'Azfār [perfume]."[691]

---

689 ...غَزَوْنَا مَعَ رَسُولِ اللَّهِ غَزْوَةَ بَلْمُصْطَلِقِ فَسَبِيْنَا كَرَائِمَ الْعَرَبِ فَطَالَتْ عَلَيْنَا الْعُزْبَةُ وَرَغِبْنَا فِي الْفِدَاءِ فَأَرَدْنَا أَنْ نَسْتَمْتِعَ وَنَعْزِلَ فَقُلْنَا نَفْعَلُ وَرَسُولُ اللَّهِ بَيْنَ أَظْهُرِنَا لَا نَسْأَلُهُ. فَسَأَلْنَا رَسُولَ اللَّهِ فَقَالَ: "لَا عَلَيْكُمْ أَنْ لَا تَفْعَلُوا مَا كَتَبَ اللَّهُ خَلْقَ نَسَمَةٍ هِيَ كَائِنَةٌ إِلَى يَوْمِ الْقِيَامَةِ إِلَّا سَتَكُونُ." Sahīh
Muslim 1438

690 ...دَخَلْتُ عَلَى أُمِّ حَبِيبَةَ زَوْجِ النَّبِيِّ فَقَالَتْ سَمِعْتُ رَسُولَ اللَّهِ يَقُولُ " لَا يَحِلُّ لِامْرَأَةٍ تُؤْمِنُ بِاللَّهِ وَالْيَوْمِ الْآخِرِ تُحِدُّ عَلَى مَيِّتٍ فَوْقَ ثَلَاثٍ، إِلَّا عَلَى زَوْجٍ أَرْبَعَةَ أَشْهُرٍ وَعَشْرًا " Sahīh al-Bukhārī 1281,
1282

691 ...قَالَ رَسُولُ اللَّهِ: "لَا تُحِدُّ عَلَى مَيِّتٍ فَوْقَ ثَلَاثٍ إِلَّا الْمَرْأَةُ تُحِدُّ عَلَى زَوْجِهَا أَرْبَعَةَ أَشْهُرٍ وَعَشْرًا وَلَا تَلْبَسُ ثَوْبًا مَصْبُوغًا إِلَّا ثَوْبَ عَصْبٍ وَلَا تَكْتَحِلُ وَلَا تَطَيَّبُ إِلَّا عِنْدَ أَدْنَى طُهْرِهَا بِنُبْذَةٍ مِنْ قُسْطٍ

In short, the recently widowed woman should wear simple clothes (not necessarily black in Islam), no make-up, no perfume, and no jewellery.

496. Are Muslims allowed to visit a grave?

Answer: Yes.

Muslim graveyards are rather plain; there are no flowers, pictures, or big tombstones, but just small head stones with the deceased's name and a verse of the Qur'an. This has to do with a warning the Prophet had issued in his last days.

The following was narrated by both 'A'isha (عائشة بِنْت أَبِي بَكْر) and by 'Abd Allah ibn 'Abbās (عَبْد الله بن عَبّاس): On his deathbed Allah's Messenger had put a sheet over his face and when he felt hot, he would remove it. When in that state [of placing and removing the sheet] he said: "May Allah's curse be on the Jews and the Christians for they built places of worship at the graves of their prophets." [By that] he intended to warn [the Muslims] from what they [i.e. Jews and Christians] had done.[692]

However, critics say that Muhammad's grave is in his mosque and that also he has a place of worship at his grave. The Prophet is buried in the *Mosque of the Prophet* - in Arabic: al-Masjid al-Nabawī (الْمَسْجِد النَّبَوِيّ) - in the city of Medina in Saudi Arabia. It is the second-holiest site in Islam after the Masjid al-Harām in Mecca where the Ka'ba is located. His companions did not bury Muhammad in the mosque in Medina, rather they buried him on the grounds of 'A'isha's house. At that time it adjoined the mosque which was expanded later during the reign of Caliph al-Walīd I to include his tomb. The first two Caliphs, 'Abū Bakr and 'Umar, are buried next to Muhammad. His wife 'A'isha is buried in the graveyard of al-Baqī' in Medina.

Sunan ibn Māja 2165 (2087) "وَأَظْفَارٍ.

692 ...قَالَ لَمَّا نَزَلَ بِرَسُولِ اللَّهِ طَفِقَ يَطْرَحُ خَمِيصَةً عَلَى وَجْهِهِ، فَإِذَا اغْتَمَّ كَشَفَهَا عَنْ وَجْهِهِ، فَقَالَ وَهُوَ كَذَلِكَ: "لَعْنَةُ اللَّهِ عَلَى الْيَهُودِ وَالنَّصَارَى، اتَّخَذُوا قُبُورَ أَنْبِيَائِهِمْ مَسَاجِدَ." يُحَذِّرُ مَا صَنَعُوا. Sahīh al-Bukhārī 3453, 3454

The tomb of Muhammad is not ornamented and around one metre high (3.3 ft). No one is allowed to see the actual grave and it cannot be seen from outside as it is cordoned off by curtains. The place is marked by a green dome, which was originally white, built by the Ottoman Turks.

Every year millions of Muslims from all around the world come to visit the Prophet's grave. However, this is exactly what Muhammad tried to prevent. 'Abū Hurayra (أَبُو هُرَيْرَة) narrated that the Prophet had said: "Do not make your houses graves, and do not make my grave a place of festivity. But invoke blessings on me, for your blessings reach me wherever you may be."[693]

In the beginning of his teachings, Muhammad even forbade his followers to visit graves – but changed this command later on. Ibn Burayda (ابن بُرَيْدة) reported on the authority of his father that the Messenger of Allah said: "I forbade you to visit graves, but you may visit them now."[694]

There is no information why the Prophet had prohibited it at first. Later, however, Allah granted him permission. 'Abū Hurayra narrated that the Apostle of Allah once visited the grave of his mother and he wept, and moved others around him to tears, and said: "I sought permission from my Lord to beg forgiveness for her but it was not granted to me, and I sought permission to visit her grave and it was granted to me so visit the graves, for that makes you mindful of death."[695]

It was narrated from 'Abū Hurayra that the Messenger of Allah had said: "Visit the graves, for they will remind you of the Hereafter."[696] I saw this sentence sprayed on the walls of a graveyard in the small village of el-Louza in Tunisia – the place from where many refugees used to take off to the Italian island of Lampedusa.

693 ...قَالَ رَسُولُ اللَّهِ: "لاَ تَجْعَلُوا بُيُوتَكُمْ قُبُورًا وَلاَ تَجْعَلُوا قَبْرِي عِيدًا وَصَلُّوا عَلَيَّ فَإِنَّ صَلاَتَكُمْ تَبْلُغُنِي حَيْثُ كُنْتُمْ." Sunan 'Abī Dāwūd 2042

694 ...قَالَ رَسُولُ اللَّهِ: "نَهَيْتُكُمْ عَنْ زِيَارَةِ الْقُبُورِ فَزُورُوهَا." Sahīh Muslim 977

695 ...قَالَ زَارَ النَّبِيُّ قَبْرَ أُمِّهِ فَبَكَى وَأَبْكَى مَنْ حَوْلَهُ فَقَالَ: "اسْتَأْذَنْتُ رَبِّي فِي أَنْ أَسْتَغْفِرَ لَهَا فَلَمْ يُؤْذَنْ لِي وَاسْتَأْذَنْتُهُ فِي أَنْ أَزُورَ قَبْرَهَا فَأُذِنَ لِي فَزُورُوا الْقُبُورَ فَإِنَّهَا تُذَكِّرُ الْمَوْتَ." Sahīh Muslim 976

696 ...قَالَ رَسُولُ اللَّهِ: "زُورُوا الْقُبُورَ فَإِنَّهَا تُذَكِّرُكُمُ الآخِرَةَ." Sunan ibn Māja 1636 (1569)

Are Muslim women allowed to visit graves or not?

There is a debate whether they are or not. The traditions of the Prophet don't give a clear answer. Some say it is okay, but others say it is reprehensible, while some others even say that it is forbidden because of the following Hadith:

'Abū Hurayra (أَبُو هُرَيْرة) narrated: "Indeed the Messenger of Allah cursed the women who visited the graves."[697]

Traditional scholars say that women are emotionally not strong enough and might break into crying and loud weeping. A Muslim man explained to me that cemeteries are usually isolated places which may not be safe for a Muslim woman if she is there alone.

Historians, on the other hand, say that this Hadith may go back to a time when Muhammad had prohibited the visiting of graveyards for all his followers: men and women. When he later changed this rule, he did not specify only men. According to this reasoning, it should be fine for women to visit graveyards.

497. What is 'Ahl al-Fatra?

Answer: Anyone who has not received the message of Islam.

In Islamic theology, the term 'Ahl al-Fatra (أَهْل الْفَتْرة) refers to anyone who has not heard of Islam or the true divine message. Fatra (interregnum) means *pause* or *interval*.

'Ahl al-Fatra are those who lived at a time or in a place that prevented them from receiving the divine message. In Islam, in a broader sense, it refers to the time between two prophets.

The 'Ahl al-Fatra includes:

- those who never received a messenger from Allah
- young children of non-Muslims who died before puberty
- old people who were senile when the message came to them
- mentally disabled people
- deaf people who could not communicate at all

---

697 ...أَنَّ رَسُولَ اللَّهِ لَعَنَ زَوَّارَاتِ الْقُبُورِ. Jāmiʿ al-Tirmidhī 1056; hasan; Sunan ibn Māja 1641 (1574); hasan

498. What happens to a person who has never heard of Islam after death?

Answer: He or she will be tested on the Day of Resurrection.

Let's start with the obvious: Non-Muslims, who knew about Islam but did not want to embrace it, will definitely go to Hell.

But if they had never heard of Islam, then they will be tested on the Day of Resurrection. These people are known as *people without messengers* – in Arabic: 'Ahl al-Fatra (أهل الفَترة). Even though they died as non-Muslims, Allah would not send them to Hell without a fair trial. If the person accept Islam and obeys Allah, he or she will be admitted to Paradise. If the person refuses Islam and disobeys, he or she will be sent to Hell.

Muslims find evidence for this in the Hadith of al-'Aswad ibn Sari' (الأْسْوَد بن سَرِيع) who reported that the Prophet had said: "There are four [who will protest] to Allah on the Day of Resurrection: the deaf man who never heard anything, the insane man, the very old man, and the man who died during the al-Fatra.

The deaf man will say: 'O Lord, Islam came but I never heard anything.'

The insane man will say: 'O Lord, Islam came but the children ran after me and threw stones at me.'

The very old man will say: 'O Lord, Islam came but I did not understand anything.'

The man who died during the al-Fatra will say: 'O Lord, no messenger from You came to me.' He will accept their promises of obedience, and then word will be sent to them to enter the Fire. By the One in Whose hand is the soul of Muhammad, if they enter it, it will be cool and safe for them.'"[698]

Note that Muhammad only talks about men in the above Hadith.

---

698 ...أَنَّ نَبِيَّ اللَّهِ قَالَ: أَرْبَعَةٌ [يحتجون] يَوْمَ الْقِيَامَةِ رَجُلٌ أَصَمُّ لا يَسْمَعُ شَيْئًا وَرَجُلٌ أَحْمَقُ وَرَجُلٌ هَرِمٌ وَرَجُلٌ مَاتَ فِي فَتْرَةٍ فَأَمَّا الأَصَمُّ فَيَقُولُ رَبِّ لَقَدْ جَاءَ الإِسْلامُ وَمَا أَسْمَعُ شَيْئًا وَأَمَّا الأَحْمَقُ فَيَقُولُ رَبِّ لَقَدْ جَاءَ الإِسْلامُ وَالصِّبْيَانُ يَحْذِفُونِي بِالْبَعْرِ وَأَمَّا الْهَرِمُ فَيَقُولُ رَبِّي لَقَدْ جَاءَ الإِسْلامُ وَمَا أَعْقِلُ شَيْئًا وَأَمَّا الَّذِي مَاتَ فِي الْفَتْرَةِ فَيَقُولُ رَبِّ مَا أَتَانِي لَكَ رَسُولٌ فَيَأْخُذُ مَوَاثِيقَهُمْ لَيُطِيعُنَّهُ فَيُرْسِلُ إِلَيْهِمْ أَنْ ادْخُلُوا النَّارَ قَالَ فَوَالَّذِي نَفْسُ مُحَمَّدٍ بِيَدِهِ لَوْ دَخَلُوهَا لَكَانَتْ عَلَيْهِمْ بَرْدًا وَسَلامًا. Sahih al-Jami', 881.

499. In Islam, is it good to pray for the deceased?

Answer: Yes.

First of all, the deceased do not hear the words of the living. This is said in sura 27 *The Ants* – in Arabic: al-Naml (سُورة النَّمْل):

| 27:80 | You cannot make the dead hear, you cannot make the deaf listen to your call when they turn their backs and leave | إِنَّكَ لَا تُسْمِعُ الْمَوْتَى وَلَا تُسْمِعُ الصُّمَّ الدُّعَاءَ إِذَا وَلَّوْا مُدْبِرِينَ |

But this does not mean that Muslims should not pray for them. On the contrary, if the children of a deceased Muslim pray for forgiveness, this could bring great benefits for the dead person. 'Abū Hurayra (أَبُو هُرَيْرَة) narrated that Allah's Messenger said: "A man will be raised in status in Paradise and will say: 'Where did this come from?' And it will be said: 'From your son's praying for forgiveness for you.'"[699]

Furthermore, size does matter. Muslims believe that the bigger the number of Muslims who join the prayer is, the more beneficial it is for the deceased.

'Ā'isha (عائشة بِنْت أَبِي بَكْر) reported that the Messenger of Allah once had said: "If a company of Muslims numbering one hundred pray over a dead person, all of them interceding for him, their intercession for him will be accepted."[700]

Furthermore, it may help if a Muslim does good things on behalf of the deceased or in the name of the deceased.

'Ā'isha narrated that a man once told the Prophet: "My mother died suddenly and I thought that if she had lived, she would have given alms. So, if I give alms now on her behalf, will she get the reward?" The Prophet replied in the affirmative: yes.[701]

---

699 ...قَالَ رَسُولُ اللَّهِ: "إِنَّ الرَّجُلَ لَتُرْفَعُ دَرَجَتُهُ فِي الْجَنَّةِ فَيَقُولُ أَنَّى هَذَا فَيُقَالُ بِاسْتِغْفَارِ وَلَدِكَ لَكَ". Sunan ibn Māja 3660

700 ...النَّبِيُّ قَالَ: "مَا مِنْ مَيِّتٍ يُصَلِّي عَلَيْهِ أُمَّةٌ مِنَ الْمُسْلِمِينَ يَبْلُغُونَ مِائَةً كُلُّهُمْ يَشْفَعُونَ لَهُ إِلاَّ شُفِّعُوا فِيهِ". Saḥīḥ Muslim 947

701 ...أَنَّ رَجُلاً، قَالَ لِلنَّبِيِّ إِنَّ أُمِّي افْتُلِتَتْ نَفْسُهَا، وَأَظُنُّهَا لَوْ تَكَلَّمَتْ تَصَدَّقَتْ، فَهَلْ لَهَا أَجْرٌ إِنْ تَصَدَّقْتُ عَنْهَا قَالَ: "نَعَمْ". Saḥīḥ al-Bukhārī 1388

'Abd Allah ibn 'Abbās (عَبْد الله بن عَبَّاس) narrated that the mother of Sa'd ibn 'Ubāda (سَعْد بن عُبادة) had died in his absence. Sa'd asked: "O Messenger of Allah! My mother died in my absence; will it be of any benefit for her if I give alms on her behalf?" The Prophet said: "Yes."

Sa'd said: "I make you a witness that I give my garden called al-Mikhrāf to charity on her behalf."[702]

500. What is *happiness* according to Islam?

Answer: There are four things: a righteous wife, a spacious abode, a good neighbour and a comfortable mount (means of transport).

Sa'd ibn 'Abī Waqqās (سَعْد بن أَبي وَقَّاص) narrated that the Messenger of Allah had said: "Four things are part of happiness: a righteous wife, a spacious abode, a good neighbour and a comfortable mount. And four things are part of misery: a bad neighbour, a bad wife, a small abode and a bad mount."[703]

What is meant by *mount* – in Arabic: al-Markab (الْمَرْكَب)? A mount is a form of transportation by which one can reach places easily and without difficulties. What was probably meant by a *mount* in the Hadith was an animal, such as a horse, mule, donkey, or camel, but nowadays that would also include cars and other modern means of transportation. You may hear Muslims say the Basmala ("In the name of Allah, …") when they enter a car or start it.

This goes back to the Qur'an, sura 16 *The Bee* – in Arabic: al-Nahl (سُورة النَّحْل):

| 16:8 | And [He created] horses, mules, and donkeys for you to ride and use for show, and other things you know nothing about. | وَالْخَيْلَ وَالْبِغَالَ وَالْحَمِيرَ لِتَرْكَبُوهَا وَزِينَةً وَيَخْلُقُ مَا لَا تَعْلَمُونَ. |

---

702 ...أَنَّ سَعْدَ بْنَ عُبَادَةَ تُوُفِّيَتْ أُمُّهُ وَهْوَ غَائِبٌ عَنْهَا، فَقَالَ يَا رَسُولَ اللَّهِ إِنَّ أُمِّي تُوُفِّيَتْ وَأَنَا غَائِبٌ عَنْهَا، أَيَنْفَعُهَا شَيْءٌ إِنْ تَصَدَّقْتُ بِهِ عَنْهَا قَالَ: "نَعَمْ." قَالَ فَإِنِّي أُشْهِدُكَ أَنَّ حَائِطِي الْمِخْرَافَ صَدَقَةٌ عَلَيْهَا. Sahīh al-Bukhārī 2756.

703 ...أَرْبَعٌ مِنَ السَّعَادَةِ: الْمَرْأَةُ الصَّالِحَةُ، وَالْمَسْكَنُ الْوَاسِعُ، وَالْجَارُ الصَّالِحُ، وَالْمَرْكَبُ الْهَنِيءُ، وَأَرْبَعٌ مِنَ الشَّقَاوَةِ: الْجَارُ السُّوءُ، وَالْمَرْأَةُ السُّوءُ، وَالْمَسْكَنُ الضَّيِّقُ، وَالْمَرْكَبُ السُّوءُ. Ahmad 1/168; Sahīh al-Jāmi' 887

What is meant by happiness in the Hadith mentioned at the begin-ning of this chapter is of course worldly happiness in the sense of comfort and wealth and not spiritual happiness.

An Egyptian Muslim explained it to me as follows:

A Muslim who suffers from a nasty wife, who has a small, shabby house, and who has no car or just a donkey will be troubled and depressed, and thus he might not find enough time to remember and praise Allah – which is the worst in Islam.

Appendix

Conversion table for names: Qur'an – Bible; Bible – Qur'an

↓ ISLAM	Arabic	Bible	↓ BIBLE	Arabic	Islam
'Ādam	آدَم	Adam	Aaron	هارُون	Hārūn
Alyasaʿ	الْيَسَع	Elisha	Abraham	إبراهيم	'Ibrāhīm
'Ayyūb	أَيُّوب	Job	Adam	آدَم	'Ādam
Dāwūd	داوُود	David	David	داوُود	Dāwūd
Dhūlkifl	ذُو الْكِفْل	Ezekiel	Eber	هُود	Hūd
Hārūn	هارُون	Aaron	Elias	إلْياس	'Ilyās
Hūd	هُود	Eber	Elisha	الْيَسَع	Alyasaʿ
'Ibrāhīm	إبراهيم	Abraham	Enoch	إدْرِس	'Idrīs
'Idrīs	إدْرِس	Enoch	Ezekiel	ذُو الْكِفْل	Dhūlkifl
'Ilyās	إلْياس	Elias	Gabriel	جِبْرِيل	Jibrīl
ʿĪsā	عِيسَى	Jesus	Isaac	إسْحاق	'Ishāq
'Ishāq	إسْحاق	Isaac	Ishmael	إسْماعِيل	'Ismāʿīl
'Ismāʿīl	إسْماعِيل	Ishmael	Jacob	يَعْقُوب	Yaʿqūb
Jibrīl	جِبْرِيل	Gabriel	Jesus	عِيسَى	ʿĪsā
Lūt	لُوط	Lot	Jethro	شُعَيْب	Shuʿayb
Mūsā	مُوسَى	Moses	Job	أَيُّوب	'Ayyūb
Nūh	نُوح	Noah	John the Baptist	يَحْيَى	Yahyā
Sālih	صالِح	*unclear*	Jonah	يُونُس	Yūnus
Shuʿayb	شُعَيْب	Jethro	Joseph	يُوسُف	Yūsuf
Sulaymān	سُلَيْمان	Solomon	Lot	لُوط	Lūt
Yaʿqūb	يَعْقُوب	Jacob	Moses	مُوسَى	Mūsā
Yahyā	يَحْيَى	John (t. Baptist)	Noah	نُوح	Nūh
Yūnus	يُونُس	Jonah	Solomon	سُلَيْمان	Sulaymān
Yūsuf	يُوسُف	Joseph	Zechariah	ذَكَرِياء	Zakarīyā'
Zakarīyā'	ذَكَرِياء	Zechariah	?	صالِح	Sālih

The main characters of this book

The characters are in alphabetical order using their English translit-
erations. The Arabic definite article *al-* (الـ) is considered as *A*.

'Abd Allah ibn 'Abbās (عَبْد الله بن عَبَّاس) - B: 619 (3 BH); D: ~ 687 (68 AH) -
commonly known as Ibn 'Abbās. Also as *the sea* (الْبَحْر) because he is
considered the greatest scholars of the first generation of Muslims.
He was the son of a wealthy man and one of the Prophet's cousins.
When Muhammad died, he was only thirteen years old. He is one of
the main transmitters of Hadiths (~ 1,660) and perhaps the first
exegete of the Qur'an. Respected by Sunni and Shia Muslims.

'Abd Allah ibn 'Amr ibn al-'Ās (عَبْد الله بن عَمرو بن الْعاص) -B: 595 (27 BH);
D: 684 (~65 AH) - was a companion of Muhammad. He was one of the
first companions to write down Hadiths, authored the first known
compilation of Hadiths and transmitted more than 700 Hadiths.

'Abd Allah ibn Mas'ūd (عَبْد الله بن مَسْعُود) - B: ~ 594 (31-37 BH); D: ~ 652 (32
AH) - was a companion of the Prophet and one of the first converts to
Islam. He was very close to the Prophet, and he thus observed and
adopted his manners. He was considered the best reciter of the
Qur'an among the companions. He became one of the best experts in
Islamic jurisprudence. He is said to have narrated 848 Hadiths.

'Abd Allah ibn 'Ubayy ibn Salūl (عَبْد الله بن أُبَيّ بن سَلُول) - B: unknown; D:
631 (~ 9/10 AH) - had several conflicts with the Prophet. Before
Muhammad had started his Islamic mission and migrated to Medina,
'Abd Allah was the most outstanding leader of the people of Medina
(then known as Yathrib). Although he "officially" embraced Islam,
Muslims call him the *Leader of the Hypocrites* (رَأْس الْمُنافِقِين).

'Abū 'Ayyūb al-'Ansārī (أَبُو أَيُّوب الْأَنْصارِئ) - B: ~ 576 (47 BH); D: ~ 671 (52 AH)
- was a companion of Muhammad from the 'Ansār who helped the
Prophet after the Hijra from Mecca to Medina in 622. He was one of
the standard-bearers of the Prophet. He died during the first Arab
siege of Constantinople. The Ottoman Turks built a mosque above
his grave in Istanbul and the neighbourhood is now called Eyüp.

'Abū Dharr al-Ghifārī (أَبُو ذَرّ الْغِفَارِيّ) - B: unkn.; D: 652 (32 AH) - was one of the very first persons who embraced Islam. He migrated with the Prophet from Mecca to Medina. He is seen by Shia Muslims as one of the followers of 'Alī ibn 'Abī Tālib. Credited with 281 traditions.

'Abū Hurayra (أَبُو هُرَيْرة) - B: 602 (21 BH); D: 679 (59 AH) - was the most prolific narrator of Hadiths - around 5,374 narrations -, though he had only spent a few years with the Prophet. He was originally from Yemen. His epithet means *Father of the Kitten*. His real name was most probably 'Abd al-Rahmān ibn Sakhr (عَبْد الرَّحْمٰن بن صَخْر).

'Abū Jahl (أَبُو جَهْل) - B: ~ 555 (68 BH); D: 624 (2 AH) - was one of the fiercest opponents of the Prophet. His original epithet was *Father of Wisdom*. However, the Prophet and his followers called him 'Abū Jahl which means *Father of Ignorance*. He was a Quraysh leader in Mecca and was killed in the first major fight between the Muslims and their Meccan enemies. His real name was 'Amr ibn Hishām (عَمْرُو بن هِشام).

'Abū Qatāda al-'Ansārī (أَبُو قَتادة الأَنْصارِيّ) - B: 606 (16 BH); D: 674 (54 AH) - was one of the companions of the Prophet and one of the 'Ansār. Full name: Hārith ibn Rabī' (حارِث بن رَبِيع).

'Abū Mas'ūd al-'Ansārī (أَبُو مَسْعُود الأَنْصارِيّ) - B: unknown; D: unknown - was one of the companions of the Prophet and a narrator of Hadiths. He was from the 'Ansār. Full name: 'Uqba ibn 'Amr (عُقْبة بن عَمْرو)

'Abū Sa'īd al-Khudrī (أَبُو سَعِيد الْخُدْرِيّ) - B: ~ 612 (10 BH); D: ~ 693 (74 AH) - was from the 'Ansār and one of the younger companions of the Prophet. He fought in many battles. He narrated 1,170 Hadiths. Shia Muslims mostly accept his narrations.

'Ahmad ibn Hanbal (أَحْمَد بن حَنْبَل الشَّيْباني) - B: 780 (164 AH); D: 855 (241 AH) - was a Muslim scholar and theologian from Baghdad. He is considered the founder of the Hanbalī School of Islamic jurisprudence, the most strict and rigid in Sunni Islam. Saudi Arabia today is following this school. He was a compiler of Hadiths. He was vehemently opposing the Mu'tazila, an Islamic theology based on reason and free will. Traditional Muslims admire him for his courage in the face of persecution and imprisonment. Legend has it that his funeral was attended by hundreds of thousands of people.

'Ā'isha bint 'Abī Bakr (عائشة بِنْت أَبِس بَكْر) - B: 614 (8 BH); D: 678 (58 AH) - commonly just known as 'Ā'isha, was one of Muhammad's wives and the daughter of 'Abū Bakr, who became the first Caliph to succeed Muhammad. She was married to the Prophet as a child and later on, she became one of the most powerful women in Arab history. She plays a major role in the division of Islam into Sunni and Shia. Furthermore, she is one of the main contributors of Hadiths (2,210 Hadiths). Her narrations deal mainly with Muhammad's private life and give some intimate details. However, they also deal with legal issues and Islamic eschatology. Shia Muslims see her role critically.

al-'Albānī (الأَلْبانِيّ) - B: 1914 (1332 AH); D: 1999 (1420 AH) - was an Islamic scholar from Albania who moved to Syria as a child. He focused on the study of hadith and evaluated thousands of narrations according to their chains of transmission. He is said to have published over 300 treatises. He became an important figure of Salafism in the 20th century. He sought to reform Islam by urging Muslims to return to a puritanical and literalist approach to the primary sources. His legacy is his constant effort to reevaluate the authenticity of the hadith. Under the regime of Hāfiz al-'Asad in Syria, he was placed under house arrest on several occasions. After his brief tenure in Saudi Arabia, he eventually moved to Jordan, where he resided until his death. His full name was Muhammad Nasr al-Dīn al-'Albānī (مُحَمّد ناصِر الدِّين الأَلْبانِيّ).

al-Barā' ibn 'Āzib (البَراء بن عازِب) - B: unknown; D: 691 (72 AH) - was a companion of the Prophet and a narrator of hadith. He belonged to the Ansār. It is said that he volunteered to fight in the first major battle, the Battle of Badr, between the Muslims and their enemies, though the Prophet Muhammad did not permit him to fight because he was only 15 years old. He plays an important role for Shia Muslims because he was a loyal supporter of 'Alī.

al-Qurtubī (القُرْطُبِيّ) - B: ~ 1214 (610 AH) - D: 1273 (671 AH) - was a traditional Islamic scholar from Cordoba (Spain). He lived in the 13th

century and was a follower of the Sunni Maliki School of jurisprudence. He later moved to Egypt where he also died. He opposed the
rationalists in Islam (Mu'tazila) and is known for his strict interpretations. He is mainly known for his commentary on the Qur'an.

al-Rāzī (رازى) - B: ~ 1149 (~ 544 AH); D: ~ 1209 (~606 AH) - was a highly
influential Persian Sunni theologian and philosopher. He was influenced by Ibn Sīnā (Avicenna) and the mystic and theologian al-
Ghazālī. His commentary on the Qur'an - al-Tafsīr al-Kabīr (التَّفْسِير
الْكَبِير) - was also called *Keys to the Unseen* - Mafātīh al-Ghayb (مَفاتِيح
الْغَيْب). It contains various philosophical ideas as well as ideas of
rationalism. Traditional scholars reject many of it. His real name was
Muhammad ibn 'Umar ibn al-Husayn (مُحَمَّد بن عُمَر بن الْحُسَيْن), but
was also known as Fakhr al-Dīn al-Rāzī (فَخْر الدِّين الرَّازِيّ).

al-Tabarī (الطَّبَرِيّ) - B: 839 (224 AH); D: 923 (310 AH) - was an influential
Persian Islamic scholar, historian and exegete of the Qur'an. He went
to Baghdad and wanted to learn from 'Ahmad ibn Hanbal – but
'Ahmad died shortly after al-Tabarī had arrived. His work on history
(تاريخ الطَّبَرِيّ) - starting from the Islamic creation (Adam) and ending
in the year 915 AD - and a commentary on the Qur'an - Tafsīr al-
Tabarī (تَفْسِير الطَّبَرِيّ) are among his most famous works. His full
name was Muhammad ibn Jarīr al-Tabarī (مُحَمَّد بن جَرير الطَّبَرِيّ).

al-Zamakhsharī (الزَّمَخْشَرِيّ) - B: 1074 (467 AH); D: 1143 (538 AH) - was a
Persian medieval Islamic scholar and authority on the Arabic language who subscribed to the Mu'tazila doctrine. His best known
work is a commentary on the Qur'an which is famous for its linguistic analysis. Full name: 'Abū al-Qāsim Mahmūd ibn 'Umar al-Zamakhsharī (أَبُو الْقاسِم مَحْمُود بن عُمَر الزَّمَخْشَرِيّ).

'Alī ibn 'Abī Tālib (عَلِيّ بن أَبي طالِب) - B: ~ 599 (~23 BH) - D: 661 (40 AH) -
commonly known as 'Alī, was the cousin and son-in-law of the
Prophet. He was married to Muhammad's daughter Fatima. They
had two sons: al-Husayn and al-Hasan. He was probably the first
male person to embrace Islam, though he was a child at that time.
'Alī is one of the most important figures in Islam and one of the reasons why Islam is divided into Sunni and Shia branches. Shia Muslims

claim that he should have been the successor of Muhammad - and not 'Abū Bakr. He ruled as the Caliph from 656 to 661.

'Anas ibn Mālik (أَنَس بن مَالِك) - B: 612 (10 BH); D: ~ 712 (93 AH) - was a companion and the most famous servant of the Prophet, thus, he lived closely with Muhammad. He is one of the major narrators/contributors of Hadiths (2,286 narrations). Furthermore, he was the last companion to die in Basra

Edward William Lane - B: 1801 (1216 AH); D: 1876 (1293 AH) - was a British orientalist and translator. He is best known for his Arabic-English Lexicon. Lane's approach was unique in that his definitions were taken from older, medieval Arabic-Arabic dictionaries. Lane was unable to finish his monumental work; he had reached the letter Qāf (ق), the 21st letter of the Arabic alphabet, when he died in 1876. His work was later finished by his great-nephew, Stanley Lane-Poole, although his contributions are generally considered to be of a lower quality compared to Edward Lane's original scholarly rigor.

Hudhayfa ibn al-Yamān (حُذَيْفة بن الْيَمَان) - B: unknown; D: ~ 656 (36 AH) - was a companion of Muhammad. His main quality was that he could keep a secret. He was Muhammad's confidant - so-called: Sahib al-Sirr (صاحِب السِّر). He is important for Shia Muslims because he was one of the main companions of 'Alī.

Ibn Hishām (ابن هشام) - B: unknown; D: 833 (218 AH) - was a historian and Islamic scholar. He edited and published the biography of Muhammad written by Ibn 'Ishāq. Although many Muslims still refer to Ibn 'Ishāq, it is actually Ibn Hishām's work because Ibn 'Ishāqs main work was lost and only parts of it survived in the works of Ibn Hishām and al-Tabarī. Ibn Hishām's work (biography) is called al-Sīra al-Nabawīya li Ibn Hishām (السِّيرة النَبَوِيَّة لِابن هشام). His full name was 'Abd al-Malik ibn Hishām (عَبْد الْمَلِك بن هشام).

Ibn 'Ishāq (ابن إسحاق) - B: ~ 703 (85 AH); D: 768 (151 AH) - was an Arab Muslim historian who collected stories about the life of the Prophet. During the reign of the Abbasid Caliph al-Mansūr (الْمَنْصُـر), Ibn 'Ishāq was asked to write about the history of Islam – which included a biography of Muhammad. It later became known as the first and most important biography of the Prophet, although critics say that parts of it lack reliable sources. Nevertheless, it is still used as the main source for Muslims to know more about the early history of Islam. It is said that there was only one copy available, which eventually got lost. A great part of it survived in the works of Ibn Hishām and in some of the works of al-Tabarī, both of whom had seen Ibn Ishāq's work before it got lost. Alfred Guillaume's English translation is a good attempt at the reconstruction of Ibn 'Ishāq's work (Oxford University Press; ISBN: 978-0196360331). His full name was 'Abū Bakr Muhammad ibn 'Ishāq (أَبُو بَكْر مُحَمَّد بن إسحاق).

Ibn Kathīr (ابن كَثِير) - B: ~ 1300 (~ 701 AH); D: 1373 (774 AH) - was an important Sunni scholar, particularly in jurisprudence as a follower of the Shāfi'ī School, during the Mamluk rule of Syria in the 14th century. He was an expert on Qur'anic exegesis; his commentary on the Qur'an incorporated relevant hadith to explain certain verses. While he is widely known for his legal affiliation with the Shāfi'ī school, his theological creed (aqidah) remains a subject of modern debate, for example, many Salafi scholars regard him as a firm adherent of the Athari (textualist) creed – heavily influenced by his teacher Ibn Taymiyya. His full name was 'Abū al-Fidā' ('Imād al-Dīn) 'Ismā'īl ibn Kathir (أَبُو الْفِداء عِماد الدِّين إسماعِيل بن كَثِير).

Ibn Taymīya (ابن تَيْمِيّة) - B: ~ 1263 (~ 661 AH); D: 1328 (728 AH) - was an Islamic scholar and theologian. He was a follower of 'Ahmad ibn Hanbal and lived during the time of the Mongol invasions. He was a very strict and conservative scholar and his works have highly influenced Salafism. Modern Islamic critics claim that his works have also inspired so-called Jihadists. Later, in Damascus, he was put in prison because of his writings. He never married and died in prison. While some sources conservatively report that at least 50,000 people attended his funeral prayer, other accounts support figures in the hundreds of thousands – with one source estimating 200,000 men and 15,000 women. Notably, at his funeral, some mourners engaged in popular piety practices (such as drinking the water used to wash his body and seeking blessings from his belongings), which were precisely the kind of innovations (bid'ah) that Ibn Taymīya had spent his life condemning. His full name was 'Ahmad ibn 'Abd al-Halīm ibn 'Abd al-Salām ibn Taymīya (أَحْمَد بن عَبْد الْحَلِيم بن عَبْد السَّلام بن تَيْمِيّة).

Jābir ibn ʿAbd Allah (جابِر بن عَبْد الله) - B: ~ 607 (~ 16 BH); D: 697 (78 AH) - was a companion of Muhammad from the 'Ansār. He came from a poor family and embraced Islam when he was a child. He narrated/ contributed about 1,540 Hadiths. Both Sunni and Shia Muslims highly respect him.

Muhammad Abdel Haleem (مُحَمَّد عَبْد الْحَلِيم) was born in Egypt in 1930 and learned the Qur'an by heart in his childhood. He was educated at Cairo University and Cambridge University. His translation of the Qur'an (Oxford University Press; 2004) was written in English and has been used for this book.

Muhammad Asad (مُحَمَّد أَسَد) - B: 1900 (1318 AH); D: 1992 (1412 AH) - was a Jewish Austro-Hungarian journalist (born Leopold Weiß) who converted to Islam and became one of the most influential European Muslims of the 20th century. He travelled extensively across Arabia and later became involved in the foundation of an independent Muslim state in India – which later became Pakistan. His translation and commentary of the Qur'an is regarded as one of the best of modern times. Since he embraced a more spiritual (abstract) understanding of Islam, traditional scholars have often criticized and rejected his work.

Saʿd ibn Muʿādh (سَعْد بن مُعاذ) - B: ~ 591 (~ 32 BH); : ~ 627 (5 AH) - was one of the most famous and heroic companions of Muhammad. He took part in all major battles of Muhammad. Following the events at the Battle of the Trench, he was chosen to be the judge in a conflict between the Prophet and the Jewish tribe Banū Qurayza. His verdict was brutal because the whole Jewish tribe was obliterated by the Muslims.

Saʿd ibn ʾAbī Waqqās (سَعْد بن أَبِي وَقّاص) - B: ~ 595 (~ 23 BH); D: ~ 674 (55 AH) - was one of the most important companions, one of the fiercest warriors and best archers of Muhammad. After the Prophet's death, he played a major role in the conquest of Persia. Later, when the first Islamic civil war had started, he withdrew from the political and military arena. It is said that he died a wealthy man.

The family tree of Muhammad

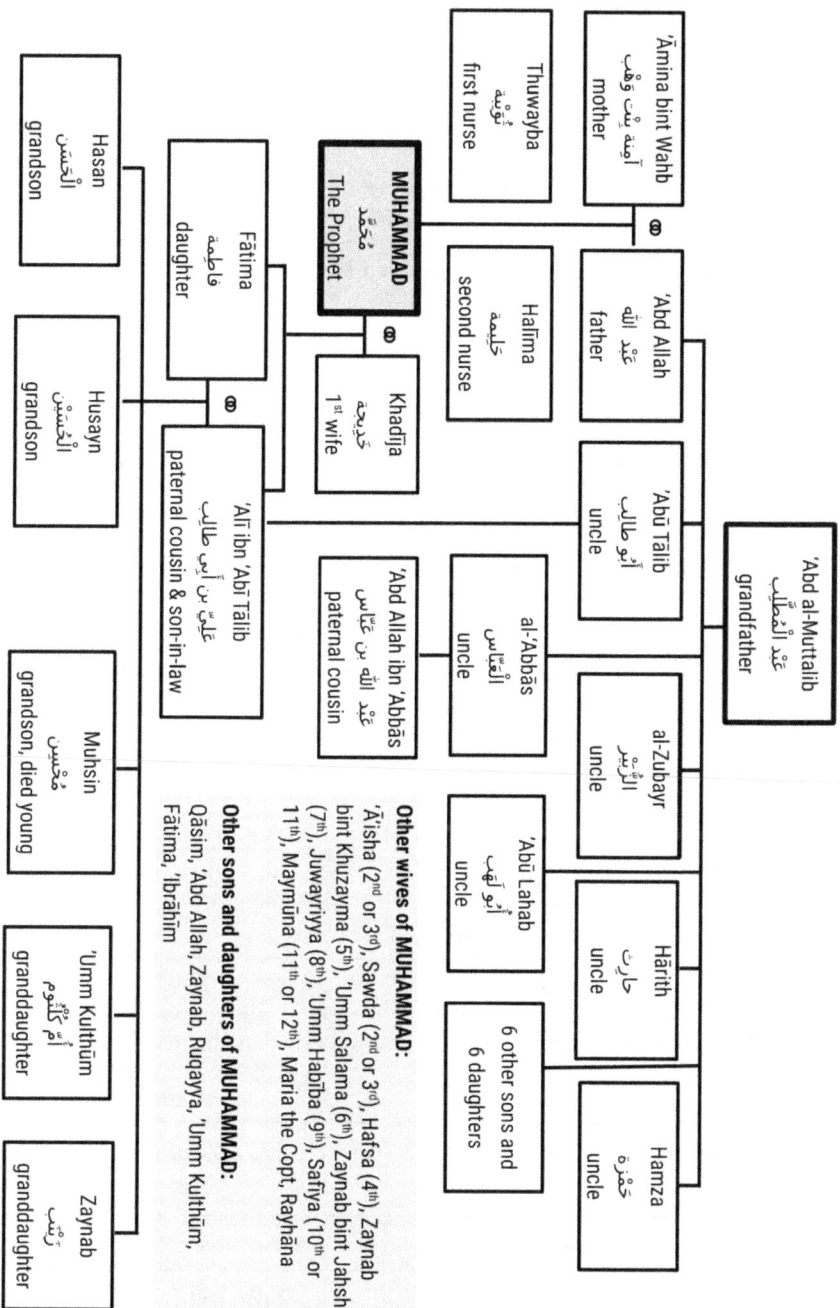

Arabic verb forms

In this book Roman numerals are used for the most common Arabic verb patterns:

I	فَعَلَ, فَعِلَ, فَعُلَ	fa'ala, fa'ila, fa'ula
	Primary meaning of the root.	
II	فَعَّلَ	fa''ala
	Strengthens the meaning of a I-verb; or makes it transitive or causative.	
III	فاعَلَ	fā'ala
	Shows the attempt to do something (try to...); describes someone doing the action in question to or with someone else.	
IV	أَفْعَلَ	'af'ala
	Makes a I-verb transitive or causative; may strengthen a I-verb.	
V	تَفَعَّلَ	tafa''ala
	Reflexive or passive meaning of a II-verb; may intensify a I-verb (very rare).	
VI	تَفاعَلَ	tafā'ala
	Reflexive form of a III-verb.	
VII	إِنْفَعَلَ	infa'ala
	Reflexive or passive meaning of a I-verb.	
VIII	إِفْتَعَلَ	ifta'ala
	Reflexive or passive meaning of a I-verb. Similar to VII.	
IX	إِفْعَلَّ	if'alla
	Reflexive meaning of a II-verb (referring to colours or physical deficiencies).	
X	إِسْتَفْعَلَ	istaf'ala
	Expresses a wish or desire; could express the reflexive form of type IV; could also denote: to regard/consider something as...	

Index

www.ingramcontent.com/pod-product-compliance
Lightning Source LLC
Chambersburg PA
CBHW061543120626
46550CB00004B/1349